Engineering and Science Math I

Brigham Young University

Multivariable Calculus
Salas

WILEY Custom
LEARNING SOLUTIONS

To order books or for customer service, please call 1(800)-CALL-WILEY (225-5945).

Printed in the United States of America.

ISBN 978-0-470-56033-4

Printed and bound by Odyssey Press Inc.

10 9 8 7 6 5 4 3

CONTENTS

TENTH EDITION

SALAS
HILLE
ETGEN

CALCULUS

ONE AND SEVERAL VARIABLES

JOHN WILEY & SONS, INC.

In fond remembrance of
EINAR HILLE

ACQUISITIONS EDITOR	Mary Kittell
PUBLISHER	Laurie Rosatone
MARKETING MANAGER	Amy Sell
EDITORIAL ASSISTANT	Danielle Amico
MARKETING ASSISTANT	Tara Martinho
SENIOR PRODUCTION EDITOR	Sandra Dumas
DESIGNER	Hope Miller
SENIOR MEDIA EDITOR	Stefanie Liebman
PRODUCTION MANAGEMENT	Suzanne Ingrao
FREELANCE DEVELOPMENTAL EDITOR	Anne Scanlan-Rohrer
COVER IMAGE	Steven Puetzer/Masterfile

This book was set in New Times Roman by Techbooks, Inc. and printed and bound by Courier(Westford). The cover was printed by Courier(Westford).

This book is printed on acid-free paper. ♾

Library of Congress Cataloging-in-Publication Data

Salas, Saturnino L.
Calculus—10th ed/Saturnino Salas, Einar Hille, Garrett Etgen.

ISBN-13 978-0471-69804-3
ISBN-10 0-471-69804-0

Printed in the United States of America
10 9 8 7 6 5 4 3 2 1

CHAPTER 13

VECTORS IN THREE-DIMENSIONAL SPACE

13.1 RECTANGULAR SPACE COORDINATES

To introduce rectangular coordinates in three-dimensional space, we begin with a plane on which we have set up a rectangular coordinate system O-xy in the usual manner. Through the point O, which we continue to call the origin, we pass a third line, perpendicular to the other two. This third line we call the z-axis. We assign coordinates to the z-axis using the same scale as used on the x- and y-axes, assigning the z-coordinate 0 to the origin O.

For later convenience we orient the z-axis according to the *right-hand rule*: if the fingers of the right hand are curled from the positive x-axis toward the positive y-axis (the short route), the thumb points along the positive z-axis. (See Figure 13.1.1.)

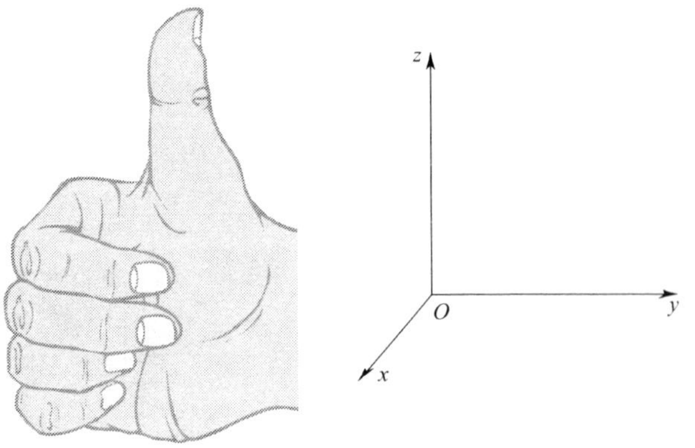

Figure 13.1.1

The point on the x-axis with x-coordinate x_0 is given space coordinates $(x_0, 0, 0)$; the point on the y-axis with y-coordinate y_0 is given space coordinates $(0, y_0, 0)$; the point on the z-axis with z-coordinate z_0 is given space coordinates $(0, 0, z_0)$.

There are now three coordinate planes; the xy-plane, the xz-plane, the yz-plane. A point P in three-dimensional space (see Figure 13.1.2) is assigned coordinates (x_0, y_0, z_0) provided that

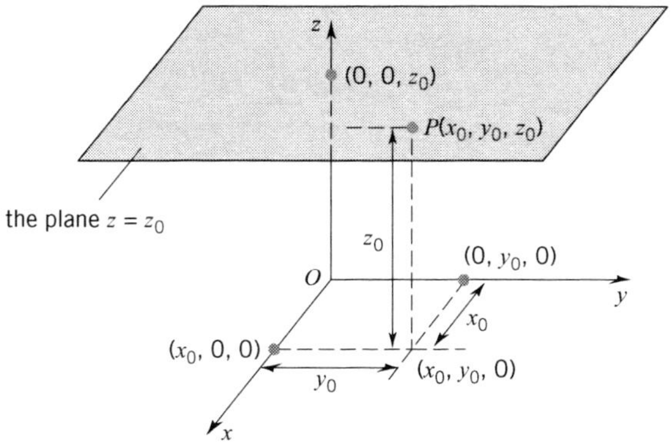

Figure 13.1.2

(1) the plane through P which is parallel to the yz-plane intersects the x-axis at $(x_0, 0, 0)$,
(2) the plane through P which is parallel to the xz-plane intersects the y-axis at $(0, y_0, 0)$,
(3) the plane through P which is parallel to the xy-plane intersects the z-axis at $(0, 0, z_0)$.

The coordinates x_0, y_0, z_0 are called the *rectangular coordinates of* P, or, in honor of Descartes, the *Cartesian coordinates of* P.

The equation $z = 0$ represents the set of all points with z-coordinate 0; this is the xy-plane. The equation $z = z_0$ represents the set of all points with z-coordinate z_0. This is the plane which is parallel to the xy-plane and intersects the z-axis at the point $(0, 0, z_0)$. (This plane with $z_0 > 0$ is pictured in Figure 13.1.2.)

Similarly, equation $y = 0$ represents the xz-plane and equation $y = y_0$ represents the plane which is parallel to the xz-plane and intersects the x-axis at the point $(0, y_0, 0)$.

In like manner, equation $x = 0$ represents the yz-plane and equation $x = x_0$ represents the plane which is parallel to the yz-plane and intersects the x-axis at the point $(x_0, 0, 0)$. (To establish these ideas in your mind, draw some figures.)

In Figure 13.1.3 we have drawn the planes $x = 1$ and $y = 3$. These planes intersect in a line which is parallel to the z-axis. The line intersects the xy-plane at the point $(1, 3, 0)$.

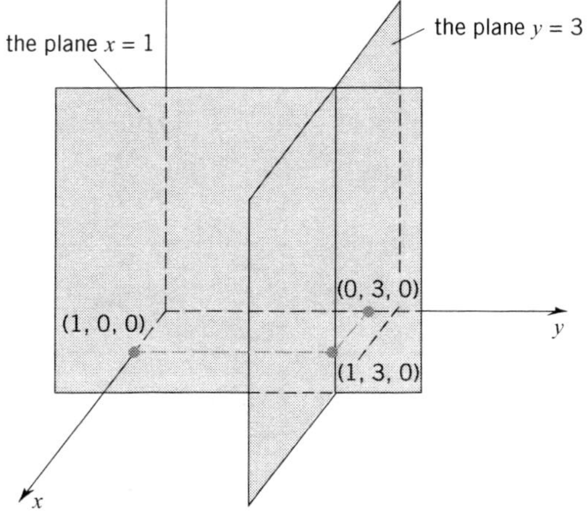

Figure 13.1.3

The Distance Formula

The distance $d(P_1, P_2)$ between two points $P_1(x_1, y_1, z_1)$ and $P_2(x_2, y_2, z_2)$ can be found by applying the Pythagorean theorem twice. With Q and R as in Figure 13.1.4, both P_1P_2R and P_1RQ form right triangles. From the first triangle

$$[d(P_1, P_2)]^2 = [d(P_1, R)]^2 + [d(R, P_2)]^2,$$

and from the second triangle

$$[d(P_1, R)]^2 = [d(Q, R)]^2 + [d(P_1, Q)]^2.$$

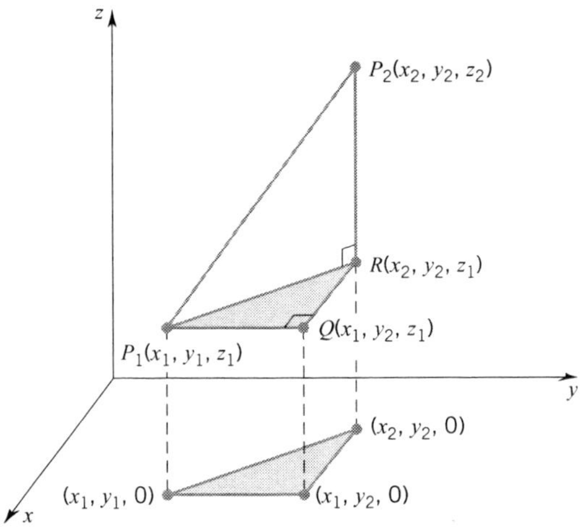

Figure 13.1.4

Combining these equations, we find that

$$\begin{aligned}[d(P_1, P_2)]^2 &= [d(Q, R)]^2 + [d(P_1, Q)]^2 + [d(R, P_2)]^2\\ &= (x_2 - x_1)^2 + (y_2 - y_1)^2 + (z_2 - z_1)^2.\end{aligned}$$

Taking square roots, we have the distance formula:

(13.1.1) $$d(P_1, P_2) = \sqrt{(x_2 - x_1)^2 + (y_2 - y_1)^2 + (z_2 - z_1)^2}.$$

The *sphere* of radius r centered at $P_0(a, b, c)$ is the set of points $P(x, y, z)$ for which $d(P, P_0) = r$. For such points $[d(P, P_0)]^2 = r^2$. Applying the distance formula, we have

(13.1.2) $$(x - a)^2 + (y - b)^2 + (z - c)^2 = r^2.$$

This is the equation of the sphere of radius r centered at $P_0(a, b, c)$. The equation

(13.1.3) $$x^2 + y^2 + z^2 = r^2$$

represents the sphere of radius r centered at the origin. The two spheres are depicted in Figure 13.1.5.

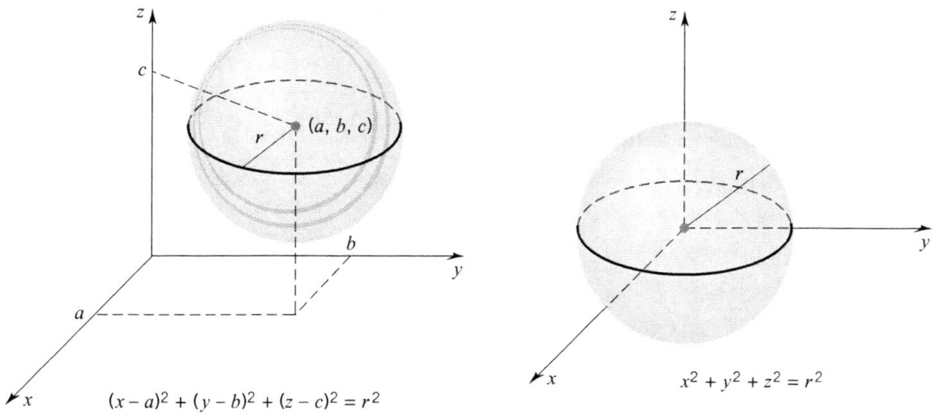

Figure 13.1.5

Example 1 The equation $(x-5)^2 + (y+2)^2 + z^2 = 9$ represents the sphere of radius 3 centered at the point $(5, -2, 0)$. ❑

Example 2 Show that the equation $x^2 + y^2 + z^2 + 6x + 2y - 4z = 11$ represents a sphere. Find the center of the sphere and the radius.

SOLUTION We write the equation as $(x^2 + 6x) + (y^2 + 2y) + (z^2 - 4z) = 11$ and complete the squares. The result,

$$(x^2 + 6x + 9) + (y^2 + 2y + 1) + (z^2 - 4z + 4) = 11 + 9 + 1 + 4 = 25,$$

can be written

$$(x+3)^2 + (y+1)^2 + (z-2)^2 = 25.$$

This equation represents the sphere of radius 5 centered at $(-3, -1, 2)$. ❑

Symmetry

You are already familiar with two kinds of symmetry: symmetry about a point and symmetry about a line. In space we can also speak of symmetry about a plane. (Figure 13.1.6.)

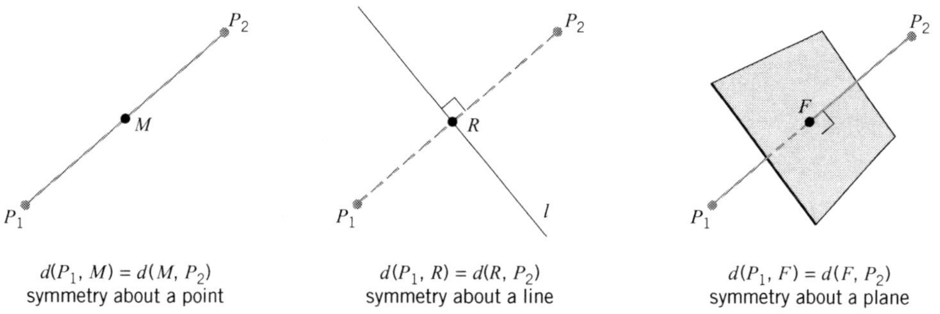

Figure 13.1.6

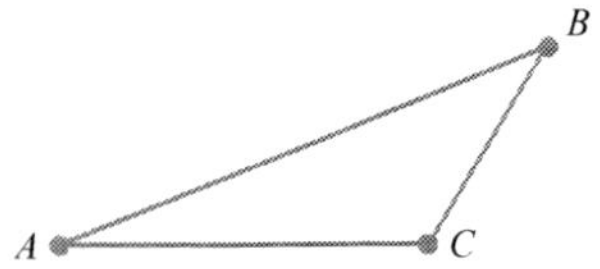

The Line Determined by Two Points

We can find the coordinates of the points of a line by using the distance formula. In general, for points A, B, C

$$d(A, B) \leq d(A, C) + d(C, B).$$

If

$$d(A, B) = d(A, C) + d(C, B),$$

we can conclude that A, B, C all lie on the same line, C between A and B.

THEOREM 13.1.4

The line l that passes through the points $A(a_1, a_2, a_3)$ and $B(b_1, b_2, b_3)$ consists of all points $P(x, y, z)$ with

$$x = a_1 + t(b_1 - a_1), \qquad y = a_2 + t(b_2 - a_2), \qquad z = a_3 + t(b_3 - a_3)$$

t ranging over the set of real numbers.

PROOF At $t = 0$, $P = A$; at $t = 1$, $P = B$. For the rest we rely on the distance formula. A straightforward calculation shows that

$$d(A, P) = |t| d(A, B) \qquad \text{and} \qquad d(P, B) = |1 - t|\, d(A, B).$$

If $0 < t < 1$, $|t| = t$ and $|1 - t| = 1 - t$. Consequently,

$$d(A, P) + d(P, B) = td(A, B) + (1 - t)d(A, B) = d(A, B).$$

The relation

$$d(A, P) + d(P, B) = d(A, B)$$

places P on l, P between A and B.

If $t > 1$, then $|t| = t$ and $|1 - t| = t - 1$. Consequently,

$$d(A, P) - d(P, B) = td(A, B) - (t - 1)d(A, B) = d(A, B).$$

The relation

$$d(A, B) + d(P, B) = d(A, P)$$

places P on l, B between A and P.

We leave it to you to show that if $t < 0$, then

$$d(P, A) + d(A, B) = d(P, B).$$

This places P on l, A between P and B. ❑

The argument used to prove Theorem 13.1.4 has some consequences worth recording.

(13.1.5) *The Line Segment* $\overline{AB}$. As t ranges from 0 to 1, the points $P(x, y, z)$ with

$$x = a_1 + t(b_1 - a_1), \qquad y = a_2 + t(b_2 - a_2), \qquad z = a_3 + t(b_3 - a_3)$$

trace out the line segment $\overline{AB}$.

PROOF As we made clear in the proof of Theorem 13.1.4, the values of t between 0 and 1 give the points P between A and B; $t = 0$ gives A and $t = 1$ gives B. ❑

(13.1.6) *The Midpoint Formula* The midpoint of $\overline{AB}$ has coordinates

$$x = \tfrac{1}{2}(a_1 + b_1), \quad y = \tfrac{1}{2}(a_2 + b_2), \quad z = \tfrac{1}{2}(a_3 + b_3).$$

PROOF For $P(x, y, z)$ as in (13.1.5)

$$d(A, P) = td(A, B).$$

For the midpoint $M(x, y, z)$ we have $t = \frac{1}{2}$. Thus

$$x = a_1 + \tfrac{1}{2}(b_1 - a_1) = \tfrac{1}{2}(a_1 + b_1)$$

$$y = a_2 + \tfrac{1}{2}(b_2 - a_2) = \tfrac{1}{2}(a_2 + b_2)$$

$$z = a_3 + \tfrac{1}{2}(b_3 - a_3) = \tfrac{1}{2}(a_3 + b_3). \quad ❑$$

EXERCISES 13.1

Exercises 1–4. Plot points A and B on a right-handed coordinate system. Then calculate the length of the line segment $\overline{AB}$ and find the midpoint.

1. $A(2, 0, 0)$, $B(0, 0, -4)$. **2.** $A(0, -2, 0)$, $B(0, 0, 6)$.

3. $A(0, -2, 5)$, $B(4, 1, 0)$. **4.** $A(4, 3, 0)$, $B(-2, 0, 6)$.

Exercises 5–10. Write an equation for the plane which passes through the point $P(3, 1, -2)$ and satisfies the given condition.

5. Parallel to the xy-plane.

6. Parallel to the xz-plane.

7. Perpendicular to the y-axis.

8. Perpendicular to the z-axis.

9. Parallel to the yz-plane.

10. Perpendicular to the x-axis.

Exercises 11–16. Write an equation for the sphere that satisfies the given conditions.

11. Centered at $P(0, 2, -1)$ with radius 3.

12. Centered at $P(1, 0, -2)$ with radius 4.

13. Centered at $P(2, 4, -4)$ and passes through the origin.

14. Centered at the origin and passes through $P(1, -2, 2)$.

15. The line segment that joins $P(0, 4, 2)$ to $Q(6, 0, 2)$ is a diameter.

16. Centered at $P(2, 3, -4)$ and tangent to the xy-plane.

Exercises 17–18. Show that the equation represents a sphere; find the center and radius.

17. $x^2 + y^2 + z^2 + 4x - 8y - 2z + 5 = 0$.

18. $3x^2 + 3y^2 + 3z^2 - 12x - 6z + 3 = 0$.

Exercises 19–30. The points $P(a, b, c)$ and $Q(2, 3, 5)$ are symmetric in the sense given. Find a, b, c.

19. About the xy-plane. **20.** About the xz-plane.

21. About the yz-plane. **22.** About the x-axis.

23. About the y-axis. **24.** About the z-axis.

25. About the origin. **26.** About the plane $x = 1$.

27. About the plane $y = -1$. **28.** About the plane $z = 4$.

29. About the point $R(0, 2, 1)$. **30.** About the point $R(4, 0, 1)$.

31. Show that the points $P(1, 2, 3)$, $Q(4, -5, 2)$, $R(0, 0, 0)$ are the vertices of a right triangle.

32. The points $A(5, -1, 3)$, $B(4, 2, 1)$, $C(2, 1, 0)$ are the midpoints of the sides of a triangle PQR. Find the vertices P, Q, R of the triangle.

Exercises 33–38. Describe the solid T.

33. $T = \{(x, y, z) : x^2 + y^2 + z^2 \le 4\}$.

34. $T = \{(x, y, z) : x^2 + y^2 + z^2 > 9\}$.

35. $T = \{(x, y, z) : 0 \le x \le 1, 0 \le y \le 2, 0 \le z \le 3\}$.

36. $T = \{(x, y, z) : |x| \le 2, |y| \le 2, |z| \le 2\}$.

37. $T = \{(x, y, z) : x^2 + y^2 \le 4, 0 \le z \le 4\}$.

38. $T = \{(x, y, z) : 4 < x^2 + y^2 + z^2 < 9\}$.

39. The point $M(1, 2, 3)$ bisects the line segment $\overline{AB}$. Find the coordinates of B given that A has coordinates 2, 3, 4.

40. Sketch a right-handed coordinate system O-xyz, choose an arbitrary point $P(a_1, a_2, a_3)$, and draw the line determined by O and P. On the line mark the following points:

(a) $Q(-a_1, -a_2, -a_3)$. (b) $R(2a_1, 2a_2, 2a_3)$.

(c) $S(-\frac{1}{2}a_1, -\frac{1}{2}a_2, -\frac{1}{2}a_3)$. (d) $T(\frac{1}{4}a_1, \frac{1}{4}a_2, \frac{1}{4}a_3)$.

41. Find the coordinates of the points P_1 and P_2 which trisect the line segment $\overline{AB}$ that joins $A(a_1, a_2, a_3)$ to $B(b_1, b_2, b_3)$.

42. Set $A(1, -2, \sqrt{2})$ and $B(2, 1, 0)$. Find the coordinates of P given that P lies on $\overline{AB}$ at a distance of 3 units from A.

On the xy-plane lines have equations of the form $Ax + By + C = 0$ with A and B not both zero. Later in this chapter we show that planes in space have equations of the form $Ax + By + Cz + D = 0$ with A, B, C not all zero.

43. Write an equation for the plane that passes through the points $(x_0, 0, 0)$, $(0, y_0, 0)$, $(0, 0, z_0)$. Assume that $x_0 y_0 z_0 \neq 0$.

44. Write an equation for the plane that passes through the xy-plane at the point $(x_0, y_0, 0)$, through the xz-plane at the point $(x_0, 0, z_0)$, through the yz-plane at the point $(0, y_0, z_0)$. Assume that $x_0 y_0 z_0 \neq 0$.

45. The line that passes through the origin and the point $P(a_1, a_2, a_3)$ intersects the plane $z = z_0$ at the point Q. Find the coordinates of Q

(i) given that $a_3 \neq 0$; (ii) given that $a_3 = 0$.

46. The line that passes through the origin O and the point $P(a_1, a_2, a_3)$ intersects the plane $x = x_0$ at the point Q. Find the coordinates of Q

(i) given that $a_1 \neq 0$; (ii) given that $a_1 = 0$.

47. The ray that emanates from the origin and passes through the point $P(a_1, a_2, a_3)$ intersects the sphere $x^2 + y^2 + z^2 = 1$ at one point. What are the coordinates of that point?

48. The line that passes through the origin and the point $P(a_1, a_2, a_3)$ intersects the unit sphere at two points. What are the coordinates of these points?

13.2 VECTORS IN THREE-DIMENSIONAL SPACE

Introduction

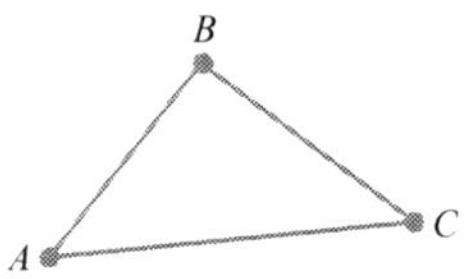

What is the area of triangle ABC in the downward direction? This question makes no sense. Area is number given in terms of square units. There is no direction to it.

Volume, temperature, mass are also directionless, and, once units of measurement have been chosen, can be specified in terms of those units by a single number.

Some quantities have direction. A move 2 feet down is not the same as a move 2 feet to the right. Flying south at 300 mph does not take you on the same path as flying east at the same speed. A force of 5 newtons to the left does not have the same effect as a force of 5 newtons to the right.

Directed quantities (such as displacement, velocity, acceleration, force) are called *vector quantities.*

To specify a vector quantity, we need to specify two elements: the magnitude of the quantity and the direction. One way to do this is to draw an arrow. Specify magnitude by the length of the arrow and indicate direction by pointing the arrow.

Arrows are ideal for geometric insight, but they are difficult to use with precision and don't lend themselves well to calculations. We can overcome these difficulties by using number triples. Number triples are easy to use with precision, lend themselves well to computation, and, once a coordinate system has been established, can be interpreted as arrows in three-dimensional space.

This takes us to the notion of vector.

Vectors

By a *vector* **a** we mean an ordered triple of real numbers:

$$\mathbf{a} = (a_1, a_2, a_3).^\dagger$$

The numbers a_1, a_2, a_3 are called the *components of* **a**.

To say that two vectors are "equal" means that they have the same components;

$$(a_1, a_2, a_3) = (b_1, b_2, b_3) \quad \text{iff} \quad a_1 = b_1,\ a_2 = b_2,\ a_3 = b_3.$$

† This is not the most general notion of vector, but it is the most useful one for our purposes. More on this later.

Vectors can be added:

(13.2.1)

for
$$\mathbf{a} = (a_1, a_2, a_3) \qquad \text{and} \qquad \mathbf{b} = (b_1, b_2, b_3)$$
we define
$$\mathbf{a} + \mathbf{b} = (a_1 + b_1, a_2 + b_2, a_3 + b_3).$$

Since the addition of real numbers is commutative and associative, vector addition is commutative and associative:

$$\mathbf{a} + \mathbf{b} = \mathbf{b} + \mathbf{a}, \qquad (\mathbf{a} + \mathbf{b}) + \mathbf{c} = \mathbf{a} + (\mathbf{b} + \mathbf{c}).$$

Vectors can be multiplied by *scalars* (real numbers):

(13.2.2)

for
$$\mathbf{a} = (a_1, a_2, a_3) \qquad \text{and} \qquad \alpha \text{ real}$$
we define
$$\alpha\,\mathbf{a} = (\alpha a_1, \alpha a_2, \alpha a_3).$$

Routine calculation shows that

$$\alpha(\mathbf{a} + \mathbf{b}) = \alpha\,\mathbf{a} + \alpha\,\mathbf{b} \qquad \text{and} \qquad (\alpha + \beta)\mathbf{a} = \alpha\,\mathbf{a} + \beta\,\mathbf{a}.$$

By the *zero vector* we mean the vector $\mathbf{0} = (0, 0, 0)$. For all vectors $\mathbf{a}$,

$$0\,\mathbf{a} = \mathbf{0} \qquad \text{and} \qquad \mathbf{a} + \mathbf{0} = \mathbf{0} + \mathbf{a} = \mathbf{a}.$$

By the vector $-\mathbf{b}$ we mean $(-1)\,\mathbf{b}$; that is,

$$-(b_1, b_2, b_3) = (-b_1, -b_2, -b_3).$$

By $\mathbf{a} - \mathbf{b}$ we mean $\mathbf{a} + (-\mathbf{b})$; that is,

$$\begin{aligned}(a_1, a_2, a_3) - (b_1, b_2, b_3) &= (a_1, a_2, a_3) + (-b_1, -b_2, -b_3)\\ &= (a_1 - b_1, a_2 - b_2, a_3 - b_3).\end{aligned}$$

Example 1 Given that $\mathbf{a} = (1, -1, 2)$, $\mathbf{b} = (2, 3, -1)$, $\mathbf{c} = (8, 7, 1)$, find **(a)** $\mathbf{a} - \mathbf{b}$. **(b)** $2\mathbf{a} + \mathbf{b}$. **(c)** $3\mathbf{a} - 7\mathbf{b}$. **(d)** $2\mathbf{a} + 3\mathbf{b} - \mathbf{c}$.

SOLUTION

(a) $\mathbf{a} - \mathbf{b} = (1, -1, 2) - (2, 3, -1) = (1 - 2, -1 - 3, 2 + 1) = (-1, -4, 3)$.

(b) $2\mathbf{a} + \mathbf{b} = 2(1, -1, 2) + (2, 3, -1) = (2, -2, 4) + (2, 3, -1) = (4, 1, 3)$.

(c) $3\mathbf{a} - 7\mathbf{b} = 3(1, -1, 2) - 7(2, 3, -1)$
$= (3, -3, 6) - (14, 21, -7) = (-11, -24, 13)$.

(d) $2\mathbf{a} + 3\mathbf{b} - \mathbf{c} = 2(1, -1, 2) + 3(2, 3, -1) - (8, 7, 1)$
$= (2, -2, 4) + (6, 9, -3) - (8, 7, 1) = (0, 0, 0) = \mathbf{0}$. ❑

Geometric Interpretation of Vectors

Vectors (as we have defined them) have geometric significance only after a coordinate system has been established. In Figure 13.2.1 we have set up a right-handed coordinate system O-xyz. Using that coordinate system, we can represent vectors by arrows in three-dimensional space.

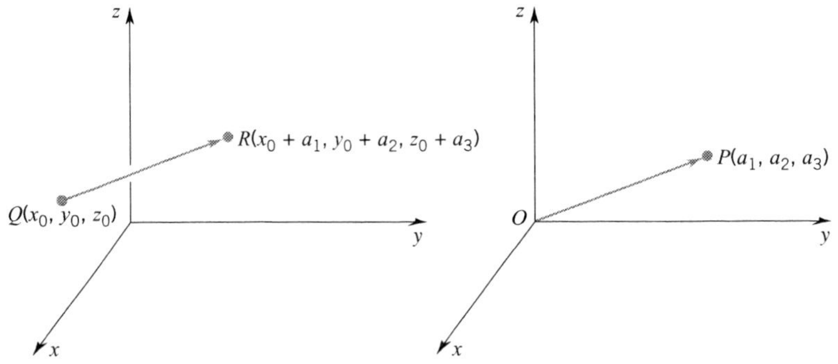

Figure 13.2.1

To represent the vector $\mathbf{a} = (a_1, a_2, a_3)$, we choose a point $Q(x_0, y_0, z_0)$ as our starting point (we can choose *any* point) and draw the arrow $\overrightarrow{QR}$ to the point $R(x_0 + a_1, y_0 + a_2, z_0 + a_3)$. If we start the arrow at the origin, we use the arrow

$$\overrightarrow{OP} \qquad \text{with} \qquad P(a_1, a_2, a_3).$$

One advantage of using $\overrightarrow{OP}$ is that there are fewer coordinates to keep track of.

Arrows $\overrightarrow{QR}$ and $\overrightarrow{OP}$ have different locations, but because they have the same length and the same direction,[†] they represent the *same* vector: the vector $\mathbf{a} = (a_1, a_2, a_3)$.

The zero vector $\mathbf{0} = (0, 0, 0)$ can be thought of as an arrow of length 0. The zero vector has no direction.

Visualizing a + b

For $\mathbf{a} = (a_1, a_2, a_3)$ and $\mathbf{b} = (b_1, b_2, b_3)$ we defined

$$\mathbf{a} + \mathbf{b} = (a_1 + b_1, a_2 + b_2, a_3 + b_3).$$

What does this mean in terms of arrows? Namely, if we have an arrow for $\mathbf{a}$ and an arrow for $\mathbf{b}$, how do we get an arrow for $\mathbf{a} + \mathbf{b}$? By proceeding as in Figure 13.2.2. For if P has coordinates (x_0, y_0, z_0), then

Q has coordinates $(x_0 + a_1, y_0 + a_2, z_0 + a_3)$ and

R has coordinates $(x_0 + a_1 + b_1, y_0 + a_2 + b_2, z_0 + a_3 + b_3)$.

Thus the arrow $\overrightarrow{PR}$ does represent $\mathbf{a} + \mathbf{b}$.

One more point. If we view $\mathbf{a}$ and $\mathbf{b}$ as emanating from the same point (Figure 13.2.3), then $\mathbf{a} + \mathbf{b}$ acts as the diagonal of the parallelogram generated by $\mathbf{a}$ and $\mathbf{b}$.

[†]That $\overrightarrow{QR}$ and $\overrightarrow{OP}$ have the same length and the same direction can be seen by noting that R is obtained from Q exactly as P is obtained from O: by adding a_1 to the first coordinate, adding a_2 to the second coordinate, adding a_3 to the third coordinate. Thus R is positioned with respect to Q exactly as P is positioned with respect to O.

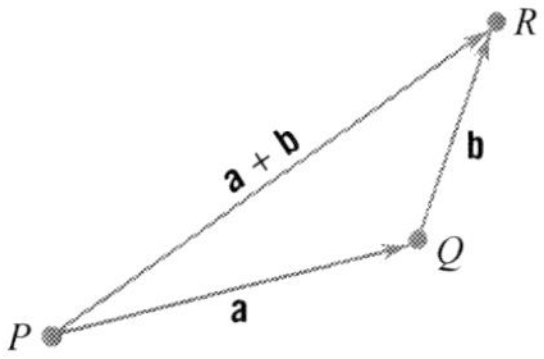

Figure 13.2.2

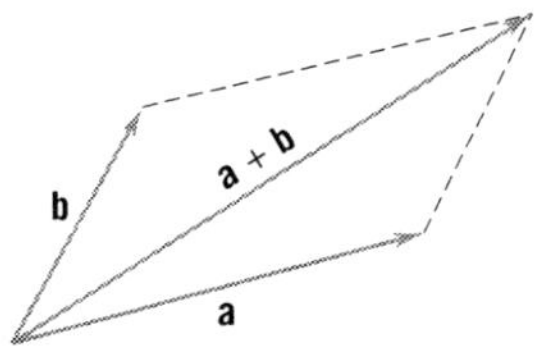

Figure 13.2.3

Norm

The properties of vectors in three dimensions are abstracted from the properties of the arrows used to represent them. Since every arrow $\overrightarrow{QR}$ used to represent the vector $\mathbf{a} = (a_1, a_2, a_3)$ has length $\sqrt{a_1^2 + a_2^2 + a_3^2}$, we can use this number as a measure of **a**.

By the *norm (magnitude, length)* of the vector $\mathbf{a} = (a_1, a_2, a_3)$ we mean the number

(13.2.3)
$$\|\mathbf{a}\| = \sqrt{a_1^2 + a_2^2 + a_3^2}.$$

The norm properties of vectors are similar to the absolute-value properties of real numbers. In particular

(13.2.4)

(1) $\|\mathbf{a}\| \geq 0$ and $\|\mathbf{a}\| = 0$ iff $\mathbf{a} = \mathbf{0}$.

(2) $\|\alpha\mathbf{a}\| = |\alpha|\ \|\mathbf{a}\|$.

(3) $\|\mathbf{a} + \mathbf{b}\| \leq \|\mathbf{a}\| + \|\mathbf{b}\|$. (the triangle inequality)

Property (1) is obvious. Property (2) is easy to verify:

$$\|\alpha\mathbf{a}\| = \sqrt{(\alpha a_1)^2 + (\alpha a_2)^2 + (\alpha a_3)^2} = |\alpha|\sqrt{a_1^2 + a_2^2 + a_3^2} = |\alpha|\ \|\mathbf{a}\|.$$

Property (3), the triangle inequality, follows from observing that the length of a side of a triangle cannot exceed the sum of the lengths of the other two sides. (Figure 13.2.4.)

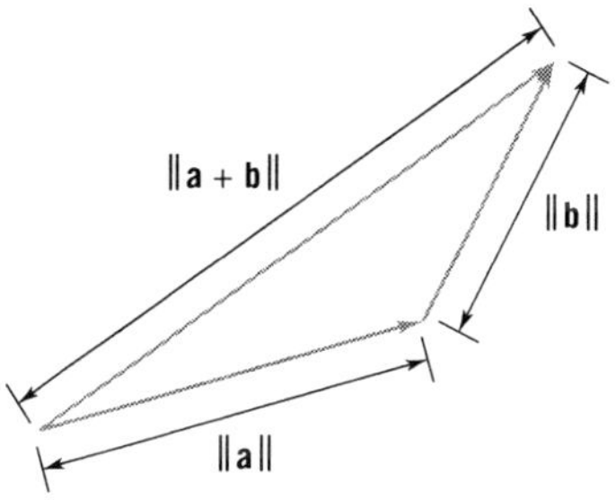

Figure 13.2.4

Example 2 Given that $\mathbf{a} = (1, -2, 3)$ and $\mathbf{b} = (-4, 1, 0)$, calculate

(a) $\|\mathbf{a}\|$. **(b)** $\|\mathbf{b}\|$. **(c)** $\|\mathbf{a} + \mathbf{b}\|$. **(d)** $\|\mathbf{a} - \mathbf{b}\|$. **(e)** $\|-7\mathbf{a}\|$.
(f) $\|2\mathbf{a} - 3\mathbf{b}\|$.

SOLUTION

(a) $\|\mathbf{a}\| = \sqrt{1^2 + (-2)^2 + 3^2} = \sqrt{1 + 4 + 9} = \sqrt{14}$.

(b) $\|\mathbf{b}\| = \sqrt{(-4)^2 + 1^2 + 0^2} = \sqrt{16 + 1 + 0} = \sqrt{17}$.

(c) $\|\mathbf{a} + \mathbf{b}\| = \|(-3, -1, 3)\| = \sqrt{(-3)^2 + (-1)^2 + 3^2} = \sqrt{9 + 1 + 9} = \sqrt{19}$.

(d) $\|\mathbf{a} - \mathbf{b}\| = \|(5, -3, 3)\| = \sqrt{5^2 + (-3)^2 + 3^2} = \sqrt{25 + 9 + 9} = \sqrt{43}$.

(e) $\|-7\mathbf{a}\| = |-7|\ \|\mathbf{a}\| = 7\sqrt{14}$.

(f) $\|2\mathbf{a} - 3\mathbf{b}\| = \|2(1, -2, 3) - 3(-4, 1, 0)\|$
$= \|(14, -7, 6)\| = \sqrt{14^2 + (-7)^2 + 6^2}$
$= \sqrt{196 + 49 + 36} = \sqrt{281}$. ❑

Scalar Multiples

Start with numbers α, β both different from 0. The triangle inequality gives

$$|\alpha + \beta| \leq |\alpha| + |\beta|.$$

If $|\alpha + \beta| = |\alpha| + |\beta|$, we can conclude that α and β have the same sign. Now start with vectors **a, b** both different from **0**. The triangle inequality gives

$$\|\mathbf{a} + \mathbf{b}\| \leq \|\mathbf{a}\| + \|\mathbf{b}\|.$$

If $\|\mathbf{a} + \mathbf{b}\| = \|\mathbf{a}\| + \|\mathbf{b}\|$, we can conclude that **a** and **b** have the same direction. To convince yourself of this, examine Figure 13.2.4.

Now start with $\mathbf{a} \neq \mathbf{0}$. If $\alpha > 0$, then, as you can check,

$$\|\mathbf{a} + \alpha\mathbf{a}\| = \|\mathbf{a}\| + \|\alpha\mathbf{a}\|.$$

It follows that, if $\alpha > 0$, the vectors **a** and $\alpha\mathbf{a}$ have the same direction. If $\alpha < 0$, then $-\alpha > 0$. Reasoning as above we see that

$$\| - \mathbf{a} + (-\alpha)(-\mathbf{a})\| = \| - \mathbf{a}\| + \| - \alpha(-\mathbf{a})\|.$$

This tells us that $-\mathbf{a}$ and $(-\alpha)(-\mathbf{a}) = \alpha\mathbf{a}$ have the same direction, and thus **a** and $\alpha\mathbf{a}$ have opposite directions.

We now have a full characterization of $\alpha\mathbf{a}$. (Obviously if $\mathbf{a} = \mathbf{0}$, then $\alpha\mathbf{a} = \mathbf{0}$. Thus we can concentrate on $\mathbf{a} \neq \mathbf{0}$.)

(13.2.5) For $\mathbf{a} \neq \mathbf{0}$, the vector $\mathbf{b} = \alpha\mathbf{a}$ is the unique vector of length $|\alpha|\|\mathbf{a}\|$, which has the direction of **a** if $\alpha > 0$ and the opposite direction if $\alpha < 0$.

Figure 13.2.5 gives some examples.

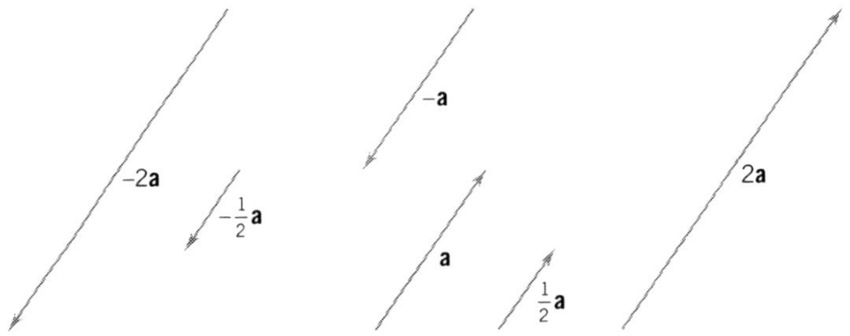

Figure 13.2.5

Since $\mathbf{a} - \mathbf{b} = \mathbf{a} + (-\mathbf{b})$, we can draw the vector $\mathbf{a} - \mathbf{b}$ by drawing $-\mathbf{b}$ and adding it to the vector **a**. (Figure 13.2.6.)

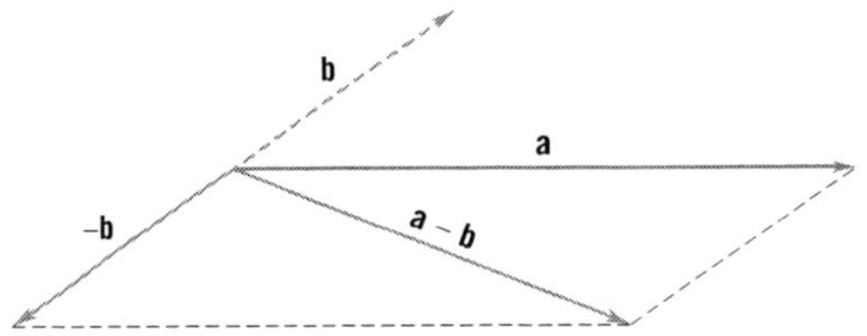

Figure 13.2.6

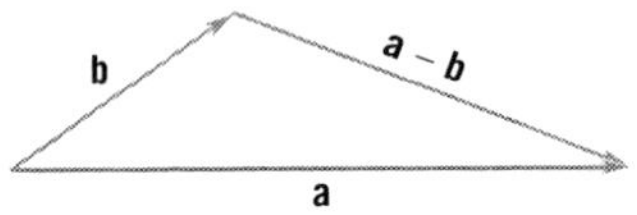

Figure 13.2.7

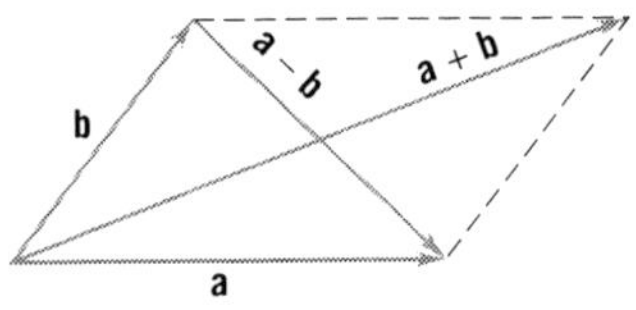

Figure 13.2.8

We can obtain the same result more easily by noting that $\mathbf{a} - \mathbf{b}$ is the vector that we must add to **b** to obtain **a**. (Figure 13.2.7.)

In Figure 13.2.8 we have drawn the parallelogram generated by **a** and **b**. The vectors $\mathbf{a} + \mathbf{b}$ and $\mathbf{a} - \mathbf{b}$ are the diagonals of the parallelogram.

Parallel Vectors

(13.2.6) For $\mathbf{a} \neq \mathbf{0}$, the vectors parallel to **a** are by definition the scalar multiples $\alpha\mathbf{a}$.

These are the vectors which have the direction of **a**, the vectors which have the direction $-\mathbf{a}$, and, since $\mathbf{0} = 0 \cdot \mathbf{a}$, the zero vector.

If $\mathbf{a} = \mathbf{0}$, the scalar multiples of **a** are all **0**.

(13.2.7) By special convention, all vectors are said to be *parallel* to **0**.

For $\mathbf{a} = (2, -2, 6)$, $\mathbf{b} = (1, -1, 3)$, $\mathbf{c} = (-1, 1, -3)$ we have

$$\mathbf{b} = \tfrac{1}{2}\mathbf{a} \qquad \text{and} \qquad \mathbf{c} = -\tfrac{1}{2}\mathbf{a}.$$

This tells us that **a** and **b** are parallel and have the same direction, whereas **a** and **c**, though parallel, have opposite directions. Figure 13.2.9 illustrates these assertions.

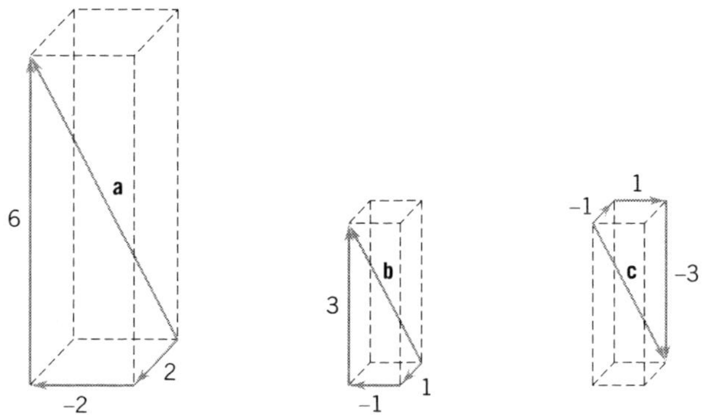

a = (2, −2, 6) **b** = (1, −1, 3) **c** = (−1, 1, −3)

some parallel vectors

Figure 13.2.9

It is easy to see that

(13.2.8) if **a** and **b** are both parallel to **c**, then every linear combination $\alpha\mathbf{a} + \beta\mathbf{b}$ is also parallel to **c**.

PROOF Suppose that **a** and **b** are parallel to **c**. If $\mathbf{c} = \mathbf{0}$, then every vector is parallel to **c** and there is nothing to prove. If $\mathbf{c} \neq \mathbf{0}$, then **a** and **b** are scalar multiples of **c**:

$$\mathbf{a} = \alpha_1\mathbf{c}, \qquad \mathbf{b} = \beta_1\mathbf{c}.$$

Then

$$\alpha\,\mathbf{a} + \beta\,\mathbf{b} = \alpha(\alpha_1\mathbf{c}) + \beta(\beta_1\mathbf{c}) = (\alpha\alpha_1 + \beta\beta_1)\mathbf{c}$$

is also parallel to **c**. ❑

Unit Vectors

Vectors of norm 1 are called *unit vectors.* For each nonzero vector **a** there is a unique unit vector $\mathbf{u_a}$ which has the direction of **a**. As we show below,

(13.2.9) $$\mathbf{u_a} = \frac{1}{\|\mathbf{a}\|}\mathbf{a} = \frac{\mathbf{a}}{\|\mathbf{a}\|}.$$

PROOF We know two things about $\mathbf{u_a}$:

$$\|\mathbf{u_a}\| = 1 \quad \text{and} \quad \mathbf{u_a} = \alpha\mathbf{a} \quad \text{for some } \alpha > 0.$$

These relations give

$$1 = \|\alpha\mathbf{a}\| = |\alpha|\,\|\mathbf{a}\| = \alpha\|\mathbf{a}\|.$$

It follows that

$$\alpha = \frac{1}{\|\mathbf{a}\|}. \quad \square$$

While

$$\mathbf{u_a} = \frac{\mathbf{a}}{\|\mathbf{a}\|}$$

is the unit vector in the direction of **a**,

$$-\mathbf{u_a} = -\frac{\mathbf{a}}{\|\mathbf{a}\|}$$

is the unit vector in the opposite direction.

We single out for attention the vectors

$$\mathbf{i} = (1, 0, 0), \qquad \mathbf{j} = (0, 1, 0), \qquad \mathbf{k} = (0, 0, 1).$$

These unit vectors (they all have norm 1) are particularly useful in calculations because every vector **a** can be expressed in a simple unique way as a linear combination of these vectors:

(13.2.10) if $\mathbf{a} = (a_1, a_2, a_3)$, then $\mathbf{a} = a_1\,\mathbf{i} + a_2\,\mathbf{j} + a_3\,\mathbf{k}$.

PROOF

$$\begin{aligned}(a_1, a_2, a_3) &= (a_1, 0, 0) + (0, a_2, 0) + (0, 0, a_3)\\ &= a_1(1, 0, 0) + a_2(0, 1, 0) + a_3(0, 0, 1)\\ &= a_1\,\mathbf{i} + a_2\,\mathbf{j} + a_3\,\mathbf{k}. \quad \square\end{aligned}$$

The components of **a**, the numbers a_1, a_2, a_3, can thus be called the **i**, **j**, **k** *components* of **a**.

Example 3 Set $\mathbf{a} = 3\mathbf{i} - \mathbf{j} + \mathbf{k}$ and $\mathbf{b} = 2\mathbf{i} + 3\mathbf{j} - \mathbf{k}$.

(a) Express $2\mathbf{a} - \mathbf{b}$ as a linear combination of **i**, **j**, **k**.

(b) Calculate $\|2\mathbf{a} - \mathbf{b}\|$.

(c) Find the unit vector $\mathbf{u_c}$ in the direction of $\mathbf{c} = 2\mathbf{a} - \mathbf{b}$.

SOLUTION

(a) $2\mathbf{a} - \mathbf{b} = 2(3\mathbf{i} - \mathbf{j} + \mathbf{k}) - (2\mathbf{i} + 3\mathbf{j} - \mathbf{k})$
$= 6\mathbf{i} - 2\mathbf{j} + 2\mathbf{k} - 2\mathbf{i} - 3\mathbf{j} + \mathbf{k} = 4\mathbf{i} - 5\mathbf{j} + 3\mathbf{k}.$

(b) $\|2\mathbf{a} - \mathbf{b}\| = \|4\mathbf{i} - 5\mathbf{j} + 3\mathbf{k}\| = \sqrt{16 + 25 + 9} = \sqrt{50} = 5\sqrt{2}.$

(c) $\mathbf{u_c} = \dfrac{2\mathbf{a} - \mathbf{b}}{\|2\mathbf{a} - \mathbf{b}\|} = \dfrac{1}{5\sqrt{2}}(4\mathbf{i} - 5\mathbf{j} + 3\mathbf{k}).$ ❑

On the Distinction Between Points and Vectors

We make a distinction between the point P with coordinates a_1, a_2, a_3 and the vector $\mathbf{a}$ with components a_1, a_2, a_3. The point P has a definite location, but it has no magnitude and no direction. The vector $\mathbf{a}$ has a definite magnitude and (unless it is the zero vector) a definite direction. However, it has no location. We can represent it by an arrow that starts at any point we choose. The vector operations that we define depend on magnitude and direction, not on location.

Vectors as Used in Plane Geometry

A vector $\mathbf{a}$ in the xy-plane is an ordered triple of the form $(a_1, a_2, 0)$. When working entirely in the xy-plane, we can drop the final zero and write $\mathbf{a} = (a_1, a_2)$. Now

$$\mathbf{0} = (0, 0) \qquad \text{and} \qquad \|\mathbf{a}\| = \sqrt{a_1^2 + a_2^2}.$$

Vector addition and multiplication by scalars reduce to

$$(a_1, a_2) + (b_1, b_2) = (a_1 + b_1, a_2 + b_2), \qquad \alpha(a_1, a_2) = (\alpha a_1, \alpha a_2).$$

In this context, we set

$$\mathbf{i} = (1, 0) \qquad \text{and} \qquad \mathbf{j} = (0, 1). \qquad \text{(There is no } \mathbf{k}.\text{)}$$

Every plane vector $\mathbf{a} = (a_1, a_2)$ can be expressed as a linear combination of these $\mathbf{i}$ and $\mathbf{j}$:

$$\mathbf{a} = (a_1, a_2) = a_1\mathbf{i} + a_2\mathbf{j}.$$

All the notions introduced for vectors in 3-space apply (with obvious modification) to vectors restricted to the xy-plane. Just drop the third component.

Remark: On the Use of Boldface to Indicate Vectors In this text we have used boldface to indicate vectors, but that is not easy to do without special equipment. Here are some other ways to indicate vectors

$$\overrightarrow{a}, \quad \underrightarrow{a}, \quad \tilde{a}, \quad \underset{\sim}{a}, \quad \hat{a}. \quad ❑$$

EXERCISES 13.2

Exercises 1–4. The vector $\mathbf{a}$ is represented by the arrow $\overrightarrow{PQ}$ with P and Q as given. Determine $\mathbf{a}$ and $\|\mathbf{a}\|$.

1. $P(1, -2, 5),\ Q(4, 2, 3).$

2. $P(4, -2, 0),\ Q(2, 4, 0).$

3. $P(0, 3, 1),\ Q(0, 1, 0).$

4. $P(-4, 0, 7),\ Q(0, 3, -1).$

Exercises 5–8. Set $\mathbf{a} = (1, -2, 3)$, $\mathbf{b} = (3, 0, -1)$, $\mathbf{c} = (-4, 2, 1)$. Then write each vector below as an ordered triple of real numbers.

5. $2\mathbf{a} - \mathbf{b}$.

6. $2\mathbf{b} + 3\mathbf{c}$.

7. $-2\mathbf{a} + \mathbf{b} - \mathbf{c}$.

8. $\mathbf{a} + 3\mathbf{b} - 2\mathbf{c}$.

Exercises 9–12. Simplify the linear combination.

9. $(2\mathbf{i} - \mathbf{j} + \mathbf{k}) + (\mathbf{i} - 3\mathbf{j} + 5\mathbf{k})$.

10. $(6\mathbf{j} - \mathbf{k}) + (3\mathbf{i} - \mathbf{j} + 2\mathbf{k})$.

11. $2(\mathbf{j} + \mathbf{k}) - 3(\mathbf{i} + \mathbf{j} - 2\mathbf{k})$.

12. $2(\mathbf{i} - \mathbf{j}) + 6(2\mathbf{i} + \mathbf{j} - 2\mathbf{k})$.

Exercises 13–18. Calculate the norm of the vector.

13. $3\mathbf{i} + 4\mathbf{j}$.

14. $\mathbf{i} - \mathbf{j}$.

15. $2\mathbf{i} + \mathbf{j} - 2\mathbf{k}$.

16. $6\mathbf{i} + 2\mathbf{j} - \mathbf{k}$.

17. $\frac{1}{2}(\mathbf{i} + 4\mathbf{j}) - (\frac{3}{2}\mathbf{i} + \mathbf{k})$.

18. $(\mathbf{i} - \mathbf{j}) + 2(\mathbf{j} - \mathbf{i}) + (\mathbf{k} - \mathbf{j})$.

19. Set

$$\mathbf{a} = \mathbf{i} - \mathbf{j} + 2\mathbf{k}, \qquad \mathbf{b} = 2\mathbf{i} - \mathbf{j} + 2\mathbf{k},$$

$$\mathbf{c} = 3\mathbf{i} - 3\mathbf{j} + 6\mathbf{k}, \qquad \mathbf{d} = -2\mathbf{i} + 2\mathbf{j} - 4\mathbf{k}.$$

(a) Which vectors are parallel?
(b) Which vectors have the same direction?
(c) Which vectors have opposite directions?

Exercises 20–23. Points $P(1, 4, -2)$ and $Q(3, -1, 1)$ are given. Find the coordinates of the point R that satisfies the given condition.

20. $\overrightarrow{QR}$ and $\overrightarrow{OP}$ represent the same vector.

21. $\overrightarrow{RQ}$ and $\overrightarrow{OP}$ represent the same vector.

22. $\overrightarrow{OP}$ represents the vector $\mathbf{a}$ and $\overrightarrow{RQ}$ represents the vector $3\mathbf{a}$.

23. $\overrightarrow{OP}$ represents the vector $\mathbf{a}$ and $\overrightarrow{RQ}$ represents the vector $-2\mathbf{a}$.

24. (*Important*) Prove the following version of the triangle inequality:

$$\big|\|\mathbf{a}\| - \|\mathbf{b}\|\big| \leq \|\mathbf{a} - \mathbf{b}\|.$$

Assume the triangle inequality as stated in (13.2.4).

Exercises 25–28. Find the unit vector in the direction of $\mathbf{a}$.

25. $\mathbf{a} = (3, -4, 0)$.

26. $\mathbf{a} = -2\mathbf{i} + 3\mathbf{j}$.

27. $\mathbf{a} = \mathbf{i} - 2\mathbf{j} + 2\mathbf{k}$.

28. $\mathbf{a} = (2, 1, 2)$.

Exercises 29–30. Find the unit vector in the direction opposite to the direction of $\mathbf{a}$.

29. $\mathbf{a} = -\mathbf{i} + 3\mathbf{j} + 2\mathbf{k}$.

30. $\mathbf{a} = 2\mathbf{i} - \mathbf{k}$.

31. Label the vector.

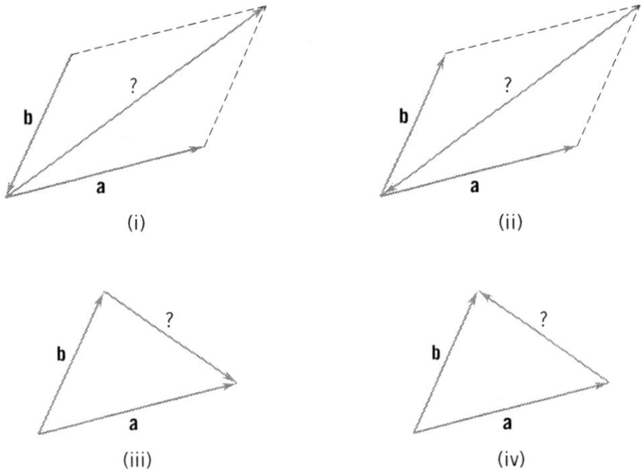

32. Set $\mathbf{a} = (1, 1, 1)$, $\mathbf{b} = (-1, 3, 2)$, $\mathbf{c} = (-3, 0, 1)$, $\mathbf{d} = (4, -1, 1)$.

(a) Express $\mathbf{a} + 2\mathbf{b} + 3\mathbf{c} + 4\mathbf{d}$ as a linear combination of $\mathbf{i}, \mathbf{j}, \mathbf{k}$.
(b) Find scalars A, B, C such that $\mathbf{d} = A\mathbf{a} + B\mathbf{b} + C\mathbf{c}$.

33. Set $\mathbf{a} = (2, 0, -1)$, $\mathbf{b} = (1, 3, 5)$, $\mathbf{c} = (-1, 1, 1)$, $\mathbf{d} = (1, 1, 6)$.

(a) Express $\mathbf{a} - 3\mathbf{b} + 2\mathbf{c} + 4\mathbf{d}$ as a linear combination of $\mathbf{i}, \mathbf{j}, \mathbf{k}$.
(b) Find scalars A, B, C such that $\mathbf{d} = A\mathbf{a} + B\mathbf{b} + C\mathbf{c}$.

34. Find α given that $3\mathbf{i} + \mathbf{j} - \mathbf{k}$ and $\alpha\mathbf{i} - 4\mathbf{j} + 4\mathbf{k}$ are parallel.

35. Find α given that $3\mathbf{i} + \mathbf{j}$ and $\alpha\mathbf{j} - \mathbf{k}$ have the same length.

36. Find the unit vector in the direction of $\mathbf{i} - 2\mathbf{j} + 2\mathbf{k}$.

37. Find α given that $\|\alpha\mathbf{i} + (\alpha - 1)\mathbf{j} + (\alpha + 1)\mathbf{k}\| = 2$.

38. Find the vector of norm 2 in the direction of $\mathbf{i} + 2\mathbf{j} - \mathbf{k}$.

39. Find the vectors of norm 2 parallel to $3\mathbf{j} + 2\mathbf{k}$.

40. Express $\mathbf{c}$ in terms of $\mathbf{a}$ and $\mathbf{b}$ given that the tip of $\mathbf{c}$ bisects the line segment shown.

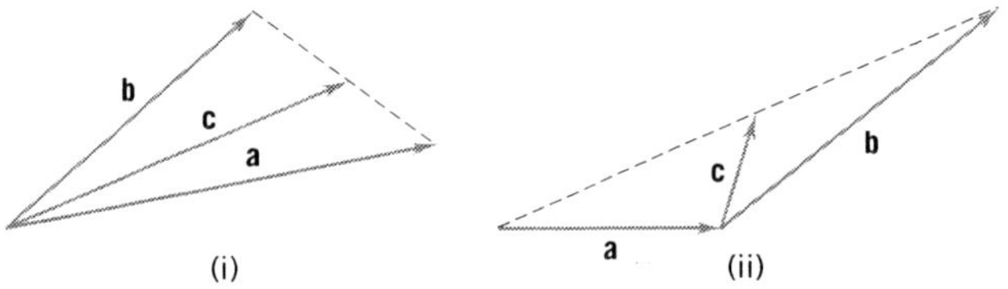

41. Let $\mathbf{a}$ and $\mathbf{b}$ be nonzero vectors such that

$$\|\mathbf{a} - \mathbf{b}\| = \|\mathbf{a} + \mathbf{b}\|.$$

(a) What can you conclude about the parallelogram generated by $\mathbf{a}$ and $\mathbf{b}$?
(b) Show that, if $\mathbf{a} = a_1\mathbf{i} + a_2\mathbf{j} + a_3\mathbf{k}$, and $\mathbf{b} = b_1\mathbf{i} + b_2\mathbf{j} + b_3\mathbf{k}$, then

$$a_1b_1 + a_2b_2 + a_3b_3 = 0.$$

42. (a) Show without reference to a figure that, if $\alpha > 0$, then

$$\|\mathbf{a} + \alpha\mathbf{a}\| = \|\mathbf{a}\| + \|\alpha\mathbf{a}\|.$$

(b) Does this equation necessarily hold for $\alpha < 0$?

43. Let P and Q be two points in space and let M be the midpoint of the line segment $\overline{PQ}$. Assume that $\overrightarrow{OP}$ represents $\mathbf{p}$, $\overrightarrow{OQ}$ represents $\mathbf{q}$, and $\overrightarrow{OM}$ represents $\mathbf{m}$. Express $\mathbf{m}$ in terms of $\mathbf{p}$ and $\mathbf{q}$.

44. Let P and Q be two points in space and let R be the point on $\overline{PQ}$ which is twice as far from P as it is from Q. Assume that $\overrightarrow{OP}$ represents $\mathbf{p}$, $\overrightarrow{OQ}$ represents $\mathbf{q}$, and $\overrightarrow{OR}$ represents $\mathbf{r}$. Express $\mathbf{r}$ as a linear combination of $\mathbf{p}$ and $\mathbf{q}$.

13.3 THE DOT PRODUCT

In this section we introduce the first of two products that we define for vectors.

Introduction

We begin with nonzero vectors

$$\mathbf{a} = a_1\,\mathbf{i} + a_2\,\mathbf{j} + a_3\,\mathbf{k}, \qquad \mathbf{b} = b_1\,\mathbf{i} + b_2\,\mathbf{j} + b_3\,\mathbf{k}$$

and view them as emanating from the same point. How can we tell from the components of these vectors whether these vectors meet at right angles? To explore this question, we draw Figure 13.3.1. By the Pythagorean theorem, **a** and **b** meet at right angles iff

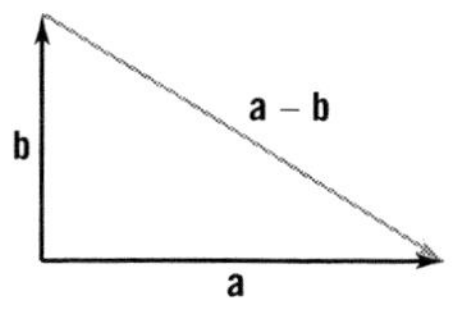

Figure 13.3.1

$$\|\mathbf{a}\|^2 + \|\mathbf{b}\|^2 = \|\mathbf{a} - \mathbf{b}\|^2.$$

In terms of components, this equation reads

$$(a_1^2 + a_2^2 + a_3^2) + (b_1^2 + b_2^2 + b_3^2) = (a_1 - b_1)^2 + (a_2 - b_2)^2 + (a_3 - b_3)^2,$$

which, as you can readily check, simplifies to

$$a_1b_1 + a_2b_2 + a_3b_3 = 0.$$

Definition of the Dot Product

The expression $a_1b_1 + a_2b_2 + a_3b_3$ is widely used in geometry and physics. It has a name, the *dot product* of **a** and **b**, and there is a special notation for it, $\mathbf{a} \cdot \mathbf{b}$. The notion is so important that it deserves a formal definition.

DEFINITION 13.3.1

For vectors

$$\mathbf{a} = a_1\,\mathbf{i} + a_2\,\mathbf{j} + a_3\,\mathbf{k} \quad \text{and} \quad \mathbf{b} = b_1\,\mathbf{i} + b_2\,\mathbf{j} + b_3\,\mathbf{k},$$

we define the *dot product* $\mathbf{a} \cdot \mathbf{b}$ by setting

$$\mathbf{a} \cdot \mathbf{b} = a_1b_1 + a_2b_2 + a_3b_3.$$

Remark For plane vectors $\mathbf{a} = a_1\,\mathbf{i} + a_2\,\mathbf{j}$ and $\mathbf{b} = b_1\,\mathbf{i} + b_2\,\mathbf{j}$

$$\mathbf{a} \cdot \mathbf{b} = a_1b_1 + a_2b_2. \quad ❑$$

Example 1 For $\mathbf{a} = 2\mathbf{i} - \mathbf{j} + 3\mathbf{k}$, $\mathbf{b} = -3\mathbf{i} + \mathbf{j} + 4\mathbf{k}$, $\mathbf{c} = \mathbf{i} + 3\mathbf{j}$, we have

$$\mathbf{a} \cdot \mathbf{b} = (2)(-3) + (-1)(1) + (3)(4) = -6 - 1 + 12 = 5,$$

$$\mathbf{a} \cdot \mathbf{c} = (2)(1) + (-1)(3) + (3)(0) = 2 - 3 = -1,$$

$$\mathbf{b} \cdot \mathbf{c} = (-3)(1) + (1)(3) + (4)(0) = -3 + 3 = 0.$$

The last equation (see the introduction) tells us that **b** and **c** meet at right angles. (Verify this by drawing a figure.) ❑

Because $\mathbf{a} \cdot \mathbf{b}$ is not a vector, but a scalar, it is sometimes called the *scalar product* of **a** and **b**. We will continue to call it the dot product and speak of "dotting **a** with **b**."

Properties of the Dot Product

If we dot a vector with itself, we obtain the square of its norm:

(13.3.2)
$$\mathbf{a} \cdot \mathbf{a} = \|\mathbf{a}\|^2.$$

PROOF

$$\mathbf{a} \cdot \mathbf{a} = a_1a_1 + a_2a_2 + a_3a_3 = a_1^2 + a_2^2 + a_3^2 = \|\mathbf{a}\|^2. \quad \square$$

The dot product of any vector with the zero vector is zero:

(13.3.3)
$$\mathbf{a} \cdot \mathbf{0} = 0, \qquad \mathbf{0} \cdot \mathbf{a} = 0.$$

PROOF

$$(a_1)(0) + (a_2)(0) + (a_3)(0) = 0, \qquad (0)(a_1) + (0)(a_2) + (0)(a_3) = 0. \quad \square$$

The dot product is commutative:

(13.3.4)
$$\mathbf{a} \cdot \mathbf{b} = \mathbf{b} \cdot \mathbf{a}$$

and scalars can be factored:

(13.3.5)
$$\alpha\mathbf{a} \cdot \beta\mathbf{b} = \alpha\beta(\mathbf{a} \cdot \mathbf{b}).$$

PROOF

$$\mathbf{a} \cdot \mathbf{b} = a_1b_1 + a_2b_2 + a_3b_3 = b_1a_1 + b_2a_2 + b_3a_3 = \mathbf{b} \cdot \mathbf{a}$$

and

$$\begin{aligned}\alpha\mathbf{a} \cdot \beta\mathbf{b} &= (\alpha a_1)(\beta b_1) + (\alpha a_2)(\beta b_2) + (\alpha a_3)(\beta b_3)\\ &= \alpha\beta(a_1b_1 + a_2b_2 + a_3b_3) = \alpha\beta(\mathbf{a} \cdot \mathbf{b}). \quad \square\end{aligned}$$

The dot product satisfies the following distributive laws:

(13.3.6)
$$\mathbf{a} \cdot (\mathbf{b} + \mathbf{c}) = \mathbf{a} \cdot \mathbf{b} + \mathbf{a} \cdot \mathbf{c}, \qquad (\mathbf{a} + \mathbf{b}) \cdot \mathbf{c} = \mathbf{a} \cdot \mathbf{c} + \mathbf{b} \cdot \mathbf{c}.$$

PROOF

$$\begin{aligned}\mathbf{a} \cdot (\mathbf{b} + \mathbf{c}) &= a_1(b_1 + c_1) + a_2(b_2 + c_2) + a_3(b_3 + c_3)\\ &= a_1b_1 + a_1c_1 + a_2b_2 + a_2c_2 + a_3b_3 + a_3c_3\\ &= (a_1b_1 + a_2b_2 + a_3b_3) + (a_1c_1 + a_2c_2 + a_3c_3)\\ &= \mathbf{a} \cdot \mathbf{b} + \mathbf{a} \cdot \mathbf{c}.\end{aligned}$$

The second distributive law can be verified in a similar manner. $\square$

Example 2 Given that

$$\|\mathbf{a}\| = 1, \quad \|\mathbf{b}\| = 3, \quad \|\mathbf{c}\| = 4, \quad \mathbf{a}\cdot\mathbf{b} = 0, \quad \mathbf{a}\cdot\mathbf{c} = 1, \quad \mathbf{b}\cdot\mathbf{c} = -2,$$

find

(a) $3\mathbf{a}\cdot(\mathbf{b}+4\mathbf{c})$.

(b) $(\mathbf{a}-\mathbf{b})\cdot(2\mathbf{a}+\mathbf{b})$.

(c) $[(\mathbf{b}\cdot\mathbf{c})\,\mathbf{a}-(\mathbf{a}\cdot\mathbf{c})\mathbf{b}]\cdot\mathbf{c}$.

SOLUTION

(a) $3\mathbf{a}\cdot(\mathbf{b}+4\mathbf{c}) = (3\mathbf{a}\cdot\mathbf{b}) + (3\mathbf{a}\cdot 4\mathbf{c}) = 3(\mathbf{a}\cdot\mathbf{b}) + 12(\mathbf{a}\cdot\mathbf{c}) = 12.$

(b)
$$\begin{aligned}(\mathbf{a}-\mathbf{b})\cdot(2\mathbf{a}+\mathbf{b}) &= (\mathbf{a}\cdot 2\mathbf{a}) + (\mathbf{a}\cdot\mathbf{b}) + (-\mathbf{b}\cdot 2\mathbf{a}) + (-\mathbf{b}\cdot\mathbf{b})\\ &= 2(\mathbf{a}\cdot\mathbf{a}) + (\mathbf{a}\cdot\mathbf{b}) - 2(\mathbf{b}\cdot\mathbf{a}) - (\mathbf{b}\cdot\mathbf{b})\\ &= 2\|\mathbf{a}\|^2 + (\mathbf{a}\cdot\mathbf{b}) - 2(\mathbf{a}\cdot\mathbf{b}) - \|\mathbf{b}\|^2\\ &= 2 + 0 - 2(0) - 9 = -7.\end{aligned}$$

(c)
$$\begin{aligned}[(\mathbf{b}\cdot\mathbf{c})\mathbf{a}-(\mathbf{a}\cdot\mathbf{c})\mathbf{b}]\cdot\mathbf{c} &= [(\mathbf{b}\cdot\mathbf{c})\mathbf{a}\cdot\mathbf{c}] - [(\mathbf{a}\cdot\mathbf{c})\mathbf{b}\cdot\mathbf{c}]\\ &= (\mathbf{b}\cdot\mathbf{c})(\mathbf{a}\cdot\mathbf{c}) - (\mathbf{a}\cdot\mathbf{c})(\mathbf{b}\cdot\mathbf{c}) = 0.\end{aligned}$$ ❑

Geometric Interpretation of the Dot Product

We begin with a triangle with sides a, b, c. (Figure 13.3.2). If θ were $\frac{1}{2}\pi$, the Pythagorean theorem would tell us that $c^2 = a^2 + b^2$. The law of cosines,

$$c^2 = a^2 + b^2 - 2ab\ \cos\theta,$$

is a generalization of the Pythagorean theorem.

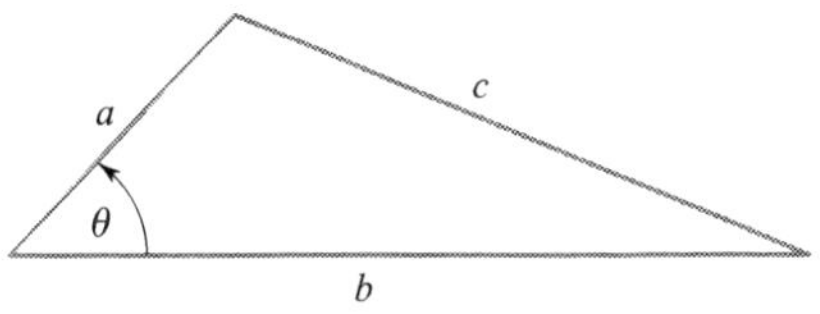

Figure 13.3.2

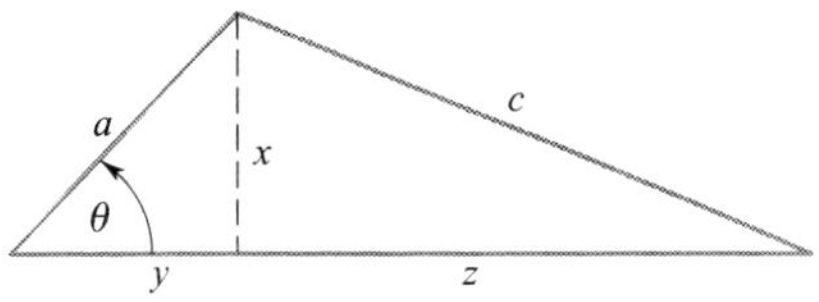

Figure 13.3.3

To derive the law of cosines, we drop a perpendicular to side b. (Figure 13.3.3.) We then have

$$c^2 = z^2 + x^2 = (b-y)^2 + x^2 = b^2 - 2by + y^2 + x^2.$$

From the figure, $y^2 + x^2 = a^2$ and $y = a\cos\theta$. Therefore

$$c^2 = a^2 + b^2 - 2ab\cos\theta$$

as asserted. (What if the angle θ is obtuse? We leave that case to you.)

Now back to dot products. If neither **a** nor **b** is zero, we can interpret $\mathbf{a}\cdot\mathbf{b}$ from the triangle in Figure 13.4.4. The lengths of the sides are $\|\mathbf{a}\|$, $\|\mathbf{b}\|$, $\|\mathbf{a}-\mathbf{b}\|$. By the law of cosines,

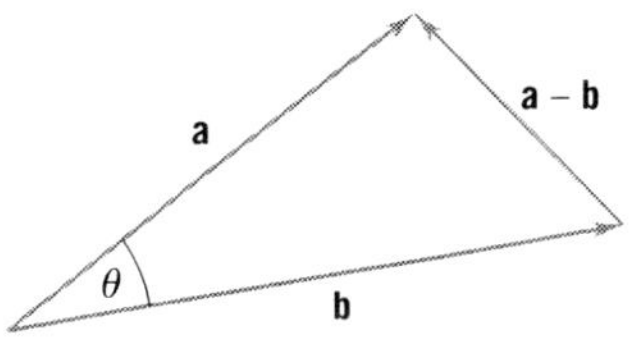

Figure 13.3.4

$$\|\mathbf{a}-\mathbf{b}\|^2 = \|\mathbf{a}\|^2 + \|\mathbf{b}\|^2 - 2\|\mathbf{a}\|\|\mathbf{b}\|\cos\theta.$$

This gives

$$\begin{aligned}2\|\mathbf{a}\|\|\mathbf{b}\|\cos\theta &= \|\mathbf{a}\|^2 + \|\mathbf{b}\|^2 - \|\mathbf{a}-\mathbf{b}\|^2\\ &= a_1^2 + a_2^2 + a_3^2 + b_1^2 + b_2^2 + b_3^2 - (a_1-b_1)^2 - (a_2-b_2)^2 - (a_3-b_3)^2\\ &= 2(a_1b_1 + a_2b_2 + a_3b_3) = 2(\mathbf{a}\cdot\mathbf{b})\end{aligned}$$

and thus

(13.3.7) $$\mathbf{a}\cdot\mathbf{b} = \|\mathbf{a}\|\,\|\mathbf{b}\|\cos\theta.$$

By convention, θ, the angle between **a** and **b**, is taken from 0 to π (in degrees from 0 to 180); no negative angles.

From (13.3.7) you can see that the dot product of two vectors depends on the norms of the vectors and on the angle between them. For vectors of a given norm, the dot product measures the extent to which the vectors agree in direction. As the difference in direction increases, the dot product decreases:

If **a** and **b** have the same direction, then $\theta = 0$ and

$$\mathbf{a}\cdot\mathbf{b} = \|\mathbf{a}\|\,\|\mathbf{b}\|; \qquad (\cos 0 = 1)$$

this is the largest possible value for $\mathbf{a}\cdot\mathbf{b}$.

If **a** and **b** meet at right angles, then $\theta = \frac{1}{2}\pi$ and

$$\mathbf{a}\cdot\mathbf{b} = 0. \qquad (\cos \tfrac{1}{2}\pi = 0)$$

If **a** and **b** have opposite directions, then $\theta = \pi$ and

$$\mathbf{a}\cdot\mathbf{b} = -\|\mathbf{a}\|\,\|\mathbf{b}\|; \qquad (\cos\pi = -1)$$

this is the least possible value for $\mathbf{a}\cdot\mathbf{b}$.

Two vectors are said to be *perpendicular* if they lie at right angles to each other or one of the vectors is the zero vector; thus, two vectors are perpendicular iff their dot product is zero.† In symbols

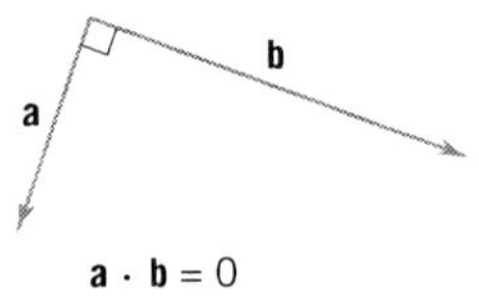

Figure 13.3.5

(13.3.8) $$\mathbf{a}\perp\mathbf{b} \quad \text{iff} \quad \mathbf{a}\cdot\mathbf{b} = 0. \qquad \text{(Figure 13.3.5)}$$

The unit vectors **i**, **j**, **k** are mutually perpendicular:

$$\mathbf{i}\cdot\mathbf{j} = \mathbf{i}\cdot\mathbf{k} = \mathbf{j}\cdot\mathbf{k} = 0.$$

Example 3 Verify that $\mathbf{a} = 2\mathbf{i} + \mathbf{j} + \mathbf{k}$ and $\mathbf{b} = \mathbf{i} + \mathbf{j} - 3\mathbf{k}$ are perpendicular.

SOLUTION

$$\mathbf{a}\cdot\mathbf{b} = (2)(1) + (1)(1) + (1)(-3) = 2 + 1 - 3 = 0. \quad ❑$$

Example 4 Find the value of α for which $(3\mathbf{i} - \alpha\mathbf{j} + \mathbf{k}) \perp (\mathbf{i} + 2\mathbf{j})$.

SOLUTION For the two vectors to be perpendicular, their dot product must be zero. Since

$$(3\mathbf{i} - \alpha\mathbf{j} + \mathbf{k})\cdot(\mathbf{i} + 2\mathbf{j}) = (3)(1) + (-\alpha)(2) + (1)(0) = 3 - 2\alpha,$$

α must be $\frac{3}{2}$. ❑

With **a** and **b** both different from zero, we can divide the equation

$$\mathbf{a}\cdot\mathbf{b} = \|\mathbf{a}\|\,\|\mathbf{b}\|\cos\theta$$

†This makes the zero vector both parallel and perpendicular to every vector. There is, however, no contradiction since we do not apply the notion of "direction" to the zero vector.

by $\|\mathbf{a}\|\,\|\mathbf{b}\|$ to obtain

$$\cos\theta = \frac{\mathbf{a}\cdot\mathbf{b}}{\|\mathbf{a}\|\,\|\mathbf{b}\|} = \frac{\mathbf{a}}{\|\mathbf{a}\|}\cdot\frac{\mathbf{b}}{\|\mathbf{b}\|}.$$

In terms of the unit vectors

$$\mathbf{u_a} = \frac{\mathbf{a}}{\|\mathbf{a}\|} \quad \text{and} \quad \mathbf{u_b} = \frac{\mathbf{b}}{\|\mathbf{b}\|},$$

we have

(13.3.9)

$$\boxed{\cos\theta = \mathbf{u_a}\cdot\mathbf{u_b}.}$$

The cosine of the angle between **a** and **b** is the dot product of the corresponding unit vectors.

Example 5 Calculate the angle between $\mathbf{a} = 2\mathbf{i} + 3\mathbf{j} + 2\mathbf{k}$ and $\mathbf{b} = \mathbf{i} + 2\mathbf{j} - \mathbf{k}$.

SOLUTION

$$\mathbf{u_a} = \frac{2\mathbf{i} + 3\mathbf{j} + 2\mathbf{k}}{\|2\mathbf{i} + 3\mathbf{j} + 2\mathbf{k}\|} = \frac{1}{\sqrt{17}}(2\mathbf{i} + 3\mathbf{j} + 2\mathbf{k})$$

$$\mathbf{u_b} = \frac{\mathbf{i} + 2\mathbf{j} - \mathbf{k}}{\|\mathbf{i} + 2\mathbf{j} - \mathbf{k}\|} = \frac{1}{\sqrt{6}}(\mathbf{i} + 2\mathbf{j} - \mathbf{k}).$$

Therefore

$$\cos\theta = \mathbf{u_a}\cdot\mathbf{u_b}\frac{1}{\sqrt{17}}\frac{1}{\sqrt{6}}[(2\mathbf{i} + 3\mathbf{j} + 2\mathbf{k})\cdot(\mathbf{i} + 2\mathbf{j} - \mathbf{k})].$$

Since

$$(2\mathbf{i} + 3\mathbf{j} + 2\mathbf{k})\cdot(\mathbf{i} + 2\mathbf{j} - \mathbf{k}) = (2)(1) + (3)(2) + (2)(-1) = 6,$$

we see that

$$\cos\theta = \frac{6}{\sqrt{17}\sqrt{6}} = \frac{1}{17}\sqrt{102} \cong \frac{10.1}{17} \cong 0.594.$$

This gives $\theta \cong 0.935$ radians, which is about 54 degrees. ❑

It is easy to see that

(13.3.10)

if **a** and **b** are both perpendicular to **c**, then every linear combination $\alpha\mathbf{a} + \beta\,\mathbf{b}$ is also perpendicular to **c**.

PROOF Suppose that **a** and **b** are both perpendicular to **c**. Then

$$\mathbf{a}\cdot\mathbf{c} = 0 \quad \text{and} \quad \mathbf{b}\cdot\mathbf{c} = 0.$$

It follows that

$$(\alpha\mathbf{a} + \beta\mathbf{b})\cdot\mathbf{c} = \alpha\underbrace{(\mathbf{a}\cdot\mathbf{c})}_{0} + \beta\underbrace{(\mathbf{b}\cdot\mathbf{c})}_{0} = 0$$

and therefore $\alpha\mathbf{a} + \beta\mathbf{b}$ is perpendicular to **c**. ❑

Projections and Components

If $\mathbf{b} \neq 0$, then every vector $\mathbf{a}$ can be written in a unique manner as the sum of a vector $\mathbf{a}_{\parallel}$ parallel to $\mathbf{b}$ and a vector $\mathbf{a}_{\perp}$ perpendicular to $\mathbf{b}$:

$$\mathbf{a} = \mathbf{a}_{\parallel} + \mathbf{a}_{\perp}. \qquad \text{(Exercise 51)}$$

The idea is illustrated in Figure 13.3.6. If $\mathbf{a}$ is parallel to $\mathbf{b}$, then $\mathbf{a}_{\parallel} = \mathbf{a}$ and $\mathbf{a}_{\perp} = \mathbf{0}$. If $\mathbf{a}$ is perpendicular to $\mathbf{b}$, then $\mathbf{a}_{\parallel} = 0$ and $\mathbf{a}_{\perp} = \mathbf{a}$.

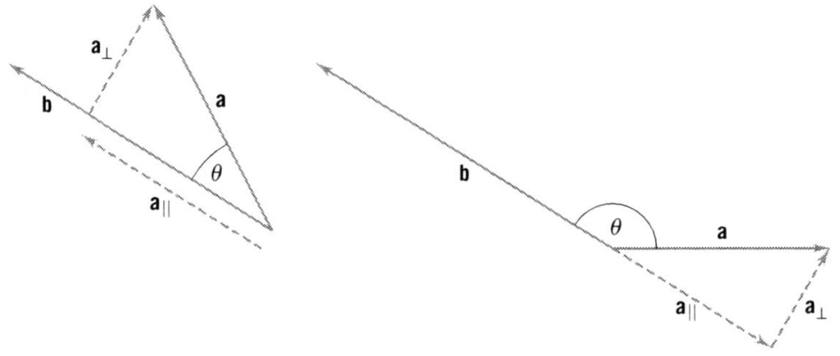

Figure 13.3.6

The vector $\mathbf{a}_{\parallel}$ (go back to Figure 13.3.6) is called the *projection of* $\mathbf{a}$ *on* $\mathbf{b}$:

$$\mathbf{a}_{\parallel} = \mathbf{proj_b}\ \mathbf{a}.$$

Since $\mathbf{proj_b}\ \mathbf{a}$ is parallel to $\mathbf{b}$, it is a scalar multiple of $\mathbf{u_b}$,

$$\mathbf{proj_b a} = \lambda\ \mathbf{u_b}.$$

The scalar λ is called the $\mathbf{b}$-*component* of $\mathbf{a}$ and is denoted by $\text{comp}_\mathbf{b}\mathbf{a}$:

(13.3.11) $$\mathbf{proj_b a} = (\text{comp}_\mathbf{b}\mathbf{a})\mathbf{u_b}.$$

The $\mathbf{b}$-component of $\mathbf{a}$ measures the "advance" of $\mathbf{a}$ in the direction of $\mathbf{b}$. In Figure 13.3.6 we used θ to indicate the angle between $\mathbf{a}$ and $\mathbf{b}$. If $0 \leq \theta < \frac{1}{2}\pi$, the projection and $\mathbf{b}$ have the same direction. If $\theta = \frac{1}{2}\pi$, the projection is $\mathbf{0}$ and the component is 0. If $\frac{1}{2}\pi < \theta \leq \pi$, the projection and $\mathbf{b}$ have opposite directions and, consequently, the component is negative.

Projections and components are readily expressed in terms of the dot product: for $\mathbf{b} \neq 0$

(13.3.12) $$\mathbf{proj_b a} = (\mathbf{a} \cdot \mathbf{u_b})\mathbf{u_b} \qquad \text{and} \qquad (\text{comp}_\mathbf{b}\mathbf{a}) = \mathbf{a} \cdot \mathbf{u_b}.$$

PROOF The second assertion follows immediately from the first. We will prove the first. We begin with the identity

$$\mathbf{a} = (\mathbf{a} \cdot \mathbf{u_b})\,\mathbf{u_b} + [\mathbf{a} - (\mathbf{a} \cdot \mathbf{u_b})\,\mathbf{u_b}].$$

Since the first vector $(\mathbf{a} \cdot \mathbf{u_b})\,\mathbf{u_b}$ is a scalar multiple of $\mathbf{b}$. it is parallel to $\mathbf{b}$. All we have to show now is that the second vector is perpendicular to $\mathbf{b}$. We do this by showing that its dot product with $\mathbf{u_b}$ is zero:

$$[\mathbf{a} - (\mathbf{a} \cdot \mathbf{u_b})\,\mathbf{u_b}] \cdot \mathbf{u_b} = (\mathbf{a} \cdot \mathbf{u_b}) - (\mathbf{a} \cdot \mathbf{u_b})(\mathbf{u_b} \cdot \mathbf{u_b}) = 0. \quad ❑$$

$\uparrow$ $\mathbf{u_b} \cdot \mathbf{u_b} = \|\mathbf{u_b}\|^2 = 1$

Example 6 Find $\text{comp}_{\mathbf{b}}\mathbf{a}$ and $\mathbf{proj}_{\mathbf{b}}\,\mathbf{a}$ given that

$$\mathbf{a} = -2\mathbf{i} + \mathbf{j} + \mathbf{k} \qquad \text{and} \qquad \mathbf{b} = 4\mathbf{i} - 3\mathbf{j} + \mathbf{k}.$$

SOLUTION Since $\|\mathbf{b}\| = \sqrt{4^2 + (-3)^2 + 1^2} = \sqrt{26}$,

$$\mathbf{u_b} = \frac{\mathbf{b}}{\|\mathbf{b}\|} = \frac{1}{\sqrt{26}}(4\mathbf{i} - 3\mathbf{j} + \mathbf{k}).$$

Thus

$$\begin{aligned}\text{comp}_{\mathbf{b}}\mathbf{a} = \mathbf{a} \cdot \mathbf{u_b} &= (-2\mathbf{i} + \mathbf{j} + \mathbf{k}) \cdot \frac{1}{\sqrt{26}}(4\mathbf{i} - 3\mathbf{j} + \mathbf{k}) \\ &= \frac{1}{\sqrt{26}}[(-2)(4) + (1)(-3) + (1)(1)] = -\frac{10}{\sqrt{26}} = -\frac{5}{13}\sqrt{26}\end{aligned}$$

and

$$\mathbf{proj}_{\mathbf{b}}\,\mathbf{a} = (\text{comp}_{\mathbf{b}}\mathbf{a})\,\mathbf{u_b} = -\tfrac{5}{13}(4\mathbf{i} - 3\mathbf{j} + \mathbf{k}). \quad \square$$

The following characterization of $\mathbf{a} \cdot \mathbf{b}$ is frequently used in physical applications:

(13.3.13)

$$\text{if } \mathbf{b} \neq \mathbf{0}, \qquad \mathbf{a} \cdot \mathbf{b} = (\text{comp}_{\mathbf{b}}\,\mathbf{a})\|\mathbf{b}\|.$$

PROOF

$$\mathbf{a} \cdot \mathbf{b} = \left(\mathbf{a} \cdot \frac{\mathbf{b}}{\|\mathbf{b}\|}\right)\|\mathbf{b}\| = (\mathbf{a} \cdot \mathbf{u_b})\|\mathbf{b}\| = (\text{comp}_{\mathbf{b}}\,\mathbf{a})\|\mathbf{b}\|. \quad \square$$

For each vector $\mathbf{a} = a_1\,\mathbf{i} + a_2\,\mathbf{j} + a_3\,\mathbf{k}$,

$$\text{comp}_{\mathbf{i}}\mathbf{a} = \mathbf{a} \cdot \mathbf{i} = a_1, \quad \text{comp}_{\mathbf{j}}\mathbf{a} = \mathbf{a} \cdot \mathbf{j} = a_2, \quad \text{comp}_{\mathbf{k}}\mathbf{a} = \mathbf{a} \cdot \mathbf{k} = a_3.$$

This agrees with our previous use of the term "component" (Section 13.2) and gives the identity

(13.3.14)

$$\mathbf{a} = (\mathbf{a} \cdot \mathbf{i})\,\mathbf{i} + (\mathbf{a} \cdot \mathbf{j})\,\mathbf{j} + (\mathbf{a} \cdot \mathbf{k})\,\mathbf{k}.$$

Direction Angles, Direction Cosines

In Figure 13.3.7 we show a nonzero vector $\mathbf{a}$ and the vectors $\mathbf{i}$, $\mathbf{j}$, $\mathbf{k}$ for convenience all started at the origin. The angles α, β, γ marked in the figure are called the *direction angles* of $\mathbf{a}$. The numbers $\cos\alpha, \cos\beta, \cos\gamma$ are called the *direction cosines.* By (13.3.7)

$$\mathbf{a} \cdot \mathbf{i} = \|\mathbf{a}\| \cos\alpha, \qquad \mathbf{a} \cdot \mathbf{j} = \|\mathbf{a}\| \cos\beta, \qquad \mathbf{a} \cdot \mathbf{k} = \|\mathbf{a}\| \cos\gamma.$$

Thus by (13.3.14)

(13.3.15)

$$\mathbf{a} = \|\mathbf{a}\|(\cos\alpha\,\mathbf{i} + \cos\beta\,\mathbf{j} + \cos\gamma\,\mathbf{k}).$$

Taking the norm of both sides, we have

$$\|\mathbf{a}\| = \|\mathbf{a}\|\sqrt{\cos^2\alpha + \cos^2\beta + \cos^2\gamma}$$

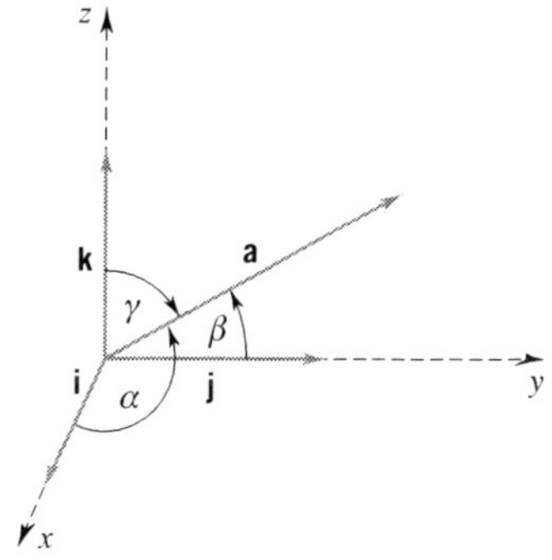

Figure 13.3.7

and therefore

(13.3.16)
$$\cos^2\alpha + \cos^2\beta + \cos^2\gamma = 1.$$

The sum of the squares of the direction cosines is always 1.

For a unit vector **u**, Equation (13.3.15) takes the form

(13.3.17)
$$\mathbf{u} = \cos\alpha\,\mathbf{i} + \cos\beta\,\mathbf{j} + \cos\gamma\,\mathbf{k}.$$

The **i**, **j**, **k** *components of a unit vector are the direction cosines.*

Example 7 Find the unit vector with direction angles
$$\alpha = \tfrac{1}{4}\pi, \quad \beta = \tfrac{2}{3}\pi, \quad \gamma = \tfrac{1}{3}\pi.$$
What is the vector of norm 4 with these same direction angles?

SOLUTION The unit vector with these direction angles is
$$\cos\tfrac{1}{4}\pi\,\mathbf{i} + \cos\tfrac{2}{3}\pi\,\mathbf{j} + \cos\tfrac{1}{3}\pi\,\mathbf{k} = \tfrac{1}{2}\sqrt{2}\,\mathbf{i} - \tfrac{1}{2}\,\mathbf{j} + \tfrac{1}{2}\,\mathbf{k}.$$
The vector of norm 4 with these direction angles is the vector
$$4(\tfrac{1}{2}\sqrt{2}\,\mathbf{i} - \tfrac{1}{2}\,\mathbf{j} + \tfrac{1}{2}\,\mathbf{k}) = 2\sqrt{2}\,\mathbf{i} - 2\,\mathbf{j} + 2\,\mathbf{k}. \quad \square$$

Example 8 Find the direction cosines and direction angles of the vector
$$\mathbf{a} = 2\mathbf{i} + 3\mathbf{j} - 6\mathbf{k}.$$

SOLUTION Since $\|\mathbf{a}\| = \sqrt{2^2 + 3^2 + (-6)^2} = 7$,
$$2 = 7\cos\alpha, \qquad 3 = 7\cos\beta, \qquad -6 = 7\cos\gamma$$
and
$$\cos\alpha = \tfrac{2}{7}, \qquad \cos\beta = \tfrac{3}{7}, \qquad \cos\gamma = -\tfrac{6}{7}.$$
Measuring the angles in radians from 0 to π, we have
$$\alpha = \arccos\tfrac{2}{7} \cong 1.28 \text{ radians}, \qquad \beta = \arccos\tfrac{3}{7} \cong 1.13 \text{ radians}$$
$$\gamma = \arccos\left(-\tfrac{6}{7}\right) \cong 2.60 \text{ radians}. \quad \square$$

Schwarz's Inequality

You know that
$$\mathbf{a}\cdot\mathbf{b} = \|\mathbf{a}\|\,\|\mathbf{b}\|\cos\theta,$$
where θ is the angle between **a** and **b**. Taking absolute values and recognizing that $|\cos\theta| \le 1$, we have *Schwarz's inequality*:

(13.3.18)
$$|\mathbf{a}\cdot\mathbf{b}| \le \|\mathbf{a}\|\,\|\mathbf{b}\|.$$

Schwarz's inequality enables us to derive the triangle inequality

$$\|\mathbf{a}+\mathbf{b}\| \leq \|\mathbf{a}\| + \|\mathbf{b}\|$$

without having to picture **a**, **b**, **a** + **b** as the sides of a triangle.

DERIVATION

$$\begin{aligned}\|\mathbf{a}+\mathbf{b}\|^2 &= (\mathbf{a}+\mathbf{b})\cdot(\mathbf{a}+\mathbf{b})\\ &= (\mathbf{a}\cdot\mathbf{a}) + (\mathbf{b}\cdot\mathbf{a}) + (\mathbf{a}\cdot\mathbf{b}) + (\mathbf{b}\cdot\mathbf{b})\\ &= \|\mathbf{a}\|^2 + 2(\mathbf{a}\cdot\mathbf{b}) + \|\mathbf{b}\|^2\\ &\leq \|\mathbf{a}\|^2 + 2|\mathbf{a}\cdot\mathbf{b}| + \|\mathbf{b}\|^2 \qquad (\mathbf{a}\cdot\mathbf{b} \leq |\mathbf{a}\cdot\mathbf{b}|)\\ &\leq \|\mathbf{a}\|^2 + 2\|\mathbf{a}\|\,\|\mathbf{b}\| + \|\mathbf{b}\|^2 = (\|\mathbf{a}\| + \|\mathbf{b}\|)^2.\end{aligned}$$

by Schwarz's inequality ⟶ (last inequality)

Taking square roots, we have

$$\|\mathbf{a}+\mathbf{b}\| \leq \|\mathbf{a}\| + \|\mathbf{b}\|. \quad ❑$$

Remark Schwarz's inequality can be obtained by purely algebraic methods. No consideration of $\cos\theta$ is required. See Exercise 54. ❑

EXERCISES 13.3

Exercises 1–6. Find $\mathbf{a}\cdot\mathbf{b}$.

1. $\mathbf{a} = (2, -3, 1)$, $\mathbf{b} = (-2, 0, 3)$.

2. $\mathbf{a} = (4, 2, -1)$, $\mathbf{b} = (-2, 2, 1)$.

3. $\mathbf{a} = (2, -4, 0)$, $\mathbf{b} = (1, \frac{1}{2}, 0)$.

4. $\mathbf{a} = (-2, 0, 5)$, $\mathbf{b} = (3, 0, 1)$.

5. $\mathbf{a} = 2\mathbf{i} + \mathbf{j} - 2\mathbf{k}$, $\mathbf{b} = \mathbf{i} + \mathbf{j} + 2\mathbf{k}$.

6. $\mathbf{a} = 2\mathbf{i} + 3\mathbf{j} + \mathbf{k}$, $\mathbf{b} = \mathbf{i} + 4\mathbf{j}$.

Exercises 7–10. Simplify.

7. $(3\mathbf{a}\cdot\mathbf{b}) - (\mathbf{a}\cdot 2\mathbf{b})$.

8. $\mathbf{a}\cdot(\mathbf{a}-\mathbf{b}) + \mathbf{b}\cdot(\mathbf{b}+\mathbf{a})$.

9. $(\mathbf{a}-\mathbf{b})\cdot\mathbf{c} + \mathbf{b}\cdot(\mathbf{c}+\mathbf{a})$.

10. $\mathbf{a}\cdot(\mathbf{a}+2\mathbf{c}) + (2\mathbf{b}-\mathbf{a})\cdot(\mathbf{a}+2\mathbf{c}) - 2\mathbf{b}\cdot(\mathbf{a}+2\mathbf{c})$.

11. Taking

$$\mathbf{a} = 2\mathbf{i} + \mathbf{j}, \qquad \mathbf{b} = 3\mathbf{i} - \mathbf{j} + 2\mathbf{k}, \qquad \mathbf{c} = 4\mathbf{i} + 3\mathbf{k},$$

calculate

(a) the three dot products $\mathbf{a}\cdot\mathbf{b}$, $\mathbf{a}\cdot\mathbf{c}$, $\mathbf{b}\cdot\mathbf{c}$;

(b) the cosines of the angles between these vectors;

(c) the component of **a** (i) in the **b** direction, (ii) in the **c** direction;

(d) the projection of **a** (i) in the **b** direction, (ii) in the **c** direction.

12. Exercise 11 for

$$\mathbf{a} = \mathbf{j} + 3\mathbf{k}, \qquad \mathbf{b} = 2\mathbf{i} - \mathbf{j} + 2\mathbf{k}, \qquad \mathbf{c} = 3\mathbf{i} - \mathbf{k}.$$

13. Find the unit vector with direction angles $\frac{1}{3}\pi$, $\frac{1}{4}\pi$, $\frac{2}{3}\pi$.

14. Find the vector of norm 2 with direction angles $\frac{1}{4}\pi$, $\frac{1}{4}\pi$, $\frac{1}{2}\pi$.

15. Find the angle between $3\mathbf{i} - \mathbf{j} - 2\mathbf{k}$ and $\mathbf{i} + 2\mathbf{j} - 3\mathbf{k}$.

16. Find the angle between $2\mathbf{i} - 3\mathbf{j} + \mathbf{k}$ and $-3\mathbf{i} + \mathbf{j} + 9\mathbf{k}$.

17. Find the direction angles of the vector $\mathbf{i} - \mathbf{j} + \sqrt{2}\mathbf{k}$.

18. Find the direction angles of the vector $\mathbf{i} - \sqrt{3}\mathbf{k}$.

Exercises 19–22. Estimate the angle between the vectors. Express your answers in radians rounded to the nearest hundredth of a radian, and in degrees to the nearest tenth of a degree.

19. $\mathbf{a} = (3, 1, -1)$, $\mathbf{b} = (-2, 1, 4)$.

20. $\mathbf{a} = (-2, -3, 0)$, $\mathbf{b} = (-6, 0, 4)$.

21. $\mathbf{a} = -\mathbf{i} + 2\mathbf{k}$, $\mathbf{b} = 3\mathbf{i} + 4\mathbf{j} - 5\mathbf{k}$.

22. $\mathbf{a} = -3\mathbf{i} + \mathbf{j} - \mathbf{k}$, $\mathbf{b} = \mathbf{i} - \mathbf{j}$.

23. Use a CAS to determine the angles and the perimeter of the triangle with vertices $P(1, 3, -2)$, $Q(3, 1, 2)$, $R(2, -3, 1)$.

Exercises 24–27. Find the direction cosines and direction angles of the vector.

24. $\mathbf{a} = (2, 6, -1)$.

25. $\mathbf{a} = (1, 2, 2)$.

26. $\mathbf{a} = 3\mathbf{i} + 5\mathbf{j} - 4\mathbf{k}$.

27. $\mathbf{a} = 3\mathbf{i} + 12\mathbf{j} + 4\mathbf{k}$.

28. Use a CAS to find the direction cosines and the direction angles of $\overrightarrow{PQ}$ for $P(5, 7, -2)$, $Q(-3, 4, 1)$.

29. Find the numbers x for which

$$2\mathbf{i} + 5\mathbf{j} + 2x\mathbf{k} \perp 6\mathbf{i} + 4\mathbf{j} - x\mathbf{k}.$$

30. Find the numbers x for which

$$(x\mathbf{i} + 11\mathbf{j} - 3\mathbf{k}) \perp (2x\mathbf{i} - x\mathbf{j} - 5\mathbf{k}).$$

31. Find the numbers x for which the angle between $\mathbf{c} = x\mathbf{i} + \mathbf{j} + \mathbf{k}$ and $\mathbf{d} = \mathbf{i} + x\mathbf{j} + \mathbf{k}$ is $\frac{1}{3}\pi$.

32. Set $\mathbf{a} = \mathbf{i} + x\mathbf{j} + \mathbf{k}$ and $\mathbf{b} = 2\mathbf{i} - \mathbf{j} + y\mathbf{k}$. Find x and y given that $\mathbf{a} \perp \mathbf{b}$ and $\|\mathbf{a}\| = \|\mathbf{b}\|$.

33. (a) Show that $\frac{1}{4}\pi$, $\frac{1}{6}\pi$, $\frac{2}{3}\pi$ cannot be the direction angles of a vector.
(b) Show that, if $\mathbf{a} = a_1\mathbf{i} + a_2\mathbf{j} + a_3\mathbf{k}$ has direction angles α, $\frac{1}{4}\pi$, $\frac{1}{4}\pi$, then $a_1 = 0$.

34. A vector has direction angles $\alpha = \pi/3$ and $\beta = \pi/4$. What are the possibilities for the third direction angle γ?

35. What are the direction angles of $-\mathbf{a}$ if the direction angles of $\mathbf{a}$ are α, β, γ?

36. Suppose that the direction angles of a vector are equal. What are the angles?

37. Find the unit vectors $\mathbf{u}$ which are perpendicular to both $\mathbf{i} + 2\mathbf{j} + \mathbf{k}$ and $3\mathbf{i} - 4\mathbf{j} + 2\mathbf{k}$.

38. Find two mutually perpendicular unit vectors that are perpendicular to $2\mathbf{i} + 3\mathbf{j}$.

39. Find the angle between the diagonal of a cube and one of the edges.

40. Find the angle between the diagonal of a cube and the diagonal of one of the faces.

41. Show that
(a) $\mathbf{proj}_\mathbf{b}\alpha\mathbf{a} = \alpha\,\mathbf{proj}_\mathbf{b}\mathbf{a}$ for all real α, and
(b) $\mathbf{proj}_\mathbf{b}(\mathbf{a} + \mathbf{c}) = \mathbf{proj}_\mathbf{b}\mathbf{a} + \mathbf{proj}_\mathbf{b}\mathbf{c}$.

42. Show that
(a) $\mathbf{proj}_{\beta\mathbf{b}}\mathbf{a} = \mathbf{proj}_\mathbf{b}\mathbf{a}$ for all real $\beta \neq 0$, but
(b) $\text{comp}_{\beta\mathbf{b}}\mathbf{a} = \begin{cases} \text{comp}_\mathbf{b}\mathbf{a}, & \text{for } \beta > 0 \\ -\text{comp}_\mathbf{b}\mathbf{a}, & \text{for } \beta < 0. \end{cases}$

43. (a) (*Important*) Let $\mathbf{a} \neq \mathbf{0}$. Show that $\mathbf{a} \cdot \mathbf{b} = \mathbf{a} \cdot \mathbf{c}$ does not necessarily imply that $\mathbf{b} = \mathbf{c}$, but only that $\mathbf{a} \perp (\mathbf{b} - \mathbf{c})$.
(b) Show that if $\mathbf{u} \cdot \mathbf{b} = \mathbf{u} \cdot \mathbf{c}$ for all unit vectors $\mathbf{u}$, then $\mathbf{b} = \mathbf{c}$.

44. What can you conclude about $\mathbf{a}$ and $\mathbf{b}$ given that
(a) $\|\mathbf{a}\|^2 + \|\mathbf{b}\|^2 = \|\mathbf{a} + \mathbf{b}\|^2$?
(b) $\|\mathbf{a}\|^2 + \|\mathbf{b}\|^2 = \|\mathbf{a} - \mathbf{b}\|^2$?
HINT: Draw figures.

45. (a) Show that for all vectors $\mathbf{a}$ and $\mathbf{b}$

$$4(\mathbf{a} \cdot \mathbf{b}) = \|\mathbf{a} + \mathbf{b}\|^2 - \|\mathbf{a} - \mathbf{b}\|^2.$$

(b) Use part (a) to verify that

$$\mathbf{a} \perp \mathbf{b} \quad \text{iff} \quad \|\mathbf{a} + \mathbf{b}\| = \|\mathbf{a} - \mathbf{b}\|.$$

(c) Show that, if $\mathbf{a}$ and $\mathbf{b}$ are nonzero vectors such that

$$(\mathbf{a} + \mathbf{b}) \perp (\mathbf{a} - \mathbf{b}) \quad \text{and} \quad \|\mathbf{a} + \mathbf{b}\| = \|\mathbf{a} - \mathbf{b}\|,$$

then the parallelogram generated by $\mathbf{a}$ and $\mathbf{b}$ is a square.

46. Under what conditions does $|\mathbf{a} \cdot \mathbf{b}| = \|\mathbf{a}\|\,\|\mathbf{b}\|$?

47. Given two vectors $\mathbf{a}$ and $\mathbf{b}$, prove the *parallelogram law*:

$$\|\mathbf{a} + \mathbf{b}\|^2 + \|\mathbf{a} - \mathbf{b}\|^2 = 2\|\mathbf{a}\|^2 + 2\|\mathbf{b}\|^2.$$

Show that the sum of the squares of the lengths of the diagonals of a parallelogram equals the sum of the squares of the lengths of the four sides. See the figure.

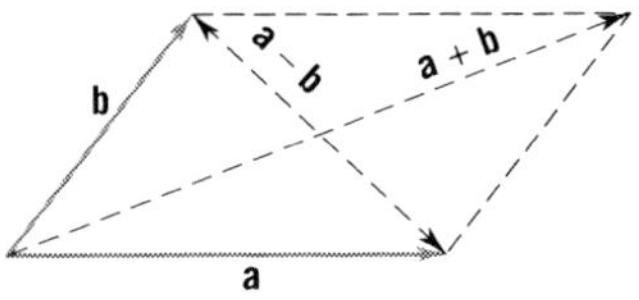

48. A *rhombus* is a parallelogram with sides of equal length. Show that the diagonals of a rhombus are perpendicular.

49. Let $\mathbf{a}$ and $\mathbf{b}$ be nonzero vectors. Show that the vector $\mathbf{c} = \|\mathbf{b}\|\mathbf{a} + \|\mathbf{a}\|\mathbf{b}$ bisects the angle between $\mathbf{a}$ and $\mathbf{b}$ in the sense that the angle between $\mathbf{a}$ and $\mathbf{c}$ equals the angle between $\mathbf{b}$ and $\mathbf{c}$.

50. Let θ be the angle between $\mathbf{a}$ and $\mathbf{b}$, and let β be a negative number. Use the dot product to express the angle between $\mathbf{a}$ and $\beta\mathbf{b}$ in terms of θ. Draw a figure to verify your answer geometrically.

51. (*Important*) Show that, if $\mathbf{b}$ is a nonzero vector, then every vector $\mathbf{a}$ can be written in a unique manner as the sum of a vector $\mathbf{a}_\parallel$ parallel to $\mathbf{b}$ and a vector $\mathbf{a}_\perp$ perpendicular to $\mathbf{b}$:

$$\mathbf{a} = \mathbf{a}_\parallel + \mathbf{a}_\perp.$$

52. Let $r = f(\theta)$ be the polar equation of a curve in the plane and let

$$\mathbf{u}_r = (\cos\theta)\mathbf{i} + (\sin\theta)\mathbf{j} \qquad \mathbf{u}_\theta = (-\sin\theta)\mathbf{i} + (\cos\theta)\mathbf{j}.$$

(a) Show that $\mathbf{u}_r$ and $\mathbf{u}_\theta$ are unit vectors and that they are perpendicular.
(b) Let $P[r, \theta]$ be a point on the curve. Show that $\mathbf{u}_r$ has the direction of $\overrightarrow{OP}$ and that $\mathbf{u}_\theta$ points 90° counterclockwise from $\mathbf{u}_r$.

53. Two points on a sphere are called *antipodal* if they are opposite endpoints of a diameter. Show that, if P_1 and P_2 are antipodal points on a sphere and Q is any other point on the sphere, then $\overrightarrow{P_1Q} \perp \overrightarrow{P_2Q}$.

54. (*Important*) Give an algebraic proof of Schwarz's inequality $|\mathbf{a} \cdot \mathbf{b}| \leq \|\mathbf{a}\|\,\|\mathbf{b}\|$. HINT: If $\mathbf{b} = 0$, the inequality is trivial; so assume $\mathbf{b} \neq \mathbf{0}$. Note that for any number λ we have $\|\mathbf{a} - \lambda\mathbf{b}\|^2 \geq 0$. First expand this inequality using the fact that $\|\mathbf{a} - \lambda\mathbf{b}\|^2 = (\mathbf{a} - \lambda\mathbf{b}) \cdot (\mathbf{a} - \lambda\mathbf{b})$. After collecting terms, make the special choice $\lambda = (\mathbf{a} \cdot \mathbf{b})/\|\mathbf{b}\|^2$ and see what happens.

■ PROJECT 13.3 Work

If a constant force **F** is applied to an object that moves in a straight line throughout a displacement **r** (see Figure A), then the work done by **F** is defined by the equation

$$W = (\text{comp}_{\mathbf{r}}\ \mathbf{F})\|\mathbf{r}\|.$$

As you'll see, this generalizes (6.5.1).

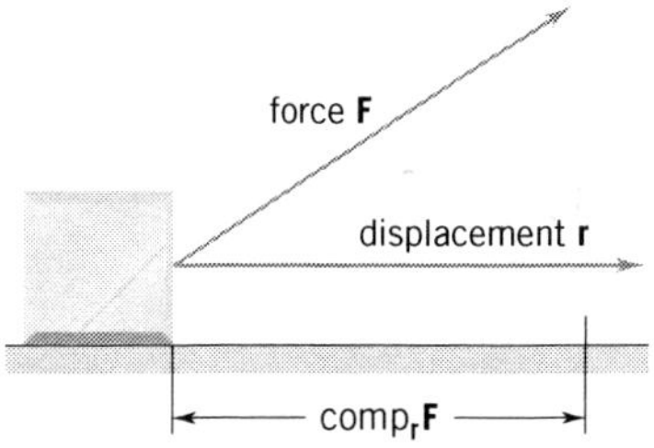

Figure A

Problem 1. A constant force **F** is applied throughout a displacement **r**.

a. Express the work done by **F** as a dot product.
b. What is the work done by **F** if $\mathbf{F} \perp \mathbf{r}$?
c. Show that the work done by $\mathbf{F} = \|\mathbf{F}\|\,\mathbf{i}$ applied throughout the displacement $\mathbf{r} = (b - a)\,\mathbf{i}$ is given by (6.5.1). (Thus we have a generalization of what we had before.)

Problem 2. A sled is pulled along level ground by a force of 15 newtons by a rope that makes an angle θ with the ground. Find the work done by the force in pulling the sled 50 meters if (a) $\theta = 0^\circ$, (b) $\theta = 30^\circ$, (c) $\theta = 45^\circ$. See Figure B.

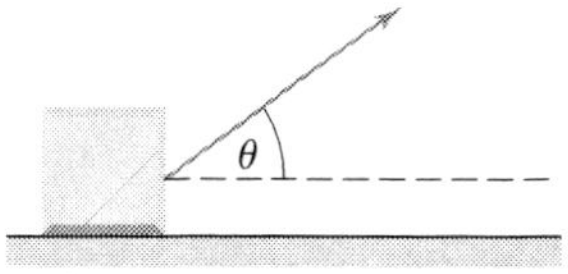

Figure B

Problem 3. Two forces, $\mathbf{F}_1$ and $\mathbf{F}_2$, are applied throughout a displacement **r** at angles θ_1 and θ_2 respectively. Compare the work done by $\mathbf{F}_1$ to that done by $\mathbf{F}_2$ if (a) $\theta_1 = -\theta_2$. (b) $\theta_1 = \pi/3$ and $\theta_2 = \pi/6$.

Problem 4. What is the total work done by a constant force **F** if the object to which it is applied moves around a triangle? Justify your answer.

■ 13.4 THE CROSS PRODUCT

Everything we have done with vectors so far (other than draw pictures) can be generalized to higher dimensions. The cross product, defined below, is particular to three-dimensional space and cannot be generalized to higher dimensions.

Definition of the Cross Product

While the dot product $\mathbf{a} \cdot \mathbf{b}$ is a scalar (and as such is sometimes called the *scalar product* of **a** and **b**), the *cross product* $\mathbf{a} \times \mathbf{b}$ is a vector (sometimes called the *vector product* of **a** and **b**). What is $\mathbf{a} \times \mathbf{b}$? We could directly write down a formula that gives the components of $\mathbf{a} \times \mathbf{b}$ in terms of the components of **a** and **b**, but at this stage that would reveal little. Instead we will begin geometrically. We will define $\mathbf{a} \times \mathbf{b}$ by giving its direction and its magnitude. For convenience, we represent **a** and **b** by arrows that emanate from the same point.

The Direction of a × b

If the vectors **a** and **b** are not parallel, they determine a plane. The vector $\mathbf{a} \times \mathbf{b}$ is perpendicular to this plane and, like the O-xyz-system of coordinate axes, is directed by the right-hand rule: if the fingers of the right hand are curled from **a** toward **b** (through the angle between **a** and **b**), then the thumb points in the direction of $\mathbf{a} \times \mathbf{b}$. (Figure 13.4.1.)

The Magnitude of a × b

If **a** and **b** are not parallel, they form the sides of a parallelogram. (See Figure 13.4.2.) The magnitude of $\mathbf{a} \times \mathbf{b}$ is the area of this parallelogram: $\|\mathbf{a}\|\,\|\mathbf{b}\|\,\sin\theta$.†

†The advantages that ensue from assigning this magnitude to $\mathbf{a} \times \mathbf{b}$ will become apparent as we go on.

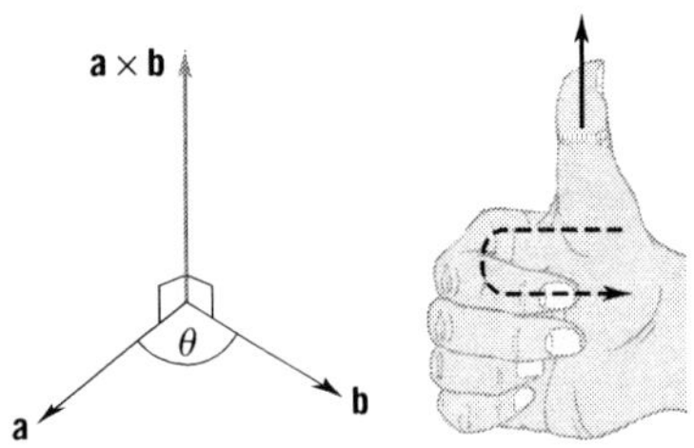

Figure 13.4.1

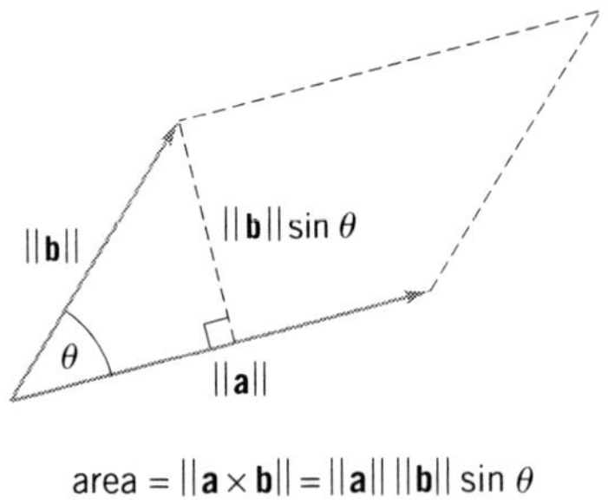

Figure 13.4.2

One more point. What if **a** and **b** are parallel? Then there is no parallelogram and we define **a** × **b** to be 0.

We summarize all this below.

> **DEFINITION 13.4.1**
>
> If **a** and **b** are not parallel, then **a** × **b** is the vector with the following properties:
>
> **1.** **a** × **b** is prependicular to the plane of **a** and **b**.
>
> **2.** **a**, **b**, **a** × **b** form a right-handed triple.
>
> **3.** $\|\mathbf{a} \times \mathbf{b}\| = \|\mathbf{a}\|\|\mathbf{b}\| \sin\theta$ where θ is the angle between **a** and **b**.
>
> If **a** and **b** are parallel, then $\mathbf{a} \times \mathbf{b} = 0$.

Right-Handed Triples

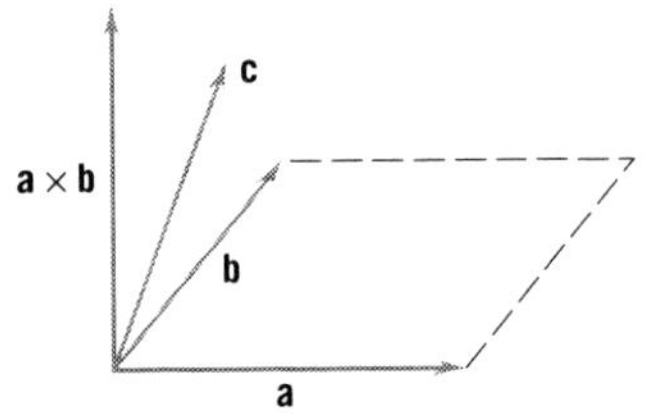

Figure 13.4.3

Start with three vectors **a**, **b**, **c** which emanate from the same point. If the vectors **a** and **b** are not parallel, they determine a plane. Points not on this plane fall into two categories: those on one side of the plane, those on the other side of the plane. The vectors **a, b, c** are said to form a *right-handed triple* provided that **c** and **a** × **b** point to the same side of the plane generated by **a** and **b**. As is clear from Figure 13.4.3,

(13.4.2) $\quad$ **a**, **b**, **c** form a right-handed triple iff $(\mathbf{a} \times \mathbf{b}) \cdot \mathbf{c} > 0.$

Properties of Right-Handed Triples

I. Since $(\mathbf{a} \times \mathbf{b}) \cdot (\mathbf{a} \times \mathbf{b}) = \|(\mathbf{a} \times \mathbf{b})\|^2 > 0$, (**a**, **b**, **a** × **b**) is a right-handed triple.

II. If (**a**, **b**, **c**) is a right-handed triple, then (**c**, **a**, **b**) and (**b**, **c**, **a**) are right-handed triples. (Figure 13.4.4.)

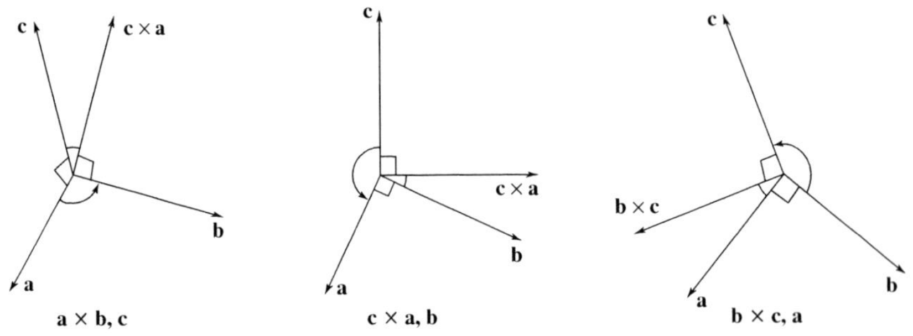

Figure 13.4.4

To maintain right-handedness, we don't have to keep the vectors in the same order, but we do have to keep them in the *same cyclic order*:

$$\mathbf{a} \to \mathbf{b} \to \mathbf{c}$$

Alter the cyclic order and you reverse the orientation

III. Multiply any of the three vectors by a positive scalar and you maintain the orientation: if $(\mathbf{a}, \mathbf{b}, \mathbf{c})$ is a right-handed triple and $\alpha > 0$, then $(\alpha\mathbf{a}, \mathbf{b}, \mathbf{c})$, $(\mathbf{a}, \alpha\mathbf{b}, \mathbf{c})$, and $(\mathbf{a}, b, \alpha\mathbf{c})$ are also right-handed triples. (Draw figures.)

Multiply any of the vectors by a negative scalar and you reverse the orientation: if $(\mathbf{a}, \mathbf{b}, \mathbf{c})$ is a right-handed triple and $\alpha < 0$, then $(\alpha\mathbf{a}, \mathbf{b}, \mathbf{c})$, $(\mathbf{a}, \alpha\mathbf{b}, \mathbf{c})$, and $(\mathbf{a}, \mathbf{b}, \alpha\mathbf{c})$ are not right-handed. (Draw figures.)

Properties of the Cross Product

The cross product is *anticommutative*:

(13.4.3)
$$\mathbf{b} \times \mathbf{a} = -(\mathbf{a} \times \mathbf{b}).$$

To see this, note that both vectors have the same norm and they can differ only in direction. Curling the right-hand fingers from **a** to **b** points the thumb in one direction; curling the fingers from **b** to **a** points the thumb in the opposite direction. (Figure 13.4.5.)

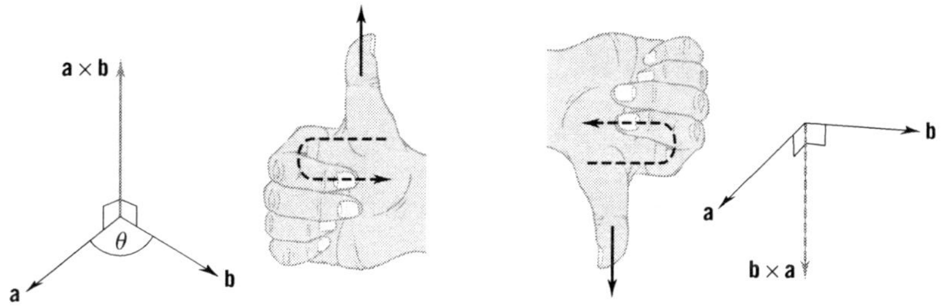

Figure 13.4.5

Scalars can be factored:

(13.4.4)
$$\alpha\mathbf{a} \times \beta\mathbf{b} = \alpha\beta(\mathbf{a} \times \mathbf{b}).$$

If α or β is zero, the result is obvious. We will assume that α and β are both nonzero. In this case the two vectors are perpendicular both to **a** and to **b** and (as you are asked to show in Exercise 35) have the same norm. Thus $\alpha\mathbf{a} \times \beta\mathbf{b} = \pm\alpha\beta(\mathbf{a} \times \mathbf{b})$. That the positive sign holds comes from noting that $\alpha\mathbf{a}$, $\beta\mathbf{b}$, $\alpha\beta(\mathbf{a} \times \mathbf{b})$ is a right-handed triple. This is obvious if α and β are both positive. If not, two of the three coefficients α, β, $\alpha\beta$ are negative and the other is positive. In this case, the first minus sign reverses the orientation of the triple and the second minus sign restores it.

Finally, there are two distributive laws, the verification of which we postpone for a moment.

(13.4.5)
$$\mathbf{a} \times (\mathbf{b} + \mathbf{c}) = (\mathbf{a} \times \mathbf{b}) + (\mathbf{a} \times \mathbf{c}),$$
$$(\mathbf{a} + \mathbf{b}) \times \mathbf{c} = (\mathbf{a} \times \mathbf{c}) + (\mathbf{b} \times \mathbf{c}).$$

The Scalar Triple Product

Earlier we saw that $(\mathbf{a}, \mathbf{b}, \mathbf{c})$ is a right-handed triple iff $(\mathbf{a} \times \mathbf{b}) \cdot \mathbf{c} > 0$. The expression $(\mathbf{a} \times \mathbf{b}) \cdot \mathbf{c}$ is called a *scalar triple product.* The absolute value of this number (it is a number, not a vector) has geometric significance. To describe it, we refer to Figure 13.4.6. There you see a parallelepiped with edges **a, b, c**. The absolute value of the scalar triple product gives the volume of that parallelepiped:

(13.4.6)
$$V = |(\mathbf{a} \times \mathbf{b}) \cdot \mathbf{c}|.$$

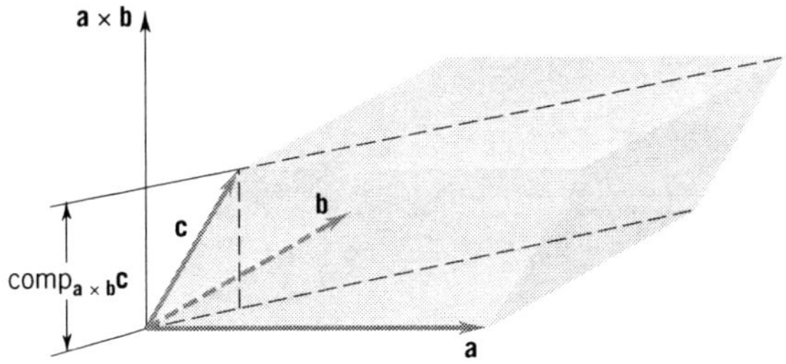

Figure 13.4.6

PROOF The area of the base is $\|\mathbf{a} \times \mathbf{b}\|$. ($\|\mathbf{a} \times \mathbf{b}\|$ was defined so that this would be the case.) The height of the parallelepiped is $|\text{comp}_{\mathbf{a}\times\mathbf{b}}\, \mathbf{c}|$. Therefore

$$V = |\text{comp}_{\mathbf{a}\times\mathbf{b}}\, \mathbf{c}|\,\|\mathbf{a} \times \mathbf{b}\| = |(\mathbf{a} \times \mathbf{b}) \cdot \mathbf{c}| \quad \square$$
(13.3.13)

Of course, we could have formed the same parallelepiped using a different base (for example, using the vectors **c** and **a**) with a correspondingly different height ($\text{comp}_{\mathbf{c}\times\mathbf{a}}\, \mathbf{b}$). Therefore,

$$|(\mathbf{a} \times \mathbf{b}) \cdot \mathbf{c}| = |(\mathbf{c} \times \mathbf{a}) \cdot \mathbf{b}| = |(\mathbf{b} \times \mathbf{c}) \cdot \mathbf{a}|.$$

Since the **a, b, c** appear in the same cyclic order, the expressions inside the absolute value signs all have the same sign. (Property II of right-handed triples.) Therefore

(13.4.7)
$$(\mathbf{a} \times \mathbf{b}) \cdot \mathbf{c} = (\mathbf{c} \times \mathbf{a}) \cdot \mathbf{b} = (\mathbf{b} \times \mathbf{c}) \cdot \mathbf{a}.$$

Verification of the Distributive Laws

We will verify the first distributive law,

$$\mathbf{a} \times (\mathbf{b} + \mathbf{c}) = (\mathbf{a} \times \mathbf{b}) + (\mathbf{a} \times \mathbf{c}).$$

The second follows readily from this one. The argument is left to you as an exercise.

Take an arbitrary vector **r** and form the dot product $[\mathbf{a} \times (\mathbf{b} + \mathbf{c})] \cdot \mathbf{r}$. We can then write

$$\begin{aligned}
[\mathbf{a} \times (\mathbf{b} + \mathbf{c})] \cdot \mathbf{r} &= (\mathbf{r} \times \mathbf{a}) \cdot (\mathbf{b} + \mathbf{c}) && (13.4.7)\\
&= [(\mathbf{r} \times \mathbf{a}) \cdot \mathbf{b}] + [(\mathbf{r} \times \mathbf{a}) \cdot \mathbf{c}]\\
&= [(\mathbf{a} \times \mathbf{b}) \cdot \mathbf{r}] + [(\mathbf{a} \times \mathbf{c}) \cdot \mathbf{r}] && (13.4.7)\\
&= [(\mathbf{a} \times \mathbf{b}) + (\mathbf{a} \times \mathbf{c})] \cdot \mathbf{r}.
\end{aligned}$$

Since this holds true for all vectors **r**, it holds true for **i**, **j**, **k** and proves that

$$\mathbf{a} \times (\mathbf{b} + \mathbf{c}) = (\mathbf{a} \times \mathbf{b}) + (\mathbf{a} \times \mathbf{c}).$$

(Both sides have the same **i**, **j**, **k** components.) ❑

The Components of $a \times b$

You have learned a lot about cross products, but you still have not seen $\mathbf{a} \times \mathbf{b}$ expressed in terms of the components of **a** and **b**. To derive the formula that does this, we need to observe one more fact, one which follows directly from the definition of cross product and the fact that our O-xyz coordinate system satisfies the right-hand rule.

(13.4.8) $$\mathbf{i} \times \mathbf{j} = \mathbf{k}, \quad \mathbf{j} \times \mathbf{k} = \mathbf{i}, \quad \mathbf{k} \times \mathbf{i} = \mathbf{j}.$$ (Figure 13.4.7)

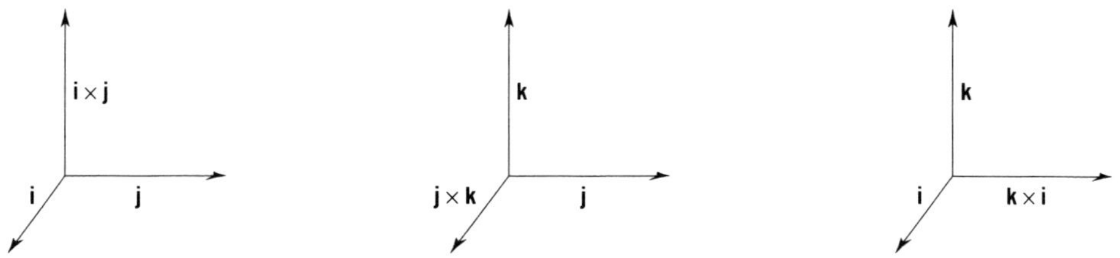

Figure 13.4.7

One way to remember these products is to arrange **i**, **j**, **k** in cyclic order, $\mathbf{i} \to \mathbf{j} \to \mathbf{k}$, and note that

[each coordinate unit vector] × [the next one] = [the third one].

THEOREM 13.4.9

For vectors $\mathbf{a} = a_1\mathbf{i} + a_2\mathbf{j} + a_3\mathbf{k}$ and $\mathbf{b} = b_1\mathbf{i} + b_2\mathbf{j} + b_3\mathbf{k}$,

$$\mathbf{a} \times \mathbf{b} = (a_2b_3 - a_3b_2)\mathbf{i} - (a_1b_3 - a_3b_1)\mathbf{j} + (a_1b_2 - a_2b_1)\mathbf{k}.$$

Those of you who have studied some linear algebra will recognize that the jumble of symbols we have just written down for $\mathbf{a} \times \mathbf{b}$ can be elegantly summarized by the use of determinants. Here is Theorem 13.4.9 stated in terms of determinants. (If you are not familiar with determinants, see Appendix A-2.)

THEOREM 13.4.9′

For vectors $\mathbf{a} = a_1\mathbf{i} + a_2\mathbf{j} + a_3\mathbf{k}$ and $\mathbf{b} = b_1\mathbf{i} + b_2\mathbf{j} + b_3\mathbf{k}$,

$$\mathbf{a} \times \mathbf{b} = \begin{vmatrix} \mathbf{i} & \mathbf{j} & \mathbf{k} \\ a_1 & a_2 & a_3 \\ b_1 & b_2 & b_3 \end{vmatrix} = \begin{vmatrix} a_2 & a_3 \\ b_2 & b_3 \end{vmatrix}\mathbf{i} - \begin{vmatrix} a_1 & a_3 \\ b_1 & b_3 \end{vmatrix}\mathbf{j} + \begin{vmatrix} a_1 & a_2 \\ b_1 & b_2 \end{vmatrix}\mathbf{k}.$$

(The 3×3 determinant with **i**, **j**, **k** in the top row is there only as a mnemonic device.)

PROOF The hard work has all been done. With what you know about cross products now, the proof is just a matter of algebraic manipulation:

$$\mathbf{a}\times\mathbf{b} = (a_1\mathbf{i}+a_2\mathbf{j}+a_3\mathbf{k})\times(b_1\mathbf{i}+b_2\mathbf{j}+b_3\mathbf{k})$$

$$= a_1b_2(\mathbf{i}\times\mathbf{j}) + a_1b_3(\mathbf{i}\times\mathbf{k}) + a_2b_1(\mathbf{j}\times\mathbf{i}) + a_2b_3(\mathbf{j}\times\mathbf{k}) + a_3b_1(\mathbf{k}\times\mathbf{i}) + a_3b_2(\mathbf{k}\times\mathbf{j})$$

↑ $\mathbf{i}\times\mathbf{i}=\mathbf{j}\times\mathbf{j}=\mathbf{k}\times\mathbf{k}=0$

$$= a_1b_2\mathbf{k} - a_1b_3\mathbf{j} - a_2b_1\mathbf{k} + a_2b_3\mathbf{i} + a_3b_1\mathbf{j} - a_3b_2\mathbf{i}$$

$$= (a_2b_3 - a_3b_2)\mathbf{i} - (a_1b_3 - a_3b_1)\mathbf{j} + (a_1b_2 - a_2b_1)\mathbf{k} \quad \text{(this proves Theorem 13.4.9)}$$

$$= \begin{vmatrix} a_2 & a_3 \\ b_2 & b_3 \end{vmatrix}\mathbf{i} - \begin{vmatrix} a_1 & a_3 \\ b_1 & b_3 \end{vmatrix}\mathbf{j} + \begin{vmatrix} a_1 & a_2 \\ b_1 & b_2 \end{vmatrix}\mathbf{k}. \quad ❑$$

Example 1 Calculate $\mathbf{a}\times\mathbf{b}$ given that $\mathbf{a}=\mathbf{i}-2\mathbf{j}+3\mathbf{k}$ and $\mathbf{b}=2\mathbf{i}+\mathbf{j}-\mathbf{k}$.

SOLUTION

$$\mathbf{a}\times\mathbf{b} = \begin{vmatrix} \mathbf{i} & \mathbf{j} & \mathbf{k} \\ 1 & -2 & 3 \\ 2 & 1 & -1 \end{vmatrix} = \begin{vmatrix} -2 & 3 \\ 1 & -1 \end{vmatrix}\mathbf{i} - \begin{vmatrix} 1 & 3 \\ 2 & -1 \end{vmatrix}\mathbf{j} + \begin{vmatrix} 1 & -2 \\ 2 & 1 \end{vmatrix}\mathbf{k}$$

$$= -\mathbf{i} + 7\mathbf{j} + 5\mathbf{k}. \quad ❑$$

Example 2 Calculate $\mathbf{a}\times\mathbf{b}$ given that $\mathbf{a}=\mathbf{i}-\mathbf{j}$ and $\mathbf{b}=\mathbf{i}+\mathbf{k}$.

SOLUTION

$$\mathbf{a}\times\mathbf{b} = \begin{vmatrix} \mathbf{i} & \mathbf{j} & \mathbf{k} \\ 1 & -1 & 0 \\ 1 & 0 & 1 \end{vmatrix} = \begin{vmatrix} -1 & 0 \\ 0 & 1 \end{vmatrix}\mathbf{i} - \begin{vmatrix} 1 & 0 \\ 1 & 1 \end{vmatrix}\mathbf{j} + \begin{vmatrix} 1 & -1 \\ 1 & 0 \end{vmatrix}\mathbf{k}$$

$$= -\mathbf{i} - \mathbf{j} + \mathbf{k}. \quad ❑$$

In Examples 1 and 2 we calculated some cross products using Theorem 13.4.9′. We can obtain the same results just by applying the distributive laws. For example, for $\mathbf{a}=\mathbf{i}-2\mathbf{j}+3\mathbf{k}$ and $\mathbf{b}=2\mathbf{i}+\mathbf{j}-\mathbf{k}$, we have

$$\mathbf{a}\times\mathbf{b} = (\mathbf{i}-2\mathbf{j}+3\mathbf{k})\times(2\mathbf{i}+\mathbf{j}-\mathbf{k})$$

$$= (\mathbf{i}\times\mathbf{j}) - (\mathbf{i}\times\mathbf{k}) - 4(\mathbf{j}\times\mathbf{i}) + 2(\mathbf{j}\times\mathbf{k}) + 6(\mathbf{j}\times\mathbf{i}) + 3(\mathbf{k}\times\mathbf{j})$$

$$= \mathbf{k} + \mathbf{j} + 4\mathbf{k} + 2\mathbf{i} + 6\mathbf{j} - 3\mathbf{i} = -\mathbf{i} + 7\mathbf{j} + 5\mathbf{k}.$$

Example 3 (*Useful*) Show that the triple scalar product can be written as a determinant:

(13.4.10)
$$(\mathbf{a}\times\mathbf{b})\cdot\mathbf{c} = \begin{vmatrix} a_1 & a_2 & a_3 \\ b_1 & b_2 & b_3 \\ c_1 & c_2 & c_3 \end{vmatrix}.$$

SOLUTION

$$(\mathbf{a}\times\mathbf{b})\cdot\mathbf{c} = \mathbf{c}\cdot(\mathbf{a}\times\mathbf{b})$$

$$= (c_1\mathbf{i}+c_2\mathbf{j}+c_3\mathbf{k})\cdot\left(\begin{vmatrix} a_2 & a_3 \\ b_2 & b_3 \end{vmatrix}\mathbf{i} - \begin{vmatrix} a_1 & a_3 \\ b_1 & b_3 \end{vmatrix}\mathbf{j} + \begin{vmatrix} a_1 & a_2 \\ b_1 & b_2 \end{vmatrix}\mathbf{k}\right)$$

$$= c_1\begin{vmatrix} a_2 & a_3 \\ b_2 & b_3 \end{vmatrix} - c_2\begin{vmatrix} a_1 & a_3 \\ b_1 & b_3 \end{vmatrix} + c_3\begin{vmatrix} a_1 & a_2 \\ b_1 & b_2 \end{vmatrix}.$$

This is the expansion of

$$\begin{vmatrix} a_1 & a_2 & a_3 \\ b_1 & b_2 & b_3 \\ c_1 & c_2 & c_3 \end{vmatrix}$$

by the elements of the third row. ❑

A Suggestion: Vectors were defined as ordered triples, and many of the early proofs were done by "breaking up" vectors into their components. This may give you the impression that the method of "breakup" and working with the components is the first thing to try when confronted with a problem that involves vectors. If it is a *computational* problem, this method may give good results. But if you have to *analyze* a situation involving vectors, particularly one in which geometry plays a role, then the "breakup" strategy is seldom the best. Think instead of using the *operations* we have defined on vectors: addition, subtraction, scalar multiplication, dot product, cross product. Being geometrically motivated, these operations are likely to provide greater understanding than breaking up everything in sight into components. ❑

Example 4 Verify *Lagrange's identity*: $\|\mathbf{a} \times \mathbf{b}\|^2 + (\mathbf{a} \cdot \mathbf{b})^2 = \|\mathbf{a}\|^2\|\mathbf{b}\|^2$.

SOLUTION We could begin by writing

$$\begin{aligned}\|\mathbf{a} \times \mathbf{b}\|^2 &= (a_2b_3 - a_3b_2)^2 + (a_1b_3 - a_3b_1)^2 + (a_1b_2 - a_2b_1)^2 \\ (\mathbf{a} \cdot \mathbf{b})^2 &= (a_1b_1 + a_2b_2 + a_3b_3)^2 \\ \|\mathbf{a}\|^2\|\mathbf{b}\|^2 &= (a_1^2 + a_2^2 + a_3^2)(b_1^2 + b_2^2 + b_3^2),\end{aligned}$$

but this would take us into a morass of arithmetic. It is much more fruitful to proceed as follows:

$$\|\mathbf{a} \times \mathbf{b}\| = \|\mathbf{a}\|\,\|\mathbf{b}\| \sin\theta \qquad \text{and} \qquad \mathbf{a} \cdot \mathbf{b} = \|\mathbf{a}\|\,\|\mathbf{b}\| \cos\theta.$$

Therefore

$$\begin{aligned}\|\mathbf{a} \times \mathbf{b}\|^2 + (\mathbf{a} \cdot \mathbf{b})^2 &= \|\mathbf{a}\|^2\|\mathbf{b}\|^2 \sin^2\theta + \|\mathbf{a}\|^2\|\mathbf{b}\|^2 \cos^2\theta \\ &= \|\mathbf{a}\|^2\|\mathbf{b}\|^2(\sin^2\theta + \cos^2\theta) = \|\mathbf{a}\|^2\|\mathbf{b}\|^2.\end{aligned}$$ ❑

Remark Lagrange's identity is one more dividend we get from the apparently arbitrary definition of $\|\mathbf{a} \times \mathbf{b}\|$. ❑

Three Additional Identities

You have seen that the cross product is not commutative. It is also not associative: the vectors $\mathbf{a} \times (\mathbf{b} \times \mathbf{c})$ and $(\mathbf{a} \times \mathbf{b}) \times \mathbf{c}$ are generally not the same. For example,

$$\mathbf{i} \times (\mathbf{i} \times \mathbf{j}) = \mathbf{i} \times \mathbf{k} = -\mathbf{j} \qquad \text{but} \qquad (\mathbf{i} \times \mathbf{i}) \times \mathbf{j} = \mathbf{0} \times \mathbf{j} = \mathbf{0}.$$

What is true instead is that

(13.4.11)

$$\begin{aligned}\mathbf{a} \times (\mathbf{b} \times \mathbf{c}) &= (\mathbf{a} \cdot \mathbf{c})\mathbf{b} - (\mathbf{a} \cdot \mathbf{b})\mathbf{c}, \\ (\mathbf{a} \times \mathbf{b}) \times \mathbf{c} &= (\mathbf{c} \cdot \mathbf{a})\mathbf{b} - (\mathbf{c} \cdot \mathbf{b})\mathbf{a}.\end{aligned}$$

There is one more identity that we want to mention:

(13.4.12) $$(\mathbf{a}\times\mathbf{b})\cdot(\mathbf{c}\times\mathbf{d}) = (\mathbf{a}\cdot\mathbf{c})(\mathbf{b}\cdot\mathbf{d}) - (\mathbf{a}\cdot\mathbf{d})(\mathbf{b}\cdot\mathbf{c}).$$

The verification of these three identities is left to you in the Exercises.

Remark Dot products and cross products appear frequently in physics and in engineering. Work is a dot product. So is the power expended by a force. Torque and angular momentum are cross products. Turn on a television set and watch the dots on the screen. How they move is determined by the laws of electromagnetism. It is all based on Maxwell's four equations. Two of them feature dot products; two of them feature cross products. ❑

EXERCISES 13.4

Exercises 1–20. Calculate.

1. $(\mathbf{i}+\mathbf{j})\times(\mathbf{i}-\mathbf{j})$.
2. $(\mathbf{i}-\mathbf{j})\times(\mathbf{j}-\mathbf{i})$.

3. $(\mathbf{i}-\mathbf{j})\times\mathbf{j}-\mathbf{k})$.
4. $\mathbf{j}\times(2\mathbf{i}-\mathbf{k})$.

5. $(2\mathbf{j}-\mathbf{k})\times(\mathbf{i}-3\mathbf{j})$.
6. $\mathbf{i}\cdot(\mathbf{j}\times\mathbf{k})$.

7. $\mathbf{j}\cdot(\mathbf{i}\times\mathbf{k})$.
8. $(\mathbf{j}\times\mathbf{i})\cdot(\mathbf{i}\times\mathbf{k})$.

9. $(\mathbf{i}\times\mathbf{j})\times\mathbf{k}$.
10. $\mathbf{k}\cdot(\mathbf{j}\times\mathbf{i})$.

11. $\mathbf{j}\cdot(\mathbf{k}\times\mathbf{i})$.
12. $\mathbf{j}\times(\mathbf{k}\times\mathbf{i})$.

13. $(\mathbf{i}+3\mathbf{j}-\mathbf{k})\times(\mathbf{i}+\mathbf{k})$.

14. $(3\mathbf{i}-2\mathbf{j}+\mathbf{k})\times(\mathbf{i}-\mathbf{j}+\mathbf{k})$.

15. $(\mathbf{i}+\mathbf{j}+\mathbf{k})\times(2\mathbf{i}+\mathbf{k})$.

16. $(2\mathbf{i}-\mathbf{k})\times(\mathbf{i}-2\mathbf{j}+2\mathbf{k})$.

17. $[2\mathbf{i}+\mathbf{j}]\cdot[(i-3\mathbf{j}+\mathbf{k})\times(4\mathbf{i}+\mathbf{k})]$.

18. $[(-2\mathbf{i}+\mathbf{j}-3\mathbf{k})\times\mathbf{i}]\times[\mathbf{i}+\mathbf{j}]$.

19. $[(\mathbf{i}-\mathbf{j})\times(\mathbf{j}-\mathbf{k})]\times[\mathbf{i}+5\mathbf{k}]$.

20. $[\mathbf{i}-\mathbf{j}]\times[(\mathbf{j}-\mathbf{k})\times(\mathbf{j}+5\mathbf{k})]$.

21. Find the unit vectors which are perpendicular to both

$$\mathbf{a} = (1, 3, -1) \quad \text{and} \quad \mathbf{b} = (2, 0, 1).$$

22. Exercise 21 for $\mathbf{a} = (1, 2, 3)$ and $\mathbf{b} = (2, 1, 1)$.

Exercises 23–26. Find a unit vector **N** which is perpendicular to the plane of P, Q, R, and find the area of triangle PQR.

23. $P(0, 1, 0)$, $Q(-1, 1, 2)$, $R(2, 1, -1)$.

24. $P(1, 2, 3)$, $Q(-1, 3, 2)$, $R(3, -1, 2)$.

25. $P(1, -1, 4)$, $Q(2, 0, 1)$, $R(0, 2, 3)$.

26. $P(2, -1, 3)$, $Q(4, 1, -1)$, $R(-3, 0, 5)$.

Exercises 27–28. Find the volume of the parallelepiped with the edges given.

27. $\mathbf{i}+\mathbf{j}$, $2\mathbf{i}-\mathbf{k}$, $3\mathbf{j}+\mathbf{k}$.

28. $\mathbf{i}-3\mathbf{j}+\mathbf{k}$, $2\mathbf{j}-\mathbf{k}$, $\mathbf{i}+\mathbf{j}-2\mathbf{k}$.

29. Given the points $O(0, 0, 0)$, $P(1, 2, 3)$, $Q(1, 1, 2)$, $R(2, 1, 1)$, find the volume of the parallelepiped with edges $\overrightarrow{OP}, \overrightarrow{OQ}, \overrightarrow{OR}$.

30. Given the points $P(1, -1, 4)$, $Q(2, 0, 1)$, $R(0, 2, 3)$, $S(3, 5, 7)$, find the volume of the parallelepiped with edges $\overrightarrow{PQ}, \overrightarrow{PR}, \overrightarrow{PS}$.

31. Express $(\mathbf{a}+\mathbf{b})\times(\mathbf{a}-\mathbf{b})$ as a scalar multiple of $\mathbf{a}\times\mathbf{b}$.

32. Earlier we verified that $\mathbf{a}\times(\mathbf{b}+\mathbf{c}) = (\mathbf{a}\times\mathbf{b}) + (\mathbf{a}\times\mathbf{c})$. Show now that

$$(\mathbf{a}+\mathbf{b})\times\mathbf{c} = (\mathbf{a}\times\mathbf{c}) + (\mathbf{b}\times\mathbf{c}).$$

33. Suppose that $\mathbf{a}\times\mathbf{i} = \mathbf{0}$ and $\mathbf{a}\times\mathbf{j} = \mathbf{0}$. What can you conclude about $\mathbf{a}$?

34. Show that if $\mathbf{a} = a_1\mathbf{i} + a_2\mathbf{j}$ and $\mathbf{b} = b_1\mathbf{i} + b_2\mathbf{j}$, then $\mathbf{a}\times\mathbf{b}$ is parallel to $\mathbf{k}$.

35. Show that $\alpha\mathbf{a}\times\beta\mathbf{b}$ and $\alpha\beta(\mathbf{a}\times\mathbf{b})$ have the same norm.

36. (a) Let **a**, **b**, **c** be distinct nonzero vectors. Show that

$$\mathbf{a}\times\mathbf{b} = \mathbf{a}\times\mathbf{c} \quad \text{iff} \quad \mathbf{a} \text{ and } \mathbf{b}-\mathbf{c} \text{ are parallel.}$$

(b) Sketch a figure depicting all the vectors **c** that satisfy the relation $\mathbf{a}\times\mathbf{b} = \mathbf{a}\times\mathbf{c}$.

37. Let **a**, **b**, **c** be vectors. Which of the following expressions make sense and which do not? Explain your answer in each case.

(a) $\mathbf{a}\cdot(\mathbf{b}\times\mathbf{c})$.
(b) $\mathbf{a}\times(\mathbf{b}\cdot\mathbf{c})$.
(c) $\mathbf{a}\cdot(\mathbf{b}\cdot\mathbf{c})$.
(d) $\mathbf{a}\times(\mathbf{b}\times\mathbf{c})$.

38. For each vector **a** determine all vectors **b** for which $(\mathbf{a}\times\mathbf{b})\cdot\mathbf{b} \neq 0$.

39. Given that **a**, **b**, **c** are nonzero vectors, find all vectors **d** for which

$$\mathbf{d}\cdot\mathbf{a} = \mathbf{d}\cdot\mathbf{b} = \mathbf{d}\cdot\mathbf{c}.$$

40. Given that **a**, **b**, **c** are mutually perpendicular, show that

$$\mathbf{a}\times(\mathbf{b}\times\mathbf{c}) = \mathbf{0}.$$

41. Let $\mathbf{a} \neq \mathbf{0}$. Show that if

$$\mathbf{a}\times\mathbf{b} = \mathbf{a}\times\mathbf{c} \quad \text{and} \quad \mathbf{a}\cdot\mathbf{b} = \mathbf{a}\cdot\mathbf{c}, \quad \text{then} \quad \mathbf{b} = \mathbf{c}.$$

42. (a) Verify the identity

$$\mathbf{a}\times(\mathbf{b}\times\mathbf{c}) = (\mathbf{a}\cdot\mathbf{c})\mathbf{b} - (\mathbf{a}\cdot\mathbf{b})\mathbf{c}.$$

HINT: Show that both sides have the same **i**, **j**, **k** components.

(b) Verify the identity

$$(\mathbf{a} \times \mathbf{b}) \times \mathbf{c} = (\mathbf{c} \cdot \mathbf{a})\mathbf{b} - (\mathbf{c} \cdot \mathbf{b})\mathbf{a}.$$

HINT: $(\mathbf{a} \times \mathbf{b}) \times \mathbf{c} = -[\mathbf{c} \times (\mathbf{a} \times \mathbf{b})]$.

(c) Finally, show that

$$(\mathbf{a} \times \mathbf{b}) \cdot (\mathbf{c} \times \mathbf{d}) = (\mathbf{a} \cdot \mathbf{c})(\mathbf{b} \cdot \mathbf{d}) - (\mathbf{a} \cdot \mathbf{d})(\mathbf{b} \cdot \mathbf{c}).$$

HINT: Set $\mathbf{c} \times \mathbf{d} = \mathbf{r}$ and use (13.4.7).

43. Let **a** and **b** be nonzero vectors with $\mathbf{a} \perp \mathbf{b}$, and set $\mathbf{c} = \mathbf{a} \times \mathbf{b}$. Express $\mathbf{c} \times \mathbf{a}$ as a multiple of **b**.

44. Given that **u** is a unit vector, prove that each vector **a** can be written as the sum of a vector parallel to **u** and a vector perpendicular to **u**:

$$\mathbf{a} = \underbrace{(\mathbf{a} \cdot \mathbf{u})\mathbf{u}}_{\text{parallel to } \mathbf{u}} + \underbrace{(\mathbf{u} \times \mathbf{a}) \times \mathbf{u}}_{\text{perpendicular to } \mathbf{u}}$$

HINT: Use Exercise 42(b).

45. Suppose **a** and **b** are vectors such that

$$\mathbf{a} \times \mathbf{b} = \mathbf{0} \quad \text{and} \quad \mathbf{a} \cdot \mathbf{b} = 0.$$

What can you conclude about a and b?

Exercises 46 and 47 relate to the tetrahedron with vertices $O(0, 0, 0)$, $P(a, 0, 0)$, $Q(0, b, 0)$, $R(0, 0, c)$ shown in the figure.

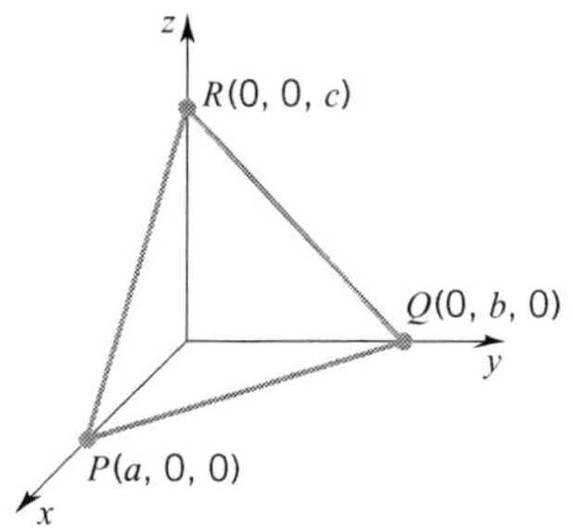

46. Derive a formula for the area D of the face of the tetrahedron with vertices P, Q, R. HINT: Extend the face to a parallelogram.

47. Let A be the area of the face opposite vertex P, let B be the area of the face opposite vertex Q, and let C be the area of the face opposite vertex R. Show that

$$A^2 + B^2 + C^2 = D^2.$$

You can think of this as a three-dimensional version of the Pythagorean theorem.

48. Which of the following dot products are equal?

$\mathbf{a} \cdot (\mathbf{b} \times \mathbf{c})$, $\mathbf{a} \cdot (\mathbf{c} \times \mathbf{b})$, $(\mathbf{a} \times \mathbf{b}) \cdot \mathbf{c}$, $(\mathbf{c} \times \mathbf{a}) \cdot \mathbf{b}$,
$(\mathbf{b} \times \mathbf{c}) \cdot \mathbf{a}$, $\mathbf{c} \cdot (\mathbf{b} \times \mathbf{a})$, $(-\mathbf{a} \times \mathbf{b}) \cdot \mathbf{c}$, $(\mathbf{a} \times -\mathbf{c}) \cdot \mathbf{b}$.

■ 13.5 LINES

Preliminary Remark In themselves vectors have no definite location, just magnitude and direction. For some applications it is convenient to assign to a vector a particular location, a particular starting point. A vector which has a particular starting point is called a *bound* vector. If **a** is a bound vector, then **a** can be represented by one and only one arrow: the arrow that has the specified magnitude, the specified direction, and the specified starting point. By writing $\mathbf{a} = \overrightarrow{PQ}$ we indicate not only that **a** has the length of $\overrightarrow{PQ}$ and the direction $\overrightarrow{PQ}$, but that **a** is bound to (attached to) the point P. In effect, then, **a** is $\overrightarrow{PQ}$. ❑

Vector Parametrizations

We begin with the idea that two distinct points determine a line. In Figure 13.5.1 we have marked two points and the line l that they determine. To obtain a vector characterization of l, we choose the vectors $\mathbf{r}_0$ and $\mathbf{d}$ as in Figure 13.5.2. The vector $\mathbf{r}_0$ is bound to the origin; the vector $\mathbf{d}$ is bound to the tip of $\mathbf{r}_0$. Since we began with two distinct points, the vector $\mathbf{d}$ is nonzero.

In Figure 13.5.3, we have drawn an additional vector **r**, bound at the origin. The vector that begins at the tip of $\mathbf{r}_0$ and ends at the tip of **r** will fall on l iff

$$\mathbf{r} - \mathbf{r}_0 \quad \text{and} \quad \mathbf{d} \quad \text{are parallel;}$$

this in turn will happen iff

$$\mathbf{r} - \mathbf{r}_0 = t\mathbf{d} \qquad \text{for some real number } t,$$

or, equivalently, iff

$$\mathbf{r} = \mathbf{r}_0 + t\mathbf{d} \qquad \text{for some real number } t.$$

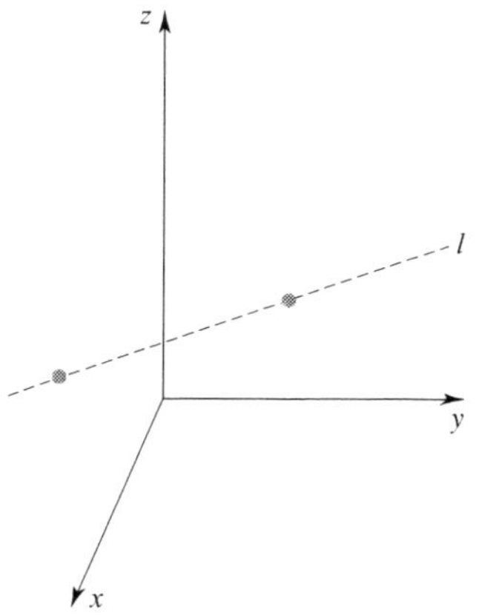

Figure 13.5.1

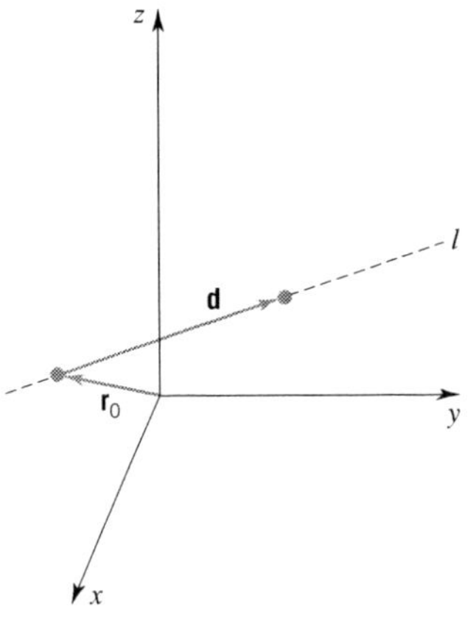

Figure 13.5.2

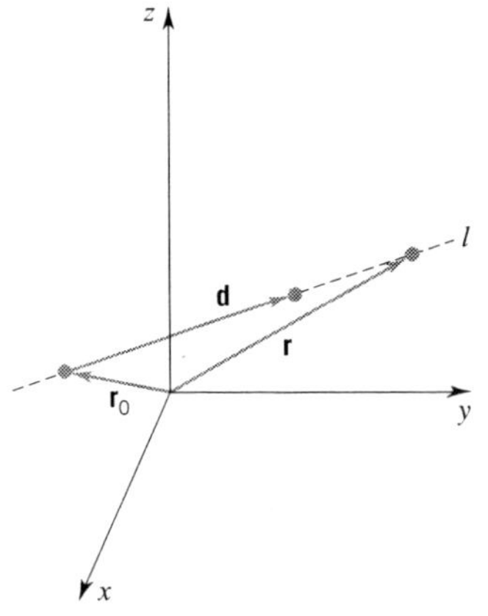

Figure 13.5.3

The vector function

(13.5.1)
$$\mathbf{r}(t) = \mathbf{r}_0 + t\mathbf{d}, \qquad t \text{ real}$$

parametrizes the line l: by varying t we vary the vector $\mathbf{r}(t)$, but the tip of $\mathbf{r}(t)$ remains on l; as t ranges over the set of real numbers, the tip of $\mathbf{r}(t)$ traces out the line l. The vector $\mathbf{d}$ is called a *direction vector* for the line.

The line that passes through the point $P(x_0, y_0, x_0)$ with direction vector $\mathbf{d} = d_1\mathbf{i} + d_2\mathbf{j} + d_3\mathbf{k}$ can be parametrized by setting

(13.5.2)
$$\mathbf{r}(t) = (x_0 + td_1)\,\mathbf{i} + (y_0 + td_2)\,\mathbf{j} + (z_0 + td_3)\,\mathbf{k}.$$

PROOF Set $\mathbf{r}_0 = \overrightarrow{OP}$. Then $\mathbf{r}_0 = x_0\mathbf{i} + y_0\mathbf{j} + z_0\mathbf{k}$. Equation (13.5.2) is equation $\mathbf{r}(t) = \mathbf{r}_0 + t\mathbf{d}$ in expanded form:

$$\begin{aligned}\mathbf{r}(t) = \mathbf{r}_0 + t\,\mathbf{d} &= (x_0\,\mathbf{i} + y_0\,\mathbf{j} + z_0\,\mathbf{k}) + t(d_1\,\mathbf{i} + d_2\,\mathbf{j} + d_3\,\mathbf{k})\\ &= (x_0 + dt_1)\,\mathbf{i} + (y_0 + td_2)\,\mathbf{j} + (z_0 + td_3)\,\mathbf{k}. \quad \square\end{aligned}$$

Example 1 Parametrize the line that passes through the point $P(1, -1, 2)$ and has direction vector $2\mathbf{i} - 3\mathbf{j} + \mathbf{k}$.

SOLUTION We set

$$\mathbf{r}_0 = \mathbf{i} - \mathbf{j} + 2\mathbf{k} \qquad \text{and} \qquad \mathbf{d} = 2\mathbf{i} - 3\mathbf{j} + \mathbf{k}.$$

Equation $\mathbf{r}(t) = \mathbf{r}_0 + t\mathbf{d}$ gives

$$\mathbf{r}(t) = (\mathbf{i} - \mathbf{j} + 2\mathbf{k}) + t(2\mathbf{i} - 3\mathbf{j} + \mathbf{k}),$$

which we write as

$$\mathbf{r}(t) = (1 + 2t)\,\mathbf{i} - (1 + 3t)\,\mathbf{j} + (2 + t)\,\mathbf{k}. \quad \square$$

Direction vectors are not unique. If $\mathbf{d}$ is a direction vector for l, then every nonzero vector parallel to $\mathbf{d}$, every vector of the form $\alpha\mathbf{d}$ with $\alpha \neq 0$, can be used as a direction vector for l: what $\mathbf{r}_0 + t\mathbf{d}$ produces at t is produced by $\mathbf{r}_0 + t(\alpha\mathbf{d})$ at t/α.

Equations

$$\mathbf{r}_0 + t\mathbf{d}, \qquad \mathbf{r}_0 + t(\tfrac{1}{2})\mathbf{d}, \qquad \mathbf{r}_0 - t(3\mathbf{d})$$

all give the same line.

Example 2 The line given by

$$\mathbf{r}(t) = (3\mathbf{i} - 2\mathbf{j} + 4\mathbf{k}) + t\left(-\tfrac{2}{3}\mathbf{i} - \tfrac{1}{9}\mathbf{j} + \tfrac{2}{9}\mathbf{k}\right)$$

can be defined more simply by setting

$$\mathbf{r}(t) = (3\mathbf{i} - 2\mathbf{j} + 4\mathbf{k}) + t(6\mathbf{i} + \mathbf{j} - 2\mathbf{k}).$$

(We multiplied the initial direction vector by -9.) ❑

If $\mathbf{d} = d_1\mathbf{i} + d_2\mathbf{j} + d_3\mathbf{k}$ is a direction vector for l, the components d_1, d_2, d_3 are called *direction numbers* for l. From what we just stated, if d_1, d_2, d_3 are direction numbers for l, then so are $\alpha d_1, \alpha d_2, \alpha d_3$ provided only that $\alpha \neq 0$.

In Example 2 we replaced the direction numbers $-\frac{2}{3}, -\frac{1}{9}, \frac{2}{9}$ by $6, 1, -2$.

Scalar Parametric Equations

It follows from (13.5.2) that the line that passes through the point $P(x_0, y_0, z_0)$ with direction numbers d_1, d_2, d_3 can be parametrized by three scalar equations:

(13.5.3) $$x(t) = x_0 + d_1 t, \qquad y(t) = y_0 + d_2 t, \qquad z(t) = z_0 + d_3 t.$$

These quantities are the **i**, **j**, **k** components of the vector $\mathbf{r}(t) = \mathbf{r}_0 + t\mathbf{d}$.

Example 3 Write scalar parametric equations for the line that passes through the point $P(-1, 4, 2)$ with direction numbers $1, 2, 3$.

SOLUTION In this case the scalar equations

$$x(t) = x_0 + d_1 t, \qquad y(t) = y_0 + d_2 t, \qquad z(t) = z_0 + d_3 t$$

take the form

$$x(t) = -1 + t, \qquad y(t) = 4 + 2t, \qquad z(t) = 2 + 3t. \quad ❑$$

Example 4 What direction numbers are displayed by the parametric equations

$$x(t) = 3 - t, \qquad y(t) = 2 + 4t, \qquad z(t) = 1 - 5t?$$

What other direction numbers could be used for the same line?

SOLUTION The direction numbers displayed are $-1, 4, -5$. Any triple of the form

$$-\alpha, 4\alpha, -5\alpha, \qquad \text{with } \alpha \neq 0$$

could be used as a set of direction numbers for that same line. ❑

Symmetric Form

If the direction numbers are all nonzero, then each of the scalar parametric equations can be solved for t:

$$t = \frac{x(t) - x_0}{d_1}, \qquad t = \frac{y(t) - y_0}{d_2}, \qquad t = \frac{z(t) - z_0}{d_3}.$$

Eliminating the parameter t, we obtain three equations:

$$\frac{x - x_0}{d_1} = \frac{y - y_0}{d_2}, \qquad \frac{y - y_0}{d_2} = \frac{z - z_0}{d_3}, \qquad \frac{x - x_0}{d_1} = \frac{z - z_0}{d_3}.$$

Any two of these equations suffice; the third is redundant and can be discarded. Rather than decide which equation to discard, we simply write

(13.5.4)

$$\frac{x - x_0}{d_1} = \frac{y - y_0}{d_2} = \frac{z - z_0}{d_3}.$$

These are the equations of a line written in *symmetric form*. The equations of a line can be written in this form only if d_1, d_2, d_3 are all different from zero.

Example 5 Write equations in symmetric form for the line that passes through the point $P(x_0, y_0, z_0)$ and $Q(x_1, y_1, z_1)$. Under what conditions are the equations valid?

SOLUTION As direction numbers we can take the triple

$$x_1 - x_0, \qquad y_1 - y_0, \qquad z_1 - z_0.$$

We can base our calculations on $P(x_0, y_0, z_0)$ and write

$$\frac{x - x_0}{x_1 - x_0} = \frac{y - y_0}{y_1 - y_0} = \frac{z - z_0}{z_1 - z_0},$$

or we can base our calculations on $Q(x_1, y_1, z_1)$ and write

$$\frac{x - x_1}{x_1 - x_0} = \frac{y - y_1}{y_1 - y_0} = \frac{z - z_1}{z_1 - z_0}.$$

Both sets of equations are valid provided that $x_1 \neq x_0, y_1 \neq y_0, z_1 \neq z_0$. ❑

Equations 13.5.4 can be used only if the direction numbers are all different from zero. If one of the direction numbers is zero, then one of the coordinates is constant. As you will see, this simplifies the algebra. Geometrically, it means that the line lies on a plane which is parallel to one of the coordinate planes.

Suppose, for example, that $d_3 = 0$. Then the scalar parametric equations take the form

$$x(t) = x_0 + d_1 t, \qquad y(t) = y_0 + d_2 t, \qquad z(t) = z_0.$$

Eliminating t, we are left with two equations:

$$\frac{x - x_0}{d_1} = \frac{y - y_0}{d_2}, \qquad z = z_0.$$

The line lies on the horizontal plane $z = z_0$ and its projection onto the xy-plane (see Figure 13.5.4) is the line l' with equation

$$\frac{x - x_0}{d_1} = \frac{y - y_0}{d_2}.$$

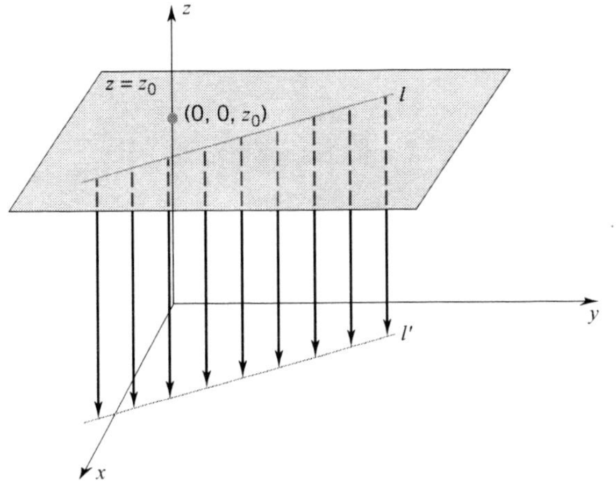

Figure 13.5.4

Intersecting Lines, Parallel Lines

Two distinct lines

$$l_1 : \mathbf{r}(t) = \mathbf{r}_0 + t\mathbf{d}, \qquad l_2 : \mathbf{R}(u) = \mathbf{R}_0 + u\mathbf{D}$$

intersect iff there are numbers t and u at which

$$\mathbf{r}(t) = \mathbf{R}(u).$$

Example 6 Find the point at which the lines

$$l_1 : \mathbf{r}(t) = (\mathbf{i} - 6\mathbf{j} + 2\mathbf{k}) + t(\mathbf{i} + 2\mathbf{j} + \mathbf{k}), \qquad l_2 : \mathbf{R}(u) = (4\mathbf{j} + \mathbf{k}) + u(2\mathbf{i} + \mathbf{j} + 2\mathbf{k})$$

intersect.

SOLUTION We set $\mathbf{r}(t) = \mathbf{R}(u)$ and solve for t and u:

$$(\mathbf{i} - 6\mathbf{j} + 2\mathbf{k}) + t(\mathbf{i} + 2\mathbf{j} + \mathbf{k}) = (4\mathbf{j} + \mathbf{k}) + u(2\mathbf{i} + \mathbf{j} + 2\mathbf{k})$$

gives

$$(1 + t)\,\mathbf{i} + (-6 + 2t)\,\mathbf{j} + (2 + t)\,\mathbf{k} = 2u\mathbf{i} + (4 + u)\,\mathbf{j} + (1 + 2u)\,\mathbf{k}$$

and therefore

$$(1 + t - 2u)\,\mathbf{i} + (-10 + 2t - u)\,\mathbf{j} + (1 + t - 2u)\,\mathbf{k} = \mathbf{0}.$$

This tells us that

$$1 + t - 2u = 0, \qquad -10 + 2t - u = 0, \qquad 1 + t - 2u = 0.$$

Note that the first and third equations are the same. Solving the first two equations simultaneously, we obtain $t = 7$, $u = 4$. As you can verify,

$$\mathbf{r}(7) = 8\mathbf{i} + 8\mathbf{j} + 9\mathbf{k} = \mathbf{R}(4).$$

The two lines intersect at the tip of this vector, the point $P(8, 8, 9)$. ❑

Remark To give a physical interpretation of the result in Example 6, think of the parameters t and u as representing time, and think of particles moving along the lines l_1 and l_2. At time $t = u = 0$, the particle on l_1 is at the point $(1, -6, 2)$ and the particle on l_2 is at the point $(0, 4, 1)$. The particle on l_1 passes through the point $P(8, 8, 9)$ at time $t = 7$, while the particle on l_2 passes through P at time $u = 4$; both particles pass through the same point P, but at different times. ❑

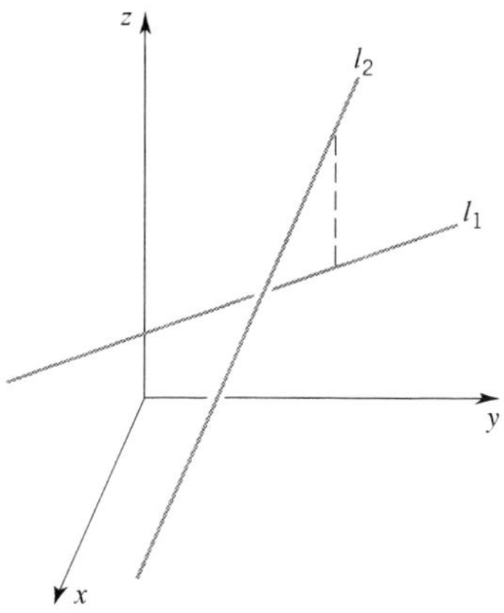

Figure 13.5.5

Lines in space are said to be *parallel* if they have parallel direction vectors. Thus if l_1 is parallel to l_2 there are two possibilities: either $l_1 = l_2$ or l_1 and l_2 lie in the same plane but do not intersect.

Lines which do not lie in the same plane are called *skew* lines. The lines marked in Figure 13.5.5 are skew. Skew lines cannot intersect (because to intersect, they would have to lie on the same plane).

If two lines l_1, l_2 intersect, we can find the angle between them by finding the angle between their direction vectors, $\mathbf{d}$ and $\mathbf{D}$. Depending on our choice of direction vectors, there are two such angles, each the supplement of the other. We choose the smaller of the two angles, the one with nonnegative cosine:

(13.5.5) $$\cos\theta = |\mathbf{u_d} \cdot \mathbf{u_D}|.$$ (Figure 13.5.6)

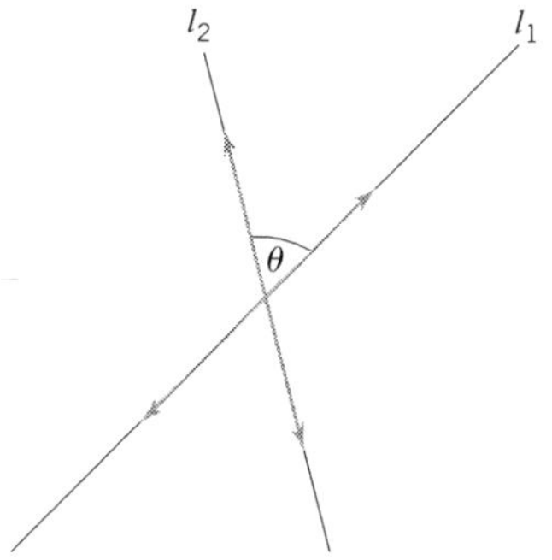

Figure 13.5.6

Example 7 Earlier we verified that the lines

$$l_1 : \mathbf{r}(t) = (\mathbf{i} - 6\mathbf{j} + 2\mathbf{k}) + t(\mathbf{i} + 2\mathbf{j} + \mathbf{k}), \qquad l_2 : \mathbf{R}(u) = (4\mathbf{j} + \mathbf{k}) + u(2\mathbf{i} + \mathbf{j} + 2\mathbf{k})$$

intersect at $P(8, 8, 9)$. What is the angle between these lines?

SOLUTION As direction vectors we can take

$$\mathbf{d} = \mathbf{i} + 2\mathbf{j} + \mathbf{k} \quad \text{and} \quad \mathbf{D} = 2\mathbf{i} + \mathbf{j} + 2\mathbf{k}.$$

Then, as you can check,

$$\mathbf{u_d} = \tfrac{1}{6}\sqrt{6}(\mathbf{i} + 2\mathbf{j} + \mathbf{k}) \quad \text{and} \quad \mathbf{u_D} = \tfrac{1}{3}(2\mathbf{i} + \mathbf{j} + 2\mathbf{k}).$$

It follows that

$$\cos\theta = |\mathbf{u_d} \cdot \mathbf{u_D}| = \tfrac{1}{3}\sqrt{6} \quad \text{and} \quad \theta \cong 0.615 \text{ radians, about } 35.26^\circ \quad ❑$$

Two intersecting lines are said to be *perpendicular* if their direction vectors are perpendicular.

Example 8 Let l_1 and l_2 be the lines of the last example. These lines intersect at $P(8, 8, 9)$. Find a vector parametrization for the line l_3 that passes through $P(8, 8, 9)$ and is perpendicular to both l_1 and l_2.

SOLUTION We are given that l_3 passes through $P(8, 8, 9)$. All we need to parametrize that line is a direction vector $\mathbf{c}$. We require that $\mathbf{c}$ be perpendicular to the direction vectors of l_1 and l_2; namely, we require that

$$\mathbf{c} \perp \mathbf{d} \text{ and } \mathbf{c} \perp \mathbf{D}, \quad \text{where} \quad \mathbf{d} = \mathbf{i} + 2\mathbf{j} + \mathbf{k} \quad \text{and} \quad \mathbf{D} = 2\mathbf{i} + \mathbf{j} + 2\mathbf{k}.$$

Since $\mathbf{d} \times \mathbf{D}$ is perpendicular to both $\mathbf{d}$ and $\mathbf{D}$, we can set

$$\mathbf{c} = \mathbf{d} \times \mathbf{D} = \begin{vmatrix} \mathbf{i} & \mathbf{j} & \mathbf{k} \\ 1 & 2 & 1 \\ 2 & 1 & 2 \end{vmatrix} = \begin{vmatrix} 2 & 1 \\ 1 & 2 \end{vmatrix}\mathbf{i} - \begin{vmatrix} 1 & 1 \\ 2 & 2 \end{vmatrix}\mathbf{j} + \begin{vmatrix} 1 & 2 \\ 2 & 1 \end{vmatrix}\mathbf{k} = 3\mathbf{i} - 3\mathbf{k}.$$

As a parametrization for l_3 we can write

$$\mathbf{s}(t) = (8\mathbf{i} + 8\mathbf{j} + 9\mathbf{k}) + t(3\mathbf{i} - 3\mathbf{k}). \quad ❑$$

Example 9

(a) Find a vector parametrization for the line

$$l : y = mx + b \quad \text{in the } xy\text{-plane.}$$

(b) Show by vector methods that

$$l_1 : y = m_1 x + b_1 \perp l_2 : y = m_2 x + b_2 \quad \text{iff} \quad m_1 m_2 = -1.$$

SOLUTION

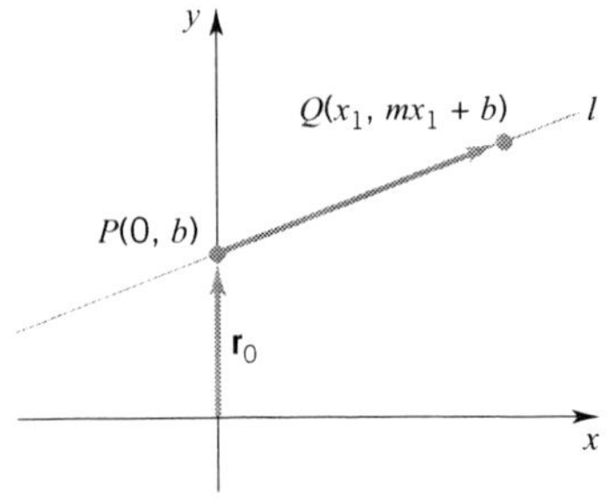

Figure 13.5.7

(a) We seek a parametrization of the form

$$\mathbf{r}(t) = \mathbf{r}_0 + t\mathbf{d}.$$

Since $P(0, b)$ lies on l, we can set

$$\mathbf{r}_0 = 0\mathbf{i} + b\mathbf{j} = b\mathbf{j}.$$

To find a direction vector, we take $x_1 \neq 0$ and note that the point $Q(x_1, mx_1 + b)$ also lies on l. (See Figure 13.5.7.) As direction numbers we can take

$$x_1 - 0 = x_1 \quad \text{and} \quad (mx_1 + b) - b = mx_1$$

or, more simply, 1 and m. This choice of direction numbers gives us the direction vector $\mathbf{d} = \mathbf{i} + m\mathbf{j}$. The vector equation

$$\mathbf{r}(t) = b\mathbf{j} + t(\mathbf{i} + m\mathbf{j})$$

parametrizes the line l.

(b) As direction vectors for l_1 and l_2 we take

$$\mathbf{d}_1 = \mathbf{i} + m_1\mathbf{j} \quad \text{and} \quad \mathbf{d}_2 = \mathbf{i} + m_2\mathbf{j}.$$

Since

$$\mathbf{d}_1 \cdot \mathbf{d}_2 = (\mathbf{i} + m_1\mathbf{j}) \cdot (\mathbf{i} + m_2\mathbf{j}) = 1 + m_1 m_2,$$

you can see that

$$\mathbf{d}_1 \cdot \mathbf{d}_2 = 0 \quad \text{iff} \quad m_1 m_2 = -1. \quad \square$$

Distance from a Point to a Line

In Figure 13.5.8 we have drawn a line l and a point P_1 not on l. We are interested in finding the distance $d(P_1, l)$ between P_1 and l.

Let P_0 be a point on l and let $\mathbf{d}$ be a direction vector for l. With P_0 and Q as shown in the figure, you can see that

$$d(P_1, l) = d(P_1, Q) = \|\overrightarrow{P_0P_1}\| \sin\theta.$$

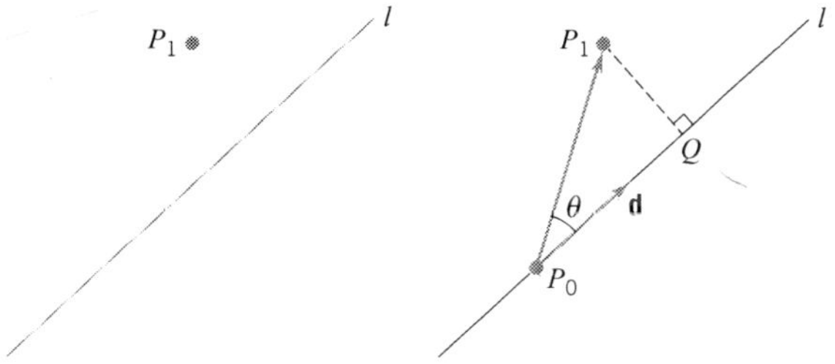

Figure 13.5.8

Since $\|\overrightarrow{P_0P_1} \times \mathbf{d}\| = \|\overrightarrow{P_0P_1}\| \|\mathbf{d}\| \sin\theta$, we have

(13.5.6)
$$d(P_1, l) = \frac{\|\overrightarrow{P_0P_1} \times \mathbf{d}\|}{\|\mathbf{d}\|}.$$

This elegant little formula gives the distance from a point P_1 to any line l in terms of any point P_0 on l and any direction vector $\mathbf{d}$ for l.

Computations based on this formula are left to the Exercises.

EXERCISES 13.5

1. Which of the points $P(1, 2, 0)$, $Q(-5, 1, 5)$, $R(-4, 2, 5)$ lie on the line

$$l : \mathbf{r}(t) = (\mathbf{i} + 2\mathbf{j}) + t(6\mathbf{i} + \mathbf{j} - 5\mathbf{k})?$$

2. Which lines are parallel?

$$l_1 : \mathbf{r}_1(t) = (\mathbf{i} + 2\mathbf{k}) + t(\mathbf{i} - 2\mathbf{j} + 3\mathbf{k}),$$

$$l_2 : \mathbf{r}_2(u) = (\mathbf{i} + 2\mathbf{k}) + u(\mathbf{i} + 2\mathbf{j} - 3\mathbf{k}),$$

$$l_3 : \mathbf{r}_3(v) = (6\mathbf{i} - \mathbf{j}) - v(2\mathbf{i} - 4\mathbf{j} + 6\mathbf{k}),$$

$$l_4 : \mathbf{r}_4(w) = (\tfrac{1}{2} + \tfrac{1}{2}w)\mathbf{i} - w\mathbf{j} - (1 + \tfrac{2}{3}w)\mathbf{k}.$$

Exercises 3–6. Find a vector parametrization for the line that satisfies the given conditions.

3. Passes through the point $P(3, 1, 0)$ and is parallel to the line $\mathbf{r}(t) = (\mathbf{i} - \mathbf{j}) + t\mathbf{k}$.

4. Passes through the point $P(1, -1, 2)$ and is parallel to the line $\mathbf{r}(t) = t(3\mathbf{i} - \mathbf{j} + \mathbf{k})$.

5. Passes through the origin and $Q(x_1, y_1, z_1)$.

6. Passes through $P(x_0, y_0, z_0)$ and $Q(x_1, y_1, z_1)$.

Exercises 7–10. Find a set of scalar parametric equations for the line that satisfies the given conditions.

7. Passes through $P(1, 0, 3)$ and $Q(2, -1, 4)$.

8. Passes through $P(x_0, y_0, z_0)$ and $Q(x_1, y_1, z_1)$.

9. Passes through $P(2, -2, 3)$ and is perpendicular to the xz-plane.

10. Passes through $P(1, 4, -3)$ and is perpendicular to the yz-plane.

11. Give a vector parametrization for the line that passes through $P(-1, 2, -3)$ and is parallel to the line $2(x + 1) = 4(y - 3) = z$.

12. Write equations in symmetric form for the line that passes through the origin and the point $P(x_0, y_0, z_0)$ with $x_0 \neq 0$, $y_0 \neq 0, z_0 \neq 0$.

Exercises 13–20. Determine whether the lines l_1 and l_2 are parallel, skew, or intersecting. If they intersect, find the point of intersection.

13. $l_1 : \mathbf{r}(t) = (3\mathbf{i} + \mathbf{j} + 5\mathbf{k}) + t(\mathbf{i} - \mathbf{j} + 2\mathbf{k})$,
$l_2 : \mathbf{R}(u) = (\mathbf{i} + 4\mathbf{j} + 2\mathbf{k}) + u(\mathbf{j} + \mathbf{k})$.

14. $l_1 : \mathbf{r}(t) = (-\mathbf{i} + 2\mathbf{j} + \mathbf{k}) + t(\mathbf{i} - 3\mathbf{j} + 2\mathbf{k})$,
$l_2 : \mathbf{R}(u) = (2\mathbf{i} - \mathbf{j}) + u(-2\mathbf{i} + 6\mathbf{j} - 4\mathbf{k})$.

15. $l_1 : x_1(t) = 3 + 2t,\ y_1(t) = -1 + 4t,\ z_1(t) = 2 - t$,
$l_2 : x_2(u) = 3 + 2u,\ y_2(u) = 2 + u,\ z_2(u) = -2 + 2u$.

16. $l_1 : x_1(l) = 1 + t,\ y_1(y) = -1 - t,\ z_1(l) = -4 + 2t$,
$l_2 : x_2(u) = 1 - u,\ y_2(u) = 1 + 3u,\ z_2(u) = -2u$.

17. $l_1 : x_1(t) = 1 - 6t,\ y_1(t) = 2 + 9t,\ z_1(t) = -3t$,
$l_2 : x_2(u) = 2 + 2u,\ y_2(u) = 3 - 3u,\ z_2(u) = u$.

18. $l_1 : x - 2 = \dfrac{y + 1}{2} = \dfrac{z - 1}{3}$,
$l_2 : \dfrac{x - 5}{3} = \dfrac{y - 1}{2} = z - 4$.

19. $l_1 : \dfrac{x - 4}{2} = \dfrac{y + 5}{4} = \dfrac{z - 1}{3}$, $\quad l_2 : x - 2 = \dfrac{y + 1}{3} = \dfrac{z}{2}$.

20. $l_1 : x_1(t) = 1 + t,\ y_1(t) = 2t,\ z_1(t) = 1 + 3t$,
$l_2 : x_2(u) = 3u,\ y_2(u) = 2u,\ z_2(u) = 2 + u$.

Exercises 21–22. Find the point where l_1 and l_2 intersect and find the angle between l_1 and l_2.

21. $l_1 : \mathbf{r}_1(t) = \mathbf{i} + t\mathbf{j}, \quad l_2 : \mathbf{r}_2(u) = \mathbf{j} + u(\mathbf{i} + \mathbf{j})$.

22. $l_1 : \mathbf{r}_1(t) = (\mathbf{i} - 4\sqrt{3}\,\mathbf{j}) + t(\mathbf{i} + \sqrt{3}\,\mathbf{j})$,
$l_2 : \mathbf{r}_2(t) = (4\mathbf{i} + 3\sqrt{3}\,\mathbf{j}) + u(\mathbf{i} - \sqrt{3}\,\mathbf{j})$.

23. Where does the line

$$\frac{x - x_0}{d_1} = \frac{y - y_0}{d_2} = \frac{z - z_0}{d_3}$$

intersect the xy-plane?

24. What can you conclude about the lines

$$\frac{x - x_0}{d_1} = \frac{y - y_0}{d_2} = \frac{z - z_0}{d_3}, \quad \frac{x - x_0}{D_1} = \frac{y - y_0}{D_2} = \frac{z - z_0}{D_3}$$

given that $d_1 D_1 + d_2 D_2 + d_3 D_3 = 0$?

25. What can you conclude about the lines

$$\frac{x - x_0}{d_1} = \frac{y - y_0}{d_2} = \frac{z - z_0}{d_3}, \quad \frac{x - x_1}{D_1} = \frac{y - y_1}{D_2} = \frac{z - z_1}{D_3}$$

given that $d_1/D_1 = d_2/D_2 = d_3/D_3$?

26. Let P_0, P_1 be two distinct points and let

$$\mathbf{r}_0 = \overrightarrow{OP_0}, \qquad \mathbf{r}_1 = \overrightarrow{OP_1}.$$

As t ranges over the set of real numbers, $\mathbf{r}(t) = \mathbf{r}_0 + t(\mathbf{r}_1 - \mathbf{r}_0)$ traces out the line determined by P_0 and P_1. Restrict t so that $\mathbf{r}(t)$ traces out only the line segment $\overline{P_0 P_1}$.

27. Find a vector parametrization for the line segment that begins at $P(2, 7, -1)$ and ends at $Q(4, 2, 3)$.

28. Restrict t so that the equations

$$x(t) = 7 - 5t, \quad y(t) = -3 + 2t, \quad z(t) = 4 - t$$

parametrize the line segment that begins at $P(12, -5, 5)$ and ends at $Q(-3, 1, 2)$.

29. Determine a unit vector $\mathbf{u}$ and the values of t for which the function

$$\mathbf{r}(t) = (6\mathbf{i} - 5\mathbf{j} + \mathbf{k}) + t\mathbf{u}$$

parametrizes the line segment that begins at $P(0, -2, 7)$ and ends at $Q(-4, 0, 11)$.

30. Suppose that the lines

$$l_1 : \mathbf{r}(t) = \mathbf{r}_0 + t\mathbf{d}, \qquad l_2 : \mathbf{R}(u) = \mathbf{R}_0 + u\mathbf{D}$$

intersect at right angles. Show that the point of intersection is the origin iff $\mathbf{r}(t) \perp \mathbf{R}(u)$ for all real numbers t and u.

31. Find scalar parametric equations for all the lines that are perpendicular to the line

$$x(t) = 1 + 2(t), \qquad y(t) = 3 - 4t, \qquad z(t) = 2 + 6t$$

and intersect that line at the point $P(3, -1, 8)$.

32. Suppose that $\mathbf{r}(t) = \mathbf{r}_0 + t\mathbf{d}$ and $\mathbf{R}(u) = \mathbf{R}_0 + u\mathbf{D}$ both parametrize the same line. (a) Show that $\mathbf{R}_0 = \mathbf{r}_0 + t_0\mathbf{d}$ for some real number t_0. (b) Then show that, for some real number α, $\mathbf{R}(u) = \mathbf{r}_0 + (t_0 + \alpha u)\,\mathbf{d}$ for all real u.

Exercises 33–34. Find the distance from $P(1, 0, 2)$ to the line specified.

33. The line through the origin parallel to $2\mathbf{i} - \mathbf{j} + 2\mathbf{k}$.

34. The line through $P_0(1, -1, 1)$ parallel to $\mathbf{i} - 2\mathbf{j} - 2\mathbf{k}$.

Exercises 35–37. Find the distance from the point to the line.

35. $P(1, 2, 3), \quad l : \mathbf{r}(t) = \mathbf{i} + 2\mathbf{k} + t(\mathbf{i} - 2\mathbf{j} + 3\mathbf{k})$.

36. $P(0, 0, 0), \quad l : \mathbf{r}(t) = \mathbf{i} + t\mathbf{j}$.

37. $P(1, 0, 1), \quad l : \mathbf{r}(t) = 2\mathbf{i} - \mathbf{j} + t(\mathbf{i} + \mathbf{j})$.

38. Find the distance from the point $P(x_0, y_0, z_0)$ to the line $y = mx + b$ in the xy-plane.

39. What is the distance from the origin: (a) to the line that joins $P(1, 1, 1)$ and $Q(2, 2, 1)$? (b) to the line segment that joins these same points? [For part (b) find the point of the line segment $\overline{PQ}$ closest to the origin and calculate its distance from the origin.]

40. Let l be the line

$$\mathbf{r}(t) = \mathbf{r}_0 + t\mathbf{d}.$$

(a) Find the scalar t_0 for which $\mathbf{r}(t_0) \perp l$.
(b) Find the parametrizations $\mathbf{R}(t) = \mathbf{R}_0 + t\mathbf{D}$ for l in which $\mathbf{R}_0 \perp l$ and $\|\mathbf{D}\| = 1$. These are called the *standard vector parametrizations* for l.

Exercises 41–42. Find the standard vector parametrizations for the line specified. (See Exercise 40.)

41. The line through $P(0, 1, -2)$ parallel to $\mathbf{i} - \mathbf{j} + 3\mathbf{k}$.

42. The line through $P(\sqrt{3}, 0, 0)$ parallel to $\mathbf{i} + \mathbf{j} + \mathbf{k}$.

43. Let A, B, C be the vertices of a triangle in the xy-plane. Given that $0 < s < 1$, determine the values of t for which the tip of

$$\overrightarrow{OA} + s\overrightarrow{AB} + t\overrightarrow{BC}$$

lies inside the triangle. HINT: Draw a diagram.

44. (*The distance between two skew lines*) Suppose that l_1 and l_2 are skew. Justify the following statement: if l_1 passes through point P with direction vector $\mathbf{d}_1$ and l_2 passes through point Q with direction vector $\mathbf{d}_2$, then the number

$$s = \frac{|\overrightarrow{PQ} \cdot (\mathbf{d}_1 \times \mathbf{d}_2)|}{\|\mathbf{d}_1 \times \mathbf{d}_2\|}$$

gives the distance between l_1 and l_2.

45. Show that the lines

$$l_1 : x_1(t) = 2 + t,\ y_1(t) = -1 + 3t,\ z_1(t) = 1 - 2t,$$
$$l_2 : x_2(u) = -1 + 4u,\ y_2(u) = 2 - u,\ z_2(u) = -3 + 2u.$$

are skew and find the distance between them.

46. Exercise 45 for

$$l_1 : x_1(t) = 1 + t,\ y_1(t) = -2 + 3t,\ z_1(t) = 4 - 2t,$$
$$l_2 : x_2(u) = 2u,\ y_2(u) = 3 + u,\ z_2(u) = -3 + 4u.$$

■ 13.6 PLANES

Ways of Specifying a Plane

How can we specify a plane? There are a number of ways of doing this: by giving three noncollinear points that lie on the plane; by giving two distinct lines that lie on the plane; by giving a line that lies on the plane and a point that lies on the plane, so long as the point does not lie on the line. There is still another way to specify a plane, and that is to give a point on the plane and a nonzero vector perpendicular to the plane.

Scalar Equation of a Plane

Figure 13.6.1 shows a plane. On it we have marked a point $P(x_0, y_0, z_0)$ and, starting at that point, a nonzero vector $\mathbf{N} = A\mathbf{i} + B\mathbf{j} + C\mathbf{k}$ perpendicular to the plane. We call $\mathbf{N}$ a *normal vector*. We can obtain an equation for the plane in terms of the coordinates of P and the components of $\mathbf{N}$.

To find such an equation we take an arbitrary point $Q(x, y, z)$ in space and form the vector

$$\overrightarrow{PQ} = (x - x_0)\mathbf{i} + (y - y_0)\mathbf{j} + (z - z_0)\mathbf{k}.$$

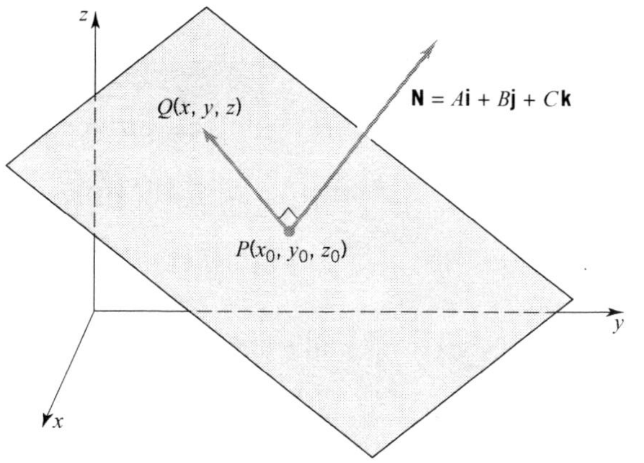

Figure 13.6.1

The point Q will lie on the given plane iff

$$\mathbf{N} \cdot \overrightarrow{PQ} = 0,$$

which is to say, iff

(13.6.1) $$A(x - x_0) + B(y - y_0) + C(z - z_0) = 0.$$

This is an equation in x, y, z for the plane that passes through the point $P(x_0, y_0, z_0)$ and has normal vector $\mathbf{N} = A\mathbf{i} + B\mathbf{j} + C\mathbf{k}$.

Remark If $\mathbf{N}$ is normal to a given plane, then so is every nonzero scalar multiple of $\mathbf{N}$. If we choose $-2\mathbf{N}$ as our normal, then (13.6.1) reads

$$-2A(x - x_0) - 2B(y - y_0) - 2C(z - z_0) = 0.$$

Canceling the -2, we have the same equation we had before. It does not matter which normal we choose. All normals give equivalent equations. ❑

We can write (13.6.1) in the form

$$Ax + By + Cz + D = 0$$

simply by setting $D = -Ax_0 - By_0 - Cz_0$.

Example 1 Write an equation for the plane that passes through the point $P(1, 0, 2)$ and has normal vector $\mathbf{N} = 3\mathbf{i} - 2\mathbf{j} + \mathbf{k}$.

SOLUTION The general equation

$$A(x - x_0) + B(y - y_0) + C(z - z_0) = 0$$

becomes

$$3(x - 1) + (-2)(y - 0) + (z - 2) = 0.$$

This simplifies to

$$3x - 2y + z - 5 = 0.$$ ❑

Example 2 Find an equation for the plane p that passes through $P(-2, 3, 5)$ and is perpendicular to the line l with parametric equations $x = -2 + t, y = 1 + 2t, z = 4$.

SOLUTION As a direction vector for l we can take $\mathbf{N} = \mathbf{i} + 2\mathbf{j}$. Since p and l are perpendicular, $\mathbf{N}$ is a normal vector for p. Thus, as an equation for p, we can write

$$(x + 2) + 2(y - 3) + 0(z - 5) = 0.$$

This simplifies to

$$x + 2y - 4 = 0.$$

The last equation looks very much like the equation of a line in the xy-plane. If the context of our discussion were the xy-plane, then the equation $x + 2y - 4 = 0$ would represent a line. In this case, however, our context is three-dimensional space. Hence, the equation $x + 2y - 4 = 0$ represents the set of all points $Q(x, y, z)$ where $x + 2y - 4 = 0$ and z is unrestricted. This set forms a vertical plane that intersects the xy-plane in the line indicated. (Figure 13.6.2.) ❑

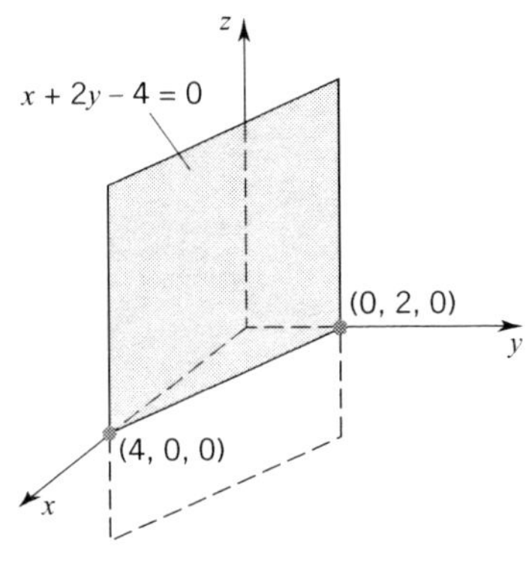

Figure 13.6.2

Example 3 Show that every equation

$$ax + by + cz + d = 0 \qquad \text{with} \qquad \sqrt{a^2 + b^2 + c^2} \neq 0$$

represents a plane in space.

SOLUTION Since $\sqrt{a^2 + b^2 + c^2} \neq 0$, the numbers a, b, c are not all zero. Therefore there exist numbers x_0, y_0, z_0 such that

$$ax_0 + by_0 + cz_0 + d = 0.^{\dagger}$$

The equation

$$ax + by + cz + d = 0$$

can now be written

$$(ax + by + cz + d) - (ax_0 + by_0 + cz_0 + d) = 0.$$

After factoring, we have

$$a(x - x_0) + b(y - y_0) + c(z - z_0) = 0.$$

This equation (and hence the initial equation) represents the plane through the point $P(x_0, y_0, z_0)$ with normal $\mathbf{N} = a\mathbf{i} + b\mathbf{j} + c\mathbf{k}$. The initial assumption that $\sqrt{a^2 + b^2 + c^2} \neq 0$ guarantees that $\mathbf{N} \neq \mathbf{0}$. ❑

Vector Equation of a Plane

We can write the equation of a plane entirely in vector notation. Set

$$\mathbf{N} = A\mathbf{i} + B\mathbf{j} + C\mathbf{k}, \qquad \mathbf{r}_0 = \overrightarrow{OP} = (x_0, y_0, z_0), \qquad \mathbf{r} = \overrightarrow{OQ} = (x, y, z).$$

Since

$$\mathbf{r}_0 = x_0\mathbf{i} + y_0\mathbf{j} + z_0\mathbf{k} \qquad \text{and} \qquad \mathbf{r} = x\mathbf{i} + y\mathbf{j} + z\mathbf{k},$$

(13.6.1) can be written

(13.6.2)

$$\boxed{\mathbf{N} \cdot (\mathbf{r} - \mathbf{r}_0) = 0.}$$

This vector equation represents the plane that passes through the tip of $\mathbf{r}_0$ and has normal $\mathbf{N}$. (Figure 13.6.3) A point $Q(x, y, z)$ lies on this plane iff the vector $\mathbf{r} = \overrightarrow{OQ} = (x, y, z)$ satisfies this vector equation.

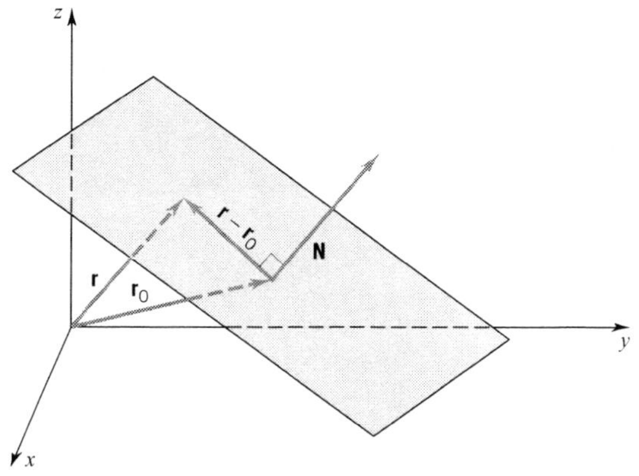

Figure 13.6.3

†Would such numbers necessarily exist if $\sqrt{a^2 + b^2 + c^2}$ were zero?

Linear Dependence

Two vectors **a** and **b** are said to be *linearly dependent* if there exist scalars s and t, not both zero, such that

$$s\mathbf{a} + t\mathbf{b} = \mathbf{0}.$$

Such vectors are called *collinear* because they are parallel and therefore, viewed as emanating from the same point, fall on the same line.

Three vectors **a, b, c** are said to be *linearly dependent* if there exist scalars s, t, u not all zero such that

$$s\mathbf{a} + t\mathbf{b} + u\mathbf{c} = \mathbf{0}.$$

Such vectors are called *coplanar* because, viewed as emanating from the same point, they fall on the same plane.

To see this, assume that

$$s\mathbf{a} + t\mathbf{b} + u\mathbf{c} = \mathbf{0}$$

s, t, u not all zero. Without loss of generality we can assume that $u \neq 0$ and write

$$\mathbf{c} = -(s/u)\,\mathbf{a} - (t/u)\,\mathbf{b}.$$

Since $\mathbf{a} \times \mathbf{b}$ is perpendicular to both **a** and **b**, we have

$$\begin{aligned}(\mathbf{a} \times \mathbf{b}) \cdot \mathbf{c} &= (\mathbf{a} \times \mathbf{b}) \cdot [-(s/u)\,\mathbf{a} - (t/u)\,\mathbf{b}] \\ &= -(s/u)[(\mathbf{a} \times \mathbf{b}) \cdot \mathbf{a}] - (t/u)[(\mathbf{a} \times \mathbf{b}) \cdot \mathbf{b}] \\ &= 0.\end{aligned}$$

But $|(\mathbf{a} \times \mathbf{b}) \cdot \mathbf{c}|$ gives the volume of the parallelepiped with edges **a, b, c**. (Figure 13.4.6) This volume can be zero only if **a, b, c** lie on the same plane. ❑

Unit Normals

If **N** is normal to a given plane, then all other normals to that plane are parallel to **N** and hence scalar multiples of **N**. In particular there are two normals of length 1:

$$\mathbf{u_N} = \frac{\mathbf{N}}{\|\mathbf{N}\|} \quad \text{and} \quad -\mathbf{u_N} = \frac{\mathbf{N}}{\|\mathbf{N}\|}.$$

These are called the *unit normals*.

Example 4 Find the unit normals for the plane $3x - 4y + 12z + 8 = 0$.

SOLUTION We can take $\mathbf{N} = 3\mathbf{i} - 4\mathbf{j} + 12\mathbf{k}$. Since

$$\|\mathbf{N}\| = \sqrt{3^2 + (-4)^2 + 12^2} = 13,$$

we have

$$\mathbf{u_N} = \tfrac{1}{13}(3\mathbf{i} - 4\mathbf{j} + 12\mathbf{k}) \quad \text{and} \quad -\mathbf{u_N} = -\tfrac{1}{13}(3\mathbf{i} - 4\mathbf{j} + 12\mathbf{k}).$$ ❑

Parallel Planes, Intersecting Planes

As must be evident to you, two planes p_1 and p_2 are parallel iff their normals are parallel. If p_1 is parallel to p_2, there are two possibilities: either $p_1 = p_2$, or p_1 and p_2 do not intersect.

If planes p_1 and p_2 intersect, we can find the angle between them by finding the angle between their normals, $\mathbf{N}_1, \mathbf{N}_2$. Depending on our choice of normals, there are two such angles, each the supplement of the other. We will choose the smaller angle, the one with nonnegative cosine:

(13.6.3)
$$\cos\theta = |\mathbf{u}_{\mathbf{N}_1} \cdot \mathbf{u}_{\mathbf{N}_2}|.$$
(Figure 13.6.4)

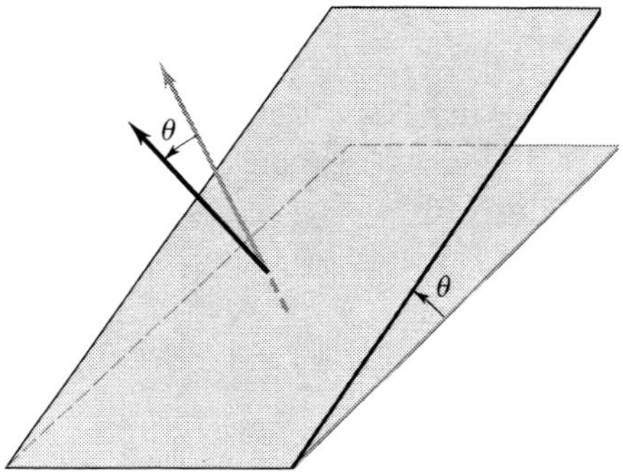

Figure 13.6.4

Example 5 Here are some planes:

$$p_1 : 2(x-1) - 3y + 5(z-2) = 0, \qquad p_2 : -4x + 6y + 10z + 24 = 0,$$
$$p_3 : 4x - 6y - 10z + 1 = 0, \qquad p_4 : 2x - 3y + 5z - 12 = 0.$$

(a) Which planes are identical?
(b) Which planes are distinct but parallel?
(c) Find the angle between p_1 and p_2.

SOLUTION

(a) p_1 and p_4 are identical, as you can verify by simplifying the equation of p_1.
(b) p_2 and p_3 are distinct but parallel. The planes are distinct since $P(0, 0, \frac{1}{10})$ lies on p_3 but not on p_2; they are parallel since the normals

$$-4\mathbf{i} + 6\mathbf{j} + 10\mathbf{k} \quad \text{and} \quad 4\mathbf{i} - 6\mathbf{j} - 10\mathbf{k}$$

are parallel.
(c) Taking

$$\mathbf{N}_1 = 2\mathbf{i} - 3\mathbf{j} + 5\mathbf{k} \quad \text{and} \quad \mathbf{N}_2 = -4\mathbf{i} + 6\mathbf{j} + 10\mathbf{k},$$

we have

$$\mathbf{u}_{\mathbf{N}_1} = \frac{1}{\sqrt{38}}(2\mathbf{i} - 3\mathbf{j} + 5\mathbf{k}) \quad \text{and} \quad \mathbf{u}_{\mathbf{N}_2} = \frac{1}{\sqrt{152}}(-4\mathbf{i} + 6\mathbf{j} + 10\mathbf{k}).$$

As you can check,

$$\cos\theta = |\mathbf{u}_{\mathbf{N}_1} \cdot \mathbf{u}_{\mathbf{N}_2}| = \frac{6}{19} \quad \text{and thus} \quad \theta \cong 1.25 \text{ radians, about } 71.59^\circ.$$

If two planes

$$p_1 : A_1x + B_1y + C_1z + D_1 = 0, \qquad p_2 : A_2x + B_2y + C_2z + D_2 = 0$$

intersect, their intersection forms some line l. To construct a vector parametrization for l, we need a point on l and a direction vector for l.

To find a point $P_0(x_0, y_0, z_0)$ on l, we need a triple x_0, y_0, z_0 that satisfies the equations of both planes. We can find such a triple by solving the two equations simultaneously.

Now the search for a direction vector. Since p_1 and p_2 intersect in a line, the normals

$$\mathbf{N}_1 = A_1\mathbf{i} + B_1\mathbf{j} + C_1\mathbf{k}, \qquad \mathbf{N}_2 = A_2\mathbf{i} + B_2\mathbf{j} + C_2\mathbf{k}$$

are not parallel. This guarantees that $\mathbf{N}_1 \times \mathbf{N}_2$ is not $\mathbf{0}$. Since l lies on both p_1 and p_2, the line l, like the vector $\mathbf{N}_1 \times \mathbf{N}_2$, is perpendicular to both $\mathbf{N}_1$ and $\mathbf{N}_2$. This makes l parallel to $\mathbf{N}_1 \times \mathbf{N}_2$. (See Figure 13.6.5.) We can therefore take $\mathbf{N}_1 \times \mathbf{N}_2$ as a direction vector for l and write

$$l : \mathbf{r}(t) = \overrightarrow{OP_0} + t(\mathbf{N}_1 \times \mathbf{N}_2).$$

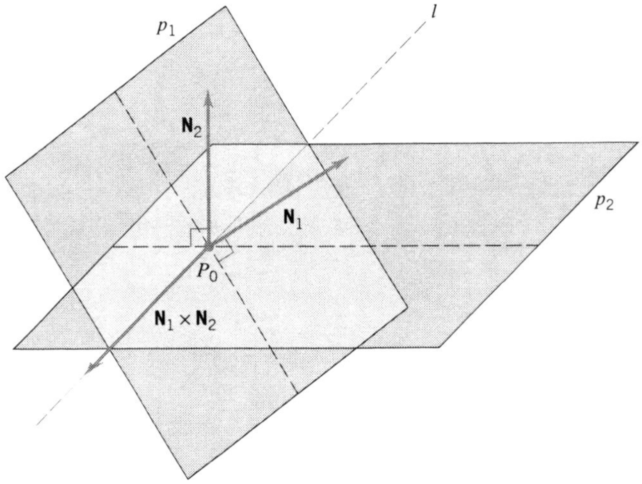

Figure 13.6.5

Example 6 Show that the planes $p_1 : 2x - 3y + 2z = 9$ and $p_2 : x + 2y - z = -4$ are not parallel and therefore intersect. Then find scalar parametric equations for the line formed by the two intersecting planes.

SOLUTION As normal vectors for p_1 and p_2, we can take $\mathbf{N}_1 = 2\mathbf{i} - 3\mathbf{j} + 2\mathbf{k}$ and $\mathbf{N}_2 = \mathbf{i} + 2\mathbf{j} - \mathbf{k}$. Since neither vector is a scalar multiple of the other, the vectors are not parallel. Therefore, p_1 and p_2 are not parallel.

As a direction vector for l, we use the vector

$$\mathbf{N}_1 \times \mathbf{N}_2 = \begin{vmatrix} \mathbf{i} & \mathbf{j} & \mathbf{k} \\ 2 & -3 & 2 \\ 1 & 2 & -1 \end{vmatrix} = -\mathbf{i} + 4\mathbf{j} + 7\mathbf{k}.$$

Now we need a point that lies on l. To find one, we solve the equations for p_1 and p_2 simultaneously. If, for example, we set $x = 0$ in the two equations, we get

$$-3y + 2z = 9$$
$$2y - z = -4.$$

Solving this pair of equations for y and z, we find that $y = 1$ and $z = 6$. Thus, the point $(0, 1, 6)$ is on l. As scalar parametric equations for l, we can write

$$x(t) = -t, \quad y(t) = 1 + 4t, \quad z(t) = 6 + 7t. \quad \square$$

The Plane Determined by Three Noncollinear Points

Suppose now that we are given three noncollinear points P_1, P_2, P_3. These points determine a plane. How can we find an equation for this plane?

First we form the vectors $\overrightarrow{P_1P_2}$, $\overrightarrow{P_1P_3}$. Since P_1, P_2, P_3 are noncollinear, the vectors are not parallel. Therefore their cross product $\overrightarrow{P_1P_2} \times \overrightarrow{P_1P_3}$ can be used as a normal for the plane. We are back in a familiar situation. We have a point of the plane, say P_1, and we have a normal vector, $\overrightarrow{P_1P_2} \times \overrightarrow{P_1P_3}$. A point P lies on the plane iff

(13.6.4) $$\overrightarrow{P_1P} \cdot (\overrightarrow{P_1P_2} \times \overrightarrow{P_1P_3}) = 0. \qquad \text{(Figure 13.6.6)}$$

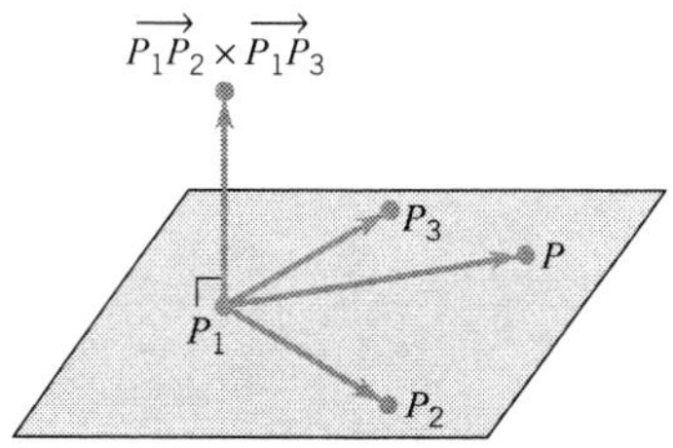

Figure 13.6.6

Example 7 Find an equation in x, y, z for the plane that passes through the points $P_1(0, 1, 1)$, $P_2(1, 0, 1)$, $P_3(1, -3, -1)$.

SOLUTION A point $P = P(x, y, z)$ lies on this plane iff

$$\overrightarrow{P_1P} \cdot (\overrightarrow{P_1P_2} \times \overrightarrow{P_1P_3}) = 0.$$

Here

$$\overrightarrow{P_1P} = x\mathbf{i} + (y-1)\mathbf{j} + (z-1)\mathbf{k}, \qquad \overrightarrow{P_1P_2} = \mathbf{i} - \mathbf{j}, \qquad \overrightarrow{P_1P_3} = \mathbf{i} - 4\mathbf{j} - 2\mathbf{k}.$$

As you can check,

$$\overrightarrow{P_1P_2} \times \overrightarrow{P_1P_3} = 2\mathbf{i} + 2\mathbf{j} - 3\mathbf{k}.$$

Thus,

$$\begin{aligned} \overrightarrow{P_1P} \cdot (\overrightarrow{P_1P_2} \times \overrightarrow{P_1P_3}) &= [x\mathbf{i} + (y-1)\mathbf{j} + (z-1)\mathbf{k}] \cdot [2\mathbf{i} + 2\mathbf{j} - 3\mathbf{k}] \\ &= 2x + 2(y-1) - 3(z-1) = 2x + 2y - 3z + 1. \end{aligned}$$

As an equation for the plane, we can use the equation

$$2x + 2y - 3z + 1 = 0. \quad \square$$

The Distance from a Point to a Plane

In Figure 13.6.7 we have drawn a plane $p : Ax + By + Cz + D = 0$ and a point $P_0(x_0, y_0, z_0)$ not on p. The distance between the point P_0 and the plane p is given by the formula

(13.6.5) $$d(P_0, p) = \frac{|Ax_0 + By_0 + Cz_0 + D|}{\sqrt{A^2 + B^2 + C^2}}.$$

PROOF Pick any point $P(x, y, z)$ in the plane. As a normal to p we can take the vector

$$\mathbf{N} = A\mathbf{i} + B\mathbf{j} + C\mathbf{k}.$$

Then

$$\mathbf{u_N} = \frac{A\mathbf{i} + B\mathbf{j} + C\mathbf{k}}{\sqrt{A^2 + B^2 + C^2}}$$

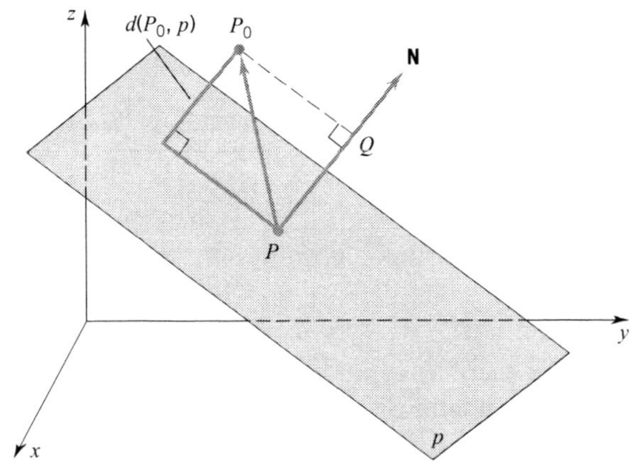

Figure 13.6.7

is the corresponding unit normal. From Figure 13.6.7

$$\begin{aligned} d(P_0, p) = d(P, Q) &= |\text{comp}_{\mathbf{N}} \overrightarrow{PP_0}| \\ &= |\overrightarrow{PP_0} \cdot \mathbf{u_N}| \\ &= \frac{|(x_0 - x)A + (y_0 - y)B + (z_0 - z)C|}{\sqrt{A^2 + B^2 + C^2}} \\ &= \frac{|Ax_0 + By_0 + Cz_0 - (Ax + By + Cz)|}{\sqrt{A^2 + B^2 + C^2}}. \end{aligned}$$

Since $P(x, y, z)$ lies on p

$$Ax + By + Cz = -D$$

and we have

$$d(P_0, p) = \frac{|Ax_0 + By_0 + Cz_0 + D|}{\sqrt{A^2 + B^2 + C^2}}. \quad \square$$

EXERCISES 13.6

1. Which of the points $P(3, 2, 1)$, $Q(2, 3, 1)$, $R(1, 4, 1)$ lie on the plane

$$3(x - 1) + 4y - 5(z + 2) = 0?$$

2. Which of the points $P(2, 1, -2)$, $Q(2, 0, 0)$, $R(4, 1, -1)$, $S(0, -1, -3)$ lie on the plane $\mathbf{N} \cdot (\mathbf{r} - \mathbf{r}_0) = 0$ given that $\mathbf{N} = \mathbf{i} - 3\mathbf{j} + \mathbf{k}$ and $\mathbf{r}_0 = 4\mathbf{i} + \mathbf{j} - \mathbf{k}$?

Exercises 3–9. Find an equation for the plane which satisfies the given conditions.

3. Passes through the point $P(2, 3, 4)$ and is perpendicular to $\mathbf{i} - 4\mathbf{j} + 3\mathbf{k}$.

4. Passes through the point $P(1, -2, 3)$ and is perpendicular to $\mathbf{j} + 2\mathbf{k}$.

5. Passes through the point $P(2, 1, 1)$ and is parallel to the plane $3x - 2y + 5z - 2 = 0$.

6. Passes through the point $P(3, -1, 5)$ and is parallel to the plane $4x + 2y - 7z + 5 = 0$.

7. Passes through the point $P(1, 3, 1)$ and contains the line $l : x = t, y = t, z = -2 + t$.

8. Passes through the point $P(2, 0, 1)$ and contains the line $l : x = 1 - 2t, y = 1 + 4t, z = 2 + t$.

9. Passes through the point $P_0(x_0, y_0, z_0)$ and is perpendicular to $\overrightarrow{OP_0}$.

Exercises 10–11. Find the unit normals for the plane.

10. $2x - 3y + 7z - 3 = 0$. **11.** $2x - y + 5z - 10 = 0$.

12. Show that the equation $x/a + y/b + z/c = 1$ represents the plane that intersects the coordinate axes at $x = a, y = b, z = c$. This is the equation of a plane in written *intercept from*.

Exercises 13–14. Write the equation of the plane in intercept form and find the points where it intersects the coordinate axes.

13. $4x + 5y - 6z = 60$. **14.** $3x - y + 4z + 2 = 0$.

Exercises 15–18. Find the angle between the planes.

15. $5(x-1)-3(y+2)+2z=0,$
$x+3(y-1)+2(z+4)=0.$

16. $2x-y+3z=5, \quad 5x+5y-z=1.$

17. $x-y+z-1=0, \quad 2x+y+3z+5=0.$

18. $4x+4y-2z=3, \quad 2x+y+z=-1.$

Exercises 19–22. Determine whether the vectors are coplanar.

19. $4\mathbf{j}-\mathbf{k}, \quad 3\mathbf{i}+\mathbf{j}+2\mathbf{k}, \quad \mathbf{0}.$

20. $\mathbf{i}, \quad \mathbf{i}-2\mathbf{j}, \quad 3\mathbf{j}+\mathbf{k}.$

21. $\mathbf{i}+\mathbf{j}+\mathbf{k}, \quad 2\mathbf{i}-\mathbf{j}, \quad 3\mathbf{i}-\mathbf{j}-\mathbf{k}.$

22. $\mathbf{j}-\mathbf{k}, \quad 3\mathbf{i}-\mathbf{j}+2\mathbf{k}, \quad 3\mathbf{i}-2\mathbf{j}+3\mathbf{k}.$

Exercises 23–26. Find the distance from the point to the plane.

23. $P(2,-1,3); \quad 2x+4y-z+1=0.$

24. $P(3,-5,2); \quad 8x-2y+z=5.$

25. $P(1,-3,5); \quad -3x+4z+5=0.$

26. $P(1,3,4); \quad x+y-2z=0.$

Exercises 27–30. Find an equation in x, y, z for the plane that passes through the given points.

27. $P_1(1,0,1), \quad P_2(2,1,0), \quad P_3(1,1,1).$

28. $P_1(1,1,1), \quad P_2(2,-2,-1), \quad P_3(0,2,1).$

29. $P_1(3,-4,1), \quad P_2(3,2,1), \quad P_3(1,1,-2).$

30. $P_1(3,2,-1), \quad P_2(3,-2,4), \quad P_3(1,-1,3).$

31. Write equations in symmetric form for the line that passes through $P_0(x_0, y_0, z_0)$ and is perpendicular to the plane $Ax+By+Cz+D=0.$

32. Find the distance between the parallel planes

$$Ax+By+Cz+D_1=0, \qquad Ax+By+Cz+D_2=0.$$

33. Show that the equations of a line in symmetric form

$$\frac{x-x_0}{d_1}=\frac{y-y_0}{d_2}=\frac{z-z_0}{d_3}$$

express the line as an intersection of two planes by finding equations for two such planes.

34. Find scalar parametric equations for the line formed by the two intersecting planes.

(a) $z=z_0, \quad y=y_0.$ (b) $x=x_0, \quad z=z_0.$

Exercises 35–36. Find a set of scalar parametric equations for the line formed by the two intersecting planes.

35. $p_1: x+2y+3z=0, \quad p_2: -3x+4y+z=0.$

36. $p_1: x+y+z+1=0, \quad p_2: x-y+z+2=0.$

Exercises 37–38. Let l be the line determined by P_1, P_2, and let p be the plane determined by Q_1, Q_2, Q_3. Where, if anywhere, does l intersect p?

37. $P_1(1,-1,2), \quad P_2(-2,3,1);$
$Q_1(2,0,-4), \quad Q_2(1,2,3), \quad Q_3(-1,2,1).$

38. $P_1(4,-3,1), \quad P_2(2,-2,3);$
$Q_1(2,0,-4), \quad Q_2(1,2,3), \quad Q_3(-1,2,1).$

39. Let l_1, l_2 be the lines that pass through the origin with direction vectors

$$\mathbf{d}_1=\mathbf{i}+2\mathbf{j}+4\mathbf{k}, \qquad \mathbf{d}_2=-\mathbf{i}-\mathbf{j}+3\mathbf{k}.$$

Find an equation for the plane that contains l_1 and l_2.

40. Show that two nonparallel lines $\mathbf{r}(t)=\mathbf{r}_0+t\mathbf{d}$ and $\mathbf{R}(t)=\mathbf{R}_0+t\mathbf{D}$ intersect iff the vectors $\mathbf{r}_0-\mathbf{R}_0$, $\mathbf{d}$, and $\mathbf{D}$ are coplanar.

41. Given that a plane contains the point P and has normal $\mathbf{N}$, describe the set of points Q on the plane for which $(\mathbf{N}+\overrightarrow{PQ})\perp(\mathbf{N}-\overrightarrow{PQ})$. HINT: Draw a figure.

42. Let **a, b, c** be three nonzero vectors which are mutually perpendicular. Prove that the vectors cannot be linearly dependent.

43. The vector $\mathbf{N}=A\mathbf{i}+B\mathbf{j}+C\mathbf{k}$ is normal to the plane $p: Ax+By+Cz+D=0$. Picture $\mathbf{N}$ as emanating from some point of p. (Which point is immaterial.) Let $P_0(x_0, y_0, z_0)$ be an arbitrary point of space and set $\alpha = Ax_0+By_0+Cz_0+D$. If $\alpha=0$, P_0 lies on p. What can you conclude about P_0 if $\alpha>0$? if $\alpha<0$?

44. If **a, b, c** are not linearly dependent, they are called *linearly independent.* For such vectors

$$s\mathbf{a}+t\mathbf{b}+u\mathbf{c}=\mathbf{0}$$

only if s, t, u are all 0.

Show that if **a, b, c** are linearly independent, then every vector **d** can be expressed as a unique linear combination of **a, b, c:**

$$\mathbf{d}=\alpha\mathbf{a}+\beta\mathbf{b}+\gamma\mathbf{c}.$$

Find α, β, γ. HINT: To find α form $\mathbf{d}\cdot(\mathbf{b}\times\mathbf{c})$.

Exercises 45–48. (*Sketching planes*) The equation of a plane p is given.

(a) Find the intercepts of p.
(b) Find the *traces* of p. (These are the lines in which p intersects the coordinate planes.)
(c) Find the unit normals.
(d) Sketch the plane.

45. $5x+4y+10z=20.$ **46.** $x+2y+3z-6=0.$

47. $3x+2z-12=0.$ **48.** $3x+2y-6=0.$

Exercises 49–51. Find an equation for the plane shown in the figure.

49. Use a CAS to draw the planes $2x+y+3z=4$ and $x+5y-2z=3$ in one figure. Then find the angle between the two planes.

50. Exercise 49 with the planes $-x-2y+4z=5$ and $2x-y-3z=1$.

51. Find an equation for the plane that passes through the point $(2,7,-3)$ and is perpendicular to the line $x=2+3t$, $y=7+t, z=-3+4t$. Use a CAS to draw the line and the plane in one figure.

52. Find an equation for the plane which passes through the point $(5,-3,-4)$ and is perpendicular to the line $x=5-t$, $y=-3+2t, z=-4-3t$. Use a CAS to draw the line and the plane in one figure.

Exercises 53–56. Find an equation for the plane shown in the figure

53.

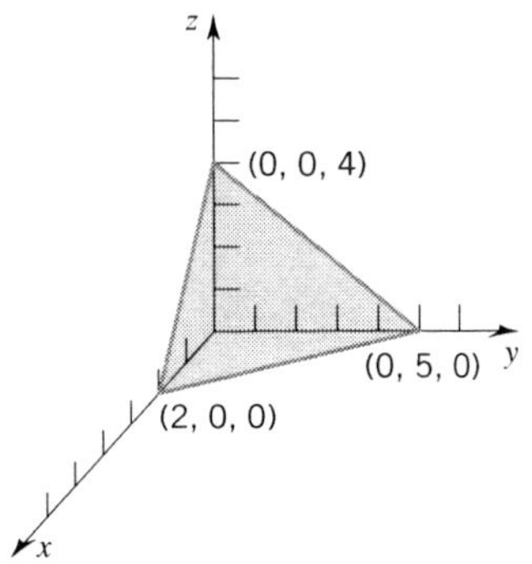

54.

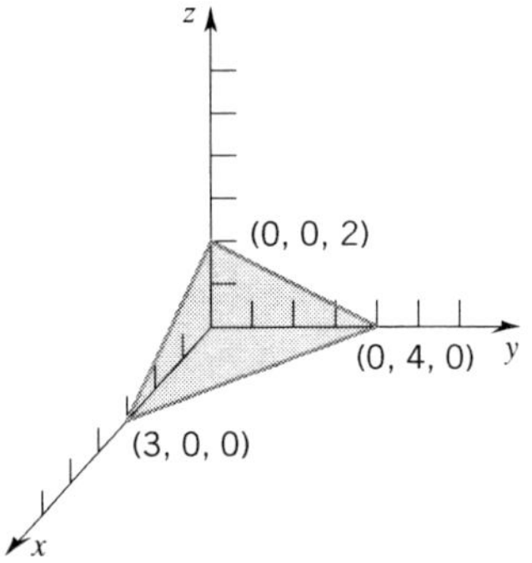

55.

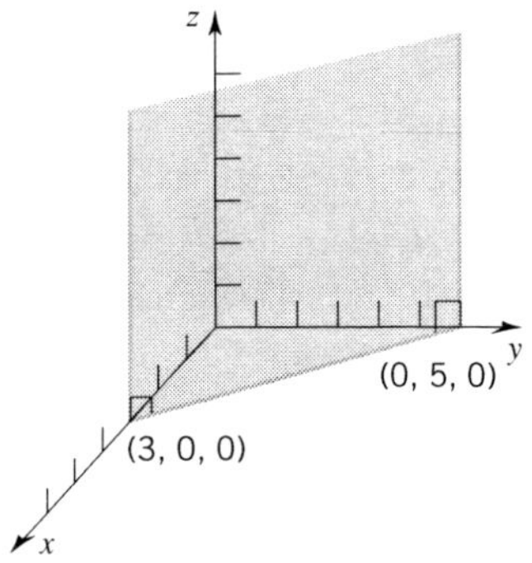

56.

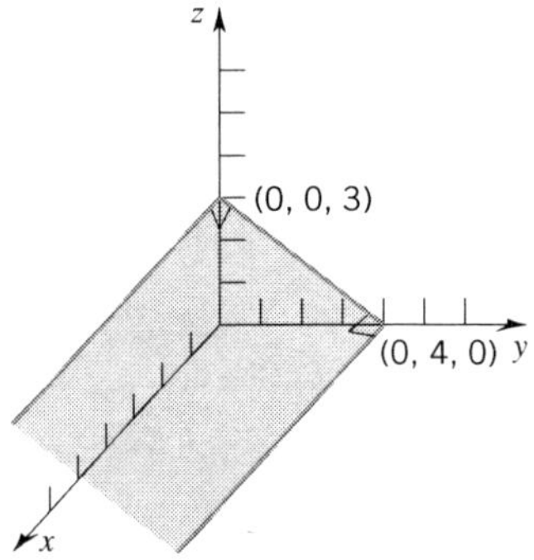

■ PROJECT 13.6 SOME GEOMETRY BY VECTOR METHODS

Try your hand at proving the following theorems by vector methods. Follow the hints if you like, but you may find it more interesting to disregard them and come up with your own proofs.

Theorem 1. The diagonals of a parallelogram are perpendicular iff the parallelogram is a rhombus.

HINT FOR PROOF With $\mathbf{a}$ and $\mathbf{b}$ as in Figure A, the diagonals are $\mathbf{a}+\mathbf{b}$ and $\mathbf{a}-\mathbf{b}$. Show that $(\mathbf{a}+\mathbf{b})\cdot(\mathbf{a}-\mathbf{b})=0$ iff $\|\mathbf{a}\|=\|\mathbf{b}\|$.

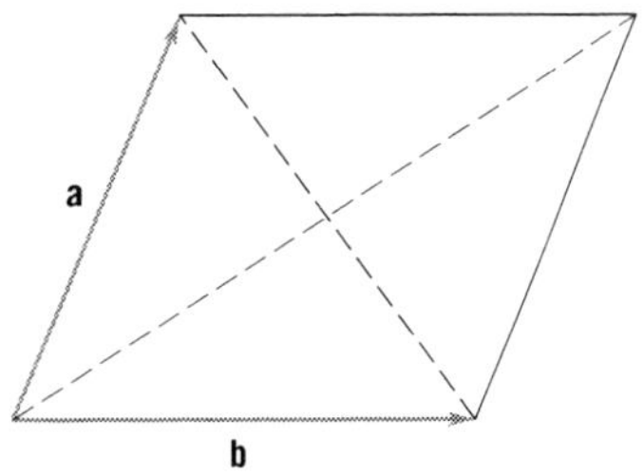

Figure A

Theorem 2. Every angle inscribed in a semicircle is a right angle.

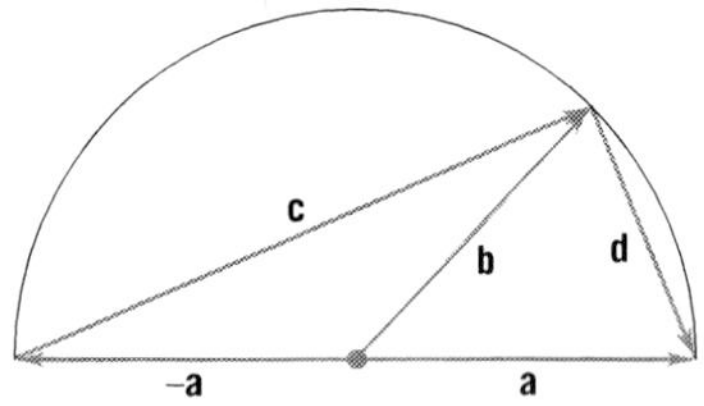

Figure B

HINT FOR PROOF Take $\mathbf{c}$ and $\mathbf{d}$ as in Figure B; express $\mathbf{c}$ and $\mathbf{d}$ in terms of $\mathbf{a}$ and $\mathbf{b}$; then show that $\mathbf{c}\cdot\mathbf{d}=0$.

Theorem 3. In a parallelogram the sum of the squares of the lengths of the diagonals equals the sum of the squares of the lengths of the sides.

HINT FOR PROOF With $\mathbf{a}$ and $\mathbf{b}$ as in Figure A, the diagonals are $\mathbf{a}+\mathbf{b}$ and $\mathbf{a}-\mathbf{b}$.

Theorem 4. The three altitudes of a triangle intersect at one point.

HINT FOR PROOF As in Figure C assume that the altitudes from P_1, and P_2 intersect at Q. Use the fact that $\overrightarrow{P_1Q} \perp \overrightarrow{OP_2}$ and $\overrightarrow{P_2Q} \perp \overrightarrow{OP_1}$ to show that $\overrightarrow{OQ} \perp \overrightarrow{P_1P_2}$.

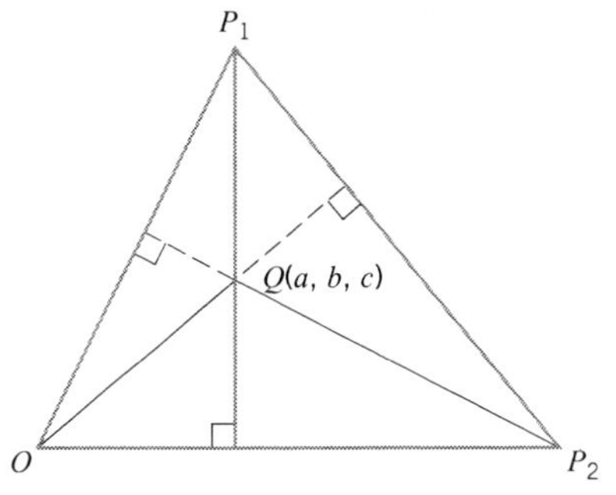

Figure C

Theorem 5. The three medians of a triangle intersect at one point.

HINT FOR PROOF With l_1, l_2, l_3 as in Figure D,

$$l_1 : \mathbf{r}_1(t) = t(\mathbf{a} + \mathbf{b}),$$
$$l_2 : \mathbf{r}_2(u) = \tfrac{1}{2}\mathbf{b} + u\left(\mathbf{a} - \tfrac{1}{2}\mathbf{b}\right),$$
$$l_3 : \mathbf{r}_3(v) = \tfrac{1}{2}\mathbf{a} + v\left(\mathbf{b} - \tfrac{1}{2}\mathbf{a}\right).$$

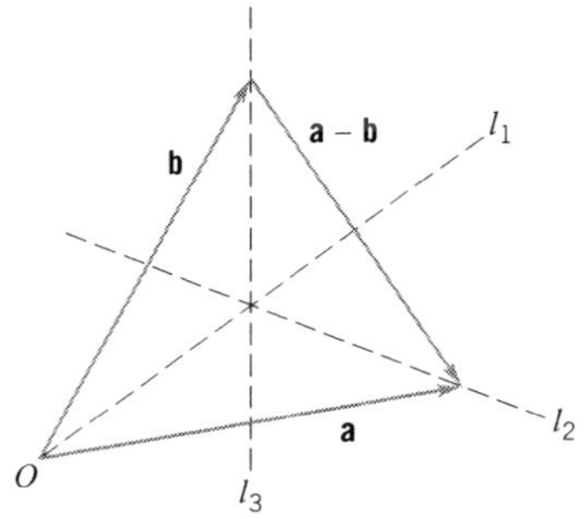

Figure D

Show that l_1 intersects both l_2 and l_3 at the same point.

Theorem 6. (The Law of Sines). If a triangle has sides **a, b, c** and opposite angles A, B, C, then

$$\frac{\sin A}{\|\mathbf{a}\|} = \frac{\sin B}{\|\mathbf{b}\|} = \frac{\sin C}{\|\mathbf{c}\|}.$$

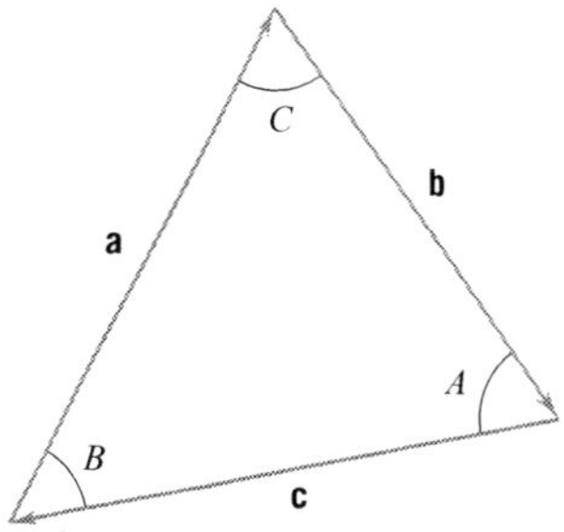

Figure E

HINT FOR PROOF With **a, b, c** as in Figure E, $\mathbf{a} + \mathbf{b} + \mathbf{c} = \mathbf{0}$. Observe then that $\mathbf{a} \times [\mathbf{a} + \mathbf{b} + \mathbf{c}] = \mathbf{0}$ and $\mathbf{b} \times [\mathbf{a} + \mathbf{b} + \mathbf{c}] = \mathbf{0}$. ❑

Theorem 7. If two planes have a point in common, then they have a line in common.

HINT FOR PROOF As equations for the two planes, take $\mathbf{n} \cdot (\mathbf{r} - \mathbf{r}_0) = 0$ and $\mathbf{N} \cdot (\mathbf{R} - \mathbf{R}_0) = 0$. If the point $P(a_1, a_2, a_3)$ lies on both planes, then the vector $\mathbf{a} = a_1\mathbf{i} + a_2\mathbf{j} + a_3\mathbf{k}$ satisfies both equations. In that case $\mathbf{n} \cdot (\mathbf{a} - \mathbf{r}_0) = 0$ and $\mathbf{N} \cdot (\mathbf{a} - \mathbf{R}_0) = 0$. Consider the line $\mathbf{r}(t) = \mathbf{a} + t(\mathbf{n} \times \mathbf{N})$.

■ 13.7 HIGHER DIMENSIONS

Vectors in three-space are number triples:

$$\mathbf{a} = (a_1, a_2, a_3).$$

We can form quadruples and quintuples:

$$(a_1, a_2, a_3, a_4), \qquad (a_1, a_2, a_3, a_4, a_5).$$

More generally, for each positive integer n we can form n-tuples:

$$(a_1, a_2, \ldots, a_n).$$

The vector algebra that we introduced for number triples can be extended to n-tuples.

For

$$\mathbf{a} = (a_1, a_2, \ldots, a_n) \qquad \text{and} \qquad \mathbf{b} = (b_1, b_2, \ldots, b_n)$$

set

$$\mathbf{a} + \mathbf{b} = (a_1 + b_1, a_2 + b_2, \dots, a_n + b_n)$$

and for each scalar α set

$$\alpha\mathbf{a} = (\alpha a_1, \alpha a_2, \dots, \alpha a_n).$$

By defining

$$\mathbf{i}_1 = (1, 0, 0, \dots, 0), \qquad \mathbf{i}_2 = (0, 1, 0, \dots, 0) \dots, \qquad \mathbf{i}_n = (0, 0, 0, \dots, 1)$$

we have

$$\mathbf{a} = (a_1, a_2, \dots, a_n) = a_1\mathbf{i}_1 + a_2\mathbf{i}_2 + \cdots + a_n\mathbf{i}_n.$$

By the *norm* of **a** we mean the number

$$\|\mathbf{a}\| = \sqrt{a_1^2 + a_2^2 + \cdot s + a_n^2}.$$

The *dot product* now reads

$$\mathbf{a} \cdot \mathbf{b} = a_1b_1 + a_2b_2 + \cdots + a_nb_n.$$

After showing that $|\mathbf{a} \cdot \mathbf{b}| \leq \|\mathbf{a}\| \, \|\mathbf{b}\|$, we can define the angle between n-tuples by setting

$$\cos\theta = \frac{|\mathbf{a} \cdot \mathbf{b}|}{\|\mathbf{a}\| \, \|\mathbf{b}\|}$$

provided that neither **a** nor **b** is the zero n-tuple

$$\mathbf{0} = (0, 0, \dots, 0).$$

In going from three dimensions to higher dimensions, we lose the capacity to draw pictures (how can we draw in n-dimensions?) and we lose the notion of cross product (there is no third direction that we can single out). For the rest, all we did with number triples we can do with n-tuples.

The study of n-tuples forms the core of *finite dimensional linear algebra*—a beautiful subject with many useful applications. There are also infinite dimensional "vector spaces." These form the core of a subject called *functional analysis*—again, a beautiful subject with interesting applications. It is very abstract, but well worth studying.

■ CHAPTER 13. REVIEW EXERCISES

1. Throughout this exercise let

$$P(3, 2, -1), \qquad Q(7, -5, 4), \qquad R(5, 6, -3).$$

(a) Find the length of the line segment $\overline{PQ}$.
(b) Find the midpoint of the line segment $\overline{QR}$.
(c) Given that Q is the midpoint of the line segment $\overline{PX}$, what are the coordinates of X?
(d) Find an equation for the sphere which passes through P and is centered at the midpoint of $\overline{PR}$.

2. Exercise 1 for $P(4, 2, -3)$, $Q(-2, 1, 4)$, $R(1, -1, -6)$.

Exercises 3–4. Write an equation for the sphere that satisfies the given conditions.

3. Centered at $(2, -3, 1)$, passes through the origin.

4. The line segment that joins $(-1, 4, 2)$ to $(3, -2, 6)$ is a diameter.

Exercises 5–6. Show that the equation represents a sphere; find the center and the radius.

5. $x^2 + y^2 + z^2 + 2x + 4y - 8z + 17 = 0$.

6. $x^2 + y^2 + z^2 - 6x + 10y - 2z + 2 = 0$.

Exercises 7–24. Set $\mathbf{a} = 3\mathbf{i} + 2\mathbf{j} - \mathbf{k}$, $\mathbf{b} = 5\mathbf{i} + 3\mathbf{j}$, $\mathbf{c} = -2\mathbf{i} + 4\mathbf{j} + \mathbf{k}$. Determine the following.

7. $\frac{1}{2}\mathbf{a}$.

8. $\mathbf{a} + 4\mathbf{b} - 3\mathbf{c}$.

9. $\mathbf{a} \cdot (\mathbf{b} + \mathbf{c})$.

10. $\|\mathbf{a} + \mathbf{b}\|$.

11. $\|\mathbf{c}\|^2$.

12. $\|\mathbf{b} \times \mathbf{b}\|$.

13. $(2\mathbf{a} - \mathbf{b}) \cdot \mathbf{c}$.

14. $\mathbf{a} \times (\mathbf{b} + \mathbf{c})$.

15. The unit vector in the direction of **a**.

16. The unit vector in the direction opposite to the direction of **c**.

17. The angle between **a** and **c**. Express your answer in radians rounded to the nearest hundredth of a radian.

18. The angle between **b** and **c**. Express your answer in degrees rounded to the nearest tenth of a degree.

19. The direction cosines and the direction angles of **a**.

20. $\text{comp}_{\mathbf{a}}\, \mathbf{b}$.

21. $\text{comp}_{\mathbf{a}}\, (\mathbf{b} \times \mathbf{c})$.

22. The unit vectors perpendicular to **a** and **c**.

23. The volume of the parallelepiped determined by **a, b, c.**

24. The area of the triangle determined by **a**, **b**, $\mathbf{a} - \mathbf{b}$.

25. The points $P(1, 1, 1)$, $Q(-2, 1, 0)$, $R(4, -2, 3)$ are given.

(a) Find scalar parametric equations for the line that passes through P and is parallel to $\overrightarrow{QR}$.

(b) Find an equation for the plane through P that is perpendicular to $\overrightarrow{PR}$.

(c) Find an equation for the plane that passes through P, Q, R.

26. The points $P(3, 2, -1)$, $Q(7, -5, 4)$, $R(5, 6, -3)$ are given.

(a) Find scalar parametric equations for the line that passes through R and is parallel to the line determined by P and Q.

(b) Find scalar parametric equations for the line that passes through R and is perpendicular to the line determined by P and Q.

(c) The lines in parts (a) and (b) determine a plane. Find an equation in rectangular coordinates for this plane.

Exercises 27–29. Determine whether the lines l_1 and l_2 are parallel, skew, or intersecting. If they intersect, find the point of intersection.

27. $l_1 : x = t, y = -t, z = -6 + 2t;\quad l_2 : x = 1 - u,$
$y = 1 + 3u, z = 2u.$

28. $l_1 : \mathbf{r}(t) = (1 - 2t)\mathbf{i} + (3 + 3t)\mathbf{j} + 5t\mathbf{k};$
$l_2 : \mathbf{R}(u) = (3 + 2u)\mathbf{i} + (1 - u)\mathbf{j} + (6 + 3u)\mathbf{k}.$

29. $l_1 : \dfrac{x-1}{2} = \dfrac{y+2}{-1}, \dfrac{z-3}{4};\quad l_2 : x + 2 = \dfrac{y-3}{3} = z.$

30. The point $P(3, 1, -2)$ and the line $l : x + 1 = y + 2 = z + 1$ are given. Find The point Q on l for which $\overrightarrow{PQ} \perp l$.

31. (a) Are the points $P(3, 2, -1)$, $Q(7, -5, 4)$, $R(5, -1, 1)$ collinear?

(b) Are the points $P(3, 2, -1)$, $Q(7, -5, 4)$, $R(5, -1, 1)$, $S(1, 2, 0)$ coplanar?

32. Where does the line

$$\frac{x+2}{3} = \frac{y-1}{2} = \frac{z+6}{1}$$

intersect the plane $2x + y - 3z + 6 = 0$?

Exercises 33–38. Write an equation for the plane that satisfies the given conditions.

33. Contains the points $P(1, -2, 1)$, $Q(2, 0, 3)$, $R(0, 1, -1)$.

34. Contains the point $P(2, 1, -3)$ and is perpendicular to the line

$$\frac{x+1}{2} = \frac{y-1}{3} = -\frac{z}{4}$$

35. Contains the point $P(1, -2, -1)$ and is parallel to the plane $3x + 2y - z = 4$.

36. Contains the point $P(3, -1, 2)$ and the line $x = 2 + 2t, y = -1 + 3t, z = -2t$.

37. Contains the line $x = -1 + 3t, y = 1 + 2t, z = 2 + 4t$ and is perpendicular to the plane $2x + y - 3z + 4 = 0$.

38. Contains the point $P(2, 1, -3)$ and the line formed by intersecting the planes

$$3x + y - z = 2, \quad 2x + y + 4z = 1.$$

39. Find the distance from the point $P(4, 6, -4)$ to the line which passes through $Q(2, 2, 1)$ and $R(4, 3, -1)$.

40. Find the distance from the point $P(2, 1, -1)$ to the plane $x - 2y + 2z + 5 = 0$.

Exercises 41–42. Find the angle between the planes.

41. $2x + y + z + 3 = 0, \quad 4z + 4y - 2z - 9 = 0.$

42. $2x - 3y + z + 2 = 0, \quad x + 4y - 5z - 6 = 0.$

Exercises 43–44. Find a set of scalar parametric equations for the line formed by intersecting the planes.

43. $3x + 5y + 2z - 4 = 0, \quad x + 2y - z - 2 = 0.$

44. $x - 2y + 2z = 1, \quad 3x - y - z = 2.$

45. Set $\mathbf{a} = 2\mathbf{i} - \mathbf{j} + 3\mathbf{k}$ and $\mathbf{b} = 3\mathbf{i} + 2\mathbf{j} - \mathbf{k}$. Find all vectors of length 4 that are perpendicular to both **a** and **b**.

46. Show that, for all vectors **a**, **b**, **c**, **d**,

$$(\mathbf{a} \times \mathbf{b}) \times (\mathbf{c} \times \mathbf{d}) = [(\mathbf{a} \times \mathbf{b}) \cdot \mathbf{d}]\mathbf{c} - [(\mathbf{a} \times \mathbf{b}) \cdot \mathbf{c}]\mathbf{d}.$$

47. Show that, for all vectors **a** and **b**,

$$(\|\mathbf{b}\|\mathbf{a} - \|\mathbf{a}\|\mathbf{b}) \perp (\|\mathbf{b}\|\mathbf{a} + \|\mathbf{a}\|\mathbf{b}).$$

48. Verify that, for all vectors **a** and **b**,

$$\|\mathbf{a} + \mathbf{b}\|^2 - \|\mathbf{a} - \mathbf{b}\|^2 = 4\mathbf{a} \cdot \mathbf{b}.$$

49. Use Exercise 46 to prove that the diagonals of a parallelogram have equal length iff the parallelogram is a rectangle.

50. Show that the midpoints of the sides of a quadrilateral are the four vertices of a parallelogram.

51. Use vector methods to show that the line segment that joins the midpoints of two sides of a triangle is parallel to the third side. Show that the length of this line segment is one-half the length of the third side.

52. The setting is the xy-plane.

(a) Verify that the line $l : Ax + By + C = 0$ can be parametrized by setting

$$\mathbf{r}(t) = (-C/A)\mathbf{i} + (B\mathbf{i} - A\mathbf{j})t$$

provided that $A \neq 0$.

(b) Show that $A\mathbf{i} + B\mathbf{j}$ is normal to l.

(c) Show that

$$d(O, l) = \frac{|C|}{\sqrt{A^2 + B^2}}$$

by vector methods.

CHAPTER 14

VECTOR CALCULUS

Functions such as

$$f(t) = 2 + 3t, \qquad f(t) = at^2 + bt + c, \qquad f(t) = \sin 2t$$

assign real numbers to real numbers. They are called *real-valued functions of a real variable*, for short, *scalar functions*. Functions such as

$$\mathbf{f}(t) = \mathbf{r}_0 + t\mathbf{d}, \qquad \mathbf{f}(t) = t^2\,\mathbf{a} + t\,\mathbf{b} + \mathbf{c}, \qquad \mathbf{f}(t) = \sin t\,\mathbf{a} + \cos t\,\mathbf{b}$$

assign vectors to real numbers. They are called *vector-valued functions of a real variable*, for short, *vector functions*.

Vector functions can be built up from scalar functions in an obvious manner. From scalar functions f_1, f_2, f_3 that share a common domain we can construct the vector function

$$\mathbf{f}(t) = f_1(t)\,\mathbf{i} + f_2(t)\,\mathbf{j} + f_3(t)\,\mathbf{k}.$$

The functions f_1, f_2, f_3 are called the *components* of $\mathbf{f}$. A number t is in the domain of $\mathbf{f}$ iff it is in the domain of each of its components.

In the examples that follow we'll define $\mathbf{f}$ by giving its components and view $\mathbf{f}(t)$ as a *radius vector*, a vector attached to the origin. Then the tip of $\mathbf{f}(t)$ has a definite position and, as t varies, traces out a path in space.

Example 1 From the scalar functions

$$f_1(t) = x_0 + d_1 t, \qquad f_2(t) = y_0 + d_2 t, \qquad f_3(t) = z_0 + d_3 t$$

we can form the vector function

$$\mathbf{f}(t) = (x_0 + d_1 t)\,\mathbf{i} + (y_0 + d_2 t)\,\mathbf{j} + (z_0 + d_3 t)\,\mathbf{k}.$$

The domain of $\mathbf{f}$ is the set of all real numbers. If d_1, d_2, d_3 are not all zero, then the radius vector $\mathbf{f}(t)$ traces out the line that passes through the point $P(x_0, y_0, z_0)$ and has the direction numbers d_1, d_2, d_3. If d_1, d_2, d_3 are all 0, then we have the constant function

$$\mathbf{f}(t) = x_0\,\mathbf{i} + y_0\,\mathbf{j} + z_0\,\mathbf{k}.$$

In this case the path traced out by $\mathbf{f}(t)$ has been reduced to a point, the point $P(x_0, y_0, z_0)$. ❑

Example 2 From the functions

$$f_1(t) = \cos t, \qquad f_2(t) = \sin t, \qquad f_3(t) = 0$$

we can form the vector function

$$\mathbf{f}(t) = \cos t\,\mathbf{i} + \sin t\,\mathbf{j}.$$

For each t

$$\|\mathbf{f}(t)\| = \sqrt{\cos^2 t + \sin^2 t} = 1.$$

Since the third component is zero, the radius vector $\mathbf{f}(t)$ lies in the xy-plane. As t increases, $\mathbf{f}(t)$ traces out the unit circle in a counterclockwise manner, effecting a complete revolution on every interval of length 2π. (Figure 14.1.1) ❑

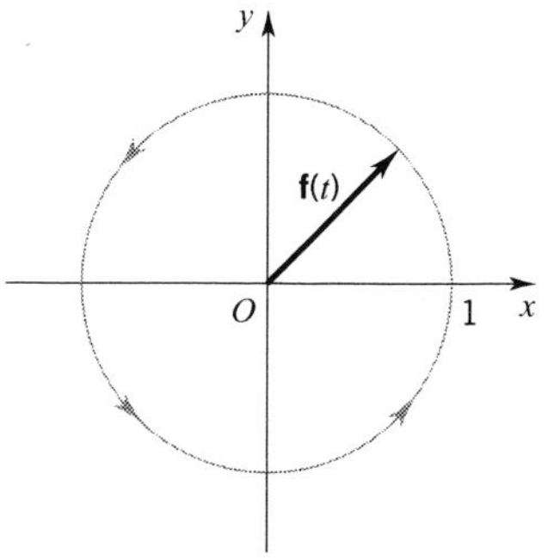

$\mathbf{f}(t) = \cos t\,\mathbf{i} + \sin t\,\mathbf{j}$

Figure 14.1.1

Example 3 Each real-valued function f defined on an interval $[a, b]$ gives rise to a vector-valued function $\mathbf{f}$ in a natural way. Setting

$$f_1(t) = t, \qquad f_2(t) = f(t), \qquad f_3(t) = 0,$$

we obtain the vector function

$$\mathbf{f}(t) = t\,\mathbf{i} + f(t)\,\mathbf{j}.$$

As t increases from a to b, the radius vector $\mathbf{f}(t)$ traces out the graph of f from left to right. See Figure 14.1.2. ❑

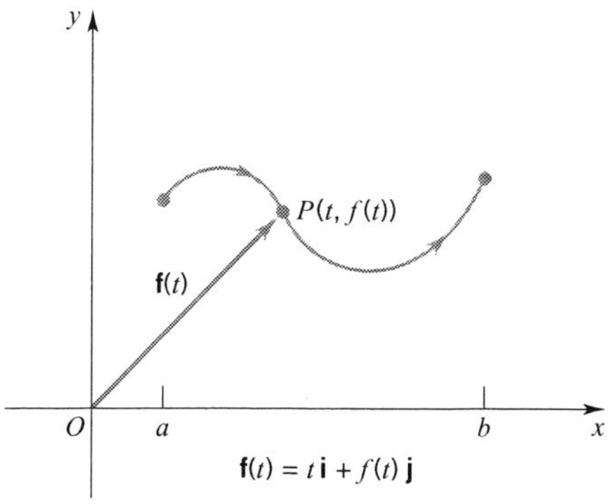

$\mathbf{f}(t) = t\,\mathbf{i} + f(t)\,\mathbf{j}$

Figure 14.1.2

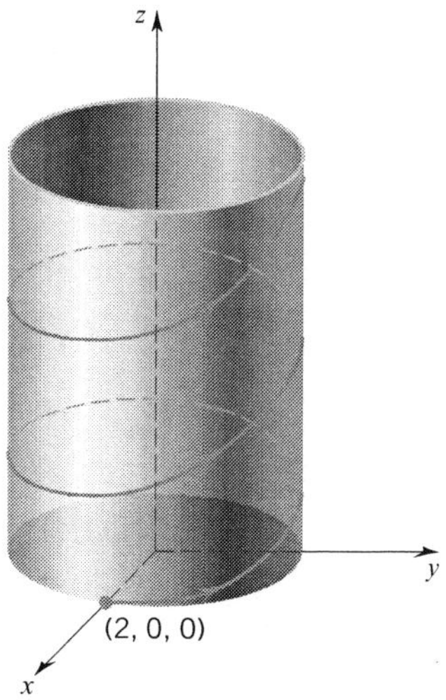

Figure 14.1.3

Example 4 From the functions

$$f_1(t) = 2\cos t, \qquad f_2(t) = 2\sin t, \qquad f_3(t) = t, \qquad t \geq 0$$

we can form the vector function

$$\mathbf{f}(t) = 2\cos t\,\mathbf{i} + 2\sin t\,\mathbf{j} + t\,\mathbf{k}, \qquad t \geq 0.$$

At $t = 0$, the tip of the radius vector $\mathbf{f}(0)$ is at the point (2, 0, 0). As t increases, the tip of $\mathbf{f}(t)$ spirals up the circular cylinder $x^2 + y^2 = 4$ (z arbitrary), effecting a complete turn on every t-interval of length 2π. Such a spiraling curve is called a *circular helix*. (Figure 14.1.3) ❑

As in the examples given, and under conditions to be spelled out later, as t ranges over the interval I, the radius vector

$$\mathbf{f}(t) = f_1(t)\,\mathbf{i} + f_2(t)\,\mathbf{j} + f_3(t)\,\mathbf{k}$$

traces out a curve C. We say that **f** *parametrizes* C. The equations

$$x = f_1(t), \qquad y = f_2(t), \qquad z = f_3(t)$$

formed from the components of **f** serve as parametric equations for C. If one of the components is identically 0 on I, for example, if **f** has the form $\mathbf{f}(t) = f_1(t)\,\mathbf{i} + f_2(t)\,\mathbf{j}$, then C is a *plane curve*; otherwise C is a space curve.

In this chapter we study the geometry of curves and then apply this geometry to obtain a useful description of curvilinear motion. But first we have to extend the limit process to vector functions, establish the notion of vector-function continuity, define vector derivative, and spell out the rules of differentiation.

■ 14.1 LIMIT, CONTINUITY, VECTOR DERIVATIVE

The Limit Process

The limit process for vector functions does not require that $\mathbf{f}(t)$ be attached to any particular point. It can be applied to any vector-valued function.

DEFINITION 14.1.1 LIMIT OF A VECTOR FUNCTION

$$\lim_{t\to t_0} \mathbf{f}(t) = \mathbf{L} \qquad \text{provided that} \qquad \lim_{t\to t_0} \|\mathbf{f}(t) - \mathbf{L}\| = 0.$$

Note that for each t in the domain of **f**, $\|\mathbf{f}(t) - \mathbf{L}\|$ is a real number, and therefore the limit on the right is the limit of a real-valued function. Thus we are still in familiar territory.

The first thing we show is that

(14.1.2) $$\text{if} \qquad \lim_{t\to t_0} \mathbf{f}(t) = \mathbf{L}, \qquad \text{then} \qquad \lim_{t\to t_0} \|\mathbf{f}(t)\| = \|\mathbf{L}\|.$$

PROOF We know that

$$0 \le \big|\|\mathbf{f}(t)\| - \|\mathbf{L}\|\big| \le \|\mathbf{f}(t) - \mathbf{L}\|. \qquad \text{(Exercise 24, Section 13.2)}$$

It follows from the pinching theorem that

$$\text{if} \qquad \lim_{t\to t_0} \|\mathbf{f}(t) - \mathbf{L}\| = 0, \qquad \text{then} \qquad \lim_{t\to t_0} \big|\|\mathbf{f}(t)\| - \|\mathbf{L}\|\big| = 0.$$

Remark The converse of (14.1.2) is false. You can see this by setting $\mathbf{f}(t) = \mathbf{k}$ and taking $\mathbf{L} = -\mathbf{k}$. ❑

We can indicate that $\lim_{t\to t_0} \mathbf{f}(t) = \mathbf{L}$ by writing

$$\text{as} \quad t \to t_0, \qquad \mathbf{f}(t) \to \mathbf{L}.$$

We will state the limit rules in this form. As you will see below, there are no surprises.

THEOREM 14.1.3 LIMIT RULES

Let **f** and **g** be vector functions and let u be a real-valued function. Suppose that, as $t \to t_0$,

$$\mathbf{f}(t) \to \mathbf{L}, \qquad \mathbf{g}(t) \to \mathbf{M}, \qquad u(t) \to A.$$

Then

$$\mathbf{f}(t) + \mathbf{g}(t) \to \mathbf{L} + \mathbf{M}, \qquad \alpha\mathbf{f}(t) + \beta\mathbf{g}(t) \to \alpha\mathbf{L} + \beta\mathbf{M},$$

$$u(t)\mathbf{f}(t) \to A\mathbf{L}, \qquad \mathbf{f}(t)\cdot\mathbf{g}(t) \to \mathbf{L}\cdot\mathbf{M}, \qquad \mathbf{f}(t)\times\mathbf{g}(t) \to \mathbf{L}\times\mathbf{M}.$$

Each of these limit rules is easy to verify. We will verify the last one. To do this, we have to show that

$$\text{as } t \to t_0, \qquad \|[\mathbf{f}(t)\times\mathbf{g}(t)] - [\mathbf{L}\times\mathbf{M}]\| \to 0.$$

We do this as follows:

$$\begin{aligned}
\|[(\mathbf{f}(t)\times\mathbf{g}(t)] - [\mathbf{L}\times\mathbf{M}]\| &= \|[\mathbf{f}(t)\times\mathbf{g}(t)] - [\mathbf{L}\times\mathbf{g}(t)] + [\mathbf{L}\times\mathbf{g}(t)] - [\mathbf{L}\times\mathbf{M}]\| \\
&= \|[(\mathbf{f}(t) - \mathbf{L})\times\mathbf{g}(t)] + [\mathbf{L}\times(\mathbf{g}(t) - \mathbf{M})]\| \qquad (13.4.5) \\
&\le \|(\mathbf{f}(t) - \mathbf{L})\times\mathbf{g}(t)\| + \|\mathbf{L}\times(\mathbf{g}(t) - \mathbf{M})\| \quad \text{(triangle inequality)} \\
&\le \|\mathbf{f}(t) - \mathbf{L}\|\ \|\mathbf{g}(t)\| + \|\mathbf{L}\|\ \|\mathbf{g}(t) - \mathbf{M}\|. \quad \text{(explain)}
\end{aligned}$$

As $t \to t_0$, $\|\mathbf{g}(t)\| \to \|\mathbf{M}\|$. [This follows from (14.1.2).] Therefore, as $t \to t_0$,

$$\|\mathbf{f}(t) - \mathbf{L}\|\ \|\mathbf{g}(t)\| + \|\mathbf{L}\|\ \|\mathbf{g}(t) - \mathbf{M}\| \to (0)\|\mathbf{M}\| + \|\mathbf{L}\|(0) = 0.$$

Since $0 \le \|\mathbf{f}(t)\times\mathbf{g}(t)] - [\mathbf{L}\times\mathbf{M}]\|$, it follows from the pinching theorem that $\|[\mathbf{f}(t)\times\mathbf{g}(t)] - [\mathbf{L}\times\mathbf{M}]\| \to 0$. ❑

The limit process can be carried out component by component: let $\mathbf{f}(t) = f_1(t)\,\mathbf{i} + f_2(t)\,\mathbf{j} + f_3(t)\,\mathbf{k}$ and let $\mathbf{L} = L_1\,\mathbf{i} + L_2\,\mathbf{j} + L_3\,\mathbf{k}$; then

(14.1.4)

$$\lim_{t\to t_0} \mathbf{f}(t) = \mathbf{L} \quad \text{iff}$$
$$\lim_{t\to t_0} f_1(t) = L_1, \qquad \lim_{t\to t_0} f_2(t) = L_2, \qquad \lim_{t\to t_0} f_3(t) = L_3.$$

PROOF

$$\begin{aligned}
\lim_{t\to t_0} \mathbf{f}(t) = \mathbf{L} \quad &\text{iff} \quad \lim_{t\to t_0} \|\mathbf{f}(t) - \mathbf{L}\| = 0 \\
&\text{iff} \quad \lim_{t\to t_0} \sqrt{[f_1(t) - L_1]^2 + [f_2(t) - L_2]^2 + [f_3(t) - L_3]^2} = 0 \\
&\text{iff} \quad \lim_{t\to t_0} f_1(t) = L_1, \quad \lim_{t\to t_0} f_2(t) = L_2, \quad \lim_{t\to t_0} f_3(t) = L_3. \quad ❑
\end{aligned}$$

Example 1 Find $\lim_{t\to 0} \mathbf{f}(t)$ given that

$$\mathbf{f}(t) = \cos(t + \pi)\,\mathbf{i} + \sin(t + \pi)\,\mathbf{j} + e^{-t^2}\mathbf{k}.$$

SOLUTION

$$\begin{aligned}\lim_{t\to 0}\mathbf{f}(t) &= \lim_{t\to 0}[\cos(t+\pi)\,\mathbf{i}+\sin(t+\pi)\,\mathbf{j}+e^{-t^2}\,\mathbf{k}]\\ &= \left[\lim_{t\to 0}\cos(t+\pi)\right]\mathbf{i}+\left[\lim_{t\to 0}\sin(t+\pi)\right]\mathbf{j}+\left[\lim_{t\to 0}e^{-t^2}\right]\mathbf{k}\\ &= (-1)\,\mathbf{i}+(0)\,\mathbf{j}+(1)\,\mathbf{k}=-\mathbf{i}+\mathbf{k}.\quad \square\end{aligned}$$

Continuity and Differentiability

As you would expect, $\mathbf{f}$ is said to be *continuous* at t_0 provided that

$$\lim_{t\to t_0}\mathbf{f}(t)=\mathbf{f}(t_0).$$

Thus, by (14.1.4), $\mathbf{f}$ is continuous at t_0 iff each component of $\mathbf{f}$ is continuous at t_0.

To differentiate $\mathbf{f}$, we form the vector $(1/h)\,[\mathbf{f}(t+h)-\mathbf{f}(t)]$ and write it as

$$\frac{\mathbf{f}(t+h)-\mathbf{f}(t)}{h}.$$

DEFINITION 14.1.5 DERIVATIVE OF A VECTOR FUNCTION

The vector function $\mathbf{f}$ is said to be *differentiable* at t provided that

$$\lim_{h\to 0}\frac{\mathbf{f}(t+h)-\mathbf{f}(t)}{h}\quad\text{exists.}$$

If this limit exists, it is called the *derivative of* $\mathbf{f}$ *at* t and is denoted by $\mathbf{f}'(t)$.

Observe first that

(14.1.6) constant functions have derivative $\mathbf{0}$.

PROOF If $\mathbf{f}(t)$ is constantly $\mathbf{c}$, then

$$\lim_{h\to 0}\frac{\mathbf{f}(t+h)-\mathbf{f}(t)}{h}=\lim_{h\to 0}\mathbf{0}=\mathbf{0}.\quad\square$$

Next we come to variable multiples of a constant vector.

(14.1.7) Functions of the form

$$\mathbf{f}(t)=u(t)\,\mathbf{c}\qquad (u\text{ differentiable})$$

have derivative

$$\mathbf{f}'(t)=u'(t)\,\mathbf{c}.$$

PROOF Note that

$$\frac{\mathbf{f}(t+h)-\mathbf{f}(t)}{h}=\frac{u(t+h)\,\mathbf{c}-u(t)\,\mathbf{c}}{\mathbf{h}}=\frac{u(t+h)-u(t)}{h}\mathbf{c}$$

and take the limit of both sides as $h\to 0$. $\square$

Thus

$$\mathbf{f}(t) = t^2\mathbf{a} \qquad \text{has derivative} \qquad \mathbf{f}'(t) = 2t\,\mathbf{a}$$

and

$$\mathbf{f}(t) = \sin \pi t(\mathbf{i} - \mathbf{j}) \qquad \text{has derivative} \qquad \mathbf{f}'(t) = \pi \cos \pi t(\mathbf{i} - \mathbf{j}). \quad \square$$

Differentiation can be carried out component by component; which is to say, if $\mathbf{f}(t) = f_1(t)\,\mathbf{i} + f_2(t)\,\mathbf{j} + f_3(t)\,\mathbf{k}$ is differentiable at t, then

$$\mathbf{f}'(t) = f_1'(t)\,\mathbf{i} + f_2'(t)\,\mathbf{j} + f_3'(t)\,\mathbf{k}.$$

PROOF

$$\begin{aligned}
\mathbf{f}'(t) &= \lim_{h\to 0} \frac{\mathbf{f}(t+h) - \mathbf{f}(t)}{h} \\
&= \lim_{h\to 0} \left[\frac{f_1(t+h) - f_1(t)}{h}\,\mathbf{i} + \frac{f_2(t+h) - f_2(t)}{h}\,\mathbf{j} + \frac{f_3(t+h) - f_3(t)}{h}\,\mathbf{k} \right] \\
&= \left[\lim_{h\to 0} \frac{f_1(1+h) - f_1(t)}{h} \right] \mathbf{i} + \left[\lim_{h\to 0} \frac{f_2(t+h) - f_2(t)}{h} \right] \mathbf{j} + \\
&\qquad \left[\lim_{h\to 0} \frac{f_3(t+h) - f_3(t)}{h} \right] \mathbf{k} \\
&= f_1'(t)\,\mathbf{i} + f_2'(t)\,\mathbf{j} + f_3'(t)\,\mathbf{k}. \quad \square
\end{aligned}$$

As with real-valued functions, if $\mathbf{f}$ is differentiable at t, then $\mathbf{f}$ is continuous at t. (Exercise 53)

Interpretations of the vector derivative and applications of vector differentiation are introduced later in the chapter. Here we limit ourselves to sample computations.

Example 2 Given that $\mathbf{f}(t) = t\,\mathbf{i} + \sqrt{t}\,\mathbf{j} - e^t\mathbf{k}$, find:

(a) the domain of $\mathbf{f}$ **(b)** $\mathbf{f}(0)$

(c) $\mathbf{f}'(t)$ **(d)** $\mathbf{f}'(0)$

(e) $\|\mathbf{f}(t)\|$ **(f)** $\mathbf{f}(t)\cdot\mathbf{f}'(t)$.

SOLUTION

(a) For a number to be in the domain of $\mathbf{f}$, it is necessary only that it be in the domain of each of the components. The domain of $\mathbf{f}$ is $[0, \infty)$.

(b) $\mathbf{f}(0) = 0\,\mathbf{i} + \sqrt{0}\,\mathbf{j} - e^0\,\mathbf{k} = -\mathbf{k}$.

(c) $\mathbf{f}'(t) = \mathbf{i} + \dfrac{1}{2\sqrt{t}}\mathbf{j} - e^t\mathbf{k}$, but only for $t > 0$. (explain)

(d) $\mathbf{f}'(0)$ does not exist.

(e) $\|\mathbf{f}(t)\| = \sqrt{t^2 + (\sqrt{t})^2 + (-e^t)^2} = \sqrt{t^2 + t + e^{2t}}, \quad t \geq 0$

(f) $\mathbf{f}(t)\cdot\mathbf{f}'(t) = (t\,\mathbf{i} + \sqrt{t}\,\mathbf{j} - e^t\,\mathbf{k})\cdot\left(\mathbf{i} + \dfrac{1}{2\sqrt{t}}\mathbf{j} - e^t\,\mathbf{k}\right)$

$$= t + \frac{1}{2} + e^{2t}, \qquad \text{but only for } t > 0. \quad \square$$

If $\mathbf{f}'$ is itself differentiable, we can calculate the second derivative $\mathbf{f}''$ and so on.

Example 3 Find $\mathbf{f}''(t)$ for $\mathbf{f}(t) = t \sin t\, \mathbf{i} + e^{-t}\, \mathbf{j} + t\, \mathbf{k}$.

SOLUTION

$$\mathbf{f}'(t) = (t \cos t + \sin t)\,\mathbf{i} - e^{-t}\mathbf{j} + \mathbf{k}$$

$$\mathbf{f}''(t) = (-t \sin t + \cos t + \cos t)\,\mathbf{i} + e^{-t}\mathbf{j} = (2\cos t - t \sin t)\,\mathbf{i} + e^{-t}\mathbf{j}. \quad \square$$

Integration

Just as we can differentiate component by component, we can integrate component by component. For $\mathbf{f}(t) = f_1(t)\,\mathbf{i} + f_2(t)\,\mathbf{j} + f_3(t)\,\mathbf{k}$ continuous on $[a, b]$, we set

(14.1.8)
$$\int_a^b \mathbf{f}(t)\,dt = \left(\int_a^b f_1(t)\,dt\right)\mathbf{i} + \left(\int_a^b f_2(t)\,dt\right)\mathbf{j} + \left(\int_a^b f_3(t)\,dt\right)\mathbf{k}.$$

Example 4 Find $\displaystyle\int_0^1 \mathbf{f}(t)\,dt$ for $\mathbf{f}(t) = t\,\mathbf{i} + \sqrt{t+1}\,\mathbf{j} - e^t\,\mathbf{k}$.

SOLUTION

$$\begin{aligned}\int_0^1 \mathbf{f}(t)\,dt &= \left(\int_0^1 t\,dt\right)\mathbf{i} + \left(\int_0^1 \sqrt{t+1}\,dt\right)\mathbf{j} + \left(\int_0^1 (-e^t)\,dt\right)\mathbf{k} \\ &= \left[\tfrac{1}{2}t^2\right]_0^1 \mathbf{i} + \left[\tfrac{2}{3}(t+1)^{3/2}\right]_0^1 \mathbf{j} + \left[-e^t\right]_0^1 \mathbf{k} \\ &= \tfrac{1}{2}\,\mathbf{i} + \tfrac{2}{3}(2\sqrt{2} - 1)\,\mathbf{j} + (1 - e)\,\mathbf{k}. \quad \square\end{aligned}$$

We can calculate indefinite integrals.

Example 5 Find $\mathbf{f}(t)$ given that

$$\mathbf{f}'(t) = 2\cos t\,\mathbf{i} - t \sin t^2\,\mathbf{j} + 2t\,\mathbf{k} \qquad \text{and} \qquad \mathbf{f}(0) = \mathbf{i} + 3\mathbf{k}.$$

SOLUTION By integrating $\mathbf{f}'(t)$, we find that

$$\mathbf{f}(t) = (2\sin t + C_1)\,\mathbf{i} + (\tfrac{1}{2}\cos t^2 + C_2)\,\mathbf{j} + (t^2 + C_3)\,\mathbf{k}$$

where C_1, C_2, C_3 are constants to be determined. Since

$$\mathbf{i} + 3\mathbf{k} = \mathbf{f}(0) = C_1\mathbf{i} + \left(\tfrac{1}{2} + C_2\right)\mathbf{j} + C_3\mathbf{k},$$

you can see that

$$C_1 = 1, \qquad C_2 = -\tfrac{1}{2}, \qquad C_3 = 3.$$

Thus

$$\mathbf{f}(t) = (2\sin t + 1)\,\mathbf{i} + \left(\tfrac{1}{2}\cos t^2 - \tfrac{1}{2}\right)\mathbf{j} + (t^2 + 3)\,\mathbf{k}. \quad \square$$

(Integration can also be carried out without direct reference to components. See Exercise 54.)

Properties of the Integral

It is clear that

(14.1.9)
$$\int_a^b [\mathbf{f}(t) + \mathbf{g}(t)]\,dt = \int_a^b \mathbf{f}(t)\,dt + \int_a^b \mathbf{g}(t)\,dt$$

and

(14.1.10) $$\int_a^b [\alpha\mathbf{f}(t)]\,dt = \alpha\int_a^b \mathbf{f}(t)\,dt \qquad \text{for every constant scalar } \alpha.$$

It is also true that

(14.1.11) $$\int_a^b [\mathbf{c}\cdot\mathbf{f}(t)]\,dt = \mathbf{c}\cdot\left(\int_a^b \mathbf{f}(t)\,dt\right) \qquad \text{for every constant vector } \mathbf{c}$$

and

(14.1.12) $$\left\|\int_a^b \mathbf{f}(t)\,dt\right\| \le \int_a^b \|\mathbf{f}(t)\|\,dt.$$

The proof of (14.1.11) is left as an exercise. (Exercise 56) Here we prove (14.1.12). It is an important inequality.

PROOF Set $\mathbf{c} = \int_a^b \mathbf{f}(t)\,dt$ and note that

$$\|\mathbf{c}\|^2 = \mathbf{c}\cdot\mathbf{c} = \mathbf{c}\cdot\int_a^b \mathbf{f}(t)\,dt$$

$$= \int_a^b [\mathbf{c}\cdot\mathbf{f}(t)]\,dt \le \int_a^b \|\mathbf{c}\|\,\|\mathbf{f}(t)\|\,dt = \|\mathbf{c}\|\int_a^b \|\mathbf{f}(t)\|\,dt.$$

by (14.1.11) ↑ ↑ by Schwarz's inequality (13.3.18)

If $\mathbf{c} \neq \mathbf{0}$, we can divide by $\|\mathbf{c}\|$ and conclude that

$$\|\mathbf{c}\| \le \int_a^b \|\mathbf{f}(t)\|\,dt.$$

If $\mathbf{c} = \mathbf{0}$, the result is obvious in the first place. ❑

EXERCISES 14.1

Exercises 1–8. Calculate the derivative.

1. $\mathbf{f}(t) = (1+2t)\,\mathbf{i} + (3-t)\,\mathbf{j} + (2+3t)\,\mathbf{k}$.

2. $\mathbf{f}(t) = 2\mathbf{i} - \cos t\,\mathbf{k}$.

3. $\mathbf{f}(t) = \sqrt{1-t}\,\mathbf{i} + \sqrt{1+t}\,\mathbf{j} + (1-t)^{-1}\,\mathbf{k}$.

4. $\mathbf{f}(t) = \arctan t(\mathbf{i}-\mathbf{j})$.

5. $\mathbf{f}(t) = \sin t\,\mathbf{i} + \cos t\,\mathbf{j} + \tan t\,\mathbf{k}$.

6. $\mathbf{f}(t) = e^t(\mathbf{i} + t\,\mathbf{j} + t^2\,\mathbf{k})$.

7. $\mathbf{f}(t) = \ln(1-t)\,\mathbf{i} + \cos t\,\mathbf{j} + t^2\,\mathbf{k}$.

8. $\mathbf{f}(t) = e^t(\mathbf{i}-\mathbf{j}) + e^{-2t}(\mathbf{j}-\mathbf{k})$.

Exercises 9–12. Calculate the second derivative

9. $\mathbf{f}(t) = 4t\,\mathbf{i} + 2t^3\,\mathbf{j} + (t^2+2t)\,\mathbf{k}$.

10. $\mathbf{f}(t) = t\sin t\,\mathbf{i} + t\cos t\,\mathbf{k}$.

11. $\mathbf{f}(t) = \cos 2t\,\mathbf{i} + \sin 2t\,\mathbf{j} + 4t\,\mathbf{k}$.

12. $\mathbf{f}(t) = \sqrt{t}\,\mathbf{i} + t\sqrt{t}\,\mathbf{j} + \ln t\,\mathbf{k}$.

13. (a) $\mathbf{r}(t) = e^{-t^2}\,\mathbf{i} + e^{-t}\,\mathbf{j}$, $\quad t_0 = 0$.

(b) $\mathbf{r}(t) = \ln(\sin t)\,\mathbf{i} + \ln(\cos t)\,\mathbf{j} + (2\sin t - 3\cot t)\,\mathbf{k}$, $t_0 = \pi/4$.

14. Find $\mathbf{r}''(t_0)$.

(a) $\mathbf{r}(t) = t^2e^{-t}\,\mathbf{i} + te^{-t}\,\mathbf{j}$, $\quad t_0 = \mathbf{0}$.

(b) $\mathbf{r}(t) = t\ln t\,\mathbf{i} + \ln^2 t\,\mathbf{j} + \sqrt{\ln t}\,\mathbf{k}$, $\quad t_0 = e$.

Exercises 15–20. Carry out the integration.

15. $\int_1^2 (\mathbf{i} + 2t\,\mathbf{j})\,dt$.

16. $\int_0^\pi (\sin t\,\mathbf{i} + \cos t\,\mathbf{j} + t\,\mathbf{k})\,dt$.

17. $\int_0^1 (e^t\,\mathbf{i} + e^{-t}\,\mathbf{j})\,dt.$

18. $\int_0^1 e^{-t}(t\,\mathbf{i} + 4e^{3t}\,\mathbf{j} + \mathbf{k})\,dt.$

19. $\int_0^1 \left(\frac{1}{1+t^2}\,\mathbf{i} + \sec^2 t\,\mathbf{j}\right)dt.$

20. $\int_1^3 \left(\frac{1}{t}\,\mathbf{i} + \frac{\ln t}{t}\,\mathbf{j} + e^{-2t}\,\mathbf{k}\right)dt.$

Exercises 21–24. Find $\lim_{t\to 0}\mathbf{f}(t)$ if it exists.

21. $\mathbf{f}(t) = \frac{\sin t}{2t}\,\mathbf{i} + e^{2t}\,\mathbf{j} + \frac{t^2}{e^t}\,\mathbf{k}.$

22. $\mathbf{f}(t) = 3(t^2-1)\,\mathbf{i} + \cos t\,\mathbf{j} + \frac{t}{|t|}\,\mathbf{k}.$

23. $\mathbf{f}(t) = t^2\,\mathbf{i} + \frac{1-\cos t}{3t}\,\mathbf{j} + \frac{t}{t+1}\,\mathbf{k}.$

24. $\mathbf{f}(t) = 3t\,\mathbf{i} + (t^2+1)\,\mathbf{j} + e^{2t}\,\mathbf{k}.$

25. Evaluate using a CAS.

(a) $\int_0^1 \left(te^t\,\mathbf{i} + te^{t^2}\mathbf{j}\right)dt.$

(b) $\int_3^8 \left(\frac{t}{t+1}\,\mathbf{i} + \frac{t}{(t+1)^2}\,\mathbf{j} + \frac{t}{(t+1)^3}\,\mathbf{k}\right)dt.$

26. Find the limit.

(a) $\lim_{t\to\pi/6} (\cos^2 t\,\mathbf{i} + \sin^2 t\,\mathbf{j} + \mathbf{k}).$

(b) $\lim_{t\to e^2} \left(t\ln t\,\mathbf{i} + \frac{\ln t}{t^2}\,\mathbf{j} + \sqrt{\ln t^2}\,\mathbf{k}\right).$

Exercises 27–34. Sketch the curve traced out by the tip of the radius vector and indicate the direction in which the curve is traversed as t increases.

27. $\mathbf{r}(t) = 2t\,\mathbf{i} + t^2\,\mathbf{j},\quad t \ge 0.$ **28.** $\mathbf{r}(t) = t^3\,\mathbf{i} + 2t\,\mathbf{j},\quad t \ge 0.$

29. $\mathbf{r}(t) = 2\sinh t\,\mathbf{i} + 2\cosh t\,\mathbf{j},\quad t \ge 0.$

30. $\mathbf{r}(t) = 3\cos t\,\mathbf{i} + 3\sin t\,\mathbf{k},\quad 0 \le t \le 2\pi.$

31. $\mathbf{r}(t) = 2\cos t\,\mathbf{i} + 3\sin t\,\mathbf{j},\quad 0 \le t \le 2\pi.$

32. $\mathbf{r}(t) = 2t\,\mathbf{i} + (5-2t)\,\mathbf{j} + 3t\,\mathbf{k},\quad t \ge 0.$

33. $\mathbf{r}(t) = (t^2+1)\,\mathbf{i} + t\,\mathbf{j} + 4k,\quad -2 \le t \le 2.$

34. $\mathbf{r}(t) = 2\cos t\,\mathbf{i} + 2\sin t\,\mathbf{j} + (2\pi - t)\,\mathbf{k},\quad 0 \le t \le 2\pi.$

Exercises 35–38. Use a graphing utility to draw the curve and indicate the direction in which the curve is traversed as t increases.

35. $\mathbf{r}(t) = 2\cos(t^2)\,\mathbf{i} + (2-\sqrt{t})\,\mathbf{j}.$

36. $\mathbf{r}(t) = e^{\cos 2t}\,\mathbf{i} + e^{-\sin t}\,\mathbf{j}.$

37. $\mathbf{r}(t) = (2-\sin 2t)\,\mathbf{i} + (3+2\cos t)\,\mathbf{j}.$

38. $\mathbf{r}(t) = (t-\sin t)\,\mathbf{i} + (1-\cos t)\,\mathbf{j}.$ (a cycloid)

Exercises 39–44. Find a vector-valued function $\mathbf{f}$ that parametrizes the curve in the direction indicated.

39. $4x^2 + 9y^2 = 36$ (a) Counterclockwise. (b) Clockwise.

40. $(x-1)^2 + y^2 = 1$ (a) Counterclockwise. (b) Clockwise.

41. $y = x^2$ (a) From left to right. (b) From right to left.

42. $y = x^3$ (a) From left to right. (b) From right to left.

43. The directed line segment from $(1, 4, -2)$ to $(3, 9, 6)$.

44. The directed line segment from $(3, 2, -5)$ to $(7, 2, 9)$.

45. Set $\mathbf{f}(t) = t\,\mathbf{i} + f(t)\,\mathbf{j}$ and calculate

$$\mathbf{f}'(t_0),\qquad \int_a^b \mathbf{f}(t)\,dt,\qquad \int_a^b \mathbf{f}'(t)\,dt$$

given that

$$f'(t_0) = m,\quad f(a) = c,\quad f(b) = d,\quad \int_c^b f(t)\,dt = A.$$

Exercises 46–49. Find $\mathbf{f}(t)$ from the information given.

46. $\mathbf{f}'(t) = t\,\mathbf{i} + t(1+t^2)^{-1/2}\mathbf{j} + te^t\,\mathbf{k}$ and $\mathbf{f}(0) = \mathbf{i} + 2\,\mathbf{j} + 3\,\mathbf{k}.$

47. $\mathbf{f}'(t) = 1 + t^2\mathbf{j}$ and $\mathbf{f}(0) = \mathbf{j} - \mathbf{k}.$

48. $\mathbf{f}'(t) = 2\mathbf{f}(t)$ and $\mathbf{f}(0) = \mathbf{i} - \mathbf{k}.$

49. $\mathbf{f}'(t) = \alpha\mathbf{f}(t)$ with α a real number and $\mathbf{f}(0) = \mathbf{c}.$

50. No ϵ, δ's have surfaced so far, but they are still there at the heart of the limit process. Give an ϵ, δ characterization of

$$\lim_{t\to t_0} \mathbf{f}(t) = \mathbf{L}.$$

51. (a) Show that, if $\mathbf{f}'(t) = \mathbf{0}$ for all t in an interval I, then $\mathbf{f}$ is a constant vector on I.

(b) Show that, if $\mathbf{f}'(t) = \mathbf{g}'(t)$ for all t in an interval I, then $\mathbf{f}$ and $\mathbf{g}$ differ by a constant vector on I.

52. Assume that, as $t \to t_0$, $\mathbf{f}(t) \to \mathbf{L}$ and $\mathbf{g}(t) \to \mathbf{M}$. Show that

$$\mathbf{f}(t)\cdot\mathbf{g}(t) \to \mathbf{L}\cdot\mathbf{M}.$$

53. Show that, if $\mathbf{f}$ is differentiable at t, then $\mathbf{f}$ is continuous at t.

54. A vector-valued function $\mathbf{G}$ is called an *antiderivative* for $\mathbf{f}$ on $[a, b]$ provided that (i) $\mathbf{G}$ is continuous on $[a, b]$ and (ii) $\mathbf{G}'(t) = \mathbf{f}(t)$ for all $t \in (a, b)$. Show that:

(a) If $\mathbf{f}$ is continuous on $[a, b]$ and $\mathbf{G}$ is an antiderivative for $\mathbf{f}$ on $[a, b]$, then

$$\int_a^b \mathbf{f}(t)\,dt = \mathbf{G}(b) - \mathbf{G}(a).$$

(b) If $\mathbf{f}$ is continuous on an interval I and $\mathbf{F}$ and $\mathbf{G}$ are antiderivatives for $\mathbf{f}$, then

$$\mathbf{F} = \mathbf{G} + \mathbf{C}$$

for some constant vector $\mathbf{C}$.

55. Is it necessarily true that

$$\int_a^b [\mathbf{f}(t)\cdot\mathbf{g}(t)]\,dt = \left[\int_a^b \mathbf{f}(t)\,dt\right]\cdot\left[\int_a^b \mathbf{g}(t)\,dt\right]?$$

56. Prove that, if $\mathbf{f}$ is continuous on $[a, b]$, then for each constant vector $\mathbf{c}$,

$$\int_a^b [\mathbf{c}\cdot\mathbf{f}(t)]\,dt = \mathbf{c}\cdot\int_a^b \mathbf{f}(t)\,dt$$

$$\int_a^b [\mathbf{c}\times\mathbf{f}(t)]\,dt = \mathbf{c}\times\int_a^b \mathbf{f}(t)\,dt.$$

57. Let $\mathbf{f}$ be a differentiable vector-valued function. Show that if $\|\mathbf{f}(t)\| \neq 0$, then

$$\frac{d}{dt}(\|\mathbf{f}(t)\|) = \frac{\mathbf{f}(t) \cdot \mathbf{f}'(t)}{\|\mathbf{f}(t)\|}.$$

58. Let $\mathbf{f}$ be a differentiable vector-valued function. Show that where $\|\mathbf{f}(t)\| \neq 0$,

$$\frac{d}{dt}\left(\frac{\mathbf{f}(t)}{\|\mathbf{f}(t)\|}\right) = \frac{\mathbf{f}'(t)}{\|\mathbf{f}(t)\|} - \frac{\mathbf{f}(t) \cdot \mathbf{f}'(t)}{\|\mathbf{f}(t)\|^3}\mathbf{f}(t).$$

■ 14.2 THE RULES OF DIFFERENTIATION

Vector functions with a common domain can be combined in many ways to form new functions. From $\mathbf{f}$ and $\mathbf{g}$ we can form the sum $\mathbf{f} + \mathbf{g}$:

$$(\mathbf{f} + \mathbf{g})(t) = \mathbf{f}(t) + \mathbf{g}(t).$$

We can form scalar multiples $\alpha\mathbf{f}$ and thus linear combinations $\alpha\mathbf{f} + \beta\mathbf{g}$:

$$(\alpha\mathbf{f})(t) = \alpha\mathbf{f}(t), \qquad (\alpha\mathbf{f} + \beta\mathbf{g})(t) = \alpha\mathbf{f}(t) + \beta\mathbf{g}(t).$$

We can form the dot product $\mathbf{f} \cdot \mathbf{g}$:

$$(\mathbf{f} \cdot \mathbf{g})(t) = \mathbf{f}(t) \cdot \mathbf{g}(t).$$

We can also form the cross product $\mathbf{f} \times \mathbf{g}$:

$$(\mathbf{f} \times \mathbf{g})(t) = \mathbf{f}(t) \times \mathbf{g}(t).$$

These operations on vector functions are simply the pointwise application of the algebraic operations on vectors that we introduced in Chapter 13.

There are two ways of bringing *scalar functions* (real-valued functions) into this mix. If a scalar function u shares a common domain with $\mathbf{f}$, we can form the product $u\mathbf{f}$:

$$(u\mathbf{f})(t) = u(t)\mathbf{f}(t).$$

If $u(t)$ is in the domain of $\mathbf{f}$ for each t in some interval, then we can form the composition $\mathbf{f} \circ u$:

$$(\mathbf{f} \circ u)(t) = \mathbf{f}(u(t)).$$

For example, with $u(t) = t^2$ and $\mathbf{f}(t) = e^t\mathbf{i} + \sin 2t\,\mathbf{j}$,

$$(u\mathbf{f})(t) = u(t)\mathbf{f}(t) = t^2e^t\mathbf{i} + t^2 \sin 2t\,\mathbf{j} \quad \text{and} \quad (\mathbf{f} \circ u)(t) = \mathbf{f}(u(t)) = e^{t^2}\mathbf{i} + \sin 2t^2\mathbf{j}.$$

It follows from Theorem 14.1.3 that if $\mathbf{f}$, $\mathbf{g}$ and u are continuous on a common domain, then $\mathbf{f} + \mathbf{g}$, $\alpha\mathbf{f}$, $\mathbf{f} \cdot \mathbf{g}$, $\mathbf{f} \times \mathbf{g}$, and $u\mathbf{f}$ are all continuous on that same set. We have yet to show the continuity of $\mathbf{f} \circ u$. The verification of that is left to you. (Exercise 36) What interests us here is that, if $\mathbf{f}$, $\mathbf{g}$ and u are differentiable, then the newly constructed functions are also differentiable and their derivatives satisfy the rules below. Here α is a scalar and $\mathbf{c}$ is a constant vector.

(14.2.1)

(1) $(\mathbf{f} + \mathbf{g})'(t) = \mathbf{f}'(t) + \mathbf{g}'(t)$.

(2) $(\alpha\mathbf{f})'(t) = \alpha\mathbf{f}'(t), \qquad (u\mathbf{c})'(t) = u'(t)\,\mathbf{c}$

(3) $(u\mathbf{f})'(t) = u(t)\mathbf{f}'(t) + u'(t)\mathbf{f}(t)$

(4) $(\mathbf{f} \cdot \mathbf{g})'(t) = [\mathbf{f}(t) \cdot \mathbf{g}'(t)] + [\mathbf{f}'(t) \cdot \mathbf{g}(t)]$

(5) $(\mathbf{f} \times \mathbf{g})'(t) = [\mathbf{f}(t) \times \mathbf{g}'(t)] + [\mathbf{f}'(t) \times \mathbf{g}(t)]$

(6) $(\mathbf{f} \circ u)'(t) = \mathbf{f}'(u(t))u'(t) = u'(t)\mathbf{f}'(u(t))$. (chain rule)

Rules (3), (4), (5) are all "product' rules and should remind you of the rule for differentiating the product of ordinary functions. Keep in mind, however, that the cross product is not commutative and therefore the order in Rule (5) is important.

In Rule (6) we first wrote the scalar part $u'(t)$ on the right so that the formula would look like the chain rule for ordinary functions. In general, $\mathbf{a}\alpha$ has the same meaning as $\alpha\mathbf{a}$.

Example 1 For $\mathbf{f}(t) = 2t^2\,\mathbf{i} - 3\mathbf{j}, \quad g(t) = \mathbf{i} + t\,\mathbf{j} + t^2\,\mathbf{k}, \quad u(t) = \frac{1}{3}t^3$

$$\mathbf{f}'(t) = 4t\,\mathbf{i}, \qquad \mathbf{g}'(t) = \mathbf{j} + 2t\,\mathbf{k}, \qquad u'(t) = t^2.$$

Therefore

(a) $(\mathbf{f}+\mathbf{g})'(t) = \mathbf{f}'(t) + \mathbf{g}'(t) = 4t\,\mathbf{i} + (\mathbf{j} + 2t\,\mathbf{k}) = 4t\,\mathbf{i} + \mathbf{j} + 2t\,\mathbf{k};$

(b) $(2\mathbf{f})'(t) = 2\mathbf{f}'(t) = 2(4t\,\mathbf{i}) = 8t\,\mathbf{i};$

(c) $(u\mathbf{f})'(t) = u(t)\mathbf{f}'(t) + u'(t)\mathbf{f}(t) = \frac{1}{3}t^3(4t\,\mathbf{i}) + t^2(2t^2\,\mathbf{i} - 3\,\mathbf{j}) = \frac{10}{3}t^4\mathbf{i} - 3t^2\,\mathbf{j};$

(d)
$$\begin{aligned}(\mathbf{f}\cdot\mathbf{g})'(t) &= [\mathbf{f}(t)\cdot\mathbf{g}'(t)] + [\mathbf{f}'(t)\cdot\mathbf{g}(t)]\\ &= [(2t^2\,\mathbf{i} - 3\,\mathbf{j})\cdot(\mathbf{j} + 2t\,\mathbf{k})] + [4t\,\mathbf{i}\cdot(\mathbf{i} + t\,\mathbf{j} + t^2\,\mathbf{k})] = -3 + 4t;\end{aligned}$$

(e)
$$\begin{aligned}(\mathbf{f}\times\mathbf{g})'(t) &= [\mathbf{f}(t)\times\mathbf{g}'(t)] + [\mathbf{f}'(t)\times\mathbf{g}(t)]\\ &= [(2t^2\,\mathbf{i} - 3\,\mathbf{j})\times(\mathbf{j} + 2t\,\mathbf{k})] + [4t\,\mathbf{i}\times(\mathbf{i} + t\,\mathbf{j} + t^2\,\mathbf{k})]\\ &= (2t^2\mathbf{k} - 4t^3\mathbf{j} - 6t\,\mathbf{i}) + (4t^2\,\mathbf{k} - 4t^3\mathbf{j}) = -6t\,\mathbf{i} - 8t^3\,\mathbf{j} + 6t^2\,\mathbf{k};\end{aligned}$$

while

$$\begin{aligned}(\mathbf{g}\times\mathbf{f})'(t) &= [\mathbf{g}(t)\times\mathbf{f}'(t)] + [\mathbf{g}'(t)\times\mathbf{f}(t)]\\ &= [(\mathbf{i} + t\,\mathbf{j} + t^2\,\mathbf{k})\times 4t\,\mathbf{i}] + [(\mathbf{j} + 2t\,\mathbf{k})\times(2t^2\,\mathbf{i} - 3\mathbf{j})]\\ &= (-4t^2\,\mathbf{k} + 4t^3\,\mathbf{j}) + (-2t^2\,\mathbf{k} + 4t^3\,\mathbf{j} + 6t\,\mathbf{i})\\ &= 6t\,\mathbf{i} + 8t^3\,\mathbf{j} - 6t^2\,\mathbf{k} = -(\mathbf{f}\times\mathbf{g})'(t);\end{aligned}$$

(f)
$$\begin{aligned}(\mathbf{f}\circ u)'(t) &= \mathbf{f}'(u(t))u'(t)\\ &= [4u(t)\,\mathbf{i}]u'(t) = \left[4\left(\tfrac{1}{3}t^3\right)\mathbf{i}\right]t^2 = \tfrac{4}{3}t^5\,\mathbf{i}. \quad \square\end{aligned}$$

Derivatives are limits and as such can be calculated component by component, and they can be calculated in a component-free manner. It follows that the rules of differentiation can be derived component by component, and they can be derived in a component-free manner. Take, for example, the differentiation rule

$$(u\mathbf{f})'(t) = u(t)\,\mathbf{f}'(t) + u'(t)\,\mathbf{f}(t).$$

COMPONENT-BY-COMPONENT DERIVATION Set

$$\mathbf{f}(t) = f_1(t)\,\mathbf{i} + f_2(t)\,\mathbf{j} + f_3(t)\,\mathbf{k}.$$

Then

$$(u\,\mathbf{f})(t) = u(t)\,\mathbf{f}(t) = u(t)f_1(t)\,\mathbf{i} + u(t)f_2(t)\,\mathbf{j} + u(t)f_3(t)\,\mathbf{k}$$

and

$$\begin{aligned}(u\,\mathbf{f})'(t) &= [u(t)f_1'(t) + u'(t)f_1(t)]\,\mathbf{i} + [u(t)f_2'(t) + u'(t)f_2(t)]\,\mathbf{j} +\\ &\qquad [u(t)f_3'(t) + u'(t)f_3(t)]\,\mathbf{k}\\ &= u(t)[f_1'(t)\,\mathbf{i} + f_2'(t)\,\mathbf{j} + f_3'(t)\,\mathbf{k}] + u'(t)[f_1(t)\,\mathbf{i} + f_2(t)\,\mathbf{j} + f_3(t)\,\mathbf{k}]\\ &= u(t)\,\mathbf{f}'(t) + u'(t)\,\mathbf{f}(t). \quad \square\end{aligned}$$

COMPONENT-FREE DERIVATION We find $(u\mathbf{f})'(t)$ by taking the limit as $h \to 0$ of the difference quotient

$$\frac{u(t+h)\mathbf{f}(t+h) - u(t)\mathbf{f}(t)}{h}.$$

By adding and subtracting $u(t+h)\mathbf{f}(t)$, we can rewrite this quotient as

$$\frac{u(t+h)\mathbf{f}(t+h) - u(t+h)\mathbf{f}(t) + u(t+h)\mathbf{f}(t) - u(t)\mathbf{f}(t)}{h}.$$

This equals

$$u(t+h)\frac{\mathbf{f}(t+h) - \mathbf{f}(t)}{h} + \frac{u(t+h) - u(t)}{h}\mathbf{f}(t).$$

As $h \to 0$,

$$u(t+h) \to u(t), \qquad \text{(differentiable functions are continuous)}$$

$$\frac{\mathbf{f}(t+h) - \mathbf{f}(t)}{h} \to \mathbf{f}'(t), \qquad \text{(definition of derivative for vector functions)}$$

$$\frac{u(t+h) - u(t)}{h} \to u'(t). \qquad \text{(definition of derivative for scalar functions)}$$

It follows from the limit rules (Theorem 14.1.3) that

$$u(t+h)\frac{\mathbf{f}(t+h) - \mathbf{f}(t)}{h} \to u(t)\mathbf{f}'(t), \qquad \frac{u(t+h) - u(t)}{h}\mathbf{f}(t) \to u'(t)\mathbf{f}(t)$$

and therefore

$$u(t+h)\frac{\mathbf{f}(t+h) - \mathbf{f}(t)}{h} + \frac{u(t+h) - u(t)}{h}\mathbf{f}(t) \to u(t)\mathbf{f}'(t) + u'(t)\mathbf{f}(t). \quad \square$$

In Leibniz's notation the rules of differentiation take the following form:

(14.2.2)

(1) $\dfrac{d}{dt}(\mathbf{f} + \mathbf{g}) = \dfrac{d\mathbf{f}}{dt} + \dfrac{d\mathbf{g}}{dt}$

(2) $\dfrac{d}{dt}(\alpha\mathbf{f}) = \alpha\dfrac{d\mathbf{f}}{dt}, \quad \dfrac{d}{dt}(u\mathbf{c}) = \dfrac{du}{dt}\mathbf{c}$

(3) $\dfrac{d}{dt}(u\mathbf{f}) = u\dfrac{d\mathbf{f}}{dt} + \dfrac{du}{dt}\mathbf{f}.$

(4) $\dfrac{d}{dt}(\mathbf{f} \cdot \mathbf{g}) = \left(\mathbf{f} \cdot \dfrac{d\mathbf{g}}{dt}\right) + \left(\dfrac{d\mathbf{f}}{dt} \cdot \mathbf{g}\right)$

(5) $\dfrac{d}{dt}(\mathbf{f} \times \mathbf{g}) = \left(\mathbf{f} \times \dfrac{d\mathbf{g}}{dt}\right) + \left(\dfrac{d\mathbf{f}}{dt} \times \mathbf{g}\right)$

(6) $\dfrac{d\mathbf{f}}{dt} = \dfrac{d\mathbf{f}}{du}\dfrac{du}{dt}.$ (chain rule)

We conclude this section with two results that will prove useful as we go on.

(14.2.3)

If $\mathbf{r}$ is a differentiable vector function of t, then the function $r = \|\mathbf{r}\|$ is differentiable where it is not zero and

$$\mathbf{r} \cdot \frac{d\mathbf{r}}{dt} = r\frac{dr}{dt}.$$

PROOF If $\mathbf{r}$ is differentiable, then $\mathbf{r}\cdot\mathbf{r} = \|\mathbf{r}\|^2 = r^2$ is differentiable. Let's assume now that $r \neq 0$. Since the square-root function is differentiable at all positive numbers and r^2 is positive, we can apply the square-root function to r^2 and conclude by the chain rule that r is itself differentiable.

To obtain the formula, we differentiate the identity $\mathbf{r}\cdot\mathbf{r} = r^2$:

$$\mathbf{r}\cdot\frac{d\mathbf{r}}{dt} + \frac{d\mathbf{r}}{dt}\cdot\mathbf{r} = 2r\frac{dr}{dt}$$

$$2\mathbf{r}\cdot\frac{d\mathbf{r}}{dt} = 2r\frac{dr}{dt}$$

$$\mathbf{r}\cdot\frac{d\mathbf{r}}{dt} = r\frac{dr}{dt}. \quad \square$$

(14.2.4) If $\mathbf{r}$ is a differentiable vector function of t, then where $r = \|\mathbf{r}\| \neq 0$

$$\frac{d}{dt}\left(\frac{\mathbf{r}}{r}\right) = \frac{1}{r^3}\left[\left(\mathbf{r}\times\frac{d\mathbf{r}}{dt}\right)\times\mathbf{r}\right].$$

PROOF The argument is somewhat delicate.

$$\begin{aligned}\frac{d}{dt}\left(\frac{\mathbf{r}}{r}\right) &= \frac{1}{r}\frac{d\mathbf{r}}{dt} - \frac{1}{r^2}\frac{dr}{dt}\mathbf{r}\\ &= \frac{1}{r^3}\left[r^2\frac{d\mathbf{r}}{dt} - r\frac{dr}{dt}\mathbf{r}\right]\\ &= \frac{1}{r^3}\left[(\mathbf{r}\cdot\mathbf{r})\frac{d\mathbf{r}}{dt} - \left(\mathbf{r}\cdot\frac{d\mathbf{r}}{dt}\right)\mathbf{r}\right] = \frac{1}{r^3}\left[\left(\mathbf{r}\times\frac{d\mathbf{r}}{dt}\right)\times\mathbf{r}\right]. \quad \square\end{aligned}$$

$(\mathbf{a}\times\mathbf{b})\times\mathbf{c} = (\mathbf{c}\cdot\mathbf{a})\mathbf{b} - (\mathbf{c}\cdot\mathbf{b})\mathbf{a}$ ↑

EXERCISES 14.2

Exercises 1–12. Calculate $\mathbf{f}'(t)$ and $\mathbf{f}''(t)$.

1. $\mathbf{f}(t) = \mathbf{a} + t\mathbf{b}$.

2. $\mathbf{f}(t) = \mathbf{a} + t\mathbf{b} + t^2\mathbf{c}$.

3. $\mathbf{f}(t) = e^{2t}\mathbf{i} - \sin t\,\mathbf{j}$.

4. $\mathbf{f}(t) = [(t^2\,\mathbf{i} - \mathbf{j})\cdot(\mathbf{i} - t^2\,\mathbf{j})]\,\mathbf{i}$.

5. $\mathbf{f}(t) = [(t^2\,\mathbf{i} - 2t\,\mathbf{j})\cdot(t\,\mathbf{i} + t^3\,\mathbf{j})]\,\mathbf{j}$.

6. $\mathbf{f}(t) = [(3t\,\mathbf{i} - t^2\,\mathbf{j} + \mathbf{k})\cdot(\mathbf{i} + t^3\,\mathbf{j} - 2t\,\mathbf{k})]\,\mathbf{k}$.

7. $\mathbf{f}(t) = (e^t\,\mathbf{i} + t\,\mathbf{k})\times(t\,\mathbf{j} + e^{-t}\,\mathbf{k})$.

8. $\mathbf{f}(t) = (\mathbf{a}\times t\,\mathbf{b}) + (\mathbf{a} + t^2\,\mathbf{b})$.

9. $\mathbf{f}(t) = (\mathbf{a}\times t\,\mathbf{b})\times(\mathbf{a} + t^2\,\mathbf{b})$.

10. $\mathbf{f}(t) = t\mathbf{g}(t^2)$.

11. $\mathbf{f}(t) = t\mathbf{g}(\sqrt{t})$.

12. $\mathbf{f}(t) = (e^{2t}\mathbf{i} + e^{-2t}\mathbf{j} + \mathbf{k})\times(e^{2t}\mathbf{i} - e^{-2t}\mathbf{j} + \mathbf{k})$.

Exercises 13–20. Calculate.

13. $\dfrac{d}{dt}[e^{\cos t}\mathbf{i} + e^{\sin t}\mathbf{j}]$.

14. $\dfrac{d^2}{dt^2}[e^t\,\cos t\,\mathbf{i} + e^t\,\sin t\,\mathbf{j}]$.

15. $\dfrac{d^2}{dt^2}[(e^t\mathbf{i} + e^{-t}\mathbf{j})\cdot(e^t\,\mathbf{i} - e^{-t}\,\mathbf{j})]$.

16. $\dfrac{d}{dt}[(\ln t\,\mathbf{i} + t\,\mathbf{j})\times(t^2\,\mathbf{j} - t\,\mathbf{k})]$.

17. $\dfrac{d}{dt}[(\mathbf{a} + t\,\mathbf{b})\times(\mathbf{c} + t\,\mathbf{d})]$.

18. $\dfrac{d}{dt}[(\mathbf{a} + t\,\mathbf{b})\times(\mathbf{a} + t\,\mathbf{b} + t^2\,\mathbf{c})]$.

19. $\dfrac{d}{dt}[(\mathbf{a} + t\,\mathbf{b})\cdot(\mathbf{c} + t\,\mathbf{d})]$.

20. $\dfrac{d}{dt}[(\mathbf{a} + t\,\mathbf{b})\cdot(\mathbf{a} + t\,\mathbf{b} + t^2\mathbf{c})]$.

Exercises 21–24. Find $\mathbf{r}(t)$ given the following information.

21. $\mathbf{r}'(t) = \mathbf{b}$ for all real t, $\quad\mathbf{r}(0) = \mathbf{a}$.

22. $\mathbf{r}''(t) = \mathbf{c}$ for all real t, $\quad\mathbf{r}'(0) = \mathbf{b}$, $\quad\mathbf{r}(0) = \mathbf{a}$.

23. $\mathbf{r}''(t) = \mathbf{a} + t\mathbf{b}$ for all real t, $\quad\mathbf{r}'(0) = \mathbf{c}$, $\quad\mathbf{r}(0) = \mathbf{d}$.

24. $\mathbf{r}''(t) = \cos 2t\,\mathbf{i} + \sin 2t\,\mathbf{j}$ for all real t,
$\mathbf{r}'(0) = 2\mathbf{i} - \frac{1}{2}\mathbf{j}$, $\quad\mathbf{r}(0) = \frac{3}{4}\,\mathbf{i} + \mathbf{j}$.

25. Show that, if $\mathbf{r}(t) = \sin t\,\mathbf{i} + \cos t\,\mathbf{j}$, then $\mathbf{r}(t)$ and $\mathbf{r}''(t)$ are parallel. Is there a value of t for which $\mathbf{r}(t)$ and $\mathbf{r}''(t)$ have the same direction?

26. Show that, if $\mathbf{r}(t) = e^{kt}\mathbf{i} + e^{-kt}\mathbf{j}$, then $\mathbf{r}(t)$ and $\mathbf{r}''(t)$ have the same direction.

27. Calculate $\mathbf{r}(t)\cdot\mathbf{r}'(t)$ and $\mathbf{r}(t)\times\mathbf{r}'(t)$ for $\mathbf{r}(t) = \cos t\,\mathbf{i} + \sin t\,\mathbf{j}$.

Exercises 28–30. Assume the rule for differentiating a cross product and show the following.

28. $(\mathbf{g}\times\mathbf{f})'(t) = -(\mathbf{f}\times\mathbf{g})'(t)$.

29. $\dfrac{d}{dt}[\mathbf{f}(t)\times\mathbf{f}'(t)] = \mathbf{f}(t)\times\mathbf{f}''(t)$.

30. $\dfrac{d}{dt}[u_1(t)\mathbf{r}_1(t)\times u_2(t)\mathbf{r}_2(t)] = u_1(t)u_2(t)\dfrac{d}{dt}[\mathbf{r}_1(t)\times\mathbf{r}_2(t)] + [\mathbf{r}_1(t)\times\mathbf{r}_2(t)]\dfrac{d}{dt}[u_1(t)u_2(t)]$.

31. Set $\mathbf{E}(t) = \mathbf{f}(t)\cdot[\mathbf{g}(t)\times\mathbf{h}(t)]$ and show that $\mathbf{E}'(t) = \mathbf{f}'(t)\cdot[\mathbf{g}(t)\times\mathbf{h}(t)] + \mathbf{f}(t)\cdot[\mathbf{g}'(t)\times\mathbf{h}(t)] + \mathbf{f}(t)\cdot[\mathbf{g}(t)\times\mathbf{h}'(t)]$.

32. Prove that, if $\mathbf{f}(t)$ is parallel to $\mathbf{f}''(t)$ for all t in some interval, then $\mathbf{f}\times\mathbf{f}'$ is constant on that interval. HINT: See Exercise 29.

33. Show that $\|\mathbf{r}(t)\|$ is constant iff $\mathbf{r}(t)\cdot\mathbf{r}'(t) = 0$ identically.

34. Derive the formula

$$(\mathbf{f}\cdot\mathbf{g})'(t) = [\mathbf{f}(t)\cdot\mathbf{g}'(t)] + [\mathbf{f}'(t)\cdot\mathbf{g}(t)]$$

(a) by appealing to components;
(b) without appealing to components.

35. Derive the formula

$$(\mathbf{f}\times\mathbf{g})'(t) = [\mathbf{f}(t)\times\mathbf{g}'(t)] + [\mathbf{f}'(t)\times\mathbf{g}(t)]$$

without appealing to components.

36. (a) Show that, if u is continuous at t_0 and $\mathbf{f}$ is continuous at $u(t_0)$, then the composition $\mathbf{f}\circ u$ is continuous at t_0.
(b) Derive the following chain rule for vector functions:

$$\frac{d\mathbf{f}}{dt} = \frac{d\mathbf{f}}{du}\frac{du}{dt}.$$

■ 14.3 CURVES

Introduction

A linear function

$$\mathbf{r}(t) = \mathbf{r}_0 + t\,\mathbf{d}, \qquad \mathbf{d}\neq\mathbf{0}$$

traces out a line, and it does so in a particular direction, the direction imparted to it by increasing t.

More generally, a differentiable vector function

$$\mathbf{r}(t) = x(t)\,\mathbf{i} + y(t)\,\mathbf{j} + z(t)\,\mathbf{k} \qquad \text{(Figure 14.3.1)}$$

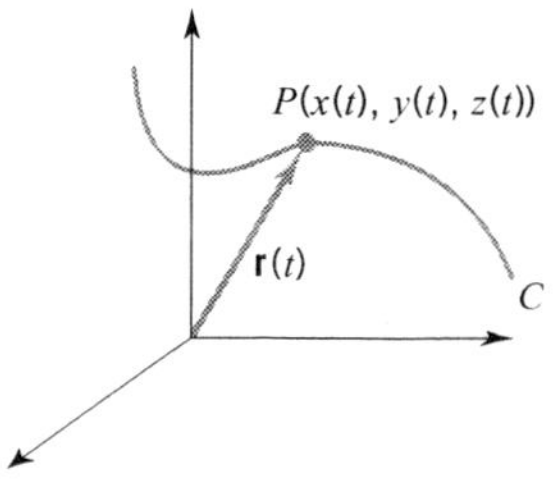

Figure 14.3.1

traces out a curved path, and it does so in a particular direction, the direction imparted to it by increasing t. The *directed path* C (called by some the *oriented path*) traced out by a differentiable vector function is called a *differentiable parametrized curve.*

We draw a distinction between the parametrized curve

$$C_1: \qquad \mathbf{r}_1(t) = \cos t\,\mathbf{i} + \sin t\,\mathbf{j}, \qquad t\in[0, 2\pi]$$

and the parametrized curve

$$C_2: \qquad \mathbf{r}_2(u) = \cos(2\pi - u)\,\mathbf{i} + \sin(2\pi - u)\,\mathbf{j}, \qquad u\in[0, 2\pi].$$

The first curve is the unit circle traversed counterclockwise; the second curve is the unit circle traversed clockwise. (Figure 14.3.2.)

For an example in space we refer to Figure 14.3.3. There you see the curve parametrized by the function

$$\mathbf{r}(t) = t\,\mathbf{i} + 2\cos t\,\mathbf{j} + 3\sin t\,\mathbf{k}, \qquad t\geq 0.$$

The direction imparted to the curve by the parametrization is indicated by the little arrows.

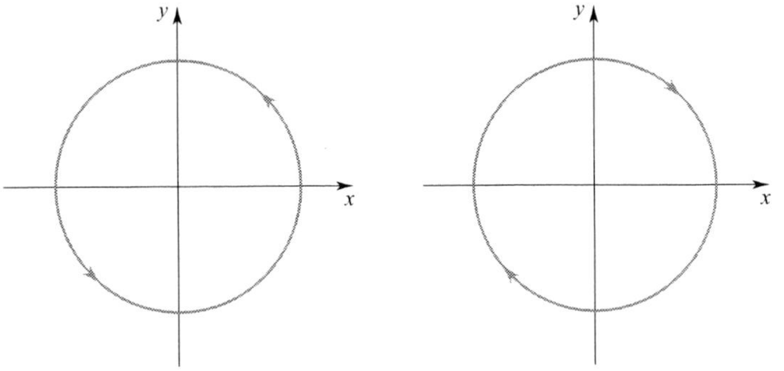

$\mathbf{r}_1(t) = \cos t\,\mathbf{i} + \sin(t)\,\mathbf{j}$ $\qquad$ $\mathbf{r}_2(t) = \cos(2\pi - u)\mathbf{i} + \sin(2\pi - u)\,\mathbf{j}$

Figure 14.3.2

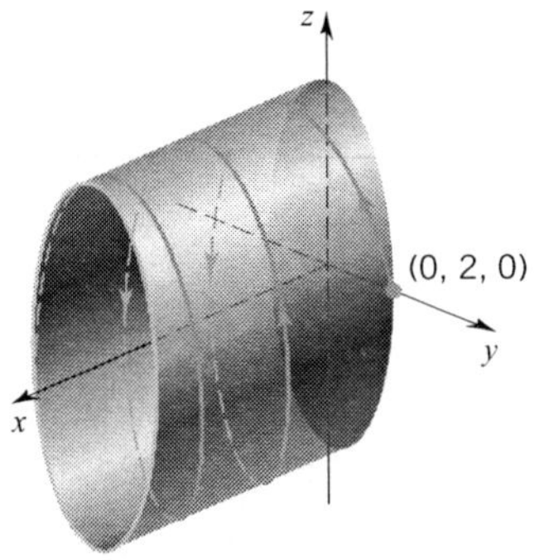

Figure 14.3.3

Tangent Vector, Tangent Line

Let's view the derivative

$$\mathbf{r}'(t) = x'(t)\,\mathbf{i} + y'(t)\,\mathbf{j} + z'(t)\,\mathbf{k}$$

geometrically. First of all,

$$\mathbf{r}'(t) = \lim_{h \to 0} \frac{\mathbf{r}(t+h) - \mathbf{r}(t)}{h}.$$

If $\mathbf{r}'(t) \neq \mathbf{0}$, then we can be sure that, for $t + h$ close enough to t, the vector

$$\mathbf{r}(t+h) - \mathbf{r}(t)$$

will not be $\mathbf{0}$. (Explain.) Consequently, we can think of the vector $\mathbf{r}(t+h) - \mathbf{r}(t)$ as pictured in Figure 14.3.4.

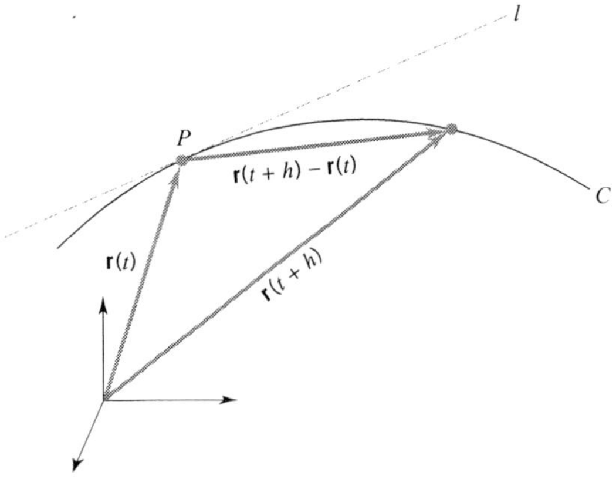

Figure 14.3.4

Let's agree that the line marked l in the figure corresponds to our intuitive notion of the tangent line at the point P. As h tends to zero, the vector

$$\mathbf{r}(t+h) - \mathbf{r}(t)$$

comes increasingly closer to serving as a direction vector for that tangent line. It may be tempting therefore to take the limiting case

$$\lim_{h \to 0} [\mathbf{r}(t+h) - \mathbf{r}(t)]$$

and call that a direction vector for the tangent line. The trouble is that this limit vector is **0**, and **0** has no direction.

We can circumvent this difficulty by replacing $\mathbf{r}(t+h)-\mathbf{r}(t)$ by a vector which, for small h, has greater length: the difference quotient

$$\frac{\mathbf{r}(t+h)-\mathbf{r}(t)}{h}.$$

For each real number $h \neq 0$, the vector $[\mathbf{r}(t+h)-\mathbf{r}(t)]/h$ is parallel to $\mathbf{r}(t+h)-\mathbf{r}(t)$, and therefore its limit,

$$\mathbf{r}'(t)=\lim_{h\to 0}\frac{\mathbf{r}(t+h)-\mathbf{r}(t)}{h},$$

which by assumption is not **0**, can be taken as a direction vector for the tangent line. Hence the following definition.

DEFINITION 14.3.1 TANGENT VECTOR

Let

$$C: \quad \mathbf{r}(t)=x(t)\,\mathbf{i}+y(t)\,\mathbf{j}+z(t)\,\mathbf{k}$$

be a differentiable curve. The vector $\mathbf{r}'(t)$, if not **0**, is said to be *tangent* to the curve C at the point $P(x(t), y(t), z(t))$.

Remark In all this we view $\mathbf{r}(t)$ as a vector bound to the origin and $\mathbf{r}'(t)$ as a vector attached to the curve at the tip of $\mathbf{r}(t)$. ❑

If $\mathbf{r}'(t)\neq\mathbf{0}$, the following question arises: what is the direction of $\mathbf{r}'(t)$? Does it point in the direction imparted by increasing t or does it point in the direction imparted by decreasing t?

Figure 14.3.5 shows a parametrized curve C and the vector $\mathbf{r}(t+h)-\mathbf{r}(t)$ with $h>0$. In this case

$$\frac{\mathbf{r}(t+h)-\mathbf{r}(t)}{h}$$

points in the direction of $\mathbf{r}(t+h)-\mathbf{r}(t)$, the direction imparted by increasing t.

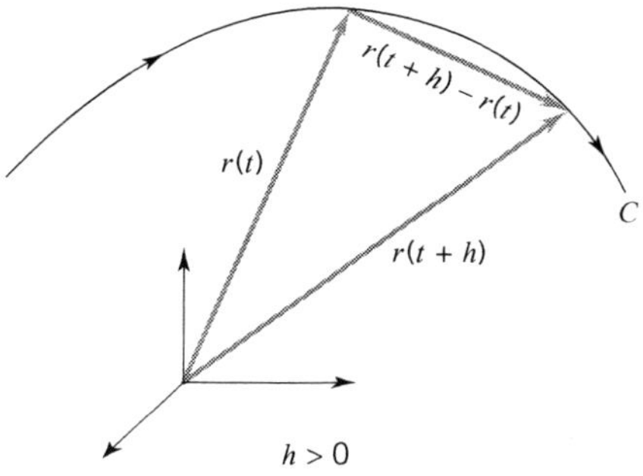

Figure 14.3.5

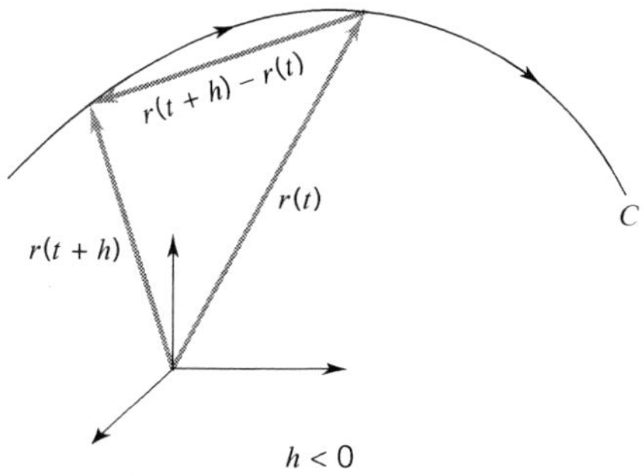

Figure 14.3.6

Figure 14.3.6 shows the vector $\mathbf{r}(t+h)-\mathbf{r}(t)$ for $h<0$. In this case, dividing by h to form the difference quotient *reverses* the direction of the vector. Thus

$$\frac{\mathbf{r}(t+h)-\mathbf{r}(t)}{h}$$

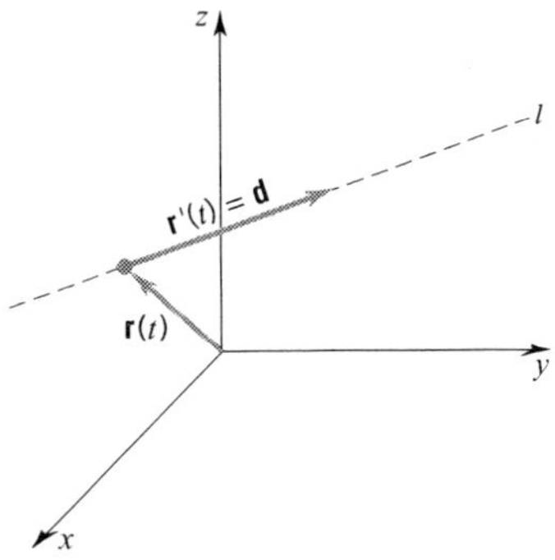

Figure 14.3.7

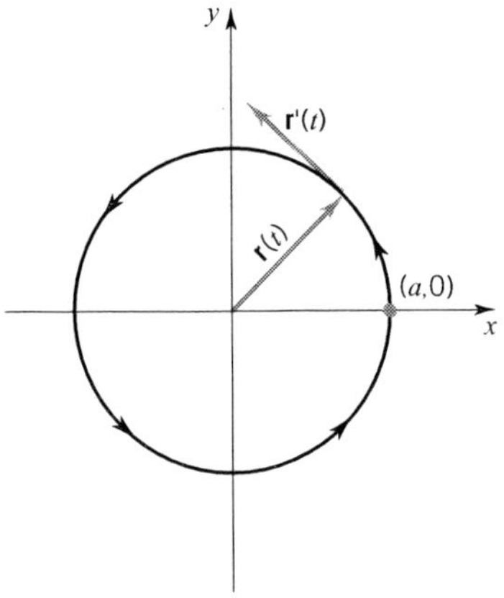

Figure 14.3.8

also points in the direction imparted by increasing t. We conclude that in each case

(14.3.2) $\mathbf{r}'(t)$ points in the direction imparted by increasing t.

For a line $y = mx + b$, the derivative $y'(x)$ is the slope of the line: $y'(x) = m$. For a parametrized line

$$l: \qquad \mathbf{r}(t) = \mathbf{r}_0 + t\,\mathbf{d}, \qquad \text{(Figure 14.3.7)}$$

the derivative $\mathbf{r}'(t)$ is the direction vector used to parametrize the line: $\mathbf{r}'(t) = \mathbf{d}$.

For a circle parametrized counterclockwise,

$$C: \qquad \mathbf{r}(t) = a\cos t\,\mathbf{i} + a\sin t\,\mathbf{j} \qquad \text{with } a > 0,$$

the tangent vector

$$\mathbf{r}'(t) = -a\sin t\,\mathbf{i} + a\cos t\,\mathbf{j} \qquad \text{(Figure 14.3.8)}$$

points in the counterclockwise direction and is perpendicular to the radius vector $\mathbf{r}(t)$.

Example 1 Find a point P on the curve

$$\mathbf{r}(t) = (1 - 2t)\,\mathbf{i} + t^2\,\mathbf{j} + 2e^{2(t-1)}\,\mathbf{k}$$

at which the tangent vector $\mathbf{r}'(t)$ is parallel to the radius vector $\mathbf{r}(t)$.

SOLUTION $\mathbf{r}'(t) = -2\,\mathbf{i} + 2t\,\mathbf{j} + 4e^{2(t-1)}\,\mathbf{k}$.

For $\mathbf{r}'(t)$ to be parallel to $\mathbf{r}(t)$ there must exist a scalar α such that

$$\mathbf{r}(t) = \alpha\mathbf{r}'(t).$$

This vector equation holds iff

$$1 - 2t = -2\alpha, \qquad t^2 = 2\alpha t, \qquad 2e^{2(t-1)} = 4\alpha e^{2(t-1)}.$$

The last scalar equation requires that $\alpha = \frac{1}{2}$. The only value of t that satisfies all three equations with $\alpha = \frac{1}{2}$ is $t = 1$. Therefore the only point at which $\mathbf{r}'(t)$ is parallel to $\mathbf{r}(t)$ is the tip of $\mathbf{r}(1)$. This is the point $P(-1, 1, 2)$. ❑

If $\mathbf{r}'(t_0) \neq \mathbf{0}$, then $\mathbf{r}'(t_0)$ is tangent to the curve at the tip of $\mathbf{r}(t_0)$. The *tangent line* at this point can be parametrized by setting

(14.3.3) $$\mathbf{R}(u) = \mathbf{r}(t_0) + u\,\mathbf{r}'(t_0).$$

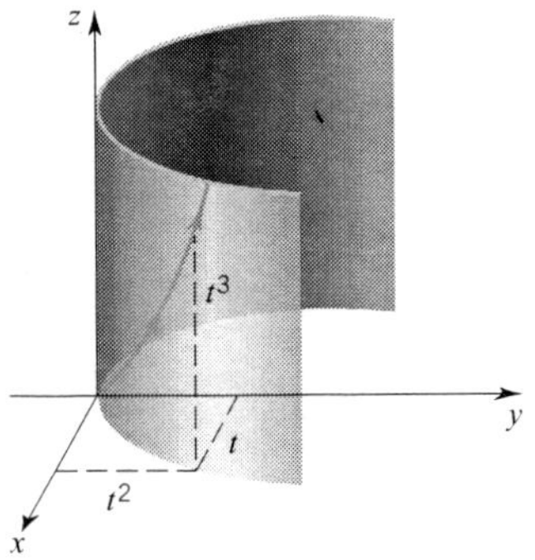

the twisted cubic, $t > 0$

Figure 14.3.9

Example 2 Find a vector tangent to the *twisted cubic*

$$\mathbf{r}(t) = t\,\mathbf{i} + t^2\,\mathbf{j} + t^3\,\mathbf{k} \qquad \text{(Figure 14.3.9)}$$

at the point $P(2, 4, 8)$, and then parametrize the tangent line at that point.

SOLUTION Here $\mathbf{r}'(t) = \mathbf{i} + 2t\,\mathbf{j} + 3t^2\,\mathbf{k}$. Since $P(2, 4, 8)$ is the tip of $\mathbf{r}(2)$, the vector

$$\mathbf{r}'(t) = \mathbf{i} + 4\mathbf{j} + 12\,\mathbf{k}$$

is tangent to the curve at the point $P(2, 4, 8)$. The vector function

$$\mathbf{R}(u) = (2\,\mathbf{i} + 4\,\mathbf{j} + 8\,\mathbf{k}) + u(\mathbf{i} + 4\,\mathbf{j} + 12\,\mathbf{k})$$

parametrizes the tangent line. ❑

Intersecting Curves

Two curves

$$C_1: \quad \mathbf{r}_1(t) = x_1(t)\,\mathbf{i} + y_1(t)\,\mathbf{j} + z_1(t)\,\mathbf{k}, \quad C_2: \quad \mathbf{r}_2(u) = x_2(u)\,\mathbf{i} + y_2(u)\,\mathbf{j} + z_2(u)\,\mathbf{k}$$

intersect iff there are numbers t and u for which

$$\mathbf{r}_1(t) = \mathbf{r}_2(u).$$

The angle between C_1 and C_2 at a point where $\mathbf{r}_1(t) = \mathbf{r}_2(u)$ is by definition the angle between the corresponding tangent vectors $\mathbf{r}_1'(t)$ and $\mathbf{r}_2'(u)$.

Example 3 Show that the circles

$$C_1: \qquad \mathbf{r}_1(t) = \cos t\,\mathbf{i} + \sin t\,\mathbf{j}, \qquad C_2: \qquad \mathbf{r}_2(u) = \cos u\,\mathbf{j} + \sin u\,\mathbf{k}$$

intersect at right angles at $P(0, 1, 0)$ and $Q(0, -1, 0)$.

SOLUTION Since $\mathbf{r}_1(\pi/2) = \mathbf{j} = \mathbf{r}_2(0)$, the curves meet at the tip of $\mathbf{j}$, which is the point $P(0, 1, 0)$. Also, since $\mathbf{r}_1(3\pi/2) = -\mathbf{j} = \mathbf{r}_2(\pi)$, the curves meet at the tip of $-\mathbf{j}$, which is the point $Q(0, -1, 0)$. Differentiation gives

$$\mathbf{r}_1'(t) = -\sin t\,\mathbf{i} + \cos t\,\mathbf{j} \qquad \text{and} \qquad \mathbf{r}_2'(u) = -\sin u\,\mathbf{j} + \cos u\,\mathbf{k}.$$

Since $\mathbf{r}_1'(\pi/2) = -\mathbf{i}$ and $\mathbf{r}_2'(0) = \mathbf{k}$, we have

$$\mathbf{r}_1'(\pi/2) \cdot \mathbf{r}_2'(0) = 0.$$

This tells us that the curves are perpendicular at $P(0, 1, 0)$. Since $\mathbf{r}_1'(3\pi/2) = \mathbf{i}$ and $\mathbf{r}_2'(\pi) = -\mathbf{k}$, we have

$$\mathbf{r}_1'(3\pi/2) \cdot \mathbf{r}_2'(\pi) = 0.$$

This tells us that the curves are perpendicular at $Q(0, -1, 0)$. The curves are shown in Figure 14.3.10. ❑

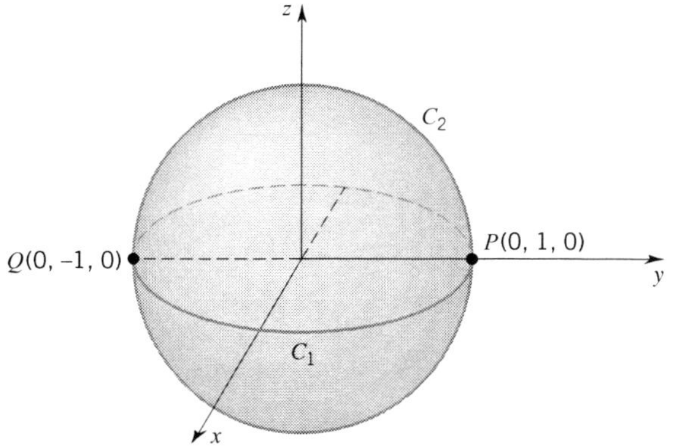

Figure 14.3.10

The Unit Tangent, the Principal Normal, the Osculating Plane

Suppose now that the curve

$$C: \qquad \mathbf{r}(t) = x(t)\,\mathbf{i} + y(t)\,\mathbf{j} + z(t)\,\mathbf{k}$$

is twice differentiable and $\mathbf{r}'(t)$ is never zero. Then at each point $P(x(t), y(t), z(t))$ of the curve, there is a *unit tangent vector*:

(14.3.4)
$$\mathbf{T}(t) = \frac{\mathbf{r}'(t)}{\|\mathbf{r}'(t)\|}.$$

Since $\|\mathbf{r}'(t)\| > 0$, $\mathbf{T}(t)$ points in the direction of $\mathbf{r}'(t)$; that is, in the direction of increasing t. Since $\|\mathbf{T}(t)\| = 1$, we have $\mathbf{T}(t) \cdot \mathbf{T}(t) = 1$. Differentiation gives

$$\mathbf{T}(t) \cdot \mathbf{T}'(t) + \mathbf{T}'(t) \cdot \mathbf{T}(t) = 0.$$

Since the dot product is commutative, we have

$$2[\mathbf{T}'(t) \cdot \mathbf{T}(t)] = 0 \qquad \text{and thus} \qquad \mathbf{T}'(t) \cdot \mathbf{T}(t) = 0.$$

At each point of the curve *the vector* $\mathbf{T}'(t)$ *is perpendicular to* $\mathbf{T}(t)$.

The vector $\mathbf{T}'(t)$ measures the rate of change of $\mathbf{T}(t)$ with respect to t. Since the norm of $\mathbf{T}(t)$ is constantly 1, $\mathbf{T}(t)$ can change only in direction. The vector $\mathbf{T}'(t)$ measures this change in direction.

If the unit tangent vector is not changing in direction (as in the case of a straight line), then $\mathbf{T}'(t) = \mathbf{0}$. If $\mathbf{T}'(t) \neq 0$, then we can form what is called the *principal normal vector*:

(14.3.5)
$$\mathbf{N}(t) = \frac{\mathbf{T}'(t)}{\|\mathbf{T}'(t)\|}.$$

This is the unit vector in the direction of $\mathbf{T}'(t)$. The *normal line* at P is the line through P parallel to the principal normal.

Figure 14.3.11 shows a curve on which we have marked several points. At each of these points we have drawn the unit tangent and the principal normal. The plane determined by these two vectors is called the *osculating plane* (literally, the "kissing plane"). This is the plane of greatest contact with the curve at the point in question. The principal normal points in the direction in which the curve is curving, that is, on the concave side of the curve.

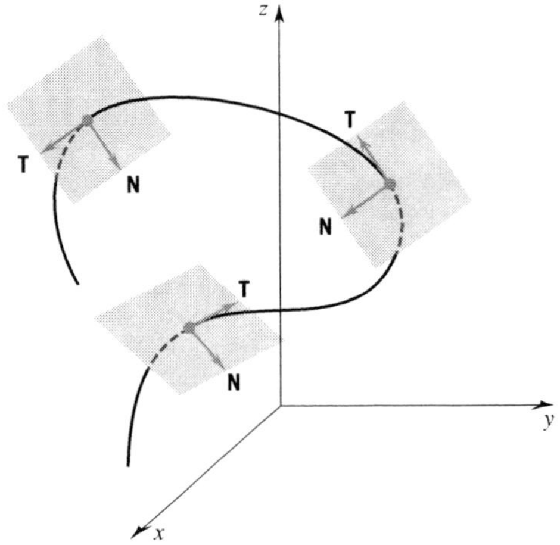

Figure 14.3.11

If a curve is a plane curve but not a straight line, then the osculating plane is simply the plane of the curve. A straight line does not have an osculating plane. There is no principal normal vector $[\mathbf{T}'(t) = \mathbf{0}]$, and there is no single plane of greatest contact. Each straight line lies on an infinite number of planes.

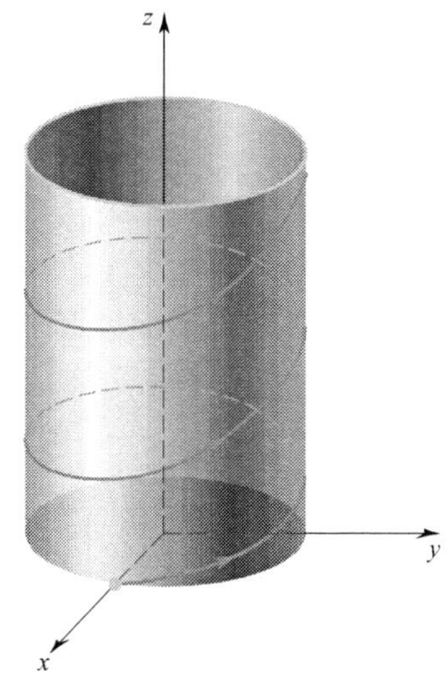

circular helix

Figure 14.3.12

Example 4 In Figure 14.3.12 you can see a curve spiraling up a circular cylinder with a constant rate of climb. The curve is called a *circular helix*. The simplest parametrization for a circular helix takes the form

$$\mathbf{r}(t) = a\cos t\,\mathbf{i} + a\sin t\,\mathbf{j} + bt\,\mathbf{k} \qquad \text{with} \quad a > 0,\ b > 0.$$

The first two components produce the rotational effect; the third component gives the rate of climb.

We will find the unit tangent, the principal normal, and then an equation for the osculating plane. Since

$$\mathbf{r}'(t) = -a\sin t\,\mathbf{i} + a\cos t\,\mathbf{j} + b\,\mathbf{k},$$

we have

$$\|\mathbf{r}'(t)\| = \sqrt{a^2\sin^2 t + a^2\cos^2 t + b^2} = \sqrt{a^2 + b^2}$$

and therefore

$$\mathbf{T}(t) = \frac{\mathbf{r}'(t)}{\|\mathbf{r}'(t)\|} = \frac{1}{\sqrt{a^2+b^2}}(-a\sin t\,\mathbf{i} + a\cos t\,\mathbf{j} + b\,\mathbf{k}).$$

This is the unit tangent vector.

The principal normal vector is the unit vector in the direction of $\mathbf{T}'(t)$. Since

$$\frac{d}{dt}(-a\ \sin t\,\mathbf{i} + a\ \cos t\,\mathbf{j} + b\mathbf{k}) = -a\cos t\,\mathbf{i} - a\sin t\,\mathbf{j} \qquad \text{and} \qquad a > 0,$$

you can see that

$$\mathbf{N}(t) = -\cos t\,\mathbf{i} - \sin t\,\mathbf{j} = -(\cos t\,\mathbf{i} + \sin t\,\mathbf{j}).$$

The principal normal is horizontal and points directly toward the z-axis.

Now let's find an equation for the osculating plane p at an arbitrary point of the curve: $P(a\cos t, a\sin t, bt)$. The cross product $\mathbf{T}(t) \times \mathbf{N}(t)$ is perpendicular to p. Therefore, as a normal for p, we can take a nonzero scalar multiple of $\mathbf{T}(t) \times \mathbf{N}(t)$. In particular, we can take

$$(a\ \sin t\,\mathbf{i} - a\ \cos t\,\mathbf{j} - b\,\mathbf{k}) \times (\cos t\,\mathbf{i} + \sin t\,\mathbf{j}).$$

As you can check, this simplifies to

$$b\sin t\,\mathbf{i} - b\cos t\,\mathbf{j} + a\,\mathbf{k}.$$

The equation for the osculating plane at the point $P(a\cos t, a\sin t, bt)$ thus takes the form

$$b\sin t(x - a\cos t) - b\cos t(y - a\sin t) + a(z - bt) = 0. \qquad (13.7.1)$$

This simplifies to

$$(b\sin t)x - (b\cos t)y + az = abt.$$

To visualize how this osculating plane changes from point to point, think of a playground spiral slide or the threaded surface on a bolt. ❑

Remark At this stage some of you may think of the unit tangent, the principal normal, and the osculating plane merely as somewhat obscure geometric niceties. They are much more than that. One of the most important notions in science is the notion of acceleration. (You can't feel velocity, but you can feel acceleration.) In curvilinear motion acceleration is a vector, a vector best understood in terms of the unit tangent **T**, the principal normal **N**, and the osculating plane p. How this is so is explained in Section 14.5. □

Reversing the Direction of a Curve

We make a distinction between the curve

$$\mathbf{r} = \mathbf{r}(t), \qquad t \in [a, b]$$

and the curve

$$\mathbf{R}(u) = \mathbf{r}(a + b - u), \qquad u \in [a, b].$$

Both vector functions trace out the same set of points (check that out), but the order has been reversed. Whereas the first curve starts at $\mathbf{r}(a)$ and ends at $\mathbf{r}(b)$, the second curve starts at $\mathbf{r}(b)$ and ends at $\mathbf{r}(a)$:

$$\mathbf{R}(a) = \mathbf{r}(a + b - a) = \mathbf{r}(b), \qquad \mathbf{R}(b) = \mathbf{r}(a + b - b) = \mathbf{r}(a).$$

The vector function

$$\mathbf{r}(t) = \cos t\,\mathbf{i} + \sin t\,\mathbf{j}, \qquad t \in [0, 2\pi]$$

gives the unit circle traversed counterclockwise, while

$$R(u) = \cos(2\pi - u)\,\mathbf{i} + \sin(2\pi - u)\,\mathbf{j}, \qquad u \in [0, 2\pi]$$

gives the unit circle traversed clockwise. You have seen this before.

The function

$$\mathbf{r}(t) = a\cos t\,\mathbf{i} + a\sin t\,\mathbf{j} + bt\,\mathbf{k}, \qquad t \in [0, 2\pi]$$

traces out one turn of a spiraling helix (Figure 14.3.13), the direction of transversal indicated by the little arrows. The function

$$\mathbf{R}(u) = a\cos(2 - u)\pi\,\mathbf{i} + a\sin(2 - u)\pi\,\mathbf{j} + b(2 - u)\pi\,\mathbf{k}, \qquad u \in [0, 2]$$

produces the same path but in the opposite direction. (Figure 14.3.14)

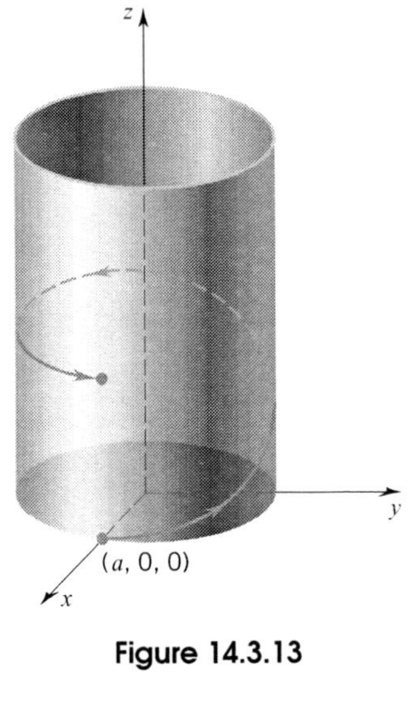

Figure 14.3.13

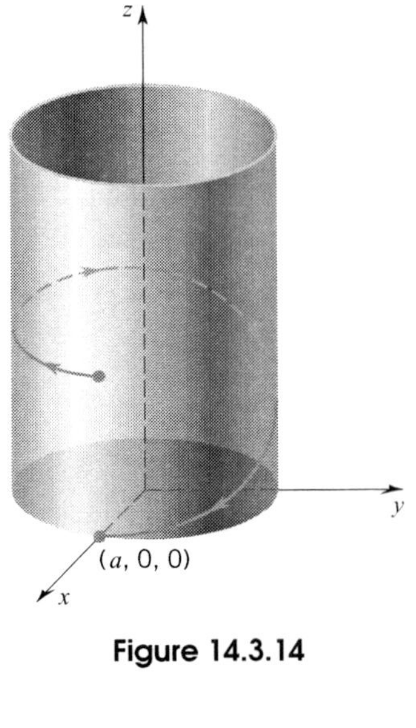

Figure 14.3.14

What happens to the unit tangent **T**, the principal normal **N**, and the osculating plane when we reverse the direction of the curve? As you are asked to show in Exercise 43, **T** is replaced by $-\mathbf{T}$, but **N** remains the same. The osculating plane also remains the same.

EXERCISES 14.3

Exercises 1–8. Find the tangent vector $\mathbf{r}'(t)$ at the indicated point and parametrize the tangent line at that point.

1. $\mathbf{r}(t) = \cos \pi t\,\mathbf{i} + \sin \pi t\,\mathbf{j} + t\,\mathbf{k}$ at $t = 2$.

2. $\mathbf{r}(t) = e^t\,\mathbf{i} + e^{-t}\,\mathbf{j} - \ln t\,\mathbf{k}$ at $t = 1$.

3. $\mathbf{r}(t) = \mathbf{a} + t\,\mathbf{b} + t^2\,\mathbf{c}$ at $t = -1$.

4. $\mathbf{r}(t) = (t+1)\,\mathbf{i} + (t^2+1)\,\mathbf{j} + (t^3+1)\,\mathbf{k}$ at $P(1, 1, 1)$.

5. $\mathbf{r}(t) = 2t^2\,\mathbf{i} + (1-t)\,\mathbf{j} + (3+2t^2)\,\mathbf{k}$ at $P(2, 0, 5)$.

6. $\mathbf{r}(t) = 3t\,\mathbf{a} + \mathbf{b} - t^2\,\mathbf{c}$ at $t = 2$.

7. $\mathbf{r}(t) = 2\cos t\,\mathbf{i} + 3\sin t\,\mathbf{j} + t\,\mathbf{k}$; $t = \pi/4$.

8. $\mathbf{r}(t) = t\sin t\,\mathbf{i} + t\cos t\,\mathbf{j} + 2t\,\mathbf{k}$; $t = \pi/2$.

9. Show that $\mathbf{r}(t) = at\,\mathbf{i} + bt^2\,\mathbf{j}$ parametrizes a parabola. Find an equation in x and y for this parabola.

10. Show that $\mathbf{r}(t) = \frac{1}{2}a(e^{\omega t} + e^{-\omega t})\,\mathbf{i} + \frac{1}{2}a(e^{\omega t} - t^{-\omega t})\,\mathbf{j}$ parametrizes the right branch ($x > 0$) of the hyperbola $x^2 - y^2 = a^2$.

11. Find (a) the points on the curve $\mathbf{r}(t) = t\,\mathbf{i} + (1+t^2)\,\mathbf{j}$ at which $\mathbf{r}(t)$ and $\mathbf{r}'(t)$ are perpendicular; (b) the points at which they have the same direction; (c) the points at which they have opposite directions.

12. Find the curve given that $\mathbf{r}'(t) = \alpha\mathbf{r}(t)$ for all real t and $\mathbf{r}(0) = \mathbf{i} + 2\mathbf{j} + 3\mathbf{k}$. (Here α is a constant.)

13. Suppose that $\mathbf{r}'(t)$ and $\mathbf{r}(t)$ are parallel for all t. Show that, if $\mathbf{r}'(t)$ is never $\mathbf{0}$, then the tangent line at each point passes through the origin.

Exercises 14–16. The curves intersect at the point given. Find the angle of intersection. Express your answer in radians.

14. $\mathbf{r}_1(t) = t\,\mathbf{i} + t^2\,\mathbf{j} + t^3\,\mathbf{k}$,
$\mathbf{r}_2(u) = \sin 2u\,\mathbf{i} + u\cos u\,\mathbf{j} + u\,\mathbf{k}$; $P(0, 0, 0)$.

15. $\mathbf{r}_1(t) = (e^t - 1)\,\mathbf{i} + 2\sin t\,\mathbf{j} + \ln(t+1)\,\mathbf{k}$,
$\mathbf{r}_2(u) = (u+1)\,\mathbf{i} + (u^2-1)\,\mathbf{j} + (u^3+1)\,\mathbf{k}$; $P(0, 0, 0)$.

16. $\mathbf{r}_1(t) = e^{-t}\,\mathbf{i} + \cos t\,\mathbf{j} + (t^2+4)\,\mathbf{k}$,
$\mathbf{r}_2(u) = (2+u)\,\mathbf{i} + u^4\,\mathbf{j} + 4u^2\,\mathbf{k}$; $P(1, 1, 4)$.

17. Find the point at which the curves

$$\mathbf{r}_1(t) = e^t\mathbf{i} + 2\sin(t + \tfrac{1}{2}\pi)\,\mathbf{j} + (t^2 - 2)\,\mathbf{k},$$
$$\mathbf{r}_2(u) = u\,\mathbf{i} + 2\,\mathbf{j} = (u^2 - 3)\,\mathbf{k}$$

intersect and find the angle of intersection.

18. Consider the vector function $\mathbf{f}(t) = t\,\mathbf{i} + f(t)\,\mathbf{j}$ formed from a differentiable real-valued function f. The vector function $\mathbf{f}$ parametrizes the graph of f.

(a) Parametrize the tangent line at $P(t_0, f(t_0))$.

(b) Show that the parametrization obtained in part (a) can be reduced to the usual equation for the tangent line:

$$y - f(t_0) = f'(t_0)(x - t_0) \quad \text{if} \quad f'(t_0) \neq 0;$$
$$y = f(t_0) \quad \text{if } f'(t_0) = 0.$$

19. Define a vector function $\mathbf{r}$ on the interval $[0, 2\pi]$ that satisfies the initial condition $\mathbf{r}(0) = a\mathbf{i}$ and, as t increases to 2π, traces out the ellipse $b^2x^2 + a^2y^2 = a^2b^2$;

(a) Once in a counterclockwise manner.

(b) Once in a clockwise manner.

(c) Twice in a counterclockwise manner.

(d) Three times in a clockwise manner.

20. Exercise 19 given that $\mathbf{r}(0) = b\,\mathbf{j}$.

Exercises 21–26. Sketch the curve, show the direction of the curve, and display both $\mathbf{r}(t)$ and $\mathbf{r}'(t)$ for the given value of t.

21. $\mathbf{r}(t) = \frac{1}{4}t^4\,\mathbf{i} + t^2\,\mathbf{j}$; $t = 2$.

22. $\mathbf{r}(t) = 2t\,\mathbf{i} + (t^2+1)\,\mathbf{j}$; $t = 4$.

23. $\mathbf{r}(t) = e^{2t}\,\mathbf{i} + e^{-4t}\,\mathbf{j}$; $t = 0$.

24. $\mathbf{r}(t) = \sin t\,\mathbf{i} - 2\cos t\,\mathbf{j}$; $t = \pi/3$.

25. $\mathbf{r}(t) = 2\cos t\,\mathbf{i} + 3\sin t\,\mathbf{j}$; $t = \pi/6$.

26. $\mathbf{r}(t) = \sec t\,\mathbf{i} + \tan t\,\mathbf{j}$, $|t| < \pi/2$; $t = \pi/4$.

Exercises 27–30. Find a vector parametrization for the curve.

27. $y^2 = x - 1$, $y \geq 1$.

28. $r = 1 - \cos\theta$, $\theta \in [0, 2\pi]$. (polar coordinates)

29. $r = \sin 3\theta$, $\theta \in [0, \pi]$. (polar coordinates)

30. $y^4 = x^3$, $y \leq 0$.

31. Find an equation in x and y for the curve $\mathbf{r}(t) = t^3\,\mathbf{i} + t^2\,\mathbf{j}$. Draw the curve. Does the curve have a tangent vector at the origin? If so, what is the unit tangent vector?

32. (a) Show that the curve

$$\mathbf{r}(t) = (t^2 - t + 1)\,\mathbf{i} + (t^3 - t + 2)\,\mathbf{j} + (\sin \pi t)\,\mathbf{k}$$

intersects itself at $P(1, 2, 0)$ by finding numbers $t_1 < t_2$ for which P is the tip of both $\mathbf{r}(t_1)$ and $\mathbf{r}(t_2)$.

(b) Find the unit tangents at $P(1, 2, 0)$, first taking $t = t_1$, then taking $t = t_2$.

33. Find the point(s) at which the twisted cubic

$$\mathbf{r}(t) = t\,\mathbf{i} + t^2\,\mathbf{j} + t^3\,\mathbf{k}$$

intersects the plane $4x + 2y + z = 24$. What is the angle of intersection between the curve and the normal to this plane?

34. (a) Find the unit tangent and the principal normal at an arbitrary point of the ellipse

$$\mathbf{r}(t) = a\cos t\,\mathbf{i} + b\sin t\,\mathbf{j}.$$

(b) Write vector equations for the tangent line and the normal line at the tip of $\mathbf{r}(\frac{1}{4}\pi)$.

Exercises 35–42. Find the unit tangent, the principal normal, and write an equation in x, y, z for the osculating plane at the point on the curve that corresponds to the indicated value of t.

35. $\mathbf{r}(t) = i + 2t\,\mathbf{j} + t^2\,\mathbf{k}; \quad t = 1.$

36. $\mathbf{r}(t) = t\,\mathbf{i} + t^2\,\mathbf{j} + 2t^2\,\mathbf{k}; \quad t = 1.$

37. $\mathbf{r}(t) = \cos 2t\,\mathbf{i} + \sin 2t\,\mathbf{j} + t\,\mathbf{k} \quad \text{at } t = \frac{1}{4}\pi.$

38. $\mathbf{r}(t) = t\,\mathbf{i} + 2t\,\mathbf{j} + t^2\,\mathbf{k} \quad \text{at } t = 2.$

39. $\mathbf{r}(t) = \sinh t\,\mathbf{i} + \cosh t\,\mathbf{j} + t\,\mathbf{k}; \quad \text{at } t = 0.$

40. $\mathbf{r}(t) = \cos 3t\,\mathbf{i} + t\,\mathbf{j} - \sin 3t\,\mathbf{k} \quad \text{at } t = \frac{1}{3}\pi.$

41. $\mathbf{r}(t) = e^t \sin t\,\mathbf{i} + e^t \cos t\,\mathbf{j} + e^t\,\mathbf{k}; \quad t = 0.$

42. $\mathbf{r}(t) = (\cos t + t \sin t)\,\mathbf{i} + (\sin t - t\cos t)\,\mathbf{j} + 2k; \quad t = \frac{1}{4}\pi.$

43. Let $\mathbf{r} = \mathbf{r}(t), t \in [a, b]$ be a differentiable curve with nonzero tangent vector $\mathbf{r}'(t)$. We know that the vector function

$$\mathbf{R}(u) = \mathbf{r}(a + b - u), \quad u \in [a, b]$$

traces out the same curve but in the opposite direction. Verify that this change of parameter changes the sign of the unit tangent but does not alter the principal normal.

44. Let $\mathbf{r}(t) = \sqrt{2}\cos t\,\mathbf{i} + \sqrt{2}\sin t\,\mathbf{j} + t\,\mathbf{k}, \quad 0 \le t \le 2\pi.$

(a) Find scalar parametric equations for the line tangent to the curve at the point $(1, 1, \frac{1}{4}\pi)$.

(b) Use a CAS to draw the curve and attach to it the tangent line found in part (a).

(c) Are there points on the curve where the tangent line is parallel to the xy-plane? If so, find them.

45. Let $\mathbf{r}(t) = \sqrt{2}\cos t\,\mathbf{i} + \sqrt{2}\sin t\,\mathbf{j} + \sin 5t\,\mathbf{k}, \quad 0 \le t \le 2\pi.$

(a) Find scalar parametric equations for the line tangent to the curve at the point $(1, 1, -\frac{1}{2}\sqrt{2})$.

(b) Use a CAS to draw the curve and attach to it the tangent line found in part (a).

(c) Are there points on the curve where the tangent line is parallel to the xy-plane? If so, find them.

46. Let $\mathbf{r}(t) = \sqrt{2}\cos t\,\mathbf{i} + \sqrt{2}\sin t\,\mathbf{j} + \ln t\,\mathbf{k}, \quad 0 \le t \le 2\pi.$

(a) Find scalar parametric equations for the line tangent to the curve at the point $(1, 1, \ln \frac{1}{4}\pi)$.

(b) Use a CAS to draw the curve and attach to it the tangent line found in part (a)

14.4 ARC LENGTH

In Section 10.7 we took up the notion of arc length and concluded on intuitive grounds that the length of the path C traced out by a pair of continuously differentiable functions

$$x = x(t), \qquad y = y(t), \qquad t \in [a, b]$$

is given by the formula

$$L(C) = \int_a^b \sqrt{[x'(t)]^2 + [y'(t)]^2}\, dt.$$

Applied to a path C in space traced out by

$$x = x(t), \qquad y = y(t), \qquad z = z(t), \qquad t \in [a, b]$$

the formula becomes

$$L(C) = \int_a^b \sqrt{[x'(t)]^2 + [y'(t)]^2 + [z'(t)]^2}\, dt.$$

In vector notation, both formulas can be written

$$L(C) = \int_a^b \|\mathbf{r}'(t)\|\, dt.$$

We will prove the result in this form, but first we must give a precise definition of arc length.

In Figure 14.4.1 we sketched the path C traced out by a continuously differentiable vector function

$$\mathbf{r} = \mathbf{r}(t), \qquad t \in [a, b].$$

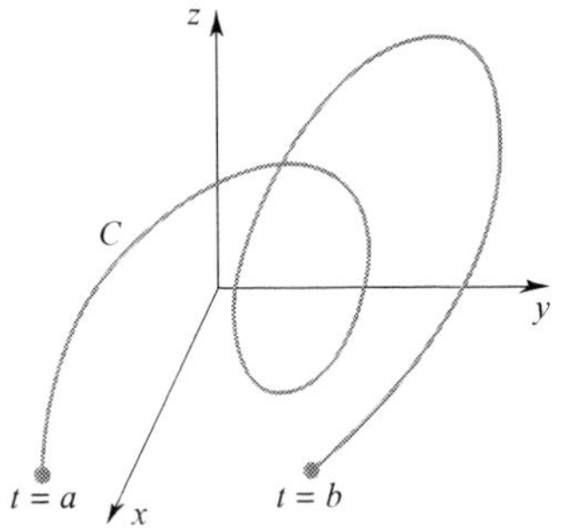

Figure 14.4.1

To decide what should be meant by the length of C, we approximate C by the union of a finite number of line segments.

Choosing a finite number of points in $[a, b]$,

$$a = t_0 < t_1 < \cdots < t_{i-1} < t_i < \cdots < t_{n-1} < t_n = b,$$

we obtain a finite number of points $P_0, P_1, \ldots, P_{i-1}, P_i, \ldots, P_{n-1}, P_n$, on C, where for each index k, P_k denotes the point $P(x(t_k), y(t_k), z(t_k))$. We join these points consecutively by line segments and call the resulting path,

$$\gamma = \overline{P_0P_1} \cup \cdots \cup \overline{P_{i-1}, P_i} \cup \cdots \cup \overline{P_{n-1}P_n},$$

a *polygonal path* inscribed in C. (Figure 14.4.2)

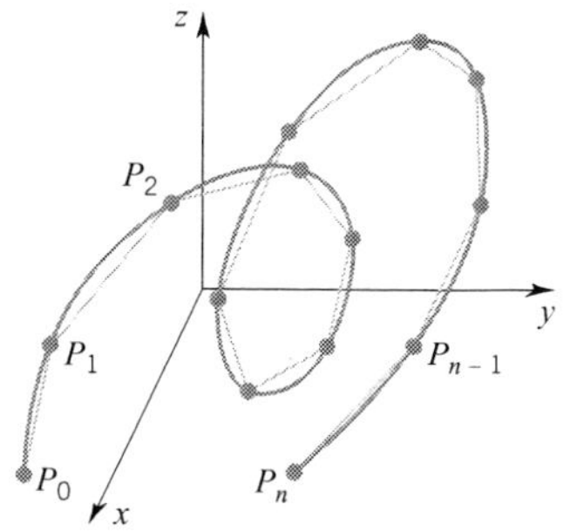

Figure 14.4.2

The length of this polygonal path is the sum of the distances between consecutive vertices:

$$L(\gamma) = d(P_0, P_1) + \cdots + d(P_{i-1}, P_i) + \cdots + d(P_{n-1}, P_n).$$

The path γ serves as an approximation to the path C. Better approximations can be obtained by adding more vertices to γ. We now ask ourselves exactly what we should require of the number that we shall call the length of C. Certainly we require that

$$L(\gamma) \leq L(C) \qquad \text{for each } \gamma \text{ inscribed in } C.$$

But that is not enough. There is another requirement that seems reasonable. If we can choose γ to approximate C as closely as we wish, then we should be able to choose γ so that $L(\gamma)$ approximates the length of C as closely as we wish; namely, for each positive number ε there should exist a polygonal path γ such that

$$L(C) - \epsilon < L(\gamma) \leq L(C).$$

In Section 11.1, we introduced the concept of least upper bound of a set of real numbers. Theorem 11.1.2 tells us that we can achieve the result we want by defining the length of C as the least upper bound of the set of all $L(\gamma)$. This is in fact what we do.

DEFINITION 14.4.1 ARC LENGTH

$$L(C) = \left\{ \begin{array}{l} \text{the least upper bound of the set of all} \\ \text{lengths of polygonal paths inscribed in } C. \end{array} \right.$$

We are now ready to establish the arc length formula.

THEOREM 14.4.2 ARC LENGTH FORMULA

Let C be the path traced out by a continuously differentiable vector function

$$\mathbf{r} = \mathbf{r}(t), \qquad t \in [a, b].$$

The length of C is given by the formula

$$L(C) = \int_a^b \|\mathbf{r}'(t)\|\, dt.$$

PROOF First we show that

$$L(C) \leq \int_a^b \|\mathbf{r}'(t)\|\, dt.$$

To do this, we begin with an arbitrary partition P of $[a, b]$:

$$P = \{a = t_0, \ldots, t_{i-1}, t_i, \ldots, t_n = b\}.$$

Such a partition gives rise to a finite number of points of C:

$$\mathbf{r}(a) = \mathbf{r}(t_0), \ldots, \mathbf{r}(t_{i-1}), \mathbf{r}(t_i), \ldots, \mathbf{r}(t_n) = \mathbf{r}(b)$$

and thus to an inscribed polygonal path of total length

$$L_P = \sum_{i=1}^{n} \|\mathbf{r}(t_i) - \mathbf{r}(t_{i-1})\|. \qquad \text{(Figure 14.4.3)}$$

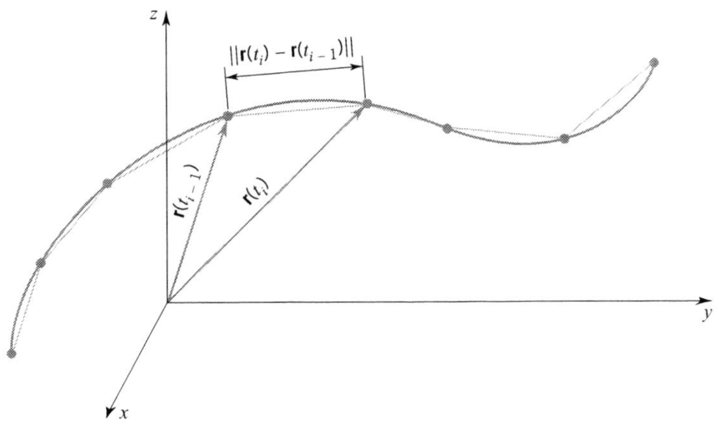

Figure 14.4.3

For each i,

$$\mathbf{r}(t_i) - \mathbf{r}(t_{i-1}) = \int_{t_{i-1}}^{t_i} \mathbf{r}'(t)dt.$$

This gives

$$\|\mathbf{r}(t_i) - \mathbf{r}(t_{i-1})\| = \left\| \int_{t_{i-1}}^{t_i} \mathbf{r}'(t)dt \right\| \overset{\text{by (14.1.10)}}{\leq} \int_{t_{i-1}}^{t_i} \|\mathbf{r}'(t)\|\, dt$$

and thus

$$L_P = \sum_{i=1}^{n} \|\mathbf{r}(t_i) - \mathbf{r}(t_{i-1})\| \leq \sum_{i=1}^{n} \int_{t_{i-1}}^{t_i} \|\mathbf{r}'(t)\|\, dt = \int_a^b \|\mathbf{r}'(t)\|\, dt.$$

Since the partition P is arbitrary, we know that the inequality

$$L_P \leq \int_a^b \|\mathbf{r}'(t)\|\, dt$$

must hold for all the L_P. This makes the integral on the right an upper bound for all the L_P. Since $L(C)$ is the *least* upper bound of all the L_P, we can conclude right now that

$$L(C) \leq \int_a^b \|\mathbf{r}'(t)\|\, dt.$$

The next step is to show that this inequality is actually an equality. To do this we need to know that arc length, *as we have defined it*, is additive. That is, with P, Q, R as in Figure 14.4.4, we need to know that the arc length from P to Q plus the arc length from Q to R equals the arc length from P to R. It is clear arc length should have this property. We must prove that it does. A proof has been placed in a supplement to this section. For the moment we shall assume that arc length is additive and continue with the proof of the arc length formula.

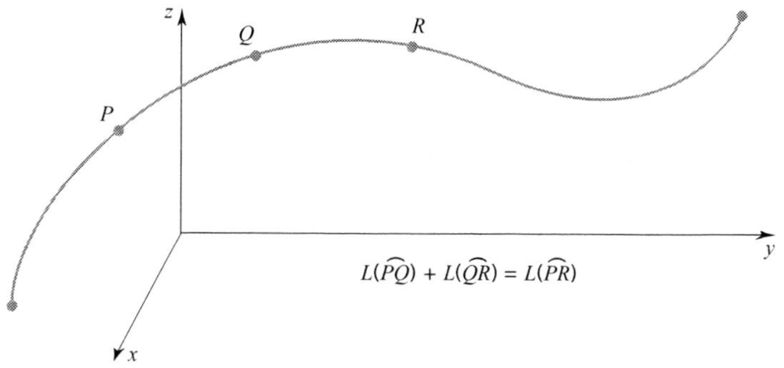

Figure 14.4.4

In Figure 14.4.5, we display the initial vector $\mathbf{r}(a)$, a general radius vector $\mathbf{r}(t)$, and a nearby vector $\mathbf{r}(t+h)$. Set

$$s(t) = \text{length of the path from } \mathbf{r}(a) \text{ to } \mathbf{r}(t).$$

Then

$$s(a) = 0 \quad \text{and} \quad s(t+h) \;=\; \text{length of the path from } \mathbf{r}(a) \text{ to } \mathbf{r}(t+h).$$

By the additivity of arc length (remember, we are assuming this for the moment),

$$s(t+h) - s(t) = \text{length of the curve from } \mathbf{r}(t) \text{ to } \mathbf{r}(t+h).$$

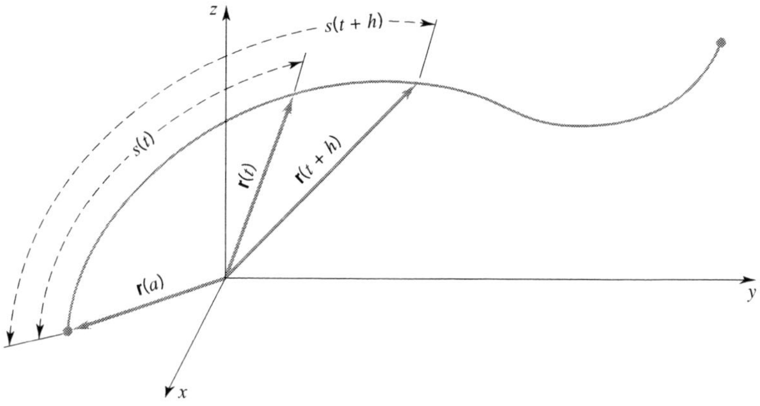

Figure 14.4.5

From what we have shown already, you can see that

$$\|\mathbf{r}(t+h) - \mathbf{r}(t)\| \le s(t+h) - s(t) \le \int_t^{t+h} \|\mathbf{r}'(u)\|\, du.$$

Dividing this inequality by h (which we are taking as positive), we get

$$\left\| \frac{\mathbf{r}(t+h) - \mathbf{r}(t)}{h} \right\| \le \frac{s(t+h) - s(t)}{h} \le \frac{1}{h} \int_t^{t+h} \|\mathbf{r}'(u)\|\, du.$$

As $h \to 0^+$, the left-hand side tends to $\|\mathbf{r}'(t)\|$ and, by the first mean-value theorem for integrals (Theorem 5.9.1), so does the right-hand side:

$$\frac{1}{h} \int_t^{t+h} \|\mathbf{r}'(u)\|\, du = \underset{\substack{\uparrow \\ c_h \in (t,\, t+h)}}{\frac{1}{h}} \|\mathbf{r}'(c_h)\|(t+h-t) = \|\mathbf{r}'(c_h)\| \to \|\mathbf{r}'(t)\|.$$

Therefore

$$\lim_{h \to 0^+} \frac{s(t+h) - s(t)}{h} = \|\mathbf{r}'(t)\|.$$

By taking $h < 0$ and proceeding in a similar manner, one can show that

$$\lim_{h\to 0^-} \frac{s(t+h)-s(t)}{h} = \|\mathbf{r}'(t)\|.$$

Therefore, we can conclude that

$$\lim_{h\to 0} \frac{s(t+h)-s(t)}{h} = \|\mathbf{r}'(t)\|$$

and so $s'(t) = \|\mathbf{r}'(t)\|$. Integrating this equation from a to t, we get

$$s(t) - s(a) = \int_a^t s'(u)du = \int_a^t \|\mathbf{r}'(u)\|\, du.$$

Since $s(a) = 0$, it follows that

$$s(t) = \int_a^t \|\mathbf{r}'(u)\|\, du.$$

The total length of C is therefore

$$s(b) = \int_a^b \|\mathbf{r}'(u)\|\, du = \int_a^b \|\mathbf{r}'(t)\|\, dt. \quad \square$$

Example 1 Find the length of the curve

$$\mathbf{r}(t) = 2t^{3/2}\,\mathbf{i} + 4t\,\mathbf{j} \qquad \text{from} \qquad t=0 \quad \text{to} \quad t=1.$$

SOLUTION

$$\mathbf{r}'(t) = 3t^{1/2}\,\mathbf{i} + 4\,\mathbf{j}.$$

$$\|\mathbf{r}'(t)\| = \sqrt{(3t^{1/2})^2 + 4^2} = \sqrt{9t+16}.$$

$$L(C) = \int_0^1 \|\mathbf{r}'(t)\|\, dt = \int_0^1 \sqrt{9t+16}\, dt$$

$$= \left[\frac{1}{9}\left(\frac{2}{3}\right)(9t+16)^{3/2}\right]_0^1 = \frac{250}{27} - \frac{128}{27} = \frac{122}{27}. \quad \square$$

Example 2 Find the length of the curve

$$\mathbf{r}(t) = 2\cos t\,\mathbf{i} + 2\sin t\,\mathbf{j} + t^2\,\mathbf{k} \qquad \text{from } t=0 \text{ to } t=\pi/2$$

and compare it to the straight-line distance between the endpoints of the curve. (See Figure 14.4.6.)

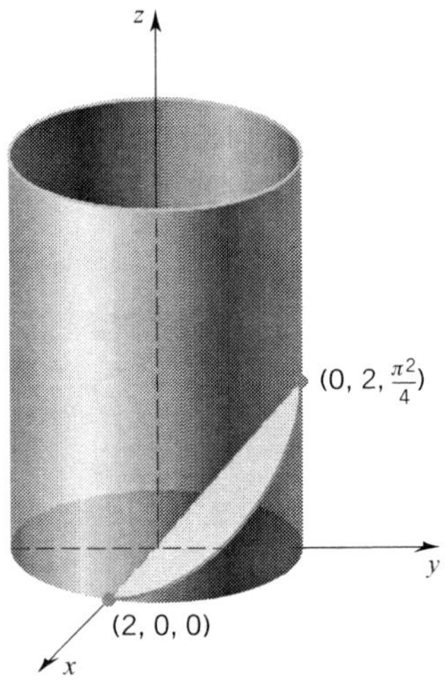

Figure 14.4.6

SOLUTION

$$\mathbf{r}'(t) = -2\sin t\,\mathbf{i} + 2\cos t\,\mathbf{j} + 2t\,\mathbf{k}.$$

$$\|\mathbf{r}'(t)\| = \sqrt{4\sin^2 t + 4\cos^2 t + 4t^2} = 2\sqrt{\sin^2 t + \cos^2 t + t^2} = 2\sqrt{1+t^2}.$$

$$L(C) = \int_0^{\pi/2} \|\mathbf{r}'(t)\| dt = \int_0^{\pi/2} 2\sqrt{1+t^2}\, dt$$

$$= \left[t\sqrt{1+t^2} + \ln\left(t + \sqrt{1+t^2}\right)\right]_0^{\pi/2} \qquad \text{(Formula 78)}$$

$$= \frac{\pi}{2}\sqrt{1+\frac{\pi^2}{4}} + \ln\left[\frac{\pi}{2} + \sqrt{1+\frac{\pi^2}{4}}\right] \cong 4.158.$$

The curve begins at $\mathbf{r}(0) = 2\,\mathbf{i}$ and ends at $\mathbf{r}(\pi/2) = 2\,\mathbf{j} + (\pi^2/4)\,\mathbf{k}$. The straight-line distance between these two points is

$$\|\mathbf{r}(\pi/2) - \mathbf{r}(0)\| = \sqrt{2^2 + 2^2 + \frac{\pi^4}{16}} \cong 3.753.$$

The curve is about 11% longer than the straight-line distance between the endpoints of the curve. ❑

Parametrizing a Curve by Arc Length

Suppose that

$$C : \mathbf{r} = \mathbf{r}(t), \qquad t \in [a, b]$$

is a continuously differentiable curve of length L with nonzero tangent vector $\mathbf{r}'(t)$. The length of C from $\mathbf{r}(a)$ to $\mathbf{r}(t)$ is

$$s(t) = \int_a^t \|\mathbf{r}'(u)\|\,du.$$

Since $ds/dt = \|\mathbf{r}'(t)\| > 0$, the function $s = s(t)$ is a one-to-one increasing function. Thus, no two points of C can lie at the same arc distance from $\mathbf{r}(a)$. It follows that for each $s \in [0, L]$, there is a unique point $\mathbf{R}(s)$ on C at arc distance s from $\mathbf{r}(a)$.

(14.4.3)

> *The function*
>
> $$\mathbf{R} = \mathbf{R}(s), \qquad s \in [0, L]$$
>
> *parametrizes C by arc length.*

Since

$$\frac{ds}{dt} = \left\|\frac{d\mathbf{r}}{dt}\right\| > 0$$

the function $s = s(t)$ has a differentiable inverse $t = t(s)$ and we can write

$$\frac{dt}{ds} = \frac{1}{\|d\mathbf{r}/dt\|}.$$

Since both $\mathbf{R}(s(t))$ and $\mathbf{r}(t)$ lie at arc distance $s(t)$ from $\mathbf{r}(a)$, $\mathbf{R}(s(t)) = \mathbf{r}(t)$. Therefore

$$\mathbf{R}(s) = \mathbf{r}(t(s)).$$

Differentiation gives

$$\frac{d\mathbf{R}}{ds} = \frac{d\mathbf{r}}{dt}\frac{dt}{ds} = \frac{d\mathbf{r}}{dt}\frac{1}{\|d\mathbf{r}/dt\|}.$$

Taking the norm of both sides, we have

$$\left\|\frac{d\mathbf{R}}{ds}\right\| = 1.$$

(14.4.4)

> Thus, for a curve parametrized by arc length, the tangent vector can change in direction but not in length: the tangent vector maintains length 1.

Example 3 Parametrize the circular helix

$$\mathbf{r}(t) = 3\cos t\,\mathbf{i} + 3\sin t\,\mathbf{j} + 4t\,\mathbf{k}, \qquad t \geq 0$$

by arc length.

SOLUTION The length of the curve from $\mathbf{r}(0)$ to $\mathbf{r}(t)$ is the number

$$s = \int_0^t \|\mathbf{r}'(u)\|du = \int_0^t \sqrt{(-3\sin u)^2 + (3\cos u)^2 + 4^2}\,du$$

$$= \int_0^t \sqrt{9+16}\,du = \int_0^t 5\,du = 5t.$$

In this case, $t = \frac{1}{5}s$. Since $\mathbf{r}(t) = \mathbf{r}(\frac{1}{5}s)$ lies at arc distance s from $\mathbf{r}(0)$, the vector function

$$\mathbf{R}(s) = \mathbf{r}(\tfrac{1}{5}s) = 3\cos\tfrac{1}{5}s\,\mathbf{i} + 3\sin\tfrac{1}{5}s\,\mathbf{j} + \tfrac{4}{5}s\,\mathbf{k}, \qquad s \geq 0$$

parametrizes the curve by arc length. As you can check $\|d\mathbf{R}/ds\| = 1$. ❑

You have seen that for a curve parametrized by arc length, the tangent vector has constant length 1. There is a partial converse to this.

(14.4.5)

> If the curve
>
> $$C : \mathbf{r} = \mathbf{r}(t), \qquad t \in [0, b]$$
>
> has tangent vector of constant length 1, then the parametrization is by arc length and the length of the curve is b.

(We called this a partial converse because for the statement to be true, we must start the parametrization at $t = 0$.)

PROOF The arc distance from $\mathbf{r}(0)$ to $\mathbf{r}(t)$ is the number

$$s = \int_0^t \left\|\frac{d\mathbf{r}}{du}\right\| du.$$

Since $\|d\mathbf{r}/dt\|$ is constantly 1,

$$s = \int_0^t 1\,du = t.$$

The parameter t is thus the arc length parameter s.

The total length of C is

$$\int_0^b 1\,du = b. \quad ❑$$

Remark More general changes of parameter are introduced in Project 14.4. ❑

EXERCISES 14.4

Exercises 1–16. Find the length of the curve.

1. $\mathbf{r}(t) = t\,\mathbf{i} + \frac{2}{3}t^{3/2}\,\mathbf{j}$ from $t = 0$ to $t = 8$.
2. $\mathbf{r}(t) = (\frac{1}{3}t^3 - t)\,\mathbf{i} + t^2\,\mathbf{j}$ from $t = 0$ to $t = 2$.
3. $\mathbf{r}(t) = a\cos t\,\mathbf{i} + a\sin t\,\mathbf{j} + bt\,\mathbf{k}$ from $t = 0$ to $t = 2\pi$.
4. $\mathbf{r}(t) = t\,\mathbf{i} + \frac{2}{3}\sqrt{2}\,t^{3/2}\,\mathbf{j} + \frac{1}{2}t^2\,\mathbf{k}$ from $t = 0$ to $t = 2$.
5. $\mathbf{r}(t) = t\,\mathbf{i} + \ln(\sec t)\,\mathbf{j} + 3\,\mathbf{k}$ from $t = 0$ to $t = \frac{1}{4}\pi$.
6. $\mathbf{r}(t) = \arctan t\,\mathbf{i} + \frac{1}{2}\ln(1 + t^2)\,\mathbf{j}$ from $t = 0$ to $t = 1$.
7. $\mathbf{r}(t) = t^3\,\mathbf{i} + t^2\,\mathbf{j}$ from $t = 0$ to $t = 1$.

8. $\mathbf{r}(t) = t\,\mathbf{i} + \mathbf{j} + (\frac{1}{6}t^3 + \frac{1}{2}t^{-1})\,\mathbf{k}$ from $t = 1$ to $t = 3$.

9. $\mathbf{r}(t) = e^t[\cos t\,\mathbf{i} + \sin t\,\mathbf{j}]$ from $t = 0$ to $t = \pi$.

10. $\mathbf{r}(t) = t^2\,\mathbf{i} + (t^2 - 2)\,\mathbf{j} + (1 - t^2)\,\mathbf{k}$ from $t = 0$ to $t = 2$.

11. $\mathbf{r}(t) = (\ln t)\,\mathbf{i} + 2t\,\mathbf{j} + t^2\,\mathbf{k}$ from $t = 1$ to $t = e$.

12. $\mathbf{r}(t) = (t\sin t + \cos t)\,\mathbf{i} + (t\cos t - \sin t)\,\mathbf{j} + 2\,\mathbf{k}$ from $t = 0$ to $t = 2$.

13. $\mathbf{r}(t) = (\cos t + t\sin t)\,\mathbf{i} + (\sin t - t\cos t)\,\mathbf{j} + \frac{1}{2}\sqrt{3}\,t^2\,\mathbf{k}$ from $t = 0$ to $t = 2\pi$.

14. $\mathbf{r}(t) = \frac{2}{3}(1 + t)^{3/2}\,\mathbf{i} + \frac{2}{3}(1 - t)^{3/2}\,\mathbf{j} + \sqrt{2}t\,\mathbf{k}$ from $t = -\frac{1}{2}$ to $t = \frac{1}{2}$.

15. $\mathbf{r}(t) = 2t\mathbf{i} + (t^2 - 2)\,\mathbf{j} + (1 - t^2)\,\mathbf{k}$ from $t = 0$ to $t = 2$.

16. $\mathbf{r}(t) = 3t\cos t\,\mathbf{i} + 3t\sin t\,\mathbf{j} + 4t\,\mathbf{k}$ from $t = 0$ to $t = 4$.

17. (*Important*) Let $\mathbf{r}(t) = x(t)\,\mathbf{i} + y(t)\,\mathbf{j} + z(t)\,\mathbf{k}$, $t \in [a, b]$, be a continuously differentiable curve. Show that, if s is the length of the curve from $\mathbf{r}(a)$ to $\mathbf{r}(t)$, then

(14.4.6) $$\frac{ds}{dt} = \sqrt{\left(\frac{dx}{dt}\right)^2 + \left(\frac{dy}{dt}\right)^2 + \left(\frac{dz}{dt}\right)^2}.$$

18. Use vector methods to show that, if $y = f(x)$ has a continuous first derivative, then the length of the graph from $x = a$ to $x = b$ is given by the integral

$$\int_a^b \sqrt{1 + [f'(x)]^2}\,dx.$$

19. (*Important*) Let $y = f(x)$, $x \in [a, b]$, be a continuously differentiable function. Show that, if s is the length of the graph from $(a, f(a))$ to $(x, f(x))$, then

(14.4.7) $$\frac{ds}{dx} = \sqrt{1 + \left(\frac{dy}{dx}\right)^2}.$$

20. Let C_1 be the curve

$$\mathbf{r}(t) = (t - \ln t)\,\mathbf{i} + (t + \ln t)\,\mathbf{j}, \qquad 1 \le t \le e$$

and let C_2 be the graph of

$$y = e^x, \qquad 0 \le x \le 1.$$

Find a relation between the length of C_1, and the length of C_2.

21. Show that the usual parametrization of the unit circle

$$\mathbf{r}(t) = \cos t\,\mathbf{i} + \sin t\,\mathbf{j}, \qquad t \in [0, 2\pi]$$

is already a parametrization by arc length.

22. Find the length of the directed line segment

$$\mathbf{r}(t) = (1 - t)\,\mathbf{a} + t\,\mathbf{b}, \qquad t \in [0, 1].$$

Then parametrize the line segment by arc length.

23. Parametrize the curve

$$\mathbf{r}(t) = (\sin t - t\cos t)\,\mathbf{i} + (\cos t + t\sin t)\,\mathbf{i} + \tfrac{1}{2}t^2\,\mathbf{k}, \quad t \ge 0$$

by arc length.

24. If you carried out Exercise 9, you found out that the curve

$$\mathbf{r}(t) = e^t[\cos t\,\mathbf{i} + \sin t\,\mathbf{j}], \qquad t \in [0, \pi]$$

has length $\sqrt{2}(e^{\pi} - 1)$. Parametrize this curve by arc length.

Exercise 25–28. Use a CAS to estimate the length of the curve.

25. $\mathbf{r}(t) = \frac{2}{5}t^{5/2}\,\mathbf{j} + t\,\mathbf{k}$ from $t = 0$ to $t = \frac{1}{2}$.

26. $\mathbf{r}(t) = t\,\mathbf{i} + \frac{1}{3}t^3\,\mathbf{j}$ from $t = 0$ to $t = 2$.

27. $\mathbf{r}(t) = 3\cos t\,\mathbf{i} + 4\sin t\,\mathbf{j} + 2\,\mathbf{k}$ from $t = 0$ to $t = 2\pi$.

28. $\mathbf{r}(t) = t\,\mathbf{i} + t^2\,\mathbf{j} + (\ln t)\,\mathbf{k}$ from $t = 1$ to $t = 4$.

29. Let $\mathbf{r}(t) = \cos t\,\mathbf{i} + \sin t\,\mathbf{j} + \sin 4t\,\mathbf{k}$, $0 \le t \le 2\pi$.

(a) Use a graphing utility to draw the curve.
(b) Use a CAS to estimate the length of the curve.

30. Let $\mathbf{r}(t) = \cos t\,\mathbf{i} + \ln(1 + t)\,\mathbf{j} + \sin t\,\mathbf{k}$, $0 \le t \le 2\pi$

(a) Use a graphing utility to draw the curve.
(b) Use a CAS to estimate the length of the curve.

■ PROJECT 14.4 MORE GENERAL CHANGES OF PARAMETER

(Although this material is cast as a project, the ideas introduced here, if not the details, constitute an integral part of the text.)

Begin with a differentiable curve

$$\mathbf{r} = \mathbf{r}(t), \qquad t \in I \qquad (I \text{ some interval})$$

with nonzero tangent vector $\mathbf{r}'(t)$. Change from parameter t to parameter u by expressing t in terms of u by a continuously differentiable function $t = \varphi(u)$ which maps some u-interval J onto the t-interval I in a one-to-one manner. Make sure that $\varphi'(u)$ does not take on the value 0: either it remains positive or it remains negative. Now form the composition

$$\mathbf{R}(u) = \mathbf{r}(\varphi(u)), \qquad u \in J.$$

Problem 1. Show that

(14.4.8) $\mathbf{r} = \mathbf{r}(t)$, $t \in I$ and $\mathbf{R} = \mathbf{R}(u)$, $u \in J$ trace out exactly the same path, in the same direction if $\varphi'(u) > 0$, but in the opposite direction if $\varphi'(u) < 0$.

Because of what you just proved

(14.4.9) we say that

$$\mathbf{r} = \mathbf{r}(t), \quad t \in I \quad \text{and} \quad \mathbf{R} = \mathbf{R}(u), \quad u \in J.$$

differ by a *sense-preserving* change of parameter if $\varphi'(u) > 0$, by a *sense-reversing* change of parameter if $\varphi'(u) < 0$.

For example, let

$$\mathbf{r}(t) = t\mathbf{i} - \cos t\mathbf{j} + \sin t\mathbf{k}, \qquad t \in [0, \pi].$$

The curve

$$\mathbf{R}(u) = \sqrt{u}\mathbf{i} - \cos\sqrt{u}\mathbf{j} + \sin\sqrt{u}\mathbf{k}, \qquad u \in [0, \pi^2]$$

differs from $\mathbf{r}$ only by a sense-preserving change of parameter: $\varphi(u) = \sqrt{u}$ maps $[0, \pi^2]$ in a one-to-one manner onto $[0, \pi]$ with $\varphi'(u) = 1/(2\sqrt{u}) > 0$. (check all this)

The curve

$$\mathbf{R}(u) = (4 - \sqrt{u})\mathbf{i} - \cos(4 - \sqrt{u})\mathbf{j} + \sin(4 - \sqrt{u})\mathbf{k}, \qquad u \in [(4 - \pi)^2, 16]$$

differs from $\mathbf{r}$ by a sense-reversing change of parameter: $\varphi(u) = 4 - \sqrt{u}$ maps $[(4 - \pi)^2, 16]$ onto $[0, \pi]$ with $\varphi'(u) = -1/(2\sqrt{u}) < 0$. (check all this)

Problem 2. Show that the unit tangent, the principal normal, and the osculating plane are left invariant (left unchanged) by a sense-preserving change of parameter.

Problem 3. What happens to the unit tangent, the principal normal, and the osculating plane if we apply a sense-reversing change of parameter?

Problem 4. Review the process by which we obtained the arc length parametrization $\mathbf{R} = \mathbf{R}(s)$. What was the function φ in that case?

Problem 5. Let

$$\mathbf{r} = \mathbf{r}(t), \quad t \in I \qquad \text{and} \qquad \mathbf{R} = \mathbf{R}(u), \quad u \in J.$$

be continuously differentiable curves with nonzero tangent vectors. Show that if $\mathbf{r}$ and $\mathbf{R}$ differ only by a sense-preserving (or a sense-reversing) change of parameter, then both curves have the same arc length.

*SUPPLEMENT TO SECTION 14.4

The Additivity of Arc Length We wish to show that with P, Q, R as in Figure 14.4.4,

$$L(\widehat{PQ}) + L(\widehat{QR}) = L(\widehat{PR}).$$

Let γ_1 be an arbitrary polygonal path inscribed in $\widehat{PQ}$ and γ_2 an arbitrary polygonal path inscribed in $\widehat{QR}$. Then $\gamma_1 \cup \gamma_2$ is a polygonal path inscribed in $\widehat{PR}$. Since

$$L(\gamma_1) + L(\gamma_2) = L(\gamma_1 \cup \gamma_2) \qquad \text{and} \qquad L(\gamma_1 \cup \gamma_2) \leq L(\widehat{PR}),$$

we have

$$L(\gamma_1) + L(\gamma_2) \leq L(\widehat{PR}) \qquad \text{and thus} \qquad L(\gamma_1) \leq L(\widehat{PR}) - L(\gamma_2).$$

Since γ_1 is arbitrary, we can conclude that $L(\widehat{PR}) - L(\gamma_2)$ is an upper bound for the set of all lengths of polygonal paths inscribed in $\widehat{PQ}$. Since $L(\widehat{PQ})$ is the *least* upper bound of this set, we have

$$L(\widehat{PQ}) \leq L(\widehat{PR}) - L(\gamma_2).$$

It follows that

$$L(\gamma_2) \leq L(\widehat{PR}) - L(\widehat{PQ}).$$

Arguing as we did with γ_1, we can conclude that

$$L(\widehat{QR}) \leq L(\widehat{PR}) - L(\widehat{PQ}).$$

This gives

$$L(\widehat{PQ}) + L(\widehat{QR}) \leq L(\widehat{PR}).$$

We now set out to prove that $L(\widehat{PR}) \leq L(\widehat{PQ}) + L(\widehat{QR})$. To do this, we need only take $\gamma = \overline{T_0T_1} \cup \ldots \cup \overline{T_{n-1}T_n}$ as an arbitrary polygonal path inscribed in $\widehat{PR}$ and show that

$$L(\gamma) \leq L(\widehat{PQ}) + L(\widehat{QR}).$$

If Q is one of the T_i, say $Q = T_k$, then

$$\gamma_1 = \overline{T_0T_1} \cup \cdots \cup \overline{T_{k-1}T_k} \qquad \text{is inscribed in } \widehat{PQ}$$

and

$$\gamma_2 = \overline{T_kT_{k+1}} \cup \cdots \cup \overline{T_{n-1}T_n} \qquad \text{is inscribed in } \widehat{QR}.$$

Moreover, $L(\gamma) = L(\gamma_1) + L(\gamma_2)$, so that

$$L(\gamma) \leq L(\widehat{PQ}) + L(\widehat{QR}).$$

If Q is none of the T_i, then Q lies between two consecutive points T_k and T_{k+1}. Set

$$\gamma' = \overline{T_0T_1} \cup \cdots \cup \overline{T_kQ} \cup \overline{QT_{k+1}} \cup \cdots \cup \overline{T_{n-1}T_n}.$$

Since

$$d(T_k, T_{k+1}) \leq d(T_k, Q) + d(Q, T_{k+1}),$$

we have

$$L(\gamma) \leq L(\gamma').$$

Proceed as before and you will see that

$$L(\gamma') \leq L(\widehat{PQ}) + L(\widehat{QR}),$$

and once again

$$L(\gamma) \leq L(\widehat{PQ}) + L(\widehat{QR}). \quad \square$$

■ 14.5 CURVILINEAR MOTION; CURVATURE

Curvilinear Motion from a Vector Viewpoint

Here we use the theory we have developed for vector-valued functions to study the motion of an object moving in space. We can describe the position of a moving object at time t by a radius vector $\mathbf{r}(t)$. As t ranges over a time interval I, the object traces out some path

$$C: \quad \mathbf{r}(t) = x(t)\,\mathbf{i} + y(t)\,\mathbf{j} + z(t)\,\mathbf{k}, \qquad t \in I. \qquad \text{(Figure 14.5.1)}$$

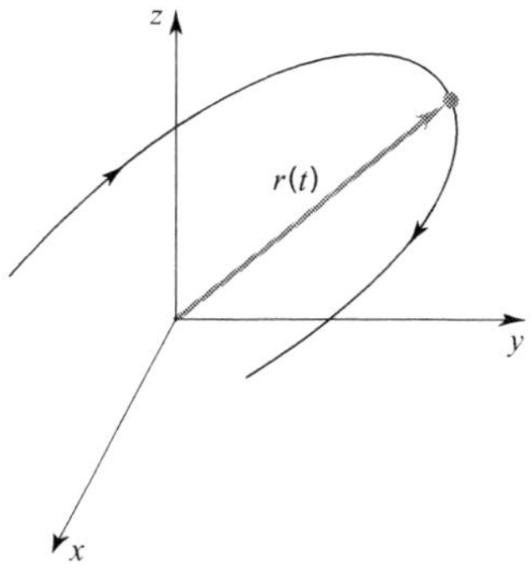

Figure 14.5.1

If $\mathbf{r}$ is twice differentiable, we can form $\mathbf{r}'(t)$ and $\mathbf{r}''(t)$. In this context these vectors have special names and special significance: $\mathbf{r}'(t)$ is called the *velocity* of the object at time t, and $\mathbf{r}''(t)$ is called the *acceleration*. In symbols, we have

(14.5.1)
$$\mathbf{r}'(t) = \mathbf{v}(t) \qquad \text{and} \qquad \mathbf{r}''(t) = \mathbf{v}'(t) = \mathbf{a}(t).$$

There should be nothing surprising about this. As before, velocity is the time rate of change of position and acceleration the time rate of change of velocity.

Since $\mathbf{v}(t) = \mathbf{r}'(t)$, the velocity vector, when not $\mathbf{0}$, is tangent to the path of the motion at the tip of $\mathbf{r}(t)$. (Section 14.3) The direction of the velocity vector at time t gives the direction of the motion at time t. (Figure 14.5.2.)

The magnitude of the velocity vector is called the *speed* of the object:

(14.5.2)
$$\|\mathbf{v}(t)\| = \text{the speed at time } t.$$

The reasoning is as follows: during a time interval $[t_0, t]$ the object moves along its path from $\mathbf{r}(t_0)$ to $\mathbf{r}(t)$ for a total distance

$$s(t) = \int_{t_0}^{t} \|\mathbf{r}'(u)\|\, du. \qquad \text{(Section 14.4)}$$

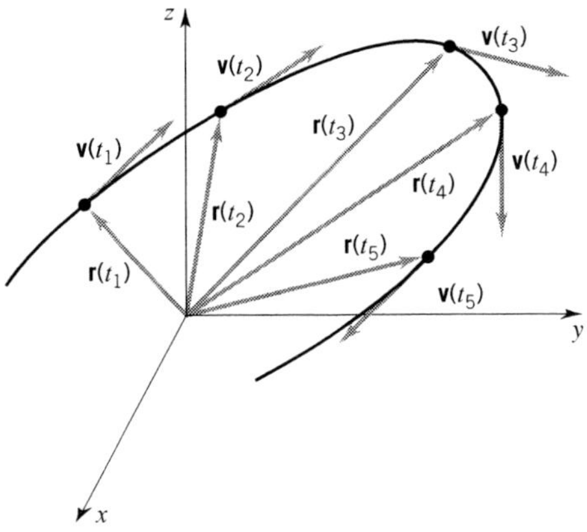

Figure 14.5.2

Differentiating with respect to t, we have

$$\frac{ds}{dt} = \|\mathbf{r}'(t)\|.$$

The magnitude of the velocity vector is thus *the rate of change of arc distance with respect to time*. This is why we call it the speed of the object.

Motion Along a Straight Line

The position at time t is given by a function of the form

$$\mathbf{r}(t) = \mathbf{r}_0 + f(t)\mathbf{d}, \qquad \mathbf{d} \neq 0.$$

The velocity and acceleration vectors are both directed along the line of the motion:

$$\mathbf{v}(t) = f'(t)\mathbf{d} \qquad \text{and} \qquad \mathbf{a}(t) = f''(t)\mathbf{d}.$$

If $\mathbf{d}$ is a unit vector, the speed is $|f'(t)|$:

$$\|\mathbf{v}(t)\| = \|f'(t)\mathbf{d}\| = |f'(t)|\;\|\mathbf{d}\| = |f'(t)|$$

and the magnitude of the acceleration is $|f''(t)|$:

$$\|\mathbf{a}(t)\| = \|f''(t)\mathbf{d}\| = |f''(t)|\;\|\mathbf{d}\| = |f''(t)|.$$

Circular Motion About the Origin

The position function can be written

$$\mathbf{r}(t) = a[\cos\theta(t)\,\mathbf{i} + \sin\theta(t)\,\mathbf{j}], \qquad a > 0 \text{ constant}.$$

Here $\theta'(t)$ gives the time rate of change of the central angle θ. If $\theta'(t) > 0$, the motion is counterclockwise; if $\theta'(t) < 0$, the motion is clockwise. We call $\theta'(t)$ the *angular velocity* and $|\theta'(t)|$ the *angular speed.*

Uniform circular motion is circular motion with constant angular speed $\omega > 0$. The position function for uniform circular motion in the counterclockwise direction can be written

$$\mathbf{r}(t) = a(\cos\omega t\;\mathbf{i} + \sin\omega t\;\mathbf{j}).$$

Differentiation gives

$$\mathbf{v}(t) = a\omega(-\sin\omega t\;\mathbf{i} + \cos\omega t\;\mathbf{j}),$$

$$\mathbf{a}(t) = -a\omega^2(\cos\omega t\;\mathbf{i} + \sin\omega t\;\mathbf{j}) = -\omega^2\mathbf{r}(t).$$

The acceleration is directed along the line of the radius vector toward the center of the circle and is therefore perpendicular to the velocity vector, which, as always, is tangential. As you can verify, the speed is $a\omega$ and the magnitude of acceleration is $a\omega^2$.

Motion along a circular helix is a combination of circular motion and motion along a straight line.

Example 1 An object moves along a circular helix (Figure 14.3.12) with position at time t given by the function

$$\mathbf{r}(t) = a\cos\omega t\,\mathbf{i} + a\sin\omega t\,\mathbf{j} + b\omega t\,\mathbf{k}. \qquad (a > 0, b > 0, \omega > 0)$$

For each time t, find

(a) the velocity of the particle; **(b)** the speed; **(c)** the acceleration;

(d) the magnitude of the acceleration;

(e) the angle between the velocity vector and the acceleration vector.

SOLUTION

(a) Velocity: $\mathbf{v}(t) = \mathbf{r}'(t) = -a\omega\sin\omega t\,\mathbf{i} + a\omega\cos\omega t\,\mathbf{j} + b\omega\,\mathbf{k}$.

(b) Speed : $\|\mathbf{v}(t)\| = \sqrt{a^2\omega^2\sin^2\omega t + a^2\omega^2\cos^2\omega t + b^2\omega^2}$

$$= \sqrt{a^2\omega^2 + b^2\omega^2} = \omega\sqrt{a^2 + b^2}.$$

(Thus the speed is constant.)

(c) Acceleration : $\mathbf{a}(t) = \mathbf{v}'(t) = -a\omega^2\cos\omega t\,\mathbf{i} - a\omega^2\sin\omega t\,\mathbf{j}$

$$= -a\omega^2(\cos\omega t\,\mathbf{i} + \sin\omega t\,\mathbf{j}).$$

(Since the speed is constant, the acceleration comes entirely from the change in direction.)

(d) Magnitude of the acceleration: $\|\mathbf{a}(t)\| = a\omega^2$.

(e) Angle between $\mathbf{v}(t)$ and $\mathbf{a}(t)$:

$$\cos\theta = \frac{\mathbf{v}(t)}{\|\mathbf{v}(t)\|}\cdot\frac{\mathbf{a}(t)}{\|\mathbf{a}(t)\|}$$

$$= \left[\frac{-a\omega\sin\omega t\,\mathbf{i} + a\omega\cos\omega t\,\mathbf{j} + b\omega\,\mathbf{k}}{\omega\sqrt{a^2+b^2}}\right]\cdot\left[\frac{-a\omega^2(\cos\omega t\,\mathbf{i} + \sin\omega t\,\mathbf{j})}{a\omega^2}\right]$$

$$= \frac{a(\sin\omega t\cos\omega t - \cos\omega t\sin\omega t)}{\sqrt{a^2+b^2}} = 0.$$

Therefore $\theta = \frac{1}{2}\pi$. (At each point the acceleration is perpendicular to the velocity.) ❑

Curvature

Let

$$C: \qquad \mathbf{r} = \mathbf{r}(t), \qquad t \in I$$

be a twice differentiable curve with nonzero tangent vector $\mathbf{r}'(t)$. At each point the curve has a unit tangent vector $\mathbf{T}$. While $\mathbf{T}$ cannot change in length, it can change in direction. At each point of the curve the change in direction of $\mathbf{T}$ per unit of arc length is given by the derivative $d\mathbf{T}/ds$. The magnitude of this change in direction per unit of arc length, the number

$$\kappa = \left\|\frac{d\mathbf{T}}{ds}\right\|,$$

is called the *curvature* of the curve.†

†The symbol κ is the Greek letter "kappa."

As you would expect,

> along a straight line the curvature is constantly zero.

PROOF At each point of a line

$$\mathbf{r}(t) = \mathbf{r}_0 + t\,\mathbf{d}$$

the unit tangent vector $\mathbf{T}$ is the vector $\mathbf{d}/\|\mathbf{d}\|$. Since $\mathbf{T}$ is constant

$$\frac{d\mathbf{T}}{ds} = \mathbf{0} \qquad \text{and} \qquad \kappa = \left\|\frac{d\mathbf{T}}{ds}\right\| = 0. \quad \square$$

The Curvature of a Plane Curve

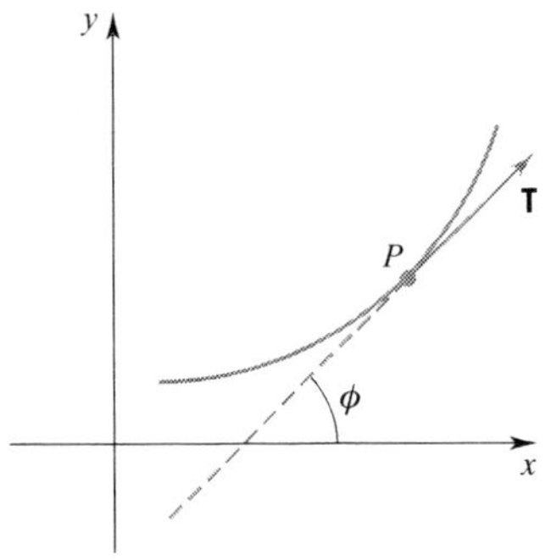

Figure 14.5.3

Figure 14.5.3 shows a plane curve. At a point P we have attached the unit tangent vector $\mathbf{T}$ and drawn the tangent line. The angle marked ϕ is the inclination of the tangent line measured in radians. As P moves along the curve, angle ϕ changes. *The curvature at P can be interpreted as the magnitude of the change in ϕ per unit of arc length.*

PROOF Since $\mathbf{T}$ has length 1, we can write

$$\mathbf{T} = \cos\phi\,\mathbf{i} + \sin\phi\,\mathbf{j}.^{\dagger}$$

Differentiation with respect to s gives

$$\frac{d\mathbf{T}}{ds} = -\sin\phi\frac{d\phi}{ds}\,\mathbf{i} + \cos\phi\frac{d\phi}{ds}\,\mathbf{j} = \frac{d\phi}{ds}(-\sin\phi\,\mathbf{i} + \cos\phi\,\mathbf{j}).$$

Taking norms we have

$$\kappa = \left\|\frac{d\mathbf{T}}{ds}\right\| = \left|\frac{d\phi}{ds}\right|\sqrt{\sin^2\phi + \cos^2\phi} = \left|\frac{d\phi}{ds}\right|. \quad \square$$

We will express the curvature κ of a plane curve

$$C: \qquad \mathbf{r}(t) = x(t)\,\mathbf{i} + y(t)\,\mathbf{j}$$

in terms of the components $x(t)$ and $y(t)$.

Suppose that C is twice differentiable. If C has nonzero tangent vector $\mathbf{r}'(t) = x'(t)\,\mathbf{i} + y'(t)\,\mathbf{j}$, then

(14.5.3)
$$\kappa = \frac{|x'(t)y''(t) - y'(t)x''(t)|}{([x'(t)]^2 + [y'(t)]^2)^{3/2}}.$$

PROOF We'll outline the argument and leave some details to you. We know that

$$\mathbf{T} = \frac{\mathbf{r}'(t)}{\|\mathbf{r}'(t)\|}.$$

Therefore

$$\frac{d\mathbf{T}}{dt} = \frac{d}{dt}\left(\frac{\mathbf{r}'(t)}{\|\mathbf{r}'(t)\|}\right).$$

---

†The direction angles are ϕ and $\frac{1}{2}\pi - \phi$. This expression for $\mathbf{T}$ follows from observing that $\cos(\frac{1}{2}\pi - \phi) = \sin\phi$.

It follows from (14.2.4) applied to $\mathbf{r}'(t)$ that

$$\frac{d\mathbf{T}}{dt} = \frac{1}{\|\mathbf{r}'(t)\|^3}[(\mathbf{r}'(t) \times \mathbf{r}''(t)) \times \mathbf{r}'(t)].$$

The relations

$$\frac{d\mathbf{T}}{dt} = \frac{d\mathbf{T}}{ds}\frac{ds}{dt} \quad \text{and} \quad \frac{ds}{dt} = \|\mathbf{r}'(t)\|$$

give

$$\frac{d\mathbf{T}}{ds} = \frac{1}{\|\mathbf{r}'(t)\|^4}[(\mathbf{r}'(t) \times \mathbf{r}''(t)) \times \mathbf{r}'(t)]$$

and

$$\kappa = \frac{1}{\|\mathbf{r}'(t)\|^4}\|(\mathbf{r}'(t) \times \mathbf{r}''(t)) \times \mathbf{r}'(t)\|.$$

Substitute

$$x'(t)\,\mathbf{i} + y'(t)\,\mathbf{j} \quad \text{for} \quad \mathbf{r}'(t) \qquad \text{and} \qquad x''(t)\,\mathbf{i} + y''(t)\,\mathbf{j} \quad \text{for} \quad \mathbf{r}''(t)$$

and you'll find out that this expression for κ gives (14.5.3). ❑

For the graph of a twice differentiable function $y = f(x)$,

(14.5.4)

$$\boxed{\kappa = \frac{|y''(x)|}{(1 + [y'(x)]^2)^{3/2}}.}$$

PROOF Parametrize the graph by setting

$$\mathbf{r}(t) = t\,\mathbf{i} + y(t)\,\mathbf{j}.$$

Here $x'(t) = 1$ and $x''(t) = 0$. Then (14.5.3) gives

$$\kappa = \frac{|y''(t)|}{(1 + [y'(t)]^2)^{3/2}}.$$

Now replace t by x. ❑

Example 2 In the case of a circle of radius r,

$$\mathbf{r}(t) = r(\cos t\,\mathbf{i} + \sin t\,\mathbf{j}),$$

we have

$$x(t) = r\cos t \quad \text{and} \quad y(t) = r\sin t.$$

Differentiation gives

$$x'(t) = -r\sin t, \qquad x''(t) = -r\cos t, \qquad y'(t) = r\cos t, \qquad y''(t) = -r\sin t.$$

It follows that

$$\kappa = \frac{|(-r\sin t)(-r\sin t) - (r\cos t)(-r\cos t)|}{[(-r\sin t)^2 + (r\cos t)^2]^{3/2}} = \frac{r^2}{r^3} = \frac{1}{r}. \quad ❑$$

We have just proved that

> along a circle of radius r the curvature is constantly $1/r$.

Hardly surprising. It is geometrically evident that along a circular path the change in direction takes place at a constant rate. Since a complete revolution entails a change of direction of 2π radians and this change is effected on a path of length $2\pi r$, the change in direction per unit of arc length is $2\pi/2\pi r = 1/r$.

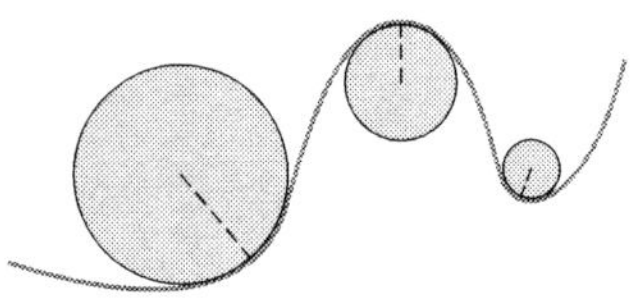

Figure 14.5.4

To say that a curve $y = f(x)$ has slope m at a point P is to say that at the point P the curve is rising or falling at the rate of a line of slope m. To say that a plane curve C has curvature $1/a$ at a point P is to say that at the point P the curve is turning at the rate of a circle of radius a. (Figure 14.5.4.) The smaller the circle, the tighter the turn and, thus, the greater the curvature.

Example 3 Calculate the curvature at each point (x, y) of the ellipse

$$\frac{x^2}{a^2} + \frac{y^2}{b^2} = 1.$$

SOLUTION We parametrize the ellipse by setting

$$\mathbf{r}(t) = a\cos t\,\mathbf{i} + b\sin t\,\mathbf{j}$$

and use (14.5.3). Here

$$x = a\cos t, \qquad y = b\sin t.$$

Therefore

$$x' = -a\sin t, \qquad x'' = -a\cos t, \qquad y' = b\cos t, \qquad y'' = -b\sin t$$

and

$$\kappa = \frac{|(-a\sin t)(-b\sin t) - (b\cos t)(-a\cos t)|}{[(-a\sin t)^2 + (b\cos t)^2]^{3/2}} = \frac{ab}{[a^2\sin^2 t + b^2\cos^2 t]^{3/2}}.$$

As you can check, the curvature at each point $P(x, y)$ can be written

$$\kappa = \frac{a^4b^4}{(b^4x^2 + a^4y^2)^{3/2}}. \quad \square$$

Calculating the Curvature of a Space Curve

The generalization of (14.5.3) to space curves

$$\mathbf{r}(t) = x(t)\,\mathbf{i} + y(t)\,\mathbf{j} + z(t)\,\mathbf{k}$$

leads to a complicated formula that is burdensome to state and burdensome to apply. Instead we go back to the definition

$$\kappa = \left\| \frac{d\mathbf{T}}{ds} \right\|.$$

Since

$$\frac{d\mathbf{T}}{dt} = \frac{d\mathbf{T}}{ds}\frac{ds}{dt},$$

we have

$$\left\|\frac{d\mathbf{T}}{dt}\right\| = \left\|\frac{d\mathbf{T}}{ds}\right\|\frac{ds}{dt} = \kappa\frac{ds}{dt}$$

and therefore

(14.5.5)
$$\boxed{\kappa = \frac{\|d\mathbf{T}/dt\|}{ds/dt}.}$$

Example 4 Calculate the curvature of the circular helix

$$\mathbf{r}(t) = a\sin t\,\mathbf{i} + a\cos t\,\mathbf{j} + t\,\mathbf{k}. \qquad (a > 0)$$

SOLUTION We will use the Leibniz notation. Here

$$\frac{d\mathbf{r}}{dt} = a\cos t\,\mathbf{i} - a\sin t\,\mathbf{j} + \mathbf{k}, \qquad \frac{ds}{dt} = \left\|\frac{d\mathbf{r}}{dt}\right\| = \sqrt{a^2+1}$$

$$\mathbf{T} = \frac{d\mathbf{r}/dt}{\|d\mathbf{r}/dt\|} = \frac{a\cos t\,\mathbf{i} - a\sin t\,\mathbf{j} + \mathbf{k}}{\sqrt{a^2+1}}$$

$$\frac{d\mathbf{T}}{dt} = \frac{-a\sin t\,\mathbf{i} - a\cos t\,\mathbf{j}}{\sqrt{a^2+1}} \quad \text{and} \quad \left\|\frac{d\mathbf{T}}{dt}\right\| = \frac{a}{\sqrt{a^2+1}}.$$

Therefore

$$\kappa = \frac{\|d\mathbf{T}/dt\|}{ds/dt} = \frac{a/\sqrt{a^2+1}}{\sqrt{a^2+1}} = \frac{a}{a^2+1}.$$

The circular helix is a curve of constant curvature. ❑

Components of Acceleration

In straight-line motion, acceleration is purely tangential; that is, the acceleration vector points along the line of the motion. In uniform circular motion, the acceleration is normal; the acceleration vector is perpendicular to the tangent vector and points along the line of the normal vector toward the center of the circle.

In general, acceleration has two components, a tangential component and a normal component. To see this, let's suppose that the position of an object at time t is given by the vector function

$$\mathbf{r}(t) = x(t)\,\mathbf{i} + y(t)\,\mathbf{j} + z(t)\,\mathbf{k}.$$

Since

$$\mathbf{T} = \frac{d\mathbf{r}/dt}{\|d\mathbf{r}/dt\|} = \frac{\mathbf{v}}{ds/dt},$$

we have

$$\mathbf{v} = \frac{ds}{dt}\mathbf{T}.$$

Differentiation gives

$$\mathbf{a} = \frac{d^2s}{dt^2}\mathbf{T} + \frac{ds}{dt}\frac{d\mathbf{T}}{dt}.$$

Observe now that

$$\frac{d\mathbf{T}}{dt} = \left\|\frac{d\mathbf{T}}{dt}\right\| \mathbf{N} = \kappa \frac{ds}{dt}\mathbf{N}.$$

(14.3.5) ↑ ↑ (14.5.5)

Substitution in the previous display gives

(14.5.6)
$$\mathbf{a} = \frac{d^2s}{dt^2}\mathbf{T} + \kappa\left(\frac{ds}{dt}\right)^2 \mathbf{N}.$$

The acceleration vector lies in the osculating plane, the plane of **T** and **N**. The tangential component of acceleration,

$$a_{\mathbf{T}} = \frac{d^2s}{dt^2},$$

depends only on the change of speed of the object; if the speed is constant, the tangential component of acceleration is zero and the acceleration is directed entirely toward the center of curvature of the path. On the other hand, the normal component of acceleration,

$$a_{\mathbf{N}} = \kappa\left(\frac{ds}{dt}\right)^2,$$

depends on both the speed of the object and the curvature of the path. At a point where the curvature is zero, the normal component of acceleration is zero and the acceleration is directed entirely along the path of motion. If the curvature is not zero, then the normal component of acceleration is a multiple of the *square* of the speed. This means, for example, that if you are in a car going around a curve at 50 miles per hour, you will feel *four times* the normal component of acceleration that you would feel going around the same curve at 25 miles per hour.

We can use (14.5.6) to obtain alternative formulas for $a_{\mathbf{T}}$, $a_{\mathbf{N}}$, and the curvature κ.

If we take the dot product of **T** with **a**, we get

$$\mathbf{T}\cdot\mathbf{a} = a_{\mathbf{T}}(\mathbf{T}\cdot\mathbf{T}) + a_{\mathbf{N}}(\mathbf{T}\cdot\mathbf{N}) = a_{\mathbf{T}}.$$

Therefore,

(14.5.7)
$$a_{\mathbf{T}} = \mathbf{T}\cdot\mathbf{a} = \frac{\mathbf{v}\cdot\mathbf{a}}{\|\mathbf{v}\|} = \frac{\mathbf{v}\cdot\mathbf{a}}{(ds/dt)}.$$

Crossing **T** with **a**, we get

$$\mathbf{T}\times\mathbf{a} = a_{\mathbf{T}}(\mathbf{T}\times\mathbf{T}) + a_{\mathbf{N}}(\mathbf{T}\times\mathbf{N}) = a_{\mathbf{N}}(\mathbf{T}\times\mathbf{N})$$

and so

$$\|\mathbf{T}\times\mathbf{a}\| = a_{\mathbf{N}}\|\mathbf{T}\times\mathbf{N}\| = a_{\mathbf{N}}\|\mathbf{T}\|\,\|\mathbf{N}\|\sin(\pi/2) = a_{\mathbf{N}}.$$

Therefore

(14.5.8)
$$a_{\mathbf{N}} = \|\mathbf{T}\times\mathbf{a}\| = \frac{\|\mathbf{v}\times\mathbf{a}\|}{\|\mathbf{v}\|} = \frac{\|\mathbf{v}\times\mathbf{a}\|}{(ds/dt)}.$$

Since $a_{\mathbf{N}} = \kappa(ds/dt)^2$, it follows that

(14.5.9)
$$\kappa = \frac{\|\mathbf{v} \times \mathbf{a}\|}{(ds/dt)^3}.$$

Example 5 The position of a moving object at time t is given by

$$\mathbf{r}(t) = \ln t\,\mathbf{i} + 2t\,\mathbf{j} + t^2\,\mathbf{k}, \qquad t > 0.$$

Find the tangential and normal components of acceleration and the curvature of the path of the object at time $t = 1$.

SOLUTION $\mathbf{r}'(t) = \mathbf{v}(t) = \dfrac{1}{t}\mathbf{i} + 2\,\mathbf{j} + 2t\,\mathbf{k}$ and $\mathbf{r}''(t) = -\dfrac{1}{t^2}\mathbf{i} + 2\,\mathbf{k}.$

At $t = 1$

$$\mathbf{v} = \mathbf{i} + 2\,\mathbf{j} + 2\,\mathbf{k} \qquad \|\mathbf{v}\| = ds/dt = \sqrt{9} = 3 \qquad \mathbf{a} = -\mathbf{i} + 2\,\mathbf{k}$$

$$a_{\mathbf{T}} = \frac{\mathbf{v}\cdot\mathbf{a}}{(ds/dt)} = \frac{-1+4}{3} = 1$$

$$a_{\mathbf{N}} = \frac{\|\mathbf{v} \times \mathbf{a}\|}{(ds/dt)} = \tfrac{1}{3}\left\| \begin{vmatrix} \mathbf{i} & \mathbf{j} & \mathbf{k} \\ 1 & 2 & 2 \\ -1 & 0 & 2 \end{vmatrix} \right\| = \tfrac{1}{3}\|4\,\mathbf{i} - 4\,\mathbf{j} + 2\,\mathbf{k}\| = \frac{\sqrt{36}}{3} = 2$$

$$\kappa = \frac{\|\mathbf{v} \times \mathbf{a}\|}{(ds/dt)^3} = \frac{\sqrt{36}}{27} = \frac{2}{9}. \quad \square$$

EXERCISES 14.5

1. A particle moves in a circle of radius a at constant speed v. Find the angular speed and the magnitude of the acceleration.

2. A particle moves so that

$$\mathbf{r}(t) = (a\cos\pi t + bt^2)\,\mathbf{i} + (a\sin\pi t - bt^2)\,\mathbf{j}.$$

Find the velocity, speed, acceleration, and the magnitude of the acceleration all at time $t = 1$.

3. A particle moves so that $\mathbf{r}(t) = at\,\mathbf{i} + b\sin at\,\mathbf{j}$. Show that the magnitude of the acceleration of the particle is proportional to its distance from the x-axis.

4. A particle moves so that $\mathbf{r}(t) = 2\,\mathbf{i} + t^2\,\mathbf{j} + (t-1)^2\,\mathbf{k}$. At what time is the speed a minimum?

Exercises 5–8. View the curve as the path of a moving object. Sketch the curve. Then calculate and draw in the acceleration vector at the points indicated.

5. $\mathbf{r}(t) = (t/\pi)\,\mathbf{i} + \cos t\,\mathbf{j}, \quad t \in [0, 2\pi]; \quad$ at $t = \frac{1}{4}\pi, \frac{1}{2}\pi, \pi$.

6. $\mathbf{r}(t) = t^3\,\mathbf{i} + t\,\mathbf{j}, \quad t$ treal; $\quad$ at $t = -\frac{1}{2}, \frac{1}{2}, 1$.

7. $\mathbf{r}(t) = \sec t\,\mathbf{i} + \tan t\,\mathbf{j}, \ t \in [-\frac{1}{4}\pi, \frac{1}{2}\pi)$; at $t = -\frac{1}{6}\pi, 0, \frac{1}{3}\pi$.

8. $\mathbf{r}(t) = \sin\pi t\,\mathbf{i} + t\,\mathbf{j}, \quad t \in [0, 2]; \quad$ at $t = \frac{1}{2}, 1, \frac{5}{4}$.

9. An object moves so that

$$\mathbf{r}(t) = x_0\,\mathbf{i} + [y_0 + (\alpha\cos\theta)t]\,\mathbf{j} + [z_0 + (\alpha\sin\theta)t - 16t^2]\,\mathbf{k}, \qquad t \geq 0.$$

Find (a) the initial position, (b) the initial velocity, (c) the initial speed, (d) the acceleration throughout the motion. Finally, (e) identify the curve.

10. A particle moves so that $\mathbf{r}(t) = 2\cos 2t\,\mathbf{i} + 3\cos t\,\mathbf{j}$. (a) Show that the particle oscillates on an arc of the parabola $4y^2 - 9x = 18$. (b) Draw the path. (c) What are the acceleration vectors at the points of zero velocity? (d) Draw these vectors at the points in question.

11. Let $\mathbf{r}(t)$ be the position vector of a moving particle. Show that $\|\mathbf{r}(t)\|$ is constant iff $\mathbf{r}(t) \perp \mathbf{r}'(t)$.

12. Let $\mathbf{r}(t)$ be the position vector of a moving particle. Show that if the speed of the particle is constant, then the velocity vector is perpendicular to the acceleration vector.

Exercises 13–20. Calculate the curvature from (14.5.4).

13. $y = e^{-x}$. **14.** $y = x^3$.

15. $y = \sqrt{x}$. **16.** $y = x - x^2$.

17. $y = \ln\sec x$. **18.** $y = \tan x$.

19. $y = \sin x$. **20.** $x^2 - y^2 = a^2$.

Exercises 21–26. Calculate the curvature at the point indicated.

21. $6y = x^3; \quad (2, \frac{4}{3})$. **22.** $2y = x^2; \quad (0, 0)$.

23. $y^2 = 2x; \quad (2, 2)$. **24.** $y = 2\sin 2x; \quad (\frac{1}{2}\pi, 2)$.

25. $y = \ln(x+1); \quad (2, \ln 3)$. **26.** $y = \sec x; \quad (\frac{1}{4}\pi, \sqrt{2})$.

27. Find the point of maximal curvature on the curve $y = \ln x$.

28. Find the curvature of the graph of $y = 3x - x^3$ at the point where the function takes on a local maximum.

Exercises 29–36. Express the curvature in terms of t.

29. $\mathbf{r}(t) = t\,\mathbf{i} + \frac{1}{2}t^2\,\mathbf{j}$.

30. $\mathbf{r}(t) = e^t\,\mathbf{i} + e^{-t}\,\mathbf{j}$.

31. $\mathbf{r}(t) = 2t\,\mathbf{i} + t^3\,\mathbf{j}$.

32. $\mathbf{r}(t) = t^2\,\mathbf{i} + t^3\,\mathbf{j}$.

33. $\mathbf{r}(t) = e^t(\cos t\,\mathbf{i} + \sin t\,\mathbf{j})$.

34. $\mathbf{r}(t) = 2\cos t\,\mathbf{i} + 3\sin t\,\mathbf{j}$.

35. $\mathbf{r}(t) = (t\cos t)\,\mathbf{i} + (t\sin t)\,\mathbf{j}$.

36. $\mathbf{r}(t) = (\cos t + t\sin t)\,\mathbf{i} + (\sin t - t\cos t)\,\mathbf{j},\ t > 0$.

37. Find the curvature of the hyperbola $xy = 1$ at the points $(1, 1)$ and $(-1, -1)$.

38. Find the curvature at the vertices of the hyperbola $x^2 - y^2 = 1$.

39. Find the curvature at each point (x, y) on the hyperbola $b^2x^2 - a^2y^2 = a^2b^2$. HINT: The vector function $\mathbf{r}(t) = a\cosh t\,\mathbf{i} + b\sinh t\,\mathbf{j}$ parametrizes the curve.

40. Find the curvature at the highest point of an arch of the cycloid

$$x(t) = r(t - \sin)t, \quad y(t) = r(1 - \cos t).$$

Exercises 41–47. Interpret $\mathbf{r}(t)$ as the position of a moving object at time t. Find the curvature of the path and determine the tangential and normal components of acceleration.

41. $\mathbf{r}(t) = e^t\cos t\,\mathbf{i} + e^t\sin t\,\mathbf{j} + e^t\,\mathbf{k}$.

42. $\mathbf{r}(t) = \sinh t\,\mathbf{i} + \cosh t\,\mathbf{j} + t\,\mathbf{k}$.

43. $\mathbf{r}(t) = \cos 2t\,\mathbf{i} + \sin 2t\,\mathbf{j} + \mathbf{k}$.

44. $\mathbf{r}(t) = 2t\,\mathbf{i} + t^2\,\mathbf{j} + \ln t\,\mathbf{k}$.

45. $\cos 3t\,\mathbf{i} + 4t\,\mathbf{j} - \sin 3t\,\mathbf{k}$.

46. $\mathbf{r}(t) = (\cos t + t\sin t)\,\mathbf{i} + (\sin t - t\cos t)\,\mathbf{j} + \frac{1}{2}\sqrt{3}t^2\,\mathbf{k}$, from $t = 0$ to $t = 2\pi$.

47. $\mathbf{r}(t) = \frac{2}{3}(1 + t)^{3/2}\,\mathbf{i} + \frac{2}{3}(1 - t)^{3/2}\,\mathbf{j} + \sqrt{2}\,t\,\mathbf{k}$.

For Exercises 48–49, interpret $\mathbf{r}(t) = 6t\,\mathbf{i} + 3t^2\,\mathbf{j} + 2t^3\,\mathbf{k}$ as the position of a moving object at time t.

48. (a) Use a graphing utility to draw the curve of motion.
(b) Use a CAS to find the maximum curvature of the curve.

49. Use a CAS to find the tangential and normal components of the acceleration of the object.

50. Show that the curvature of a polar curve $r = f(\theta)$ is given by

$$\kappa = \frac{|[f(\theta)]^2 + 2[f'(\theta)]^2 - f(\theta)f''(\theta)|}{([f(\theta)]^2 + [f'(\theta)]^2)^{3/2}}.$$

51. Find the curvature of the logarithmic spiral $r = e^{a\theta}$. Take $a > 0$.

52. Find the curvature of the spiral of Archimedes $r = a\theta$. Take $a > 0$.

53. Express the curvature of the cardioid $r = a(1 - \cos\theta)$ in terms of r.

54. Find the curvature of the petal curve $r = a\sin 2\theta$, $a > 0$.

■ PROJECT 14.5A Transition Curves

In the design of an automobile fender, engineers face the problem of connecting curved pieces in a smooth and elegant manner. In this context problems of the following sort arise.

The total curve of a fender is to be made up of two pieces, each bounded by the graph of a cubic polynomial. The first piece p is to begin at the point $(1, 3)$ and end at the point $(3, 7)$. This requires that $p(1) = 3$ and $p(3) = 7$. The second piece q is to meet the first piece at the point $(3, 7)$ and end at the point $(9, -2)$. This requires that $q(3) = 7$ and $q(9) = -2$. The two pieces must meet smoothly. This requires that $p'(3) = q'(3)$ and $p''(3) = q''(3)$. Finally, the fender must be straight at the ends. This requires that $p''(1) = 0$ and $q''(9) = 0$. A curve that meets such requirements is called a *cubic spline*.

Problem 1. Let

$$p(x) = ax^3 + bx^2 + cx + d \quad \text{and}$$
$$q(x) = \alpha x^3 + \beta x^2 + \gamma x + \delta.$$

Write the system of equations generated by the conditions specified above and use a CAS to find a solution to the system.

Problem 2. Set

$$F(x) = \begin{cases} p(x), & 1 \le x \le 3 \\ q(x), & 3 \le x \le 9. \end{cases}$$

Show that F, F', and F'' are continuous on $[1, 9]$. Does F have continuous curvature? Sketch the graph of F using a graphing utility.

Problem 3. You are given the data in the table:

x	3	4	6
y	10	15	35

a. Define a cubic polynomial p on $[3, 4]$ and a cubic polynomial q on $[4, 6]$ that satisfy the data in the table.

b. Write the 8×8 system of equations as in Problem 1.

c. Use a CAS to solve the system.

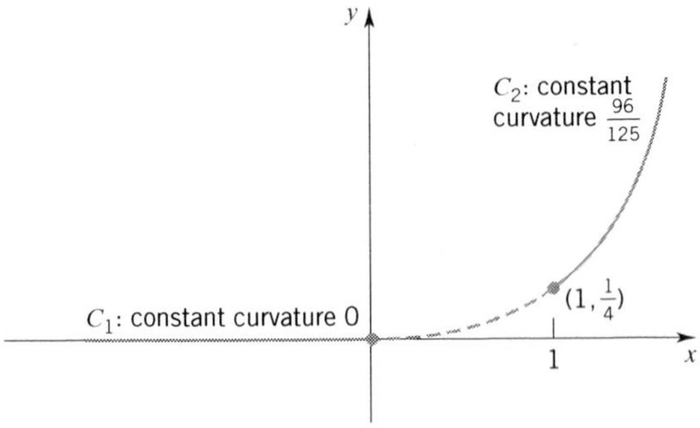

When engineers lay railroad track, they cannot allow any abrupt changes in curvature. To join a straight away that ends at a point P to a curved track that begins at a point Q, they need to lay some *transitional track* that has zero curvature at P and the curvature of the second piece at Q.

Problem 4. Find an arc of the form $y = Cx^n$, $x \in [0, 1]$ that joins the arcs C_1 and C_2 in the figure without any discontinuities in curvature.

■ PROJECT 14.5B The Frenet Formulas

A space curve bends in two ways. It bends in the osculating plane (the plane of the unit tangent **T** and the principal normal **N**) and it bends away from that plane. The first form of bending is measured by the change in **T** per unit of arc length. The magnitude of this change is the curvature κ. The second form of bending is measured by the change in $\mathbf{T} \times \mathbf{N}$ per unit of arc length. Here we examine both forms of bending.

The figure shows a space curve. At a point of the curve we have drawn the unit tangent, **T**, the principal normal, **N**, and the unit vector $\mathbf{B} = \mathbf{T} \times \mathbf{N}$, which, being normal to both **T** and **N**, is called the *binormal*. At each point of the curve, the vectors **T**, **N**, **B** form what is called the *Frenet frame*, a set of mutually perpendicular vectors that, in the order given, form a right-handed coordinate system.

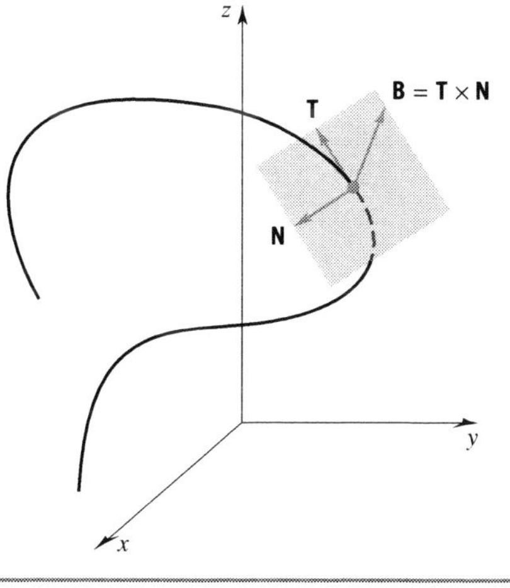

Problem 1. Show that

$$\frac{d\mathbf{T}}{ds} = \kappa\mathbf{N}.$$

Problem 2. Show that $d\mathbf{B}/ds$ is parallel to **N**, and therefore there is a scalar τ† for which

$$\frac{d\mathbf{B}}{ds} = \tau\mathbf{N}.$$

HINT: Since **B** has constant length one, $d\mathbf{B}/ds \perp \mathbf{B}$. Show that $d\mathbf{B}/ds \perp \mathbf{T}$ by carrying out the differentiation

$$\frac{d\mathbf{B}}{ds} = \frac{d}{ds}(\mathbf{T} \times \mathbf{N}).$$

Problem 3. Now show that

$$\frac{d\mathbf{N}}{ds} = -\kappa\mathbf{T} - \tau\mathbf{B}.$$

HINT: Since **T**, **N**, **B** form a right handed system of mutually perpendicular unit vectors, we can show that

$$\mathbf{N} \times \mathbf{B} = \mathbf{T} \qquad \text{and} \qquad \mathbf{B} \times \mathbf{T} = \mathbf{N}.$$

You can assume these relations.

Problem 4. The scalar τ is called the *torsion* of the curve. Give a geometric interpretation to $|\tau|$.

† τ is the Greek letter "tau."

■ 14.6 VECTOR CALCULUS IN MECHANICS

The tools we have developed in the preceding sections have their premier application in Newtonian mechanics, the study of bodies in motion subject to Newton's laws. The heart of Newton's mechanics is his second law of motion:

$$\text{force} = \text{mass} \times \text{acceleration}.$$

We have worked with Newton's second law, but only in a very restricted context: motion along a coordinate line under the influence of a force directed along that same line. In that special setting, Newton's law was written as a scalar equation: $F = ma$. In general, objects do not move along straight lines (they move along curved paths) and the forces on them vary in direction. What happens to Newton's second law then? It becomes the vector equation

$$\mathbf{F} = m\mathbf{a}.$$

This is Newton's second law in its full glory.

An Introduction to Vector Mechanics

We are now ready to work with Newton's second law of motion in its vector form: $\mathbf{F} = m\mathbf{a}$. Since at each time t we have $\mathbf{a}(t) = \mathbf{r}''(t)$, Newton's law can be written

$$\mathbf{F}(t) = m\,\mathbf{a}(t) = m\,\mathbf{r}''(t). \tag{14.6.1}$$

This is a second-order differential equation.

When objects are moving, certain quantities (positions, velocities, and so on) are continually changing. This can make a situation difficult to grasp. In these circumstances it is particularly satisfying to find quantities that do not change. Such quantities are said to be *conserved*. (These conserved quantities are called the *constants of the motion*.) Mathematically we can determine whether a quantity is conserved by looking at its derivative with respect to time (the time derivative): *The quantity is conserved (is constant) iff its time derivative remains zero*. A *conservation law* is the assertion that in a given context a certain quantity does not change.

Momentum

We start with the idea of momentum. The *momentum* $\mathbf{p}$ of an object is the mass of the object times the velocity of the object:

$$\mathbf{p} = m\mathbf{v}.$$

To indicate the time dependence we write

$$\mathbf{p}(t) = m\mathbf{v}(t) = m\mathbf{r}'(t). \tag{14.6.2}$$

Assume that the mass of the object is constant. Then differentiation gives

$$\mathbf{p}'(t) = m\mathbf{r}''(t) = \mathbf{F}(t).$$

Thus, *the time derivative of the momentum of an object is the net force on the object*. If the net force on an object is continually zero, the momentum $\mathbf{p}(t)$ is constant. This is the law of *conservation of momentum*:

(14.6.3) If the net force on an object is continually zero, then the momentum of the object is conserved.

Angular Momentum

The angular momentum of an object about any given point is a vector quantity that is intended to measure the extent to which the object is circling about that point. If the position of the object at time t is given by the radius vector $\mathbf{r}(t)$, then the object's *angular momentum about the origin* is defined by the formula

(14.6.4)
$$\mathbf{L}(t) = \mathbf{r}(t) \times \mathbf{p}(t) = \mathbf{r}(t) \times m\mathbf{v}(t).$$

At each time t of a motion, $\mathbf{L}(t)$ is perpendicular to $\mathbf{r}(t)$, perpendicular to $\mathbf{v}(t)$, and directed so that $\mathbf{r}(t), \mathbf{v}(t), \mathbf{L}(t)$ form a right-handed triple. The magnitude of $\mathbf{L}(t)$ is given by the relation

$$\|\mathbf{L}(t)\| = \|\mathbf{r}(t)\|\,\|m\mathbf{v}(t)\|\sin\theta(t)$$

where $\theta(t)$ is the angle between $\mathbf{r}(t)$ and $\mathbf{v}(t)$. (All this, of course, comes from the definition of the cross product.)

If $\mathbf{r}(t)$ and $\mathbf{v}(t)$ are not zero, then we can express $\mathbf{v}(t)$ as a vector parallel to $\mathbf{r}(t)$ plus a vector perpendicular to $\mathbf{r}(t)$:

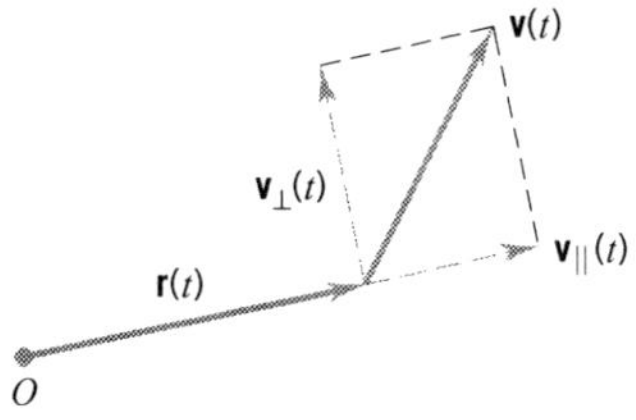

Figure 14.6.1

$$\mathbf{v}(t) = \mathbf{v}_{\parallel}(t) + \mathbf{v}_{\perp}(t).$$ (See Figure 14.6.1.)

Thus

$$\begin{aligned}\mathbf{L}(t) &= \mathbf{r}(t) \times m\mathbf{v}(t)\\ &= \mathbf{r}(t) \times m[\mathbf{v}_{\parallel}(t) + \mathbf{v}_{\perp}(t)]\\ &= \underbrace{[\mathbf{r}(t) \times m\mathbf{v}_{\parallel}(t)]}_{0} + [\mathbf{r}(t) \times m\mathbf{v}_{\perp}(t)]\\ &= \mathbf{r}(t) \times m\mathbf{v}_{\perp}(t).\end{aligned}$$

The component of velocity that is parallel to the radius vector contributes nothing to angular momentum. *The angular momentum comes entirely from the component of velocity that is perpendicular to the radius vector.*

Example 1 In uniform circular motion about the origin,

$$\mathbf{r}(t) = a(\cos\omega t\,\mathbf{i} + \sin\omega t\,\mathbf{j}),$$

the velocity vector $\mathbf{v}(t)$ is always perpendicular to the radius vector $\mathbf{r}(t)$. In this case all of $\mathbf{v}(t)$ contributes to the angular momentum.

We can calculate $\mathbf{L}(t)$ as follows:

$$\begin{aligned}\mathbf{L}(t) &= \mathbf{r}(t) \times m\mathbf{v}(t)\\ &= [a(\cos\omega t\,\mathbf{i} + \sin\omega t\,\mathbf{j})] \times [ma(-\omega\sin\omega t\,\mathbf{i} + \omega\cos\omega t\,\mathbf{j})]\\ &= ma^2\omega(\cos^2\omega t + \sin^2\omega t)\,\mathbf{k} = ma^2\,\omega\,\mathbf{k}.\end{aligned}$$

The angular momentum is constant and is perpendicular to the xy-plane. If the motion is counterclockwise (if $\omega > 0$), then the angular momentum points up from the xy-plane. If the motion is clockwise (if $\omega < 0$), then the angular momentum points down from the xy-plane. (This is the right-handedness of the cross product coming in.) ❑

Example 2 In uniform straight-line motion with constant velocity $\mathbf{d}$,

$$\mathbf{r}(t) = \mathbf{r}_0 + t\mathbf{d},$$

we have

$$\mathbf{L}(t) = \mathbf{r}(t) \times m\mathbf{v}(t) = (\mathbf{r}_0 + t\mathbf{d}) \times m\mathbf{d} = m(\mathbf{r}_0 \times \mathbf{d}).$$

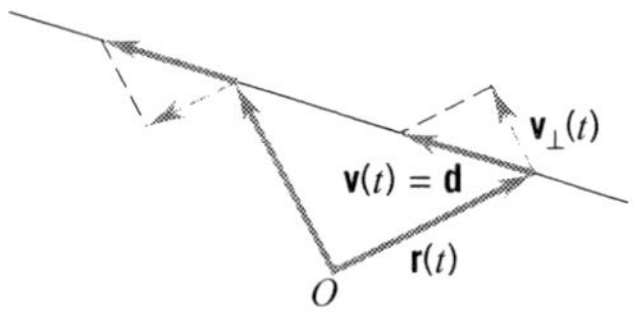

Figure 14.6.2

Here again the angular momentum is constant, but all is not quite so simple as it seems. In Figure 14.6.2 you can see the radius vector $\mathbf{r}(t)$, the velocity vector $\mathbf{v}(t) = \mathbf{d}$, and the part of the velocity vector that gives rise to angular momentum, the part perpendicular to $\mathbf{r}(t)$. As before, we have called this $\mathbf{v}_{\perp}(t)$. While $\mathbf{v}(t)$ is constant, $\mathbf{v}_{\perp}(t)$ is not constant. What happens here is that $\mathbf{r}(t)$ and $\mathbf{v}_{\perp}(t)$ vary in such a way that the cross product

$$\mathbf{L}(t) = \mathbf{r}(t) \times m\mathbf{v}_{\perp}(t)$$

remains constant. If the line of motion passes through the origin, then $\mathbf{v}(t)$ is parallel to $\mathbf{r}(t)$, $\mathbf{v}_{\perp}(t)$ is zero, and the angular momentum is zero. ❑

Torque

How the angular momentum of an object changes in time depends on the force acting on the object and on the position of the object relative to the origin that we are using. Since $\mathbf{L}(t) = \mathbf{r}(t) \times m\mathbf{r}'(t)$,

$$\mathbf{L}'(t) = [\mathbf{r}(t) \times m\mathbf{r}''(t)] + \underbrace{[\mathbf{r}'(t) \times m\mathbf{r}'(t)]}_{0} = \mathbf{r}(t) \times \mathbf{F}(t).$$

The cross product

(14.6.5) $$\tau(t) = \mathbf{r}(t) \times \mathbf{F}(t)$$

is called the *torque* about the origin[†]

Since $\mathbf{L}'(t) = \tau(t)$, we have the following conservation law:

(14.6.6) If the net torque on an object is continually zero, then the angular momentum of the object is conserved.

A force $\mathbf{F} = \mathbf{F}(t)$ is called a *central force (radial force)* if $\mathbf{F}(t)$ is always parallel to $\mathbf{r}(t)$. (Gravitational force, for example, is a central force.) For a central force, the cross product $\mathbf{r}(t) \times \mathbf{F}(t)$ is always zero. Thus a central force produces no torque about the origin. As you will see, this places severe restrictions on the kind of motion possible under a central force.

THEOREM 14.6.7

If an object moves under a central force and has constant angular momentum $\mathbf{L}$ different from zero, then:

1. The object is confined to the plane that passes through the origin and is perpendicular to $\mathbf{L}$.
2. The radius vector of the object sweeps out equal areas in equal times.

(This theorem plays an important role in astronomy and is embodied in Kepler's three celebrated laws of planetary motion. We will study Kepler's laws in Section *14.7.)

[†]The symbol τ is the Greek letter "tau". The word *torque* comes from the Latin word *torquere*, "to twist."

PROOF OF THEOREM 14.6.7 The first assertion is easy to verify: all the radius vectors pass through the origin, and (by the very definition of angular momentum) they are all perpendicular to the constant vector **L**.

To verify the second assertion, we introduce a right-handed coordinate system O-xyz setting the xy-plane as the plane of the motion, the positive z-axis pointing along **L**. On the xy-plane we introduce polar coordinates r, θ. Thus, at time t, the object has some position $[r(t), \theta(t)]$.

Let's denote by $A(t)$ the area swept out by the radius vector from some fixed time t_0 up to time t. Our task is to show that $A'(t)$ is constant.

The area swept out during the time interval $[t, t+h]$ is simply

$$A(t+h) - A(t).$$

Assuming that the motion takes place in the direction of increasing polar angle θ (see Figure 14.6.3), we have with obvious notation,

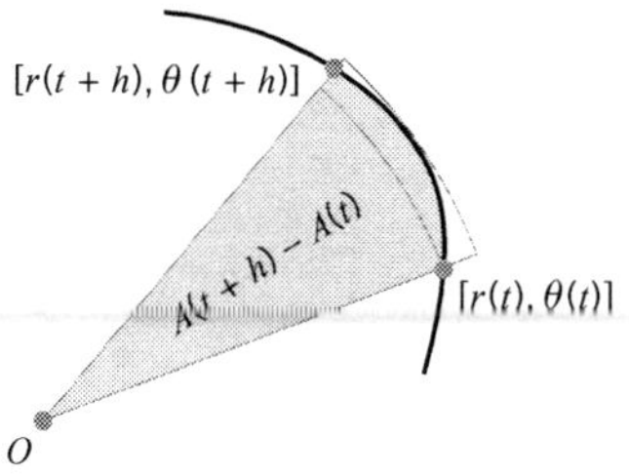

Figure 14.6.3

$$\underbrace{\tfrac{1}{2}\min\,[r(t)]^2 \cdot [\theta(t+h) - \theta(t)]}_{\text{area of inner sector}} \le A(t+h) - A(t) \le \underbrace{\tfrac{1}{2}\max\,[r(t)]^2 \cdot [\theta(t+h) - \theta(t)]}_{\text{area of outer sector}}.$$

Divide through by h, take the limit as h tends to 0, and you will see that

$$(*) \qquad A'(t) = \tfrac{1}{2}[r(t)]^2\theta'(t).$$

Note that

$$\begin{aligned}\mathbf{r}(t) &= r(t)[\cos\theta(t)\,\mathbf{i} + \sin\theta(t)\,\mathbf{j}]\\ \mathbf{v}(t) &= r'(t)[\cos\theta(t)\,\mathbf{i} + \sin\theta(t)\,\mathbf{j}] + r(t)\theta'(t)[-\sin\theta(t)\,\mathbf{i} + \cos\theta(t)\,\mathbf{j}]\\ &= [r'(t)\cos\theta(t) - r(t)\theta'(t)\sin\theta(t)]\,\mathbf{i} + [r'(t)\sin\theta(t) + r(t)\theta'(t)\cos\theta(t)]\,\mathbf{j}\end{aligned}$$

A calculation that you can carry out yourself shows that

$$\mathbf{L} = \mathbf{r}(t) \times m\mathbf{v}(t) = mr^2(t)\theta'(t)\mathbf{k}.$$

Since **L** is constant, $r^2(t)\theta'(t)$ is constant. Thus, by $(*)$, $A'(t)$ is constant:

$$A'(t) = L/2m \qquad \text{where} \qquad L = \|\mathbf{L}\|. \quad \square$$

Initial-Value Problems

In physics one tries to make predictions about the future on the basis of current information and a knowledge of the forces at work. In the case of an object in motion, the task can be to determine $\mathbf{r}(t)$ for all t given the force and some "initial conditions." Frequently the initial conditions give the position and velocity of the object at some time t_0. The problem then is to solve the differential equation

$$\mathbf{F} = m\mathbf{r}''$$

subject to conditions of the form

$$\mathbf{r}(t_0) = \mathbf{r}_0, \qquad \mathbf{v}(t_0) = \mathbf{v}_0.$$

Such problems are known as initial-value problems. (You saw initial-value problems in several contexts earlier in the text.)

By far the simplest problem of this sort concerns a *free particle*, an object on which there is no net force.

Example 3 At time t_0 a free particle has position $\mathbf{r}(t_0) = \mathbf{r}_0$ and velocity $\mathbf{v}(t_0) = \mathbf{v}_0$. Find $\mathbf{r}(t)$ for all t.

SOLUTION Since there is no net force on the object, the acceleration is zero and the velocity is constant. Since $\mathbf{v}(t_0) = \mathbf{v}_0$,

$$\mathbf{v}(t) = \mathbf{v}_0 \qquad \text{for all } t.$$

Integration with respect to t gives

$$\mathbf{r}(t) = t\mathbf{v}_0 + \mathbf{c},$$

where $\mathbf{c}$, the constant of integration, is a vector that we can determine from the initial position. The initial position $\mathbf{r}(t_0) = \mathbf{r}_0$ gives

$$\mathbf{r}_0 = t_0\mathbf{v}_0 + \mathbf{c} \qquad \text{and therefore} \qquad \mathbf{c} = \mathbf{r}_0 - t_0\mathbf{v}_0.$$

Using this value for $\mathbf{c}$ in our equation for $\mathbf{r}(t)$, we have

$$\mathbf{r}(t) = t\mathbf{v}_0 + (\mathbf{r}_0 - t_0\mathbf{v}_0),$$

which we write as

$$\mathbf{r}(t) = \mathbf{r}_0 + (t - t_0)\mathbf{v}_0.$$

This is the equation of a straight line with direction vector $\mathbf{v}_0$. Free particles travel in straight lines with constant velocity. (We have tacitly assumed that $\mathbf{v}_0 \neq \mathbf{0}$. If $\mathbf{v}_0 = \mathbf{0}$, the particle remains at rest at $\mathbf{r}_0$.) ❑

Example 4 An object of mass m is subject to a force of the form

$$\mathbf{F}(t) = -m\omega^2\mathbf{r}(t) \qquad \text{with} \qquad \omega > 0.$$

Find $\mathbf{r}(t)$ for all t given that

$$\mathbf{r}(0) = a\,\mathbf{i} \qquad \text{and} \qquad \mathbf{v}(0) = \omega a\,\mathbf{j} \qquad \text{with} \qquad a > 0.$$

SOLUTION The force is a vector version of the restoring force exerted by a linear spring (Hooke's law). Since the force is central, the angular momentum of the object, $\mathbf{L}(t) = \mathbf{r}(t) \times m\mathbf{v}(t)$, is conserved. So $\mathbf{L}(t)$ is constantly equal to the value it had at time $t = 0$; for all t;

$$\mathbf{L}(t) = \mathbf{L}(0) = \mathbf{r}(0) \times m\mathbf{v}(0) = a\,\mathbf{i} \times m\omega a\,\mathbf{j} = ma^2\omega\,\mathbf{k}.$$

From our earlier discussion (Theorem 14.6.7) we can conclude that the motion takes place in the plane that passes through the origin and is perpendicular to $\mathbf{k}$. This is the xy-plane. Thus we can write

$$\mathbf{r}(t) = x(t)\,\mathbf{i} + y(t)\,\mathbf{j}.$$

Since $\mathbf{F}(t) = m\mathbf{r}''(t)$, the force equation can be written $\mathbf{r}''(t) = -\omega^2\mathbf{r}(t)$. In terms of components we have

$$x''(t) = -\omega^2 x(t), \qquad y''(t) = -\omega^2 y(t).$$

These are the equations of simple harmonic motion. As you saw in Chapter 9, the general solutions of these equations can be written

$$x(t) = A_1 \sin(\omega t + \phi_1), \qquad y(t) = A_2 \sin(\omega t + \phi_2).$$

To evaluate the constants, we use the initial conditions. The condition $\mathbf{r}(0) = a\,\mathbf{i}$ indicates that $x(0) = a$ and $y(0) = 0$. Therefore

$$(*) \qquad A_1 \sin\phi_1 = a \qquad A_2 \sin\phi_2 = 0.$$

The condition $\mathbf{v}(0) = \omega a\mathbf{j}$ indicates that $x'(0) = 0$ and $y'(0) = \omega a$. Since

$$x'(t) = \omega A_1 \cos(\omega t + \phi_1) \qquad \text{and} \qquad y'(t) = \omega A_2 \cos(\omega t + \phi_2),$$

we have

$$(**) \qquad \omega A_1 \cos\phi_1 = 0, \qquad \omega A_2 \cos\phi_2 = \omega a.$$

Conditions $(*)$ and $(**)$ are met by setting $A_1 = a$, $A_2 = a$, $\phi_1 = \frac{1}{2}\pi$, $\phi_2 = 0$. Thus

$$x(t) = a\sin(\omega t + \tfrac{1}{2}\pi) = a\cos\omega t, \qquad y(t) = a\sin\omega t.$$

The vector equation reads

$$\mathbf{r}(t) = a\cos\omega t\,\mathbf{i} + a\sin\omega t\,\mathbf{j}.$$

The object moves about the origin in a circle of radius a with constant angular velocity ω. ❑

Example 5 A particle of charge q in a magnetic field $\mathbf{B}$ is subject to the force

$$\mathbf{F}(t) = \frac{q}{c}[\mathbf{v}(t) \times \mathbf{B}(t)]$$

where c is the speed of light and $\mathbf{v}$ is the velocity of the particle. Given that $\mathbf{r}(0) = \mathbf{r}_0$ and $\mathbf{v}(0) = \mathbf{v}_0$, find the path of the particle in the constant magnetic field $\mathbf{B}(t) = B_0\mathbf{k}$, $B_0 \neq 0$.

SOLUTION There is no conservation law that we can conveniently appeal to here. Neither momentum nor angular momentum is conserved: the force is not zero and it is not central. We start directly from Newton's law $\mathbf{F} = m\mathbf{r}''$.

Since $\mathbf{r}'' = \mathbf{v}'$, we have

$$m\mathbf{v}'(t) = \frac{q}{c}[\mathbf{v}(t) \times B_0\mathbf{k}],$$

which we can write as

$$\mathbf{v}'(t) = \frac{qB_0}{mc}[\mathbf{v}(t) \times \mathbf{k}].$$

To simplify notation, we set $qB_0/mc = \omega$. We then have

$$\mathbf{v}'(t) = \omega[\mathbf{v}(t) \times \mathbf{k}].$$

Placing $\mathbf{v}(t) = v_1(t)\,\mathbf{i} + v_2(t)\,\mathbf{j} + v_3(t)\,\mathbf{k}$ in this last equation and working out the cross product, we find that

$$v_1'(t)\,\mathbf{i} + v_2'(t)\,\mathbf{j} + v_3'(t)\,\mathbf{k} = \omega[v_2(t)\,\mathbf{i} - v_1(t)\,\mathbf{j}].$$

This gives the scalar equations

$$v_1'(t) = \omega v_2(t), \qquad v_2'(t) = -\omega v_1(t), \qquad v_3'(t) = 0.$$

The last equation is trivial. It says that v_3 is constant:

$$v_3(t) = C.$$

The equations for v_1 and v_2 are linked together. We can get an equation that involves only v_1 by differentiating the first equation:

$$v_1''(t) = \omega v_2'(t) = -\omega^2 v_1(t).$$

As we know from our earlier work, this gives

$$v_1(t) = A_1\sin(\omega t + \phi_1).$$

Since $v_1'(t) = \omega v_2(t)$, we have

$$v_2(t) = \frac{v_1'(t)}{\omega} = \frac{A_1\omega}{\omega}\cos(\omega t + \phi_1) = A_1\cos(\omega t + \phi_1).$$

Therefore

$$\mathbf{v}(t) = A_1 \sin(\omega t + \phi_1)\,\mathbf{i} + A_1 \cos(\omega t + \phi_1)\,\mathbf{j} + C\mathbf{k}.$$

A final integration with respect to t gives

$$\mathbf{r}(t) = \left[-\frac{A_1}{\omega}\cos(\omega t + \phi_1) + D_1\right]\mathbf{i} + \left[\frac{A_1}{\omega}\sin(\omega t + \phi_1) + D_2\right]\mathbf{j} + [Ct + D_3]\mathbf{k}$$

where D_1, D_2, D_3 are constants of integration. All six constants of integration—$A_1, \phi_1, C, D_1, D_2, D_3$—can be evaluated from the initial conditions. We will not pursue this. What is important here is that the path of the particle is a circular helix with axis parallel to $\mathbf{B}$, in this case parallel to $\mathbf{k}$. You should be able to see this from the equation for $\mathbf{r}(t)$: the z-component of $\mathbf{r}$ varies linearly with t from the value D_3, while the x- and y-components represent uniform motion with angular velocity ω in a circle of radius $|A_1/\omega|$ around the center (D_1, D_2). ❑

(Physicists express the behavior just found by saying that charged particles *spiral around* the magnetic field lines. Qualitatively, this behavior still holds even if the magnetic field lines are "bent," as is the case with the earth's magnetic field. Many charged particles become trapped by the earth's magnetic field. They keep spiraling around the magnetic field lines that run from pole to pole.)

EXERCISES 14.6

1. An object of mass m moves so that

$$\mathbf{r}(t) = \tfrac{1}{2}a(e^{\omega t} + e^{-\omega t})\,\mathbf{i} + \tfrac{1}{2}b(e^{\omega t} - e^{-\omega t})\,\mathbf{j}.$$

(a) What is the velocity at $t = 0$? (b) Show that the acceleration vector is a constant positive multiple of the radius vector. (This shows that the force is central and repelling.) (c) What does (b) imply about the angular momentum and the torque? Verify your answers by direct calculation.

2. (a) An object moves so that

$$\mathbf{r}(t) = a_1 e^{bt}\mathbf{i} + a_2 e^{bt}\mathbf{j} + a_3 e^{bt}\mathbf{k}.$$

Show that, if $b > 0$, the object experiences a repelling central force.

(b) An object moves so that

$$\mathbf{r}(t) = \sin t\,\mathbf{i} + \cos t\,\mathbf{j} + (\sin t + \cos t)\,\mathbf{k}.$$

Show that the object experiences an attracting central force.

(c) Calculate the angular momentum $\mathbf{L}(t)$ for the motion in part (b).

3. A constant force of magnitude α directed upward from the xy-plane is continually applied to an object of mass m. Given that the object starts at time 0 at the point $P(0, y_0, z_0)$ with initial velocity $2\mathbf{j}$, find: (a) the velocity of the object t seconds later; (b) the speed of the object t seconds later; (c) the momentum of the object t seconds later; (d) the path followed by the object, both in vector form and in Cartesian coordinates.

4. Show that, if the force on an object is always perpendicular to the velocity of the object, then the *speed* of the object is constant. (This tells us that the speed of a charged particle in a magnetic field is constant.)

5. Find the force required to propel a particle of mass m so that $\mathbf{r}(t) = t\,\mathbf{j} + t^2\,\mathbf{k}$.

6. Show that for an object of constant velocity, the angular momentum is constant.

7. At each point $P(x(t), y(t), z(t))$ of its motion, an object of mass m is subject to a force

$$\mathbf{F}(t) = m\pi^2[a\cos\pi t\,\mathbf{i} + b\sin\pi t\,\mathbf{j}]. \qquad (a > 0, b > 0).$$

Given that $\mathbf{v}(0) = -\pi b\,\mathbf{j} + \mathbf{k}$ and $\mathbf{r}(0) = b\,\mathbf{j}$, find the following at time $t = 1$:

(a) The velocity. (b) The speed.
(c) The acceleration. (d) The momentum.
(e) The angular momentum. (f) The torque.

8. If an object of mass m moves with velocity $\mathbf{v}(t)$ subject to a force $\mathbf{F}(t)$, the scalar product

(14.6.8) $$\mathbf{F}(t)\cdot\mathbf{v}(t)$$

is called the *power* (expended by the force) and the number

(14.6.9) $$\tfrac{1}{2}m[v(t)]^2$$

is called the *kinetic energy* of the object. Show that the time rate of change of the kinetic energy of an object is the power expended on it:

(14.6.10) $$\frac{d}{dt}\left(\tfrac{1}{2}m[v(t)]^2\right) = \mathbf{F}(t)\cdot\mathbf{v}(t).$$

9. Two particles of equal mass m, one with constant velocity $\mathbf{v}$ and the other at rest, collide elastically (i.e., the kinetic energy of the system is conserved) and go off in different directions. Show that the two particles go off at right angles.

10. (*Elliptic harmonic motion*) Show that if the force on a particle of mass m is of the form

$$\mathbf{F}(t) = -m\omega^2\mathbf{r}(t),$$

then the path of the particle may be written

$$\mathbf{r}(t) = \cos\omega t\;\mathbf{A} + \sin\omega t\;\mathbf{B}$$

where $\mathbf{A}$ and $\mathbf{B}$ are constant vectors. Give the physical significance of $\mathbf{A}$ and $\mathbf{B}$ and specify conditions on $\mathbf{A}$ and $\mathbf{B}$ that restrict the particle to a circular path.
HINT: The solutions of the differential equation

$$x''(t) = -\omega^2 x(t)$$

can all be written in the form

$$x(t) = A\cos\omega t + B\sin\omega t. \qquad \text{(Chapter 9)}$$

11. A particle moves with constant acceleration $\mathbf{a}$. Show that the path of the particle lies entirely in some plane. Find a vector equation for this plane.

12. In Example 5 we stated that the path

$$\mathbf{r}(t) = \left[-\frac{A_1}{\omega}\cos(\omega t + \phi_1) + D_1\right]\mathbf{i} + \left[\frac{A_1}{\omega}\sin(\omega t + \phi_1) + D_2\right]\mathbf{j} + [Ct + D_3]\mathbf{k}$$

was a circular helix. Set $\omega = -1$ and show that, if $\mathbf{r}(0) = a\mathbf{i}$ and $\mathbf{v}(0) = a\mathbf{j} + b\mathbf{k}$, then the path takes the form

$$\mathbf{r}(t) = a\cos t\;\mathbf{i} + a\sin t\;\mathbf{j} + bt\;\mathbf{k},$$

the circular helix of Example 4, Section 14.3.

13. A charged particle in a time-independent electric field $\mathbf{E}$ experiences the force $q\mathbf{E}$, where q is the charge of the particle. Assume that the field has the constant value $\mathbf{E} = E_0\mathbf{k}$ and find the path of the particle given that $\mathbf{r}(0) = \mathbf{i}$ and $\mathbf{v}(0) = \mathbf{j}$.

14. (*Important*) A wheel is rotating about an axle with angular speed ω. Let $\boldsymbol{\omega}$ be the *angular velocity vector*, the vector of length ω that points along the axis of the wheel in such a direction that, observed from the tip of $\boldsymbol{\omega}$, the wheel rotates counterclockwise. Take the origin as the center of the wheel and let $\mathbf{r}$ be the vector from the origin to a point P on the rim of the wheel. Express the velocity $\mathbf{v}$ of P in terms of $\boldsymbol{\omega}$ and $\mathbf{r}$.

15. Solve the initial-value problem

$$\mathbf{F}(t) = m\mathbf{r}''(t) = t\,\mathbf{i} + t^2\,\mathbf{j}, \qquad \mathbf{r}_0 = \mathbf{r}(0) = \mathbf{i}\,,$$
$$\mathbf{v}_0 = \mathbf{v}(0) = \mathbf{k}.$$

16. Solve the initial-value problem

$$\mathbf{F}(t) = m\mathbf{r}''(t) = -m\beta^2 z(t)\mathbf{k}, \qquad \mathbf{r}_0 = \mathbf{r}(0) = \mathbf{k},$$
$$\mathbf{v}_0 = \mathbf{v}(0) = 0.$$

[Here $z(t)$ is the z-component of $\mathbf{r}(t)$.]

17. An object of mass m moves subject to the force

$$\mathbf{F}(\mathbf{r}) = 4r^2\mathbf{r}$$

where $\mathbf{r} = \mathbf{r}(t)$ is the position of the object. Suppose $\mathbf{r}(0) = 0$ and $\mathbf{v}(0) = 2\mathbf{u}$, where $\mathbf{u}$ is a unit vector. Show that at each time t the speed v of the object satisfies the relation

$$v = \sqrt{4 + \frac{2}{m}r^4}.$$

HINT: Examine the quantity $\frac{1}{2}mv^2 - r^4$ (This is the *energy* of the object, a notion we will take up in Chapter 18.)

■ *14.7 PLANETARY MOTION

Tycho Brahe, Johannes Kepler

In the middle of the sixteenth century the arguments on planetary motion persisted. Was Copernicus right? Did the planets move in circles about the sun? Perhaps not. But wasn't the earth the center of the universe?

In 1576, with the generous support of his king, the Danish astronomer Tycho Brahe built an elaborate astronomical observatory on the isle of Hveen and began his painstaking observations. For more than twenty years he looked through his telescopes and recorded what he saw. He was a meticulous observer, but he could draw no definite conclusions.

In 1599 the German astronomer-mathematician Johannes Kepler began his study of Brahe's voluminous tables. For a year and a half Brahe and Kepler worked together. Then Brahe died and Kepler went on wrestling with the data. His persistence paid off. By 1619 Kepler had made three stupendous discoveries, known today as *Kepler's laws of planetary motion*:

> **I.** Each planet moves in a plane, not in a circle, but in an elliptical orbit with the sun at one focus.
> **II.** The radius vector from the sun to the planet sweeps out equal areas in equal times.
> **III.** The square of the period of the motion varies directly as the cube of the major semiaxis, and the constant of proportionality is the same for all the planets.

What Kepler formulated empirically, Newton was able to explain. Each of these laws, Newton showed, was deducible from his laws of motion and his law of gravitation.

Newton's Second Law of Motion for Extended Three-Dimensional Objects

Imagine an object that consists of n particles with masses $m_1, m_2, \ldots, m_n$ located at $\mathbf{r}_1, \mathbf{r}_2, \ldots \mathbf{r}_n$.[†] The total mass M of the object is the sum of the masses of the constituent particles:

$$M = m_1 + \cdots + m_n.$$

The center of mass of the object is the point $\mathbf{R}_M$ where

$$M\,\mathbf{R}_M = m_1\mathbf{r}_1 + \cdots + m_n\mathbf{r}_n.$$

The total force $\mathbf{F}_{\text{TOT}}$ on the object is the sum of all the forces that act on the particles that constitute the object:

$$\mathbf{F}_{\text{TOT}} = \mathbf{F}_1 + \cdots + \mathbf{F}_n.$$

Since $\mathbf{F}_1 = m_1\mathbf{r}_1'', \cdots, \mathbf{F}_n = m_n\mathbf{r}_n''$, we have

$$\mathbf{F}_{\text{TOT}} = m_1\mathbf{r}_1'' + \cdots + m_n\mathbf{r}_n'',$$

which we can write as

$$\mathbf{F}_{\text{TOT}} = M\,\mathbf{R}_M''.$$

The total force on an extended object is thus the total mass of the object times the acceleration of the center of mass.

We can simplify this still further. The forces that act between the constituent particles, the so-called internal forces, cancel in pairs: if particle 23 tugs at particle 71 in a certain direction with a certain strength, then particle 71 tugs at particle 23 in the opposite direction with the same strength. (Newton's third law: To every action there is an equal and opposite reaction.) Therefore, in calculating the total force on our object, we can disregard the internal forces and simply add up the external forces. $\mathbf{F}_{\text{TOT}} = \mathbf{F}_{\text{TOT}}^{(\text{Ext})}$ and Newton's second law takes the form

(*14.7.1)
$$\boxed{\mathbf{F}_{\text{TOT}}^{(\text{Ext})} = M\,\mathbf{R}_M''.}$$

The total external force on an extended three-dimensional object is thus the total mass of the object times the acceleration of the center of mass.

[†]The case of a continuously distributed mass is taken up in Chapter 17.

When an external force is applied to an extended object, we cannot predict the reaction of all the constituent particles, but we can predict the reaction of the center of mass. The center of mass will react to the force as if it were a particle with all the mass concentrated there. Suppose, for example, that a bomb is dropped from an airplane. The center of mass, "feeling" only the force of gravity (we are neglecting air resistance), falls in a parabolic arc toward the ground even if the bomb explodes at a thousand meters and individual pieces fly every which way. The forces of explosion are internal and do not affect the motion of the center of mass.

Some Preliminary Comments about the Planets

Roughly speaking, a planet is a massive object in the form of a ball with the center of mass at the center. In what follows, when we refer to the position of a planet, you are to understand that we really mean the position of the center of mass of the planet. Two other points require comment. First, we will write our equations as if the sun affected the motion of the planet, but not vice versa: we will assume that the sun stays put and that the planet moves. Really, each affects the other. Our viewpoint is justified by the immense difference in mass between the planets and the sun. In the case of the earth and the sun, for example, a reasonable analogy is to imagine a tug of war in space between someone who weighs three pounds and someone who weighs a million pounds: to a good approximation, the million-pound person does not move. The second point is that the planet is affected not only by the pull from the sun, but also by the gravitational pulls from the other planets and all the other celestial bodies. But these forces are much smaller, and they tend to cancel. We will ignore them. (Our results are only approximations, but they prove to be very good approximations.)

A Derivation of Kepler's Laws from Newton's Laws of Motion and His Law of Gravitation

The gravitational force exerted by the sun on a planet can be written in vector form as

$$(*) \qquad \mathbf{F}(\mathbf{r}) = -G\frac{mM}{r^3}\mathbf{r}.$$

Here m is the mass of the planet, M is the mass of the sun, G is the universal gravitational constant, $\mathbf{r}$ is the vector from the center of the sun to the center of the planet, and r is the magnitude of $\mathbf{r}$. (Thus we are placing the sun at the origin of our coordinate system; namely, we are using what is known as a *heliocentric* coordinate system, from *hēlios*, the Greek word for "sun".)

Let's make sure that $(*)$ conforms to our earlier characterization of gravitational force. First of all, because of the minus sign, the direction is toward the origin, where the sun is located. Taking norms we have

$$\|\mathbf{F}(\mathbf{r})\| = \frac{GmM}{r^3}\|\mathbf{r}\| = \frac{GmM}{r^2}. \qquad \uparrow\ \|\mathbf{r}\| = r$$

Thus the magnitude of the force is as expected: it does vary directly as the product of the masses and inversely as the square of the distance between them. So we are back in familiar territory.

We will derive Kepler's laws in a somewhat piecemeal manner. Since the force on the planet is a central force, $\mathbf{L}$, the angular momentum of the planet, is conserved. (Section 14.6.) If $\mathbf{L}$ were zero, we would have

$$\|\mathbf{L}\| = L = m\|\mathbf{r}\|\ \|\mathbf{v}\| \sin\theta = 0.$$

This would mean that either $\mathbf{r} = \mathbf{0}$, $\mathbf{v} = \mathbf{0}$, or $\sin\theta = 0$. The first equation would place the planet at the center of the sun. The second equation could hold only if the planet stopped. The third equation could hold only if the planet moved directly toward the sun or directly away from the sun. We can be thankful that none of those things happen.

Since the planet moves under a central force and $\mathbf{L}$ is not zero, *the planet stays on the plane that passes through the center of the sun and is perpendicular to* $\mathbf{L}$, and the radius vector does sweep out equal areas in equal times. (We know all this from Theorem 14.6.7.)

Now we go on to show that the path is an ellipse with the sun at one focus.† The equation of motion of a planet of mass m can be written

$$m\,\mathbf{a}(t) = -GmM\frac{\mathbf{r}(t)}{[r(t)]^3}.$$

Clearly m drops out of the equation. Setting $GM = \rho$ and suppressing the explicit dependence on t, we have

$$\mathbf{a} = -\rho\frac{\mathbf{r}}{r^3},$$

which gives

$$(**) \qquad \frac{\mathbf{r}}{r^3} = -\frac{1}{\rho}\mathbf{a} = -\frac{1}{\rho}\frac{d\mathbf{v}}{dt}.$$

From (14.2.4) we know that in general

$$\frac{d}{dt}\left(\frac{\mathbf{r}}{r}\right) = (\mathbf{r}\times\mathbf{v})\times\frac{\mathbf{r}}{r^3}.$$

Since $\mathbf{L} = \mathbf{r}\times m\mathbf{v}$, we have

$$\frac{d}{dt}\left(\frac{\mathbf{r}}{r}\right) = \frac{\mathbf{L}}{m}\times\frac{\mathbf{r}}{r^3}.$$

Inserting $(**)$, we see that

$$\frac{d}{dt}\left(\frac{\mathbf{r}}{r}\right) = \frac{\mathbf{L}}{m}\times\left(-\frac{1}{\rho}\frac{d\mathbf{v}}{dt}\right) = \frac{d\mathbf{v}}{dt}\times\frac{\mathbf{L}}{m\rho} = \frac{d}{dt}\left(\mathbf{v}\times\frac{\mathbf{L}}{m\rho}\right)$$

$\mathbf{L}$, m, ρ are all constant

and therefore

$$\frac{d}{dt}\left[\left(\mathbf{v}\times\frac{\mathbf{L}}{m\rho}\right) - \frac{\mathbf{r}}{r}\right] = \mathbf{0}.$$

Integration with respect to t gives

$$(***) \qquad \left(\mathbf{v}\times\frac{\mathbf{L}}{m\rho}\right) - \frac{\mathbf{r}}{r} = \mathbf{e}$$

where $\mathbf{e}$ is a constant vector that depends on the initial conditions. Dotting both sides with $\mathbf{r}$, we have

$$\mathbf{r}\cdot\left(\mathbf{v}\times\frac{\mathbf{L}}{m\rho}\right) - \frac{\mathbf{r}\cdot\mathbf{r}}{r} = \mathbf{r}\cdot\mathbf{e}.$$

†If some of the steps seem unanticipated to you, you should realize that we are discussing one of the most celebrated physical problems in history and there have been three hundred years to think of ingenious ways to deal with it. The argument we give here follows the lines of the excellent discussion that appears in Harry Pollard's *Celestial Mechanics*, Mathematical Association of America (1976).

Since

$$\mathbf{r}\cdot\left(\mathbf{v}\times\frac{\mathbf{L}}{m\rho}\right)=\frac{\mathbf{L}}{m\rho}\cdot(\mathbf{r}\times\mathbf{v})=\frac{\mathbf{L}}{m\rho}\cdot\frac{\mathbf{L}}{m}=\frac{L^2}{m^2\rho}\qquad\text{and}\qquad\frac{\mathbf{r}\cdot\mathbf{r}}{r}=\frac{r^2}{r}=r,$$

we find that

$$\frac{L^2}{m^2\rho}-r=\mathbf{r}\cdot\mathbf{e},$$

which we write as

$$r+(\mathbf{r}\cdot\mathbf{e})=\frac{L^2}{m^2\rho}.\qquad\text{(orbit equation)}$$

If $\mathbf{e}=0$, the orbit is a circle:

$$r=\frac{L^2}{m^2\rho}.$$

This is a possibility that requires very special initial conditions, conditions not met by any of the planets in our solar system. In our solar system at least, $\mathbf{e}\neq\mathbf{0}$.

Given that $\mathbf{e}\neq\mathbf{0}$, we can write the orbit equation as

(*14.7.2)
$$r(1+e\cos\theta)=\frac{L^2}{m^2\rho}$$

where $e=\|\mathbf{e}\|$ and θ is the angle between $\mathbf{r}$ and $\mathbf{e}$. We are almost through. Since $\mathbf{v}\times\mathbf{L}$ and $\mathbf{r}$ are both perpendicular to $\mathbf{L}$, we know from $(***)$ that $\mathbf{e}$ is perpendicular to $\mathbf{L}$. Therefore, in the plane of $\mathbf{e}$ and $\mathbf{r}$ (see Figure 14.7.1) we can interpret r and θ as the usual polar coordinates. The orbit equation [(14.7.2)] is then a polar equation. We refer you to Project 10.3, where it is shown that an equation of the form (14.7.2) represents a conic section with focus at the origin, which is to say *focus at the sun*. Accordingly, the conic section can be a parabola, a hyperbola, or an ellipse. The repetitiveness of planetary motion rules out the parabola and the hyperbola. *The orbit is an ellipse.*

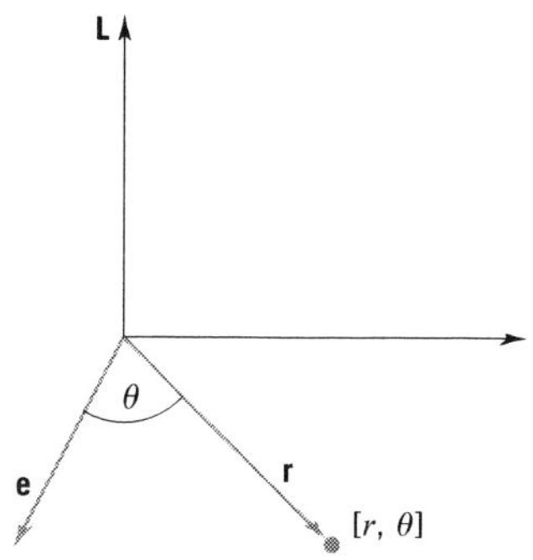

Figure 14.7.1

Finally, we will verify Kepler's third law: The square of the period of the motion varies directly as the cube of the major semiaxis, and the constant of proportionality is the same for all planets.

The elliptic orbit has an equation of the form

$$r(1+e\cos\theta)=ed\qquad\text{with}\qquad 0<e<1,\qquad d>0.$$

Rewriting this equation in rectangular coordinates $(x=r\cos\theta,\ y=r\sin\theta)$, we get

$$\frac{(x+c)^2}{a^2}+\frac{y^2}{a^2-c^2}=1,\qquad\text{where}\qquad a=\frac{ed}{1-e^2}\qquad\text{and}\qquad c=\frac{e^2d}{1-e^2}.$$

The lengths of the major and minor semiaxes are as follows:

$$a=\frac{ed}{1-e^2}\qquad\text{and}\qquad b=\sqrt{a^2-c^2}=a\sqrt{1-e^2}.$$

Denote the period of revolution by T. Since the radius vector sweeps out area at the constant rate of $L/2m$ (we know this from the proof of Theorem 14.6.7)

$$\left(\frac{L}{2m}\right)T=\text{area of the ellipse}=\pi ab=\pi a^2\sqrt{1-e^2}.$$

Thus

$$T=\frac{2\pi ma^2\sqrt{1-e^2}}{L}\qquad\text{and}\qquad T^2=\frac{4\pi^2m^2a^4(1-e^2)}{L^2}.$$

From (14.7.2) we know that

$$ed = \frac{L^2}{m^2\rho} = \frac{L^2}{m^2GM} \qquad \text{and therefore} \qquad \frac{m^2}{L^2} = \frac{1}{edGM}.$$

It follows that

$$T^2 = \frac{4\pi^2a^4(1-e^2)}{edGM} = \frac{4\pi^2a^4(1-e^2)}{a(1-e^2)GM} = \frac{4\pi^2}{GM}a^3.$$

$$\uparrow\ ed = a(1-e^2)$$

T^2 does vary directly with a^3, and the constant of proportionality $4\pi^2/GM$ is the same for all planets.

EXERCISES 14.7

1. Kepler's third law can be stated as follows: For each planet the square of the period of revolution varies directly as the cube of the planet's average distance from the sun, and the constant of proportionality is the same for all planets. A *year* on a given planet is the time taken by the planet to make one circuit around the sun. Thus, a year on a planet is the period of revolution of that planet. Given that on average Venus is 0.72 times as far from the sun as the earth, how does the length of a "Venus year" compare with the length of an "earth year"?

2. Verify by differentiation with respect to time t that if the acceleration of a planet is given by

$$\mathbf{a} = -\rho\frac{\mathbf{r}}{r^3},$$

then the energy $E = \frac{1}{2}mv^2 - \dfrac{m\rho}{r}$ is constant.

3. Given that a planet moves in a plane, its motion can be described by rectangular coordinates (x, y) or polar coordinates $[r, \theta]$, with the origin at the sun. The kinetic energy of a planet is

$$\frac{1}{2}mv^2 = \frac{1}{2}m\left[\left(\frac{dx}{dt}\right)^2 + \left(\frac{dy}{dt}\right)^2\right].$$

Show that in polar coordinates

$$\frac{1}{2}mv^2 = \frac{1}{2}m\left[\left(\frac{dr}{dt}\right)^2 + r^2\left(\frac{d\theta}{dt}\right)^2\right].$$

4. We have seen that the energy of a planet

$$E = \frac{1}{2}mv^2 - \frac{m\rho}{r}$$

is constant (Exercise 2). Setting $dr/dt = \dot{r}$, $d\theta/dt = \dot{\theta}$, and using Exercise 3, we have

$$E = \frac{1}{2}m(\dot{r}^2 + r^2\dot{\theta}^2) - \frac{m\rho}{r}.$$

We also know that the angular momentum $\mathbf{L}$ is constant and that $L = mr^2\dot{\theta}$. Use this fact to verify that

$$E = \frac{L^2}{2m}\left\{\frac{1}{r^2} + \frac{1}{r^4}\left(\frac{dr}{d\theta}\right)^2\right\} - \frac{m\rho}{r}.$$

Since E is a constant, this is a differential equation for r as a function of θ.

5. Show that the function

$$r = \frac{a}{1 + e\cos\theta} \quad \text{with} \quad a = \frac{L^2}{m^2\rho} \quad \text{and} \quad e^2 = \frac{2Ea}{m\rho} + 1$$

satisfies the equation derived in Exercise 4.

CHAPTER 14. REVIEW EXERCISES

Exercises 1–4. Calculate the first and second derivatives.

1. $\mathbf{f}(t) = 3t^2\,\mathbf{i} - 5t^3\,\mathbf{j}$.

2. $\mathbf{f}(t) = e^{2t}\,\mathbf{i} + \ln(t^2+1)\,\mathbf{j}$.

3. $\mathbf{f}(t) = e^t\cos t\,\mathbf{i} - \cos 2t\,\mathbf{j} + 3\,\mathbf{k}$.

4. $\mathbf{f}(t) = \sinh t\,\mathbf{i} - t^2e^{-t}\,\mathbf{j} + \cosh t\,\mathbf{k}$.

Exercises 5–6. Evaluate.

5. $\displaystyle\int_0^2 [2t\,\mathbf{i} + (t^2-1)\,\mathbf{j}]\,dt$.

6. $\displaystyle\int_0^{\pi} [\sin 2t\,\mathbf{i} + 2\cos t\,\mathbf{j} + \sqrt{t}\,\mathbf{k}]\,dt$.

Exercises 7–10. Sketch the curve traced out by the tip of the radius vector and indicate the direction in which the curve is traversed as t increases.

7. $\mathbf{r}(t) = 2t^2\,\mathbf{i} - t\,\mathbf{j}$, $\quad t \geq 0$.

8. $\mathbf{r}(t) = e^{-t}\,\mathbf{i} + 2e^{2t}\,\mathbf{j}$, $\quad t$ real.

9. $\mathbf{r}(t) = t\,\mathbf{i} + 3\sin t\,\mathbf{j} + 4\cos t\,\mathbf{k}$, $\quad 0 \leq t \leq 2\pi$.

10. $\mathbf{r}(t) = t\,\mathbf{i} + t\,\mathbf{j} + \sin t\,\mathbf{k}$, $\quad t \geq 0$.

11. Define a vector function $\mathbf{r}$ on the interval $[0, 2\pi]$ that traces out the ellipse $16x^2 + 4y^2 = 64$ in the manner indicated.

(a) Once in the counterclockwise direction starting at the point $(0, 4)$.

(b) Twice in the clockwise direction starting at the point $(-2, 0)$.

12. Define a vector function $\mathbf{r}$ that traces out the directed line segment from $(1, 1, -2)$ to $(3, 5, 4)$.

13. Find $\mathbf{f}(t)$ given that $\mathbf{f}'(t) = t^2\,\mathbf{i} + (e^{2t} + 1)\,\mathbf{j} + \sqrt{1+2t}\,\mathbf{k}$ and $\mathbf{f}(0) = \mathbf{i} - 3\,\mathbf{j} + 3\,\mathbf{k}$.

14. Find $\mathbf{f}(t)$ given that $\mathbf{f}'(t) = -\mathbf{f}(t)$ for all t and $\mathbf{f}(0) = \mathbf{i} + 2\mathbf{k}$.

Exercises 15–18. Calculate $\mathbf{f}'(t)$.

15. $\mathbf{f}(t) = 3(2t\,\mathbf{i} + t^4\,\mathbf{j} - \mathbf{k}) + 4(t^2\,\mathbf{i} + \mathbf{j} - 3t\,\mathbf{k})$.

16. $\mathbf{f}(t) = [(e^{2t}\,\mathbf{i} + e^{-2t}\,\mathbf{j} + t\,\mathbf{k}) \cdot (e^{-t}\,\mathbf{i} + e^{2t}\,\mathbf{j})]\,\mathbf{j}$.

17. $\mathbf{f}(t) = (t\,\mathbf{i} + t^2\,\mathbf{j} - (1/t)\,\mathbf{k}) \times ([1/t]\,\mathbf{i} + t^3\,\mathbf{j} + 2t\,\mathbf{k})$.

18. $\mathbf{f}(t) = [(t^3\,\mathbf{i} + t^2\,\mathbf{j} + t\,\mathbf{k}) \cdot (\cos t\,\mathbf{i} + \sin t\,\mathbf{j} + 3\cos t\,\mathbf{k})]\,\mathbf{k}$.

19. An object moves along a curve C in such a manner that the tangent vector $\mathbf{r}'(t)$ is always $2\mathbf{r}(t)$. Find parametric equations for C given that $\mathbf{r}(0) = (1, 2, 1)$. Sketch the curve.

20. Set $\mathbf{F}(t) = e^{2t}\,\mathbf{i} + e^{-2t}\,\mathbf{j}$. Show that $\mathbf{F}(t)$ and $\mathbf{F}''(t)$ are parallel for all t. Is there a value of t for which $\mathbf{F}$ and $\mathbf{F}'$ have the same direction?

Exercises 21–22. Find the tangent vector $\mathbf{r}'(t)$ at the indicated point and parametrize the tangent line at that point.

21. $\mathbf{r}(t) = (t^2 + 2t + 1)\,\mathbf{i} + (3t + 1)\,\mathbf{j} + (t^3 + t + 1)\,\mathbf{k}$ at $P(1, 1, 1)$.

22. $\mathbf{r}(t) = \sin 2t\,\mathbf{i} + \cos 2t\,\mathbf{j} + t\,\mathbf{k}$ at $t = \pi/3$.

23. Show that the curves

$$\mathbf{r}_1(t) = 2t\,\mathbf{i} + t^2\,\mathbf{j} + t\,\mathbf{k}, \quad \mathbf{r}_2(u) = (1-u)\mathbf{i} + (2-u^2)\,\mathbf{j} + u^2\,\mathbf{k}$$

intersect at the point $(2, 1, 1)$ and find the angle of intersection. Express your answer in radians.

24. Find the points, if any, on the curve $\mathbf{r}(t) = t^2\,\mathbf{i} + (1-t^2)\,\mathbf{j} - t^2\,\mathbf{k}$ at which $\mathbf{r}(t)$ and the line tangent to the curve meet at right angles.

Exercises 25–26. Sketch the curve showing the direction of the curve and displaying both $\mathbf{r}(t)$ and $\mathbf{r}'(t)$ at the value of t indicated.

25. $\mathbf{r}(t) = t\,\mathbf{i} + e^{2t}\,\mathbf{j}$; $t = 0$.

26. $\mathbf{r}(t) = 2\sin t\,\mathbf{i} - 3\cos t\,\mathbf{j}$; $t = \pi/6$.

27. Find the unit tangent and principal normal for the elliptical helix

$$\mathbf{r}(t) = (\cos t + t\sin t)\,\mathbf{i} + (\sin t - t\cos t)\,\mathbf{j} + \tfrac{1}{2}\sqrt{3}\,t^2\,\mathbf{k}.$$

28. Show that along the circular helix $\mathbf{r}(t) = a\cos t\,\mathbf{i} + a\sin t\,\mathbf{j} + bt\,\mathbf{k}$. the angle between $\mathbf{k}$ and the tangent vector $\mathbf{r}'(t)$ remains constant.

Exercises 29–30. Find the unit tangent, the principal normal, and write an equation in x, y, z for the osculating plane at the point on the curve that corresponds to the indicated value of t.

29. $\mathbf{r}(t) = 2t\,\mathbf{i} + \ln t\,\mathbf{j} - t^2\,\mathbf{k}$; $t = 1$.

30. $\mathbf{r}(t) = \cos t\,\mathbf{i} + \cos t\,\mathbf{j} - \sqrt{2}\sin t\,\mathbf{k}$; $t = \pi/4$.

Exercises 31–34. Find the length of the curve.

31. $\mathbf{r}(t) = 2t\,\mathbf{i} + \frac{2}{3}t^{3/2}\,\mathbf{j}$ from $t = 0$ to $t = 5$.

32. $\mathbf{r}(t) = e^t\mathbf{i} + e^{-t}\mathbf{j} - t\sqrt{2}\,\mathbf{k}$ from $t = 0$ to $t = \ln 3$.

33. $\mathbf{r}(t) = \sinh t\,\mathbf{i} + \cosh t\,\mathbf{j} + t\,\mathbf{k}$ from $t = 0$ to $t = 1$.

34. $\mathbf{r}(t) = \cos t\,\mathbf{i} + \sin t\,\mathbf{j} + \cosh t\,\mathbf{k}$ from $t = 0$ to $t = \ln 2$.

35. Set $\mathbf{r}(t) = \cos t\,\mathbf{i} + \sin t\,\mathbf{j} + \frac{2}{3}t^{3/2}\mathbf{k}$.

(a) Determine the arc length s from $\mathbf{r}(0)$ to $\mathbf{r}(t)$ by evaluating the integral

$$s = \int_0^t \sqrt{(dx/du)^2 + (dy/du)^2 + (dz/du)^2}\,du.$$

(b) Use the relation found in part (a) to express t as a function of s, $t = \varphi(s)$, and find $\mathbf{R}(s) = \mathbf{r}(\varphi(s))$.

(c) Show that $\|\mathbf{R}'(s)\| = 1$.

36. A particle moves so that $\mathbf{r}(t) = \cos t\,\mathbf{i} + \sin t\,\mathbf{j} - \cos 2t\,\mathbf{k}$. Find the velocity, speed, acceleration, and the magnitude of the acceleration at time t.

37. Find the position, velocity, and speed of an object with initial velocity $\mathbf{v}_0 = \mathbf{k}$, initial position $\mathbf{r}_0 = \mathbf{i}$, and acceleration $\mathbf{a}(t) = -\cos t\,\mathbf{i} - \sin t\,\mathbf{j}$.

38. A particle moves along a path of the form $\mathbf{r}(t) = f(t)\mathbf{i} + f^2(t)\mathbf{j}$ where f is a twice differentiable function. What condition on f ensures that the acceleration vector remains perpendicular to the path of the motion?

Exercises 39–44. Calculate the curvature.

39. $y = x^{3/2}$.

40. $y = \cos 2x$.

41. $x(t) = 2e^{-t}$, $y(t) = e^{-2t}$.

42. $x(t) = \frac{1}{3}t^3$, $y(t) = \frac{1}{2}t^2$.

43. $\mathbf{r}(t) = \cos 3t\,\mathbf{i} - 4t\,\mathbf{j} + \sin 3t\,\mathbf{k}$.

44. $\mathbf{r}(t) = t\,\mathbf{i} + \frac{2}{3}\sqrt{2}\,t^{3/2}\mathbf{j} + \frac{1}{2}t^2\mathbf{k}$.

45. Show that the curvature at each point (x, y) of the catenary $y = a\cosh(x/a)$ the curvature is a/y^2.

46. An object moves at constant speed.

(a) Show that the acceleration vector $\mathbf{a}$ remains perpendicular to the velocity vector $\mathbf{v}$.

(b) Express the curvature of the path of the motion in terms of $\|\mathbf{v}\|$ and $\|\mathbf{a}\|$.

Exercises 47–48. Interpret $\mathbf{r}(t)$ as the position of a moving object at time t. Find the curvature of the path and determine the tangential and normal components of acceleration.

47. $\mathbf{r}(t) = \frac{4}{5}\cos t\,\mathbf{i} - \frac{3}{5}\cos t\,\mathbf{j} + (1 + \sin t)\,\mathbf{k}$.

48. $\mathbf{r}(t) = 2t\,\mathbf{i} + t^2\mathbf{j} + \frac{1}{3}t^3\mathbf{k}$.

CHAPTER 15 FUNCTIONS OF SEVERAL VARIABLES

15.1 ELEMENTARY EXAMPLES

First a remark on notation. Points $P(x, y)$ of the xy-plane will be written (x, y) and points $P(x, y, z)$ of three-space will be written (x, y, z).

Let D be a nonempty subset of the xy-plane. A function f that assigns a real number $f(x, y)$ to each point in D is called a *real-valued function of two variables*. The set D is called the *domain of f*, and the set of all values $f(x, y)$ is called the *range of f*.

Example 1 Take D as the entire xy-plane and to each point (x, y) assign the number

$$f(x, y) = xy. \quad \square$$

Example 2 Take D as the set of all points (x, y) with $y \neq 0$. To each such point assign the number

$$f(x, y) = \arctan\left(\frac{x}{y}\right). \quad \square$$

Example 3 Take D as the *open unit disk*: $D = \{(x, y) : x^2 + y^2 < 1\}$. The set consists of all points which lie inside the *unit circle* $x^2 + y^2 < 1$; the circle itself is not part of the set.† To each point (x, y) in D assign the number

$$f(x, y) = \frac{1}{\sqrt{1 - (x^2 + y^2)}}. \quad \square$$

Now let D be a nonempty subset of three-space. A function f that assigns a real number $f(x, y, z)$ to each point (x, y, z) in D is called a *real-valued function of three variables*. The set D is called the *domain of f*, and the set of all values $f(x, y, z)$ is called the *range of f*.

†The *closed unit disk* $D = \{x^2 + y^2 \leq 1\}$ consists of all points which lie on or inside the unit circle; the circle is part of the set.

Example 4 Take D as all of three-space and to each point (x, y, z) assign the number

$$f(x, y, z) = xyz\ . \quad \square$$

Example 5 Take D as the set of all points (x, y, z) with $z \neq x + y$. (Thus D consists of all points not on the plane $x + y - z = 0$.) To each point of D assign the number

$$f(x, y, z) = \cos\left(\frac{1}{x + y - z}\right). \quad \square$$

Example 6 Take D as the *open unit ball*: $D = \{(x, y, z) : x^2 + y^2 + z^2 < 1\}$. This set consists of all points which lie inside the *unit sphere* $x^2 + y^2 + z^2 < 1$; the sphere itself is not part of the set.† To each point (x, y, z) in D assign the number

$$f(x, y, z) = \frac{1}{\sqrt{1 - (x^2 + y^2 + z^2)}}. \quad \square$$

Functions of several variables arise naturally in very elementary settings.

$f(x, y) = \sqrt{x^2 + y^2}$ gives the distance between (x, y) and the origin;
$f(x, y) = xy$ gives the area of a rectangle of dimensions x, y; and
$f(x, y) = 2(x + y)$ gives the perimeter.
$f(x, y, z) = \sqrt{x^2 + y^2 + z^2}$ gives the distance between (x, y, z) and the origin;
$f(x, y, z) = xyz$ gives the volume of a rectangular solid of dimensions x, y, z; and
$f(x, y, z) = 2(xy + xz + yz)$ gives the total surface area.

Many notions in the physical sciences and the social sciences are conveniently expressed by functions of several variables. Some examples follow.

A mass M exerts a gravitational force on a mass m. According to the *law of universal gravitation*, if M is located at the origin of our coordinate system and m is located at (x, y, z), then the magnitude of the gravitational force is given by the function

$$F(x, y, z) = \frac{GmM}{x^2 + y^2 + z^2} \qquad \text{(3 variables: } x, y, z\text{)}$$

where G is the universal gravitational constant.

According to the *ideal gas law*, the pressure P of a gas enclosed in a container varies directly with the temperature T of the gas and varies inversely with the volume V of the container. Thus P is given by a function of the form

$$P(T, V) = k\,\frac{T}{V}. \qquad \text{(2 variables: } T, V\text{)}$$

An investment A_0 is made at continuous compounding at interest rate r. Over time t the investment grows to have value

$$A(t, r) = A_0 e^{rt}. \qquad \text{(2 variables: } r, t\text{)}$$

You saw this in Section 7.6.

†The *closed unit ball* $D = \{(x, y, z) : x^2 + y^2 + z^2 \leq 1\}$ consists of all points which lie on or inside the unit sphere; the sphere is part of the set.

Remark The notion of function does not stop at three variables. As you heat a metal slab, its overall temperature increases. The function f that gives the temperature T at $P(x, y, z)$ at time t is a function of four variables:

$$T = f(x, y, z, t).$$

In Section 13.7 we introduced the algebra of n-tuples. By assigning a real number $f(x_1, x_2, \ldots, x_n)$ to each n-tuple $(x_1, x_2, \ldots, x_n)$ we create a real-valued function of n variables.

In this text we'll concentrate on the basics: functions of one variable, two variables, three variables. Once you have a firm grasp of this material, you can readily go on to more complicated settings. ❑

If the domain of a function of several variables is not explicitly given, it is to be understood that the domain is the maximal set of points for which the definition generates a real number. Thus, in the case of

$$f(x, y) = \frac{1}{x - y},$$

the domain is understood to be all points (x, y) with $y \neq x$; that is, all points of the plane not on the line $y = x$. In the case of

$$g(x, y, z) = \arcsin(x + y + z),$$

the domain is understood to be all points (x, y, z) with $-1 \leq x + y + z \leq 1$. This set is the slab bounded by the parallel planes

$$x + y + z = -1 \qquad \text{and} \qquad x + y + z = 1.$$

To say that a function is *bounded* is to say that its range is bounded. Since the function

$$f(x, y) = \frac{1}{x - y}$$

takes on all values other than 0, its range is $(-\infty, 0) \cup (0, \infty)$. The function is unbounded. In the case of

$$g(x, y, z) = \arcsin(x + y + z),$$

the range is the closed interval $[-\frac{1}{2}\pi, \frac{1}{2}\pi]$. This function is bounded, below by $-\frac{1}{2}\pi$ and above by $\frac{1}{2}\pi$.

Example 7 Find the domain and range of the function $f(x, y) = \dfrac{1}{\sqrt{4x^2 - y^2}}$.

SOLUTION A point (x, y) is in the domain of f iff $4x^2 - y^2 > 0$. This occurs iff

$$y^2 < 4x^2 \qquad \text{and thus iff} \qquad -2|x| < y < 2|x|.$$

The domain of f is the region shaded in Figure 15.1.1. It consists of all points of the xy-plane that lie between the graph of $y = -2|x|$ and the graph of $y = 2|x|$. On this set $\sqrt{4x^2 - y^2}$ takes on all positive values, and so does its reciprocal $f(x, y)$. The range of f is $(0, \infty)$. ❑

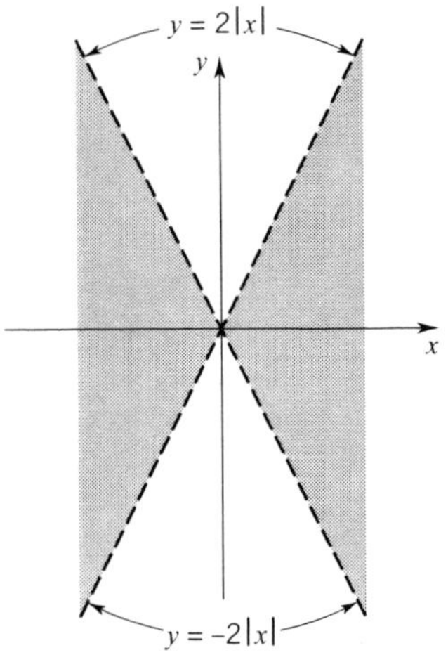

Figure 15.1.1

EXERCISES 15.1

Exercises 1–22. Find the domain and range of the function.

1. $f(x, y) = \sqrt{xy}$.
2. $f(x, y) = \sqrt{1 - xy}$.

3. $f(x, y) = \dfrac{1}{x + y}$.
4. $f(x, y) = \dfrac{1}{x^2 + y^2}$.

5. $f(x, y) = \dfrac{e^x - e^y}{e^x + e^y}$.
6. $f(x, y) = \dfrac{x^2}{x^2 + y^2}$.

7. $f(x, y) = \ln xy$.
8. $f(x, y) = \ln(1 - xy)$.

9. $f(x, y) = \dfrac{1}{\sqrt{y - x^2}}$.
10. $f(x, y) = \dfrac{\sqrt{9 - x^2}}{1 + \sqrt{1 - y^2}}$.

11. $f(x, y) = \sqrt{9 - x^2} - \sqrt{4 - y^2}$.

12. $f(x, y, z) = \cos x + \cos y + \cos z$.

13. $f(x, y, z) = \dfrac{x + y + z}{|x + y + z|}$.
14. $f(x, y, z) = \dfrac{z^2}{x^2 - y^2}$.

15. $f(x, y, z) = -\dfrac{z^2}{\sqrt{x^2 - y^2}}$.
16. $f(x, y, z) = \dfrac{z}{x - y}$.

17. $f(x, y) = \dfrac{2}{\sqrt{9 - (x^2 + y^2)}}$.

18. $f(x, y, z) = \ln(|x + 2y + 3z| + 1)$.

19. $f(x, y, z) = \ln(x + 2y + 3z)$.

20. $f(x, y, z) = e^{\sqrt{4-(x^2+y^2+z^2)}}$.

21. $f(x, y, z) = e^{-(x^2+y^2+z^2)}$.

22. $f(x, y, z) = \dfrac{\sqrt{1 - x^2} + \sqrt{4 - y^2}}{1 + \sqrt{9 - z^2}}$.

23. Let $f(x) = \sqrt{x}$, $g(x, y) = \sqrt{x}$, $h(x, y, z) = \sqrt{x}$. Determine the domain and range of each function and compare the results.

24. Determine the domain and range of each of the functions and compare the results.
(a) $f(x, y) = \cos \pi x \sin \pi y$ (b) $g(x, y, z) = \cos \pi x \sin \pi y$

Exercises 25–30. Take $h \neq 0$ and form the difference quotients

$$\frac{f(x + h, y) - f(x, y)}{h} \quad \text{and} \quad \frac{f(x, y + h) - f(x, y)}{y}.$$

Fix x and y and calculate the limits of these quotients as $h \to 0$.

25. $f(x, y) = 2x^2 - y$.
26. $f(x, y) = xy + 2y$.

27. $f(x, y) = 3x - xy + 2y^2$
28. $f(x, y) = x \sin y$.

29. $f(x, y) = \cos(xy)$.
30. $f(x, y) = x^2 e^y$.

31. Express as a function of two variables.

(a) The volume of a box of base area A and height y.
(b) The volume of a right circular cylinder of base radius x and height y.
(c) The area of a parallelogram formed by the vectors $2\,\mathbf{i}$ and $x\,\mathbf{i} + y\,\mathbf{j}$.

32. Express as a function of three variables.

(a) The surface area of a box with no top and with sides of lengths x, y, z.
(b) The angle between the vectors $\mathbf{i} + \mathbf{j}$, $x\,\mathbf{i} + y\,\mathbf{j} + z\,\mathbf{k}$.
(c) The volume of the parallelepiped formed by the vectors $\mathbf{i}$, $\mathbf{i} + \mathbf{j}$, $x\,\mathbf{i} + y\,\mathbf{j} + z\,\mathbf{k}$.

33. A closed box is to have a total surface area of 20 square feet. Express the volume V of the box as a function of the length l and the height h.

34. An open box is to contain a volume of 12 cubic meters. Given that the material for the sides of the box costs \$2 per square meter and the material for the bottom costs \$4 per square meter, express the total cost C of the box as a function of the length l and width w.

35. A petrochemical company is designing a cylindrical tank with hemispherical ends to be used in the transportation of its products. (See the figure.) Express the volume of the tank as a function of the radius r and the length h of the cylindrical portion.

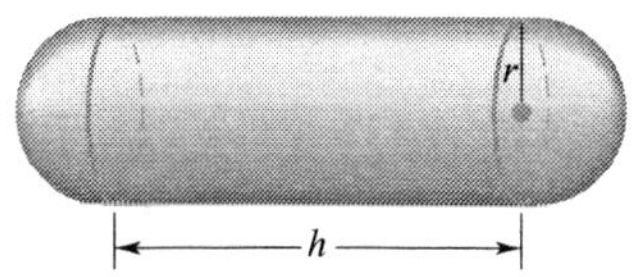

36. A 10-foot section of gutter is to be made from a 12-inch-wide strip of metal by folding up strips of length x on each side so that they make an angle θ with the bottom of the gutter. (See the figure.) Express the area of the trapezoidal cross section as a function of x and θ.

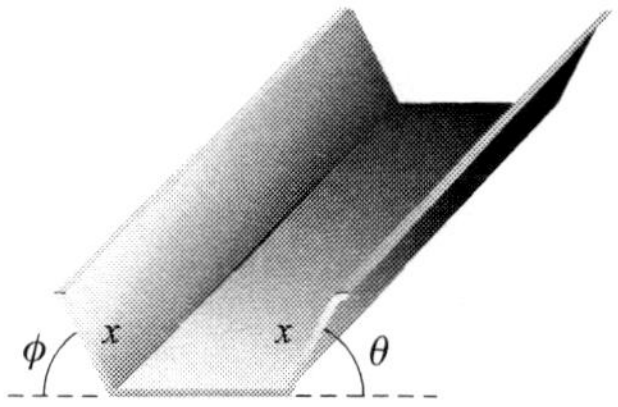

■ 15.2 A BRIEF CATALOGUE OF THE QUADRIC SURFACES; PROJECTIONS

The curves in the xy-plane defined by equations in x and y of the second degree are the conic sections: circle, ellipse, parabola, hyperbola. The surfaces in three-dimensional space defined by equations in x, y, z of the second degree,

$$(*) \qquad Ax^2 + By^2 + Cz^2 + Dxy + Exz + Fyz + Hx + Iy + Jz + K = 0,$$

are called the *quadric surfaces*. Equation (∗) contains terms in xy, xz, yz. These terms can be eliminated by a suitable change of coordinates. Thus, for our purposes, the quadric surfaces are given by equations of the form

$$Ax^2 + By^2 + Cz^2 + Dx + Ey + Fz + H = 0$$

with A, B, C not all zero. (If A, B, C are all zero, we don't have an equation of the second degree.)

The quadric surfaces can be viewed as the three-space analogs of the conic sections. They fall into nine distinct types.†

1. The ellipsoid.
2. The hyperboloid of one sheet.
3. The hyperboloid of two sheets.
4. The elliptic cone.
5. The elliptic paraboloid.
6. The hyperbolic paraboloid.
7. The parabolic cylinder.
8. The elliptic cylinder.
9. The hyperbolic cylinder.

As you go on with calculus in three-space, you will encounter these surfaces time and time again. Here we give you a picture of each one, together with its equation in standard form and some information about its special properties. These are some of the things to look for:

(a) The *intercepts* (the points at which the surface intersects the coordinate axes).
(b) The *traces* (the intersections with the coordinate planes).
(c) The *sections* (the intersections with planes in general).
(d) The *center* (some quadrics have a center; some do not).
(e) *Symmetry.*
(f) *Boundedness, unboundedness.*

Throughout this section you can take a, b, c as positive constants.

The Ellipsoid

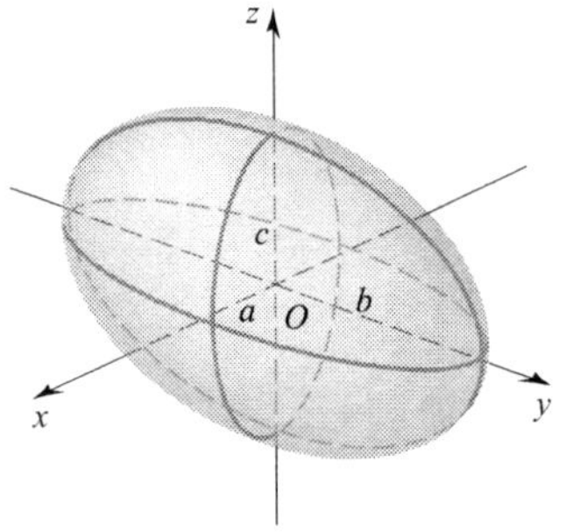

ellipsoid

Figure 15.2.1

$$\frac{x^2}{a^2} + \frac{y^2}{b^2} + \frac{z^2}{c^2} = 1. \qquad \text{(Figure 15.2.1)}$$

The ellipsoid is centered at the origin and is symmetric about the three coordinate axes. It intersects the coordinate axes at six points: $(\pm a, 0, 0)$, $(0, \pm b, 0)$, $(0, 0, \pm c)$. These points are called the *vertices*. The surface is bounded, being contained in the ball $x^2 + y^2 + z^2 \leq a^2 + b^2 + c^2$. All three traces are ellipses; thus, for example, the trace in the xy-plane (the set $z = 0$) is the ellipse

$$\frac{x^2}{a^2} + \frac{y^2}{b^2} = 1.$$

†There is no reason to commit these surfaces to memory. We are creating a catalogue to which you can refer as needed. You'll become familiar with these surfaces by working with them.

Sections parallel to the coordinate planes are also ellipses; for example, taking $y = y_0$, we have

$$\frac{x^2}{a^2} + \frac{z^2}{c^2} = 1 - \frac{y_0^2}{b^2}.$$

This ellipse is the intersection of the ellipsoid with the plane $y = y_0$. The numbers a, b, c are called the *semiaxes* of the ellipsoid. If two of the semiaxes are equal, then we have an *ellipsoid of revolution*. (If, for example, $a = c$, then all sections parallel to the xz-plane are circles and the surface can be obtained by revolving the trace in the xy-plane about the y-axis.) If all three semiaxes are equal, the surface is a *sphere*.

The Hyperboloid of One Sheet

$$\frac{x^2}{a^2} + \frac{y^2}{b^2} - \frac{z^2}{c^2} = 1. \qquad \text{(Figure 15.2.2)}$$

The surface is unbounded. It is centered at the origin and is symmetric about the three coordinate planes. The surface intersects the coordinate axes at four points: $(\pm a, 0, 0)$, $(0, \pm b, 0)$. The trace in the xy-plane (set $z = 0$) is the ellipse

$$\frac{x^2}{a^2} + \frac{y^2}{b^2} = 1.$$

Sections parallel to the xy-plane are ellipses. The trace in the xz-plane (set $y = 0$) is the hyperbola

$$\frac{x^2}{a^2} - \frac{z^2}{c^2} = 1,$$

and the trace in the yz-plane (set $x = 0$) is the hyperbola

$$\frac{y^2}{b^2} - \frac{z^2}{c^2} = 1.$$

Sections parallel to the xz-plane and the yz-plane are hyperbolas. If $a = b$, sections parallel to the xy-plane are circles and we have a *hyperboloid of revolution*.

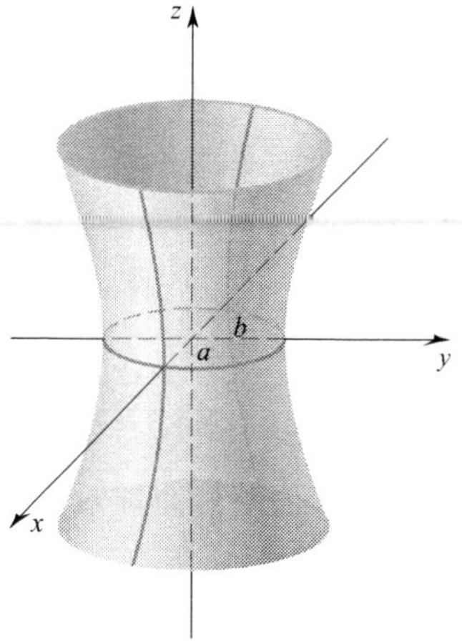

hyperboloid of one sheet

Figure 15.2.2

The Hyperboloid of Two Sheets

$$\frac{x^2}{a^2} + \frac{y^2}{b^2} - \frac{z^2}{c^2} = -1. \qquad \text{(Figure 15.2.3)}$$

The surface intersects the coordinate axes only at the two vertices $(0, 0, \pm c)$. The surface consists of two parts: one for which $z \geq c$, another for which $z \leq -c$. We can see this by rewriting the equation as

$$\frac{x^2}{a^2} + \frac{y^2}{b^2} = \frac{z^2}{c^2} - 1.$$

The equation requires

$$\frac{z^2}{c^2} - 1 \geq 0, \qquad z^2 \geq c^2, \qquad |z| \geq c.$$

Each of the two parts is unbounded. Sections parallel to the xy-plane are ellipses: setting $z = z_0$ with $|z_0| \geq c$, we have

$$\frac{x^2}{a^2} + \frac{y^2}{b^2} = \frac{z_0^2}{c^2} - 1.$$

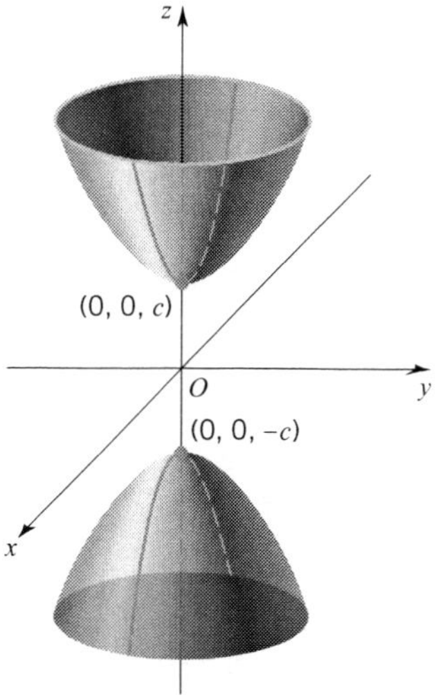

hyperboloid of two sheets

Figure 15.2.3

If $a = b$, then all sections parallel to the xy-plane are circles and we have a hyperboloid of revolution. Sections parallel to the other coordinate planes are hyperbolas; for example, setting $y = y_0$, we have

$$\frac{z^2}{c^2} - \frac{x^2}{a^2} = 1 + \frac{y_0^2}{b^2}.$$

The entire surface is symmetric about the three coordinate planes and is centered at the origin.

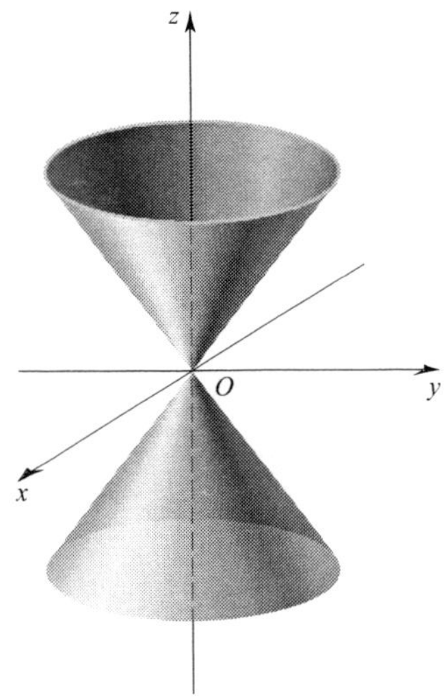

elliptic cone

Figure 15.2.4

The Elliptic Cone

$$\frac{x^2}{a^2} + \frac{y^2}{b^2} = z^2. \qquad \text{(Figure 15.2.4)}$$

The surface intersects the coordinate axes only at the origin. The surface is unbounded. Once again there is symmetry about the three coordinate planes. The trace in the xz-plane is a pair of intersecting lines: $z = \pm x/a$. The trace in the yz-plane is also a pair of intersecting lines: $z = \pm y/b$. The trace in the xy-plane is just the origin. Sections parallel to the xy-plane are ellipses. If $a = b$, these sections are circles and we have a surface of revolution, what is commonly called a *double circular cone* or simply a *cone*. The upper and lower portions of the cone are called *nappes*.

We come now to the *paraboloids*. The equations in standard form will involve x^2 and y^2, but then z instead of z^2.

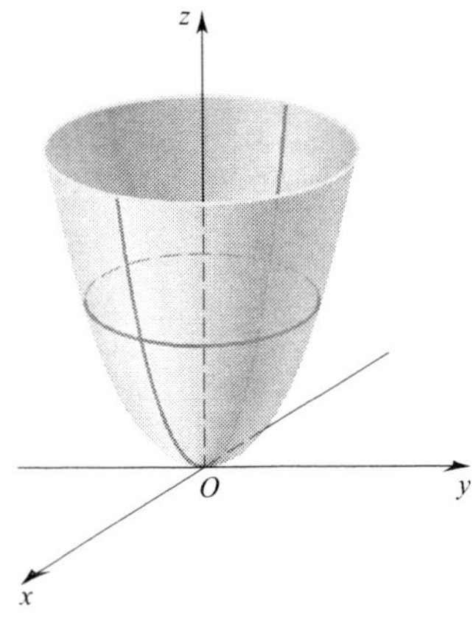

elliptic paraboloid

Figure 15.2.5

The Elliptic Paraboloid

$$\frac{x^2}{a^2} + \frac{y^2}{b^2} = z. \qquad \text{(Figure 15.2.5)}$$

The surface does not extend below the xy-plane; it is unbounded above. The origin is called the *vertex*. Sections parallel to the xy-plane are ellipses; sections parallel to the other coordinate planes are parabolas. Hence the term "elliptic paraboloid." The surface is symmetric about the xz-plane and about the yz-plane. It is also symmetric about the z-axis. If $a = b$, then the surface is a *paraboloid of revolution*.

The Hyperbolic Paraboloid

$$\frac{x^2}{a^2} - \frac{y^2}{b^2} = z. \qquad \text{(Figure 15.2.6)}$$

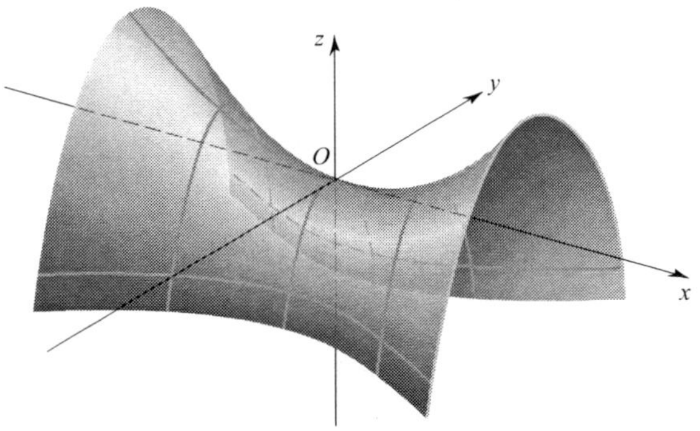

hyperbolic paraboloid

Figure 15.2.6

Here there is symmetry about the xz-plane and yz-plane. Sections parallel to the xy-plane are hyperbolas; sections parallel to the other coordinate planes are parabolas. Hence the term "hyperbolic paraboloid." The origin is a minimum point for the trace in the xz-plane but a maximum point for the trace in the yz-plane. The origin is called a *minimax* or *saddle point* of the surface.

The rest of the quadric surfaces are *cylinders*. The term deserves definition. Take any plane curve C. All the lines through C that are perpendicular to the plane of C form a surface. Such a surface is called a *cylinder*, the cylinder with *base curve* C. The perpendicular lines are known as the *generators* of the cylinder.

If the base curve lies in the xy-plane (or in a plane parallel to the xy-plane), then the generators of the cylinder are parallel to the z-axis. In such a case the equation of the cylinder involves only x and y. The z-coordinate is left unrestricted; it can take on all values.

There are three basic types of quadric cylinders. We give you their equations in standard form: base curve in the xy-plane, generators parallel to the z-axis.

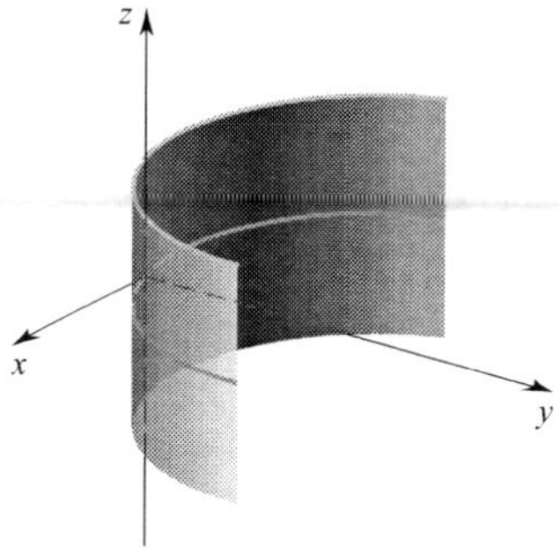

parabolic cylinder

Figure 15.2.7

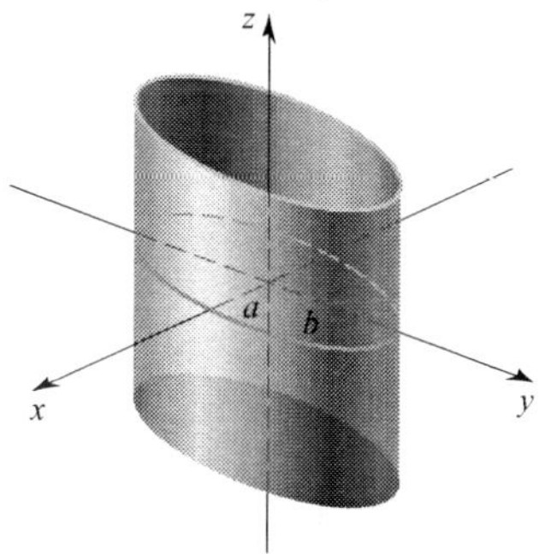

elliptic cylinder

Figure 15.2.8

The Parabolic Cylinder

$$x^2 = 4cy. \qquad \text{(Figure 15.2.7)}$$

This surface is formed by all lines that pass through the parabola $x^2 = 4cy$ and are perpendicular to the xy-plane.

The Elliptic Cylinder

$$\frac{x^2}{a^2} + \frac{y^2}{b^2} = 1. \qquad \text{(Figure 15.2.8)}$$

The surface is formed by all lines that pass through the ellipse

$$\frac{x^2}{a^2} + \frac{y^2}{b^2} = 1$$

and are perpendicular to the xy-plane. If $a = b$, we have the common *right circular cylinder*.

The Hyperbolic Cylinder

$$\frac{x^2}{a^2} - \frac{y^2}{b^2} = 1. \qquad \text{(Figure 15.2.9)}$$

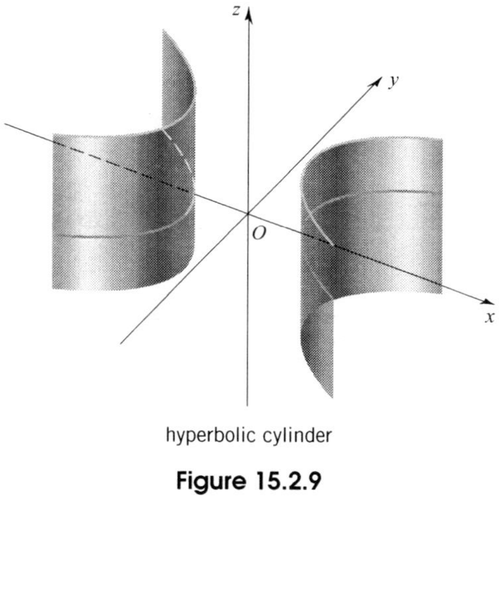

hyperbolic cylinder

Figure 15.2.9

The surface has two parts, each generated by a branch of the hyperbola

$$\frac{x^2}{a^2} - \frac{y^2}{b^2} = 1.$$

Projections

Suppose that $S_1 : z = f(x, y)$ and $S_2 : z = g(x, y)$ are surfaces in three-space that intersect in a space curve C. (See Figure 15.2.10.)

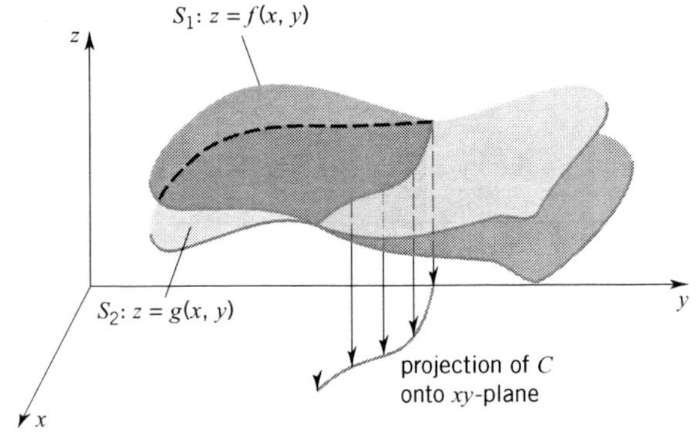

Figure 15.2.10

The curve C is the set of all points (x, y, z) with

$$z = f(x, y) \qquad \text{and} \qquad z = g(x, y).$$

The set of all points (x, y, z) with

$$f(x, y) = g(x, y) \qquad \text{(Here } z \text{ is unrestricted.)}$$

is the vertical cylinder that passes through C.

The set of all points $(x, y, 0)$ with

$$f(x, y) = g(x, y) \qquad \text{(Here } z = 0.)$$

is called the *projection of C onto the xy-plane.* In Figure 15.2.10 it appears as the curve in the xy-plane that lies directly below C.

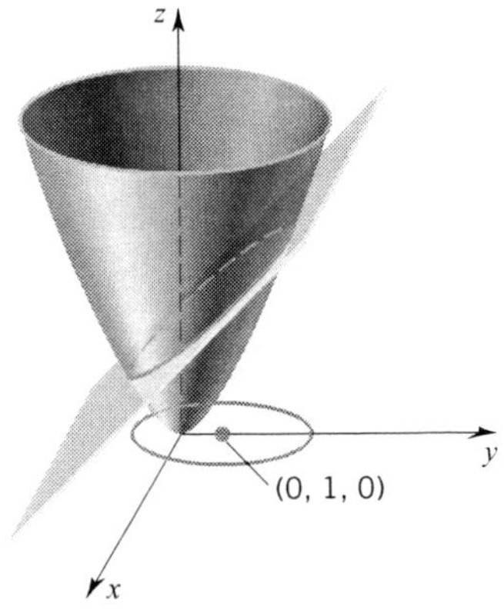

Figure 15.2.11

Example 1 The paraboloid of revolution $z = x^2 + y^2$ and the plane

$$z = 2y + 3$$

intersect in a curve C. See Figure 15.2.11. The projection of this curve onto the xy-plane is the set of all points $(x, y, 0)$ with

$$x^2 + y^2 = 2y + 3.$$

This equation can be written

$$x^2 + (y - 1)^2 = 4.$$

The projection of C onto the xy-plane is the circle of radius 2 centered at $(0, 1, 0)$. ❑

EXERCISES 15.2

Exercises 1–12. Identify the surface.

1. $x^2 + 4y^2 - 16z^2 = 0.$

2. $x^2 + 4y^2 + 16z^2 - 12 = 0.$

3. $x - 4y^2 = 0.$

4. $x^2 - 4y^2 - 2z = 0.$

5. $5x^2 + 2y^2 - 6z^2 - 10 = 0.$

6. $2x^2 + 4y^2 - 1 = 0.$

7. $x^2 + y^2 + z^2 - 4 = 0.$

8. $5x^2 + 2y^2 - 6z^2 + 10 = 0.$

9. $x^2 + 2y^2 - 4z = 0.$ **10.** $2x^2 - 3y^2 - 6 = 0.$

11. $x - y^2 + 2z^2 = 0.$ **12.** $x - y^2 - 6z^2 = 0.$

Exercises 13–24. Sketch the cylinder.

13. $25y^2 + 4z^2 - 100 = 0.$ **14.** $25x^2 + 4y^2 - 100 = 0.$

15. $y^2 - z = 0.$ **16.** $x^2 - y + 1 = 0.$

17. $y^2 + z = 0.$ **18.** $25x^2 - 9y^2 - 225 = 0.$

19. $x^2 + y^2 = 9.$ **20.** $\dfrac{x^2}{4} + \dfrac{y^2}{9} = 1.$

21. $y^2 - 4x^2 = 4.$ **22.** $z = x^2.$

23. $y = x^2 + 1.$

24. $(x - 1)^2 + (y - 1)^2 = 1.$

Exercises 25–38. Identify the surface and find the traces. Then sketch the surface.

25. $9x^2 + 4y^2 - 36z = 0.$

26. $9x^2 + 4y^2 + 36z^2 - 36 = 0.$

27. $9x^2 + 4y^2 - 36z^2 = 0.$

28. $9x^2 + 4y^2 - 36z^2 - 36 = 0.$

29. $9x^2 + 4y^2 - 36z^2 + 36 = 0.$

30. $9x^2 - 4y^2 - 36z = 0.$

31. $9x^2 - 4y^2 - 36z^2 = 36.$

32. $4x^2 + 4z^2 - 36y^2 - 36 = 0.$

33. $4x^2 + 9z^2 - 36y = 0.$

34. $9x^2 + 4z^2 - 36y^2 = 0.$

35. $9y^2 - 4x^2 - 36z^2 - 36 = 0.$

36. $9y^2 + 4z^2 - 36x = 0.$ **37.** $x^2 + y^2 - 4z = 0.$

38. $36x^2 + 9y^2 + 4z^2 - 36 = 0.$

39. Identify all possibilities for the surface

$$z = Ax^2 + By^2$$

taking (a) $AB > 0$. (b) $AB < 0$. (c) $AB = 0$.

40. Find the planes of symmetry for the cylinder $x - 4y^2 = 0$.

41. Write an equation for the surface obtained by revolving the parabola $4z - y^2 = 0$ about the z-axis.

42. The hyperbola $c^2y^2 - b^2z^2 - b^2c^2 = 0$ is revolved about the z-axis. Find an equation for the resulting surface.

43. (a) The equation

$$\sqrt{x^2 + y^2} = kz \qquad \text{with } k > 0$$

represents the upper nappe of a cone, vertex at the origin. The positive z-axis is the axis of symmetry. Describe the section in the plane $z = z_0$, $z_0 > 0$.

(b) Let S be a nappe of a cone, vertex at the origin. Write an equation for S given that

(i) the negative z-axis is the axis of symmetry and the section in the plane $z = -2$ is a circle of radius 6;

(ii) the positive y-axis is the axis of symmetry and the section in the plane $y = 3$ is a circle of radius 1.

44. Form the elliptic paraboloid

$$x^2 + \frac{y^2}{b^2} = z.$$

(a) Describe the section in the plane $z = 1$.

(b) What happens to this section as b tends to infinity?

(c) What happens to the paraboloid as b tends to infinity?

Exercises 45–52. The surfaces intersect in a space curve C. Determine the projection of C onto the xy-plane.

45. The planes $x + 2y + 3z = 6$ and $x + y - 2z = 6$.

46. The planes $x - 2y + z = 4$ and $3x + y - 2z = 1$.

47. The sphere $x^2 + y^2 + (z - 1)^2 = \frac{3}{2}$ and the hyperboloid $x^2 + y^2 - z^2 = 1$.

48. The sphere $x^2 + y^2 + (z - 2)^2 = 2$ and the cone $x^2 + y^2 = z^2$.

49. The paraboloids $x^2 + y^2 + z = 4$ and $x^2 + 3y^2 = z$.

50. The cylinder $y^2 + z - 4 = 0$ and the paraboloid $x^2 + 3y^2 = z$.

51. The cone $x^2 + y^2 = z^2$ and the plane $y + z = 2$.

52. The cone $x^2 + y^2 = z^2$ and the plane $y + 2z = 2$.

53. The ellipsoid $\dfrac{x^2}{a^2} + \dfrac{y^2}{b^2} + \dfrac{z^2}{c^2} = 1$ can be parametrized by the vector function of two variables

$$\mathbf{r}(u, v) = a\cos u \cos v\,\mathbf{i} + b\cos u \sin v\,\mathbf{j} + c\sin u\,\mathbf{k}.$$

(a) Verify that $\mathbf{r}$ parametrizes the ellipsoid given.

(b) Use a graphing utility to draw the ellipsoid with $a = 3$, $b = 4$, $c = 2$.

(c) Experiment with other values of a, b, c to see how the ellipsoid changes shape. How would you choose a, b, c to obtain a sphere?

54. The hyperboloid of one sheet $\dfrac{x^2}{a^2} + \dfrac{y^2}{b^2} - \dfrac{z^2}{c^2} = 1$ can be parametrized by the vector function of two variables

$$\mathbf{r}(u, v) = a\sec u \cos v\,\mathbf{i} + b\sec u \sin v\,\mathbf{j} + c\tan u\,\mathbf{k}.$$

(a) Verify that $\mathbf{r}$ parametrizes the hyperboloid given.

(b) Use a graphing utility to draw the hyperboloid with $a = 2$, $b = 3$, $c = 4$.

(c) Experiment with other values of a, b, c to see how the hyperboloid changes shape.

55. The elliptic cone $\dfrac{x^2}{a^2} + \dfrac{y^2}{b^2} = \dfrac{z^2}{c^2}$ can be parametrized by the vector function of two variables

$$\mathbf{r}(u, v) = av\cos u\,\mathbf{i} + b\,v\sin u\,\mathbf{j} + cv\,\mathbf{k}.$$

(a) Verify that $\mathbf{r}$ parametrizes the elliptic cone given.

(b) Use a graphing utility to draw the elliptic cone with $a = 1, b = 2, c = 3$.

(c) Experiment with other values of a, b, c to see how the cone changes shape. In particular, what effect does c have on the cone?

■ 15.3 GRAPHS; LEVEL CURVES AND LEVEL SURFACES

We begin with a function f of two variables defined on a subset D of the xy-plane. By the *graph of f*, we mean the set of all points (x, y, z) with

$$z = f(x, y), \qquad (x, y) \in D.$$

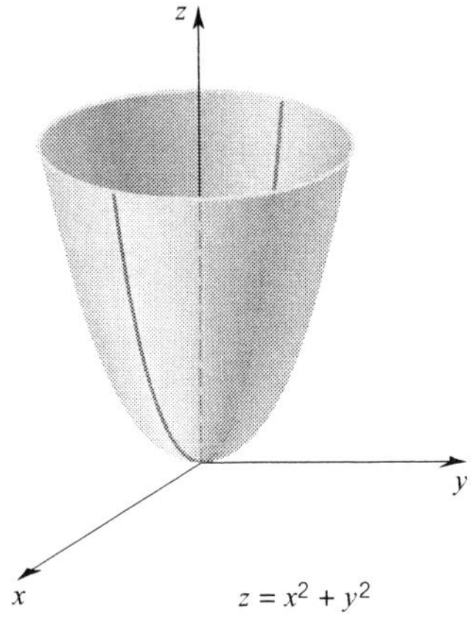

Figure 15.3.1

Example 1 In the case of $f(x, y) = x^2 + y^2$, the domain is the entire plane. The graph of f is the paraboloid of revolution

$$z = x^2 + y^2.$$

This surface can be generated by revolving the parabola

$$z = x^2 \qquad \text{(which lies in the } xz\text{-plane)}$$

about the z-axis. See Figure 15.3.1. ❑

Example 2 Let a, b, c be positive constants. The domain of the function

$$g(x, y) = c - ax - by$$

is the entire xy-plane. The graph of g is the plane

$$z = c - ax - by. \qquad \text{(Figure 15.3.2)}$$

The intercepts of this plane are $x = c/a$, $y = c/b$, $z = c$. ❑

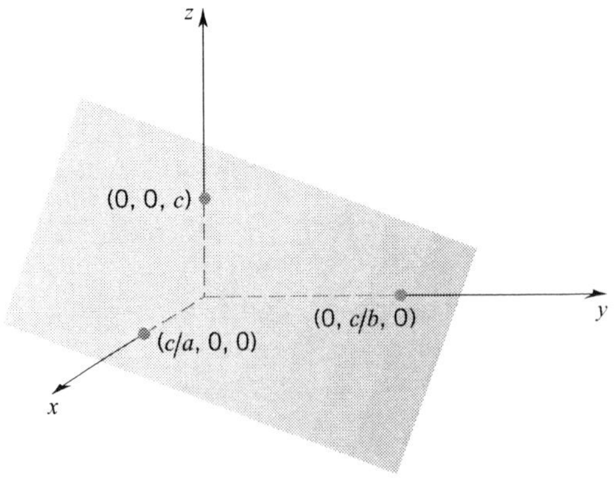

Figure 15.3.2

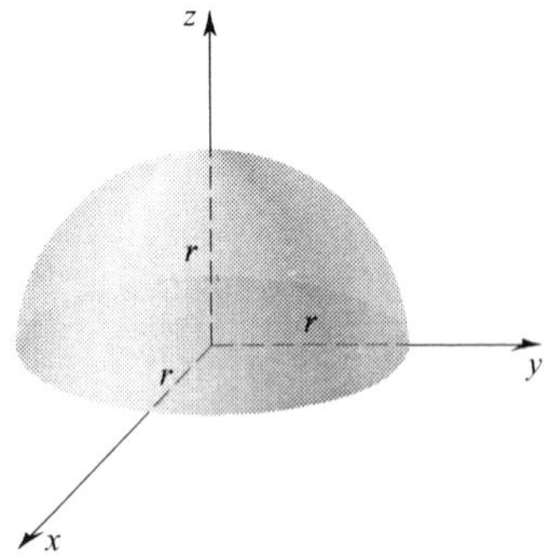

Figure 15.3.3

Example 3 The function $f(x, y) = \sqrt{r^2 - (x^2 + y^2)}$, $r > 0$ is defined only on the closed disk $x^2 + y^2 \leq r^2$. The graph of this function is the surface

$$z = \sqrt{r^2 - (x^2 + y^2)}. \qquad \text{(Figure 15.3.3)}$$

This is the upper half of the sphere

$$x^2 + y^2 + z^2 = r^2. \quad \square$$

Example 4 The function $f(xy) = xy$ is simple enough, but its graph, the surface $z = xy$, is quite difficult to draw. It is a "saddle-shaped" surface, the hyperbolic paraboloid

$$z = \frac{x^2}{2} - \frac{y^2}{2}{}^{\dagger}$$

rotated $\frac{1}{4}\pi$ radians in the counterclockwise direction. ☐

Level Curves

In practice, the graph of a function of two variables is difficult to visualize and difficult to draw. Moreover, if drawn, the drawing is often difficult to interpret. Computer-generated graphics can be useful in resolving these matters. We will provide some illustration of this later in the section.

Here we discuss an approach which we take from the mapmaker. In mapping mountainous terrain, it is common practice to sketch curves that join points of constant elevation. A collection of such curves, called a topographic map, gives a good idea of the altitude variations in a region and suggests the shape of mountains and valleys. (See Figure 15.3.4.)

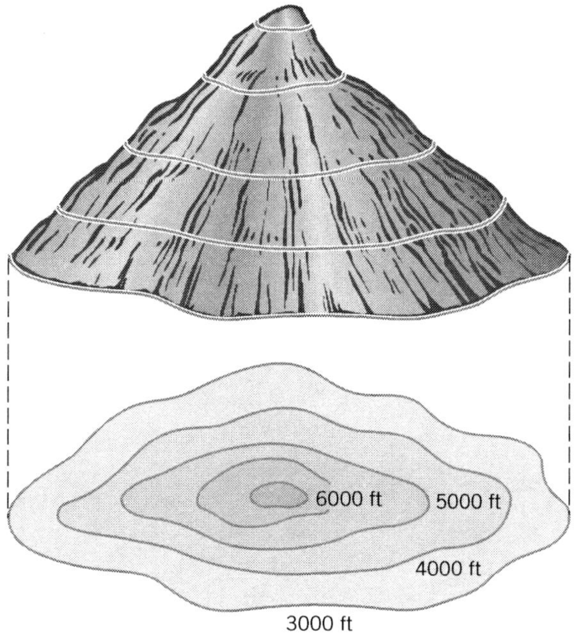

Figure 15.3.4

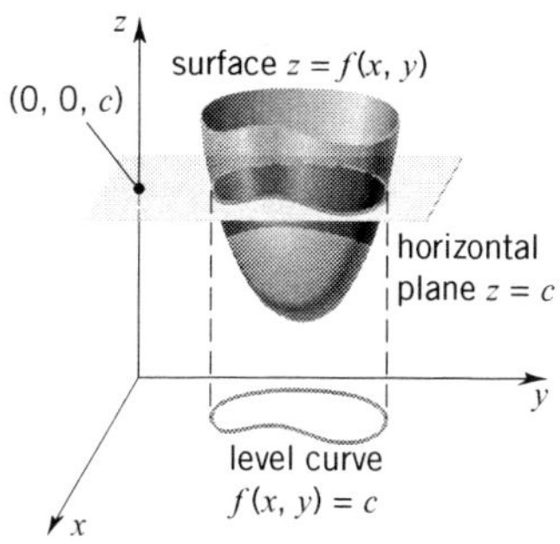

Figure 15.3.5

We can apply this technique to functions of two variables. Suppose that f is a nonconstant function defined on some portion of the xy-plane. If c is a value in the range of f, then we can sketch the curve $f(x, y) = c$. Such a curve is called a *level curve* for f. It can be obtained by intersecting the graph of f with the horizontal plane $z = c$ and then projecting that intersection onto the xy-plane. (See Figure 15.3.5.)

†For rotations, see Appendix A-1.

The level curve $f(x, y) = c$ lies entirely in the domain of f, and on this curve f is constantly c. A collection of level curves, well drawn and labeled, can lead to a good view of the overall behavior of a function.

Example 5 We return to the function $f(x, y) = x^2 + y^2$. (See Figure 15.3.1.) The level curves are circles centered at the origin:

$$x^2 + y^2 = c, \qquad c \geq 0. \qquad \text{(Figure 15.3.6)}$$

The function has the value c on the circle of radius $\sqrt{c}$ centered at the origin. At the origin, the function has the value 0. ❑

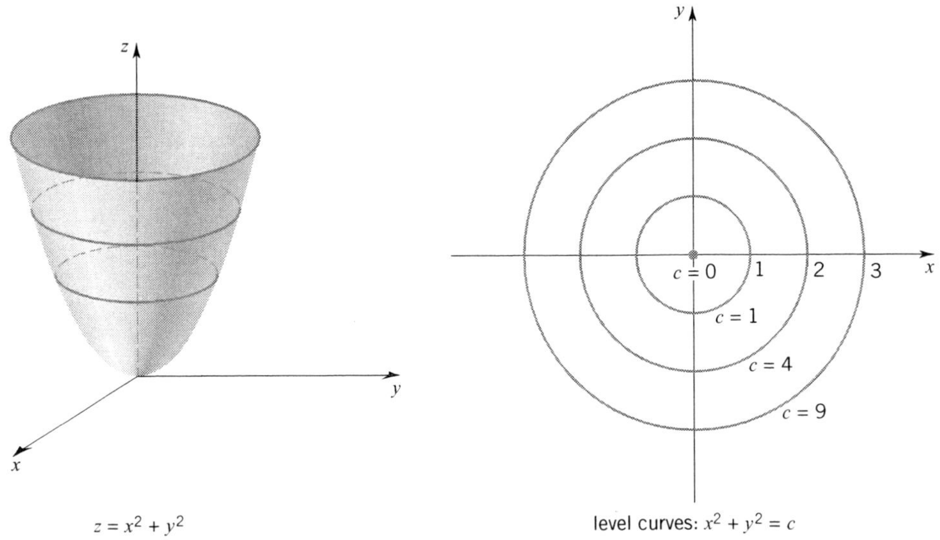

Figure 15.3.6

Example 6 The graph of the function $g(x, y) = 4 - x - y$ is a plane. The level curves are parallel lines of the form $4 - x - y = c$.

The surface and the level curves are indicated in Figure 15.3.7. ❑

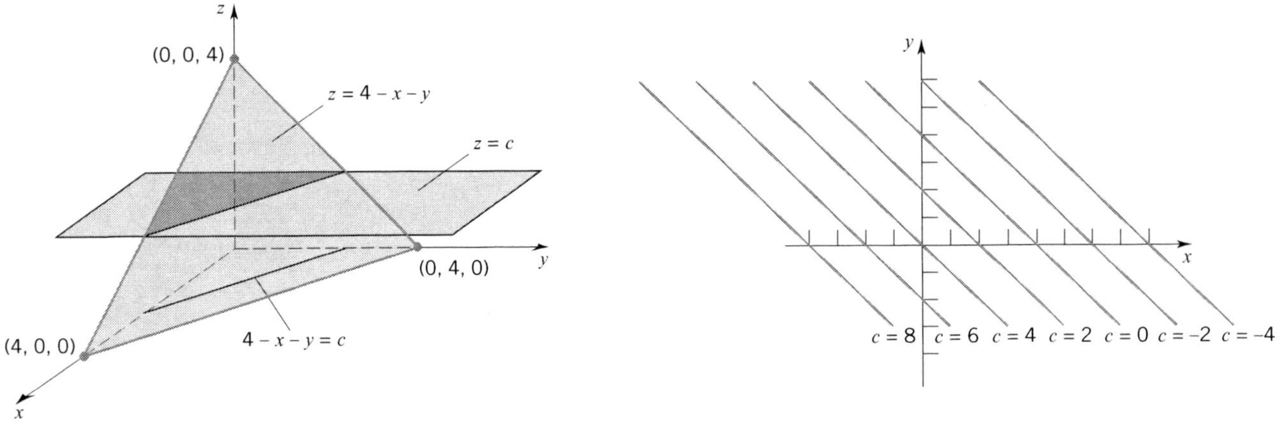

Figure 15.3.7

Example 7 Set

$$h(x, y) = \begin{cases} \sqrt{x^2 + y^2}, & x \geq 0 \\ |y|, & x < 0. \end{cases}$$

For $x \geq 0$, $h(x, y)$ is the distance from (x, y) to the origin. For $x < 0$, $h(x, y)$ is the distance from (x, y) to the x-axis. The level curves are indicated in Figure 15.3.8. The 0-level curve is the nonpositive x-axis. The other level curves are horseshoe-shaped: pairs of horizontal rays capped on the right by semicircles. ❑

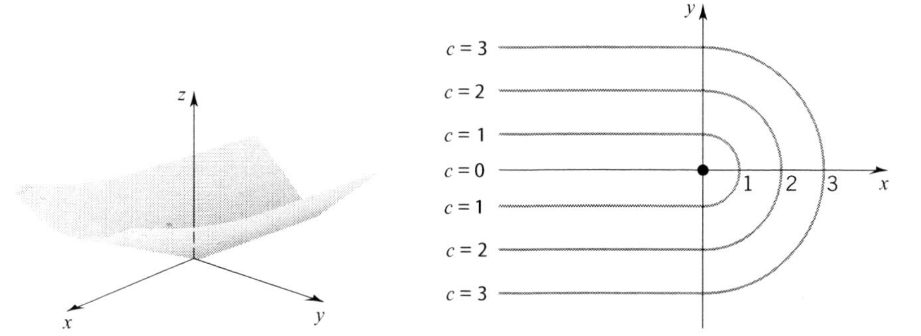

Figure 15.3.8

Example 8 Let's return to the function $f(x, y) = xy$. Earlier we noted that the graph is a saddled-shaped surface. You can visualize the surface from the few level curves sketched in Figure 15.3.9. The 0-level curve, $xy = 0$, consists of the two coordinate axes. The other level curves, $xy = c$ with $c \neq 0$, are hyperbolas. ❑

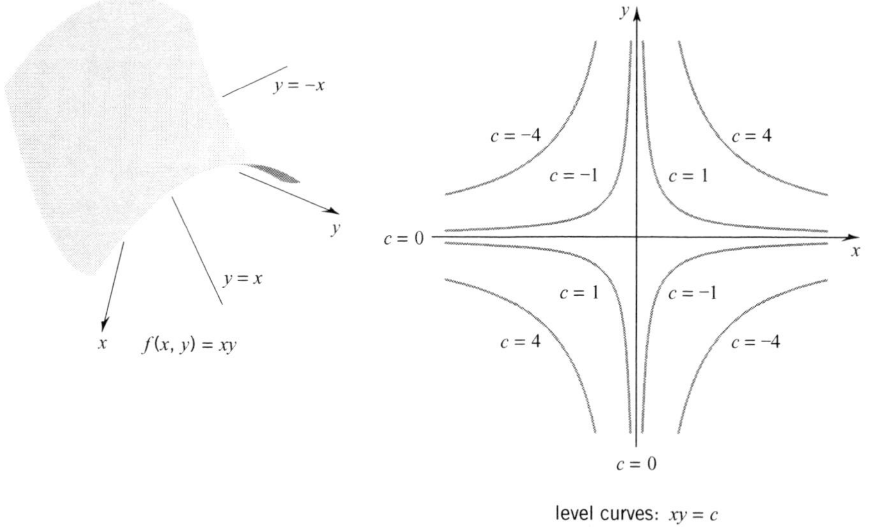

Figure 15.3.9

Computer-Generated Graphs

The preceding examples illustrate how difficult it is to sketch an accurate graph of a function of two variables. But powerful help is at hand. Three-dimensional graphing programs for modern computers make it possible to visualize even quite complicated surfaces. These programs allow the user to view a surface from different perspectives, and they show level curves and sections in various planes. Examples of computer-generated graphs are shown in Figure 15.3.10 and in the Exercises.

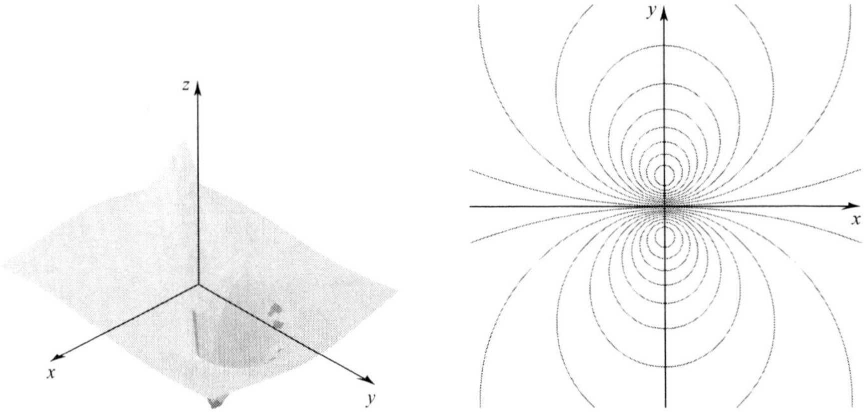

$f(x, y) = \dfrac{-3y}{x^2 + y^2 + 1}$ (*a*) level curves: $-3y = c(x^2 + y^2 + 1)$

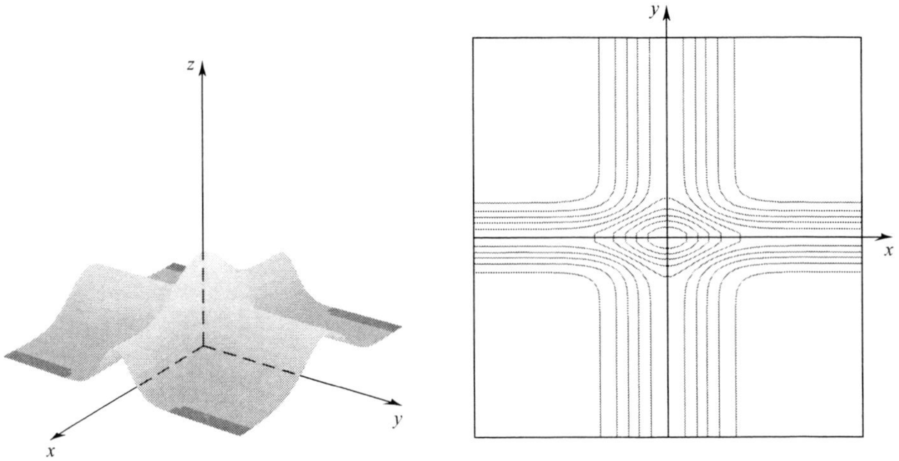

$f(x, y) = e^{-x^2} + e^{-4y^2}$ (*b*) level curves: $e^{-x^2} + e^{-4y^2} = c$

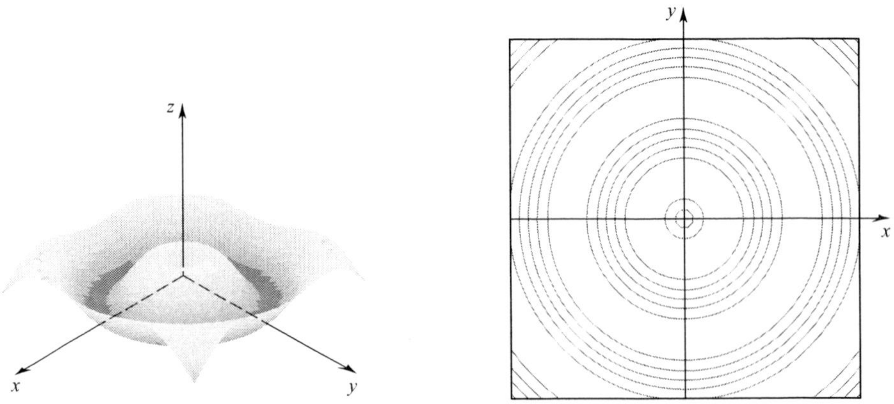

$f(x, y) = \sin\sqrt{x^2 + y^2}$ (*c*) level curves: $\sin\sqrt{x^2 + y^2} = c$

Figure 15.3.10

Level Surfaces

While drawing graphs for functions of two variables is quite difficult, drawing graphs for functions of three variables is actually impossible. To draw such figures we would need four dimensions at our disposal; the domain itself takes up three dimensions.

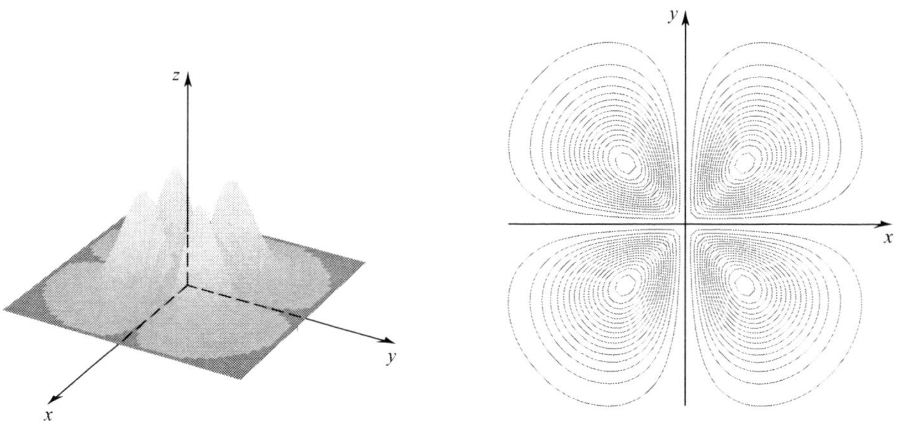

$f(x, y) = \dfrac{x^2 y^2 e^{-x^2-y^2}}{x^2 + y^2}$ (*d*) level curves: $x^2 y^2 e^{-x^2-y^2} = c(x^2 + y^2)$

Figure 15.3.10 ***Continued***

One can try to visualize the behavior of a function of three variables, $w = f(x, y, z)$, by examining the *level surfaces* of f. These are the subsets of the domain of f with equations of the form

$$f(x, y, z) = c$$

where c is a value in the range of f.

Level surfaces are usually difficult to draw. Nevertheless, a knowledge of what they are can be helpful. Here we restrict ourselves to a few simple examples.

Example 9 For the function $f(x, y, z) = Ax + By + Cz$, the level surfaces are parallel planes

$$Ax + By + Cz = c. \quad \square$$

Example 10 For the function $g(x, y, z) = \sqrt{x^2 + y^2 + z^2}$, the level surfaces are concentric spheres

$$x^2 + y^2 + z^2 = c^2. \quad \square$$

Example 11 As our final example we take the function

$$f(x, y, z) = \frac{|z|}{x^2 + y^2}.$$

We extend this function to the origin by defining it to be zero there. At other points of the z-axis we leave f undefined. $\square$

In the first place note that f takes on only nonnegative values. Since f is zero only at $z = 0$, the 0-level surface is the xy-plane. To find the other level surfaces, we take $c > 0$ and set $f(x, y, z) = c$. This gives

$$\frac{|z|}{x^2 + y^2} = c \qquad \text{and thus} \qquad |z| = c(x^2 + y^2).$$

(See Figure 15.3.11.) Each level surface is a double paraboloid of revolution.[†]

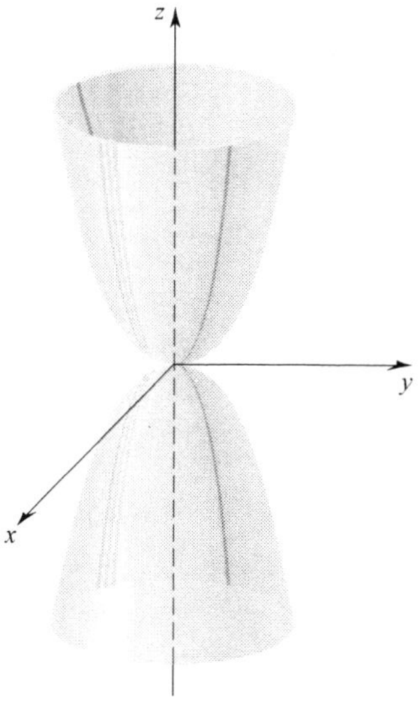

level surface: $|z| = c(x^2 + y^2)$, $(c > 0)$

Figure 15.3.11

[†] A paraboloid (Figure 15.2.5) together with its reflection in the xy-plane.

EXERCISES 15.3

Exercises 1–18. Identify the level curves $f(x, y) = c$ and sketch the curves corresponding to the indicated values of c.

1. $f(x, y) = x - y; \quad c = -2, 0, 2.$

2. $f(x, y) = 2x - y; \quad c = -2, 0, 2.$

3. $f(x, y) = x^2 - y; \quad c = -1, 0, 1, 2.$

4. $f(x, y) = \dfrac{1}{x - y^2}; \quad c = -2, -1, 1, 2.$

5. $f(x, y) = \dfrac{x}{x + y}; \quad c = -1, 0, 1, 2.$

6. $f(x, y) = \dfrac{y}{x^2}; \quad c = -1, 0, 1, 2.$

7. $f(x, y) = x^3 - y; \quad c = -1, 0, 1, 2.$

8. $f(x, y) = e^{xy}; \quad c = \frac{1}{2}, 1, 2, 3.$

9. $f(x, y) = x^2 - y^2; \quad c = -2, -1, 0, 1, 2.$

10. $f(x, y) = x^2; \quad c = 0, 1, 4, 9.$

11. $f(x, y) = y^2; \quad c = 0, 1, 4, 9.$

12. $f(x, y) = x(y - 1); \quad c = -2, -1, 0, 1, 2.$

13. $f(x, y) = \ln(x^2 + y^2); \quad c = -1, 0, 1.$

14. $f(x, y) = \ln\left(\dfrac{y}{x^2}\right); \quad c = -2, -1, 0, 1, 2.$

15. $f(x, y) = \dfrac{\ln y}{x^2}; \quad c = -2, -1, 0, 1, 2.$

16. $f(x, y) = x^2 y^2; \quad c = -4, -1, 0, 1, 4.$

17. $f(x, y) = \dfrac{x^2}{x^2 + y^2}; \quad c = 0, \frac{1}{4}, \frac{1}{2}.$

18. $f(x, y) = \dfrac{\ln y}{x}; \quad c = -2, -1, 0, 1, 2.$

Exercises 19–24. Identify the c-level surface and sketch it.

19. $f(x, y, z) = x + 2y + 3z, \quad c = 0.$

20. $f(x, y, z) = x^2 + y^2, \quad c = 4.$

21. $f(x, y, z) = z(x^2 + y^2)^{-1/2}, \quad c = 1.$

22. $f(x, y, z) = x^2/4 + y^2/6 + z^2/9, \quad c = 1.$

23. $f(x, y, z) = 4x^2 + 9y^2 - 72z, \quad c = 0.$

24. $f(x, y, z) = z^2 - 36x^2 - 9y^2, \quad c = 1.$

25. Identify the c-level surfaces of

$$f(x, y, z) = x^2 + y^2 - z^2$$

taking (i) $c < 0$, (ii) $c = 0$, (iii) $c > 0$.

26. Identify the c-level surfaces of

$$f(x, y, z) = 9x^2 - 4y^2 + 36z^2$$

taking (i) $c < 0$, (ii) $c = 0$, (iii) $c > 0$.

Exercises 27–30. Find an equation for the level curve that contains the point P.

27. $f(x, y) = 1 - 4x^2 - y^2; \quad P(0, 1).$

28. $f(x, y) = (x^2 + y^2)e^{xy}; \quad P(1, 0).$

29. $f(x, y) = y^2 \arctan x; \quad P(1, 2).$

30. $f(x, y) = (x^2 + y)\ln[2 - x + e^y]; \quad P(2, 1).$

Exercises 31–32. Find an equation for the level surface of f that contains the point P.

31. $f(x, y, z) = x^2 + 2y^2 - 2xyz; \quad P(-1, 2, 1).$

32. $f(x, y, z) = \sqrt{x^2 + y^2} - \ln z; \quad P(3, 4, e).$

33. Use a graphing utility to draw (i) the surface and (ii) some level curves.

(a) $f(x, y) = 3x + y^3.$ [b] $f(x, y) = \dfrac{x^2 + 1}{y^2 + 4}.$

34. Use a graphing utility to draw the c-level surfaces for the indicated values of c.

(a) $f(x, y, z) = x + 2y + 4z; \quad c = 0, 4, 8.$

(b) $f(x, y, z) = \dfrac{x + y}{1 + z^2}; \quad c = -2, 0, 2.$

35. Use a CAS to find the level curve/surface at the point P.

(a) $f(x, y) = \dfrac{3x + 2y + 1}{4x^2 + 9}; \quad P(2, 4).$

(b) $f(x, y, z) = x^2 + 2y^2 - z^2; \quad P(2, -3, 1).$

36. Use a CAS to draw the surface and some level curves.

(a) $f(x, y) = (x^2 - y^2)e^{(-x^2 - y^2)}; \quad -2 \le x \le 2,$ $-2 \le y \le 2.$

(b) $f(x, y) = xy^3 - yx^3; \quad -5 \le x \le 5, \quad -5 \le y \le 5.$

37. The magnitude of the gravitational force exerted by a body of mass M situated at the origin on a body of mass m located at the point (x, y, z) is given by the function

$$F(x, y, z) = \frac{GmM}{x^2 + y^2 + z^2}$$

where G is the universal gravitational constant. What are the level surfaces? What is the physical significance of these surfaces?

38. The strength E of an electric field at a point (x, y, z) due to an infinitely long charged wire lying along the y-axis is given by the function

$$E(x, y, z) = \frac{k}{\sqrt{x^2 + z^2}}$$

where k is a positive constant. Describe the level surfaces of E.

39. A metal solid occupies a region in three-space. The temperature T (in °C) at the point (x, y, z) in the solid is inversely proportional to its distance from the origin.

(a) Express T as a function of x, y, z.

(b) Describe the level surfaces and sketch a few of them. NOTE: The level surfaces of T are known as *isothermals*; at all points of an isothermal the temperature is the same.

(c) Suppose the temperature at the point $(1, 2, 1)$ is $50°$. What is the temperature at the point $(4, 0, 3)$?

40. The function

$$V(x, y) = \frac{k}{\sqrt{r^2 - x^2 - y^2}},$$

where k and r are positive constants, gives the electric potential (in volts) at a point (x, y) in the xy-plane. Describe the level curves of V and sketch a representative set. NOTE: The level curves of V are called the *equipotential curves*; all points on an equipotential curve have the same electric potential.

Exercises 41–46. A function is given and a set of level curves is shown. Surfaces **A–F** are the graphs of these functions in some order. Match the surface to the function.

41. $f(x, y) = y^2 - y^3$.

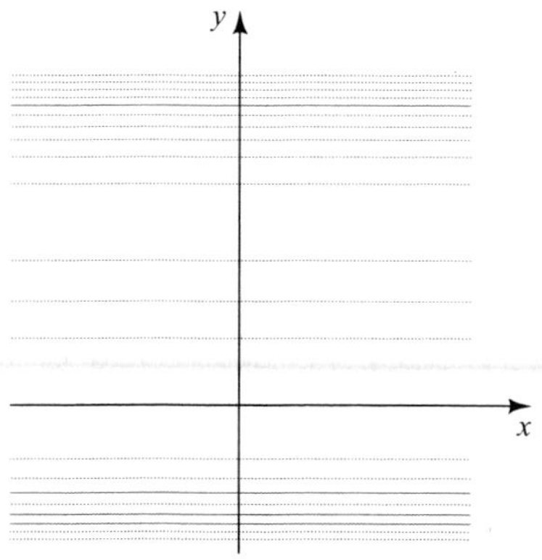

42. $f(x, y) = \sin x,\ 0 \le x \le 2\pi$.

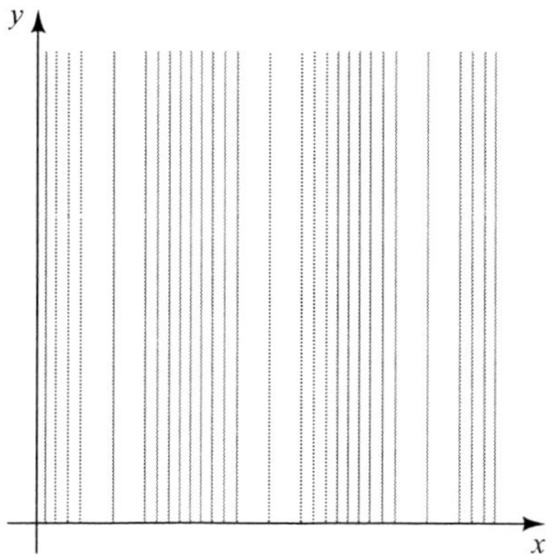

43. $f(x, y) = \cos\sqrt{x^2 + y^2},\ -10 \le x \le 10,\ -10 \le y \le 10$.

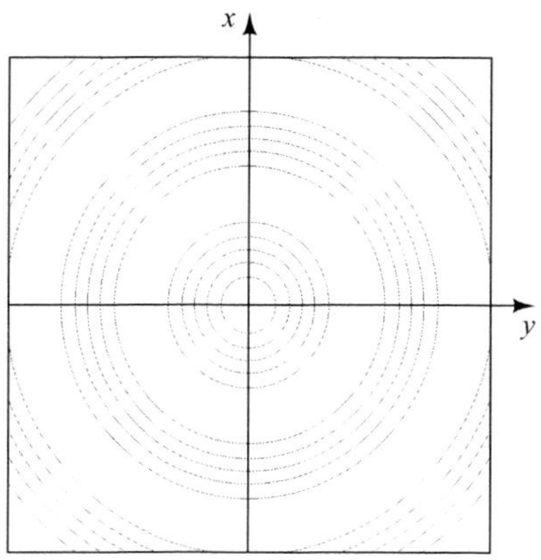

44. $f(x, y) = 2x^2 + 4y^2$.

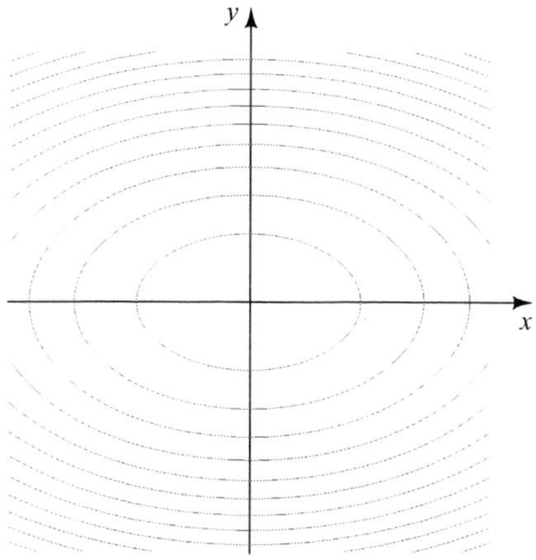

45. $f(x, y) = xye^{-(x^2+y^2)/2}$.

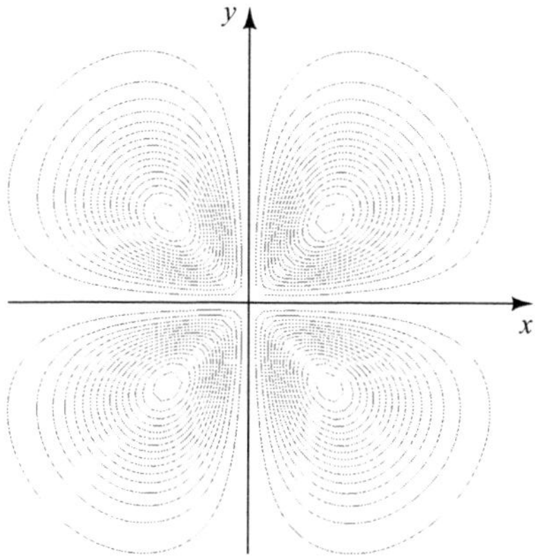

46. $f(x, y) = \sin x \sin y$.

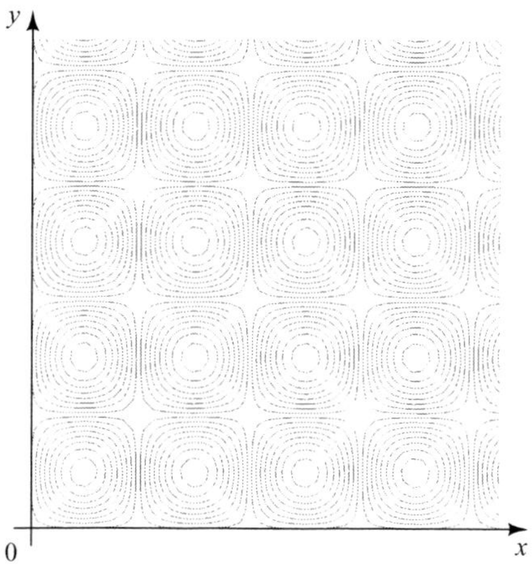

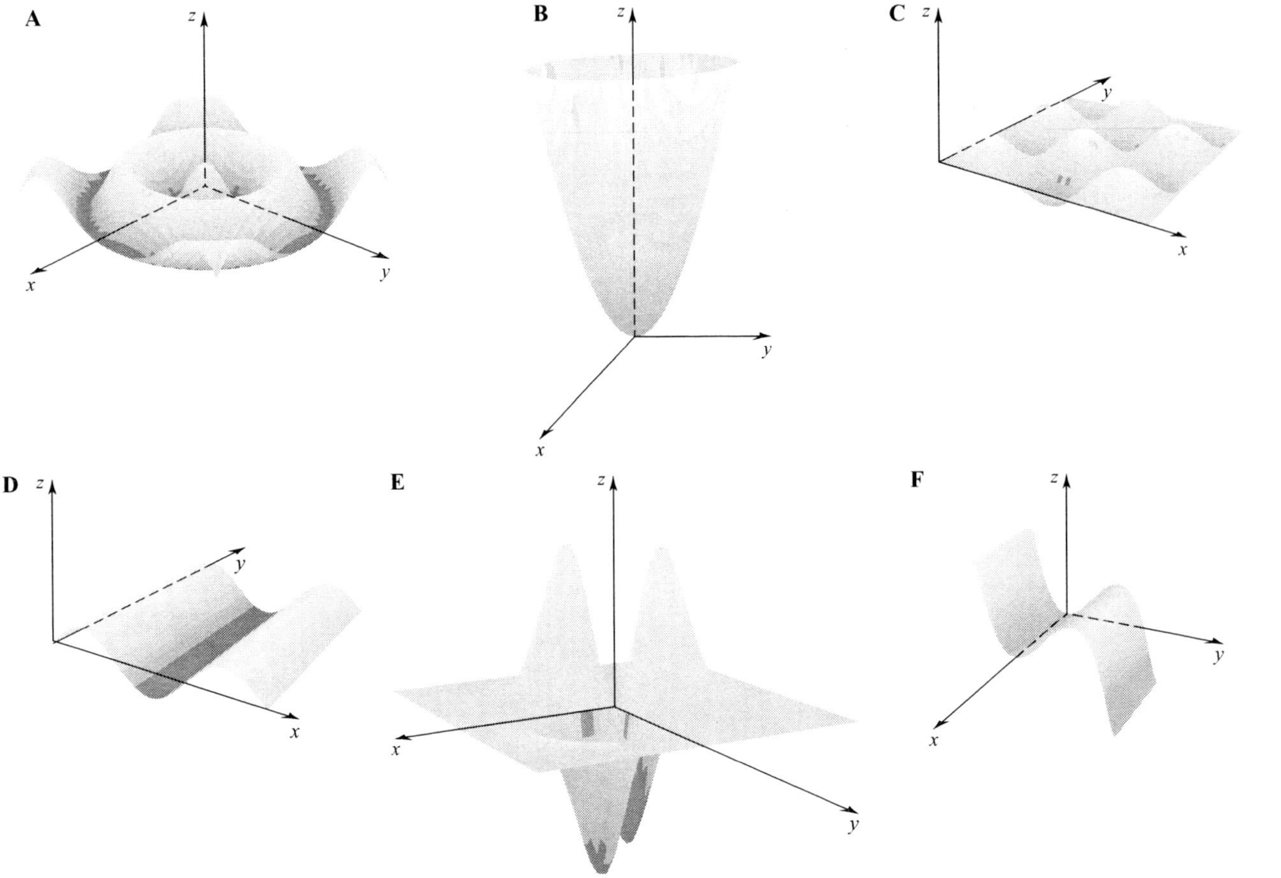

■ PROJECT 15.3 Level Curves and Surfaces

Computer systems such as Derive, Maple, and Mathematica can be used to map the level curves of a function $f = f(x, y)$. In this project you are asked to map the level curves of a function given over a rectangle and then you are asked to "visualize" the surface $z = f(x, y)$. For example, the level curves of

$$f(x, y) = x^2y^2e^{-(x^2+y^2)}$$

on the rectangle $-3 \leq x \leq 3$, $-3 \leq y \leq 3$ look like this.

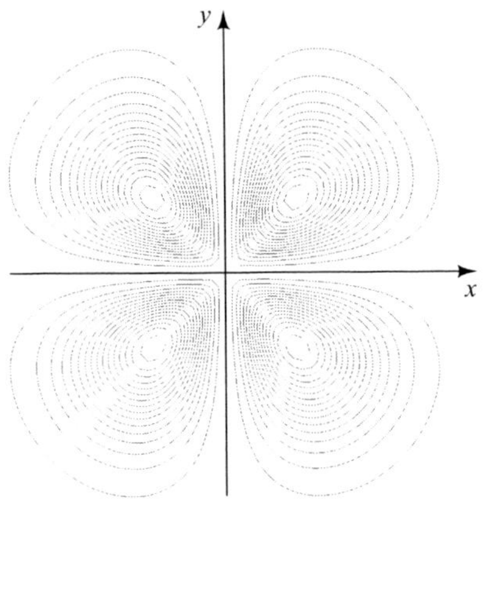

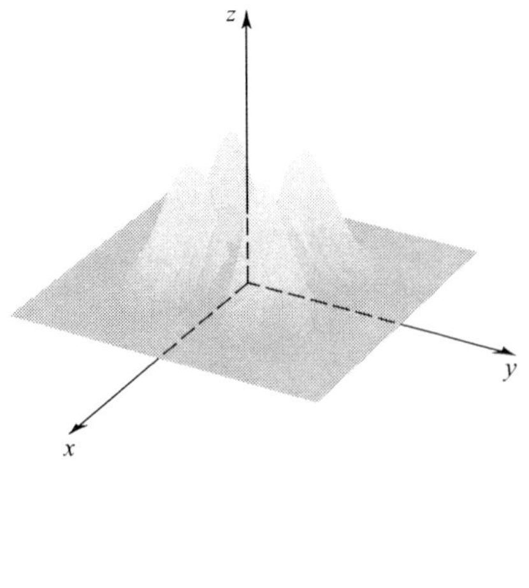

This map of the level curves suggests that the surface $z = f(x, y)$ has either "peaks" or "pits" symmetrically placed in the four quadrants. The computer-generated graph confirms this conjecture.

Problem 1. Map the level curves of $f(x, y) = \dfrac{1}{x^2 + y^2}$ over the rectangle $-3 \leq x \leq 3$, $-3 \leq y \leq 3$. Try to visualize the graph of f from your map of the level curves. Then sketch the surface $z = f(x, y)$ to confirm your visualization.

Problem 2. Problem 1 for the $f(x, y) = \dfrac{2y}{x^2 + y^2 + 1}$ over the rectangle $-5 \le x \le 5, -5 \le y \le 5$.

Problem 3. Problem 1 for $f(x, y) = \cos x \cos y e^{-\frac{1}{4}(x^2+y^2)^{1/2}}$ over the rectangle $-2\pi \le x \le 2\pi, -2\pi \le y \le 2\pi$.

Problem 4. Problem 1 for $f(x, y) = -\dfrac{xy}{e^{x^2+y^2}}$ over the rectangle $-2 \le x \le 2, -2 \le y \le 2$.

15.4 PARTIAL DERIVATIVES

Functions of Two Variables

Let f be a function of x and y; take for example

$$f(x, y) = 3x^2 y - 5x \cos \pi y.$$

The *partial derivative of f with respect to x* is the function f_x obtained by differentiating f with respect to x, keeping y fixed. In this case

$$f_x(x, y) = 6xy - 5 \cos \pi y.$$

The *partial derivative of f with respect to y* is the function f_y obtained by differentiating f with respect to y, keeping x fixed. In this case

$$f_y(x, y) = 3x^2 + 5\pi x \sin \pi y.$$

These partial derivatives are limits:

DEFINITION 15.4.1 PARTIAL DERIVATIVES (*two variables*)

Let f be a function of two variables x, y. The partial derivatives of f with respect to x and with respect to y are the functions f_x and f_y defined by setting

$$f_x(x, y) = \lim_{h \to 0} \frac{f(x + h, y) - f(x, y)}{h}$$

$$f_y(x, y) = \lim_{h \to 0} \frac{f(x, y + h) - f(x, y)}{h}$$

provided these limits exist.

Example 1 For the function $f(x, y) = x \arctan xy$

$$f_x(x, y) = x\frac{y}{1 + (xy)^2} + \arctan xy = \frac{xy}{1 + x^2y^2} + \arctan xy$$

$$f_y(x, y) = x\frac{x}{1 + (xy)^2} = \frac{x^2}{1 + x^2y^2}. \quad \square$$

In the one-variable case, $f'(x_0)$ gives the rate of change of $f(x)$ with respect to x at $x = x_0$. In the two-variable case, *$f_x(x_0, y_0)$ gives the rate of change of $f(x, y_0)$ with respect to x at $x = x_0$, and $f_y(x_0, y_0)$ gives the rate of change of $f(x_0, y)$ with respect to y at $y = y_0$.*

Example 2 For the function $f(x, y) = e^{xy} + \ln(x^2 + y)$,

$$f_x(x, y) = ye^{xy} + \frac{2x}{x^2 + y} \quad \text{and} \quad f_y(x, y) = xe^{xy} + \frac{1}{x^2 + y}.$$

The number

$$f_x(2, 1) = e^2 + \frac{4}{4+1} = e^2 + \frac{4}{5}$$

gives the rate of change with respect to x of the function

$$f(x, 1) = e^x + \ln(x^2 + 1) \qquad \text{at } x = 2;$$

the number

$$f_y(2, 1) = 2\,e^2 + \frac{1}{4+1} = 2\,e^2 + \frac{1}{5}$$

gives the rate of change with respect to y of the function

$$f(2, y) = e^{2y} + \ln(4 + y) \qquad \text{at } y = 1. \quad \square$$

A Geometric Interpretation

In Figure 15.4.1 we have sketched a surface $z = f(x, y)$ which you can take as everywhere defined. Through the surface we have passed a plane $y = y_0$ parallel to the xz-plane. The plane $y = y_0$ intersects the surface in a curve, the y_0-section of the surface.

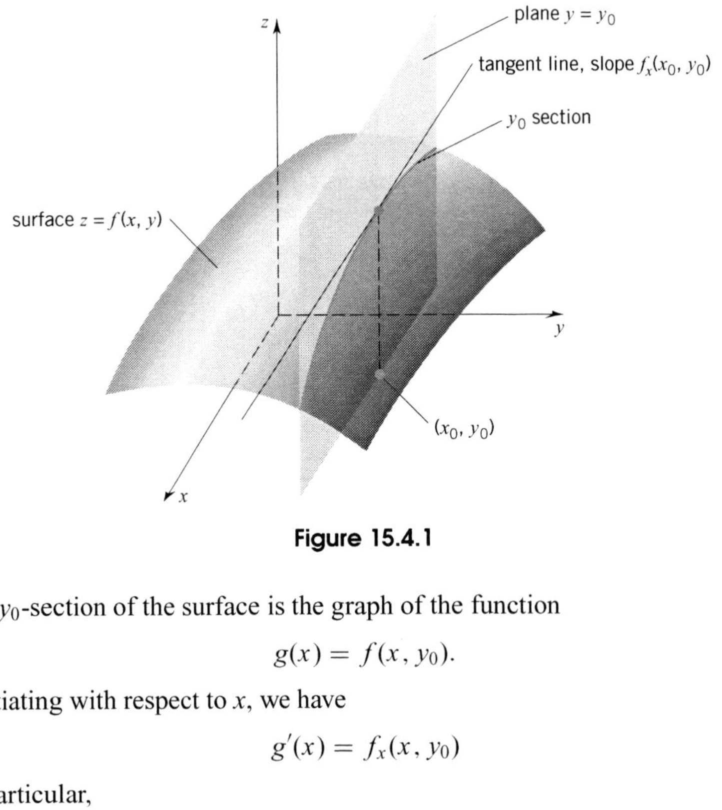

Figure 15.4.1

The y_0-section of the surface is the graph of the function

$$g(x) = f(x, y_0).$$

Differentiating with respect to x, we have

$$g'(x) = f_x(x, y_0)$$

and, in particular,

$$g'(x_0) = f_x(x_0, y_0).$$

The number $f_x(x_0, y_0)$ is thus the slope of the y_0-section of the surface $z = f(x, y)$ at the point $P(x_0, y_0, f(x_0, y_0))$.

The other partial derivative f_y can be given a similar interpretation. In Figure 15.4.2 you can see the same surface $z = f(x, y)$, this time sliced by a plane $x = x_0$ parallel to the yz-plane. The plane $x = x_0$ intersects the surface in a curve, the x_0-section of the surface.

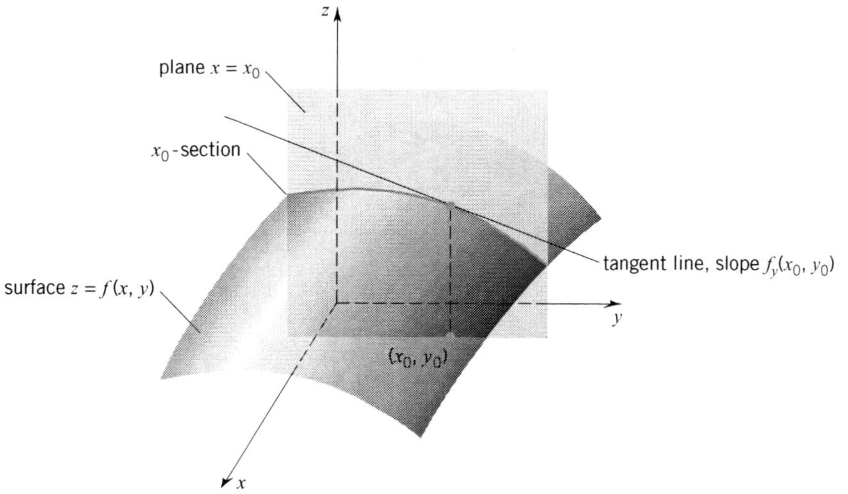

Figure 15.4.2

The x_0-section of the surface is the graph of the function

$$h(y) = f(x_0, y).$$

Differentiating, this time with respect to y, we have

$$h'(y) = f_y(x_0, y)$$

and thus

$$h'(y_0) = f_y(x_0, y_0).$$

The number $f_y(x_0, y_0)$ is the slope of the x_0-section of the surface $z = f(x, y)$ at the point $P(x_0, y_0, f(x_0, y_0))$.

Functions of Three Variables

In the case of a function of three variables, you can look for three partial derivatives: the partial with respect to x, the partial with respect to y, and the partial with respect to z. These partials,

$$f_x(x, y, z), \qquad f_y(x, y, z), \qquad f_z(x, y, z),$$

are defined as follows.

DEFINITION 15.4.2 PARTIAL DERIVATIVES (*three variables*)

Let f be a function of three variables x, y, z. The partial derivatives of f with respect to x, with respect to y, and with respect to z are the functions f_x, f_y, f_z defined by setting

$$f_x(x, y, z) = \lim_{h \to 0} \frac{f(x + h, y, z) - f(x, y, z)}{h}$$

$$f_y(x, y, z) = \lim_{h \to 0} \frac{f(x, y + h, z) - f(x, y, z)}{h}$$

$$f_z(x, y, z) = \lim_{h \to 0} \frac{f(x, y, z + h) - f(x, y, z)}{h}$$

provided these limits exist.

Each partial can be found by differentiating with respect to the subscript variable, keeping the other two variables fixed.

Example 3 For the function $f(x, y, z) = xy^2z^3$

$$f_x(x, y, z) = y^2z^3, \quad f_y(x, y, z) = 2xyz^3, \quad f_z(x, y, z) = 3xy^2z^2.$$

In particular,

$$f_x(1, -2, -1) = -4, \quad f_y(1, -2, -1) = 4, \quad f_z(1, -2, -1) = 12. \quad \square$$

Example 4 For $g(x, y, z) = x^2e^{y/z}$

$$g_x(x, y, z) = 2x\, e^{y/z}, \quad g_y(x, y, z) = \frac{x^2}{z}e^{y/z}, \quad g_z(x, y, z) = -\frac{x^2y}{z^2}e^{y/z}. \quad \square$$

Example 5 For a function of the form $f(x, y, z) = F(x, y)G(y, z)$

$$f_x(x, y, z) = F_x(x, y)G(y, z),$$

$$f_y(x, y, z) = F(x, y)G_y(y, z) + F_y(x, y)G(y, z),$$

$$f_z(x, y, z) = F(x, y)G_z(y, z). \quad \square$$

The number $f_x(x_0, y_0, z_0)$ gives the rate of change of $f(x, y_0, z_0)$ with respect to x at $x = x_0$; $f_y(x_0, y_0, z_0)$ gives the rate of change of $f(x_0, y, z_0)$ with respect to y at $y = y_0$; $f_z(x_0, y_0, z_0)$ gives the rate of change of $f(x_0, y_0, z)$ with respect to z at $z = z_0$.

Example 6 The function $f(x, y, z) = xy^2 - yz^2$ has partial derivatives

$$f_x(x, y, z) = y^2, \quad f_y(x, y, z) = 2xy - z^2, \quad f_z(x, y, z) = -2yz.$$

The number $f_x(1, 2, 3) = 4$ gives the rate of change with respect to x of the function

$$f(x, 2, 3) = 4x - 18 \qquad \text{at } x = 1;$$

$f_y(1, 2, 3) = -5$ gives the rate of change with respect to y of the function

$$f(1, y, 3) = y^2 - 9y \qquad \text{at } y = 2.$$

$f_z(1, 2, 3) = -12$ gives the rate of change with respect to z of the function

$$f(1, 2, z) = 4 - 2z^2 \qquad \text{at } z = 3. \quad \square$$

Remark Partial differentiation is easily extended to functions of more than three variables. For a function f of n variables, $x_1, x_2, \ldots, x_n$, we define the partial derivative of f with respect to the kth variable x_k by setting

$$f_{x_k}(x_1, x_2, \cdots, x_n) = \lim_{h \to 0} \frac{f(x_1, \cdots, x_{k-1}, x_k + h, x_{k+1}, \cdots, x_n) - f(x_1, \cdots, x_k, \cdots, x_n)}{h}. \quad \square$$

Other Notations

There is no need to restrict ourselves to variables x, y, z. Where more convenient, we use other letters.

Example 7 The volume of the frustum of a cone (Figure 15.4.3) is given by the function

$$V(R, r, h) = \tfrac{1}{3}\pi h(R^2 + Rr + r^2).$$

Given that the volume is changing, find the rate of change of the volume with respect to each of its dimensions if the other dimensions are held constant. Determine these rates of change when $R = 8$, $r = 4$, and $h = 6$.

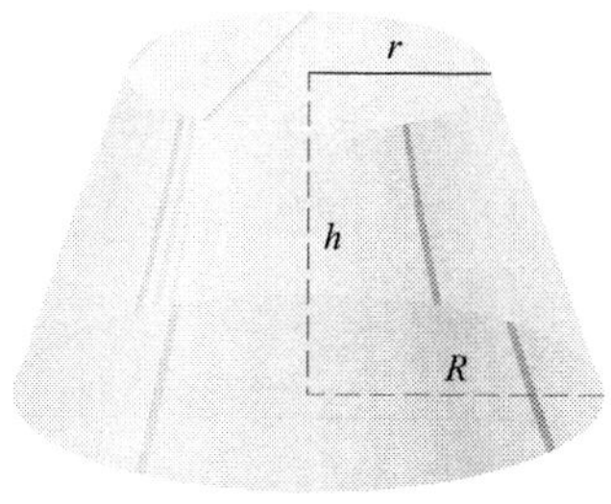

frustum of a cone

Figure 15.4.3

SOLUTION The partial derivatives of V with respect to R, with respect to r, and with respect to h are as follows:

$$V_R(R, r, h) = \tfrac{1}{3}\pi h(2R + r),$$
$$V_r(R, r, h) = \tfrac{1}{3}\pi h(R + 2r),$$
$$V_h(R, r, h) = \tfrac{1}{3}\pi(R^2 + Rr + r^2).$$

When $R = 8$, $r = 4$, and $h = 6$,

the rate of change of V with respect to R is $V_R(8, 4, 6) = 40\pi$,
the rate of change of V with respect to r is $V_r(8, 4, 6) = 32\pi$,
the rate of change of V with respect to h is $V_h(8, 4, 6) = \frac{112}{3}\pi$. ❑

The subscript notation is not the only one used in partial differentiation. A variant of Leibniz's double-*d* notation is also commonly used. In this notation the partials f_x, f_y, f_z are denoted by

$$\frac{\partial f}{\partial x}, \quad \frac{\partial f}{\partial y}, \quad \frac{\partial f}{\partial z}.$$

Thus, for

$$f(x, y, z) = x^3y^2z + \sin xy$$

we have

$$\frac{\partial f}{\partial x}(x, y, z) = 3x^2y^2z + y\cos xy, \qquad \frac{\partial f}{\partial y}(x, y, z) = 2x^2yz + x\cos xy,$$
$$\frac{\partial f}{\partial z}(x, y, z) = x^3y^2,$$

or more simply,

$$\frac{\partial f}{\partial x} = 3x^2y^2z + y\cos xy, \qquad \frac{\partial f}{\partial y} = 2x^3yz + x\cos xy, \qquad \frac{\partial f}{\partial z} = x^3y^2.$$

We can also write

$$\frac{\partial}{\partial x}(x^3y^2z + \sin xy) = 3x^2y^2z + y\cos xy,$$
$$\frac{\partial}{\partial y}(x^3y^2z + \sin xy) = 2x^3yz + x\cos xy, \qquad \frac{\partial}{\partial z}(x^3y^2z + \sin xy) = x^3y^2.$$

Of course, this notation is not restricted to the letters x, y, z. For instance, we can write

$$\frac{\partial}{\partial r}(r^2\cos\theta + e^{\theta r}) = 2r\cos\theta + \theta e^{\theta r}, \qquad \frac{\partial}{\partial\theta}(r^2\cos\theta + e^{\theta r}) = -r^2\sin\theta + re^{\theta r}.$$

For the function $\rho = \sin 2\theta \cos 3\phi$,

$$\frac{\partial \rho}{\partial \theta} = 2\cos 2\theta \cos 3\phi \quad \text{and} \quad \frac{\partial \rho}{\partial \phi} = -3\sin 2\theta \sin 3\phi.$$

EXERCISES 15.4

Exercises 1–28. Calculate the partial derivatives.

1. $f(x, y) = 3x^2 - xy + y$. **2.** $g(x, y) = x^2 e^{-y}$.

3. $\rho = \sin\phi\cos\theta$. **4.** $\rho = \sin^2(\theta - \phi)$.

5. $f(x, y) = e^{x-y} - e^{y-x}$. **6.** $z = \sqrt{x^2 - 3y}$.

7. $g(x, y) = \dfrac{Ax + By}{Cx + Dy}$. **8.** $u = \dfrac{e^z}{xy^2}$.

9. $u = xy + yz + zx$. **10.** $z = Ax^2 + Bxy + Cy^2$.

11. $f(x, y, z) = z\sin(x - y)$.

12. $g(u, v, w) = \ln(u^2 + vw - w^2)$.

13. $\rho = e^{\theta+\phi}\cos(\theta - \phi)$.

14. $f(x, y) = (x + y)\sin(x - y)$.

15. $f(x, y) = x^2 y \sec xy$.

16. $g(x, y) = \arctan(2x + y)$.

17. $h(x, y) = \dfrac{x}{x^2 + y^2}$. **18.** $z = \ln\sqrt{x^2 + y^2}$.

19. $f(x, y) = \dfrac{x\sin y}{y\cos x}$. **20.** $f(x, y, z) = e^{xy}\sin xz$.

21. $h(x, y) = [f(x)]^2 g(y)$. **22.** $h(x, y) = e^{f(x)g(y)}$.

23. $f(x, y, z) = z^{xy^2}$.

24. $h(x, y, z) = [f(x, y)]^3[g(x, z)]^2$.

25. $h(r, \theta, t) = r^2 e^{2t}\cos(\theta - t)$.

26. $u = \ln(x/y) - ye^{xz}$.

27. $f(x, y, z) = z\arctan(y/x)$.

28. $w = xy\sin z - yz\sin x$.

29. Find $f_x(0, e)$ and $f_y(0, e)$ given that $f(x, y) = e^x \ln y$.

30. Find $g_x(0, \frac{1}{4}\pi)$ and $g_y(0, \frac{1}{4}\pi)$ given that

$$g(x, y) = e^{-x}\sin(x + 2y).$$

31. Find $f_x(1, 2)$ and $f_y(1, 2)$ given that $f(x, y) = \dfrac{x}{x + y}$.

32. Find $g_x(1, 2)$ and $g_y(1, 2)$ given that $g(x, y) = \dfrac{x}{x + y^2}$.

Exercises 33–38. Find $f_x(x, y)$ and $f_y(x, y)$ by forming the appropriate difference quotient and taking the limit as h tends to zero.

33. $f(x, y) = x^2 y$. **34.** $f(x, y) = y^2$.

35. $f(x, y) = \ln(x^2 y)$. **36.** $f(x, y) = \dfrac{1}{x + 4y}$.

37. $f(x, y) = \dfrac{1}{x - y}$. **38.** $f(x, y) = e^{2x+3y}$.

Exercises 39–40. Find $f_x(x, y, z)$, $f_y(x, y, z)$, $f_z(x, y, z)$ by forming the appropriate difference quotient and taking the limit as h tends to zero.

39. $f(x, y, z) = xy^2 z$. **40.** $f(x, y, z) = \dfrac{x^2 y}{z}$.

41. The intersection of a surface $z = f(x, y)$ with a plane $y = y_0$ is a curve C in space. The slope of the tangent line to C at the point $P(x_0, y_0, f(x_0, y_0))$ is $f_x(x_0, y_0)$. (Figure 15.4.1.)

(a) Show that the tangent line can be specified by the following two equations:

$$y = y_0, \qquad z - z_0 = f_x(x_0, y_0)(x - x_0).$$

(b) Now let C be the curve formed by intersecting the surface $z = f(x, y)$ with the plane $x = x_0$. Derive equations that specify the line tangent to C at the point $P(x_0, y_0, f(x_0, y_0))$. (Figure 15.4.2.)

Exercises 42–43. Set $z = x^2 + y^2$ and let C be the curve in which the surface intersects the given plane. Find equations that specify the line tangent to C at the point P.

42. Plane $y = 3$; $P(1, 3, 10)$.

43. Plane $x = 2$; $P(2, 1, 5)$.

Exercises 44–45. Set

$$z = \frac{x^2}{y^2 - 3}$$

and let C be the curve in which the surface intersects the given plane. Find equations that specify the line tangent to C at the point P.

44. Plane $x = 3$; $P(3, 2, 9)$. **45.** Plane $y = 2$; $P(3, 2, 9)$.

46. The surface $x = \sqrt{4 - x^2 - y^2}$ is a hemisphere of radius 2 centered at the origin.

(a) The line l_1 is tangent at the point $(1, 1, \sqrt{2})$ to the curve in which the hemisphere intersects the plane $x = 1$. Find equations that specify l_1.

(b) The line l_2 is tangent at the point $(1, 1, \sqrt{2})$ to the curve in which the hemisphere intersects the plane $y = 1$. Find equations that specify l_2.

(c) The tangent lines l_1 and l_2 determine a plane. Find an equation for this plane. [This plane can be viewed as tangent to the surface at the point $(1, 1, \sqrt{2})$.]

47. Set $f(x, y) = 3x^2 - 6xy + 2y^3$. Use a graphing utility to draw the graph of f near the point $P(1, 2)$.

(a) Use a CAS to find $m_x = \partial f/\partial x$ at P. Use a graphing utility to draw the graph of $z = f(x, 2)$ showing the line through P with slope m_x.

(b) Use a CAS to find $m_y = \partial f/\partial y$ at P. Use a graphing utility to draw the graph of $z = f(1, y)$ showing the line through P with slope m_y.

48. Exercise 47 with $f(x, y) = \dfrac{x - y}{x^2 + y^2}$ and $P(1, 2)$.

Exercises 49–52. Show that the functions u and v satisfy the *Cauchy-Riemann equations*

$$u_x(x, y) = v_y(x, y) \quad \text{and} \quad u_y(x, y) = -v_x(x, y).$$

These equations arise in the study of functions of a complex variable and are of fundamental importance in that setting.

49. $u(x, y) = x^2 - y^2$; $v(x, y) = 2xy$.

50. $u(x, y) = e^x \cos y$; $v(x, y) = e^x \sin y$.

51. $u(x, y) = \frac{1}{2}\ln(x^2 + y^2)$; $v(x, y) = \arctan \dfrac{y}{x}$.

52. $u(x, y) = \dfrac{x}{x^2 + y^2}$; $v(x, y) = \dfrac{-y}{x^2 + y^2}$.

53. Assume that f is a function defined on a set D in the xy-plane, and assume that the partial derivatives exist throughout D.

(a) Suppose that $f_x(x, y) = 0$ for all $(x, y) \in D$. What can you conclude about f?

(b) Suppose that $f_y(x, y) = 0$ for all $(x, y) \in D$. What can you conclude about f?

54. The law of cosines for a triangle can be written

$$a^2 = b^2 + c^2 - 2bc\cos\theta.$$

At time t_0, $b_0 = 10$ inches, $c_0 = 15$ inches, $\theta_0 = \frac{1}{3}\pi$ radians.

(a) Find a_0 (the length a at time t_0).

(b) Find the rate of change of a with respect to b at time t_0 given that c and θ remain constant.

(c) Use the rate you found in part (b) to estimate by a differential the change in a that results from a 1-inch decrease in b.

(d) Find the rate of change of a with respect to θ at time t_0 given that b and c remain constant.

(e) Find the rate of change of c with respect to θ at time t_0 given that a and b remain constant.

55. The area of a triangle is given by the formula

$$A = \tfrac{1}{2}bc\sin\theta.$$

At time t_0, $b_0 = 10$ inches, $c_0 = 15$ inches, $\theta_0 = \frac{1}{3}\pi$ radians.

(a) Find the area of the triangle at time t_0.

(b) Find the rate of change of the area with respect to b at time t_0 given that c and θ remain constant.

(c) Find the rate of change of the area with respect to θ at time t_0 given that b and c remain constant.

(d) Use the rate you found in part (c) to estimate by a differential the change in area that results from a 1° increase in θ.

(e) Find the rate of change of c with respect to b at time t_0 given that the area and θ remain constant.

56. Let f be a function of x and y that satisfies a relation of the form

$$\frac{\partial f}{\partial x} = kf, \qquad k \text{ a constant.}$$

Show that

$$f(x, y) = g(y)e^{kx},$$

where g is some function of y.

57. Let $z = f(x, y)$ be a function everywhere defined.

(a) Find a vector function that parametrizes the y_0-section of the graph. (Figure 15.4.1.) Find a vector function that parametrizes the line tangent to the y_0-section at the point $P(x_0, y_0, f(x_0, y_0))$. See Exercise 41.

(b) Find a vector function that parametrizes the x_0-section of the graph. (See Figure 14.5.2.) Find a vector function that parametrizes the line tangent to the x_0-section at the point $P(x_0, y_0, f(x_0, y_0))$.

(c) Show that the equation of the plane determined by the tangent lines found in parts (a) and (b) can be written

$$z - f(x_0, y_0) = (x - x_0)\frac{\partial f}{\partial x}(x_0, y_0) + (y - y_0)\frac{\partial f}{\partial y}(x_0, y_0).$$

58. (*A chain rule*) Let f be a function of x and y with partial derivatives f_x and f_y, and let g be a differentiable function of a single variable defined on the range of f. Form the composition $h(x, y) = g(f(x, y))$ and show that

$$h_x(x, y) = g'(f(x, y))f_x(x, y) \quad \text{and} \quad h_y(x, y) = g'(f(x, y))f_y(x, y).$$

Setting $u = f(x, y)$, we have in Leibniz's notation

$$\frac{\partial h}{\partial x} = \frac{dg}{du}\frac{\partial u}{\partial x} \quad \text{and} \quad \frac{\partial h}{\partial y} = \frac{dg}{du}\frac{\partial u}{\partial y}.$$

59. Let g be a differentiable function of a single variable everywhere defined. Use Exercise 58 to verify the following results.

(a) If a and b are constants and $w = g(ax + by)$, then

$$b\frac{\partial w}{\partial x} = a\frac{\partial w}{\partial y}.$$

(b) If m and n are nonzero integers and $w = g(x^m y^n)$, then

$$nx\frac{\partial w}{\partial x} = my\frac{\partial w}{\partial y}.$$

60. Given that $x = r\cos\theta$ and $y = r\sin\theta$, find

$$\frac{\partial x}{\partial r}\frac{\partial y}{\partial \theta} - \frac{\partial x}{\partial \theta}\frac{\partial y}{\partial r}.$$

61. For a gas confined in a container, the ideal gas law states that the pressure P is related to the volume V and the temperature T by an equation of the form

$$P = k\frac{T}{V}$$

where k is a positive constant. Show that

$$V\frac{\partial P}{\partial V} = -P \quad \text{and} \quad V\frac{\partial P}{\partial V} + T\frac{\partial P}{\partial T} = 0.$$

62. Three resistances R_1, R_2, R_3 connected in parallel in an electrical circuit produce a resistance R that is given by the formula

$$\frac{1}{R} = \frac{1}{R_1} + \frac{1}{R_2} + \frac{1}{R_3}.$$

Find $\partial R/\partial R_1$.

■ 15.5 OPEN AND CLOSED SETS

A *neighborhood* of a real number x_0 is by definition a set of the form $\{x : |x - x_0| < \delta\}$ where δ is a positive number. This is just an open interval centered at x_0:

$$(x_0 - \delta, x_0 + \delta).$$

If we remove x_0 from the set, we obtain the set

$$(x_0 - \delta, x_0) \cup (x_0, x_0 + \delta).$$

Such a set is called a *deleted neighborhood* of x_0.

From your study of one-variable calculus you know that for a function to have a limit at x_0 it must be defined at least on a deleted neighborhood of x_0, and for it to be continuous or differentiable at x_0 it must be defined at least on a full neighborhood of x_0.

To pave the way for the calculus of functions of several variables, we will extend the notions of neighborhood and deleted neighborhood to higher dimensions and, in so doing, obtain access to other fruitful ideas.

Points in the domain of a function of several variables can be written in vector notation. In the two-variable case, set

$$\mathbf{x} = (x, y),$$

and, in the three-variable case, set

$$\mathbf{x} = (x, y, z).$$

The vector notation enables us to treat the two cases together.

In this section we introduce five important notions:

(1) Neighborhood of a point.

(2) Interior of a set.

(3) Boundary of a set.

(4) Open set.

(5) Closed set.

For our purposes, the fundamental notion here is "neighborhood of a point." The other four notions can be derived from it.

DEFINITION 15.5.1 NEIGHBORHOOD OF A POINT

A *neighborhood* of a point $\mathbf{x}_0$ is a set of the form

$$\{\mathbf{x} : \|\mathbf{x} - \mathbf{x}_0\| < \delta\}$$

where δ is some number greater than zero.

In the plane, a neighborhood of $\mathbf{x}_0 = (x_0, y_0)$ consists of all the points inside a disk centered at (x_0, y_0). In three-space, a neighborhood of $\mathbf{x}_0 = (x_0, z_0, z_0)$ consists of all the points inside a ball centered at (x_0, y_0, z_0). See Figure 15.5.1.

DEFINITION 15.5.2 THE INTERIOR OF A SET

A point $\mathbf{x}_0$ is said to be an *interior point* of the set S if the set S contains some neighborhood of $\mathbf{x}_0$. The set of all interior points of S is called the *interior* of S.

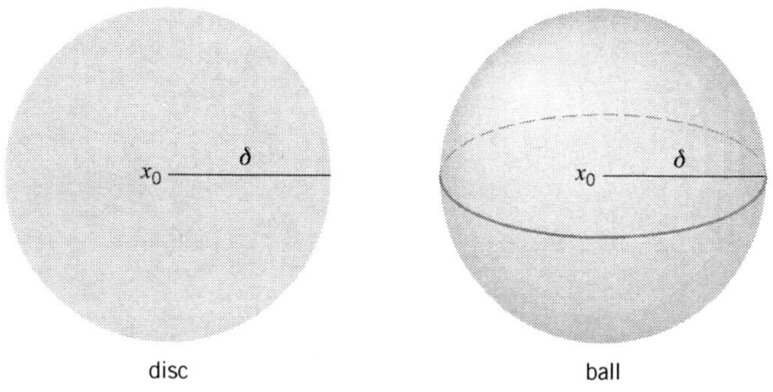

Figure 15.5.1

Example 1 Let Ω be the plane set shown in Figure 15.5.2. The point marked $\mathbf{x}_1$ is an interior point of Ω because Ω contains a neighborhood of $\mathbf{x}_1$. The point $\mathbf{x}_2$ is not an interior point of Ω because *no* neighborhood of $\mathbf{x}_2$ is completely contained in Ω. (Every neighborhood of $\mathbf{x}_2$ has points that do not lie in Ω.) ❑

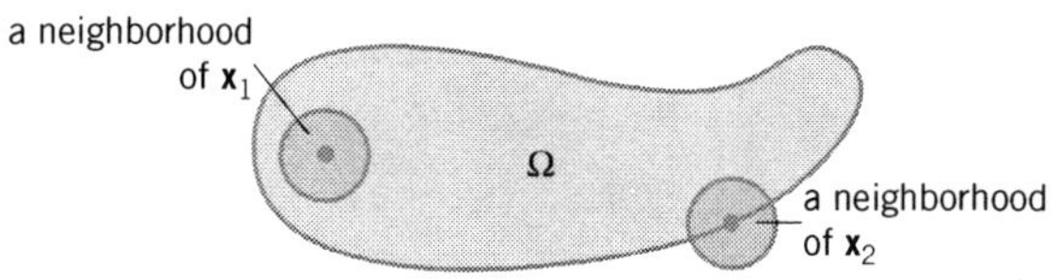

Figure 15.5.2

DEFINITION 15.5.3 THE BOUNDARY OF A SET

A point $\mathbf{x}_0$ is said to be a *boundary point* of the set S if every neighborhood of $\mathbf{x}_0$ contains points that are in S and points that are not in S. The set of all boundary points of S is called the *boundary* of S.

Example 2 The point marked $\mathbf{x}_2$ in Figure 15.5.2 is a boundary point of Ω: each neighborhood of $\mathbf{x}_2$ contains points in Ω and points not in Ω. ❑

DEFINITION 15.5.4 OPEN SET

A set S is said to be *open* if it contains a neighborhood of each of its points.

Thus

(1) A set S is open provided that each of its points is an interior point.

(2) A set S is open provided that it contains no boundary points.

DEFINITION 15.5.5 CLOSED SET

A set S is said to be *closed* if it contains its boundary.

Here are some examples of sets that are open, sets that are closed, and sets that are neither open nor closed:

Two-Dimensional Examples

The sets

$$S_1 = \{(x, y) : 1 < x < 2, 1 < y < 2\},$$
$$S_2 = \{(x, y) : 3 \le x \le 4, 1 \le y \le 2\},$$
$$S_3 = \{(x, y) : 5 \le x \le 6, 1 < y < 2\}$$

are displayed in Figure 15.5.3. S_1 is the inside of the first square. S_1 is open because it contains a neighborhood of each of its points. S_2 is the inside of the second square together with the four bounding line segments. S_2 is closed because it contains its entire boundary. S_3 is the inside of the last square together with the two vertical bounding line segments. S_3 is not open because it contains part of its boundary, and it is not closed because it does not contain all of its boundary.

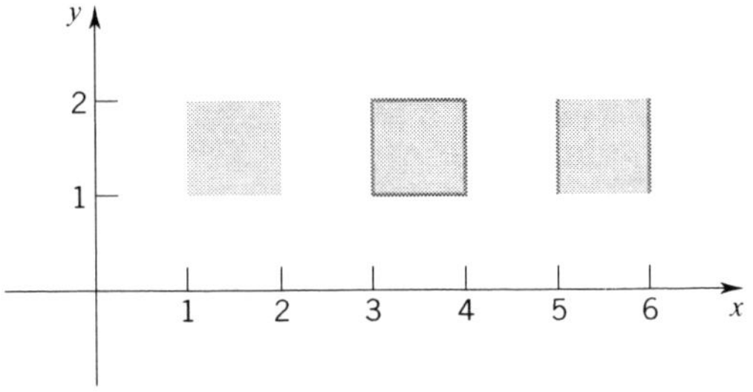

Figure 15.5.3

Three-Dimensional Examples

We now examine some three-dimensional sets:

$$S_1 = \{(x, y, z) : z > x^2 + y^2\},$$
$$S_2 = \{(x, y, z) : z \ge x^2 + y^2\},$$
$$S_3 = \left\{(x, y, z) : 1 \ge \frac{x^2 + y^2}{z}\right\}.$$

The boundary of each of these sets is the paraboloid of revolution

$$z = x^2 + y^2. \qquad \text{(Figure 15.5.4)}$$

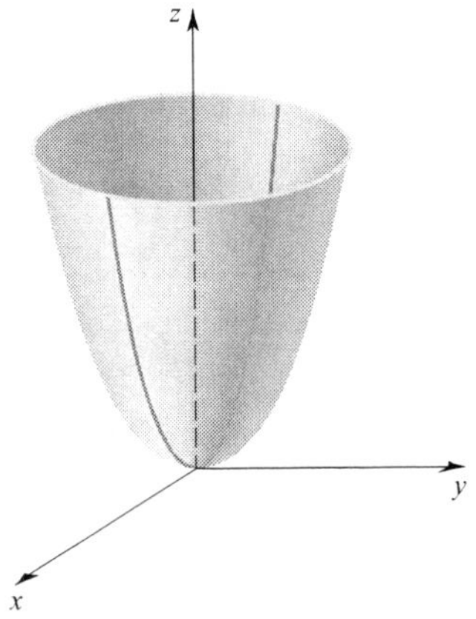

$z = x^2 + y^2$

Figure 15.5.4

The first set consists of all points above this surface. This set is open because, if a point is above this surface, then all points sufficiently close to it are also above this surface. Thus the set contains a neighborhood of each of its points. The second set is closed because it contains all of its boundary. The third set is neither open nor closed. It is not open because it contains some boundary points; for example, it contains the point (1, 1, 2). It is not closed because it fails to contain the boundary point (0, 0, 0).

A Final Remark A neighborhood of $\mathbf{x}_0$ is a set of the form

$$\{\mathbf{x} : \|\mathbf{x} - \mathbf{x}_0\| < \delta\}.$$

If we remove $\mathbf{x}_0$ from the set, we have the set

$$\{\mathbf{x} : 0 < \|\mathbf{x} - \mathbf{x}_0\| < \delta\}.$$

Such a set is called a *deleted neighborhood* of $\mathbf{x}_0$. (We will use deleted neighborhoods in the next section to support the definition of limit.) ❑

EXERCISES 15.5

Exercises 1–10. Specify the interior and the boundary of the set. State whether the set is open, closed, or neither. Then sketch the set.

1. $\{(x, y) : 2 \le x \le 4,\ 1 \le y \le 3\}$.

2. $\{(x, y) : 2 < x < 4,\ 1 < y < 3\}$.

3. $\{(x, y) : 1 < x^2 + y^2 < 4\}$.

4. $\{(x, y) : 1 \le x^2 \le 4\}$.

5. $\{(x, y) : 1 < x^2 \le 4\}$.

6. $\{(x, y) : y < x^2\}$.

7. $\{(x, y) : y \le x^2\}$.

8. $\{(x, y, z) : 1 \le x \le 2,\ 1 \le y \le 2,\ 1 \le z < 2\}$.

9. $\{(x, y, z) : x^2 + y^2 \le 1,\ 0 \le z \le 4\}$.

10. $\{(x, y, z) : (x-1)^2 + (y-1)^2 + (z-1)^2 < \frac{1}{4}\}$.

11. Let $S = \{\mathbf{x}_1, \mathbf{x}_2, \ldots, \mathbf{x}_n\}$ be a nonempty, finite set of points. (a) What is the interior of S? (b) What is the boundary of S? (c) Is S open, closed, or neither?

All the notions introduced in this section can be applied to sets of real numbers: write x for $\mathbf{x}$ and $|x|$ for $\|\mathbf{x}\|$. As indicated earlier, a *neighborhood* of a number x_0, a set of the form

$$\{x : |x - x_0| < \delta\} \qquad \text{with } \delta > 0,$$

is just the open interval $(x_0 - \delta, x_0 + \delta)$.

Exercises 12–19. Specify the interior and boundary of the set. State whether the set is open, closed, or neither.

12. $\{x : 1 < x < 3\}$.

13. $\{x : 1 \le x \le 3\}$.

14. $\{x : 1 \le x < 3\}$.

15. $\{x : x > 1\}$.

16. $\{x : x \le -1\}$.

17. $\{x : x < -1 \text{ or } x \ge 1\}$.

18. The set of positive integers: $\{1, 2, 3, \ldots, n, \ldots\}$.

19. The set of reciprocals: $\{1, 1/2, 1/3, \ldots, 1/n \ldots\}$.

20. Let $\emptyset$ be the empty set. Let X be the real line, the entire plane, or, in the three-dimensional case, all of three-space. For each subset A of X, let $X - A$ be the set of all points $\mathbf{x} \in X$ such that $\mathbf{x} \notin A$.

(a) Show that $\emptyset$ is both open and closed.

(b) Show that X is both open and closed. (It can be shown that $\emptyset$ and X are the only subsets of X that are both open and closed.)

(c) Let U be a subset of X. Show that U is open iff $X - U$ is closed.

(d) Let F be a subset of X. Show that F is closed iff $X - F$ is open.

■ 15.6 LIMITS AND CONTINUITY; EQUALITY OF MIXED PARTIALS

The Basic Notions

The limit process used in taking partial derivatives involved nothing new because in each instance all but one of the variables remained fixed. In this section we take up limits of the form

$$\lim_{(x,y)\to(x_0,y_0)} f(x, y) \qquad \text{and} \qquad \lim_{(x,y,z)\to(x_0,y_0,z_0)} f(x, y, z).$$

To avoid having to treat the two- and three-variable cases separately, we will write instead

$$\lim_{\mathbf{x}\to\mathbf{x}_0} f(\mathbf{x}).$$

This gives us both the two-variable case [set $\mathbf{x} = (x, y)$ and $\mathbf{x}_0 = (x_0, y_0)$] and the three-variable case [set $\mathbf{x} = (x, y, z)$ and $\mathbf{x}_0 = (x_0, y_0, z_0)$].

To take the limit of $f(\mathbf{x})$ as $\mathbf{x}$ tends to $\mathbf{x}_0$, we do not need f to be defined at $\mathbf{x}_0$ itself, but we do need f to be defined at points $\mathbf{x}$ close to $\mathbf{x}_0$. At this stage, we will assume that f is defined at all points $\mathbf{x}$ in some deleted neighborhood of $\mathbf{x}_0$ (f may or may not be defined at $\mathbf{x}_0$). This will guarantee that we can form $f(\mathbf{x})$ for all $\mathbf{x} \ne \mathbf{x}_0$ that are "sufficiently close" to $\mathbf{x}_0$. This approach is consistent with our approach to limits of functions of one variable in Chapter 2.

To say that

$$\lim_{\mathbf{x}\to\mathbf{x}_0} f(\mathbf{x}) = L$$

is to say that for $\mathbf{x}$ sufficiently close to $\mathbf{x}_0$ but different from $\mathbf{x}_0$, the number $f(\mathbf{x})$ is close to L; or, to put it another way, as $\|\mathbf{x} - \mathbf{x}_0\|$ tends to zero but remains different from zero, $|f(\mathbf{x}) - L|$ tends to zero. The ϵ, δ definition is a direct generalization of the ϵ, δ definition in the single-variable case.

DEFINITION 15.6.1 THE LIMIT OF A FUNCTION OF SEVERAL VARIABLES

Let f be a function defined at least on some deleted neighborhood of $\mathbf{x}_0$.

$$\lim_{\mathbf{x}\to\mathbf{x}_0} f(x) = L$$

provided that for each $\epsilon > 0$ there exists a $\delta > 0$ such that

$$\text{if} \quad 0 < \|\mathbf{x} - \mathbf{x}_0\| < \delta, \quad \text{then} \quad |f(\mathbf{x}) - L| < \epsilon.$$

Example 1 We will show that the function $f(x, y) = \dfrac{xy + y^3}{x^2 + y^2}$ does not have a limit at (0, 0). Note that f is not defined at (0, 0) but is defined for all $(x, y) \neq (0, 0)$.

Along the obvious paths to (0, 0), the coordinate axes, the limiting value is 0:
Along the x-axis, $y = 0$; thus, $f(x, y) = f(x, 0) = 0$ and $\lim_{x\to 0} f(x, 0) = \lim_{x\to 0} 0 = 0$.
Along the y-axis, $x = 0$; thus, $f(x, y) = f(0, y) = y$ and $\lim_{y\to 0} f(0, y) = \lim_{y\to 0} y = 0$.

Along the line $y = 2x$, however, the limiting value is $\frac{2}{5}$:

$$f(x, y) = f(x, 2x) = \frac{2x^2 + 8x^3}{x^2 + 4x^2} = \frac{2 + 8x}{5} \to \frac{2}{5} \quad \text{as} \quad x \to 0.$$

There is nothing special about the line $y = 2x$ here. For example, as you can verify, $f(x, y) \to -\frac{1}{2}$ as $(x, y) \to (0, 0)$ along the line $y = -x$. These different modes of approach are illustrated in Figure 15.6.1.

We have shown that not all paths to (0, 0) yield the same limiting value. It follows that f does not have a limit at (0, 0). ❑

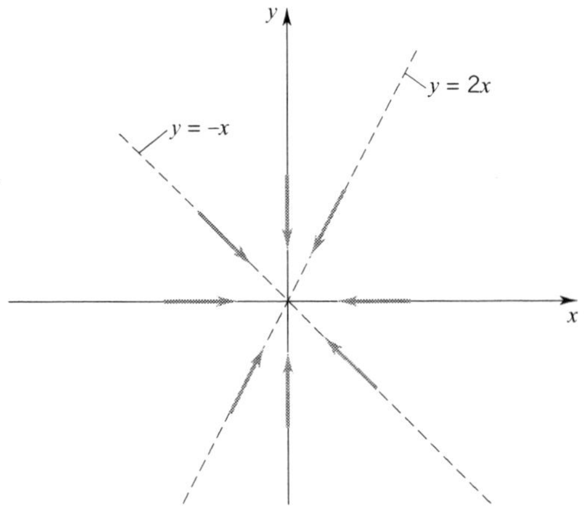

Figure 15.6.1

Example 2 Show that the function $g(x, y) = \dfrac{x^2 y}{x^4 + y^2}$ has limiting value 0 as $(x, y) \to (0, 0)$ along *any* line through the origin, but

$$\lim_{(x,y)\to(0,0)} g(x, y)$$

still does not exist. Note that the domain of g is all $(x, y) \neq (0, 0)$.

SOLUTION As in Example 1, it is easy to verify that $g(x, y) \to 0$ as $(x, y) \to (0, 0)$ along the coordinate axes. If we let $y = mx$, then

$$g(x, y) = g(x, mx) = \frac{mx^3}{x^4 + m^2x^2} = \frac{mx}{x^2 + m^2} \qquad (x \neq 0)$$

and

$$\lim_{x \to 0} g(x, mx) = \lim_{x \to 0} \frac{mx}{x^2 + m^2} = 0.$$

Therefore, $g(x, y) \to 0$ as $(x, y) \to (0, 0)$ along any line through the origin.

Now suppose that $(x, y) \to (0, 0)$ along the parabola $y = x^2$. Then we have

$$g(x, y) = g(x, x^2) = \frac{x^4}{x^4 + x^4} = \frac{1}{2}$$

and

$$\lim_{x \to 0} g(x, x^2) = \lim_{x \to 0} \frac{1}{2} = \frac{1}{2}.$$

Thus, $g(x, y) \to \frac{1}{2}$ as $(x, y) \to (0, 0)$ along the parabola $y = x^2$. (Figure 15.6.2.)

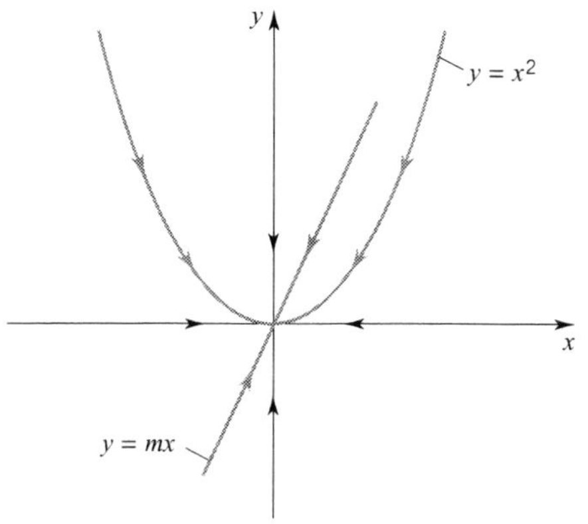

Figure 15.6.2

Since not all paths to (0, 0) yield the same limiting value, we conclude that g does not have a limit at (0, 0). ❑

As in the one-variable case, the limit (if it exists) is unique. Moreover, if

$$\lim_{\mathbf{x} \to \mathbf{x}_0} f(\mathbf{x}) = L \qquad \text{and} \qquad \lim_{\mathbf{x} \to \mathbf{x}_0} g(\mathbf{x}) = M,$$

then

$$\lim_{\mathbf{x} \to \mathbf{x}_0} [f(\mathbf{x}) + g(\mathbf{x})] = L + M, \qquad \lim_{\mathbf{x} \to \mathbf{x}_0} [f(\mathbf{x})g(\mathbf{x})] = LM,$$

and if $M \neq 0$

$$\lim_{\mathbf{x} \to \mathbf{x}_0} [f(\mathbf{x})/g(\mathbf{x})] = L/M.$$

These results are not hard to derive. You can do it simply by imitating the corresponding arguments in the one-variable case.

Suppose now that $\mathbf{x}_0$ is an interior point of the domain of f. To say that f is *continuous* at $\mathbf{x}_0$ is to say that

(15.6.2)
$$\lim_{\mathbf{x} \to \mathbf{x}_0} f(\mathbf{x}) = f(\mathbf{x}_0).$$

For the two-variable case we can write

$$\lim_{(x,y)\to(x_0,y_0)} f(x, y) = f(x_0, y_0)$$

and for three variables,

$$\lim_{(x,y,z)\to(x_0,y_0,z_0)} f(x, y, z) = f(x_0, y_0, z_0).$$

Another way to indicate that f is continuous at $\mathbf{x}_0$ is to write

(15.6.3) $$\lim_{\mathbf{h}\to 0} f(\mathbf{x}_0 + \mathbf{h}) = f(\mathbf{x}_0).$$

To say that f is *continuous on an open set S* is to say that f is continuous at all points of S.

Some Examples of Continuous Functions

Polynomials in several variables, for example,

$$P(x, y) = x^2y + 3x^3y^4 - x + 2y \qquad \text{and} \qquad Q(x, y, z) = 6x^3z - yz^3 + 2xyz$$

are everywhere continuous. In the two-variable case, that means continuity at each point of the xy-plane, and in the three-variable case, continuity at each point of three-space.

Rational functions (quotients of polynomials) are continuous everywhere except where the denominator is zero. Thus

$$f(x, y) = \frac{2x - y}{x^2 + y^2}$$

is continuous at each point of the xy-plane other than the origin (0, 0);

$$g(x, y) = \frac{x^4}{x - y}$$

is continuous except on the line $y = x$;

$$h(x, y) = \frac{1}{x^2 - y}$$

is continuous except on the parabola $y = x^2$;

$$F(x, y, z) = \frac{2x}{x^2 + y^2 + z^2}$$

is continuous at each point of three-space other than the origin (0, 0, 0);

$$G(x, y, z) = \frac{x^5 - y}{ax + by + cz},$$

where a, b, c are constants, is continuous except on the plane $ax + by + cz = 0$.

You can construct more elaborate continuous functions by forming composites: take, for example,

$$f(x, y, z) = \arctan\left(\frac{xz^2}{x + y}\right), \qquad g(x, y, z) = \sqrt{x^2 + y^4 + z^6}, \qquad h(x, y, z) = \sin xyz.$$

The first function is continuous except along the vertical plane $x + y = 0$. The other two functions are continuous at each point of space. The continuity of such composites follows from a simple theorem that we now state and prove. In the theorem, g is a function of several variables, but f is a function of a single variable.

THEOREM 15.6.4 THE CONTINUITY OF COMPOSITE FUNCTIONS

If g is continuous at the point $\mathbf{x}_0$ and f is continuous at the number $g(\mathbf{x}_0)$, then the composition $f \circ g$ is continuous at the point $\mathbf{x}_0$.

PROOF We begin with $\epsilon > 0$. We must show that there exists a $\delta > 0$ such that

$$\text{if} \quad \|\mathbf{x} - \mathbf{x}_0\| < \delta, \quad \text{then} \quad |f(g(\mathbf{x})) - f(g(\mathbf{x}_0))| < \epsilon.$$

From the continuity of f at $g(\mathbf{x}_0)$, we know that there exists a $\delta_1 > 0$ such that

$$\text{if} \quad |u - g(\mathbf{x}_0)| < \delta_1, \quad \text{then} \quad |f(u) - f(g(\mathbf{x}_0))| < \epsilon.$$

From the continuity of g at $\mathbf{x}_0$, we know that there exists a $\delta > 0$ such that

$$\text{if} \quad \|\mathbf{x} - \mathbf{x}_0\| < \delta, \quad \text{then} \quad |g(\mathbf{x}) - g(\mathbf{x}_0)| < \delta_1.$$

This last δ obviously works; namely,

$$\text{if} \quad \|\mathbf{x} - \mathbf{x}_0\| < \delta, \quad \text{then} \quad |g(x) - g(\mathbf{x}_0)| < \delta_1,$$

and therefore

$$|f(g(\mathbf{x})) - f(g(\mathbf{x}_0))| < \epsilon. \quad \square$$

Continuity in Each Variable Separately

A *continuous function of several variables is continuous in each of its variables separately*. In the two-variable case, this means that, if

$$\lim_{(x,y)\to(x_0,y_0)} f(x, y) = f(x_0, y_0),$$

then

$$\lim_{x\to x_0} f(x, y_0) = f(x_0, y_0) \quad \text{and} \quad \lim_{y\to y_0} f(x_0, y) = f(x_0, y_0).$$

(This is not hard to prove.) The converse is false. *It is possible for a function to be continuous in each variable separately and yet fail to be continuous as a function of several variables*. You can see this is in the next example.

Example 3 We set

$$f(x, y) = \begin{cases} \dfrac{2xy}{x^2 + y^2}, & (x, y) \neq (0, 0) \\ 0, & (x, y) = (0, 0). \end{cases}$$

Since $f(x, 0) = 0$ for all x and $f(0, y) = 0$ for all y,

$$\lim_{x\to 0} f(x, 0) = 0 = f(0, 0) \quad \text{and} \quad \lim_{y\to 0} f(0, y) = 0 = f(0, 0).$$

Thus, at the point (0,0), f is continuous in x and continuous in y. As a function of two variables, however, f is not continuous at $(0, 0)$. One way to see this is to note that we can approach $(0, 0)$ as closely as we wish by points of the form (t, t) with $t \neq 0$ (that

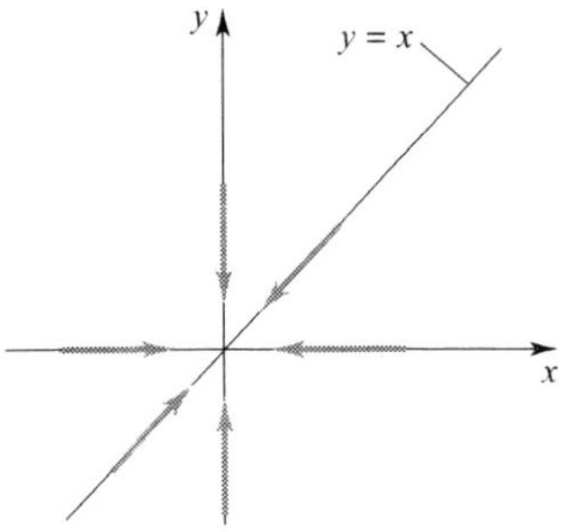

Figure 15.6.3

is, along the line $y = x$). (See Figure 15.6.3.) At such points f takes on the value 1:

$$f(t, t) = \frac{2t^2}{t^2 + t^2} = 1.$$

Hence, f cannot tend to $f(0, 0) = 0$ as required. ❑

Continuity and Partial Differentiability

For functions of a single variable the existence of the derivative guarantees continuity. (Theorem 3.1.3.). *For functions of several variables the existence of partial derivatives does not guarantee continuity.*†

To show this, we can use the same function

$$f(x, y) = \begin{cases} \dfrac{2xy}{x^2 + y^2}, & (x, y) \neq (0, 0) \\ 0, & (x, y) = (0, 0). \end{cases}$$

Since both $f(x, 0)$ and $f(0, y)$ are constantly zero, both partials exist (and are zero) at $(0, 0)$, and yet, as you saw, the function is discontinuous at $(0, 0)$.

It is not hard to understand how a function can have partial derivatives and yet fail to be continuous. The existence of $\partial f/\partial x$ at (x_0, y_0) depends on the behavior of f only at points of the form $(x_0 + h, y_0)$. Similarly, the existence of $\partial f/\partial y$ at (x_0, y_0) depends on the behavior of f only at points of the form $(x_0, y_0 + k)$. On the other hand, continuity at (x_0, y_0) depends on the behavior of f at points of the more general form $(x_0 + h, y_0 + k)$. More briefly, we can put it this way: *the existence of a partial derivative depends on the behavior of the function along a line segment parallel to one of the axes, whereas continuity depends on the behavior of the function in all directions.*

Derivatives of Higher Order; Equality of Mixed Partials

Suppose that f is a function of x and y with first partials f_x and f_y. These are again functions of x and y and may themselves possess partial derivatives: $(f_x)_x$, $(f_x)_y$, $(f_y)_x$, $(f_y)_y$. These functions are called the *second-order partials*. If $z = f(x, y)$, we use the following notations for second-order partials

$$f_{xx} = (f_x)_x = \frac{\partial}{\partial x}\left(\frac{\partial f}{\partial x}\right) = \frac{\partial^2 f}{\partial x^2} = \frac{\partial^2 z}{\partial x^2},$$

$$f_{xy} = (f_x)_y = \frac{\partial}{\partial y}\left(\frac{\partial f}{\partial x}\right) = \frac{\partial^2 f}{\partial y \partial x} = \frac{\partial^2 z}{\partial y \partial x},$$

$$f_{yx} = (f_y)_x = \frac{\partial}{\partial x}\left(\frac{\partial f}{\partial y}\right) = \frac{\partial^2 f}{\partial x \partial y} = \frac{\partial^2 z}{\partial x \partial y},$$

$$f_{yy} = (f_y)_y = \frac{\partial}{\partial y}\left(\frac{\partial f}{\partial y}\right) = \frac{\partial^2 f}{\partial y^2} = \frac{\partial^2 z}{\partial y^2}.$$

Note that there are two "mixed" partials: $f_{xy}(\partial^2 f/\partial y \partial x)$ and $f_{yx}(\partial^2 f/\partial x \partial y)$. The first of these is obtained by differentiating first with respect to x and then with respect to y. The second is obtained by differentiating first with respect to y and then with respect to x.

†See, however, Exercise 32.

Example 4 The function $f(x, y) = \sin x^2 y$ has first partials

$$\frac{\partial f}{\partial x} = 2xy\cos x^2 y \qquad \text{and} \qquad \frac{\partial f}{\partial y} = x^2 \cos x^2 y.$$

The second-order partials are

$$\frac{\partial^2 f}{\partial x^2} = -4x^2y^2 \sin x^2 y + 2y\cos x^2 y, \qquad \frac{\partial^2 f}{\partial y \partial x} = -2x^3 y \sin x^2 y + 2x\cos x^2 y,$$

$$\frac{\partial^2 f}{\partial x \partial y} = -2x^3 y \sin x^2 y + 2x\cos x^2 y, \qquad \frac{\partial^2 f}{\partial y^2} = -x^4 \sin x^2 y. \quad \square$$

Example 5 Setting $f(x, y) = \ln(x^2 + y^3)$, we have

$$\frac{\partial f}{\partial x} = \frac{2x}{x^2 + y^3} \qquad \text{and} \qquad \frac{\partial f}{\partial y} = \frac{3y^2}{x^2 + y^3}.$$

The second-order partials are

$$\frac{\partial^2 f}{\partial x^2} = \frac{(x^2 + y^3)2 - 2x(2x)}{(x^2 + y^3)^2} = \frac{2(y^3 - x^2)}{(x^2 + y^3)^2},$$

$$\frac{\partial^2 f}{\partial y \partial x} = \frac{-2x(3y^2)}{(x^2 + y^3)^2} = -\frac{6xy^2}{(x^2 + y^3)^2},$$

$$\frac{\partial^2 f}{\partial x \partial y} = \frac{-3y^2(2x)}{(x^2 + y^3)^2} = -\frac{6xy^2}{(x^2 + y^3)^2},$$

$$\frac{\partial^2 f}{\partial y^2} = \frac{(x^2 + y^3)6y - 3y^2(3y^2)}{(x^2 + y^3)^2} = \frac{3y(2x^2 - y^3)}{(x^2 + y^3)^2}. \quad \square$$

Perhaps you noticed that in both examples

$$\frac{\partial^2 f}{\partial y \partial x} = \frac{\partial^2 f}{\partial x \partial y}.$$

Since in neither case is f symmetric in x and y, this inequality of the mixed partials is not due to symmetry. Actually it is due to continuity. It can be proved that

(15.6.5)

$$\frac{\partial^2 f}{\partial y \partial x} = \frac{\partial^2 f}{\partial x \partial y}$$

on every open set on which f and the partials

$$\frac{\partial f}{\partial x}, \quad \frac{\partial f}{\partial y}, \quad \frac{\partial^2 f}{\partial y \partial x}, \quad \frac{\partial^2 f}{\partial x \partial y}$$

are continuous.[†]

In the case of a function of three variables, you can look for three first partials

$$\frac{\partial f}{\partial x}, \quad \frac{\partial f}{\partial y}, \quad \frac{\partial f}{\partial z}$$

[†]For a proof, consult a text on advanced calculus.

and nine second partials

$$\frac{\partial^2 f}{\partial^2 x}, \frac{\partial^2 f}{\partial x \partial y}, \frac{\partial^2 f}{\partial x \partial z}, \quad \frac{\partial^2 f}{\partial y \partial x}, \frac{\partial^2 f}{\partial^2 y}, \frac{\partial^2 f}{\partial y \partial z}, \quad \frac{\partial^2 f}{\partial z \partial x}, \frac{\partial^2 f}{\partial z \partial y}, \frac{\partial^2 f}{\partial^2 z}.$$

Here again, there is equality of mixed partials

$$\frac{\partial^2 f}{\partial y \partial x} = \frac{\partial^2 f}{\partial x \partial y}, \quad \frac{\partial^2 f}{\partial z \partial x} = \frac{\partial^2 f}{\partial x \partial z}, \quad \frac{\partial^2 f}{\partial y \partial z} = \frac{\partial^2 f}{\partial z \partial y}$$

on every open set on which f, its first partials, and its mixed partials are continuous.

Example 6 Set $f(x, y, z) = xe^y \sin \pi z$. Here

$$\frac{\partial f}{\partial x} = e^y \sin \pi z \qquad \frac{\partial f}{\partial y} = xe^y \sin \pi z \qquad \frac{\partial f}{\partial z} = \pi xe^y \cos \pi z$$

$$\frac{\partial^2 f}{\partial x^2} = 0 \qquad \frac{\partial^2 f}{\partial y^2} = xe^y \sin \pi z \qquad \frac{\partial^2 f}{\partial z^2} = -\pi^2 xe^y \sin \pi z$$

$$\frac{\partial^2 f}{\partial y \partial x} = e^y \sin \pi z = \frac{\partial^2 f}{\partial x \partial y} \qquad \frac{\partial^2 f}{\partial z \partial x} = \pi e^y \cos \pi z = \frac{\partial^2 f}{\partial x \partial z}$$

$$\frac{\partial^2 f}{\partial y \partial z} = \pi xe^y \cos \pi z = \frac{\partial^2 f}{\partial z \partial y}. \quad \square$$

EXERCISES 15.6

Exercises 1–20. Calculate the second-order partial derivatives. (Treat A, B, C, D as constants.)

1. $f(x, y) = Ax^2 + 2Bxy + Cy^2$.

2. $f(x, y) = Ax^3 + Bx^2y + Cxy^2$.

3. $f(x, y) = Ax + By + Ce^{xy}$.

4. $f(x, y) = x^2 \cos y + y^2 \sin x$.

5. $f(x, y, z) = (x + y^2 + z^3)^2$.

6. $f(x, y) = \sqrt{x + y^2}$.

7. $f(x, y) = \ln\left(\dfrac{x}{x + y}\right)$.

8. $f(x, y) = \dfrac{Ax + By}{Cx + Dy}$.

9. $f(x, y, z) = (x + y)(y + z)(z + x)$.

10. $f(x, y, z) = \arctan xyz$.

11. $f(x, y) = x^y$.

12. $f(x, y, z) = \sin(x + z^y)$.

13. $f(x, y) = xe^y + ye^x$.

14. $f(x, y) = \arctan(y/x)$.

15. $f(x, y) = \ln\sqrt{x^2 + y^2}$.

16. $f(x, y) = \sin x^3y^2$.

17. $f(x, y) = \cos^2 xy$.

18. $f(x, y) = e^{xy^2}$.

19. $f(x, y, z) = xy \sin z - xz \sin y$.

20. $f(x, y, z) = xe^y + ye^z + ze^x$.

21. Show that

$$\text{for } u = \frac{xy}{x + y}, \qquad x^2\frac{\partial^2 u}{\partial x^2} + 2xy\frac{\partial^2 u}{\partial x \partial y} + y^2\frac{\partial^2 u}{\partial y^2} = 0.$$

22. Show that for f of the form specified below,

$$\frac{\partial^2 f}{\partial y \partial x} = \frac{\partial^2 f}{\partial x \partial y}.$$

(a) $f(x, y) = g(x) + h(y)$ with g and h differentiable.

(b) $f(x, y) = g(x)h(y)$ with g and h differentiable.

(c) $f(x, y)$ a polynomial in x and y.

HINT for part (c): Check each term $x^m y^n$ separately.

23. Let f be a function of x and y with everywhere continuous second partials. Is it possible that

(a) $\dfrac{\partial f}{\partial x} = x + y$ and $\dfrac{\partial f}{\partial y} = y - x$?

(b) $\dfrac{\partial f}{\partial x} = xy$ and $\dfrac{\partial y}{\partial y} = xy$?

24. Let g be a twice-differentiable function of one variable and set

$$h(x, y) = g(x + y) + g(x - y).$$

Show that

$$\frac{\partial^2 h}{\partial x^2} = \frac{\partial^2 h}{\partial y^2}.$$

HINT: Use the chain rule of Exercise 58, Section 15.4.

25. Let f be a function of x and y with third-order partials

$$\frac{\partial^3 f}{\partial x^2 \partial y} = \frac{\partial}{\partial x}\left(\frac{\partial^2 f}{\partial x \partial y}\right) \quad \text{and} \quad \frac{\partial^3 f}{\partial y \partial x^2} = \frac{\partial}{\partial y}\left(\frac{\partial^2 f}{\partial x^2}\right).$$

Show that, if all the partials are continuous, then

$$\frac{\partial^3 f}{\partial x^2 \partial y} = \frac{\partial^2 f}{\partial y \partial x^2}.$$

26. Show that the following functions do not have a limit as $(x, y) \to (0, 0)$.

(a) $f(x, y) = \dfrac{x^2 - y^2}{x^2 + y^2}$. (b) $f(x, y) = \dfrac{y^2}{x^2 + y^2}$.

Exercises 27–28. Evaluate the limit of the function as (x, y) approaches the origin along the path indicated.

(a) The x-axis. (b) The y-axis.
(c) The line $y = mx$. (d) The spiral $r = \theta, \theta > 0$.
(e) The differentiable curve $y = f(x)$ with $f(0) = 0$.
(f) The arc $r = \sin 3\theta$, $\frac{1}{6}\pi < \theta < \frac{1}{3}\pi$.
(g) The path $\mathbf{r}(t) = \dfrac{1}{t}\mathbf{i} + \dfrac{\sin t}{t}\mathbf{j}$, $t > 0$.

27. $f(x, y) = \dfrac{xy}{x^2 + y^2}$.

28. $f(x, y) = \dfrac{xy^2}{(x^2 + y^2)^{3/2}}$.

29. Set

$$g(x, y) = \begin{cases} \dfrac{x^2y^2}{x^4 + y^4}, & (x, y) \neq (0, 0) \\ 0, & (x, y) = (0, 0). \end{cases}$$

(a) Show that $\partial g/\partial x$ and $\partial g/\partial y$ both exist at $(0, 0)$. What are their values at $(0, 0)$?
(b) Show that $\displaystyle\lim_{(x,y)\to(0,0)} g(x, y)$ does not exist.

30. Set

$$f(x, y) = \frac{x - y^4}{x^3 - y^4}.$$

Determine whether or not f has a limit at $(1, 1)$.
HINT: Let (x, y) tend to $(1, 1)$ along the line $x = 1$ and along the line $y = 1$.

31. Set

$$f(x, y) = \begin{cases} \dfrac{xy(y^2 - x^2)}{x^2 + y^2}, & (x, y) \neq (0, 0) \\ 0, & (x, y) = (0, 0). \end{cases}$$

It can be shown that some of the second partials are discontinuous at $(0, 0)$. Show that

$$\frac{\partial^2 f}{\partial y \partial x}(0, 0) \neq \frac{\partial^2 f}{\partial x \partial y}(0, 0).$$

32. If a function of several variables has all its first partials at a point, then it is continuous in each variable separately at that point. Show, for example, that if f_x exists at (x_0, y_0), then f is continuous in x at (x_0, y_0).

33. Let f be a function of x and y which has continuous first and second partial derivatives throughout some open set D in the plane. Suppose that $f_{xy}(x, y) = 0$ for all $(x, y) \in D$. What can you conclude about f?

34. Use a graphing utility to draw the graph of the function of Exercise 26(a) on the square $-2 \leq x \leq 2$, $-2 \leq y \leq 2$. The figure should show that the limit as $(x, y) \to (0, 0)$ along the y-axis is 1 and the limit as $(x, y) \to (0, 0)$ along the y-axis is -1.

35. Use a graphing utility to draw the graph of the function of Exercise 26(b) on the square $-2 \leq x \leq 2$, $-2 \leq y \leq 2$. The figure should show that the limit as $(x, y) \to (0, 0)$ along the x-axis is 0 and the limit as $(x, y) \to (0, 0)$ along the y-axis is 1.

36. Use a graphing utility to draw the graph of the function of Exercise 27 on the square $-2 \leq x \leq 2$, $-2 \leq y \leq 2$. The figure should show that the limit as $(x, y) \to (0, 0)$ along the coordinate axes is 0 and the limit as $(x, y) \to (0, 0)$ along the line $y = x$ is $\frac{1}{2}$.

PROJECT 15.6 Partial Differential Equations

The differential equations that we have studied so far are *ordinary differential equations*. They involve only ordinary derivatives, derivatives of functions of one variable. Here we examine some *partial differential equations*, the most prominent of which are equations that relate two or more of the partial derivatives of an unknown function of several variables.

Partial differential equations play an enormous role in science because the description of most natural phenomena is based on models that involve functions of several variables. For example, the partial differential equation known as the Schrödinger[†] equation is viewed by many physicists as the cornerstone of quantum mechanics. Below we introduce two equations of classical physics which have found broad applications in science and engineering.

[†]Introduced in 1926 by the Austrian theoretical physicist Erwin Schrödinger (1881–1961).

Problem 1. Show that the given function satisfies the corresponding differential equation.

a. $u = \dfrac{x^2y^2}{x + y}$; $\quad x\dfrac{\partial u}{\partial x} + y\dfrac{\partial u}{\partial y} = 3u.$

b. $u = x^2y + y^2z + z^2x$; $\quad \dfrac{\partial u}{\partial x} + \dfrac{\partial u}{\partial y} + \dfrac{\partial u}{\partial z} = (x + y + z)^2.$

Laplace's Equation.[††] The partial differential equation

$$\frac{\partial^2 f}{\partial x^2} + \frac{\partial^2 f}{\partial y^2} = 0$$

[††]Named after the French mathematician Pierre-Simon Laplace (1749–1827). Laplace wrote two monumental works: one on celestial mechanics, the other on probability theory. He also made major contributions to the theory of differential equations.

is known as *Laplace's equation in two dimensions.* It is used to describe potentials and steady-state temperature distributions in the plane. In three dimensions Laplace's equation reads

$$\frac{\partial^2 f}{\partial x^2} + \frac{\partial^2 f}{\partial y^2} + \frac{\partial^2 f}{\partial z^2} = 0.$$

This equation is satisfied by gravitational and electrostatic potentials and by steady-state temperature distributions in space. Functions that satisfy Laplace's equation are called *harmonic* functions.

Problem 2.

a. Show that the functions below satisfy Laplace's equation in two dimensions.

 (i) $f(x, y) = x^3 - 3xy^2$.

 (ii) $f(x, y) = \cos x \sinh y + \sin x \cosh y$.

 (iii) $f(x, y) = \ln \sqrt{x^2 + y^2}$.

b. Show that the functions below satisfy Laplace's equation in three dimensions.

 (i) $f(x, y, z) = \dfrac{1}{\sqrt{x^2 + y^2 + z^2}}$.

 (ii) $f(x, y, z) = e^{x+y} \cos \sqrt{2}\, z$.

The Wave Equation The partial differential equation

$$\frac{\partial^2 f}{\partial t^2} - c^2 \frac{\partial^2 f}{\partial x^2} = 0$$

where c is a positive constant is known as the *wave equation.* It arises in the study of phenomena that involve the propagation of waves in a continuous medium. Studies of water waves, sound waves, and light waves are all based on this equation. The wave equation is also used in the study of mechanical vibrations.

Problem 3. Show that the functions below satisfy the wave equation.

a. $f(x, t) = (Ax + B)(Ct + D)$.

b. $f(x, t) = \sin(x + ct) \cos(2x + 2ct)$.

c. $f(x, t) = \ln(x + ct)$.

d. $f(x, t) = (Ae^{kx} + Be^{-kx})(Ce^{ckt} + De^{-ckt})$.

Problem 4. Let $f(x, t) = g(x + ct) + h(x - ct)$ where g and h are any two twice differentiable functions. Show that f is a solution of the wave equation. (This is the most general form of solution for the wave equation.)

CHAPTER 15. REVIEW EXERCISES

Exercises 1–4. Find the domain and range of the function.

1. $f(x, y) = \dfrac{1}{\sqrt{y - x^2}}$. **2.** $f(x, y) = e^{-(x^2+y^2)}$.

3. $f(x, y, z) = \sqrt{z - x^2 - y^2}$.

4. $f(x, y, z) = \ln(x + 2y + z)$.

5. Express as a function of two variables x and y.

 (a) The volume of a circular cone of radius x and height y.

 (b) The volume of a box of length x height y given that the box is twice as long as it is wide.

 (c) The angle between the vectors $\mathbf{i} + 2\mathbf{j}$ and $x\,\mathbf{i} + y\,\mathbf{j}$.

6. A rectangular box is inscribed in the ellipsoid $(x^2/a^2) + (y^2/b^2) + (z^2/c^2) = 1$. The sides of the box are parallel to the coordinate planes and the vertices of the box are on the ellipsoid. Express the volume of the box as a function of x and y.

Exercises 7–12. Identify the surface and find the traces. Then sketch the surface.

7. $4x^2 + 9y^2 + 36z^2 = 36$. **8.** $4z^2 - x^2 - y^2 = 4$.

9. $z = y^2 - x^2$. **10.** $4x^2 + 9z^2 = y$.

11. $x^2 = y^2 + z^2$. **12.** $z^2 = 9x^2 + 4y^2 - 36$.

Exercises 13–16. Sketch the cylinder.

13. $x^2 + z^2 = 4$. **14.** $y - x^2 = 1$.

15. $4y^2 + 9z^2 - 36 = 0$. **16.** $(y - 1)^2 + (z - 1)^2 = 1$.

Exercises 17–20. Identify the level curves $f(x, y) = c$ and sketch the curves corresponding to the indicated values of c.

17. $f(x, y) = 2x^2 + 3y^2$; $c = 0, 6, 12$.

18. $f(x, y) = \sqrt{x^2 + y^2 - 4}$; $c = 0, 1, 2, \sqrt{5}$.

19. $f(x, y) = \dfrac{x}{y^2}$; $c = -4, -1, 1, 4$.

20. $f(x, y) = e^{x^2+y^2}$; $c = e, e^4, e^9$.

Exercises 21–22. Identify the c-level surface and sketch it.

21. $f(x, y, z) = 2x + y + 3z$; $c = 6$.

22. $f(x, y, z) = x^2 + y^2 + 4z^2$; $c = 16$.

23. Set $f(x, y) = (y^2 + 1)\, e^x$. Find an equation for the level curve that passes through the point indicated

 (a) $P(0, 0)$. (b) $P(\ln 2, 1)$. (c) $P(1, -1)$.

24. Set $f(x, y, z) = x^2 \cos yz$. Find an equation for the level surface that passes through the point indicated.

 (a) $P(2, 0, 1)$. (b) $P(1, \pi, -1)$. (c) $P(4, \pi, \frac{1}{2})$.

Exercises 25–26. Find $f_x(x, y)$ and $f_y(x, y)$ by forming the appropriate difference quotient and taking the limit as h tends to 0.

25. $f(x, y) = x^2 + 2xy$. **26.** $f(x, y) = y^2 \cos 2x$.

Exercises 27–36. Calculate the first-order partial derivatives.

27. $f(x, y) = x^2 y - 2xy^3$. **28.** $g(x, y) = \dfrac{x}{\sqrt{x^2 + y^2}}$.

29. $z = x^2 \sin xy^2$. **30.** $f(x, y) = e^{xy} \ln(y/x)$.

31. $h(x, y) = e^{-x} \cos(2x - y)$.

32. $u = y^2 \sec x + x^2 \tan y$.

33. $f(x, y, z) = \dfrac{2xy}{x + y + z}$. **34.** $w = x \arctan(y - z)$.

35. $g(x, y, z) = \ln \sqrt{x^2 + y^2 + z^2}$.

36. $h(u, v, w) = e^{uv} \sin uw$.

Exercises 37–42. Calculate the second-order partial derivatives.

37. $f(x, y) = x^3y^2 - 4xy^3 + 2x - y$.

38. $g(x, y) = x^2 \ln(y - x)$.

39. $g(x, y) = xy \sin(xy)$. **40.** $f(x, y) = x^2 e^{x/y}$.

41. $f(x, y, z) = x^2 e^{2y} \cos(2z + 1)$.

42. $g(x, y, z) = 2x^2yz^3 + e^{xyz}$.

Exercises 43–44. The surface $z = 2x^2 + 3xy$ intersects the plane in a curve C. Give parametric equations for the line tangent to C at the point indicated.

43. Plane $y = 2$; $P(1, 2, 8)$. **44.** Plane $x = 2$; $P(2, -1, 2)$.

45. The surface $z = \sqrt{20 - 2x^2 - 3y^2}$ is the top half of an ellipsoid centered at the origin.

(a) The surface intersects the plane $x = 2$ in a curve C_1. Write scalar parametric equations for the line tangent to C_1 at the point $(2, 1, 3)$.

(b) The surface intersects the plane $y = 1$ in a curve C_2. Write scalar parametric equations for the line tangent to C_2 at the point $(2, 1, 3)$.

(c) The lines found in (a) and (b) determine a plane. Write an equation in (x, y, z) for this plane.

Exercises 46–50. Specify the interior and the boundary of the set. State whether the set is open, closed, or neither. Then sketch the set.

46. $\{(x, y) : \ 0 \le x \le 3, 2 < y \le 5\}$.

47. $\{(x, y) : \ 0 < x^2 + y^2 < 4\}$.

48. $\{(x, y) : \ x + y \ge 4\}$.

49. $\{(x, y, z) : \ y^2 + z^2 \le 4, \ 0 \le x \le 2, \ y \ge 0, z \ge 0\}$.

50. $\{(x, y, z) : \ 0 \le x^2 + y^2 \le z < 4\}$.

51. Let g be a twice differentiable function of one variable and set $f(x, y) = g(xy)$.

(a) Show that

$$x\frac{\partial f}{\partial x} - y\frac{\partial f}{\partial y} = 0.$$

(b) Show that

$$x^2\frac{\partial^2 f}{\partial x^2} - y^2\frac{\partial^2 f}{\partial y^2} = 0.$$

52. Show that $f(x, y) = \arctan(y/x)$ satisfies Laplace's equation $f_{xx} + f_{yy} = 0$.

53. Is there a function f of x and y with everywhere continuous second partials such that

$$\frac{\partial f}{\partial x} = xe^{xy} \quad \text{and} \quad \frac{\partial f}{\partial y} = ye^{xy}?$$

54. Set $f(x, y) = \dfrac{2x^2y}{x^4 + y^2}$. Evaluate the limit of $f(x, y)$ as (x, y) approaches the origin along

(a) the x-axis; (b) the y-axis;

(c) the line $y = mx$; (d) the parabola $y = ax^2$.

Does $\lim_{(x,y)\to(0,0)} f(x, y)$ exist?

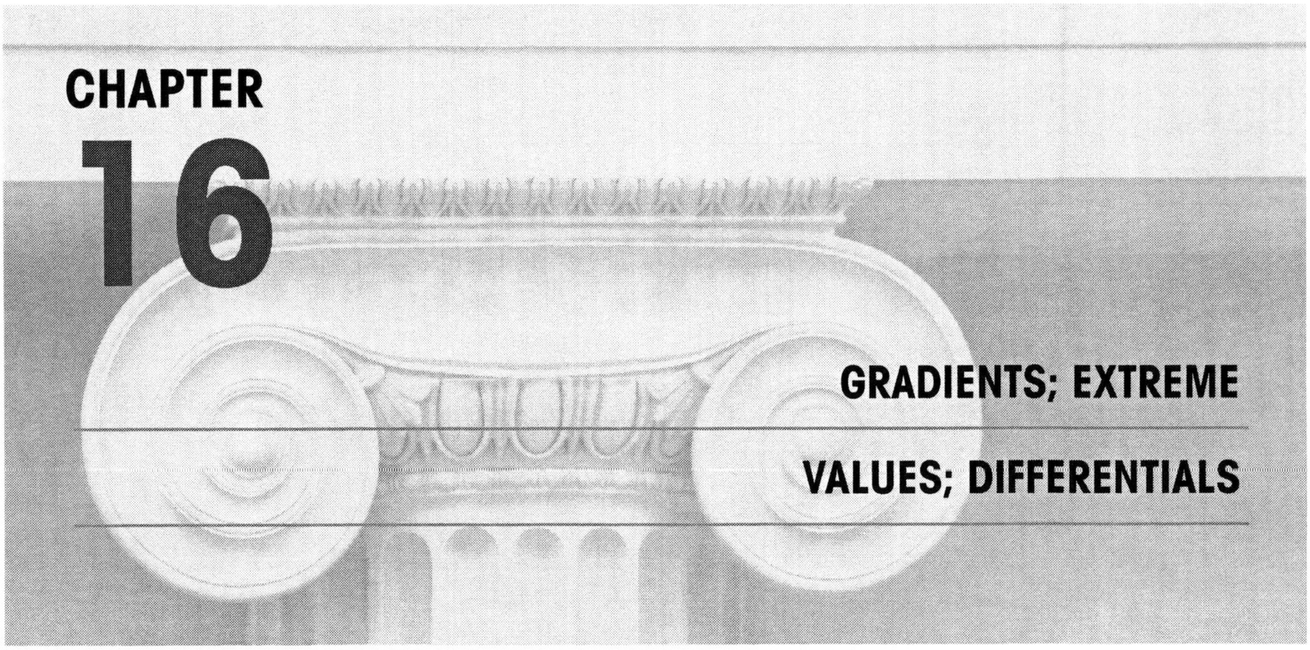

CHAPTER 16 GRADIENTS; EXTREME VALUES; DIFFERENTIALS

16.1 DIFFERENTIABILITY AND GRADIENT

The Notion of Differentiability

Our object here is to extend the notion of differentiability from real-valued functions of one variable to real-valued functions of several variables. Partial derivatives alone do not fulfill this role because they reflect behavior only along paths parallel to the coordinate axes.

In the one-variable case we formed the difference quotient

$$\frac{f(x+h)-f(x)}{h}$$

and called f differentiable at x provided that this quotient had a limit as h tended to zero. In the multivariable case we can still form the difference

$$f(\mathbf{x}+\mathbf{h})-f(\mathbf{x}),$$

but the "quotient"

$$\frac{f(\mathbf{x}+\mathbf{h})-f(\mathbf{x})}{\mathbf{h}}$$

is not defined because it makes no sense to divide by a vector $\mathbf{h}$.

We can get around this difficulty by going back to an idea introduced in the Exercises for Section 4.11. We review the idea here.

Let g be a real-valued function of a single variable defined at least on some open interval that contains the number 0. We say that $g(h)$ is *little-o*(h) (read "little oh of h") and write $g(h)=o(h)$ to indicate that $g(h)$ is so small compared to h that

$$\lim_{h\to 0}\frac{g(h)}{h}=0 \qquad \text{or equivalently that} \qquad \lim_{h\to 0}\frac{g(h)}{|h|}=0.$$

We will use the second formulation, the one with $|h|$ in the denominator.

For a function of one variable, the following statements are equivalent:

$$\lim_{h\to 0} \frac{f(x+h)-f(x)}{h} = f'(x)$$

$$\lim_{h\to 0} \frac{[f(x+h)-f(x)]-f'(x)h}{h} = 0$$

$$\lim_{h\to 0} \frac{[f(x+h)-f(x)]-f'(x)h}{|h|} = 0$$

$$[f(x+h)-f(x)]-f'(x)h = o(h)$$

$$[f(x+h)-f(x)] = f'(x)h + o(h).$$

Thus, for a function of one variable, the derivative of f at x is the unique number $f'(x)$ such that

$$f(x+h)-f(x) = f'(x)h + o(h).$$

It is this view of the derivative that inspires the notion of differentiability in the multi-variable case.

Let g be a function of several variables defined at least in some neighborhood of $\mathbf{0}$. We say that $g(\mathbf{h})$ is $o(\mathbf{h})$ and write $g(\mathbf{h}) = o(\mathbf{h})$ to indicate that

$$\lim_{\mathbf{h}\to \mathbf{0}} \frac{g(\mathbf{h})}{\|\mathbf{h}\|} = 0.$$

Now let f be a function of several variables *defined at least in some neighborhood of* $\mathbf{x}$. [In the three-variable case, $\mathbf{x} = (x, y, z)$; in the two-variable case, $\mathbf{x} = (x, y)$.]

DEFINITION 16.1.1 DIFFERENTIABILITY

We say that f is *differentiable at* $\mathbf{x}$ provided that there exists a vector $\mathbf{y}$ such that

$$f(\mathbf{x}+\mathbf{h}) - f(\mathbf{x}) = \mathbf{y}\cdot\mathbf{h} + o(\mathbf{h}).$$

It is not hard to show that, if such a vector $\mathbf{y}$ exists, it is unique. (Exercise 41) We call this unique vector *the gradient of f at* $\mathbf{x}$ and denote it by $\nabla f(\mathbf{x})$.[†]

DEFINITION 16.1.2 GRADIENT

Let f be differentiable at $\mathbf{x}$. The *gradient of f at* $\mathbf{x}$ is the unique vector $\nabla f(\mathbf{x})$ such that

$$f(\mathbf{x}+\mathbf{h}) - f(\mathbf{x}) = \nabla f(\mathbf{x})\cdot\mathbf{h} + o(\mathbf{h}).$$

The similarities between the one-variable case,

$$f(x+h)-f(x) = f'(x)h + o(h),$$

[†]The symbol ∇, an inverted capital delta, is called a *nabla* and is read "del." The gradient of f is sometimes written grad f.

and the multivariable case,

$$f(\mathbf{x}+\mathbf{h}) - f(\mathbf{x}) = \nabla f(\mathbf{x}) \cdot \mathbf{h} + o(\mathbf{h}),$$

are obvious. We point to the differences. There are essentially two of them:

(1) While the derivative $f'(x)$ is a number, the gradient $\nabla f(\mathbf{x})$ is a vector.

(2) While $f'(x)h$ is the ordinary product of two real numbers, $\nabla f(\mathbf{x}) \cdot \mathbf{h}$ is the dot product of two vectors.

Calculating Gradients

First we calculate some gradients by applying the definition directly. In the two-variable case we write

$$\nabla f(\mathbf{x}) = \nabla f(x, y) \qquad \text{and} \qquad \mathbf{h} = (h_1, h_2)$$

and in the three-variable case,

$$\nabla f(\mathbf{x}) = \nabla f(x, y, z) \qquad \text{and} \qquad \mathbf{h} = (h_1, h_2, h_3).$$

Example 1 For the function $f(x, y) = x^2 + y^2$.

$$\begin{aligned} f(\mathbf{x}+\mathbf{h}) - f(\mathbf{x}) &= f(x+h_1, y+h_2) - f(x, y) \\ &= \left[(x+h_1)^2 + (y+h_2)^2\right] - \left[x^2 + y^2\right] \\ &= [2xh_1 + 2yh_2] + \left[h_1^2 + h_2^2\right] \\ &= [2x\,\mathbf{i} + 2y\,\mathbf{j}] \cdot \mathbf{h} + \|\mathbf{h}\|^2. \end{aligned}$$

The remainder $g(\mathbf{h}) = \|\mathbf{h}\|^2$ is $o(\mathbf{h})$:

$$\text{as } \mathbf{h} \to \mathbf{0}, \qquad \frac{\|\mathbf{h}\|^2}{\|\mathbf{h}\|} = \|\mathbf{h}\| \to \mathbf{0}.$$

Thus,

$$\nabla f(\mathbf{x}) = \nabla f(x, y) = 2x\,\mathbf{i} + 2y\,\mathbf{j}. \quad ❑$$

Example 2 For the function $f(x, y, z) = 2xy - 3z^2$.

$$\begin{aligned} f(\mathbf{x}+\mathbf{h}) - f(\mathbf{x}) &= f(x+h_1, y+h_2, z+h_3) - f(x, y, z) \\ &= 2(x+h_1)(y+h_2) - 3(z+h_3)^2 - [2xy - 3z^2] \\ &= 2xh_2 + 2yh_1 + 2h_1h_2 - 6zh_3 - 3h_3^2 \\ &= (2y\,\mathbf{i} + 2x\,\mathbf{j} - 6z\,\mathbf{k}) \cdot (h_1\,\mathbf{i} + h_2\,\mathbf{j} + h_3\,\mathbf{k}) + 2h_1h_2 - 3h_3^2 \\ &= (2y\,\mathbf{i} + 2x\,\mathbf{j} - 6z\,\mathbf{k}) \cdot \mathbf{h} + 2h_1h_2 - 3h_3^2. \end{aligned}$$

Now we show that the remainder $g(\mathbf{h}) = 2h_1h_2 - 3h_3^2$ is $o(\mathbf{h})$. Note that

$$g(\mathbf{h}) = (2h_2\,\mathbf{i} - 3h_3\,\mathbf{k}) \cdot (h_1\,\mathbf{i} + h_2\,\mathbf{j} + h_3\,\mathbf{k}) = (2h_2\,\mathbf{i} - 3h_3\,\mathbf{k}) \cdot \mathbf{h}.$$

By Schwarz's inequality (13.3.18),

$$g(\mathbf{h}) \le \|(2h_2\,\mathbf{i} - 3h_3\,\mathbf{k})\|\,\|\mathbf{h}\|.$$

Dividing by $\|\mathbf{h}\|$ we have

$$\frac{g(\mathbf{h})}{\|\mathbf{h}\|} \leq \|(2h_2\,\mathbf{i} - 3h_3\,\mathbf{k})\| \leq \|2h_2\,\mathbf{i}\| + \|3h_3\,\mathbf{k}\| = 2|h_2| + 3|h_3|.$$

As $\mathbf{h} \to \mathbf{0}$,

$$h_2 \to 0,\ h_3 \to 0, \qquad 2|h_2| + 3|h_3| \to 0, \qquad \text{and} \qquad \frac{g(\mathbf{h})}{\|\mathbf{h}\|} \to 0.$$

Since $g(\mathbf{h}) = o(\mathbf{h})$,

$$\nabla f(\mathbf{x}) = 2y\,\mathbf{i} + 2x\,\mathbf{j} - 6z\,\mathbf{k}. \quad \square$$

As you just saw, the calculation of a gradient by direct application of the definition is a rather laborious process. The following theorem relates the gradient of a function to its partial derivatives and enables us to calculate gradients with much less effort.

THEOREM 16.1.3

If f has continuous first partials in a neighborhood of $\mathbf{x}$, then f is differentiable at $\mathbf{x}$ and

$$\nabla f(\mathbf{x}) = \frac{\partial f}{\partial x}(\mathbf{x})\,\mathbf{i} + \frac{\partial f}{\partial y}(\mathbf{x})\,\mathbf{j} + \frac{\partial f}{\partial z}(\mathbf{x})\,\mathbf{k}.$$

For two variables

$$\nabla f(\mathbf{x}) = \frac{\partial f}{\partial x}(\mathbf{x})\,\mathbf{i} + \frac{\partial f}{\partial y}(\mathbf{x})\,\mathbf{j}.$$

The proof of this theorem is somewhat difficult. A proof in the two-variable case is given in a supplement to this section.

We return to the functions of Examples 1 and 2 and this time calculate the gradients by using the partial derivatives. For $f(x, y) = x^2 + y^2$, $\partial f/\partial x = 2x$ and $\partial f/\partial y = 2y$. Since these partials are continuous,

$$\nabla f(\mathbf{x}) = 2x\,\mathbf{i} + 2y\,\mathbf{j}.$$

For $f(x, y, z) = 2xy - 3z^2$, $\partial f/\partial x = 2y$, $\partial f/\partial y = 2x$, and $\partial f/\partial z = -6z$. Since these partials are continuous,

$$\nabla f(\mathbf{x}) = 2y\,\mathbf{i} + 2x\,\mathbf{j} - 6z\,\mathbf{k}.$$

These are the results we obtained before.

Example 3 For $f(x, y) = x\,e^y - y\,e^x$, we have

$$\frac{\partial f}{\partial x}(x, y) = e^y - y\,e^x, \qquad \frac{\partial f}{\partial y}(x, y) = x\,e^y - e^x$$

and therefore

$$\nabla f(x, y) = (e^y - y\,e^x)\,\mathbf{i} + (x\,e^y - e^x)\,\mathbf{j}. \quad \square$$

When there is no reason to emphasize the point of evaluation, we don't write

$$\nabla f(\mathbf{x}) \qquad \text{or} \qquad \nabla f(x, y) \qquad \text{or} \qquad \nabla f(x, y, z)$$

but simply ∇f. Thus for the function

$$f(x, y) = x\,e^y - y\,e^x$$

we write

$$\frac{\partial f}{\partial x} = e^y - y\,e^x, \qquad \frac{\partial f}{\partial x} = x\,e^y - e^x$$

and

$$\nabla f = (e^y - y\,e^x)\,\mathbf{i} + (x\,e^y - e^x)\,\mathbf{j}. \quad \square$$

Example 4 For $f(x, y, z) = \sin xy^2z^3$

$$\frac{\partial f}{\partial x} = y^2z^3 \cos xy^2z^3, \qquad \frac{\partial f}{\partial y} = 2xyz^3 \cos xy^2z^3, \qquad \frac{\partial f}{\partial z} = 3xy^2z^2 \cos xy^2z^3$$

and

$$\nabla f = yz^2 \cos xy^2z^3[yz\,\mathbf{i} + 2xz\,\mathbf{j} + 3xy\,\mathbf{k}]. \quad \square$$

Example 5 Set

$$f(x, y, z) = x \sin \pi y + y \cos \pi z.$$

Evaluate ∇f at $(0, 1, 2)$.

SOLUTION Here

$$\frac{\partial f}{\partial x} = \sin \pi y, \qquad \frac{\partial f}{\partial y} = \pi x \cos \pi y + \cos \pi z, \qquad \frac{\partial f}{\partial z} = -\pi y \sin \pi z.$$

At $(0, 1, 2)$,

$$\frac{\partial f}{\partial x} = 0, \qquad \frac{\partial f}{\partial y} = 1, \qquad \frac{\partial f}{\partial z} = 0. \qquad \text{Therefore} \qquad \nabla f(0, 1, 2) = \mathbf{j}. \quad \square$$

Of special interest for later work are the powers of r where, as usual,

$$r = \|\mathbf{r}\| \qquad \text{and} \qquad \mathbf{r} = x\,\mathbf{i} + y\,\mathbf{j} + z\,\mathbf{k}.$$

We begin by showing that, for $r \neq 0$,

(16.1.4)
$$\nabla r = \frac{\mathbf{r}}{r} \qquad \text{and} \qquad \nabla\left(\frac{1}{r}\right) = -\frac{\mathbf{r}}{r^3}.$$

PROOF

$$\begin{aligned}
\nabla r &= \nabla(x^2 + y^2 + z^2)^{1/2} \\
&= \frac{\partial}{\partial x}(x^2 + y^2 + z^2)^{1/2}\,\mathbf{i} + \frac{\partial}{\partial y}(x^2 + y^2 + z^2)^{1/2}\,\mathbf{j} + \frac{\partial}{\partial z}(x^2 + y^2 + z^2)^{1/2}\,\mathbf{k} \\
&= \frac{x}{(x^2 + y^2 + z^2)^{1/2}}\,\mathbf{i} + \frac{y}{(x^2 + y^2 + z^2)^{1/2}}\,\mathbf{j} + \frac{z}{(x^2 + y^2 + z^2)^{1/2}}\,\mathbf{k} \\
&= \frac{1}{(x^2 + y^2 + z^2)^{1/2}}(x\,\mathbf{i} + y\,\mathbf{j} + z\,\mathbf{k}) = \frac{\mathbf{r}}{r}.
\end{aligned}$$

$$\begin{aligned}\nabla\left(\frac{1}{r}\right) &= \nabla(x^2+y^2+z^2)^{-1/2}\\ &= \frac{\partial}{\partial x}(x^2+y^2+z^2)^{-1/2}\,\mathbf{i}+\frac{\partial}{\partial y}(x^2+y^2+z^2)^{-1/2}\,\mathbf{j}+\frac{\partial}{\partial z}(x^2+y^2+z^2)^{-1/2}\,\mathbf{k}\\ &= -\frac{x}{(x^2+y^2+z^2)^{3/2}}\,\mathbf{i}-\frac{y}{(x^2+y^2+z^2)^{3/2}}\,\mathbf{j}-\frac{z}{(x^2+y^2+z^2)^{3/2}}\,\mathbf{k}\\ &= -\frac{1}{(x^2+y^2+z^2)^{3/2}}(x\,\mathbf{i}+y\,\mathbf{j}+z\,\mathbf{k}) = -\frac{\mathbf{r}}{r^3}.\quad \square\end{aligned}$$

The formulas we just derived can be generalized. As you are asked to show in the Exercises, for each integer n and all $\mathbf{r} \neq \mathbf{0}$,

(16.1.5)

$$\nabla r^n = nr^{n-2}\,\mathbf{r}.$$

(If n is positive and even, the result also holds at $\mathbf{r} = \mathbf{0}$.)

Differentiability Implies Continuity

As in the one-variable case, differentiability implies continuity:

(16.1.6)

if f is differentiable at $\mathbf{x}$, then f is continuous at $\mathbf{x}$.

To see this, write

$$f(\mathbf{x}+\mathbf{h}) - f(\mathbf{x}) = \nabla f(\mathbf{x})\cdot\mathbf{h} + o(\mathbf{h})$$

and note that

$$|f(\mathbf{x}+\mathbf{h}) - f(\mathbf{x})| = |\nabla f(\mathbf{x})\cdot\mathbf{h} + o(\mathbf{h})| \leq |\nabla f(\mathbf{x})\cdot\mathbf{h}| + |o(\mathbf{h})|. \quad \text{(triangle inequality)}$$

As $\mathbf{h} \to \mathbf{0}$,

$$|\nabla f(\mathbf{x})\cdot\mathbf{h}| \leq \|\nabla f(\mathbf{x})\|\,\|\mathbf{h}\| \to 0 \quad \text{and} \quad |o(\mathbf{h})| \to 0.$$

(Schwarz's inequality for the first inequality; Exercise 42 for $|o(\mathbf{h})| \to 0$.)

It follows that

$$f(\mathbf{x}+\mathbf{h}) - f(\mathbf{x}) \to 0 \quad \text{and therefore} \quad f(\mathbf{x}+\mathbf{h}) \to f(\mathbf{x}).\quad \square$$

EXERCISES 16.1

Exercises 1–16. Find the gradient.

1. $f(x, y) = 3x^2 - xy + y$.

2. $f(x, y) = Ax^2 + Bxy + Cy^2$.

3. $f(x, y) = xe^{xy}$.

4. $f(x, y) = \dfrac{x-y}{x^2+y^2}$.

5. $f(x, y) = 2xy^2 \sin(x^2+1)$.

6. $f(x, y) = \ln(x^2+y^2)$.

7. $f(x, y) = e^{x-y} - e^{y-x}$.

8. $f(x, y) = \dfrac{Ax+By}{Cx+Dy}$.

9. $f(x, y, z) = x^2y + y^2z + z^2x$.

10. $f(x, y, z) = \sqrt{x^2+y^2+z^2}$.

11. $f(x, y, z) = x^2ye^{-z}$.

12. $f(x, y, z) = xyz\ln(x+y+z)$.

13. $f(x, y, z) = e^{x+2y}\cos(z^2+1)$.

14. $f(x, y, z) = e^{yz^2/x^3}$.

15. $f(x, y, z) = \sin(2xy) + \ln(x^2z)$.

16. $f(x, y, z) = x^2y/z - 3xz^4$.

Exercises 17–26. Find the gradient at P.

17. $f(x, y) = 2x^2 - 3xy + 4y^2$; $P(2, 3)$.

18. $f(x, y) = 2x(x - y)^{-1}$; $P(3, 1)$.

19. $f(x, y) = \ln(x^2 + y^2)$; $P(2, 1)$.

20. $f(x, y) = x \arctan(y/x)$; $P(1, 1)$.

21. $f(x, y) = x \sin(xy)$; $P(1, \pi/2)$.

22. $f(x, y) = xye^{-(x^2+y^2)}$; $P(1, -1)$.

23. $f(x, y, z) = e^{-x} \sin(z + 2y)$; $P(0, \frac{1}{4}\pi, \frac{1}{4}\pi)$.

24. $f(x, y, z) = (x - y) \cos \pi z$; $P(1, 0, \frac{1}{2})$.

25. $f(x, y, z) = x - \sqrt{y^2 + z^2}$; $P(2, -3, 4)$.

26. $f(x, y, z) = \cos(xyz^2)$; $P(\pi, \frac{1}{4}, -1)$.

Exercises 27–28. Use a CAS to find the gradient at P.

27. (a) $f(x, y) = xy^2e^{-xy}$; $P(0, 2)$.

(b) $f(x, y) = \sin(2x + y) - \cos(x - 2y)$; $P(\pi/4, \pi/6)$.

(c) $f(x, y) = x - y \ln(x^2y)$; $P(1, e)$.

28. (a) $f(x, y, z) = \sqrt{x + y^2 - z^3}$; $P(1, 2, -3)$.

(b) $f(x, y, z) = \dfrac{xy}{x - y + z}$; $P(1, -2, 3)$.

(c) $f(x, y, z) = x \sin(z \ln y)$; $P(1, e^2, \pi/6)$.

Exercises 29–32. Obtain the gradient directly from Definition 16.1.2.

29. $f(x, y) = 3x^2 - xy + y$. **30.** $f(x, y) = \frac{1}{2}x^2 + 2xy + y^2$.

31. $f(x, y, z) = x^2y + y^2z + z^2x$.

32. $f(x, y, z) = 2x^2y - \dfrac{1}{z}$.

Exercises 33–36. Find the functions with gradient $\mathbf{F}$.

33. $\mathbf{F}(x, y) = 2xy\,\mathbf{i} + (1 + x^2)\,\mathbf{j}$.

34. $\mathbf{F}(x, y) = (2xy + x)\,\mathbf{i} + (x^2 + y)\,\mathbf{j}$.

35. $\mathbf{F}(x, y) = (x + \sin y)\,\mathbf{i} + (x \cos y - 2y)\,\mathbf{j}$.

36. $\mathbf{F}(x, y, z) = yz\,\mathbf{i} + (xz + 2yz)\,\mathbf{j} + (xy + y^2)\,\mathbf{k}$.

37. Find (a) $\nabla(\ln r)$, (b) $\nabla(\sin r)$, (c) $\nabla(e^r)$ taking $r = \sqrt{x^2 + y^2 + z^2}$.

38. Derive (16.1.5).

39. Set $f(x, y) = 1 + x^2 + y^2$.

(a) Find the points (x, y) (if any) at which $\nabla f(x, y) = \mathbf{0}$.

(b) Sketch the graph of the surface $z = f(x, y)$.

(c) What can you say about the surface at the point(s) found in part (a)?

40. Exercise 39 for $f(x, y) = \sqrt{4 - x^2 - y^2}$.

41. (a) Show that, if $\mathbf{c} \cdot \mathbf{h}$ is $o(\mathbf{h})$, then $\mathbf{c} = \mathbf{0}$. HINT: First set $\mathbf{h} = h\,\mathbf{i}$, then set $\mathbf{h} = h\,\mathbf{j}$, then $\mathbf{h} = h\,\mathbf{k}$.

(b) Show that, if

$$f(\mathbf{x} + \mathbf{h}) - f(\mathbf{x}) = \mathbf{y} \cdot \mathbf{h} + o(\mathbf{h})$$

and

$$f(\mathbf{x} + \mathbf{h}) - f(\mathbf{x}) = \mathbf{z} \cdot \mathbf{h} + o(\mathbf{h}),$$

then

$$\mathbf{y} = \mathbf{z}.$$

42. Show that if $g(\mathbf{h})$ is $o(\mathbf{h})$, then

$$\lim_{\mathbf{h} \to \mathbf{0}} g(\mathbf{h}) = 0.$$

43. Set

$$f(x, y) = \begin{cases} \dfrac{2xy}{x^2 + y^2}, & (x, y) \neq (0, 0) \\ 0, & (x, y) = (0, 0). \end{cases}$$

(a) Show that f is not differentiable at $(0, 0)$.

(b) In Section 15.6 you saw that the first partials $\partial f/\partial x$ and $\partial f/\partial y$ exist at $(0, 0)$. Since these partials obviously exist at every other point of the plane, we can conclude from Theorem 16.1.3 that at least one of these partials is not continuous in a neighborhood of $(0, 0)$. Show that $\partial f/\partial x$ is discontinuous at $(0, 0)$.

*SUPPLEMENT TO SECTION 16.1

PROOF OF THEOREM 16.1.3

We prove the theorem in the two-variable case. A similar argument yields a proof in the three-variable case, but there the details are more burdensome.

In the two-variable case

$$f(\mathbf{x} + \mathbf{h}) - f(\mathbf{x}) = f(x + h_1, y + h_2) - f(x, y).$$

Adding and subtracting $f(x, y + h_2)$, we have

$$(1) \quad f(\mathbf{x} + \mathbf{h}) - f(\mathbf{x}) = [f(x + h_1, y + h_2) - f(x, y + h_2)] + [f(x, y + h_2) - f(x, y)].$$

By the mean-value theorem for functions of one variable, we know that there are numbers θ_1 and θ_2 between 0 and 1 for which

$$f(x + h_1, y + h_2) - f(x, y + h_2) = \frac{\partial f}{\partial x}(x + \theta_1 h_1, y + h_2)h_1$$

and

$$f(x, y + h_2) - f(x, y) = \frac{\partial f}{\partial y}(x, y + \theta_2 h_2)\, h_2. \qquad \text{(Exercise 42, Section 4.1)}$$

By the continuity of $\partial f/\partial x$,

$$\frac{\partial f}{\partial x}(x + \theta_1 h_1, y + h_2) = \frac{\partial f}{\partial x}(x, y) + \epsilon_1(\mathbf{h})$$

where

$$\epsilon_1(\mathbf{h}) \to 0 \quad \text{as} \quad \mathbf{h} \to 0.^{\dagger}$$

By the continuity of $\partial f/\partial y$,

$$\frac{\partial f}{\partial x}(x, y + \theta_2 h_2) = \frac{\partial f}{\partial x}(x, y) + \epsilon_2(\mathbf{h})$$

where

$$\epsilon_2(\mathbf{h}) \to 0 \qquad \text{as} \qquad \mathbf{h} \to 0.$$

Substituting these expressions into (1), we find that

$$\begin{aligned}
f(\mathbf{x} + \mathbf{h}) - f(\mathbf{x}) &= \left[\frac{\partial f}{\partial x}(x, y) + \epsilon_1(\mathbf{h})\right] h_1 + \left[\frac{\partial f}{\partial y}(x, y) + \epsilon_2(\mathbf{h})\right] h_2 \\
&= \left[\frac{\partial f}{\partial x}(x, y) + \epsilon_1(\mathbf{h})\right](\mathbf{i} \cdot \mathbf{h}) + \left[\frac{\partial f}{\partial y}(x, y) + \epsilon_2(\mathbf{h})\right](\mathbf{j} \cdot \mathbf{h}) \\
&= \left[\frac{\partial f}{\partial x}(x, y)\,\mathbf{i} + \epsilon_1(\mathbf{h})\,\mathbf{i}\right] \cdot \mathbf{h} + \left[\frac{\partial f}{\partial y}(x, y)\,\mathbf{j} + \epsilon_2(\mathbf{h})\,\mathbf{j}\right] \cdot \mathbf{h} \\
&= \left[\frac{\partial f}{\partial x}(x, y)\,\mathbf{i} + \frac{\partial f}{\partial y}(x, y)\,\mathbf{j}\right] \cdot \mathbf{h} + [\epsilon_1(\mathbf{h})\,\mathbf{i} + \epsilon_2(\mathbf{h})\,\mathbf{j}] \cdot \mathbf{h}.
\end{aligned}$$

To complete the proof of the theorem, we need only show that

$$(2) \qquad [\epsilon_1(\mathbf{h})\,\mathbf{i} + \epsilon_2(\mathbf{h})\,\mathbf{j}] \cdot \mathbf{h} = o(\mathbf{h}).$$

From Schwarz's inequality, $|\mathbf{a} \cdot \mathbf{b}| \le \|\mathbf{a}\|\, \|\mathbf{b}\|$, we know that

$$|[\epsilon_1(\mathbf{h})\,\mathbf{i} + \epsilon_2(\mathbf{h})\,\mathbf{j}] \cdot \mathbf{h}| \le \|\epsilon_1(\mathbf{h})\,\mathbf{i} + \epsilon_2(\mathbf{h})\,\mathbf{j}\|\, \|\mathbf{h}\|.$$

It follows that

$$\frac{|[\epsilon_1(\mathbf{h})\,\mathbf{i} + \epsilon_2(\mathbf{h})\,\mathbf{j}] \cdot \mathbf{h}|}{\|\mathbf{h}\|} \le \|\epsilon_1(\mathbf{h})\,\mathbf{i} + \epsilon_2(\mathbf{h})\,\mathbf{j}\| \le \|\epsilon_1(\mathbf{h})\,\mathbf{i}\| + \|\epsilon_2(\mathbf{h})\,\mathbf{j}\| = |\epsilon_1(\mathbf{h})| + |\epsilon_2(\mathbf{h})|.$$

↑ by the triangle inequality

As $\mathbf{h} \to \mathbf{0}$, the expression on the right tends to 0. This shows that (2) holds and completes the proof of the theorem. ❑

---

†

$$\epsilon_1(\mathbf{h}) = \frac{\partial f}{\partial x}(x + \theta_1 h_1, y + h_2) - \frac{\partial f}{\partial x}(x, y) \to 0$$

since, by the continuity of $\partial f/\partial x$,

$$\frac{\partial f}{\partial x}(x + \theta_1 h_1, y + h_2) \to \frac{\partial f}{\partial x}(x, y).$$

16.2 GRADIENTS AND DIRECTIONAL DERIVATIVES

Some Elementary Formulas

In many respects gradients behave just as derivatives do in the one-variable case. In particular, if $\nabla f(\mathbf{x})$ and $\nabla g(\mathbf{x})$ exist, then $\nabla[f(\mathbf{x})+g(\mathbf{x})]$, $\nabla[\alpha f(\mathbf{x})]$, and $\nabla[f(\mathbf{x})g(\mathbf{x})]$ all exist, and

(16.2.1)

$$\begin{aligned}\nabla[f(\mathbf{x})+g(\mathbf{x})] &= \nabla f(\mathbf{x})+\nabla g(\mathbf{x}),\\ \nabla[\alpha f(\mathbf{x})] &= \alpha\nabla f(\mathbf{x}),\\ \nabla[f(\mathbf{x})g(\mathbf{x})] &= f(\mathbf{x})\nabla g(\mathbf{x})+g(\mathbf{x})\nabla f(\mathbf{x}).\end{aligned}$$

The first two formulas are easy to derive. To derive the third formula, let's assume that $\nabla f(\mathbf{x})$ and $\nabla g(\mathbf{x})$ both exist. Our task is to show that

$$f(\mathbf{x}+\mathbf{h})g(\mathbf{x}+\mathbf{h})-f(\mathbf{x})g(\mathbf{x})=[f(\mathbf{x})\nabla g(\mathbf{x})+g(\mathbf{x})\nabla f(\mathbf{x})]\cdot\mathbf{h}+o(\mathbf{h}).$$

We now sketch how this can be done. We leave it to you to justify each step. The key to proving a product rule is to add and subtract an appropriate expression. (See, for instance, the proof of product rule, Theorem 3.2.6.) Starting from

$$f(\mathbf{x}+\mathbf{h})g(\mathbf{x}+\mathbf{h})-f(\mathbf{x})g(\mathbf{x}),$$

we add and subtract the term $f(\mathbf{x})g(\mathbf{x}+\mathbf{h})$. This gives

$$\begin{aligned}&[f(\mathbf{x}+\mathbf{h})g(\mathbf{x}+\mathbf{h})-f(\mathbf{x})g(\mathbf{x}+\mathbf{h})]+[f(\mathbf{x})g(\mathbf{x}+\mathbf{h})-f(\mathbf{x})g(\mathbf{x})]\\ &=[f(\mathbf{x}+\mathbf{h})-f(\mathbf{x})]g(\mathbf{x}+\mathbf{h})+f(\mathbf{x})[g(\mathbf{x}+\mathbf{h})-g(\mathbf{x})]\\ &=[\nabla f(\mathbf{x})\cdot\mathbf{h}+o(\mathbf{h})]g(\mathbf{x}+\mathbf{h})+f(\mathbf{x})[\nabla g(\mathbf{x})\cdot\mathbf{h}+o(\mathbf{h})]\\ &=g(\mathbf{x}+\mathbf{h})\nabla f(\mathbf{x})\cdot\mathbf{h}+f(\mathbf{x})\nabla g(\mathbf{x})\cdot\mathbf{h}+o(\mathbf{h}) \qquad \text{(Exercise 30)}\\ &=g(\mathbf{x})\nabla f(\mathbf{x})\cdot\mathbf{h}+f(\mathbf{x})\nabla g(\mathbf{x})\cdot\mathbf{h}+[g(\mathbf{x}+\mathbf{h})-g(\mathbf{x})]\nabla f(\mathbf{x})\cdot\mathbf{h}+o(\mathbf{h})\\ &=[g(\mathbf{x})\nabla f(\mathbf{x})+f(\mathbf{x})\nabla g(\mathbf{x})]\cdot\mathbf{h}+o(\mathbf{h}). \qquad \text{(Exercise 30)} \quad \square\end{aligned}$$

In Exercise 43, you are asked to derive this formula from Theorem 16.1.3.

Directional Derivatives

Here we take up an idea that generalizes the notion of partial derivative. Its connection with gradients will be made clear as we go on. We begin by recalling the definitions of the first partial derivatives:

(two variables)

$$\frac{\partial f}{\partial x}(x,y)=\lim_{h\to 0}\frac{f(x+h,y)-f(x,y)}{h}$$

$$\frac{\partial f}{\partial y}(x,y)=\lim_{h\to 0}\frac{f(x,y+h)-f(x,y)}{h}.$$

(three variables)

$$\frac{\partial f}{\partial x}(x,y,z)=\lim_{h\to 0}\frac{f(x+h,y,z)-f(x,y,z)}{h}$$

$$\frac{\partial f}{\partial y}(x,y,z)=\lim_{h\to 0}\frac{f(x,y+h,z)-f(x,y,z)}{h}$$

$$\frac{\partial f}{\partial z}(x,y,z)=\lim_{h\to 0}\frac{f(x,y,z+h)-f(x,y,z)}{h}.$$

Expressed in vector notation, these definitions take the form

$(\mathbf{x} = (x, y))$

$$\frac{\partial f}{\partial x}(\mathbf{x}) = \lim_{h\to 0} \frac{f(\mathbf{x} + h\,\mathbf{i}) - f(\mathbf{x})}{h}$$

$$\frac{\partial f}{\partial y}(\mathbf{x}) = \lim_{h\to 0} \frac{f(\mathbf{x} + h\,\mathbf{j}) - f(\mathbf{x})}{h}.$$

$(\mathbf{x} = (x, y, z))$

$$\frac{\partial f}{\partial x}(\mathbf{x}) = \lim_{h\to 0} \frac{f(\mathbf{x} + h\,\mathbf{i}) - f(\mathbf{x})}{h}$$

$$\frac{\partial f}{\partial y}(\mathbf{x}) = \lim_{h\to 0} \frac{f(\mathbf{x} + h\,\mathbf{j}) - f(\mathbf{x})}{h}$$

$$\frac{\partial f}{\partial z}(\mathbf{x}) = \lim_{h\to 0} \frac{f(\mathbf{x} + h\,\mathbf{k}) - f(\mathbf{x})}{h}.$$

Each partial is thus the limit of a quotient

$$\frac{f(\mathbf{x} + h\mathbf{u}) - f(\mathbf{x})}{h}$$

where **u** is one of the unit vectors **i**, **j**, **k**. There is no reason to be so restrictive on **u**. If f is defined in a neighborhood of **x**, then, for small h, the difference quotient

$$\frac{f(\mathbf{x} + h\mathbf{u}) - f(\mathbf{x})}{h}$$

is defined for every unit vector **u**.

DEFINITION 16.2.2 DIRECTIONAL DERIVATIVE

For each unit vector **u**, the limit

$$f'_u(\mathbf{x}) = \lim_{h\to 0} \frac{f(\mathbf{x} + h\mathbf{u}) - f(\mathbf{x})}{h},$$

if it exists, is called the *directional derivative of f at* **x** *in the direction* **u**.

Note that each partial derivative $\partial f/\partial x$, $\partial f/\partial y$, $\partial f/\partial z$ is itself a directional derivative.

(16.2.3) $$\frac{\partial f}{\partial x}(\mathbf{x}) = f'_{\mathbf{i}}(\mathbf{x}), \qquad \frac{\partial f}{\partial y}(\mathbf{x}) = f'_{\mathbf{j}}(\mathbf{x}), \qquad \frac{\partial f}{\partial z}(\mathbf{x}) = f'_{\mathbf{k}}(\mathbf{x}).$$

As you know, the partials of f give the rates of change of f in the **i**, **j**, **k** directions. The directional derivative $f'_{\mathbf{u}}$ gives *the rate of change of f in the direction* **u**.

A geometric interpretation of the directional derivative for a function of two variables can be obtained from Figure 16.2.1. Fix a point (x, y) in the domain of f and let **u** be a unit vector in the xy-plane with initial point (x, y). The plane p which contains **u** and is perpendicular to the xy-plane intersects the surface $z = f(x, y)$ in a curve C. The directional derivative $f'_{\mathbf{u}}(\mathbf{x})$ is the slope of the line tangent to C at the point $(x, y, f(x, y))$.

Remark So far we have defined directional derivatives only for unit vectors **u**. Now let **a** be any nonzero vector. By directional derivative in the direction **a** we mean the directional derivative $f'_{\mathbf{u}}$ where **u** is the unit vector in the direction of **a**. ❑

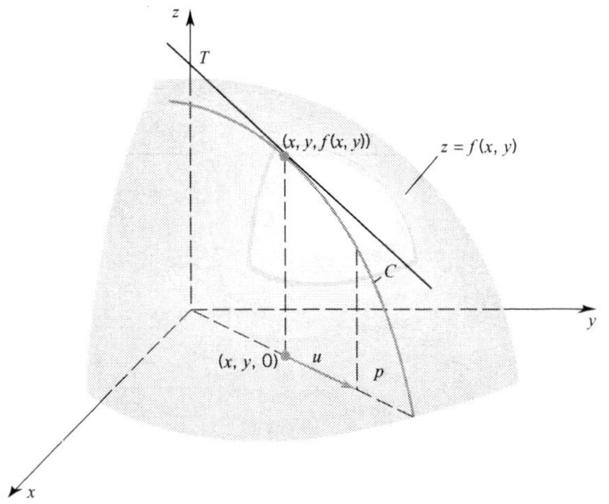

Figure 16.2.1

There is an important connection between the gradient at **x** and the directional derivatives at **x**.

THEOREM 16.2.4

If f is differentiable at **x**, then f has a directional derivative at **x** in every direction, and for each unit vector **u**

$$f'_{\mathbf{u}}(\mathbf{x}) = \nabla f(\mathbf{x}) \cdot \mathbf{u}.$$

PROOF Assume that f is differentiable at **x** and let **u** be any unit vector. The differentiability at **x** tells us that $\nabla f(\mathbf{x})$ exists and

$$f(\mathbf{x} + h\mathbf{u}) - f(\mathbf{x}) = \nabla f(\mathbf{x}) \cdot h\,\mathbf{u} + o(h\mathbf{u}).$$

Division by h gives

$$\frac{f(\mathbf{x} + h\mathbf{u}) - f(\mathbf{x})}{h} = \nabla f(\mathbf{x}) \cdot \mathbf{u} + \frac{o(h\mathbf{u})}{h}.$$

We leave it to you to show that

$$\frac{o(h\mathbf{u})}{h} \to 0$$

and therefore

$$\frac{f(\mathbf{x} + h\mathbf{u}) - f(\mathbf{x})}{h} \to \nabla f(\mathbf{x}) \cdot \mathbf{u}. \quad \square$$

In Theorem 16.1.3 we stated that, *if f has continuous first partials in a neighborhood of* **x**, *then f is differentiable at* **x** *and*

$$\nabla f(\mathbf{x}) = \frac{\partial f}{\partial x}(\mathbf{x})\,\mathbf{i} + \frac{\partial f}{\partial y}(\mathbf{x})\,\mathbf{j} + \frac{\partial f}{\partial z}(\mathbf{x})\,\mathbf{k}.$$

For two variables

$$\nabla f(x) = \frac{\partial f}{\partial x}(\mathbf{x})\,\mathbf{i} + \frac{\partial f}{\partial y}(\mathbf{x})\,\mathbf{j}.$$

The next theorem shows that these formulas for $\nabla f(\mathbf{x})$ hold wherever f is differentiable.

THEOREM 16.2.5

If f is differentiable at $\mathbf{x}$, then all the first partial derivatives of f exist at $\mathbf{x}$ and

$$\nabla f(\mathbf{x}) = \frac{\partial f}{\partial x}(\mathbf{x})\,\mathbf{i} + \frac{\partial f}{\partial y}(\mathbf{x})\,\mathbf{j} + \frac{\partial f}{\partial z}(\mathbf{x})\,\mathbf{k}.$$

For two variables

$$\nabla f(\mathbf{x}) = \frac{\partial f}{\partial x}(\mathbf{x})\,\mathbf{i} + \frac{\partial f}{\partial y}(\mathbf{x})\,\mathbf{j}.$$

PROOF It is sufficient to prove the theorem for the case $\mathbf{x} = (x, y, z)$. Assume that f is differentiable at $\mathbf{x}$. Then $\nabla f(\mathbf{x})$ exists and we can write

$$\nabla f(\mathbf{x}) = [\nabla f(\mathbf{x}) \cdot \mathbf{i}]\,\mathbf{i} + [\nabla f(\mathbf{x}) \cdot \mathbf{j}]\,\mathbf{j} + [\nabla f(\mathbf{x}) \cdot \mathbf{k}]\,\mathbf{k}. \tag{13.3.14}$$

The result follows from observing that

$$\nabla f(\mathbf{x}) \cdot \mathbf{i} \overset{(16.2.4)}{=} f'_{\mathbf{i}}(\mathbf{x}) \overset{(16.2.3)}{=} \frac{\partial f}{\partial x}(\mathbf{x})$$

$$\nabla f(\mathbf{x}) \cdot \mathbf{j} = f'_{\mathbf{j}}(\mathbf{x}) = \frac{\partial f}{\partial y}(\mathbf{x})$$

$$\nabla f(\mathbf{x}) \cdot \mathbf{k} = f'_{\mathbf{k}}(\mathbf{x}) = \frac{\partial f}{\partial z}(\mathbf{x}). \quad \square$$

Example 1 Find the directional derivative of the function $f(x, y) = x^2 + y^2$ at the point (1, 2) in the direction of the vector $2\,\mathbf{i} - 3\,\mathbf{j}$.

SOLUTION Note that $2\,\mathbf{i} - 3\,\mathbf{j}$ is not a unit vector; its norm is $\sqrt{13}$. The unit vector in the direction of $2\,\mathbf{i} - 3\,\mathbf{j}$ is the vector

$$\mathbf{u} = \frac{1}{\sqrt{13}}(2\,\mathbf{i} - 3\,\mathbf{j}).$$

Since $\nabla f = 2x\,\mathbf{i} + 2y\,\mathbf{j}$, $\nabla f(1, 2) = 2\,\mathbf{i} + 4\,\mathbf{j}$. By Theorem 16.2.4,

$$f'_{\mathbf{u}}(1, 2) = \nabla f(1, 2) \cdot \mathbf{u} = (2\,\mathbf{i} + 4\,\mathbf{j}) \cdot \frac{1}{\sqrt{13}}(2\,\mathbf{i} - 3\,\mathbf{j}) = \frac{-8}{\sqrt{13}} \cong -2.219. \quad \square$$

Example 2 Find the directional derivative of the function

$$f(x, y, z) = 2xz^2 \cos \pi y$$

at the point $P(1, 2, -1)$ toward the point $Q(2, 1, 3)$.

SOLUTION The vector from P to Q is the vector $\overrightarrow{PQ} = \mathbf{i} - \mathbf{j} + 4\,\mathbf{k}$. The unit vector in this direction is the vector

$$\mathbf{u} = \frac{1}{3\sqrt{2}}(\mathbf{i} - \mathbf{j} + 4\,\mathbf{k}).$$

In this case

$$\frac{\partial f}{\partial x} = 2z^2 \cos \pi y, \qquad \frac{\partial f}{\partial y} = -2\pi x z^2 \sin \pi y, \qquad \frac{\partial f}{\partial z} = 4xz \cos \pi y$$

so that

$$\frac{\partial f}{\partial x}(1, 2, -1) = 2, \qquad \frac{\partial f}{\partial y}(1, 2, -1) = 0, \qquad \frac{\partial f}{\partial z}(1, 2, -1) = -4.$$

Therefore $\nabla f(1, 2, -1) = 2\mathbf{i} - 4\mathbf{k}$ and

$$f'_{\mathbf{u}}(1, 2, -1) = \nabla f(1, 2, -1) \cdot \mathbf{u} = (2\mathbf{i} - 4\mathbf{k}) \cdot \frac{1}{3\sqrt{2}}(\mathbf{i} - \mathbf{j} + 4\mathbf{k})$$

$$= -\frac{14}{3\sqrt{2}} \cong -3.30. \quad \square$$

You know that for each unit vector $\mathbf{u}$

$$f'_{\mathbf{u}}(\mathbf{x}) = \nabla f(\mathbf{x}) \cdot \mathbf{u}.$$

By (13.3.13),

$$\nabla f(\mathbf{x}) \cdot \mathbf{u} = (\text{comp}_{\mathbf{u}} \nabla f(\mathbf{x}))\|\mathbf{u}\| = \text{comp}_{\mathbf{u}} \nabla f(\mathbf{x}).$$

$\|\mathbf{u}\| = 1$ ⟶ (arrow to $=$)

Therefore

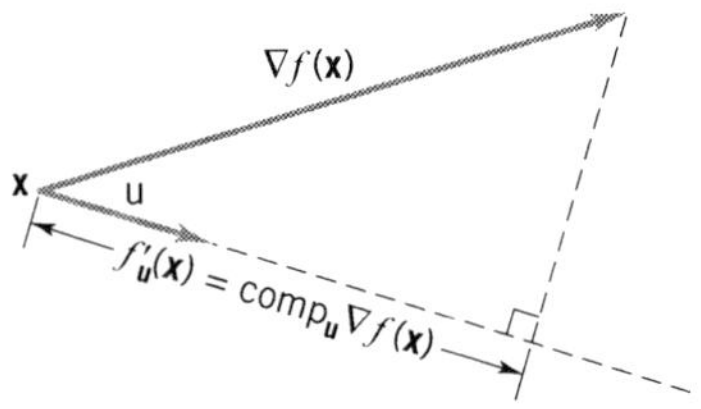

Figure 16.2.2

(16.2.6)

$$\boxed{f'_{\mathbf{u}}(\mathbf{x}) = \text{comp}_{\mathbf{u}} \nabla f(\mathbf{x}).}$$

This tells us that *the directional derivative in a direction* **u** *is the component of the gradient vector in that direction.* (Figure 16.2.2.)

If $\nabla f(\mathbf{x}) \neq 0$, then

$$f'_{\mathbf{u}}(\mathbf{x}) = \nabla f(\mathbf{x}) \cdot \mathbf{u} = \|\nabla f(\mathbf{x})\| \, \|\mathbf{u}\| \cos\theta = \|\nabla f(\mathbf{x})\| \cos\theta$$

(13.3.7) $\qquad \|\mathbf{u}\| = 1$

where θ is the angle between $\nabla f(\mathbf{x})$ and $\mathbf{u}$. Since $-1 \leq \cos\theta \leq 1$ we have

$$-\|\nabla f(\mathbf{x})\| \leq f'_{\mathbf{u}}(\mathbf{x}) \leq \|\nabla f(\mathbf{x})\| \qquad \text{for all directions } \mathbf{u}.$$

If $\mathbf{u}$ points in the direction of $\nabla f(\mathbf{x})$, then

$$f'_{\mathbf{u}}(\mathbf{x}) = \|\nabla f(\mathbf{x})\|; \qquad (\theta = 0, \cos\theta = 1)$$

if $\mathbf{u}$ points in the direction of $-\nabla f(\mathbf{x})$, then

$$f'_{\mathbf{u}}(\mathbf{x}) = -\|\nabla f(\mathbf{x})\|. \qquad (\theta = \pi, \cos\theta = -1)$$

Since the directional derivative gives the rate of change of the function in that direction, it is clear that

(16.2.7) from each point $\mathbf{x}$ of the domain, a differentiable function f increases most rapidly in the direction of the gradient (the rate of change at $\mathbf{x}$ being $\|\nabla f(\mathbf{x})\|$); the function decreases most rapidly in the opposite direction (the rate of change at $\mathbf{x}$ being $-\|\nabla f(\mathbf{x})\|$).

Example 3 The graph of the function $f(x, y) = \sqrt{1 - (x^2 + y^2)}$ is the upper half of the unit sphere $x^2 + y^2 + z^2 = 1$. The function is defined on the closed unit disk $x^2 + y^2 \leq 1$ but differentiable only on the open unit disk.

In Figure 16.2.3 we have marked a point (x, y) and drawn the corresponding radius vector $\mathbf{r} = x\,\mathbf{i} + y\,\mathbf{j}$. The gradient

$$\nabla f(x, y) = \frac{-x}{\sqrt{1 - (x^2 + y^2)}}\,\mathbf{i} + \frac{-y}{\sqrt{1 - (x^2 + y^2)}}\,\mathbf{j}$$

is a negative multiple of $\mathbf{r}$:

$$\nabla f(x, y) = -\frac{1}{\sqrt{1 - (x^2 + y^2)}}(x\,\mathbf{i} + y\,\mathbf{j}) = -\frac{1}{\sqrt{1 - (x^2 + y^2)}}\,\mathbf{r}.$$

Since $\mathbf{r}$ points from the origin to (x, y), the gradient points from (x, y) to the origin. This means that f increases most rapidly toward the origin. This is borne out by the observation that along the hemispherical surface the path of steepest ascent from the point $P(x, y, f(x, y))$ is the "great circle route to the North Pole." ❑

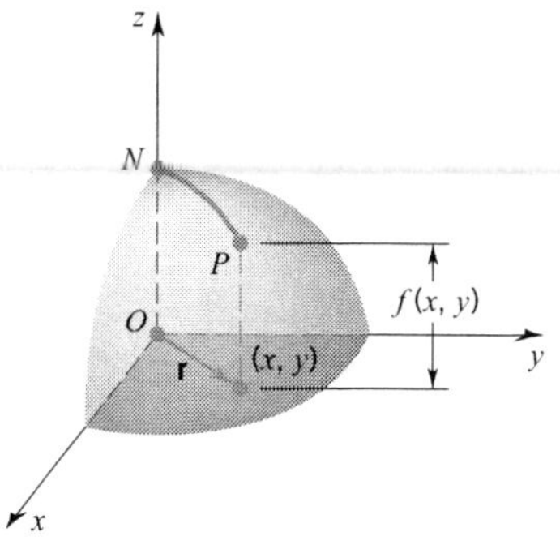

$f(x, y) = \sqrt{1 - (x^2 + y^2)}$

Figure 16.2.3

Example 4 Suppose that the temperature at each point of a metal plate is given by the function

$$T(x, y) = e^x \cos y + e^y \cos x.$$

(a) In what direction does the temperature increase most rapidly at the point $(0, 0)$? What is this rate of increase?

(b) In what direction does the temperature decrease most rapidly at $(0, 0)$?

SOLUTION

$$\nabla T(x, y) = \frac{\partial T}{\partial x}(x, y)\,\mathbf{i} + \frac{\partial T}{\partial y}(x, y)\,\mathbf{j}$$
$$= (e^x \cos y - e^y \sin x)\,\mathbf{i} + (e^y \cos x - e^x \sin y)\,\mathbf{j}.$$

(a) At $(0, 0)$ the temperature increases most rapidly in the direction of the gradient

$$\nabla T(0, 0) = \mathbf{i} + \mathbf{j}.$$

This rate of increase is

$$\|\nabla T(0, 0)\| = \|\mathbf{i} + \mathbf{j}\| = \sqrt{2}.$$

(b) The temperature decreases most rapidly in the direction of

$$-\nabla T(0, 0) = -\mathbf{i} - \mathbf{j}.$$ ❑

Example 5 Suppose that the mass density (mass per unit volume) of a metal ball centered at the origin is given by the function

$$\lambda(x, y, z) = ke^{-(x^2+y^2+z^2)}, \qquad k \text{ a positive constant.}$$

(a) In what direction does the density increase most rapidly at the point (x, y, z)? What is this rate of density increase?

(b) In what direction does the density decrease most rapidly?

(c) What are the rates of density change at (x, y, z) in the $\mathbf{i}, \mathbf{j}, \mathbf{k}$ directions?

SOLUTION

$$\nabla\lambda(x, y, z) = \frac{\partial\lambda}{\partial x}(x, y, z)\,\mathbf{i} + \frac{\partial\lambda}{\partial y}(x, y, z)\,\mathbf{j} + \frac{\partial\lambda}{\partial z}(x, y, z)\,\mathbf{k}$$

$$= -2ke^{-(x^2+y^2+z^2)}[x\,\mathbf{i} + y\,\mathbf{j} + z\,\mathbf{k}].$$

Since $\lambda(x, y, z) = ke^{-(x^2+y^2+z^2)}$, we have

$$\nabla\lambda(x, y, z) = -2\lambda(x, y, z)\,\mathbf{r}.$$

From this, we see that the gradient points from (x, y, z) in the direction opposite to that of the radius vector.

(a) The density increases most rapidly directly toward the origin. The rate of increase is

$$\|\nabla\lambda(x, y, z)\| = 2\lambda(x, y, z)\|\mathbf{r}\| = 2\lambda(x, y, z)\sqrt{x^2 + y^2 + z^2}.$$

(b) The density decreases most rapidly directly away from the origin.

(c) The rates of density change in the $\mathbf{i}$, $\mathbf{j}$, $\mathbf{k}$ directions are given by the directional derivatives

$$\lambda'_{\mathbf{i}}(x, y, z) = \nabla\lambda(x, y, z)\cdot\mathbf{i} = -2x\lambda(x, y, z),$$

$$\lambda'_{\mathbf{j}}(x, y, z) = \nabla\lambda(x, y, z)\cdot\mathbf{j} = -2y\lambda(x, y, z),$$

$$\lambda'_{\mathbf{k}}(x, y, z) = \nabla\lambda(x, y, z)\cdot\mathbf{k} = -2z\lambda(x, y, z).$$

These are just the first partials of λ. ❑

Example 6 Suppose that the temperature at each point of a metal plate is given by the function

$$T(x, y) = 1 + x^2 - y^2.$$

Find the path followed by a heat-seeking particle that originates at $(-2, 1)$.

SOLUTION The particle moves in the direction of the gradient vector

$$\nabla T = 2x\,\mathbf{i} - 2y\,\mathbf{j}.$$

We want the curve

$$C : \mathbf{r}(t) = x(t)\mathbf{i} + y(t)\mathbf{j},$$

which begins at $(-2, 1)$ and at each point has tangent vector in the direction of ∇T. We can satisfy the first condition by setting

$$x(0) = -2, \qquad y(0) = 1.$$

We can satisfy the second condition by setting

$$x'(t) = 2x(t), \qquad y'(t) = -2y(t). \qquad \text{(explain)}$$

These differential equations, together with initial conditions at $t = 0$, imply that

$$x(t) = -2e^{2t}, \qquad y(t) = e^{-2t}. \qquad \text{(Section 7.6)}$$

We can eliminate the parameter t by noting that

$$x(t)y(t) = (-2e^{2t})(e^{-2t}) = -2.$$

In terms of just x and y we have

$$xy = -2.$$

The particle moves from the point $(-2, 1)$ along the left branch of the hyperbola $xy = -2$ in the direction of decreasing x. (Figure 16.2.4.)

The level curves, *isothermals* of the temperature distribution T, are also hyperbolas. As you can verify, the path of the object is perpendicular to each of the isothermals $x^2 - y^2 = c - 1$. ❑

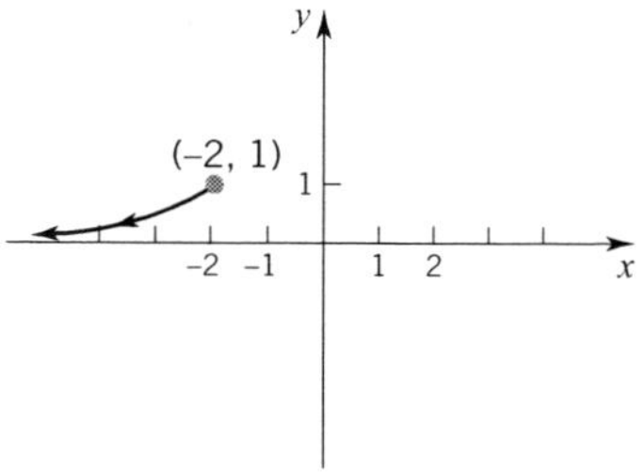

Figure 16.2.4

Remark The pair of differential equations

$$x'(t) = 2x(t), \qquad y'(t) = -2y(t)$$

can be set as a single differential equation in x and y: the relation

$$\frac{y'(t)}{x'(t)} = -\frac{y(t)}{x(t)} \quad \text{gives} \quad \frac{dy}{dx} = -\frac{y}{x}.$$

This equation is readily solved directly:

$$\frac{1}{y}\frac{dy}{dx} = -\frac{1}{x}$$

$$\ln|y| = -\ln|x| + C$$

$$\ln|x| + \ln|y| = C$$

$$\ln|xy| = C.$$

Thus xy is constant:

$$xy = k.$$

Since the curve passes through the point $(-2, 1)$, $k = -2$ and once again we have the curve

$$xy = -2.$$

You will be called on to use this method of solution in some of the Exercises. ❑

EXERCISES 16.2

Exercises 1–14. Find the directional derivative at the point P in the direction indicated.

1. $f(x, y) = x^2 + 3y^2$ at $P(1, 1)$ in the direction of $\mathbf{i} - \mathbf{j}$.

2. $f(x, y) = x + \sin(x + y)$ at $P(0, 0)$ in the direction of $2\,\mathbf{i} + \mathbf{j}$.

3. $f(x, y) = x\,e^y - y\,e^x$ at $P(1, 0)$ in the direction of $3\,\mathbf{i} + 4\,\mathbf{j}$.

4. $f(x, y) = \dfrac{2x}{x - y}$ at $P(1, 0)$ in the direction of $\mathbf{i} - \sqrt{3}\,\mathbf{j}$.

5. $f(x, y) = \dfrac{ax + by}{x + y}$ at $P(1, 1)$ in the direction of $\mathbf{i} - \mathbf{j}$.

6. $f(x, y) = \dfrac{x + y}{cx + dy}$ at $P(1, 1)$ in the direction of $c\,\mathbf{i} - d\,\mathbf{j}$.

7. $f(x, y) = \ln(x^2 + y^2)$ at $P(0, 1)$ in the direction of $8\,\mathbf{i} + \mathbf{j}$.

8. $f(x, y) = x^2y + \tan y$ at $P(-1, \pi/4)$ in the direction of $\mathbf{i} - 2\,\mathbf{j}$.

9. $f(x, y, z) = xy + yz + zx$ at $P(1, -1, 1)$ in the direction of $\mathbf{i} + 2\,\mathbf{j} + \mathbf{k}$.

10. $f(x, y, z) = x^2y + y^2z + z^2x$ at $P(1, 0, 1)$ in the direction of $3\,\mathbf{j} - \mathbf{k}$.

11. $f(x, y, z) = (x + y^2 + z^3)^2$ at $P(1, -1, 1)$ in the direction of $\mathbf{i} + \mathbf{j}$.

12. $f(x, y, z) = Ax^2 + Bxyz + Cy^2$ at $P(1, 2, 1)$ in the direction of $A\mathbf{i} + B\,\mathbf{j} + C\,\mathbf{k}$.

13. $f(x, y, z) = x\arctan(y + z)$ at $P(1, 0, 1)$ in the direction of $\mathbf{i} + \mathbf{j} - \mathbf{k}$.

14. $f(x, y, z) = xy^2\cos z - 2yz^2\sin\pi x + 3zx^2$ at $P(0, -1, \pi)$ in the direction of $2\,\mathbf{i} - \mathbf{j} + 2\,\mathbf{k}$.

15. Find the directional derivative of $f(x, y) = \ln\sqrt{x^2 + y^2}$ at $(x, y) \neq (0, 0)$ toward the origin.

16. Find the directional derivative of $f(x, y) = (x - 1)y^2e^{xy}$ at $(0, 1)$ toward the point $(-1, 3)$.

17. Find the directional derivative of $f(x, y) = Ax^2 + 2Bxy + Cy^2$ at (a, b) toward (b, a) (a) if $a > b$; (b) if $a < b$.

18. Find the directional derivative of $f(x, y, z) = z \ln(x/y)$ at $(1, 1, 2)$ toward the point $(2, 2, 1)$.

19. Find the directional derivative of $f(x, y, z) = xe^{y^2-z^2}$ at $(1, 2, -2)$ in the direction of increasing t along the path

$$\mathbf{r}(t) = t\,\mathbf{i} + 2\cos(t-1)\,\mathbf{j} - 2e^{t-1}\,\mathbf{k}.$$

20. Find the directional derivative of $f(x, y, z) = x^2 + yz$ at $(1, -3, 2)$ in the direction of increasing t along the path

$$\mathbf{r}(t) = t^2\,\mathbf{i} + 3t\,\mathbf{j} + (1 - t^3)\,\mathbf{k}.$$

21. Find the directional derivatives of $f(x, y, z) = x^2 + 2xyz - yz^2$ at $(1, 1, 2)$ in the directions parallel to the line

$$\frac{x-1}{2} = y - 1 = \frac{z-2}{-3}.$$

22. Find the directional derivatives of $f(x, y, z) - e^x \cos \pi yz$ at $(0, 1, \frac{1}{2})$ in the directions parallel to the line in which the planes $x + y - z = 5$ and $4x - y - z = 2$ intersect.

Exercises 23–26. Find the unit vector in the direction in which f increases most rapidly at P and give the rate of change of f in that direction; find the unit vector in the direction in which f decreases most rapidly at P and give the rate of change of f in that direction.

23. $f(x, y) = y^2e^{2x}$; $P(0, 1)$.

24. $f(x, y) = x + \sin(x + 2y)$; $P(0, 0)$.

25. $f(x, y, z) = \sqrt{x^2 + y^2 + z^2}$; $P(1, -2, 1)$.

26. $f(x, y, z) = x^2z\,e^y + xz^2$; $P(1, \ln 2, 2)$.

27. Let $f = f(x)$ be a differentiable function of one variable. What is the gradient of f at x_0? What is the geometric significance of the direction of this gradient?

28. Suppose that f is differentiable at (x_0, y_0) and $\nabla f(x_0, y_0) \neq \mathbf{0}$. Calculate the rate of change of f in the direction of

$$\frac{\partial f}{\partial y}(x_0, y_0)\,\mathbf{i} - \frac{\partial f}{\partial x}(x_0, y_0)\,\mathbf{j}.$$

Give a geometric interpretation to your answer.

29. Let

$$f(x, y) = \sqrt{x^2 + y^2}.$$

(a) Show that $\partial f/\partial x$ is not defined at $(0, 0)$.
(b) Is f differentiable at $(0, 0)$?

30. Verify that, if g is continuous at $\mathbf{x}$, then
(a) $g(\mathbf{x} + \mathbf{h})\,o(\mathbf{h}) = o(\mathbf{h})$ and
(b) $[g(\mathbf{x} + \mathbf{h}) - g(\mathbf{x})]\nabla f(\mathbf{x}) \cdot \mathbf{h} = o(\mathbf{h})$.

31. Given the density function $\lambda(x, y) = 48 - \frac{4}{3}x^2 - 3y^2$, find the rate of density change (a) at $(1, -1)$ in the direction of the most rapid density decrease; (b) at $(1, 2)$ in the $\mathbf{i}$ direction; (c) at (2,2) in the direction away from the origin.

32. The intensity of light in a neighborhood of the point $(-2, 1)$ is given by a function of the form $I(x, y) = A - 2x^2 - y^2$. Find the path followed by a light-seeking particle that originates at the center of the neighborhood.

33. Determine the path of steepest descent along the surface $z = x^2 + 3y^2$ from each of the following points: (a) $(1, 1, 4)$; (b) $(1, -2, 13)$.

34. Determine the path of steepest ascent along hyperbolic paraboloid $z = \frac{1}{2}x^2 - y^2$ from each of the following points: (a) $(-1, 1, -\frac{1}{2})$; (b) $(1, 0, \frac{1}{2})$.

35. Determine the path of steepest descent along the surface $z = a^2x^2 + b^2y^2$ from the point $(a, b, a^4 + b^4)$.

36. The temperature in a neighborhood of the origin is given by a function of the form

$$T(x, y) = T_0 + e^y \sin x.$$

Find the path followed by a heat-fleeing particle that originates at the origin.

37. The temperature in a neighborhood of the point $(\frac{1}{4}\pi, 0)$ is given by the function

$$T(x, y) = \sqrt{2}e^{-y} \cos x.$$

Find the path followed by a heat-seeking particle that originates at the center of the neighborhood.

38. Determine the path of steepest descent along the surface $z = A + x + 2y - x^2 - 3y^2$ from the point $(0, 0, A)$.

39. Set $f(x, y) = 3x^2 + y$.
(a) Find

$$\lim_{h \to 0} \frac{f(x(2+h), y(2+h)) - f(2, 4)}{h}$$

given that $x(t) = t$ and $y(t) = t^2$. (These functions parametrize the parabola $y = x^2$.)
(b) Find

$$\lim_{h \to 0} \frac{f(x(4+h), y(4+h)) - f(2, 4)}{h}$$

given that $x(t) = \frac{1}{4}(t + 4)$ and $y(t) = t$. (These functions parametrize the line $y = 4x - 4$.)
(c) Calculate the directional derivative of f at $(2, 4)$ in the direction of $\mathbf{i} + 4\mathbf{j}$.
(d) Observe that $\mathbf{i} + 4\mathbf{j}$ is a direction vector for the line $y = 4x - 4$ and that this line is tangent to the parabola $y = x^2$ at $(2, 4)$. Explain then why the computations in (a), (b), (c) yield different values.

40. According to Newton's law of gravitation, the force exerted on a particle of mass m located at the point (x, y, z) by a particle of mass M located at the origin is given by

$$\mathbf{F}(x, y, z) = -\frac{GMm}{r^3}\mathbf{r}$$

where $\mathbf{r} = x\,\mathbf{i} + y\,\mathbf{j} + z\,\mathbf{k}$, $r = \|\mathbf{r}\|$, and G is the universal gravitational constant. Show that $\mathbf{F}$ is the gradient of the function

$$f(x, y, z) = \frac{GMm}{r}.$$

41. Let $\mathbf{u}$ be a unit vector in the plane attached to the origin, and let θ be the angle measured counterclockwise from the positive x-axis to $\mathbf{u}$. Let f be a differentiable function of two variables.

(a) Show that $f'_{\mathbf{u}}(x, y) = \frac{\partial f}{\partial x}\cos\theta + \frac{\partial f}{\partial y}\sin\theta$.

(b) Set $f(x, y) = x^3 + 2xy - xy^2, \theta = 2\pi/3$. Find $f'_{\mathbf{u}}(-1, 2)$.

42. Refer to Exercise 41. Let $f(x, y) = x^2e^{2y}$ and $\theta = 5\pi/4$. Find $f'_u(x, y)$ and $f'_u(2, \ln 2)$.

43. Assume that both f and g have continuous first partials in a neighborhood of $\mathbf{x}$. Derive the product rule

$$\nabla[f(\mathbf{x})g(\mathbf{x})] = f(\mathbf{x})\nabla g(\mathbf{x}) + g(\mathbf{x}) + g(\mathbf{x})\nabla f(\mathbf{x})$$

from Theorem 16.1.3.

44. Assume that $\nabla f(\mathbf{x})$ and $\nabla g(\mathbf{x})$ both exist, and that $g(\mathbf{x}) \neq 0$. Derive the quotient rule

$$\nabla\left[\frac{f(\mathbf{x})}{g(\mathbf{x})}\right] = \frac{g(\mathbf{x})\nabla f(\mathbf{x}) - f(\mathbf{x})\nabla g(\mathbf{x})}{g^2(\mathbf{x})}.$$

45. Assume that $\nabla f(\mathbf{x})$ exists. Prove that, for each integer n,

$$\nabla f^n(\mathbf{x}) = nf^{n-1}(\mathbf{x})\nabla f(\mathbf{x}).$$

Does this result hold if n is replaced by an arbitrary real number?

16.3 THE MEAN-VALUE THEOREM; THE CHAIN RULE

The Mean-Value Theorem

You have seen the important role played by the mean-value theorem in the calculus of functions of one variable. Here we take up the analogous result for functions of several variables. Let $\mathbf{a}$ and $\mathbf{b}$ be points (either in the plane or in three-space); by $\overline{\mathbf{ab}}$ we mean the line segment that joins point $\mathbf{a}$ to point $\mathbf{b}$.

> **THEOREM 16.3.1 THE MEAN-VALUE THEOREM (SEVERAL VARIABLES)**
>
> If f is differentiable at each point of the line segment $\overline{\mathbf{ab}}$, then there exists on that line segment a point $\mathbf{c}$ between $\mathbf{a}$ and $\mathbf{b}$ such that
>
> $$f(\mathbf{b}) - f(\mathbf{a}) = \nabla f(\mathbf{c}) \cdot (\mathbf{b} - \mathbf{a}).$$

PROOF As t ranges from 0 to 1, $\mathbf{a} + t(\mathbf{b} - \mathbf{a})$ traces out the line segment $\overline{\mathbf{ab}}$. The idea of the proof is to apply the one-variable mean-value theorem to the function

$$g(t) = f(\mathbf{a} + t[\mathbf{b} - \mathbf{a}]), \qquad t \in [0, 1].$$

To show that g is differentiable on the open interval $(0, 1)$, we take $t \in (0, 1)$ and form

$$\begin{aligned} g(t+h) - g(t) &= f(\mathbf{a} + (t+h)[\mathbf{b} - \mathbf{a}]) - f(\mathbf{a} + t[\mathbf{b} - \mathbf{a}]) \\ &= f(\mathbf{a} + t[\mathbf{b} - \mathbf{a}] + h[\mathbf{b} - \mathbf{a}]) - f(\mathbf{a} + t[\mathbf{b} - \mathbf{a}]) \\ &= \nabla f(\mathbf{a} + t[\mathbf{b} - \mathbf{a}]) \cdot h[\mathbf{b} - \mathbf{a}] + o(h[\mathbf{b} - \mathbf{a}]). \end{aligned}$$

Since

$$\nabla f(\mathbf{a} + t[\mathbf{b} + \mathbf{a}]) \cdot h(\mathbf{b} - \mathbf{a}) = [\nabla f(\mathbf{a} + t[\mathbf{b} - \mathbf{a}]) \cdot (\mathbf{b} - \mathbf{a})]h$$

and the $o(h[\mathbf{b} - \mathbf{a}])$ term is obviously $o(h)$, we can write

$$g(t+h) - g(t) = [\nabla f(\mathbf{a} + t[\mathbf{b} - \mathbf{a}]) \cdot (\mathbf{b} - \mathbf{a})]h + o(h).$$

Dividing both sides by h, we see that g is differentiable and

$$g'(t) = \nabla f(\mathbf{a} + t[\mathbf{b} - \mathbf{a}]) \cdot (\mathbf{b} - \mathbf{a}).$$

The function g is clearly continuous at 0 and at 1. Applying the one-variable mean-value theorem to g, we can conclude that there exists a number t_0 between 0 and

1 such that

$$(*) \qquad g(1) - g(0) = g'(t_0)(1 - 0).$$

Since $g(1) = f(\mathbf{b}), g(0) = f(\mathbf{a})$, and $g'(t_0) = \nabla f(\mathbf{a} + t_0[\mathbf{b} - \mathbf{a}]) \cdot (\mathbf{b} - \mathbf{a})$, condition $(*)$ gives

$$f(\mathbf{b}) - f(\mathbf{a}) = \nabla f(\mathbf{a} + t_0[\mathbf{b} - \mathbf{a}]) \cdot (\mathbf{b} - \mathbf{a}).$$

Setting $\mathbf{c} = \mathbf{a} + t_0[\mathbf{b} - \mathbf{a}]$, we have

$$f(\mathbf{b}) - f(\mathbf{a}) = \nabla f(\mathbf{c}) \cdot (\mathbf{b} - \mathbf{a}). \quad \square$$

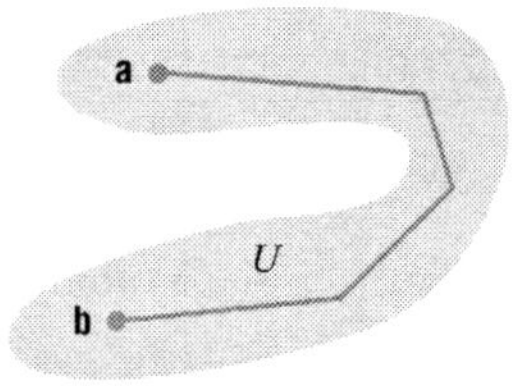

U is connected

Figure 16.3.1

A nonempty open set U (in the plane or in three-space) is said to be *connected* if any two points of U can be joined by a polygonal path that lies entirely in U. You can see such a set pictured in Figure 16.3.1.

The set shown in Figure 16.3.2 is the union of two disjoint open sets. The set is open but not connected: it is impossible to join **a** and **b** by a polygonal path that lies within the set.

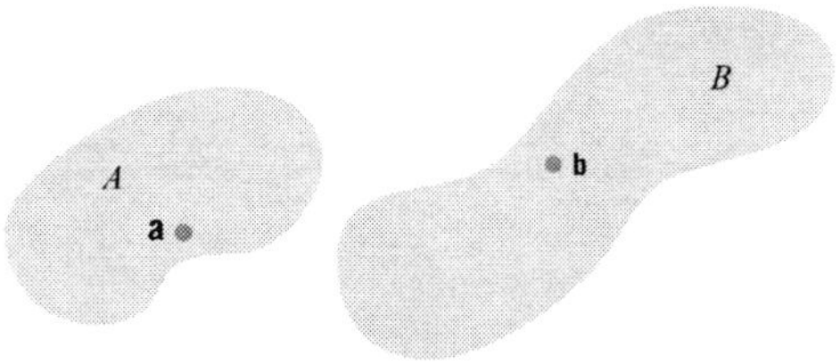

$U = A \cup B$ is not connected

Figure 16.3.2

In Chapter 4 you saw that, if $f'(x) = 0$ for all x in an open interval I, then f is constant on I. We have a similar result for functions of several variables.

> **THEOREM 16.3.2**
>
> Let U be an open connected set and let f be a differentiable function on U.
>
> If $\nabla f(\mathbf{x}) = \mathbf{0}$ for all $\mathbf{x}$ in U, then f is constant on U.

PROOF Let **a** and **b** be any two points in U. Since U is connected, we can join these points by a polygonal path with vertices $\mathbf{a} = \mathbf{c}_0, \mathbf{c}_1, \mathbf{c}_2, \ldots, \mathbf{c}_{n-1}, \mathbf{c}_n = \mathbf{b}$. (Figure 16.3.3.) By the mean-value theorem (Theorem 16.3.1) there exist points

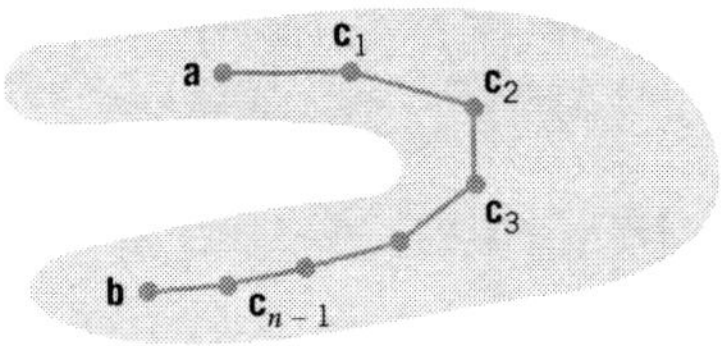

Figure 16.3.3

$\mathbf{c}_1^*$ between $\mathbf{c}_0$ and $\mathbf{c}_1$	such that	$f(\mathbf{c}_1) - f(\mathbf{c}_0) = \nabla f(\mathbf{c}_1^*) \cdot (\mathbf{c}_1 - \mathbf{c}_0)$,
$\mathbf{c}_2^*$ between $\mathbf{c}_1$ and $\mathbf{c}_2$	such that	$f(\mathbf{c}_2) - f(\mathbf{c}_1) = \nabla f(\mathbf{c}_2^*) \cdot (\mathbf{c}_2 - \mathbf{c}_1)$,
$\vdots$		$\vdots$
$\mathbf{c}_n^*$ between $\mathbf{c}_{n-1}$ and $\mathbf{c}_n$	such that	$f(\mathbf{c}_n) - f(\mathbf{c}_{n-1}) = \nabla f(\mathbf{c}_n^*) \cdot (\mathbf{c}_n - \mathbf{c}_{n-1})$.

If $\nabla f(\mathbf{x}) = 0$ for all $\mathbf{x}$ in U, then

$$f(\mathbf{c}_1) - f(\mathbf{c}_0) = 0, \qquad f(\mathbf{c}_2) - f(\mathbf{c}_1) = 0, \ \cdots, \qquad f(\mathbf{c}_n) - f(\mathbf{c}_{n-1}) = 0.$$

This shows that

$$f(\mathbf{a}) = f(\mathbf{c}_0) = f(\mathbf{c}_1) = f(\mathbf{c}_2) = \cdots = f(\mathbf{c}_{n-1}) = f(\mathbf{c}_n) = f(\mathbf{b}).$$

Since $\mathbf{a}$ and $\mathbf{b}$ are arbitrary points of U, f must be constant on U. ❑

THEOREM 16.3.3

Let U be an open connected set and let f and g be functions differentiable on U.

If $\nabla f(\mathbf{x}) = \nabla g(\mathbf{x})$ for all $\mathbf{x}$ in U, then f and g differ by a constant on U.

PROOF If $\nabla f(\mathbf{x}) = \nabla g(\mathbf{x})$ for all $\mathbf{x}$ in U, then

$$\nabla[f(\mathbf{x}) - g(\mathbf{x})] = \nabla f(\mathbf{x}) - \nabla g(\mathbf{x}) = 0 \qquad \text{for all } \mathbf{x} \text{ in } U.$$

By Theorem 16.3.2, $f - g$ must be constant on U. ❑

The Chain Rule

You are by now thoroughly familiar with the chain rule for functions of a single variable (Theorem 3.5.6): If g is differentiable at x and f is differentiable at $g(x)$, then

$$\frac{d}{dx}(f[g(x)]) = f'[g(x)]g'(x).$$

Here we obtain generalizations of the chain rule for functions of several variables.

A vector-valued function is said to be *continuous* provided that its components are continuous. If $f = f(x, y, z)$ is a scalar-valued function (a real-valued function), then its gradient ∇f is a vector-valued function. We say that f is *continuously differentiable* on an *open set* U if f is differentiable on U and ∇f is continuous on U.

If a curve $\mathbf{r}$ lies in the domain of f, then we can form the composition

$$(f \circ \mathbf{r})(t) = f(\mathbf{r}(t)).$$

The composition $f \circ \mathbf{r}$ is a real-valued function of the real variable t. The numbers $f(\mathbf{r}(t))$ are the values taken on by f *along the curve* $\mathbf{r}$. For example, let

$$f(x, y) = \tfrac{1}{3}(x^3 + y^3) \qquad \text{and} \qquad \mathbf{r}(t) = a\cos t\,\mathbf{i} + b\sin t\,\mathbf{j}.$$

Then, with $x(t) = a\cos t$ and $y(t) = b\sin t$, we have

$$f(\mathbf{r}(t)) = \tfrac{1}{3}(a^3\cos^3 t + b^3\sin^3 t).$$

The chain rule gives a formula for calculating the derivative of the composition $f \circ \mathbf{r}$.

THEOREM 16.3.4 THE CHAIN RULE

If f is continuously differentiable on an open set U and $\mathbf{r} = \mathbf{r}(t)$ is a differentiable curve that lies in U, then the composition $f \circ \mathbf{r}$ is differentiable and

$$\frac{d}{dt}[f(\mathbf{r}(t))] = \nabla f(\mathbf{r}(t)) \cdot \mathbf{r}'(t).$$

PROOF We will show that

$$\lim_{h \to 0} \frac{f(\mathbf{r}(t+h)) - f(\mathbf{r}(t))}{h} = \nabla f(\mathbf{r}(t)) \cdot \mathbf{r}'(t).$$

For $h \neq 0$ and sufficiently small, the line segment that joins $\mathbf{r}(t)$ to $\mathbf{r}(t+h)$ lies entirely in U. This we know because U is open and $\mathbf{r}$ is continuous. (See Figure 16.3.4.) For such h, the mean-value theorem assures us that there exists a point $\mathbf{c}(h)$ between $\mathbf{r}(t)$ and $\mathbf{r}(t+h)$ such that

$$f(\mathbf{r}(t+h)) - f(\mathbf{r}(t)) = \nabla f(\mathbf{c}(h)) \cdot [\mathbf{r}(t+h) - \mathbf{r}(t)].$$

Dividing both sides by h, we have

$$\frac{f(\mathbf{r}(t+h)) - f(\mathbf{r}(t))}{h} = \nabla f(\mathbf{c}(h)) \cdot \left[\frac{\mathbf{r}(t+h) - \mathbf{r}(t)}{h}\right].$$

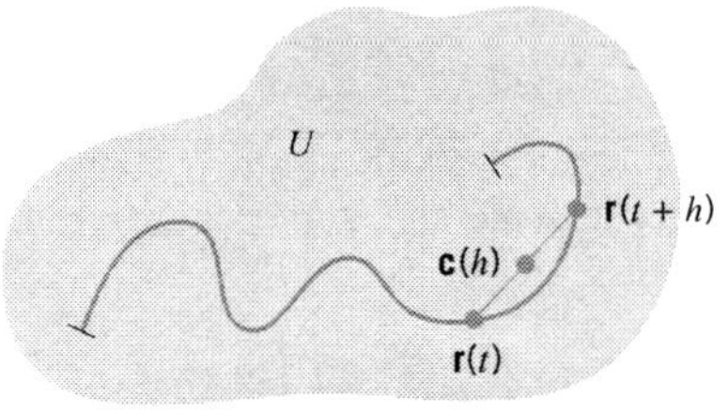

Figure 16.3.4

As h tends to zero, $\mathbf{c}(h)$ tends to $\mathbf{r}(t)$ and, by the continuity of ∇f,

$$\nabla f(\mathbf{c}(h)) \to \nabla f(\mathbf{r}(t)).$$

Since

$$\frac{\mathbf{r}(t+h) - \mathbf{r}(t)}{h} \to \mathbf{r}'(t),$$

the result follows. ❑

Example 1 Use the chain rule to find the rate of change of

$$f(x, y) = \tfrac{1}{3}(x^3 + y^3)$$

with respect to t along the ellipse $\mathbf{r}(t) = a \cos t\, \mathbf{i} + b \sin t\, \mathbf{j}$.

SOLUTION The rate of change of f with respect to t along the curve $\mathbf{r}$ is the derivative

$$\frac{d}{dt}[f(\mathbf{r}(t))].$$

By the chain rule (Theorem 16.3.4),

$$\frac{d}{dt}[f(\mathbf{r}(t))] = \nabla f(\mathbf{r}(t)) \cdot \mathbf{r}'(t).$$

Here

$$\nabla f = x^2\,\mathbf{i} + y^2\,\mathbf{j}.$$

With $x(t) = a\cos t$ and $y(t) = b\sin t$, we have

$$\nabla f(\mathbf{r}(t)) = a^2\cos^2 t\,\mathbf{i} + b^2\sin^2 t\,\mathbf{j}.$$

Since $\mathbf{r}'(t) = -a\sin t\,\mathbf{i} + b\cos t\,\mathbf{j}$,

$$\begin{aligned}\frac{d}{dt}[f(\mathbf{r}(t))] &= \nabla f(\mathbf{r}(t)) \cdot \mathbf{r}'(t)\\ &= (a^2\cos^2 t\,\mathbf{i} + b^2\sin^2 t\,\mathbf{j}) \cdot (-a\sin t\,\mathbf{i} + b\cos t\,\mathbf{j})\\ &= -a^3\sin t\cos^2 t + b^3\sin^2 t\cos t\\ &= \sin t\cos t(b^3\sin t - a^3\cos t). \quad \square\end{aligned}$$

Remark Note that we could have obtained the same result without invoking Theorem 16.3.4 by first forming $f(\mathbf{r}(t))$ and then differentiating with respect to t. As you saw in the calculations carried out before the statement of the theorem,

$$f(\mathbf{r}(t)) = \tfrac{1}{3}(a^3\cos^3 t + b^3\sin^3 t).$$

Differentiation gives

$$\begin{aligned}\frac{d}{dt}[f(\mathbf{r}(t))] &= \tfrac{1}{3}[3a^3(\cos^2 t)(-\sin t) + 3b^3\sin^2 t\cos t]\\ &= \sin t\cos t(b^3\sin t - a^3\cos t). \quad \square\end{aligned}$$

Example 2 Use the chain rule to find the rate of change of

$$f(x, y, z) = x^2 y + z\cos x$$

with respect to t along the twisted cubic $\mathbf{r}(t) = t\,\mathbf{i} + t^2\,\mathbf{j} + t^3\,\mathbf{k}$.

SOLUTION Once again we use the relation

$$\frac{d}{dt}[f(\mathbf{r}(t))] = \nabla f(\mathbf{r}(t)) \cdot \mathbf{r}'(t).$$

This time

$$\nabla f = (2xy - z\sin x)\,\mathbf{i} + x^2\,\mathbf{j} + \cos x\,\mathbf{k}.$$

Since $x(t) = t$, $y(t) = t^2$, $z(t) = t^3$,

$$\nabla f(\mathbf{r}(t)) = (2t^3 - t^3\sin t)\,\mathbf{i} + t^2\,\mathbf{j} + \cos t\,\mathbf{k}.$$

Since $\mathbf{r}'(t) = \mathbf{i} + 2t\,\mathbf{j} + 3t^2\,\mathbf{k}$,

$$\begin{aligned}\frac{d}{dt}[(\mathbf{r}(t))] &= \nabla f(\mathbf{r}(t)) \cdot \mathbf{r}'(t)\\ &= [(2t^3 - t^3\sin t)\,\mathbf{i} + t^2\,\mathbf{j} + \cos t\,\mathbf{k}] \cdot [\mathbf{i} + 2t\,\mathbf{j} + 3t^2\,\mathbf{k}]\\ &= 2t^3 - t^3\sin t + 2t^3 + 3t^2\cos t\\ &= 4t^3 - t^3\sin t + 3t^2\cos t.\end{aligned}$$

You can check this answer by first forming $f(\mathbf{r}(t))$ and then differentiating. $\square$

Another Formulation of Theorem 16.3.4

The chain rule for functions of one variable,

$$\frac{d}{dt}[u(x(t))] = u'(x(t))x'(t),$$

can be written

$$\frac{du}{dt} = \frac{du}{dx}\frac{dx}{dt}.$$

In a similar manner, the relation

$$\frac{d}{dt}[u(\mathbf{r}(t))] = \nabla u(\mathbf{r}(t)) \cdot \mathbf{r}'(t)$$

can be written

(1) $$\frac{du}{dt} = \nabla u \cdot \frac{d\mathbf{r}}{dt}.$$

Since

$$\nabla u = \frac{\partial u}{\partial x}\mathbf{i} + \frac{\partial u}{\partial y}\mathbf{j} + \frac{\partial u}{\partial z}\mathbf{k} \quad \text{and} \quad \frac{d\mathbf{r}}{dt} = \frac{dx}{dt}\mathbf{i} + \frac{dy}{dt}\mathbf{j} + \frac{dz}{dt}\mathbf{k},$$

(1) gives

(16.3.5) $$\frac{du}{dt} = \frac{\partial u}{\partial x}\frac{dx}{dt} + \frac{\partial u}{\partial y}\frac{dy}{dt} + \frac{\partial u}{\partial z}\frac{dz}{dt}.$$

In the two-variable case, the z-term drops out and we have

(16.3.6) $$\frac{du}{dt} = \frac{\partial u}{\partial x}\frac{dx}{dt} + \frac{\partial u}{\partial y}\frac{dy}{dt}.$$

Example 3 Find du/dt given that $u = x^2 - y^2$ and $x = t^2 - 1$, $y = 3\sin \pi t$.

SOLUTION Here we are in the two-variable case

$$\frac{du}{dt} = \frac{\partial u}{\partial x}\frac{dx}{dt} + \frac{\partial u}{\partial y}\frac{dy}{dt}.$$

Since

$$\frac{\partial u}{\partial x} = 2x, \qquad \frac{\partial u}{\partial y} = -2y \quad \text{and} \quad \frac{dx}{dt} = 2t, \qquad \frac{dy}{dt} = 3\pi \cos \pi t,$$

we have

$$\begin{aligned}\frac{du}{dt} &= (2x)(2t) + (-2y)(3\pi \cos \pi t)\\ &= 2(t^2 - 1)(2t) + (-2)(3\sin \pi t)(3\pi \cos \pi t)\\ &= 4t^3 - 4t - 18\pi \sin \pi t \cos \pi t.\end{aligned}$$

You can obtain this same result by first writing u directly as a function of t and then differentiating:

$$u = x^2 - y^2 = (t^2 - 1)^2 - (3\sin \pi t)^2$$

so that

$$\frac{du}{dt} = 2(t^2 - 1)2t - 2(3\sin \pi t)3\pi \cos \pi t = 4t^3 - 4t - 18\pi \sin \pi t \cos \pi t. \quad \square$$

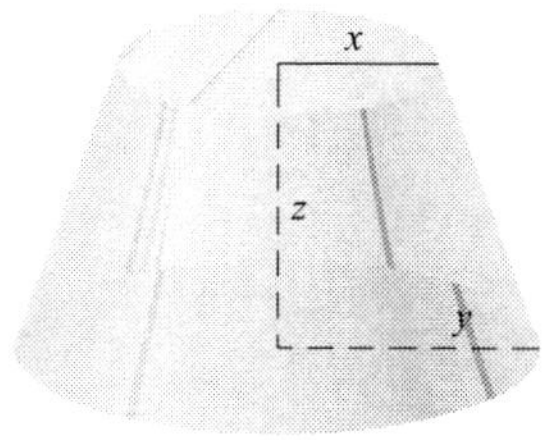

Figure 16.3.5

Example 4 A solid is in the shape of a frustum of a right circular cone. (Figure 16.3.5.) Given that the upper radius x decreases at the rate of 2 inches per minute, the lower radius y increases at the rate of 3 inches per minute, and the height z decreases at the rate of 4 inches per minute, at what rate is the volume V changing at the instant the upper radius is 10 inches, the lower radius is 12 inches, and the height is 18 inches?

SOLUTION With x, y, z as given,

$$V = \frac{1}{3}\pi z(x^2 + xy + y^2). \qquad \text{(Exercise 39, Section 6.2)}$$

Here

$$\frac{\partial V}{\partial x} = \frac{1}{3}\pi z(2x + y), \qquad \frac{\partial V}{\partial y} = \frac{1}{3}\pi z(x + 2y), \qquad \frac{\partial V}{\partial z} = \frac{1}{3}\pi(x^2 + xy + y^2).$$

Since

$$\frac{dV}{dt} = \frac{\partial V}{\partial x}\frac{dx}{dt} + \frac{\partial V}{\partial y}\frac{dy}{dt} + \frac{\partial V}{\partial z}\frac{dz}{dt},$$

we have

$$\frac{dV}{dt} = \frac{1}{3}\pi z(2x + y)\frac{dx}{dt} + \frac{1}{3}\pi z(x + 2y)\frac{dy}{dt} + \frac{1}{3}\pi(x^2 + xy + y^2)\frac{dz}{dt}.$$

Set

$$x = 10, \qquad y = 12, \qquad z = 18, \qquad \frac{dx}{dt} = -2, \qquad \frac{dy}{dt} = 3, \qquad \frac{dz}{dt} = -4,$$

and you will find that

$$\frac{dV}{dt} = -\frac{772}{3}\pi \cong -808.4.$$

The volume decreases at the rate of approximately 808 cubic inches per minute. □

Differentiating Other Composites

The chain rule (Theorem 16.3.4) spawns many rules of differentiation. Two are stated in (16.3.5) and (16.3.6). More are stated here; more in the Exercises.

First of all, if

$$u = u(x, y) \qquad \text{where} \qquad x = x(s, t) \qquad \text{and} \qquad y = y(s, t),$$

then

(16.3.7)
$$\frac{\partial u}{\partial s} = \frac{\partial u}{\partial x}\frac{\partial x}{\partial s} + \frac{\partial u}{\partial y}\frac{\partial y}{\partial s} \qquad \text{and} \qquad \frac{\partial u}{\partial t} = \frac{\partial u}{\partial x}\frac{\partial x}{\partial t} + \frac{\partial u}{\partial y}\frac{\partial y}{\partial t}.$$

To obtain the first equation, keep t fixed and differentiate u with respect to s according to (16.3.6); to obtain the second equation, keep s fixed and differentiate u with respect to t.

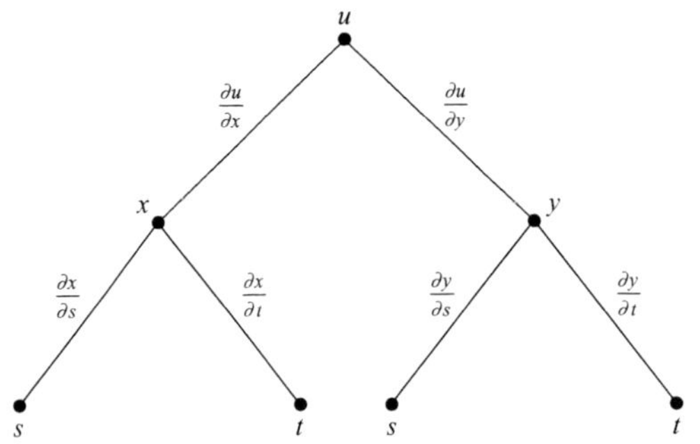

Figure 16.3.6

In Figure 16.3.6 we have drawn a *tree diagram* for (16.3.7). We construct such a tree by branching at each stage from a function to all the variables that directly determine it. Each path starting at u and ending at a variable determines a product of (partial) derivatives. The partial derivative of u with respect to each variable is the sum of the products generated by all the direct paths to that variable.

Example 5 Let $u = x^2 - 2xy + 2y^3$ where $x = s^2 \ln t$ and $y = 2st^3$. Determine $\partial u/\partial s$ and $\partial u/\partial t$.

SOLUTION Here u is a function of two variables, x and y, each of which is itself a function of two variables, s and t. Thus (16.3.7) applies:

$$\begin{aligned}\frac{\partial u}{\partial s} &= \frac{\partial u}{\partial x}\frac{\partial x}{\partial s} + \frac{\partial u}{\partial y}\frac{\partial y}{\partial s}\\ &= (2x - 2y)(2s \ln t) + (-2x + 6y^2)2t^3.\end{aligned}$$

The result can be expressed entirely in terms of s and t by using the fact that $x = s^2 \ln t$ and $y = 2st^3$. This substitution gives

$$\frac{\partial u}{\partial s} = (2s^2 \ln t - 4st^3)(2s \ln t) + (-2s^2 \ln t + 24s^2t^6)\,2t^3.$$

Similarly,

$$\begin{aligned}\frac{\partial u}{\partial t} &= \frac{\partial u}{\partial x}\frac{\partial x}{\partial t} + \frac{\partial u}{\partial y}\frac{\partial y}{\partial t}\\ &= (2s^2 \ln t - 4st^3)\left(\frac{s^2}{t}\right) + (-2s^2 \ln t + 24s^2t^6)\,6st^2.\end{aligned}$$ ❑

Suppose now that u is a function of three variables:

$$u = u(x, y, z) \qquad \text{where} \qquad x = x(s, t), \qquad y = y(s, t), \qquad z = z(s, t).$$

A tree diagram for the partials of u appears in Figure 16.3.7. The partials of u with respect to s and t can be read from the diagram:

(16.3.8)
$$\frac{\partial u}{\partial s} = \frac{\partial u}{\partial x}\frac{\partial x}{\partial s} + \frac{\partial u}{\partial y}\frac{\partial y}{\partial s} + \frac{\partial u}{\partial z}\frac{\partial z}{\partial s}, \qquad \frac{\partial u}{\partial t} = \frac{\partial u}{\partial x}\frac{\partial x}{\partial t} + \frac{\partial u}{\partial y}\frac{\partial y}{\partial t} + \frac{\partial u}{\partial z}\frac{\partial z}{\partial t}.$$

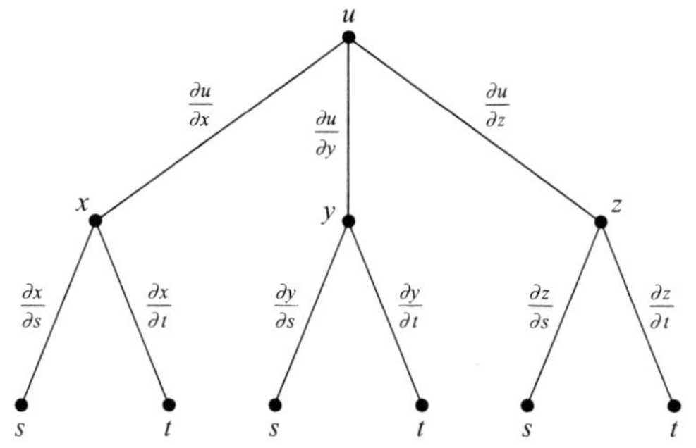

Figure 16.3.7

Example 6 Let $u = x^2y^3e^{xz}$ where $x = s^2 + t^2$, $y = 2st$, $z = s\ln t$. Determine $\partial u/\partial s$.

SOLUTION In this case u is a function of three variables, x, y, z, each of which is a function of two variables, s and t. Thus (16.3.8) applies. Therefore

$$\begin{aligned}\frac{\partial u}{\partial s} &= \frac{\partial u}{\partial x}\frac{\partial x}{\partial s} + \frac{\partial u}{\partial y}\frac{\partial y}{\partial s} + \frac{\partial u}{\partial z}\frac{\partial z}{\partial s}\\ &= (2xy^3e^{xz} + x^2y^3ze^{xz})\,2s + (3x^2y^2e^{xz})\,2t + (x^3y^3e^{xz})\ln t.\end{aligned}$$

The result can be expressed entirely in terms of s and t by using the fact that $x = s^2 + t^2$, $y = 2st$, $z = s\ln t$. ❑

Implicit Differentiation

We return to implicit differentiation, a technique we introduced in Section 3.7.

Suppose that $u = u(x, y)$ is a continuously differentiable function. If y is a differentiable function of x that satisfies $u(x, y) = 0$, then we can find the derivative of y with respect to x without first having to express y *explicitly* in terms of x. The process by which we do this is called *implicit differentiation.*

The process is based on (16.3.6). To be able to apply that formula, we introduce a new variable t by setting $x = t$. We then have

$$u = u(x, y) \qquad \text{with} \qquad x = t \qquad \text{and} \qquad y = y(t).$$

Formula (16.3.6) states that

$$\frac{du}{dt} = \frac{\partial u}{\partial x}\frac{dx}{dt} + \frac{\partial u}{\partial y}\frac{dy}{dt}.$$

Since $u(x(t), y(t)) = 0$ for all t under consideration, $du/dt = 0$ for such t. Since $x = t$, we have $dx/dt = 1$ and $dy/dt = dy/dx$. Therefore,

$$0 = \frac{\partial u}{\partial x} + \frac{\partial u}{\partial y}\frac{dy}{dx}.$$

For points (x, y) where $\partial u/\partial y \neq 0$

$$\frac{dy}{dx} = -\frac{\partial u/\partial x}{\partial u/\partial y}.$$

The result can be summarized as follows:

(16.3.9) If $u = u(x, y)$ is continuously differentiable, and y is a differentiable function of x that satisfies the equation $u(x, y) = 0$, then at all points (x, y) where $\partial u/\partial y \neq 0$,

$$\frac{dy}{dx} = -\frac{\partial u/\partial x}{\partial u/\partial y}.$$

Example 7 Suppose that y is a differentiable function of x that satisfies the equation

$$u(x, y) = 2x^2y - y^3 + 1 - x - 2y = 0.$$

Since

$$\frac{\partial u}{\partial x} = 4xy - 1 \qquad \text{and} \qquad \frac{\partial u}{\partial y} = 2x^2 - 3y^2 - 2,$$

we know that

$$\frac{dy}{dx} = -\frac{4xy - 1}{2x^2 - 3y^2 - 2}.$$

We obtained this result without involving partial derivatives in Chapter 3. (Section 3.7, Example 2) ❑

We can use implicit differentiation to obtain the partial derivatives of functions of more than one variable.

(16.3.10) If $u = u(x, y, z)$ is continuously differentiable, and $z = z(x, y)$ is a differentiable function that satisfies the equation $u(x, y, z) = 0$, then at all points (x, y, z) where $\partial u/\partial z \neq 0$,

$$\frac{\partial z}{\partial x} = -\frac{\partial u/\partial x}{\partial u/\partial z} \qquad \text{and} \qquad \frac{\partial z}{\partial y} = -\frac{\partial u/\partial y}{\partial u/\partial z}.$$

PROOF We write

$$u = u(x, y, z) \qquad \text{with} \qquad x = s, \qquad y = t, \qquad z = z(s, t)$$

and note that

$$\frac{\partial u}{\partial s} = \frac{\partial u}{\partial x}\frac{\partial x}{\partial s} + \frac{\partial u}{\partial y}\frac{\partial y}{\partial s} + \frac{\partial u}{\partial z}\frac{\partial z}{\partial s}.$$

Since $u(s, t, z(s, t)) = 0$, $\partial u/\partial s = 0$. Since $\partial x/\partial s = 1$ and $\partial y/\partial s = 0$, we have

$$0 = \frac{\partial u}{\partial x}(1) + \frac{\partial u}{\partial y}(0) + \frac{\partial u}{\partial z}\frac{\partial z}{\partial s} = \frac{\partial u}{\partial x} + \frac{\partial u}{\partial z}\frac{\partial z}{\partial s} = \frac{\partial u}{\partial x} + \underbrace{\frac{\partial u}{\partial z}\frac{\partial z}{\partial x}}_{x = s}.$$

At those points (x, y, z) where $\partial u/\partial z \neq 0$,

$$\frac{\partial z}{\partial x} = -\frac{\partial u/\partial x}{\partial u/\partial z}.$$

The formula for $\partial z/\partial y$ can be obtained in a similar manner. ❑

EXERCISES 16.3

1. Let $f(x, y) = x^3 - xy$. Set $\mathbf{a} = (0, 1)$ and $\mathbf{b} = (1, 3)$. Find a point $\mathbf{c}$ on the line segment $\overline{\mathbf{ab}}$ for which

$$f(\mathbf{b}) - f(\mathbf{a}) = \nabla f(\mathbf{c}) \cdot (\mathbf{b} - \mathbf{a}).$$

2. Let $f(x, y, z) = 4xz - y^2 + z^2$. Set $\mathbf{a} = (0, 1, 1)$ and $\mathbf{b} = (1, 3, 2)$. Find a point $\mathbf{c}$ on the line segment $\overline{\mathbf{ab}}$ for which

$$f(\mathbf{b}) - f(\mathbf{a}) = \nabla f(\mathbf{c}) \cdot (\mathbf{b} - \mathbf{a}).$$

3. (a) Find f if $\nabla f(x, y, z) = a_1\mathbf{i} + a_2\mathbf{j} + a_3\mathbf{k}$ for all (x, y, z).
(b) What can you conclude about f and g if $\nabla f(x, y, z) - \nabla g(x, y, z) = a_1\mathbf{i} + a_2\mathbf{j} + a_3\mathbf{k}$ for all (x, y, z)?

4. *(Rolle's theorem for functions of several variables)* Show that, if f is differentiable at each point of the line segment $\overline{\mathbf{ab}}$ and $f(\mathbf{a}) = f(\mathbf{b})$, then there exists a point $\mathbf{c}$ between $\mathbf{a}$ and $\mathbf{b}$ for which $\nabla f(\mathbf{c}) \perp (\mathbf{b} - \mathbf{a})$.

5. Let $U = \{\mathbf{x} : \|\mathbf{x}\| \neq 1\}$. Define f on U by setting

$$f(\mathbf{x}) = \begin{cases} 0, & \|\mathbf{x}\| < 1 \\ 1, & \|\mathbf{x}\| > 1. \end{cases}$$

(a) Note that $\nabla f(\mathbf{x}) = 0$ for all $\mathbf{x}$ in U, but f is not constant on U. Explain how this does not contradict Theorem 16.3.2.
(b) Define a function g on U different from f such that $\nabla f(\mathbf{x}) = \nabla g(\mathbf{x})$ for all $\mathbf{x}$ in U and $f - g$ is (i) constant on U, (ii) not constant on U.

6. A set of points is said to be *convex* provided that every pair of points in the set can be joined by a line segment that lies entirely within the set. Show that, if $\|\nabla f(\mathbf{x})\| \leq M$ for all $\mathbf{x}$ in some convex set Ω then

$$|f(\mathbf{x}_1) - f(\mathbf{x}_2)| \leq M\|\mathbf{x}_1 - \mathbf{x}_2\| \qquad \text{for all } \mathbf{x}_1 \text{ and } \mathbf{x}_2 \text{ in } \Omega.$$

Exercises 7–16. Find the rate of change of f with respect to t along the curve.

7. $f(x, y) = x^2 y, \quad \mathbf{r}(t) = e^t\,\mathbf{i} + e^{-t}\,\mathbf{j}$.

8. $f(x, y) = x - y, \quad \mathbf{r}(t) = at\,\mathbf{i} + b\cos at\,\mathbf{j}$.

9. $f(x, y) = \arctan(y^2 - x^2), \quad \mathbf{r}(t) = \sin t\,\mathbf{i} + \cos t\,\mathbf{j}$.

10. $f(x, y) = \ln(2x^2 + y^3), \quad \mathbf{r}(t) = e^{2t}\,\mathbf{i} + t^{1/3}\,\mathbf{j}$.

11. $f(x, y) = x\,e^y + y\,e^{-x}, \quad \mathbf{r}(t) = (\ln t)\,\mathbf{i} + t(\ln t)\,\mathbf{j}$.

12. $f(x, y, z) = \ln(x^2 + y^2 + z^2)$,
$\mathbf{r}(t) = \sin t\,\mathbf{i} + \cos t\,\mathbf{j} + e^{2t}\,\mathbf{k}$.

13. $f(x, y, z) = xy - yz, \quad \mathbf{r}(t) = t\,\mathbf{i} + t^2\,\mathbf{j} + t^3\,\mathbf{k}$.

14. $f(x, y, z) = x^2 + y^2$,
$\mathbf{r}(t) = a\cos\omega t\,\mathbf{i} + b\sin\omega t\,\mathbf{j} + b\omega t\,\mathbf{k}$.

15. $f(x, y, z) = x^2 + y^2 + z$,
$\mathbf{r}(t) = a\cos\omega t\,\mathbf{i} + b\sin\omega t\,\mathbf{j} + b\omega t\,\mathbf{k}$.

16. $f(x, y, z) = y^2\sin(x + z), \quad \mathbf{r}(t) = 2t\,\mathbf{i} + \cos t\,\mathbf{j} + t^3\,\mathbf{k}$.

Exercises 17–24. Find du/dt by applying (16.3.5) or (16.3.6).

17. $u = x^2 - 3xy + 2y^2; \quad x = \cos t, y = \sin t$.

18. $u = x + 4\sqrt{xy} - 3y; \quad x = t^3, y = t^{-1} \quad (t > 0)$.

19. $u = e^x \sin y + e^y \sin x; \quad x = \frac{1}{2}t, y = 2t$.

20. $u = 2x^2 - xy + y^2; \quad x = \cos 2t, y = \sin t$.

21. $u = e^x \sin y; \quad x = t^2, y = \pi t$.

22. $u = z\ln\left(\frac{y}{x}\right); \quad x = t^2 + 1, y = \sqrt{t}, z = te^t$.

23. $u = xy + yz + zx; \quad x = t^2, y = t(1 - t), z = (1 - t)^2$.

24. $u = x\sin\pi y - z\cos\pi x; \quad x = t^2, y = 1 - t, z = 1 - t^2$.

25. The radius of a right circular cone is increasing at the rate of 3 inches per second and the height is decreasing at the rate of 2 inches per second. At what rate is the volume of the cone changing at the instant the height is 20 inches and the radius is 14 inches?

26. The radius of a right circular cylinder is decreasing at the rate of 2 centimeters per second and the height is increasing at the rate of 3 centimeters per second. At what rate is the volume of the cylinder changing at the instant the radius is 13 centimeters and the height is 18 centimeters?

27. If the lengths of two sides of a triangle are x and y, and θ is the angle between the two sides, then the area A of the triangle is given by $A = \frac{1}{2}xy\sin\theta$. See the figure. If the sides are each increasing at the rate of 3 inches per second and θ is decreasing at the rate of 0.10 radians per second, how fast is the area changing at the instant $x = 1.5$ feet, $y = 2$ feet, $\theta = 1$ radian?

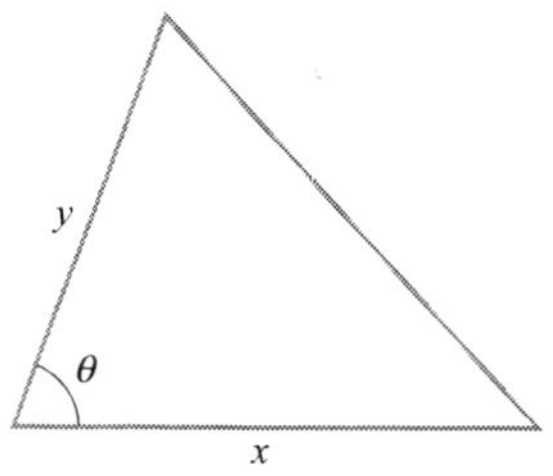

28. An object is moving along the curve in which the paraboloid $z = x^2 + \frac{1}{4}y^2$ intersects the circular cylinder $x^2 + y^2 = 13$. If the x-coordinate is increasing at the rate of 5 centimeters per second, how fast is the z-coordinate changing at the instant $x = 2$ centimeters and $y = 3$ centimeters?

Exercises 29–34. Find $\partial u/\partial s$ and $\partial u/\partial t$.

29. $u = x^2 - xy; \quad x = s\cos t, y = t\sin s$.

30. $u = \sin(x - y) + \cos(x + y); \quad x = st, y = s^2 - t^2$.

31. $u = x^2\tan y; \quad x = s^2 t, y = s + t^2$.

32. $u = z^2\sec xy; \quad x = 2st, y = s - t^2, z = s^2 t$.

33. $u = x^2 - xy + z^2; \quad x = s\cos t, y = \sin(t - s)$,
$z = t\sin s$.

34. $u = x\,e^{yz^2}; \quad x = \ln st, y = t^3, z = s^2 + t^2$.

35. An object moves so that at time t it has position $\mathbf{r}(t) = x(t)\,\mathbf{i} + y(t)\,\mathbf{j} + z(t)\,\mathbf{k}$. Show that

$$\frac{d}{dt}[f(\mathbf{r}(t))]$$

is the directional derivative of f in the direction of the motion times the speed of the object.

36. *(Important)* Set $r = \|\mathbf{r}\|$ where $\mathbf{r} = x\,\mathbf{i} + y\,\mathbf{j} + z\,\mathbf{k}$. If f is a continuously differentiable function of r, then

(16.3.11) $$\nabla[f(r)] = f'(r)\frac{\mathbf{r}}{r} \quad \text{where } r \neq 0.$$

Exercises 37–39. Calculate the following gradients taking $r = \|\mathbf{r}\|$.

37. (a) $\nabla(\sin r)$. (b) $\nabla(r \sin r)$.

38. (a) $\nabla(r \ln r)$. (b) $\nabla(e^{1-r^2})$.

39. (a) $\nabla\left(\dfrac{\sin r}{r}\right)$. (b) $\nabla\left(\dfrac{r}{\sin r}\right)$.

40. (a) Draw a tree diagram for du/dt given that $u = u(x, y)$ where $x = x(s)$, $y = y(s)$, and $s = s(t)$.

(b) Calculate du/dt.

41. Set $u = u(x, y, z)$ where

$$x = x(w, t), \quad y = y(w, t), \quad z = z(w, t),$$
$$w = w(r, s), \quad t = t(r, s).$$

(a) Draw a tree diagram for the partials of u.

(b) Calculate $\partial u/\partial r$ *and* $\partial u/\partial s$.

42. Set $u = u(x, y, z, w)$ where

$$x = x(r, s, t), \quad y = y(s, t, v), \quad z = z(r, t),$$
$$w = w(r, s, t, v).$$

(a) Draw a tree diagram for the partials of u.

(b) Calculate $\partial u/\partial r$ *and* $\partial u/\partial v$.

Higher Derivatives

43. Let $u = u(x, y)$, where $x = x(t)$ and $y = y(t)$, and assume that these functions have continuous second derivatives.

Show that

$$\frac{d^2u}{dt^2} = \frac{\partial^2 u}{\partial x^2}\left(\frac{dx}{dt}\right)^2 + 2\frac{\partial^2 u}{\partial x \partial y}\frac{dx}{dt}\frac{dy}{dt} + \frac{\partial^2 u}{\partial y^2}\left(\frac{dy}{dt}\right)^2 + \frac{\partial u}{\partial x}\frac{d^2x}{dt^2} + \frac{\partial u}{\partial y}\frac{d^2y}{dt^2}.$$

44. Let $u = u(x, y)$, where $x = x(s, t)$ and $y = y(s, t)$, and assume that all these functions have continuous second partials. Show that

$$\frac{d^2u}{ds^2} = \frac{\partial^2 u}{\partial x^2}\left(\frac{\partial x}{\partial s}\right)^2 + 2\frac{\partial^2 u}{\partial x \partial y}\frac{\partial x}{\partial s}\frac{\partial y}{\partial s} + \frac{\partial^2 u}{\partial y^2}\left(\frac{\partial y}{\partial s}\right)^2 + \frac{\partial u}{\partial x}\frac{\partial^2 x}{\partial s^2} + \frac{\partial u}{\partial y}\frac{\partial^2 y}{\partial s^2}.$$

Polar Coordinates

45. Assume that $u = u(x, y)$ is differentiable.

(a) Show that the change of variables to polar coordinates $x = r\cos\theta$ and $y = r\sin\theta$ gives

$$\frac{\partial u}{\partial r} = \frac{\partial u}{\partial x}\cos\theta + \frac{\partial u}{\partial y}\sin\theta,$$
$$\frac{\partial u}{\partial \theta} = -\frac{\partial u}{\partial x}r\sin\theta + \frac{\partial u}{\partial y}r\cos\theta.$$

(b) Express

$$\left(\frac{\partial u}{\partial r}\right)^2 + \frac{1}{r^2}\left(\frac{\partial u}{\partial \theta}\right)^2$$

entirely in terms of $\partial u/\partial x$ and $\partial u/\partial y$.

46. Let w be a function of polar coordinates r and θ. Then w can be expressed in rectangular coordinates by using

$$x = r\cos\theta \quad \text{and} \quad y = r\sin\theta.$$

(a) Using the first part of Exercise 45, verify that

$$\frac{\partial w}{\partial x} = \frac{\partial w}{\partial r}\cos\theta - \frac{1}{r}\frac{\partial w}{\partial \theta}\sin\theta,$$
$$\frac{\partial w}{\partial y} = \frac{\partial w}{\partial r}\sin\theta + \frac{1}{r}\frac{\partial w}{\partial \theta}\cos\theta.$$

(b) Deduce from part (a) that

$$\frac{\partial r}{\partial x} = \cos\theta, \qquad \frac{\partial r}{\partial y}\sin\theta;$$
$$\frac{\partial \theta}{\partial x} = -\frac{1}{r}\sin\theta, \qquad \frac{\partial \theta}{\partial y} = \frac{1}{r}\cos\theta.$$

(c) Find the fallacy in the following argument:

$$x = r\cos\theta, \qquad r = \frac{x}{\cos\theta}, \qquad \frac{\partial r}{\partial x} = \frac{1}{\cos\theta}.$$

47. *(The gradient in polar coordinates)* Let $u = u(x, y)$ be differentiable. Show that if u is written in terms of polar coordinates, then

$$\nabla u = \frac{\partial u}{\partial r}\mathbf{e}_r + \frac{1}{r}\frac{\partial u}{\partial \theta}\mathbf{e}_\theta$$

where

$$\mathbf{e}_r = \cos\theta\,\mathbf{i} + \sin\theta\,\mathbf{j} \quad \text{and} \quad \mathbf{e}_\theta = -\sin\theta\,\mathbf{i} + \cos\theta\,\mathbf{j}.$$

Exercises 48–49. Use the formula given in Exercise 47 to express the gradient of u in polar coordinates.

48. $u(x, y) = x^2 + y^2$. **49.** $u(x, y) = x^2 - xy + y^2$.

50. Let $u = u(x, y)$, where $x = r\cos\theta$ and $y = r\sin\theta$, and assume that u has continuous second partials. Derive a formula for $\partial^2 u/\partial r \partial\theta$.

51. *(The Laplace operator in polar coordinates).* Assume that $u = u(x, y)$ has continuous second partials. Show that

$$\frac{\partial^2 u}{\partial x^2} + \frac{\partial^2 u}{\partial y^2} = \frac{\partial^2 u}{\partial r^2} + \frac{1}{r^2}\frac{\partial^2 u}{\partial \theta^2} + \frac{1}{r}\frac{\partial u}{\partial r}.$$

Exercises 52–55. Assume that y is a differentiable function of x which satisfies the equation. Obtain dy/dx by implicit differentiation.

52. $x^2 - 2xy + y^4 = 4$.

53. $x e^y + y e^x - 2x^2 y = 0$.

54. $x^{2/3} + y^{2/3} = a^{2/3}$. ($a$ a constant)

55. $x\cos xy + y\cos x = 2$.

Exercises 56–57. Assume that z is a differentiable function of (x, y) which satisfies the given equation. Obtain $\partial z/\partial x$ and $\partial x/\partial y$ by implicit differentiation.

56. $z^4 + x^2z^3 + y^2 + xy = 2.$

57. $\cos xyz + \ln(x^2 + y^2 + z^2) = 0.$

58. *(A chain rule for vector-valued functions)* Suppose that

$$\mathbf{u}(x, y) = u_1(x, y)\,\mathbf{i} + u_2(x, y)\,\mathbf{j}; \quad x = x(t), \; y = y(t).$$

(a) Show that

$$\textbf{(16.3.12)} \qquad \frac{d\mathbf{u}}{dt} = \frac{\partial \mathbf{u}}{\partial x}\frac{dx}{dt} + \frac{\partial \mathbf{u}}{\partial y}\frac{dy}{dt}$$

where

$$\frac{\partial \mathbf{u}}{\partial x} = \frac{\partial u_1}{\partial x}\mathbf{i} + \frac{\partial u_2}{\partial x}\mathbf{j} \quad \text{and} \quad \frac{\partial \mathbf{u}}{\partial y} = \frac{\partial u_1}{\partial y}\mathbf{i} + \frac{\partial u_2}{\partial y}\mathbf{j}.$$

(b) Let

$$\mathbf{u} = e^x \cos y\,\mathbf{i} + e^x \sin y\,\mathbf{j}; \quad x = \tfrac{1}{2}t^2, \quad y = \pi t.$$

Calculate $d\mathbf{u}/dt$ (i) by applying (16.3.12), (ii) by forming $\mathbf{u}(t)$ directly.

59. Set

$$\mathbf{u}(x, y) = u_1(x, y)\,\mathbf{i} + u_2(x, y)\,\mathbf{j}; \quad x = x(s, t),\; y = y(s, t).$$

Find $\partial\mathbf{u}/\partial s$ and $\partial\mathbf{u}/\partial t$.

60. Set

$$\mathbf{u}(x, y, z) = u_1(x, y, z)\,\mathbf{i} + u_2(x, y, z)\,\mathbf{j} + u_3(x, y, z)\,\mathbf{k}$$

with

$$x = x(t), \quad y = y(t), \quad z = z(t).$$

Derive a formula for $d\mathbf{u}/dt$ analogous to (16.3.12).

*SUPPLEMENT TO SECTION 16.3

THE INTERMEDIATE-VALUE THEOREM

You have seen that a function of a single variable which is continuous on an interval skips no values. (The intermediate-value theorem, Theorem 2.6.1.) There is an analogous result for functions of several variables.

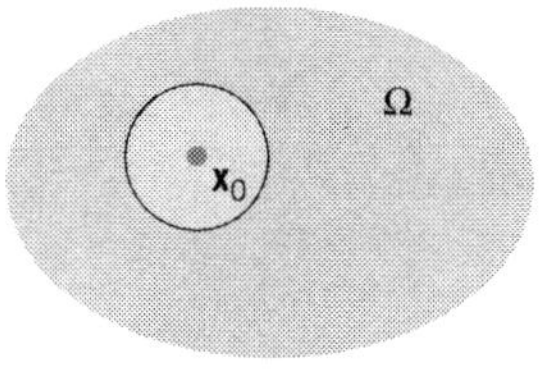

Figure 16.3.8

Suppose that f is continuous on a set S. If $\mathbf{x}_0$ is an interior point of S, then all points $\mathbf{x}$ sufficiently close to $\mathbf{x}_0$ are in S and, by definition, f is continuous at $\mathbf{x}_0$ provided that

$$\text{as } \mathbf{x} \text{ approaches } \mathbf{x}_0, \qquad f(\mathbf{x}) \text{ approaches } f(\mathbf{x}_0). \qquad \text{(Figure 16.3.8)}$$

If $\mathbf{x}_0$ is a boundary point of S, then we have to modify the definition and say: f is continuous at $\mathbf{x}_0$ provided that

$$\text{as } \mathbf{x} \text{ approaches } \mathbf{x}_0 \text{ from } \textit{within } S, \qquad f(\mathbf{x}) \text{ approaches } f(\mathbf{x}_0). \quad \text{(Figure 16.3.9)}$$

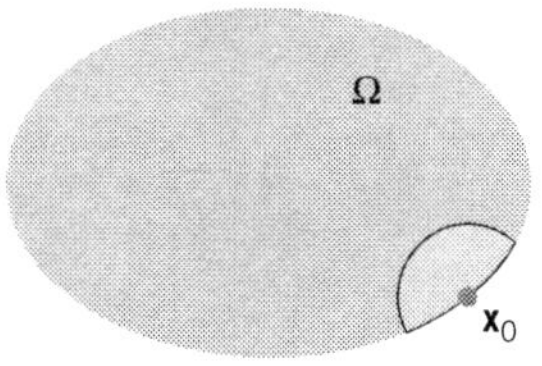

Figure 16.3.9

THEOREM 16.3.13 THE INTERMEDIATE-VALUE THEOREM

Let S be an open connected set or an open connected set to which are adjoined some or all of its boundary points. Suppose that f is continuous on S and A, B, C are real numbers with $A < C < B$. If, somewhere in S, f takes on the value A and, somewhere in S, f takes on the value B, then, somewhere in S, f takes on the value C.

PROOF Let $\mathbf{a}$ and $\mathbf{b}$ be points in S for which

$$f(\mathbf{a}) = A \qquad \text{and} \qquad f(\mathbf{b}) = B.$$

We must show that there exists a point $\mathbf{c}$ in S for which $f(\mathbf{c}) = C$.

Let U be the interior of S and assume first that $\mathbf{a}$ and $\mathbf{b}$ are in U. Since U is an open connected set, there is polygonal path γ in U that joins $\mathbf{a}$ to $\mathbf{b}$. Let $\mathbf{r} = \mathbf{r}(t)$, $a \le t \le b$, be a continuous parametrization of the path γ with $\mathbf{r}(a) = \mathbf{a}$ and $\mathbf{r}(b) = \mathbf{b}$. Since $\mathbf{r}$ is continuous, the composition

$$g(t) = f(\mathbf{r}(t))$$

is also continuous on $[a, b]$. Since

$$g(a) = f(\mathbf{r}(a)) = A \quad \text{and} \quad g(b) = f(\mathbf{r}(b)) = B,$$

we know from Theorem 2.6.1 that there is a number c in $[a, b]$ for which $g(c) = C$. Setting $\mathbf{c} = \mathbf{r}(c)$ we have $f(\mathbf{c}) = C$.

Now let $\mathbf{a}$ and $\mathbf{b}$ be *any* two points in S for which

$$f(\mathbf{a}) = A \quad \text{and} \quad f(\mathbf{b}) = B.$$

Since $\mathbf{a}$ and/or $\mathbf{b}$ may be boundary points, we proceed as follows. We take ϵ small enough that

$$A + \epsilon < C < B - \epsilon.$$

Since boundary points can be approached as closely as we wish by interior points, we know from the continuity of f that there exist interior points $\mathbf{x}_1, \mathbf{x}_2$ for which

$$f(\mathbf{x}_1) < A + \epsilon \quad \text{and} \quad B - \epsilon < f(\mathbf{x}_2).$$

Then $f(\mathbf{x}_1) < C < f(\mathbf{x}_2)$ and the result follows by the argument used above, this time applied to $\mathbf{x}_1$ and $\mathbf{x}_2$. ❑

16.4 THE GRADIENT AS A NORMAL; TANGENT LINES AND TANGENT PLANES

Functions of Two Variables

We begin with a nonconstant function $f = f(x, y)$ that is continuously differentiable. (*Remember:* That means f is differentiable and its gradient ∇f is continuous.) You have seen that at each point of the domain, the gradient vector, if not $\mathbf{0}$, points in the direction of the most rapid increase of f. Here we show that

(16.4.1) at each point of the domain, the gradient vector ∇f, if not $\mathbf{0}$, is perpendicular to the level curve of f that passes through that point.

PROOF We choose a point (x_0, y_0) in the domain and assume that $\nabla f(x_0, y_0) \neq \mathbf{0}$. The level curve through this point has equation

$$f(x, y) = c \quad \text{where} \quad c = f(x_0, y_0).$$

Under our assumptions on f, this curve can be parametrized in a neighborhood of (x_0, y_0) by a continuously differentiable vector function

$$\mathbf{r}(t) = x(t)\,\mathbf{i} + y(t)\,\mathbf{j} \qquad t \in I$$

with nonzero tangent vector $\mathbf{r}'(t)$.[†]

Now take t_0 such that

$$\mathbf{r}(t_0) = x_0\,\mathbf{i} + y_0\,\mathbf{j} = (x_0, y_0).$$

We will show that

$$\nabla f(\mathbf{r}(t_0)) \perp \mathbf{r}'(t_0).$$

[†]This follows from a result of advanced calculus known as the *implicit function theorem*.

Since f is constantly c on the curve, we have

$$f(\mathbf{r}(t)) = c \qquad \text{for all } t \in I.$$

For such t

$$\frac{d}{dt}[f(\mathbf{r}(t))] = \nabla f(\mathbf{r}(t)) \cdot \mathbf{r}'(t) = 0.$$

(Theorem 16.3.4)

In particular,

$$\nabla f(\mathbf{r}(t_0)) \cdot \mathbf{r}'(t_0) = 0,$$

and thus

$$\nabla f(\mathbf{r}(t_0)) \perp \mathbf{r}'(t_0). \quad \square$$

Figure 16.4.1 illustrates the result.

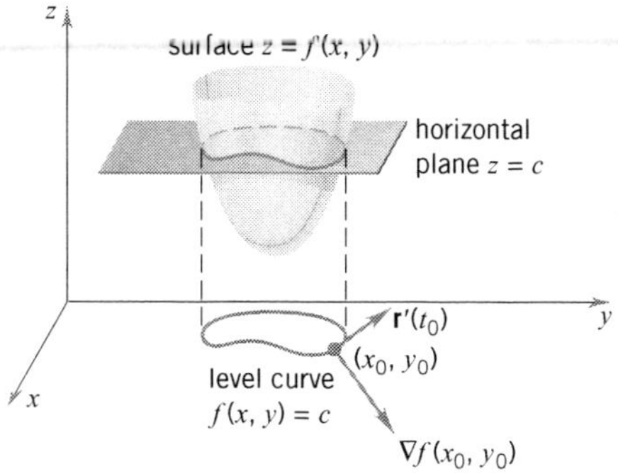

Figure 16.4.1

Example 1 For the function $f(x, y) = x^2 + y^2$ the level curves are concentric circles:

$$x^2 + y^2 = c.$$

At each point $(x, y) \neq (0, 0)$ the gradient vector

$$\Delta f(x, y) = 2x\,\mathbf{i} + 2y\,\mathbf{j} = 2\,\mathbf{r}$$

points away from the origin along the line of the radius vector and is thus perpendicular to the circle in question. At the origin the level curve is reduced to a point and the gradient is simply $\mathbf{0}$. See Figure 16.4.2. $\square$

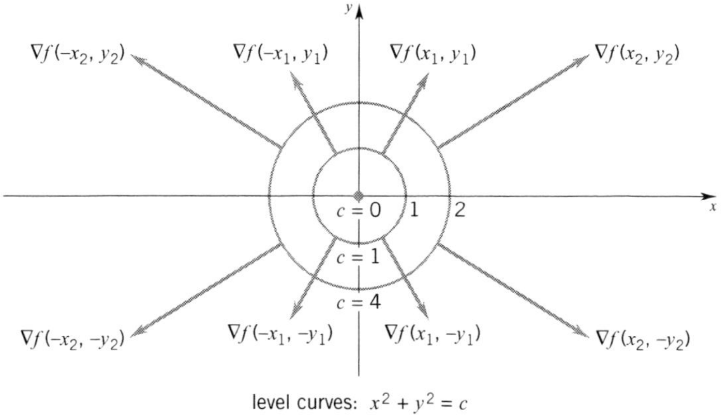

Figure 16.4.2

Consider now a curve in the xy-plane

$$C: f(x, y) = c.$$

As before, we assume that f is nonconstant and continuously differentiable. Let's suppose that (x_0, y_0) lies on the curve and $\nabla f(x_0, y_0) \neq \mathbf{0}$.

We can view C as the c-level curve of f and conclude from (16.4.1) that the gradient

(16.4.2) $$\nabla f(x_0, y_0) = \frac{\partial f}{\partial x}(x_0, y_0)\,\mathbf{i} + \frac{\partial f}{\partial y}(x_0, y_0)\,\mathbf{j}$$

is perpendicular to C at (x_0, y_0). We call it a *normal vector.*

The vector

(16.4.3) $$\mathbf{t}(x_0, y_0) = \frac{\partial f}{\partial y}(x_0, y_0)\,\mathbf{i} - \frac{\partial f}{\partial x}(x_0, y_0)\,\mathbf{j}$$

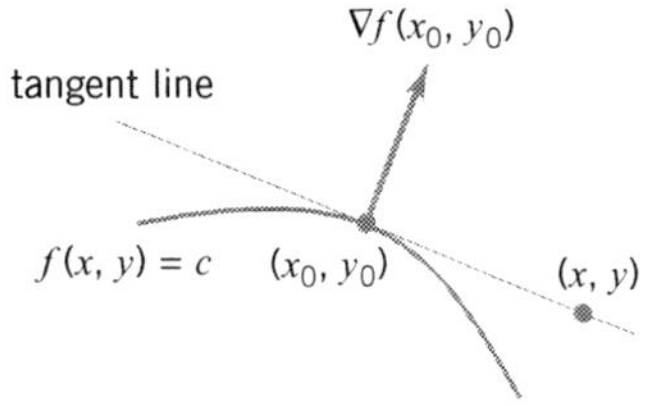

Figure 16.4.3

is perpendicular to the gradient:

$$\nabla f(x_0, y_0) \cdot \mathbf{t}(x_0, y_0) = \frac{\partial f}{\partial x}(x_0, y_0)\frac{\partial f}{\partial y}(x_0, y_0) - \frac{\partial f}{\partial y}(x_0, y_0)\frac{\partial f}{\partial x}(x_0, y_0) = 0.$$

It is therefore a *tangent vector.*

The line through (x_0, y_0) perpendicular to the gradient is the tangent line. To obtain an equation for the tangent line, we refer to Figure 16.4.3. A point (x, y) will lie on the tangent line iff

$$[(x - x_0)\,\mathbf{i} + (y - y_0)\,\mathbf{j}] \cdot \nabla f(x_0, y_0) = 0;$$

that is, iff

(16.4.4) $$\frac{\partial f}{\partial x}(x_0, y_0)(x - x_0) + \frac{\partial f}{\partial y}(x_0, y_0)(y - y_0) = 0.$$

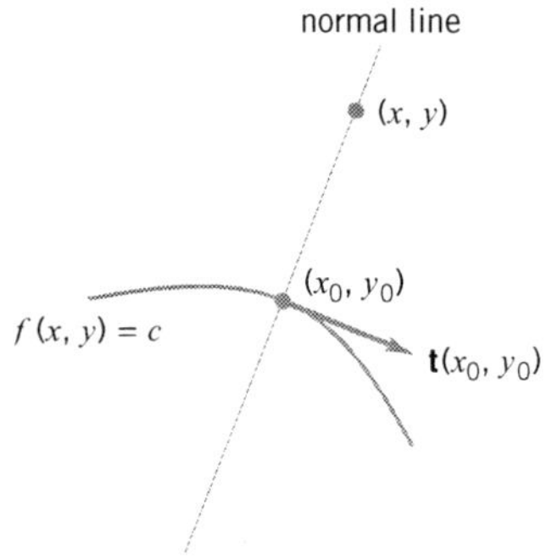

Figure 16.4.4

This is an equation for the *tangent line.*

The line through (x_0, y_0) perpendicular to the tangent vector $\mathbf{t}(x_0, y_0)$ is the normal line. (Figure 16.4.4.) A point (x, y) will lie on the normal line iff

$$[(x - x_0)\,\mathbf{i} + (y - y_0)\,\mathbf{j}] \cdot \mathbf{t}(x_0, y_0) = 0;$$

that is, iff

(16.4.5) $$\frac{\partial f}{\partial y}(x_0, y_0)(x - x_0) - \frac{\partial f}{\partial x}(x_0, y_0)(y - y_0) = 0.$$

This is an equation for the *normal line.*

Example 2 Let C be the plane curve

$$x^2 + 2y^3 = xy + 4.$$

Find a tangent vector and a normal vector at the point (2, 1). Then write equations for the tangent line and normal line at that point.

SOLUTION Set $f(x, y) = x^2 + 2y^3 - xy$. Note that C is the level curve $f(x, y) = 4$.

$$\nabla f = (2x - y)\,\mathbf{i} + (6y^2 - x)\,\mathbf{j} \qquad \text{and} \qquad \nabla f(2, 1) = 3\,\mathbf{i} + 4\,\mathbf{j}.$$

Therefore, we have

normal vector $\nabla f(2, 1) = 3\,\mathbf{i} + 4\,\mathbf{j}$, tangent vector $\mathbf{t}(2, 1) = 4\,\mathbf{i} - 3\,\mathbf{j}$

equation of tangent line $3(x - 2) + 4(y - 1) = 0$, $(y = -\frac{3}{4}x + \frac{5}{2})$

equation of normal line $4(x - 2) - 3(y - 1) = 0$. $(y = \frac{4}{3}x - \frac{5}{3})$ ❑

Functions of Three Variables

Here, instead of level curves, we have level surfaces, but the results are similar. If $f = f(x, y, z)$ is nonconstant and continuously differentiable, then

(16.4.6) at each point of the domain, the gradient vector, if not $\mathbf{0}$, is perpendicular to the level surface that passes through that point.

PROOF We choose a point $\mathbf{x}_0 = (x_0, y_0, z_0)$ in the domain and assume that $\nabla f(x_0, y_0, z_0) \neq \mathbf{0}$. The level surface through this point has equation

$$f(x, y, z) = c \qquad \text{where} \qquad c = f(x_0, y_0, z_0).$$

We suppose now that

$$\mathbf{r}(t) = x(t)\,\mathbf{i} + y(t)\,\mathbf{j} + z(t)\,\mathbf{k}, \qquad t \in I$$

is a differentiable curve that lies on this surface and passes through the point $\mathbf{x}_0 = (x_0, y_0, z_0)$. We choose t_0 so that

$$\mathbf{r}(t_0) = \mathbf{x_0} = (x_0, y_0, z_0)$$

and suppose that $\mathbf{r}'(t_0) \neq \mathbf{0}$.

Since the curve lies on the given surface, we have

$$f(\mathbf{r}(t)) = c \qquad \text{for all } t \in I.$$

For such t

$$\frac{d}{dt}[f(\mathbf{r}(t))] = \nabla f(\mathbf{r}(t)) \cdot \mathbf{r}'(t) = 0.$$

In particular,

$$\nabla f(\mathbf{r}(t_0)) \cdot \mathbf{r}'(t_0) = 0.$$

The gradient vector

$$\nabla f(\mathbf{r}(t_0)) = \nabla f(\mathbf{x}_0) = \nabla f(x_0, y_0, z_0)$$

is thus perpendicular to the curve in question.

This same argument applies to *every* differentiable curve that lies on this level surface and passes through the point $\mathbf{x}_0 = (x_0, y_0, z_0)$ with nonzero tangent vector. (See Figure 16.4.5.) Consequently, $\nabla f(\mathbf{x}_0)$ must be perpendicular to the surface itself. ❑

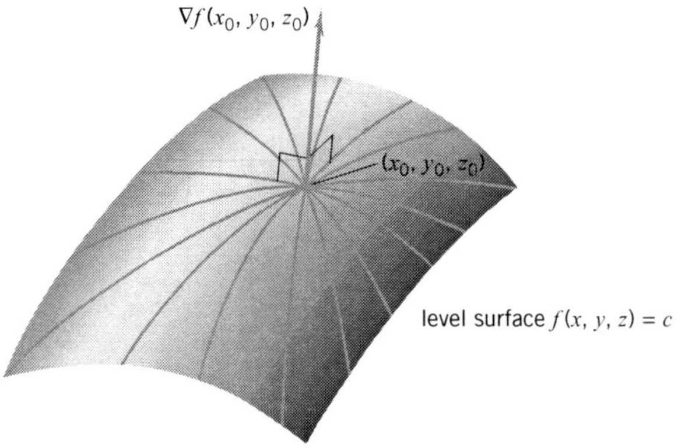

The gradient vector $\nabla f(x_0, y_0, z_0)$ is perpendicular to the level surface at (x_0, y_0, z_0)

Figure 16.4.5

Example 3 For the function $f(x, y, z) = x^2 + y^2 + z^2$ the level surfaces are concentric spheres:

$$x^2 + y^2 + z^2 = c.$$

At each point $(x, y, z) \neq (0, 0, 0)$, the gradient vector

$$\nabla f(x, y, z) = 2x\,\mathbf{i} + 2y\,\mathbf{j} + 2z\,\mathbf{k} = 2\,\mathbf{r}$$

points away from the origin along the line of the radius vector and is thus perpendicular to the sphere in question. At the origin the level surface is reduced to a point and the gradient is $\mathbf{0}$. ❑

The *tangent plane* for a surface

$$f(x, y, z) = c$$

at a point $\mathbf{x}_0 = (x_0, y_0, z_0)$ is the plane through $\mathbf{x}_0$ with normal $\nabla f(\mathbf{x}_0)$. See Figure 16.4.6.

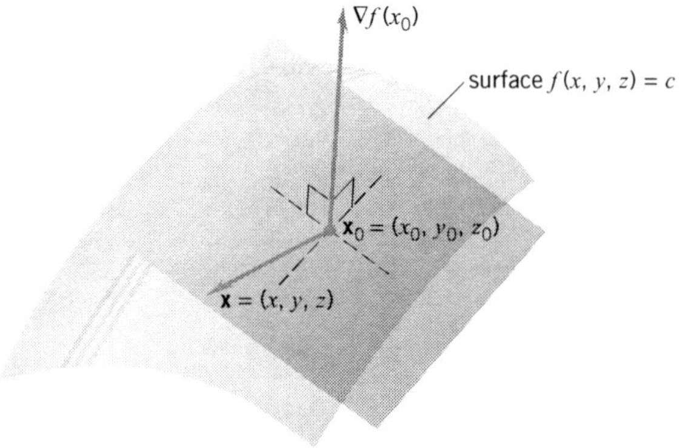

tangent plane to a surface $f(x, y, z) = c$

Figure 16.4.6

The tangent plane at a point $\mathbf{x}_0$ is the plane through $\mathbf{x}_0$ that best approximates the surface in a neighborhood of $\mathbf{x}_0$. (We return to this later.)

A point $\mathbf{x}$ lies on the tangent plane through $\mathbf{x}_0$ iff

(16.4.7)
$$\nabla f(\mathbf{x}_0) \cdot (\mathbf{x} - \mathbf{x}_0) = 0.$$
(Figure 16.4.6)

This is an equation for the tangent plane in vector notation. In Cartesian coordinates the equation takes the form

(16.4.8)
$$\frac{\partial f}{\partial x}(x_0, y_0, z_0)(x - x_0) + \frac{\partial f}{\partial y}(x_0, y_0, z_0)(y - y_0) + \frac{\partial f}{\partial z}(x_0, y_0, z_0)(z - z_0) = 0.$$

The *normal line* to the surface $f(x, y, z) = c$ at a point $\mathbf{x}_0 = (x_0, y_0, z_0)$ on the surface is the line which passes through (x_0, y_0, z_0) parallel to $\nabla f(\mathbf{x}_0)$. Thus, $\nabla f(\mathbf{x}_0)$ is a direction vector for the normal line and

(16.4.9)
$$\mathbf{r}(t) = \mathbf{r}_0 + \nabla f(\mathbf{x}_0)\, t \quad (\mathbf{r}_0 = x_0\,\mathbf{i} + y_0\,\mathbf{j} + z_0\,\mathbf{k})$$

is a vector equation for the line. In scalar parametric form, equations for the normal line can be written

(16.4.10)
$$x = x_0 + \frac{\partial f}{\partial x}(x_0, y_0, z_0)\,t,$$
$$y = y_0 + \frac{\partial f}{\partial y}(x_0, y_0, z_0)\,t,$$
$$z = z_0 + \frac{\partial f}{\partial z}(x_0, y_0, z_0)\,t.$$

Example 4 Find an equation for the plane tangent to the surface

$$xy + yz + zx = 11 \qquad \text{at the point } (1, 2, 3).$$

SOLUTION The surface is of the form

$$f(x, y, z) = c \qquad \text{with} \qquad f(x, y, z) = xy + yz + zx \qquad \text{and} \qquad c = 11.$$

Observe that

$$\frac{\partial f}{\partial x} = y + z, \qquad \frac{\partial f}{\partial y} = x + z, \qquad \frac{\partial f}{\partial z} = x + y.$$

At the point $(1, 2, 3)$

$$\frac{\partial f}{\partial x} = 5, \qquad \frac{\partial f}{\partial y} = 4, \qquad \frac{\partial f}{\partial z} = 3.$$

The equation for the tangent plane can therefore be written

$$5(x - 1) + 4(y - 2) + 3(z - 3) = 0.$$

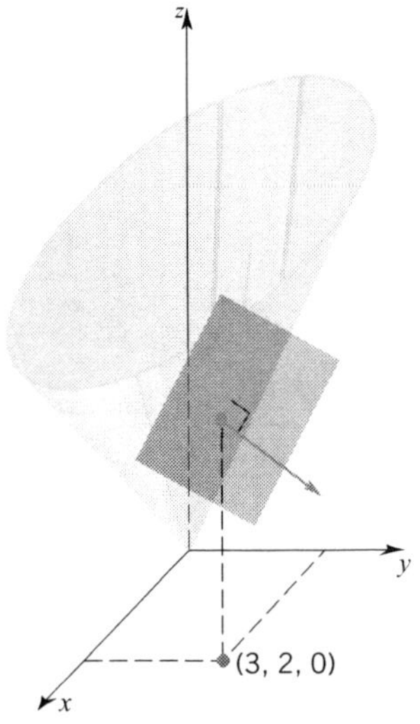

Figure 16.4.7

This simplifies to

$$5x + 4y + 3z - 22 = 0. \quad \square$$

Example 5 Find an equation for the plane tangent to the elliptic cone

$$x^2 + 4y^2 = z^2 \qquad \text{(Figure 16.4.7)}$$

at the point (3, 2, 5) and give scalar parametric equations for the normal line.

SOLUTION The surface is of the form $f(x, y, z) = c$ with

$$f(x, y, z) = x^2 + 4y^2 - z^2 \quad \text{and} \quad c = 0.$$

The partial derivatives of f are

$$\frac{\partial f}{\partial x} = 2x, \quad \frac{\partial f}{\partial y} = 8y, \quad \frac{\partial f}{\partial z} = -2z$$

and

$$\nabla f = 2x\,\mathbf{i} + 8y\,\mathbf{j} - 2z\,\mathbf{k}.$$

The vector $\nabla f(3, 2, 5) = 6\,\mathbf{i} + 16\,\mathbf{j} - 10\,\mathbf{k}$ is normal to the cone at the point (3, 2, 5). Note that $\frac{1}{2}\nabla f(3, 2, 5) = 3\,\mathbf{i} + 8\,\mathbf{j} - 5\,\mathbf{k}$ is also normal to the cone and is a little easier to work with.

The equation for the tangent plane can be written

$$3(x - 3) + 8(y - 2) - 5(z - 5) = 0.$$

The equation simplifies to

$$3x + 8y - 5z = 0.$$

Note that this plane passes through the origin. The following are scalar parametric equations for the normal line:

$$x = 3 + 3t, \quad y = 2 + 8t, \quad z = 5 - 5t. \quad \square$$

Example 6 The curve $\mathbf{r}(t) = \frac{1}{2}t^2\,\mathbf{i} + 4t^{-1}\,\mathbf{j} + (\frac{1}{2}t - t^2)\,\mathbf{k}$ intersects the hyperbolic paraboloid $x^2 - 4y^2 - 4z = 0$ at the point $(2, 2, -3)$. What is the angle of intersection?

SOLUTION We want the angle ϕ between the tangent vector of the curve and the tangent plane of the surface at the point of intersection. (Figure 16.4.8)

A simple calculation shows that the curve passes through the point $(2, 2, -3)$ at $t = 2$. Since $\mathbf{r}'(t) = t\,\mathbf{i} - 4t^{-2}\,\mathbf{j} + (\frac{1}{2} - 2t)\,\mathbf{k}$, we have

$$\mathbf{r}'(2) = 2\,\mathbf{i} - \mathbf{j} - \tfrac{7}{2}\,\mathbf{k}.$$

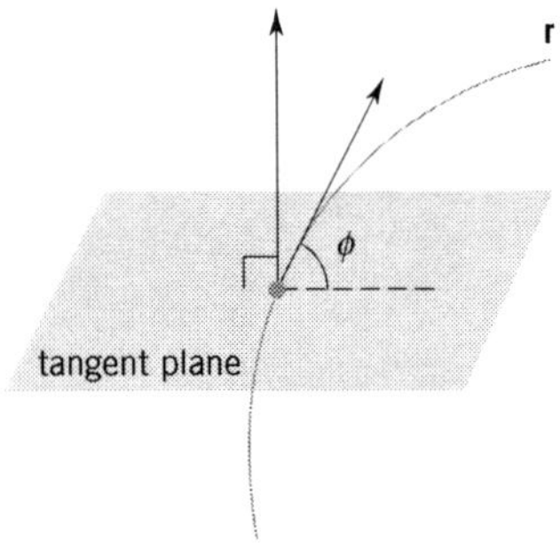

Figure 16.4.8

Now set

$$f(x, y, z) = x^2 - 4y^2 - 4z.$$

This function has gradient $2x\,\mathbf{i} - 8y\,\mathbf{j} - 4\,\mathbf{k}$. At the point $(2, 2 - 3)$,

$$\nabla f = 4\,\mathbf{i} - 16\,\mathbf{j} - 4\,\mathbf{k}.$$

Now let θ be the angle between $\mathbf{r}'(2)$ and this gradient. By (13.4.9),

$$\cos\theta = \frac{\mathbf{r}'(2)}{\|\mathbf{r}'(2)\|} \cdot \frac{\nabla f}{\|\nabla f\|} = \frac{19}{414}\sqrt{138} \cong 0.539$$

so that θ is approximately 1 radian. Since the gradient is normal to the tangent plane,

$$\phi = \tfrac{1}{2}\pi - \theta \cong 1.57 - 1.00 = 0.57 \text{ radians.} \quad \square$$

A surface of the form $z = g(x, y)$ can be written in the form

$$f(x, y, z) = 0$$

by setting

$$f(x, y, z) = g(x, y) - z.$$

If g is differentiable, so is f. Moreover,

$$\frac{\partial f}{\partial x}(x, y, z) = \frac{\partial g}{\partial x}(x, y), \qquad \frac{\partial f}{\partial y}(x, y, z) = \frac{\partial g}{\partial y}(x, y), \qquad \frac{\partial f}{\partial z}(x, y, z) = -1.$$

By (16.4.8) the tangent plane at (x_0, y_0, z_0) has equation

$$\frac{\partial g}{\partial x}(x_0, y_0)(x - x_0) + \frac{\partial g}{\partial y}(x_0, y_0)(y - y_0) + (-1)(z - z_0) = 0,$$

which we can rewrite as

(16.4.11) $$z - z_0 = \frac{\partial g}{\partial x}(x_0, y_0)(x - x_0) + \frac{\partial g}{\partial y}(x_0, y_0)(y - y_0).$$

If $\nabla g(x_0, y_0) = \mathbf{0}$, then both partials of g are zero at (x_0, y_0) and the equation reduces to

$$z = z_0.$$

In this case the tangent plane is *horizontal.*

Scalar parametric equations for the line normal to the surface $z = g(x, y)$ at the point (x_0, y_0, z_0) can be written

(16.4.12) $$x = x_0 + \frac{\partial g}{\partial x}(x_0, y_0)\,t, \qquad y = y_0 + \frac{\partial g}{\partial y}(x_0, y_0)\,t, \qquad z = z_0 + (-1)\,t.$$

Example 7 Find an equation for the tangent plane and symmetric equations for the line normal to the surface.

$$z = \ln(x^2 + y^2)$$

at the point $(-2, 1, \ln 5)$.

SOLUTION Set $g(x, y) = \ln(x^2 + y^2)$. The partial derivatives of g are

$$\frac{\partial g}{\partial x}(x, y) = \frac{2x}{x^2 + y^2}, \qquad \frac{\partial g}{\partial y}(x, y) = \frac{2y}{x^2 + y^2}.$$

Where $x = -2$ and $y = 1$,

$$\frac{\partial g}{\partial x} = -\frac{4}{5}, \qquad \frac{\partial g}{\partial y} = \frac{2}{5}.$$

Therefore, at the point $(-2, 1, \ln 5)$, the tangent plane has equation

$$z - \ln 5 = -\frac{4}{5}(x+2) + \frac{2}{5}(y-1).$$

The symmetric equations for the normal line can be written

$$\frac{x+2}{-\frac{4}{5}} = \frac{y-1}{\frac{2}{5}} = \frac{z - \ln 5}{-1}. \quad \square$$

Example 8 At what points of the surface $z = 3xy - x^3 - y^3$ is the tangent plane horizontal?

SOLUTION The function $g(x, y) = 3xy - x^3 - y^3$ has first partials

$$\frac{\partial g}{\partial x}(x, y) = 3y - 3x^2, \qquad \frac{\partial g}{\partial y}(x, y) = 3x - 3y^2.$$

We set these partial derivatives equal to 0 and solve the resulting system of equations for x and y:

$$3y - 3x^2 = 0 \quad \text{simplifies to} \quad y - x^2 = 0$$
$$3x - 3y^2 = 0 \quad \text{simplifies to} \quad x - y^2 = 0.$$

From the first equation, we get $y = x^2$. Substituting this into the second equation, we have $x - x^4 = 0$ and thus

$$x(1 - x^3) = 0.$$

Therefore, $x = 0$ (which implies that $y = 0$), or $x = 1$ (which implies that $y = 1$). Thus, the partials are both zero only at $(0, 0)$ and $(1, 1)$. The surface has a horizontal tangent plane only at the points $(0, 0, 0)$ and $(1, 1, 1)$. The surface and some level curves have been sketched in Figure 16.4.9. $\square$

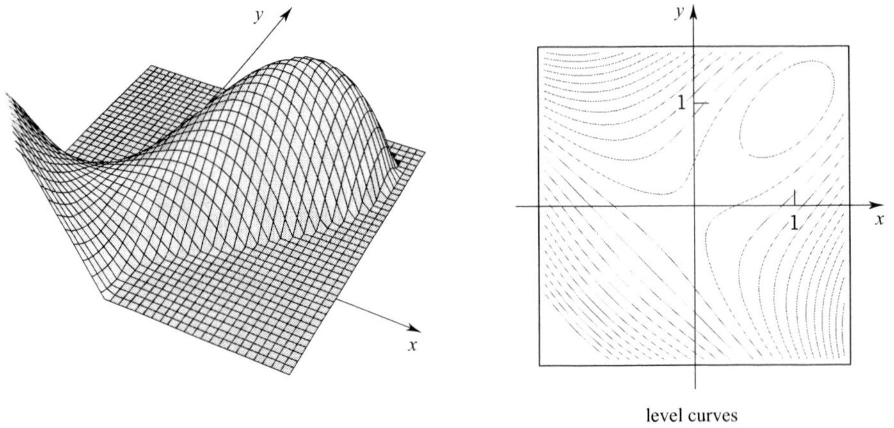

Figure 16.4.9

EXERCISES 16.4

Exercises 1–8. Find a normal vector and a tangent vector at the point P. Write an equation for the tangent line and an equation for the normal line.

1. $x^2 + xy + y^2 = 3$; $P(-1, -1)$.

2. $(y - x)^2 = 2x$; $P(2, 4)$.

3. $(x^2 + y^2)^2 = 9(x^2 - y^2)$; $P(\sqrt{2}, 1)$.

4. $x^3 + y^3 = 9$; $P(1, 2)$.

5. $xy^2 - 2x^2 + y + 5x = 6$; $P(4, 2)$.

6. $x^5 + y^5 = 2x^3$; $P(1, 1)$.

7. $2x^3 - x^2y^2 = 3x - y - 7$; $P(1, -2)$.

8. $x^3 + y^2 + 2x = 6$; $P(-1, 3)$.

9. Find the slope of the curve $x^2y = a^2(a - y)$ at the point $(0, a)$.

Exercises 10–18. Find an equation for the tangent plane at the point P and scalar parametric equations for the normal line.

10. $z = (x^2 + y^2)^2$; $P(1, 1, 4)$.

11. $x^3 + y^3 = 3xyz$; $P(1, 2, \frac{3}{2})$.

12. $xy^2 + 2z^2 = 12$; $P(1, 2, 2)$.

13. $z = axy$; $P(1, 1/a, 1)$.

14. $\sqrt{x} + \sqrt{y} + \sqrt{z} = 4$; $P(1, 4, 1)$.

15. $z = \sin x + \sin y + \sin(x + y)$; $P(0, 0, 0)$.

16. $z = x^2 + xy + y^2 - 6x + 2$; $P(4, -2, -10)$.

17. $b^2c^2x^2 - a^2c^2y^2 - a^2b^2z^2 = a^2b^2c^2$; $P(x_0, y_0, z_0)$.

18. $z = \sin(x \cos y)$; $P(1, \frac{1}{2}\pi, 0)$.

Exercises 19–23. Find the point(s) on the surface at which the tangent plane is horizontal.

19. $xy + a^3x^{-1} + b^3y^{-1} - z = 0$.

20. $z = 4x + 2y - x^2 + xy - y^2$.

21. $z = xy$.

22. $x + y + z + xy - x^2 - y^2 = 0$.

23. $z - 2x^2 - 2xy + y^2 + 5x - 3y + 2 = 0$.

24. (a) Find the *upper unit normal* (the unit normal with positive $\mathbf{k}$ component) for the surface $z = xy$ at the point $(1, 1, 1)$.
(b) Find the *lower unit normal* (the unit normal with negative $\mathbf{k}$ component) for the surface $z = 1/x - 1/y$ at the point $(1, 1, 0)$.

25. Let $f = f(x, y, z)$ be continuously differentiable. Write equations in symmetric form for the line normal to the surface $f(x, y, z) = c$ at the point (x_0, y_0, z_0).

26. Show that in the case of a surface of the form $z = xf(x/y)$ with f continuously differentiable, all the tangent planes have a point in common.

27. Given that the surfaces $F(x, y, z) = 0$ and $G(x, y, z) = 0$ intersect at right angles in a curve γ, what condition must be satisfied by the partial derivatives of F and G on γ?

28. Show that, for all planes tangent to the surface $\sqrt{x} + \sqrt{y} + \sqrt{z} = \sqrt{a}$, the sum of the intercepts is the same.

29. Show that all pyramids formed by the coordinate planes and a plane tangent to the surface $xyz = a^3$ have the same volume. What is this volume?

30. Show that, for all planes tangent to the surface $x^{2/3} + y^{2/3} + z^{2/3} = a^{2/3}$, the sum of the squares of the intercepts is the same.

31. The curve $\mathbf{r}(t) = 2t\,\mathbf{i} + 3t^{-1}\,\mathbf{j} - 2t^2\,\mathbf{k}$ and the ellipsoid $x^2 + y^2 + 3z^2 = 25$ intersect at $(2, 3, -2)$. What is the angle of intersection?

32. Show that the curve $\mathbf{r}(t) = \frac{3}{2}(t^2 + 1)\,\mathbf{i} + (t^4 + 1)\,\mathbf{j} + t^3\,\mathbf{k}$ is perpendicular to the ellipsoid $x^2 + 2y^2 + 3z^2 = 20$ at the point $(3, 2, 1)$.

33. The surfaces $x^2y^2 + 2x + z^3 = 16$ and $3x^2 + y^2 - 2z = 9$ intersect in a curve that passes through the point $(2, 1, 2)$. What are the equations of the respective tangent planes for the two surfaces at this point?

34. Show that the sphere $x^2 + y^2 + z^2 - 8x - 8y - 6z + 24 = 0$ is tangent to the ellipsoid $x^2 + 3y^3 + 2z^2 = 9$ at the point $(2, 1, 1)$.

35. Show that the sphere $x^2 + y^2 + z^2 - 4y - 2z + 2 = 0$ is perpendicular to the paraboloid $3x^2 + 2y^2 - 2z = 1$ at the point $(1, 1, 2)$.

36. Show that the following surfaces are mutually perpendicular:

$$xy = az^2, \quad x^2 + y^2 + z^2 = b, \quad z^2 + 2x^2 = c(z^2 + 2y^2).$$

37. The surface $S: z = x^2 + 3y^2 + 2$ intersects the vertical plane $p: 3x + 4y + 6 = 0$ in a space curve C.
(a) Let C_1 be the projection of C onto the xy-plane. Find an equation for C_1.
(b) Find a parametrization $\mathbf{r}(t) = x(t)\,\mathbf{i} + y(t)\,\mathbf{j} + z(t)\,\mathbf{k}$ for C setting $x(t) = 4t - 2$.
(c) Find a parametrization $\mathbf{R}(s) = \mathbf{R}_0 + s\mathbf{d}$ for the line l tangent to C at the point $(2, -3, 33)$.
(d) Find an equation for the plane p_1 tangent to S at the point $(2, -3, 33)$.
(e) Find a parametrization $\mathbf{r}(t) = x(t)\,\mathbf{i} + y(t)\,\mathbf{j} + z(t)\,\mathbf{k}$ for the line l' formed by the intersection of p with p_1 taking $x(t) = t$. What is the relation between l and l'?

38. Set $f(x, y) = \dfrac{x^2 - 2y}{x^2 + y^2}$. The level curve $f(x, y) = \frac{2}{5}$ passes through the point $P(2, 1)$.
(a) Find a normal vector at P and scalar parametric equations for the normal line at P.
(b) Find scalar parametric equations for the tangent line at P.
(c) Use a graphing utility to display the level curve, the normal line, and the tangent line all in one figure.

39. Set $f(x, y, z) = x^2 + (y - 1)^2 + z^2$. The level surface $f(x, y, z) = 6$ passes through the point $P(1, 2, 2)$.

(a) Find a normal vector at P and scalar parametric equations for the normal line at P.

(b) Find an equation for the tangent plane at P.

(c) Use a graphing utility to display the level surface, the normal line, and the tangent plane all in one figure.

40. Set $f(x, y) = \frac{3}{2}x - \frac{1}{2}x^3 - xy^2 + 1$.

(a) Use a graphing utility to draw the surface $z = f(x, y)$.

(b) Draw the level curves of the surface and use these to estimate the points where the surface has a horizontal tangent plane.

(c) Calculate ∇f and find the points where $\nabla f(x, y) = \mathbf{0}$. Compare your answers here with your estimates in part (b).

41. Exercise 40 for $f(x, y) = x^4 - y^4 - 2x^2 + 2y^2 + 2$.

42. Exercise 40 for $f(x, y) = 8xye^{-(x^2+y^2)}$.

16.5 LOCAL EXTREME VALUES

In Chapter 4 we discussed local extreme values for a function of one variable. Here we take up the same subject for functions of several variables. The ideas are similar.

DEFINITION 16.5.1 LOCAL EXTREME VALUES

Suppose that f is a function of several variables and $\mathbf{x}_0$ is an interior point of the domain.

The function f is said to have a *local maximum at* $\mathbf{x}_0$ provided that

$$f(\mathbf{x}_0) \geq f(\mathbf{x}) \qquad \text{for all } \mathbf{x} \text{ in some neighborhood of } \mathbf{x}_0.$$

The function f is said to have a *local minimum at* $\mathbf{x}_0$ provided that

$$f(\mathbf{x}_0) \leq f(\mathbf{x}) \qquad \text{for all } \mathbf{x} \text{ in some neighborhood of } \mathbf{x}_0.$$

The local maxima and minima of f comprise the *local extreme values* of f.

In the one-variable case we know that if f has local extreme value at x_0, then

$$f'(x_0) = 0 \qquad \text{or} \qquad f'(x_0) \text{ does not exist.}$$

We have a similar result for functions of several variables.

THEOREM 16.5.2

If f has a local extreme value at $\mathbf{x}_0$, then

$$\nabla f(\mathbf{x}_0) = 0 \qquad \text{or} \qquad \nabla f(\mathbf{x}_0) \text{ does not exist.}$$

PROOF We assume that f has a local extreme value at $\mathbf{x}_0$ and that f is differentiable at $\mathbf{x}_0$ [namely, that $\nabla f(\mathbf{x}_0)$ exists]. We need to show that $\nabla f_0(\mathbf{x}_0) = \mathbf{0}$. For simplicity we set $\mathbf{x}_0 = (x_0, y_0)$. The three-variable case is similar.

Since f has a local extreme value at (x_0, y_0), the function $g(x) = f(x, y_0)$ has a local extreme value at x_0. Since f is differentiable at (x_0, y_0), g is differentiable at x_0. Therefore

$$g'(x_0) = \frac{\partial f}{\partial x}(x_0, y_0) = 0.$$

Similarly, the function $h(y) = f(x_0, y)$ has a local extreme value at y_0 and, being differentiable there, satisfies the relation

$$h'(y_0) = \frac{\partial f}{\partial y}(x_0, y_0) = 0.$$

The gradient is $\mathbf{0}$ since both partials are 0. ❑

The interior points of the domain at which the gradient is zero or the gradient does not exist constitute the *critical points*. By Theorem 16.5.2 these are the only points that can give rise to local extreme values.

Although the ideas introduced so far are completely general, their application to functions of more than two variables is generally laborious. We restrict ourselves mostly to functions of two variables. Not only are the computations less formidable, but also we can make use of our geometric intuition.

Two Variables

We suppose for the moment that $f = f(x, y)$ is defined on an open connected set and is continuously differentiable there. The graph of f is a surface

$$z = f(x, y).$$

Where f has a local maximum, the surface has a local high point. Where f has a local minimum, the surface has a local low point. Where f has either a local maximum or a local minimum, the gradient is $\mathbf{0}$ and therefore the tangent plane is horizontal. See Figure 16.5.1.

A zero gradient signals the possibility of a local extreme value; it does not guarantee it. For example, in the case of the saddle-shaped surface of Figure 16.5.2, there is a horizontal tangent plane at the origin and therefore the gradient is zero there, yet the origin gives neither a local maximum nor a local minimum.

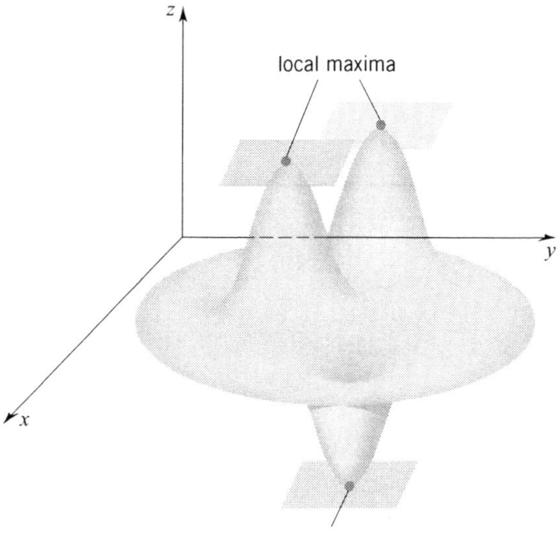

Figure 16.5.1

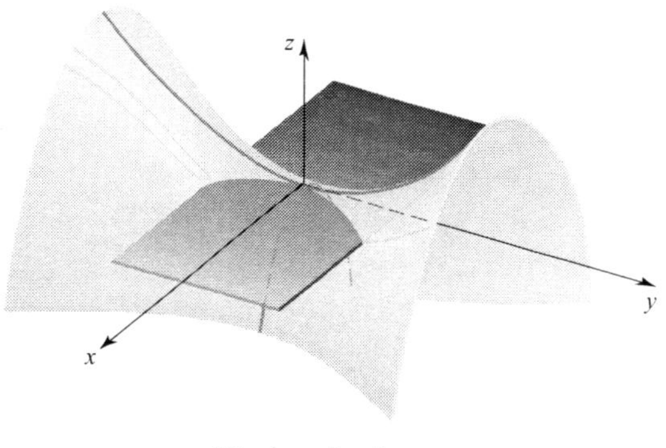

Figure 16.5.2

Critical points at which the gradient is zero are called *stationary points*. The stationary points that do not give rise to local extreme values are called *saddle points*.

Remark *Critical points, stationary points,* and *saddle points* are terms to be kept firmly in mind. ❑

In Examples 1 and 2 we test some differentiable functions for local extreme values. The functions being differentiable, the only critical points are stationary points.

Example 1 The function $f(x, y) = 2x^2 + y^2 - xy - 7y$ has gradient

$$\nabla f(x, y) = (4x - y)\,\mathbf{i} + (2y - x - 7)\,\mathbf{j}.$$

To find the stationary points, we set $\nabla f(x, y) = \mathbf{0}$. This gives

$$4x - y = 0 \qquad \text{and} \qquad 2y - x - 7 = 0.$$

The only simultaneous solution to these equations is $x = 1, y = 4$. The point $(1, 4)$ is therefore the only stationary point.

Now we compare the value of f at $(1, 4)$ with the values of f at nearby points $(1 + h, 4 + k)$:

$$\begin{aligned} f(1, 4) &= 2 + 16 - 4 - 28 = -14, \\ f(1 + h, 4 + k) &= 2(1 + h)^2 + (4 + k)^2 - (1 + h)(4 + k) - 7(4 + k) \\ &= 2 + 4h + 2h^2 + 16 + 8k + k^2 - 4 - 4h - k - hk - 28 - 7k \\ &= 2h^2 + k^2 - hk - 14. \end{aligned}$$

The difference

$$\begin{aligned} f(1 + h, 4 + k) - f(1, 4) &= 2h^2 + k^2 - hk \\ &= h^2 + (h^2 - hk + k^2) \\ &\geq h^2 + (h^2 - 2|h||k| + k^2) \\ &= h^2 + (|h| - |k|)^2 \geq 0. \end{aligned}$$

Thus, $f(1 + h, 4 + k) \geq f(1, 4)$ for all small h and k (in fact, for all real h and k).† It follows that f has a local minimum at $(1, 4)$. This local minimum is -14. ❑

Example 2 The function $f(x, y) = y^2 - xy + 2x + y + 1$ has gradient

$$\nabla f(x, y) = (2 - y)\,\mathbf{i} + (2y - x + 1)\,\mathbf{j}.$$

The gradient is $\mathbf{0}$ where

$$2 - y = 0 \qquad \text{and} \qquad 2y - x + 1 = 0.$$

The only simultaneous solution to these equations is $x = 5, y = 2$. The point $(5, 2)$ is the only stationary point.

We now compare the value of f at $(5, 2)$ with the values of f at nearby points $(5 + h, 2 + k)$:

$$\begin{aligned} f(5, 2) &= 4 - 10 + 10 + 2 + 1 = 7, \\ f(5 + h, 2 + k) &= (2 + k)^2 - (5 + h)(2 + k) + 2(5 + h) + (2 + k) + 1 \\ &= 4 + 4k + k^2 - 10 - 2h - 5k - hk + 10 + 2h + 2 + k + 1 \\ &= k^2 - hk + 7. \end{aligned}$$

† Another way to see that $2h^2 + k^2 - hk$ is nonnegative is to complete the square:

$$2h^2 + k^2 - hk = \tfrac{1}{4}h^2 - hk + k^2 + \tfrac{7}{4}h^2 = (\tfrac{1}{2}h - k)^2 + \tfrac{7}{4}h^2 \geq 0.$$

The difference

$$d = f(5+h, 2+k) - f(5,2) = k^2 - hk = k(k-h)$$

does not keep a constant sign for small h and k. (See Figure 16.5.3.) Therefore the point (5, 2) is a saddle point. ❑

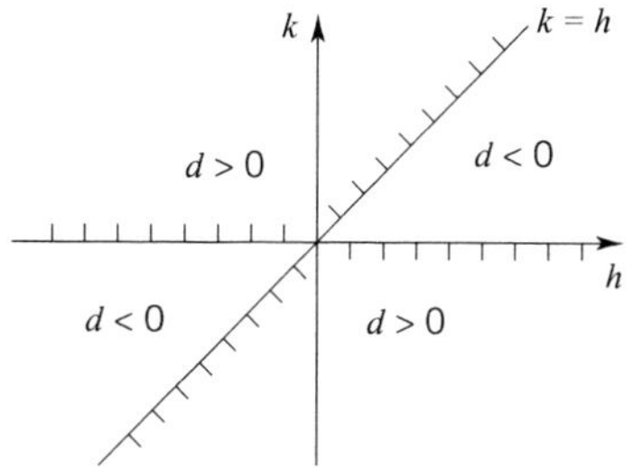

Figure 16.5.3

Example 3 The function $f(x,y) = 1 + \sqrt{x^2+y^2}$ is everywhere defined and everywhere continuous. The graph is the upper nappe of a right circular cone. (See Figure 16.5.4.) The number $f(0,0) = 1$ is obviously a local minimum.

Since the partials

$$\frac{\partial f}{\partial x} = \frac{x}{\sqrt{x^2+y^2}}, \qquad \frac{\partial f}{\partial y} = \frac{y}{\sqrt{x^2+y^2}}$$

are not defined at (0, 0), the gradient is not defined at (0, 0). (Theorem 16.2.5) The point (0, 0) is thus a critical point, but not a stationary point. At (0, 0, 1) the surface comes to a sharp point and there is no tangent plane. ❑

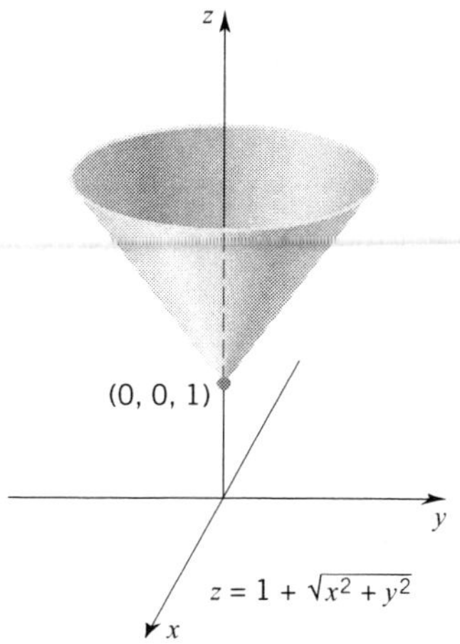

Figure 16.5.4

Second-Partials Test

Suppose that g is a function of one variable and $g'(x_0) = 0$. Then, according to the second-derivative test (Theorem 4.3.5), g has

a local minimum at x_0 if $g''(x_0) > 0$,

a local maximum at x_0 if $g''(x_0) < 0$.

We have a similar test for functions of two variables. Not surprisingly, the test is somewhat more complicated to state and definitely more difficult to prove. We will omit the proof.†

THEOREM 16.5.3 THE SECOND-PARTIALS TEST

Suppose that f has continuous second-order partial derivatives in a neighborhood of (x_0, y_0) and $\nabla f(x_0, y_0) = 0$. Set

$$A = \frac{\partial^2 f}{\partial x^2}(x_0, y_0) \qquad B = \frac{\partial^2 f}{\partial y \partial x}(x_0, y_0), \qquad C = \frac{\partial^2 f}{\partial y^2}(x_0, y_0)$$

and form the *discriminant* $D = AC - B^2$.

1. If $D < 0$, then (x_0, y_0) is a saddle point.
2. If $D > 0$, then f has

a local minimum at (x_0, y_0) if $A > 0$,

a local maximum at (x_0, y_0) if $A < 0$.

The test is geometrically evident for functions of the form

$$f(x,y) = \tfrac{1}{2}ax^2 + \tfrac{1}{2}cy^2. \qquad (a \neq 0, c \neq 0)$$

†You can find a proof in most texts on advanced calculus.

The graph of such a function is a paraboloid:

$$z = \tfrac{1}{2}ax^2 + \tfrac{1}{2}cy^2. \qquad \text{(Section 15.2)}$$

The gradient is **0** at the origin (0, 0):

$$A = \frac{\partial^2 f}{\partial x^2}(0,0) = a, \qquad B = \frac{\partial^2 f}{\partial y \partial x}(0,0) = 0, \qquad C = \frac{\partial^2 f}{\partial y^2}(0,0) = c.$$

Thus $D = AC - B^2 = ac$. If $D < 0$, then a and c have opposite signs and (0, 0) is a saddle point. (Figure 16.5.5)

Suppose now that $D > 0$. If $a > 0$, then $c > 0$ and the surface has a low point; if $a < 0$, then $c < 0$ and the surface has a high point.

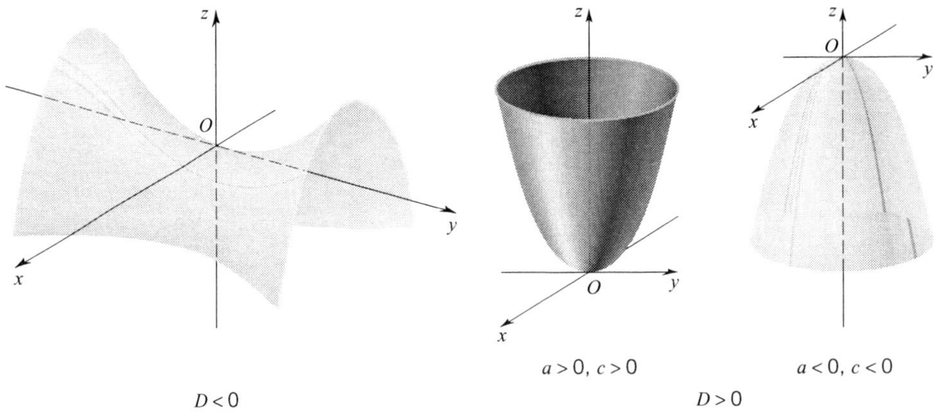

Figure 16.5.5

Below we apply the second-partials test to a variety of functions.

Example 4 In Example 1 we saw that the point (1, 4) is the only stationary point of the function

$$f(x, y) = 2x^2 + y^2 - xy - 7y.$$

The first partials of f are

$$\frac{\partial f}{\partial x} = 4x - y, \qquad \frac{\partial f}{\partial y} = 2y - x - 7.$$

The second partials are constant:

$$\frac{\partial^2 f}{\partial x^2} = 4, \qquad \frac{\partial^2 f}{\partial y \partial x} = -1, \qquad \frac{\partial^2 f}{\partial y^2} = 2.$$

Thus, $A = 4$, $B = -1$, $C = 2$, and $D = AC - B^2 = 7 > 0$. Since $A > 0$, it follows from the second-partials test that

$$f(1, 4) = 2 + 16 - 4 - 28 = -14$$

is a local minimum. ❑

Example 5 The function $f(x, y) = -\frac{1}{4}x^4 + \frac{2}{3}x^3 + 4xy - y^2$ has partial derivatives

$$\frac{\partial f}{\partial x} = -x^3 + 2x^2 + 4y, \qquad \frac{\partial f}{\partial y} = 4x - 2y.$$

Setting both partials equal to zero, we have

$$-x^3 + 2x^2 + 4y = 0, \qquad 4x - 2y = 0.$$

From the second equation we get $y = 2x$. Substituting $y = 2x$ into the first equation, we have

$$-x^3 + 2x^2 + 8x = -x(x^2 - 2x - 8) = -x(x - 4)(x + 2) = 0.$$

The solutions to this equation are $x = 0, x = 4, x = -2$. The stationary points are $(0, 0), (4, 8), (-2, -4)$.

The second partials are

$$\frac{\partial^2 f}{\partial x^2} = -3x^2 + 4x, \qquad \frac{\partial^2 f}{\partial x \partial y} = 4, \qquad \frac{\partial^2 f}{\partial y^2} = -2.$$

The application of the second-partials test is outlined below.

Point	A	B	C	D	Result
(0, 0)	0	4	−2	−16	Saddle point
(4, 8)	−32	4	−2	48	Local maximum
(−2, −4)	−20	4	−2	24	Local maximum

The surface and its level curves are sketched in Figure 16.5.6. ❑

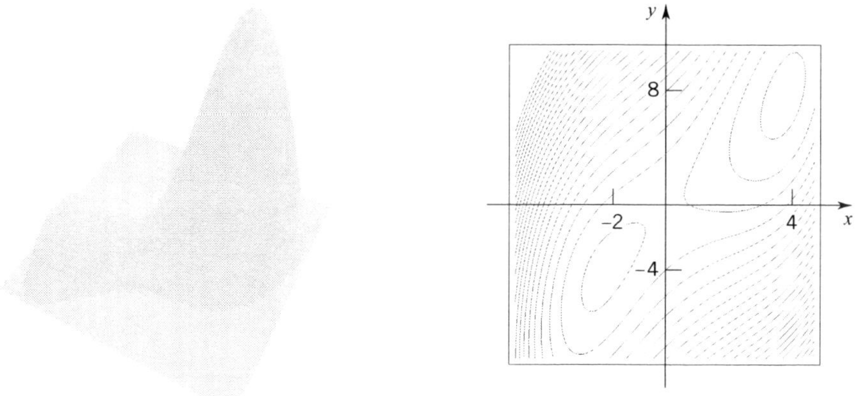

level curves

Figure 16.5.6

Example 6 For the function $f(x, y) = -xye^{-(x^2+y^2)/2}$

$$\frac{\partial f}{\partial x} = -y\,e^{-(x^2+y^2)/2} + x^2 y\,e^{-(x^2+y^2)/2} = y(x^2 - 1)\,e^{-(x^2+y^2)/2}$$

$$\frac{\partial f}{\partial y} = -x\,e^{-(x^2+y^2)/2} + xy^2 e^{-(x^2+y^2)/2} = x(y^2 - 1)e^{-(x^2+y^2)/2}$$

$$\nabla f(x, y) = e^{-(x^2+y^2)/2}\,[y(x^2 - 1)\,\mathbf{i} + x(y^2 - 1)\,\mathbf{j}].$$

Since $e^{-(x^2+y^2)/2} \neq 0$, $\nabla f(x, y) = \mathbf{0}$ iff

$$y(x^2 - 1) = 0 \qquad \text{and} \qquad x(y^2 - 1) = 0.$$

The simultaneous solutions to these equations are $x = 0, y = 0; x = \pm 1, y = \pm 1$. Thus, $(0, 0), (1, 1), (1, -1), (-1, 1), (-1, -1)$ are the only stationary points.

As you can check, the second-partial derivatives are

$$\frac{\partial^2 f}{\partial x^2} = xy(3 - x^2)\,e^{-(x^2+y^2)/2}, \qquad \frac{\partial^2 f}{\partial y^2} = xy(3 - y^2)\,e^{-(x^2+y^2)/2},$$

$$\frac{\partial^2 f}{\partial y \partial x} = (x^2 - 1)(1 - y^2)\,e^{-(x^2+y^2)/2}.$$

The data needed for the second-partials test are recorded in the following table.

Point	A	B	C	D	Result
$(0, 0)$	0	-1	0	-1	Saddle point
$(1, 1)$	$2e^{-1}$	0	$2e^{-1}$	$4e^{-2}$	Local minimum
$(1, -1)$	$-2e^{-1}$	0	$-2e-1$	$4e^{-2}$	Local maximum
$(-1, 1)$	$-2e^{-1}$	0	$-2e^{-1}$	$4e^{-2}$	Local maximum
$(-1, -1)$	$2e^{-1}$	0	$2e^{-1}$	$4e^{-2}$	Local minimum

A computer-generated graph of the function is shown in Figure 16.5.7. ❑

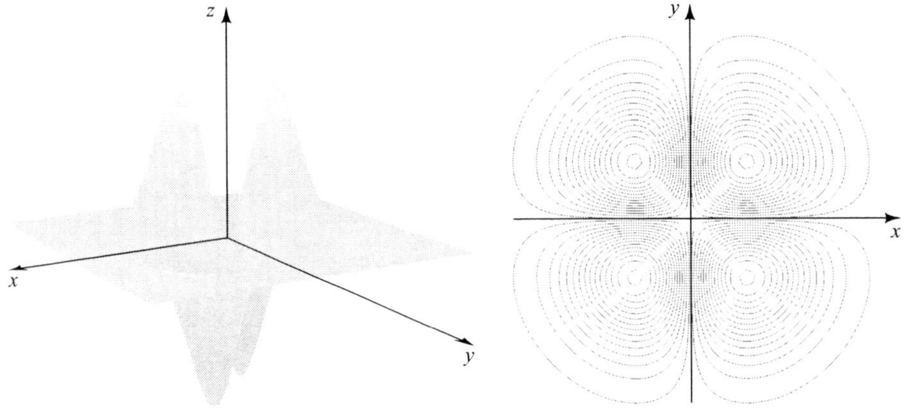

level curves of $f(x, y) = -xye^{-(x^2+y^2)/2}$

Figure 16.5.7

The second-derivative test for a function of one variable applies to points x_0 where $g'(x_0) = 0$ but $g''(x_0) \neq 0$, If $g''(x_0) = 0$, the second-derivative test provides no information. The second-partials test suffers from a similar limitation. It applies to points (x_0, y_0) where $\nabla f(x_0, y_0) = \mathbf{0}$ and $D \neq 0$. If $D = 0$, the second-partials test provides no information.

Consider, for example, the functions

$$f(x, y) = x^4 + y^4, \qquad g(x, y) = -(x^4 + y^4), \qquad h(x, y) = x^4 - y^4.$$

Each of these functions has zero gradient at the origin, and, as you can check, in each case $D = 0$. Yet,

(1) for f, $(0, 0)$ gives a local minimum;

(2) for g, $(0, 0)$ gives a local maximum;

(3) for h, $(0, 0)$ is a saddle point.

Statements (1) and (2) are obvious. To confirm (3), note that $h(0, 0) = 0$, but in every neighborhood of (0,0) the function h takes on both positive and negative values:

$$h(x, 0) > 0 \quad \text{for } x \neq 0, \quad \text{while} \quad h(0, y) < 0 \quad \text{for } y \neq 0. \quad \square$$

EXERCISES 16.5

Exercises 1–4. Find the stationary points and use the method illustrated in Examples 1 and 2 to determine the local extreme values.

1. $f(x, y) = 2x - x^2 - y^2$.

2. $f(x, y) = 2x + 2y - x^2 + y^2 + 5$.

3. $f(x, y) = x^2 + xy + y^2 + 3x + 1$.

4. $f(x, y) = x^3 - 3x + y$.

Exercises 5–24. Find the stationary points and the local extreme values.

5. $f(x, y) = x^2 + xy + y^2 - 6x + 2$.

6. $f(x, y) = x^2 + 2xy + 3y^2 + 2x + 10y + 1$.

7. $f(x, y) = x^3 - 6xy + y^3$.

8. $f(x, y) = 3x^2 + xy - y^2 + 5x - 5y + 4$.

9. $f(x, y) = x^3 + y^2 - 6xy + 6x + 3y - 2$.

10. $f(x, y) = x^2 - 2xy + 2y^2 - 3x + 5y$.

11. $f(x, y) = x \sin y$.

12. $f(x, y) = y + x \sin y$.

13. $f(x, y) = (x + y)(xy + 1)$.

14. $f(x, y) = xy^{-1} - yx^{-1}$.

15. $f(x, y) = xy + x^{-1} + 8y^{-1}$.

16. $f(x, y) = x^2 - 2xy - y^2 + 1$.

17. $f(x, y) = xy + x^{-1} + y^{-1}$.

18. $f(x, y) = (x - y)(xy - 1)$.

19. $f(x, y) = \dfrac{-2x}{x^2 + y^2 + 1}$.

20. $f(x, y) = (x - 3) \ln xy$.

21. $f(x, y) = x^4 - 2x^2 + y^2 - 2$.

22. $f(x, y) = (x^2 + y^2)e^{x^2 - y^2}$.

23. $f(x, y) = \sin x \sin y, \quad 0 < x < 2\pi, \quad 0 < y < 2\pi$.

24. $f(x, y) = \cos x \cosh y, \quad -2\pi < x < 2\pi$.

25. Let $f(x, y) = x^2 + kxy + y^2$, k a constant.

(a) Show that f has a stationary point at (0, 0) no matter what value is assigned to k.

(b) For what values of k will f have a saddle point at (0, 0)?

(c) For what values of k will f have a local minimum at (0, 0)?

(d) For what values of k is the second-partials test inconclusive?

26. Exercise 25 for the function

$$f(x, y) = x^2 + kxy + 4y^2, \qquad k \text{ a constant}.$$

27. Find the point in the plane $2x - y + 2z = 16$ that is closest to the origin and calculate the distance from the origin to this point. Check your answer by using (13.6.5).

28. Find the point in the plane $3x - 4y + 2z + 32 = 0$ that is closest to the point $P(-1, 2, 4)$ and calculate the distance from P to this point. Check your answer by using (13.6.5).

29. What point on the elliptic cone $z = \sqrt{x^2 + 2y^2}$ is closest to the point (1, 2, 0)?

30. Find the maximum volume for a rectangular solid inscribed in the sphere

$$x^2 + y^2 + z^2 = a^2.$$

Exercises 31–32. Suppose that f is a differentiable function of one variable defined on an interval. If f takes on a local maximum at two points, then f takes on a local minimum somewhere in between. If f takes on a local minimum at two points, then somewhere in between it takes on a local maximum. These results do not extend to functions of several variables.

31. Set $f(x, y) = 4xy - x^4 - y^4 + 1$.

(a) Use a graphing utility to draw the graph of f and some level curves.

(b) Your drawings should show that f has a local maximum at (1, 1) and at (−1, −1), a saddle point at (0, 0), but no local minima.

(c) Verify the results suggested in part (b) by applying the methods of this section.

32. Set $f(x, y) = x^4 - 2x^2 + y^2 + 1$.

(a) Use a graphing utility to draw the graph of f and some level curves.

(b) Your drawings should show that f has a local maximum at (1, 0) and at (−1, 0), a saddle point at (0, 0), but no local maxima.

(c) Verify the results suggested in part (b) by applying the methods of this section.

Exercises 33–36. Use a graphing utility to draw the graph of f and some level curves. Locate the stationary points, if any, and at each stationary point state whether f has a local maximum, a local minimum, or a stationary point.

33. $f(x, y) = 3xy - x^3 - y^3 + 2$.

34. $f(x, y) = (x^2 + 2y^2)e^{-(x^2+y^2)}$.

35. $f(x, y) = \dfrac{-2x}{x^2 + y^2 + 1}$.

36. $f(x, y) = \sin x + \sin y - \cos(x + y); \quad x, y \in [0, 3\pi]$.

16.6 ABSOLUTE EXTREME VALUES

Whether or not a function of several variables has a local extreme value at some point $\mathbf{x}_0$ depends on the behavior of the function on only a neighborhood of $\mathbf{x}_0$. Absolute extreme values, which we define below, depend on the behavior of the function on its entire domain.

DEFINITION 16.6.1 ABSOLUTE EXTREME VALUES

Suppose that f is a function of several variables.

f is said to have an *absolute maximum at* $\mathbf{x}_0$ provided that

$$f(\mathbf{x}_0) \geq f(\mathbf{x}) \qquad \text{for all } \mathbf{x} \text{ in the domain of } f;$$

f is said to have an *absolute minimum at* $\mathbf{x}_0$ provided that

$$f(\mathbf{x}_0) \leq f(\mathbf{x}) \qquad \text{for all } \mathbf{x} \text{ in the domain of } f.$$

In Chapter 2 we stated that a function of one variable that is continuous on a bounded closed interval takes on both an absolute maximum and an absolute minimum. (Theorem 2.6.2) In a moment we'll generalize on this, but first we need to extend the notion of boundedness from sets of real numbers to sets of higher dimensions.

DEFINITION 16.6.2

A subset S of the plane or three-space is said to be *bounded* provided there exists a positive number R such that

$$\|\mathbf{x}\| \leq R \qquad \text{for all } \mathbf{x} \in S.$$

Thus a set on the plane or in three-space is bounded iff it is contained in some ball of finite radius.

THEOREM 16.6.3 THE EXTREME-VALUE THEOREM

If f is continuous on a closed and bounded set D, then on that set f takes on an absolute maximum and an absolute minimum.

Two Variables

To find the local extreme values, we need to test only the interior points. To find the absolute extreme values, we also have to test the boundary points. This usually requires special methods. One approach is to try to parametrize the boundary by some vector function $\mathbf{r} = \mathbf{r}(t)$ and then work with the function of one variable $f(\mathbf{r}(t))$. This is the approach we take in this section. Another approach is introduced in Section 16.7.

The procedure we use for finding the absolute extreme values can be outlined as follows:

1. Determine the critical points. These are the interior points at which the gradient is zero (the stationary points) and the interior points at which the gradient does not exist.

2. Determine the points on the boundary that can possibly give rise to extreme values. At this stage this is a one-variable process.
3. Evaluate f at the points found in Steps 1 and 2.
4. The greatest of the numbers found in Step 3 is the absolute maximum; the least is the absolute minimum.

Example 1 Find the absolute extreme values taken on by the function

$$f(x, y) = x^2 + y^2 - 2x - 2y + 4$$

on the closed disk $D = \{(x, y) : x^2 + y^2 \leq 9\}$. (Figure 16.6.1)

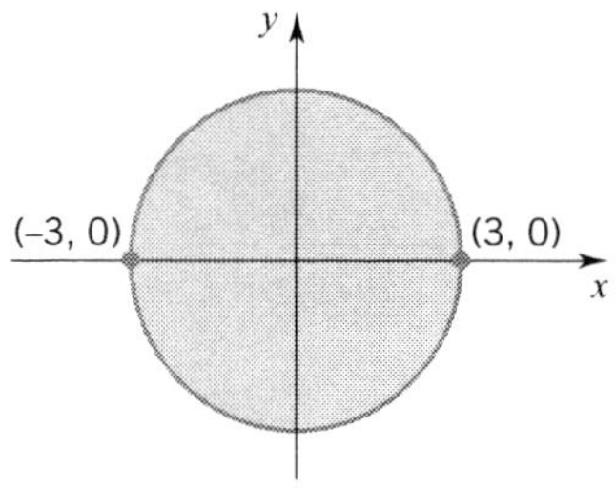

Figure 16.6.1

SOLUTION The region D is a bounded closed set and the function f, being continuous everywhere, is continuous on D. Therefore, we know that f takes on an absolute maximum on D and an absolute minimum.

First we find the critical points. The gradient of f,

$$\nabla f(x, y) = (2x - 2)\,\mathbf{i} + (2y - 2)\,\mathbf{j},$$

is defined throughout the open disk. The gradient is $\mathbf{0}$ only where

$$2x - 2 = 0 \qquad \text{and} \qquad 2y - 2 = 0.$$

These equations give $x = 1$, $y = 1$. The point $(1, 1)$ is the only stationary point.

Now we look for extreme values on the boundary of D. The boundary can be parametrized by the equations

$$x = 3\cos t, \quad y = 3\sin t, \quad (\text{or } \mathbf{r}(t) = 3\cos t\,\mathbf{i} + 3\sin t\,\mathbf{j}),\ 0 \leq t \leq 2\pi$$

The values of f on the boundary are given by the function

$$\begin{aligned} F(t) = f(\mathbf{r}(t)) &= 9\cos^2 t + 9\sin^2 t - 6\cos t - 6\sin t + 4 \\ &= 13 - 6\cos t - 6\sin t, \qquad 0 \leq t \leq 2\pi. \end{aligned}$$

Since F is a real-valued function continuous on a bounded closed interval, it has an absolute maximum and an absolute minimum. (Theorem 2.6.2) To find the critical numbers for F, we differentiate:

$$F'(t) = 6\sin t - 6\cos t.$$

Setting $F'(t) = 0$, we get

$$\sin t = \cos t.$$

The solutions of this equation within the open interval $(0, 2\pi)$ are $t = \pi/4$ and $t = 5\pi/4$. We must also check the endpoints of the interval: $t = 0$ and $t = 2\pi$.

The only values of t that can possibly give rise to an extreme value are $t = 0$, $t = \pi/4$, $t = 5\pi/4$, $t = 2\pi$. At these values of t we have

$$\begin{aligned} F(0) = F(2\pi) &= f(3, 0) = 7, \\ F(\pi/4) &= f(\tfrac{3}{2}\sqrt{2}, \tfrac{3}{2}\sqrt{2}) = 13 - 6\sqrt{2} \cong 4.51, \\ F(5\pi/4) &= f(-\tfrac{3}{2}\sqrt{2}, -\tfrac{3}{2}\sqrt{2}) = 13 + 6\sqrt{2} \cong 21.49. \end{aligned}$$

At the only stationary point, the point $(1, 1)$, the function takes on the value 2: $f(1, 1) = 2$.

Thus, the absolute maximum is $13 + 6\sqrt{2}$ and the absolute minimum is 2. ❑

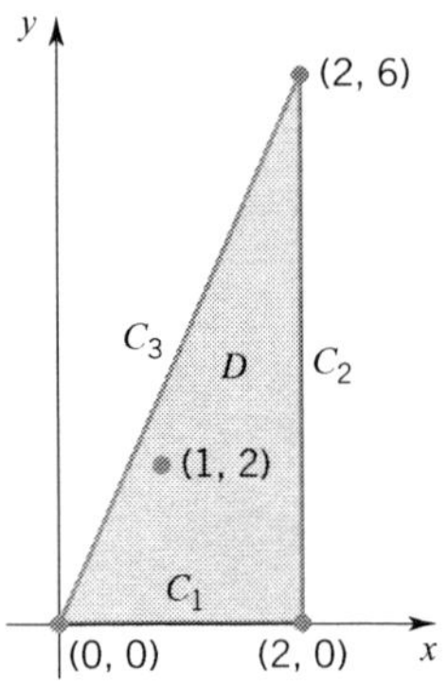

Figure 16.6.2

Example 2 Find the absolute extreme values of the function

$$f(x, y) = 4xy - x^2 - y^2 - 6x$$

on the triangular region $D = \{(x, y) : 0 \le x \le 2, 0 \le y \le 3x\}$. (Figure 16.6.2)

SOLUTION Since f is continuous and D is a bounded closed set, we know that f takes on an absolute maximum and an absolute minimum.

First we find the critical points of f. The gradient of f,

$$\nabla f = (4y - 2x - 6)\,\mathbf{i} + (4x - 2y)\,\mathbf{j},$$

is defined everywhere. The gradient is $\mathbf{0}$ where

$$4y - 2x - 6 = 0 \quad \text{and} \quad 4x - 2y = 0.$$

Solving these equations simultaneously, we get $x = 1$, $y = 2$. The only stationary point in D is the point $(1, 2)$.

Now we look for extreme values on the boundary. We write each side of the triangle in the form $\mathbf{r} = \mathbf{r}(t)$ and then analyze $f(\mathbf{r}(t))$. With C_1, C_2, C_3 as in the figure, we have

$$C_1 : \mathbf{r}_1(t) = t\,\mathbf{i}, \qquad t \in [0, 2];$$
$$C_2 : \mathbf{r}_2(t) = 2\,\mathbf{i} + t\,\mathbf{j}, \qquad t \in [0, 6];$$
$$C_3 : \mathbf{r}_3(t) = t\,\mathbf{i} + 3t\,\mathbf{j}, \qquad t \in [0, 2].$$

The values of f on these line segments are given by the functions

$$f_1(t) = f(\mathbf{r}_1(t)) = -t^2 - 6t, \qquad t \in [0, 2];$$
$$f_2(t) = f(\mathbf{r}_2(t)) = -(t - 4)^2, \qquad t \in [0, 6];$$
$$f_3(t) = f(\mathbf{r}_3(t)) = 2t^2 - 6t, \qquad t \in [0, 2].$$

As you can check, f_1 has no critical points in $(0, 2)$, f_2 has a critical point at $t = 4$, and f_3 has a critical point at $t = \frac{3}{2}$. Evaluating these functions at the endpoints of their domains and at the critical points for f_2 and f_3, we find that

$$f_1(0) = f_3(0) = f(0, 0) = 0$$
$$f_1(2) = f_2(0) = f(2, 0) = -16$$
$$f_2(6) = f_3(3) = f(2, 6) = -4$$
$$f_2(4) = f(2, 4) = 0$$
$$f_3(\tfrac{3}{2}) = f(\tfrac{3}{2}, \tfrac{9}{2}) = -\tfrac{9}{2}.$$

At the only stationary point, the point $(1, 2)$, f takes on the value $-3 : f(1, 2) = -3$.

Thus the absolute maximum is 0, and the absolute minimum is -16. ❑

Whether or not a function takes on an absolute extreme value on a set which is not bounded or not closed has to be decided on a case-by-case basis.

Example 3 The rectangle $\{(x, y) : 0 \le x \le a, -b \le y \le b\}$ is a bounded closed subset of the plane. The function

$$f(x, y) = 1 + \sqrt{x^2 + y^2},$$

being everywhere continuous, is continuous on this rectangle. Thus we can be sure that f takes on both an absolute maximum and an absolute minimum on this set. The absolute maximum is taken on at the points $(a, -b)$ and (a, b), the points of the rectangle farthest away from the origin. The value of f at these points is $1 + \sqrt{a^2 + b^2}$. The absolute minimum is taken on at the origin $(0, 0)$. The value there is 1.

Now let's continue with the same function but apply it instead to the rectangle

$$\{(x, y) : 0 < x \leq a, \ -b \leq y \leq b\}.$$

This rectangle is bounded but not closed. On this set f takes on an absolute maximum (the same maximum as before and at the same points), but it takes on no absolute minimum (the origin is not in the set).

Finally, on the entire plane (which is closed but not bounded), f takes on an absolute minimum (1 at the origin) but no maximum. ❑

Example 4 Here we work with the function

$$f(x, y) = xy + \frac{1}{x} + \frac{1}{y}; \qquad x > 0, \ y > 0.$$

The domain of f is the first quadrant, a set which is open and unbounded. Differentiation shows that the gradient is $\mathbf{0}$ only at the point $(1, 1)$. Thus $(1, 1)$ is the only stationary point. The second-partials test reveals that $f(1, 1) = 3$ is a local minimum. (You can check these assertions by making the calculations yourself.)

Question: Does f take on values less than 3?

To answer this question, we break up the first quadrant into two parts: a closed and bounded part Ω that contains the point $(1, 1)$ and an unbounded part on which $f(x, y)$ is clearly greater than 3. Such a break up is indicated in Figure 16.6.3.

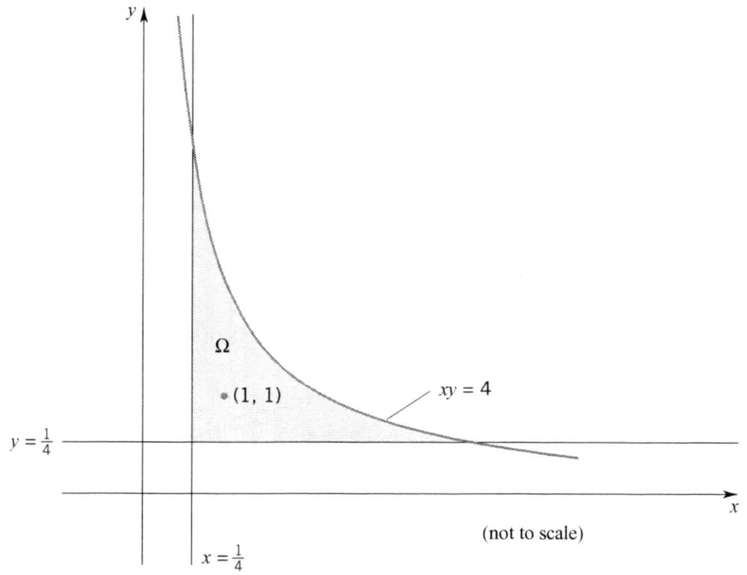

Figure 16.6.3

At points outside Ω

$$xy > 4, \qquad x < \tfrac{1}{4}, \qquad \text{or} \quad y < \tfrac{1}{4}.$$

Thus outside Ω

$$f(x, y) = xy + \frac{1}{x} + \frac{1}{y}$$

is greater than 4. If f takes on values less than 3, it doesn't do it outside Ω.

Now let's look at what happens on Ω. Since Ω is closed and bounded, and f is continuous, the function does take on an absolute minimum on Ω. It can't do so on the boundary because on the boundary $f(x, y)$ is at least 4 and $f(1, 1) = 3$. Thus the minimum value of f is taken on in the interior of Ω. This minimum value is therefore a local minimum, and as such must be taken on at a stationary point. Since (1, 1) is the only stationary point, the absolute minimum on Ω must be 3. Since outside of Ω, $f(x, y) > 4$, $f(1, 1)$ is the absolute minimum of f on its entire domain. The question has been answered: f does not take on values less than 3. ❑

EXERCISES 16.6

Exercises 1–18. Find the absolute extreme values taken on by f on the set indicated.

1. $f(x, y) = 2x^2 + y^2 - 4x - 2y + 2;\quad 0 \le x \le 2,\ 0 \le y \le 2x.$

2. $f(x, y) = 2 - 3x + 2y;$ the closed region enclosed by the triangle with vertices (0, 0), (4, 0), (0, 6).

3. $f(x, y) = x^2 + xy + y^2 - 6x - 1;\quad 0 \le x \le 5,\ -3 \le y \le 0.$

4. $f(x, y) = x^2 + 2xy + 3y^2;\quad |x| \le 2, |y| \le 2.$

5. $f(x, y) = x^2 + y^2 + 3xy + 2;\quad x^2 + y^2 \le 4.$

6. $f(x, y) = y(x - 3);\quad x^2 + y^2 \le 9.$

7. $f(x, y) = (x - 1)^2 + (y - 1)^2;\quad x^2 + y^2 \le 4.$

8. $f(x, y) = 3 + x - y + xy;$ the closed region enclosed by $y = x^2$ and $y = 4$.

9. $f(x, y) = \dfrac{-2x}{x^2 + y^2 + 1};\quad |x| \le 2, |y| \le 2.$

10. $f(x, y) = \dfrac{-2x}{x^2 + y^2 + 1};\quad 0 \le x \le 2, -x \le y \le x.$

11. $f(x, y) = (4x - 2x^2)\cos y;\quad 0 \le x \le 2,\ -\pi/4 \le y \le \pi/4.$

12. $f(x, y) = (x - 3)^2 + y^2;\quad 0 \le x \le 4, x^2 \le y \le 4x.$

13. $f(x, y) = x^3 - 3xy - y^3;\quad 2 \le x \le 2, x \le y \le 1.$

14. $f(x, y) = (x - 4)^2 + y^2;\quad 0 \le x \le 2, x^3 \le y \le 4x.$

15. $f(x, y) = \dfrac{-2y}{x^2 + y^2 + 1};\quad x^2 + y^2 \le 4.$

16. $f(x, y) = x^2 + 4y^2 + x - 2y;$ the closed region enclosed by the ellipse $\frac{1}{4}x^2 + y = 1$.

17. $f(x, y) = x^2 - 2xy + y^2;\quad 0 \le x \le 6, 0 \le y \le 12 - 2x.$

18. $f(x, y) = \dfrac{1}{\sqrt{x^2 + y^2}};\quad 1 \le x \le 3, 1 \le y \le 4.$

19. Find positive numbers x, y, z such that $x + y + z = 18$ and xyz is a maximum. HINT: Maximize $f(x, y) = xy(18 - x - y)$ on the triangular region bounded by the positive x- and y-axes and the line $x + y = 18$.

20. Find positive numbers x, y, z such that $x + y + z = 30$ and xyz^2 is a maximum. HINT: Maximize $f(y, z) = (30 - y - z)yz^2$ on the triangular region bounded by the positive y- and z-axes and the line $y + z = 30$.

21. Find the maximum volume for a rectangular solid in the first octant ($x \ge 0, y \ge 0, z \ge 0$) with one vertex at the origin and opposite vertex on the plane $x + y + z = 1$.

22. Find the maximum volume for a rectangular solid in the first octant with one vertex at the origin and the opposite vertex on the plane

$$\frac{x}{a} + \frac{y}{b} + \frac{z}{c} = 1.$$

23. Define $f(x, y) = \frac{1}{4}x^2 - \frac{1}{9}y^2$ on the closed unit disk. Find
(a) the stationary points,
(b) the local extreme values,
(c) the absolute extreme values.

24. Let n be an integer greater than 2 and set

$$f(x, y) = ax^n + cy^n, \quad \text{taking } ac \ne 0.$$

(a) Find the stationary points.
(b) Find the discriminant at each stationary point.
(c) Find the local and absolute extreme values given that
(i) $a > 0, c > 0$.
(ii) $a < 0, c < 0$.
(iii) $a > 0, c < 0$.

25. Show that a closed rectangular box of maximum volume having prescribed surface area S is a cube.

26. If an open rectangular box has a prescribed surface area S, what dimensions yield the maximum volume?

27. Find the point with the property that the sum of the squares of its distances from $P_1(x_1, y_1)$, $P_2(x_2, y_2)$, $P_3(x_3, y_3)$ is an absolute minimum.

28. A bakery produces two types of bread, one at a cost of 50 cents per loaf, the other at a cost of 60 cents per loaf. Assume that if the first bread is sold at x cents a loaf and the second at y cents a loaf, then the number of loaves that can be sold each week is given by the formulas

$$N_1 = 250(y - x), \quad N_2 = 32,000 + 250(x - 2y).$$

Determine x and y for maximum profit.

29. A pentagon is composed of a rectangle surmounted by an isosceles triangle (see the figure). Given that the perimeter of the pentagon has a fixed value P, find the dimensions for maximum area.

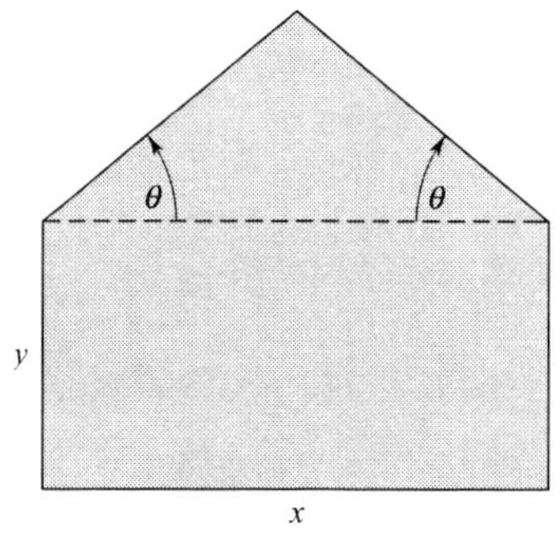

30. Let $f(x, y) = ax^2 + bxy + cy^2$ taking $abc \neq 0$.

(a) Find the discriminant D.

(b) Find the stationary points and local extreme values if $D \neq 0$.

(c) Suppose that $D = 0$. Find the stationary points and the local and absolute extreme values given that

(i) $a > 0, c > 0$.
(ii) $a < 0, c < 0$.

31. Find the distance between the lines $x = \frac{1}{2}y = \frac{1}{3}z$ and $x = y - 2 = z$.

32. A petrochemical company is designing a cylindrical tank with hemispherical ends to be used in transporting its products. If the volume of the tank is to be 10,000 cubic meters, what dimensions should be used to minimize the amount of metal required?

33. According to U.S. Postal Service regulations, the length plus the girth (the perimeter of a cross section) of a package cannot exceed 108 inches. (See the figure.)

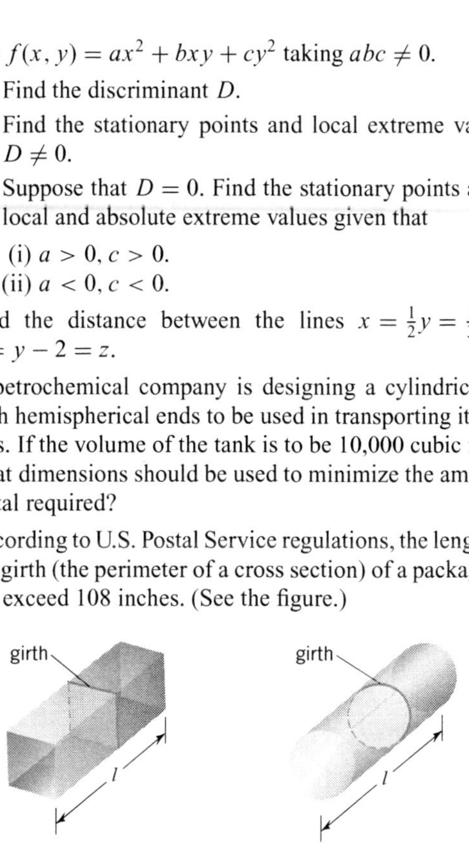

(a) Find the dimensions of the rectangular box of maximum volume that is acceptable for mailing.

(b) Find the dimensions of the cylindrical tube of maximum volume that is acceptable for mailing.

34. Find the volume of the largest rectangular box with edges parallel to the coordinate axes that can be inscribed in the ellipsoid

$$4x^2 + 9y^2 + 36z^2 = 36.$$

35. A 10-foot section of gutter is to be made from a 12-inch-wide strip of metal by folding up strips of length x on each side so that they make an angle θ with the bottom of the gutter. (See the figure.) Determine values for x and θ that will maximize the cross-sectional area of the gutter.

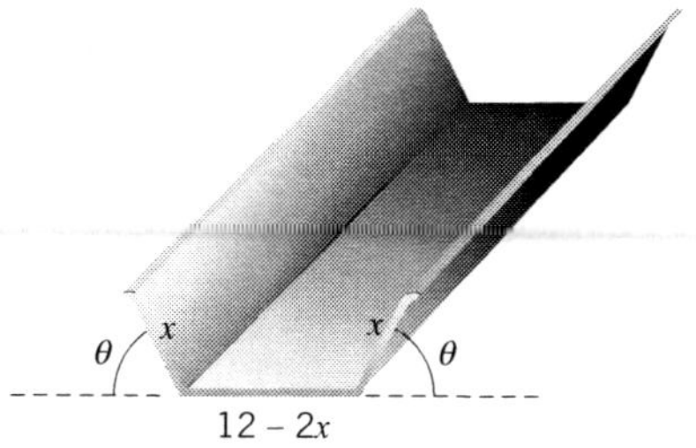

36. Find the dimensions of the most economical open-top rectangular crate 96 cubic meters in volume given that the base costs 30 cents per square meter and the sides cost 10 cents per square meter.

37. (*The method of least squares*) In this exercise we illustrate an important method of fitting a curve to a collection of points. Consider three points

$$(x_1, y_1) = (0, 2), \quad (x_2, y_2) = (1, -5), \quad (x_3, y_3) = (2, 4).$$

(a) Find the line $y = mx + b$ that minimizes the sum of the squares of the vertical distances $d_i = |y_i - (mx_i + b)|$ from these points to the line.

(b) Find the parabola $y = \alpha x^2 + \beta$ that minimizes the sum of the squares of the vertical distances $d_i = |y_i - (\alpha x_i^2 + \beta)|$ from the points to the parabola.

38. Exercise 37 taking

$$(x_1, y_1) = (-1, 2), (x_2, y_2) = (0, -1), (x_3, y_3) = (1, 1).$$

■ 16.7 MAXIMA AND MINIMA WITH SIDE CONDITIONS

(What we call *side conditions* are often called *constraints*.)

When we ask for the distance from a point $P(x_0, y_0)$ to a line $l: Ax + By + C = 0$, we are asking for the minimum value of

$$f(x, y) = \sqrt{(x - x_0)^2 + (y - y_0)^2}$$

with (x, y) subject to the side condition $Ax + By + C = 0$. When we ask for the distance from a point $P(x_0, y_0, z_0)$ to a plane p: $Ax + By + Cz + D = 0$, we are asking for a minimum value of

$$f(x, y, z) = \sqrt{(x - x_0)^2 + (y - y_0)^2 + (z - z_0)^2}$$

with (x, y, z) subject to the side condition $Ax + By + Cz + D = 0$.

We have already treated these particular problems by special techniques. Our interest here is to present techniques for handling problems of this sort in general. In the two-variable case, the problems will take the form of maximizing (or minimizing) some expression $f(x, y)$ subject to a side condition $g(x, y) = 0$. In the three-variable case, we will seek to maximize (or minimize) some expression $f(x, y, z)$ subject to a side condition $g(x, y, z) = 0$. We begin with two simple examples.

Example 1 Maximize the product xy subject to the side condition $x + y - 1 = 0$.

SOLUTION The condition $x + y - 1 = 0$ gives $y = 1 - x$. The original problem can therefore be solved simply by maximizing the product $h(x) = x(1 - x)$. The derivative $h'(x) = 1 - 2x$ is 0 only at $x = \frac{1}{2}$. Since $h''(x) = -2 < 0$, we know from the second-derivative test that $h(\frac{1}{2}) = \frac{1}{2}(1 - \frac{1}{2}) = \frac{1}{4}$ is the desired maximum. ❑

Example 2 Find the maximum volume of a rectangular solid given that the sum of the lengths of its edges is $12a$.

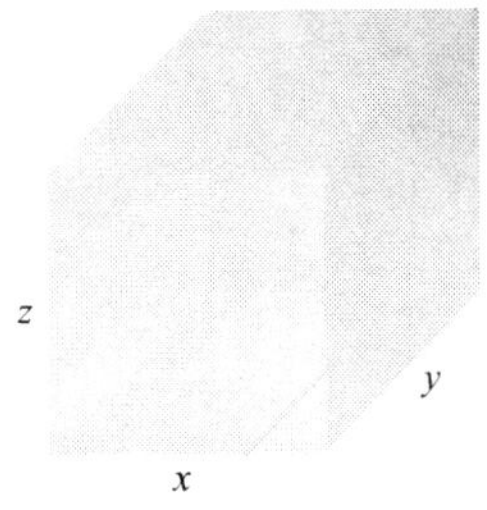

Figure 16.7.1

SOLUTION We denote the dimensions of the solid by x, y, z. (Figure 16.7.1.) The volume is given by

$$V = xyz.$$

The stipulation on the edges requires that

$$4(x + y + z) = 12a.$$

Solving this last equation for z, we find that

$$z = 3a - (x + y).$$

Substituting this expression for z in the volume formula, we have

$$V = xy[3a - (x + y)].$$

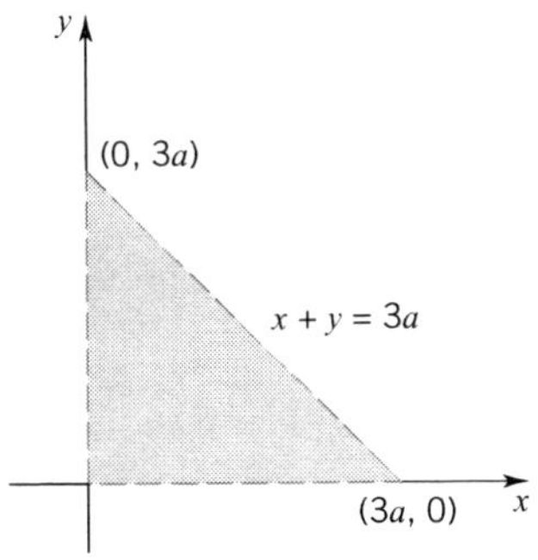

Figure 16.7.2

Since x, y, V cannot be negative, the function V is defined only on the triangular region shown in Figure 16.7.2. Since $V = 0$ on the boundary of the region, the maximum value of V is taken on somewhere inside the triangle.

Differentiation gives

$$\frac{\partial V}{\partial x} = xy(-1) + y[3a - (x + y)] = 3ay - 2xy - y^2,$$

$$\frac{\partial V}{\partial y} = xy(-1) + x[3a - (x + y)] = 3ax - x^2 - 2xy.$$

Setting both partials equal to zero, we have

$$(3a - 2x - y)y = 0 \qquad \text{and} \qquad (3a - x - 2y)x = 0.$$

Since x and y are assumed positive, we can divide by x and y and get

$$3a - 2x - y = 0 \qquad \text{and} \qquad 3a - x - 2y = 0.$$

Solving these equations simultaneously, we find that $x = y = a$. The point (a, a), which does lie within the triangle, is the only stationary point. The value of V at that point is a^3. The conditions of the problem make it clear that this is a maximum. (If you are skeptical, you can confirm this by appealing to the second-partials test.) ❑

The last two problems were easy. They were easy *in part* because the side conditions were such that we could solve for one of the variables in terms of the other(s). In general this is not possible and a more sophisticated approach is required.

The Method of Lagrange

We begin with what looks like a detour. To avoid having to make separate statements for the two- and three-variable cases, we will use vector notation.

Throughout the discussion f will be a function of two or three variables which is continuously differentiable on some open set U. We take

$$C : \mathbf{r} = \mathbf{r}(t), \quad t \in I$$

to be a curve that lies entirely in U and has at each point a nonzero tangent vector $\mathbf{r}'(t)$. The basic result is this:

(16.7.1) if $\mathbf{x}_0$ maximizes (or minimizes) $f(\mathbf{x})$ on C, then $\nabla f(\mathbf{x}_0)$ is perpendicular to C at $\mathbf{x}_0$.

PROOF Assume that $\mathbf{x}_0$ maximizes (or minimizes) $f(\mathbf{x})$ on C. Choose t_0, so that

$$\mathbf{r}(t_0) = \mathbf{x}_0.$$

The composition $f(\mathbf{r}(t))$ has a maximum (or minimum) at t_0. Consequently, its derivative,

$$\frac{d}{dt}[f(\mathbf{r}(t))] = \nabla f(\mathbf{r}(t)) \cdot \mathbf{r}'(t),$$

must be zero at t_0:

$$0 = \nabla f(\mathbf{r}(t_0)) \cdot \mathbf{r}'(t_0) = \nabla f(\mathbf{x}_0) \cdot \mathbf{r}'(t_0).$$

This shows that

$$\nabla f(\mathbf{x}_0) \perp \mathbf{r}'(t_0).$$

Since $\mathbf{r}'(t_0)$ is tangent to C at $\mathbf{x}_0$, $\nabla f(\mathbf{x}_0)$ is perpendicular to C at $\mathbf{x}_0$. ❑

We are now ready for side-condition problems. Suppose that g is a continuously differentiable function of two or three variables defined on a subset of the domain of f. Lagrange made the following observation:†

(16.7.2) if $\mathbf{x}_0$ maximizes (or minimizes) $f(\mathbf{x})$ subject to the side condition $g(\mathbf{x}) = 0$, then $\nabla f(\mathbf{x}_0)$ and $\nabla g(\mathbf{x}_0)$ are parallel. Thus, if $\nabla g(\mathbf{x}_0) \neq \mathbf{0}$, then there exists a scalar λ such that

$$\nabla f(\mathbf{x}_0) = \lambda \nabla g(\mathbf{x}_0).$$

Such a scalar λ has come to be called a *Lagrange multiplier*.

PROOF OF (16.7.2) Let's suppose that $\mathbf{x}_0$ maximizes (or minimizes) $f(\mathbf{x})$ subject to the side condition $g(\mathbf{x}) = 0$. If $\nabla g(\mathbf{x}_0) = \mathbf{0}$, the result is trivially true: every vector is parallel to the zero vector. We suppose therefore that $\nabla g(\mathbf{x}_0) \neq \mathbf{0}$.

In the two-variable case we have

$$\mathbf{x}_0 = (x_0, y_0) \qquad \text{and} \qquad \text{the side condition} \qquad g(x, y) = 0.$$

†Another contribution of the French mathematician Joseph Louis Lagrange.

The side condition defines a curve C that has a nonzero tangent vector at (x_0, y_0).† Since (x_0, y_0) maximizes (or minimizes) $f(x, y)$ on C, we know from (16.7.1) that $\nabla f(x_0, y_0)$ is perpendicular to C at (x_0, y_0). By (16.4.2), $\nabla g(x_0, y_0)$ is also perpendicular to C at (x_0, y_0). The two gradients are therefore parallel. See Figure 16.7.3.

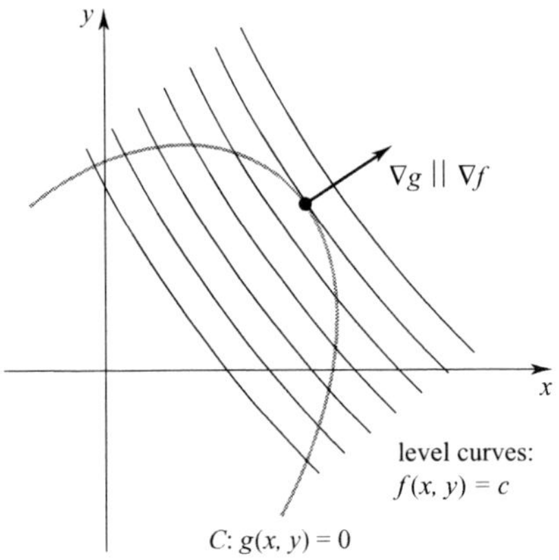

Figure 16.7.3

In the three-variable case we have

$$\mathbf{x}_0 = (x_0, y_0, z_0) \qquad \text{and} \qquad \text{the side condition} \qquad g(x, y, z) = 0.$$

The side condition defines a surface Γ that lies in the domain of f. Now let C be a curve that lies on Γ and passes through (x_0, y_0, z_0) with nonzero tangent vector. We know that (x_0, y_0, z_0) maximizes (or minimizes) $f(x, y, z)$ on C. Consequently, $\nabla f(x_0, y_0, z_0)$ is perpendicular to C at (x_0, y_0, z_0). Since this is true for each such curve C, $\nabla f(x_0, y_0, z_0)$ must be perpendicular to Γ itself. But since Γ is a level surface for g and (x_0, y_0, z_0) lies on Γ, $\nabla g(x_0, y_0, z_0)$ is also perpendicular to Γ. [(16.4.6)] It follows that $\nabla f(x_0, y_0, z_0)$ and $\nabla g(x_0, y_0, z_0)$ are parallel. ❑

We come now to some problems that are susceptible to Lagrange's method. In each case ∇g is not $\mathbf{0}$ where g is 0 and therefore we can focus entirely on those points $\mathbf{x}$ that satisfy the Lagrange condition

$$\nabla f(\mathbf{x}) = \lambda \nabla g(\mathbf{x}). \qquad (16.7.2)$$

Example 3 Maximize and minimize

$$f(x, y) = xy \qquad \text{on the unit circle} \qquad x^2 + y^2 = 1.$$

SOLUTION Since f is continuous and the unit circle is closed and bounded, it is clear that both a maximum and a minimum exist. (Section 16.6)

To apply Lagrange's method, we set

$$g(x, y) = x^2 + y^2 - 1.$$

We want to maximize and minimize

$$f(x, y) = xy \qquad \text{subject to the side condition } g(x, y) = 0.$$

† $\mathbf{t}(x_0, y_0) = \dfrac{\partial g}{\partial y}(x_0, y_0)\,\mathbf{i} - \dfrac{\partial g}{\partial x}(x_0, y_0)\,\mathbf{j} \neq \mathbf{0}$. (16.4.3)

The gradients are

$$\nabla f(x, y) = y\,\mathbf{i} + x\,\mathbf{j}, \qquad \nabla g(x, y) = 2x\,\mathbf{i} + 2y\,\mathbf{j}.$$

Setting $\nabla f(x, y) = \lambda \nabla g(x, y)$, we have

$$y = 2\lambda x, \qquad x = 2\lambda y.$$

Multiplying the first equation by y and the second equation by x, we find that

$$y^2 = 2\lambda xy, \qquad x^2 = 2\lambda xy$$

and therefore

$$y^2 = x^2.$$

The side condition $x^2 + y^2 = 1$ implies that $2x^2 = 1$ and therefore $x = \pm\frac{1}{2}\sqrt{2}$. The only points that can give rise to an extreme value are

$$(\tfrac{1}{2}\sqrt{2}, \tfrac{1}{2}\sqrt{2}), \qquad (\tfrac{1}{2}\sqrt{2}, -\tfrac{1}{2}\sqrt{2}), \qquad (-\tfrac{1}{2}\sqrt{2}, \tfrac{1}{2}\sqrt{2}), \qquad (-\tfrac{1}{2}\sqrt{2}, -\tfrac{1}{2}\sqrt{2}).$$

At the first and fourth points f takes on the value $\frac{1}{2}$. At the second and third points f takes on the value $-\frac{1}{2}$. Clearly then, $\frac{1}{2}$ is the maximum value and $-\frac{1}{2}$ the minimum value. ❑

Example 4 Find the minimum value taken on by the function

$$f(x, y) = x^2 + (y-2)^2 \qquad \text{on the hyperbola} \qquad x^2 - y^2 = 1.$$

SOLUTION Note that the expression $f(x, y) = x^2 + (y-2)^2$ gives the square of the distance between the points $(0, 2)$ and (x, y). Therefore, the problem asks us to minimize the square of the distance from the point $(0, 2)$ to the hyperbola, and this minimum value clearly exists. Note, also, that there is no maximum value. See Figure 16.7.4.

Now set

$$g(x, y) = x^2 - y^2 - 1.$$

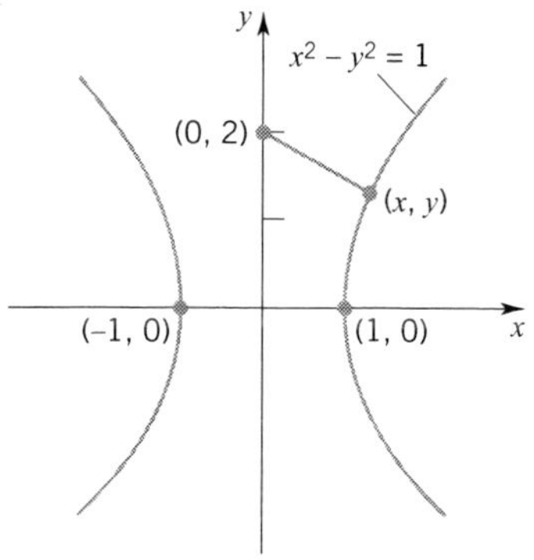

Figure 16.7.4

We want to minimize

$$f(x, y) = x^2 + (y-2)^2 \qquad \text{subject to the side condition} \qquad g(x, y) = 0.$$

Here

$$\nabla f(x, y) = 2x\,\mathbf{i} + 2(y-2)\,\mathbf{j}, \qquad \nabla g(x, y) = 2x\,\mathbf{i} - 2y\,\mathbf{j}.$$

The Lagrange condition $\nabla f(x, y) = \lambda \nabla g(x, y)$ gives

$$2x = 2\lambda x, \qquad 2(y-2) = -2\lambda y,$$

which we can simplify to

$$x = \lambda x, \qquad y - 2 = -\lambda y.$$

The side condition $x^2 - y^2 = 1$ shows that x cannot be zero. Dividing $x = \lambda x$ by x, we get $\lambda = 1$. This means that $y - 2 = -y$ and therefore $y = 1$. With $y = 1$, the side condition gives $x = \pm\sqrt{2}$. The points to be checked are therefore $(-\sqrt{2}, 1)$ and $(\sqrt{2}, 1)$. At each of these points f takes on the value 3. This is the desired minimum. ❑

Remark The last problem could have been solved more simply by rewriting the side condition as $x^2 = 1 + y^2$ and eliminating x from $f(x, y)$ by substitution. Then it would have been simply a matter of minimizing the function $h(y) = 1 + y^2 + (y-2)^2 = 2y^2 - 4y + 5$. ❑

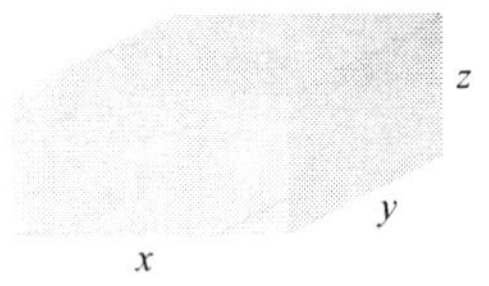

Figure 16.7.5

Example 5 A rectangular box without a top is to have a volume of 12 cubic feet. Find the dimensions of the box that will have minimum surface area.

SOLUTION With the dimensions indicated in Figure 16.7.5, the surface area is given by the expression

$$S = xy + 2xz + 2yz.$$

We want to minimize S subject to the side condition $xyz = 12$ with $x > 0, y > 0, z > 0$.

We begin by setting

$$g(x, y, z) = xyz - 12$$

so that the side condition becomes $g(x, y, z) = 0$. We seek those triples (x, y, z) that simultaneously satisfy the Lagrange condition

$$\nabla f(x, y, z) = \lambda \nabla g(x, y, z) \qquad \text{and the side condition} \qquad g(x, y, z) = 0.$$

The gradients are

$$\nabla f = (y + 2z)\,\mathbf{i} + (x + 2z)\,\mathbf{j} + (2x + 2y)\,\mathbf{k}, \qquad \nabla g = yz\,\mathbf{i} + xz\,\mathbf{j} + xy\,\mathbf{k}.$$

The Lagrange condition gives

$$y + 2z = \lambda yz, \qquad x + 2z = \lambda xz, \qquad 2x + 2y = \lambda xy.$$

Multiplying the first equation by x, the second by $-y$, and adding the resulting equations, we get

$$2z(x - y) = 0.$$

Since $z \neq 0$, it follows that $y = x$. Replacing y by x in the third equation yields the equation

$$4x = \lambda x^2.$$

Since $x \neq 0$, we conclude that $x = 4/\lambda$, and since $y = x$, $y = 4/\lambda$. We can now solve either the first or second equation for z in terms of λ. The result is $z = 2/\lambda$.

Finally, substituting $x = y = 4/\lambda$ and $z = 2/\lambda$ into the side condition, we get

$$\left(\frac{4}{\lambda}\right)\left(\frac{4}{\lambda}\right)\left(\frac{2}{\lambda}\right) = 12 \qquad \text{which implies} \qquad \lambda^3 = \frac{8}{3} \qquad \text{and therefore} \qquad \lambda = \frac{2}{\sqrt[3]{3}}.$$

With $\lambda = 2/\sqrt[3]{3}$, we find that $x = y = 2\sqrt[3]{3}$ and $z = \sqrt[3]{3}$. The dimensions that minimize the surface area are

$$\text{length} = 2\sqrt[3]{3}, \qquad \text{width} = 2\sqrt[3]{3}, \qquad \text{height} = \sqrt[3]{3}. \quad \square$$

Example 6 Show that, of all the triangles inscribed in a circle of radius R, the equilateral triangle has the largest perimeter.

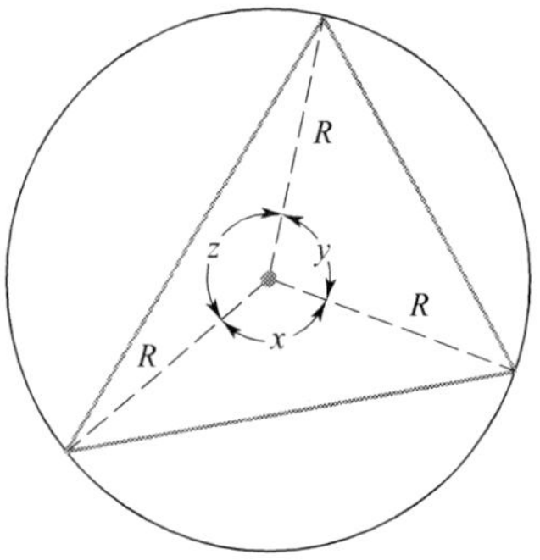

Figure 16.7.6

SOLUTION It is intuitively clear that this maximum exists and geometrically clear that the triangle that offers this maximum contains the center of the circle in its interior or on its boundary. As in Figure 16.7.6, we denote by x, y, z the central angles that subtend the three sides. As you can verify by trigonometry, the perimeter of the triangle is given by the function.

$$f(x, y, z) = 2R(\sin \tfrac{1}{2}x + \sin \tfrac{1}{2}y + \sin \tfrac{1}{2}z).$$

As a side condition we have

$$g(x, y, z) = x + y + z - 2\pi = 0.$$

To maximize the perimeter, we form the gradients

$$\nabla f(x, y, z) = R(\cos \tfrac{1}{2}x\,\mathbf{i} + \cos \tfrac{1}{2}y\,\mathbf{j} + \cos \tfrac{1}{2}z\,\mathbf{k}), \qquad \nabla g(x, y, z) = \mathbf{i} + \mathbf{j} + \mathbf{k}.$$

The Lagrange condition $\nabla f(x, y, z) = \lambda \nabla g(x, y, z)$ gives

$$\lambda = R\cos \tfrac{1}{2}x, \qquad \lambda = R\cos \tfrac{1}{2}y, \qquad \lambda = R\cos \tfrac{1}{2}z,$$

and therefore

$$\cos \tfrac{1}{2}x = \cos \tfrac{1}{2}y = \cos \tfrac{1}{2}z.$$

With x, y, z all in $(0, \pi]$, we can conclude that $x = y = z$. Since the central angles are equal, the sides are equal. The triangle is therefore equilateral. ❑

An Application of the Cross Product

The Lagrange condition can be replaced by a cross-product equation. Points that satisfy the equation $\nabla f = \lambda \nabla g$ satisfy the equation

(16.7.3)

$$\boxed{\nabla f \times \nabla g = \mathbf{0}.}$$

If f and g are functions of two variables,

$$\nabla f \times \nabla g = \begin{vmatrix} \mathbf{i} & \mathbf{j} & \mathbf{k} \\ f_x & f_y & 0 \\ g_x & g_y & 0 \end{vmatrix} = (f_x g_y - f_y g_x)\,\mathbf{k}.$$

Thus, in two variables, the condition $\nabla f \times \nabla g = \mathbf{0}$ gives

(16.7.4)

$$\boxed{\frac{\partial f}{\partial x}\frac{\partial g}{\partial y} - \frac{\partial f}{\partial y}\frac{\partial g}{\partial x} = 0.}$$

Example 7 Maximize and minimize $f(x, y) = xy$ on the unit circle $x^2 + y^2 = 1$.

SOLUTION This problem was solved earlier by the method of Lagrange. (Example 3) This time we will use (16.7.4) instead.

As before, we set

$$g(x, y) = x^2 + y^2 - 1,$$

so that the side condition takes the form $g(x, y) = 0$. Since

$$\frac{\partial f}{\partial x} = y, \quad \frac{\partial f}{\partial y} = x \qquad \text{and} \qquad \frac{\partial g}{\partial x} = 2x, \quad \frac{\partial g}{\partial y} = 2y,$$

(16.7.4) gives

$$y(2y) - x(2x) = 0 \qquad \text{which simplifies to} \qquad x^2 = y^2.$$

As before, the side condition $x^2 + y^2 = 1$ implies that $2x^2 = 1$ and therefore $x = \pm\frac{1}{2}\sqrt{2}$. The points under consideration are

$$(\tfrac{1}{2}\sqrt{2}, \tfrac{1}{2}\sqrt{2}), \qquad (\tfrac{1}{2}\sqrt{2}, -\tfrac{1}{2}\sqrt{2}), \qquad (-\tfrac{1}{2}\sqrt{2}, \tfrac{1}{2}\sqrt{2}), \qquad (-\tfrac{1}{2}\sqrt{2}, -\tfrac{1}{2}\sqrt{2}).$$

As you saw in Example 3, f takes on its maximum value $\frac{1}{2}$ at the first and fourth points, and its minimum value $-\frac{1}{2}$ at the second and third points. ❑

In three variables the computations demanded by the cross-product equation are often quite complicated, and it is usually easier to follow the method of Lagrange.

EXERCISES 16.7

1. Minimize $x^2 + y^2$ on the hyperbola $xy = 1$.

2. Maximize xy on the ellipse $b^2x^2 + a^2y^2 = a^2b^2$.

3. Minimize xy on the ellipse $b^2x^2 + a^2y^2 = a^2b^2$.

4. Minimize xy^2 on the unit circle $x^2 + y^2 = 1$.

5. Maximize xy^2 on the ellipse $b^2x^2 + a^2y^2 = a^2b^2$.

6. Maximize $x + y$ on the curve $x^4 + y^4 = 1$.

7. Maximize $x^2 + y^2$ on the curve $x^4 + 7x^2y^2 + y^4 = 1$.

8. Minimize xyz on the unit sphere $x^2 + y^2 + z^2 = 1$.

9. Maximize xyz on the ellipsoid $x^2/a^2 + y^2/b^2 + z^2/c^2 = 1$.

10. Minimize $x + 2y + 4z$ on the sphere $x^2 + y^2 + z^2 = 7$.

11. Maximize $2x + 3y + 5z$ on the sphere $x^2 + y^2 + z^2 = 19$.

12. Minimize $x^4 + y^4 + z^4$ on the plane $x + y + z = 1$.

13. Maximize the volume of a rectangular solid in the first octant with one vertex at the origin and opposite vertex on the plane $x/a + y/b + z/c = 1$. (Take $a > 0, b > 0, c > 0$.)

14. Show that the square has the largest area of all the rectangles with a given perimeter.

15. Find the distance from the point $(0, 1)$ to the parabola $x^2 = 4y$.

16. Find the distance from the point $(p, 4p)$ to the parabola $y^2 = 2px$.

17. Find the points on the sphere $x^2 + y^2 + z^2 = 1$ that are closest to and farthest from the point $(2, 1, 2)$.

18. Let x, y, z be the angles of a triangle. Determine the maximum value of $f(x, y, z) = \sin x \sin y \sin z$.

19. Maximize $f(x, y, z) = 3x - 2y + z$ on the sphere $x^2 + y^2 + z^2 = 14$.

20. A rectangular box has three of its faces on the coordinate planes and one vertex in the first octant on the paraboloid $z = 4 - x^2 - y^2$. Determine the maximum volume of the box.

21. Use the method of Lagrange to find the distance from the origin to the plane with equation $Ax + By + Cz + D = 0$.

22. Maximize the volume of a rectangular solid given that the sum of the areas of the six faces is $6a^2$.

23. Within a triangle there is a point P such that the sum of the squares of the distances from P to the sides of the triangle is a minimum. Find this minimum.

24. Show that of all the triangles inscribed in a fixed circle, the equilateral one has the largest: (a) product of the lengths of the sides; (b) sum of the squares of the lengths of the sides.

25. The curve $x^3 - y^3 = 1$ is asymptotic to the line $y = x$. Find the point(s) on the curve $x^3 - y^3 = 1$ farthest from the line $y = x$.

26. A plane passes through the point (a, b, c). Find its intercepts with the coordinate axes if the volume of the solid bounded by the plane and the coordinate planes is to be a minimum.

27. Show that, of all the triangles with a given perimeter, the equilateral triangle has the largest area. HINT: Area $= \sqrt{s(s-a)(s-b)(s-c)}$, where s represents the semiperimeter $s = \frac{1}{2}(a + b + c)$.

28. Show that the rectangular box of maximum volume that can be inscribed in the sphere $x^2 + y^2 + z^2 = a^2$ is a cube.

29. Determine the maximum value of $f(x, y) = (xy)^{1/2}$ given that x and y are nonnegative numbers and $x + y = k$, k a constant. Then show that if x and y are nonnegative numbers,

$$(xy)^{1/2} \le \tfrac{1}{2}(x + y).$$

30. (a) Determine the maximum value of $f(x, y, z) = (xyz)^{1/3}$ given that x, y, and z are nonnegative numbers and $x + y + z = k$, k a constant.

(b) Use the result in part (a) to show that if x, y, and z are nonnegative numbers, then

$$(xyz)^{1/3} \le \tfrac{1}{3}(x + y + z).$$

31. Let $x_1, x_2, \ldots, x_n$ be nonnegative numbers such that $x_1 + x_2 + \cdots + x_n = k$, k a constant. Prove that

$$(x_1x_2\cdots x_n)^{1/n} \le \tfrac{1}{n}(x_1 + x_2 + \cdots + x_n).$$

Thus, for n nonnegative numbers, the *geometric mean is less than or equal to the arithmetic mean.*

32. (a) Maximize and (b) minimize xy^2z on the sphere $x^2 + y^2 + z^2 = 1$.

33. A soft-drink manufacturer wants to design an aluminum can in the shape of a right circular cylinder to hold a given volume V (measured in cubic inches). If the objective is to minimize the amount of aluminum needed (top, sides, and bottom), what dimensions should be used?

Exercises 34–42. Use the Lagrange method to give alternative solutions to following exercises of Section 16.6.

34. Exercise 19.

35. Exercise 22.

36. Exercise 20.

37. Exercise 25.

38. Exercise 26.

39. Exercise 32.

40. Exercise 33.

41. Exercise 34.

42. Exercise 36.

43. A manufacturer can produce three distinct products in quantities Q_1, Q_2, Q_3 and thereby derive a profit $p(Q_1, Q_2, Q_3) = 2Q_1 + 8Q_2 + 24Q_3$. Find the values of Q_1, Q_2, Q_3 that maximize profit given that production is subject to the constraint $Q_1^2 + 2Q_2^2 + 4Q_3^2 = 4.5 \times 10^9$.

44. Find the volume of the largest rectangular box that can be inscribed in the ellipsoid

$$\frac{x^2}{a^2} + \frac{y^2}{b^2} + \frac{z^2}{c^2} = 1$$

if the edges of the box are parallel to the coordinate planes.

■ PROJECT 16.7 Maxima and Minima with Two Side Conditions

The Lagrange method can be extended to problems with two side conditions. If $\mathbf{x}_0$ gives rise to a maximum (or minimum) of $f(\mathbf{x})$ subject to the two side conditions $g(\mathbf{x}) = \mathbf{0}$ and $h(\mathbf{x}) = \mathbf{0}$, and if $\nabla g(\mathbf{x}_0)$, $\nabla h(\mathbf{x}_0)$ are nonzero and nonparallel, then there exist scalars λ and μ such that

$$\nabla f(\mathbf{x}_0) = \lambda \nabla g(\mathbf{x}_0) + \mu \nabla h(\mathbf{x}_0).$$

Assume this result and solve the following problems.

Problem 1. Find the extreme values of

$$f(x, y, z) = xy + z^2$$

subject to the side conditions:

$$x^2 + y^2 + z^2 = 4 \quad \text{and} \quad y - x = 0.$$

Problem 2. The planes $x + 2y + 3z = 0$ and $2x + 3y + z = 4$ intersect in a straight line. Find the point on that line that is closest to the origin.

Problem 3. The plane $x + y - z + 1 = 0$ intersects the upper nappe of the cone $z^2 = x^2 + y^2$ in an ellipse. Find the points on this ellipse that are closest to and farthest from the origin.

■ 16.8 DIFFERENTIALS

We begin by reviewing the one-variable case. If f is differentiable at x, then for small h, the increment

$$\Delta f = f(x + h) - f(x)$$

can be approximated by the differential

$$df = f'(x)h.$$

For a geometric view of Δf and df, see Figure 16.8.1. We write

$$\Delta f \cong df.$$

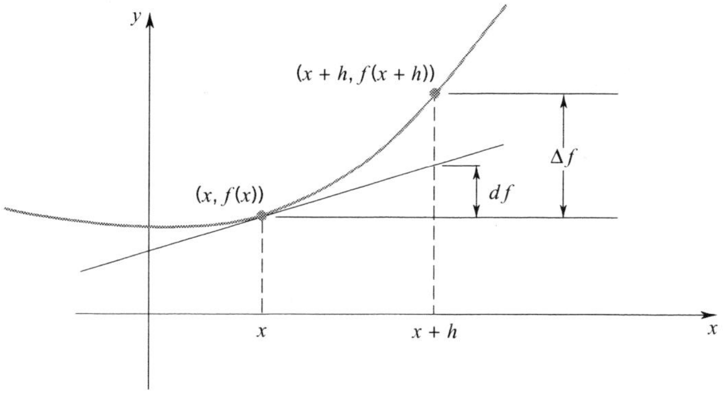

Figure 16.8.1

How good is this approximation? It is good enough that the ratio

$$\frac{\Delta f - df}{|h|}$$

tends to 0 as h tends to 0.

The differential of a function of several variables, defined in an analogous manner, plays a similar approximating role. Let's suppose that f, now a function of several variables, is differentiable at $\mathbf{x}$. The difference

(16.8.1) $$\Delta f = f(\mathbf{x} + \mathbf{h}) - f(\mathbf{x})$$

is called the *increment* of f, and the dot product

(16.8.2) $$df = \nabla f(\mathbf{x}) \cdot \mathbf{h}$$

is called the *differential* (more formally, the *total differential*). As in the one-variable case, for small $\mathbf{h}$, the differential and the increment are approximately equal:

(16.8.3) $$\Delta f \cong df.$$

How approximately equal are they? Enough so that the ratio

$$\frac{\Delta f - df}{\|\mathbf{h}\|}$$

tends to 0 as $\mathbf{h}$ tends to $\mathbf{0}$. How do we know this? We know that

$$f(\mathbf{x} + \mathbf{h}) - f(\mathbf{x}) = \nabla f(\mathbf{x}) \cdot \mathbf{h} + o(\mathbf{h})$$

and therefore

$$[f(\mathbf{x} + \mathbf{h})] - f(\mathbf{x})] - \nabla f(\mathbf{x}) \cdot \mathbf{h} = o(\mathbf{h}).$$

This tells us that

$$\frac{\overbrace{[f(\mathbf{x} + \mathbf{h}) - f(\mathbf{x})]}^{\Delta f} - \overbrace{\nabla f(\mathbf{x}) \cdot \mathbf{h}}^{df}}{\|\mathbf{h}\|} \to 0 \text{ as } \mathbf{h} \to \mathbf{0}. \qquad \text{(Section 16.1)}$$

In the two-variable case we set $\mathbf{x} = (x, y)$ and $\mathbf{h} = (\Delta x, \Delta y)$. The increment $\Delta f = f(\mathbf{x} + \mathbf{h}) - f(\mathbf{x})$ then takes the form

$$\Delta f = f(x + \Delta x, y + \Delta y) - f(x, y),$$

and the differential $df = \Delta f(\mathbf{x}) \cdot \mathbf{h}$ takes the form

$$df = \frac{\partial f}{\partial x}(x, y)\Delta x + \frac{\partial f}{\partial y}(x, y)\Delta y.$$

By suppressing the point of evaluation, we can write

(16.8.4) $$df = \frac{\partial f}{\partial x}\Delta x + \frac{\partial f}{\partial y}\Delta y.$$

The approximation $\Delta f \cong df$ is illustrated in Figure 16.8.2. There we have represented f as a surface $z = f(x, y)$. Through a point $P(x_0, y_0, f(x_0, y_0))$ we have drawn the tangent plane. *The difference $df - \Delta f$ is the vertical separation between this tangent plane and the surface as measured at the point* $(x_0 + \Delta x, y_0 + \Delta y)$.

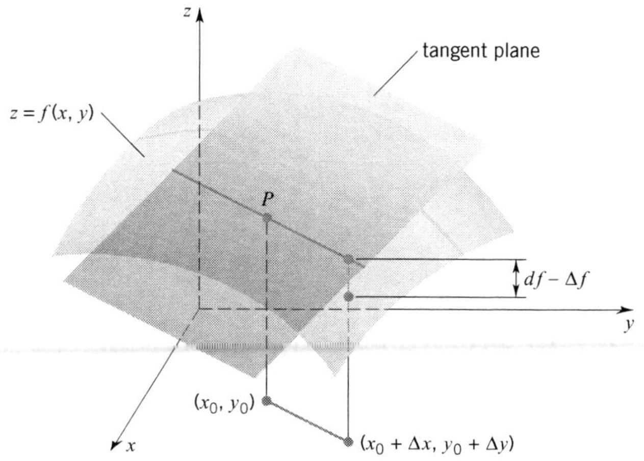

Figure 16.8.2

PROOF The tangent plane at P has equation

$$z - f(x_0, y_0) = \frac{\partial f}{\partial x}(x_0, y_0)(x - x_0) + \frac{\partial f}{\partial y}(x_0, y_0)(y - y_0).$$

On this plane the z-coordinate of the point above $(x_0 + \Delta x, y_0 + \Delta y)$ is

$$f(x_0, y_0) + \frac{\partial f}{\partial x}(x_0, y_0)\Delta x + \frac{\partial f}{\partial y}(x_0, y_0)\Delta y. \qquad \text{(Check this.)}$$

On the surface the z-coordinate of the point above $(x_0 + \Delta x, y_0 + \Delta y)$ is

$$f(x_0 + \Delta x, y_0 + \Delta y).$$

The difference between these two,

$$\left[f(x_0, y_0) + \frac{\partial f}{\partial x}(x_0, y_0)\Delta x + \frac{\partial f}{\partial y}(x_0, y_0)\Delta y\right] - [f(x_0 + \Delta x, y_0 + \Delta y)],$$

can be written as

$$\left[\frac{\partial f}{\partial x}(x_0, y_0)\Delta x + \frac{\partial f}{\partial y}(x_0, y_0)\Delta y\right] - [f(x_0 + \Delta x, y_0 + \Delta y) - f(x_0, y_0)].$$

This is just $df - \Delta f$.

The quantity $df - \Delta f$ is positive if, as in Figure 16.8.2, the tangent plane lies above the surface. It is negative if the tangent plane lies below the surface. ❑

For the three-variable case we set $\mathbf{x} = (x, y, z)$ and $\mathbf{h} = (\Delta x, \Delta y, \Delta z)$. The increment becomes

$$\Delta f = f(x + \Delta x, y + \Delta y, z + \Delta z) - f(x, y, z),$$

and the approximating differential becomes

$$df = \frac{\partial f}{\partial x}(x, y, z)\Delta x + \frac{\partial f}{\partial y}(x, y, z)\Delta y + \frac{\partial f}{\partial z}(x, y, z)\Delta z.$$

Suppressing the point of evaluation, we have

(16.8.5)
$$df = \frac{\partial f}{\partial x}\Delta x + \frac{\partial f}{\partial y}\Delta y + \frac{\partial f}{\partial z}\Delta z.$$

To illustrate the use of differentials, we begin with a rectangle of sides x and y. The area is given by

$$A(x, y) = xy.$$

An increase in the dimensions of the rectangle to $x + \Delta x$ and $y + \Delta y$ produces a change in area

$$\begin{aligned} \Delta A &= (x + \Delta x)(y + \Delta y) - xy \\ &= (xy + x\,\Delta y + y\,\Delta x + \Delta x\,\Delta y) - xy \\ &= x\,\Delta y + y\,\Delta x + \Delta x\,\Delta y. \end{aligned}$$

The differential estimate for this change in area is

$$dA = \frac{\partial A}{\partial x}\Delta x + \frac{\partial A}{\partial y}\Delta y = y\,\Delta x + x\,\Delta y. \qquad \text{(Figure 16.8.3)}$$

The error of our estimate, the difference between the actual change and the estimated change, is the difference $\Delta A - dA = \Delta x\,\Delta y$.

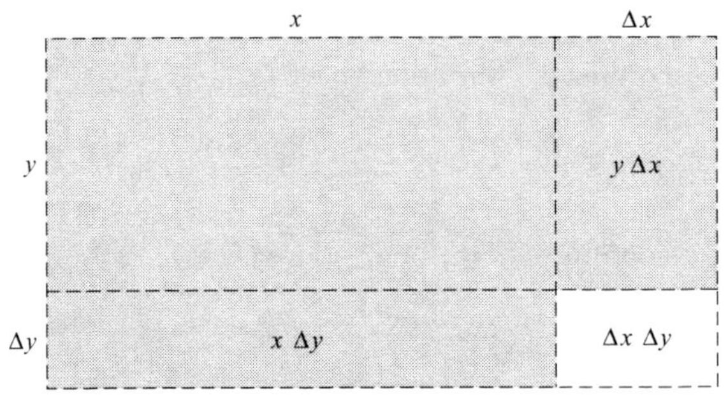

Figure 16.8.3

Example 1 Given that $f(x, y) = yx^{2/5} + x\sqrt{y}$, estimate by a differential the change in the value of f from (32, 16) to (32.1, 16.3).

SOLUTION Since

$$\frac{\partial f}{\partial x} = \frac{2y}{5}\left(\frac{1}{x}\right)^{3/5} + \sqrt{y} \qquad \text{and} \qquad \frac{\partial f}{\partial y} = x^{2/5} + \frac{x}{2\sqrt{y}},$$

we have

$$df = \left[\frac{2y}{5}\left(\frac{1}{x}\right)^{3/5} + \sqrt{y}\right]\Delta x + \left[x^{2/5} + \frac{x}{2\sqrt{y}}\right]\Delta y.$$

At $x = 32$, $y = 16$, $\Delta x = 0.1$, $\Delta y = 0.3$,

$$df = \left[\frac{32}{5}\left(\frac{1}{32}\right)^{3/5} + \sqrt{16}\right](0.1) + \left[32^{2/5} + \frac{32}{2\sqrt{16}}\right](0.3) = 2.88.$$

The change increases the value of f by approximately 2.88. ❑

Example 2 Use a differential to estimate $\sqrt{27}\,\sqrt[3]{1021}$.

SOLUTION We know $\sqrt{25}$ and $\sqrt[3]{1000}$. We need an estimate for the increase of

$$f(x, y) = \sqrt{x}\,\sqrt[3]{y} = x^{1/2}y^{1/3}$$

from $x = 25$, $y = 1000$ to $x = 27$, $y = 1021$. The differential is

$$df = \tfrac{1}{2}x^{-1/2}y^{1/3}\Delta x + \tfrac{1}{3}x^{1/2}y^{-2/3}\Delta y.$$

With $x = 25$, $y = 1000$, $\Delta x = 2$, $\Delta y = 21$, df becomes

$$(\tfrac{1}{2}\cdot 25^{-1/2}\cdot 1000^{1/3})\,2 + (\tfrac{1}{3}\cdot 25^{1/2}\cdot 1000^{-2/3})\,21 = 2.35.$$

The change increases the value of the function by about 2.35. It follows that

$$\sqrt{27}\sqrt[3]{1021} \cong \sqrt{25}\sqrt[3]{1000} + 2.35 = 52.35.$$

(Our calculator gives $\sqrt{27}\sqrt[3]{1021} \cong 52.323$.) ❑

Example 3 Estimate by a differential the change in the volume of the frustum of a right circular cone if the upper radius r is decreased from 3 to 2.7 centimeters, the base radius R is increased from 8 to 8.1 centimeters, and the height h is increased from 6 to 6.3 centimeters.

SOLUTION Since $V(r, R, h) = \frac{1}{3}\pi h(R^2 + Rr + r^2)$, we have

$$dV = \tfrac{1}{3}\pi h(R + 2r)\Delta r + \tfrac{1}{3}\pi h(2R + r)\Delta R + \tfrac{1}{3}\pi(R^2 + Rr + r^2)\Delta h.$$

At $r = 3$, $R = 8$, $h = 6$, $\Delta r = -0.3$, $\Delta R = 0.1$, and $\Delta h = 0.3$,

$$dV = (28\pi)(-0.3) + (38\pi)(0.1) + \tfrac{1}{3}(97\pi)(0.3) = 5.1\pi \cong 16.02.$$

According to our differential estimate, the volume increases by about 16 cubic centimeters. ❑

EXERCISES 16.8

Exercises 1–12. Find the differential df.

1. $f(x, y) = x^3y - x^2y^2$.

2. $f(x, y, z) = xy + yz + xz$.

3. $f(x, y) = x\cos y - y\cos x$.

4. $f(x, y, z) = x^2y\,e^{2z}$.

5. $f(x, y, z) = x - y\tan z$.

6. $f(x, y) = (x - y)\ln(x + y)$.

7. $f(x, y, z) = \dfrac{xy}{x^2 + y^2 + z^2}$.

8. $f(x, y) = \ln(x^2 + y^2) + x\,e^{xy}$.

9. $f(x, y) = \sin(x + y) + \sin(x - y)$.

10. $f(x, y) = x\ln\left[\dfrac{1 + y}{1 - y}\right]$.

11. $f(x, y, z) = y^2e^{xz} + x\ln z$.

12. $f(x, y) = xy\,e^{-(x^2+y^2)}$.

13. Calculate Δu and du for $u = x^2 - 3xy + 2y^2$ at $x = 2$, $y = -3$, $\Delta x = -0.3$, $\Delta y = 0.2$.

14. Calculate du for $u = (x + y)\sqrt{x - y}$ at $x = 6$, $y = 2$, $\Delta x = \frac{1}{4}$, $\Delta y = -\frac{1}{2}$.

15. Calculate Δu and du for $u = x^2z - 2yz^2 + 3xyz$ at $x = 2$, $y = 1$, $z = 3$, $\Delta x = 0.1$, $\Delta y = 0.3$, $\Delta z = -0.2$.

16. Calculate du for

$$u = \frac{xy}{\sqrt{x^2 + y^2 + z^2}}$$

at $x = 1, y = 3, z = -2, \Delta x = \frac{1}{2}, \Delta y = \frac{1}{4}, \Delta z = -\frac{1}{4}$.

Exercises 17–20. Use differentials to find the approximate value.

17. $\sqrt{125\sqrt[4]{17}}$.

18. $(1 - \sqrt{10})(1 + \sqrt{24})$.

19. $\sin \frac{6}{7}\pi \cos \frac{1}{5}\pi$.

20. $\sqrt{8} \tan \frac{5}{16}\pi$.

Exercises 21–24. Use differentials to approximate the value of f at the point P.

21. $f(x, y) = x^2 e^{xy}$; $P(2.9, 0.01)$.

22. $f(x, y, z) = x^2 y \cos \pi z$; $P(2.12, 2.29, 3.02)$.

23. $f(x, y, z) = x \arctan yz$; $P(2.94, 1.1, 0.92)$.

24. $f(x, y) = \sqrt{x^2 + y^2}$; $P(3.06, 3.88)$.

25. Given that $z = (x - y)(x + y)^{-1}$, use dz to find the approximate change in z if x is increased from 4 to $4\frac{1}{10}$ and y is increased from 2 to $2\frac{1}{10}$. What is the exact change?

26. Estimate by a differential the change in the volume of a right circular cylinder if the height is increased from 12 to 12.2 inches and the radius is decreased from 8 to 7.7 inches.

27. Estimate the change in the total surface area for the cylinder of Exercise 26.

28. Use a differential to estimate the change in $T = x^2 \cos \pi z - y^2 \sin \pi z$ from $x = 2, y = 2, z = 2$ to $x = 2.1, y = 1.9, z = 2.2$.

29. Estimate the surface area of a closed rectangular box of the following dimensions: length 9.98 inches, width 5.88 inches, height 4.08 inches.

30. Estimate the volume of a right circular cone of base radius 7.2 centimeters and height 10.15 centimeters.

31. The dimensions of a closed rectangular box change from length 12, width 8, height 6 to length 12.02, width 7.95, height 6.03.

(a) Use a differential to approximate the change in volume.

(b) Calculate the exact change in volume.

32. Use the dimensions of the rectangular box of Exercise 31.

(a) Approximate the change in the surface area using a differential.

(b) Calculate the exact change in the surface area.

33. The function $T(x, y, z) = 100 - x^2 - y^2 - z^2 + 2xyz$ is defined at all points in space. Use a differential to approximate the difference between $T(1, 3, 4)$ and $T(1.15, 2.90, 4.10)$.

34. A closed rectangular box 4 feet long, 2 feet wide, 3 feet high is covered by a coat of paint $\frac{1}{16}$ inch thick. Estimate by a differential the amount of paint on the box.

35. The radius of a right circular cylinder of height h is increased from r to $r + \Delta r$.

(a) Determine the exact change in h that will keep the volume constant. Then estimate this change in h by using a differential.

(b) Determine the exact change in h that will keep the total surface area constant. Then estimate this change in h by using a differential.

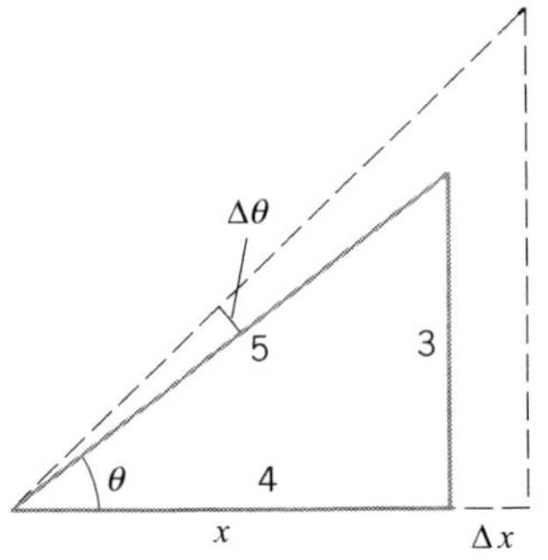

36. The figure shows a right triangle.

(a) Estimate by a differential the change in the area of the triangle if x is increased to $x + \Delta x$ and θ is increased to $\theta + \Delta\theta$.

(b) What is the actual change?

(c) Suppose that x and θ change by the same amount; that is, suppose $\Delta x = \Delta\theta$. Is the area more sensitive to the change in x or the change in θ?

37. The figure shows an isosceles triangle of area $A = \frac{1}{2}x^2 \sin\theta$.

(a) Estimate by a differential the change in the area of the triangle if x is increased to $x + \Delta x$ and θ is increased to $\theta + \Delta\theta$.

(b) Suppose that x and θ change by the same amount: $\Delta x = \Delta\theta$. Is the area more affected by the change in x or the change in θ?

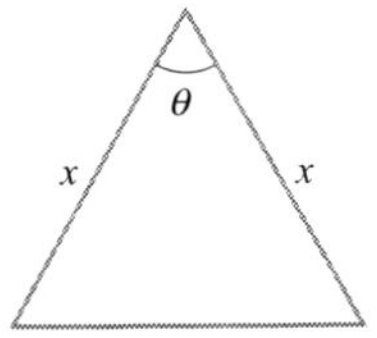

38. A closed rectangular box is measured to be 5 feet long, 3 feet wide, 3.5 feet high. Assume that each measurement is accurate within $\frac{1}{12}$ inch. Estimate by a differential the largest possible error in the calculated value (a) of the volume of the box, (b) of the surface area of the box.

39. The specific gravity s of a solid is given by the formula $s = A(A - W)^{-1}$ where A is the weight of the solid in air and W is the weight of the object in water. Given that A is measured to be 9 pounds (within a tolerance of 0.01 pounds) and W is measured to be 5 pounds (within a tolerance of 0.02 pounds), estimate by a differential the largest possible error in the calculated value of s.

40. We return to the notion of specific gravity as introduced in Exercise 39. Suppose that A and W are measured within the same tolerance; that is, suppose that $\Delta A = \Delta W$. Is s more sensitive to an error in the measurement of A or to an error in the measurement of W?

16.9 RECONSTRUCTING A FUNCTION FROM ITS GRADIENT

This section has three parts. In Part 1 we show how to find $f(x, y)$ given its gradient

$$\nabla f(x, y) = \frac{\partial f}{\partial x}(x, y)\,\mathbf{i} + \frac{\partial f}{\partial y}(x, y)\,\mathbf{j}.$$

In Part 2 we show that, although all gradients $\nabla f(x, y)$ are expressions of the form

$$P(x, y)\,\mathbf{i} + Q(x, y)\,\mathbf{j}$$

(set $P = \partial f/\partial x$ and $Q = \partial f/\partial y$), not all such expressions are gradients. In Part 3 we tackle the problem of recognizing which expressions $P(x, y)\,\mathbf{i} + Q(x, y)\,\mathbf{j}$ are actually gradients.

Part 1

Example 1 Find f given that $\nabla f(x, y) = (4x^3y^3 - 3x^2)\,\mathbf{i} + (3x^4y^2 + \cos 2y)\,\mathbf{j}$.

SOLUTION The first partial derivatives of f are

$$\frac{\partial f}{\partial x}(x, y) = 4x^3y^3 - 3x^2, \qquad \frac{\partial f}{\partial y}(x, y) = 3x^4y^2 + \cos 2y.$$

Integrating $\partial f/\partial x$ with respect to x, treating y as a constant, we find that

$$(*) \qquad f(x, y) = x^4y^3 - x^3 + \phi(y)$$

where ϕ is an unknown function of y. Here $\phi(y)$, being independent of x, acts as the constant of integration. Differentiation with respect to y gives

$$\frac{\partial f}{\partial y}(x, y) = 3x^4y^2 + \phi'(y).$$

Equating the two expressions for $\partial f/\partial y$, we have

$$3x^4y^2 + \phi'(y) = 3x^4y^2 + \cos 2y.$$

This implies that

$$\phi'(y) = \cos 2y \qquad \text{and therefore} \qquad \phi(y) = \tfrac{1}{2}\sin 2y + C. \quad (C \text{ an arbitrary constant})$$

By $(*)$,

$$f(x, y) = x^4y^3 - x^3 + \tfrac{1}{2}\sin 2y + C$$

where C is an arbitrary constant. ❑

Remark In Example 1 we began by integrating $\partial f/\partial x$ with respect to x. We can begin by integrating $\partial f/\partial y$ with respect to y.

$$\frac{\partial f}{\partial y}(x, y) = 3x^4y^2 + \cos 2y \qquad \text{gives} \qquad f(x, y) = x^4y^3 + \tfrac{1}{2}\sin 2y + \psi(x)$$

where ψ is an unknown function of x. Differentiating with respect to x, we have

$$\frac{\partial f}{\partial x}(x, y) = 4x^3y^3 + \psi'(x).$$

Equating the two expressions for $\partial f/\partial x$, we see that

$$4x^3y^3 + \psi'(x) = 4x^3y^3 - 3x^2$$
$$\psi'(x) = -3x^2$$
$$\psi(x) = -x^3 + C$$

and consequently

$$f(x, y) = x^4y^3 + \tfrac{1}{2}\sin 2y - x^3 + C.$$

Changing the order of two terms, we have

$$f(x, y) = x^4y^3 - x^3 + \tfrac{1}{2}\sin 2y + C,$$

the answer we had before. ❑

You can regard the function

$$f(x, y) = x^4y^3 - x^3 + \tfrac{1}{2}\sin 2y + C$$

as the *general solution* of the vector differential equation

$$\nabla f(x, y) = (4x^3y^2 - 3x^2)\,\mathbf{i} + (3x^4y^2 + \cos 2y)\,\mathbf{j}.$$

Each *particular solution* can be obtained by assigning a particular value to the constant C.

Example 2 Find f given that

$$\nabla f(x, y) = \left(\sqrt{y} - \frac{y}{2\sqrt{x}} + 2x\right)\mathbf{i} + \left(\frac{x}{2\sqrt{y}} - \sqrt{x} + 1\right)\mathbf{j}.$$

SOLUTION Here

$$\frac{\partial f}{\partial x}(x, y) = \sqrt{y} - \frac{y}{2\sqrt{x}} + 2x, \qquad \frac{\partial f}{\partial y}(x, y) = \frac{x}{2\sqrt{y}} - \sqrt{x} + 1.$$

Integrating $\partial f/\partial x$ with respect to x, we have

$$f(x, y) = x\sqrt{y} - y\sqrt{x} + x^2 + \phi(y)$$

with $\phi(y)$ independent of x. Differentiation with respect to y gives

$$\frac{\partial f}{\partial y}(x, y) = \frac{x}{2\sqrt{y}} - \sqrt{x} + \phi'(y).$$

The two equations for $\partial f/\partial y$ can be reconciled only by having

$$\phi'(y) = 1 \quad \text{and thus} \quad \phi(y) = y + C.$$

This means that

$$f(x, y) = x\sqrt{y} - y\sqrt{x} + x^2 + y + C. \quad ❑$$

Part 2

The next example shows that not all linear combinations $P(x, y)\,\mathbf{i} + Q(x, y)\,\mathbf{j}$ are gradients.

Example 3 We show that $y\,\mathbf{i} - x\,\mathbf{j}$ is not a gradient.

SOLUTION Suppose on the contrary that it is a gradient. Then there exists a function f such that

$$\nabla f(x, y) = y\,\mathbf{i} - x\,\mathbf{j}.$$

This implies that

$$\frac{\partial f}{\partial x}(x, y) = y, \qquad \frac{\partial f}{\partial y}(x, y) = -x \qquad \text{and} \qquad \frac{\partial^2 f}{\partial y\,\partial x}(x, y) = 1, \qquad \frac{\partial^2 f}{\partial x\,\partial y}(x, y) = -1.$$

Since the four partials are continuous, we can conclude from (15.6.5) that

$$\frac{\partial^2 f}{\partial y \partial x}(x, y) = \frac{\partial^2 f}{\partial x \partial y}(x, y).$$

But by looking at our results, we see that in this case

$$\frac{\partial^2 f}{\partial y \partial x}(x, y) \neq \frac{\partial^2 f}{\partial x \partial y}(x, y).$$

The assumption that $y\,\mathbf{i} - x\,\mathbf{j}$ is a gradient has led to a contradiction. We can conclude that $y\,\mathbf{i} - x\,\mathbf{j}$ is not a gradient. ❑

Part 3

We come now to the problem of recognizing which linear combinations

$$P(x, y)\,\mathbf{i} + Q(x, y)\,\mathbf{j}$$

are actually gradients. But first we need to review some ideas and establish some terminology.

As indicated earlier (Section 16.3), an open set (in the plane or in three-space) is said to be *connected* if each pair of points of the set can be joined by a polygonal path that lies entirely within the set. An open connected set will be called an *open region*. A curve

$$C : \mathbf{r} = \mathbf{r}(t), \qquad t \in [a, b]$$

is said to be *closed* if it begins and ends at the same point:

$$\mathbf{r}(a) = \mathbf{r}(b).$$

It is said to be *simple* if it does not intersect itself:

$$a < t_1 < t_2 < b \qquad \text{implies} \qquad \mathbf{r}(t_1) \neq \mathbf{r}(t_2).$$

These notions are illustrated in Figure 16.9.1.

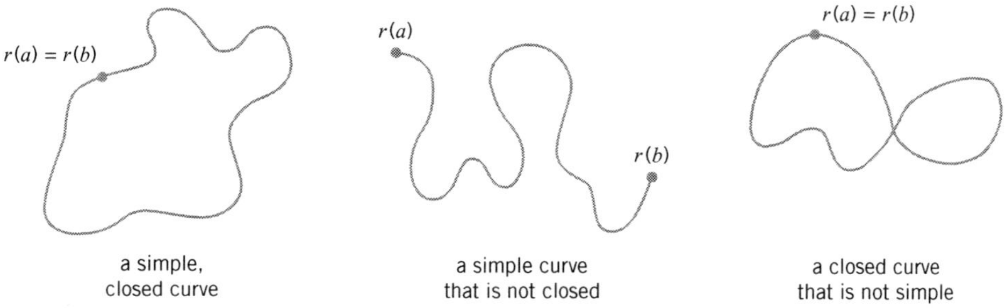

Figure 16.9.1

As is intuitively clear (Figure 16.9.2), a simple closed curve in the plane separates the plane into two disjoint open connected sets: a bounded inner region consisting of all points surrounded by the curve and an unbounded outer region consisting of all points not surrounded by the curve.

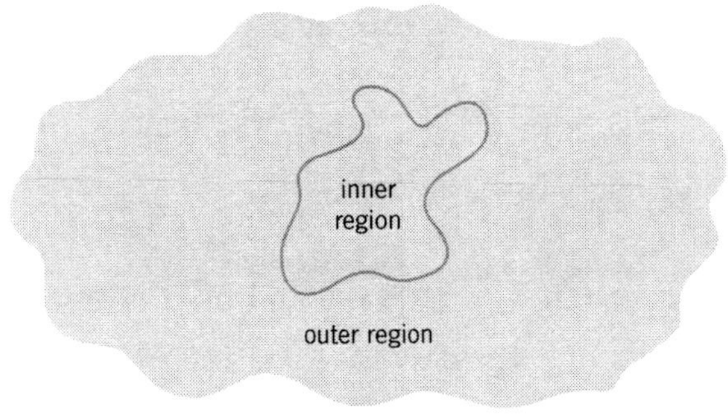

Figure 16.9.2

Finally, we come to a notion we will need in our work with gradients:

(16.9.1) Let Ω be an open region of the plane. Ω is said to be *simply connected* if, for every simple closed curve C in Ω, the inner region of C is contained in Ω.

The first two regions in Figure 16.9.3 are simply connected. The annular region is not simply connected; the annular region contains the simple closed curve drawn there, but it does not contain all of the inner region of that curve.

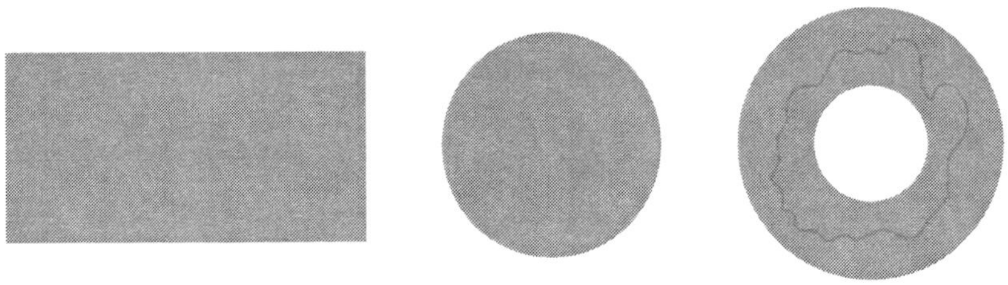

Figure 16.9.3

THEOREM 16.9.2

Let P and Q be functions of two variables, each continuously differentiable on a simply connected open region Ω. The linear combination $P(x, y)\mathbf{i} + Q(x, y)\mathbf{j}$ is a gradient on Ω iff

$$\frac{\partial P}{\partial y}(x, y) = \frac{\partial Q}{\partial x}(x, y) \qquad \text{for all } (x, y) \in \Omega.$$

A complete proof of this theorem for a general region Ω is complicated. We will prove the result under the additional assumption that Ω has the form of an open rectangle with sides parallel to the coordinate axes.

Suppose that $P(x, y)\mathbf{i} + Q(x, y)\mathbf{j}$ is a gradient on this open rectangle Ω, say,

$$\nabla f(x, y) = P(x, y)\mathbf{i} + Q(x, y)\mathbf{j}.$$

Since

$$\nabla f(x, y) = \frac{\partial f}{\partial x}(x, y)\,\mathbf{i} + \frac{\partial f}{\partial y}(x, y)\,\mathbf{j},$$

we have

$$P = \frac{\partial f}{\partial x} \qquad \text{and} \qquad Q = \frac{\partial f}{\partial y}.$$

Since P and Q have continuous first partials, f has continuous second partials. Thus, according to (15.6.5), the mixed partials are equal and we have

$$\frac{\partial P}{\partial y} = \frac{\partial^2 f}{\partial y \partial x} = \frac{\partial^2 f}{\partial x \partial y} = \frac{\partial Q}{\partial x}.$$

Conversely, suppose that

$$\frac{\partial P}{\partial y}(x, y) = \frac{\partial Q}{\partial x}(x, y) \qquad \text{for all} \qquad (x, y) \in \Omega.$$

We must show that $P(x, y)\,\mathbf{i} + Q(x, y)\,\mathbf{j}$ is a gradient on Ω. To do this, we choose a point (x_0, y_0) in Ω and form the function

$$f(x, y) = \int_{x_0}^{x} P(u, y_0)\,du + \int_{y_0}^{y} Q(x, v)\,dv, \qquad (x, y) \in \Omega.$$

[If you want to visualize f, you can refer to Figure 16.9.4. The function P is being integrated along the horizontal line segment that joins (x_0, y_0) to (x, y_0), and Q is being integrated along the vertical line segment that joins (x, y_0) to (x, y). Our assumptions on Ω guarantee that these line segments remain in Ω.]

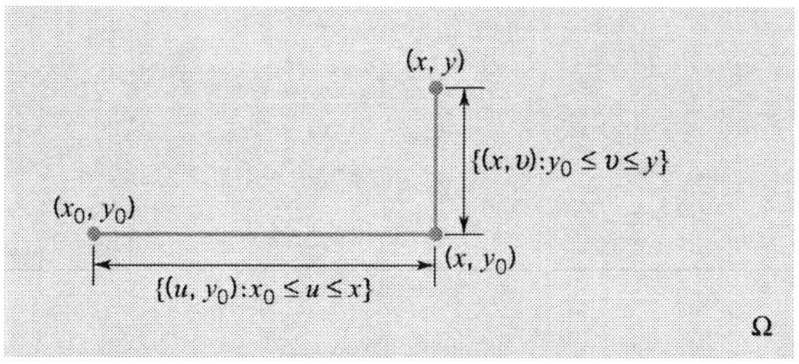

Figure 16.9.4

The first integral is independent of y. Hence

$$\frac{\partial f}{\partial y}(x, y) = \frac{\partial}{\partial y}\left(\int_{y_0}^{y} Q(x, v)\,dv\right) = Q(x, y).$$

The last equality holds because we are differentiating an integral with respect to its upper limit. (Theorem 5.3.5) Differentiating f with respect to x we have

$$\frac{\partial f}{\partial x}(x, y) = \frac{\partial}{\partial x}\left(\int_{x_0}^{x} P(u, y_0)\,du\right) + \frac{\partial}{\partial x}\left(\int_{y_0}^{y} Q(x, v)\,dv\right).$$

The first term is $P(x, y_0)$, since once again we are differentiating with respect to the upper limit. In the second term the variable x appears in the integrand. It can be shown that, since Q and $\partial Q/\partial x$ are continuous,

$$\frac{\partial}{\partial x}\left(\int_{y_0}^{y} Q(x, v)\,dv\right) = \int_{y_0}^{y} \frac{\partial Q}{\partial x}(x, v)\,dv.^{\dagger}$$

Anticipating this result, we have

$$\frac{\partial f}{\partial x}(x, y) = P(x, y_0) + \int_{y_0}^{y} \frac{\partial Q}{\partial x}(x, v)\,dv = P(x, y_0) + \int_{y_0}^{y} \frac{\partial P}{\partial y}(x, v)\,dv$$

explain ⟶

$$= P(x,y_0) + P(x,y) - P(x,y_0) = P(x,y).$$

We have now shown that

$$P(x, y) = \frac{\partial f}{\partial x}(x, y) \qquad \text{and} \qquad Q(x, y) = \frac{\partial f}{\partial y}(x, y) \qquad \text{for all } (x, y) \in \Omega.$$

It follows that $P(x, y)\,\mathbf{i} + Q(x, y)\,\mathbf{j}$ is the gradient of f on Ω. ❑

Example 4 The vector functions

$$\mathbf{F}(x, y) = 2x \sin y\,\mathbf{i} + x^2 \cos y\,\mathbf{j} \qquad \text{and} \qquad \mathbf{G}(x, y) = xy\,\mathbf{i} + \tfrac{1}{2}(x+1)^2 y^2\,\mathbf{j}$$

are both defined everywhere. The first vector function is the gradient of a function that is defined everywhere: for $P(x, y) = 2x \sin y$ and $Q(x, y) = x^2 \cos y$,

$$\frac{\partial P}{\partial y}(x, y) = 2x \cos y = \frac{\partial Q}{\partial x} \qquad \text{for all } (x, y).$$

As you can check, $F(x, y) = \nabla f(x, y)$ where $f(x, y) = x^2 \sin y + C$.

The vector function $\mathbf{G}$ is not a gradient: for $P(x, y) = xy$ and $Q(x, y) = \frac{1}{2}(x+1)^2 y^2$

$$\frac{\partial P}{\partial y}(x, y) = x \qquad \text{and} \qquad \frac{\partial Q}{\partial x}(x, y) = (x+1)y^2.$$

Thus,

$$\frac{\partial P}{\partial y}(x, y) \neq \frac{\partial Q}{\partial x}(x, y). \quad ❑$$

Example 5 The vector function $\mathbf{F}$ defined on the *punctured disk* $0 < x^2 + y^2 < 1$ by setting

$$\mathbf{F}(x, y) = \frac{y}{x^2 + y^2}\,\mathbf{i} - \frac{x}{x^2 + y^2}\,\mathbf{j}$$

satisfies the relation

$$\frac{\partial P}{\partial y}(x, y) = \frac{\partial Q}{\partial x}(x, y) \qquad \text{on the punctured disk.}$$

(Check this out.) Nevertheless, as you will see in Chapter 18,[††] $\mathbf{F}$ is not a gradient on that set. The punctured disk is not simply connected and therefore Theorem 16.9.2 does not apply. ❑

[†] The validity of this equality is the subject of Exercise 58, Section 17.3.

[††] Section 18.2, Exercise 28.

EXERCISES 16.9

Exercises 1–16. Determine whether or not the vector function is a gradient. If so, find all the functions with that gradient.

1. $xy^2\,\mathbf{i} + x^2y\,\mathbf{j}$.
2. $x\,\mathbf{i} + y\,\mathbf{j}$.
3. $y\,\mathbf{i} + x\,\mathbf{j}$.
4. $(x^2 + y)\,\mathbf{i} + (y^3 + x)\,\mathbf{j}$.
5. $(y^3 + x)\,\mathbf{i} + (x^2 + y)\,\mathbf{j}$.
6. $(y^2e^x - y)\,\mathbf{i} + (2ye^x - x)\,\mathbf{j}$.
7. $(\cos x - y\sin x)\,\mathbf{i} + \cos x\,\mathbf{j}$.
8. $(1 + e^y)\,\mathbf{i} + (x\,e^y + y^2)\,\mathbf{j}$.
9. $e^x\cos y^2\,\mathbf{i} - 2y\,e^x\sin y^2\,\mathbf{j}$.
10. $e^x\cos y\,\mathbf{i} + e^x\sin y\,\mathbf{j}$.
11. $ye^x(1 + x)\,\mathbf{i} + (x\,e^x - e^{-y})\,\mathbf{j}$.
12. $(e^x + 2xy)\,\mathbf{i} + (x^2 + \sin y)\,\mathbf{j}$.
13. $(x\,e^{xy} + x^2)\,\mathbf{i} + (y\,e^{xy} - 2y)\,\mathbf{j}$.
14. $(y\sin x + xy\cos x)\,\mathbf{i} + (x\sin x + 2y + 1)\,\mathbf{j}$.
15. $(1 + y^2 + xy^2)\,\mathbf{i} + (x^2y + y + 2xy + 1)\,\mathbf{j}$.
16. $\left[2\ln(3y) + \dfrac{1}{x}\right]\mathbf{i} + \left[\dfrac{2x}{y} + y^2\right]\mathbf{j}$.

Exercises 17–20. Find all functions with this gradient.

17. $\dfrac{x}{\sqrt{x^2 + y^2}}\,\mathbf{i} + \dfrac{y}{\sqrt{x^2 + y^2}}\,\mathbf{j}$.

18. $(x\tan y + \sec^2 x)\,\mathbf{i} + (\frac{1}{2}x^2\sec^2 y + \pi y)\,\mathbf{j}$.

19. $(x^2\arcsin y)\,\mathbf{i} + \left(\dfrac{x^3}{3\sqrt{1 - y^2}} - \ln y\right)\mathbf{j}$.

20. $\left(\dfrac{\arctan y}{\sqrt{1 - x^2}} + \dfrac{x}{y}\right)\mathbf{i} + \left(\dfrac{\arcsin x}{1 + y^2} - \dfrac{x^2}{2y^2} + 1\right)\mathbf{j}$.

21. Use a CAS to determine whether $\mathbf{F}$ is a gradient.
(a) $\mathbf{F}(x, y) = (y - 2xy + y^2)\,\mathbf{i} + (x - x^2 + 2xy)\,\mathbf{j}$.
(b) $\mathbf{F}(x, y) = [2xy^2\cos(x^2 - y)]\,\mathbf{i} + [-y^2\cos(x^2 - y) + 2y\sin(x^2 - y)]\,\mathbf{j}$.
(c) $\mathbf{F}(x, y) = 2xy(y - x)e^{-x^2y}\,\mathbf{i} + x^2(x - y)e^{-x^2y}\,\mathbf{j}$.

22. (a) Use a CAS to find f up to an additive constant.

$$\nabla f = [(1 - 2xy[x - y])e^{-x^2y}]\,\mathbf{i} + [-(1 + x^2[x - y])e^{-x^2y}]\,\mathbf{j}.$$

(b) Use a CAS to find f given that $f\left(\frac{\pi}{3}, \frac{\pi}{4}\right) = 6$ and

$$\nabla f = [\cos(x + y) + \sin(x - y)]\,\mathbf{i} + [\cos(x + y) - \sin(x - y)]\,\mathbf{j}.$$

23. Find the general solution of the differential equation $\nabla f(x, y) = f(x, y)\,\mathbf{i} + f(x, y)\,\mathbf{j}$.

24. Given that g and its first and second partials are everywhere continuous, find the general solution of the differential equation $\nabla f(x, y) = e^{g(x,y)}[g_x(x, y)\,\mathbf{i} + g_y(x, y)\,\mathbf{j}]$.

Theorem 16.9.2 has a three-dimensional analog. In particular we can show that, if P, Q, R are continuously differentiable on an open rectangular box S, then the vector function

$$P(x, y, z)\,\mathbf{i} + Q(x, y, z)\,\mathbf{j} + R(x, y, z)\,\mathbf{k}$$

is a gradient on S iff

$$\frac{\partial P}{\partial y} = \frac{\partial Q}{\partial x}, \quad \frac{\partial P}{\partial z} = \frac{\partial R}{\partial x}, \quad \frac{\partial Q}{\partial z} = \frac{\partial R}{\partial y} \quad \text{throughout S.}$$

25. (a) Verify that $2x\,\mathbf{i} + z\,\mathbf{j} + y\,\mathbf{k}$ is the gradient of a function f that is everywhere defined.
(b) Deduce from the relation $\partial f/\partial x = 2x$ that $f(x, y, z) = x^2 + g(y, z)$.
(c) Verify then that $\partial f/\partial y = z$ gives $g(y, z) = zy + h(z)$ and finally that $\partial f/\partial z = y$ gives $h(z) = C$.
(d) What is $f(x, y, z)$?

Exercises 26–30. Determine whether the vector function is a gradient and, if so, find all functions f with that gradient.

26. $yz\,\mathbf{i} + xz\,\mathbf{j} + xy\,\mathbf{k}$.
27. $(2x + y)\,\mathbf{i} + (2y + x + z)\,\mathbf{j} + (y - 2z)\,\mathbf{k}$.
28. $(2x\sin 2y\cos z)\,\mathbf{i} + (2x^2\cos 2y\cos z)\,\mathbf{j} - (x^2\sin 2y\sin z)\,\mathbf{k}$.
29. $(y^2z^3 + 1)\,\mathbf{i} + (2xyz^3 + y)\,\mathbf{j} + (3xy^2z^2 + 1)\,\mathbf{k}$.
30. $\left[\dfrac{y}{z} - e^z\right]\mathbf{i} + \left[\dfrac{x}{z} + 1\right]\mathbf{j} - \left[xe^z + \dfrac{xy}{z^2}\right]\mathbf{k}$.

31. Show that the gravitational force function

$$\mathbf{F}(\mathbf{r}) = -G\frac{mM}{r^3}\mathbf{r} \qquad (\mathbf{r} = x\,\mathbf{i} + y\,\mathbf{j} + z\,\mathbf{k})$$

is a gradient.

32. Verify that every vector function of the form

$$\mathbf{h}(\mathbf{r}) = kr^n\,\mathbf{r} \qquad (k \text{ constant},\ n \text{ an integer})$$

is a gradient.

CHAPTER 16 REVIEW EXERCISES

Exercises 1–6. Find the gradient.

1. $f(x, y) = 2x^2 - 4xy + y^3$.
2. $f(x, y) = \dfrac{xy}{x^2 + y^2}$.
3. $f(x, y) = e^{xy}\tan 2x$.
4. $f(x, y, z) = \ln\sqrt{x^2 + y^2 + z^2}$.
5. $f(x, y, z) = x^2e^{-yz}\sec z$.
6. $f(x, y, z) = e^{-3z}(\sin xy - \cos y)$.

Exercises 7–10. Find the directional derivative at the point P in the direction indicated.

7. $f(x, y) = x^2 - 2xy$ at $P(1, -2)$ in the direction of $\mathbf{i} + 2\mathbf{j}$.

8. $f(x, y) = xe^{xy}$ at $P(2, 0)$ in the direction of $\mathbf{i} + \sqrt{3}\,\mathbf{j}$.

9. $f(x, y, z) = xy^2 + 2yz + 3zx^2$ at $P(1, -2, 3)$ in the direction of $\frac{1}{3}\mathbf{i} - \frac{2}{3}\mathbf{j} + \frac{2}{3}\mathbf{k}$.

10. $f(x, y, z) = \ln(x^2 + y^2 + z^2)$ at $P(1, 2, 3)$ in the direction of $\mathbf{i} - \mathbf{j} + \mathbf{k}$.

11. Find the directional derivative of $f(x, y) = 3x^2 - 2xy^2 + 1$ at $(3, -2)$ toward the origin.

12. Find the directional derivative of $f(x, y, z) = xy^2z - 3xyz$ at $(1, -1, 2)$ in the direction of increasing t along the path $\mathbf{r}(t) = t\,\mathbf{i} + \cos\pi t\,\mathbf{j} + 2e^{t-1}\,\mathbf{k}$.

13. Find the directional derivatives of $f(x, y, z) = \sqrt{x^2 + y^2 + z^2}$ at $(3, -1, 4)$ in the directions parallel to the line

$$\frac{x-3}{4} = \frac{y+1}{-3} = z - 4.$$

14. Find the directional derivative of $f(x, y) = e^{2x}(\cos y - \sin y)$ at the point $(\frac{1}{2}, -\frac{1}{2}\pi)$ in the direction in which f increases most rapidly.

15. Find the directional derivative of $f(x, y, z) = \sin xyz$ at the point $(\frac{1}{2}, \frac{1}{3}, \pi)$ in the direction in which f decreases most rapidly.

16. The intensity of light in a neighborhood of the point (4, 3) is given by the function

$$I(x, y) = 10 - x^2 - 3y^2.$$

Find the path of a light-seeking particle that originates at the center of the neighborhood.

17. The temperature in a neighborhood of the origin is given by the function

$$T(x, y) = 100 + e^{-x}\cos y.$$

Find the path of a heat-fleeing particle that originates at the origin.

18. Determine the path of steepest descent along the surface $z = 4x^2 + y^2$ from each of the following points: (a) $(1, 1, 5)$; (b) $(1, -2, 8)$.

Exercises 19–20. Find the unit vector in the direction in which f increases most rapidly at P and give the rate of the change of f in that direction.

19. $f(x, y) = e^x \arctan y$; $P(0, 1)$.

20. $f(x, y, z) = \dfrac{x - z}{y + z}$; $P(-1, 1, 3)$.

Exercises 21–23. Find the rate of change of f with respect to t along the curve.

21. $f(x, y) = 2x^2 - 3y^3$; $\mathbf{r}(t) = \sqrt{t}\,\mathbf{i} + e^{2t}\,\mathbf{j}$.

22. $f(x, y) = \sin x + \cos xy$; $\mathbf{r}(t) = t^2\,\mathbf{i} + \mathbf{j}$.

23. $f(x, y, z) = \dfrac{x}{y} - \dfrac{z}{x}$; $\mathbf{r}(t) = \sin t\,\mathbf{i} + \cos t\,\mathbf{j} + \tan t\,\mathbf{k}$.

Exercises 24–26. Find du/dt.

24. $u(x, y) = \arctan xy$; $x = \tan t,\ y = e^{2t}$.

25. $u(x, y) = 3xy^2 - x^2$; $x = t^2 + 2t,\ y = 3t$.

26. $u(x, y, z) = \dfrac{1}{\sqrt{x^2 + y^2 + z^2}}$; $x = \cos t,\ y = \sin t,\ z = t$.

27. A triangle has sides x and y, and included angle θ. Given that x and y increase at the rate of 2 inches per second but the area of the triangle is kept constant, at what rate is θ changing when $x = 4$ inches, $y = 5$ inches, and $\theta = \pi/3$ radians?

28. View the trunk of a tree as a right circular cylinder. Suppose that a certain tree grows in such a manner that the radius increases at the rate of 4 centimeters per year and the height increases at the rate of 1.5 meters per year. At what rate is the volume of the trunk changing when the radius is 12 centimeters and the height is 10 meters?

29. Assume that $u = u(x, y)$ is differentiable, and set $x = s + t$, $y = s - t$. Show that

$$\left(\frac{\partial u}{\partial x}\right)^2 - \left(\frac{\partial u}{\partial y}\right)^2 = \frac{\partial u}{\partial s}\frac{\partial u}{\partial t}.$$

30. Assume that $u = u(x, y)$ has continuous second partials. Show that if $x = e^s\cos t$ and $y = e^s \sin t$, then

$$\frac{\partial^2 u}{\partial x^2} + \frac{\partial^2 u}{\partial y^2} = e^{-2s}\left[\frac{\partial^2 u}{\partial s^2} + \frac{\partial^2 u}{\partial t^2}\right].$$

Exercises 31–32. Find a normal vector and a tangent vector at the point P. Write scalar parametric equations for the tangent line and the normal line.

31. $x^3 - 3x^2y + y^2 = 5$; $P(1, -1)$.

32. $\cos\pi xy = -\frac{1}{2}$; $P(\frac{1}{3}, 2)$.

Exercises 33–36. Write an equation for the tangent plane and scalar parametric equations for the normal line at the point P.

33. $z = x^{1/2} + y^{1/2}$; $P(1, 1, 2)$.

34. $x^2 + y^2 + z^2 = 9$; $P(1, 2, -2)$.

35. $z^3 + xyz - 2 = 0$; $P(1, 1, 1)$.

36. $z = e^{3x}\sin 3y$; $P(0, \pi/6, 1)$.

37. Show that the hyperboloids $x^2 + 2y^2 - 4z^2 = 8$ and $4x^2 - y^2 + 2z^2 = 14$ are mutually perpendicular at the point $(2, 2, 1)$.

38. Show that every line normal to the sphere $x^2 + y^2 + z^2 = a^2$ passes through the origin.

Exercises 39–44. Find the stationary points and the local extreme values.

39. $f(x, y) = x^2y - 2xy + 2y^2 - 15y - 2$.

40. $f(x, y) = 3x^2 - 3xy^2 + y^3 + 3y^2$.

41. $f(x, y) = x^3 + y^3 - 18xy$.

42. $f(x, y) = x^3 + y^2 - 6x^2 + y - 4$.

43. $f(x, y) = (x - y)(1 - xy)$.

44. $f(x, y) = xy^2e^{-(x^2+y^2)/2}$.

Exercises 45–48. Find the absolute extreme values taken on by f on the set indicated.

45. $f(x, y) = x^2 + y^2 - 2x + 2y + 2$; $x^2 + y^2 \leq 4$.

46. $f(x, y) = 2x^2 - 4x + y^2 - 4y + 3$; the closed triangular region bounded by the lines $x = 0$, $y = 2$, $y = 2x$.

47. $f(x, y) = 4x^2 - xy + y^2 + y$; $x^2 + \frac{1}{4}y^2 \leq 1$.

48. $f(x, y) = x^4 + 2y^3$; $x^2 + y^2 \leq 1$.

49. Find the point of the plane $3x + 2y - z = 5$ that is closest to the point $P(1, -2, 3)$. What is the distance from the point P to the plane?

50. Maximize $3x - 2y + z$ on the sphere $x^2 + y^2 + z^2 = 14$.

51. Find the maximum and minimum values of $f(x, y, z) = x + y - z$ on the ellipsoid

$$\frac{x^2}{4} + \frac{y^2}{4} + z^2 = 1.$$

52. Closed rectangular boxes 16 cubic feet in volume are to be constructed from three types of metal. The cost of the metal for the bottom of the box is \$0.50 per square foot, for the sides of the box \$0.25 per square foot, for the top \$0.10 per square foot. Find the dimensions that minimize cost of material.

Exercises 53–56. Find the differential df.

53. $f(x, y) = 3x^3 - 5x^2y^2 + 2x - y$.

54. $f(x, y) = y \tan x^2 - 2xy^2 + 3$.

55. $f(x, y, z) = \dfrac{xyz}{x + y + z}$.

56. $f(x, y, z) = e^{yz} - \ln(y^2 + xz)$.

Exercises 57–58. Use differentials to find the approximate value.

57. $e^{0.02}\sqrt{15.2 + (1.01)^3}$. **58.** $\sqrt[3]{64.5}\cos^2(28°)$.

59. A silo is in the shape of a right circular cylinder 22 feet high and 10 feet in diameter. The top and lateral surface are to be given a coat of paint 0.01 inches thick. Estimate by a differential the amount of paint required. Express your answer in gallons. (There are 231 cubic inches in a gallon.)

Exercises 60–63. Determine whether or not the vector function is a gradient. If so, find all the functions with that gradient.

60. $(6x^2y^2 - 8xy + 2x)\,\mathbf{i} + (4x^3y - 4x^2 - 8)\,\mathbf{j}$.

61. $(2xy + 3 - y\sin x)\,\mathbf{i} + (x^2 + 2y + 1 + \cos x)\,\mathbf{j}$.

62. $(xy^2 + 2y^2)\,\mathbf{i} + (2y^3 - x^2y + 2x)\,\mathbf{j}$.

63. $(e^y \sin z + 2x)\,\mathbf{i} + (xe^y \sin z - y^2)\,\mathbf{j} + xe^y \cos z\,\mathbf{k}$.

CHAPTER 17

DOUBLE AND TRIPLE INTEGRALS

We began with ordinary integrals

$$\int_a^b f(x)\,dx,$$

which, with $b > a$, we can write as

$$\int_{[a,b]} f(x)\,dx.$$

Here we will study double integrals

$$\iint_{\Omega} f(x, y)\,dx\,dy$$

where Ω is a region in the xy-plane and, a little later, triple integrals

$$\iiint_{T} f(x, y, z)\,dx\,dy\,dz$$

where T is a solid in three-dimensional space. Our first step is to introduce some new notation.

17.1 MULTIPLE-SIGMA NOTATION

In an ordinary sequence $a_1, a_2, \ldots,$ each term a_i is indexed by a single integer. The sum of all the a_i from $i = 1$ to $i = m$ is then denoted by

$$\sum_{i=1}^{m} a_i.$$

When two indices are involved, say,

$$a_{ij} = 2^i 5^j, \qquad a_{ij} = \frac{2i}{5+j}, \qquad a_{ij} = (1+i)^j,$$

we use double-sigma notation. By

(17.1.1)
$$\sum_{i=1}^{m}\sum_{j=1}^{n} a_{ij}$$

we mean *the sum of all the a_{ij} where i ranges from* 1 *to m and j ranges from* 1 *to n*. For example,

$$\sum_{i=1}^{3}\sum_{j=1}^{2} 2^i 5^j = 2\cdot 5 + 2\cdot 5^2 + 2^2\cdot 5 + 2^2\cdot 5^2 + 2^3\cdot 5 + 2^3\cdot 5^2 = 420.$$

Since addition is associative and commutative, we can add the terms of (17.1.1) in any order we choose. Usually we set

(17.1.2)
$$\sum_{i=1}^{m}\sum_{j=1}^{n} a_{ij} = \sum_{i=1}^{m}\left(\sum_{j=1}^{n} a_{ij}\right).$$

We can expand the expression on the right by expanding first with respect to i and then with respect to j:

$$\begin{aligned}\sum_{i=1}^{m}\left(\sum_{j=1}^{n} a_{ij}\right) &= \sum_{j=1}^{n} a_{1j} + \sum_{j=1}^{n} a_{2j} + \cdots + \sum_{j=1}^{n} a_{mj}\\ &= (a_{11}+a_{12}+\cdots+a_{1n}) + (a_{21}+a_{22}+\cdots+a_{2n}) +\\ &\quad \cdots + (a_{m1}+a_{m2}+\cdots+a_{mn}),\end{aligned}$$

or we can expand first with respect to j and then with respect to i:

$$\begin{aligned}\sum_{i=1}^{m}\left(\sum_{j=1}^{n} a_{ij}\right) &= \sum_{i=1}^{m}(a_{i1}+a_{i2}+\cdots+a_{in})\\ &= (a_{11}+a_{12}+\cdots+a_{1n}) + (a_{21}+a_{22}+\cdots+a_{2n}) +\\ &\quad \cdots + (a_{m1}+a_{m2}+\cdots+a_{mn}).\end{aligned}$$

The result is the same.

For example, we can write

$$\begin{aligned}\sum_{i=1}^{3}\left(\sum_{j=1}^{2} a_{ij}\right) &= \sum_{j=1}^{2} a_{1j} + \sum_{j=1}^{2} a_{2j} + \sum_{j=1}^{2} a_{3j}\\ &= (a_{11}+a_{12}) + (a_{21}+a_{22}) + (a_{31}+a_{32}),\end{aligned}$$

or we can write

$$\sum_{i=1}^{3}\left(\sum_{j=1}^{2} a_{ij}\right) = \sum_{i=1}^{3}(a_{i1}+a_{i2}) = (a_{11}+a_{12}) + (a_{21}+a_{22}) + (a_{31}+a_{32}).$$

Since constants can be factored through single sums, they can also be factored through double sums:

(17.1.3)
$$\sum_{i=1}^{m}\sum_{j=1}^{n} \alpha a_{ij} = \alpha\sum_{i=1}^{m}\sum_{j=1}^{n} a_{ij}.$$

Also,

(17.1.4) $$\sum_{i=1}^{m}\sum_{j=1}^{n}(a_{ij}+b_{ij}) = \sum_{i=1}^{m}\sum_{j=1}^{n}a_{ij} + \sum_{i=1}^{m}\sum_{j=1}^{n}b_{ij}.$$

Double sums in which each term a_{ij} appears as a product $b_i c_j$ can be expressed as the product of two single sums:

(17.1.5) $$\sum_{i=1}^{m}\sum_{j=1}^{n}b_i c_j = \left(\sum_{i=1}^{m}b_i\right)\left(\sum_{j=1}^{n}c_j\right).$$

PROOF Set

$$B = \sum_{i=1}^{m}b_i, \quad C\sum_{j=1}^{n}c_j.$$

and note that

$$\sum_{i=1}^{m}\sum_{j=1}^{n}b_i c_i = \sum_{i=1}^{m}\left(\sum_{j=1}^{n}b_i c_j\right) \overset{\dagger}{=} \sum_{i=1}^{m}b_i\left(\sum_{j=1}^{n}c_j\right) = \sum_{i=1}^{m}b_i C$$

$$= C\sum_{i=1}^{m}b_i = CB = BC. \quad \square$$

For example,

$$\sum_{i=1}^{3}\sum_{j=1}^{2}2^i 5^j = \left(\sum_{i=1}^{3}2^i\right)\left(\sum_{j=1}^{2}5^j\right) = (2+2^2+2^3)(5+5^2) = (14)(30) = 420.$$

Triple-sigma notation is used when three indices are involved. The sum of all the a_{ijk} where i ranges from 1 to m, j from 1 to n, and k from 1 to q can be written

(17.1.6) $$\sum_{i=1}^{m}\sum_{j=1}^{n}\sum_{k=1}^{q}a_{ijk}.$$

Multiple sums appear in the following sections. We introduced them here so as to avoid lengthy asides later.

† Since b_i is independent of j, it can be factored through the j-summation.

EXERCISES 17.1

Exercises 1–4. Evaluate the sum.

1. $\sum_{i=1}^{3}\sum_{j=1}^{3}2^{i-1}3^{j+1}$.

2. $\sum_{i=1}^{4}\sum_{j=1}^{2}(1+i)^j$.

3. $\sum_{i=1}^{4}\sum_{j=1}^{3}(i^2+3i)(j-2)$.

4. $\sum_{i=1}^{3}\sum_{j=1}^{2}\sum_{k=1}^{3}\dfrac{2i}{k+j^2}$.

For Exercises 5–16, let

$P_1 = \{x_0, x_1, \ldots, x_m\}$ be a partition of $[a_1, a_2]$,
$P_2 = \{y_0, y_1, \ldots, y_n\}$ be a partition of $[b_1, b_2]$,
$P_3 = \{z_0, z_1, \ldots, z_q\}$ be a partition of $[c_1, c_2]$,

and let

$$\Delta x_i = x_i - x_{i-1}, \quad \Delta y_j = y_j - y_{j-1}, \quad \Delta z_k = z_k - z_{k-1}.$$

Exercises 5–16. Evaluate the sum.

5. $\sum_{i=1}^{m} \Delta x_i.$

6. $\sum_{j=1}^{n} \Delta y_j.$

7. $\sum_{i=1}^{m}\sum_{j=1}^{n} \Delta x_i \Delta y_j.$

8. $\sum_{j=1}^{n}\sum_{k=1}^{q} \Delta y_j \Delta z_k.$

9. $\sum_{i=1}^{m} (x_i + x_{i-1})\Delta x_i.$

10. $\sum_{j=1}^{n} \frac{1}{2}(y_j^2 + y_j y_{j-1} + y_{j-1}^2)\Delta y_j.$

11. $\sum_{i=1}^{m}\sum_{j=1}^{n} (x_i + x_{i-1})\Delta x_i \Delta y_j.$

12. $\sum_{i=1}^{m}\sum_{j=1}^{n} (y_j + y_{j-1})\Delta x_i \Delta y_j.$

13. $\sum_{i=1}^{m}\sum_{j=1}^{n} (2\Delta x_i - 3\Delta y_j).$

14. $\sum_{i=1}^{m}\sum_{j=1}^{n} (3\Delta x_i - 2\Delta y_j).$

15. $\sum_{i=1}^{m}\sum_{j=1}^{n}\sum_{k=1}^{q} \Delta x_i \Delta y_j \Delta z_k.$

16. $\sum_{i=1}^{m}\sum_{j=1}^{n}\sum_{k=1}^{q} (x_i + x_{i-1})\Delta x_i \Delta y_j \Delta z_k.$

17. Evaluate

$$\sum_{i=1}^{m}\sum_{j=1}^{n}\sum_{k=1}^{n} \delta_{ijk}\, a_{ijk} \quad \text{where} \quad \delta_{ijk} = \begin{cases} 1, & \text{if } i = j = k \\ 0, & \text{otherwise.} \end{cases}$$

18. Show that any sum written in double-sigma notation can be expressed in single-sigma notation.

■ 17.2 DOUBLE INTEGRALS

The Double Integral over a Rectangle

We start with a function f continuous on a rectangle

$$R : a \le x \le b, \quad c \le y \le d. \qquad \text{(Figure 17.2.1)}$$

We want to define the double integral of f over R:

$$\iint_R f(x, y)\, dx\, dy.$$

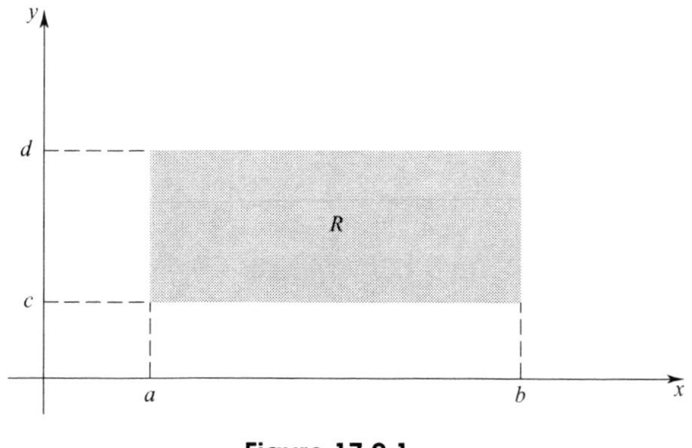

Figure 17.2.1

To define the integral

$$\int_a^b f(x)\, dx,$$

we introduced some auxiliary notions: partition P of $[a, b]$, upper sum $U_f(P)$, and lower sum $L_f(P)$. We then defined

$$\int_a^b f(x)\, dx$$

as the unique number I that satisfies the inequality

$$L_f(P) \le I \le U_f(P) \qquad \text{for all partitions } P \text{ of } [a, b].$$

We will follow exactly the same procedure to define the double integral

$$\iint_R f(x, y)\,dx\,dy.$$

First we explain what we mean by a partition of the rectangle R. We begin with a partition

$$P_1 = \{x_0, x_1, \ldots, x_m\} \qquad \text{of} \qquad [a, b].$$

and a partition

$$P_2 = \{y_0, y_1, \ldots, y_n\} \qquad \text{of} \qquad [c, d].$$

The set

$$P = P_1 \times P_2 = \{(x_i, y_j) : x_i \in P_1, y_j \in P_2\}^\dagger$$

is called a *partition of R*. (See Figure 17.2.2.) The set P consists of all the grid points (x_i, y_j).

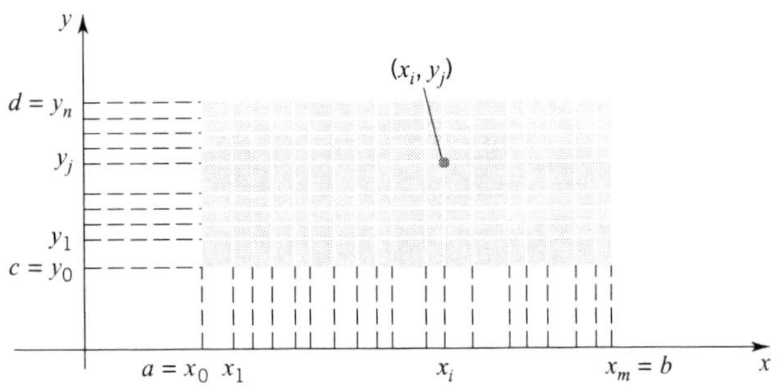

Figure 17.2.2

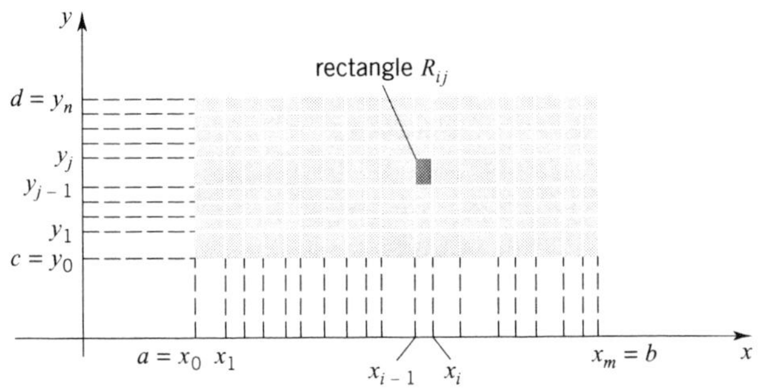

Figure 17.2.3

Using the partition P, we break up R into $m \times n$ nonoverlapping rectangles

$$R_{ij}: \quad x_{i-1} \le x \le x_i, y_{j-1} \le y \le y_j, \qquad \text{(Figure 17.2.3)}$$

where $1 \le i \le m$, $1 \le j \le n$. On each rectangle R_{ij}, the function f takes on a maximum value M_{ij} and a minimum value m_{ij}. We know this because f is continuous and R_{ij} is closed and bounded. (Section 16.6) The sum of all the products

$$M_{ij}(\text{area of } R_{ij}) = M_{ij}(x_i - x_{i-1})(y_j - y_{j-1}) = M_{ij}\,\Delta x_i\,\Delta y_j$$

is called the *P upper sum* for f:

(17.2.1)
$$U_f(P) = \sum_{i=1}^{m}\sum_{j=1}^{n} M_{ij}(\text{area of } R_{ij}) = \sum_{i=1}^{m}\sum_{j=1}^{n} M_{ij}\,\Delta x_i\,\Delta y_j.$$

The sum of all the products

$$m_{ij}(\text{area of } R_{ij}) = m_{ij}(x_i - x_{i-1})(y_j - y_{j-1}) = m_{ij}\,\Delta x_i\,\Delta y_j$$

† $P_1 \times P_2$ is called the *Cartesian product* of P_1 and P_2. More generally, for arbitrary sets A and B, $A \times B$ is, by definition, the set of all ordered pairs (a, b) with $a \in A$ and $b \in B$.

is called the P *lower sum* for f:

(17.2.2) $$L_f(P) = \sum_{i=1}^{m}\sum_{j=1}^{n} m_{ij}(\text{area of } R_{ij}) = \sum_{i=1}^{m}\sum_{j=1}^{n} m_{ij}\,\Delta x_i\,\Delta y_j.$$

Example 1 Set $f(x, y) = x + y - 2$ on the rectangle

$$R: \quad 1 \le x \le 4, \ 1 \le y \le 3.$$

As a partition of $[1, 4]$, take

$$P_1 = \{1, 2, 3, 4\}$$

and as a partition of $[1, 3]$, take

$$P_2 = \{1, \tfrac{3}{2}, 3\}.$$

The partition $P = P_1 \times P_2$ breaks up the initial rectangle into the six rectangles marked in Figure 17.2.4. On each rectangle R_{ij}, the function f takes on its maximum value M_{ij} at the point (x_i, y_j), the corner farthest from the origin:

$$M_{ij} = f(x_i, y_j) = x_i + y_j - 2.$$

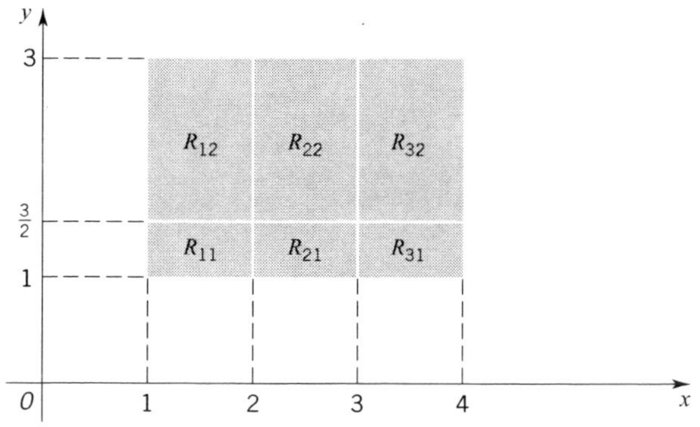

Figure 17.2.4

Therefore

$$\begin{aligned} U_f(P) &= M_{11}(\text{area of } R_{11}) + M_{12}(\text{area of } R_{12}) + M_{21}(\text{area of } R_{21}) \\ &\quad + M_{22}(\text{area of } R_{22}) + M_{31}(\text{area of } R_{31}) + M_{32}(\text{area of } R_{32}) \\ &= \tfrac{3}{2}(\tfrac{1}{2}) + 3(\tfrac{3}{2}) + \tfrac{5}{2}(\tfrac{1}{2}) + 4(\tfrac{3}{2}) + \tfrac{7}{2}(\tfrac{1}{2}) + 5(\tfrac{3}{2}) = \tfrac{87}{4}. \end{aligned}$$

On each rectangle R_{ij}, f takes on its minimum value m_{ij} at the point (x_{i-1}, y_{j-1}), the corner closest to the origin:

$$m_{ij} = f(x_{i-1}, y_{j-1}) = x_{i-1} + y_{j-1} - 2.$$

Therefore

$$\begin{aligned} L_f(P) &= m_{11}(\text{area of } R_{11}) + m_{12}(\text{area of } R_{12}) + m_{21}(\text{area of } R_{21}) \\ &\quad + m_{22}(\text{area of } R_{22}) + m_{31}(\text{area of } R_{31}) + m_{32}(\text{area of } R_{32}) \\ &= 0(\tfrac{1}{2}) + \tfrac{1}{2}(\tfrac{3}{2}) + 1(\tfrac{1}{2}) + \tfrac{3}{2}(\tfrac{3}{2}) + 2(\tfrac{1}{2}) + \tfrac{5}{2}(\tfrac{3}{2}) = \tfrac{33}{4}. \end{aligned}$$ ❑

We return to the general situation. As in the one-variable case, it can be shown that if f is continuous, then there exists one and only one number I that satisfies the inequality

$$L_f(P) \le I \le U_f(P) \qquad \text{for all partitions } P \text{ of } R.$$

DEFINITION 17.2.3 THE DOUBLE INTEGRAL OVER A RECTANGLE *R*

Let f be continuous on a closed rectangle R. The unique number I that satisfies the inequality

$$L_f(P) \le I \le U_f(P) \qquad \text{for all partitions } P \text{ of } R$$

is called the *double integral* of f over R, and is denoted by

$$\iint_R f(x, y)\,dx\,dy.^\dagger$$

The Double Integral as a Volume

If f is continuous and nonnegative on the rectangle R, the equation

$$z = f(x, y)$$

represents a surface that lies above R. (See Figure 17.2.5.) In this case the double integral

$$\iint_R f(x, y)\,dx\,dy$$

gives the volume of the solid that is bounded below by R and bounded above by the surface $z = f(x, y)$.

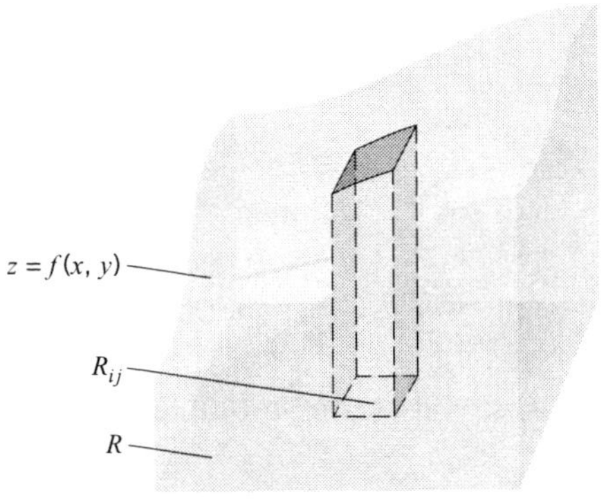

Figure 17.2.5

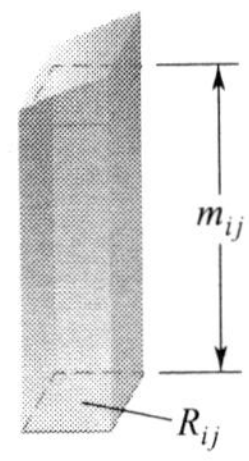

Figure 17.2.6

To see this, consider a partition P of R. P breaks up R into subrectangles R_{ij} and thus the entire solid T into parts T_{ij}. Since T_{ij} contains a rectangular solid with base R_{ij} and height m_{ij} (Figure 17.2.6), we must have

$$m_{ij}\ (\text{area of } R_{ij}) \le \text{volume of } T_{ij}.$$

†The double integral $\iint_R f(x, y)\,dx\,dy$ can be written $\iint_R f(x, y)\,dA$.

Since T_{ij} is contained in a rectangular solid with base R_{ij} and height M_{ij} (Figure 17.2.7), we must have

$$\text{volume of } T_{ij} \leq M_{ij} \text{ (area of } R_{ij}).$$

In short, for each pair of indices i and j, we must have

$$m_{ij}(\text{area of } R_{ij}) \leq \text{ volume of } T_{ij} \leq M_{ij} \text{ (area of } R_{ij}).$$

Adding up these inequalities, we can conclude that

$$L_f(P) \leq \text{ volume of } T \leq U_f(P).$$

Since P is arbitrary, the volume of T must be the double integral:

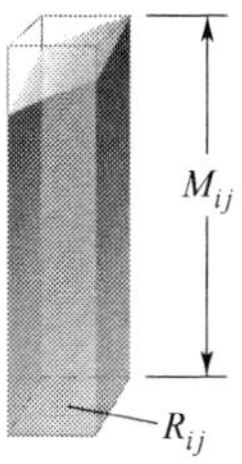

Figure 17.2.7

(17.2.4)
$$\text{volume of } T = \iint_R f(x, y)\, dx\, dy.$$

The double integral

$$\iint_R 1\, dx\, dy = \iint_R dx\, dy$$

gives the volume of a solid of constant height 1 erected over R. In square units this is just the area of R:

(17.2.5)
$$\text{area of } R = \iint_R dx\, dy.$$

Some Calculations

Double integrals are generally calculated by techniques that we will take up later. It is possible, however, to evaluate simple double integrals directly from the definition.

Example 2 Evaluate

$$\iint_R \alpha\, dx\, dy$$

where α is a constant and R is the rectangle

$$R: \quad a \leq x \leq b, \ c \leq y \leq d.$$

SOLUTION Here $f(x, y) = \alpha$ for all $(x, y) \in R$.

We begin with $P_1 = \{x_0, x_1, \ldots, x_m\}$ as an arbitrary partition of the interval $[a, b]$ and $P_2 = \{y_0, y_1, \ldots, y_n\}$ as an arbitrary partition of $[c, d]$. This gives

$$P = P_1 \times P_2 = \{(x_i, y_j) : x_i \in P_1, y_j \in P_2\}$$

as an arbitrary partition of R. On each rectangle R_{ij}, f has constant value α. Therefore we have $M_{ij} = \alpha$ and $m_{ij} = \alpha$ throughout. Thus

$$U_f(P) = \sum_{i=1}^{m} \sum_{j=1}^{n} \alpha \Delta x_i \Delta y_j = \alpha \left(\sum_{i=1}^{m} \Delta x_i \right) \left(\sum_{j=1}^{n} \Delta y_j \right) = \alpha(b - a)(d - c).$$

Similarly,

$$L_f(P) = \alpha(b-a)(d-c).$$

The inequality

$$L_f(P) \le I \le U_f(P) \qquad \text{for all } P$$

forces

$$\alpha(b-a)(d-c) \le I \le \alpha(b-a)(d-c).$$

The only number I that can satisfy this inequality is

$$I = \alpha(b-a)(d-c).$$

Therefore

$$\iint\limits_R f(x, y)\, dx\, dy = \alpha(b-a)(d-c). \quad ❑$$

Remark If $\alpha > 0$.

$$\iint\limits_R \alpha\, dx\, dy = \alpha(b-a)(d-c)$$

gives the volume of the rectangular solid of constant height α erected over the rectangle R. (Figure 17.2.8.) ❑

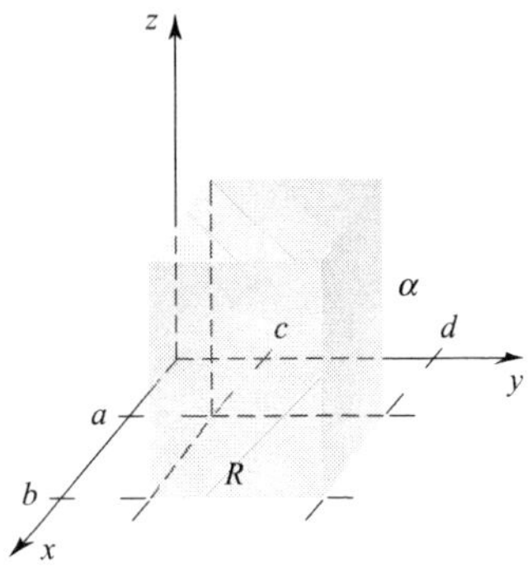

Figure 17.2.8

Example 3 Evaluate

$$\iint\limits_R (x + y - 2)\, dx\, dy,$$

where R is the rectangle: $1 \le x \le 4$, $1 \le y \le 3$.

SOLUTION With $P_1 = \{x_0, x_1, \ldots, x_m\}$ as an arbitrary partition of the interval $[1, 4]$ and $P_2 = \{y_0, y_1, \ldots, y_n\}$ as an arbitrary partition of $[1, 3]$, we have

$$P_1 \times P_2 = \{(x_i, y_j) : x_i \in P_1, y_j \in P_2\}$$

as an arbitrary partition of R. On each rectangle $R_{ij} : x_{i-1} \le x \le x_i, y_{j-1} \le y \le y_j$, the function

$$f(x, y) = x + y - 2$$

has a maximum $M_{ij} = x_i + y_j - 2$ and a minimum $m_{ij} = x_{i-1} + y_{j-1} - 2$. Thus

$$L_f(P) = \sum_{i=1}^{m}\sum_{j=1}^{n}(x_{i-1} + y_{j-1} - 2)\Delta x_i \Delta y_i$$

$$U_f(P) = \sum_{i=1}^{m}\sum_{j=1}^{n}(x_i + y_j - 2)\Delta x_i \Delta y_j.$$

For each pair of indices i and j

$$x_{i-1} + y_{j-1} - 2 \le \tfrac{1}{2}(x_i + x_{i-1}) + \tfrac{1}{2}(y_j + y_{j-1}) - 2 \le x_i + y_j - 2. \qquad \text{(explain)}$$

Adding up these inequalities, we have

$$L_f(P) \le \sum_{i=1}^{m}\sum_{j=1}^{n}[\tfrac{1}{2}(x_i + x_{i-1}) + \tfrac{1}{2}(y_j + y_{j-1}) - 2]\Delta x_i \Delta y_j \le U_f(P).$$

The double sum in the middle can be written

$$\sum_{i=1}^{m}\sum_{j=1}^{n}\tfrac{1}{2}(x_i + x_{i-1})\Delta x_i \Delta y_j + \sum_{i=1}^{m}\sum_{j=1}^{n}\tfrac{1}{2}(y_j + y_{j-1})\Delta x_i \Delta y_j - \sum_{i=1}^{m}\sum_{j=1}^{n}2\Delta x_i \Delta y_j.$$

Since $\Delta x_i = x_i - x_{i-1}$, the first of these double sums reduces to

$$\begin{aligned}\sum_{i=1}^{m}\sum_{j=1}^{n}\tfrac{1}{2}(x_i^2 - x_{i-1}^2)\Delta y_j &= \tfrac{1}{2}\left(\sum_{i=1}^{m}(x_i^2 - x_{i-1}^2)\right)\left(\sum_{j=1}^{n}\Delta y_j\right)\\ &= \tfrac{1}{2}(16-1)(3-1) = 15.\end{aligned}$$

The second double sum reduces to

$$\begin{aligned}\sum_{i=1}^{m}\sum_{j=1}^{n}\tfrac{1}{2}\Delta x_i(y_j^2 - y_{j-1}^2) &= \tfrac{1}{2}\left(\sum_{i=1}^{m}\Delta x_i\right)\left(\sum_{j=1}^{n}(y_j^2 - y_{j-1}^2)\right)\\ &= \tfrac{1}{2}(4-1)(9-1)(9-1) = 12.\end{aligned}$$

The third double sum reduces to

$$-\sum_{i=1}^{m}\sum_{j=1}^{n}2\Delta x_i \Delta y_j = -2\left(\sum_{i=1}^{m}\Delta x_i\right)\left(\sum_{j=1}^{n}\Delta y_j\right) = -2(4-1)(3-1) = -12.$$

The sum of these three numbers, $15 + 12 - 12 = 15$, satisfies the inequality

$$L_f(P) \le 15 \le U_f(P) \qquad \text{for arbitrary } P.$$

Therefore

$$\iint_R (x + y - 2)\,dx\,dy = 15. \quad ❑$$

Remark Since $f(x, y) = x + y - 2$ is nonnegative on the rectangle R, the double integral gives the volume of the prism bounded above by the plane $z = x + y - 2$ and below by the rectangle R. See Figure 17.2.9. ❑

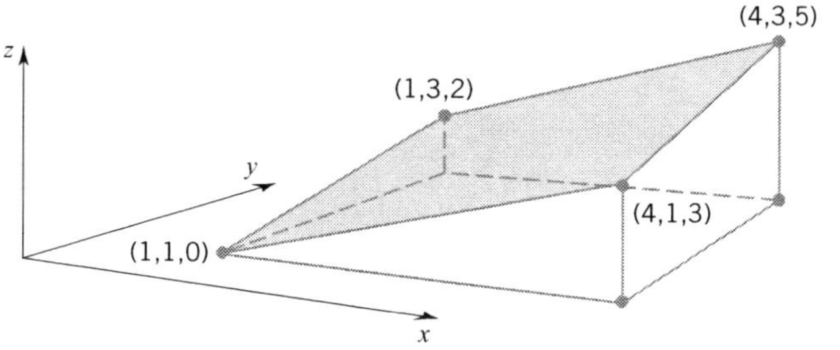

Figure 17.2.9

The Double Integral over a Region

We start with a closed and bounded set Ω in the xy-plane such as that depicted in Figure 17.2.10. We assume that Ω is a *basic region*; that is, we assume that Ω is a connected set (see Section 16.3) the total boundary of which consists of a finite number of continuous arcs of the form $y = \phi(x)$, $x = \psi(y)$. See, for example, Figure 17.2.11.

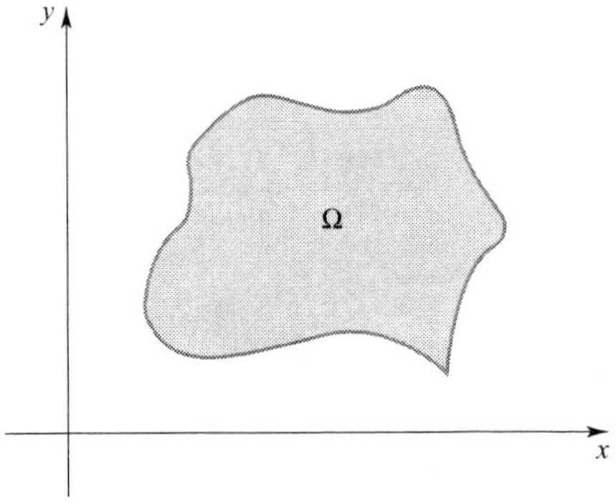

Figure 17.2.10

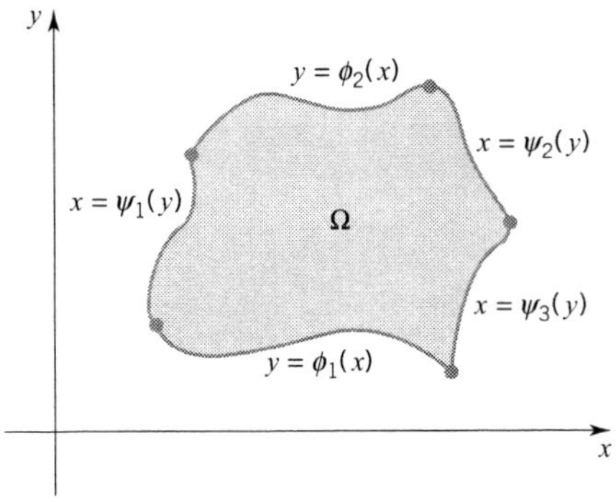

Figure 17.2.11

Now let f be a function continuous on Ω. We want to define the double integral

$$\iint_{\Omega} f(x, y)\, dx\, dy.$$

To do this, we enclose Ω by a rectangle R with sides parallel to the coordinate axes as in Figure 17.2.12. We extend f to all of R by setting f equal to 0 outside Ω. This extended function, which we continue to call f, is bounded on R, and it is continuous on all of R except possibly at the boundary of Ω. In spite of these possible discontinuities, it can be shown that f is still integrable on R; that is, there still exists a unique number I such that

$$L_f(P) \le I \le U_f(P) \qquad \text{for all partitions } P \text{ of } R.$$

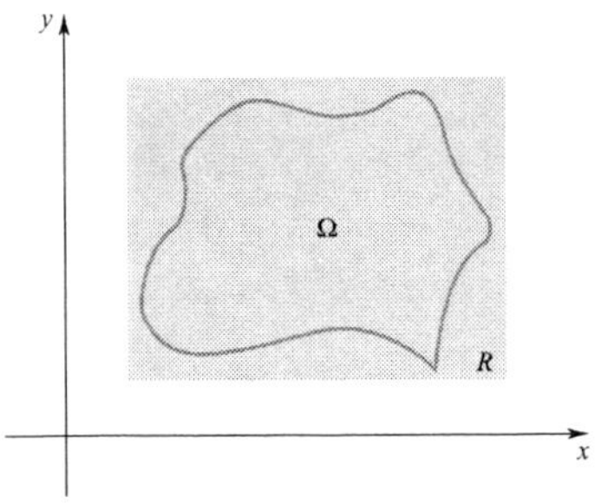

Figure 17.2.12

(We will not attempt to prove this.) This number I is by definition the double integral

$$\iint_{R} f(x, y)\, dx\, dy.$$

As you have probably guessed by now, we define the double integral over Ω by setting

(17.2.6)
$$\iint_{\Omega} f(x, y)\, dx\, dy = \iint_{R} f(x, y)\, dx\, dy.$$

Figure 17.2.13

If f is continuous and nonnegative over Ω, the extended f is nonnegative on all of R. (Figure 17.2.13.) The double integral gives the volume of the solid bounded above by the surface $z = f(x, y)$ and bounded below by the rectangle R. But since the surface has height 0 outside of Ω, the volume outside Ω is 0. It follows that

$$\iint_{\Omega} f(x, y)\, dx\, dy$$

gives the volume of the solid T bounded above by $z = f(x, y)$ and bounded below by Ω:

(17.2.7)
$$\text{volume of } T = \iint_{\Omega} f(x, y)\,dx\,dy.$$

The double integral

$$\iint_{\Omega} 1\,dx\,dy = \iint_{\Omega} dx\,dy$$

gives the volume of a solid of constant height 1 erected over Ω. In square units this is the area of Ω:

(17.2.8)
$$\text{area of } \Omega = \iint_{\Omega} dx\,dy.$$

Below we list four elementary properties of the double integral. They are all analogous to what you saw in the one-variable case. As specified above, the Ω referred to is a basic region. The functions f and g are assumed to be continuous on Ω.

I. *Linearity*: The double integral of a linear combination is the linear combination of the double integrals:

$$\iint_{\Omega} [\alpha f(x, y) + \beta g(x, y)]\,dx\,dy = \alpha \iint_{\Omega} f(x, y)\,dx\,dy + \beta \iint_{\Omega} g(x, y)\,dx\,dy.$$

II. *Order*: The double integral preserves order:

$$\text{if } f \geq 0 \text{ on } \Omega, \text{ then } \iint_{\Omega} f(x, y)\,dx\,dy \geq 0;$$

$$\text{if } f \leq g \text{ on } \Omega, \text{ then } \iint_{\Omega} f(x, y)\,dx\,dy \leq \iint_{\Omega} g(x, y)\,dx\,dy.$$

III. *Additivity*: If Ω is broken up into a finite number of nonoverlapping basic regions $\Omega_1, \ldots, \Omega_n$, then

$$\iint_{\Omega} f(x, y)\,dx\,dy = \iint_{\Omega_1} f(x, y)\,dx\,dy + \cdots + \iint_{\Omega_n} f(x, y)\,dx\,dy.$$

See, for example, Figure 17.2.14.

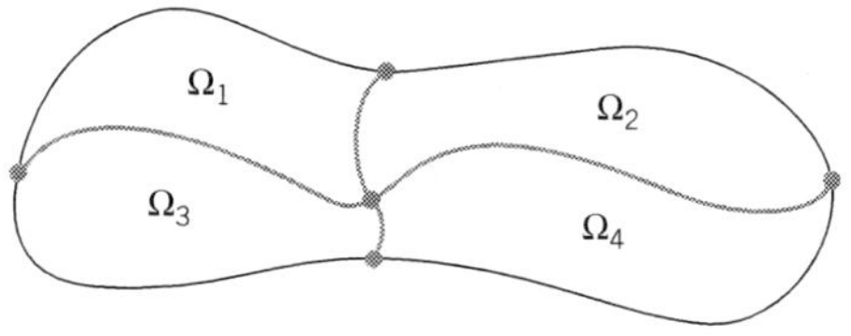

$$\iint_{\Omega} f(x, y)\,dxdy = \iint_{\Omega_1} f(x, y)\,dxdy + \iint_{\Omega_2} f(x, y)\,dxdy + \iint_{\Omega_3} f(x, y)\,dxdy + \iint_{\Omega_4} f(x, y)\,dxdy$$

Figure 17.2.14

IV. *Mean-value condition*: There is a point (x_0, y_0) in Ω for which

$$\iint_\Omega f(x, y)\, dx\, dy = f(x_0, y_0) \cdot (\text{area of } \Omega).$$

We call $f(x_0, y_0)$ *the average value of f on* Ω.

The notion of average introduced in Property IV enables us to write

(17.2.9)
$$\iint_\Omega f(x, y)\, dx\, dy = \begin{pmatrix} \text{the average value} \\ \text{of } f \text{ on } \Omega \end{pmatrix} \cdot (\text{area of } \Omega).$$

This is a powerful, intuitive way of viewing the double integral. We will capitalize on it as we go on.

THEOREM 17.2.10 THE MEAN-VALUE THEOREM FOR DOUBLE INTEGRALS

Let f and g be functions continuous on a basic region Ω. If g is nonnegative on Ω, then there exists a point (x_0, y_0) in Ω for which

$$\iint_\Omega f(x, y) g(x, y)\, dx\, dy = f(x_0, y_0) \iint_\Omega g(x, y)\, dx\, dy.^\dagger$$

We call $f(x_0, y_0)$ the *g-weighted average of f on* Ω.

PROOF Since f is continuous on Ω, and Ω is closed and bounded, we know that f takes on a minimum value m and a maximum value M. Since g is nonnegative on Ω,

$$mg(x, y) \le f(x, y)\, g(x, y) \le Mg(x, y) \qquad \text{for all } (x, y) \text{ in } \Omega.$$

Therefore (by Property II)

$$\iint_\Omega m\, g(x, y)\, dx\, dy \le \iint_\Omega f(x, y)\, g(x, y)\, dx\, dy \le \iint_\Omega M\, g(x, y)\, dx\, dy,$$

and (by Property I)

$$(*) \qquad m \iint_\Omega g(x, y)\, dx\, dy \le \iint_\Omega f(x, y) g(x, y)\, dx\, dy \le M \iint_\Omega g(x, y)\, dx\, dy.$$

We know that $\iint_\Omega g(x, y)\, dx\, dy \ge 0$ (again, by Property II). If $\iint_\Omega g(x, y)\, dx\, dy = 0$, then by $(*)$ we have $\iint_\Omega f(x, y) g(x, y)\, dx\, dy = 0$ and the theorem holds for all choices of (x_0, y_0) in Ω. If $\iint_\Omega g(x, y)\, dx\, dy > 0$, then

$$m \le \frac{\iint_\Omega f(x, y)\, g(x, y)\, dx\, dy}{\iint_\Omega g(x, y)\, dx\, dy} \le M,$$

†Property IV is this equation with g constantly 1.

and, by the intermediate-value theorem (given in the supplement to Section 16.3), there exists a point (x_0, y_0) in Ω for which

$$f(x_0, y_0) = \frac{\iint_\Omega f(x, y)g(x, y)\,dx\,dy}{\iint_\Omega g(x, y)\,dx\,dy}.$$

Obviously then,

$$f(x_0, y_0)\iint_\Omega g(x, y)\,dx\,dy = \iint_\Omega f(x, y)g(x, y)\,dx\,dy. \quad \square$$

EXERCISES 17.2

For Exercises 1–3, take

$$f(x, y) = x + 2y \quad \text{on} \quad R: 0 \le x \le 2,\ 0 \le y \le 1.$$

and let P be the partition $P = P_1 \times P_2$.

1. Find $L_f(P)$ and $U_f(P)$ given that $P_1 = \{0, 1, \frac{3}{2}, 2\}$ and $P_2 = \{0, \frac{1}{2}, 1\}$.

2. Find $L_f(P)$ and $U_f(P)$ given that $P_1 = \{0, \frac{1}{2}, 1, \frac{3}{2}, 2\}$ and $P_2 = \{0, \frac{1}{4}, \frac{1}{2}, \frac{3}{4}, 1\}$.

3. (a) Find $L_f(P)$ and $U_f(P)$ given that

$$P_1 = \{x_0, x_1, \ldots, x_m\}$$

is an arbitrary partition of $[0, 2]$, and

$$P_2 = \{y_0, y_1, \ldots, y_n\}$$

is an arbitary partition of $[0, 1]$.

(b) Use your answer to part (a) to evaluate the double integral

$$\iint_R (x + 2y)\,dx\,dy$$

and give a geometric interpretation to your answer.

For Exercises 4–6, take

$$f(x, y) = x - y \quad \text{on} \quad R: 0 \le x \le 1, 0 \le y \le 1.$$

and let P be the partition $P = P_1 \times P_2$.

4. Find $L_f(P)$ and $U_f(P)$ given that $P_1 = \{0, \frac{1}{2}, \frac{3}{4}, 1\}$ and that $P_2 = \{0, \frac{1}{2}, 1\}$.

5. Find $L_f(P)$ and $U_f(P)$ given that $P_1 = \{0, \frac{1}{4}, \frac{1}{2}, \frac{3}{4}, 1\}$ and $P_2 = \{0, \frac{1}{3}, \frac{2}{3}, 1\}$.

6. (a) Find $L_f(P)$ and $U_f(P)$ given that

$$P_1 = \{x_0, x_1, \ldots, x_m\} \quad \text{and} \quad P_2 = \{y_0, y_1, \ldots, y_n\}$$

are arbitrary partitions of $[0, 1]$.

(b) Use your answers in part (a) to evaluate the double integral

$$\iint_R (x - y)\,dx\,dy.$$

For Exercises 7–9, take $R: 0 \le x \le b, 0 \le y \le d$ and let $P = P_1 \times P_2$ where

$$P_1 = \{x_0, x_1, \ldots, x_m\} \quad \text{is an arbitrary partition of } [0, b],$$
$$P_2 = \{y_0, y_1, \ldots, y_n\} \quad \text{is an arbitrary partition of } [0, d].$$

7. (a) Find $L_f(P)$ and $U_f(P)$ for $f(x, y) = 4xy$.

(b) Calculate

$$\iint_R 4xy\,dx\,dy.$$

HINT: $4x_{i-1}y_{j-1} \le (x_i + x_{i-1})(y_j + y_{j-1}) \le 4x_iy_j$.

8. (a) Find $L_f(P)$ and $U_f(P)$ for $f(x, y) = 3(x^2 + y^2)$.

(b) Calculate

$$\iint_R 3(x^2 + y^2)\,dx\,dy.$$

HINT: If $0 \le s \le t$, then $3s^2 \le t^2 + ts + s^2 \le 3t^2$.

9. (a) Find $L_f(P)$ and $U_f(P)$ for $f(x, y) = 3(x^2 - y^2)$.

(b) Calculate

$$\iint_R 3(x^2 - y^2)\,dx\,dy.$$

10. Let $f = f(x, y)$ be continuous on the rectangle R: $a \le x \le b, c \le y \le d$. Suppose that $L_f(P) = U_f(P)$ for some partition P of R. What can you conclude about f? What is

$$\iint_R f(x, y)\,dx\,dy?$$

11. Let $\phi = \phi(x)$ be continuous and nonnegative on the interval $[a, b]$ and set

$$\Omega = \{(x, y) : a \le x \le b, 0 \le y \le \phi(x)\}.$$

Compare

$$\iint_\Omega dx\,dy \quad \text{to} \quad \int_a^b \phi(x)\,dx.$$

12. Begin with a function f that is continuous on a closed bounded region Ω. Now surround Ω by a rectangle R as in Figure 17.2.12 and extend f to all of R by defining f to be 0 outside of Ω. Explain how the extended f can fail to be continuous on the boundary of Ω although the original function f, being continuous on all of Ω, was continuous on the boundary of Ω.

13. Suppose that f is continuous on a disk Ω centered at (x_0, y_0) and assume that

$$\iint_R f(x, y)\,dx\,dy = 0$$

for every rectangle R contained in Ω. Show that $f(x_0, y_0) = 0$.

14. Calculate the average value of $f(x, y) = x + 2y$ on the rectangle $R: 0 \le x \le 2,\ 0 \le y \le 1$. HINT: See Exercise 3.

15. Calculate the average value of $f(x, y) = 4xy$ on the rectangle $R: 0 \le x \le 2,\ 0 \le y \le 3$. HINT: See Exercise 7.

16. Calculate the average value of $f(x, y) = x^2 + y^2$ on the rectangle $R: 0 \le x \le b, 0 \le y \le d$. HINT: See Exercise 8.

17. Let f be continuous on a closed bounded region Ω and let (x_0, y_0) be a point in the interior of Ω. Let D_r be the closed disk with center (x_0, y_0) and radius r. Show that

$$\lim_{r\to 0} \frac{1}{\pi r^2} \iint_{D_r} f(x, y)\,dx\,dy = f(x_0, y_0).$$

18. Let $f(x, y) = \sin(x + y)$ on $R: 0 \le x \le 1, 0 \le y \le 1$. Show that

$$0 \le \iint_R \sin(x + y)\,dx\,dy \le 1.$$

Exercises 19–21. These integrals represent the volumes of recognizable solids. Evaluate these integrals.

19. $\iint_\Omega \sqrt{4 - x^2 - y^2}\,dx\,dy$ where Ω is the quarter disk $x^2 + y^2 \le 4, x \ge 0, y \ge 0$.

20. $\iint_\Omega 8 - 4\sqrt{x^2 + y^2}\,dx\,dy$ where Ω is the disk $x^2 + y^2 \le 4$.

21. $\iint_\Omega (6 - 2x - 3y)\,dx\,dy$ where Ω is the triangular region bounded by the coordinate axes and the line $2x + 3y = 6$.

22. Set $f(x, y) = 3y^2 - 2x$ on the rectangle $R: 2 \le x \le 5$, $1 \le y \le 3$. Let P_1 be a regular partition of [2, 5] with $n = 100$ subintervals, let P_2 be a regular partition of [1, 3] with $m = 200$ subintervals, and let $P = P_1 \times P_2$.

(a) Use a CAS to find $L_f(P)$ and $U_f(P)$.

(b) Find $L_f(P)$ and $U_f(P)$ for several values of $n > 100, m > 200$.

(c) Estimate $\iint_R f(x, y)\,dx\,dy$.

■ 17.3 THE EVALUATION OF DOUBLE INTEGRALS BY REPEATED INTEGRALS

The Reduction Formulas

If an integral

$$\int_a^b f(x)\,dx$$

proves difficult to evaluate, it is not because of the interval $[a, b]$ but because of the integrand f. Difficulty in evaluating a double integral

$$\iint_\Omega f(x, y)\,dx\,dy$$

can come from two sources: from the integrand f or from the base region Ω. Even such a simple-looking integral as $\iint_\Omega 1\,dx\,dy$ is difficult to evaluate if Ω has a complicated structure.

In this section we introduce a technique for evaluating double integrals of continuous functions over regions of Type I or Type II as depicted in Figure 17.3.1. In each case the region Ω is a basic region and so we know that the double integral exists. The fundamental idea of this section is that double integrals over such regions can each be reduced to a pair of ordinary integrals.

Type I Region The *projection* of Ω onto the x-axis is a closed interval $[a, b]$ and Ω consists of all points (x, y) with

$$a \le x \le b \quad \text{and} \quad \phi_1(x) \le y \le \phi_2(x).$$

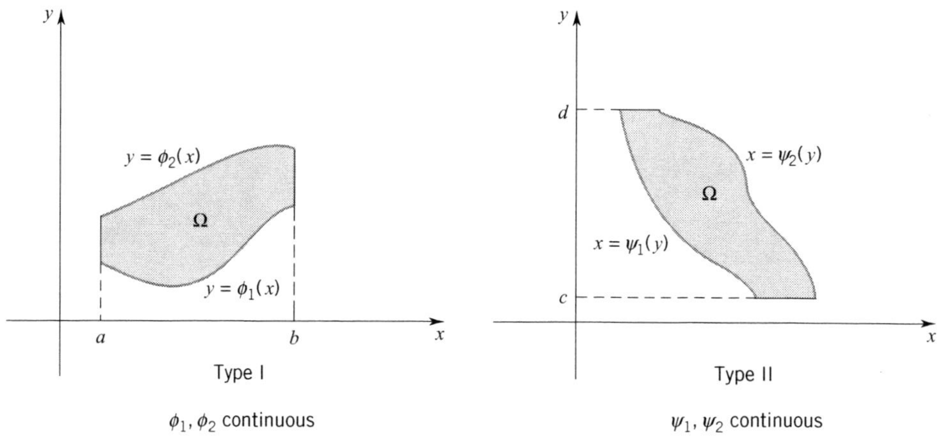

Figure 17.3.1

In this case

(17.3.1)
$$\iint_{\Omega} f(x, y)\,dx\,dy = \int_a^b \left(\int_{\phi_1(x)}^{\phi_2(x)} f(x, y)\,dy\right) dx.$$

Here we first calculate

$$\int_{\phi_1(x)}^{\phi_2(x)} f(x, y)\,dy$$

by integrating $f(x, y)$ with respect to y from $y = \phi_1(x)$ to $y = \phi_2(x)$. The resulting expression is a function of x alone, which we then integrate with respect to x from $x = a$ to $x = b$.

Type II Region The *projection* of Ω onto the y-axis is a closed interval $[c, d]$ and Ω consists of all points (x, y) with

$$c \le y \le d \qquad \text{and} \qquad \psi_1(y) \le x \le \psi_2(y).$$

In this case

(17.3.2)
$$\iint_{\Omega} f(x, y)\,dx\,dy = \int_c^d \left(\int_{\psi_1(y)}^{\psi_2(y)} f(x, y)\,dy\right) dy.$$

This time we first calculate

$$\int_{\psi_1(y)}^{\psi_2(y)} f(x, y)\,dx$$

by integrating $f(x, y)$ with respect to x from $x = \psi_1(y)$ to $x = \psi_2(y)$. The resulting expression is a function of y alone, which we can then integrate with respect to y from $y = c$ to $y = d$.

The integrals on the right-hand sides of (17.3.1) and (17.3.2) are called *repeated integrals*.

The Reduction Formulas Viewed Geometrically

Suppose that f is nonnegative and Ω is a region of Type I. The double integral over Ω gives the volume of the solid T bounded above by the surface $z = f(x, y)$ and bounded below by the region Ω:

$$(1) \qquad \iint_{\Omega} f(x, y)\,dx\,dy = \text{volume of } T. \qquad \text{(Figure 17.3.2)}$$

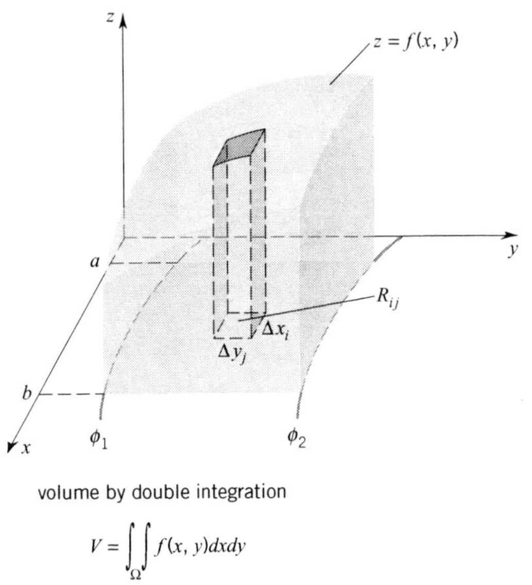

Figure 17.3.2

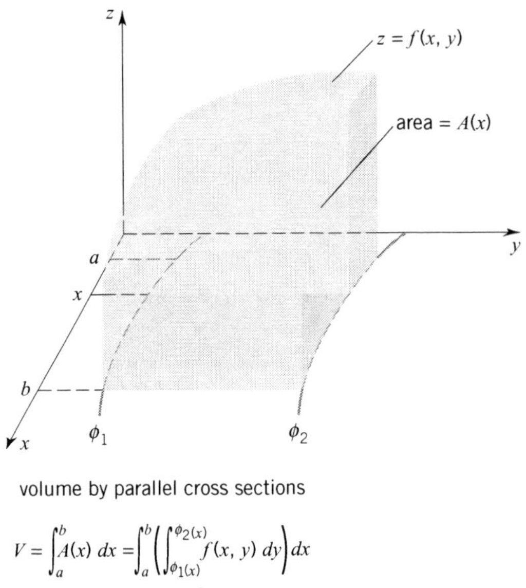

Figure 17.3.3

We can also calculate the volume of T by the method of parallel cross sections. (Section 6.2) As in Figure 17.3.3, let $A(x)$ be the area of the cross section which consists of all points of T which have first coordinate x. Then by (6.2.1),

$$\int_a^b A(x)\,dx = \text{volume of } T.$$

Since

$$A(x) = \int_{\phi_1(x)}^{\phi_2(x)} f(x, y)\,dy,$$

we have

$$(2) \qquad \int_a^b \left(\int_{\phi_1(x)}^{\phi_2(x)} f(x, y)\,dy\right) dx = \text{volume of } T.$$

Combining (1) with (2), we have the first reduction formula

$$\iint_{\Omega} f(x, y)\,dx\,dy = \int_a^b \left(\int_{\phi_1(x)}^{\phi_2(x)} f(x, y)\,dy\right) dx.$$

The other reduction formula can be obtained in a similar manner.

Remark Note that our argument was a very loose one and certainly not a proof. How do we know, for example, that the "volume" obtained by double integration is the same as the "volume" obtained by the method of parallel cross sections? Intuitively it seems evident, but actually it is quite difficult to prove. The result follows from what is known as Fubini's theorem.† ❑

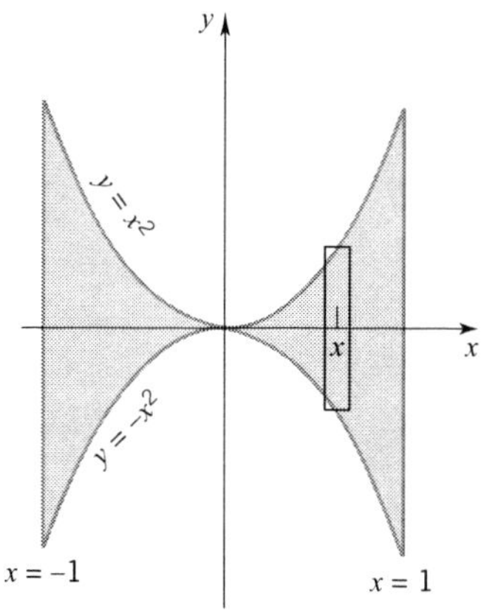

Figure 17.3.4

Computations

Example 1 Evaluate $\iint_\Omega (x^4 - 2y)\,dx\,dy$ with Ω as in Figure 17.3.4.

SOLUTION By projecting Ω onto the x-axis, we obtain the interval $[-1, 1]$. The region Ω consists of all points (x, y) with

$$-1 \le x \le 1 \qquad \text{and} \qquad -x^2 \le y \le x^2.$$

This is a region of Type I. By (17.3.1),

$$\begin{aligned}\iint_\Omega (x^4 - 2y)\,dx\,dy &= \int_{-1}^{1}\left(\int_{-x^2}^{x^2}[x^4 - 2y]\,dy\right)dx\\ &= \int_{-1}^{1}\left[x^4y - y^2\right]_{-x^2}^{x^2}dx\\ &= \int_{-1}^{1}\left[(x^6 - x^4) - (-x^6 - x^4)\right]dx\\ &= \int_{-1}^{1} 2x^6\,dx = \left[\tfrac{2}{7}x^7\right]_{-1}^{1} = \tfrac{4}{7}. \quad ❑\end{aligned}$$

Example 2 Evaluate $\iint_\Omega (xy - y^3)\,dx\,dy$ with Ω as in Figure 17.3.5.

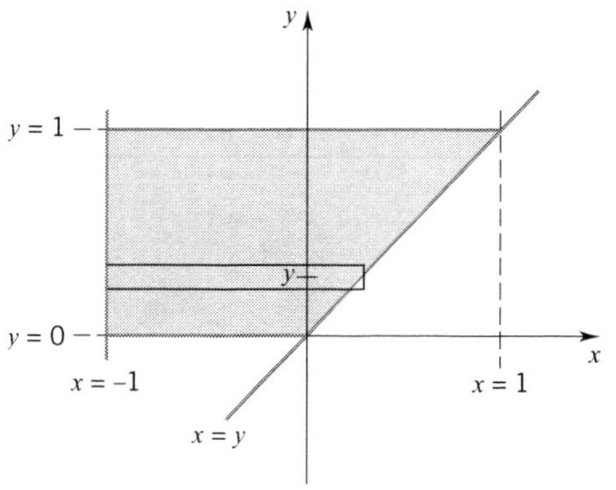

Figure 17.3.5

SOLUTION By projecting Ω onto the y-axis, we obtain the interval $[0, 1]$. The region Ω consists of all points (x, y) with

$$0 \le y \le 1 \qquad \text{and} \qquad -1 \le x \le y.$$

†After the Italian mathematician Guido Fubini (1879–1943).

This is a region of Type II. By (17.3.2),

$$\iint_{\Omega} (xy - y^3)\,dx\,dy = \int_0^1 \left(\int_{-1}^{y} (xy - y^3)\,dx \right) dy$$

$$= \int_0^1 \left[\tfrac{1}{2}x^2 y - xy^3 \right]_{-1}^{y} dy$$

$$= \int_0^1 \left[\left(\tfrac{1}{2}y^3 - y^4\right) - \left(\tfrac{1}{2}y + y^3\right) \right] dy$$

$$= \int_0^1 \left(-\tfrac{1}{2}y^3 - y^4 - \tfrac{1}{2}y \right) dy$$

$$= \left[-\tfrac{1}{8}y^4 - \tfrac{1}{5}y^5 - \tfrac{1}{4}y^2 \right]_0^1 = -\tfrac{23}{40}.$$

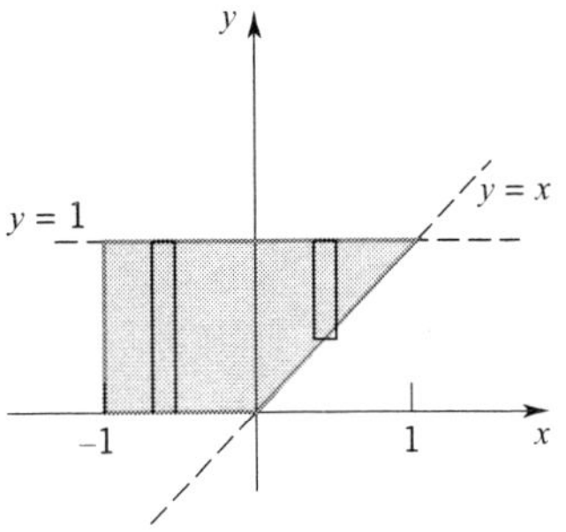

We can also project Ω onto the x-axis and express Ω as a region of Type I, but then the lower boundary is defined piecewise (see the figure) and the calculations are somewhat more complicated: setting

$$\phi(x) = \begin{cases} 0, & -1 \le x \le 0 \\ x, & 0 \le x \le 1, \end{cases}$$

we have Ω as the set of all points (x, y) with

$$-1 \le x \le 1 \qquad \text{and} \qquad \phi(x) \le y \le 1;$$

thus

$$\iint_{\Omega} (xy - y^3)\,dx\,dy = \int_{-1}^{1} \left(\int_{\phi(x)}^{1} (xy - y^3)\,dy \right) dx$$

$$= \int_{-1}^{0} \left(\int_{\phi(x)}^{1} (xy - y^3)\,dy \right) dx + \int_{0}^{1} \left(\int_{\phi(x)}^{1} (xy - y^3)\,dy \right) dx$$

$$= \int_{-1}^{0} \left(\int_{0}^{1} (xy - y^3)\,dy \right) dx + \int_{0}^{1} \left(\int_{x}^{1} (xy - y^3)\,dy \right) dx$$

as you can check ⟶

$$= \left(-\tfrac{1}{2}\right) + \left(-\tfrac{3}{40}\right) = -\tfrac{23}{40}.$$

Repeated integrals

$$\int_a^b \left(\int_{\phi_1(x)}^{\phi_2(x)} f(x, y)\,dy \right) dx \qquad \text{and} \qquad \int_c^d \left(\int_{\psi_1(y)}^{\psi_2(y)} f(x, y)\,dx \right) dy$$

can be written in more compact form by omitting the large parentheses. From now on we will simply write

$$\int_a^b \int_{\phi_1(x)}^{\phi_2(x)} f(x, y)\,dy\,dx \qquad \text{and} \qquad \int_c^d \int_{\psi_1(y)}^{\psi_2(y)} f(x, y)\,dx\,dy.$$

Example 3 Evaluate $\iint_{\Omega} (x^{1/2} - y^2)\,dx\,dy$ with Ω as in Figure 17.3.6.

SOLUTION The projection of Ω onto the x-axis is the closed interval [0, 1], and Ω can be characterized as the set of all (x, y) with

$$0 \le x \le 1 \qquad \text{and} \qquad x^2 \le y \le x^{1/4}.$$

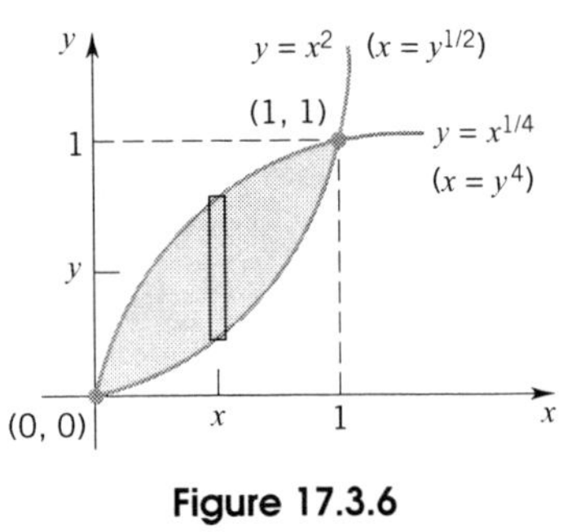

Figure 17.3.6

Therefore

$$\iint_{\Omega} (x^{1/2} - y^2)\,dx\,dy = \int_0^1 \int_{x^2}^{x^{1/4}} (x^{1/2} - y^2)\,dy\,dx$$

$$= \int_0^1 \left[x^{1/2}y - \tfrac{1}{3}y^3\right]_{x^2}^{x^{1/4}} dx$$

$$= \int_0^1 \left(\tfrac{2}{3}x^{3/4} - x^{5/2} + \tfrac{1}{3}x^6\right) dx$$

$$= \left[\tfrac{8}{21}x^{7/4} - \tfrac{2}{7}x^{7/2} + \tfrac{1}{21}x^7\right]_0^1 = \tfrac{8}{21} - \tfrac{2}{7} + \tfrac{1}{21} = \tfrac{1}{7}.$$

We can also integrate in the other order. The projection of Ω onto the y-axis is the closed interval $[0, 1]$, and Ω can be characterized as the set of all (x, y) with

$$0 \le y \le 1 \qquad \text{and} \qquad y^4 \le x \le y^{1/2}.$$

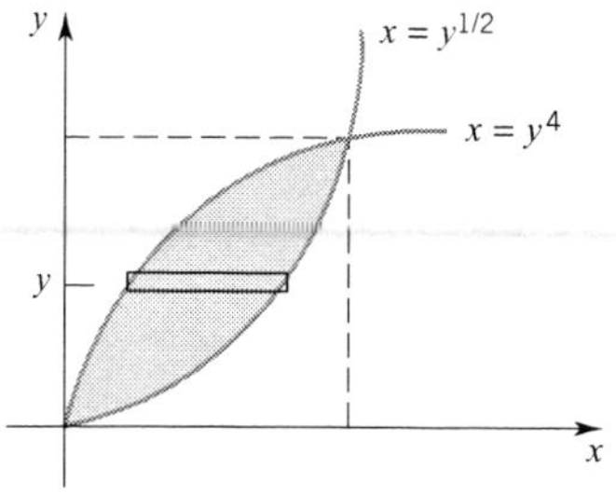

This gives the same result:

$$\iint_{\Omega} (x^{1/2} - y^2)\,dx\,dy = \int_0^1 \int_{y^4}^{y^{1/2}} (x^{1/2} - y^2)\,dx\,dy$$

$$= \int_0^1 \left[\tfrac{2}{3}x^{3/2} - y^2x\right]_{y^4}^{y^{1/2}} dy$$

$$= \int_0^1 \left(\tfrac{2}{3}y^{3/4} - y^{5/2} + \tfrac{1}{3}y^6\right) dy$$

$$= \left[\tfrac{8}{21}y^{7/4} - \tfrac{2}{7}y^{7/2} + \tfrac{1}{21}y^7\right]_0^1 = \tfrac{8}{21} - \tfrac{2}{7} + \tfrac{1}{21} = \tfrac{1}{7}. \quad \square$$

Example 4 Use double integration to calculate the area of the region Ω encolsed by

$$y = x^2 \qquad \text{and} \qquad x + y = 2.$$

SOLUTION The region Ω is pictured in Figure 17.3.7. Its area is given by the double integral

$$\iint_{\Omega} dx\,dy.$$

We project Ω onto the x-axis and write the boundaries as functions of x:

$$y = x^2, \quad y = 2 - x.$$

Ω is the set of all (x, y) with $-2 \le x \le 1$ and $x^2 \le y \le 2 - x$. Therefore

$$\iint_{\Omega} dx\,dy = \int_{-2}^{1} \int_{x^2}^{2-x} dy\,dx = \int_{-2}^{1} (2 - x - x^2)\,dx = \left[2x - \tfrac{1}{2}x^2 - \tfrac{1}{3}x^3\right]_{-2}^{1}$$

$$= (2 - \tfrac{1}{2} - \tfrac{1}{3}) - (-4 - 2 + \tfrac{8}{3}) = \tfrac{9}{2}.$$

We can also project Ω onto the y-axis and write the boundaries as functions of y, but then the calculations become more complicated. As illustrated in Figure 17.3.8, Ω is the set of all (x, y) with

$$0 \le y \le 4 \qquad \text{and} \qquad -\sqrt{y} \le x \le \psi(y)$$

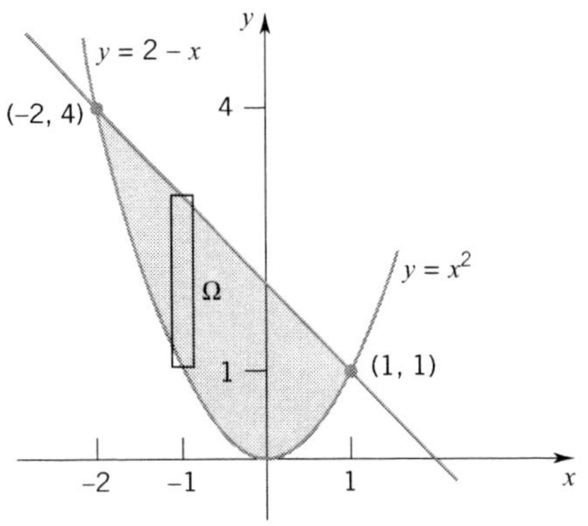

Figure 17.3.7

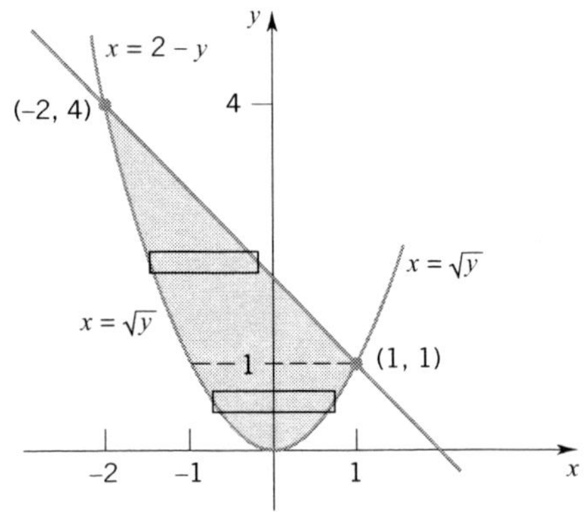

Figure 17.3.8

where

$$\psi(y) = \begin{cases} \sqrt{y}, & 0 \le y \le 1 \\ 2 - y, & 1 \le y \le 4. \end{cases}$$

Therefore

$$\iint_{\Omega} dx\,dy = \int_0^1 \int_{-\sqrt{y}}^{\sqrt{y}} dx\,dy + \int_1^4 \int_{-\sqrt{y}}^{2-y} dx\,dy.$$

As you can check, the sum of the integrals is $\frac{9}{2}$.

Symmetry in Double Integration

First we go back to the one-variable case. (Section 5.8) Let's suppose that g is continuous on an interval which is symmetric about the origin, say $[-a, a]$.

$$\text{If } g \text{ is odd,} \qquad \text{then} \qquad \int_{-a}^{a} g(x)\,dx = 0.$$

$$\text{If } g \text{ is even,} \qquad \text{then} \qquad \int_{-a}^{a} g(x)\,dx = 2\int_0^a g(x)\,dx.$$

We have similar results for double integrals.

Suppose that Ω is symmetric about the y-axis.

If f is odd in x $[f(-x, y) = -f(x, y)]$, then $\displaystyle\iint_{\Omega} f(x, y)\,dx\,dy = 0.$

If f is even in x $[f(-x, y) = -f(x, y)]$, then $\displaystyle\iint_{\Omega} f(x, y)\,dx\,dy = 2\iint_{\substack{\text{right half}\\ \text{of } \Omega}} f(x, y)\,dx\,dy.$

Suppose that Ω is symmetric about the x-axis.

If f is odd in y $[f(x, -y) = -f(x, y)]$, then $\displaystyle\iint_{\Omega} f(x, y)\,dx\,dy = 0.$

If f is even in y $[f(x, -y) = -f(x, y)]$, then $\displaystyle\iint_{\Omega} f(x, y)\,dx\,dy = 2\iint_{\substack{\text{upper half}\\ \text{of } \Omega}} f(x, y)\,dx\,dy.$

By way of example, we integrate $f(x, y) = 2x - \sin x^2 y$ over the region Ω depicted in Figure 17.3.9. First of all

$$\iint_{\Omega} (2x - \sin x^2 y)\, dx\, dy = \iint_{\Omega} 2x\, dx\, dy - \iint_{\Omega} \sin x^2 y\, dx\, dy.$$

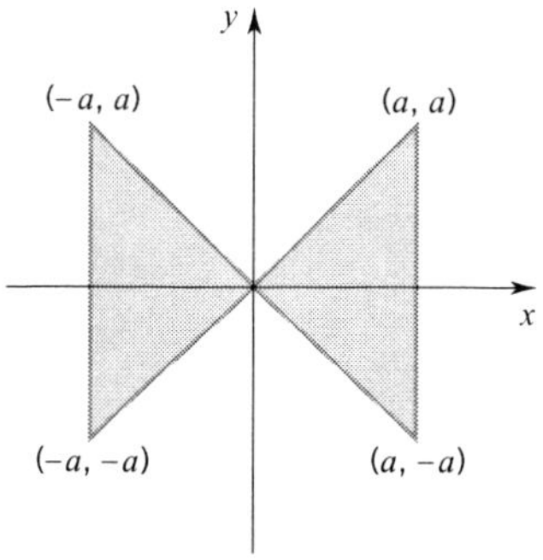

Figure 17.3.9

The symmetry of Ω about the y-axis gives

$$\iint_{\Omega} 2x\, dx\, dy = 0. \qquad \text{(the integrand is odd in } x\text{)}$$

The symmetry of Ω about the x-axis gives

$$\iint_{\Omega} \sin x^2 y\, dx\, dy = 0. \qquad \text{(the integrand is odd in } y\text{)}$$

Therefore

$$\iint_{\Omega} (2x - \sin x^2 y)\, dx\, dy = 0.$$

Let's go back to Example 1 and reevaluate

$$\iint_{\Omega} (x^4 - 2y)\, dx\, dy,$$

this time capitalizing on the symmetry of the base region Ω. Note that

$$\underbrace{\iint_{\Omega} 2y\, dx\, dy = 0}_{\text{symmetry about } x\text{-axis}} \quad \text{and} \quad \iint_{\Omega} x^4\, dx\, dy \overset{\text{symmetry about } y\text{-axis}}{=} 2 \iint_{\substack{\text{right half} \\ \text{of } \Omega}} x^4\, dx\, dy \overset{\text{symmetry about } x\text{-axis}}{=} 4 \iint_{\substack{\text{upper part of} \\ \text{right half of } \Omega}} x^4 dx\, dy.$$

Therefore

$$\iint_{\Omega} (x^4 - 2y)\, dx\, dy = 4 \int_0^1 \int_0^{x^2} x^4\, dy\, dx = 4 \int_0^1 x^6\, dx = \tfrac{4}{7}.$$

Example 5 Calculate the volume within the cylinder $x^2 + y^2 = b^2$ between the planes $y + z = a$ and $z = 0$ given that $a \geq b > 0$.

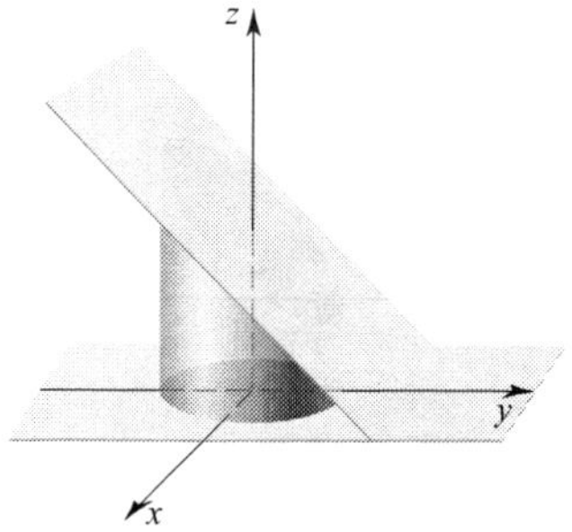

Figure 17.3.10

SOLUTION See Figure 17.3.10. The solid in question is bounded below by the disk

$$\Omega: \quad 0 \leq x^2 + y^2 \leq b^2$$

and above by the plane

$$z = a - y.$$

The volume is given by the double integral

$$\iint_{\Omega} (a - y)\, dx\, dy.$$

Since Ω is symmetric about the x-axis,

$$\iint_{\Omega} y\, dx\, dy = 0.$$

Thus

$$\iint_{\Omega} (a-y)\,dx\,dy = \iint_{\Omega} a\,dx\,dy = a\iint_{\Omega} dx\,dy = a(\text{area of }\Omega) = \pi ab^2. \quad \square$$

Concluding Remarks

When two orders of integration are possible, one order may be easy to carry out, while the other may present serious difficulties. Take as an example the double integral

$$\iint_{\Omega} \cos \tfrac{1}{2}\pi x^2\,dx\,dy$$

with Ω an in Figure 17.3.11. Projection onto the x-axis leads to

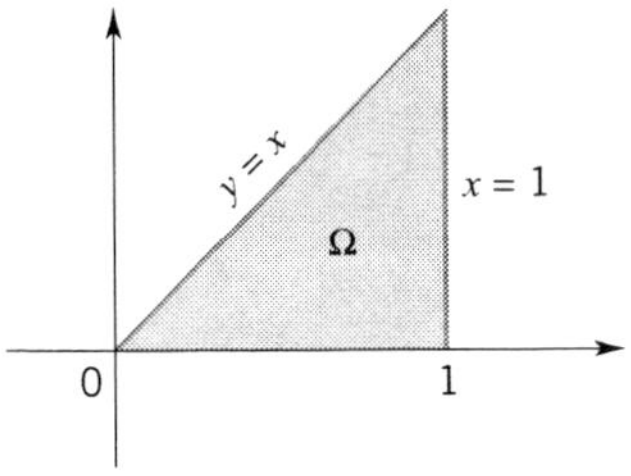

Figure 17.3.11

$$\int_0^1 \int_0^x \cos \tfrac{1}{2}\pi x^2\,dy\,dx.$$

Projection onto the y-axis leads to

$$\int_0^1 \int_y^1 \cos \tfrac{1}{2}\pi x^2\,dx\,dy.$$

The first expression is easy to evaluate:

$$\begin{aligned}\int_0^1 \int_0^x \cos \tfrac{1}{2}\pi x^2\,dy\,dx &= \int_0^1 \left(\int_0^x \cos \tfrac{1}{2}\pi x^2\,dy\right) dx\\ &= \int_0^1 \left[y \cos \tfrac{1}{2}\pi x^2\right]_0^x dx = \int_0^1 x \cos \tfrac{1}{2}\pi x^2\,dx\\ &= \left[\frac{1}{\pi} \sin \frac{1}{2}\pi x^2\right]_0^1 = \frac{1}{\pi}.\end{aligned}$$

The second expression is not as easy to evaluate:

$$\int_0^1 \int_y^1 \cos \tfrac{1}{2}\pi x^2\,dx\,dy = \int_0^1 \left(\int_y^1 \cos \tfrac{1}{2}\pi x^2\,dx\right) dy,$$

and $\cos \frac{1}{2}\pi x^2$ does not have an elementary antiderivative.

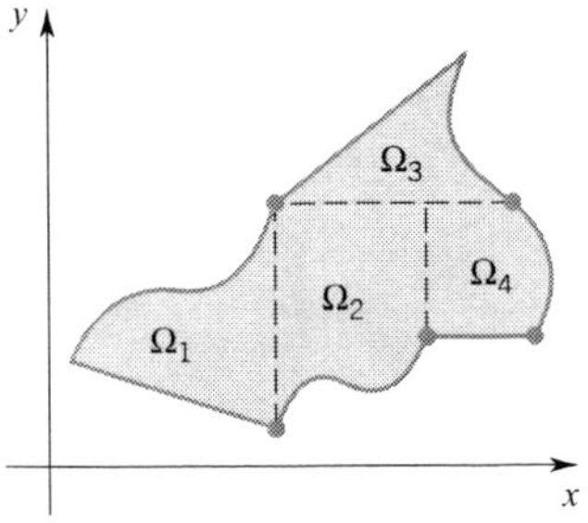

Figure 17.3.12

Finally, if Ω, the region of integration, is neither of Type I nor of Type II, it may be possible to break it up into a finite number of regions $\Omega_1, \ldots, \Omega_n$, each of which is of Type I or Type II. (See Figure 17.3.12.) Since the double integral is additive,

$$\iint_{\Omega_1} f(x,y)\,dx\,dy + \cdots + \iint_{\Omega_4} f(x,y)\,dx\,dy = \iint_{\Omega} f(x,y)\,dx\,dy.$$

Each of the integrals on the left can be evaluated by the methods of this section.

EXERCISES 17.3

Exercises 1–3. Evaluate for $\Omega : 0 \le x \le 1, 0 \le y \le 3$.

1. $\iint_\Omega x^2\,dx\,dy$.

2. $\iint_\Omega e^{x+y}\,dx\,dy$.

3. $\iint_\Omega xy^2\,dx\,dy$.

Exercises 4–6. Evaluate for $\Omega : 0 \le x \le 1, 0 \le y \le x$.

4. $\iint_\Omega x^3 y\,dx\,dy$.

5. $\iint_\Omega xy^3\,dx\,dy$.

6. $\iint_\Omega x^2y^2\,dx\,dy$.

Exercises 7–9. Evaluate the integral taking $\Omega : 0 \le x \le \frac{1}{2}\pi$, $0 \le y \le \frac{1}{2}\pi$.

7. $\iint_\Omega \sin(x+y)\,dx\,dy$.

8. $\iint_\Omega \cos(x+y)\,dx\,dy$.

9. $\iint_\Omega (1+xy)\,dx\,dy$.

Exercises 10–18. Evaluate the double integral.

10. $\iint_\Omega (x+3y^3)\,dx\,dy$, $\quad \Omega : 0 \le x^2+y^2 \le 1$.

11. $\iint_\Omega \sqrt{xy}\,dx\,dy$, $\quad \Omega : 0 \le y \le 1, y^2 \le x \le y$.

12. $\iint_\Omega ye^x\,dx\,dy$, $\quad \Omega : 0 \le y \le 1, 0 \le x \le y^2$.

13. $\iint_\Omega (4-y^2)\,dx\,dy$, Ω the bounded region between $y^2 = 2x$ and $y^2 = 8 - 2x$.

14. $\iint_\Omega (x^4+y^2)\,dx\,dy$, Ω the bounded region between $y = x^3$ and $y = x^2$.

15. $\iint_\Omega (3xy^3 - y)\,dx\,dy$, Ω the region between $y = |x|$ and $y = -|x|, x \in [-1, 1]$.

16. $\iint_\Omega e^{-y^2/2}\,dx\,dy$, Ω the triangular region bounded by the y-axis, $2y = x$, $y = 1$.

17. $\iint_\Omega e^{x^2}\,dx\,dy$, Ω the triangular region bounded by the x-axis, $2y = x$, $x = 2$.

18. $\iint_\Omega (x+y)\,dx\,dy$, Ω the region between $y = x^3$ and $y = x^4, x \in [-1, 1]$.

Exercises 19–24. Sketch the region Ω that gives rise to the repeated integral and change the order of integration.

19. $\int_0^1 \int_{x^4}^{x^2} f(x,y)\,dy\,dx$.

20. $\int_0^1 \int_0^{y^2} f(x,y)\,dx\,dy$.

21. $\int_0^1 \int_{-y}^{y} f(x,y)\,dx\,dy$.

22. $\int_{1/2}^1 \int_{x^3}^{x} f(x,y)\,dy\,dx$.

23. $\int_1^4 \int_x^{2x} f(x,y)\,dy\,dx$.

24. $\int_1^3 \int_{-x}^{x^2} f(x,y)\,dy\,dx$.

Exercises 25–28. Calculate by double integration the area of the bounded region determined by the curves.

25. $x^2 = 4y, \quad 2y - x - 4 = 0$.

26. $y = x, \quad x = 4y - y^2$.

27. $y = x, \quad 4y^3 = x^2$.

28. $x + y = 5, \quad xy = 6$.

Exercises 29–32. Sketch the region Ω that gives rise to the repeated integral, change the order of integration, and then evaluate.

29. $\int_0^1 \int_{\sqrt{x}}^1 \sin\left(\frac{y^3+1}{2}\right) dy\,dx$.

30. $\int_{-1}^0 \int_{-\sqrt{y+1}}^{\sqrt{y+1}} x^2\,dx\,dy$.

31. $\int_1^2 \int_0^{\ln y} e^{-x}\,dx\,dy$.

32. $\int_0^1 \int_{x^2}^1 \frac{x^3}{\sqrt{x^4+y^2}}\,dy\,dx$.

33. Find the area of the first quadrant region bounded by $xy = 2, y = 1, y = x + 1$.

34. Find the volume of the solid bounded above by $z = x + y$ and below by the triangular region with vertices (0, 0), (0, 1), (1, 0).

35. Find the volume of the solid bounded by $\frac{1}{2}x + \frac{1}{3}y + \frac{1}{4}z = 1$ and the coordinate planes.

36. Find the volume of the solid bounded above by the plane $z = 2x + 3y$ and below by the unit square

$$0 \le x \le 1, \qquad 0 \le y \le 1.$$

37. Find the volume of the solid bounded above by $z = x^3y$ and below by the triangular region with vertices (0, 0), (2, 0), (0, 1).

38. Find the volume under the paraboloid $z = x^2 + y^2$ within the cylinder $x^2 + y^2 \le 1, z \ge 0$.

39. Find the volume of the solid bounded above by the plane $z = 2x + 1$ and below by the disk $(x-1)^2 + y^2 \le 1$.

40. Find the volume of the solid bounded above by $z = 4 - y^2 - \frac{1}{4}x^2$ and below by the disk $(y-1)^2 + x^2 \le 1$.

41. Find the volume of the solid in the first octant ($x \ge 0$, $y \ge 0, z \ge 0$) bounded by $z = x^2 + y^2$, the plane $x + y = 1$, and the coordinate planes.

42. Find the volume of the solid bounded by the circular cylinder $x^2 + y^2 = 1$, the plane $z = 0$, and the plane $x + z = 1$.

43. Find the volume of the solid in the first octant bounded above by $z = x^2 + 3y^2$, below by the xy-plane, and on the sides by the cylinder $y = x^2$ and the plane $y = x$.

44. Find the volume of the solid bounded above by the surface $z = 1 + xy$ and below by the triangular region with vertices $(1, 1), (4, 1), (3, 2)$.

45. Find the volume of the solid in the first octant bounded by the cylinders $x^2 + y^2 = a^2, x^2 + z^2 = a^2$.

46. Find the volume of the tetrahedron bounded by the coordinate planes and the plane

$$\frac{x}{a} + \frac{y}{b} + \frac{z}{c} = 1, \qquad a,b,c > 0.$$

Exercises 47–50. Evaluate.

47. $\int_0^1 \int_y^1 e^{y/x}\, dx\, dy.$

48. $\int_0^1 \int_0^{\arccos y} e^{\sin x}\, dx\, dy.$

49. $\int_0^1 \int_x^1 x^2 e^{y^4}\, dy\, dx.$

50. $\int_0^1 \int_x^1 e^{y^2}\, dy\, dx.$

Exercises 51–54. Calculate the average value of f over Ω.

51. $f(x, y) = x^2 y;\quad \Omega: -1 \le x \le 1,\ 0 \le y \le 4.$

52. $f(x, y) = xy;\quad \Omega: 0 \le x \le 1,\ 0 \le y \le \sqrt{1 - x^2}.$

53. $f(x, y) = \dfrac{1}{xy};\quad \Omega: \ln 2 \le x \le 2\ln 2,$
$\ln 2 \le y \le 2\ln 2.$

54. $f(x, y) = e^{x+y};\quad \Omega: 0 \le x \le 1,\ x - 1 \le y \le x + 1.$

55. (*Separated variables over a rectangle*) Let R be the rectangle $a \le x \le b, c \le y \le d$. Show that, if f is continuous on $[a, b]$ and g is continuous on $[c, d]$, then

(17.3.3)
$$\iint_R f(x)g(y)\, dx\, dy = \left[\int_a^b f(x)\, dx\right] \cdot \left[\int_c^d g(y)\, dy\right].$$

56. Given that $f(-x, -y) = -f(x, y)$ for all (x, y) in Ω, what form of symmetry in Ω will ensure that the double integral of f over Ω is zero?

57. Let Ω be the triangular region with vertices $(0, 0), (0, 1), (1, 1)$. Show that

$$\text{if} \quad \int_0^1 f(x)\, dx = 0, \quad \text{then} \quad \iint_\Omega f(x)f(y)\, dx\, dy = 0.$$

58. (*Differentiation under the integral sign*) If f and $\partial f/\partial x$ are continuous, then the function

$$H(t) = \int_a^b \frac{\partial f}{\partial x}(t, y)\, dy$$

can be shown to be continuous. Use the identity

$$\int_0^x \int_a^b \frac{\partial f}{\partial x}(t, y)\, dy\, dt = \int_a^b \int_0^x \frac{\partial f}{\partial x}(t, y)\, dt\, dy$$

to verify that

$$\frac{d}{dx}\left[\int_a^b f(x, y)\, dy\right] = \int_a^b \frac{\partial f}{\partial x}(x, y)\, dy.$$

59. We integrate over regions of Type I by setting

$$\iint_\Omega f(x, y)\, dx\, dy = \int_a^b \int_{\phi_1(x)}^{\phi_2(x)} f(x, y)\, dy\, dx.$$

Here f is assumed to be continuous on Ω and ϕ_1, ϕ_2 are assumed to be continuous on $[a, b]$. Show that the function

$$F(x) = \int_{\phi_1(x)}^{\phi_2(x)} f(x, y)\, dy$$

is continuous on $[a, b]$.

60. Use a CAS to evaluate the expression.

(a) $\int_{-1}^3 \int_2^5 x e^{-xy}\, dy\, dx.$ (b) $\int_3^7 \int_1^4 \dfrac{xy}{x^2 + y^2}\, dy\, dx.$

61. Sketch the region Ω bounded by $y = x^2 - 2x + 2$ and $y = 1 + \sqrt{x - 1}$. Find the area of Ω by integrating

(a) first with respect to y and then with respect to x;
(b) first with respect to x and then with respect to y.

62. Sketch the region Ω bounded by $x - 2y = 0, x + y = 3, y = 0$. Use a CAS to calculate

$$\iint_\Omega \sqrt{2x + y}\, dx\, dy$$

by integrating

(a) first with respect to x and then with respect to y;
(b) first with respect to y and then with respect to x.

17.4 THE DOUBLE INTEGRAL AS THE LIMIT OF RIEMANN SUMS; POLAR COORDINATES

In the one-variable case we can write the integral as the limit of Riemann sums:

$$\int_a^b f(x)\, dx = \lim_{\max \Delta x \to 0} \sum_{i=1}^n f(x_i^*)\Delta x_i.$$

The same approach works with double integrals. To explain it, we need to explain what we mean by the *diameter of a set*.

Suppose that S is a bounded closed set (on the line, in the plane, or in three-space). For any two points P and Q of S, we can measure their separation, $d(P, Q)$. The maximal separation between points of S is called the *diameter of S:*

$$\text{diam } S = \max_{P,Q\in S} d(P, Q).^{\dagger}$$

For a circle, a circular disk, a sphere, or a ball, this sense of diameter agrees with the usual one. Figure 17.4.1 gives some other examples.

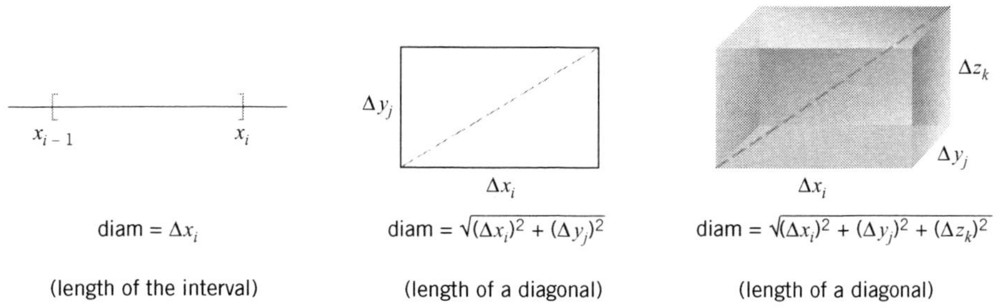

Figure 17.4.1

We start with a basic plane region Ω and decompose it into a finite number of basic subregions $\Omega_1, \ldots, \Omega_n$. (See Figure 17.4.2.) If f is continuous on Ω, then f is continuous on each Ω_i. Now from each Ω_i we pick an arbitrary point (x_i^*, y_i^*) and form the *Riemann sum*

$$\sum_{i=1}^{n} f(x_i^*, y_i^*)(\text{area of } \Omega_i).$$

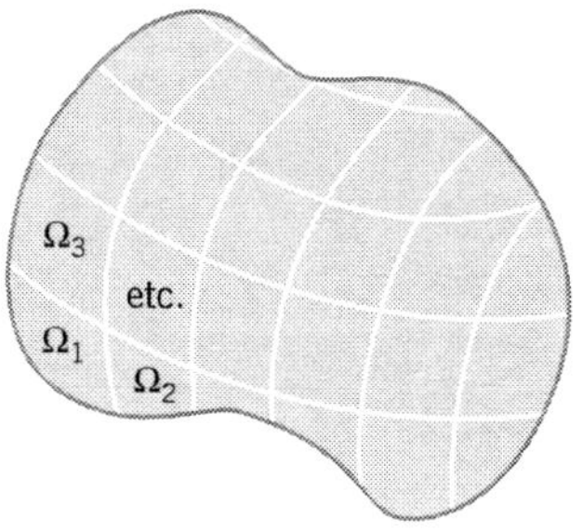

Figure 17.4.2

As you would expect, the double integral over Ω can be obtained as the limit of such sums; namely, given any $\epsilon > 0$, there exists $\delta > 0$ such that, if the diameters of the Ω_i are all less than δ, then

$$\left| \sum_{i=1}^{n} f(x_i^*, y_i^*)(\text{area of } \Omega_i) - \iint_{\Omega} f(x, y)\, dx\, dy \right| < \epsilon$$

no matter how the (x_i^*, y_i^*) are chosen within the Ω_i. We express this by writing

(17.4.1)
$$\iint_{\Omega} f(x, y)\, dx\, dy = \lim_{\text{diam } \Omega_i \to 0} \sum_{i=1}^{n} f(x_i^*, y_i^*)(\text{area of } \Omega_i).$$

---

†If a set S is bounded, it is contained in some ball, which in turn has some finite diameter D. The set of all distances between points of S, being bounded above by D, has a least upper bound. This least upper bound is called the *diameter* of S:

$$\text{diam } S = \underset{P,Q\in S}{\text{lub}}\; d(P, Q).$$

It can be shown that, if S is bounded and closed (which is the case we are dealing with), then this least upper bound is attained, and therefore we can set

$$\text{diam } S = \max_{P,Q\in S} d(P, Q).$$

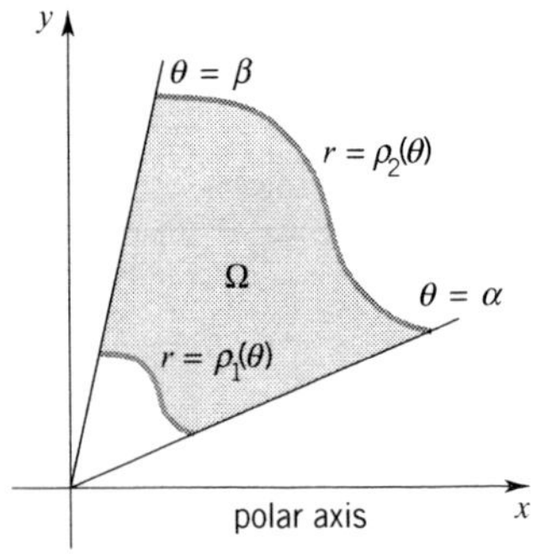

Figure 17.4.3

Evaluating Double Integrals Using Polar Coordinates

Here we explain how to calculate double integrals

$$\iint_{\Omega} f(x, y)\, dx\, dy$$

using polar coordinates $[r, \theta]$. Throughout we take $r \geq 0$.

We will work with the type of region shown in Figure 17.4.3. The region Ω is then the set of all points (x, y) which have polar coordinates $[r, \theta]$ in the set

$$\Gamma: \quad \alpha \leq \theta \leq \beta, \qquad \rho_1(\theta) \leq r \leq \rho_2(\theta).$$

Here $0 \leq \alpha < \beta \leq 2\pi$.

You already know how to calculate the area of Ω. By (10.4.2),

$$\text{area of } \Omega = \int_{\alpha}^{\beta} \tfrac{1}{2}\left([\rho_2(\theta)]^2 - [\rho_1(\theta)]^2\right) d\theta.$$

We can write this as a double integral over Γ:

(17.4.2)
$$\text{area of } \Omega = \iint_{\Gamma} r\, dr d\theta.$$

PROOF Simply note that

$$\tfrac{1}{2}([\rho_2(\theta)]^2 - [\rho_1(\theta)]^2) = \int_{\rho_1(\theta)}^{\rho_2(\theta)} r\, dr$$

and therefore

$$\text{area of } \Omega = \int_{\alpha}^{\beta} \int_{\rho_1(\theta)}^{\rho_2(\theta)} r\, dr\, d\theta = \iint_{\Gamma} r\, dr d\theta. \quad \square$$

Now let's suppose that f is some function continuous at each point (x, y) of Ω. Then the composition

$$F(r, \theta) = f(r\cos\theta, r\sin\theta)$$

is continuous at each point $[r, \theta]$ of Γ. We will show that

(17.4.3)
$$\iint_{\Omega} f(x, y)\, dx\, dy \iint_{\Gamma} f(r\cos\theta, r\sin\theta)\, r\, dr d\theta.$$
(note the extra r)

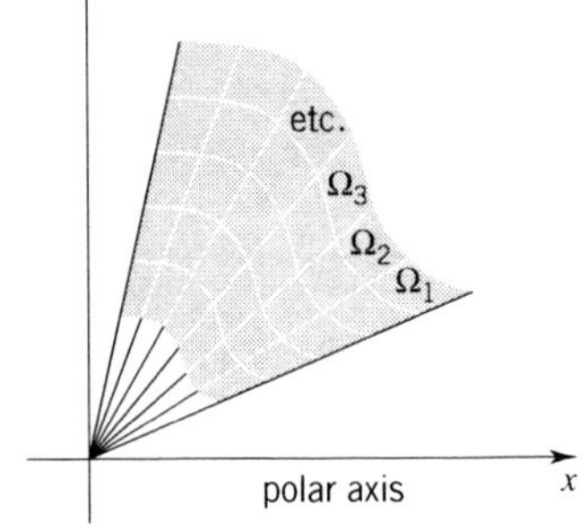

Figure 17.4.4

PROOF Our first step is to place a grid on Ω by using a finite number of rays $\theta = \theta_j$ and a finite number of continuous curves $r = \rho_k(\theta)$ in the manner of Figure 17.4.4. This grid decomposes Ω into a finite number of regions

$$\Omega_1, \ldots, \Omega_n$$

with polar coordinates in sets $\Gamma_1, \ldots, \Gamma_n$. Note that by (17.4.2)

$$\text{area of each } \Omega_i = \iint_{\Gamma_i} r\, dr d\theta.$$

Writing $F(r, \theta)$ for $f(r\cos\theta, r\sin\theta)$, we have

$$\iint_{\Gamma} F(r,\theta)\, r\, dr d\theta \underset{\text{additivity}}{=} \sum_{i=1}^{n} \iint_{\Gamma_i} F(r,\theta)\, r\, dr d\theta$$

$$\underset{\substack{\text{for some } [r_i^*, \theta_i^*] \in \Gamma_i \\ \text{(Theorem 17.2.10)}}}{=} \sum_{i=1}^{n} F(r_i^*, \theta_i^*) \iint_{\Gamma_i} r\, dr d\theta$$

$$= \sum_{i=1}^{n} F(r_i^*, \theta_i^*)(\text{area of } \Omega_i)$$

$$\underset{\text{with } x_i^* = r_i^* \cos\theta_i^*,\ y_i^* = r_i^* \sin\theta_i^*}{=} \sum_{i=1}^{n} f(x_i^*, y_i^*)(\text{area of } \Omega_i).$$

This last expression is a Riemann sum for the double integral

$$\iint_{\Omega} f(x, y)\, dx\, dy.$$

As such, by (17.4.1), it differs from that integral by less than any preassigned positive ϵ provided only that the diameters of all the Ω_i are sufficiently small. This we can guarantee by making our grid sufficiently fine. ❑

Example 1 Use polar coordinates to evaluate $\iint_{\Omega} xy\, dx\, dy$ where Ω is the portion of the unit disk that lies in the first quadrant.

SOLUTION Ω is the set of all points (x, y) which have polar coordinates $[r, \theta]$ in the set

$$\Gamma: \quad 0 \le \theta \le \tfrac{1}{2}\pi, \qquad 0 \le r \le 1.$$

Therefore

$$\iint_{\Omega} xy\, dx\, dy = \iint_{\Gamma} (r\cos\theta)(r\sin\theta)\, r\, dr d\theta$$

$$= \int_0^{\pi/2} \int_0^1 r^3 \cos\theta \sin\theta\, dr d\theta \underset{\text{check this}}{=} \tfrac{1}{8}. \quad ❑$$

Example 2 Use polar coordinates to calculate the volume of a sphere of radius R.

SOLUTION In rectangular coordinates,

$$V = 2 \iint_{\Omega} \sqrt{R^2 - (x^2 + y^2)}\, dx\, dy$$

where Ω is the disk of radius R centered at the origin. (Verify this.) Ω is the set of all points which have polar coordinates in the set

$$\Gamma: \quad 0 \le \theta \le 2\pi, \qquad 0 \le r \le R.$$

Therefore

$$V = 2\iint_{\Gamma} \sqrt{R^2 - r^2}\, r\, dr d\theta = 2\int_0^{2\pi}\int_0^R \sqrt{R^2 - r^2}\, r\, dr\, d\theta = \tfrac{4}{3}\pi R^3. \quad \square$$

check this ⟶

Example 3 Find the volume of the solid bounded above by the cone $z = 2 - \sqrt{x^2 + y^2}$ and below by the disk $\Omega : (x - 1)^2 + y^2 \le 1$. (See Figure 17.4.5.)

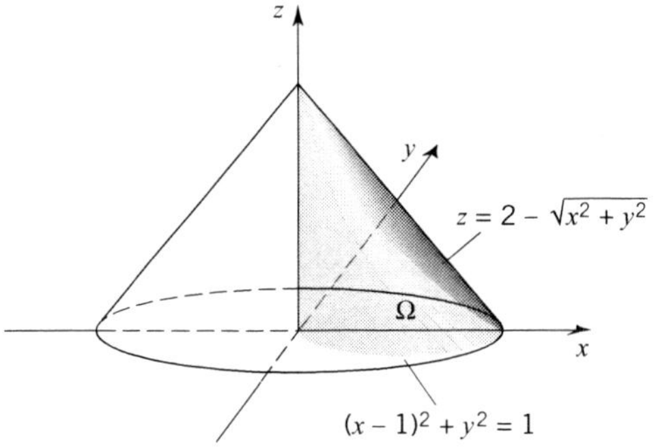

Figure 17.4.5

SOLUTION

$$V = \iint_{\Omega} (2 - \sqrt{x^2 + y^2})\, dx\, dy = 2\iint_{\Omega} dx\, dy - \iint_{\Omega} \sqrt{x^2 + y^2}\, dx\, dy.$$

The first integral is $2\times$ (area of Ω) $= 2\pi$. We evaluate the second integral by changing to polar coordinates.

The equation $(x - 1)^2 + y^2 = 1$ simplifies to $x^2 + y^2 = 2x$. In polar coordinates this becomes $r^2 = 2r\cos\theta$, which simplifies to $r = 2\cos\theta$. The disk Ω is the set of all points with polar coordinates in the set

$$\Gamma : -\tfrac{1}{2}\pi \le \theta \le \tfrac{1}{2}\pi,\ 0 \le r \le 2\cos\theta.$$

Therefore

$$\iint_{\Omega} \sqrt{x^2 + y^2}\, dx\, dy = \iint_{\Gamma} r^2 dr d\theta = \int_{-\pi/2}^{\pi/2}\int_0^{2\cos\theta} r^2\, dr\, d\theta = \tfrac{32}{9}.$$

Check this. ⟶

It follows that

$$V = 2\pi - \tfrac{32}{9} \cong 2.73. \quad \square$$

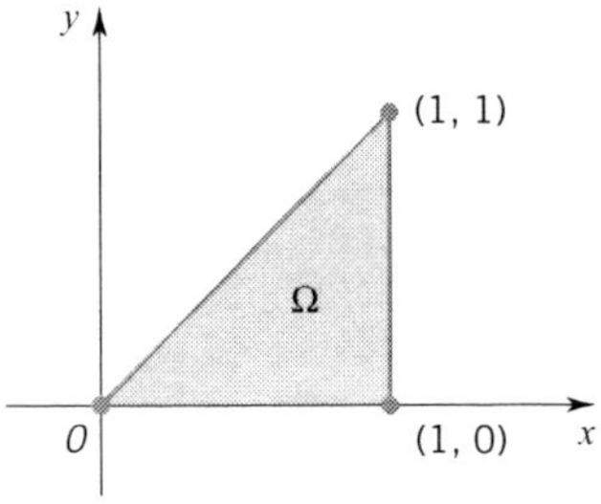

Figure 17.4.6

Example 4 Evaluate $\displaystyle\iint_{\Omega} \frac{1}{(1 + x^2 + y^2)^{3/2}}\, dx\, dy$ where Ω is the triangular region shown in Figure 17.4.6.

SOLUTION The vertical side of the triangle is part of the line $x = 1$. In polar coordinates this is $r\cos\theta = 1$, which can be written $r = \sec\theta$. Therefore

$$\iint_{\Omega} \frac{1}{(1 + x^2 + y^2)^{3/2}}\, dx\, dy = \iint_{\Gamma} \frac{r}{(1 + r^2)^{3/2}}\, dr d\theta$$

where

$$\Gamma: \quad 0 \leq \theta \leq \pi/4, \qquad 0 \leq r \leq \sec\,\theta. \qquad \text{(Figure 17.4.7)}$$

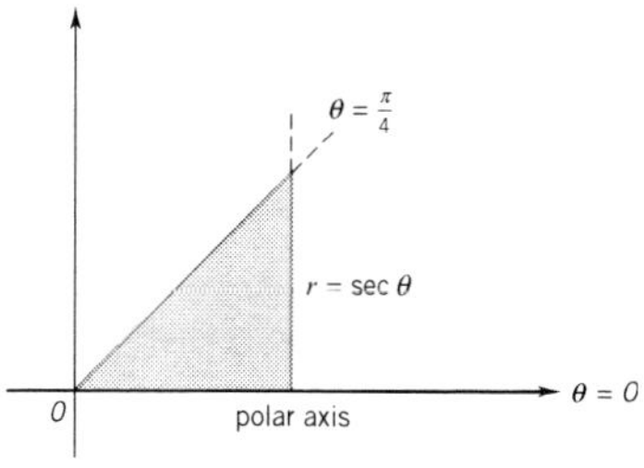

Figure 17.4.7

The double integral over Γ reduces to

$$\int_0^{\pi/4}\int_0^{\sec\theta} \frac{r}{(1+r^2)^{3/2}}\,dr\,d\theta = \int_0^{\pi/4}\left[\frac{-1}{\sqrt{1+r^2}}\right]_0^{\sec\,\theta} d\theta$$

$$= \int_0^{\pi/4}\left(1 - \frac{1}{\sqrt{1+\sec^2\theta}}\right) d\theta.$$

For $\theta \in [0, \pi/4]$

$$\frac{1}{\sqrt{1+\sec^2\theta}} = \frac{\cos\theta}{\sqrt{\cos^2\theta+1}} = \frac{\cos\theta}{\sqrt{2-\sin^2\theta}}.$$

Therefore the integral can be written

$$\int_0^{\pi/4}\left(1 - \frac{\cos\theta}{\sqrt{2-\sin^2\theta}}\right) d\theta = \left[\theta - \arcsin\left(\frac{\sin\theta}{\sqrt{2}}\right)\right]_0^{\pi/4} = \frac{\pi}{4} - \frac{\pi}{6} = \frac{\pi}{12}. \quad \square$$

(7.7.4) ⟶↑

The function $f(x) = e^{-x^2}$ has no elementary antiderivative. Nevertheless, by taking a circuitous route and then using polar coordinates, we can show that

(17.4.4)

$$\int_{-\infty}^{\infty} e^{-x^2}\,dx = \sqrt{\pi}.^{\dagger}$$

PROOF The circular disk $D_b : x^2 + y^2 \leq b^2$ is the set of all (x, y) with polar coordinates $[r, \theta]$ in the set $\Gamma : 0 \leq \theta \leq 2\pi, 0 \leq r \leq b$. Therefore

$$\iint_{D_b} e^{-(x^2+y^2)}\,dx\,dy = \iint_{\Gamma} e^{-r^2}\,r\,dr\,d\theta = \int_0^{2\pi}\int_0^{b} e^{-r^2} r\,dr\,d\theta$$

$$= \int_0^{2\pi} \tfrac{1}{2}(1 - e^{-b^2})\,d\theta = \pi(1 - e^{-b^2}).$$

Let S_a be the square $-a \leq x \leq a, -a \leq y \leq a$. Since $D_a \subseteq S_a \subseteq D_{2a}$ and $e^{-(x^2+y^2)}$ is positive,

$$\iint_{D_a} e^{-x^2+y^2}\,dx\,dy \leq \iint_{S_a} e^{-(x^2+y^2)}\,dx\,dy \leq \iint_{D_{2a}} e^{-(x^2+y^2)}\,dx\,dy.$$

It follows that

$$\pi(1 - e^{-a^2}) \leq \iint_{S_a} e^{-(x^2+y^2)}\,dx\,dy \leq \pi(1 - e^{-4a^2}).$$

† This integral comes up frequently in probability theory and plays an important role in the branch of physics called "statistical mechanics." Since this is a well-known integral, we know that it exists. We can therefore calculate it by integrating from $-a$ to a and taking the limit as $a \to \infty$. In a roundabout way this is what we do.

As $a \to \infty$, $\pi(1 - e^{-a^2}) \to \pi$ and $\pi(1 - e^{-4a^2}) \to \pi$. Therefore

$$\lim_{a\to\infty} \iint_{S_a} e^{-(x^2+y^2)}\,dx\,dy = \pi.$$

But

$$\begin{aligned}\iint_{S_a} e^{-(x^2+y^2)}\,dx\,dy &= \int_{-a}^{a}\int_{-a}^{a} e^{-(x^2+y^2)}\,dx\,dy \\ &= \int_{-a}^{a}\int_{-a}^{a} e^{-x^2}\cdot e^{-y^2}\,dx\,dy \\ &= \left(\int_{-a}^{a} e^{-x^2}\,dx\right)\left(\int_{-a}^{a} e^{-y^2}\,dy\right) = \left(\int_{-a}^{a} e^{-x^2}\,dx\right)^2.\end{aligned}$$

Therefore

$$\lim_{a\to\infty}\int_{-a}^{a} e^{-x^2}\,dx = \lim_{a\to\infty}\left(\iint_{S_a} e^{-(x^2+y^2)}\,dx\,dy\right)^{1/2} = \sqrt{\pi}.\quad ❑$$

EXERCISES 17.4

Exercises 1–4. Calculate.

1. $\displaystyle\int_0^{\pi/2}\int_0^{\sin\theta} r\cos\theta\,dr\,d\theta.$

2. $\displaystyle\int_0^{\pi/4}\int_0^{\cos 2\theta} r\,dr\,d\theta.$

3. $\displaystyle\int_0^{\pi/2}\int_0^{3\sin\theta} r^2 dr\,d\theta.$

4. $\displaystyle\int_{-\pi/3}^{2\pi/3}\int_0^{2\cos\theta} r\sin\theta\,dr\,d\theta.$

5. Integrate $f(x, y) = \cos(x^2 + y^2)$
(a) over the closed unit disk;
(b) over the annular region $1 \le x^2 + y^2 \le 4$.

6. Integrate $f(x, y) = \sin(\sqrt{x^2 + y^2})$
(a) over the closed unit disk;
(b) over the annular region $1 \le x^2 + y^2 \le 4$.

7. Integrate $f(x, y) = x + y$
(a) over the region $0 \le x^2 + y^2 \le 1, \quad x \ge 0, y \ge 0$;
(b) over the region $1 \le x^2 + y^2 \le 4, \quad x \ge 0, y \ge 0$.

8. Integrate $f(x, y) = \sqrt{x^2 + y^2}$ over the triangular region with vertices $(0, 0), (1, 0), (1, \sqrt{3})$.

Exercises 9–16. Calculate using polar coordinates.

9. $\displaystyle\int_{-1}^{1}\int_0^{\sqrt{1-y^2}} \sqrt{x^2 + y^2}\,dx\,dy.$

10. $\displaystyle\int_0^{2}\int_0^{\sqrt{4-x^2}} \sqrt{x^2 + y^2}\,dy\,dx.$

11. $\displaystyle\int_{1/2}^{1}\int_0^{\sqrt{1-x^2}} dy\,dx.$

12. $\displaystyle\int_0^{1/2}\int_0^{\sqrt{1-x^2}} xy\sqrt{x^2 + y^2}\,dy\,dx.$

13. $\displaystyle\int_0^{1}\int_0^{\sqrt{1-x^2}} \sin\sqrt{x^2 + y^2}\,dy\,dx.$

14. $\displaystyle\int_{-1}^{1}\int_{-\sqrt{1-y^2}}^{\sqrt{1-y^2}} e^{-(x^2+y^2)}\,dx\,dy.$

15. $\displaystyle\int_0^{2}\int_0^{\sqrt{2x-x^2}} x\,dy\,dx.$

16. $\displaystyle\int_0^{1}\int_{-\sqrt{x-x^2}}^{\sqrt{x-x^2}} (x^2 + y^2)\,dy\,dx.$

Exercises 17–22. Find the area of the region by double integration.

17. One leaf of the petal curve $r = 3\sin 3\theta$.

18. The region enclosed by the cardioid $r = 2(1 - \cos\theta)$.

19. The region inside the circle $r = 4\cos\theta$ but outside the circle $r = 2$.

20. The region inside the large loop but outside the small loop of the limaçon $r = 1 + 2\cos\theta$.

21. The region enclosed by the lemniscate $r^2 = 4\cos 2\theta$.

22. The region inside the circle $r = 3\cos\theta$ but outside the cardioid $r = 1 + \cos\theta$.

23. Find the volume of the solid bounded above by the plane $z = y + b$, below by the xy-plane, and on the sides by the circular cylinder $x^2 + y^2 = b^2$.

24. Find the volume of the solid bounded below by the xy-plane and above by the paraboloid $z = 1 - (x^2 + y^2)$.

25. Find the volume of the ellipsoid

$$x^2/4 + y^2/4 + z^2/3 = 1.$$

26. Find the volume of the solid bounded below by the xy-plane and above by the surface $x^2 + y^2 + z^6 = 5$.

27. Find the volume of the solid bounded below by the xy-plane, above by the spherical surface $x^2 + y^2 + z^2 = 4$, and on the sides by the cylinder $x^2 + y^2 = 1$.

28. Find the volume of the solid bounded above by the surface $z = 1 - (x^2 + y^2)$, below by the xy-plane, and on the sides by the cylinder $x^2 + y^2 - x = 0$.

29. Find the volume of the solid bounded above by the plane $z = 2x$ and below by the disk $(x - 1)^2 + y^2 \leq 1$.

30. Find the volume of the solid bounded above by the cone $z^2 = x^2 + y^2$ and below by the region Ω which lies inside the curve $x^2 + y^2 = 2ax$. Take $a > 0$.

31. Find the volume of the solid bounded above by the ellipsoid of revolution $b^2x^2 + b^2y^2 + a^2z^2 = a^2b^2$, below by the xy-plane, and on the sides by the cylinder $x^2 + y^2 - ay = 0$.

32. A cylindrical hole of radius r is drilled through the center of a sphere of radius R.

(a) Determine the volume of the material that has been removed from the sphere.

(b) Determine the volume of the ring-shaped solid that remains.

33. Sketch the petal curve $r = 2\cos 2\theta$. Find the area of a petal.

34. Let $I = \iint_{\Omega} e^{x^2+y^2}\,dx\,dy$ where Ω is the annular region between the circles $x^2 + y^2 = 4$ and $x^2 + y^2 = 16$. Evaluate this integral by changing to polar coordinates.

■ 17.5 FURTHER APPLICATIONS OF THE DOUBLE INTEGRAL

A thin plane distribution of matter (we call it a *plate*) is laid out in the xy-plane in the form of a basic region Ω. If the mass density of the plate (the mass per unit area) is a constant λ, then the total mass M of the plate is simply the density λ times the area of the plate:

$$M = \lambda \times \text{ the area of } \Omega.$$

If the density varies continuously from point to point, say $\lambda = \lambda(x, y)$, then the mass of the plate is the average density of the plate times the area of the plate:

$$M = \text{average density } \times \text{ the area of } \Omega.$$

This is a double integral:

(17.5.1)
$$M = \iint_{\Omega} \lambda(x, y)\,dx\,dy.$$

The Center of Mass of a Plate

The center of mass x_M of a rod is a density-weighted average of position taken over the interval occupied by the rod:

$$x_M M = \int_a^b x\,\lambda(x)\,dx.$$ [This you have seen: (5.9.5).]

The coordinates of the center of mass of a plate (x_M, y_M) are determined by two density-weighted averages of position, each taken over the region occupied by the plate:

(17.5.2)
$$x_M M = \iint_{\Omega} x\,\lambda(x, y)\,dx\,dy, \qquad y_M M = \iint_{\Omega} y\,\lambda(x, y)\,dx\,dy.$$

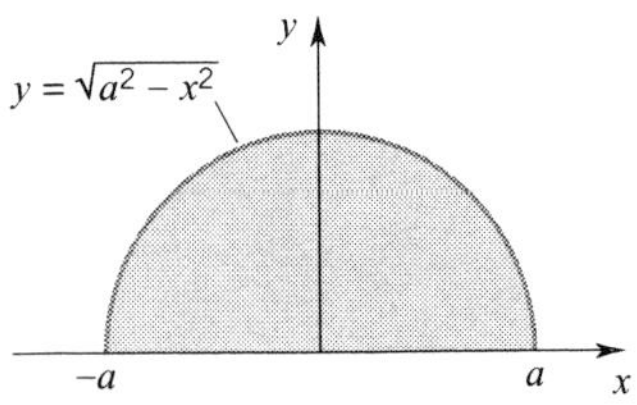

Figure 17.5.1

Example 1 A plate is in the form of a half-disk of radius a. Find the mass of the plate and the center of mass given that the mass density of the plate is directly proportional to the distance from the midpoint of the straight edge of the plate.

SOLUTION Place the plate over the region $\Omega : -a \le x \le a, 0 \le y\sqrt{a^2 - x^2}$. (Figure 17.5.1.) The mass density can then be written $\lambda(x, y) = k\sqrt{x^2 + y^2}$ where $k > 0$ is the constant of proportionality. Now

$$M = \iint_{\Omega} k\sqrt{x^2 + y^2}\, dx\, dy = \int_0^{\pi}\int_0^{a} (kr)r\, dr\, d\theta = k\left(\int_0^{\pi} 1\, d\theta\right)\left(\int_0^{a} r^2 dr\right)$$

change to polar coordinates ↑

$$= k(\pi)(\tfrac{1}{3}a^3) = \tfrac{1}{3}ka^3\pi.$$

$$x_M M = \iint_{\Omega} x(k\sqrt{x^2 + y^2})\, dx\, dy \qquad y_M M = \iint_{\Omega} y(k\sqrt{x^2 + y^2})\, dx\, dy.$$

Note that $x_M M = 0$ since Ω is symmetric about the y-axis and the integrand is odd in x. Thus, $x_M = 0$. Now let's find y_M.

$$y_M M = \iint_{\Omega} y(k\sqrt{x^2 + y^2})\, dx\, dy = \int_0^{\pi}\int_0^{a} (r\sin\theta)(kr)r\, dr\, d\theta$$

$$= k\left(\int_0^{\pi} \sin\theta\, d\theta\right)\left(\int_0^{a} r^3\, dr\right)$$

$$= k(2)(\tfrac{1}{4}a^4) = \tfrac{1}{2}ka^4.$$

Since $M = \frac{1}{3}ka^3\pi$, $y_M = (\frac{1}{2}ka^4)/(\frac{1}{3}ka^3\pi) = 3a/2\pi$. The center of mass of the plate is at the point $(0, 3a/2\pi) \cong (0, 0.48a)$. ❑

Centroids

If the plate is homogeneous, then the mass density λ is constantly M/A where A is the area of the base region Ω. In this case the center of mass of the plate falls on the *centroid* of the base region (a notion with which you are already familiar). The centroid $(\overline{x}, \overline{y})$ depends only on the geometry of Ω:

$$\overline{x}M = \iint_{\Omega} x(M/A)\, dx\, dy = (M/A)\iint_{\Omega} x\, dx\, dy,$$

$$\overline{y}M = \iint_{\Omega} y(M/A)\, dx\, dy = (M/A)\iint_{\Omega} y\, dx\, dy.$$

Dividing by M and multiplying through by A, we have

(17.5.3)
$$\overline{x}A = \iint_{\Omega} x\, dx\, dy, \quad \overline{y}A = \iint_{\Omega} y\, dx\, dy.$$

Thus, in the sense of (17.2.9), $\overline{x}$ is the average x-coordinate on Ω and $\overline{y}$ is the average y-coordinate. The mass of the plate does not enter into this at all.

Example 2 Find the centroid of the region

$$\Omega : a \leq x \leq b, \phi_1(x) \leq y \leq \phi_2(x). \qquad \text{(Figure 17.5.2)}$$

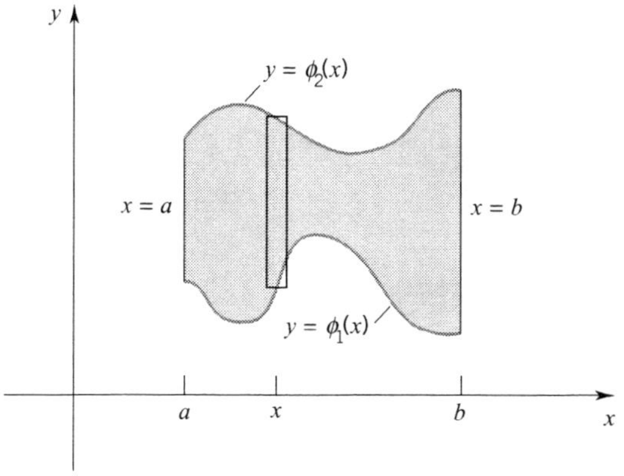

Figure 17.5.2

SOLUTION

$$\overline{x}A = \iint_{\Omega} x\,dx\,dy = \int_a^b \int_{\phi_1(x)}^{\phi_2(x)} x\,dy\,dx = \int_a^b x[\phi_2(x) - \phi_1(x)]\,dx;$$

$$\overline{y}A = \iint_{\Omega} y\,dx\,dy = \int_a^b \int_{\phi_1(x)}^{\phi_2(x)} y\,dy\,dx = \int_a^b \tfrac{1}{2}([\phi_2(x)]^2 - [\phi_1(x)]^2)\,dx.$$

These are the formulas for the centroid that we developed in Section 6.4. Having calculated many centroids there, we won't do so here. ❑

Kinetic Energy and Moment of Inertia

A particle of mass m at a distance r from a given line rotates about that line (called the *axis of rotation*) with angular speed ω. The speed v of the particle is then $r\omega$, and the kinetic energy is given by the formula

$$\text{KE} = \tfrac{1}{2}mv^2 = \tfrac{1}{2}mr^2\omega^2.$$

Imagine now a rigid body composed of a finite number of point masses m_i located at distances r_i from some fixed line. If the rigid body rotates about that line with angular speed ω, then all the point masses rotate about that same line with that same angular speed ω. The kinetic energy of the body can be obtained by adding up the kinetic energies of all the individual particles:

$$\text{KE} = \sum_i \tfrac{1}{2}m_i r_i^2 \omega^2 = \tfrac{1}{2}\left(\sum_i m_i r_i^2\right)\omega^2.$$

The expression in parentheses is called the *moment of inertia* (or *rotational inertia*) of the body and is denoted by the letter I:

(17.5.4)
$$I = \sum_i m_i r_i^2.$$

In straight-line motion all parts of a rigid body move at the same speed, and we have

$$\text{KE} = \tfrac{1}{2}Mv^2 \qquad \text{where } M = \text{ total mass and } v = \text{speed.}$$

In pure rotation all parts of a rigid body move at the same angular speed and we have

$$\text{KE} = \tfrac{1}{2}I\omega^2 \qquad \text{where } I = \text{total moment of inertia and } \omega = \text{angular speed.}$$

The Moment of Inertia of a Plate

Suppose that a plate in the shape of a basic region Ω rotates about a line. The moment of inertia of the plate about that axis of rotation is given by the formula

(17.5.5)
$$I = \iint_{\Omega} \lambda(x, y)[r(x, y)]^2 \, dx\, dy$$

where $\lambda = \lambda(x, y)$ is the mass density function and $r(x, y)$ is the distance from the axis to the point (x, y).

DERIVATION OF (17.5.5) Decompose the plate into n pieces in the form of basic regions $\Omega_1, \ldots, \Omega_n$. From each Ω_i choose a point (x_i^*, y_i^*) and view all the mass of the ith piece as concentrated there. The moment of inertia of this piece is then approximately

$$\underbrace{[\lambda(x_i^*, y_i^*)(\text{area of } \Omega_i)]}_{\text{approx. mass of piece}} \; \underbrace{[r(x_i^*, y_i^*)]^2}_{(\text{approx. distance})^2} = \lambda(x_i^*, y_i^*)[r(x_i^*, y_i^*)]^2(\text{area of } \Omega_i).$$

The sum of these approximations,

$$\sum_{i=1}^{n} \lambda(x_i^*, y_i^*)[r(x_i^*, y_i^*)]^2(\text{area of } \Omega_i),$$

is a Riemann sum for the double integral

$$\iint_{\Omega} \lambda(x, y)[r(x, y)]^2 \, dx\, dy.$$

As the maximum diameter of the Ω_i tends to zero, the Riemann sum tends to this integral. ❑

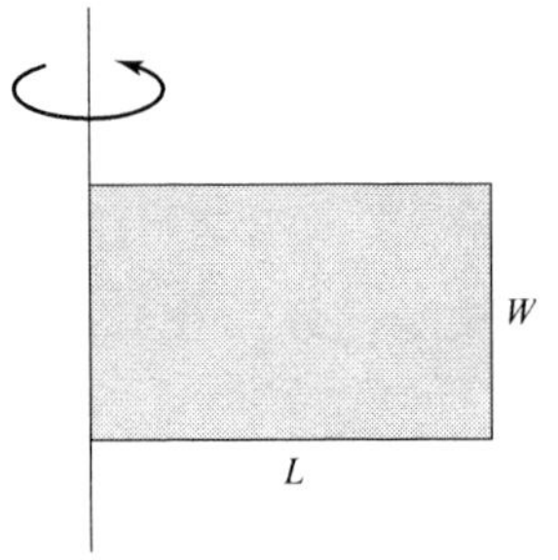

Figure 17.5.3

Example 3 A rectangular plate of mass M, length L, width W rotates about the line shown in Figure 17.5.3. Find the moment of inertia of the plate about that line: **(a)** given that the plate has uniform mass density; **(b)** given that the mass density of the plate varies directly as the square of the distance from the rightmost side.

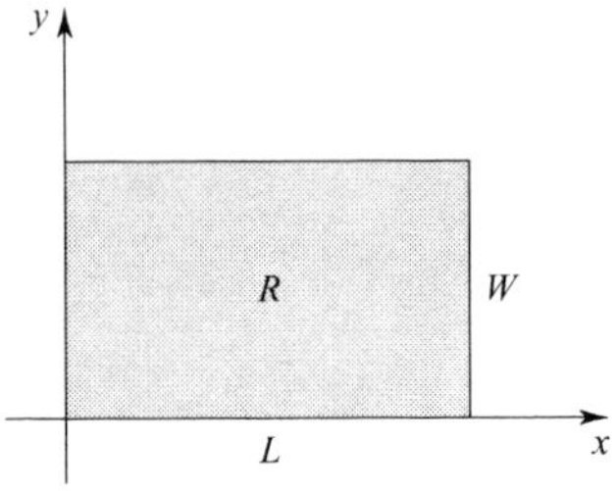

Figure 17.5.4

SOLUTION Coordinatize the plate as in Figure 17.5.4 and call the base region R.

(a) Here $\lambda(x, y) = M/LW$ and $r(x, y) = x$. Thus

$$I = \iint_{R} \frac{M}{LW}x^2 \, dx\, dy = \frac{M}{LW}\int_0^W \int_0^L x^2 \, dx\, dy$$

$$= \frac{M}{LW} W \int_0^L x^2 \, dx = \frac{M}{L}(\tfrac{1}{3}L^3) = \tfrac{1}{3}ML^2.$$

(b) In this case $\lambda(x, y) = k(L - x)^2$, but we still have $r(x, y) = x$. Therefore

$$I = \iint_R k(L-x)^2 x^2\, dx\, dy = k\int_0^W \int_0^L (L-x)^2 x^2\, dx\, dy$$

$$= kW\int_0^L (L^2x^2 - 2Lx^3 + x^4)\, dx = \tfrac{1}{30}kL^5W.$$

We can eliminate the constant of proportionality k by noting that

$$M = \iint_R k(L-x)^2\, dx\, dy = k\int_0^W \int_0^L (L-x)^2\, dx\, dy$$

$$= kW\Big[-\tfrac{1}{3}(L-x)^3\Big]_0^L = \tfrac{1}{3}kWL^3.$$

Therefore

$$k = \frac{3M}{WL^3} \qquad \text{and} \qquad I = \frac{1}{30}\left(\frac{3M}{WL^3}\right)L^5W = \frac{1}{10}ML^2. \quad \square$$

Radius of Gyration

If the mass M of an object is all concentrated at a distance r from a given line, then the moment of inertia about that line is given by the product Mr^2.

Suppose now that we have a plate of mass M (actually any object of mass M will do here), and suppose that l is some line. The object has some moment of inertia I about l. Its *radius of gyration* about l is the distance K for which

$$I = MK^2.$$

Namely, the radius of gyration about l is the distance from l at which all the mass of the object would have to be concentrated to effect the same moment of inertia. The formula for radius of gyration K is usually written

(17.5.6) $$K = \sqrt{I/M}.$$

Example 4 A homogeneous circular plate of mass M and radius R rotates about an axle that passes through the center of the plate and is perpendicular to the plate. Calculate the moment of inertia and the radius of gyration.

SOLUTION Take the axle as the z-axis and let the plate rest on the circular region $\Omega : x^2 + y^2 \le R^2$. (Figure 17.5.5) The density of the plate is $M/A = M/\pi R^2$ and $r(x, y) = \sqrt{x^2 + y^2}$. Hence

$$I = \iint_\Omega \frac{M}{\pi R^2}(x^2 + y^2)\, dx\, dy = \frac{M}{\pi R^2}\int_0^{2\pi}\int_0^R r^3\, dr\, d\theta = \tfrac{1}{2}MR^2.$$

In this case the radius of gyration $K = \sqrt{I/M}$ is $R/\sqrt{2}$.

The circular plate of radius R has the same moment of inertia about the central axle as a circular wire of the same mass with radius $R/\sqrt{2}$. $\square$

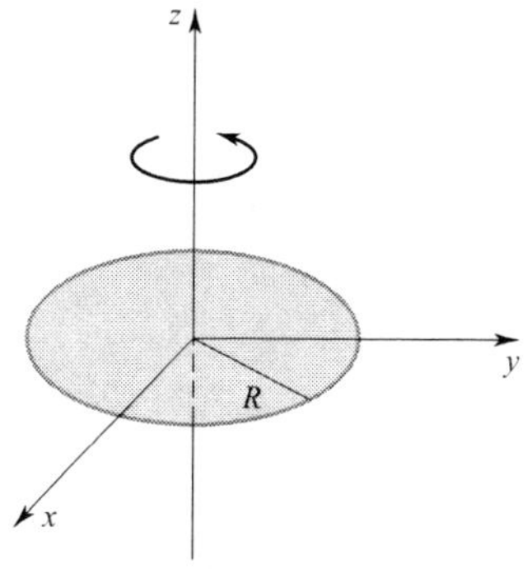

Figure 17.5.5

The Parallel Axis Theorem

Suppose we have an object of mass M and a line l_M that passes through the center of mass (x_M, y_M). The object has moment of inertia about that line; call it I_M. If l is a line parallel to l_M, then the object has moment of inertia about l; call that I. The parallel axis theorem states that

(17.5.7) $$I = I_M + d^2 M$$

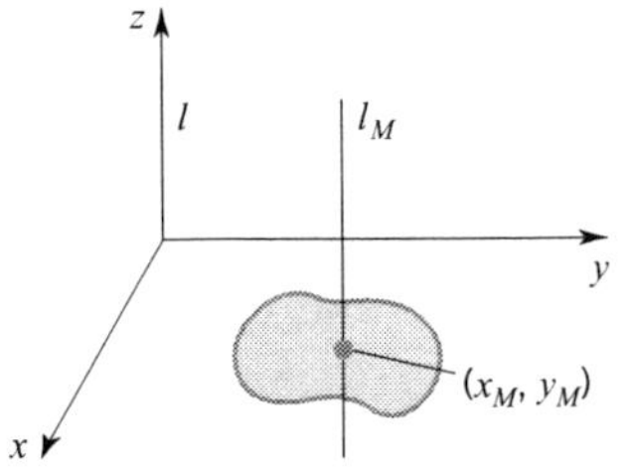

Figure 17.5.6

where d is the distance between the axes.

We prove the theorem under somewhat restrictive assumptions. We assume that the object is a plate of mass M in the shape of a basic region Ω, and assume that l_M is perpendicular to the plate. We call l the z-axis and place the plate on the xy-plane. (See Figure 17.5.6.) Denoting the points of Ω by (x, y), we have

$$\begin{aligned} I - I_M &= \iint_\Omega \lambda(x,y)(x^2+y^2)\,dx\,dy - \iint_\Omega \lambda(x,y)[(x-x_M)^2+(y-y_M)^2]\,dx\,dy \\ &= \iint_\Omega \lambda(x,y)[2x_M x + 2y_M y - (x_M^2+y_M^2)]\,dx\,dy \\ &= 2x_M \iint_\Omega x\lambda(x,y)\,dx\,dy + 2y_M \iint_\Omega y\lambda(x,y)\,dx\,dy \\ &\quad -(x_M^2+y_M^2)\iint_\Omega \lambda(x,y)\,dx\,dy \\ &= 2x_M^2 + 2y_M^2 M - (x_M^2+y_M^2)M = (x_M^2+y_M^2)M = d^2 M. \quad \square \end{aligned}$$

An obvious consequence of the parallel axis theorem is that $I_M \le I$ for all lines l parallel to l_M. To minimize the moment of inertia, we must pass the axis of rotation through the center of mass.

EXERCISES 17.5

Exercises 1–10. Find the mass and center of mass of the plate that occupies the region and has mass density λ.

1. $\Omega: -1 \le x \le 1, \quad 0 \le y \le 1, \quad \lambda(x,y) = x^2.$

2. $\Omega: 0 \le x \le 1, \quad 0 \le y \le \sqrt{x}, \quad \lambda(x,y) = x + y.$

3. $\Omega: 0 \le x \le 1, \quad x^2 \le y \le 1, \quad \lambda(x,y) = xy.$

4. $\Omega: 0 \le x \le \pi, \quad 0 \le y \le \sin x, \quad \lambda(x,y) = y.$

5. $\Omega: 0 \le x \le 8, \quad 0 \le y \le \sqrt[3]{x}, \quad \lambda(x,y) = y^2.$

6. $\Omega: 0 \le x \le a, \quad 0 \le y \le \sqrt{a^2 - x^2}, \quad \lambda(x,y) = xy.$

7. Ω : the triangular region with vertices $(0,0), (1,2), (1,3)$; $\lambda(x,y) = xy$.

8. Ω: the triangular region in the first quadrant bounded by $x = 0, y = 0, 3x + 2y = 6$; $\lambda(x,y) = x + y$.

9. Ω: the region bounded by the cardioid $r = 1 + \cos\theta$; λ is the distance to the pole.

10. Ω: the region inside the circle $r = 2\sin\theta$ but outside the circle $r = 1$; $\lambda(x,y) = y$.

In the exercises that follow, I_x, I_y, I_z denote the moments of inertia about the x, y, z axes.

11. A rectangular plate of mass M, length L, and width W is placed on the xy-plane with center at the origin, long sides parallel to the x-axis. (We assume here that $L \ge W$.) Find I_x, I_y, I_z if the plate is homogeneous. Determine the corresponding radii of gyration K_x, K_y, K_z.

12. Verify that I_x, I_y, I_z are unchanged if the mass density of the plate of Exercise 11 varies directly as the distance from the leftmost side.

13. Determine the center of mass of the plate of Exercise 11 if the mass density varies as in Exercise 12.

14. Show that for any plate in the xy-plane

$$I_z = I_x + I_y.$$

How are the corresponding radii of gyration K_x, K_y, K_z related?

15. A homogeneous plate of mass M in the form of a quarter-disk of radius R is placed in the xy-plane as in the figure. Find I_x, I_y, I_z and the corresponding radii of gyration.

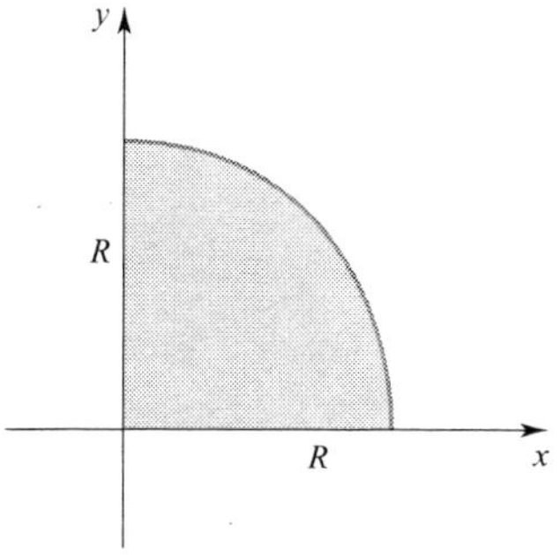

16. A plate in the xy-plane undergoes a rotation in that plane about its center of mass. Show that I_z remains unchanged.

17. A homogeneous disk of mass M and radius R is to be placed on the xy-plane so that it has moment of inertia I_0 about the z-axis. Where should the disk be placed?

18. A homogeneous plate of mass density λ occupies the region under the curve $y = f(x)$ from $x = a$ to $x = b$. Show that

$$I_x = \tfrac{1}{3}\lambda \int_a^b [f(x)]^3\, dx \qquad \text{and} \qquad I_y = \lambda \int_a^b x^2 f(x)\, dx.$$

19. A homogeneous plate of mass M in the form of an elliptical quadrant is placed on the xy-plane. (See the figure.) Find I_x, I_y, I_z.

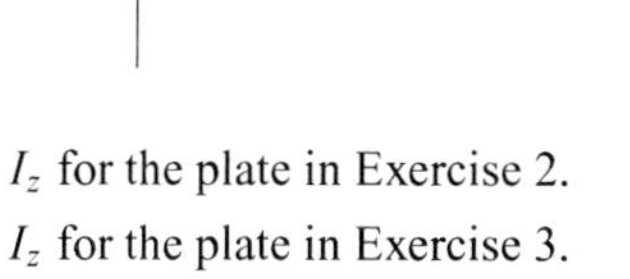

20. Find I_x, I_y, I_z for the plate in Exercise 2.

21. Find I_x, I_y, I_z for the plate in Exercise 3.

22. Find I_x, I_y, I_z for the plate in Exercise 5.

23. Find I_x, I_y, I_z for the plate in Exercise 9.

24. A plate of varying density occupies the region $\Omega = \Omega_1 \cup \Omega_2$ shown in the figure. Find the center of mass of the plate given that the Ω_1 piece has mass M_1 and center of mass (x_1, y_1), and the Ω_2 piece has mass M_2 and center of mass (x_2, y_2).

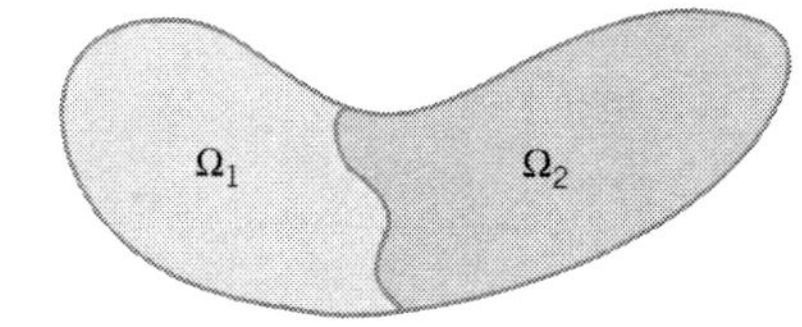

25. A homogeneous plate of mass M is in the form of a ring. (See the figure.) Calculate the moment of inertia of the plate:
(a) about a diameter;
(b) about a tangent to the inner circle;
(c) about a tangent to the outer circle.

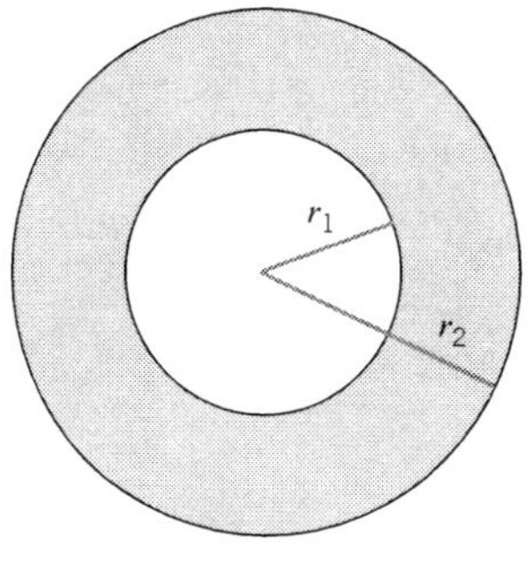

26. Find the moment of inertia of a homogeneous circular wire of mass M and radius r:
(a) about a diameter;
(b) about a tangent. HINT: Use the previous exercise.

27. The plate of Exercise 25 rotates about the axis that is perpendicular to the plate and passes through the center. Find the moment of inertia.

28. Prove the parallel axis theorem for the case where the line through the center of mass lies in the plane of the plate.

29. A plate of mass M has the form of a half-disk Ω, $-R \le x \le R, 0 \le y \le \sqrt{R^2 - x^2}$. Find the center of mass given that the mass density varies directly as the distance from the curved boundary.

30. Find I_x, I_y, I_z for the plate of Exercise 29.

31. A plate of mass M is in the form of a disk of radius R. Given that the mass density of the plate varies directly as the distance from a point P on the boundary of the plate, locate the center of mass.

32. The edges of a plate of mass M form a right triangle of base b, height h. Given that the mass density of the plate varies directly as the square of the distance from the vertex of the right angle, locate the center of mass of the plate.

33. Use double integrals to justify the additivity assumption we made about centroids in Chapter 6, (6.4.1).

34. A plate occupies the triangular region with vertices (0, 0), (0, 1), (2, 1). The mass density is given by the function $\lambda(x, y) = x + y$. Calculate (a) the center of mass of the plate, and (b) the moments of inertia I_x and I_y.

17.6 TRIPLE INTEGRALS

Now that you are familiar with double integrals

$$\iint_{\Omega} f(x, y)\, dx\, dy,$$

you will find it easy to understand triple integrals

$$\iiint_{T} f(x, y, z)\, dx\, dy\, dz.$$

Basically the only difference is that, instead of working with functions of two variables continuous on a plane region Ω, we will be working with functions of three variables continuous on some portion T of three-space.

The Triple Integral over a Box

For double integration we began with a rectangle

$$R: \quad a_1 \le x \le a_2, \; b_1 \le y \le b_2.$$

For triple integration we begin with a *box* (a rectangular solid)

$$\Pi: \quad a_1 \le x \le a_2, \; b_1 \le y \le b_2, \; c_1 \le z \le c_2. \qquad \text{(Figure 17.6.1)}$$

To partition this box, we first partition the edges. Taking

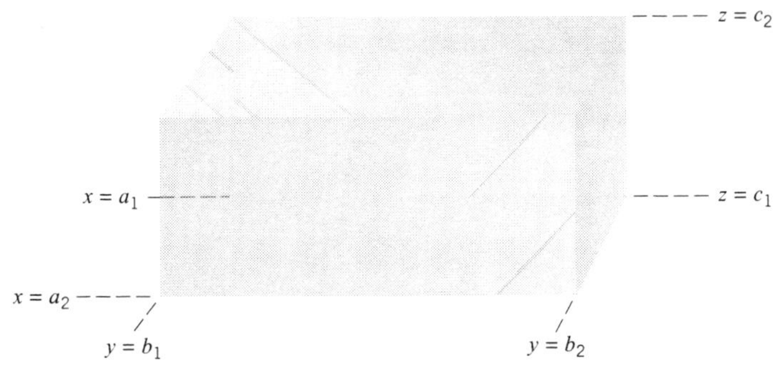

Figure 17.6.1

$$P_1 = \{x_0, \ldots, x_m\} \quad \text{as a partition of } [a_1, a_2],$$
$$P_2 = \{y_0, \ldots, y_n\} \quad \text{as a partition of } [b_1, b_2],$$
$$P_3 = \{z_0, \ldots, z_q\} \quad \text{as a partition of } [c_1, c_2],$$

we form the set

$$P = P_1 \times P_2 \times P_3 = \{(x_i, y_j, z_k) : x_i \in P_1, y_j \in P_2, z_k \in P_3\}.^{\dagger}$$

We call this a *partition of* Π. The partition P breaks up Π into $m \times n \times q$ nonoverlapping boxes

$$\Pi_{ijk}: \quad x_{i-1} \le x \le x_i, \qquad y_{j-1} \le y \le y_j, \qquad z_{k-1} \le z \le z_k.$$

† $P_1 \times P_2 \times P_3$ is called the *Cartesian product* of P_1, P_2, P_3.

A typical such box is pictured in Figured 17.6.2.

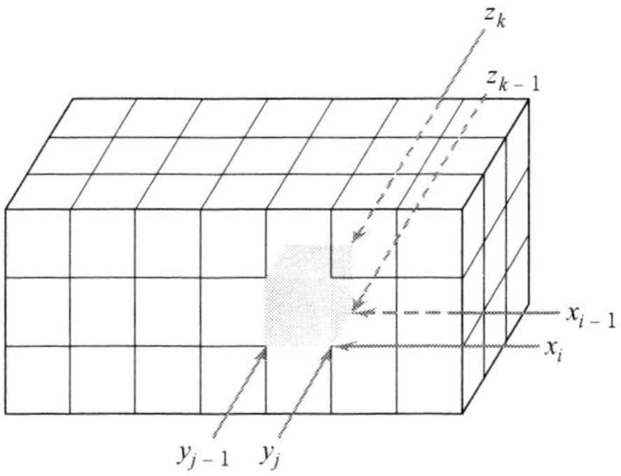

Figure 17.6.2

Assume that f is a function continuous on Π. Taking

$$M_{ijk} \text{ as the maximum value of } f \text{ on } \Pi_{ijk}$$

and

$$m_{ijk} \text{ as the minimum value of } f \text{ on } \Pi_{ijk},$$

we form the *upper sum*

$$U_f(P) = \sum_{i=1}^{m}\sum_{j=1}^{n}\sum_{k=1}^{q} M_{ijk} \,(\text{volume of } \Pi_{ijk}) = \sum_{i=1}^{m}\sum_{j=1}^{n}\sum_{k=1}^{q} M_{ijk}\Delta_{x_i}\Delta_{y_j}\Delta_{z_k}$$

and the *lower sum*

$$L_f(P) = \sum_{i=1}^{m}\sum_{j=1}^{n}\sum_{k=1}^{q} m_{ijk} \,(\text{volume of } \Pi_{ijk}) = \sum_{i=1}^{m}\sum_{j=1}^{n}\sum_{k=1}^{q} m_{ijk}\Delta_{x_i}\Delta_{y_j}\Delta_{z_k}.$$

As in the case of functions of one and two variables, it turns out that, with f continuous on Π, there is one and only one number I that satisfies the inequality

$$L_f(P) \le I \le U_f(P) \qquad \text{for all partitions } P \text{ of } \Pi.$$

DEFINITION 17.6.1 THE TRIPLE INTEGRAL OVER A BOX Π

Let f be continuous on a closed box Π. The unique number I that satisfies the inequality

$$L_f(P) \le I \le U_f(P) \qquad \text{for all partitions } P \text{ of } \Pi$$

is called the *triple integral* of f over Π and is denoted by

$$\iiint\limits_{\Pi} f(x, y, z)\,dxdydz^{\dagger}$$

†The triple integral can be written $\iiint\limits_{\Pi} f(x, y, z)\,dV$.

The Triple Integral over a More General Solid

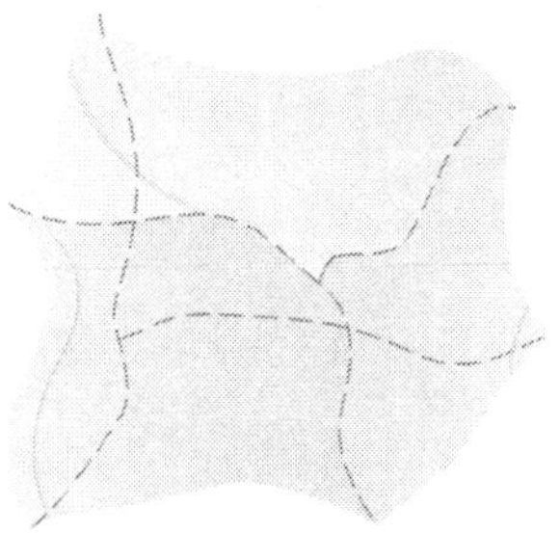

Figure 17.6.3

We start with a three-dimensional, bounded, closed, connected set T. We assume that T is a *basic solid*; that is, we assume that the boundary of T consists of a finite number of continuous surfaces $z = \alpha(x, y)$, $y = \beta(x, z)$, $x = \gamma(y, z)$. See, for example, Figure 17.6.3.

Now let's suppose that f is some function continuous on T. To define the triple integral of f over T, we first encase T in a rectangular box Π with sides parallel to the coordinate planes. (Figure 17.6.4.) We then extend f to all of Π by defining f to be zero outside of T. This extended function f is bounded on Π, and it is continuous on all of Π except possibly at the boundary of T. In spite of these possible discontinuities, f is still integrable over Π; that is, there still exists a unique number I such that

$$L_f(P) \leq I \leq U_f(P) \qquad \text{for all partitions } P \text{ of } \Pi.$$

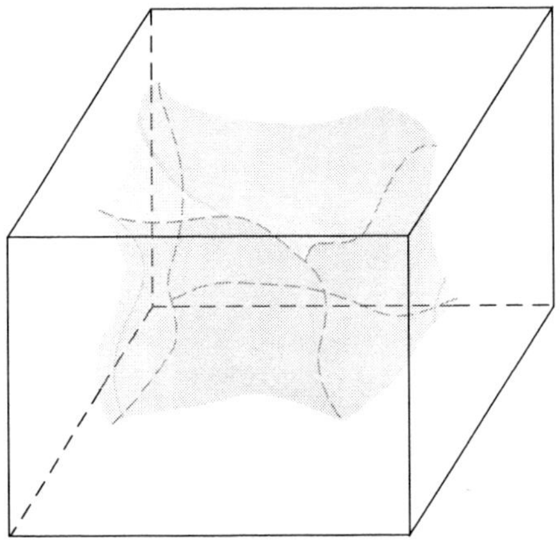

Figure 17.6.4

(We will not attempt to prove this.) The number I is by definition the triple integral

$$\iiint_{\Pi} f(x, y, z)\, dx\, dy\, dz.$$

We define the triple integral over T by setting

(17.6.2)
$$\iiint_{T} f(x, y, z)\, dx\, dy\, dz = \iiint_{\Pi} f(x, y, z)\, dx\, dy\, dz.$$

Volume as a Triple Integral

The simplest triple integral of interest is the triple integral of the function that is constantly 1 on T. This gives the volume of T:

(17.6.3)
$$\text{volume of } T = \iiint_{T} dx\, dy\, dz.$$

PROOF Set $f(x, y, z) = 1$ for all (x, y, z) in T. Encase T in a box Π. Define f to be zero outside of T. An arbitrary partition P of Π breaks up T into little boxes Π_{ijk}. Note that

$$L_f(P) = \text{the sum of the volumes of all the } \Pi_{ijk} \text{ that are contained in } T$$
$$U_f(P) = \text{the sum of the volumes of all the } \Pi_{ijk} \text{ that intersect } T.$$

It follows that

$$L_f(P) \leq \text{the volume of } T \leq U_f(P).$$

The arbitrariness of P gives the formula. ❑

Some Properties of the Triple Integral

Below we give without proof the elementary properties of triple integrals analogous to what you saw in the one- and two-variable cases. Assume throughout that T is a basic solid. The functions f and g are assumed to be continuous on T.

I. *Linearity:*

$$\iiint_T [\alpha f(x, y, z) + \beta g(x, y, z)]\, dx\, dy\, dz$$
$$= \alpha \iiint_T f(x, y, z)\, dx\, dy\, dz + \beta \iiint_T g(x, y, z)\, dx\, dy\, dz.$$

II. *Order:*

$$\text{if } f \geq 0 \text{ on } T, \quad \text{then} \quad \iiint_T f(x, y, z)\, dx\, dy\, dz \geq 0;$$

$$\text{if } f \leq g \text{ on } T, \quad \text{then} \quad \iiint_T f(x, y, z)\, dx\, dy\, dz \leq \iiint_T g(x, y, z)\, dx\, dy\, dz.$$

III. *Additivity*: If T is broken up into a finite number of basic solids $T_1, \ldots, T_n$, then

$$\iiint_T f(x, y, z)\, dx\, dy\, dz = \iiint_{T_1} f(x, y, z)\, dx\, dy\, dz + \cdots + \iiint_{T_n} f(x, y, z)\, dx\, dy\, dz.$$

IV. *Mean-value condition*: There is a point (x_0, y_0, z_0) in T for which

$$\iiint_T f(x, y, z)\, dx\, dy\, dz = f(x_0, y_0, z_0) \cdot (\text{volume of } T).$$

We call $f(x_0, y_0, z_0)$ *the average value of f on T.*

This notion of average enables us to write

(17.6.4)
$$\iiint_T f(x, y, z)\, dx\, dy\, dz = \begin{pmatrix} \text{the average value} \\ \text{of } f \text{ on } T \end{pmatrix} \cdot (\text{volume of } T).$$

We can also take weighted averages: if f and g are continuous and g is nonnegative on T, then there is a point (x_0, y_0, z_0) in T for which

(17.6.5)
$$\iiint_T f(x, y, z)\, g(x, y, z)\, dx\, dy\, dz = f(x_0, y_0, z_0) \iiint_T g(x, y, z)\, dx\, dy\, dz.$$

As you would expect, we call $f(x_0, y_0, z_0)$ *the g-weighted average of f on T.*

The formulas for mass, center of mass, and moments of inertia derived in the previous section for two-dimensional plates are easily extended to three-dimensional objects.

Suppose that T is an object in the form of a basic solid. If T has constant mass density λ (here density is mass per unit volume), then the mass of T is the density λ times the volume of T:

$$M = \lambda V.$$

If the mass density varies continuously over T, say, $\lambda = \lambda(x, y, z)$, then *the mass of T is the average density of T times the volume of T.* This is a triple integral

(17.6.6)
$$M = \iiint_T \lambda(x, y, z)\, dx\, dy\, dz.$$

The coordinates of the center of mass (x_M, y_M, z_M) are density-weighted averages of position, each taken over the portion of space occupied by the solid.

(17.6.7)
$$x_M M = \iiint_T x\lambda(x, y, z)\, dx\, dy\, dz, \qquad \text{etc.}$$

If the object T is homogeneous (constant mass density M/V), then the center of mass of T depends only on the geometry of T and falls on the centroid $(\bar{x}, \bar{y}, \bar{z})$ of the space occupied by T. The density is irrelevant. The coordinates of the centroid are simple averages over T:

(17.6.8)
$$\bar{x} V = \iiint_T x\, dx\, dy\, dz, \qquad \text{etc.}$$

The moment of inertia of T about a line is given by the formula

(17.6.9)
$$I = \iiint_T \lambda(x, y, z)[r(x, y, z)]^2\, dx\, dy\, dz.$$

Here $\lambda(x, y, z)$ is the mass density of T at (x, y, z) and $r(x, y, z)$ is the distance of (x, y, z) from the line in question. The moments of inertia about the x, y, z axes are again denoted by I_x, I_y, I_z.

All of this should be readily understandable. Techniques for evaluating triple integrals are introduced in the next three sections.

EXERCISES 17.6

1. Let $f(x, y)$ be a function continuous and nonnegative on a basic region Ω and set

$$T = \{(x, y, z) : (x, y) \in \Omega, \quad 0 \le z \le f(x, y)\}.$$

Compare

$$\iiint_T dx\,dy\,dz \qquad \text{to} \qquad \iint_\Omega f(x, y)\,dx\,dy.$$

2. Set $f(x, y, z) = xyz$ on $\Pi: \quad 0 \le x \le 1, 0 \le y \le 1, 0 \le z \le 1$ and take P as the partition $P_1 \times P_2 \times P_3$.

(a) Find $L_f(P)$ and $U_f(P)$ given that

$$P_1 = \{x_0, \dots, x_m\}, \quad P_2 = \{y_0, \dots, y_n\},$$
$$P_3 = \{z_0, \dots, z_q\}$$

are arbitrary partitions of [0, 1].

(b) Use your answer to part (a) to calculate

$$\iiint_\Pi xyz\,dx\,dy\,dz.$$

3. Set $\Pi : a_1 \le x \le a_2, b_1 \le y \le b_2, c_1 \le z \le c_2$. Show that

$$\iiint_\Pi \alpha\,dx\,dy\,dz = \alpha(a_2 - a_1)(b_2 - b_1)(c_2 - c_1).$$

4. Find the average value of $f(x, y, z) = xyz$ over the box defined in Exercise 2.

5. Set $\Pi : 0 \le x \le a, 0 \le y \le b, 0 \le z \le c$. Calculate

$$\iiint_\Pi xy\,dx\,dy\,dz.$$

6. Let T be a basic solid of varying mass density $\lambda = \lambda(x, y, z)$. The moment of inertia of T about the xy-plane is defined by setting

$$I_{xy} = \iiint_T \lambda(x, y, z) z^2\,dx\,dy\,dz.$$

The other moments of inertia, I_{xz} and I_{yz}, are defined in a similar manner. Express I_x, I_y, I_z in terms of the plane moments of inertia.

7. A box $\Pi_1 : \quad 0 \le x \le 2a, 0 \le y \le 2b, 0 \le z \le 2c$ is cut away from a larger box $\Pi_0 : 0 \le x \le 2A, 0 \le y \le 2B, 0 \le z \le 2C$. Locate the centroid of the remaining solid.

8. Show that, if f is continuous and nonnegative on a basic solid T, then the triple integral of f over T is nonnegative.

9. The box $\Pi : \quad 0 \le x \le a, 0 \le y \le a, 0 \le z \le a$ is a cube. Find the mass of the cube if the density varies directly as the distance from the face on the xy-plane.

10. Locate the center of mass of the cube of Exercise 9.

11. Find the moment of inertia I_z of the cube of Exercise 9.

12. Let $f(x, y, z) = 3y^2 - 2x + z$ on the box $B : 2 \le x \le 5, 1 \le y \le 3, 3 \le z \le 4$. Let P_1 be a regular partition of [2, 5] with $k = 10$ subintervals, let P_2 be a regular partition of $[1, 3]$ with $m = 20$ subintervals, let P_3 be a regular partition of $[3, 4]$ with $n = 15$ subintervals, and let $P = P_1 \times P_2 \times P_3$.

(a) Use a CAS to find $L_f(P)$ and $U_f(P)$.

(b) Investigate $L_f(P)$ and $U_f(P)$ for values of $k > 100$, $m > 200$ and $n > 150$.

(c) Estimate $\iiint_B f(x, y, z)\,dx\,dy\,dz$.

■ 17.7 REDUCTION TO REPEATED INTEGRALS

In this section we give no proofs. You can assume that all the solids that appear are basic solids and all the functions that you encounter are continuous.

In Figure 17.7.1 we have sketched a solid T. The projection of T onto the xy-plane has been labeled Ω_{xy}. The solid T is then the set of all (x, y, z) with

$$(x, y) \in \Omega_{xy} \qquad \text{and} \qquad \psi_1(x, y) \le z \le \psi_2(x, y).$$

The triple integral over T can be evaluated by setting

$$(*) \qquad \iiint_T f(x, y, z)\,dx\,dy\,dz = \iint_{\Omega_{xy}} \left(\int_{\psi_2(x,y)}^{\psi_2(x,y)} f(x, y, z)\,dz \right) dx\,dy.$$

Moving to Figure 17.7.2, we see that in this case Ω_{xy} is the region

$$a_1 \le x \le a_2, \qquad \phi_1(x) \le y \le \phi_2(x)$$

and T itself is the set of all (x, y, z) with

$$a_1 \le x \le a_2, \qquad \phi_1(x) \le y \le \phi_2(x), \qquad \psi_1(x, y) \le z \le \psi_2(x, y).$$

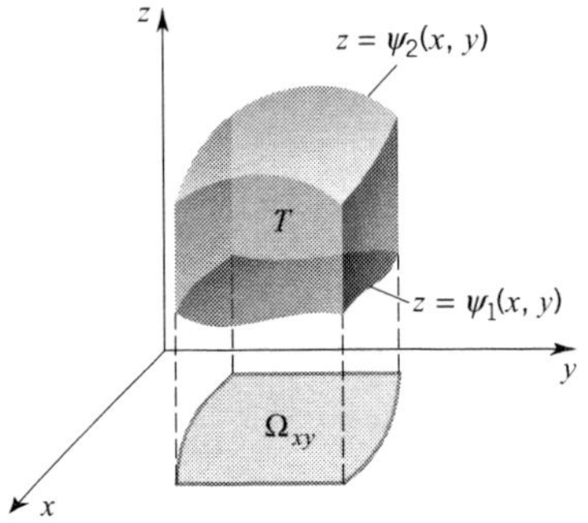

Figure 17.7.1

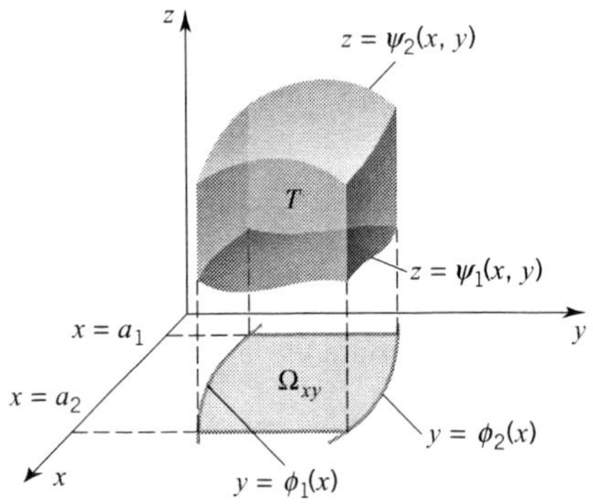

Figure 17.7.2

The triple integral over T can then be expressed by three ordinary integrals:

$$\iiint_T f(x, y, z)\, dx\, dy\, dz = \int_{a_1}^{a_2} \left[\int_{\phi_1(x)}^{\phi_2(x)} \left(\int_{\psi_1(x,y)}^{\psi_2(x,y)} f(x, y, z)\, dz \right) dy \right] dx.$$

It is customary to omit the brackets and parentheses and write

(17.7.1) $$\iiint_T f(x, y, z)\, dx\, dy\, dz = \int_{a_1}^{a_2} \int_{\phi_1(x)}^{\phi_2(x)} \int_{\psi_1(x,y)}^{\psi_2(x,y)} f(x, y, z)\, dz\, dy\, dx.$$ †

Here we first integrate with respect to z [from $z = \psi_1(x, y)$ to $z = \psi_2(x, y)$], then with respect to y [from $y = \phi_1(x)$ to $y = \phi_2(x)$], and finally with respect to x [from $x = a_1$ to $x = a_2$].

There is nothing special about this order of integration. Other orders of integration are possible and in some cases more convenient. Suppose, for example, that the projection of T onto the xz-plane is a region of the form

$$\Omega_{xz}: \quad a_1 \le z \le a_2, \; \phi_1(z) \le x \le \phi_2(z).$$

If T is the set of all (x, y, z) with

$$a_1 \le z \le a_2, \qquad \phi_1(z) \le x \le \phi_2(z), \qquad \psi_1(x, z) \le y \le \psi_2(x, z),$$

then

$$\iiint_T f(x, y, z)\, dx\, dy\, dz = \int_{a_1}^{a_2} \int_{\phi_1(z)}^{\phi_2(z)} \int_{\psi_1(x,z)}^{\psi_2(x,z)} f(x, y, z)\, dy\, dx\, dz.$$

† This formula is (∗) taken one step further. Usually we skip the double-integral stage and go directly to three integrals.

In this case we integrate first with respect to y, then with respect to x, and finally with respect to z. Still four other orders of integration are possible.

Example 1 Evaluate the expression $\int_0^2 \int_0^x \int_0^{4-x^2} xyz\,dz\,dy\,dx.$

SOLUTION

$$\begin{aligned}
\int_0^2 \int_0^x \int_0^{4-x^2} xyz\,dz\,dy\,dx &= \int_0^2 \int_0^x \left(\int_0^{4-x^2} xyz\,dz \right) dy\,dx \\
&= \int_0^2 \int_0^x \left(\left[\tfrac{1}{2}xyz^2 \right]_0^{4-x^2} \right) dy\,dx \\
&= \tfrac{1}{2} \int_0^2 \int_0^x x(4-x^2)^2 y\,dy\,dx \\
&= \tfrac{1}{2} \int_0^2 \left(\int_0^x x(4-x^2)^2 y\,dy \right) dx \\
&= \tfrac{1}{2} \int_0^2 \left(\left[\tfrac{1}{2}x(4-x^2)^2 y^2 \right]_0^x \right) dx \\
&= \tfrac{1}{4} \int_0^2 x^3(4-x^2)^2\,dx = \tfrac{1}{4} \int_0^2 x^3(16-8x^2+x^4)\,dx \\
&= \tfrac{1}{4}\left[4x^4 - \tfrac{8}{6}x^6 + \tfrac{1}{8}x^8 \right]_0^2 = \tfrac{8}{3}. \quad \square
\end{aligned}$$

Remark The solid determined by the limits of integration in Example 1 is the solid T in the first octant bounded by the parabolic cylinder $z = 4 - x^2$, the plane $z = 0$, the plane $y = x$, and the plane $y = 0$. This solid is shown in Figure 17.7.3. ❑

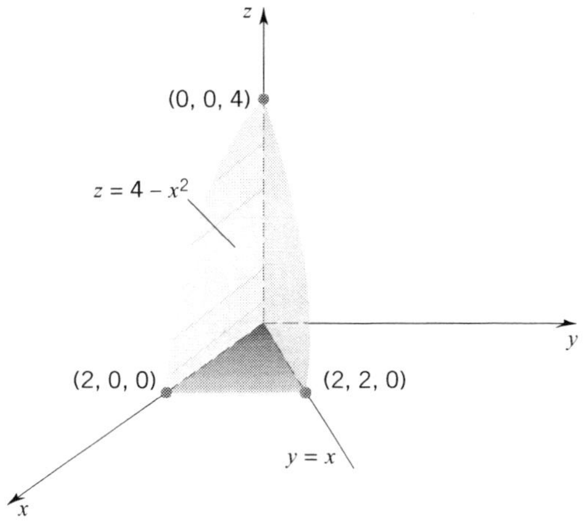

Figure 17.7.3

Example 2 Use triple integration to find the volume of the tetrahedron T shown in Figure 17.7.4. Then find the coordinates of the centroid.

SOLUTION The volume of T is given by the triple integral

$$V = \iiint_T dx\,dy\,dz.$$

To evaluate this triple integral, we can project T onto any one of the three coordinate planes. We will project onto the xy-plane. The base region is then the triangular region

$$\Omega_{xy} : 0 \le x \le 1, 0 \le y \le 1 - x. \qquad \text{(Figure 17.7.5)}$$

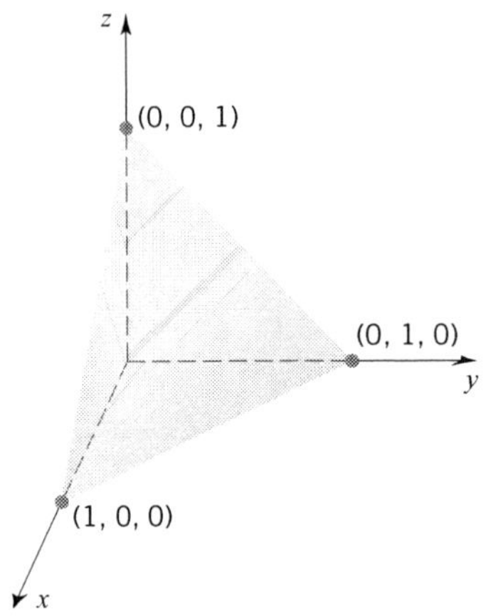

Figure 17.7.4

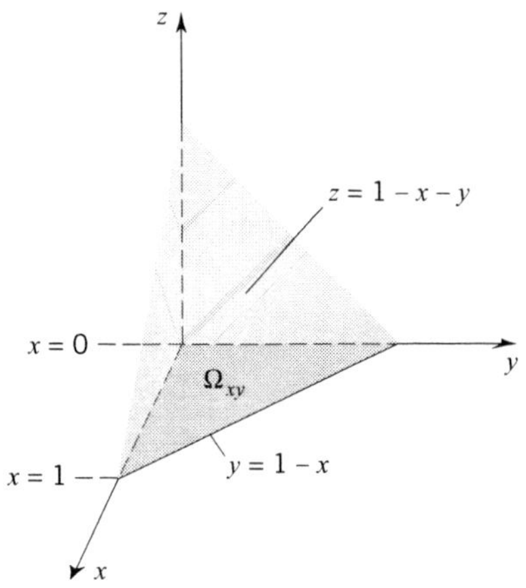

Figure 17.7.5

Since the inclined face is part of the plane $z = 1 - x - y$, we have T as the set of all (x, y, z) with

$$0 \le x \le 1, \qquad 0 \le y \le 1 - x, \qquad 0 \le z \le 1 - x - y.$$

It follows that

$$V = \iiint_T dx\,dy\,dz = \int_0^1 \int_0^{1-x} \int_0^{1-x-y} dz\,dy\,dx$$

$$= \int_0^1 \int_0^{1-x} (1 - x - y)\,dy\,dx$$

$$= \int_0^1 \left[(1-x)y - \tfrac{1}{2}y^2\right]_0^{1-x} dx$$

$$= \int_0^1 \tfrac{1}{2}(1-x)^2\,dx = \left[-\tfrac{1}{6}(1-x)^3\right]_0^1 = \tfrac{1}{6}.$$

By symmetry, $\overline{x} = \overline{y} = \overline{z}$. We can calculate $\overline{x}$ as follows:

$$\overline{x}\,V = \iiint_T x\,dx\,dy\,dz = \int_0^1 \int_0^{1-x} \int_0^{1-x-y} x\,dz\,dy\,dx = \tfrac{1}{24}.$$

check this ↑

Since $V = \frac{1}{6}$, we have $\overline{x} = \frac{1}{4}$. The centroid is the point $\left(\frac{1}{4}, \frac{1}{4}, \frac{1}{4}\right)$. ❑

Example 3 Find the mass of a solid right circular cylinder of radius r and height h given that the mass density varies directly with distance from the lower base.

SOLUTION Call the solid T. In the setup of Figure 17.7.6, we can characterize T by the following inequalities:

$$-r \le x \le r, \qquad -\sqrt{r^2 - x^2} \le y \le \sqrt{r^2 - x^2}, \qquad 0 \le z \le h.$$

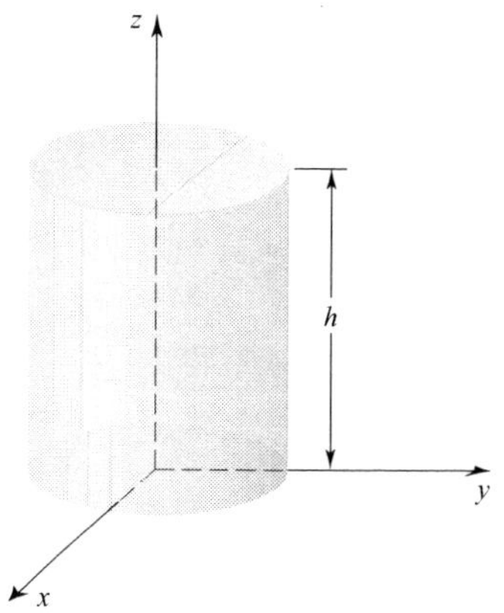

Figure 17.7.6

The first two inequalities define the base region Ω_{xy}. Since the density varies directly with the distance from the lower base, we have $\lambda(x, y, z) = kz$ where $k > 0$ is the constant of proportionality. Then

$$\begin{aligned} M &= \iiint_T kz\, dx\, dy\, dz \\ &= \int_{-r}^{r} \int_{-\sqrt{r^2-x^2}}^{\sqrt{r^2-x^2}} \int_0^h kz\, dz\, dy\, dx \\ &= \int_{-r}^{r} \int_{-\sqrt{r^2-x^2}}^{\sqrt{r^2-x^2}} \tfrac{1}{2}kh^2\, dy\, dx \\ &= 4\int_0^r \int_0^{\sqrt{r^2-x^2}} \tfrac{1}{2}\, kh^2\, dy\, dx \qquad \text{(by the symmetry)} \\ &= 2kh^2 \int_0^r \sqrt{r^2 - x^2}\, dx. \\ &= 2kh^2 \underbrace{\int_0^r \sqrt{r^2 - x^2}\, dx}_{\text{area of quarter disk}} = 2kh^2\left(\tfrac{1}{4}\pi r^2\right) = \tfrac{1}{2}kh^2 r^2 \pi. \quad ❑ \end{aligned}$$

Remark In Example 3 we would have profited by not skipping the double-integral stage; namely, we could have written

$$\begin{aligned} M &= \iint_{\Omega_{xy}} \left(\int_0^h kz\, dz\right) dx\, dy = \iint_{\Omega_{xy}} \tfrac{1}{2}kh^2 dx\, dy \\ &= \tfrac{1}{2}kh^2(\text{area of } \Omega_{xy}) = \tfrac{1}{2}kh^2 r^2 \pi. \quad ❑ \end{aligned}$$

Example 4 Integrate $f(x, y, z) = yz$ over the first-octant solid bounded by the coordinate planes and the ellipsoid

$$\frac{x^2}{a^2} + \frac{y^2}{b^2} + \frac{z^2}{c^2} = 1.$$

SOLUTION Call the solid T. The upper boundary of T has equation

$$z = \psi(x, y) = \frac{c}{ab}\sqrt{a^2b^2 - b^2x^2 - a^2y^2}.$$

This surface intersects the xy-plane in the curve

$$y = \phi(x) = \frac{b}{a}\sqrt{a^2 - x^2}.$$

We take

$$\Omega_{xy}: \quad 0 \le x \le a, \qquad 0 \le y \le \phi(x)$$

as the base region (see Figure 17.7.7) and characterize T as the set of all (x, y, z) with

$$0 \leq x \leq a, \qquad 0 \leq y \leq \phi(x), \qquad 0 \leq z \leq \psi(x, y).$$

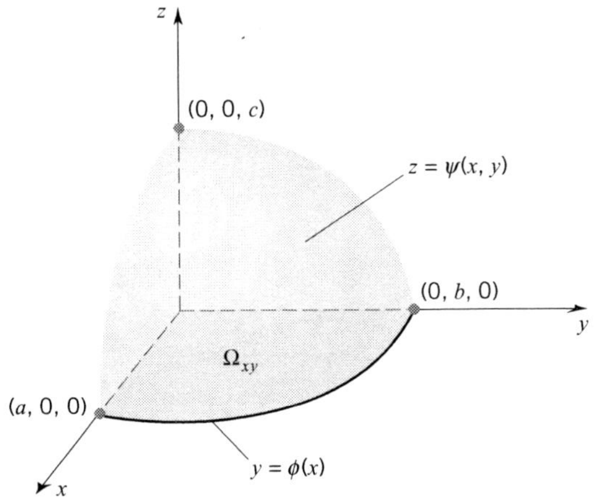

Figure 17.7.7

We can calculate the triple integral by evaluating

$$\int_0^a \int_0^{\phi(x)} \int_0^{\psi(x,y)} yz \, dz \, dy \, dx.$$

A straightforward (but somewhat lengthy) computation that you can carry out gives the answer of $\frac{1}{15}ab^2c^2$.

ANOTHER SOLUTION This time we carry out the integration in a different order. In Figure 17.7.8 you can see the same solid projected this time onto the yz-plane. In terms of y and z, the curved surface has equation

$$x = \Psi(y, z) = \frac{a}{bc}\sqrt{b^2c^2 - c^2y^2 - b^2z^2}.$$

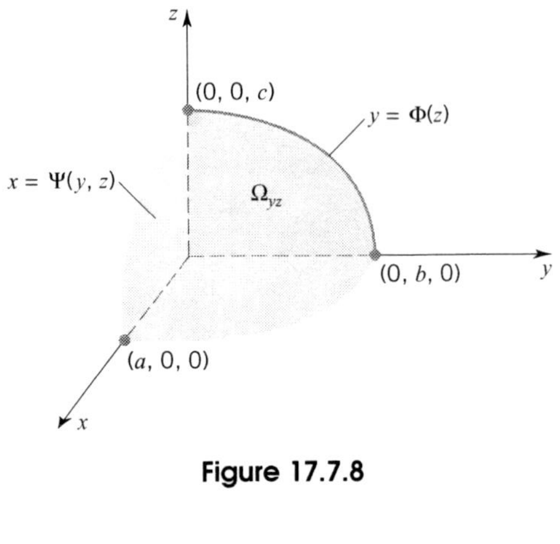

Figure 17.7.8

This surface intersects the yz-plane in the curve

$$y = \Phi(z) = \frac{b}{c}\sqrt{c^2 - z^2}.$$

We can take

$$\Omega_{yz}: \quad 0 \le z \le c, \quad 0 \le y \le \Phi(z)$$

as the base region and characterize T as the set of all (x, y, z) with

$$0 \le z \le c, \quad 0 \le y \le \Phi(z), \quad 0 \le x \le \Psi(y, z).$$

This leads to the repeated integral

$$\int_0^c \int_0^{\Phi(z)} \int_0^{\Psi(y,z)} yz\ dx\, dy\, dz,$$

which, as you can check, also gives $\frac{1}{15}ab^2c^2$. ❑

Example 5 Use triple integration to find the volume of the solid T bounded above by the parabolic cylinder $z = 4 - y^2$ and bounded below by the elliptic paraboloid $z = x^2 + 3y^2$.

SOLUTION Solving the two equations simultaneously, we have

$$4 - y^2 = x^2 + 3y^2 \qquad \text{and thus} \qquad x^2 + 4y^2 = 4.$$

This tells us that the two surfaces intersect in a space curve that lies on the elliptic cylinder $x^2 + 4y^2 = 4$. The projection of this intersection onto the xy-plane is the ellipse $x^2 + 4y^2 = 4$. (See Figure 17.7.9.)

The projection of T onto the xy-plane is the region

$$\Omega_{xy}: \quad -2 \le x \le 2, -\tfrac{1}{2}\sqrt{4 - x^2} \le y \le \tfrac{1}{2}\sqrt{4 - x^2}.$$

The solid T is then the set of all (x, y, z) with

$$-2 \le x \le 2, \quad -\tfrac{1}{2}\sqrt{4 - x^2} \le y \le \tfrac{1}{2}\sqrt{4 - x^2}, \quad x^2 + 3y^2 \le z \le 4 - y^2.$$

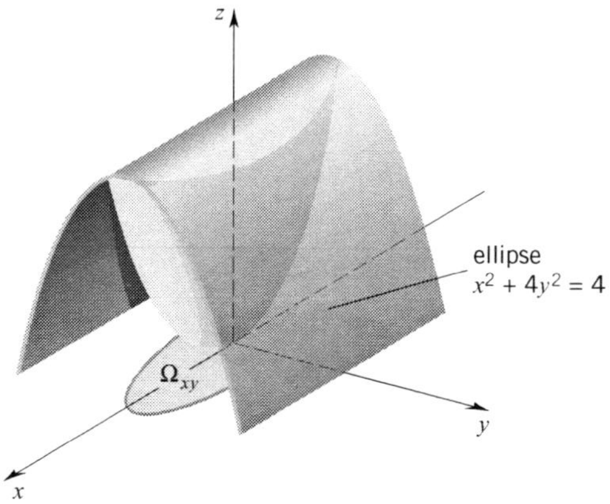

Figure 17.7.9

The volume of T is now easily obtained:

$$V = \int_{-2}^{2} \int_{-\frac{1}{2}\sqrt{4-x^2}}^{\frac{1}{2}\sqrt{4-x^2}} \int_{x^2+3y^2}^{4-y^2} dz\, dy\, dx$$

$$= 4 \int_0^2 \int_0^{\frac{1}{2}\sqrt{4-x^2}} \int_{x^2+3y^2}^{4-y^2} dz\, dy\, dx = 4\pi. \quad ❑$$

explain (points to the factor 4) ; check this (points to 4π)

EXERCISES 17.7

Exercises 1–10. Evaluate.

1. $\int_0^a \int_0^b \int_0^c dx\,dy\,dz.$ **2.** $\int_0^1 \int_0^x \int_0^y y\,dz\,dy\,dx.$

3. $\int_0^1 \int_1^{2y} \int_0^x (x+2z)\,dz\,dx\,dy.$

4. $\int_0^1 \int_{1-x}^{1+x} \int_0^{xy} 4z\,dz\,dy\,dx.$

5. $\int_0^2 \int_{-1}^1 \int_1^3 (z-xy)\,dz\,dy\,dx.$

6. $\int_0^2 \int_{-1}^1 \int_1^3 (z-xz)\,dy\,dx\,dz.$

7. $\int_0^{\pi/2} \int_0^1 \int_0^{\sqrt{1-x^2}} x\cos z\,dy\,dx\,dz.$

8. $\int_{-1}^2 \int_1^{y-2} \int_e^{e^2} \frac{x+y}{z}\,dz\,dx\,dy.$

9. $\int_1^2 \int_y^{y^2} \int_0^{\ln x} y\,e^z\,dz\,dx\,dy.$

10. $\int_0^{\pi/2} \int_0^{\pi/2} \int_0^1 e^z \cos x \sin y\,dz\,dy\,dx.$

11. (*Separated variables over a box*) Set $\Pi: a_1 \le x \le a_2$, $b_1 \le y \le b_2$, $c_1 \le z \le c_2$. Show that, if f is continuous on $[a_1, a_2]$, g is continuous on $[b_1, b_2]$, and h is continuous on $[c_1, c_2]$, then

(17.7.2)
$$\iiint_\Pi f(x)g(y)h(z)\,dx\,dy\,dz = \left(\int_{a_1}^{a_2} f(x)\,dx\right)\left(\int_{b_1}^{b_2} g(y)\,dy\right)\left(\int_{c_1}^{c_2} h(z)\,dz\right).$$

Exercises 12–13. Evaluate the triple integral, taking $\Pi: 0 \le x \le 1,\ 0 \le y \le 2,\ 0 \le z \le 3.$

12. $\iiint_\Pi x^3y^2z\,dx\,dy\,dz.$ **13.** $\iiint_\Pi x^2y^2z^2\,dx\,dy\,dz.$

Exercises 14–16. The mass density of the box $\Pi: 0 \le x \le a$, $0 \le y \le b,\ 0 \le z \le c$ varies directly as the product xyz.

14. Calculate the mass of Π.

15. Locate the center of mass.

16. Determine the moment of inertia of Π about: (a) the vertical line that passes through the point (a,b,c); (b) the vertical line that passes through the center of mass.

Exercises 17–20. A homogeneous solid T of mass M consists of all points (x,y,z) with $0 \le x \le 1,\ 0 \le y \le 1, 0 \le z \le 1-y$.

17. Sketch T. **18.** Find the volume of T.

19. Locate the center of mass.

20. Find the moments of inertia of T about the coordinate axes.

Exercises 21–26. Express by repeated integrals. Do not evaluate.

21. The mass of a ball $x^2+y^2+z^2 \le r^2$ given that the density varies directly with the distance from the outer shell.

22. The mass of the solid bounded above by $z=1$ and bounded below by $z=\sqrt{x^2+y^2}$ given that the density varies directly with the distance from the origin. Identify the solid.

23. The volume of the solid bounded above by the parabolic cylinder $z=1-y^2$, below by the plane $2x+3y+z+10=0$, and on the sides by the circular cylinder $x^2+y^2-x=0$.

24. The volume of the solid bounded above by the paraboloid $z=4-x^2-y^2$ and bounded below by the parabolic cylinder $z=2+y^2$.

25. The mass of the solid bounded by the elliptic paraboloids $z=4-x^2-\frac{1}{4}y^2$ and $z=3x^2+\frac{1}{4}y^2$ given that the density varies directly with the vertical distance from the lower surface.

26. The mass of the solid bounded by the paraboloid $x=z^2+2y^2$ and the parabolic cylinder $x=4-z^2$ given that the density varies directly with the distance from the z-axis.

Exercises 27–32. Evaluate the triple integral.

27. $\iiint_T (x^2z+y)\,dx\,dy\,dz$ where T is the solid bounded by the planes $x=0, x=1, y=1, y=3, z=0, z=2$.

28. $\iiint_T 2ye^x\,dx\,dy\,dz.$ where T is the solid given by $0 \le y \le 1,\ 0 \le x \le y,\ 0 \le z \le x+y$.

29. $\iiint_T x^2y^2z^2\,dx\,dy\,dz$, where T is the solid bounded by the planes $z=y+1,\ y+z=1,\ x=0, x=1,\ z=0$.

30. $\iiint_T xy\,dx\,dy\,dz$ where T is the first-octant solid bounded by the coordinate planes and the upper half of the sphere $x^2+y^2+z^2=4$.

31. $\iiint_T y^2\,dx\,dy\,dz$ where T is the tetrahedron in the first octant bounded by the coordinate planes and the plane $2x+3y+z=6$.

32. $\iiint_T y^2\,dx\,dy\,dz$ where T is the solid in the first octant bounded by the cylinders $x^2+y=1,\ z^2+y=1$.

33. Find the volume of the first-octant solid bounded by the planes $z=x,\ y-x=2$, and the cylinder $y=x^2$. Where is the centroid?

34. Find the mass of a block in the shape of a unit cube given that the density varies directly (a) with the distance from one of the faces; (b) with the square of the distance from one of the vertices.

35. Find the volume and the centroid of the solid bounded above by the cylindrical surface $x^2 + z = 4$, below by plane $x + z = 2$, and on the sides by the planes $y = 0$ and $y = 3$.

36. Show that, if $(\bar{x}, \bar{y}, \bar{z})$ is the centroid of a solid T, then

$$\iiint_T (x - \bar{x})\, dx\, dy\, dz = 0,$$

$$\iiint_T (y - \bar{y})\, dx\, dy\, dz = 0,$$

$$\iiint_T (z - \bar{z})\, dx\, dy\, dz = 0.$$

37. Taking a, b, c as positive, find the volume of the tetrahedron with vertices $(0, 0, 0), (a, 0, 0), (0, b, 0), (0, 0, c)$. Where is the centroid?

38. A homogeneous solid of mass M in the form and position of the tetrahedron of Figure 17.7.4 rotates about the z-axis. Find the moment of inertia I_z.

39. A homogeneous box of mass M occupies the set of all points (x, y, z) where

$$0 \le x \le a, \qquad 0 \le y \le b, \qquad 0 \le z \le c.$$

Calculate the moment of inertia of the box

(a) about the z-axis;

(b) about the line that passes through the center of the box and is parallel to the z-axis;

(c) about the line that passes through the center of the $x = 0$ face and is parallel to the z-axis.

40. Where is the centroid of the solid bounded above by the plane $z = 1 + x + y$, below by the plane $z = -2$, and on the sides by the planes $x = 1,\ x = 2,\ y = 1,\ y = 2$?

41. Let T be the solid bounded above by the plane $z = y$, below by the xy-plane, on the sides by the planes $x = 0$, $x = 1,\ y = 1$. Find the mass of T given that the density varies directly with the square of the distance from the origin. Where is the center of mass?

42. What can you conclude about T given that

$$\iiint_T f(x, y, z)\, dx\, dy\, dz = 0$$

(a) for every continuous function f that is odd in x?

(b) for every continuous function f that is odd in y?

(c) for every continuous function f that is odd in z?

(d) for every continuous function f that satisfies the relation $f(-x, -y, -z) = -f(x, y, z)$?

43. (a) Integrate $f(x, y, z) = x + y^3 + z$ over the unit ball centered at the origin.

(b) Integrate $f(x, y, z) = a_1x + a_2y + a_3z + a_4$ over the unit ball centered at the origin.

44. Integrate $f(x, y, z) = x^2y^2$ over the solid bounded above by the cylinder $y^2 + z = 4$, below by the plane $y + z = 2$, and on the sides by the planes $x = 0$ and $x = 2$.

45. Use triple integrals to find the volume enclosed by the sphere $x^2 + y^2 + z^2 = a^2$.

46. Use triple integrals to find the volume enclosed by the ellipsoid

$$\frac{x^2}{a^2} + \frac{y^2}{b^2} + \frac{z^2}{c^2} = 1.$$

47. Find the mass of the solid in Example 5 given that the density varies directly with $|x|$.

48. Find the volume of the solid bounded by the paraboloids $z = 2 - x^2 - y^2$ and $z = x^2 + y^2$.

49. Find the mass and the center of mass of the solid of Exercise 35 given that the density varies directly with $1 + y$.

50. Let T be a solid with volume

$$V = \iiint_T dx\, dy\, dz = \int_0^2 \int_0^{9-x^2} \int_0^{2-x} dz\, dy\, dx.$$

Sketch T and fill in the blanks.

(a) $V = \int_\square^\square \int_\square^\square \int_\square^\square dy\, dx\, dz.$

(b) $V = \int_\square^\square \int_\square^\square \int_\square^\square dy\, dz\, dx.$

(c) $V = \int_0^5 \int_\square^\square \int_\square^\square dz\, dx\, dy + \int_5^9 \int_\square^\square \int_\square^\square dz\, dx\, dy.$

51. Let T be a solid with volume

$$V = \iiint_T dx\, dy\, dz = \int_0^3 \int_0^{6-x} \int_0^{2x} dz\, dy\, dx.$$

Sketch T and fill in the blanks.

(a) $V = \int_\square^\square \int_\square^\square \int_\square^\square dy\, dx\, dz.$

(b) $V = \int_\square^\square \int_\square^\square \int_\square^\square dy\, dz\, dx.$

(c) $V = \int_0^6 \int_\square^\square \int_\square^\square dx\, dy\, dz + \int_\square^\square \int_\square^\square \int_\square^\square dx\, dy\, dz.$

Exercises 52–54. Let V be the volume of the solid T enclosed by the parabolic cylinder $y = 4 - z^2$ and the cylinder $y = |x|$. Let $\Omega_{xy}, \Omega_{yz}, \Omega_{xz}$ be the projections of T onto the xy-, yz-, and xz-planes, respectively. Fill in the blanks.

52. (a) $V = \iint_{\Omega_{xy}} \square\, dx\, dy.$

(b) $V = \iint_{\Omega_{xy}} \left(\int_\square^\square dz\right) dx\, dy.$

(c) $V = \int_{\square}^{\square}\int_{\square}^{\square}\int_{\square}^{\square} dz\,dy\,dx.$

(d) $V = \int_{\square}^{\square}\int_{\square}^{\square}\int_{\square}^{\square} dz\,dx\,dy.$

53. (a) $V = \iint_{\Omega_{yz}} \square\, dy\,dz.$

(b) $V = \iint_{\Omega_{yz}} \left(\int_{\square}^{\square} dx\right) dy\,dz.$

(c) $V = \int_{\square}^{\square}\int_{\square}^{\square}\int_{\square}^{\square} dx\,dz\,dy.$

(d) $V = \int_{\square}^{\square}\int_{\square}^{\square}\int_{\square}^{\square} dx\,dy\,dz.$

54. (a) $V = \iint_{\Omega_{xz}} \square\, dx\,dz.$

(b) $V = \iint_{\Omega_{xz}} \left(\int_{\square}^{\square} dy\right) dx\,dz.$

(c) $V = \int_{\square}^{\square}\int_{\square}^{\square}\int_{\square}^{\square} dy\,dx\,dz.$

(d) $V = \int_{-2}^{0}\int_{\square}^{\square}\int_{\square}^{\square} dy\,dz\,dx + \int_{0}^{2}\int_{\square}^{\square}\int_{\square}^{\square} dy\,dz\,dx.$

55. Use a CAS to evaluate the triple integrals.

(a) $\int_{2}^{4}\int_{3}^{5}\int_{1}^{2} \frac{\ln xy}{z}\, dz\,dy\,dx.$

(b) $\int_{0}^{4}\int_{1}^{2}\int_{0}^{3} x\sqrt{yz}\, dz\,dy\,dx.$

56. Use a CAS to find the volume of the solid bounded by the xy-plane, the yz-plane, the plane $3x + 6y - 2z = 6$, and the elliptic paraboloid $y = 36 - 9x^2 - 4z^2$.

■ 17.8 CYLINDRICAL COORDINATES

Introduction to Cylindrical Coordinates

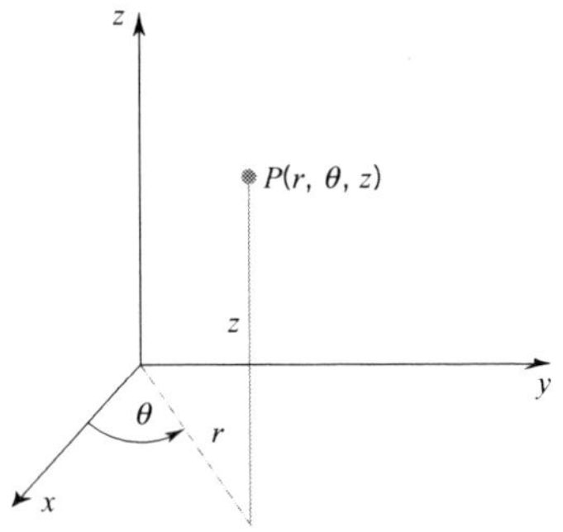

cylindrical coordinates (r, θ, z): $r \geq 0$, $0 \leq \theta \leq 2\pi$, z real

Figure 17.8.1

The cylindrical coordinates (r, θ, z) of a point P in xyz-space are shown geometrically in Figure 17.8.1. The first two coordinates, r and θ, are the usual plane polar coordinates except that r is taken to be nonnegative and θ is restricted to the interval $[0, 2\pi]$.† The third coordinate is the third rectangular coordinate z.

In rectangular coordinates, the coordinate surfaces

$$x = x_0, \qquad y = y_0, \qquad z = z_0$$

are three mutually perpendicular planes. In cylindrical coordinates, the coordinate surfaces take the form

$$r = r_0, \qquad \theta = \theta_0, \qquad z = z_0. \qquad \text{(Figure 17.8.2)}$$

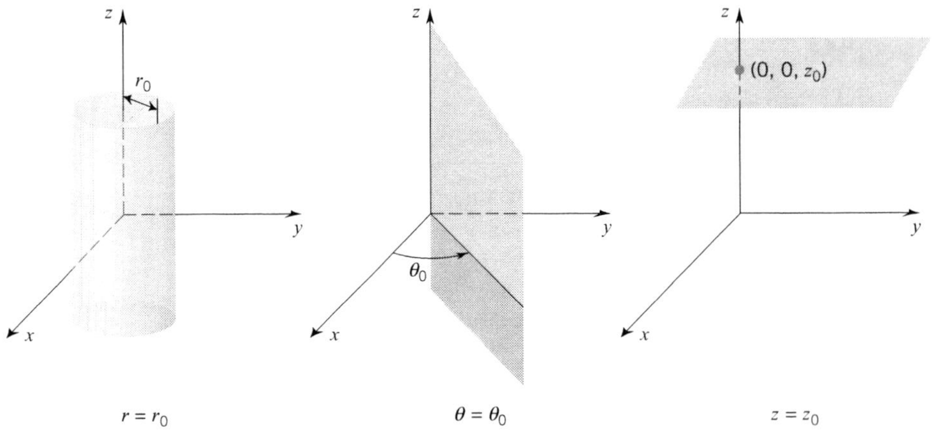

Figure 17.8.2

†By allowing θ to take on both 0 and 2π, we lose uniqueness but we gain flexibility and convenience.

The surface $r = r_0$ is a right circular cylinder of radius r_0. The central axis of the cylinder is the z-axis. The surface $\theta = \theta_0$ is a vertical half-plane hinged at the z-axis. The plane stands at an angle of θ_0 radians from the positive x-axis. The last coordinate surface is the plane $z = z_0$.

The point P with rectangular coordinates (x_0, y_0, z_0) lies on the plane $x = x_0$, on the plane $y = y_0$, and on the plane $z = z_0$. P is at the intersection of these three planes.

The point P with cylindrical coordinates (r_0, θ_0, z_0) lies on the cylinder $r = r_0$, on the vertical half-plane $\theta = \theta_0$, and on the horizontal plane $z = z_0$. P is at the intersection of these three surfaces.

Changing from cylindrical coordinates to rectangular coordinates is easy:

$$x = r\cos\theta, \qquad y = r\sin\theta, \qquad z = z.$$

Changing from rectangular coordinates to cylindrical coordinates requires more care:

$$r = \sqrt{x^2 + y^2}, \qquad \tan\theta = \frac{y}{x}, \qquad z = z$$

except for cases where $x = 0$. Points where $x = 0$ require case-by-case attention. (Exercises 17–20.)

The solids in xyz-space easiest to describe in cylindrical coordinates are the *cylindrical wedges*. Such a wedge is pictured in Figure 17.8.3. The wedge consists of all points (x, y, z) with cylindrical coordinates (r, θ, z) in the box

$$\Pi: \quad a_1 \le r \le a_2, \qquad b_1 \le \theta \le b_2, \qquad c_1 \le z \le c_2.$$

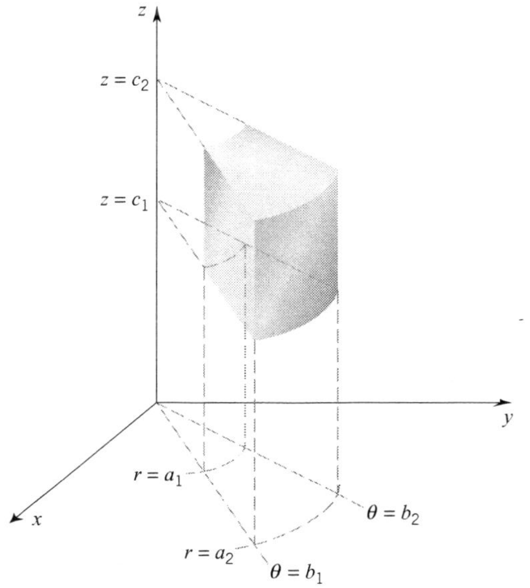

a cylindrical wedge

Figure 17.8.3

Evaluating Triple Integrals Using Cylindrical Coordinates

Suppose that T is some basic solid in xyz-space, not necessarily a wedge. If T is the set of all (x, y, z) with cylindrical coordinates in some basic solid S in

$r\theta z$-space, then

(17.8.1)
$$\iiint_T f(x, y, z)\,dx\,dy\,dz = \iiint_S f(r\cos\theta, r\sin\theta, z)\,r\,dr\,d\theta\,dz.$$

DERIVATION OF (17.8.1) We will carry out the argument on the assumption that T is projectable onto some basic region Ω_{xy} of the xy-plane. (It is for such solids that the formula is most useful.) T has some lower boundary $z = \psi_1(x, y)$ and some upper boundary $z = \psi_2(x, y)$. T is then the set of all (x, y, z) with

$$(x, y) \in \Omega_{xy} \qquad \text{and} \qquad \psi_1(x, y) \le z \le \psi_2(x, y).$$

The region Ω_{xy} has polar coordinates in some set $\Omega_{r\theta}$ (which we assume is a basic region). Then S is the set of all (r, θ, z) with

$$[r, \theta] \in \Omega_{r\theta} \qquad \text{and} \qquad \psi_1(r\cos\theta, r\sin\theta) \le z \le \psi_2(r\cos\theta, r\sin\theta).$$

Therefore

$$\iiint_T f(x, y, z)\,dx\,dy\,dz = \iint_{\Omega_{xy}} \left(\int_{\psi_1(x,y)}^{\psi_2(x,y)} f(x, y, z)\,dz\right) dx\,dy$$

$$\underset{(17.4.3)}{=} \iint_{\Omega_{r\theta}} \left(\int_{\psi_1(r\cos\theta,\, r\sin\theta)}^{\psi_2(r\cos\theta,\, r\sin\theta)} f(r\cos\theta, r\sin\theta, z)\,dz\right) r\,dr\,d\theta$$

$$= \iiint_S f(r\cos\theta, r\sin\theta, z)\,r\,dr\,d\theta\,dz. \quad \square$$

Volume Formula

If $f(x, y, z) = 1$ for all (x, y, z) in T, then (17.8.1) reduces to

$$\iiint_T dx\,dy\,dz = \iiint_S r\,dr\,d\theta\,dz.$$

The triple integral on the left is the volume of T. In summary, if T is a basic solid in xyz-space and the cylindrical coordinates of T constitute a basic solid S in $r\theta z$-space, then the volume of T is given by the formula

(17.8.2)
$$V = \iiint_S r\,dr\,d\theta\,dz.$$

Calculations

Cylindrical coordinates are particularly useful in cases where there is an axis of symmetry. The axis of symmetry is then taken as the z-axis.

Example 1 Use cylindrical coordinates to calculate

$$\iiint_T (x^2 + y^2)\,dx\,dy\,dz$$

for

$$T: \quad -2 \le x \le 2,\ -\sqrt{4 - x^2} \le y \le \sqrt{4 - x^2},\ 0 \le z \le 4 - x^2 - y^2.$$

SOLUTION The solid is bounded above by the paraboloid of revolution $z = 4 - x^2 - y^2$ and below by the xy-plane. (See Figure 17.8.4.) Since the solid is symmetric about the z-axis, the solid has a simpler representation in cylindrical coordinates:

$$S: \quad 0 \le r \le 2,\ 0 \le \theta \le 2\pi,\ 0 \le z \le 4 - r^2.$$

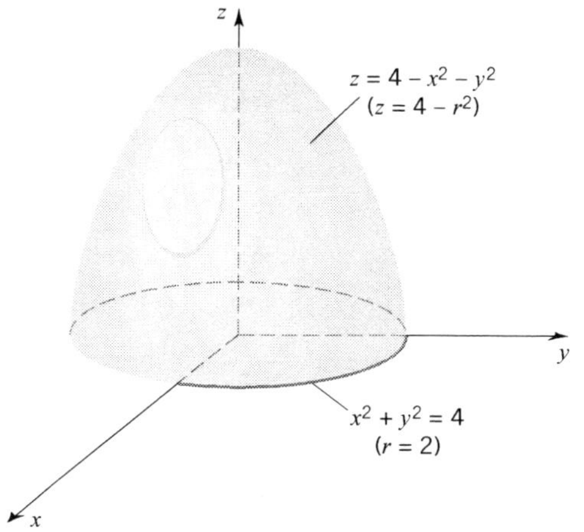

Figure 17.8.4

Now we can replace the integral over T by an integral over S:

$$\iiint_T (x^2 + y^2)\,dx\,dy\,dz = \iiint_S r^2\, r\,dr\,d\theta\,dz = \int_0^{2\pi}\int_0^2\int_0^{4-r^2} r^3\,dz\,dr\,d\theta$$

$$= \int_0^{2\pi}\int_0^2 \left[r^3 z\right]_0^{4-r^2} dr\,d\theta = \int_0^{2\pi}\int_0^2 (4r^3 - r^5)\,dr\,d\theta$$

$$= \int_0^{2\pi} \left[r^4 - \tfrac{1}{6}r^6\right]_0^2 d\theta$$

$$= \tfrac{16}{3}\int_0^{2\pi} d\theta = \tfrac{32}{3}\pi. \quad \square$$

Example 2 Find the mass of a solid right circular cylinder T of radius R and height h given that the density varies directly with the distance from the axis of the cylinder.

SOLUTION Place the cylinder T on the xy-plane so that the axis of T coincides with the z-axis. The density function then takes the form $\lambda(x, y, z) = k\sqrt{x^2 + y^2}$, and T consists of all points (x, y, z) with cylindrical coordinates (r, θ, z) in the set

$$S: \quad 0 \le r \le R, \quad 0 \le \theta \le 2\pi, \quad 0 \le z \le h.$$

Therefore

$$M = \iiint_T k\sqrt{x^2+y^2}\,dx\,dy\,dz = \iiint_S (kr)\,r\,dr\,d\theta\,dz$$

$$= k\int_0^R \int_0^{2\pi} \int_0^h r^2\,dz\,d\theta\,dr = \tfrac{2}{3}k\pi R^3 h. \quad \square$$

↑ check this

Example 3 Use cylindrical coordinates to find the volume of the solid T bounded above by the plane $z = y$ and below by the paraboloid $z = x^2 + y^2$.

SOLUTION In cylindrical coordinates the plane has equation $z = r\sin\theta$ and the paraboloid has equation $z = r^2$. Solving these two equations simultaneously, we have $r = \sin\theta$. This tells us that the two surfaces intersect in a space curve that lies along the circular cylinder $r = \sin\theta$. The projection of this intersection onto the xy-plane is the circle with polar equation $r = \sin\theta$. (See Figure 17.8.5.) The base region Ω_{xy} is thus the set of all (x, y) with polar coordinates in the set

$$0 \le \theta \le \pi, \qquad 0 \le r \le \sin\theta.$$

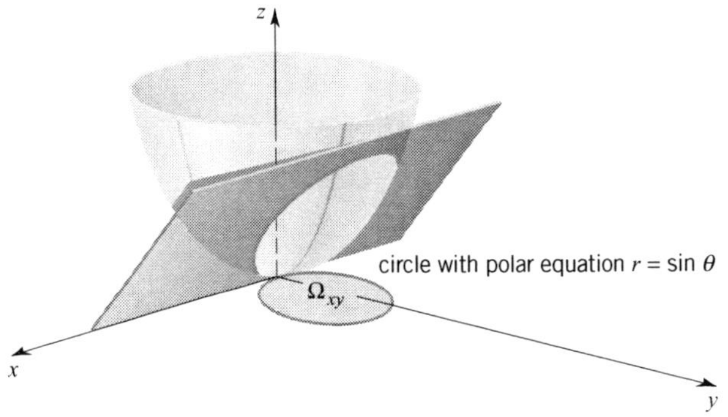

Figure 17.8.5

T itself is the set of all (x, y, z) with cylindrical coordinates in the set

$$S: \quad 0 \le \theta \le \pi, \quad 0 \le r \le \sin\theta, \quad r^2 \le z \le r\sin\theta. \qquad \text{(check this)}$$

Therefore,

$$V = \iiint_T dx\,dy\,dz = \iiint_S r\,dr\,d\theta\,dz$$

$$= \int_0^\pi \int_0^{\sin\theta} \int_{r^2}^{r\sin\theta} r\,dz\,dr\,d\theta$$

$$= \int_0^\pi \int_0^{\sin\theta} (r^2\sin\theta - r^3)\,dr\,d\theta$$

$$= \int_0^\pi \left[\tfrac{1}{3}r^3\sin\theta - \tfrac{1}{4}r^4\right]_0^{\sin\theta} d\theta$$

$$= \tfrac{1}{12}\int_0^\pi \sin^4\theta\,d\theta = \tfrac{1}{12}\left(\tfrac{3}{8}\pi\right) = \tfrac{1}{32}\pi. \quad \square$$

↑ (Section 8.3)

Example 4 Locate the centroid of the solid in Example 3.

SOLUTION Since T is symmetric about the yz-plane, we see that $\overline{x} = 0$. To get $\overline{y}$ we begin as usual:

$$\overline{y}V = \iiint_T y\,dx\,dy\,dz = \iiint_S (r\sin\theta)\,r\,dr d\theta\,dz$$

$$= \int_0^{\pi}\int_0^{\sin\theta}\int_{r^2}^{r\sin\theta} r^2\sin\theta\,dz\,dr\,d\theta$$

$$= \int_0^{\pi}\int_0^{\sin\theta} (r^3\sin^2\theta - r^4\sin\theta)\,dr\,d\theta$$

$$= \int_0^{\pi}\left[\tfrac{1}{4}r^4\sin^2\theta - \tfrac{1}{5}r^5\sin\theta\right]_0^{\sin\theta} d\theta$$

$$= \tfrac{1}{20}\int_0^{\pi}\sin^6\theta d\theta = \tfrac{1}{20}(\tfrac{5}{16}\pi) = \tfrac{1}{64}\pi.$$

(Section 8.3)

Since $V = \frac{1}{32}\pi$, we have $\overline{y} = \frac{1}{2}$. Now for $\overline{z}$:

$$\overline{z}V = \iiint_T z\,dx\,dy\,dz$$

$$= \iiint_S zr\;dr d\theta dz$$

$$= \int_0^{\pi}\int_0^{\sin\theta}\int_{r^2}^{r\sin\theta} zr\,dz\,dr\,d\theta = \cdots = \tfrac{1}{24}\int_0^{\pi}\sin^6\theta d\theta = \tfrac{1}{24}(\tfrac{5}{16}\pi) = \tfrac{5}{384}\pi.$$

Details are left to you

Division by $V = \frac{1}{32}\pi$ gives $\overline{z} = \frac{5}{12}$. The centroid is thus the point $(0, \frac{1}{2}, \frac{5}{12})$. ❑

EXERCISES 17.8

Exercises 1–6. Express in cylindrical coordinates and sketch the surface.

1. $x^2 + y^2 = z^2 = 9$.

2. $x^2 + y^2 = 4$.

3. $z = 2\sqrt{x^2 + y^2}$.

4. $x = 4z$.

5. $4x^2 + 4y^2 - z^2 = 0$.

6. $y^2 + z^2 = 8$.

Exercises 7–10. The volume of a solid T is given in cylindrical coordinates. Sketch T and evaluate the repeated integral.

7. $\displaystyle\int_0^{\pi/2}\int_0^2\int_0^{4-r^2} r\,dz\,dr\,d\theta.$

8. $\displaystyle\int_0^{\pi/4}\int_0^1\int_0^{\sqrt{1-r^2}} r\,dz\,dr\,d\theta.$

9. $\displaystyle\int_0^{2\pi}\int_0^2\int_0^{r^2} r\,dz\,dr\,d\theta.$

10. $\displaystyle\int_0^3\int_0^{2\pi}\int_r^3 r\;dz\,d\theta\,dr.$

Exercises 11–16. Evaluate using cylindrical coordinates.

11. $\displaystyle\iiint_T dx\,dy\,dz;\quad T: 0 \le x \le 1, 0 \le y \le \sqrt{1-x^2},$ $0 \le z \le \sqrt{4-(x^2+y^2)}$.

12. $\displaystyle\iiint_T z^3\,dx\,dy\,dz;\quad T: -1 \le x \le 1, 0 \le y \le \sqrt{1-x^2},$ $\sqrt{x^2+y^2} \le z \le 1$.

13. $\displaystyle\iiint_T \frac{1}{\sqrt{x^2+y^2}}\,dx\,dy\,dz;\quad T: 0 \le x \le \sqrt{9-y^2},$ $0 \le y \le 3, 0 \le z \le \sqrt{9-(x^2-y^2)}$.

14. $\iiint_T z\,dx\,dy\,dz;\quad T: 0 \le x \le 1, 0 \le y \le \sqrt{1-x^2},$
$0 \le z \le \sqrt{1-x^2-y^2}.$

15. $\iiint_T \sin(x^2+y^2)\,dx\,dy\,dz;\quad T: 0 \le x \le 1,$
$0 \le y \le \sqrt{1-x^2}, 0 \le z \le 2.$

16. $\iiint_T \sqrt{x^2+y^2}\,dx\,dy\,dz;\quad T: -1 \le x \le 1,$
$-\sqrt{1-x^2} \le y \le \sqrt{1-x^2}, x^2+y^2 \le z \le 2-(x^2+y^2).$

Exercises 17–20. Equations

$$r = \sqrt{x^2+y^2}, \qquad \tan\theta = \frac{y}{x}, \qquad z = z$$

do not assign cylindrical coordinates to the points (x, y, z) where $x = 0$. Find cylindrical coordinates for the point with the given rectangular coordinates.

17. $x = 0, y = 1, z = 2.$ **18.** $x = 0, y = 1, z = -2.$

19. $x = 0, y = -1, z = 2.$ **20.** $x = 0, y = 0, z = 0.$

21. Find the volume of the solid bounded above by the cone $z^2 = x^2 + y^2$, below by the xy-plane, and on the sides by the cylinder $x^2 + y^2 = 2ax$. Take $a > 0$.

22. Find the volume of the solid bounded by the paraboloid of revolution $x^2 + y^2 = az$, the xy-plane, and the cylinder $x^2 + y^2 = 2ax$. Take $a > 0$.

23. Find the volume of the solid bounded above by the surface $z = a - \sqrt{x^2+y^2}$, below by the xy-plane, and on the sides by the cylinder $x^2 + y^2 = ax$. Take $a > 0$.

24. Find the volume of the solid bounded above by the plane $2z = 4 + x$, below by the xy-plane, and on the sides by the cylinder $x^2 + y^2 = 2x$.

25. Find the volume of the solid bounded by the paraboloid $z = x^2 + y^2$ and the plane $z = x$.

26. Find the volume of the solid bounded above by $x^2 + y^2 + z^2 = 25$ and below by $z = \sqrt{x^2+y^2} + 1$.

27. Find the volume of the "ice cream cone" bounded below by the half-cone $z = \sqrt{3(x^2+y^2)}$ and above by the unit sphere $x^2 + y^2 + z^2 = 1$.

28. Find the volume of the solid bounded by the hyperboloid $z^2 = a^2 + x^2 + y^2$ and by the upper nappe of the cone $z^2 = 2(x^2 + y^2)$.

29. Find the volume of the solid that is bounded below by the xy-plane and lies inside the sphere $x^2 + y^2 + z^2 = 9$ but outside the cylinder $x^2 + y^2 = 1$.

30. Find the volume of the solid that lies between the cylinders $x^2 + y^2 = 1$ and $x^2 + y^2 = 4$, and is bounded above by the ellipsoid $x^2 + y^2 + 4z^2 = 36$ and below by the xy-plane.

For Exercises 31–33 let T be a solid right circular cylinder of base radius R and height h. Assume that the mass density varies directly with the distance from one of the bases.

31. Use cylindrical coordinates to find the mass M of T.

32. Locate the center of mass of T.

33. Find the moment of inertia of T about the axis of the cylinder.

34. Let T be a homogeneous right circular cylinder of mass M, base radius R, and height h. Find the moment of inertia of the cylinder about: (a) the central axis; (b) a line that lies in the plane of one of the bases and passes through the center of that base; (c) a line that passes through the center of the cylinder and is parallel to the bases.

For Exercises 35–38 let T be a homogeneous solid right circular cone of mass M, base radius R, and height h.

35. Use cylindrical coordinates to verify that the volume of the cone is given by the formula $V = \frac{1}{3}\pi R^2 h$.

36. Locate the center of mass.

37. Find the moment of inertia about the axis of the cone.

38. Find the moment of inertia about a line that passes through the vertex and is parallel to the base.

For Exercises 39–41 let T be the solid bounded above by the paraboloid $z = 1 - (x^2 + y^2)$ and bounded below by the xy-plane.

39. Use cylindrical coordinates to find the volume of T.

40. Find the mass of T if the density varies directly with the distance from the xy-plane.

41. Find the mass of T if the density varies directly with the square of the distance from the origin.

17.9 THE TRIPLE INTEGRAL AS THE LIMIT OF RIEMANN SUMS; SPHERICAL COORDINATES

The Triple Integral as the Limit of Riemann Sums

You have seen that single integrals and double integrals can be obtained as limits of Riemann sums. The same holds true for triple integrals.

Start with a basic solid T in xyz-space and decompose it into a finite number of basic solids $T_1 \ldots, T_n$. If f is continuous on T, then f is continuous on each T_i. From each T_i pick an arbitrary point (x_i^*, y_i^*, z_i^*) and form the *Riemann sum*

$$\sum_{i=1}^{n} f(x_i^*, y_i^*, z_i^*)(\text{volume of } T_i).$$

As you would expect, the triple integral over T is the limit of such sums; namely, given any $\epsilon > 0$, there exists a $\delta > 0$ such that, if the diameters of the T_i are all less than δ, then

$$\left|\sum_{i=1}^{n} f(x_i^*, y_i^*, z_i^*)(\text{volume of } T_i) - \iiint_T f(x, y, z)\,dx\,dy\,dz\right| < \epsilon$$

no matter how the (x_i^*, y_i^*, z_i^*) are chosen within the T_i. We express this by writing

(17.9.1) $$\iiint_T f(x, y, z)\,dx\,dy\,dz = \lim_{\text{diam}\,T_i \to 0} \sum_{i=1}^{n} f(x_i^*, y_i^*, z_i^*)(\text{volume of } T_i).$$

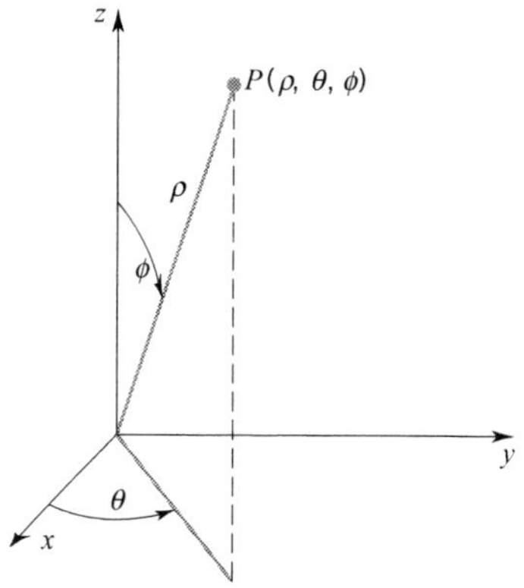

spherical coordinates (ρ, θ, ϕ): $\rho \geq 0,\ 0 \leq \theta \leq 2\pi,\ 0 \leq \phi \leq \pi$

Figure 17.9.1

Introduction to Spherical Coordinates

The spherical coordinates (ρ, θ, ϕ) of a point P in xyz-space are shown geometrically in Figure 17.9.1. The first coordinate ρ is the distance from P to the origin; thus $\rho \geq 0$. The second coordinate, the angle marked θ, is the second coordinate of cylindrical coordinates; θ ranges from 0 to 2π. We call θ the *longitude.* The third coordinate, the angle marked ϕ, ranges only from 0 to π. We call ϕ the *colatitude*, or more simply the *polar angle.* (The complement of ϕ would be the *latitude* on a globe.)

The coordinate surfaces

$$\rho = \rho_0, \qquad \theta = \theta_0, \qquad \phi = \phi_0$$

are shown in Figure 17.9.2. The surface $\rho = \rho_0$ is a sphere; the radius is ρ_0 and the center is the origin. The second surface, $\theta = \theta_0$, is the same as in cylindrical coordinates: the vertical half-plane hinged at the z-axis and standing at an angle of θ_0 radians from the positive x-axis. The surface $\phi = \phi_0$ requires detailed explanation. If $0 < \phi_0 < \frac{1}{2}\pi$ or $\frac{1}{2}\pi < \phi_0 < \pi$, the surface is the nappe of a cone; it is generated by revolving about the z-axis any ray that emerges from the origin at an angle of ϕ_0 radians from the positive z-axis. The surface $\phi = \frac{1}{2}\pi$ is the xy-plane. (The nappe of the cone has opened up

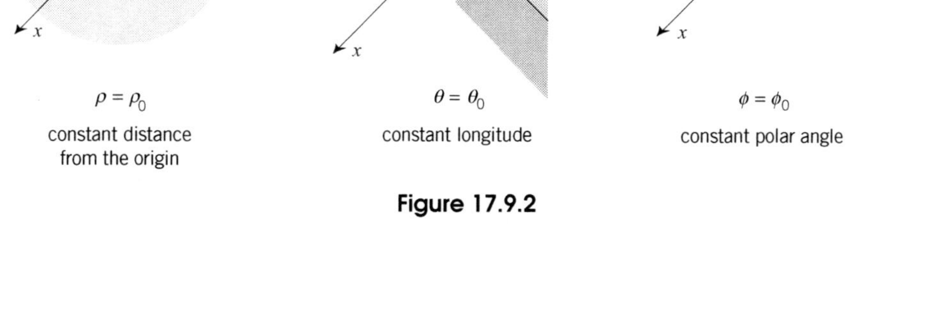

$\rho = \rho_0$ constant distance from the origin

$\theta = \theta_0$ constant longitude

$\phi = \phi_0$ constant polar angle

Figure 17.9.2

completely.) The equation $\phi = 0$ gives the nonnegative z-axis, and the equation $\phi = \pi$ gives the nonpositive z-axis. (When $\phi = 0$ or $\phi = \pi$, the nappe of the cone has closed up completely.)

The point P with spherical coordinates $(\rho_0, \theta_0, \phi_0)$ is located at the intersection of the three surfaces $\rho = \rho_0, \theta = \theta_0, \phi = \phi_0$.

Rectangular coordinates (x, y, z) are related to spherical coordinates (ρ, θ, ϕ) by the following equations:

$$x = \rho \sin\phi \cos\theta, \qquad y = \rho \sin\phi \sin\theta, \qquad z = \rho \cos\phi.$$

You can verify these relations by referring to Figure 17.9.3. (Note that the factor $\rho \sin\phi$ appearing in the first two equations is the r of cylindrical coordinates: $r = \rho \sin\phi$.) Conversely, excluding the points where $x = 0$, we have

$$\rho = \sqrt{x^2 + y^2 + z^2}, \qquad \tan\theta = \frac{y}{x}, \qquad \cos\phi = \frac{z}{\sqrt{x^2 + y^2 + z^2}}.$$

The Volume of a Spherical Wedge

Figure 17.9.4 shows a *spherical wedge* W in xyz-space. The wedge W consists of all points (x, y, z) which have spherical coordinates in the box

$$\Pi: \quad a_1 \le \rho \le a_2, \qquad b_1 \le \theta \le b_2, \qquad c_1 \le \phi \le c_2.$$

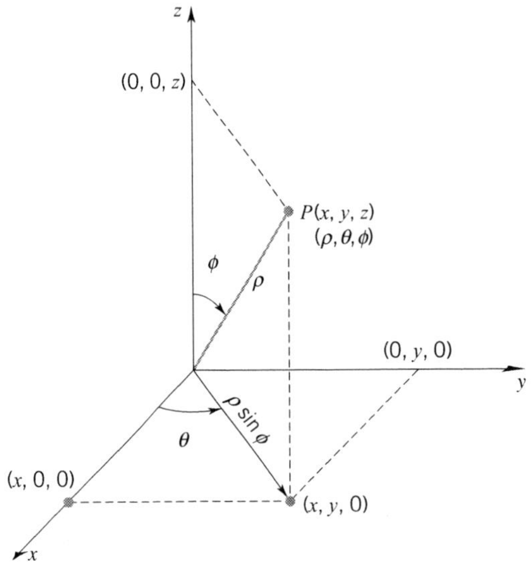

Figure 17.9.3

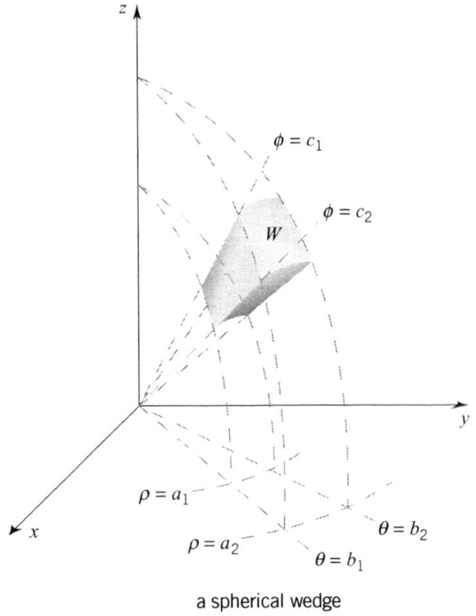

Figure 17.9.4

The volume of this wedge is given by the formula

(17.9.2)
$$V = \iiint_{\Pi} \rho^2 \sin\phi \, d\rho \, d\theta \, d\phi.$$

PROOF Note first that W is part of a solid of revolution. One way to obtain W is to rotate the $\theta = b_1$ face of W, call it Ω, about the z-axis for $b_2 - b_1$ radians. (See Figure 17.9.4.) On that face ρ and $\alpha = \frac{1}{2}\pi - \phi$ play the role of polar coordinates. (See Figure 17.9.5.) In the setup of Figure 17.9.5 the face Ω is the set of all (X, z) with polar coordinates $[\rho, \alpha]$ in the set $\Gamma : a_1 \leq \rho \leq a_2, \frac{1}{2}\pi - c_2 \leq \alpha \leq \frac{1}{2}\pi - c_1$. The centroid of Ω is at a distance $\overline{X}$ from the z-axis where

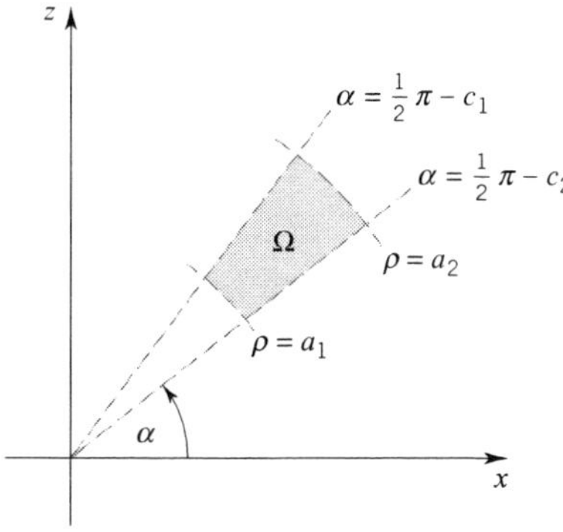

Figure 17.9.5

$$\overline{X}(\text{area of }\Omega) \iint_{\Omega} X\, dXdz = \iint_{\Gamma} \rho^2 \cos\alpha\, d\rho d\alpha$$

This follow from (17.4.3) together with the fact that here $[\rho, \alpha]$ play the role of polar coordinates.

$$= \left(\int_{a_1}^{a_2} \rho^2 d\rho\right)\left(\int_{\frac{1}{2}\pi - c_2}^{\frac{1}{2}\pi - c_1} \cos\alpha\, d\alpha\right)$$

$$= \left(\int_{a_1}^{a_2} \rho^2 d\rho\right)\left(\int_{c_1}^{c_2} \sin\phi\, d\phi\right).$$

$\phi = \frac{1}{2}\pi - \alpha$

As the face Ω is rotated from $\theta = b_1$ to $\theta = b_2$, the centroid travels through a circular arc of length

$$s = (b_2 - b_1)\overline{X} = (b_2 - b_1)\frac{1}{\text{area of }\Omega}\left(\int_{a_1}^{a_2} \rho^2 d\rho\right)\left(\int_{c_1}^{c_2} \sin\phi\, d\phi\right).$$

From Pappus's theorem on volumes, we know that

$$\text{the volume of } W = s(\text{area of }\Omega) = (b_2 - b_1)\left(\int_{a_1}^{a_2} \rho^2 d\rho\right)(\sin\phi\, d\phi)$$

$$= \left(\int_{b_1}^{b_2} d\theta\right)\left(\int_{a_1}^{a_2} \rho^2 d\rho\right)\left(\int_{c_1}^{c_2} \sin\phi\, d\phi\right)$$

$$= \int_{a_1}^{a_2}\int_{b_1}^{b_2}\int_{c_1}^{c_2} \rho^2 \sin\phi\, d\phi\, d\theta\, d\rho$$

$$= \iiint_{\Pi} \rho^2 \sin\phi\, d\rho d\theta d\phi. \quad \square$$

Evaluating Triple Integrals Using Spherical Coordinates

Suppose that T is a basic solid in xyz-space with spherical coordinates in some basic solid S of $\rho\theta\phi$-space. Then

(17.9.3)
$$\iiint_T f(x, y, z)\, dx\, dy\, dz = \iiint_S f(\rho\sin\phi\cos\theta, \rho\sin\phi\sin\theta, \rho\cos\phi)\, \rho^2 \sin\phi\, d\rho d\theta d\phi.$$

DERIVATION OF (17.9.3) Assume first that T is a spherical wedge W. The solid S is then a box Π. Now decompose Π into n boxes $\Pi_1, \ldots, \Pi_n$. This induces a subdivision of W into n spherical wedges $W_1, \ldots, W_n$.

Writing $F(\rho, \theta, \phi)$ for $f(\rho\sin\phi\cos\theta, \rho\sin\phi\sin\theta, \rho\cos\phi)$ to save space, we have

$$\begin{aligned}\iiint_\Pi F(\rho, \theta, \phi)\, \rho^2 \sin\phi\, d\rho d\theta d\phi &= \sum_{i=1}^{n} \iiint_{\Pi_i} F(\rho, \theta, \phi)\, \rho^2 \sin\phi\, d\rho d\theta d\phi \quad \text{(additivity)}\\ &= \sum_{i=1}^{n} F(\rho_i^*, \theta_i^*, \phi_i^*) \iiint_{\Pi_i} \rho^2 \sin\phi\, d\rho d\theta d\phi \quad \text{(for some } (\rho_i^*, \theta_i^*, \phi_i^*) \in \Pi_i \text{ (by 17.6.5))}\\ &= \sum_{i=1}^{n} F(\rho_i^*, \theta_i^*, \phi_i^*)\,(\text{volume of } W_i) \quad \text{((17.9.2) applied to } \Pi_i)\\ &= \sum_{i=1}^{n} f(x_i^*, y_i^*, z_i^*)\,(\text{volume of } W_i).\end{aligned}$$

$x_i^* = \rho_i^* \sin\phi_i^* \cos_i^*$,
$y_i^* = \rho_i^*, \sin\phi_i^* \sin\theta_i^*$,
$z_i^* = \rho_i^* \cos\phi_i^*$

This last expression is a Riemann sum for

$$\iiint_W f(x, y, z)\, dx\, dy\, dz$$

and, as such, by (17.9.1), will differ from that integral by less than any preassigned positive number ϵ provided only that the diameters of all the W_i are sufficiently small. This we can guarantee by making the diameters of all the Π_i sufficiently small.

This verifies the formula for the case where T is a spherical wedge. The more general case is left to you. HINT: Encase T in a wedge W and define f to be zero outside of T. ❑

Volume Formula

If $f(x, y, z) = 1$ for all (x, y, z) in T, then the change-of-variables formula reduces to

$$\iiint_T dx\, dy\, dz = \iiint_S \rho^2 \sin\phi\, d\rho d\theta d\phi.$$

The integral on the left is the volume of T. It follows that the volume of T is given by the formula

(17.9.4)
$$V = \iiint_S \rho^2 \sin\phi \, d\rho \, d\theta \, d\phi.$$

Calculations

Spherical coordinates are commonly used in applications where there is a center of symmetry. The center of symmetry is then taken as the origin.

Example 1 Calculate the mass M of a solid ball of radius 1 given that the density varies directly with the square of the distance from the center of the ball.

SOLUTION Center the ball at the origin. The ball, call it T, is now the set of all (x, y, z) with spherical coordinates (ρ, θ, ϕ) in the box

$$S: \quad 0 \le \rho \le 1, \quad 0 \le \theta \le 2\pi, \quad 0 \le \phi \le \pi. \qquad \text{(Figure 17.9.6)}$$

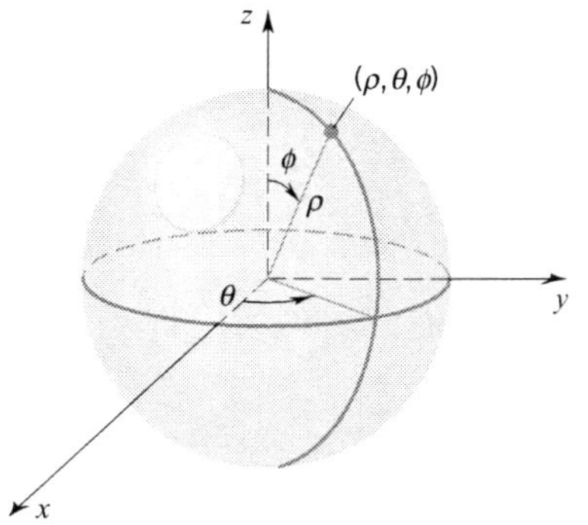

Figure 17.9.6

Therefore

$$M = \iiint_T k(x^2 + y^2 + z^2) \, dx \, dy \, dz$$
$$= \iiint_S (k\rho^2)\rho^2 \sin\phi \, d\rho \, d\theta \, d\phi = k \int_0^{\pi} \int_0^{2\pi} \int_0^1 \rho^4 \sin\phi \, d\rho \, d\theta \, d\phi$$
$$= k\left(\int_0^{\pi} \sin\phi \, d\phi\right)\left(\int_0^{2\pi} d\theta\right)\left(\int_0^1 \rho^4 d\rho\right) = k(2)(2\pi)(\tfrac{1}{5}) = \tfrac{4}{5}k\pi. \quad ❑$$

Example 2 Find the volume of the solid bounded above by the cone $z^2 = x^2 + y^2$, below by the xy-plane, and on the sides by the hemisphere $z = \sqrt{4 - x^2 - y^2}$. (See Figure 17.9.7.)

SOLUTION Call the solid T. In terms of spherical coordinates, the hemisphere is given by $\rho = 2, 0 \le \phi \le \pi/2$. As you can verify, the hemisphere and the cone intersect in a circle which lies on the plane $z = \sqrt{2}$ and is centered on the z-axis. For points on

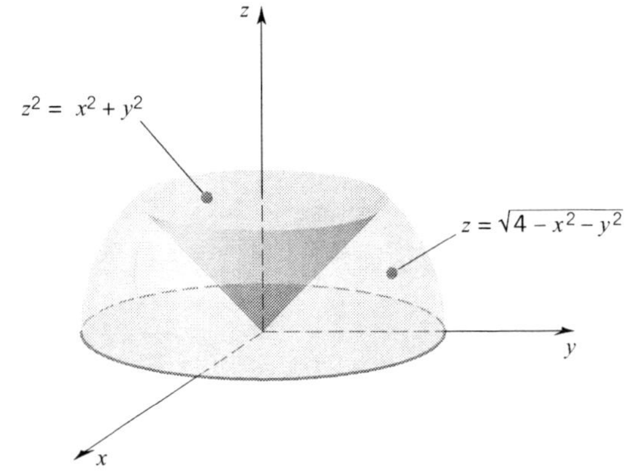

Figure 17.9.7

this circle, the angle ϕ is $\pi/4$. (Verify this.) It follows that the solid T is the set of all (x, y, z) with spherical coordinates (ρ, θ, ϕ) in the set

$$S: \quad 0 \le \rho \le 2, \qquad 0 \le \theta \le 2\pi, \qquad \pi/4 \le \phi \le \pi/2.$$

Thus,

$$V = \iiint_T dx\,dy\,dz = \iiint_S \rho^2 \sin\phi \, d\rho\, d\phi\, d\theta$$

$$= \int_{\pi/4}^{\pi/2} \int_0^{2\pi} \int_0^2 \rho^2 \sin\phi \, d\rho\, d\theta\, d\phi = \left(\int_{\pi/4}^{\pi/2} \sin\phi\, d\phi\right)\left(\int_0^{2\pi} d\theta\right)\left(\int_0^2 \rho^2 d\rho\right)$$

$$= (\sqrt{2}/2)(2\pi)(\tfrac{8}{3}) = \frac{8\pi\sqrt{2}}{3} \cong 11.85. \quad ❑$$

Example 3 Find the volume of the solid T enclosed by the surface

$$(x^2 + y^2 + z^2)^2 = 2z(x^2 + y^2).$$

SOLUTION In spherical coordinates the bounding surface takes the form

$$\rho = 2\sin^2\phi\cos\phi. \qquad \text{(check this out)}$$

This equation places no restriction on θ; thus θ can range from 0 to 2π. Since ρ remains nonnegative, ϕ can range only from 0 to $\frac{1}{2}\phi$. Thus the solid T is the set of all (x, y, z) with spherical coordinates (ρ, θ, ϕ) in the set

$$S: \quad 0 \le \theta \le 2\pi, \qquad 0 \le \phi \le \tfrac{1}{2}\pi, \qquad 0 \le \rho \le 2\sin^2\phi\cos\phi.$$

The rest is straightforward:

$$V = \iiint_T dx\,dy\,dz = \iiint_S \rho^2 \sin\phi\, d\rho\, d\theta\, d\phi$$

$$= \int_0^{2\pi}\int_0^{\pi/2}\int_0^{2\sin^2\phi\cos\phi} \rho^2 \sin\phi\, d\rho\, d\phi\, d\theta = \int_0^{2\pi}\int_0^{\pi/2} \tfrac{8}{3}\sin^7\phi\cos^3\phi\, d\phi\, d\theta$$

$$= \tfrac{8}{3}\left(\int_0^{2\pi} d\theta\right)\left(\int_0^{\pi/2} (\sin^7\phi\cos\phi - \sin^9\phi\cos\phi)\, d\phi\right)$$

$$= \tfrac{8}{3}(2\pi)(\tfrac{1}{40}) = \tfrac{2}{15}\pi \cong 0.42. \quad ❑$$

EXERCISES 17.9

1. Find the spherical coordinates (ρ, θ, ϕ) of the point with rectangular coordinates $(1, 1, 1)$.

2. Find the rectangular coordinates of the point with spherical coordinates $\left(2, \frac{1}{6}\pi, \frac{1}{4}\pi\right)$.

3. Find the rectangular coordinates of the point with spherical coordinates $\left(3, \frac{1}{3}\pi, \frac{1}{6}\pi\right)$.

4. Find the spherical coordinates of the point with cylindrical coordinates $\left(2, \frac{2}{3}\pi, 6\right)$.

5. Find the spherical coordinates of the point with rectangular coordinates $\left(2, 2, \frac{2}{3}\sqrt{6}\right)$.

6. Find the spherical coordinates of the point with rectangular coordinates $(2\sqrt{2}, -2\sqrt{2}, -4\sqrt{3})$.

7. Find the rectangular coordinates of the point with spherical coordinates $(3, \pi/2, 0)$.

8. Find the spherical coordinates of the point with rectangular coordinates (a) $(0, 3, 4)$, (b) $(0, -3, 4)$.

Exercises 9–14. Equations are given in spherical coordinates. Interpret each one geometrically.

9. $\rho \sin\phi = 1$.

10. $\sin\phi = 1$.

11. $\cos\phi = -\frac{1}{2}\sqrt{2}$.

12. $\tan\theta = 1$.

13. $\rho\cos\phi = 1$.

14. $\rho = \cos\phi$.

Exercises 15–18. Each expression represents the volume of a solid as calculated in spherical coordinates. Sketch the solid and carry out the integration.

15. $\displaystyle\int_0^{2\pi}\int_0^{\pi}\int_0^{2} \rho^2 \sin\phi \, d\rho \, d\phi \, d\theta.$

16. $\displaystyle\int_0^{\pi/4}\int_0^{\pi/2}\int_0^{1} \rho^2 \sin\phi \, d\rho \, d\phi \, d\theta.$

17. $\displaystyle\int_{\pi/6}^{\pi/2}\int_0^{\pi/2}\int_0^{3} \rho^2 \sin\phi \, d\rho \, d\theta \, d\phi.$

18. $\displaystyle\int_0^{\pi/4}\int_0^{2\pi}\int_0^{\sec\varphi} \rho^2 \sin\phi \, d\rho \, d\theta \, d\phi.$

Exercises 19–22. Evaluate using spherical coordinates.

19. $\displaystyle\iiint_T dx\,dy\,dz; \quad T: 0 \le x \le 1, 0 \le y \le \sqrt{1-x^2},$
$\sqrt{x^2+y^2} \le z \le \sqrt{2-(x^2+y^2)}.$

20. $\displaystyle\iiint_T (x^2+y^2+z^2)\,dx\,dy\,dz;$

$$T: 0 \le x \le \sqrt{4-y^2}, 0 \le y \le 2,$$
$$\sqrt{x^2+y^2} \le z \le \sqrt{4-x^2-y^2}.$$

21. $\displaystyle\iiint_T z\sqrt{x^2+y^2+z^2}\,dx\,dy\,dz;$

$$T: 0 \le x \le \sqrt{9-y^2}, 0 \le y \le 3,$$
$$0 \le z \le \sqrt{9-(x^2+y^2)}.$$

22. $\displaystyle\iiint_T \frac{1}{(x^2+y^2+z^2)}\,dx\,dy\,dz;$

$$T: 0 \le x \le 1, 0 \le y \le \sqrt{1-x^2},$$
$$0 \le z \le \sqrt{1-x^2-y^2}.$$

23. Derive the formula for the volume of a sphere of radius R using spherical coordinates.

24. Express cylindrical coordinates in terms of spherical coordinates.

25. A wedge is cut from a ball of radius R by two planes that meet in a diameter. Find the volume of the wedge if the angle between the planes is α radians.

26. Find the mass of a ball of radius R given that the density varies directly with the distance from the boundary.

27. Find the mass of a right circular cone of base radius r and height h given that the density varies directly with the distance from the vertex.

28. Use spherical coordinates to dervie the formula for the volume of a right circular cone of base radius r and height h.

For Exercises 29 and 30 let T be a homogeneous ball of mass M and radius R.

29. Calculate the moment of inertia (a) about a diameter; (b) about a tangent line.

30. Locate the center of mass of the upper half given that the center of the ball is at the origin.

For Exercises 31 and 32, let T be a homogeneous solid bounded by two concentric spherical shells, an outer shell of radius R_2, and an inner shell of radius R_1.

31. (a) Calculate the moment of inertia about a diameter.
(b) Use your result in part (a) to determine the moment of inertia of a spherical shell of radius R and mass M about a diameter.
(c) What is the moment of inertia of that same shell about a tangent line?

32. (a) Locate the center of mass of the upper half of T given that the center of T is at the origin.
(b) Use your result in part (a) to locate the center of mass of a homogeneous hemispherical shell of radius R.

33. Find the volume of the solid common to the sphere $\rho = a$ and the cone $\phi = \alpha$. Take $\alpha \in \left(0, \frac{1}{2}\pi\right)$.

34. Let T be the solid bounded below by the half-cone $z = \sqrt{x^2+y^2}$ and above by the spherical surface

$x^2 + y^2 + z^2 = 1$. Use spherical coordinates to evaluate

$$\iiint_T e^{(x^2+y^2+z^2)^{3/2}}\, dx\, dy\, dz.$$

35. (a) Find an equation in spherical coordinates for the sphere $x^2 + y^2 + (z - R)^2 = R^2$.
(b) Express the upper half of the ball $x^2 + y^2 + (z - R)^2 \leq R^2$ by inequalities in spherical coordinates.

36. Find the mass of the ball $\rho \leq 2R\cos\phi$ given that the density varies directly (a) with ρ; (b) with $\rho\sin\phi$; (c) with $\rho\cos^2\theta\sin\phi$.

37. Find the volume of the solid common to the spheres $\rho = 2\sqrt{2}\cos\phi$ and $\rho = 2$.

38. Find the volume of the solid enclosed by the surface $\rho = 1 - \cos\phi$.

39. Finish the derivation begun for (17.9.3).

40. (*Gravitational attraction*) Let T be a basic solid and let (a, b, c) be a point not in T. Show that, if T has continuously varying mass density $\lambda = \lambda(x, y, z)$, then T attracts a point mass m at (a, b, c) with a force

$$\mathbf{F} = \iiint_T Gm\lambda\,(x, y, z)\,\mathbf{f}(x, y, z)\, dx\, dy\, dz, \quad \text{where}$$

$$\mathbf{f}(x, y, z) = \frac{[(x-a)\,\mathbf{i} + (y-b)\,\mathbf{j} + (z-c)\,\mathbf{k}]}{[(x-a)^2 + (y-b)^2 + (z-c)^2]^{3/2}}.$$

[Assume that a point mass m_1 at P_1 attracts a point mass m_2 at P_2 with a force $\mathbf{F} = -(Gm_1m_2/r^3)\mathbf{r}$, where $\mathbf{r}$ is the vector $\overrightarrow{P_1P_2}$. Interpret the triple integral component by component.]

41. Let T be the upper half of the ball $x^2 + y^2 + (z - R)^2 \leq R^2$. Given that T is homogeneous and has mass M, find the gravitational force exerted by T on a point mass m located at the origin. (Note Exercise 40.)

42. A point mass m is placed on the axis of a homogeneous solid right circular cylinder at a distance α from the nearest base of the cylinder. Find the gravitational force exerted by the cylinder on the point mass given that the cylinder has base radius R, height h, and mass M. (Note Exercise 40.)

■ 17.10 JACOBIANS; CHANGING VARIABLES IN MULTIPLE INTEGRATION

During the course of the last few sections you have met several formulas for changing variables in multiple integration: to polar coordinates, to cylindrical coordinates, to spherical coordinates. The purpose of this section is to bring some unity into that material and provide an overall view of the change-of-variables process.

We begin with a consideration of area. Figure 17.10.1 shows a basic region Γ in a plane that we are calling the uv-plane. (In this plane we denote the abscissa of a point by u and the ordinate by v.) Suppose that

$$x = x(u, v), \qquad y = y(u, v)$$

are continuously differentiable functions on the region Γ. As (u, v) ranges over Γ, the point (x, y), $(x(u, v), y(u, v))$ generates a region Ω in the xy-plane. If the mapping

$$(u, v) \to (x, y)$$

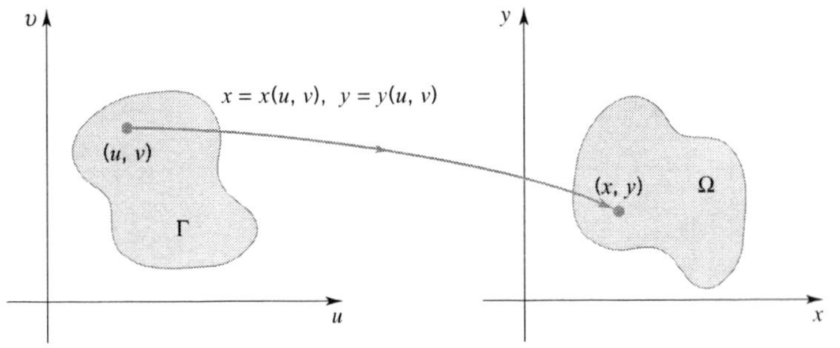

Figure 17.10.1

is one-to-one on the interior of Γ, and the *Jacobian*

$$J(u, v) = \begin{vmatrix} \dfrac{\partial x}{\partial u} & \dfrac{\partial y}{\partial u} \\ \dfrac{\partial x}{\partial v} & \dfrac{\partial y}{\partial v} \end{vmatrix} = \frac{\partial x}{\partial u}\frac{\partial y}{\partial v} - \frac{\partial x}{\partial v}\frac{\partial y}{\partial u},$$

is never zero on the interior of Γ, then

(17.10.1)
$$\text{area of } \Omega = \iint_{\Gamma} |J(u, v)|\, du dv.$$

It is very difficult to prove this assertion without making additional assumptions. A proof valid for all cases of practical interest is given in the supplement to Section 18.5. At this point we simply assume this area formula and go on from there.

Suppose now that we want to integrate some continuous function $f = f(x, y)$ over Ω. If this proves difficult to do directly, then we can change variables to u, v and try to integrate over Γ instead. It follows from (17.10.1) that

(17.10.2)
$$\iint_{\Omega} f(x, y)\, dx\, dy = \iint_{\Gamma} f(x(u, v), y(u, v)\, |J(u, v)|\, du dv.$$

The derivation of this formula from (17.10.1) follows the usual lines. Break up Γ into n little basic regions $\Gamma_1, \ldots, \Gamma_n$. These induce a decomposition of Ω into n little basic regions $\Omega_1, \ldots, \Omega_n$. We can then write

$$\iint_{\Gamma} f(x(u, v), y(u, v))|J(u, v)|du dv = \sum_{i=1}^{n} \iint_{\Gamma_i} f(x(u, v), y(u, v))\, |J(u, v)|\, du dv$$

additivity

$$= \sum_{i=1}^{n} f(x(u_i^*, v_i^*), y(u_i^*, v_i^*)) \iint_{\Gamma_i} |J(u, v)|\, du dv$$

Theorem 17.2.10 applied to Γ_i

$$= \sum_{i=1}^{n} f(x_i^*, y_i^*) \iint_{\Gamma_i} |J(u, v)| du dv$$

set $x_i^* = x(u_i^*, v_i^*), y_i^* = y(u_i^*, v_i^*)$

$$= \sum_{i=1}^{n} f(x_i^*, y_i^*)(\text{area of } \Omega_i).$$

(17.10.1) applied to Γ_i

This last expression is a Riemann sum for

$$\iint_{\Omega} f(x, y)\, dx\, dy$$

and tends to that integral as the maximum diameter of the Ω_i tends to zero. We can ensure this by letting the maximum diameter of the Γ_i tend to zero. ❑

Example 1 Evaluate

$$\iint_{\Omega} (x+y)^2\, dx\, dy$$

where Ω is the parallelogram bounded by the lines

$$x+y=0, \qquad x+y=1, \qquad 2x-y=0, \qquad 2x-y=3.$$

SOLUTION The parallelogram is shown in Figure 17.10.2. The boundaries suggest that we set

$$u = x+y, \qquad v = 2x-y.$$

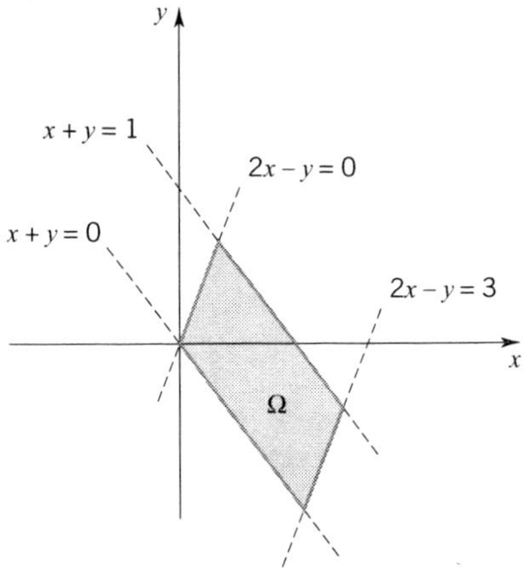

Figure 17.10.2

We want x and y in terms of u and v. Since

$$u+v=(x+y)+(2x-y)=3x \quad \text{and} \quad 2u-v=(2x+2y)-(2x-y)=3y,$$

we have

$$x = \frac{u+v}{3}, \qquad y = \frac{2u-v}{3}.$$

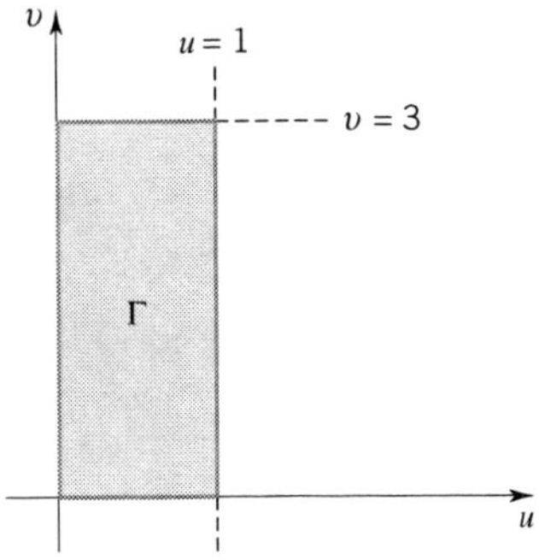

Figure 17.10.3

This transformation maps the rectangle Γ of Figure 17.10.3 onto Ω with Jacobian

$$J(u,v) = \begin{vmatrix} \dfrac{\partial}{\partial u}\left(\dfrac{u+v}{3}\right) & \dfrac{\partial}{\partial u}\left(\dfrac{2u-v}{3}\right) \\ \dfrac{\partial}{\partial v}\left(\dfrac{u+v}{3}\right) & \dfrac{\partial}{\partial v}\left(\dfrac{2u-v}{3}\right) \end{vmatrix} = \begin{vmatrix} \frac{1}{3} & \frac{2}{3} \\ \frac{1}{3} & -\frac{1}{3} \end{vmatrix} = -\tfrac{1}{3}.$$

Therefore

$$\iint_{\Omega} (x+y)^2\, dx\, dy = \iint_{\Omega} u^2 |J(u,v)|\, du dv$$

$$= \tfrac{1}{3} \int_0^3 \int_0^1 u^2 du\, dv$$

$$= \tfrac{1}{3}\left(\int_0^3 dv\right)\left(\int_0^1 u^2 du\right) = \tfrac{1}{3}(3)\tfrac{1}{3} = \tfrac{1}{3}. \quad \square$$

Example 2 Evaluate

$$\iint_{\Omega} xy\,dx\,dy$$

where Ω is the first-quadrant region bounded by the curves

$$x^2+y^2=4, \qquad x^2+y^2=9, \qquad x^2-y^2=1, \qquad x^2-y^2=4.$$

SOLUTION The region is shown in Figure 17.10.4. The boundaries suggest that we set

$$u=x^2+y^2, \qquad v=x^2-y^2.$$

We want x and y in terms of u and v. Since

$$u+v=2x^2 \qquad \text{and} \qquad u-v=2y^2,$$

we have

$$x=\sqrt{\frac{u+v}{2}}, \qquad y=\sqrt{\frac{u-v}{2}}.$$

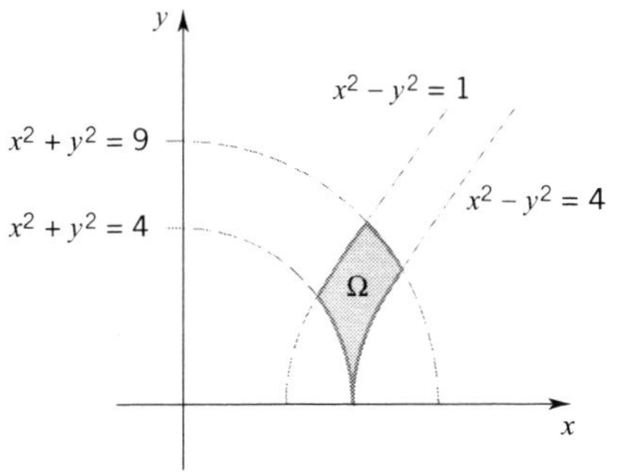

Figure 17.10.4

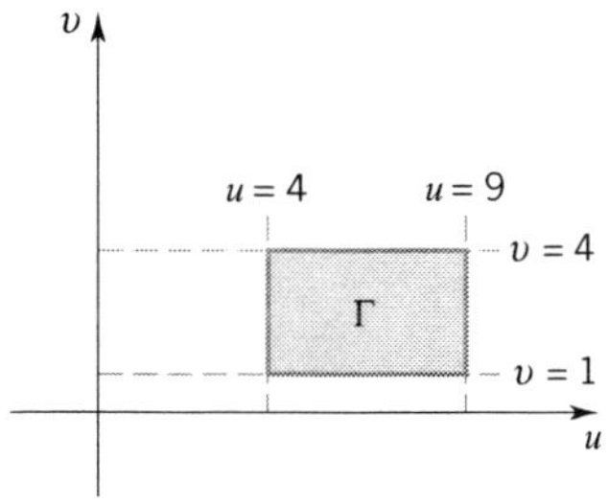

Figure 17.10.5

The transformation maps the rectangle Γ of Figure 17.10.5 onto Ω with Jacobian

$$J(u,v)=\begin{vmatrix} \dfrac{\partial}{\partial u}\left(\sqrt{\dfrac{u+v}{2}}\right) & \dfrac{\partial}{\partial u}\left(\sqrt{\dfrac{u-v}{2}}\right) \\ \dfrac{\partial}{\partial v}\left(\sqrt{\dfrac{u+v}{2}}\right) & \dfrac{\partial}{\partial v}\left(\sqrt{\dfrac{u-v}{2}}\right) \end{vmatrix} \overset{\text{check this}}{=} -\frac{1}{4\sqrt{u^2-v^2}}.$$

Therefore

$$\iint_{\Omega} xy\,dx\,dy = \iint_{\Gamma}\left(\sqrt{\frac{u+v}{2}}\right)\left(\sqrt{\frac{u-v}{2}}\right)\left(\frac{1}{4\sqrt{u^2-v^2}}\right)dudv$$

$$=\iint_{\Gamma}\frac{1}{8}dudv=\frac{1}{8}(\text{area of }\Gamma)=\frac{15}{8}. \quad \square$$

In Section 17.4 you saw the formula for changing variables from rectangular coordinates (x, y) to polar coordinates $[r, \theta]$. The formula reads

$$\iint_{\Omega} f(x,y)\,dx\,dy=\iint_{\Gamma} f(r\cos\theta, r\sin\theta)\,r\,drd\theta. \qquad (17.4.3)$$

The factor r in the double integral over Γ is the Jacobian of the transformation $x = r\cos\theta$, $y = r\sin\theta$:

$$J(r,\theta) = \begin{vmatrix} \dfrac{\partial}{\partial r}(r\cos\theta) & \dfrac{\partial}{\partial r}(r\sin\theta) \\ \dfrac{\partial}{\partial\theta}(r\cos\theta) & \dfrac{\partial}{\partial\theta}(r\sin\theta) \end{vmatrix} = \begin{vmatrix} \cos\theta & \sin\theta \\ -r\sin\theta & r\cos\theta \end{vmatrix} = r(\cos^2\theta + \sin^2\theta) = r.$$

As you can see, (17.4.3) is a special case of (17.10.2).

When changing variables in a triple integral, we make three coordinate changes:

$$x = x(u, v, w), \qquad y = y(u, v, w) \qquad z = z(u, v, w).$$

If these functions carry a basic solid Γ onto a solid T, then, under conditions analogous to those in the two-dimensional case,

$$\text{volume of } T = \iiint_{\Gamma} |J(u, v, w)| du dv dw$$

where now the Jacobian† is a three-by-three determinant:

$$J(u,v,w) = \begin{vmatrix} \dfrac{\partial x}{\partial u} & \dfrac{\partial y}{\partial u} & \dfrac{\partial z}{\partial u} \\ \dfrac{\partial x}{\partial v} & \dfrac{\partial y}{\partial v} & \dfrac{\partial z}{\partial v} \\ \dfrac{\partial x}{\partial w} & \dfrac{\partial y}{\partial w} & \dfrac{\partial z}{\partial w} \end{vmatrix}$$

$$= \frac{\partial x}{\partial u}\begin{vmatrix} \dfrac{\partial y}{\partial v} & \dfrac{\partial z}{\partial v} \\ \dfrac{\partial y}{\partial w} & \dfrac{\partial z}{\partial w} \end{vmatrix} - \frac{\partial x}{\partial v}\begin{vmatrix} \dfrac{\partial y}{\partial u} & \dfrac{\partial z}{\partial u} \\ \dfrac{\partial y}{\partial w} & \dfrac{\partial z}{\partial w} \end{vmatrix} + \frac{\partial x}{\partial w}\begin{vmatrix} \dfrac{\partial y}{\partial u} & \dfrac{\partial z}{\partial u} \\ \dfrac{\partial y}{\partial v} & \dfrac{\partial z}{\partial v} \end{vmatrix}$$

In this case the change of variables formula reads

$$\iiint_{T} f(x, y, z)\, dx\, dy\, dz =$$
$$\iiint_{\Gamma} f(x(u, v, w), y(u, v, w), z(u, v, w))\, |J(u, v, w)|\, du\, dv\, dw.$$

†The study of these functional determinants goes back to a memoir by the German mathematician C.G. Jacobi, 1804–1851.

EXERCISES 17.10

Exercises 1–9. Find the Jacobian of the transformation.

1. $x = au + bv, \quad y = cu + dv$. (linear transformation)

2. $x = u\cos\theta - v\sin\theta$, $y = u\sin\theta + v\cos\theta$. (rotation by θ)

3. $x = uv, \quad y = u^2 + v^2$.

4. $x = u\ln v, \quad y = uv$.

5. $x = uv^2, \quad y = u^2v$.

6. $x = u - \ln v, \quad y = \ln u + v$.

7. $x = au, y = bv, \quad z = cw$.

8. $x = v + w, \quad y = u + w, \quad z = u + v$.

9. $x = (1 + w\cos v)\cos u, \quad y = (1 + w\cos v)\sin u,$ $z = w\sin v$.

10. To change a triple integral in rectangular coordinates to a triple integral in cylindrical coordinates, we introduce the magnification factor r. (Formula 17.8.1.) Verify that

$$r = |J(r, \theta, z)|$$

where $J(r, \theta, z)$ is the Jacobian of the transformation

$$x = r\cos\theta, \qquad y = r\sin\theta, \qquad z = z.$$

11. To change a triple integral in rectangular coordinates to a triple integral in spherical coordinates, we introduce the magnification factor $\rho^2 \sin\phi$. (Formula 17.9.3.) Verify that

$$\rho^2 \sin\phi = |J(\rho, \theta, \phi)|$$

where $J(\rho, \theta, \phi)$ is the Jacobian of the transformation

$$x = \rho \sin\phi \cos\theta, \qquad y = \rho \sin\phi \sin\theta, \qquad z = \rho \cos\phi.$$

12. Every linear transformation

$$x = au + bv, \qquad y = cu + dv \qquad \text{with} \qquad ad - bc \neq 0$$

maps lines of the uv-plane onto lines of the xy-plane. Find the image (a) of a vertical line $u = u_0$; (b) of a horizontal line $v = v_0$.

For Exercises 13–15, take Ω as the parallelogram bounded by

$$x + y = 0,\ x + y = 1,\ x - y = 0,\ x - y = 2.$$

Evaluate.

13. $\iint_\Omega (x^2 - y^2)\,dx\,dy.$ **14.** $\iint_\Omega 4xy\,dx\,dy.$

15. $\iint_\Omega (x - y)\cos[\pi(x - y)]\,dx\,dy.$

For Exercises 16–18 take Ω as the parallelogram bounded by

$$x - y = 0, \quad x - y = \pi, \quad x + 2y = 0, \quad x + 2y = \tfrac{1}{2}\pi.$$

Evaluate.

16. $\iint_\Omega (x + y)\,dx\,dy.$

17. $\iint_\Omega \sin(x - y)\cos(x + 2y)\,dx\,dy.$

18. $\iint_\Omega \sin 3x\,dx\,dy.$

19. Let Ω be the first-quadrant region bounded by the curves $xy = 1, xy = 4, y = x, y = 4x$. (a) Determine the area of Ω and (b) locate the centroid.

20. Show that the ellipse $b^2x^2 + a^2y^2 = a^2b^2$ has area πab by setting $x = ar\cos\theta, y = br\sin\theta$.

21. A homogeneous plate in the xy-plane is in the form of a parallelogram. The parallelogram is bounded by the lines $x + y = 0, x + y = 1, 3x - 2y = 0, 3x - 2y = 2$. Calculate the moments of inertia of the plate about the three coordinate axes. Express your answers in terms of the mass of the plate.

22. Calculate the area of the region Ω bounded by the curves

$$x^2 - 2xy + y^2 + x + y = 0, \qquad x + y + 4 = 0.$$

HINT: Set $u = x - y, v = x + y$.

23. Calculate the area of the region Ω bounded by the curves

$$x^2 - 4xy + 4y^2 - 2x - y - 1 = 0, \qquad y = \tfrac{2}{5}.$$

24. Locate the centroid of the region of Exercise 22.

25. Calculate the area of the region Ω enclosed by the curve

$$11x^2 + 4\sqrt{3}xy + 7y^2 - 1 = 0.$$

HINT: Use a rotation $x = u\cos\theta - v\sin\theta$, $y = u\sin\theta + v\cos\theta$ such that the resulting uv-equation has no uv-term.

26. Evaluate

$$\int_{-\infty}^{\infty}\int_{-\infty}^{\infty} \frac{e^{-(x-y)^2}}{1 + (x + y)^2}\,dx\,dy$$

by integrating over the square $S_a : -a \leq x \leq a$, $-a \leq y \leq a$ and taking the limit as $a \to \infty$. HINT: Set $u = x - y, v = x + y$ and see (17.4.4).

For Exercises 27–30 let T be the solid ellipsoid

$$x^2/a^2 + y^2/b^2 + z^2/c^2 \leq 1.$$

27. Calculate the volume of T by setting

$$x = a\rho\sin\phi\cos\theta,\ y = b\rho\sin\phi\sin\theta,\ z = c\rho\cos\phi.$$

28. Locate the centroid of the upper half of T.

29. View the upper half of T as a homogeneous solid of mass M. Find the moments of inertia of this solid about the coordinate axes.

30. Evaluate

$$\iiint_T \left(\frac{x^2}{a^2} + \frac{y^2}{b^2} + \frac{z^2}{c^2}\right) dx\,dy\,dz.$$

■ PROJECT 17.10 Generalized Polar Coordinates

Recall the equations that transform polar coordinates to rectangular coordinates:

$$x = r\cos\theta, \qquad y = r\sin\theta.$$

In this project, we investigate a generalization of these equations, and we apply the generalized polar coordinates to the problem of finding the area of regions enclosed by curves given in rectangular coordinates.

Let a, b, and α be fixed positive numbers, and let (x, y) be related to (r, θ) by the equations

(1) $$x = ar\,(\cos\theta)^\alpha, \quad y = br\,(\sin\theta)^\alpha.$$

Problem 1.

a. Show that the mapping defined by (1) carries the polar region $\Gamma : 0 \leq r < \infty, 0 \leq \phi = \pi/2$ onto the first quadrant in the xy-plane. HINT: Find a point $[r, \theta]$ that maps onto (x, y) given that $x \geq 0$ and $y \geq 0$.

b. Show that the mapping is one-to-one on the interior of Γ.

Problem 2. Determine the Jacobian of the mapping defined by (1).

Problem 3. The curve $x^{2/3} + y^{2/3} = a^{2/3}$, $a > 0$, is called an *astroid.*

a. Use a graphing utility to draw the astroid for several values of a.

b. Calculate the area enclosed by the astroid in the first quadrant by setting $x = ar\cos^3\theta$, $y = ar\sin^3\theta$.

c. What is the entire area enclosed by the astroid?

Problem 4. Consider the curve

$$\left(\frac{x}{a}\right)^{1/4} + \left(\frac{y}{b}\right)^{1/4} = 1.$$

a. Use a graphing utility to draw this curve in the cases $a = 3, b = 2$ and $a = 2, b = 3$.

b. Calculate the area enclosed by the curve in the first quadrant by setting $x = ar\cos^8\theta$, $y = br\sin^8\theta$.

CHAPTER 17. REVIEW EXERCISES

Exercises 1–10. Evaluate.

1. $\displaystyle\int_0^1\int_y^{\sqrt{y}} xy^2\,dx\,dy.$

2. $\displaystyle\int_0^1\int_{-y}^{y} e^{x+y}\,dx\,dy.$

3. $\displaystyle\int_0^1\int_x^{3x} 2ye^{x^3}\,dy\,dx.$

4. $\displaystyle\int_1^2\int_0^{\ln x} xe^{y}\,dy\,dx.$

5. $\displaystyle\int_0^{\pi/4}\int_0^{2\sin\theta} r\cos\theta\,dr\,d\theta.$

6. $\displaystyle\int_{-1}^{2}\int_0^{4}\int_0^{1} xyz\,dx\,dy\,dz.$

7. $\displaystyle\int_0^2\int_0^{2-3x}\int_0^{x+y} x\,dz\,dy\,dx.$

8. $\displaystyle\int_0^{\pi/2}\int_z^{\pi/2}\int_0^{\sin z} 3x^2\sin y\,dx\,dy\,dz.$

9. $\displaystyle\int_{-\pi/2}^{0}\int_0^{2\sin\theta}\int_0^{r^2} r^2\cos\theta\,dz\,dr\,d\theta.$

10. $\displaystyle\int_{-\pi/6}^{\pi/2}\int_0^{\pi/2}\int_0^{1} \rho^3\sin\varphi\cos\varphi\,d\rho\,d\theta\,d\varphi.$

Exercises 11–14. Sketch the region that gives rise to the repeated integral, change the order of integration, and then evaluate.

11. $\displaystyle\int_0^1\int_y^1 e^{x^2}\,dx\,dy.$

12. $\displaystyle\int_0^2\int_{\frac{1}{2}x}^{1} \cos y^2\,dy\,dx.$

13. $\displaystyle\int_0^1\int_0^{\sqrt{1-x^2}} \frac{1}{\sqrt{1-y^2}}\,dy\,dx.$

14. $\displaystyle\int_0^1\int_0^{1-x} y\cos(x+y)\,dy\,dx.$

Exercises 15–22. Evaluate.

15. $\displaystyle\iint_\Omega xy\,dx\,dy;\ \Omega: 0 \le x^2+y^2 \le 1,\quad x, y \ge 0.$

16. $\displaystyle\iint_\Omega (x-y)\,dx\,dy;$ Ω the region between the curves $y^2 = 3x$ and $y^2 = 4 - x$.

17. $\displaystyle\iint_\Omega (x^2-xy)\,dx\,dy;$ Ω the region between the curves $y = x$ and $y = 3x - x^2$.

18. $\displaystyle\iint_\Omega x(x-1)e^{xy}\,dx\,dy;$ Ω the triangular region in the first quadrant bounded by $x = 0$, $y = 0$, and $x + y = 2$.

19. $\displaystyle\iiint_T xyz\,dx\,dy\,dz;$ T the solid bounded by the cylinder $z = 2 - y^2$ and the planes $x = 0$, $y = 0$, $y = x$.

20. $\displaystyle\iiint_T z\,dx\,dy\,dz;$ T the solid bounded by the planes $x = 0$, $y = 0$, $z = 0$, $y + z = 1$, $x + z = 1$.

21. $\displaystyle\iiint_T xy\,dx\,dy\,dz;$ T the solid in the first octant bounded by the coordinate planes and the hemisphere $z = \sqrt{4 - x^2 - y^2}$.

22. $\displaystyle\iiint_T (x^2+2z)\,dx\,dy\,dz;$ T the solid bounded by the planes $z = 0$ and $y + z = 4$, and the cylinder $y = x^2$.

Exercises 23–24. Use polar coordinates to evaluate the integral.

23. $\displaystyle\int_0^2\int_0^{\sqrt{4-y^2}} e^{\sqrt{x^2+y^2}}\,dx\,dy.$

24. $\displaystyle\int_{-1}^{1}\int_0^{\sqrt{1-x^2}} \arctan(y/x)\,dy\,dx.$

25. Find the volume of the solid bounded by the paraboloid $z = 9 - x^2 - y^2$ and the xy-plane.

26. Find the volume of the solid bounded above by the paraboloid $z = 2 - x^2 - y^2$ and below by the region between the curves $y = x^2$ and $x = y^2$ in the xy-plane.

27. Find the volume of the solid in the first octant bounded by $z = x^2 + y^2$, $x + y = 1$, and the coordinate planes.

28. Find the volume of the solid in the first octant bounded by the cylinder $x^2 + y^2 = 9$ and the planes $z = y$ and $z = 0$.

Exercises 29–32. Find the mass and center of mass of the plate that occupies the region Ω and has mass density λ.

29. $\Omega: -\pi/2 \le x \le \pi/2,\ 0 \le y \le \cos x;\ \lambda(x, y) = y.$

30. Ω : the region between the curves $y = x$ and $y = \sqrt{x}$; $\lambda(x, y) = 2x$.

31. Ω: the region in the first quadrant between the circles $x^2 + y^2 = r^2$ and $x^2 + y^2 = R^2$, $0 < r < R$; $\lambda(x, y) = x^2 + y^2$

32. Ω: the upper half of the cardioid $r = 2(1 + \cos\theta)$; λ is the distance to the pole.

33. A homogeneous plate is in the shape of an isosceles triangle of base b and height h.

(a) Find the centroid of the plate.

(b) Find the moment of inertia about the base.

(c) Find the moment of inertia about the axis of symmetry of the triangle.

34. A plate is in the shape of the upper half of the annular region between $x^2 + y^2 = r^2$ and $x^2 + y^2 = R^2$, $0 < r < R$. The mass density is inversely proportional to the distance from the origin.

(a) Find the mass and center of mass of the plate.

(b) Find the moment of inertia about the x-axis.

(c) Find the moment of inertia about the y-axis.

Exercises 35–42. Use triple integrals to find the volume of the solid. Use rectangular, cylindrical, or spherical coordinates, whichever seems appropriate.

35. The solid bounded above by the plane $2x + 2y - z + 1 = 0$, on the sides by the planes $y = x$, $x = 2$, $y = 0$, and below by $z = 0$.

36. The solid bounded above by the paraboloid $z = 4x^2 + 4y^2$, below by the plane $z = -1$, and on the sides by the cylinders $y = x^2$ and $y = x$.

37. The solid bounded above by the elliptic paraboloid $z = 12 - x^2 - 2y^2$ and below by the elliptic paraboloid $z = 2x^2 + y^2$.

38. The solid in the first octant inside the cylinder $y^2 + z^2 = 1$ and bounded by the plane $2x + y + z = 2$.

39. The solid bounded above by the sphere $x^2 + y^2 + z^2 = 4$ and below by the plane $z = 1$.

40. The solid in the first octant bounded by the cylinder $x^2 + z = 16$, the coordinate planes, and the plane $3x + 4y = 12$.

41. The solid that lies outside the cone $z = \sqrt{x^2 + y^2}$ and inside the hemisphere $z = \sqrt{1 - x^2 - y^2}$.

42. The solid that lies above the cone $z = \sqrt{x^2 + y^2}$ and below the hemisphere $z = \sqrt{1 - x^2 - y^2}$.

43. A homogeneous solid in the first octant is bounded by the cylinders $x^2 + z^2 = 1$ and $y^2 + z^2 = 1$.

(a) Find the centroid of the solid.

(b) Find I_z.

44. A homogeneous solid is bounded above by the cone $z = \sqrt{x^2 + y^2}$ and below by the paraboloid $z = x^2 + y^2$.

(a) Find the centroid of the solid.

(b) Find I_z.

45. A solid is in the shape of a right circular cylinder of height h and radius r. The mass density at each point P of the solid is equal to the square of the distance from P to the axis of the cylinder.

(a) Find the mass of the solid.

(b) Find the center of mass.

46. A solid is in the shape of a hemisphere of radius r. The mass density at each point P of the solid varies directly as the distance from P to the axis of the hemisphere.

(a) Find the mass of the solid.

(b) Find the center of mass.

47. A solid is bounded below by the cone $z = \sqrt{x^2 + y^2}$ and above by the plane $z = 1$. The mass density at each point P of the solid varies directly as the distance from P to the z-axis.

(a) Find the mass of the solid.

(b) Find the center of mass.

(c) Find I_z.

Exercises 48–50. Find the Jacobian of the transformation.

48. $x = u^2 - v^2, \quad y = 2uv.$

49. $x = e^u \cos v, \quad y = e^u \sin v.$

50. $x = u^2 + 2vw, \quad y = v^2 + 2uw, \quad z = uvw.$

Exercises 51–52. Evaluate.

51. $\displaystyle\iint_{\Omega} \sin\left(\frac{y - x}{y + x}\right) dx\,dy$; Ω the region in the first quadrant bounded by the lines $x + y = 1$ and $x + y = 2$.
[Set $x = \frac{1}{2}(v - u), \; y = \frac{1}{2}(v + u)$.]

52. $\displaystyle\iiint_{T} dx\,dy\,dz$; T the solid that lies between the paraboloids $z = x^2 + y^2$ and $z = 4x^2 + 4y^2$, and between the planes $z = 1$ and $z = 4$.
[Set $x = (r/u)\cos\theta, \; y = (r/u)\sin\theta, \; z = r^2$.]

CHAPTER 18

LINE INTEGRALS AND SURFACE INTEGRALS

In this chapter we will study integration over curves and integration over surfaces. At the heart of this subject lie three great integration theorems: *Green's theorem, Gauss's theorem* (commonly known as the *divergence theorem*), and *Stokes's theorem*.

All three theorems are ultimately based on *The Fundamental Theorem of Integral Calculus*, and all can be cast in the same general form:

an integral over a set S = a related integral over the boundary of S.

A word about terminology. Suppose that S is some subset of the plane or of three-dimensional space. A function that assigns a scalar to each point of S (say, the temperature at that point or the mass density at that point) is known in science as a *scalar field*. A function that assigns a vector to each point of S (say, the wind velocity at that point or the gradient of a function f at that point) is called a *vector field*. We will be using this "field" language throughout.

18.1 LINE INTEGRALS

We are led to the definition of *line integral* by the notion of work.

The Work Done by a Varying Force over a Curved Path

The work done by a constant force $\mathbf{F}$ on an object that moves along a straight line is, by definition, the component of $\mathbf{F}$ in the direction of the displacement multiplied by the length of the displacement vector $\mathbf{r}$ (Project 13.3):

$$W = (\text{comp}_{\text{d}}\,\mathbf{F})\|\mathbf{r}\|.$$

We can write this more briefly as a dot product:

(18.1.1) $$W = \mathbf{F} \cdot \mathbf{r}$$

This elementary notion of work is useful, but it is not sufficient. Consider, for example, an object that moves through a magnetic field or a gravitational field. The path of the motion is usually not a straight line but a curve, and the force, rather than remaining constant, tends to vary from point to point. What we want now is a notion of work that applies to this more general situation.

Let's suppose that an object moves along a curve

$$C: \mathbf{r}(u) = x(u)\,\mathbf{i} + y(u)\,\mathbf{j} + z(u)\,\mathbf{k}, \quad u \in [a, b]$$

subject to continuous force $\mathbf{F}$. (The vector field $\mathbf{F}$ may vary from point to point, not only in magnitude but also in direction.) We will suppose that the curve is *smooth*; namely, we will suppose that the tangent vector $\mathbf{r}'$ is continuous and never zero. What we want to do here is define the total work done by $\mathbf{F}$ along the curve C.

To decide how to do this, we begin by focusing on what happens over a short parameter interval $[u, u+h]$. As an estimate for the work done over this interval we can use the dot product

$$\mathbf{F}(\mathbf{r}(u)) \cdot [\mathbf{r}(u+h) - \mathbf{r}(u)].$$

In making this estimate, we are evaluating the force vector $\mathbf{F}$ at $\mathbf{r}(u)$ and we are replacing the curved path from $\mathbf{r}(u)$ to $\mathbf{r}(u+h)$ by the line segment from $\mathbf{r}(u)$ to $\mathbf{r}(u+h)$. (See Figure 18.1.1.) If we set

$$W(u) = \text{total work done by } \mathbf{F} \text{ from } \mathbf{r}(a) \text{ to } \mathbf{r}(u), \text{ and}$$

$$W(u+h) = \text{total work done by } \mathbf{F} \text{ from } \mathbf{r}(a) \text{ to } \mathbf{r}(u+h),$$

then the work done by $\mathbf{F}$ from $\mathbf{r}(u)$ to $\mathbf{r}(u+h)$ must be the difference

$$W(u+h) - W(u).$$

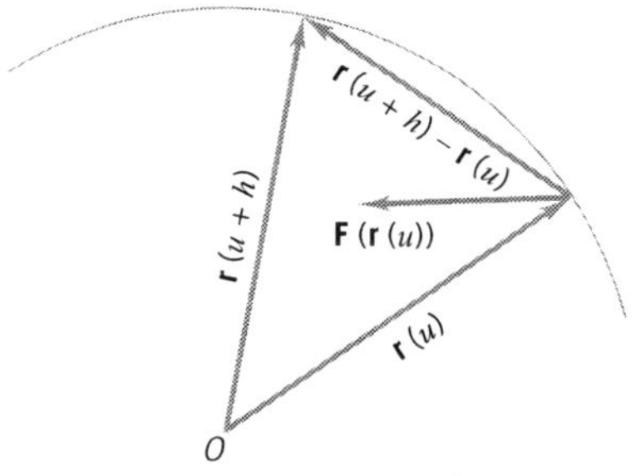

Figure 18.1.1

Bringing our estimate into play, we are led to the approximate equation

$$W(u+h) - W(u) \cong \mathbf{F}(\mathbf{r}(u)) \cdot [\mathbf{r}(u+h) - \mathbf{r}(u)],$$

which, upon division by h, becomes

$$\frac{W(u+h) - W(u)}{h} \cong \mathbf{F}(\mathbf{r}(u)) \cdot \frac{[\mathbf{r}(u+h) - \mathbf{r}(u)]}{h}.$$

The quotients here are average rates of change, and the equation is only an approximate one. The notion of work is made precise by requiring that both sides have exactly the same limit as h tends to zero; in other words, by requiring that

$$W'(u) = \mathbf{F}(\mathbf{r}(u)) \cdot \mathbf{r}'(u).$$

The rest is now determined. Since

$$W(a) = 0 \qquad \text{and} \qquad W(b) = \text{total work done by } \mathbf{F} \text{ on } C,$$

we have:

$$\text{total work done by } \mathbf{F} \text{ on } C = W(b) - W(a) = \int_a^b W'(u)\,du = \int_a^b [\mathbf{F}(\mathbf{r}(u)) \cdot \mathbf{r}'(u)]\,du.$$

In short, we have arrived at the following notion of work:

(18.1.2)

$$W = \int_a^b [\mathbf{F}(\mathbf{r}(u)) \cdot \mathbf{r}'(u)]\,du.$$

Example 1 Determine the work done by the force

$$\mathbf{F}(x, y, z) = xy\,\mathbf{i} + 2\,\mathbf{j} + 4z\,\mathbf{k}$$

along the circular helix $C : \mathbf{r}(u) = \cos u\,\mathbf{i} + \sin u\,\mathbf{j} + u\,\mathbf{k}$, from $u = 0$ to $u = 2\pi$.

SOLUTION Here $x(u) = \cos u,\ y(u) = \sin u,\ z(u) = u.$

$$\mathbf{F}(\mathbf{r}(u)) = \cos u \sin u\,\mathbf{i} + 2\,\mathbf{j} + 4u\,\mathbf{k}$$

$$\mathbf{r}'(u) = -\sin u\,\mathbf{i} + \cos u\,\mathbf{j} + \mathbf{k}$$

$$\mathbf{F}(\mathbf{r}(u)) \cdot \mathbf{r}'(u) = -\sin^2 u \cos u + 2\cos u + 4u.$$

Therefore

$$W = \int_0^{2\pi} (-\sin^2 u \cos u + 2\cos u + 4u)\,du$$

$$= \left[-\tfrac{1}{3}\sin^3 u + 2\sin u + 2u^2\right]_0^{2\pi} = 8\pi^2. \quad \square$$

Line Integrals

The integral on the right of (18.1.2) can be calculated not only for a force function **F** but for any vector field **h** continuous on C.

DEFINITION 18.1.3 LINE INTEGRAL

Let $\mathbf{h}(x, y, z) = h_1(x, y, z)\,\mathbf{i} + h_2(x, y, z)\,\mathbf{j} + h_3(x, y, z)\,\mathbf{k}$ be a vector field that is continuous on a smooth curve

$$C : \mathbf{r}(u) = x(u)\,\mathbf{i} + y(u)\,\mathbf{j} + z(u)\,\mathbf{k}, \qquad u \in [a, b].$$

The *line integral* of **h** over C is the number

$$\int_C (\mathbf{h})(\mathbf{r}) \cdot \mathbf{dr} = \int_a^b [\mathbf{h}(\mathbf{r}(u)) \cdot \mathbf{r}'(u)]\,du.$$

Note that, while we speak of integrating over C, we actually carry out the calculations over the parameter set $[a, b]$. If our definition of line integral is to make sense, the line integral as defined must be independent of the particular parametrization chosen for C. Within the limitations spelled out as follows, this is indeed the case:

THEOREM 18.1.4

Let **h** be a vector field that is continuous on a smooth curve C. The line integral

$$\int_C \mathbf{h}(\mathbf{r}) \cdot \mathbf{dr} = \int_a^b [\mathbf{h}(\mathbf{r}(u)) \cdot \mathbf{r}'(u)]\, du$$

is left invariant by every *direction-preserving* change of parameter.†

PROOF Suppose that ϕ maps $[c, d]$ onto $[a, b]$ and that ϕ' is positive and continuous on $[c, d]$. We must show that the line integral over C as parametrized by

$$\mathbf{R}(w) = \mathbf{r}(\phi(w)), \qquad w \in [c, d]$$

equals the line integral over C as parametrized by **r**. The argument is straightforward:

$$\begin{aligned}\int_c \mathbf{h}(\mathbf{R}) \cdot \mathbf{dR} &= \int_c^d [\mathbf{h}(\mathbf{R}(w)) \cdot \mathbf{R}'(w)]\, dw \\ &= \int_c^d [\mathbf{h}(\mathbf{r}(\phi(w))) \cdot \mathbf{r}'(\phi(w))\phi'(w)]\, dw \\ &= \int_c^d [\mathbf{h}(\mathbf{r}(\phi(w))) \cdot \mathbf{r}'(\phi(w))]\phi'(w)\, dw \\ &= \int_a^b [\mathbf{h}(\mathbf{r}(u)) \cdot \mathbf{r}'(u)]\, du = \int_C \mathbf{h}(\mathbf{r}) \cdot \mathbf{dr}. \quad \square\end{aligned}$$

Set $u = \phi(w)$, $du = \phi'(w)\, dw$.
At $w = c$, $u = a$; at $w = d$, $u = b$.

Example 2 Calculate $\int_C \mathbf{h}(\mathbf{r}) \cdot \mathbf{dr}$ given that

$$\mathbf{h}(x, y) = xy\,\mathbf{i} + y^2\,\mathbf{j} \qquad \text{and} \qquad C: \quad \mathbf{r}(u) = u\,\mathbf{i} + u^2\,\mathbf{j},\ u \in [0, 1].$$

SOLUTION Here $x(u) = u$, $y(u) = u^2$ and

$$\begin{aligned}\mathbf{h}(\mathbf{r}(u)) \cdot \mathbf{r}'(u) &= [x(u)y(u)\,\mathbf{i} + [y(u)]^2\,\mathbf{j}] \cdot [x'(u)\,\mathbf{i} + y'(u)\,\mathbf{j}] \\ &= x(u)y(u)x'(u) + [y(u)]^2 y'(u) \\ &= u(u^2)(1) + u^4(2u) = u^3 + 2u^5.\end{aligned}$$

$$\int_C \mathbf{h}(\mathbf{r}) \cdot \mathbf{dr} = \int_0^1 (u^3 + 2u^5)\, du = \left[\tfrac{1}{4}u^4 + \tfrac{1}{3}u^6\right]_0^1 = \tfrac{7}{12}. \quad \square$$

Example 3 Integrate the vector field $\mathbf{h}(x, y, z) = xy\,\mathbf{i} + yz\,\mathbf{j} + xz\,\mathbf{k}$ over the twisted cubic $\mathbf{r}(u) = u\,\mathbf{i} + u^2\,\mathbf{j} + u^3\,\mathbf{k}$ from $(-1, 1, -1)$ to $(1, 1, 1)$.

SOLUTION The path of integration begins at $u = -1$ and ends at $u = 1$. In this case

$$x(u) = u, \qquad y(u) = u^2, \qquad z(u) = u^3.$$

†Changes of parameter were explained in Project 14.4.

Therefore

$$\begin{aligned}\mathbf{h}(\mathbf{r}(u))\cdot\mathbf{r}'(u) &= [x(u)y(u)\,\mathbf{i} + y(u)z(u)\,\mathbf{j} + x(u)z(u)\,\mathbf{k}]\cdot[x'(u)\,\mathbf{i} + y'(u)\,\mathbf{j} + z'(u)\,\mathbf{k}]\\ &= x(u)y(u)x'(u) + y(u)z(u)y'(u) + x(u)z(u)z'(u)\\ &= u(u^2)(1) + u^2(u^3)2u + u(u^3)3u^2\\ &= u^3 + 5u^6.\end{aligned}$$

$$\int_C \mathbf{h}(\mathbf{r})\cdot d\mathbf{r} = \int_{-1}^{1}(u^3 + 5u^6)\,du = \left[\tfrac{1}{4}u^4 + \tfrac{5}{7}u^7\right]_{-1}^{1} = \tfrac{10}{7}. \quad \square$$

If a curve C is not smooth but is made up of a finite number of adjoining smooth pieces $C_1, C_2, \ldots, C_n$, then we define the integral over C as the sum of the integrals over the C_i:

(18.1.5)
$$\int_C = \int_{C_1} + \int_{C_2} + \cdots + \int_{C_n}.$$

Such a curve is said to be *piecewise smooth.* Figure 18.1.2 gives some examples.

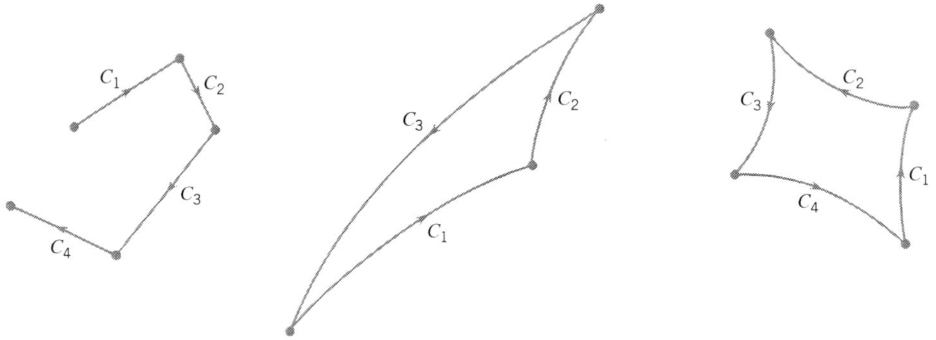

Figure 18.1.2

All polygonal paths are piecewise-smooth curves. In the next example we integrate over a triangle. We do this by integrating over each of the sides and then adding up the results. Observe that the directed line segment that begins at **a** and ends at **b** can be parametrized by setting

$$\mathbf{r}(u) = (1-u)\,\mathbf{a} + u\,\mathbf{b}, \qquad u \in [0, 1].$$

Example 4 Evaluate the line integral $\int_C \mathbf{h}(\mathbf{r})\cdot d\mathbf{r}$ if $\mathbf{h}(x, y) = e^y\,\mathbf{i} - \sin \pi x\,\mathbf{j}$ and C is the triangle with vertices $(1, 0)$, $(0, 1)$, $(-1, 0)$ traversed counterclockwise.

SOLUTION The path C is made up of the three directed line segments:

$$\begin{aligned} C_1&: \quad \mathbf{r}(u) = (1-u)\,\mathbf{i} + u\,\mathbf{j},\ u \in [0, 1],\\ C_2&: \quad \mathbf{r}(u) = (1-u)\,\mathbf{j} + u\,(-\mathbf{i}) = -u\,\mathbf{i} + (1-u)\,\mathbf{j},\ u \in [0, 1],\\ C_3&: \quad \mathbf{r}(u) = (1-u)(-\mathbf{i}) + u\,\mathbf{i} = (2u-1)\,\mathbf{i},\ u \in [0, 1].\end{aligned}$$

C_1 joins $(1, 0)$ to $(0, 1)$; C_2 joins $(0, 1)$ to $(-1, 0)$; C_3 joins $(-1, 0)$ to $(1, 0)$. See Figure 18.1.3.

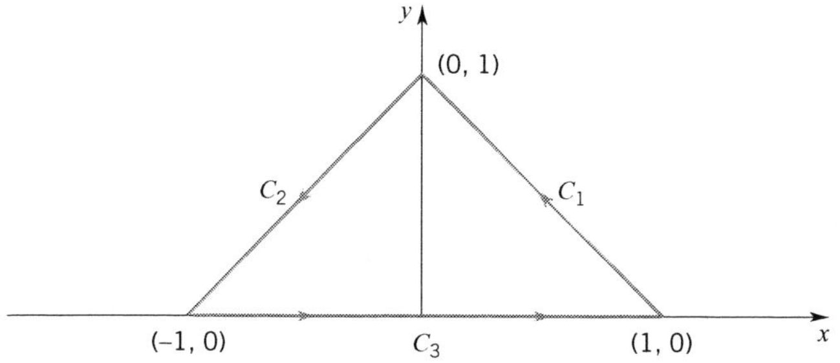

Figure 18.1.3

As you can verify,

$$\int_{C_1} \mathbf{h}(\mathbf{r}) \cdot \mathbf{dr} = \int_0^1 \left[e^{y(u)}x'(u) - \sin[\pi x(u)]y'(u)\right] du$$

$$= \int_0^1 \left[-e^u - \sin[\pi(1-u)]\right] du = 1 - e - \frac{2}{\pi};$$

$$\int_{C_2} \mathbf{h}(\mathbf{r}) \cdot \mathbf{dr} = \int_0^1 \left[e^{y(u)}x'(u) - \sin[\pi x(u)]y'(u)\right] du$$

$$= \int_0^1 \left[-e^{1-u} + \sin(-\pi u)\right] du = 1 - e - \frac{2}{\pi};$$

$$\int_{C_3} \mathbf{h}(\mathbf{r}) \cdot \mathbf{dr} = \int_0^1 \left[e^{y(u)}x'(u) - \sin[\pi x(u)]y'(u)\right] du = \int_0^1 2\,du = 2.$$

The integral over the triangle is the sum of these integrals:

$$\int_C \mathbf{h}(\mathbf{r}) \cdot \mathbf{dr} = \left(1 - e - \frac{2}{\pi}\right) + \left(1 - e - \frac{2}{\pi}\right) + 2 = 4 - 2e - \frac{4}{\pi} \cong -2.71. \quad \square$$

When we integrate over a parametrized curve, we integrate in the direction determined by the parametrization. If we integrate in the opposite direction, our answer is altered by a factor of -1. To be precise, let C be a piecewise-smooth curve and let $-C$ denote the same path traversed in the *opposite direction.* (See Figure 18.1.4.) If C is parametrized by a vector function $\mathbf{r}$ defined on $[a, b]$, then $-C$ can be parametrized by setting

$$\mathbf{R}(w) = \mathbf{r}(a + b - w), \qquad w \in [a, b]. \qquad \text{(Section 14.3)}$$

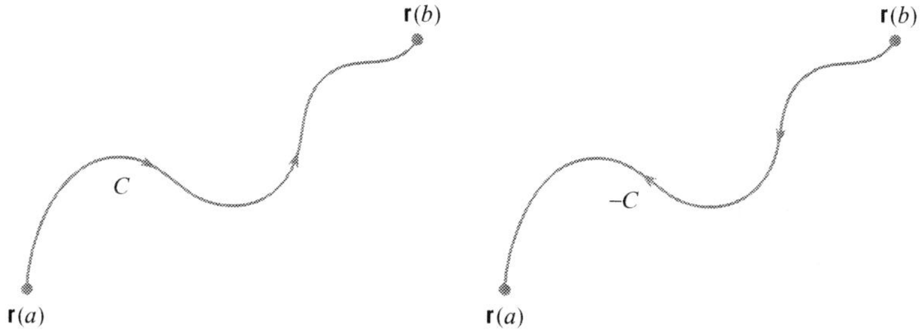

Figure 18.1.4

Our assertion is that

(18.1.6) $$\int_{-C} \mathbf{h}(\mathbf{R}) \cdot \mathbf{dR} = -\int_C \mathbf{h}(\mathbf{r}) \cdot \mathbf{dr},$$

or, more briefly, that

(18.1.7) $$\int_{-C} = -\int_C .$$

We leave the proof of this to you.

We were led to the definition of line integral by the notion of work. It follows from (18.1.2) that if a force $\mathbf{F}$ is continually applied to an object that moves over a piecewise-smooth curve C, then the work done by $\mathbf{F}$ is the line integral of $\mathbf{F}$ over C:

(18.1.8) $$W = \int_C \mathbf{F}(\mathbf{r}) \cdot \mathbf{dr}.$$

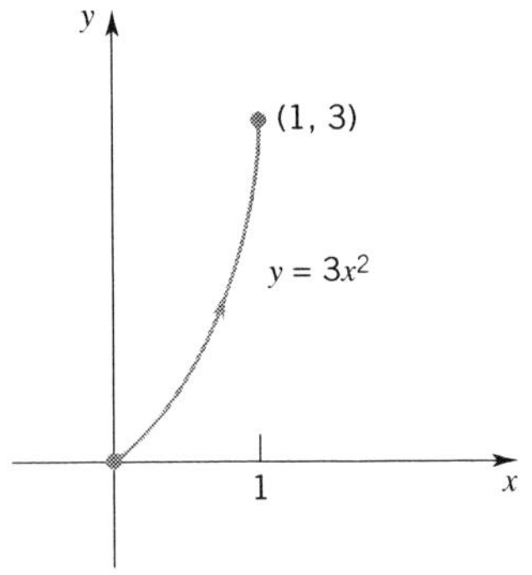

Figure 18.1.5

Example 5 An object, acted on by various forces, moves along the parabola $y = 3x^2$ from the origin to the point (1, 3). (Figure 18.1.5.) One of the forces acting on the object is $\mathbf{F}(x, y) = x^3\,\mathbf{i} + y\,\mathbf{j}$. Calculate the work done by $\mathbf{F}$.

SOLUTION We can parametrize the path by setting

$$C : \mathbf{r}(u) = u\,\mathbf{i} + 3u^2\,\mathbf{j}, \qquad u \in [0, 1].$$

Here $x(u) = u$, $y(u) = 3u^2$ and

$$\mathbf{F}(\mathbf{r}(u)) \cdot \mathbf{r}'(u) = [x(u)]^3 x'(u) + y(u)y'(u) = u^3(1) + 3u^2(6u) = 19u^3.$$

It follows that

$$W = \int_C \mathbf{F}(\mathbf{r}) \cdot \mathbf{dr} = \int_0^1 19u^3 = \tfrac{19}{4}. \quad ❑$$

If an object of mass m moves so that at time t it has position $\mathbf{r}(t)$, then, from Newton's second law, $\mathbf{F} = m\mathbf{a}$, we can conclude that the total force on the object at time t is given by the equation

$$\mathbf{F} = m\,\mathbf{a} = m\,\mathbf{r}''(t).$$

Example 6 An object of mass m moves from time $t = 0$ to $t = 1$ so that its position at time t is given by the vector function

$$\mathbf{r}(t) = \alpha t^2\,\mathbf{i} + \sin\beta t\,\mathbf{j} + \cos\beta t\,\mathbf{k}, \qquad \alpha, \beta \text{ constant.}$$

Find the total force acting on the object at time t and calculate the total work done by this force.

SOLUTION Differentiation gives

$$\mathbf{r}'(t) = 2\alpha t\,\mathbf{i} + \beta\cos\beta t\,\mathbf{j} - \beta\sin\beta t\,\mathbf{k}, \qquad \mathbf{r}''(t) = 2\alpha\,\mathbf{i} - \beta^2\sin\beta t\,\mathbf{j} - \beta^2\cos\beta t\,\mathbf{k}.$$

The total force $\mathbf{F}(t)$ on the object at time t is therefore

$$\mathbf{F}(t) = m\,\mathbf{r}''(t) = m(2\alpha\,\mathbf{i} - \beta^2 \sin\beta t\,\mathbf{j} - \beta^2 \cos\beta t\,\mathbf{k}).$$

We can calculate the total work done by this force by integrating the force over the curve

$$C : \mathbf{r}(t) = \alpha t^2\,\mathbf{i} + \sin\beta t\,\mathbf{j} + \cos\beta t\,\mathbf{k},\ t \in [0, 1].$$

We leave it to you to verify that

$$W = \int_0^1 [m\mathbf{r}''(t)\cdot\mathbf{r}'(t)]\,dt = m\int_0^1 4\alpha^2 t\,dt = 2\alpha^2 m. \quad \square$$

EXERCISES 18.1

1. Integrate $\mathbf{h}(x, y) = y\,\mathbf{i} + x\,\mathbf{j}$ over the indicated path:
 (a) $\mathbf{r}(u) = u\,\mathbf{i} + u^2\,\mathbf{j}, \quad u \in [0, 1]$.
 (b) $\mathbf{r}(u) = u^3\,\mathbf{i} - 2u\,\mathbf{j}, \quad u \in [0, 1]$.
2. Integrate $\mathbf{h}(x, y) = x\,\mathbf{i} + y\,\mathbf{j}$ over the paths of Exercise 1.
3. Integrate $\mathbf{h}(x, y) = y\,\mathbf{i} + x\,\mathbf{j}$ over the unit circle traversed clockwise.
4. Integrate $\mathbf{h}(x, y) = xy^2\,\mathbf{i} + 2\,\mathbf{j}$ over the indicated path:
 (a) $\mathbf{r}(u) = e^u\,\mathbf{i} + e^{-u}\,\mathbf{j}, \quad u \in [0, 1]$.
 (b) $\mathbf{r}(u) = (1 - u)\,\mathbf{i}, \quad u \in [0, 2]$.
5. Integrate $\mathbf{h}(x, y) = (x - y)\,\mathbf{i} + xy\,\mathbf{j}$ over the indicated path:
 (a) the line segment from $(2, 3)$ to $(1, 2)$.
 (b) the line segment from $(1, 2)$ to $(2, 3)$.
6. Integrate $\mathbf{h}(x, y) = x^{-1}y^{-2}\,\mathbf{i} + x^{-2}y^{-1}\,\mathbf{j}$ over the indicated path:
 (a) $\mathbf{r}(u) = \sqrt{u}\,\mathbf{i} + \sqrt{1 + u}\,\mathbf{j}, \quad u \in [1, 4]$.
 (b) the line segment from $(1, 1)$ to $(2, 2)$.
7. Integrate $\mathbf{h}(x, y) = y\,\mathbf{i} - x\,\mathbf{j}$ over the triangle with vertices $(-2, 0), (2, 0), (0, 2)$ traversed counterclockwise.
8. Integrate $\mathbf{h}(x, y) = e^{x-y}\,\mathbf{i} + e^{x+y}\,\mathbf{j}$ over the line segment from $(-1, 1)$ to $(1, 2)$.
9. Integrate $\mathbf{h}(x, y) = (x + y)\,\mathbf{i} + (y^2 - x)\,\mathbf{j}$ over the closed curve that begins at $(-1, 0)$, goes along the x-axis to $(1, 0)$, and returns to $(-1, 0)$ by the upper part of the unit circle.
10. Integrate $\mathbf{h}(x, y) = 3x^2y\,\mathbf{i} + (x^3 + 2y)\,\mathbf{j}$ over the square with vertices $(0, 0), (1, 0), (1, 1), (0, 1)$ traversed counterclockwise.
11. Integrate $\mathbf{h}(x, y, z) = yz\,\mathbf{i} + x^2\,\mathbf{j} + xz\,\mathbf{k}$ over the indicated path:
 (a) the line segment from $(0, 0, 0)$ to $(1, 1, 1)$.
 (b) $\mathbf{r}(u) = u\,\mathbf{i} + u^2\,\mathbf{j} + u^3\,\mathbf{k}, \quad u \in [0, 1]$.
12. Integrate $\mathbf{h}(x, y, z) = e^x\,\mathbf{i} + e^y\,\mathbf{j} + e^z\,\mathbf{k}$ over the paths of Exercise 11.
13. Integrate $\mathbf{h}(x, y, z) = \cos x\,\mathbf{i} + \sin y\,\mathbf{j} + yz\,\mathbf{k}$ over the indicated path:
 (a) the line segment from $(0, 0, 0)$ to $(2, 3, -1)$.
 (b) $\mathbf{r}(u) = u^2\,\mathbf{i} - u^3\,\mathbf{j} + u\,\mathbf{k}, \quad u \in [0, 1]$.
14. Integrate $\mathbf{h}(x, y, z) = xy\,\mathbf{i} + x^2z\,\mathbf{j} + xyz\,\mathbf{k}$ over the indicated path:
 (a) the line segment from $(0, 0, 0)$ to $(2, -1, 1)$.
 (b) $\mathbf{r}(u) = e^u\,\mathbf{i} + e^{-u}\,\mathbf{j} + u\,\mathbf{k}, \quad u \in [0, 1]$.
15. An object moves along the parabola $y = x^2$ from $(0, 0)$ to $(2, 4)$. One of the forces acting on the object is $\mathbf{F}(x, y) = (x + 2y)\,\mathbf{i} + (2x + y)\,\mathbf{j}$. Calculate the work done by $\mathbf{F}$.
16. An object moves along the polygonal path that connects $(0, 0), (1, 0), (1, 1), (0, 1)$ in the order indicated. One of the forces acting on the object is $\mathbf{F}(x, y) = x\cos y\,\mathbf{i} - y\sin x\,\mathbf{j}$. Calculate the work done by $\mathbf{F}$.
17. An object moves along the straight line from $(0, 1, 4)$ to $(1, 0, -4)$. One of the forces acting on the object is $\mathbf{F}(x, y, z) = x\,\mathbf{i} + xy\,\mathbf{j} + xyz\,\mathbf{k}$. Calculate the work done by $\mathbf{F}$.
18. An object moves along the polygonal path that connects $(0, 0, 0), (1, 0, 0), (1, 1, 0), (1, 1, 1)$ in the order indicated. One of the forces acting on the object is $\mathbf{F}(x, y, z) = yz\,\mathbf{i} + xz\,\mathbf{j} + xy\,\mathbf{k}$. Calculate the work done by $\mathbf{F}$.
19. An object moves along the circular helix $\mathbf{r}(u) = \cos u\,\mathbf{i} + \sin u\,\mathbf{j} + u\,\mathbf{k}$ from $(1, 0, 0)$ to $(1, 0, 2\pi)$. One of the forces acting on the object is $\mathbf{F}(x, y, z) = x^2\,\mathbf{i} + xy\,\mathbf{j} + z^2\,\mathbf{k}$. Calculate the work done by $\mathbf{F}$.
20. A mass m, moving in a force field, traces out a circular arc at constant speed. Show that the force field does no work. Give a physical explanation for this.
21. Let $C : \mathbf{r} = \mathbf{r}(u),\ u \in [a, b]$ be a smooth curve and $\mathbf{q}$ a fixed vector. Show that

$$\int_C \mathbf{q}\cdot d\mathbf{r} = \mathbf{q}\cdot[\mathbf{r}(b) - \mathbf{r}(a)]$$

$$\int_C \mathbf{r}\cdot d\mathbf{r} = \frac{\|\mathbf{r}(b)\|^2 - \|\mathbf{r}(a)\|^2}{2}.$$

22. The accompanying figure shows three paths from $(1, 0)$ to $(-1, 0)$. Calculate the line integral of

$$\mathbf{h}(x, y) = x^2\,\mathbf{i} + y\,\mathbf{j}$$

(a) over the straight-line path; (b) over the rectangular path; (c) over the semicircular path.

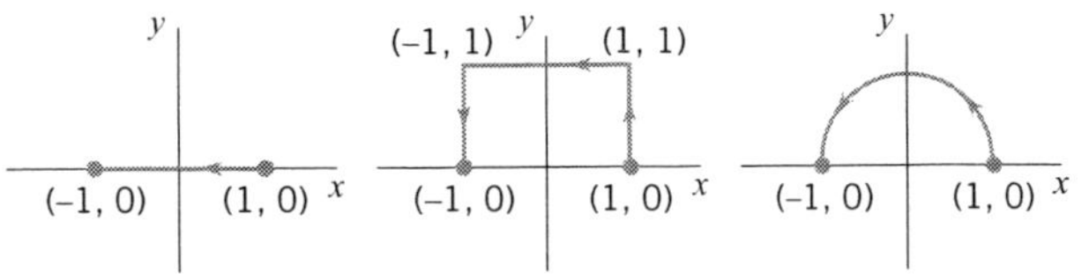

C_1: straight-line path C_2: rectangular path C_3: semicircular path

23. Let f be a continuous real-valued function of a real variable. Show that, if

$$\mathbf{f}(x, y, z) = f(x)\,\mathbf{i} \quad \text{and} \quad C : \mathbf{r}(u) = u\,\mathbf{i},\, u \in [1, b],$$

then

$$\int_C \mathbf{f}(\mathbf{r}) \cdot d\mathbf{r} = \int_a^b f(u)\,du.$$

24. (*Linearity*) Show that, if **f** and **g** are continuous vector fields and C is piecewise smooth, then

(18.1.9)
$$\int_C [\alpha\,\mathbf{f}(\mathbf{r}) + \beta\,\mathbf{g}(\mathbf{r})] \cdot d\mathbf{r} = \alpha \int_C \mathbf{f}(\mathbf{r}) \cdot d\mathbf{r} + \beta \int_C \mathbf{g}(\mathbf{r}) \cdot d\mathbf{r}$$

for all real α, β.

25. The force $\mathbf{F}(x, y) = -\frac{1}{2}[y\,\mathbf{i} - x\,\mathbf{j}]$ is continually applied to an object that orbits an ellipse in standard position. Find a relation between the work done during each orbit and the area of the ellipse.

26. An object of mass m moves from time $t = 0$ to $t = 1$ so that its position at time t is given by the vector function

$$\mathbf{r}(t) = \alpha t\,\mathbf{i} + \beta t^2\,\mathbf{j}, \; \alpha, \beta \text{ constant.}$$

Find the total force acting on the object at time t and calculate the work done by that force during the time interval $[0, 1]$.

27. Exercise 26 for $\mathbf{r}(t) = \alpha t\,\mathbf{i} + \beta t^2\,\mathbf{j} + \gamma t^3\,\mathbf{k}$.

28. (*Important*) The *circulation* of a vector field **v** around a directed closed curve C is by definition the line integral

$$\int_C \mathbf{v}(\mathbf{r}) \cdot d\mathbf{r}.$$

Let **v** be the velocity field of a fluid in counterclockwise circular motion about the z-axis with constant angular speed ω.

(a) Verify that $\mathbf{v}(\mathbf{r}) = \omega\,\mathbf{k} \times \mathbf{r}$.

(b) Show that the circulation of **v** around any circle C in the xy-plane with center at the origin is $\pm 2\omega$ times the area of the circle.

29. Let **v** be the velocity field of a fluid that moves radially from the origin; $\mathbf{v} = f(x, y)\mathbf{r}$. What is the circulation of **v** around a circle C centered at the origin?

30. A long uniformly-charged wire positioned along the z-axis creates a force field. A charged particle at the point $(x, y) \neq (0, 0)$ of the xy-plane is subjected to a force of the form

$$\mathbf{F}(x, y) = k\frac{x\,\mathbf{i} + y\,\mathbf{j}}{x^2 + y^2}, \qquad k \text{ a constant}$$

Find the work done by **F** given that the particle traverses the indicated path

(a) The line segment from $(1, 0)$ to $(1, 2)$.

(b) The line segment from $(0, 1)$ to $(1, 1)$.

31. An object is subject to a force $\mathbf{F}(x, y, z) = k\,\mathbf{r}/r^3$, k a constant, where as usual $\mathbf{r} = x\,\mathbf{i} + y\,\mathbf{j} + z\,\mathbf{k}$ and $r = \|\mathbf{r}\|$. Find the work done by **F** given that the object tranverses the path described.

(a) The line segment from $(1, 0, 2)$ to $(1, 3, 2)$.

(b) Some arc from $(3, 4, 0)$ to $(0, 4, 3)$ on the sphere $r = 5$.

32. An object moves from **a** to **b** in a force field $\mathbf{F} = k\,\mathbf{r}/r^3$, k a constant. What is the work done by **F**?

33. An object traverses the curve $y = \alpha x(1 - x)$ from $(0, 0)$ to $(1, 0)$ subject to the force $\mathbf{F}(x, y) = (y^2 + 1)\,\mathbf{i} + (x + y)\,\mathbf{j}$. What value of α minimizes the work done by **F**?

34. Suppose that f is a scalar field with a gradient ∇f which is everywhere continuous. In anticipation of Section 18.2 show that $\int_C \nabla f(\mathbf{r}) \cdot d\mathbf{r} = f(\mathbf{r}(b)) - f(\mathbf{r}(a))$ where C is the curve $\mathbf{r} = \mathbf{r}(u)$, $a \le u \le b$.

■ 18.2 THE FUNDAMENTAL THEOREM FOR LINE INTEGRALS

In general, if we integrate a vector field **h** from one point to another, the value of the line integral depends on the path chosen. There is, however, an important exception. If the vector field is a *gradient field*,

$$\mathbf{h} = \nabla f,$$

then the value of the line integral depends only on the endpoints of the path, not on the path itself. The details are spelled out in the following theorem.

THEOREM 18.2.1 THE FUNDAMENTAL THEOREM FOR LINE INTEGRALS

Let $C: \mathbf{r} = \mathbf{r}(u), u \in [a, b]$, be a piecewise-smooth curve that begins at $\mathbf{a} = \mathbf{r}(a)$ and ends at $\mathbf{b} = \mathbf{r}(b)$. If the scalar field f is continuously differentiable on an open set that contains the curve C, then

$$\int_C \nabla f(\mathbf{r}) \cdot \mathbf{dr} = f(\mathbf{b}) - f(\mathbf{a}).$$

PROOF If C is smooth,

$$\int_C \nabla f(\mathbf{r}) \cdot \mathbf{dr} = \int_a^b [\nabla f(\mathbf{r}(u)) \cdot \mathbf{r}'(u)]\, du$$

$$= \int_a^b \frac{d}{du}[f(\mathbf{r}(u))]\, du \quad \text{(chain rule (16.3.4))}$$

$$= f(\mathbf{r}(b)) - f(\mathbf{r}(a)) = f(\mathbf{b}) - f(\mathbf{a}).$$

If C is not smooth but only piecewise smooth, then we break up C into smooth pieces

$$C = C_1 \cup C_2 \cup \cdots \cup C_n.$$

With obvious notation,

$$\int_C \nabla f(\mathbf{r}) \cdot \mathbf{dr} = \int_{C_1} \nabla f(\mathbf{r}) \cdot \mathbf{dr} + \int_{C_2} \nabla f(\mathbf{r}) \cdot \mathbf{dr} + \cdots + \int_{C_n} \nabla f(\mathbf{r}) \cdot \mathbf{dr}$$

$$= [f(\mathbf{a}_1) - f(\mathbf{a}_0)] + [f(\mathbf{a}_2) - f(\mathbf{a}_1)] + \cdots + [f(\mathbf{a}_n) - f(\mathbf{a}_{n-1})]$$

$$= f(\mathbf{a}_n) - f(\mathbf{a}_0) = f(\mathbf{b}) - f(\mathbf{a}). \quad \square$$

The theorem we just proved has an important corollary:

(18.2.2) If the curve C is closed [that is, if $\mathbf{b} = \mathbf{a}$], then

$$\int_C \nabla f(\mathbf{r}) \cdot \mathbf{dr} = 0.$$

Example 1 Integrate the vector field $\mathbf{h}(x, y) = y^2\,\mathbf{i} + (2xy - e^{2y})\,\mathbf{j}$ over the circular arc

$$C: \quad \mathbf{r}(u) = \cos u\,\mathbf{i} + \sin u\,\mathbf{j}, \; u \in [0, \tfrac{1}{2}\pi].$$

SOLUTION First we try to determine whether $\mathbf{h}$ is a gradient. We do this by applying Theorem 16.9.2.

Note that $\mathbf{h}(x, y)$ has the form $P(x, y)\,\mathbf{i} + Q(x, y)\,\mathbf{j}$ with

$$P(x, y) = y^2 \quad \text{and} \quad Q(x, y) = 2xy - e^{2y}.$$

Since P and Q are continuously differentiable everywhere and

$$\frac{\partial P}{\partial y} = 2y = \frac{\partial Q}{\partial x},$$

we can conclude that $\mathbf{h}$ is a gradient. Therefore, since the integral depends only on the endpoints of C, not on C itself, we can simplify the computations by integrating over the line segment C_1 that joins these same endpoints. (See Figure 18.2.1.)

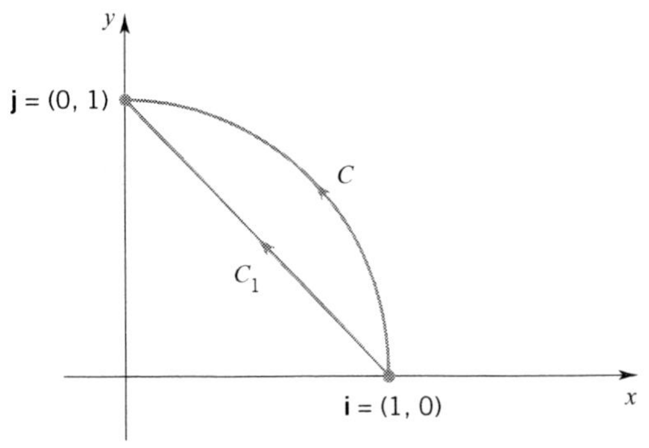

Figure 18.2.1

We parametrize C_1 by setting

$$\mathbf{r}(u) = (1-u)\,\mathbf{i} + u\,\mathbf{j}, \qquad u \in [0, 1].$$

We then have

$$\begin{aligned}\int_C \mathbf{h}(\mathbf{r}) \cdot d\mathbf{r} &= \int_{C_1} \mathbf{h}(\mathbf{r}) \cdot d\mathbf{r} \\ &= \int_0^1 [\mathbf{h}(\mathbf{r}(u)) \cdot \mathbf{r}'(u)]\, du \\ &= \int_0^1 \Big[[y(u)]^2 x'(u) + [2x(u)y(u) - e^{2y(u)}]y'(u)\Big] du \\ &= \int_0^1 \Big[u^2(-1) + [2(1-u)u - e^{2u}](1)\Big] du \\ &= \int_0^1 \Big[2u - 3u^2 - e^{2u}\Big] du = \Big[u^2 - u^3 - \tfrac{1}{2}e^{2u}\Big]_0^1 \\ &= \tfrac{1}{2} - \tfrac{1}{2}e^2.\end{aligned}$$

ALTERNATIVE SOLUTION Once we recognize that $\mathbf{h}(x, y) = y^2\,\mathbf{i} + (2xy - e^{2y})\,\mathbf{j}$ is a gradient ∇f, we can try to determine $f(x, y)$ by the methods of Section 16.9. Since

$$\frac{\partial f}{\partial x} = y^2 \qquad \text{and} \qquad \frac{\partial f}{\partial y} = 2xy - e^{2y},$$

we have

$$f(x, y) = xy^2 + \phi(y) \qquad \text{and therefore} \qquad \frac{\partial f}{\partial y} = 2xy + \phi'(y).$$

The two expressions for $\partial f/\partial y$ can be reconciled only if

$$\phi'(y) = -e^{2y} \qquad \text{and thus} \qquad \phi(y) = -\tfrac{1}{2}e^{2y} + K. \qquad (K \text{ an arbitrary constant})$$

Each function

$$f(x, y) = xy^2 - \tfrac{1}{2}e^{2y} + K$$

has gradient $\mathbf{h}$. No matter what value we assign to K,

$$\int_C \mathbf{h}(\mathbf{r}) \cdot d\mathbf{r} = f(0, 1) - f(1, 0) = (-\tfrac{1}{2}e^2) - (-\tfrac{1}{2}) = \tfrac{1}{2} - \tfrac{1}{2}e^2. \quad \square$$

Example 2 Evaluate the line integral $\int_C \mathbf{h}(\mathbf{r}) \cdot \mathbf{dr}$ where C is the square with vertices $(0, 0), (1, 0), (1, 1), (0, 1)$ traversed counterclockwise (Figure 18.2.2) and

$$\mathbf{h}(x, y) = (3x^2y + xy^2 - 1)\,\mathbf{i} + (x^3 + x^2y + 4y^3)\,\mathbf{j}.$$

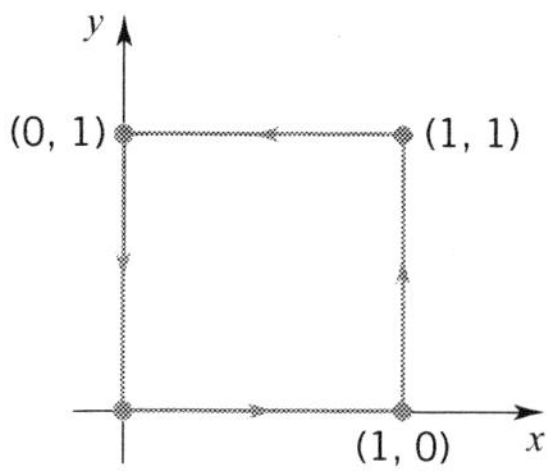

Figure 18.2.2

SOLUTION First we try to determine whether $\mathbf{h}$ is a gradient. The functions

$$P(x, y) = 3x^2y + xy^2 - 1 \qquad \text{and} \qquad Q(x, y) = x^3 + x^2y + 4y^3$$

are continuously differentiable everywhere, and

$$\frac{\partial P}{\partial y} = 3x^2 + 2xy = \frac{\partial Q}{\partial x}.$$

Therefore $\mathbf{h}$ is the gradient of a function f. By (18.2.2),

$$\int_C \mathbf{h}(\mathbf{r}) \cdot \mathbf{dr} = \int_C \nabla f(\mathbf{r}) \cdot \mathbf{dr} = 0. \quad \square$$

Example 3 Evaluate the line integral $\int_C \mathbf{h}(\mathbf{r}) \cdot \mathbf{dr}$, where C is the unit circle

$$C : \mathbf{r}(u) = \cos u\,\mathbf{i} + \sin u\,\mathbf{j}, \qquad u \in [0, 2\pi]$$

and

$$\mathbf{h}(x, y) = (y^2 + y)\,\mathbf{i} + (2xy - e^{2y})\,\mathbf{j}.$$

SOLUTION Although $(y^2 + y)\,\mathbf{i} + (2xy - e^{2y})\,\mathbf{j}$ is not a gradient $[\partial P/\partial y \neq \partial Q/\partial x]$, part of it,

$$y^2\,\mathbf{i} + (2xy - e^{2y})\,\mathbf{j},$$

is a gradient. (Example 1.) Therefore, we can write $\mathbf{h}$ as

$$\begin{aligned}\mathbf{h}(x, y) = (y^2 + y)\,\mathbf{i} + (2xy - e^{2y})\,\mathbf{j} &= [y^2\,\mathbf{i} + (2xy - e^{2y})\,\mathbf{j}] + y\,\mathbf{i} \\ &= \nabla f(x, y) + \mathbf{g}(x, y)\end{aligned}$$

where $g(x, y) = y\,\mathbf{i}$. Now

$$\int_C \mathbf{h}(\mathbf{r}) \cdot \mathbf{dr} = \int_C \nabla f(\mathbf{r}) \cdot \mathbf{dr} + \int_C \mathbf{g}(\mathbf{r}) \cdot \mathbf{dr}.$$

Since we are integrating over a closed curve, the contribution of the gradient part is 0. The contribution of the remaining part is

$$\int_C \mathbf{g}(\mathbf{r}) \cdot \mathbf{dr} = \int_0^{2\pi} [\mathbf{g}(\mathbf{r}(u)) \cdot \mathbf{r}'(u)]\,du = \int_0^{2\pi} y(u)x'(u)\,du = \int_0^{2\pi} -\sin^2 u\,du = -\pi.$$

Therefore $\int_C \mathbf{h}(\mathbf{r}) \cdot \mathbf{dr} = -\pi$. $\square$

EXERCISES 18.2

Exercises 1–11. Determine whether $\mathbf{h}$ is a gradient and then calculate the line integral of $\mathbf{h}$ over the indicated curve.

1. $\mathbf{h}(x, y) = x\,\mathbf{i} + y\,\mathbf{j}$; $\mathbf{r}(u) = a\cos u\,\mathbf{i} + b\sin u\,\mathbf{j}$, $u \in [0, 2\pi]$.

2. $\mathbf{h}(x, y) = (x + y)\,\mathbf{i} + y\,\mathbf{j}$; the curve of Exercise 1.

3. $\mathbf{h}(x, y) = \cos\pi y\,\mathbf{i} - \pi x\sin\pi y\,\mathbf{j}$; $\mathbf{r}(u) = u^2\,\mathbf{i} - u^3\,\mathbf{j}$, $u \in [0, 1]$.

4. $\mathbf{h}(x, y) = (x^2 - y)\,\mathbf{i} + (y^2 - x)\,\mathbf{j}$; the curve of Exercise 1.

5. $\mathbf{h}(x, y) = xy^2\,\mathbf{i} + x^2y\,\mathbf{j}$; $\mathbf{r}(u) = u \sin \pi u\,\mathbf{i} + \cos \pi u^2\,\mathbf{j}$, $u \in [0, 1]$.

6. $\mathbf{h}(x, y) = (1 + e^y)\,\mathbf{i} + (x e^y - x)\,\mathbf{j}$; the square with vertices $(-1, -1), (1, -1), (1, 1), (-1, 1)$ traversed counterclockwise.

7. $\mathbf{h}(x, y) = (2xy - y^2)\,\mathbf{i} + (x^2 - 2xy)\,\mathbf{j}$; $\mathbf{r}(u) = \cos u\,\mathbf{i} + \sin u\,\mathbf{j}$, $u \in [0, \pi]$.

8. $\mathbf{h}(x, y) = 3x(x^2 + y^4)^{1/2}\,\mathbf{i} + 6y^3(x^2 + y^4)^{1/2}\,\mathbf{j}$; the circular arc $y = (1 - x^2)^{1/2}$ from $(1, 0)$ to $(-1, 0)$.

9. $\mathbf{h}(x, y) = 3x(x^2 + y^4)^{1/2}\,\mathbf{i} + 6y^3(x^2 + y^4)^{1/2}\,\mathbf{j}$; the arc $y = -(1 - x^2)^{1/2}$ from $(-1, 0)$ to $(1, 0)$.

10. $\mathbf{h}(x, y) = 2xy \sinh x^2y\,\mathbf{i} + x^2 \sinh x^2y\,\mathbf{j}$; the curve of Exercise 1.

11. $\mathbf{h}(x, y) = (2x \cosh y - y)\,\mathbf{i} + (x^2 \sinh y - y)\,\mathbf{j}$; the square of Exercise 6.

Exercises 12–15. Verify that $\mathbf{h}$ is a gradient. Then evaluate the line integral of $\mathbf{h}$ over the indicated curve C in two ways: (a) by carrying out the integration; (b) by finding f such that $\nabla f = \mathbf{h}$ and evaluating f at the endpoints of C.

12. $\mathbf{h}(x, y) = xy^2\,\mathbf{i} + yx^2\,\mathbf{j}$; $\mathbf{r}(u) = u\,\mathbf{i} + u^2\,\mathbf{j}$, $u \in [0, 2]$.

13. $\mathbf{h}(x, y) = (3x^2y^3 + 2x)\,\mathbf{i} + (3x^3y^2 - 4y)\,\mathbf{j}$; $\mathbf{r}(u) = u\,\mathbf{i} + e^u\,\mathbf{j}$, $u \in [0, 1]$.

14. $\mathbf{h}(x, y) = (2x \sin y - e^x)\,\mathbf{i} + (x^2 \cos y)\,\mathbf{j}$; $\mathbf{r}(u) = \cos u\,\mathbf{i} + u\,\mathbf{j}$, $u \in [0, \pi]$.

15. $\mathbf{h}(x, y) = (e^{2y} - 2xy)\,\mathbf{i} + (2xe^{2y} - x^2 + 1)\,\mathbf{j}$; $\mathbf{r}(u) = ue^u\,\mathbf{i} + (1 + u)\,\mathbf{j}$, $u \in [0, 1]$.

Exercises 16–20. Use the three-dimensional analog of Theorem 16.9.2 given in Exercises 16.9 to show that the vector function $\mathbf{h}$ is a gradient. Then evaluate the line integral of $\mathbf{h}$ over the indicated curve.

16. $\mathbf{h}(x, y, z) = y^2z^3\,\mathbf{i} + 2xyz^3\,\mathbf{j} + 3xy^2z^2\,\mathbf{k}$; $\mathbf{r}(u) = u^2\,\mathbf{i} + u^4\,\mathbf{j} + u^6\,\mathbf{k}$, $u \in [0, 1]$.

17. $\mathbf{h}(x, y, z) = (2xz + \sin y)\,\mathbf{i} + x \cos y\,\mathbf{j} + x^2\,\mathbf{k}$; $\mathbf{r}(u) = \cos u\,\mathbf{i} + \sin u\,\mathbf{j} + u\,\mathbf{k}$, $u \in [0, 2\pi]$.

18. $\mathbf{h}(x, y, z) = \pi yz \cos \pi x\,\mathbf{i} + z \sin \pi x\,\mathbf{j} + y \sin \pi x\,\mathbf{k}$; $\mathbf{r}(u) = \cos u\,\mathbf{i} + \sin u\,\mathbf{j} + u\,\mathbf{k}$, $u \in [0, \pi/3]$.

19. $\mathbf{h}(x, y, z) = (2xy + z^2)\,\mathbf{i} + x^2\,\mathbf{j} + 2xz\,\mathbf{k}$; $\mathbf{r}(u) = 2u\,\mathbf{i} + (u^2 + 2)\,\mathbf{j} - u\,\mathbf{k}$, $u \in [0, 1]$.

20. $\mathbf{h}(x, y, z) = e^{-x} \ln y\,\mathbf{i} - e^{-x}/y\,\mathbf{j} + 3z^2\,\mathbf{k}$; $\mathbf{r}(u) = (u + 1)\,\mathbf{i} + e^{2u}\,\mathbf{j} + (u^2 + 1)\,\mathbf{k}$, $u \in [0, 1]$.

21. Calculate the work done by the force $\mathbf{F}(x, y) = (x + e^{2y})\,\mathbf{i} + (2y + 2xe^{2y})\,\mathbf{j}$ applied to an object that traverses the curve $\mathbf{r}(u) = 3 \cos u\,\mathbf{i} + 4 \sin u\,\mathbf{j}$, $u \in [0, 2\pi]$.

22. Calculate the work done by the force $\mathbf{F}(x, y, z) = (2x \ln y - yz)\,\mathbf{i} + [(x^2/y) - xz]\,\mathbf{j} - xy\,\mathbf{k}$ applied to an object that moves in a straight path from $(1, 2, 1)$ to $(3, 2, 2)$.

23. If g is a continuously differentiable real-valued function defined on $[a, b]$, then by the fundamental theorem of integral calculus

$$\int_a^b g'(u)\,du = g(b) - g(a).$$

Show that this result is included in Theorem 18.2.1.

24. Let $\mathbf{r} = x\,\mathbf{i} + y\,\mathbf{j} + z\,\mathbf{k}$ and set $r = \|\mathbf{r}\|$. The central force field

$$\mathbf{F}(\mathbf{r}) = k\frac{\mathbf{r}}{r^n}, \qquad n \text{ a positive integer}$$

is a gradient field ∇f. Find f given that (a) $n = 2$, (b) $n \neq 2$.

25. Let $\mathbf{r} = x\,\mathbf{i} + y\,\mathbf{j} + z\,\mathbf{k}$ and set $r = \|\mathbf{r}\|$. The vector field

$$\mathbf{F}(\mathbf{r}) = k\,r\,\mathbf{r}, \qquad k \text{ a positive constant}$$

is directed away from the origin, and as you can check, the magnitude of $\mathbf{F}$ at $\mathbf{r}$ is proportional to r^2. Show that $\mathbf{F}$ is a gradient field by finding a scalar field f such that $\nabla f = \mathbf{F}$.

26. Let $\mathbf{r} = x\,\mathbf{i} + y\,\mathbf{j} + z\,\mathbf{k}$ and set $r = \|\mathbf{r}\|$. Suppose that $\mathbf{F}(\mathbf{r}) = g(r^2)\,\mathbf{r}$ where g is a continuous real-valued function defined on $[0, \infty)$. Show that $\mathbf{F}$ is a gradient field by finding a scalar field f such that $\nabla f = \mathbf{F}$.

27. Let $\mathbf{r} = x\,\mathbf{i} + y\,\mathbf{j} + z\,\mathbf{k}$ and set $r = \|\mathbf{r}\|$. The function

$$\mathbf{F}(\mathbf{r}) = -\frac{mG}{r^3}\,\mathbf{r} \quad \text{where } G \text{ is the gravitational constant}$$

gives the gravitational force exerted by a unit mass at the origin on a mass m located at $\mathbf{r}$. What is the work done by $\mathbf{F}$ if m moves from $\mathbf{r}_1$ to $\mathbf{r}_2$?

28. Set

$$P(x, y) = \frac{y}{x^2 + y^2} \quad \text{and} \quad Q(x, y) = -\frac{x}{x^2 + y^2}$$

on *the punctured unit disk* $\Omega : 0 < x^2 + y^2 < 1$.

(a) Verify that P and Q are continuously differentiable on Ω and that

$$\frac{\partial P}{\partial y}(x, y) = \frac{\partial Q}{\partial x}(x, y) \quad \text{for all } (x, y) \in \Omega.$$

(b) Verify that, in spite of (a), the vector field $\mathbf{h}(x, y) = P(x, y)\,\mathbf{i} + Q(x, y)\,\mathbf{j}$ is not a gradient on Ω. HINT: Integrate $\mathbf{h}$ over a circle of radius less than 1 centered at the origin.

(c) Show that part (b) does not contradict Theorem 16.9.2.

29. The gravitational force acting on an object of mass m at a height z above the surface of the earth is given by

$$\mathbf{F}(x, y, z) = -\frac{mGr_0^2}{(r_0 + z)^2}\,\mathbf{k}$$

where G is the gravitational constant and r_0 is the radius of the earth. Show that $\mathbf{F}$ is a gradient field and find f such that $\nabla f = \mathbf{F}$.

30. A rocket of mass m falls to the earth from a height of 300 miles. How much work is done by the gravitational force? Use Exercise 29 and assume that the radius of the earth is 4000 miles.

■ 18.3 WORK-ENERGY FORMULA; CONSERVATION OF MECHANICAL ENERGY

Suppose that a continuous force field $\mathbf{F} = \mathbf{F}(\mathbf{r})$ accelerates a mass m from $\mathbf{r}(\alpha) = \mathbf{a}$ to $\mathbf{r}(\beta) = \mathbf{b}$ along some smooth curve C. The object undergoes a change in kinetic energy:

$$\tfrac{1}{2}m[v(\beta)]^2 - \tfrac{1}{2}m[v(\alpha)]^2.$$

The force does a certain amount of work W. How are these quantities related? They are equal:

(18.3.1)
$$W = \tfrac{1}{2}m[v(\beta)]^2 - \tfrac{1}{2}m[v(\alpha)]^2.$$

This relation is called the *work–energy formula.*

DERIVATION OF THE WORK–ENERGY FORMULA We parametrize the path of the motion by the time parameter t:

$$C: \quad \mathbf{r} = \mathbf{r}(t), \qquad t \in [\alpha, \beta]$$

where $\mathbf{r}(\alpha) = \mathbf{a}$ and $\mathbf{r}(\beta) = \mathbf{b}$. The work done by $\mathbf{F}$ is given by the formula

$$W = \int_C \mathbf{F}(\mathbf{r}) \cdot d\mathbf{r} = \int_\alpha^\beta [\mathbf{F}(\mathbf{r}(t)) \cdot \mathbf{r}'(t)]\,dt.$$

From Newton's second law of motion, we know that at time t,

$$\mathbf{F}(\mathbf{r}(t)) = m\mathbf{a}(t) = m\mathbf{r}''(t).$$

It follows that

$$\begin{aligned}\mathbf{F}(\mathbf{r}(t)) \cdot \mathbf{r}'(t) &= m\mathbf{r}''(t) \cdot \mathbf{r}'(t)\\ &= \frac{d}{dt}\left[\frac{1}{2}m[\mathbf{r}'(t) \cdot \mathbf{r}'(t)]\right] = \frac{d}{dt}\left[\frac{1}{2}m\|\mathbf{r}'(t)\|^2\right] = \frac{d}{dt}\left[\frac{1}{2}m[v(t)]^2\right].\end{aligned}$$

Substituting this last expression into the work integral, we see that

$$W = \int_\alpha^\beta \frac{d}{dt}\left(\frac{1}{2}m[v(\beta)]^2\right)dt = \frac{1}{2}m[v(\beta)]^2 - \frac{1}{2}m[v(\alpha)]^2$$

as asserted. ❑

Conservative Force Fields

In general, if an object moves from one point to another, the work done (and hence the change in kinetic energy) depends on the path of the motion. There is, however, an important exception: if the force field is a gradient field,

$$\mathbf{F} = \nabla f,$$

then the work done (and hence the change in kinetic energy) depends only on the endpoints of the path, not on the path itself. (This follows directly from the fundamental theorem for line integrals.) A force field that is a gradient field is called a *conservative field.*

Since the line integral over a closed path is zero, *the work done by a conservative field over a closed path is always zero. An object that passes through a given point with a certain kinetic energy returns to that same point with exactly the same kinetic energy.*

Potential Energy Functions

Suppose that **F** is a conservative force field. It is then a gradient field. Then $-\mathbf{F}$ is also a gradient field. The functions U for which $\nabla U = -\mathbf{F}$ are called *potential energy functions* for **F**.

The Conservation of Mechanical Energy

Suppose that **F** is a conservative force field: $\mathbf{F} = -\nabla U$. In our derivation of the work–energy formula we showed that

$$\frac{d}{dt}\left(\tfrac{1}{2}m[v(t)]^2\right) = \mathbf{F}(\mathbf{r}(t)) \cdot \mathbf{r}'(t).$$

Since

$$\frac{d}{dt}[U(\mathbf{r}(t))] = \nabla U(\mathbf{r}(t)) \cdot \mathbf{r}'(t) = -\mathbf{F}(\mathbf{r}(t)) \cdot \mathbf{r}'(t),$$

we have

$$\frac{d}{dt}\left[\tfrac{1}{2}m[v(t)]^2 + U(\mathbf{r}(t))\right] = 0,$$

and therefore

$$\underbrace{\tfrac{1}{2}m[v(t)]^2}_{\text{KE}} + \underbrace{U(\mathbf{r}(t))}_{\text{PE}} = \text{a constant.}$$

As an object moves in a conservative force field, its kinetic energy can vary and its potential energy can vary, but the sum of these two quantities remains constant. We call this constant *the total mechanical energy.*

The total mechanical energy is usually denoted by the letter E. The law of conservation of mechanical energy can then be written

(18.3.2)
$$\tfrac{1}{2}mv^2 + U = E.$$

The conservation of energy is one of the cornerstones of physics. Here we have been talking about mechanical energy. There are other forms of energy and other energy conservation laws.

Differences in Potential Energy

Potential energy at a particular point has no physical significance. Only differences in potential energy are significant:

$$U(\mathbf{b}) - U(\mathbf{a}) = \int_C -\mathbf{F}(\mathbf{r}) \cdot d\mathbf{r}$$

is the work required to move from $\mathbf{r} = \mathbf{a}$ to $\mathbf{r} = \mathbf{b}$ *against* the force field **F**.

Example 1 A planet moves in the gravitational field of the sun,

$$\mathbf{F}(\mathbf{r}) = -\rho m \frac{\mathbf{r}}{r^3}$$

where ρ is a positive constant and m is the mass of the planet. Show that the force field is conservative, find a potential energy function, and determine the total energy of the planet. How does the planet's speed vary with the planet's distance from the sun?

SOLUTION The field is conservative since

$$\mathbf{F}(\mathbf{r}) = -\rho m \frac{\mathbf{r}}{r^3} = \nabla\left(\frac{\rho m}{r}\right). \qquad \text{(check this out)}$$

As a potential energy function we can use

$$U(\mathbf{r}) = -\frac{\rho m}{r}.$$

The total energy of the planet is the constant

$$E = \tfrac{1}{2}mv^2 - \frac{\rho m}{r}.$$

(You met this quantity before: Exercises 2 and 4 of Section 14.7.)

Solving the energy equation for v, we have

$$v = \sqrt{\frac{2E}{m} + \frac{2\rho}{r}}.$$

As r decreases, $2\rho/r$ increases, and v increases; as r increases, $2\rho/r$ decreases, and v decreases. Thus every planet speeds up as it comes near the sun and slows down as it moves away. The same holds true for Halley's comet. The fact that it slows down as it gets farther away helps explain why it comes back. The simplicity of all this is a testimony of the power of the principle of energy conservation. ❑

EXERCISES 18.3

1. Let f be a continuous real-valued function of the real variable x. Show that the force field $\mathbf{F}(x, y, z) = f(x)\,\mathbf{i}$ is conservative and the potential functions for $\mathbf{F}$ are (except for notation) the antiderivatives of $-f$.

2. A particle with electric charge e and velocity $\mathbf{v}$ moves in a magnetic field $\mathbf{B}$ experiencing the force

$$\mathbf{F} = \frac{e}{c}[\mathbf{v} \times \mathbf{B}]. \qquad (c \text{ is the velocity of light})$$

$\mathbf{F}$ is not a gradient — it can't be, depending as it does on the *velocity* of the particle. Still, we can find a conserved quantity; the *kinetic energy* $\frac{1}{2}mv^2$. Show by differentiation with respect to t that this quantity is constant. (Assume Newton's second law.)

3. An object is subject to a constant force in the direction of $-\mathbf{k}$: $\mathbf{F} = -\alpha\,\mathbf{k}$ with $\alpha > 0$. Find a potential energy function for $\mathbf{F}$, and use energy conservation to show that the speed of the object at time t_2 is related to that at time t_1 by the equation

$$v(t_2) = \sqrt{[v(t_1)]^2 + \frac{2\alpha}{m}[z(t_1) - z(t_2)]}$$

where $z(t_1)$ and $z(t_2)$ are the z-coordinates of the object at times t_1 and t_2. (This analysis is sometimes used to model the behavior of an object in the gravitational field near the surface of the earth.)

4. (*Escape velocity*) An object is to be fired straight up from the surface of the earth. Assume that the only force acting on the object is the gravitational pull of the earth and determine the initial speed v_0 necessary to send the object off to infinity.

HINT: Appeal to conservation of energy and use the idea that the object is to arrive at infinity with zero speed.

5. (a) Justify the statement that a conservative force field $\mathbf{F}$ always acts so as to encourage motion toward regions of lower potential energy U.

(b) Evaluate $\mathbf{F}$ at a point where U has a minimum.

6. A harmonic oscillator has a restoring force $\mathbf{F} = -\lambda x\mathbf{i}$. The associated potential is $U(x, y, z) = -\frac{1}{2}\lambda x^2$, and the constant total energy is

$$E = \tfrac{1}{2}mv^2 + U(x, y, z) = \tfrac{1}{2}mv^2 + \tfrac{1}{2}\lambda x^2.$$

Given that $x(0) = 2$ and $x'(0) = 1$, calculate the maximum speed of the oscillator and the maximum value of x.

7. The *equipotential surfaces* of a conservative field $\mathbf{F}$ are the surfaces where the potential energy is constant. Show that: (a) the speed of an object in such a field is constant on every equipotential surface; and (b) at each point of such a surface the force field is perpendicular to the surface.

8. Suppose a force field $\mathbf{F}$ is directed away from the origin with a magnitude that is inversely proportional to the distance from the origin. Show that $\mathbf{F}$ is a conservative field.

9. Let $\mathbf{F}$ be the inverse-square force field:

$$\mathbf{F}(x, y, z) = k\frac{x\,\mathbf{i} + y\,\mathbf{j} + z\,\mathbf{k}}{(x^2 + y^2 + z^2)^{3/2}}$$

and let C be any curve on the unit sphere $x^2 + y^2 + z^2 = 1$. Show that the work done by $\mathbf{F}$ in moving an object along C is 0. Explain this result.

■ 18.4 ANOTHER NOTATION FOR LINE INTEGRALS; LINE INTEGRALS WITH RESPECT TO ARC LENGTH

If $\mathbf{h}(x, y, z) = P(x, y, z)\,\mathbf{i} + Q(x, y, z)\,\mathbf{j} + R(x, y, z)\,\mathbf{k}$, the line integral

$$\int_C \mathbf{h}(\mathbf{r}) \cdot \mathbf{dr} \qquad \text{can be written} \qquad \int_C P(x, y, z)\,dx + Q(x, y, z)\,dy + R(x, y, z)\,dz.$$

The notation arises as follows. With

$$C:\quad \mathbf{r}(u) = x(u)\,\mathbf{i} + y(u)\,\mathbf{j} + z(u)\,\mathbf{k}, \qquad u \in [a, b]$$

the line integral

$$\int_C \mathbf{h}(\mathbf{r}) \cdot \mathbf{dr} = \int_a^b [\mathbf{h}(\mathbf{r}(u)) \cdot \mathbf{r}'(u)]\,du$$

expands to

$$\int_a^b \{P[x(u), y(u), z(u)]x'(u) + Q[x(u), y(u), z(u)]y'(u) + R[x(u), y(u), z(u)]z'(u)\}\,du.$$

Now set

$$\int_C P(x, y, z)\,dx = \int_a^b P[x(u), y(u), z(u)]\,x'(u)\,du,$$

$$\int_C Q(x, y, z)\,dy = \int_a^b Q[x(u), y(u), z(u)]\,y'(u)\,du,$$

$$\int_C R(x, y, z)\,dz = \int_a^b R[x(u), y(u), z(u)]\,z'(u)\,du.$$

Writing the sum of these integrals as

$$\int_C P(x, y, z)\,dx + Q(x, y, z)\,dy + R(x, y, z)\,dz,$$

we have

$$\int_C P(x, y, z)\,dx + Q(x, y, z)\,dy + R(x, y, z)\,dz = \int_C \mathbf{h}(\mathbf{r}) \cdot \mathbf{dr}.$$

If C lies in the xy-plane and $\mathbf{h}(x, y) = P(x, y)\,\mathbf{i} + Q(x, y)\,\mathbf{j}$, then the line integral reduces to

$$\int_C P(x, y)\,dx + Q(x, y)\,dy.$$

Example 1 Evaluate $\int_C x^2y\,dx + xy\,dy$ where C is

(a) the straight-line path from $(1, 0)$ to $(0, 1)$,
(b) the circular path $y = \sqrt{1 - x^2}$ from $(1, 0)$ to $(0, 1)$,
(c) the polygonal path from $(1, 0)$ to $(1, 1)$ to $(0, 1)$.

(As you'll see, the results are different.)

SOLUTION

(a) The straight-line path from (1, 0) to (0, 1) can be parametrized by

$$\mathbf{r}(u) = (1-u)\,\mathbf{i} + u\,\mathbf{j}, \qquad 0 \le u \le 1.$$

Therefore

$$\begin{aligned}\int_C x^2y\,dx + xy\,dy &= \int_0^1 [x^2(u)y(u)x'(u) + x(u)y(u)y'(u)]\,du\\ &= \int_0^1 [(1-u)^2u(-1) + (1-u)u]\,du\\ &= \int_0^1 (u^2-u^3)\,du = \left[\tfrac{1}{3}u^3 - \tfrac{1}{4}u^4\right]_0^1 = \tfrac{1}{12}.\end{aligned}$$

(b) We parametrize the path $y = \sqrt{1-x^2}$ from (1, 0) to (0, 1) by setting

$$\mathbf{r}(u) = \cos u\,\mathbf{i} + \sin u\,\mathbf{j}, \qquad 0 \le u \le \pi/2.$$

Therefore

$$\begin{aligned}\int_C x^2y\,dx + xy\,dy &= \int_0^{\pi/2} [x^2(u)y(u)x'(u) + x(u)y(u)y'(u)]\,du\\ &= \int_0^{\pi/2} [\cos^2 u \sin u(-\sin u) + \cos u \sin u(\cos u)]\,du\\ &= \int_0^{\pi/2} [-\cos^2 u \sin^2 u + \cos^2 u \sin u]\,du\\ &= -\int_0^{\pi/2} \tfrac{1}{4}\sin^2 2u\,du + \int_0^{\pi/2} \cos^2 u \sin u\,du\\ &= -\tfrac{1}{8}\int_0^{\pi/2} (1-\cos 4u)\,du + \left[-\tfrac{1}{3}\cos^3 u\right]_0^{\pi/2}\\ &= -\tfrac{1}{8}\left[u - \tfrac{1}{4}\sin 4u\right]_0^{\pi/2} + \tfrac{1}{3} = \tfrac{1}{3} - \tfrac{\pi}{16}.\end{aligned}$$

(c) The polygonal path (1, 0), (1, 1), (0, 1) is made up of the two line segments

$$C_1 : \mathbf{r}(u) = \mathbf{i} + u\,\mathbf{j},\ 0 \le u \le 1 \qquad \text{and} \qquad C_2 : \mathbf{r}(u) = (1-u)\,\mathbf{i} + \mathbf{j},\ 0 \le u \le 1.$$

$$\int_{C_1} x^2y\,dx + xy\,dy = \int_{C_1} xy\,dy = \int_0^1 x(u)y(u)y'(u)\,du = \int_0^1 u\,du = \tfrac{1}{2}$$

$$\begin{aligned}\int_{C_2} x^2y\,dx + xy\,dy = \int_{C_2} x^2y\,dx &= \int_0^1 x^2(u)y(u)x'(u)\,du\\ &= \int_0^1 -(1-u)^2du = -\tfrac{1}{3}.\end{aligned}$$

Therefore,

$$\int_C x^2y\,dx + xy\,dy = \int_{C_1} x^2y\,dx + xy\,dy + \int_{C_2} x^2y\,dx + xy\,dy = \tfrac{1}{2} - \tfrac{1}{3} = \tfrac{1}{6}. \quad \square$$

Line Integrals with Respect to Arc Length

Suppose that f is a scalar field continuous on a piecewise-smooth curve

$$C: \mathbf{r}(u) = x(u)\,\mathbf{i} + y(u)\,\mathbf{j} + z(u)\,\mathbf{k}, \qquad u \in [a, b].$$

If $s(u)$ is the length of the curve from the tip of $\mathbf{r}(a)$ to the tip of $\mathbf{r}(u)$, then, as you have seen,

$$s'(u) = \|\mathbf{r}'(u)\| = \sqrt{[x'(u)]^2 + [y'(u)]^2 + [z'(u)]^2}.$$

The line integral of f over C *with respect to arc length s* is defined by setting

(18.4.1)
$$\int_C f(\mathbf{r})\,ds = \int_a^b f(\mathbf{r}(u))\,s'(u)\,du.$$

In xyz-notation we have

$$\int_C f(x, y, z)\,ds = \int_a^b f(x(u), y(u), z(u))\,s'(u)\,du,$$

which, in the two-dimensional case, becomes

$$\int_C f(x, y)\,ds = \int_a^b f(x(u), y(u))\,s'(u)\,du.$$

Suppose now that C represents a thin wire (a material curve) of varying mass density $\lambda = \lambda(\mathbf{r})$. (Here mass density is mass per unit length.) The *length* of the wire can be written

(18.4.2)
$$L = \int_C ds.$$

The *mass* of the wire is given by

(18.4.3)
$$M = \int_C \lambda(\mathbf{r})\,ds,$$

and the *center of mass* $\mathbf{r}_M$ can be obtained from the vector equation

(18.4.4)
$$\mathbf{r}_M M = \int_C \mathbf{r}\,\lambda(\mathbf{r})\,ds.$$

The equivalent scalar equations read

$$x_M M = \int_C x\lambda(\mathbf{r})\,ds, \qquad y_M M = \int_C y\lambda(\mathbf{r})\,ds, \qquad z_M M = \int_C z\lambda(\mathbf{r})\,ds.$$

Finally, the *moment of inertia* about an axis is given by the formula

(18.4.5)

$$I = \int_C \lambda(\mathbf{r})[R(\mathbf{r})]^2 ds$$

where $R(\mathbf{r})$ is the distance from the axis to the tip of $\mathbf{r}$.

Example 2 The mass density of a semicircular wire of radius a varies directly as the distance from the diameter that joins the two endpoints of the wire. **(a)** Find the mass of the wire. **(b)** Locate the center of mass. **(c)** Determine the moment of inertia of the wire about the diameter.

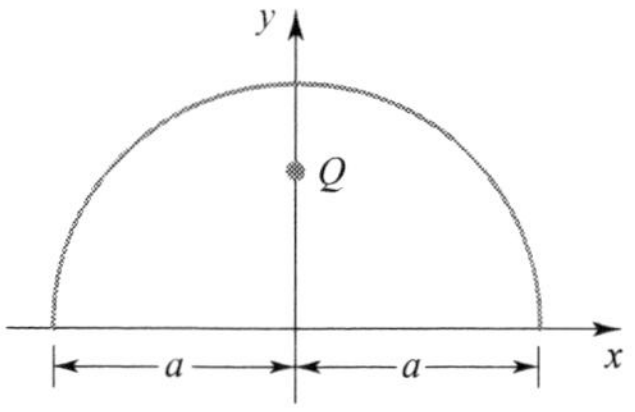

Figure 18.4.1

SOLUTION **(a)** Placed as in Figure 18.4.1, the wire can be parametrized by

$$\mathbf{r}(u) = a\cos u\,\mathbf{i} + a\sin u\,\mathbf{j}, \qquad u \in [0, \pi]$$

and the mass density function can be written $\lambda(x, y) = ky$.

$$\mathbf{r}'(u) = -a\sin u\,\mathbf{i} + a\cos u\,\mathbf{j} \quad \text{gives} \quad s'(u) = \|\mathbf{r}'(u)\| = a.$$

Therefore

(a)
$$M = \int_C \lambda(x, y)\,ds = \int_C ky\,ds$$
$$= \int_0^{\pi} ky(u)s'(u)\,du$$
$$= \int_0^{\pi} k(a\sin u)\,a\,du = ka^2 \int_0^{\pi} \sin u\,du = 2ka^2.$$

(b) By the symmetry of the configuration, $x_M = 0$. To find y_M we have to integrate:

$$y_M M = \int_C y\lambda(x, y)\,ds = \int_C ky^2 ds$$
$$= \int_0^{\pi} k[y(u)]^2 s'(u)\,du$$
$$= \int_0^{\pi} k(a\sin u)^2 a\,du = ka^3 \int_0^{\pi} \sin^2 u\,du = \tfrac{1}{2}ka^3\pi.$$

Since $M = 2ka^2$, we have $y_M = (\frac{1}{2}ka^3\pi)/(2ka^2) = \frac{1}{4}a\pi$. The center of mass Q lies on the perpendicular bisector of the wire at a distance $\frac{1}{4}a\pi$ from the diameter. (See Figure 18.4.1.) The center of mass does not lie on the wire.

(c) Now let's find the moment of inertia about the diameter:

$$I = \int_C \lambda(x, y)[R(x, y)]^2 ds = \int_C (ky)y^2 ds$$
$$= \int_C k[y(u)]^3 s'(u)\,du$$
$$= \int_0^{\pi} k(a\sin u)^3 a\,du$$
$$= ka^4 \int_0^{\pi} \sin^3 u\,du = \tfrac{4}{3}ka^4.$$

It is customary to express I in terms of M. With $M = 2ka^2$, we have

$$I = \tfrac{2}{3}(2ka^2)a^2 = \tfrac{2}{3}Ma^2. \quad \square$$

EXERCISES 18.4

Exercises 1–4. Evaluate

$$\int_C (x - 2y)dx + 2x\,dy$$

over the given path C from $(0, 0)$ to $(1, 2)$.

1. The straight-line path.

2. The parabolic path $y = 2x^2$.

3. The polygonal path $(0, 0), (1, 0), (1, 2)$.

4. The polygonal path $(0, 0), (0, 2), (1, 2)$.

Exercises 5–8. Evaluate

$$\int_C y\,dx + xy\,dy$$

over the given path C from $(0, 0)$ to $(2, 1)$.

5. The parabolic path $x = 2y^2$.

6. The straight-line path.

7. The polygonal path $(0, 0), (0, 1), (2, 1)$.

8. The cubic path $x = 2y^3$.

Exercises 9–12. Evaluate

$$\int_C y^2\,dx + (xy - x^2)\,dy$$

where C is the path given from $(0, 0)$ to $(2, 4)$.

9. The straight-line path.

10. The parabolic path $y = x^2$.

11. The parabolic path $y^2 = 8x$.

12. The polygonal path $(0, 0), (2, 0), (2, 4)$.

Exercises 13–16. Evaluate

$$\int_C (y^2 + 2x + 1)\,dx + (2xy + 4y - 1)\,dy$$

where C is the path given from $(0, 0)$ to $(1, 1)$.

13. The straight-line path.

14. The parabolic path $y = x^2$.

15. The cubic path $y = x^3$.

16. The polygonal path $(0, 0), (4, 0), (4, 2), (1, 1)$.

Exercises 17–20. Evaluate

$$\int_C y\,dx + 2z\,dy + x\,dz$$

where C is the path given from $(0, 0, 0)$ to $(1, 1, 1)$.

17. The straight-line path.

18. $\mathbf{r}(u) = u\,\mathbf{i} + u^2\,\mathbf{j} + u^3\,\mathbf{k}$.

19. The polygonal path $(0, 0, 0), (0, 0, 1), (0, 1, 1), (1, 1, 1)$.

20. The polygonal path $(0, 0, 0), (1, 0, 0), (1, 1, 0), (1, 1, 1)$.

Exercises 21–24. Evaluate

$$\int_C xy\,dx + 2z\,dy + (y + z)\,dz$$

where C is the path given from $(0, 0, 0)$ to $(2, 2, 8)$.

21. The straight-line path.

22. The polygonal path $(0, 0, 0), (2, 0, 0), (2, 2, 0), (2, 2, 8)$.

23. The parabolic path $\mathbf{r}(u) = u\,\mathbf{i} + u\,\mathbf{j} + 2u^2\,\mathbf{k}$.

24. The polygonal path $(0, 0, 0), (2, 2, 2), (2, 2, 8)$.

25. Evaluate $\int_C x^2y\,dx + y\,dy + xz\,dz$ where C is the intersection of the cylinder $y - 2z^2 = 1$ with the plane $z = x + 1$ traversed from $(0, 3, 1)$ to $(1, 9, 2)$.

26. Evaluate $\int_C y\,dx + yz\,dy + z(x - 1)\,dz$ where C is the intersection of the sphere $x^2 + y^2 + z^2 = 4$ with the cylinder $(x - 1)^2 + y^2 = 1$ traversed from $(2, 0, 0)$ to $(0, 0, 2)$.

27. Let $\mathbf{h}$ be the vector field

$$\mathbf{h}(x, y) = (x^2 + 6xy - 2y^2)\,\mathbf{i} + (3x^2 - 4xy + 2y)\,\mathbf{j}.$$

(a) Show that $\mathbf{h}$ is a gradient field.

(b) What is the value of

$$\int_C (x^2 + 6xy - 2y^2)\,dx + (3x^2 - 4xy + 2y)\,dy$$

for every piecewise-smooth C (i) from $(3, 0)$ to $(0, 4)$? (ii) from $(4, 0)$ to $(0, 3)$?

28. Let $\mathbf{h}$ be the vector field

$$\mathbf{h}(x, y, z) = (2xy + z^2)\,\mathbf{i} + (x^2 - 2yz)\,\mathbf{j} + (2xz - y^2)\,\mathbf{k}.$$

(a) Show that $\mathbf{h}$ is a gradient field.

(b) What is the value of

$$\int_C (2xy + z^2)\,dx + (x^2 - 2yz)\,dy + (2xz - y^2)\,dz$$

for every piecewise-smooth curve C (i) from $(1, 0, 1)$ to $(3, 2, -1)$? (ii) from $(3, 2, -1)$ to $(1, 0, 1)$?

29. A wire in the shape of the quarter-circle

$$C : \mathbf{r}(u) = a(\cos u\,\mathbf{i} + \sin u\,\mathbf{j}), \quad u \in [0, \tfrac{1}{2}\pi]$$

has varying mass density $\lambda(x, y) = k(x + y)$ where k is a positive constant.

(a) Find the total mass of the wire and locate the center of mass.

(b) What is the moment of inertia of the wire about the x-axis?

30. Find the moment of inertia of a homogeneous circular wire of radius a and mass M (a) about a diameter; (b) about the axis that passes through the center of the circle and is perpendicular to the plane of the wire.

31. Find the moment of inertia of the wire of Exercise 29
(a) about the z-axis; (b) about the line $y = x$.

32. A wire of constant mass density k has the form

$$\mathbf{r}(u) = (1 - \cos u)\,\mathbf{i} + (u - \sin u)\,\mathbf{j}, \quad u \in [0, 2\pi].$$

(a) Determine the mass of the wire.
(b) Locate the center of mass.

33. A homogeneous wire of mass M winds around the z-axis as

$$C: \quad \mathbf{r}(u) = a\cos u\,\mathbf{i} + a\sin u\,\mathbf{j} + bu\,\mathbf{k}, \quad u \in [0, 2\pi].$$

(a) Find the length of the wire.
(b) Locate the center of mass.
(c) Determine the moments of inertia of the wire about the coordinate axes.

34. A homogeneous wire of mass M is of the form

$$C: \quad \mathbf{r}(u) = u\,\mathbf{i} + u^2\,\mathbf{j} + \tfrac{2}{3}u^3\,\mathbf{k}, \quad u \in [0, a].$$

(a) Find the length of the wire.
(b) Locate the center of mass.
(c) Determine the moment of inertia of the wire about the z-axis.

35. Calculate the mass of the wire of Exercise 33 given that the mass density varies directly as the square of the distance from the origin.

36. Show that

(18.4.6) $$\int_C \mathbf{h}(\mathbf{r}) \cdot d\mathbf{r} = \int_C [\mathbf{h}(\mathbf{r}) \cdot \mathbf{T}(\mathbf{r})]\, ds$$

where $\mathbf{T}$ is the unit tangent vector.

■ 18.5 GREEN'S THEOREM

Green's theorem is the first of the three integration theorems heralded at the beginning of this chapter.

A *Jordan curve* (named after the French mathematician Camille Jordan) is a plane curve which is both closed and simple. Thus circles, ellipses, and triangles are Jordan curves; figure eights are not.

Figure 18.5.1 depicts a closed region Ω, the total boundary of which is a Jordan curve C. Such a region is called a *Jordan region*. We know how to integrate over Ω, and if the boundary C is piecewise smooth, we know how to integrate over C. Green's theorem expresses a double integral over Ω as a line integral over C.

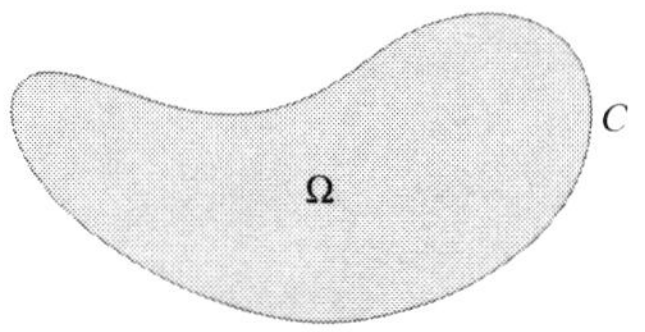

Figure 18.5.1

THEOREM 18.5.1 GREEN'S THEOREM†

Let Ω be a Jordan region with a piecewise-smooth boundary C. If P and Q are scalar fields continuously differentiable on an open set that contains Ω, then

$$\iint_\Omega \left[\frac{\partial Q}{\partial x}(x, y) - \frac{\partial P}{\partial y}(x, y)\right] dxdy = \oint_C P(x, y)\,dx + Q(x, y)\,dy$$

where the integral on the right is the line integral taken over C in the counterclockwise direction.‡

We will prove the theorem only for special cases. First of all we assume that Ω is an *elementary region*, a region that is both of Type I and Type II as defined in Section 17.3. For simplicity we take Ω as in Figure 18.5.2.

†The result was established in 1828 by the English mathematician George Green (1793–1841).

‡Counterclockwise as viewed from $z > 0$ in a right-handed coordinate system. The integral over C in the clockwise direction is written $\oint_C$.

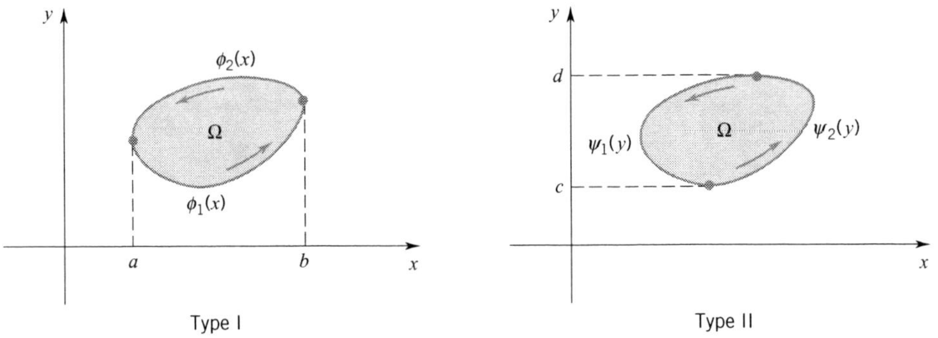

Ω is an elementary region: it is both of Type I and Type II

Figure 18.5.2

Ω being of Type I, we can show that

(1) $$\oint_C P(x, y)\,dx = \iint_\Omega -\frac{\partial P}{\partial y}(x, y)\,dxdy.$$

In the first place

$$\iint_\Omega -\frac{\partial P}{\partial y}(x, y)\,dxdy = -\int_a^b \int_{\phi_1(x)}^{\phi_2(x)} \frac{\partial P}{\partial y}(x, y)\,dy\,dx$$

by the fundamental theorem of integral calculus

$$= -\int_a^b \{P[x, \phi_2(x)] - P[x, \phi_1(x)]\}\,dx$$

(∗) $$= \int_a^b P[x, \phi_1(x)]\,dx - \int_a^b P[x, \phi_2(x)]\,dx.$$

The graph of ϕ_1 parametrized from left to right is the curve

$$C_1: \quad \mathbf{r}_1(u) = u\,\mathbf{i} + \phi_1(u)\,\mathbf{j}, \qquad u \in [a, b];$$

the graph of ϕ_2, also parametrized from left to right, is the curve

$$C_2: \quad \mathbf{r}_2(u) = u\,\mathbf{i} + \phi_2(u)\,\mathbf{j}, \qquad u \in [a, b].$$

Since C traversed counterclockwise consists of C_1 followed by $-C_2$ (C_2 traversed from right to left), you can see that

$$\oint_C P(x, y)\,dx = \int_{C_1} P(x, y)\,dx - \int_{C_2} P(x, y)\,dx$$

$$= \int_a^b P[u, \phi_1(u)]\,du - \int_a^b P[u, \phi_2(u)]\,du.$$

Since u is a dummy variable, it can be replaced by x. Comparison with (∗) proves (1).

We leave it to you to verify that

$$\oint_C Q(x, y)\,dy = \iint_\Omega \frac{\partial Q}{\partial x}(x, y)\,dxdy$$

by using the fact that Ω is of Type II. This completes the proof of the theorem for Ω as in Figure 18.5.2.

A slight modification of this argument applies to elementary regions which are bordered entirely or in part by line segments parallel to the coordinate axes.

Figure 18.5.3 shows a Jordan region that is not elementary but can be broken up into two elementary regions. (See Figure 18.5.4.) Green's theorem applied to the elementary parts tells us that

$$\iint_{\Omega_1} \left(\frac{\partial Q}{\partial x} - \frac{\partial P}{\partial y}\right) dxdy = \oint_{\text{bdry of } \Omega_1} Pdx + Qdy,$$

$$\iint_{\Omega_2} \left(\frac{\partial Q}{\partial x} - \frac{\partial P}{\partial y}\right) dxdy = \oint_{\text{bdry of } \Omega_2} Pdx + Qdy.$$

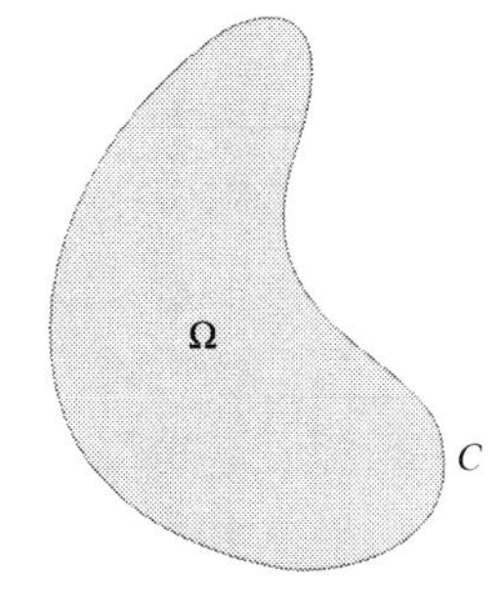

Figure 18.5.3

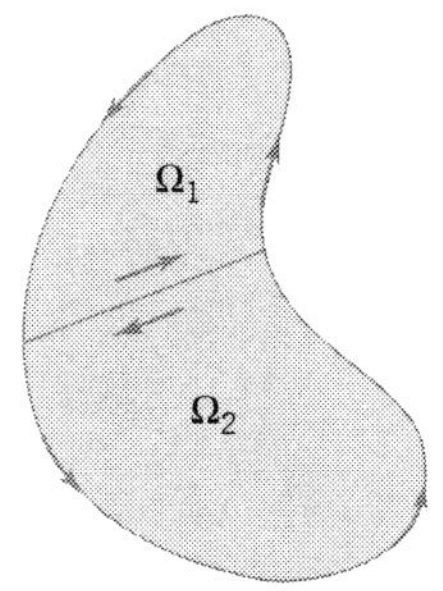

Figure 18.5.4

We now add these equations. The sum of the double integrals is, by additivity, the double integral over Ω. The sum of the line integrals is the integral over C (see the figure) plus the integrals over the crosscut. Since the crosscut is traversed twice and in opposite directions, the total contribution of the crosscut is zero and therefore Green's theorem holds:

$$\iint_{\Omega} \left(\frac{\partial Q}{\partial x} - \frac{\partial P}{\partial y}\right) dxdy = \oint_C Pdx + Qdy.$$

This same argument can be extended to a Jordan region Ω that breaks up into n elementary regions $\Omega_1, \ldots, \Omega_n$. (Figure 18.5.5 gives an example with $n = 4$.) The double integrals over the Ω_i add up to the double integral over Ω, and, since the line integrals over the crosscuts cancel, the line integrals over the boundaries of the Ω_i add up to the line integral over C. (This is as far as we will carry the proof of Green's theorem. It is far enough to cover all the Jordan regions we encounter in practice.) ❑

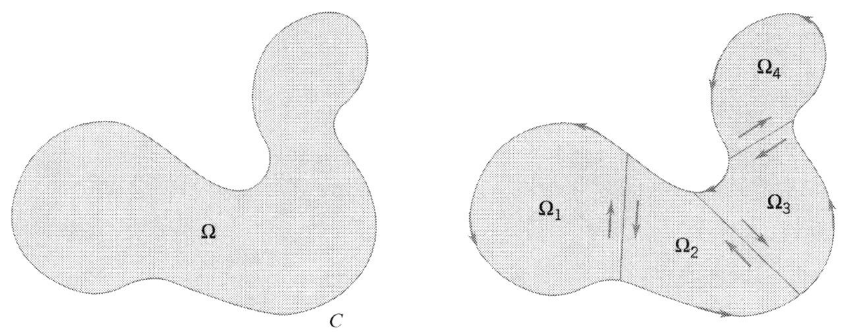

Figure 18.5.5

Example 1 Use Green's theorem to evaluate

$$\oint_C (3x^2 + y)\, dx + (2x + y^3)\, dy \qquad \text{(Figure 18.5.6)}$$

where C is the circle $x^2 + y^2 = a^2$.

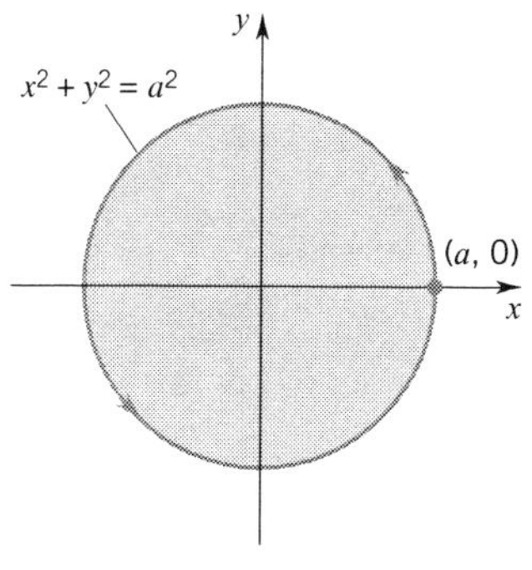

Figure 18.5.6

SOLUTION Let Ω be the closed disk $0 \le x^2 + y^2 \le a^2$. With

$$P(x, y) = 3x^2 + y \quad \text{and} \quad Q(x, y) = 2x + y^3,$$

we have

$$\frac{\partial P}{\partial y} = 1, \quad \frac{\partial Q}{\partial x} = 2, \quad \text{and} \quad \frac{\partial Q}{\partial x} - \frac{\partial P}{\partial y} = 2 - 1 = 1.$$

By Green's theorem

$$\oint_C (3x^2 + y)\,dx + (2x + y^3)\,dy = \iint_\Omega 1\,dxdy = \text{area of } \Omega = \pi a^2. \quad ❑$$

Remark The line integral in Example 1 could have been calculated directly as follows: The circle $x^2 + y^2 = a^2$ can be parametrized counterclockwise by setting

$$x = a\cos u, \qquad y = a\sin u, \qquad 0 \le u \le 2\pi.$$

Thus

$$\oint_C (3x^2 + y)\,dx + (2x + y^3)\,dy$$

$$= \int_0^{2\pi} [(3a^2\cos^2 u + a\sin u)(-a\sin u) + (2a\cos u + a^3\sin^3 u)(a\cos u)]\,du$$

$$= \int_0^{2\pi} [-3a^3\cos^2 u \sin u - a^2\sin^2 u + 2a^2\cos^2 u + a^4\sin^3 u\cos u]\,du,$$

which, as you can verify, also yields πa^2. In this case, at least, Green's theorem gives us a more direct route to the answer. ❑

Example 2 Use Green's theorem to evaluate

$$\oint_C (1 + 10xy + y^2)\,dx + (6xy + 5x^2)\,dy \qquad \text{(Figure 18.5.7)}$$

where C is the square with vertices $(0, 0)$, $(a, 0)$, (a, a), $(0, a)$.

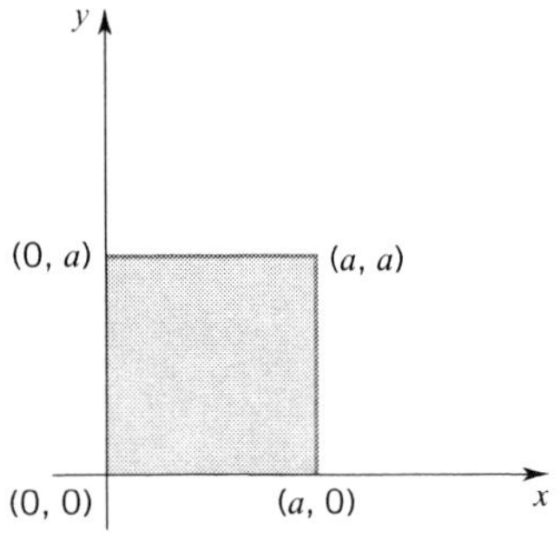

Figure 18.5.7

SOLUTION Let Ω be the square region enclosed by C. With

$$P(x, y) = 1 + 10xy + y^2 \qquad \text{and} \qquad Q(x, y) = 6xy + 5x^2,$$

we have

$$\frac{\partial P}{\partial y} = 10x + 2y, \qquad \frac{\partial Q}{\partial x} = 6y + 10x, \qquad \frac{\partial Q}{\partial x} - \frac{\partial P}{\partial y} = 4y.$$

By Green's theorem,

$$\oint_C (1 + 10xy + y^2)\,dx + (6xy + 5x^2)\,dy = \iint_\Omega 4y\,dxdy$$

$$= \int_0^a \int_0^a 4y\,dx\,dy$$

$$= \left(\int_0^a dx\right)\left(\int_0^a 4y\,dy\right)$$

$$= (a)(2a^2) = 2a^3.$$

ALTERNATIVE SOLUTION By (17.5.3),

$$\iint_\Omega y\,dxdy = \bar{y}(\text{area of } \Omega)$$

where $\overline{y}$ is the y-coordinate of the centroid of Ω. Since $\overline{y} = \frac{1}{2}a$, it is evident that

$$\iint_{\Omega} 4y\, dxdy = 4\overline{y}\,(\text{area of } \Omega) = 4(\tfrac{1}{2}a)a^2 = 2a^3. \quad \square$$

Example 3 Use Green's theorem to evaluate

$$\oint_C e^x \sin y\, dx + e^x \cos y\, dy$$

where C is the closed curve consisting of the semicircle $y = \sqrt{1-x^2}$ and the interval $[-1, 1]$. (See Figure 18.5.8.)

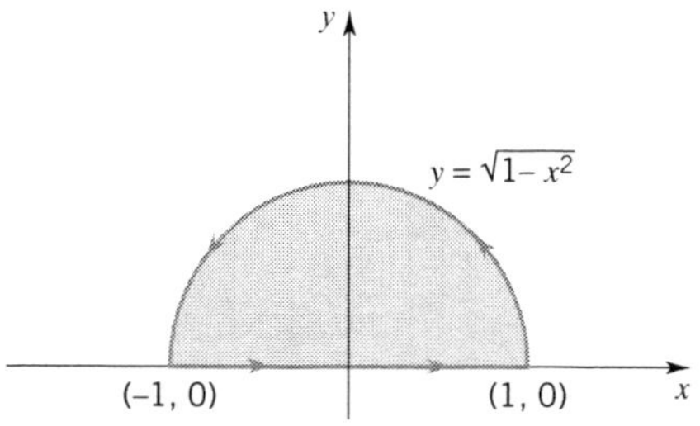

Figure 18.5.8

SOLUTION The curve bounds the closed semicircular disk $\Omega : x^2 + y^2 \leq 1, y \geq 0$.

$$\frac{\partial P}{\partial y} = e^x \cos y, \qquad \frac{\partial Q}{\partial x} = e^x \cos y. \qquad \text{Therefore} \qquad \frac{\partial Q}{\partial x} - \frac{\partial P}{\partial y} = 0.$$

By Green's theorem,

$$\oint_C e^x \sin y\, dx + e^x \cos y\, dy = \iint_{\Omega} 0\, dxdy = 0.$$

To see the power of Green's theorem, try to evaluate this line integral directly. $\square$

Green's theorem enables us to calculate the area of a Jordan region by integrating over the boundary of the region.

(18.5.2)

> The area of a Jordan region with boundary C is given by each of the following integrals:
>
> $$\oint_C -y\, dx, \qquad \oint_C x\, dy, \qquad \tfrac{1}{2}\oint_C -y\, dx + x\, dy.$$

PROOF Let Ω be the region enclosed by C. In the first integral

$$P(x, y) = -y, \qquad Q(x, y) = 0.$$

Therefore

$$\frac{\partial P}{\partial y} = -1, \qquad \frac{\partial Q}{\partial x} = 0, \qquad \text{and} \qquad \frac{\partial Q}{\partial x} - \frac{\partial P}{\partial y} = 1.$$

Thus by Green's theorem

$$\oint_C -y\,dx = \iint_\Omega 1\,dxdy = \text{area of } \Omega.$$

That the second integral also gives the area of Ω can be verified in a similar manner.

You can see the validity of the third formula by observing that

$$\oint_C -y\,dx + \oint_C x\,dy = \text{twice the area of } \Omega. \quad ❑$$

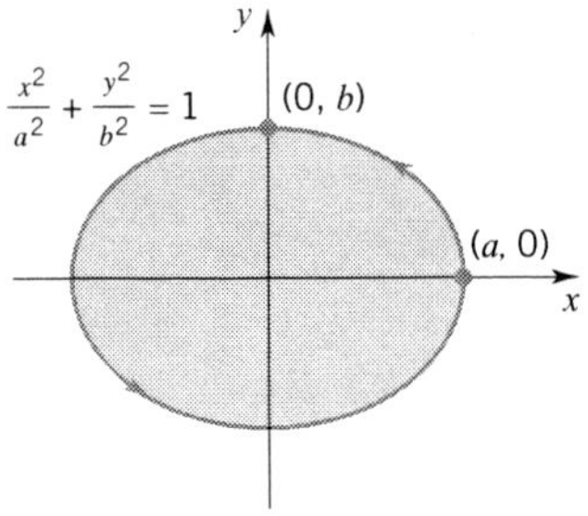

Figure 18.5.9

Example 4 Show that the area of the region Ω enclosed by the ellipse

$$\frac{x^2}{a^2} + \frac{y^2}{b^2} = 1 \qquad \text{(Figure 18.5.9)}$$

is πab.

SOLUTION The ellipse is directed counterclockwise by the parametrization

$$x = a\ \cos u,\ y = b \sin u, \qquad 0 \le u \le 2\pi.$$

Although the third integral in (18.5.2) appears to be the most complicated of the three, it is in this case the simplest to use.

$$\begin{aligned}\text{area of } \Omega &= \tfrac{1}{2}\oint_C -y\,dx + xdy\\ &= \tfrac{1}{2}\int_0^{2\pi} [-(b\sin u)(-a\sin u) + (a\cos u)(b\cos u)]\,du\\ &= \tfrac{1}{2}ab\int_0^{2\pi} du = \pi ab. \quad ❑\end{aligned}$$

Example 5 Let Ω be a Jordan region of area A with a piecewise-smooth boundary C. Show that the coordinates of the centroid of Ω are given by the formulas

$$\bar{x}A = \tfrac{1}{2}\oint_C x^2 dy, \qquad \bar{y}A = -\tfrac{1}{2}\oint_C y^2 dx.$$

SOLUTION

$$\tfrac{1}{2}\oint_C x^2 dy = \tfrac{1}{2}\iint_\Omega 2x\,dxdy = \iint_\Omega x\,dxdy = \bar{x}A,$$

by Green's theorem

$$-\tfrac{1}{2}\oint_C y^2 dx = -\tfrac{1}{2}\iint_\Omega (-2y)\,dxdy = \iint_\Omega y\,dxdy = \bar{y}A. \quad ❑$$

Regions Bounded by Two or More Jordan Curves

(All the curves that appear here are assumed to be piecewise smooth.)

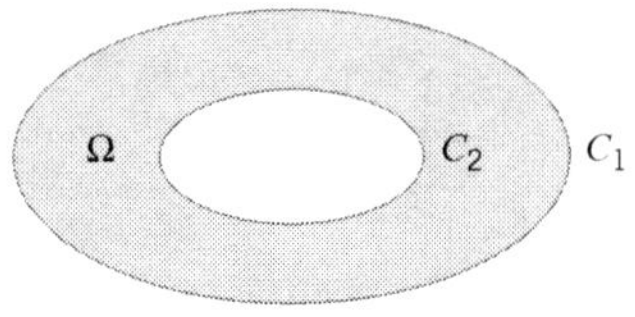

Figure 18.5.10

Figure 18.5.10 shows an annular region Ω. The region is not a Jordan region: the boundary consists of two Jordan curves C_1 and C_2. We cannot apply Green's theorem to Ω directly, but we can break up Ω into two Jordan regions as in Figure 18.5.11 and then apply Green's theorem to each piece. With Ω_1 and Ω_2 as in Figure 18.5.11,

$$\iint_{\Omega_1} \left(\frac{\partial Q}{\partial x} - \frac{\partial P}{\partial y}\right) dxdy = \oint_{\text{bdry of } \Omega_1} P\,dx + Q\,dy,$$

$$\iint_{\Omega_2} \left(\frac{\partial Q}{\partial x} - \frac{\partial P}{\partial y}\right) dxdy = \oint_{\text{bdry of } \Omega_2} Pdx + Q\,dy.$$

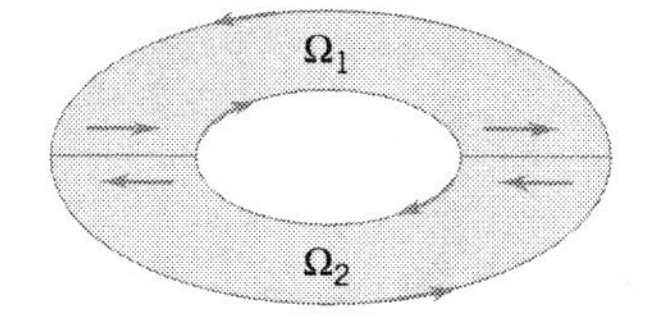

Figure 18.5.11

When we add the double integrals, we get the double integral over Ω. When we add the line integrals, the integrals over the crosscuts cancel and we are left with the *counter-clockwise integral* over C_1 and the *clockwise integral* over C_2. (See the figure.) Thus, for the annular region,

(18.5.3) $$\iint_{\Omega} \left(\frac{\partial Q}{\partial x} - \frac{\partial P}{\partial y}\right) dxdy = \oint_{C_1} P\,dx + Q\,dy + \oint_{C_2} P\,dx + Q\,dy.$$

If $\partial Q/\partial x = \partial P/\partial y$ throughout Ω, then the double integral on the left is 0, and the sum of the integrals on the right is also 0. Therefore

(18.5.4) if $\partial Q/\partial x = \partial P/\partial y$ throughout Ω, then

$$\oint_{C_1} P\,dx + Q\,dy = \oint_{C_2} P\,dx + Q\,dy.$$

Example 6 Let C_1 be a Jordan curve that does not pass through the origin (0, 0). Show that

$$\oint_{C_1} -\frac{y}{x^2+y^2}dx + \frac{x}{x^2+y^2}dy = \begin{cases} 0 & \text{if } C_1 \text{ does not enclose the origin} \\ 2\pi & \text{if } C_1 \text{ does enclose the origin.} \end{cases}$$

SOLUTION In this case

$$\frac{\partial P}{\partial y} = \frac{\partial}{\partial y}\left(-\frac{y}{x^2+y^2}\right) = -\left[\frac{(x^2+y^2)1 - 2y^2}{(x^2+y^2)^2}\right] = \frac{y^2-x^2}{(x^2+y^2)^2},$$

$$\frac{\partial Q}{\partial x} = \frac{\partial}{\partial x}\left(\frac{x}{x^2+y^2}\right) = \frac{(x^2+x^2)1 - 2x^2}{(x^2+y^2)^2} = \frac{y^2-x^2}{(x^2+y^2)^2}.$$

Thus

$$\frac{\partial Q}{\partial x} = \frac{\partial P}{\partial y} \quad \text{except at the origin.}$$

If C_1 does not enclose the origin, then $\partial Q/\partial x - \partial P/\partial y = 0$ throughout the region enclosed by C_1, and, by Green's theorem, the line integral is 0.

If C_1 does enclose the origin, we draw within the inner region of C_1 a small circle centered at the origin

$$C_2: \; x^2 + y^2 = a^2. \qquad \text{(Figure 18.5.12)}$$

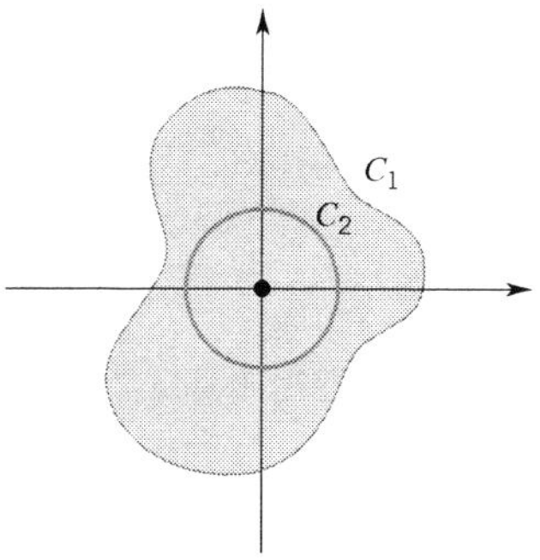

Figure 18.5.12

Since $\partial Q/\partial x - \partial P/\partial y = 0$ on the annular region bounded by C_1 and C_2, we know from (18.5.4) that the line integral over C_1 equals the line integral over C_2. All we have to show now is that the line integral over C_2 is 2π. This is straightforward. Parametrizing the circle by

$$\mathbf{r}(u) = a\cos u\,\mathbf{i} + a\sin u\,\mathbf{j} \qquad \text{with} \qquad u \in [0, 2\pi],$$

we have

$$\oint_{C_2} -\frac{y}{x^2+y^2}\,dx + \frac{x}{x^2+y^2}\,dy = \int_0^{2\pi} (\sin^2 u + \cos^2 u)\,du = \int_0^{2\pi} du = 2\pi. \quad \square$$

check this ↑

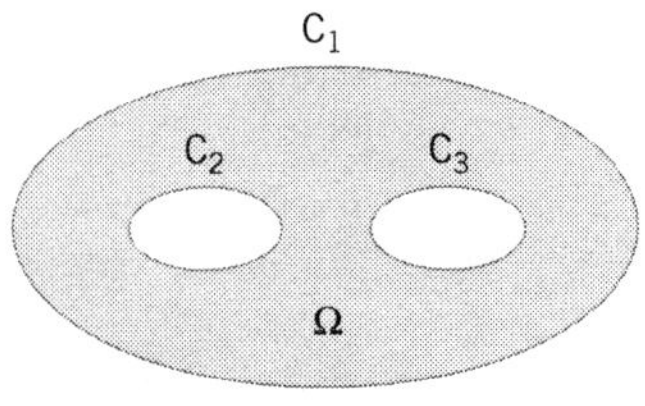

Figure 18.5.13

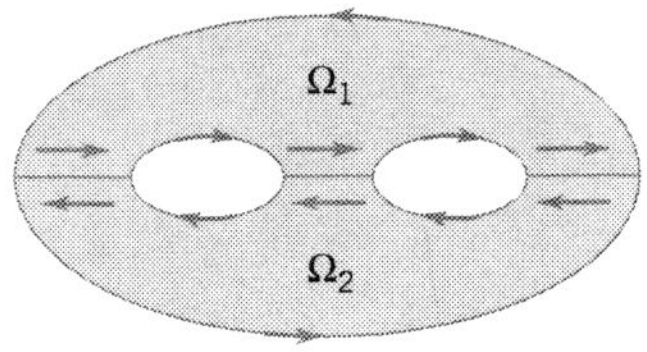

Figure 18.5.14

Figure 18.5.13 shows a region bounded by three Jordan curves: C_2 and C_3, each exterior to the other, both within C_1. For such a region Green's theorem gives

$$\iint_\Omega \left(\frac{\partial Q}{\partial x} - \frac{\partial P}{\partial y}\right) dxdy = \oint_{C_1} P\,dx + Q\,dy + \oint_{C_2} P\,dx + Q\,dy + \oint_{C_3} P\,dx + Q\,dy.$$

To see this, break up Ω into two regions by making the crosscuts shown in Figure 18.5.14.

The general formula for configurations of this type reads

$$\iint_\Omega \left(\frac{\partial Q}{\partial y} - \frac{\partial P}{\partial x}\right) dx\,dy = \oint_{C_1} P\,dx + Q\,dy + \sum_{i=2}^{n} \oint_{C_i} P\,dx + Q\,dy.$$

EXERCISES 18.5

Exercises 1–4. Evaluate the line integral (a) directly; and (b) by applying Green's theorem.

1. $\oint_C xy\,dx + x^2\,dy$; where C is the triangle with vertices $(0, 0), (0, 1), (1, 1)$.

2. $\oint_C x^2y\,dx + 2y^2\,dy$; where C is the square with vertices $(0, 0), (1, 0), (1, 1), (0, 1)$.

3. $\oint_C (3x^2 + y)\,dx + (2x + y^3)\,dy$; $\quad C: 9x^2 + 4y^2 = 36$.

4. $\oint_C y^2 dx + x^2\,dy$; where C is the boundary of the region that lies between the curves $y = x$ and $y = x^2$.

Exercises 5–16. Evaluate by Green's theorem.

5. $\oint_C 3y\,dx + 5x\,dy$; $\quad C: x^2 + y^2 = 1$.

6. $\oint_C 5x\,dx + 3y\,dy$; $\quad C: (x-1)^2 + (y+1)^2 = 1$.

7. $\oint_C x^2\,dy$; where C is the rectangle with vertices $(0, 0)$, $(a, 0), (a, b), (0, b)$.

8. $\oint_C y^2\,dx$; where C is the rectangle of Exercise 7.

9. $\oint_C (3xy + y^2)\,dx + (2xy + 5x^2)\,dy$;
$C: (x-1)^2 + (y+2)^2 = 1$.

10. $\oint_C (xy + 3y^2)\,dx + (5xy + 2x^2)\,dy$;
$C: (x-1)^2 + (y+2)^2 = 1$.

11. $\oint_C (2x^2 + xy - y^2)\,dx + (3x^2 - xy + 2y^2)\,dy$;
$C: (x-a)^2 + y^2 = r^2$.

12. $\oint_C (x^2 - 2xy + 3y^2)\,dx + (5x + 1)\,dy$;
$C: x^2 + (y-b)^2 = r^2$.

13. $\oint_C e^x \sin y\,dx + e^x \cos y\,dy$;
$C: (x-a)^2 + (y-b)^2 = r^2$.

14. $\oint_C e^x \cos y\,dx + e^x \sin y\,dy$ where C is the rectangle with vertices $(0, 0), (1, 0), (1, \pi), (0, \pi)$.

15. $\oint_C 2xy\,dx + x^2\,dy$ where C is the cardioid $r = 1 - \cos\theta, \theta \in [0, 2\pi]$.

16. $\oint_C y^2\,dx + 2xy\,dy$ where C is the first quadrant loop of the petal curve $r = 2\sin 2\theta$.

Exercises 17–18. Find the area enclosed by the curve by integrating over the curve.

17. The circle $x^2 + y^2 = a^2$.

18. The astroid $x^{2/3} + y^{2/3} = a^{2/3}$.

19. Sketch the region Ω bounded by the curves $xy = 4$ and $x + y = 5$. Then use Green's theorem to find the area of Ω.

20. Sketch the region Ω bounded by the curves $y^2 - x^2 = 5$ and $y = 3$. Then use Green's theorem to find the area of Ω.

21. Let C be a piecewise-smooth Jordan curve. Calculate

$$\oint_C (ay + b)\,dx + (cx + d)\,dy$$

given that the area enclosed by C is A.

22. Calculate

$$\oint_C \mathbf{F}(\mathbf{r}) \cdot \mathbf{dr}$$

given that $\mathbf{F}(x, y) = 2y\,\mathbf{i} - 3x\,\mathbf{j}$ and C is the astroid $x^{2/3} + y^{2/3} = a^{2/3}$.

23. Use Green's theorem to find the area under one arch of the cycloid

$$x(\theta) = R(\theta - \sin\theta), \quad y(\theta) = R(1 - \cos\theta).$$

24. Find the Jordan curve C that maximizes the line integral

$$\oint_C y^3 dx + (3x - x^3)\,dy.$$

25. Complete the proof of Green's theorem for the elementary region of Figure 18.5.2 by showing that

$$\oint_C Q(x, y)\,dy = \iint_\Omega \frac{\partial Q}{\partial x}(x, y)\,dxdy.$$

26. Suppose that f and g have continuous first-partial derivatives on a simply connected open region Ω. Show that if C is any piecewise-smooth simple closed curve in Ω, then

$$\oint_C [f(\mathbf{r})\nabla g(\mathbf{r}) + g(\mathbf{r})\nabla f(\mathbf{r})] \cdot \mathbf{dr} = 0.$$

27. Suppose that Ω is a simply connected open region on which f is *harmonic*:

$$\frac{\partial^2 f}{\partial x^2} + \frac{\partial^2 f}{\partial y^2} = 0.$$

Show that if C is any piecewise-smooth simple closed curve in Ω, then

$$\int_C \frac{\partial f}{\partial y}\,dx - \frac{\partial f}{\partial x}\,dy = 0.$$

28. Let Ω be a plate of constant mass density λ in the form of a Jordan region with a piecewise-smooth boundary C. Show that the moments of inertia of the plate about the coordinate axes are given by the formulas

(18.5.5) $$I_x = -\frac{\lambda}{3}\oint_C y^3 dx, \quad I_y = \frac{\lambda}{3}\oint_C x^3 dy.$$

29. Let P and Q be continuously differentiable functions on the region Ω of Figure 18.5.13. Given that $\partial P/\partial y = \partial Q/\partial x$ on Ω, find a relation between the line integrals

$$\oint_{C_1} P\,dx + Q\,dy, \quad \oint_{C_2} P\,dx + Q\,dy,$$
$$\oint_{C_3} P\,dx + Q\,dy.$$

30. Show that, if $f = f(x)$ and $g = g(y)$ are everywhere continuously differentiable, then

$$\oint_C f(x)\,dx + g(y)\,dy = 0$$

for all piecewise-smooth Jordan curves C.

31. Let C be a piecewise-smooth Jordan curve that does not pass through the origin. Evaluate

$$\oint_C \frac{x}{x^2 + y^2}\,dx + \frac{y}{x^2 + y^2}\,dy$$

(a) if C does not enclose the origin.
(b) if C does enclose the origin.

32. Let C be a piecewise-smooth Jordan curve that does not pass through the origin. Evaluate

$$\oint_C -\frac{y^3}{(x^2 + y^2)^2}\,dx + \frac{xy^2}{(x^2 + y^2)^2}\,dy$$

(a) if C does not enclose the origin.
(b) if C does enclose the origin.

33. Let $\mathbf{v}$ be a vector field continuously differentiable on the entire plane. Use Green's theorem to verify that if $\mathbf{v}$ is a gradient field [$\mathbf{v} = \nabla\phi$], then

$$\oint_C \mathbf{v} \cdot \mathbf{dr} = 0$$

for every piecewise-smooth Jordan curve C.

34. Let C be the line segment from the point (x_1, y_1) to the point (x_2, y_2). Show that

$$\int_C -y\,dx + x\,dy = x_1y_2 - x_2y_1.$$

35. Let $(x_1, y_1), (x_2, y_2), \ldots, (x_n, y_n)$ be the vertices of a polygon in counterclockwise order. Show that the area of the polygon is given by the sum

$$A = \tfrac{1}{2}[(x_1y_2 - x_2y_1) + (x_2y_3 - x_3y_2) + \ldots$$
$$+ (x_{n-1}y_n - x_ny_{n-1}) + (x_ny_n - x_1y_n)].$$

36. Use the formula of Exercise 35 to find the area of:

(a) the triangle with vertices (0, 0), (2, 1), (1, 4).
(b) the pentagon with vertices (0 ,0), (3, 1), (2, 4), (0, 6), (−1, 2).

*SUPPLEMENT TO SECTION 18.5

A JUSTIFICATION OF THE JACOBIAN AREA FORMULA

We based the change of variables for double integrals on the Jacobian area formula [(17.10.1)]. Green's theorem enables us to derive this formula under the conditions spelled out as follows:

Let Γ be a Jordan region in the uv-plane with a piecewise-smooth boundary C_Γ. A vector function $\mathbf{r}(u, v) = x(u, v)\,\mathbf{i} + y(u, v)\,\mathbf{j}$ with continuous second partials maps Γ onto a region Ω of the xy-plane. If $\mathbf{r}$ is one-to-one on the interior of Γ and the Jacobian J of the components of $\mathbf{r}$ is different from zero on the interior of Γ, then

$$\text{area of } \Omega = \iint_\Gamma |J(u, v)|\, du dv.$$

PROOF Suppose that C_Γ is parametrized by $u = u(t)$, $v = v(t)$ with $t \in [a, b]$. Then the boundary of Ω is a piecewise-smooth curve C given by

$$\mathbf{r}[u(t), v(t)] = x[u(t), v(t)]\,\mathbf{i} + y[u(t), v(t)]\,\mathbf{j}, \qquad t \in [a, b].$$

By Green's theorem

$$\begin{aligned}
\text{area of } \Omega = \oint_C x\,dy &= \left| \int_a^b x[u(t), v(t)] \frac{d}{dt}(y[u(t), v(t)])dt \right| \\
&= \left| \int_a^b x[u(t), v(t)] \left(\frac{\partial y}{\partial u}[u(t), v(t)]u'(t) + \frac{\partial y}{\partial v}[u(t), v(t)]v'(t) \right) dt \right| \\
&= \left| \int_a^b \left(x[u(t), v(t)] \frac{\partial y}{\partial u}[u(t), v(t)]u'(t) + x[u(t), v(t)] \frac{\partial y}{\partial v}[u(t), v(t)]v'(t) \right) dt \right| \\
&= \left| \int_{C_\Gamma} x \frac{\partial y}{\partial u} du + x \frac{\partial y}{\partial v} dv \right| \\
&\overset{\text{again by Green's theorem}}{=} \left| \iint_\Gamma \left[\frac{\partial}{\partial u}\left(x \frac{\partial y}{\partial v} \right) - \frac{\partial}{\partial v}\left(x \frac{\partial y}{\partial u} \right) \right] du dv \right|.
\end{aligned}$$

$$\begin{aligned}
\frac{\partial}{\partial u}\left(x \frac{\partial y}{\partial v} \right) - \frac{\partial}{\partial v}\left(x \frac{\partial y}{\partial u} \right) &= \frac{\partial x}{\partial u}\frac{\partial y}{\partial v} + x \frac{\partial^2 y}{\partial u \partial v} - \frac{\partial x}{\partial v}\frac{\partial y}{\partial u} - x \frac{\partial^2 y}{\partial v \partial u} \\
&= \frac{\partial x}{\partial u}\frac{\partial y}{\partial v} - \frac{\partial x}{\partial v}\frac{\partial y}{\partial u} = J(u, v).
\end{aligned}$$

Therefore

$$\text{area of } \Omega = \left| \iint_\Gamma J(u, v) du dv \right| = \iint_\Gamma |J(u, v)| du dv,$$

the final equality holding because $J(u, v)$ cannot change sign on Γ. ❑

■ 18.6 PARAMETRIZED SURFACES; SURFACE AREA

You have seen that a space curve can be parametrized by a vector function $\mathbf{r} = \mathbf{r}(u)$ where u ranges over some interval I of the u-axis. (Figure 18.6.1.) In an analogous manner, we can parametrize a surface S in space by a vector function $\mathbf{r} = \mathbf{r}(u, v)$ where (u, v) ranges over some region Ω of the uv-plane. (Figure 18.6.2.)

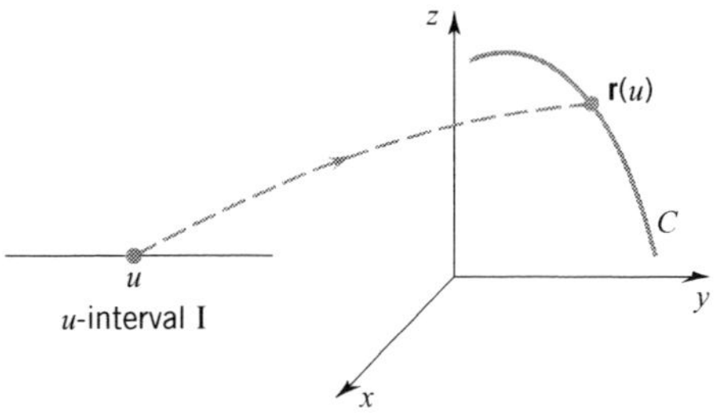

Figure 18.6.1

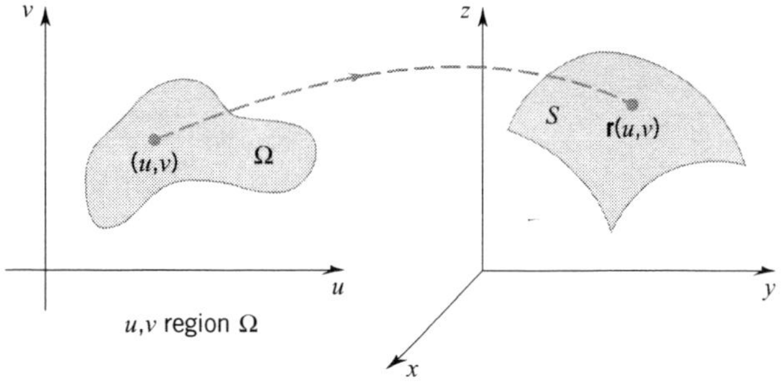

Figure 18.6.2

Example 1 (*The graph of a function*) Just as the graph of a function

$$y = f(x), \qquad x \in [a, b]$$

can be parametrized by setting

$$\mathbf{r}(u) = u\,\mathbf{i} + f(u)\,\mathbf{j}, \qquad u \in [a, b],$$

the graph of a function

$$z = f(x, y), \qquad (x, y) \in \Omega$$

can be parametrized by setting

$$\mathbf{r}(u, v) = u\,\mathbf{i} + v\,\mathbf{j} + f(u, v)\,\mathbf{k}, \qquad (u, v) \in \Omega.$$

As (u, v) ranges over Ω, the tip of $\mathbf{r}(u, v)$ traces out a surface. This surface is the graph of f. ❑

Example 2 (*A plane*) If two vectors $\mathbf{a}$ and $\mathbf{b}$ are not parallel, then the set of all linear combinations $u\mathbf{a} + v\mathbf{b}$ generate a plane p_0 that passes through the origin. We can parametrize this plane by setting

$$\mathbf{r}(u, v) = u\,\mathbf{a} + v\,\mathbf{b}, \qquad u, v \text{ real}.$$

The plane p that is parallel to p_0 and passes through the tip of $\mathbf{c}$ can be parametrized by setting

$$\mathbf{r}(u, v) = u\,\mathbf{a} + v\,\mathbf{b} + \mathbf{c}, \qquad u, v \text{ real}.$$

Note that the plane contains the lines

$$l_1 : \mathbf{r}(u, 0) = u\,\mathbf{a} + \mathbf{c} \quad \text{and} \quad l_2 : \mathbf{r}(0, v) = v\,\mathbf{b} + \mathbf{c}. \quad ❑$$

Example 3 (*A sphere*) The sphere of radius a centered at the origin can be parametrized by setting

$$\mathbf{r}(u, v) = a\cos u \cos v\,\mathbf{i} + a \sin u \cos v\,\mathbf{j} + a \sin v\,\mathbf{k}$$

with (u, v) ranging over the rectangle $R : 0 \le u \le 2\pi,\ -\frac{1}{2}\pi \le v \le \frac{1}{2}\pi$.

To derive this parametrization, we refer to Figure 18.6.3. The points of latitude v (see the figure) form a circle of radius $a \cos v$ on the horizontal plane $z = a \sin v$.

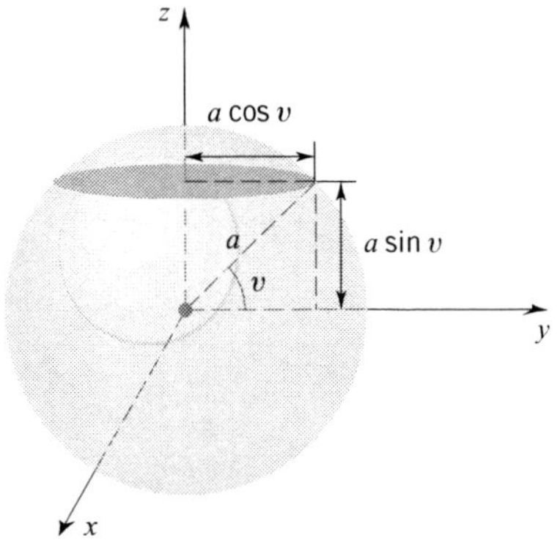

Figure 18.6.3

This circle can be parametrized by setting

$$\mathbf{R}(u) = a \cos v(\cos u\,\mathbf{i} + \sin u\,\mathbf{j}) + a \sin v\,\mathbf{k}, \quad u \in [0, 2\pi].$$

This expands to give

$$\mathbf{R}(u) = a \cos u \cos v\,\mathbf{i} + a \sin u \cos v\,\mathbf{j} + a \sin v\,\mathbf{k}, \quad u \in [0, 2\pi].$$

Letting v range from $-\frac{1}{2}\pi$ to $\frac{1}{2}\pi$, we obtain the entire sphere.

The xyz-equation for this same sphere is $x^2 + y^2 + z^2 = a^2$. It is easy to verify that the parametrization satisfies this equation:

$$\begin{aligned} x^2 + y^2 + z^2 &= a^2 \cos^2 u \cos^2 v + a^2 \sin^2 u \cos^2 v + a^2 \sin^2 v \\ &= a^2(\cos^2 u + \sin^2 u) \cos^2 v + a^2 \sin^2 v \\ &= a^2(\cos^2 v + \sin^2 v) = a^2. \quad \square \end{aligned}$$

Example 4 (*A cone*) Figure 18.6.4 shows a right circular cone with vertex semiangle α and slant height s. The points of slant height v (see the figure) form a circle of radius

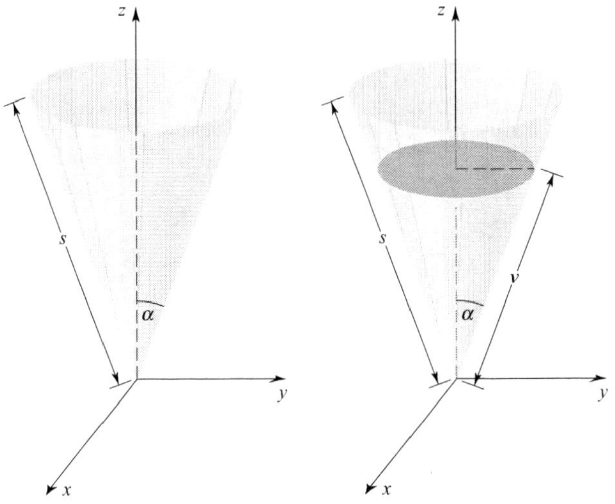

Figure 18.6.4

$v \sin\alpha$ on the horizontal plane $z = v\cos\alpha$. This circle can be parametrized by setting

$$\begin{aligned}\mathbf{R}(u) &= v\sin\alpha(\cos u\,\mathbf{i} + \sin u\,\mathbf{j}) + v\cos\alpha\,\mathbf{k}\\ &= v\cos u\sin\alpha\,\mathbf{i} + v\sin u\sin\alpha\,\mathbf{j} + v\cos\alpha\,\mathbf{k}, \qquad u \in [0, 2\pi].\end{aligned}$$

Since we can obtain the entire cone by letting v range from 0 to s, the cone is parametrized by setting

$$\mathbf{r}(u, v) = v\cos u\sin\alpha\,\mathbf{i} + v\sin u\sin\alpha\,\mathbf{j} + v\cos\alpha\,\mathbf{k},$$

with $0 \le u \le 2\pi$, $0 \le v \le s$. ❑

Example 5 (*A spiral ramp*) A rod of length l initially resting on the x-axis and attached at one end to the z-axis sweeps out a surface by rotating about the z-axis at constant rate ω while climbing at a constant rate b. The surface is pictured in Figure 18.6.5.

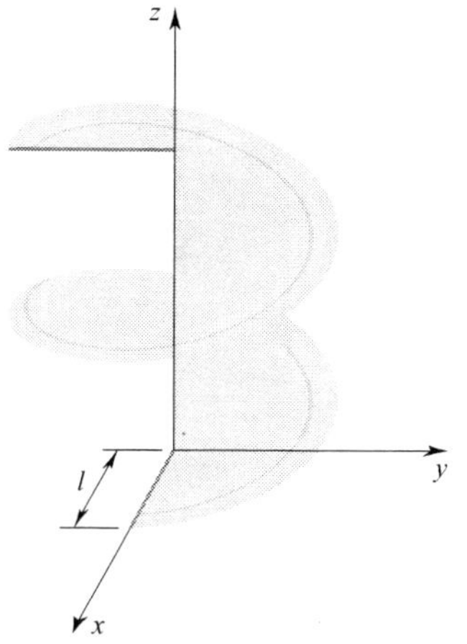

Figure 18.6.5

To parametrize this surface, we mark the point of the rod at a distance u from the z-axis ($0 \le u \le l$) and ask for the position of this point at time v. At time v the rod will have climbed a distance bv and rotated through an angle ωv. Thus the point will be found at the tip of the vector

$$u(\cos\omega v\,\mathbf{i} + \sin\omega v\,\mathbf{j}) + bv\,\mathbf{k} = u\cos\omega v\,\mathbf{i} + u\sin\omega v\,\mathbf{j} + bv\,\mathbf{k}.$$

The entire surface can be parametrized by setting

$$\mathbf{r}(u, v) = u\cos\omega v\,\mathbf{i} + u\sin\omega v\,\mathbf{j} + bv\,\mathbf{k} \qquad \text{with } 0 \le u \le l,\ v \ge 0.$$ ❑

The Fundamental Vector Product

Let S be a surface parametrized by a differentiable vector function

$$\mathbf{r} = \mathbf{r}(u, v) = x(u, v)\,\mathbf{i} + y(u, v)\,\mathbf{j} + z(u, v)\,\mathbf{k}.$$

For simplicity, let us suppose that (u, v) varies over the open rectangle $R : a < u < b$, $c < v < d$. Since $\mathbf{r}$ is a function of u and v, we can form the partial with respect to u,

$$\mathbf{r}'_u = \frac{\partial x}{\partial u}\mathbf{i} + \frac{\partial y}{\partial u}\mathbf{j} + \frac{\partial z}{\partial u}\mathbf{k},$$

and we can form the partial with respect to v,

$$\mathbf{r}'_v = \frac{\partial x}{\partial v}\mathbf{i} + \frac{\partial y}{\partial v}\mathbf{j} + \frac{\partial z}{\partial v}\mathbf{k},$$

Now let (u_0, v_0) be a point of R for which

$$\mathbf{r}'_u(u_0, v_0) \times \mathbf{r}'_v(u_0, v_0) \ne \mathbf{0}.$$

(The reason for this condition will be apparent as we go on.) The vector function

$$\mathbf{r}_1(u) = \mathbf{r}(u, v_0), \qquad u \in (a, b)$$

(here we are keeping v fixed at v_0) traces out a differentiable curve C_1 that lies on S. (Figure 18.6.6.) The vector function

$$\mathbf{r}_2(v) = \mathbf{r}(u_0, v), \qquad v \in (c, d)$$

(this time we are keeping u fixed at u_0) traces out a differentiable curve C_2 that also lies on S. Both curves pass through the tip of $\mathbf{r}(u_0, v_0)$:

$$C_1 \text{ with tangent vector } \mathbf{r}'_1(u_0) = \mathbf{r}'_u(u_0, v_0),$$

$$C_2 \text{ with tangent vector } \mathbf{r}'_2(v_0) = \mathbf{r}'_v(u_0, v_0).$$

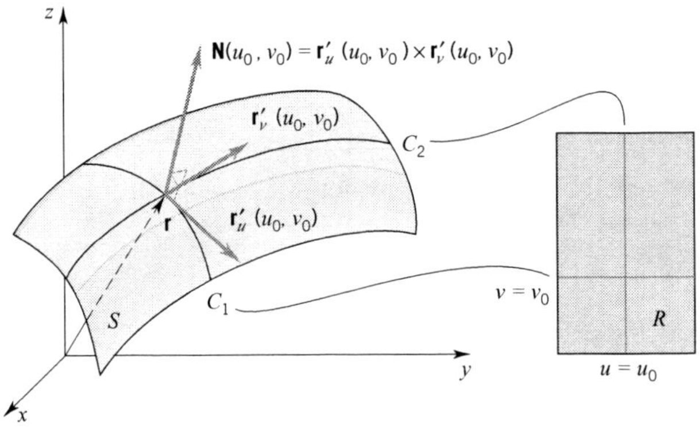

Figure 18.6.6

The cross product $\mathbf{N}(u_0, v_0) = \mathbf{r}'_u(u_0, v_0) \times \mathbf{r}'_v(u_0, v_0)$, which we have assumed to be different from zero, is perpendicular to both curves at the tip of $\mathbf{r}\,(u_0, v_0)$ and can be taken as a normal to the surface at that point. We record the result as follows:

(18.6.1) If S is the surface given by a differentiable function $\mathbf{r} = \mathbf{r}\,(u, v)$, then the vector $\mathbf{N}\,(u, v) = \mathbf{r}'_u(u, v) \times \mathbf{r}'_v(u, v)$ is perpendicular to the surface at the tip of $\mathbf{r}\,(u, v)$ and, if different from zero, can be taken as a normal to the surface at this point.

The cross product

$$\mathbf{N} = \mathbf{r}'_u \times \mathbf{r}'_v = \begin{vmatrix} \mathbf{i} & \mathbf{j} & \mathbf{k} \\ \dfrac{\partial x}{\partial u} & \dfrac{\partial y}{\partial u} & \dfrac{\partial z}{\partial u} \\ \dfrac{\partial x}{\partial v} & \dfrac{\partial y}{\partial v} & \dfrac{\partial z}{\partial v} \end{vmatrix}$$

is called the *fundamental vector product* of the surface.

Example 6 For the plane $\mathbf{r}\,(u, v) = u\,\mathbf{a} + v\,\mathbf{b} + \mathbf{c}$ we have

$$\mathbf{r}'_u(u, v) = \mathbf{a}, \quad \mathbf{r}'_v(u, v) = \mathbf{b} \quad \text{and therefore} \quad \mathbf{N}\,(u, v) = \mathbf{a} \times \mathbf{b}.$$

The vector $\mathbf{a} \times \mathbf{b}$ is normal to the plane. ❑

Example 7 We parametrized the sphere $x^2 + y^2 + z^2 = a^2$ by setting

$$\mathbf{r}\,(u, v) = a \cos u \cos v\,\mathbf{i} + a \sin u \cos v\,\mathbf{j} + a \sin v\,\mathbf{k}$$

with $0 \le u \le 2\pi$, $-\frac{1}{2}\pi \le v \le \frac{1}{2}\pi$. In this case

$$\mathbf{r}'_u(u, v) = -a \sin u \cos v\,\mathbf{i} + a \cos u \cos v\,\mathbf{j}$$

and

$$\mathbf{r}'_v(u, v) = -a \cos u \sin v\,\mathbf{i} - a \sin u \sin v\,\mathbf{j} + a \cos v\,\mathbf{k}.$$

Thus

$$\mathbf{N}(u,v) = \begin{vmatrix} \mathbf{i} & \mathbf{j} & \mathbf{k} \\ -a\sin u\cos v & a\cos u\cos v & 0 \\ -a\cos u\sin v & -a\sin u\sin v & a\cos v \end{vmatrix}$$

$$= a\cos v(a\cos u\cos v\,\mathbf{i} + a\sin u\cos v\,\mathbf{j} + a\sin v\,\mathbf{k}).$$

check this ↴

$$= a\cos v\,\mathbf{r}(u,v).$$

The fundamental vector product of a sphere, being perpendicular to the sphere, is parallel to the radius vector $\mathbf{r}(u,v)$. ❑

The Area of a Parametrized Surface

A linear function

$$\mathbf{r}(u,v) = u\,\mathbf{a} + v\,\mathbf{b} + \mathbf{c} \qquad \text{(}\mathbf{a}\text{ and }\mathbf{b}\text{ not parallel)}$$

parametrizes a plane p. Horizontal lines from the uv-plane, lines with equations of the form $v = v_0$, are mapped onto lines parallel to **a**, and vertical lines, $u = u_0$, are mapped onto lines parallel to **b**:

$$\mathbf{r}(u,v_0) = \underset{\uparrow\ \text{direction vector}}{u\,\mathbf{a}} + \underbrace{v_0\,\mathbf{b} + \mathbf{c}}_{\text{constant}}, \qquad \mathbf{r}(u_0,v) = \underset{\uparrow\ \text{direction vector}}{v\,\mathbf{b}} + \underbrace{u_0\,\mathbf{a} + \mathbf{c}}_{\text{constant}}.$$

Thus a rectangle R in the uv-plane with sides parallel to the u and v axes,

$$R: u_1 \le u \le u_2, \qquad v_1 \le v \le v_2, \qquad \text{(see Figure 18.6.7)}$$

is mapped onto a parallelogram on p with sides parallel to **a** and **b**. What is important to us here is that, as shown below,

$$\text{the area of the parallelogram} = \|\mathbf{a}\times\mathbf{b}\| \cdot (\text{the area of } R).$$

The sides of the parallelogram are given by the vectors

$$\mathbf{r}(u_2,v_1) - \mathbf{r}(u_1,v_1) = (u_2\,\mathbf{a} + v_1\,\mathbf{b} + \mathbf{c}) - (u_1\,\mathbf{a} + v_1\,\mathbf{b} + \mathbf{c}) = (u_2 - u_1)\,\mathbf{a},$$

$$\mathbf{r}(u_1,v_2) - \mathbf{r}(u_1,v_1) = (u_1\,\mathbf{a} + v_2\,\mathbf{b} + \mathbf{c}) - (u_1\,\mathbf{a} + v_1\,\mathbf{b} + \mathbf{c}) = (v_2 - v_1)\,\mathbf{b}.$$

The area of the parallelogram is

$$\|(u_2 - u_1)\mathbf{a} \times (v_2 - v_1)\mathbf{b}\| = \|\mathbf{a}\times\mathbf{b}\|(u_2 - u_1)(v_2 - v_1)$$

$$= \|\mathbf{a}\times\mathbf{b}\| \cdot (\text{area of } R).$$

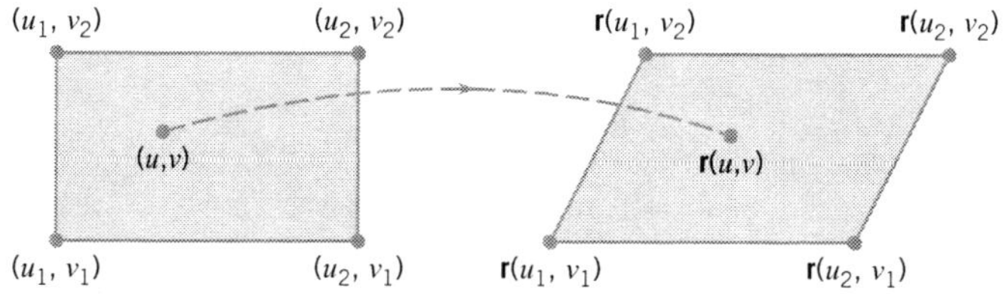

Figure 18.6.7

We summarize as follows:

(18.6.2) Let R be a rectangle in the uv-plane with sides parallel to the coordinate axes. If **a** and **b** are not parallel, the linear function

$$\mathbf{r}(u, v) = u\,\mathbf{a} + v\,\mathbf{b} + \mathbf{c}, \qquad (u, v) \in R$$

parametrizes a parallelogram with sides parallel to **a** and **b**, and

$$\text{the area of the parallelogram} = \|\mathbf{a} \times \mathbf{b}\| \cdot (\text{the area of } R.)$$

More generally, let's suppose that we have a surface S parametrized by a continuously differentiable function

$$\mathbf{r} = \mathbf{r}(u, v), \qquad (u, v) \in \Omega.$$

We assume that Ω is a basic region in the uv-plane and that r is one-to-one on the interior of Ω. (We don't want **r** to cover parts of S more than once.) Also we assume that the fundamental vector product $\mathbf{N} = \mathbf{r}'_u \times \mathbf{r}'_v$ is never zero on the interior of Ω. (We can then use it as a normal.) Under these conditions we call S a *smooth surface* and define

(18.6.3)
$$\text{area of } S = \iint_{\Omega} \|\mathbf{N}(u, v)\|\, du dv.$$

We show the reasoning behind this definition in the case where Ω is a rectangle R with sides parallel to the coordinate axes. We begin by breaking up R into n little rectangles $R_1, \ldots, R_n$. This induces a decomposition of S into little pieces $S_1, \ldots S_n$. Taking (u_i^*, v_i^*) as the center of R_i, we have the tip of $\mathbf{r}(u_i^*, v_i^*)$ in S_i. Since the vector $\mathbf{r}'_u(u_i^*, v_i^*) \times \mathbf{r}'_v(u_i^*, v_i^*)$ is normal to the surface at the tip of $\mathbf{r}(u_i^*, v_i^*)$, we can parametrize the tangent plane at this point by the linear function

$$\mathbf{f}(u, v) = u\,\mathbf{r}'_u(u_i^*, v_i^*) + v\,\mathbf{r}'_v(u_i^*, v_i^*) + [\mathbf{r}(u_i^*, v_i^*) - u_i^*\,\mathbf{r}'_u(u_i^*, v_i^*) - v_i^*\,\mathbf{r}'_v(u_i^*, v_i^*)].$$

(Check that this linear function gives the right plane.) S_i is the portion of S that corresponds to R_i. The portion of the tangent plane that corresponds to this same R_i is a parallelogram with area

$$\|\mathbf{r}'_u(u_i^*, v_i^*) \times \mathbf{r}'_v(u_i^*, v_i^*)\| \cdot (\text{area of } R_i) = \|\mathbf{N}(u_i^*, v_i^*)\| \cdot (\text{area of } R_i). \qquad [\text{by } (18.6.2)]$$

Taking this as our estimate for the area of S_i, we have

$$\text{area of } S = \sum_{i=1}^{n} \text{area of } S_i \cong \sum_{i=1}^{n} \|\mathbf{N}(u_i^*, v_i^*)\| \cdot (\text{area of } R_i).$$

This is a Riemann sum for

$$\iint_{R} \|\mathbf{N}(u, v)\|\, du dv$$

and tends to this integral as the maximal diameter of the R_i tends to zero.

To make sure that (18.6.3) does not violate our previously established notion of area, we must verify that it gives the expected result both for plane regions and for surfaces of revolution. This is done in Examples 9 and 10. By way of introduction we begin with the sphere.

Example 8 (*The surface area of a sphere*) The function

$$\mathbf{r}(u, v) = a\cos u \cos v\,\mathbf{i} + a\sin u \cos v\,\mathbf{j} + a\sin v\,\mathbf{k},$$

with (u, v) ranging over the set Ω: $0 \le u \le 2\pi$, $-\frac{1}{2}\pi \le v \le \frac{1}{2}\pi$, parametrizes a sphere of radius a. For this parametrization

$$\underset{\text{Example 7}}{\mathbf{N}(u, v) = a\cos v\,\mathbf{r}(u, v)} \qquad \text{and} \qquad \underset{-\frac{1}{2}\pi \le v \le \frac{1}{2}\pi}{\|\mathbf{N}(u, v)\| = a^2|\cos v| = a^2\cos v}.$$

According to the new formula,

$$\begin{aligned}\text{area of the sphere} &= \iint_{\Omega} a^2 \cos v\, du\, dv \\ &= \int_0^{2\pi}\left(\int_{-\frac{1}{2}\pi}^{\frac{1}{2}\pi} a^2\cos v\, dv\right) du = 2\pi a^2 \int_{-\frac{1}{2}\pi}^{\frac{1}{2}\pi} \cos v\, dv = 4\pi a^2,\end{aligned}$$

which, as you know, is correct. ❑

Example 9 (*The area of a plane region*) If S is a plane region Ω, then S can be parametrized by setting

$$\mathbf{r}(u, v) = u\,\mathbf{i} + v\,\mathbf{j}, \quad (u, v) \in \Omega.$$

Here $\mathbf{N}(u, v) = \mathbf{r}'_u(u, v) \times \mathbf{r}'_v(u, v) = \mathbf{i} \times \mathbf{j} = \mathbf{k}$ and $\|\mathbf{N}(u, v)\| = 1$. In this case (18.6.3) reduces to the familiar formulas

$$A = \iint_{\Omega} du\, dv. \quad ❑$$

Example 10 (*The area of a surface of revolution*) Let S be the surface generated by revolving about the x-axis the graph of the function

$$y = f(x), \qquad x \in [a, b]. \qquad \text{(Figure 18.6.8)}$$

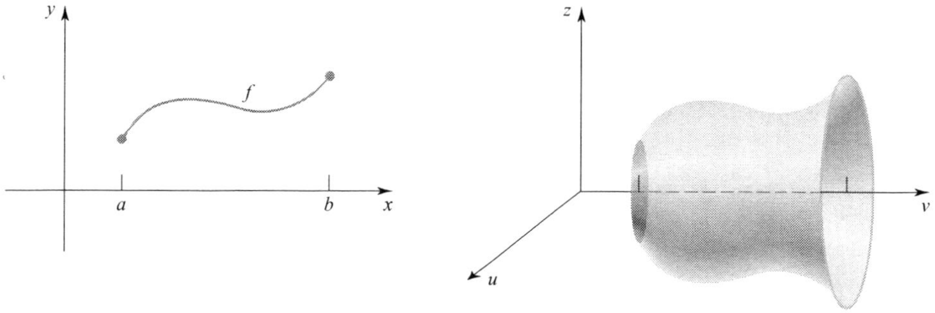

Figure 18.6.8

We assume that f is positive and continuously differentiable. We can parametrize S by setting

$$\mathbf{r}(u, v) = v\,\mathbf{i} + f(v)\cos u\,\mathbf{j} + f(v)\sin u\,\mathbf{k}$$

with (u, v) ranging over the set Ω: $0 \le u \le 2\pi$, $a \le v \le b$. (We leave it to you to verify that this is right.) In this case

$$\mathbf{N}(u,v) = \mathbf{r}'_u(u,v) \times \mathbf{r}'_v(u,v) = \begin{vmatrix} \mathbf{i} & \mathbf{j} & \mathbf{k} \\ 0 & -f(v)\sin u & f(v)\cos u \\ 1 & f'(v)\cos u & f'(v)\sin u \end{vmatrix}$$

$$= -f(v)f'(v)\,\mathbf{i} + f(v)\cos u\,\mathbf{j} + f(v)\sin u\,\mathbf{k}.$$

$$\|\mathbf{N}(u,v)\| = f(v)\sqrt{[f'(v)]^2+1}.$$

$$\text{area of } S = \iint_\Omega f(v)\sqrt{[f'(v)]^2+1}\,du\,dv$$

$$= \int_0^{2\pi}\left(\int_a^b f(v)\sqrt{[f'(v)]^2+1}\,dv\right)du = \int_a^b 2\pi f(v)\sqrt{[f'(v)]^2+1}\,dv.$$

This is in agreement with (10.9.3) ❑

Example 11 (*Spiral ramp*) One turn of the spiral ramp of Example 5 is the surface

$$S: \quad \mathbf{r}(u,v) = u\cos\omega v\,\mathbf{i} + u\sin\omega v\,\mathbf{j} + bv\,\mathbf{k}$$

with (u, v) ranging over the set Ω: $0 \le u \le l$, $0 \le v \le 2\pi/\omega$. In this case

$$\mathbf{r}'_u(u,v) = \cos\omega v\,\mathbf{i} + \sin\omega v\,\mathbf{j}, \qquad \mathbf{r}'_v(u,v) = -\omega u\sin\omega v\,\mathbf{i} + \omega u\cos\omega v\,\mathbf{j} + b\,\mathbf{k}.$$

Therefore

$$\mathbf{N}(u,v) = \begin{vmatrix} \mathbf{i} & \mathbf{j} & \mathbf{k} \\ \cos\omega v & \sin\omega v & 0 \\ -\omega u\sin\omega v & \omega u\cos\omega v & b \end{vmatrix} = b\sin\omega v\,\mathbf{i} - b\cos\omega v\,\mathbf{j} + \omega u\,\mathbf{k},$$

$$\|\mathbf{N}(u,v)\| = \sqrt{b^2+\omega^2u^2},$$

$$\text{area of } S = \iint_\Omega \sqrt{b^2+\omega^2u^2}\,du\,dv$$

$$= \int_0^{2\pi/\omega}\left(\int_0^l \sqrt{b^2+\omega^2u^2}\,du\right)dv = \frac{2\pi}{\omega}\int_0^l \sqrt{b^2+\omega^2u^2}\,du.$$

The integral can be evaluated by setting $u = (b/\omega)\tan x$. ❑

The Area of a Surface $z = f(x, y)$

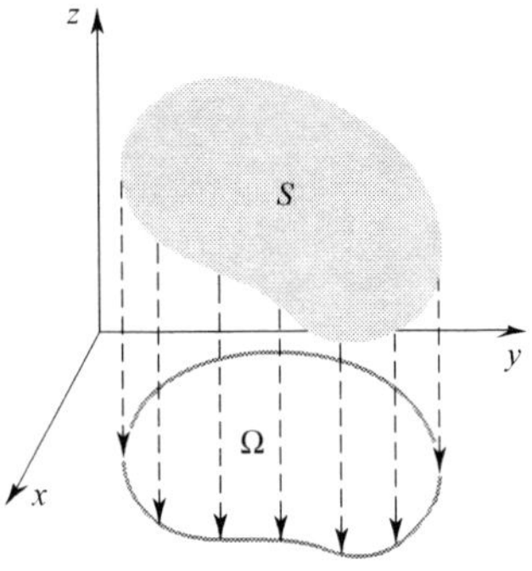

Figure 18.6.9

Figure 18.6.9 shows a surface that projects onto a basic region Ω of the xy-plane. Above each point (x, y) of Ω there is one and only one point of S. The surface S is then the graph of a function

$$z = f(x,y), \qquad (x,y) \in \Omega.$$

As we show, if f is continuously differentiable, then

(18.6.4)
$$\text{area of } S = \iint_\Omega \sqrt{[f_x(x,y)]^2 + [f_y(x,y)]^2 + 1}\,dx\,dy.$$

DERIVATION OF (18.6.4) We can parametrize S by setting

$$\mathbf{r}(u, v) = u\,\mathbf{i} + v\,\mathbf{j} + f(u, v)\,\mathbf{k}, \qquad (u, v) \in \Omega.$$

We may just as well use x and y and write

$$\mathbf{r}(x, y) = x\,\mathbf{i} + y\,\mathbf{j} + f(x, y)\,\mathbf{k}, \quad (x, y) \in \Omega.$$

$$\mathbf{r}'_x(x, y) = \mathbf{i} + f_x(x, y)\,\mathbf{k} \quad \text{and} \quad \mathbf{r}'_y(x, y) = \mathbf{j} + f_y(x, y)\,\mathbf{k}.$$

$$\mathbf{N}(x, y) = \begin{vmatrix} \mathbf{i} & \mathbf{j} & \mathbf{k} \\ 1 & 0 & f_x(x, y) \\ 0 & 1 & f_y(x, y) \end{vmatrix} = -f_x(x, y)\,\mathbf{i} - f_y(x, y)\,\mathbf{j} + \mathbf{k}.$$

Therefore $\|\mathbf{N}(x, y)\| = \sqrt{[f_x(x, y)]^2 + [f_y(x, y)]^2 + 1}$ and the formula is verified. ❑

Example 12 Find the surface area of that part of the parabolic cylinder $z = y^2$ that lies over the triangle with vertices (0, 0), (0, 1), (1, 1) in the xy-plane.

SOLUTION Here $f(x, y) = y^2$ so that

$$f_x(x, y) = 0, \qquad f_y(x, y) = 2y.$$

The base triangle can be expressed by writing

$$\Omega\colon 0 \le y \le 1, \qquad 0 \le x \le y.$$

The surface has area

$$A = \iint_\Omega \sqrt{[f_x(x, y)]^2 + [f_y(x, y)]^2 + 1}\, dx\, dy$$

$$= \int_0^1 \int_0^y \sqrt{4y^2 + 1}\, dx dy$$

$$= \int_0^1 y\sqrt{4y^2 + 1}\, dy = \left[\tfrac{1}{12}(4y^2 + 1)^{3/2}\right]_0^1 = \tfrac{1}{12}(5\sqrt{5} - 1). \quad ❑$$

Example 13 Find the surface area of that part of the hyperbolic paraboloid $z = xy$ that lies inside the cylinder $x^2 + y^2 = a^2$. See Figure 18.6.10.

SOLUTION Here $f(x, y) = xy$, so that $f_x(x, y) = y, \quad f_y(x, y) = x$. The formula gives

$$A = \iint_\Omega \sqrt{y^2 + x^2 + 1}\, dx dy.$$

In polar coordinates the base region takes the form

$$\Gamma\colon 0 \le r \le a, \qquad 0 \le \theta \le 2\pi.$$

Thus we have

$$A = \iint_\Gamma \sqrt{r^2 + 1}\; r\, dr d\theta = \int_0^{2\pi} \int_0^a \sqrt{r^2 + 1}\; r\, dr\, d\theta = \tfrac{2}{3}\pi[(a^2 + 1)^{3/2} - 1]. \quad ❑$$

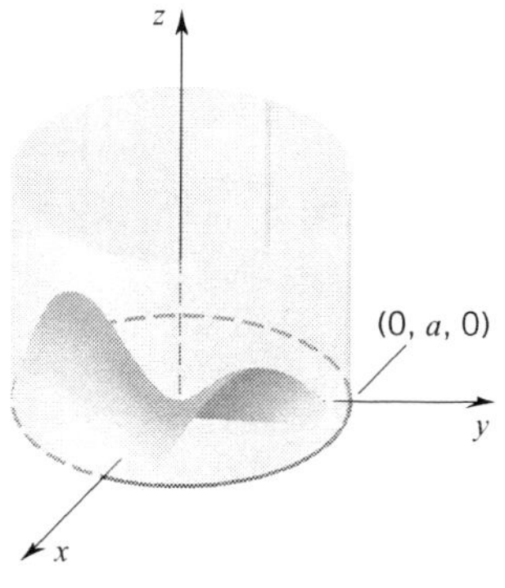

Figure 18.6.10

There is an elegant version of this last area formula [(18.6.4)] that is geometrically vivid. We know that the vector

$$\mathbf{r}'_x(x, y) \times \mathbf{r}'_y(x, y) = -f_x(x, y)\,\mathbf{i} - f_y(x, y)\,\mathbf{j} + \mathbf{k}$$

is normal to the surface at the point $(x, y, f(x, y))$. The unit vector in that direction, the vector

$$\mathbf{n}(x, y) = \frac{-f_x(x, y)\,\mathbf{i} - f_y(x, y)\,\mathbf{j} + \mathbf{k}}{\sqrt{[f_x(x, y)]^2 + [f_y(x, y)]^2 + 1}},$$

is called the *upper unit normal.* (It is the unit normal with positive **k**-component.)

Now let $\gamma(x, y)$ be the angle between $\mathbf{n}(x, y)$ and $\mathbf{k}$. (Figure 18.6.11.) Since $\mathbf{n}(x, y)$ and $\mathbf{k}$ are both unit vectors,

$$\cos[\gamma(x, y)] = \mathbf{n}(x, y) \cdot \mathbf{k} = \frac{1}{\sqrt{[f_x(x, y)]^2 + [f_y(x, y)]^2 + 1}}.$$

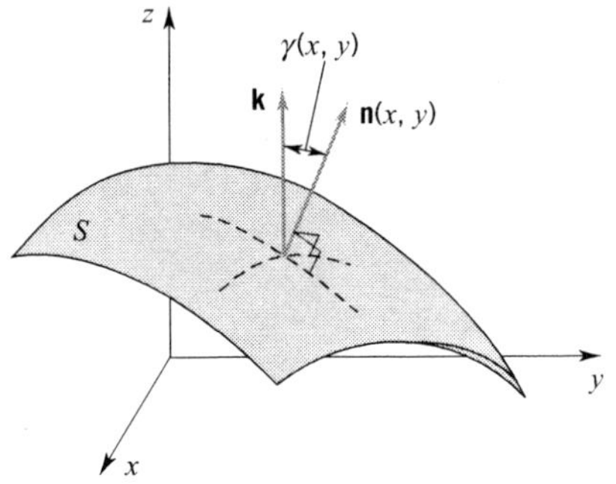

Figure 18.6.11

Taking reciprocals, we have

$$\sec[\gamma(x, y)] = \sqrt{[f_x(x, y)]^2 + [f_y(x, y)]^2 + 1}.$$

Area formula (18.6.4) can therefore be written

(18.6.5)
$$A = \iint_{\Omega} \sec[\gamma(x, y)]\, dxdy.$$

EXERCISES 18.6

Exercises 1–4. Calculate the fundamental vector product.

1. $\mathbf{r}(u, v) = (u^2 - v^2)\,\mathbf{i} + (u^2 + v^2)\,\mathbf{j} + 2uv\,\mathbf{k}$.

2. $\mathbf{r}(u, v) = u\cos v\,\mathbf{i} + u\sin v\,\mathbf{j} + \mathbf{k}$.

3. $\mathbf{r}(u, v) = (u + v)\,\mathbf{i} + (u + v)\,\mathbf{j} + (u - v)\,\mathbf{k}$.

4. $\mathbf{r}(u, v) = \cos u \sin v\,\mathbf{i} + \sin u \cos v\,\mathbf{j} + u\,\mathbf{k}$.

Exercises 5–10. Find a parametric representation for the surface.

5. The upper half of the ellipsoid $4x^2 + 9y^2 + z^2 = 36$.

6. The part of the cylinder $x^2 + y^2 = 4$ that lies between the planes $z = 1$ and $z = 4$.

7. The part of the sphere $x^2 + y^2 + z^2 = 4$ that lies above the plane $z = \sqrt{2}$.

8. The part of the plane $z = x + 2$ that lies inside the cylinder $x^2 + y^2 = 1$.

9. $y = g(x, z)$, $(x, z) \in \Omega$.

10. $x = h(y, z)$, $(y, z) \in \Gamma$.

Exercises 11–13. Find an equation in x,y,z for the surface and identify the surface.

11. $\mathbf{r}(u, v) = a\cos u \cos v\,\mathbf{i} + b\sin u \cos v\,\mathbf{j} + c\sin v\,\mathbf{k}$; $0 \le u \le 2\pi$, $-\frac{1}{2}\pi \le v \le \frac{1}{2}\pi$.

12. $\mathbf{r}(u, v) = au\cos v\,\mathbf{i} + bu\sin v\,\mathbf{j} + u^2\,\mathbf{k}$; $0 \le u$, $0 \le v \le 2\pi$.

13. $\mathbf{r}(u, v) = au\cosh v\,\mathbf{i} + bu\sinh v\,\mathbf{j} + u^2\,\mathbf{k}$; u real, v real.

14. Use a graphing utility to draw the surface of

(a) Exercise 11 with $a = 4, b = 3, c = 2$; experiment with other values of a, b, c.

(b) Exercise 12 with $a = 3, b = 2$; experiment with other values of a and b.

(c) Exercise 13 with $a = 3, b = 2$; experiment with viewpoints to obtain a good view of the surface and try other values of a and b.

15. The graph of a continuously differentiable function $y = f(x), x \in [a, b]$ is revolved about the y-axis. Parametrize the surface given that $a \geq 0$.

16. Show that the area of the surface of Exercise 15 is given by the formula

$$A = \int_a^b 2\pi x\sqrt{1 + [f'(x)]^2}\, dx.$$

17. A plane p intersects the xy-plane at an angle γ. (Draw a figure.) Find the area of the region Γ on p given that the projection of Γ onto the xy-plane is a region Ω of area A_Ω.

18. Determine the area of the portion of the plane $x + y + z = a$ that lies within the cylinder $x^2 + y^2 = b^2$.

19. Find the area of the part of the plane $bcx + acy + abz = abc$ that lies within the first octant.

20. Find the area of the surface $z^2 = x^2 + y^2$ from $z = 0$ to $z = 1$.

21. Find the area of the surface $z = x^2 + y^2$ from $z = 0$ to $z = 4$.

Exercises 22–28. Calculate the area of the surface

22. $z^2 = 2xy \quad$ with $\quad 0 \leq x \leq a, 0 \leq y \leq b, z \geq 0$.

23. $z = a^2 - (x^2 + y^2) \quad$ with $\quad \frac{1}{4}a^2 \leq x^2 + y^2 \leq a^2$.

24. $3z^2 = (x + y)^3 \quad$ with $\quad x + y \leq 2, x \geq 0, y \geq 0$.

25. $3z = x^{3/2} + y^{3/2} \quad$ with $\quad 0 \leq x \leq 1, 0 \leq y \leq x$.

26. $z = y^2 \quad$ with $\quad 0 \leq x \leq 1, 0 \leq y \leq 1$.

27. $x^2 + y^2 + z^2 - 4z = 0 \quad$ with $\quad 0 \leq 3(x^2 + y^2) \leq z^2$, $z \geq 2$.

28. $x^2 + y^2 + z^2 - 2az = 0 \quad$ with $\quad 0 \leq x^2 + y^2 \leq bz$. Assume $a > b > 0$.

29. (a) Find a formula for the area of a surface that is projectable onto a region Ω of the yz-plane; say,

$$S\colon x = g(y, z), \quad (y, z) \in \Omega.$$

Assume that g is continuously differentiable.

(b) Find a formula for the area of a surface that is projectable onto a region Ω of the xz-plane; say,

$$S\colon y = h(x, z), \quad (x, z) \in \Omega.$$

Assume that h is continuously differentiable.

30. (a) Determine the fundamental vector product for the cylindrical surface

$$\mathbf{r}(u, v) = a\cos u\,\mathbf{i} + a\sin u\,\mathbf{j} + v\,\mathbf{k};$$
$$0 \leq u \leq 2\pi, \; 0 \leq v \leq l.$$

(b) Use your answer to part (a) to find the area of the surface.

31. (a) Determine the fundamental vector product for the cone of Example 4:

$$\mathbf{r}(u, v) = v\cos u\sin\alpha\,\mathbf{i} + v\sin u\sin\alpha\,\mathbf{j} + v\cos\alpha\,\mathbf{k};$$
$$0 \leq u \leq 2\pi, \; 0 \leq v \leq s.$$

(b) Use your answer to part (a) to calculate the area of the cone.

32. (a) Show that $\mathbf{r}(u) = a\cos u\sin v\,\mathbf{i} + a\sin u\sin v\,\mathbf{j} + b\cos v\,\mathbf{k}, \; 0 \leq u \leq 2\pi, \; 0 \leq v \leq \pi$, parametrizes the ellipsoid of revolution

$$\frac{x^2}{a^2} + \frac{y^2}{a^2} + \frac{z^2}{b^2} = 1.$$

(b) Use a graphing utility to draw the surface with $a = 3, \; b = 4$; experiment with other values of a and b.

(c) Show that the surface area of the ellipsoid is given by the formula

$$A = 2\pi a\int_0^\pi \sin v\sqrt{b^2\sin^2 v + a^2\cos^2 v}\, dv.$$

33. (a) Show that $\mathbf{r}(u) = a\cos u\cosh v\,\mathbf{i} + b\sin u\cosh v\,\mathbf{j} + c\sinh v\,\mathbf{k}, \; 0 \leq u \leq 2\pi, \; v$, real, parametrizes the hyperboloid of one sheet

$$\frac{x^2}{a^2} + \frac{y^2}{b^2} - \frac{z^2}{c^2} = 1.$$

(b) Use a graphing utility to draw the surface with $a = 3, \; b = 2, \; c = 4$; experiment with other values of a, b, c.

(c) Set up a double integral for the surface area of the part of the hyperboloid that lies between the planes $z = -3$ and $z = 3$. Take $a = 3, b = 2, c = 4$.

34. (a) Show that $\mathbf{r}(u) = a\cos u\sinh v\,\mathbf{i} + b\sin u\sinh v\,\mathbf{j} + c\cosh v\,\mathbf{k}$, with $0 \leq u \leq 2\pi, \; v$, real, parametrizes the hyperboloid of two sheets

$$\frac{x^2}{a^2} + \frac{y^2}{b^2} - \frac{z^2}{c^2} = -1.$$

(b) Use a graphing utility to draw the surface with $a = 3, b = 2, c = 4$; experiment with other values of a, b, c.

(c) Explain why your graph shows only the upper surface of the hyperboloid. Change the parametrization so that your graph displays the lower half of the surface.

35. Let Ω be a plane region in space and let A_1, A_2, A_3 be the areas of the projections of Ω onto the three coordinate planes. Express the area of Ω in terms of A_1, A_2, A_3.

36. Let S be a surface given in cylindrical coordinates by an equation of the form $z = f(r, \theta), \; (r, \theta) \in \Omega$. Show that if f is continuously differentiable, then

$$\text{area of } S = \iint_\Omega \sqrt{r^2[f_r(r, \theta)]^2 + [(f_\theta(r, \theta))]^2 + r^2}\, dr\, d\theta$$

provided the integrand is never zero on the interior of Ω.

37. The following surfaces are given in cylindrical coordinates. Find the surface area.

(a) $z = r + \theta; \quad 0 \leq r \leq 1, \quad 0 \leq \theta \leq \pi$.

(b) $z = r\,e^\theta; \quad 0 \leq r \leq a, \quad 0 \leq \theta \leq 2\pi$.

38. Show that, for a flat surface S that is part of the xy-plane, (18.6.3) gives

$$\text{area of } S = \iint_\Omega |J(u, v)|\, du\, dv$$

where J is the Jacobian of the components of a vector function which is defined on some region Ω and parametrizes S. Except for notation this is (17.10.1).

18.7 SURFACE INTEGRALS

The Mass of a Material Surface

Imagine a thin distribution of matter spread out over a surface S. We call this a *material surface.*

If the mass density (the mass per unit area) is a constant λ throughout, then the total mass of the material surface is the density λ times the area of S:

$$M = \lambda(\text{area of } S).$$

If, however, the mass density varies continuously from point to point, $\lambda = \lambda(x, y, z)$, then the total mass must be calculated by integration.

To develop the appropriate integral, we suppose that

$$S\colon\ \mathbf{r} = \mathbf{r}(u, v) = x(u, v)\,\mathbf{i} + y(u, v)\,\mathbf{j} + z(u, v)\,\mathbf{k}, \qquad (u, v) \in \Omega$$

is a smooth surface, a surface that meets the conditions for area formula (18.6.3).[†] Our first step is to break up Ω into n little basic regions $\Omega_1, \ldots, \Omega_n$. This decomposes the surface into n little pieces $S_1, \ldots, S_n$. The area of S_i is given by the integral

$$\iint_{\Omega_i} \|\mathbf{N}(u, v)\|\, du dv. \qquad [(18.6.3)]$$

By the mean-value therorem for double integrals, there exists a point (u_i^*, v_i^*) in Ω_i for which

$$\iint_{\Omega_i} \|\mathbf{N}(u, v)\|\, du dv = \|\mathbf{N}(u_i^*, v_i^*)\|(\text{area of } \Omega_i).$$

It follows that

$$\text{area of } S_i = \|\mathbf{N}(u_i^*, v_i^*)\|(\text{area of } \Omega_i).$$

Since the point (u_i^*, v_i^*) is in Ω_i, the tip of $\mathbf{r}(u_i^*, v_i^*)$ is on S_i. The mass density at this point is $\lambda[\mathbf{r}(u_i^*, v_i^*)]$. If S_i is small (which we can guarantee by choosing Ω_i small), then the mass density on S_i is approximately the same throughout. Thus we can estimate M_i, the mass contribution of S_i, by writing

$$M_i \cong \lambda[\mathbf{r}(u_i^*, v_i^*)](\text{area of } S_i) = \lambda[\mathbf{r}(u_i^*, v_i^*)]\, \|\mathbf{N}(u_i^*, v_i^*)\|(\text{area of } \Omega_i).$$

Adding up these estimates, we have an estimate for the total mass of the surface:

$$\begin{aligned} M &\cong \sum_{i=1}^{n} \lambda[\mathbf{r}(u_i^*, v_i^*)]\, \|\mathbf{N}(u_i^*, v_i^*)\|(\text{area of } \Omega_i) \\ &= \sum_{i=1}^{n} \lambda[x(u_i^*, v_i^*), y(u_i^*, v_i^*), z(u_i^*, v_i^*)\|\mathbf{N}(u_i^*, v_i^*)\|(\text{area of } \Omega_i)]. \end{aligned}$$

This last expression is a Riemann sum for

$$\iint_{\Omega} \lambda[x(u, v), y(u, v), z(u, v)]\, \|\mathbf{N}(u, v)\|\, du dv.$$

[†]We repeat the conditions here: $\mathbf{r}$ is continuously differentiable; Ω is a basic region in the uv-plane; $\mathbf{r}$ is one-to-one on the interior of Ω; $\mathbf{N} = \mathbf{r}'_u \times \mathbf{r}'_v$ is never zero on the interior of Ω.

and tends to this integral as the maximal diameter of the Ω_i tends to zero. We can conclude that

(18.7.1)

$$M = \iint_{\Omega} \lambda[x(u, v), y(u, v), z(u, v)] \, \|\mathbf{N}(u, v)\| \, du dv.$$

Surface Integrals

The double integral in (18.7.1) can be calculated not only for a mass density function λ but for any scalar field H continuous over S. We call this integral *the surface integral of H over S* and write

(18.7.2)

$$\iint_{S} H(x, y, z) \, d\sigma = \iint_{\Omega} H[x(u, v), y(u, v), \, z(u, v)] \, \|\mathbf{N}(u, v)\| \, du dv.$$

Note that, if $H(x, y, z)$ is identically 1, then the right-hand side of (18.7.2) gives the area of S. Thus

(18.7.3)

$$\iint_{S} d\sigma = \text{area of } S.$$

Example 1 Let $\mathbf{a} = a_1\,\mathbf{i} + a_2\,\mathbf{j} + a_3\,\mathbf{k}$ and $\mathbf{b} = b_1\,\mathbf{i} + b_2\,\mathbf{j} + b_3\,\mathbf{k}$ be nonzero vectors. Calculate

$$\iint_{S} xy \, d\sigma \qquad \text{where} \qquad S: \quad \mathbf{r}(u, v) = u\,\mathbf{a} + v\,\mathbf{b}; \quad 0 \le u \le 1, \quad 0 \le v \le 1.$$

SOLUTION Call the parameter set Ω. Then

$$\iint_{S} xy \, d\sigma = \iint_{\Omega} x(u, v) y(u, v) \|\mathbf{N}(u, v)\| \, du dv.$$

A simple calculation shows that $\|\mathbf{N}(u, v)\| = \|\mathbf{a} \times \mathbf{b}\|$. Thus

$$\iint_{S} xy \, d\sigma = \|\mathbf{a} \times \mathbf{b}\| \iint_{\Omega} x(u, v) y(u, v) \, du dv.$$

To find $x(u, v)$ and $y(u, v)$, we need the **i** and **j** components of $\mathbf{r}(u, v)$. We can get these as follows:

$$\begin{aligned}\mathbf{r}(u, v) = u\,\mathbf{a} + v\,\mathbf{b} &= u(a_1\,\mathbf{i} + a_2\,\mathbf{j} + a_3\,\mathbf{k}) + v(b_1\,\mathbf{i} + b_2\,\mathbf{j} + b_3\,\mathbf{k}) \\ &= (a_1 u + b_1 v)\,\mathbf{i} + (a_2 u + b_2 v)\,\mathbf{j} + (a_3 u + b_3 v)\,\mathbf{k}.\end{aligned}$$

Therefore $x(u, v) = a_1 u + b_1 v$ and $y(u, v) = a_2 u + b_2 v$. We can now write

$$\begin{aligned}\iint_{S} xy \, d\sigma &= \|\mathbf{a} \times \mathbf{b}\| \iint_{\Omega} (a_1 u + b_1 v)(a_2 u + b_2 v) \, du dv \\ &= \|\mathbf{a} \times \mathbf{b}\| \int_0^1 \left(\int_0^1 \left[a_1 a_2 u^2 + (a_1 b_2 + b_1 a_2) uv + b_1 b_2 v^2 \right] du \right) dv \\ &= \|\mathbf{a} \times \mathbf{b}\| \left[\tfrac{1}{3} a_1 a_2 + \tfrac{1}{4}(a_1 b_2 + b_1 a_2) + \tfrac{1}{3} b_1 b_2 \right]. \quad \square\end{aligned}$$

check this⟶

Example 2 Calculate

$$\iint_S \sqrt{x^2 + y^2}\, d\sigma$$

where S is the spiral ramp of Example 11, Section 18.6:

$$S: \qquad \mathbf{r}(u, v) = u\cos\omega v\,\mathbf{i} + u\sin\omega v\,\mathbf{j} + bv\,\mathbf{k}; \quad 0 \le u \le l, \quad 0 \le v \le 2\pi/\omega.$$

SOLUTION Call the parameter set Ω. As you saw in Example 11 of Section 18.6,

$$\|\mathbf{N}(u, v)\| = \sqrt{b^2 + \omega^2 u^2}.$$

Therefore

$$\begin{aligned}
\iint_S \sqrt{x^2 + y^2}\, d\sigma &= \iint_\Omega \sqrt{[x(u, v)]^2 + [y(u, v)]^2}\; \|\mathbf{N}(u, v)\|\, du dv \\
&= \iint_\Omega \sqrt{u^2\cos^2\omega v + u^2\sin^2\omega v}\; \sqrt{b^2 + \omega^2 u^2}\, du dv \\
&\underset{u \ge 0 \text{ on } \Omega}{=} \iint_\Omega u\sqrt{b^2 + \omega^2 u^2}\, du dv \\
&= \int_0^{2\pi/\omega}\left(\int_0^l u\sqrt{b^2 + \omega^2 u^2}\, du\right) dv \\
&= \frac{2\pi}{\omega}\int_0^l u\sqrt{b^2 + \omega^2 u^2}\, du = \frac{2\pi}{3\omega^3}\left[(b^2 + \omega^2 l^2)^{3/2} - b^3\right]. \quad \square
\end{aligned}$$

Like the other integrals you have studied, the surface integral satisfies a mean-value condition; namely, if the scalar field H is continuous, then there is a point (x_0, y_0, z_0) on S for which

$$\iint_S H(x, y, z)\, d\sigma = H(x_0, y_0, z_0)(\text{area of } S).$$

We call $H(x_0, y_0, z_0)$ *the average value of H on S*. Thus we can write

(18.7.4)
$$\iint_S H(x, y, z)\, d\sigma = \begin{pmatrix}\text{average value} \\ \text{of } H \text{ on } S\end{pmatrix} \cdot (\text{area of } S).$$

We can also take weighted averages: if H and G are continuous on S and G is nonnegative on S, then there is a point (x_0, y_0, z_0) on S for which

(18.7.5)
$$\iint_S H(x, y, z)G(x, y, z)\, d\sigma = H(x_0, y_0, z_0)\iint_S G(x, y, z)\, d\sigma.$$

As you would expect, we call $H(x_0, y_0, z_0)$ *the G-weighted average of H on S*.

The coordinates of the centroid $(\bar{x}, \bar{y}, \bar{z})$ of a surface are simply averages taken over the surface: for a surface S of area A,

$$\bar{x}A = \iint_S x\, d\sigma, \qquad \bar{y}A = \iint_S y\, d\sigma, \qquad \bar{z}A = \iint_S z\, d\sigma.$$

In the case of a material surface of mass density $\lambda = \lambda(x, y, z)$, the coordinates of the center of mass (x_M, y_M, z_M) are density-weighted averages: for a surface S of total mass M,

$$x_M M = \iint_S x\lambda(x, y, z)\,d\sigma, \quad y_M M = \iint_S y\lambda(x, y, z)\,d\sigma, \quad z_M M = \iint_S z\lambda(x, y, z)\,d\sigma.$$

Example 3 Locate the center of mass of a material surface in the form of a hemispherical shell $x^2 + y^2 + z^2 = a^2$ with $z \geq 0$ given that the mass density is directly proportional to the distance from the xy-plane. See Figure 18.7.1.

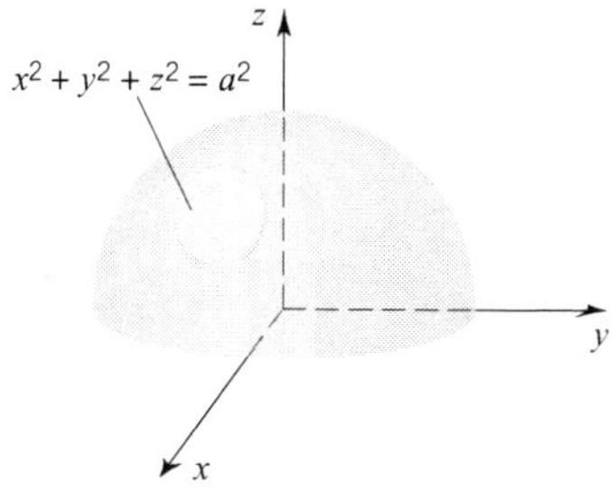

Figure 18.7.1

SOLUTION The surface S can be parametrized by the function

$$\mathbf{r}(u, v) = a\cos u \cos v\,\mathbf{i} + a \sin u \cos v\,\mathbf{j} + a \sin v\,\mathbf{k}; \qquad 0 \leq u \leq 2\pi, 0 \leq v \leq \tfrac{1}{2}\pi.$$

Call the parameter set Ω and recall that $\|\mathbf{N}(u, v)\| = a^2 \cos v$. (Example 8, Section 18.6.) The density function can be written $\lambda(x, y, z) = kz$ where k is the constant of proportionality. We can calculate the mass as follows:

$$\begin{aligned} M = \iint_S \lambda(x, y, z)\,d\sigma = k\iint_S z\,d\sigma &= k\iint_\Omega z(u, v)\|\mathbf{N}(u, v)\|\,du dv \\ &= k\int_0^{2\pi}\left(\int_0^{\pi/2}(a \sin v)(a^2\cos v)\,dv\right)du \\ &= 2\pi k a^3 \int_0^{\pi/2} \sin v\,\cos v\,dv = \pi k a^3. \end{aligned}$$

By symmetry $x_M = 0$ and $y_M = 0$. To find z_M we write

$$\begin{aligned} z_M M = \iint_S z\lambda(x, y, z)\,d\sigma &= k\iint_S z^2 d\sigma \\ &= k\iint_\Omega [z(u, v)]^2\|\mathbf{N}(u, v)\|\,du dv \\ &= k\int_0^{2\pi}\left(\int_0^{\pi/2}(a^2\sin^2 v)(a^2\cos v)\,dv\right)du \\ &= 2\pi k a^4\int_0^{\pi/2}\sin^2 v \cos v\,dv = \tfrac{2}{3}\pi k a^4. \end{aligned}$$

Since $M = \pi k a^3$, we see that $z_M = \frac{2}{3}\pi k a^4/M = \frac{2}{3}a$. The center of mass is the point $(0, 0, \frac{2}{3}a)$. ❑

Suppose that a material surface S rotates about an axis. The moment of inertia of the surface about that axis is given by the formula

(18.7.6)
$$I = \iint_S \lambda(x, y, z)[R(x, y, z)]^2\,d\sigma$$

where $\lambda = \lambda(x, y, z)$ is the mass density function and $R(x, y, z)$ is the distance from the axis to the point (x, y, z). (As usual, the moments of inertia about the x, y, z axes are denoted by I_x, I_y, I_z.)

Example 4 A homogeneous material surface of mass density 1 has the shape and position of the spherical shell

$$x^2 + y^2 + z^2 = a^2. \qquad \text{(Figure 18.7.2)}$$

Calculate the moment of inertia of this material surface about the z-axis.

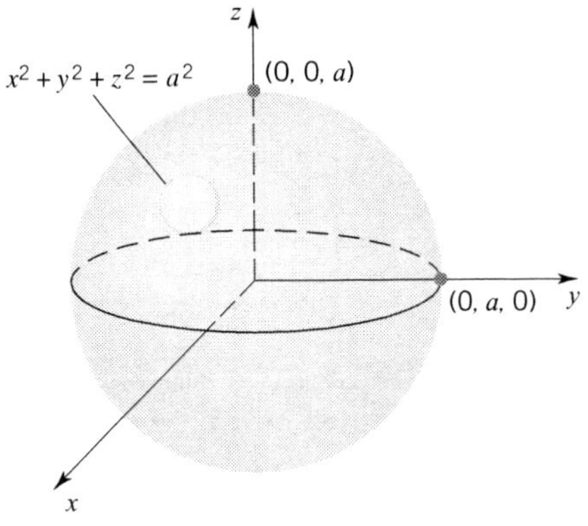

Figure 18.7.2

SOLUTION We parametrize S by setting

$$\mathbf{r}(u, v) = a\cos u \cos v\,\mathbf{i} + a\sin u \cos v\,\mathbf{j} + a\sin v\,\mathbf{k}; \quad 0 \le u \le 2\pi,\ -\tfrac{1}{2}\pi \le v \le \tfrac{1}{2}\pi.$$

Call the parameter set Ω and recall that $\|\mathbf{N}(u, v)\| = a^2 \cos v$. We can calculate the moment of inertia as follows:

$$\begin{aligned}
I_z = \iint_S (1)(x^2 + y^2)\,d\sigma &= \iint_\Omega \left([x(u, v)]^2 + [y(u, v)]^2\right)\|\mathbf{N}(u, v)\|\,d\sigma \\
&= \iint_\Omega (a^2\cos^2 v)(a^2 \cos v)\,du\,dv \\
&= a^4 \int_0^{2\pi}\left(\int_{-\pi/2}^{\pi/2} \cos^3 v\,dv\right) du \\
&= 2\pi a^4 \int_{-\pi/2}^{\pi/2} \cos^3 v\,dv = \tfrac{8}{3}\pi a^4.
\end{aligned}$$

↑ check this

Since the surface has mass $M = A = 4\pi a^2$, it follows that $I_z = \frac{2}{3}Ma^2$. ❑

A surface

$$S: \quad z = f(x, y), \quad (x, y) \in \Omega$$

can be parametrized by the function

$$\mathbf{r}(x, y) = x\,\mathbf{i} + y\,\mathbf{j} + f(x, y)\,\mathbf{k}, \qquad (x, y) \in \Omega.$$

As you saw in Section 18.6, $\|\mathbf{N}(x, y)\| = \sec[\gamma(x, y)]$ where $\gamma(x, y)$ is the angle between $\mathbf{k}$ and the upper unit normal. Therefore, for any scalar field H continuous on S,

(18.7.7)
$$\iint_S H(x, y, z)\,d\sigma = \iint_\Omega H(x, y, z)\sec[\gamma(x, y)]\,dx\,dy.$$

To evaluate this last integral, we use the fact that

$$\sec[\gamma(x, y)] = \sqrt{[f_x(x, y)]^2 + [f_y(x, y)]^2 + 1}. \qquad \text{(Section 18.6)}$$

Example 5 Calculate

$$\iint_S \sqrt{x^2 + y^2}\, d\sigma \qquad \text{with} \qquad S: z = xy,\ 0 \le x^2 + y^2 \le 1.$$

SOLUTION The base region Ω is the unit disk. The function $z = f(x, y) = xy$ has partial derivatives $f_x(x, y) = y$, $f_y(x, y) = x$. Therefore

$$\sec[\gamma(x, y)] = \sqrt{y^2 + x^2 + 1} = \sqrt{x^2 + y^2 + 1}$$

and

$$\iint_S \sqrt{x^2 + y^2}\, d\sigma = \iint_\Omega \sqrt{x^2 + y^2}\sqrt{x^2 + y^2 + 1}\, dxdy.$$

We evaluate this last integral by changing to polar coordinates. The region Ω is the set of all (x, y) with polar coordinates $[r, \theta]$ in the set

$$\Gamma: \quad 0 \le \theta \le 2\pi, \quad 0 \le r \le 1.$$

Therefore

$$\begin{aligned}
\iint_S \sqrt{x^2 + y^2}\, d\sigma = \iint_\Gamma r\sqrt{r^2 + 1}\; r\, dr d\theta &= \int_0^{2\pi} \left(\int_0^1 r^2\sqrt{r^2 + 1}\, dr\right) d\theta \\
&= 2\pi \int_0^1 r^2\sqrt{r^2 + 1}\, dr \\
&= 2\pi \int_0^{\pi/4} \tan^2\phi \sec^3\phi\, d\phi \qquad (r = \tan\phi) \\
&= 2\pi \int_0^{\pi/4} [\sec^5\phi - \sec^3\phi]\, d\phi \\
&= \tfrac{1}{4}\pi[3\sqrt{2} - \ln(\sqrt{2} + 1)]. \quad \square
\end{aligned}$$

The Flux of a Vector Field

Suppose that

$$S: \mathbf{r} = \mathbf{r}(u, v), \quad (u, v) \in \Omega$$

is a smooth surface with a unit normal $\mathbf{n} = \mathbf{n}(x, y, z)$ that is continuous on all of S. Such a surface is called an *oriented surface*. Note that an oriented surface has two sides: the side with normal $\mathbf{n}$ and the side with normal $-\mathbf{n}$.[†] If $\mathbf{v} = \mathbf{v}(x, y, z)$ is a vector field continuous on S, then we can form the surface integral

(18.7.8)
$$\iint_S (\mathbf{v} \cdot \mathbf{n})\, d\sigma = \iint_S [\mathbf{v}(x, y, z) \cdot \mathbf{n}(x, y, z)]\, d\sigma.$$

This surface integral is called *the flux of* $\mathbf{v}$ *across* S *in the direction of* $\mathbf{n}$.

[†] Not all surfaces have two sides. In Exercise 41 we exhibit a surface (the Möbius band) which has only one side.

Note that the flux across a surface depends on the choice of unit normal. If $-\mathbf{n}$ is chosen instead of $\mathbf{n}$, the sign of the flux is reversed:

$$\iint_S (\mathbf{v} \cdot [-\mathbf{n}])\, d\sigma = \iint_S -(\mathbf{v} \cdot \mathbf{n})\, d\sigma = -\iint_S (\mathbf{v} \cdot \mathbf{n})\, d\sigma.$$

Example 6 Calculate the flux of the vector field $\mathbf{v}(x, y, z) = x\,\mathbf{i} + y\,\mathbf{j}$ across the sphere $S: x^2 + y^2 + z^2 = a^2$ in the outward direction. (Figure 18.7.3.)

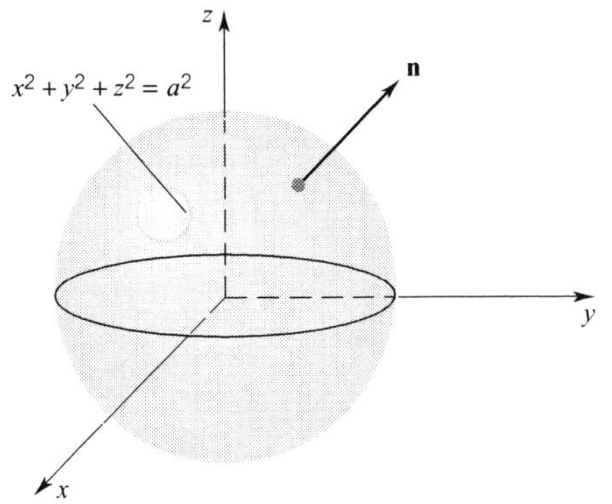

Figure 18.7.3

SOLUTION The outward unit normal is the vector

$$\mathbf{n}(x, y, z) = \frac{1}{a}(x\,\mathbf{i} + y\,\mathbf{j} + z\,\mathbf{k}).$$

Here

$$\mathbf{v} \cdot \mathbf{n} = (x\,\mathbf{i} + y\,\mathbf{j}) \cdot \frac{1}{a}(x\,\mathbf{i} + y\,\mathbf{j} + z\,\mathbf{k}) = \frac{1}{a}(x^2 + y^2).$$

Therefore

$$\text{flux out of } S = \frac{1}{a} \iint_S (x^2 + y^2)\, d\sigma.$$

To evaluate this integral we use the usual parametrization

$$\mathbf{r}(u, v) = a \cos u \cos v\,\mathbf{i} + a \sin u \cos v\,\mathbf{j} + a \sin v\,\mathbf{k}; \qquad 0 \le u \le 2\pi,\ -\tfrac{1}{2}\pi \le v \le \tfrac{1}{2}\pi.$$

Recall that $\|\mathbf{N}(u, v)\| = a^2 \cos v$. Thus

$$\begin{aligned}
\text{flux out of } S &= \frac{1}{a} \iint_\Omega ([x(u, v)]^2 + [y(u, v)]^2)\, \|\mathbf{N}(u, v)\|\, du dv \\
&= \frac{1}{a} \iint_\Omega (a^2 \cos^2 u \cos^2 v + a^2 \sin^2 u \cos^2 v)(a^2 \cos v)\, du dv \\
&= a^3 \iint_\Omega \cos^3 v\, du dv \\
&= a^3 \int_0^{2\pi} \left(\int_{-\pi/2}^{\pi/2} \cos^3 v dv \right) du = 2\pi a^3 \int_{-\pi/2}^{\pi/2} \cos^3 v dv = \tfrac{8}{3}\pi a^3. \quad \square
\end{aligned}$$

If S is the graph of a function $z = f(x, y)$, $(x, y) \in \Omega$ and $\mathbf{n}$ is the upper unit normal, then the flux of the vector field $\mathbf{v} = v_1\,\mathbf{i} + v_2\mathbf{j} + v_3\,\mathbf{k}$ across S in the direction of **n** is

(18.7.9)

$$\iint_S (\mathbf{v}\cdot\mathbf{n})\,d\sigma = \iint_\Omega (-v_1 f_x - v_2 f_y + v_3)\,dx\,dy.$$

PROOF From Section 18.6 we know that

$$\mathbf{n} = \frac{-f_x\,\mathbf{i} - f_y\,\mathbf{j} + \mathbf{k}}{\sqrt{(f_x)^2 + (f_y)^2 + 1}} = (-f_x\,\mathbf{i} - f_y\,\mathbf{j} + \mathbf{k})\cos\gamma$$

where γ is the angle between **n** and **k.** Thus $\mathbf{v}\cdot\mathbf{n} = (-v_1 f_x - v_2 f_y + v_3)\cos\gamma$ and

$$\iint_S (\mathbf{v}\cdot\mathbf{n})\,d\sigma = \iint_\Omega (\mathbf{v}\cdot\mathbf{n})\sec\gamma\,dx\,dy = \iint_\Omega (-v_1 f_x - v_2 f_y + v_3)\,dx\,dy. \quad \square$$

Example 7 Let S be the part of the paraboloid $z = 1 - (x^2 + y^2)$ that lies above the unit disk Ω. Calculate the flux of $\mathbf{v} = x\,\mathbf{i} + y\,\mathbf{j} + z\,\mathbf{k}$ across this surface in the direction of the upper unit normal. (See Figure 18.7.4.)

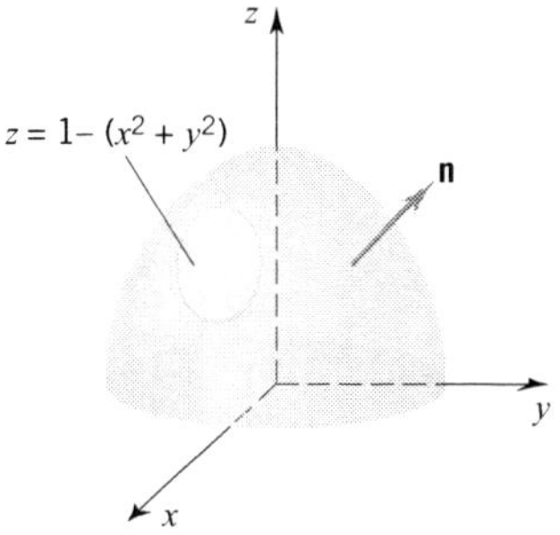

Figure 18.7.4

SOLUTION

$$f(x,y) = 1 - (x^2 + y^2); \qquad f_x = -2x, \qquad f_y = -2y.$$

$$\begin{aligned}\text{flux} &= \iint_\Omega (-v_1 f_x - v_2 f_y + v_3)\,dx\,dy \\ &= \iint_\Omega [(-x)(-2x) - y(-2y) + 1 - (x^2 + y^2)]\,dx\,dy \\ &= \iint_\Omega (1 + x^2 + y^2)\,dx\,dy = \int_0^{2\pi}\left(\int_0^1 (1 + r^2)r\,dr\right)d\theta = \tfrac{3}{2}\pi. \quad \square\end{aligned}$$

in polar coordinates

The flux out of (or into) a *closed piecewise-smooth oriented surface* (a closed surface that consists of a finite number of smooth pieces joined together at the boundaries and oriented in a consistent manner) can be evaluated by integrating over each smooth piece and adding up the results.

Example 8 Calculate the total flux of $\mathbf{v}(x,y,z) = xy\,\mathbf{i} + 4yz^2\,\mathbf{j} + yz\,\mathbf{k}$ out of the unit cube: $0 \le x \le 1, 0 \le y \le 1, 0 \le z \le 1$. (Figure 18.7.5.)

SOLUTION The total flux is the sum of the fluxes across the faces of the cube:

Face	n	v · n	Flux
$x = 0$	$-\mathbf{i}$	$-xy = 0$	0
$x = 1$	$\mathbf{i}$	$xy = y$	$\frac{1}{2}$
$y = 0$	$-\mathbf{j}$	$-4yz^2 = 0$	0
$y = 1$	$\mathbf{j}$	$yz^2 = 4z^2$	$\frac{4}{3}$
$z = 0$	$-\mathbf{k}$	$-yz = 0$	0
$z = 1$	$\mathbf{k}$	$yz = y$	$\frac{1}{2}$

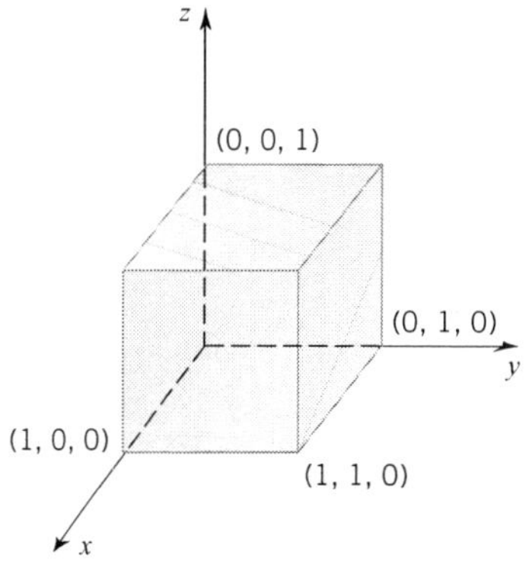

Figure 18.7.5

The total flux is $\frac{1}{2} + \frac{4}{3} + \frac{1}{2} = \frac{7}{3}$. $\square$

Flux plays an important role in the study of fluid motion. Imagine a surface S within a fluid and choose a unit normal $\mathbf{n}$. Take $\mathbf{v}$ as the velocity of the fluid that passes through S. You can expect $\mathbf{v}$ to vary from point to point, but, for simplicity, let's assume that $\mathbf{v}$ does not change with time. (Such a time-independent flow is said to be *steady state*.) The flux of $\mathbf{v}$ across S is the average component of $\mathbf{v}$ in the direction of $\mathbf{n}$ times the area of the surface S. This is just the volume of fluid that passes through S in unit time, from the $-\mathbf{n}$ side of S to the $\mathbf{n}$ side of S. If S is a closed surface (such as a cube, a sphere, or an ellipsoid) and $\mathbf{n}$ is chosen as the *outer unit normal*, then the flux across S gives the volume of fluid that flows *out* through S in unit time; if $\mathbf{n}$ is chosen as the *inner unit normal*, then the flux gives the volume of liquid that flows *in* through S in unit time.

EXERCISES 18.7

Exercises 1–6. Evaluate taking $S: z = \frac{1}{2}y^2; 0 \le x \le 1, 0 \le y \le 1$.

1. $\iint_S d\sigma$.

2. $\iint_S x^2\, d\sigma$.

3. $\iint_S 3y\, d\sigma$.

4. $\iint_S (x - y)\, d\sigma$.

5. $\iint_S \sqrt{2z}\, d\sigma$.

6. $\iint_S \sqrt{1 + y^2}\, d\sigma$.

Exercises 7–12. Evaluate.

7. $\iint_S xy\, d\sigma$; S the first-octant part of the plane $x + 2y + 3z = 6$.

8. $\iint_S xyz\, d\sigma$; S the first-octant part of the plane $x + y + z = 1$.

9. $\iint_S x^2 z\, d\sigma$; S that part of the cylinder $x^2 + z^2 = 1$ which lies between the planes $y = 0$ and $y = 2$, and is above the xy-plane.

10. $\iint_S (x^2 + y^2 + z^2)\, d\sigma$; S that part of the plane $z = x + 2$ which lies inside the cylinder $x^2 + y^2 = 1$.

11. $\iint_S (x^2 + y^2)\, d\sigma$; S the hemisphere $z = \sqrt{1 - (x^2 + y^2)}$.

12. $\iint_S (x^2 + y^2)\, d\sigma$; S that part of the paraboloid $z = 1 - x^2 - y^2$ which lies above the xy-plane.

Exercises 13–15. Find the mass of a triangular material surface with vertices $(a, 0, 0), (0, a, 0), (0, 0, a)$ given that the mass density varies as indicated. Take $a > 0$.

13. $\lambda(x, y, z) = k$.

14. $\lambda(x, y, z) = k(x + y)$.

15. $\lambda(x, y, z) = kx^2$.

16. Locate the centroid of the triangular region of Exercises 13–15.

17. Locate the centroid of the hemisphere $x^2 + y^2 + z^2 = a^2$, $z \ge 0$.

For Exercises 18–19, let S be the parallelogram given by

$$\mathbf{r}(u, v) = (u + v)\,\mathbf{i} + (u - v)\,\mathbf{j} + u\,\mathbf{k}; \quad 0 \le u \le 1, 0 \le v \le 1.$$

18. Find the area of S.

19. Determine the flux of $\mathbf{v} = x\,\mathbf{i} - y\,\mathbf{j}$ across S in the direction of the fundamental vector product.

20. Find the mass of the material surface $S: z = 1 - \frac{1}{2}(x^2 + y^2)$ with $0 \le x \le 1, 0 \le y \le 1$ given that the density at each point (x, y, z) is proportional to xy.

Exercises 21–23. Calculate the flux out of the sphere

$$x^2 + y^2 + z^2 = a^2.$$

21. $\mathbf{v} = z\,\mathbf{k}$.

22. $\mathbf{v} = x\,\mathbf{i} + y\,\mathbf{j} + z\,\mathbf{k}$.

23. $\mathbf{v} = y\,\mathbf{i} - x\,\mathbf{j}$.

24. A homogeneous plate of mass density 1 is in the form of the parallelogram of Exercises 18–19. Determine the moments of inertia about the coordinate axes: I_x, I_y, I_z.

Exercises 25–27. Determine the flux across the triangular region with vertices $(a, 0, 0), (0, a, 0), (0, 0, a)$ in the direction of the upper unit normal. (Take $a > 0$.)

25. $\mathbf{v} = x\,\mathbf{i} + y\,\mathbf{j} + z\,\mathbf{k}$.

26. $\mathbf{v} = (x + z)\,\mathbf{k}$.

27. $\mathbf{v} = x^2\,\mathbf{i} - y^2\,\mathbf{j}$.

Exercises 28–30. Determine the flux across $S: z = xy$ with $0 \le x \le 1, 0 \le y \le 2$ in the direction of the upper unit normal.

28. $\mathbf{v} = -xy^2\,\mathbf{i} + z\,\mathbf{j}$.

29. $\mathbf{v} = xz\,\mathbf{j} - xy\,\mathbf{k}$.

30. $\mathbf{v} = x^2 y\,\mathbf{i} + z^2\,\mathbf{k}$.

31. Calculate the flux of $\mathbf{v} = x\,\mathbf{i} + y\,\mathbf{j} + z\mathbf{k}$ out of the cylindrical surface

$$S: \mathbf{r}(u, v) = a\,\cos u\,\mathbf{i} + a\sin u\,\mathbf{j} + v\,\mathbf{k}; \quad 0 \le u \le 2\pi, 0 \le v \le l.$$

32. (*The gravitational field*) A mass M located at the origin exerts an attractive force

$$\mathbf{F}(\mathbf{r}) = -G\frac{mM}{r^3}\mathbf{r}$$

on a mass m located at the tip of the radius vector $\mathbf{r} = x\,\mathbf{i} + y\,\mathbf{j} + z\,\mathbf{k}$. Find the flux of $\mathbf{F}$ into the sphere $x^2 + y^2 + z^2 = a^2$.

Exercises 33–36. Find the flux across $S: z = \frac{2}{3}(x^{3/2} + y^{3/2})$ with $0 \le x \le 1$, $0 \le y \le 1 - x$ in the direction of the upper unit normal.

33. $\mathbf{v} = x\,\mathbf{i} - y\,\mathbf{j} + \frac{3}{2}z\,\mathbf{k}$.

34. $\mathbf{v} = x^2\,\mathbf{i}$.

35. $\mathbf{v} = y^2\,\mathbf{j}$.

36. $\mathbf{v} = y\,\mathbf{i} - \sqrt{xy}\,\mathbf{j}$.

37. The cone

$$\mathbf{r}(u, v) = v\cos u \sin\alpha\,\mathbf{i} + v\sin u\sin\alpha\,\mathbf{j} + v\cos\alpha\,\mathbf{k},$$
$$0 \le u \le 2\pi, \quad 0 \le v \le s,$$

has surface area $A = \pi s^2 \sin\alpha$. Locate the centroid.

Exercises 38–40. The mass density of a material conical surface $z = \sqrt{x^2 + y^2}$ with $0 \le z \le 1$ varies directly as the distance from the z-axis.

38. Find the mass of the surface.

39. Locate the center of mass.

40. Determine the moments of inertia about the coordinate axes: (*a*) I_x. (*b*) I_y. (*c*) I_z.

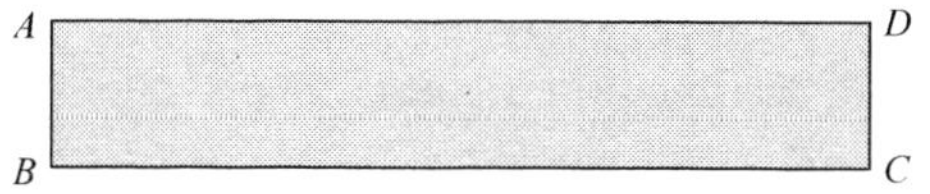

41. You have seen that, if S is a smooth oriented surface immersed in a fluid of velocity $\mathbf{v}$, then the flux

$$\iint_S (\mathbf{v}\cdot\mathbf{n})\,d\sigma$$

is the volume of fluid that passes through S in unit time from the **-n** side of S to the **n** side of S. This requires that S be a two-sided surface. There are, however, one-sided surfaces; for example, the Möbius band. To construct a material Möbius band, start with a piece of paper in the form of the rectangle in the figure. Now give the piece of paper a single twist and join the two far edges together so that C coincides with A and D coincides with B. (a) Convince yourself that this surface is one-sided and therefore the notion of flux cannot be applied to it. (b) The surface is not smooth because it is impossible to erect a unit normal $\mathbf{n}$ that varies continuously over the entire surface. Convince yourself of this as follows: Erect a unit normal $\mathbf{n}$ at some point P and make a circuit of the surface with $\mathbf{n}$. Note that, as $\mathbf{n}$ returns to P, the direction of $\mathbf{n}$ has been reversed.

Exercises 42–44. Assume that the parallelogram of Exercises 18 and 19 is a material surface with a mass density that varies directly as the square of the distance from the x-axis.

42. Determine the mass.

43. Find the x-coordinate of the center of mass.

44. Find the moment of inertia about the z-axis.

45. Calculate the total flux of $\mathbf{v}(x, y, z) = y\,\mathbf{i} - x\,\mathbf{j}$ out of the solid bounded on the sides by the cylinder $x^2 + y^2 = 1$ and above and below by the planes $z = 1$ and $z = 0$. HINT: Draw a figure.

46. Calculate the total flux of $\mathbf{v}(x, y, z) = y\,\mathbf{i} - x\,\mathbf{j}$ out of the solid bounded above by $z = 4$ and below by $z = x^2 + y^2$.

47. Calculate the total flux of $\mathbf{v}(x, y, z) = x\,\mathbf{i} + y\,\mathbf{i} + z\,\mathbf{k}$ out of the solid bounded above by $z = \sqrt{2 - (x^2 + y^2)}$ and below by $z = x^2 + y^2$.

48. Calculate the total flux of $\mathbf{v}(x, y, z) = xz\,\mathbf{i} + 4xyz^2\,\mathbf{j} + 2z\,\mathbf{k}$ out of the unit cube: $0 \le x \le 1$, $0 \le y \le 1$, $0 \le z \le 1$.

18.8 THE VECTOR DIFFERENTIAL OPERATOR ∇

Divergence $\nabla \cdot \mathbf{v}$, Curl $\nabla \times \mathbf{v}$

The *vector differential operator* ∇ is defined formally by setting

(18.8.1)
$$\nabla = \frac{\partial}{\partial x}\mathbf{i} + \frac{\partial}{\partial y}\mathbf{j} + \frac{\partial}{\partial z}\mathbf{k}.$$

By "formally," we mean that this is not an ordinary vector. Its "components" are differentiation symbols. As the term "operator" suggests, ∇ is to be thought of as something that "operates" on things. What sorts of things? Scalar fields and vector fields.

Suppose that f is a differentiable scalar field. Then ∇ operates on f as follows:

$$\nabla f = \left(\frac{\partial}{\partial x}\mathbf{i} + \frac{\partial}{\partial y}\mathbf{j} + \frac{\partial}{\partial z}\mathbf{k}\right) f = \frac{\partial f}{\partial x}\mathbf{i} + \frac{\partial f}{\partial y}\mathbf{j} + \frac{\partial f}{\partial z}\mathbf{k}.$$

This is just the *gradient* of f, with which you are already familiar.

How does ∇ operate on vector fields? In two ways. If $\mathbf{v} = v_1\,\mathbf{i} + v_2\,\mathbf{j} + v_3\,\mathbf{k}$ is a differentiable vector field, then, by definition,

(18.8.2)
$$\nabla \cdot \mathbf{v} = \frac{\partial v_1}{\partial x} + \frac{\partial v_2}{\partial y} + \frac{\partial v_3}{\partial z}$$

and

(18.8.3)
$$\nabla \times \mathbf{v} = \begin{vmatrix} \mathbf{i} & \mathbf{j} & \mathbf{k} \\ \dfrac{\partial}{\partial x} & \dfrac{\partial}{\partial y} & \dfrac{\partial}{\partial z} \\ v_1 & v_2 & v_3 \end{vmatrix}$$
$$= \left(\frac{\partial v_3}{\partial y} - \frac{\partial v_2}{\partial z}\right)\mathbf{i} + \left(\frac{\partial v_1}{\partial z} - \frac{\partial v_3}{\partial x}\right)\mathbf{j} + \left(\frac{\partial v_2}{\partial x} - \frac{\partial v_1}{\partial y}\right)\mathbf{k}.$$

The first "product," $\nabla \cdot \mathbf{v}$, defined in imitation of the ordinary dot product, is called the *divergence* of $\mathbf{v}$:

$$\nabla \cdot \mathbf{v} = \operatorname{div} \mathbf{v}.$$

The second "product," $\nabla \times \mathbf{v}$, defined in imitation of the ordinary cross product, is called the *curl* of $\mathbf{v}$:

$$\nabla \times \mathbf{v} = \operatorname{curl} \mathbf{v}.$$

Interpretation of Divergence and Curl

Suppose we know the divergence of a field and also the curl. What does that tell us? For definitive answers we must wait for the divergence theorem and Stokes's theorem, but, in a preliminary way, we can give you some rough answers right now.

View $\mathbf{v}$ as the velocity field of some fluid. The divergence of $\mathbf{v}$ at a point P gives us an indication of whether the fluid tends to accumulate near P (negative divergence) or tends to move away from P (positive divergence). In the first case, P is sometimes called a *sink*, and in the second case, it is called a *source*. The curl at P measures the rotational tendency of the fluid.

Example 1 Set

$$\mathbf{v}(x, y, z) = \alpha\,\mathbf{r} = \alpha x\,\mathbf{i} + \alpha y\,\mathbf{j} + \alpha z\,\mathbf{k}. \qquad (\alpha \text{ a constant})$$

The divergence is

$$\nabla \cdot \mathbf{v} = \alpha\frac{\partial x}{\partial x} + \alpha\frac{\partial y}{\partial y} + \alpha\frac{\partial z}{\partial z} = 3\alpha.$$

The curl is

$$\nabla \times \mathbf{v} = \begin{vmatrix} \mathbf{i} & \mathbf{j} & \mathbf{k} \\ \dfrac{\partial}{\partial x} & \dfrac{\partial}{\partial y} & \dfrac{\partial}{\partial z} \\ \alpha x & \alpha y & \alpha z \end{vmatrix} = \alpha \begin{vmatrix} \mathbf{i} & \mathbf{j} & \mathbf{k} \\ \dfrac{\partial}{\partial x} & \dfrac{\partial}{\partial y} & \dfrac{\partial}{\partial z} \\ x & y & z \end{vmatrix} = 0$$

because the partial derivatives that appear in the expanded determinant

$$\frac{\partial y}{\partial x}, \qquad \frac{\partial x}{\partial y}, \qquad \text{etc.,}$$

are all zero. ❑

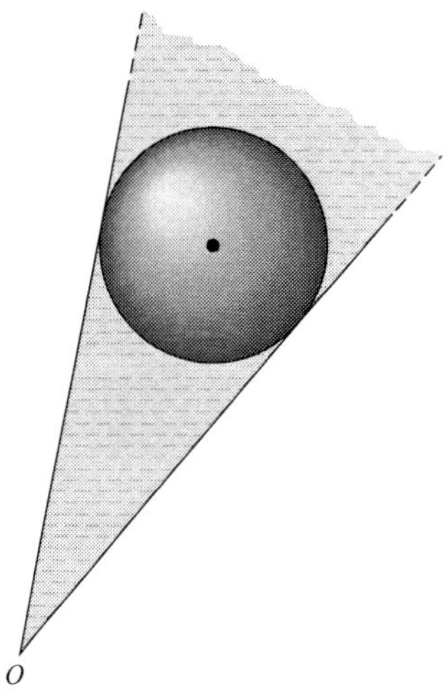

Figure 18.8.1

The field of Example 1

$$\mathbf{v}(x, y, z) = \alpha(x\,\mathbf{i} + y\,\mathbf{j} + z\,\mathbf{k}) = \alpha\,\mathbf{r}$$

can be viewed as the velocity field of a fluid in radial motion—toward the origin if $\alpha < 0$, away from the origin if $\alpha > 0$. Figure 18.8.1 shows a point (x, y, z), a spherical neighborhood of that point, and a cone emanating from the origin that is tangent to the boundary of the neighborhood.

Note two things: all the fluid in the cone stays in the cone, and the speed of the fluid is proportional to its distance from the origin. Therefore, if the divergence 3α is negative, then α is negative, the motion is toward the origin, and the neighborhood *gains fluid* because the fluid coming in is moving more quickly than the fluid going out. (Also, the entry area is larger than the exit area.) If, however, the divergence 3α is positive, then α is positive, the motion is away from the origin, and the neighborhood *loses fluid* because the fluid coming in is moving more slowly than the fluid going out. (Also, the entry area is smaller than the exit area.)

Since the motion is radial, the fluid has no rotational tendency whatsoever, and we would expect the curl to be identically zero. It is.

Example 2 Set

$$\mathbf{v}(x, y, z) = -\omega y\,\mathbf{i} + \omega x\,\mathbf{j}. \qquad (\omega \text{ a positive constant})$$

The divergence is

$$\nabla \cdot \mathbf{v} = -\omega\frac{\partial y}{\partial x} + \omega\frac{\partial x}{\partial y} = 0 + 0 = 0.$$

The curl is

$$\nabla \times \mathbf{v} = \begin{vmatrix} \mathbf{i} & \mathbf{j} & \mathbf{k} \\ \dfrac{\partial}{\partial x} & \dfrac{\partial}{\partial y} & \dfrac{\partial}{\partial z} \\ -\omega y & \omega x & 0 \end{vmatrix} = \left(\omega\frac{\partial x}{\partial x} + \omega\frac{\partial y}{\partial y}\right)\mathbf{k} = 2\omega\,\mathbf{k}. \quad ❑$$

The field of Example 2,

$$\mathbf{v}(x, y, z) = -\omega y\,\mathbf{i} + \omega x\,\mathbf{j},$$

is the velocity field of uniform counterclockwise rotation about the z-axis with angular speed ω. You can see this by noting that $\mathbf{v}$ is perpendicular to $\mathbf{r} = x\,\mathbf{i} + y\,\mathbf{j} + z\,\mathbf{k}$:

$$\mathbf{v} \cdot \mathbf{r} = (-\omega y\,\mathbf{i} + x\,\mathbf{j}) \cdot (x\,\mathbf{i} + y\,\mathbf{j} + z\,\mathbf{k}) = -\omega yx + \omega xy = 0$$

and the speed at each point is ωR where R is the radius of rotation:

$$v = \sqrt{\omega^2 y^2 + \omega^2 x^2} = \omega\sqrt{x^2 + y^2} = \omega R.$$

How is the curl, $2\omega\,\mathbf{k}$, related to the rotation? The angular velocity vector (see Exercise 14, Section 14.6) is the vector $\boldsymbol{\omega} = \omega\,\mathbf{k}$. In this case, then, the curl of $\mathbf{v}$ is twice the angular velocity vector.

With this rotation no neighborhood gains any fluid and no neighborhood loses any fluid. As we saw, the divergence is identically zero.

Basic Identities

THEOREM 18.8.4 THE CURL OF A GRADIENT IS ZERO

If f is a scalar field with continuous second partials, then

$$\nabla \times (\nabla f) = \mathbf{0}.$$

PROOF

$$\nabla \times (\nabla f) = \begin{vmatrix} \mathbf{i} & \mathbf{j} & \mathbf{k} \\ \dfrac{\partial}{\partial x} & \dfrac{\partial}{\partial y} & \dfrac{\partial}{\partial z} \\ \dfrac{\partial f}{\partial x} & \dfrac{\partial f}{\partial y} & \dfrac{\partial f}{\partial z} \end{vmatrix} =$$

$$\left(\frac{\partial^2 f}{\partial y \partial z} - \frac{\partial^2 f}{\partial z \partial y}\right)\mathbf{i} + \left(\frac{\partial^2 f}{\partial z \partial x} - \frac{\partial^2 f}{\partial x \partial z}\right)\mathbf{j} + \left(\frac{\partial^2 f}{\partial x \partial y} - \frac{\partial^2 f}{\partial y \partial x}\right)\mathbf{k} = \mathbf{0}.$$ ❑

THEOREM 18.8.5 THE DIVERGENCE OF A CURL IS ZERO

If the components of the vector field $\mathbf{v} = v_1\,\mathbf{i} + v_2\,\mathbf{j} + v_3\,\mathbf{k}$ have continuous second partials, then

$$\nabla \cdot (\nabla \times \mathbf{v}) = 0.$$

PROOF Again the key is the equality of the mixed partials:

$$\nabla \cdot (\nabla \times \mathbf{v}) = \frac{\partial}{\partial x}\left(\frac{\partial v_3}{\partial y} - \frac{\partial v_2}{\partial z}\right) + \frac{\partial}{\partial y}\left(\frac{\partial v_1}{\partial z} - \frac{\partial v_3}{\partial x}\right) + \frac{\partial}{\partial z}\left(\frac{\partial v_2}{\partial x} - \frac{\partial v_1}{\partial y}\right) = 0,$$

since for each component v_i the mixed partials cancel. Try it for v_1. ❑

The next two identities are product rules. Here f is a scalar field and $\mathbf{v}$ is a vector field.

(18.8.6) $$\nabla \cdot (f\mathbf{v}) = (\nabla f) \cdot \mathbf{v} + f(\nabla \cdot \mathbf{v}). \qquad [\text{div}(f\mathbf{v}) = (\text{grad } f) \cdot \mathbf{v} + f(\text{div } \mathbf{v})]$$

(18.8.7) $$\nabla \times (f\mathbf{v}) = (\nabla f) \times \mathbf{v} + f(\nabla \times \mathbf{v}). \quad [\text{curl}(f\mathbf{v}) = (\text{grad } f) \times \mathbf{v} + f(\text{curl } \mathbf{v})]$$

The verification of these identities is left to you in the Exercises.

As usual, set $\mathbf{r} = x\,\mathbf{i} + y\,\mathbf{j} + z\,\mathbf{k}$ and $r = \|\mathbf{r}\|$. From Example 1 we know that $\nabla \cdot \mathbf{r} = 3$ and $\nabla \times \mathbf{r} = \mathbf{0}$ at all points of space. Now we can show that if n is an integer, then, for all $\mathbf{r} \neq \mathbf{0}$,

(18.8.8) $$\nabla \cdot (r^n\, \mathbf{r}) = (n+3)r^n \qquad \text{and} \qquad \nabla \times (r^n\, \mathbf{r}) = \mathbf{0}.^{\dagger}$$

PROOF Earlier we showed that $\nabla r^n = nr^{n-2}\,\mathbf{r}$. [(16.1.5)] Applying (18.8.6), we have

$$\begin{aligned}\nabla \cdot (r^n \mathbf{r}) &= \nabla r^n \cdot \mathbf{r} + r^n(\nabla \cdot \mathbf{r})\\ &= (nr^{n-2}\mathbf{r}) \cdot \mathbf{r} + r^n(3)\\ &= nr^{n-2}(\mathbf{r}\cdot\mathbf{r}) + 3r^n = nr^n + 3r^n = (n+3)r^n.\end{aligned}$$

That $\nabla \times (r^n \mathbf{r}) = \mathbf{0}$ follows from the fact that $r^n\mathbf{r}$ is a gradient:

$$\nabla\left(\frac{r^{n+2}}{n+2}\right) = r^n\mathbf{r}.$$

We know that gradients have $\mathbf{0}$ curl. ❑

The Laplacian

From the operator ∇ we can construct other operators, the most important of which is the Laplacian $\nabla^2 = \nabla \cdot \nabla$. The Laplacian (named after the French mathematician Pierre-Simon Laplace) operates on scalar fields according to the following rule:

(18.8.9) $$\nabla^2 f = \nabla \cdot (\nabla f) = \frac{\partial^2 f}{\partial x^2} + \frac{\partial^2 f}{\partial y^2} + \frac{\partial^2 f}{\partial z^2}.^{\ddagger}$$

Example 3 If $f(x, y, z) = x^2 + y^2 + z^2$, then

$$\begin{aligned}\nabla^2 f &= \frac{\partial^2}{\partial x^2}(x^2+y^2+z^2) + \frac{\partial^2}{\partial y^2}(x^2+y^2+z^2) + \frac{\partial^2}{\partial z^2}(x^2+y^2+z^2)\\ &= 2+2+2 = 6.\end{aligned}$$ ❑

Example 4 If $f(x, y, z) = e^{xyz}$, then

$$\begin{aligned}\nabla^2 f &= \frac{\partial}{\partial x^2}(e^{xyz}) + \frac{\partial^2}{\partial y^2}(e^{xyz}) + \frac{\partial^2}{\partial z^2}(e^{xyz})\\ &= \frac{\partial}{\partial x}(yz\, e^{xyz}) + \frac{\partial}{\partial y}(xz\, e^{xyz}) + \frac{\partial}{\partial z}(xy\, e^{xyz})\\ &= y^2z^2\, e^{xyz} + x^2z^2e^{xyz} + x^2y^2e^{xyz}\\ &= (y^2z^2 + x^2z^2 + x^2y^2)e^{xyz}.\end{aligned}$$ ❑

Example 5 To calculate $\nabla^2(\sin r) = \nabla^2(\sin\sqrt{x^2+y^2+z^2})$, we could write

$$\frac{\partial^2}{\partial x^2}(\sin\sqrt{x^2+y^2+z^2}) + \frac{\partial^2}{\partial y^2}(\sin\sqrt{x^2+y^2+z^2}) + \frac{\partial^2}{\partial z^2}(\sin\sqrt{x^2+y^2+z^2})$$

† If n is positive and even, these formulas also hold at $\mathbf{r} = \mathbf{0}$.

‡ In some texts you will see the Laplacian of f written Δf. Unfortunately this can be misread as the increment of f.

and proceed from there. The calculations are straightforward but lengthy. We will proceed in a different way.

Recall that

$$\nabla^2 f = \nabla \cdot \nabla f \quad (18.8.9) \qquad \nabla \cdot (f\mathbf{v}) = (\nabla f)\cdot \mathbf{v} + f(\nabla \cdot \mathbf{v}) \quad (18.8.6)$$

$$\nabla f(r) = f'(r)r^{-1}\mathbf{r} \quad (16.3.11) \qquad \nabla \cdot (r^n \mathbf{r}) = (n+3)r^n. \quad (18.8.8)$$

Using these relations, we have

$$\begin{aligned}\nabla^2(\sin r) = \nabla \cdot (\nabla \sin r) &= \nabla \cdot [(\cos r) r^{-1}\mathbf{r}] \\ &= [(\nabla \cos r)\cdot r^{-1}\mathbf{r}] + \cos r\,(\nabla \cdot r^{-1}\mathbf{r}) \\ &= \{(-\sin r) r^{-1}\mathbf{r}]\cdot r^{-1}\mathbf{r}\} + (\cos r)(2r^{-1}) \\ &= -\sin r + 2r^{-1}\cos r.\end{aligned}$$

We leave it to you to verify each step. It takes practice to become familiar with these operations. ❑

EXERCISES 18.8

Exercises 1–12. Calculate the divergence $\nabla \cdot \mathbf{v}$ and the curl $\nabla \times \mathbf{v}$.

1. $\mathbf{v}(x, y) = x\,\mathbf{i} + y\,\mathbf{j}$.

2. $\mathbf{v}(x, y) = y\,\mathbf{i} + x\,\mathbf{j}$.

3. $\mathbf{v}(x, y) = \dfrac{x}{x^2+y^2}\,\mathbf{i} + \dfrac{y}{x^2+y^2}\,\mathbf{j}$.

4. $\mathbf{v}(x, y) = \dfrac{y}{x^2+y^2}\,\mathbf{i} + \dfrac{x}{x^2+y^2}\,\mathbf{j}$.

5. $\mathbf{v}(x, y, z) = x\,\mathbf{i} + 2y\,\mathbf{j} + 3z\,\mathbf{k}$.

6. $\mathbf{v}(x, y, z) = yz\,\mathbf{i} + xz\,\mathbf{j} + xy\,\mathbf{k}$.

7. $\mathbf{v}(x, y, z) = xyz\,\mathbf{i} + xz\,\mathbf{j} + z\,\mathbf{k}$.

8. $\mathbf{v}(x, y, z) = x^2y\,\mathbf{i} + y^2z\,\mathbf{j} + xy^2\,\mathbf{k}$.

9. $\mathbf{v}(\mathbf{r}) = r^{-2}\mathbf{r}$.

10. $\mathbf{v}(\mathbf{r}) = e^r\mathbf{r}$.

11. $\mathbf{v}(\mathbf{r}) = e^{r^2}(\mathbf{i} + \mathbf{j} + \mathbf{k})$.

12. $\mathbf{v}(\mathbf{r}) = e^{y^2}\,\mathbf{i} + e^{z^2}\,\mathbf{j} + e^{x^2}\,\mathbf{k}$.

13. Suppose that f is a differentiable function of one variable and $\mathbf{v}(x, y, z) = f(x)\,\mathbf{i}$. Determine $\nabla \cdot \mathbf{v}$ and $\nabla \times \mathbf{v}$.

14. Show that, if $\mathbf{v}$ is a differentiable vector field of the form $\mathbf{v}(\mathbf{r}) = f(x)\,\mathbf{i} + g(y)\,\mathbf{j} + h(z)\,\mathbf{k}$, then $\nabla \times \mathbf{v} = \mathbf{0}$.

15. Show that divergence and curl are *linear* operators:

$$\nabla \cdot (\alpha\mathbf{u} + \beta\mathbf{v}) = \alpha(\nabla \cdot \mathbf{u}) + \beta(\nabla \cdot \mathbf{v}) \quad \text{and}$$
$$\nabla \times (\alpha\mathbf{u} + \beta\mathbf{v}) = \alpha(\nabla \times \mathbf{u}) + \beta(\nabla \times \mathbf{v}).$$

16. (*Important*) Show that the gravitational field

$$\mathbf{F}(\mathbf{r}) = -\frac{GmM}{r^3}\mathbf{r}$$

has zero divergence and zero curl at each $\mathbf{r} \neq \mathbf{0}$.

A vector field with zero divergence ($\nabla \cdot \mathbf{v} = 0$) is said to be *solenoidal*, from the Greek word for "tubular." Exercise 16 shows that the gravitational field is solenoidal. If $\mathbf{v}$ is the velocity field of some fluid and $\nabla \cdot \mathbf{v} = 0$ in a solid T in three-dimensional space, then $\mathbf{v}$ has no sources or sinks within T.

17. Show that the vector field $\mathbf{v}(x, y, z) = (2x + y + 2z)\,\mathbf{i} + (x + 4y - 3z)\,\mathbf{j} + (2x - 3y - 6z)\,\mathbf{k}$ is solenoidal.

18. Show that $\mathbf{v}(x, y, z) = 3x^2\,\mathbf{i} - y^2\,\mathbf{j} + (2yz - 6xz)\,\mathbf{k}$ is solenoidal.

A vector field with zero curl ($\nabla \times \mathbf{v} = 0$) is said to be *irrotational*. Exercise 16 shows that the gravitational field is irrotational. If $\mathbf{v}$ is the velocity field of some fluid, then $\nabla \times \mathbf{v}$ measures the tendency of the fluid to "curl" or rotate about an axis. That $\nabla \times \mathbf{v} = \mathbf{0}$ can be taken to mean that the fluid tends to move in a straight line.

19. Show that the vector field $\mathbf{v}(x, y, z) = x\,\mathbf{i} + y\,\mathbf{j} - 2z\,\mathbf{k}$ is irrotational.

20. Show that the vector field of Exercise 17 is irrotational.

Exercises 21–26. Calculate the Laplacian $\nabla^2 f$.

21. $f(x, y, z) = x^4 + y^4 + z^4$.

22. $f(x, y, z) = xyz$.

23. $f(x, y, z) = x^2y^3z^4$.

24. $f(\mathbf{r}) = \cos r$.

25. $f(\mathbf{r}) = e^r$.

26. $f(\mathbf{r}) = \ln r$.

27. Given a vector field $\mathbf{u}$, the operator $\mathbf{u}\cdot\nabla$ is defined by setting

$$(\mathbf{u}\cdot\nabla)f = \mathbf{u}\cdot\nabla f = u_1\frac{\partial f}{\partial x} + u_2\frac{\partial f}{\partial y} + u_3\frac{\partial f}{\partial z}.$$

Calculate $(\mathbf{r}\cdot\nabla)f$: (a) for $f(\mathbf{r}) = r^2$, (b) for $f(\mathbf{r}) = 1/r$.

28. (Based on Exercise 27) We can also apply $\mathbf{u}\cdot\nabla$ to a vector field $\mathbf{v}$ by applying it to each component. By definition

$$(\mathbf{u}\cdot\nabla)\mathbf{v} = (\mathbf{u}\cdot\nabla v_1)\,\mathbf{i} + (\mathbf{u}\cdot\nabla v_2)\,\mathbf{j} + (\mathbf{u}\cdot\nabla v_3)\,\mathbf{k}.$$

(a) Calculate $(\mathbf{u}\cdot\nabla)\,\mathbf{r}$ for an arbitrary vector field $\mathbf{u}$.

(b) Calculate $(\mathbf{r}\cdot\nabla)\,\mathbf{u}$ given that $\mathbf{u} = yz\,\mathbf{i} + xz\,\mathbf{j} + xy\,\mathbf{k}$.

29. Show that, if $f(\mathbf{r}) = g(r)$ and g is twice differentiable, then

$$\nabla^2 f = g''(r) + 2r^{-1}g'(r).$$

30. Verify the following identities.

(a) $\nabla \cdot (f\mathbf{v}) = (\nabla f) \cdot \mathbf{v} + f(\nabla \cdot \mathbf{v})$.

(b) $\nabla \times (f\mathbf{v}) = (\nabla f) \times \mathbf{v} + f(\nabla \times \mathbf{v})$.

(c) $\nabla \times (\nabla \times \mathbf{v}) = \nabla(\nabla \cdot \mathbf{v}) - \nabla^2 \mathbf{v}$, where

$$\nabla^2 \mathbf{v} = (\nabla^2 v_1)\,\mathbf{i} + (\nabla^2 v_2)\,\mathbf{j} + (\nabla^2 v_3)\,\mathbf{k}.$$

HINT: Begin part (c) by writing out the ith component of each side.

Exercises 31–32. Equation

$$\nabla^2 f = \frac{\partial^2 f}{\partial x^2} + \frac{\partial^2 f}{\partial y^2} + \frac{\partial^2 f}{\partial z^2} = 0$$

is called *Laplace's equation in three dimensions.* A scalar field $f = f(x, y, z)$ which has continuous second partials and satisfies Laplace's equation on some solid T is said to be *harmonic* on T.

31. Show that the scalar field

$$f(x, y, z) = x^2 + 2y^2 - 3z^2 + xy + 2xz - 3yz$$

is everywhere harmonic.

32. Show that the scalar field

$$f(x, y, z) = \frac{1}{\sqrt{x^2 + y^2 + z^2}}$$

is harmonic on every solid T that excludes the origin. Up to a constant factor, f is a potential function for the gravitational field.

33. For what nonzero integers n is $f(\mathbf{r}) = r^n$ harmonic on every solid T that excludes the origin?

34. Show that if $f = f(x, y, z)$ satisfies Laplace's equation, then its gradient field is both solenoidal and irrotational.

■ 18.9 THE DIVERGENCE THEOREM

Let Ω be a Jordan region with a piecewise-smooth boundary C, and let P and Q be continuously differentiable scalar fields on an open set that contains Ω. Green's theorem allows us to express a double integral over Ω as a line integral over C:

$$\iint_{\Omega} \left(\frac{\partial Q}{\partial x} - \frac{\partial P}{\partial y}\right) dxdy = \oint_C P\,dx + Q\,dy.$$

In vector terms Green's theorem can be written:

(18.9.1)
$$\iint_{\Omega} (\nabla \cdot \mathbf{v})\,dxdy = \oint_C (\mathbf{v} \cdot \mathbf{n})\,ds.$$

Here $\mathbf{n}$ is the outer unit normal and the integral on the right is taken with respect to arc length. (Section 18.4.)

PROOF Set $\mathbf{v} = Q\,\mathbf{i} - P\,\mathbf{j}$. Then

$$\iint_{\Omega} (\nabla \cdot \mathbf{v})\,dxdy = \iint_{\Omega} \left(\frac{\partial Q}{\partial x} - \frac{\partial P}{\partial y}\right) dxdy.$$

All we have to show then is that

$$\oint_C (\mathbf{v} \cdot \mathbf{n})\,ds = \oint_C P dx + Q\,dy.$$

For C traversed counterclockwise, $\mathbf{n} = \mathbf{T} \times \mathbf{k}$ where $\mathbf{T}$ is the unit tangent vector. (Draw a figure.) Thus

$$\mathbf{v} \cdot \mathbf{n} = \mathbf{v} \cdot (\mathbf{T} \times \mathbf{k}) = (-\mathbf{v}) \cdot (\mathbf{k} \times \mathbf{T}) = (-\mathbf{v} \times \mathbf{k}) \cdot \mathbf{T}$$

↑ $\mathbf{a} \cdot (\mathbf{b} \times \mathbf{c}) = (\mathbf{a} \times \mathbf{b}) \cdot \mathbf{c}$

Since $-\mathbf{v} \times \mathbf{k} = (P\mathbf{j} - Q\mathbf{i}) \times \mathbf{k} = P\,\mathbf{i} + Q\,\mathbf{j}$, we have $\mathbf{v} \cdot \mathbf{n} = (P\,\mathbf{i} + Q\,\mathbf{j}) \cdot \mathbf{T}$.

Therefore

$$\oint_C (\mathbf{v}\cdot\mathbf{n})\,ds = \oint_C [(P\mathbf{i}+Q\mathbf{j})\cdot\mathbf{T}]\,ds \underset{(18.4.6)}{=} \oint_C (P\mathbf{i}+Q\mathbf{j})\cdot d\mathbf{r} = \oint_C P\,dx + Q\,dy. \quad \square$$

Green's theorem expressed as (18.9.1) has a higher dimensional analog that is known as the divergence theorem.[†]

THEOREM 18.9.2 THE DIVERGENCE THEOREM

Let T be a solid bounded by a closed oriented surface S which, if not smooth, is piecewise smooth. If the vector field $\mathbf{v} = \mathbf{v}(x, y, z)$ is continuously differentiable throughout T, then

$$\iiint_T (\nabla\cdot\mathbf{v})\,dx\,dy\,dz = \iint_S (\mathbf{v}\cdot\mathbf{n})\,d\sigma$$

where $\mathbf{n}$ is the outer unit normal.

PROOF We will carry out the proof under the assumption that S is smooth and that any line parallel to a coordinate axis intersects S at most twice.

Our first step is to express the outer unit normal $\mathbf{n}$ in terms of its direction cosines.

$$\mathbf{n} = \cos\alpha_1\,\mathbf{i} + \cos\alpha_2\,\mathbf{j} + \cos\alpha_3\,\mathbf{k}.$$

Then, for $\mathbf{v} = v_1\,\mathbf{i} + v_2\,\mathbf{j} + v_3\mathbf{k}$,

$$\mathbf{v}\cdot\mathbf{n} = v_1\cos\alpha_1 + v_2\cos\alpha_2 + v_3\cos\alpha_3.$$

The idea of the proof is to show that

(1) $$\iint_S v_1\cos\alpha_1\,d\sigma = \iiint_T \frac{\partial v_1}{\partial x}\,dx\,dy\,dz,$$

(2) $$\iint_S v_2\cos\alpha_2\,d\sigma = \iiint_T \frac{\partial v_2}{\partial y}\,dx\,dy\,dz,$$

(3) $$\iint_S v_3\cos\alpha_3\,d\sigma = \iiint_T \frac{\partial v_3}{\partial z}\,dx\,dy\,dz.$$

All three equations can be verified in much the same manner. We will carry out the details only for the third equation.

Let Ω_{xy} be the projection of T onto the xy-plane. (See Figure 18.9.1.) If $(x, y) \in \Omega_{xy}$, then, by assumption, the vertical line through (x, y) intersects S in at most two points, an upper point P^+ and a lower point P^-. (If the vertical line intersects S at only one point P, we set $P = P^+ = P^-$.) As (x, y) ranges over Ω_{xy}, the upper point P^+ describes a surface

$$S^+ : \quad z = f^+(x, y), \quad (x, y) \in \Omega_{xy} \qquad \text{(See the figure.)}$$

[†]This is also called Gauss's theorem after the German mathematician Carl Friedrich Gauss (1777–1855). Often referred to as "The Prince of Mathematicians," Gauss is regarded by many as one of the greatest geniuses of all time.

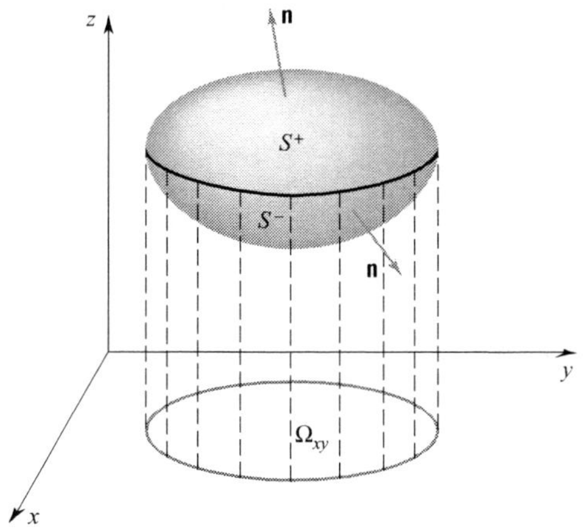

Figure 18.9.1

and the lower point describes a surface

$$S^-: \quad z = f^-(x, y), \quad (x, y) \in \Omega_{xy}.$$

By our assumptions, f^+ and f^- are continuously differentiable, $S = S^+ \cup S^-$, and the solid T is the set of all points (x, y, z) with

$$f^-(x, y) \le z \le f^+(x, y), \quad (x, y) \in \Omega_{xy}.$$

Now let λ be the angle between the positive z-axis and the upper unit normal. On S^+ the outer unit normal **n** is the upper unit normal. Thus on S^+,

$$\lambda = \alpha_3 \qquad \text{and} \qquad \cos\alpha_3 \sec\gamma = 1.$$

On S^- the outer unit normal **n** is the lower unit normal. In this case,

$$\lambda = \pi - \alpha_3 \qquad \text{and} \qquad \cos\alpha_3 \sec\gamma = -1.$$

Thus,

$$\iint_{S^+} v_3 \cos\alpha_3\, d\sigma \underset{(18.7.7)}{=} \iint_{\Omega_{xy}} v_3 \cos\alpha_3 \sec\gamma\, dxdy = \iint_{\Omega_{xy}} v_3[x, y, f^+(x, y)]\, dxdy$$

and

$$\iint_{S^-} v_3 \cos\alpha_3\, d\sigma = \iint_{\Omega_{xy}} v_3 \cos\alpha_3 \sec\gamma\, dxdy = -\iint_{\Omega_{xy}} v_3[x, y, f^-(x, y)]\, dxdy.$$

It follows that

$$\begin{aligned}
\iint_S v_3 \cos\alpha_3\, d\sigma &= \iint_{S^+} v_3 \cos\alpha_3\, d\sigma + \iint_{S^-} v_3 \cos\alpha_3\, d\sigma \\
&= \iint_{\Omega_{xy}} (v_3[x, y, f^+(x, y)] - v_3[x, y, f^-(x, y)])\, dxdy \\
&= \iint_{\Omega_{xy}} \left(\int_{f^-(xy)}^{f^+(x,y)} \frac{\partial v_3}{\partial z}(x, y, z)\, dz \right) dxdy \\
&= \iiint_T \frac{\partial v_3}{\partial z}(x, y, z)\, dxdydz.
\end{aligned}$$

This confirms (3). Equation (2) can be confirmed by projection onto the xz-plane; (1) can be confirmed by projection onto the yz-plane. ❑

Divergence as Outward Flux per Unit Volume

Choose a point P and surround it by a closed ball N_ϵ of radius ϵ. According to the divergence theorem,

$$\iiint_{N_\epsilon} (\nabla \cdot \mathbf{v})\, dxdydz = \text{flux of } \mathbf{v} \text{ out of } N_\epsilon.$$

Thus

$$(\text{average divergence of } \mathbf{v} \text{ on } N_\epsilon)\,(\text{volume of } N_\epsilon) = \text{flux of } \mathbf{v} \text{ out of } N_\epsilon$$

and

$$\text{average divergence of } \mathbf{v} \text{ on } N_\epsilon = \frac{\text{flux of } \mathbf{v} \text{ out of } N_\epsilon}{\text{volume of } N_\epsilon}.$$

Taking the limit of both sides as ϵ shrinks to 0, we have

$$\text{divergence of } \mathbf{v} \text{ at } P = \lim_{\epsilon \to 0^+} \frac{\text{flux of } \mathbf{v} \text{ out of } N_\epsilon}{\text{volume of } N_\epsilon}.$$

In this sense *divergence is outward flux per unit volume.*

Think of $\mathbf{v}$ as the velocity of a fluid. As suggested in Section 18.8, negative divergence at P signals an accumulation of fluid near P:

$$\nabla \cdot \mathbf{v} < 0 \text{ at } P \Longrightarrow \text{flux out of } N_\epsilon < 0 \Longrightarrow \text{net flow into } N_\epsilon.$$

Positive divergence at P signals a flow of liquid away from P:

$$\nabla \cdot \mathbf{v} > 0 \text{ at } P \Longrightarrow \text{flux out of } N_\epsilon > 0 \Longrightarrow \text{net flow out of } N_\epsilon.$$

Points at which the divergence is negative are called *sinks*; points at which the divergence is positive are called *sources*. If the divergence of $\mathbf{v}$ is 0 throughout, then the flow has no sinks and no sources and $\mathbf{v}$ is called *solenoidal*. (Exercises 18.8.)

Solids Bounded by Two or More Closed Surfaces

The divergence theorem, stated for solids bounded by a single closed oriented surface, can be extended to solids bounded by several closed surfaces. Suppose, for example, that we start with a solid bounded by a closed oriented surface S_1 and extract from the interior of that solid a solid bounded by a closed oriented surface S_2. The remaining solid T has a boundary S which consists of two pieces: an outer piece S_1 and an inner piece S_2. See Figure 18.9.2. The key here is to note that the *outer* normal for T points *out* of S_1 but *into* S_2. The divergence theorem can be proved for T by slicing T into two pieces T_1 and T_2 as in Figure 18.9.3 and applying the divergence theorem to each piece:

$$\iiint_{T_1} (\nabla \cdot \mathbf{v})\, dxdydz = \iint_{\text{bdry of } T_1} (\mathbf{v} \cdot \mathbf{n})\, d\sigma,$$

$$\iiint_{T_2} (\nabla \cdot \mathbf{v})\, dxdydz = \iint_{\text{bdry of } T_2} (\mathbf{v} \cdot \mathbf{n})\, d\sigma.$$

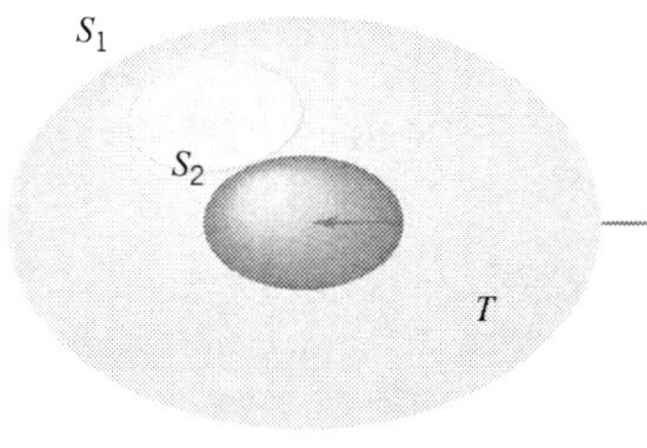

Figure 18.9.2

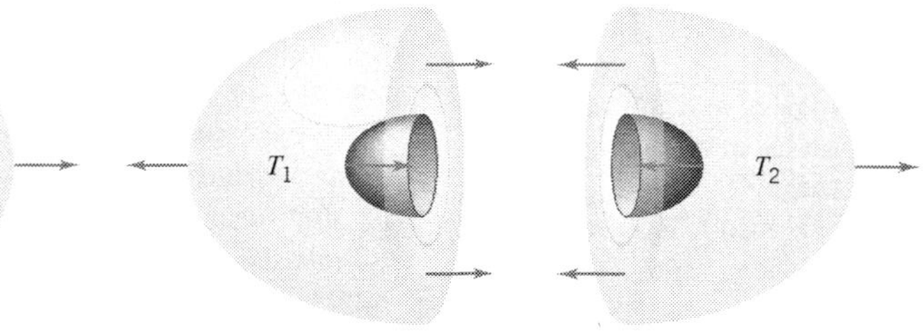

Figure 18.9.3

The triple integrals over T_1 and T_2 add up to the triple integral over T. When the surface integrals are added together, the integrals along the common cut cancel (because the normals are in opposite directions), and therefore only the integrals over S_1 and S_2 remain. Thus the surface integrals add up to the surface integral over $S = S_1 \cup S_2$ and the divergence theorem still holds:

$$\iiint_T (\nabla \cdot \mathbf{v})\, dxdydz = \iint_S (\mathbf{v} \cdot \mathbf{n})\, d\sigma.$$

EXERCISES 18.9

Exercises 1–4. Apply the divergence theorem to calculate the flux of $\mathbf{v}$ out of the unit ball $x^2 + y^2 + z^2 = 1$.

1. $\mathbf{v}(x, y, z) = x\,\mathbf{i} + y\,\mathbf{j} + z\,\mathbf{k}$.

2. $\mathbf{v}(x, y, z) = (1 - x)\,\mathbf{i} + (2 - y)\,\mathbf{j} + (3 - z)\,\mathbf{k}$.

3. $\mathbf{v}(x, y, z) = x^2\,\mathbf{i} + y^2\,\mathbf{j} + z^2\,\mathbf{k}$.

4. $\mathbf{v}(x, y, z) = (1 - x^2)\,\mathbf{i} + y^2\,\mathbf{j} + z\,\mathbf{k}$.

Exercises 5–8. Verify the divergence theorem on the unit cube $0 \le x \le 1, 0 \le y \le 1, 0 \le z \le 1$ for the given $\mathbf{v}$.

5. $\mathbf{v}(x, y, z) = x\,\mathbf{i} + y\,\mathbf{j} + z\,\mathbf{k}$.

6. $\mathbf{v}(x, y, z) = xy\,\mathbf{i} + yz\,\mathbf{j} + xz\,\mathbf{k}$.

7. $\mathbf{v}(x, y, z) = x^2\,\mathbf{i} - xz\,\mathbf{j} + z^2\,\mathbf{k}$.

8. $\mathbf{v}(x, y, z) = x\,\mathbf{i} + xy\,\mathbf{j} + xyz\,\mathbf{k}$.

Exercises 9–14. Use the divergence theorem to find the total flux out of the given solid.

9. $\mathbf{v}(x, y, z) = x\,\mathbf{i} + 2y^2\,\mathbf{j} + 3z^2\,\mathbf{k}$; $x^2 + y^2 \le 9,\ 0 \le z \le 1$.

10. $\mathbf{v}(x, y, z) = xy\,\mathbf{i} + yz\,\mathbf{j} + xz\,\mathbf{k}$; $\quad 0 \le x \le 1$, $0 \le y \le 1 - x$, $\quad 0 \le z \le 1 - x - y$.

11. $\mathbf{v}(x, y, z) = x^2\,\mathbf{i} + xy\,\mathbf{j} - 2xz\,\mathbf{k}$; $\quad 0 \le x \le 1$, $0 \le y \le 1 - x$, $\quad 0 \le z \le 1 - x - y$.

12. $\mathbf{v}(x, y, z) = (2xy + 2z)\,\mathbf{i} + (y^2 + 1)\,\mathbf{j} - (x + y)\,\mathbf{k}$; $0 \le x \le 4$, $\quad 0 \le y \le 4 - x$, $\quad 0 \le z \le 4 - x - y$.

13. $\mathbf{v}(x, y, z) = x^2\,\mathbf{i} + y^2\,\mathbf{j} + z^2\,\mathbf{k}$; the cylinder $x^2 + y^2 \le 4$, $\quad 0 \le z \le 4$, including the top and base.

14. $\mathbf{v}(x, y, z) = 2x\,\mathbf{i} + xy\,\mathbf{j} + xz\,\mathbf{k}$; the ball $x^2 + y^2 + z^2 \le 4$.

Exercises 15–16. Calculate the total flux of $\mathbf{v}(x, y, z) = 2xy\,\mathbf{i} + y^2\,\mathbf{j} + 3yz\,\mathbf{k}$ out of the given solid.

15. The ball: $x^2 + y^2 + z^2 \le a^2$.

16. The cube: $0 \le x \le a$, $\quad 0 \le y \le a$, $\quad 0 \le z \le a$.

17. What is the flux of $\mathbf{v}(x, y, z) = Ax\,\mathbf{i} + By\,\mathbf{j} + Cz\,\mathbf{k}$ out of a solid of volume V?

18. Let T be a basic solid with a piecewise-smooth boundary. Show that if f is harmonic on T (defined in Exercises 18.8), then the flux of ∇f out of T is zero.

19. Let S be a closed smooth surface with continuous unit normal $\mathbf{n} = \mathbf{n}(x, y, z)$. Show that

$$\iint_S \mathbf{n}\, d\sigma = \left(\iint_S n_1\, d\sigma\right)\mathbf{i} + \left(\iint_S n_2\, d\sigma\right)\mathbf{j} + \left(\iint_S n_3\, d\sigma\right)\mathbf{k} = \mathbf{0}.$$

20. Let T be a solid with a piecewise-smooth boundary S and let $\mathbf{n}$ be the outer unit normal.

(a) Verify the identity $\nabla \cdot (f\nabla f) = \|\nabla f\|^2 + f(\nabla^2 f)$ and show that, if f is harmonic on T, then

$$\iint_S (f f_{\mathbf{n}}')\, d\sigma = \iiint_T \|\nabla f\|^2\, dxdydz$$

where $f_{\mathbf{n}}'$ is the directional derivative $\nabla f \cdot \mathbf{n}$.

(b) Show that, if g is continuously differentiable on T, then

$$\iint_S (g f_{\mathbf{n}}')\, d\sigma = \iiint_T [(\nabla g \cdot \nabla f) + g(\nabla^2 f)]\, dxdydz.$$

21. Let T be a solid with a piecewise-smooth boundary. Show that if f and g have continuous second partials, then the flux of $\nabla f \times \nabla g$ out of T is zero.

22. Let T be a solid with a piecewise-smooth boundary S. Express the volume of T as a surface integral over S.

23. Suppose that a solid T (boundary S, outer unit normal $\mathbf{n}$) is immersed in a fluid. The fluid exerts a pressure $p = p(x, y, z)$ at each point of S, and therefore the solid T experiences a force. The total force on the solid due to the pressure distribution is given by the surface integral

$$\mathbf{F} = -\iint_S p\,\mathbf{n}\,d\sigma.$$

(The formula says that the force on the solid is the average pressure against S times the area of S.) Now choose a coordinate system with the z-axis vertical and assume that the fluid fills a region of space to the level $z = c$. The depth of a point (x, y, z) is then $c - z$ and we have $p(x, y, z) = \rho(c - z)$, where ρ is the weight density of the fluid (the weight per unit volume). Apply the divergence theorem to each component of $\mathbf{F}$ to show that $\mathbf{F} = W\,\mathbf{k}$ where W is the weight of the fluid displaced by the solid. We call this the *buoyant force* on the solid. (This shows that the object is not pushed from side to side by the pressure and verifies the *principle of Archimedes:* that the buoyant force on an object at rest in a fluid equals the weight of the fluid displaced.)

24. If $\mathbf{F}$ is a force applied at the tip of a radius vector $\mathbf{r}$, then the *torque*, or twisting strength, of $\mathbf{F}$ about the origin is given by the cross product $\boldsymbol{\tau} = \mathbf{r} \times \mathbf{F}$. From physics we learn that the total torque on the solid T of Exercise 23 is given by the formula

$$\boldsymbol{\tau}_{\text{Tot}} = -\iint_S [\mathbf{r} \times \rho(c - z)\,\mathbf{n}]\,d\sigma.$$

Use the divergence theorem to find the components of $\boldsymbol{\tau}_{\text{Tot}}$ and show that $\boldsymbol{\tau}_{\text{Tot}} = \bar{\mathbf{r}} \times \mathbf{F}$ where $\mathbf{F}$ is the buoyant force $W\,\mathbf{k}$ and $\bar{\mathbf{r}}$ is the centroid of T. (This indicates that for calculating the twisting effect of the buoyant force we can view this force as being applied at the centroid. This is very important in ship design. Imagine, for example, a totally submerged submarine. While the buoyant force acts upward through the centroid of the submarine, gravity acts downward through the center of mass. Suppose the submarine should tilt a bit to one side as depicted in the figure. If the centroid lies above the center of mass, then the buoyant force acts to restore the submarine to an upright position. If, however, the centroid lies below the center of mass, then disaster. Once the submarine has tilted a bit, the buoyant force will make it tilt further. This kind of analysis also applies to surface ships,

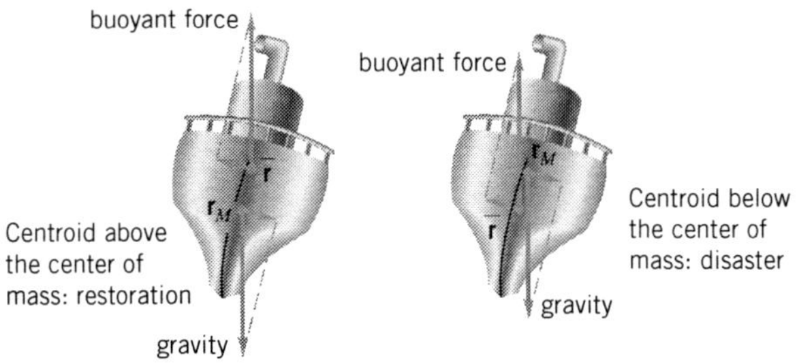

but in this case the buoyant force acts upward through *the centroid of the portion of the ship that is submerged.* This point is called the *center of flotation.* One must design and load a ship to keep the center of flotation above the center of mass. Putting a lot of heavy cargo on the deck, for instance, tends to raise the center of mass and destabilize the ship.)

■ PROJECT 18.9 Static Charges

Consider a point charge q somewhere in space. This charge creates around itself an *electric field* $\mathbf{E}$, which in turn exerts an electric force on every other nearby charge. If we center our coordinate system at q, then the electric field at the point $\mathbf{r}$ can be written

$$\mathbf{E}(\mathbf{r}) = q\frac{\mathbf{r}}{r^3}.$$

This result is found experimentally. Note that this field has the same form as a gravitational field.

Problem 1. Show that $\nabla \cdot \mathbf{E} = 0$ for all $\mathbf{r} \neq 0$.

We are interested in the flux of $\mathbf{E}$ out of a closed surface S. We assume that S does not pass through q.

Problem 2. Suppose that the charge q is outside S. Then $\mathbf{E}$ is continuously differentiable on the region T bounded by S. Use the divergence theorem to show that

$$\text{flux of } \mathbf{E} \text{ out of } S = 0.$$

If q is inside S, then the divergence theorem does not apply to T directly because $\mathbf{E}$ is not differentiable on all of T. We can circumvent this difficulty by surrounding q by a small sphere S_a of radius a and applying the divergence theorem to the region T' bounded on the outside by S and on the inside by S_a. See the figure.

Since $\mathbf{E}$ is continuously differentiable on T',

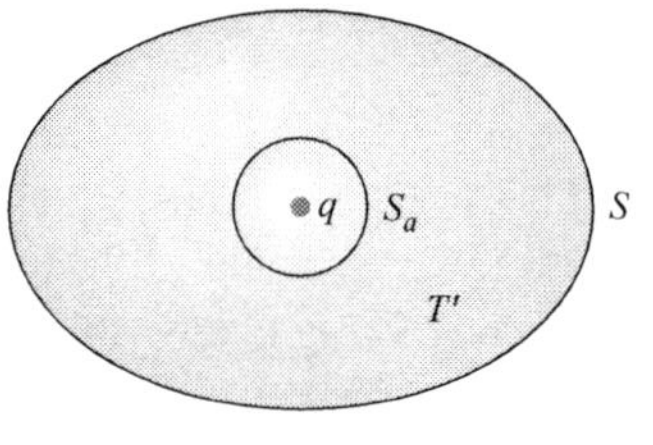

$$\iiint_T (\nabla \cdot \mathbf{E})\,dx\,dy\,dz = \text{flux of } \mathbf{E} \text{ out of } S + \text{flux of } \mathbf{E} \text{ into } S_a$$
$$= \text{flux of } \mathbf{E} \text{ out of } S - \text{flux of } \mathbf{E} \text{ out of } S_a.$$

Since $\nabla \cdot \mathbf{E} = 0$ on T', it follows that

$$\text{flux of } \mathbf{E} \text{ out of } S = \text{flux of } \mathbf{E} \text{ out of } S_a.$$

Problem 3. Show that: flux out of $S_a = 4\pi q$.

Thus, if $\mathbf{E}$ is the electric field of a point charge q and S is a closed surface that does not pass through q, then

$$\text{flux of } \mathbf{E} \text{ out of } S = \begin{cases} 0 & \text{if } q \text{ is outside } S \\ 4\pi q & \text{if } q \text{ is inside } S. \end{cases}$$

■ 18.10 STOKES'S THEOREM

We return to Green's theorem

$$\iint_{\Omega} \left(\frac{\partial Q}{\partial x} - \frac{\partial P}{\partial y} \right) dx dy = \oint_C P\,dx + Q\,dy.$$

Setting $\mathbf{v} = P\,\mathbf{i} + Q\,\mathbf{j} + R\,\mathbf{k}$, we have

$$(\nabla \times \mathbf{v}) \cdot \mathbf{k} = \begin{vmatrix} \mathbf{i} & \mathbf{j} & \mathbf{k} \\ \dfrac{\partial}{\partial x} & \dfrac{\partial}{\partial y} & \dfrac{\partial}{\partial z} \\ P & Q & R \end{vmatrix} \cdot \mathbf{k} = \frac{\partial Q}{\partial x} - \frac{\partial P}{\partial y}.$$

Thus in terms of $\mathbf{v}$, Green's theorem can be written

$$\iint_{\Omega} [(\nabla \times \mathbf{v}) \cdot \mathbf{k}]\, dx dy = \oint_C \mathbf{v}(\mathbf{r}) \cdot \mathbf{dr}.$$

Since any plane can be coordinatized as the xy-plane, this result can be phrased as follows: Let S be a flat surface in space bounded by a Jordan curve C. If $\mathbf{v}$ is continuously differentiable on S, then

$$\iint_S [(\nabla \times \mathbf{v}) \cdot \mathbf{n}]\, d\sigma = \oint_C \mathbf{v}(\mathbf{r}) \cdot \mathbf{dr}.$$

where $\mathbf{n}$ is a unit normal for S and the line integral is taken in the *positive sense*, meaning in the direction of the unit tangent $\mathbf{T}$ for which $\mathbf{T} \times \mathbf{n}$ points away from the surface. See Figure 18.10.1. (An observer marching along C with the same orientation as $\mathbf{n}$ keeps the surface to his left.) The symbol $\oint_C$ denotes this line integral.

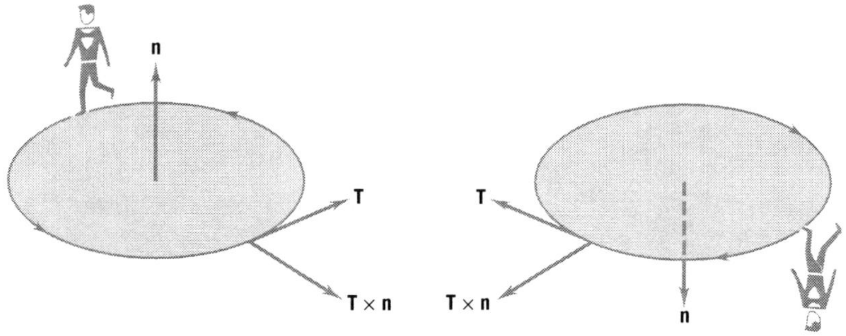

Figure 18.10.1

Figure 18.10.2 shows a *polyhedral surface* S bounded by a closed polygonal path C. The surface S consists of a finite number of flat faces $S_1, \ldots, S_n$ with polygonal boundaries $C_1, \ldots, C_n$ and unit normals $\mathbf{n}_1, \ldots, \mathbf{n}_n$. We choose these unit normals in a consistent manner; that is, they emanate from the same side of the surface. Now let $\mathbf{n} = \mathbf{n}(x, y, z)$ be a vector function of norm 1 which is $\mathbf{n}_1$ on S_1, $\mathbf{n}_2$ on S_2, $\mathbf{n}_3$ on S_3, etc. It is immaterial how $\mathbf{n}$ is defined on the line segments that join the different faces. Suppose now that $\mathbf{v} = \mathbf{v}(x, y, z)$ is a vector function continuously differentiable on an open set that contains S. Then

$$\iint_S [(\nabla \times \mathbf{v}) \cdot \mathbf{n}]\, d\sigma = \sum_{i=1}^{n} \iint_{S_i} [(\nabla \times \mathbf{v}) \cdot \mathbf{n}]\, d\sigma = \sum_{i=1}^{n} \oint_{C_i} \mathbf{v}(\mathbf{r}) \cdot \mathbf{dr},$$

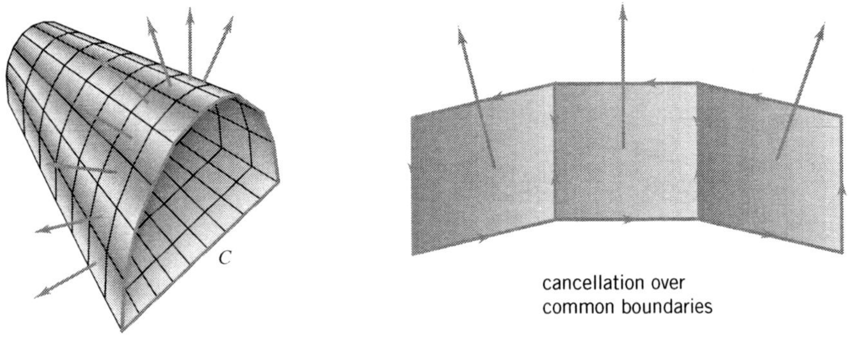

Figure 18.10.2

the integral over C_i being taken in the positive sense with respect to $\mathbf{n}_i$. Now when we add these line integrals, we find that all the line segments that make up the C_i but are not part of C are traversed twice and in opposite directions. (See the figure.) Thus these line segments contribute nothing to the sum of the line integrals and we are left with the integral around C. It follows that for a polyhedral surface S with boundary C

$$\iint_S [(\nabla \times \mathbf{v}) \cdot \mathbf{n}]\, d\sigma = \oint_C \mathbf{v}(\mathbf{r}) \cdot \mathbf{dr}.$$

This result can be extended to smooth oriented surfaces with smooth bounding curves (see Figure 18.10.3) by approximating these configurations by polyhedral configurations of the type considered and using a limit process. In an admittedly informal way we have arrived at Stokes's theorem.

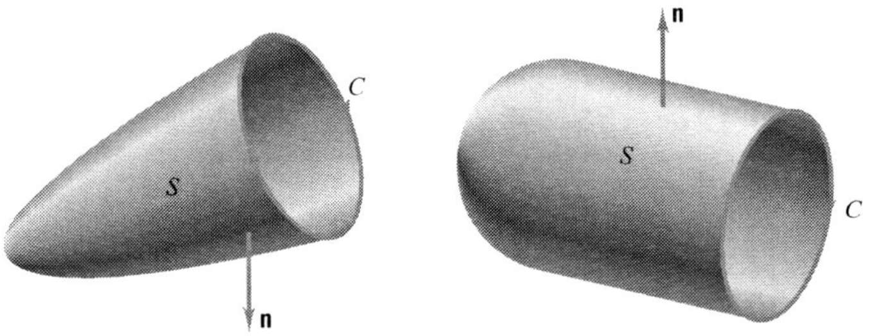

Figure 18.10.3

THEOREM 18.10.1 STOKES'S THEOREM†

Let S be a smooth oriented surface with a smooth bounding curve C. If $\mathbf{v} = \mathbf{v}(x, y, z)$ is a continuously differentiable vector field on an open set that contains S, then

$$\iint_S [(\nabla \times \mathbf{v}) \cdot \mathbf{n}]\, d\sigma = \oint_C \mathbf{v}(\mathbf{r}) \cdot \mathbf{dr}$$

where $\mathbf{n} = \mathbf{n}(x, y, z)$ is a unit normal that varies continuously on S and the line integral is taken in the positive sense with respect to $\mathbf{n}$.

†The result was announced publicly for the first time by George Gabriel Stokes (1819–1903), an Irish mathematician and physicist who, like Green, was a Cambridge professor.

Example 1 Verify Stokes's theorem for

$$\mathbf{v} = -3y\,\mathbf{i} + 3x\,\mathbf{j} + z^4\,\mathbf{k},$$

taking S as the portion of the ellipsoid $2x^2 + 2y^2 + z^2 = 1$ that lies above the plane $z = 1/\sqrt{2}$. (Figure 18.10.4.)

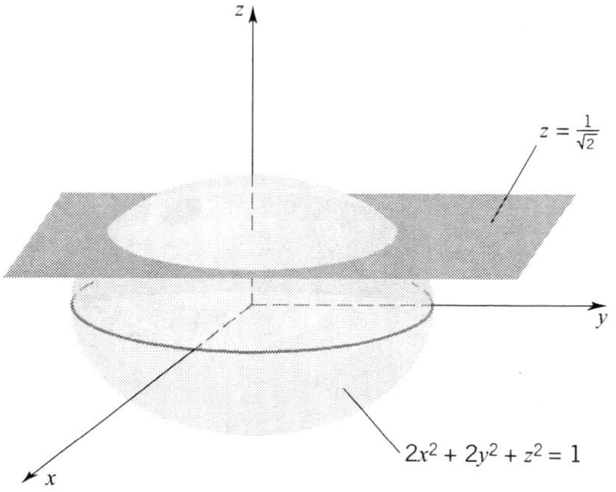

Figure 18.10.4

SOLUTION A little algebra shows that S is the graph of the function

$$f(x, y) = \sqrt{1 - 2(x^2 + y^2)}$$

with (x, y) restricted to the disk $\Omega : x^2 + y^2 \le \frac{1}{4}$.

$$\nabla \times \mathbf{v} = \begin{vmatrix} \mathbf{i} & \mathbf{j} & \mathbf{k} \\ \dfrac{\partial}{\partial x} & \dfrac{\partial}{\partial y} & \dfrac{\partial}{\partial z} \\ -3y & 3x & z^4 \end{vmatrix} = \left[\frac{\partial}{\partial x}(3x) + \frac{\partial}{\partial y}(3y)\right]\mathbf{k} = 6\,\mathbf{k}.$$

Taking $\mathbf{n}$ as the upper unit normal, we have

$$\iint_S [(\nabla \times \mathbf{v}) \cdot \mathbf{n}]\, d\sigma = \iint_S (6\,\mathbf{k} \cdot \mathbf{n})\, d\sigma$$

$$= \iint_\Omega (-(0)f_x - (0)f_y + 6)\, dx dy$$

(18.7.9)

$$= \iint_\Omega 6\, dx dy = 6\,(\text{area of } \Omega) = 6(\tfrac{1}{4}\pi) = \tfrac{3}{2}\pi.$$

The bounding curve C is the set of all (x, y, z) with $x^2 + y^2 = \frac{1}{4}$ and $z = 1/\sqrt{2}$. We can parametrize C by setting

$$\mathbf{r}(u) = \tfrac{1}{2}\cos u\,\mathbf{i} + \tfrac{1}{2}\sin u\,\mathbf{j} + \frac{1}{\sqrt{2}}\mathbf{k}, \qquad u \in [0, 2\pi].$$

Since $\mathbf{n}$ is the upper unit normal, this parametrization gives C in the positive sense.

Thus

$$\oint_C \mathbf{v}(\mathbf{r})\cdot d\mathbf{r} = \int_0^{2\pi} (-\tfrac{3}{2}\sin u\,\mathbf{i} + \tfrac{3}{2}\cos u\,\mathbf{j} + \tfrac{1}{4}\mathbf{k})\cdot(-\tfrac{1}{2}\sin u\,\mathbf{i} + \tfrac{1}{2}\cos u\,\mathbf{j})\,du$$

$$= \int_0^{2\pi} (\tfrac{3}{4}\sin^2 u + \tfrac{3}{4}\cos^2 u)\,du = \int_0^{2\pi} \tfrac{3}{4}\,du = \tfrac{3}{2}\pi.$$

This is the value we obtained for the surface integral. ❑

Example 2 Verify Stokes's theorem for

$$\mathbf{v} = z^2\,\mathbf{i} - 2x\,\mathbf{j} + y^3\,\mathbf{k},$$

taking S as the upper half of the unit sphere $x^2 + y^2 + z^2 = 1$.

SOLUTION We use the upper unit normal $\mathbf{n} = x\,\mathbf{i} + y\,\mathbf{j} + z\,\mathbf{k}$:

$$\nabla \times \mathbf{v} = \begin{vmatrix} \mathbf{i} & \mathbf{j} & \mathbf{k} \\ \dfrac{\partial}{\partial x} & \dfrac{\partial}{\partial y} & \dfrac{\partial}{\partial z} \\ z^2 & -2x & y^3 \end{vmatrix} = 3y^2\,\mathbf{i} + 2z\,\mathbf{j} - 2\,\mathbf{k}.$$

Therefore

$$\iint_S [(\nabla\times\mathbf{v})\cdot\mathbf{n}]\,d\sigma = \iint_S [(3y^2\,\mathbf{i} + 2z\,\mathbf{j} - 2\,\mathbf{k})\cdot(x\,\mathbf{i} + y\,\mathbf{j} + z\,\mathbf{k})]\,d\sigma$$

$$= \iint_S (3xy^2 + 2yz - 2z)\,d\sigma$$

$$= \iint_S 3xy^2\,d\sigma + \iint_S 2yz\,d\sigma - \iint_S 2z\,d\sigma.$$

The first integral is zero because S is symmetric about the yz-plane and the integrand is odd with respect to x. The second integral is zero because S is symmetric about the xz-plane and the integrand is odd with respect to y. Thus

$$\iint_S [(\nabla\times\mathbf{v})\cdot\mathbf{n}]\,d\sigma = -\iint_S 2z\,d\sigma = -2\bar{z}(\text{area of } S) = -2(\tfrac{1}{2})2\pi = -2\pi.$$

Exercise 17, Section 18.7 ↑

This is also the value of the integral along the bounding base circle taken in the positive sense: $\mathbf{r}(u) = \cos u\,\mathbf{i} + \sin u\,\mathbf{j}$, $u \in [0, 2\pi]$, and

$$\oint_C \mathbf{v}(\mathbf{r})\cdot d\mathbf{r} = \oint_C z^2 dx - 2x\,dy = -2\oint_C x\,dy$$

$$= -2\int_0^{2\pi} \cos^2 u\,du = -2\pi. \quad ❑$$

Earlier you saw that the curl of a gradient is zero. Using Stokes's theorem, we can prove a partial converse.

(18.10.2) If a vector field $\mathbf{v} = \mathbf{v}(x, y, z)$ is continuously differentiable on an open convex† set U and $\nabla\times\mathbf{v} = \mathbf{0}$ on all of U, then $\mathbf{v}$ is the gradient of some scalar field ϕ defined on U.

† *A* set U is said to be *convex* 0 if, for each pair of points $p, q \in U$, the line segment $\overline{pq}$ lies entirely in U.

PROOF Choose a point **a** in U, and for each point x in U, define

$$\phi(\mathbf{x}) = \int_{\mathbf{a}}^{\mathbf{x}} \mathbf{v}(\mathbf{r}) \cdot \mathbf{dr}.$$

(This is the line integral from **a** to **x** taken along the line segment that joins these two points. We know that this line segment lies in U because U is convex.)

Since U is open, $\mathbf{x}+\mathbf{h}$ is in U for all **h** sufficiently small. Assume then that **h** is sufficiently small for $\mathbf{x}+\mathbf{h}$ to be in U. Since U is convex, the triangular region with vertices at **a**, **x**, $\mathbf{x}+\mathbf{h}$ lies in U. (See Figure 18.10.5.) Since $\nabla \times \mathbf{v} = \mathbf{0}$ on U, we can conclude from Stokes's theorem that

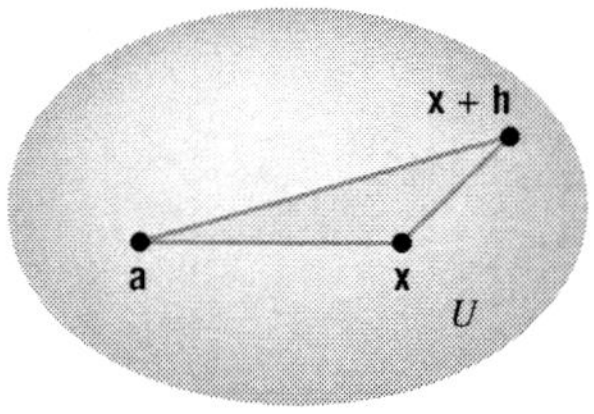

Figure 18.10.5

$$\int_{\mathbf{a}}^{\mathbf{x}} \mathbf{v}(\mathbf{r}) \cdot \mathbf{dr} + \int_{\mathbf{x}}^{\mathbf{x}+\mathbf{h}} \mathbf{v}(\mathbf{r}) \cdot \mathbf{dr} + \int_{\mathbf{x}+\mathbf{h}}^{\mathbf{a}} \mathbf{v}(\mathbf{r}) \cdot \mathbf{dr} = 0.$$

Therefore

$$\int_{\mathbf{x}}^{\mathbf{x}+\mathbf{h}} \mathbf{v}(\mathbf{r}) \cdot \mathbf{dr} = -\int_{\mathbf{x}+\mathbf{h}}^{\mathbf{a}} \mathbf{v}(\mathbf{r}) \cdot \mathbf{dr} - \int_{\mathbf{a}}^{\mathbf{x}} \mathbf{v}(\mathbf{r}) \cdot \mathbf{dr} = \int_{\mathbf{a}}^{\mathbf{x}+\mathbf{h}} \mathbf{v}(\mathbf{r}) \cdot \mathbf{dr} - \int_{\mathbf{a}}^{\mathbf{x}} \mathbf{v}(\mathbf{r}) \cdot \mathbf{dr}.$$

By our definition of ϕ, we have

$$\phi(\mathbf{x}+\mathbf{h}) - \phi(\mathbf{x}) = \int_{\mathbf{x}}^{\mathbf{x}+\mathbf{h}} \mathbf{v}(\mathbf{r}) \cdot \mathbf{dr}.$$

We can parametrize the line segment from **x** to $\mathbf{x}+\mathbf{h}$ by $\mathbf{r}(u) = \mathbf{x} + u\,\mathbf{h}$ with $u \in [0, 1]$. Therefore

$$\begin{aligned} \phi(\mathbf{x}+\mathbf{h}) - \phi(\mathbf{x}) &= \int_0^1 [\mathbf{v}(\mathbf{r}(u)) \cdot \mathbf{r}'(u)]\, du \\ &= \int_0^1 [\mathbf{v}(\mathbf{r}(u)) \cdot \mathbf{h}]\, du \\ \text{Theorem 5.9.1} \longrightarrow &= \mathbf{v}(\mathbf{r}(u_0)) \cdot \mathbf{h} \qquad \text{for some } u_0 \text{ in } [0, 1] \\ &= \mathbf{v}(\mathbf{x}+u_0\mathbf{h}) \cdot \mathbf{h} = \mathbf{v}(\mathbf{x}) \cdot \mathbf{h} + [\mathbf{v}(\mathbf{x}+u_0\mathbf{h}) - \mathbf{v}(\mathbf{x})] \cdot \mathbf{h}. \end{aligned}$$

The fact that $\mathbf{v} = \nabla\phi$ follows from observing that $[\mathbf{v}(\mathbf{x}+u_0\mathbf{h}) - \mathbf{v}(\mathbf{x})] \cdot \mathbf{h}$ is $o(\mathbf{h})$:

$$\begin{aligned} \frac{|[\mathbf{v}(\mathbf{x}+u_0\mathbf{h}) - \mathbf{v}(\mathbf{x})] \cdot \mathbf{h}|}{\|\mathbf{h}\|} &\le \frac{\|\mathbf{v}(\mathbf{x}+u_0\mathbf{h}) - \mathbf{v}(\mathbf{x})\|\;\|\mathbf{h}\|}{\|\mathbf{h}\|} \\ &= \|\mathbf{v}(\mathbf{x}+u_0\mathbf{h}) - \mathbf{v}(\mathbf{x})\| \to 0 \end{aligned}$$

as $\mathbf{h} \to \mathbf{0}$. ❑

The Normal Component of $\nabla \times \mathbf{v}$ as Circulation per Unit Area; Irrotational Flow

Interpret $\mathbf{v} = \mathbf{v}(x, y, z)$ as the velocity of a fluid flow. In Section 18.8 we stated that $\nabla \times \mathbf{v}$ measures the rotational tendency of the fluid. Now we can be more precise.

Take a point P within the flow and choose a unit vector **n**. Let D_ϵ be the ϵ-disk that is centered at P and is perpendicular to **n**. Let C_ϵ be the circular boundary of D_ϵ directed in the positive sense with respect to **n**. (See Figure 18.10.6.) By Stokes's theorem,

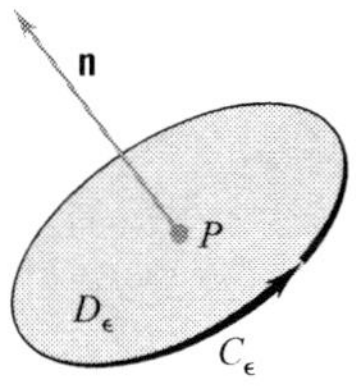

Figure 18.10.6

$$\iint_{D_\epsilon} [(\nabla \times \mathbf{n}) \cdot n]\, d\sigma = \oint_{C_\epsilon} \mathbf{v}(\mathbf{r}) \cdot \mathbf{dr}.$$

The line integral on the right is called *the circulation* of **v** around C_ϵ. Thus we can say that

$$\begin{pmatrix}\text{the average } \mathbf{n}\text{-component of} \\ \nabla \times \mathbf{v} \text{ on } D_\epsilon\end{pmatrix} (\text{the area of } D_\epsilon) = \text{the circulation of } \mathbf{v} \text{ around } C_\epsilon.$$

It follows that

$$\text{the average } \mathbf{n}\text{-component of } \nabla \times \mathbf{v} \text{ on } D_\epsilon = \frac{\text{the circulation of } \mathbf{v} \text{ around } C_\epsilon}{\text{the area of } D_\epsilon}.$$

Taking the limit as ϵ shrinks to 0, you can see that

$$\text{the } \mathbf{n}\text{-component of } \nabla \times \mathbf{v} \text{ at } P = \lim_{\epsilon \to 0^+} \frac{\text{the circulation of } \mathbf{v} \text{ around } C_\epsilon}{\text{the area of } D_\epsilon}.$$

At each point P the component of $\nabla \times \mathbf{v}$ *in any direction* **n** *is the circulation of* **v** *per unit area in the plane normal to* **n**. *If* $\nabla \times \mathbf{v} = 0$ *identically, the fluid has no rotational tendency, and the flow is called irrotational.*

Remark Flux and circulation apply to vector fields where no material substance is flowing. Electromagnetic phenomena result from the action and interaction of two vector fields: the electric field E and the magnetic field B. The four fundamental laws of electromagnetism can be stated as equations that give the flux and circulation of these two fields. ❑

EXERCISES 18.10

Exercises 1–4. Let S be the upper half of the unit sphere $x^2 + y^2 + z^2 = 1$ and take **n** as the upper unit normal. Find

$$\iint_S [(\nabla \times \mathbf{v}) \cdot \mathbf{n}]\, d\sigma$$

(a) by direct calculation; (b) by Stokes's theorem.

1. $\mathbf{v}(x, y, z) = x\,\mathbf{i} + y\,\mathbf{j} = z\,\mathbf{k}$.

2. $\mathbf{v}(x, y, z) = y\,\mathbf{i} - x\,\mathbf{j} + z\,\mathbf{k}$.

3. $\mathbf{v}(x, y, z) = z^2\,\mathbf{i} + 2x\,\mathbf{j} - y^3\,\mathbf{k}$.

4. $\mathbf{v}(x, y, z) = 6xz\,\mathbf{i} - x^2\,\mathbf{j} - 3y^2\,\mathbf{k}$.

Exercises 5–7. Let S be the triangular surface with vertices $(2, 0, 0)$, $(0, 2, 0)$, $(0, 0, 2)$ and take **n** as the upper unit normal. Find

$$\iint_S [(\nabla \times \mathbf{v}) \cdot \mathbf{n}]\, d\sigma$$

(a) by direct calculation; (b) by Stokes's theorem.

5. $\mathbf{v}(x, y, z) = 2z\,\mathbf{i} - y\,\mathbf{j} + x\,\mathbf{k}$.

6. $\mathbf{v}(x, y, z) = (x^2 + y^2)\,\mathbf{i} + y^2\,\mathbf{j} + (x^2 + z^2)\,\mathbf{k}$.

7. $\mathbf{v}(x, y, z) = x^4\,\mathbf{i} + xy\,\mathbf{j} + z^4\,\mathbf{k}$.

8. Show that if $\mathbf{v} = \mathbf{v}(x, y, z)$ is continuously differentiable everywhere and its curl is identically zero, then

$$\int_C \mathbf{v}(\mathbf{r}) \cdot d\mathbf{r} = 0 \text{ for every smooth closed curve } C.$$

9. Let $\mathbf{v} = y\,\mathbf{i} + z\,\mathbf{j} + x^2y^2\,\mathbf{k}$ and let S be the surface $z = x^2 + y^2$ from $z = 0$ to $z = 4$. Calculate the flux of $\nabla \times \mathbf{v}$ in the direction of the lower unit normal **n**.

10. Let $\mathbf{v} = \frac{1}{2}y\,\mathbf{i} + 2xz\,\mathbf{j} - 3x\,\mathbf{k}$ and let S be the surface $y = 1 - (x^2 + z^2)$ from $y = -8$ to $y = 1$. Calculate the flux of $\nabla \times \mathbf{v}$ in the direction of the unit normal **n** with positive **j**-component.

11. Let $\mathbf{v} = 2x\,\mathbf{i} + 2y\,\mathbf{j} + x^2y^2z^2\,\mathbf{k}$ and let S be the lower half of the ellipsoid.

$$\frac{x^2}{4} + \frac{y^2}{9} + \frac{z^2}{27} = 1.$$

Calculate the flux of $\nabla \times \mathbf{v}$ in the direction of the upper unit normal **n**.

12. Let S be a smooth closed surface and let $\mathbf{v} = \mathbf{v}(x, y, z)$ be a vector field with second partials continuous on an open convex set that contains S. Show that

$$\iint_S [(\nabla \times \mathbf{v}) \cdot \mathbf{n}]\, d\sigma = 0$$

where $\mathbf{n} = \mathbf{n}(x, y, z)$ is the outer unit normal.

13. The upper half of the ellipsoid $\frac{1}{2}x^2 + \frac{1}{2}y^2 + z^2 = 1$ intersects the cylinder $x^2 + y^2 - y = 0$ in a curve C. Calculate the circulation of $\mathbf{v} = y^3\,\mathbf{i} + (xy + 3xy^2)\,\mathbf{j} + z^4\,\mathbf{k}$ around C by using Stokes's theorem.

14. The sphere $x^2 + y^2 + z^2 = a^2$ intersects the plane $x + 2y + z = 0$ in a curve C. Calculate the circulation of $\mathbf{v} = 2y\,\mathbf{i} - z\,\mathbf{j} + 2x\,\mathbf{k}$ about C by using Stokes's theorem.

15. The paraboloid $z = x^2 + y^2$ intersects the plane $z = y$ in a curve C. Calculate the circulation of $\mathbf{v} = 2z\,\mathbf{i} + x\,\mathbf{j} + y\,\mathbf{k}$ about C using Stokes's theorem.

16. The cylinder $x^2 + y^2 = b^2$ intersects the plane $y + z = a^2$ in a curve C. Assume $a^2 \geq b > 0$. Calculate the circulation of $\mathbf{v} = xy\,\mathbf{i} + yz\,\mathbf{j} + xz\,\mathbf{k}$ about C using Stokes's theorem.

17. Let S be a smooth oriented surface with a smooth bounding curve C and let $\mathbf{a}$ be a fixed vector. Show that

$$\iint_S (2\mathbf{a} \cdot \mathbf{n})\, d\sigma = \oint_C (\mathbf{a} \times \mathbf{r}) \cdot \mathbf{dr}$$

where $\mathbf{n} = \mathbf{n}(x, y, z)$ is a unit normal vector that varies continuously over S and the line integral is taken in the positive sense with respect to $\mathbf{n}$.

18. Let S be a smooth oriented surface with smooth bounding curve C. Show that, if ϕ and ψ are sufficiently differentiable scalar fields, then

$$\iint_S [(\nabla\phi \times \nabla\psi) \cdot \mathbf{n}]\, d\sigma = \oint_C (\phi\nabla\psi) \cdot \mathbf{dr}$$

where $\mathbf{n} = \mathbf{n}(x, y, z)$ is a unit normal that varies continuously on S and the line integral is taken in the positive sense with respect to $\mathbf{n}$.

19. Let S be a smooth oriented surface with a smooth plane bounding curve C and let $\mathbf{v} = \mathbf{v}(x, y, z)$ be a vector field with second partials continuous on an open convex set that contains S. If S does not cross the plane of C, then Stokes's theorem for S follows readily from the divergence theorem and Green's theorem. Carry out the argument.

20. Our derivation of Stokes's theorem was admittedly nonrigorous. The following version (18.10.3) of Stokes's theorem lends itself more readily to rigorous proof.
Give a detailed proof of the theorem. HINT: Set $\mathbf{v} = v_1\,\mathbf{i} + v_2\,\mathbf{j} + v_3\,\mathbf{k}$. Then

$$\iint_S [(\nabla \times \mathbf{v}) \cdot \mathbf{n}]\, d\sigma = \iint_S [(\nabla \times v_1\,\mathbf{i}) \cdot \mathbf{n}]\, d\sigma$$
$$+ \iint_S [(\nabla \times v_2\,\mathbf{j}) \cdot n]\, d\sigma + \iint_S [(\nabla \times v_3\,\mathbf{k}) \cdot \mathbf{n}]\, d\sigma$$

and

$$\oint_C \mathbf{v(r)} \cdot \mathbf{dr} = \int_C v_1\, dx + \int_C v_2\, dy + \int_C v_3\, dz.$$

Show that

$$\iint_S [(\nabla \times v_1\,\mathbf{i}) \cdot \mathbf{n}]\, d\sigma = \int_C v_1\, dx$$

by showing that both integrals can be written

$$\iint_\Gamma \left[\frac{\partial v_1}{\partial u}\frac{\partial x}{\partial v} - \frac{\partial v_1}{\partial v}\frac{\partial x}{\partial u}\right] dudv.$$

A similar argument (no need to carry it out) equates the integrals for v_2 and v_3 and proves the theorem.

THEOREM 18.10.3

Let Γ be a Jordan region in the uv-plane with a piecewise-smooth boundary, C_Γ given in a counterclockwise sense by a pair of functions $u = u(t)$, $v = v(t)$ with $t \in [a, b]$. Let $\mathbf{R}(u, v) = x(u, v)\,\mathbf{i} + y(u, v)\,\mathbf{j} + z(u, v)\,\mathbf{k}$ be a vector function with continuous second partials on Γ. Assume that $\mathbf{R}$ is one-to-one on Γ and that the fundamental vector product $\mathbf{N} = \mathbf{R}'_u \times \mathbf{R}'_v$, is never zero. The surface S: $\mathbf{R} = \mathbf{R}(u, v)$, $(u, v) \in \Gamma$ is a smooth oriented surface bounded by the oriented space curve $C : \mathbf{r}(t) = \mathbf{R}(u(t), v(t))$, $t \in [a, b]$. If $\mathbf{v} = \mathbf{v}(x, y, z)$ is a vector field continuously differentiable on S, then

$$\iint_S [(\nabla \times \mathbf{v}) \cdot \mathbf{n}]\, d\sigma = \oint_C \mathbf{v(r)} \cdot \mathbf{dr}$$

where $\mathbf{n}$ is the unit normal in the direction of the fundamental vector product.

■ CHAPTER 18. REVIEW EXERCISES

1. Integrate $\mathbf{h}(x, y) = x^2y\,\mathbf{i} - xy\,\mathbf{j}$ over the indicated path:
(a) the line segment from (0,0) to (1,1).
(b) $\mathbf{r}(u) = u^2\,\mathbf{i} + u^3\,\mathbf{j}$, $0 \leq u \leq 1$.

2. Integrate $\mathbf{h}(x, y) = x^3\,\mathbf{i} + y^3\,\mathbf{j}$ over the indicated path:
(a) $\mathbf{r}(u) = \cos u\,\mathbf{i} + \sin u\,\mathbf{j}$, $\quad 0 \leq u \leq \pi/2$.
(b) $\mathbf{r}(u) = \cos^3 u\,\mathbf{i} + \sin^3 u\,\mathbf{j}$, $\quad 0 \leq u \leq \pi/2$.

3. Integrate $\mathbf{h}(x, y) = (2xy^2 + x)\,\mathbf{i} + (2x^2y - 1)\,\mathbf{j}$ over the indicated path:
(a) the line segment from $(-1, 2)$ to (2,4).
(b) the polygonal path from $(-1, 2)$ to (0,0) to (2,4).
(c) the line segment from $(-1, 2)$ to (0,0), followed by the parabolic path $y = x^2$ from (0,0) to (2,4).

4. Integrate $\mathbf{h}(x, y) = \dfrac{-y}{x^2 + y^2}\,\mathbf{i} + \dfrac{x}{x^2 + y^2}\,\mathbf{j}$ over the indicated path:

(a) the arc of the semicircle $y = \sqrt{4 - x^2}$ from (2,0) to $(-\sqrt{2}, \sqrt{2})$.

(b) the line segment from (2, 0) to $(-\sqrt{2}, \sqrt{2})$.

(c) the polygonal path that connects $(2, 0), (2, \sqrt{2}), (-\sqrt{2}, \sqrt{2})$ in that order.

5. Integrate $\mathbf{h}(x, y, z) = \sin y\,\mathbf{i} + xe^{xy}\,\mathbf{j} + \sin z\,\mathbf{k}$ over the curve

$$\mathbf{r}(u) = u^2\,\mathbf{i} + u\,\mathbf{j} + u^3\,\mathbf{k},\ 0 \le u \le 3.$$

6. Integrate $\mathbf{h}(x, y, z) = x^2\,\mathbf{i} + xy\,\mathbf{j} + z^2\,\mathbf{k}$ over the curve

$$\mathbf{r}(u) = \cos u\,\mathbf{i} + \sin u\,\mathbf{j} + u^2\,\mathbf{k},\ 0 \le u \le \pi/2.$$

7. An object moves along the twisted cubic $\mathbf{r}(u) = u\,\mathbf{i} + u^2\,\mathbf{j} + u^3\,\mathbf{k}$ from $(-1, 1, -1)$ to (2,4,8). One of the forces acting on the object is $\mathbf{F}(x, y, z) = xy\,\mathbf{i} + yz\,\mathbf{j} + xz\,\mathbf{k}$. Calculate the work done by $\mathbf{F}$.

8. An object moves along the cycloid $\mathbf{r}(u) = (u - \sin u)\,\mathbf{i} + (1 - \cos u)\,\mathbf{j}$ from (0,0) to $(2\pi, 0)$. One of the forces acting on the object is $\mathbf{F}(x, y) = x\,\mathbf{i} + (y - 2)\,\mathbf{j}$. Calculate the work done by $\mathbf{F}$.

9. The force exerted by a charged particle at the origin on a charged particle at a point (x, y, z) can be written

$$\mathbf{F}(x, y, z) = C\frac{(x\,\mathbf{i} + y\,\mathbf{j} + z\,\mathbf{k})}{\sqrt{x^2 + y^2 + z^2}}, \qquad C \text{ a constant.}$$

Find the work done by $\mathbf{F}$ applied to a particle that moves in a straight line from (1,0,0) to (3,0,4).

10. An object moves through a force field $\mathbf{F}$ in such a way that the velocity vector at each point (x, y, z) is orthogonal to $\mathbf{F}(x, y, z)$. Show that the work done by $\mathbf{F}$ is 0.

Exercises 11–13. Verify that $\mathbf{h}$ is a gradient. Then evaluate the line integral of $\mathbf{h}$ over the indicated curve C in two ways: (a) by carrying out the integration; (b) by applying the fundamental theorem for line integrals.

11. $\mathbf{h}(x, y) = (ye^{xy} + 2x)\,\mathbf{i} + (xe^{xy} - 2y)\,\mathbf{j}$;
$C: \mathbf{r}(u) = u\,\mathbf{i} + u^2\,\mathbf{j},\ 0 \le u \le 2.$

12. $\mathbf{h}(x, y) = (2xy^2 + 2y)\,\mathbf{i} + (2x^2y + 2x)\,\mathbf{j}$;
$C:\ \mathbf{r}(u) = 3u\,\mathbf{i} + (1 + 4u)\,\mathbf{j},\ 0 \le u \le 1.$

13. $\mathbf{h}(x, y, z) = 4x^3y^3z^2\,\mathbf{i} + 3x^4y^2z^2\,\mathbf{j} + 2x^4y^3z\,\mathbf{k}$.
$C:\ \mathbf{r}(u) = u\,\mathbf{i} + u^2\,\mathbf{j} + u^3\,\mathbf{k},\ 0 \le u \le 1.$

14. Evaluate $\int_C y^2dx + (x^2 - xy)\,dy$ where C is the path given from (0, 0) to (2, 8):

(a) the straight-line path.

(b) the polygonal path (0,0) to (2, 0) to (2, 8).

(c) the cubic path $y = x^3$.

15. Evaluate $\int_C 2xy^{1/2}\,dx + yx^{1/2}\,dy$ where C is the path given from (1, 0) to (0, 1):

(a) the straight-line path.

(b) the polygonal path (1, 0) (1, 1), (0, 1).

(c) the quarter-circle $y = \sqrt{1 - x^2}$.

16. Evaluate $\int_C z\,dx + x\,dy + y\,dz$ where C is the circular helix $\mathbf{r}(u) = a\cos u\,\mathbf{i} + a\sin u\,\mathbf{j} + u\,\mathbf{k}$, from $u = 0$ to $u = 2\pi$.

17. Evaluate $\int_C ye^{xy}dx + \cos x\ dy + (xy/z)\,dz$ where C is the twisted cubic $\mathbf{r}(u) = u\,\mathbf{i} + u^2\,\mathbf{j} + u^3\,\mathbf{k}$, from $u = 0$ to $u = 2$.

18. A wire in the shape of the semicircle

$$\mathbf{r}(u) = \cos u\,\mathbf{i} + \sin u\,\mathbf{j}, \qquad u \in [0, \pi]$$

has constant mass density k.

(a) Find the total mass of the wire and locate the center of mass.

(b) Find the moment of inertia of the wire about the y-axis.

Exercises 19–20. Evaluate the line integral (a) directly; (b) by applying Green's theorem.

19. $\oint_C xy^2\,dx - x^2y\,dy$ where C is the boundary of the region that lies between the curves $y = x^2$ and $y^2 = x$.

20. $\oint_C (x^2 + y^2)\,dx + (x^2 - y^2)\,dy$ where C is the unit circle $x^2 + y^2 = 1$.

Exercises 21–26. Evaluate the line integral using Green's theorem.

21. $\oint_C (x - 2y^2)\,dx + 2xy\,dy$ where C is the rectangle with vertices (0, 0), (2, 0), (2, 1), (0, 1).

22. $\oint_C xy\,dx + (\tfrac{1}{2}x^2 + xy)\,dy$ where C is the upper half of the ellipse $x^2 + 4y^2 = 1$ together with the interval $[-1, 1]$.

23. $\oint_C \ln(x^2 + y^2)\,dx + \ln(x^2 + y^2)\,dy$ where C is the boundary of the upper half of the annular region bounded by the circles $x^2 + y^2 = 1$ and $x^2 + y^2 = 4$.

24. $\oint_C (1/y)\,dx + (1/x)\,dy$ where C is the boundary of the region enclosed by the x-axis, the line $x = 4$, and the curve $y = \sqrt{x}$.

25. $\oint_C y^2dx$ where C is the cardioid $r = 1 + \sin\theta,\ \theta \in [0, 2\pi]$.

26. $\oint_C e^y\cos x\ dx - e^y\sin x\ dy$ where C is the rectangle with vertices $(0, 0), (\pi/2, 0), (\pi/2, 1), (0, 1)$.

Exercises 27–28. Use Green's theorem to find the area of the region bounded by the curves.

27. $y = 4 - x^2$ and $y = 0$.

28. $xy = 3$ and $x + y = 4$.

Exercises 29–32. Calculate the area of the surface.

29. The part of the sphere $x^2 + y^2 + z^2 = 4$ that lies inside the cylinder $x^2 + y^2 = 2x$.

30. The part of the plane $x + y + 2z = 4$ that lies inside the cylinder $x^2 + y^2 = 4$.

31. The part of the cone $z = \sqrt{x^2 + y^2}$ that lies between the planes $z = 0$ and $z = 3$.

32. The part of the hyperbolic paraboloid $z = 2xy$ that lies inside the cylinder $x^2 + y^2 = 9$.

Exercises 33–36. Evaluate.

33. $\iint_S yz\, d\sigma$; S that part of the plane $z = y + 4$ which lies inside the cylinder $x^2 + y^2 = 1$.

34. $\iint_S xz\, d\sigma$; S the first-octant part of the plane $x + y + z = 1$.

35. $\iint_S (x^2 + y^2 + z^2)\, d\sigma$; S the cylindrical surface $y^2 + z^2 = 4$, from $x = 0$ to $x = 2$, together with capping circular disks.

36. $\iint_S xz\, d\sigma$; S that part of the cylinder $x^2 + y^2 = 4$ which lies between the planes $z = 0$ and $z = 1$.

Exercises 37–40. Calculate the divergence $\nabla \cdot \mathbf{v}$ and the curl $\nabla \times \mathbf{v}$.

37. $\mathbf{v}(x, y) = x^2\,\mathbf{i} + 2xy\,\mathbf{j}$.

38. $\mathbf{v}(x, y) = \dfrac{x}{x^2 + y^2}\,\mathbf{i} + \dfrac{y}{x^2 + y^2}\,\mathbf{j}$.

39. $\mathbf{v}(x, y, z) = x\,\mathbf{i} + xz\,\mathbf{j} + xyz\,\mathbf{k}$.

40. $\mathbf{v}(x, y, z) = xyz\,\mathbf{i} - \cos xy\,\mathbf{j} + \sin xy\,\mathbf{k}$

41. Verify the divergence theorem on the unit cube: $0 \le x \le 1, 0 \le y \le 1, 0 \le z \le 1$ for the vector field $\mathbf{v}(x, y, z) = xz\,\mathbf{i} - xy\,\mathbf{j} + yz\,\mathbf{k}$.

42. Verify the divergence theorem on the surface $S: y^2 + z^2 = 1, 0 \le x \le 4$ for the vector field $\mathbf{v}(x, y, z) = (x + z)\,\mathbf{i} + (y + z)\,\mathbf{j} + (x + z)\,\mathbf{k}$.

43. Calculate the total flux of $\mathbf{v}(x, y, z) = 2x\,\mathbf{i} + xz\,\mathbf{j} + z^2\,\mathbf{k}$ out of the solid bounded by the paraboloid $z = 9 - x^2 - y^2$ and the xy-plane.

44. Calculate the total flux of $\mathbf{v}(x, y, z) = x^2\,\mathbf{i} - xz\,\mathbf{j} + z^2\,\mathbf{k}$ out of the cube $0 \le x \le a,\ 0 \le y \le a, 0 \le z \le a$.

45. Let S be the hemisphere $z = \sqrt{4 - x^2 - y^2}$ and take $\mathbf{n}$ as the upper unit normal. Set $\mathbf{v}(x, y, z) = z\,\mathbf{i} + x\,\mathbf{j} + y\,\mathbf{k}$ and find

$$\iint_S [(\nabla \times \mathbf{v}) \cdot \mathbf{n}]\, d\sigma$$

(a) by direct calculation; (b) by Stokes's theorem.

46. Let S be that part of the paraboloid $z = 9 - x^2 - y^2$ for which $z \ge 0$ and take $\mathbf{n}$ as the upper unit normal. Let $\mathbf{v}(x, y, z) = z^3\,\mathbf{i} + x\,\mathbf{j} + y^2\,\mathbf{k}$ and find

$$\iint_S [(\nabla \times \mathbf{v}) \cdot \mathbf{n}]\, d\sigma$$

(a) by direct calculation; (b) by Stokes's theorem.

CHAPTER 13

SECTION 13.1

1.

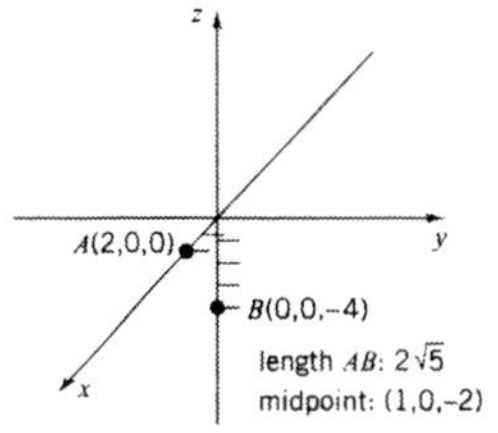

3.

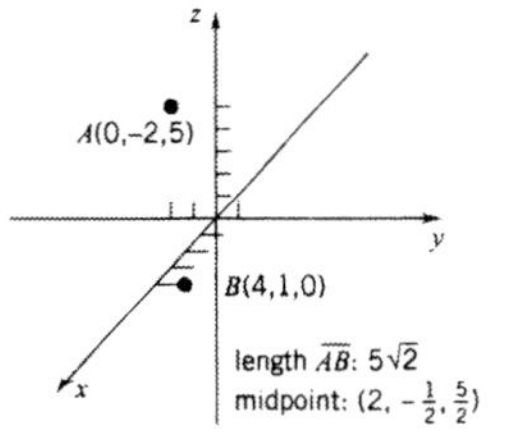

5. $z = -2$ 7. $y = 1$ 9. $x = 3$

11. $x^2 + (y-2)^2 + (z+1)^2 = 9$ 13. $(x-2)^2 + (y-4)^2 + (z+4)^2 = 36$ 15. $(x-3)^2 + (y-2)^2 + (z-2)^2 = 13$

17. center $(-2, 4, 1)$, radius 4   19. $(2, 3, -5)$ 21. $(-2, 3, 5)$ 23. $(-2, 3, -5)$ 25. $(-2, -3, -5)$

27. $(2, -5, 5)$ 29. $(-2, 1, -3)$ 31. $d(P, R) = \sqrt{14}$, $d(Q, R) = \sqrt{45}$, $d(P, Q) = \sqrt{59}$, $[d(P, R)]^2 + [d(Q, R)]^2 = [d(P, Q)]^2$

33. The sphere of radius 2 centered at the origin, together with its interior

35. A rectangular box with sides on the coordinate planes and dimensions $1 \times 2 \times 3$, together with its interior

37. A circular cylinder with base the circle $x^2 + y^2 = 4$ and height 4, together with its interior

39. $(0, 1, 2)$ 41. $\left(\frac{2a_1 + b_1}{2}, \frac{2a_2 + b_2}{2}, \frac{2a_3 + b_3}{2}\right)$, $\left(\frac{a_1 + 2b_1}{2}, \frac{a_2 + 2b_2}{2}, \frac{a_3 + 2b_3}{2}\right)$ 43. $\frac{x}{x_0} + \frac{y}{y_0} + \frac{z}{z_0} = 1$

45. (i) $\left(\frac{a_1}{a_3}z_0, \frac{a_2}{a_3}z_0, z_0\right)$ (ii) If $z_0 \neq 0$, the line does not intersect the plane. If $z_0 = 0$, the line lies in the plane.

47. $\left(\frac{a_1}{\sqrt{a_1^2 + a_2^2 + a_3^2}}, \frac{a_2}{\sqrt{a_1^2 + a_2^2 + a_3^2}}, \frac{a_3}{\sqrt{a_1^2 + a_2^2 + a_3^2}}\right)$

SECTION 13.2

1. $(3, 4, -2)$, $\sqrt{29}$ 3. $(0, -2, -1)$, $\sqrt{5}$ 5. $(-1, -4, 7)$ 7. $(5, 2, -8)$ 9. $3\mathbf{i} - 4\mathbf{j} + 6\mathbf{k}$ 11. $-3\mathbf{i} - \mathbf{j} + 8\mathbf{k}$

13. 5 15. 3 17. $\sqrt{6}$ 19. (a) a, c, d (b) a, c (c) a and c both have direction opposite to d 21. $R(2, -5, 3)$

23. $R(1, -9, 5)$ 25. $\left(\frac{3}{5}, -\frac{4}{5}, 0\right)$ 27. $\frac{1}{3}\mathbf{i} - \frac{2}{3}\mathbf{j} + \frac{2}{3}\mathbf{k}$ 29. $\frac{1}{\sqrt{14}}\mathbf{i} - \frac{3}{\sqrt{14}}\mathbf{j} - \frac{2}{\sqrt{14}}\mathbf{k}$

31. (i) $\mathbf{a} - \mathbf{b}$ (ii) $-(\mathbf{a} + \mathbf{b})$ (iii) $\mathbf{a} - \mathbf{b}$ (iv) $\mathbf{b} - \mathbf{a}$ 33. (a) $\mathbf{i} - 3\mathbf{j} + 10\mathbf{k}$ (b) $A = -2, B = \frac{3}{2}, C = -\frac{7}{2}$

35. $\alpha = \pm 3$ 37. $\alpha = \pm\frac{1}{3}\sqrt{6}$ 39. $\pm\frac{2}{13}\sqrt{13}(3\mathbf{j} + 2\mathbf{k})$

41. (a) the parallelogram is a rectangle
(b) simplify $\sqrt{(a_1 - b_1)^2 + (a_2 - b_2)^2 + (a_3 - b_3)^2} = \sqrt{(a_1 + b_1)^2 + (a_2 + b_2)^2 + (a_3 + b_3)^2}$

43. $\mathbf{m} = \mathbf{p} + \frac{1}{2}(\mathbf{q} - \mathbf{p})$

SECTION 13.3

1. -1 3. 0 5. -1 7. $\mathbf{a} \cdot \mathbf{b}$ 9. $\mathbf{a} \cdot (\mathbf{b} + \mathbf{c})$

11. (a) $\mathbf{a} \cdot \mathbf{b} = 5$, $\mathbf{a} \cdot \mathbf{c} = 8$, $\mathbf{b} \cdot \mathbf{c} = 18$ (b) $\cos\sphericalangle(\mathbf{a}, \mathbf{b}) = \frac{1}{14}\sqrt{70}$, $\cos\sphericalangle(\mathbf{a}, \mathbf{c}) = \frac{8}{25}\sqrt{5}$, $\cos\sphericalangle(\mathbf{b}, \mathbf{c}) = \frac{9}{35}\sqrt{14}$
(c) $\text{comp}_{\mathbf{b}}\mathbf{a} = \frac{5}{14}\sqrt{14}$, $\text{comp}_{\mathbf{c}}\mathbf{a} = \frac{8}{5}$ (d) $\text{proj}_{\mathbf{b}}\mathbf{a} = \frac{5}{14}(3\mathbf{i} - \mathbf{j} + 2\mathbf{k})$, $\text{proj}_{\mathbf{c}}\mathbf{a} = \frac{8}{25}(4\mathbf{i} + 3\mathbf{k})$ 13. $\frac{1}{2}\mathbf{i} + \frac{1}{2}\sqrt{2}\mathbf{j} - \frac{1}{2}\mathbf{k}$ 15. $\frac{1}{3}\pi$

17. $\frac{1}{3}\pi, \frac{2}{3}\pi, \frac{1}{4}\pi$ 19. 2.2 radians, or 126.3° 21. 2.5 radians, or 145.3°

23. angles: 38.51°, 95.52°, 45.97°; perimeter: $P \cong 15.924$ 25. $\cos\alpha = \frac{1}{3}, \cos\beta = \frac{2}{3}, \cos\gamma = \frac{2}{3}$; $\alpha \cong 70.5°, \beta \cong 48.2°, \gamma \cong 48.2°$

27. $\cos\alpha = \frac{3}{13}, \cos\beta = \frac{12}{13}, \cos\gamma = \frac{4}{13}$; $\alpha \cong 76.7°, \beta \cong 22.6°, \gamma \cong 72.1°$ 29. $x = \pm 4$ 31. $x = 0, x = 4$

35. $\pi - \alpha, \pi - \beta, \pi - \gamma$ 37. $\mathbf{u} = \pm\frac{1}{165}\sqrt{165}(8\mathbf{i} + \mathbf{j} - 10\mathbf{k})$ 39. $\theta = \cos^{-1}\left(\frac{1}{3}\sqrt{3}\right) \cong 0.96$ radians

SECTION 13.4

1. $-2\mathbf{k}$ 3. $\mathbf{i} + \mathbf{j} + \mathbf{k}$ 5. $-3\mathbf{i} - \mathbf{j} - 2\mathbf{k}$ 7. -1 9. 0 11. 1 13. $3\mathbf{i} - 2\mathbf{j} - 3\mathbf{k}$ 15. $\mathbf{i} + \mathbf{j} - 2\mathbf{k}$ 17. -3

19. $5\mathbf{i} - 4\mathbf{j} - \mathbf{k}$ 21. $\left(\frac{1}{\sqrt{6}}, \frac{-1}{\sqrt{6}}, \frac{-2}{\sqrt{6}}\right), \left(\frac{-1}{\sqrt{6}}, \frac{1}{\sqrt{6}}, \frac{2}{\sqrt{6}}\right)$ 23. $\mathbf{N} = 3\mathbf{j}$; area $= \frac{3}{2}$ 25. $\mathbf{N} = 8\mathbf{i} + 4\mathbf{j} + 4\mathbf{k}$; area $= 2\sqrt{6}$ 27. 1

29. 2 31. $-2(\mathbf{a} \times \mathbf{b})$ 33. $\mathbf{a} = \mathbf{0}$

37. (a) makes sense; dot product of two vectors (b) does not make sense; $(\mathbf{b} \cdot \mathbf{c})$ is a number
(c) does not make sense; $(\mathbf{b} \cdot \mathbf{c})$ is a number (d) makes sense; cross product of two vectors

39. $\mathbf{d} = \lambda[(\mathbf{a} - \mathbf{b}) \times (\mathbf{b} - \mathbf{c})]$ 43. $\mathbf{c} \times \mathbf{a} = \|\mathbf{a}\|^2\mathbf{b}$ 45. either $\mathbf{a} = \mathbf{0}$ or $\mathbf{b} = \mathbf{0}$

SECTION 13.5

1. P and Q 3. $\mathbf{r}(t) = (3\,\mathbf{i} + \mathbf{j}) + t\,\mathbf{k}$ 5. $\mathbf{r}(t) = t(x_i\mathbf{i} + y_1\,\mathbf{j} + z_1\,\mathbf{k})$ 7. $x(t) = 1 + t,\ \ y(t) = -t,\ \ z(t) = 3 + t$

9. $x(t) = 2,\ \ y(t) = t,\ \ z(t) = 3$ 11. $\mathbf{r}(t) = (-\mathbf{i} + 2\,\mathbf{j} - 3\,\mathbf{k}) + t(2\,\mathbf{i} + \mathbf{j} + 4\,\mathbf{k})$ 13. intersect at $(1, 3, 1)$

15. skew 17. parallel 19. skew 21. $P(1, 2, 0),\ \ \frac{1}{4}\pi$ rad 23. $(x_0 - [d_1/d_3]z_0, y_0 - [d_2/d_3]z_0, 0)$

25. The lines are parallel. 27. $\mathbf{r}(t) = (2\,\mathbf{i} + 7\,\mathbf{j} - \mathbf{k}) + t(2\,\mathbf{i} - 5\,\mathbf{j} + 4\,\mathbf{k}),\ \ 0 \le t \le 1$ 29. $\mathbf{u} = -\frac{2}{3}\mathbf{i} + \frac{1}{3}\mathbf{j} + \frac{2}{3}\mathbf{k},\ \ 9 \le t \le 15$

31. triples of the form $X(u) = 3 + au,\ Y(u) = -1 + bu,\ Z(u) = 8 + cu$ with $2a - 4b + 6c = 0$ 33. 1 35. $\sqrt{69/14} \cong 2.22$

37. $\sqrt{3} \cong 1.73$ 39. (a) 1 (b) $\sqrt{3}$ 41. $\mathbf{r}(t) = \frac{1}{11}(7\,\mathbf{i} + 4\,\mathbf{j} - \mathbf{k}) \pm t[\frac{1}{11}\sqrt{11}(\mathbf{i} - \mathbf{j} + 3\,\mathbf{k})]$ 43. $0 < t < s$ 45. $d(l_1, l_2) = \dfrac{10}{\sqrt{285}}$

SECTION 13.6

1. Q 3. $x - 4y + 3z - 2 = 0$ 5. $3x - 2y + 5z - 9 = 0$ 7. $y - z - 2 = 0$ 9. $x_0(x - x_0) + y_0(y - y_0) + z_0(z - z_0) = 0$

11. $\dfrac{1}{\sqrt{30}}(2\,\mathbf{i} - \mathbf{j} + 5\,\mathbf{k}),\ \ -\dfrac{1}{\sqrt{30}}(2\,\mathbf{i} - \mathbf{j} + 5\,\mathbf{k})$ 13. $\dfrac{1}{15}x + \dfrac{1}{12}y - \dfrac{1}{10}z = 1$ 15. $\frac{1}{2}\pi$ 17. $\cos\theta = \frac{2}{21}\sqrt{42} \cong 0.617,\ \ \theta \cong 0.91$ rad

19. coplanar 21. not coplanar 23. $\dfrac{2}{\sqrt{21}}$ 25. $\frac{22}{5}$ 27. $x + z = 2$ 29. $3x - 4z - 5 = 0$

31. $\dfrac{x - x_0}{A} = \dfrac{y - y_0}{B} = \dfrac{z - z_0}{C}$ 33. $(x - x_0)/d_1 = (y - y_0)/d_2,\ \ (y - y_0)/d_2 = (z - z_0)/d_3$ 35. $x(t) = t,\ \ y(t) = t,\ \ z(t) = -t$

37. $P(-\frac{19}{14}, \frac{15}{7}, \frac{17}{14})$ 39. $10x - 7y + z = 0$ 41. circle centered at P with radius $\|\mathbf{N}\|$

43. If $\alpha > 0$, then P_1 lies on the same side of the plane as the tip of $\mathbf{N}$;
if $\alpha < 0$, then P_1 and the tip of $\mathbf{N}$ lie on opposite sides of the plane

45. (a) $(4, 0, 0), (0, 5, 0), (0, 0, 2)$
(b) $5x + 4y = 20,\ x + 2z = 4,\ 2y + 5z = 10$
(c) $\pm\frac{1}{\sqrt{141}}(5\,\mathbf{i} + 4\,\mathbf{j} + 10\,\mathbf{k})$
(d)

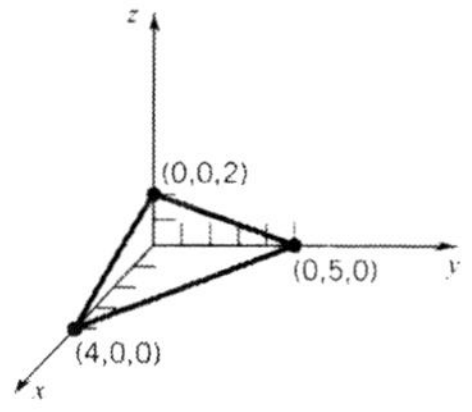

47. (a) $(4, 0, 0), (0, 0, 6)$, no y-intercept
(b) $x = 4,\ 3x + 2z = 12,\ z = 6$
(c) $\pm\frac{1}{\sqrt{13}}(3\,\mathbf{i} + 2\,\mathbf{k})$
(d)

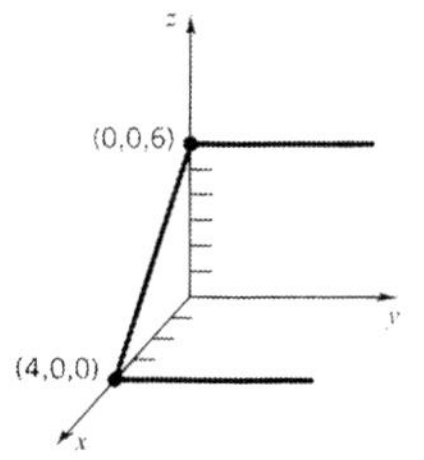

49. $\cos\theta = \dfrac{1}{2\sqrt{105}},\ \ \theta \cong 1.52$ rad 51. $3x + y + 4z = 1$ 53. $10x + 4y + 5z = 20$ 55. $5x + 3y = 15$

Review Exercises

1. (a) $3/\sqrt{10}$ (b) $(6, \frac{1}{2}, \frac{1}{2})$ (c) $(11, -12, 9)$ (d) $(x - 4)^2 + (y - 4)^2 + (z + 2)^2 = 6$

3. $(x - 2)^2 + (y + 3)^2 + (z - 1)^2 = 14$ 5. center $(-1, 2, 4)$, radius 2 7. $\frac{3}{2}\mathbf{i} + \mathbf{j} - \frac{1}{2}\mathbf{k}$ 9. 22 11. 21 13. 0

15. $\dfrac{1}{\sqrt{14}}(3\,\mathbf{i} + 2\,\mathbf{j} - \mathbf{k})$ 17. 1.51 radians 19. direction cosines: $3/\sqrt{14}, 2/\sqrt{14}, -1/\sqrt{14}$; direction angles (radians) 0.64, 1.01, 1.84

21. $-\dfrac{27}{\sqrt{14}} \cong -7.22$ 23. 27 cubic units 25. (a) $x = 1 + 6t,\ y = 1 - 3t,\ z = 1 + 3t$ (b) $3x - 3y + 2z = 2$ (c) $x - y - 3z + 3 = 0$

27. intersect at $(2, -2, -2)$ 29. skew 31. (a) no (b) yes 33. $2x - z = 1$ 35. $3x + 2y - z = 0$

37. $10x - 17y + z + 25 = 0$ 39. 3 units 41. $\theta \cong 0.822$ radians 43. $x = -2 - 9t,\ y = 2 + 5t,\ z = t$

45. $\pm\dfrac{4}{\sqrt{195}}(-5\,\mathbf{i} + 11\,\mathbf{j} + 7\,\mathbf{k})$

CHAPTER 14

SECTION 14.1

1. $\mathbf{f}'(t) = 2\,\mathbf{i} - \mathbf{j} + 3\,\mathbf{k}$ 3. $\mathbf{f}'(t) = -\dfrac{1}{2\sqrt{1-t}}\mathbf{i} + \dfrac{1}{2\sqrt{1+t}}\mathbf{j} + \dfrac{1}{(1-t)^2}\mathbf{k}$ 5. $\mathbf{f}'(t) = \cos t\,\mathbf{i} - \sin t\,\mathbf{j} + \sec^2 t\,\mathbf{k}$.

7. $-\dfrac{1}{1-t}\mathbf{i} - \sin t\,\mathbf{j} + 2t\,\mathbf{k}$ 9. $12t\,\mathbf{j} + 2\,\mathbf{k}$ 11. $-4\cos 2t\,\mathbf{i} - 4\sin 2t\,\mathbf{j}$ 13. (a) $-\mathbf{j}$ (b) $\mathbf{i} - \mathbf{j} + \frac{5}{\sqrt{2}}\,\mathbf{k}$ 15. $\mathbf{i} + 3\,\mathbf{j}$

17. $(e-1)\,\mathbf{i} + (1 - 1/e)\,\mathbf{k}$ 19. $\dfrac{\pi}{4}\,\mathbf{i} + \tan(1)\,\mathbf{j}$ 21. $\frac{1}{2}\,\mathbf{i} + \mathbf{j}$ 23. $0\,\mathbf{i} + 0\,\mathbf{j} + 0\,\mathbf{k} = \mathbf{0}$

25. (a) $\mathbf{i} + \frac{e-1}{2}\,\mathbf{j}$ (b) $\left[5 + \ln\left(\frac{4}{9}\right)\right]\mathbf{i} + \left[\frac{-5}{36} + \ln\left(\frac{9}{4}\right)\right]\mathbf{j} + \frac{295}{2592}\,\mathbf{k}$

27.

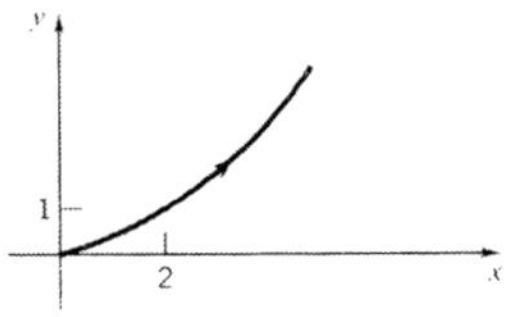

29.

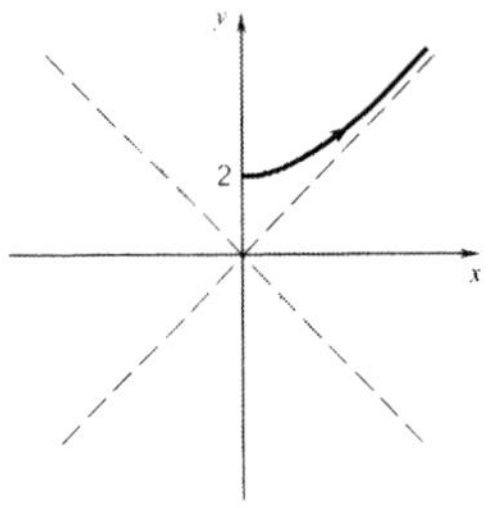

31.

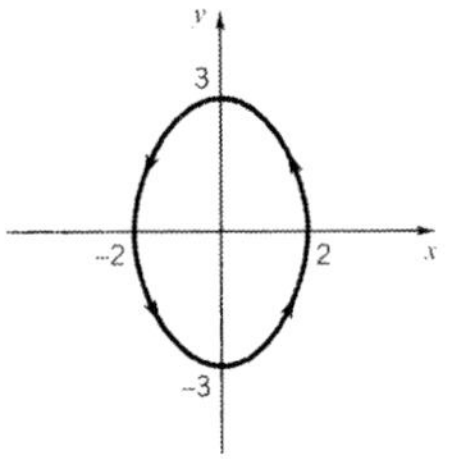

33.

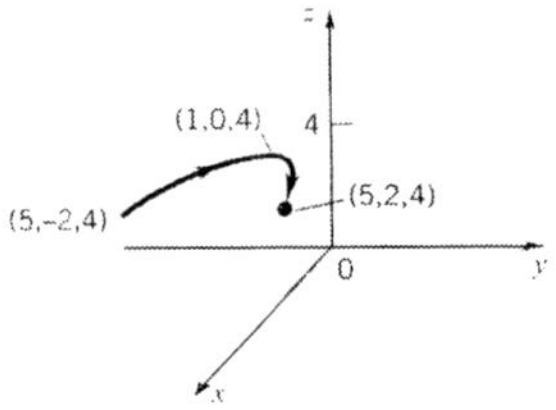

35.

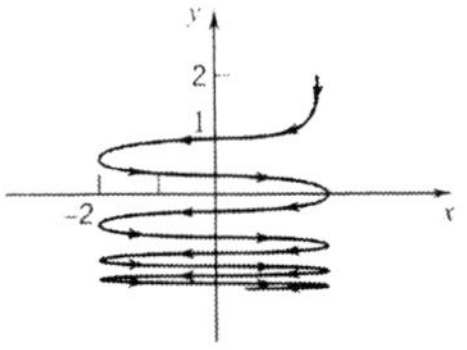

37.

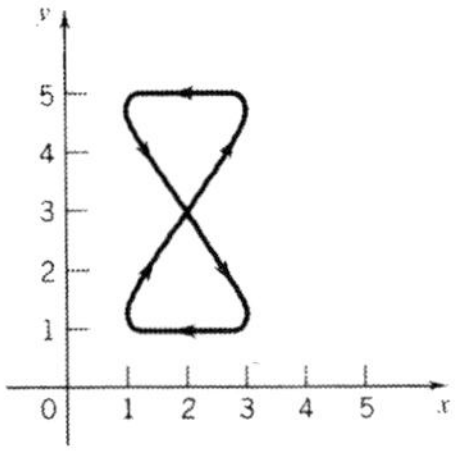

39. (a) $\mathbf{f}(t) = 3\cos t\,\mathbf{i} + 2\sin t\,\mathbf{j}$ (b) $\mathbf{f}(t) = 3\cos t\,\mathbf{i} - 2\sin t\,\mathbf{j}$ 41. (a) $\mathbf{f}(t) = t\,\mathbf{i} + t^2\,\mathbf{j}$ (b) $\mathbf{f}(t) = -t\,\mathbf{i} + t^2\,\mathbf{j}$

43. $\mathbf{f}(t) = (1 + 2t)\,\mathbf{i} + (4 + 5t)\,\mathbf{j} + (-2 + 8t)\,\mathbf{k},\ 0 \le t \le 1$

45. $\mathbf{f}'(t_0) = \mathbf{i} + m\,\mathbf{j}$ $\displaystyle\int_a^b \mathbf{f}(t)\,dt = \tfrac{1}{2}(b^2 - a^2)\,\mathbf{i} + A\,\mathbf{j},$ $\displaystyle\int_a^b \mathbf{f}'(t)\,dt = (b-a)\,\mathbf{i} + (d-c)\,\mathbf{j}$ 47. $\mathbf{f}(t) = t\,\mathbf{i} + \left(\frac{1}{3}t^3 + 1\right)\mathbf{j} - \mathbf{k}$ 49. $\mathbf{f}(t) = e^{\alpha t}\mathbf{c}$

55. no; as a counterexample set $\mathbf{f}(t) = \mathbf{i} = \mathbf{g}(t)$

SECTION 14.2

1. $\mathbf{f}'(t) = \mathbf{b},\quad \mathbf{f}''(t) = \mathbf{0}$ 3. $\mathbf{f}'(t) = 2e^{2t}\,\mathbf{i} - \cos t\,\mathbf{j},\quad \mathbf{f}''(t) = 4e^{2t}\mathbf{i} + \sin t\,\mathbf{j}$ 5. $\mathbf{f}'(t) = (3t^2 - 8t^3)\,\mathbf{j},\ \mathbf{f}''(t) = (6t - 24t^2)\,\mathbf{j}$

7. $\mathbf{f}'(t) = -2t\,\mathbf{i} + e^t(t+1)\,\mathbf{k},\quad \mathbf{f}''(t) = -2\,\mathbf{i} + e^t(t+2)\,\mathbf{k}$

9. $\mathbf{f}'(t) = (\mathbf{a} \times t\mathbf{b}) \times 2t\mathbf{b} + (\mathbf{a} \times \mathbf{b}) \times (\mathbf{a} + t^2\mathbf{b})$
$\mathbf{f}''(t) = (\mathbf{a} \times t\mathbf{b}) \times 2\mathbf{b} + 2(\mathbf{a} \times \mathbf{b}) \times (2t\,\mathbf{b})$

11. $\mathbf{f}'(t) = \frac{1}{2}\sqrt{t}\,\mathbf{g}'(\sqrt{t}) + \mathbf{g}(\sqrt{t}),\quad \mathbf{f}''(t) = \frac{1}{4}\mathbf{g}''(\sqrt{t}) + \frac{3}{4}(1/\sqrt{t})\mathbf{g}'(\sqrt{t})$ 13. $-\sin t e^{\cos t}\mathbf{i} + \cos t e^{\sin t}\mathbf{j}$ 15. $4e^{2t} - 4e^{-2t}$

17. $(\mathbf{a} \times \mathbf{d}) + (\mathbf{b} \times \mathbf{c}) + 2t(\mathbf{b} \times \mathbf{d})$ 19. $(\mathbf{a} \cdot \mathbf{d}) + (\mathbf{b} \cdot \mathbf{c}) + 2t(\mathbf{b} \cdot \mathbf{d})$ 21. $\mathbf{r}(t) = \mathbf{a} + t\mathbf{b}$ 23. $\mathbf{r}(t) = \frac{1}{2}t^2\mathbf{a} + \frac{1}{6}t^3\mathbf{b} + t\mathbf{c} + \mathbf{d}$

25. $\mathbf{r}''(t) = -\sin t\,\mathbf{i} - \cos t\,\mathbf{j} = -\mathbf{r}(t)$; no. 27. $\mathbf{r}(t) \cdot \mathbf{r}'(t) = 0,\quad \mathbf{r}(t) \times \mathbf{r}'(t) = \mathbf{k}$

SECTION 14.3

1. $\pi\mathbf{j} + \mathbf{k},\quad \mathbf{R}(u) = (\mathbf{i} + 2\,\mathbf{k}) + u(\pi\mathbf{j} + \mathbf{k})$ 3. $\mathbf{b} - 2\mathbf{c},\quad \mathbf{R}(u) = (\mathbf{a} - \mathbf{b} + \mathbf{c}) + u(\mathbf{b} - 2\,\mathbf{c})$

5. $4\,\mathbf{i} - \mathbf{j} + 4\,\mathbf{k},\quad \mathbf{R}(u) = (2\,\mathbf{i} + 5\,\mathbf{k}) + u(4\,\mathbf{i} - \mathbf{j} + 4\,\mathbf{k})$

7. $-\sqrt{2}\,\mathbf{i}+\dfrac{3\sqrt{2}}{2}\,\mathbf{j}+\mathbf{k},\quad \mathbf{R}(u)=\left(\sqrt{2}\,\mathbf{i}+\dfrac{3\sqrt{2}}{2}\mathbf{j}+\dfrac{\pi}{4}\mathbf{k}\right)+u\left(-\sqrt{2}\,\mathbf{i}+\dfrac{3\sqrt{2}}{2}\mathbf{j}+\mathbf{k}\right)$

9. $a^2y=bx^2$ 11. (a) $P(0,1)$ (b) $P(1,2)$ (c) $P(-1,2)$ 15. $\pi/2\cong 1.57$

17. $P(1,2,-2)$; $\cos^{-1}\left(\frac{1}{5}\sqrt{5}\right)\cong 1.11$ rad 19. (a) $\mathbf{r}(t)=a\cos t\,\mathbf{i}+b\sin t\,\mathbf{j}$ (b) $\mathbf{r}(t)=a\cos t\,\mathbf{i}-b\sin t\,\mathbf{j}$ (c) $\mathbf{r}(t)=a\cos 2t\,\mathbf{i}+b\sin 2t\,\mathbf{j}$ (d) $\mathbf{r}(t)=a\cos 3t\,\mathbf{i}-b\sin 3t\,\mathbf{j}$

21. $\mathbf{r}'(t)=t^3\mathbf{i}+2t\,\mathbf{j}$

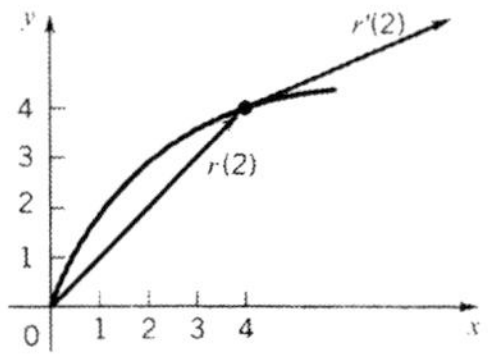

23. $\mathbf{r}'(t)=2e^{2t}\mathbf{i}-4e^{-4t}\mathbf{j}$

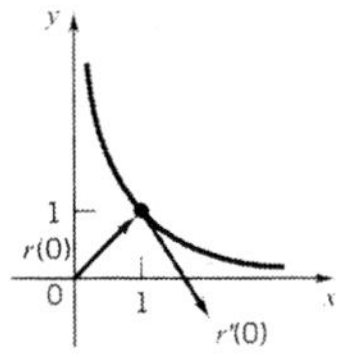

25. $\mathbf{r}'(t)=-2\sin t\,\mathbf{i}+3\cos t\,\mathbf{j}$

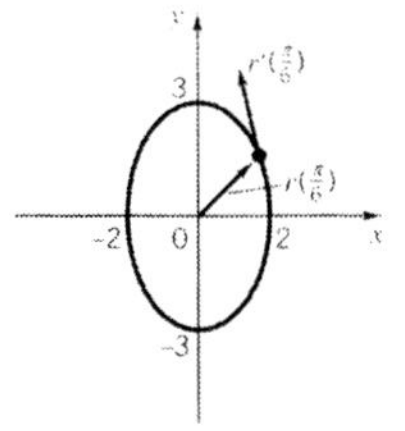

27. $\mathbf{r}(t)=(t^2+1)\,\mathbf{i}+t\,\mathbf{j},\quad t\geq 1$; or, $\mathbf{r}(t)=\sec^2 t\,\mathbf{i}+\tan t\,\mathbf{j},\quad t\in\left[\frac{1}{4}\pi,\frac{1}{2}\pi\right)$ 29. $\mathbf{r}(t)=\cos t\sin 3t\,\mathbf{i}+\sin t\sin 3t\,\mathbf{j},\quad t\in[0,\pi]$

31.

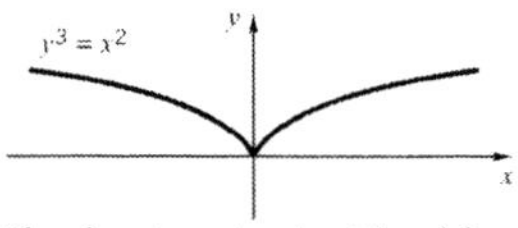

There is no tangent vector at the origin

33. $(2,4,8)$; $\cos^{-1}\left(\dfrac{24}{\sqrt{21}\sqrt{161}}\right)\cong 1.15$ rad

35. $\mathbf{T}(1)=\dfrac{1}{\sqrt{2}}\mathbf{j}+\dfrac{1}{\sqrt{2}}\mathbf{k},\quad \mathbf{N}(1)=\dfrac{-1}{\sqrt{2}}\mathbf{j}+\dfrac{1}{\sqrt{2}}\mathbf{k},\quad x-1=0$ 37. $\frac{1}{5}\sqrt{5}(-2\,\mathbf{i}+\mathbf{k}),\quad -\mathbf{j},\quad x+2z=\frac{1}{2}\pi$

39. $\mathbf{T}(0)=\dfrac{1}{\sqrt{2}}\mathbf{i}+\dfrac{1}{\sqrt{2}}\mathbf{k},\quad \mathbf{N}(0)=\mathbf{j},\quad x-z=0$

41. $\mathbf{T}(0)=\dfrac{1}{\sqrt{3}}\mathbf{i}+\dfrac{1}{\sqrt{3}}\mathbf{j}+\dfrac{1}{\sqrt{3}}\mathbf{k},\quad \mathbf{N}(0)=\dfrac{1}{\sqrt{2}}\mathbf{i}-\dfrac{1}{\sqrt{2}}\mathbf{j},\quad x+y-2z+1=0$

45. (a) $x=1-t,\ y=1+t,\ z=-\dfrac{\sqrt{2}}{2}-\dfrac{5\sqrt{2}}{2}t$

(c) the tangent line is parallel to the xy-plane at the points where $t=\dfrac{(2n+1)\pi}{10},\ n=0,1,2,\ldots,9.$

SECTION 14.4

1. $\frac{52}{3}$ 3. $2\pi\sqrt{a^2+b^2}$ 5. $\ln(1+\sqrt{2})$ 7. $\frac{1}{27}(13\sqrt{13}-8)$ 9. $\sqrt{2}(e^{\pi}-1)$ 11. e^2 13. $4\pi^2$

15. $6+\frac{1}{2}\sqrt{2}\ln(2\sqrt{2}+3)$ 23. $s=\dfrac{\sqrt{2}}{2}t^2,\quad t=2^{1/4}\sqrt{s},\quad \mathbf{R}(u)=(\sin u-u\cos u)\,\mathbf{i}+(\cos u+u\sin u)\,\mathbf{j}+\dfrac{1}{2}u^2\mathbf{k}$ where $u=2^{1/4}\sqrt{s}$

25. 0.5077 27. 22.0939 29. (b) $L\cong 17.6286$

SECTION 14.5

1. $v/a,\ v^2/a$ 3. $\|\mathbf{r}''(t)\|=a^2|b\sin at|=a^2|y(t)|$

5. $y=\cos\pi x,\quad 0\leq x\leq 2$

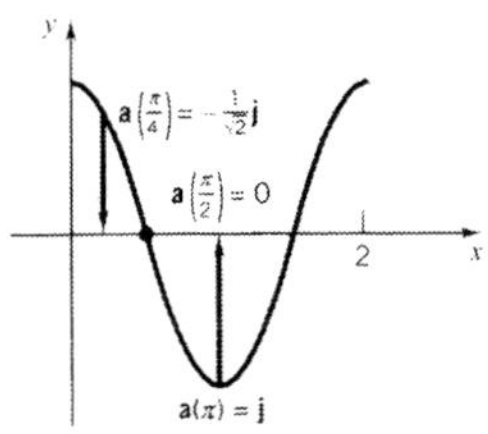

7. $x=\sqrt{1+y^2},\quad y\geq -1$

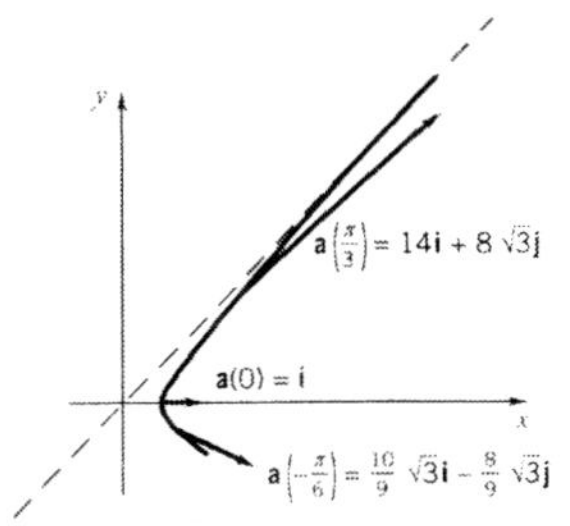

9. (a) (x_0, y_0, z_0) (b) $\alpha \cos\theta\, \mathbf{j} + \alpha \sin\theta\, \mathbf{k}$ (c) $|\alpha|$ (d) $-32\mathbf{k}$
(e) arc from parabola $z = z_0 + (\tan\theta)(y - y_0) - 16(y - y_0)^2/(\alpha^2 \cos^2\theta)$ in the plane $x = x_0$

13. $\dfrac{e^{-x}}{(1+e^{-2x})^{3/2}}$ 15. $\dfrac{2}{(1+4x)^{3/2}}$ 17. $|\cos x|$ 19. $\dfrac{|\sin x|}{(1+\cos^2 x)^{3/2}}$ 21. $2/5^{3/2}$ 23. $1/5^{3/2}$ 25. $3/10^{3/2}$

27. $\left(\frac{1}{2}\sqrt{2}, \frac{1}{2}\ln\frac{1}{2}\right)$ 29. $\dfrac{1}{(1+t^2)^{3/2}}$ 31. $\dfrac{12|t|}{(4+9t^4)^{3/2}}$ 33. $\frac{1}{2}\sqrt{2}\, e^{-1}$ 35. $\dfrac{2+t^2}{(1+t^2)^{3/2}}$ 37. $1/\sqrt{2}$ 39. $\dfrac{a^4 b^4}{(b^4 x^2 + a^4 y^2)^{3/2}}$

41. $\kappa = \frac{1}{3}\sqrt{2}\, e^{-t}, \quad a_{\mathrm{T}} = \sqrt{3}\, e^t, \quad a_{\mathrm{N}} = \sqrt{2}\, e^t$ 43. $\kappa = 1, \quad a_{\mathrm{T}} = 0, \quad a_{\mathrm{N}} = 4$ 45. $\kappa = 9/24, \quad a_{\mathrm{T}} = 0, \quad a_{\mathrm{N}} = 9$

47. $\kappa = \dfrac{1}{8}\sqrt{\dfrac{2}{1-t^2}}$; $a_{\mathrm{T}} = 0$; $a_{\mathrm{N}} = \dfrac{1}{2}\sqrt{\dfrac{2}{1-t^2}}$ 49. $a_{\mathrm{T}} = \dfrac{6t+12t^3}{\sqrt{1+t^2+t^4}}$; $a_{\mathrm{N}} = 6\sqrt{\dfrac{1+4t^2+t^4}{1+t^2+t^4}}$ 51. $\dfrac{e^{-a\theta}}{\sqrt{1+a^2}}$

53. $\dfrac{3}{2\sqrt{2a^2(1-\cos\theta)}} = \dfrac{3}{2\sqrt{2ar}}$

SECTION 14.6

1. (a) $\mathbf{r}'(0) = b\omega\, \mathbf{j}$ (b) $\mathbf{r}''(t) = \omega^2 \mathbf{r}(t)$ (c) The torque is **0** and the angular momentum is constant.

3. (a) $\mathbf{v}(t) = 2\,\mathbf{j} + (\alpha/m)t\,\mathbf{k}$ (b) $v(t) = (1/m)\sqrt{4m^2 + \alpha^2 t^2}$ (c) $\mathbf{p}(t) = 2m\,\mathbf{j} + \alpha t\,\mathbf{k}$
(d) $\mathbf{r}(t_1) = [2t + y_0]\,\mathbf{j} + [(\alpha/2m)t^2 + z_0]\mathbf{k}, \quad t \geq 0, \quad z = (\alpha/8m)(y - y_0)^2 + z_0, \quad y \geq y_0, \quad x = 0$

5. $\mathbf{F}(t) = 2m\mathbf{k}$ 7. (a) $\pi b\,\mathbf{j} + \mathbf{k}$ (b) $\sqrt{\pi^2 b^2 + 1}$ (c) $-\pi^2 a\,\mathbf{i}$ (d) $m(\pi b\,\mathbf{j} + \mathbf{k})$
(e) $m[b(1-\pi)\,\mathbf{i} - 2a\,\mathbf{j} + 2\pi ab\,\mathbf{k}]$ (f) $-m\pi^2 a[\mathbf{j} - b\,\mathbf{k}]$

11. An equation of the plane can be written

$$[\mathbf{a} \times \mathbf{v}(0)] \cdot [\mathbf{r} - \mathbf{r}(0)] = 0.$$

[If either v(0) or **a** is zero, the motion is restricted to a straight line; if both of these vectors are zero, the particle remains at its initial position r(0).]

13. $\mathbf{r}(t) = \mathbf{i} + t\,\mathbf{j} + (qE_0/2m)t^2\mathbf{k}$ 15. $\mathbf{r}(t) = (1 + t^3/6m)\,\mathbf{i} + (t^4/12m)\,\mathbf{j} + t\,\mathbf{k}$.

SECTION 14.7

1. about 61.1% of an earth year 3. set $x = r\cos\theta, \quad y = r\sin\theta$

Review Exercises

1. $\mathbf{f}'(t) = 6t\,\mathbf{i} - 15t^2\,\mathbf{j}; \quad \mathbf{f}''(t) = 6\,\mathbf{i} - 30\,\mathbf{j}$ 3. $\mathbf{f}'(t) = (e^t\cos t - e^t \sin t)\,\mathbf{i} + 2\sin 2t\,\mathbf{j}; \quad \mathbf{f}''(t) = -2e^t \sin t\,\mathbf{i} + 4\cos 2t\,\mathbf{j}$ 5. $4\mathbf{i} + \frac{2}{3}\mathbf{j}$

7.

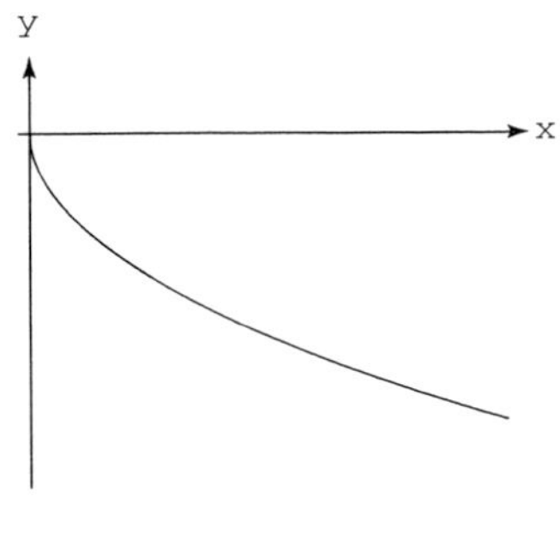

9.

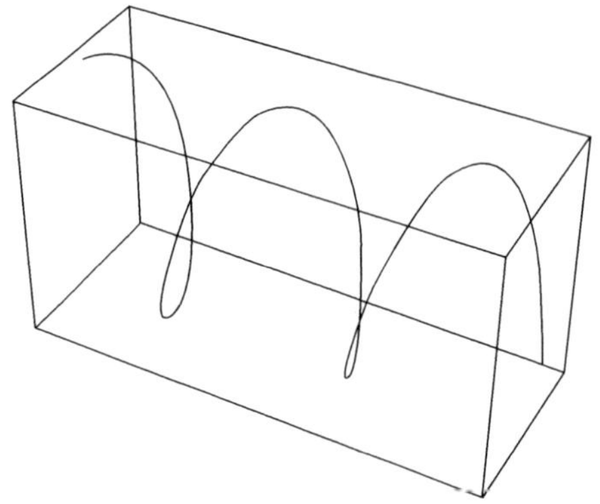

11. (a) $\mathbf{r}(t) = 2\cos\left(t + \frac{1}{2}\pi\right)\,\mathbf{i} + 4\sin\left(t + \frac{1}{2}\pi\right)\,\mathbf{j}, \quad 0 \leq t \leq 2\pi$ (b) $\mathbf{r}(t) = 2\cos(\pi - 2t)\,\mathbf{i} + 4\sin(\pi - 2t)\,\mathbf{j}, \quad 0 \leq t \leq 2\pi$

13. $\mathbf{f}(t) = \left(\frac{1}{3}t^3 + 1\right)\,\mathbf{i} + \left(\frac{1}{2}e^{2t} + t - \frac{7}{2}\right)\,\mathbf{j} + \left[\frac{1}{3}(1+2t)^{3/2} + \frac{8}{3}\right]\mathbf{k}$ 15. $\mathbf{f}'(t) = (6 + 8t)\,\mathbf{i} + 12t^3\mathbf{j} - 12\,\mathbf{k}$

17. $\mathbf{f}'(t) = (6t^2 + 2t)\,\mathbf{i} + (4t - 2t^{-3})\,\mathbf{j} + (4t^3 - 1)\,\mathbf{k}$ 19. $x = e^{2t}, y = 2e^{2t}, z = e^{2t}$, or $x = u, y = 2u, z = u, u > 0$, a line

21. $\mathbf{r}'(0) = 2\,\mathbf{i} + 3\,\mathbf{j} + \mathbf{k}; \quad x = 1 + 2t, y = 1 + 3t, z = 1 + t$ 23. $\mathbf{r}_1(1) = \mathbf{r}_2(-1); \quad \theta = \pi/2$

25.

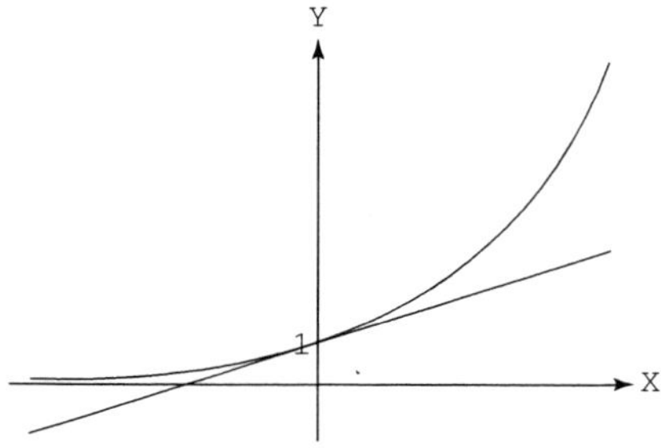

27. $\mathbf{T}(t) = \frac{1}{2}\cos t\,\mathbf{i} + \frac{1}{2}\sin t\,\mathbf{j} + \frac{1}{2}\sqrt{3}t\mathbf{k}$, $\mathbf{N}(t) = -\sin t\,\mathbf{i} + \cos t\,\mathbf{j}$

29. $\mathbf{T}(1) = \frac{2}{3}\mathbf{i} + \frac{1}{3}\mathbf{j} - \frac{2}{3}\mathbf{k}$, $\mathbf{N}(1) = -\frac{1}{3}\mathbf{i} - \frac{2}{3}\mathbf{j} - \frac{2}{3}\mathbf{k}$; $2x - 2y + z = 3$ 31. $\frac{38}{3}$ 33. $\sqrt{2}\sinh 1$

35. (a) $s = \frac{2}{3}(1+t)^{3/2} - \frac{2}{3}$ (b) $t = \left(\frac{3}{2}s + 1\right)^{2/3} - 1$

(c) $\mathbf{R}(s) = \cos\left[\left(\frac{3}{2}s+1\right)^{2/3} - 1\right]\mathbf{i} + \sin\left[\left(\frac{3}{2}s+1\right)^{2/3} - 1\right]\mathbf{j} + \frac{2}{3}\left[\left(\frac{3}{2}s+1\right)^{2/3} - 1\right]^{3/2}\mathbf{k}$

37. $\mathbf{r}(t) = \cos t\,\mathbf{i} + (\sin t - t)\,\mathbf{j} + t\,\mathbf{k}$, $\mathbf{v}(t) = -\sin t\,\mathbf{i} + (\cos t - 1)\,\mathbf{j} + \mathbf{k}$, $\|\mathbf{r}'(t)\| = \sqrt{3 - 2\cos t}$

39. $\kappa = \dfrac{6}{\sqrt{x}(4+9x)^{3/2}}$ 41. $\kappa = \dfrac{e^{2t}}{2(e^{2t}+1)^{3/2}}$ 43. $\kappa = 9/25$ 47. $\kappa = 1$, $a_T = 0$, $a_N = 1$

CHAPTER 15

SECTION 15.1

1. dom (f) = the first and third quadrants, including the axes; range $(f) = [0, \infty)$

3. dom (f) = the set of all points (x, y) not on the line $y = -x$; range $(f) = (-\infty, 0) \cup (0, \infty)$

5. dom (f) = the entire plane; range $(f) = (-1, 1)$

7. dom (f) = the first and third quadrants, excluding the axes; range $(f) = (-\infty, \infty)$

9. dom (f) = the set of all points (x, y) with $x^2 < y$; in other words, the set of all points of the plane above the parabola $y = x^2$; range $(f) = (0, \infty)$

11. dom (f) = the set of all points (x, y) with $-3 \le x \le 3$, $-2 \le y \le 2$ (a rectangle); range $(f) = [-2, 3]$

13. dom (f) = the set of all points (x, y, z) not on the plane $x + y + z = 0$; range $(f) = \{-1, 1\}$

15. dom (f) = the set of all points (x, y, z) with $|y| < |x|$; range $(f) = (-\infty, 0]$

17. dom (f) = the set of all points (x, y) such that $x^2 + y^2 < 9$; in other words, the set of all points of the plane inside the circle $x^2 + y^2 = 9$; range $(f) = \left[\frac{2}{3}, \infty\right)$

19. dom (f) = the set of all points (x, y, z) with $x + 2y + 3z > 0$; in other words, the set of all points in space that lie on the same side of the plane $x + 2y + 3z = 0$ as the point $(1, 1, 1)$; range $(f) = (-\infty, \infty)$

21. dom (f) = all of space; range $(f) = (0, 1]$

23. dom $(f) = \{x : x \ge 0\}$; range $(f) = [0, \infty)$
dom $(g) = \{(x, y) : x \ge 0,\ y \text{ real}\}$; range $(g) = [0, \infty)$
dom $(h) = \{x, y, z) : x \ge 0,\ y, z \text{ real}\}$; range $(h) = [0, \infty)$

25. $\lim\limits_{h\to 0} \dfrac{f(x+h, y) - f(x, y)}{h} = 4x$; $\lim\limits_{h\to 0} \dfrac{f(x, y+h) - f(x, y)}{h} = -1$

27. $\lim\limits_{h\to 0} \dfrac{f(x+h, y) - f(x, y)}{h} = 3 - y$; $\lim\limits_{h\to 0} \dfrac{f(x, y+h) - f(x, y)}{h} = -x + 4y$

29. $\lim\limits_{h\to 0} \dfrac{f(x+h, y) - f(x, y)}{h} = -y\sin(xy)$; $\lim\limits_{h\to 0} \dfrac{f(x, y+h) - f(x, y)}{h} = -x\sin(xy)$

31. (a) $f(x, y) = x^2 y$ (b) $f(x, y) = \pi x^2 y$ (c) $f(x, y) = 2|y|$ 33. $V = \dfrac{lh(10 - lh)}{l + h}$ 35. $V = \pi r^2 h + \frac{4}{3}\pi r^3$

SECTION 15.2

1. an elliptic cone 3. a parabolic cylinder 5. a hyperboloid of one sheet 7. sphere of radius 2 centered at the origin

9. an elliptic paraboloid 11. a hyperbolic paraboloid

13.
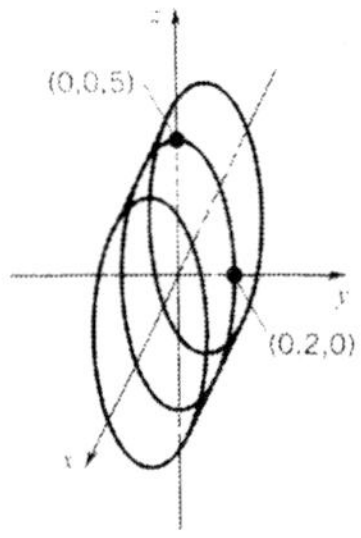

15.
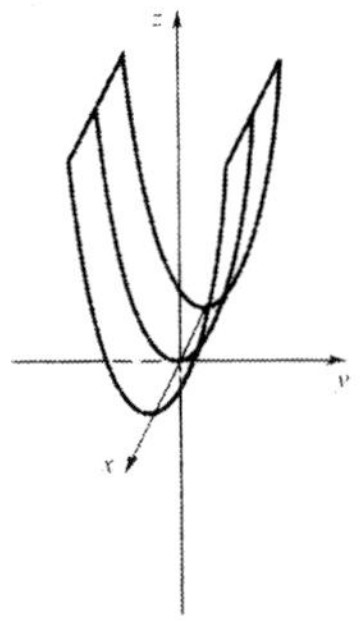

17.
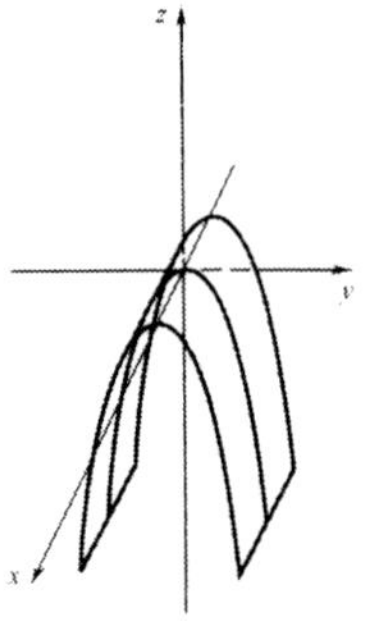

19.
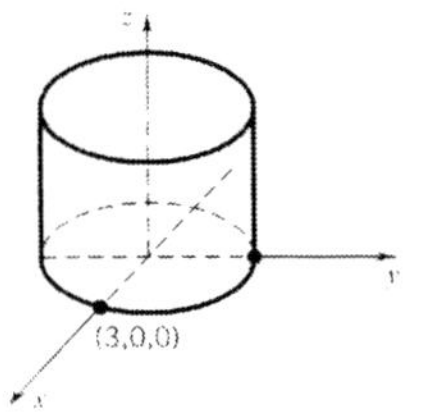

21.
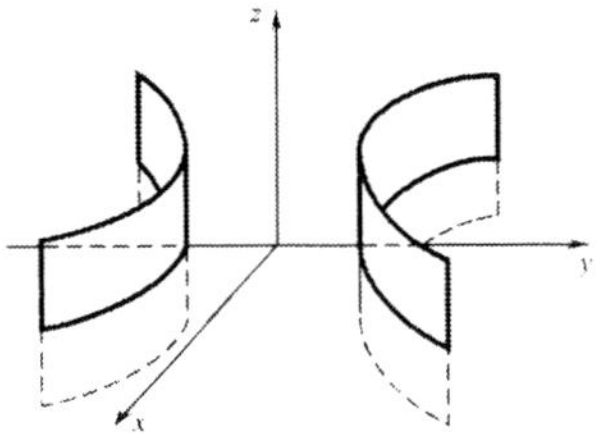

23.
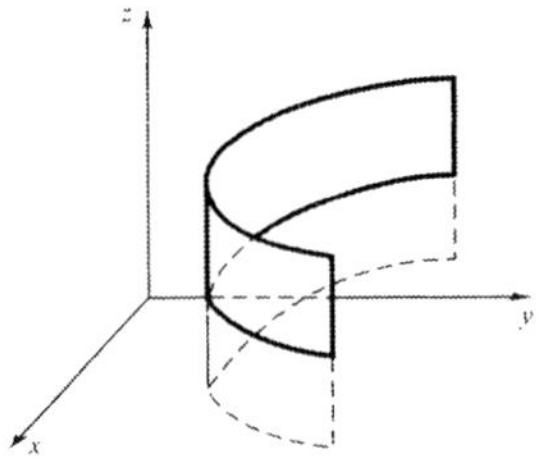

25. elliptic paraboloid, xy-trace: the origin, xz-trace: the parabola $x^2 = 4z$, yz-trace: the parabola $y^2 = 9z$, surface has the form of Figure 14.2.5

27. an elliptic cone, xy-trace: the origin, xz-trace: the lines $x = \pm 2z$, yz-trace: the lines $y = \pm 3z$, surface has the form of Figure 14.2.4

29. a hyperboloid of two sheets, xy-trace: none, xz-trace: the hyperbola $4z^2 - x^2 = 4$, yz-trace: the hyperbola $9z^2 - y^2 = 9$, surface has the form of Figure 14.2.3

31. hyperboloid of two sheets, xy-trace: the hyperbola $\frac{x^2}{4} - \frac{y^2}{9} = 1$, xz-trace: the hyperbola $\frac{y^2}{4} - z^2 = 1$, yz-trace: none, see Figure 14.2.3 for an example

33. elliptic paraboloid, xz-trace: the origin, yz-trace: the parabola $z^2 = 4y$, xy-trace: the parabola $x^2 = 9y$, surface has the form of Figure 14.2.5

35. hyperboloid of two sheets, xy-trace: the hyperbola $\frac{y^2}{4} - \frac{x^2}{9} = 1$, xz-trace: none, yz-trace: the hyperbola $\frac{y^2}{4} - z^2 = 1$, see Figure 14.2.3 for an example

37. paraboloid of revolution, xy-trace: the origin, xz-trace: the parabola $x^2 = 4z$, yz-trace: the parabola $y^2 = 4z$, surface has the form of Figure 14.2.5.

39. (a) an elliptic paraboloid (opening up if A and B are both positive, opening down if A and B are both negative)
(b) a hyperbolic paraboloid (c) the xy-plane if A and B are both zero; otherwise, a parabolic cylinder

41. $x^2 + y^2 - 4z = 0$ (paraboloid of revolution) 43. (a) a circle (b) (i) $\sqrt{x^2 + y^2} = -3z$ (ii) $\sqrt{x^2 + z^2} = \frac{1}{3}y$

45. the line $5x + 7y = 30$ 47. the circle $x^2 + y^2 = \frac{5}{4}$ 49. the ellipse $x^2 + 2y^2 = 2$ 51. the parabola $x^2 = -4(y - 1)$

53. Set $\frac{x}{a} = \cos u \cos v$, $\frac{y}{b} = \cos u \sin v$, $\frac{z}{c} = \sin u$. 55. Set $\frac{x}{a} = v \cos u$, $\frac{y}{b} = v \sin u$, $\frac{z}{c} = v$

SECTION 15.3

1. lines of slope 1 : $y = x - c$

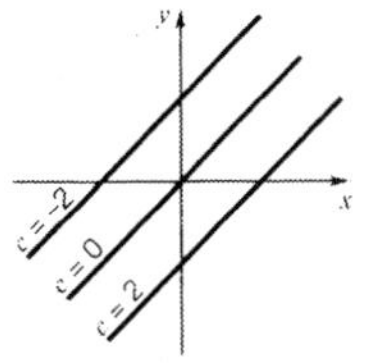

3. parabolas, $y = x^2 - c$

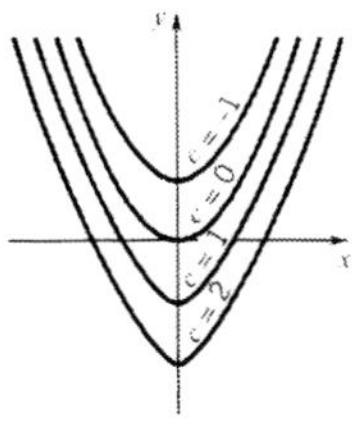

5. the y-axis and the lines $y = \left(\frac{1-c}{c}\right)x$, the origin omitted throughout

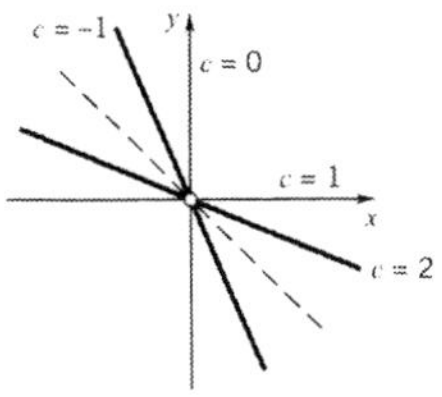

7. the cubics $y = x^3 - c$

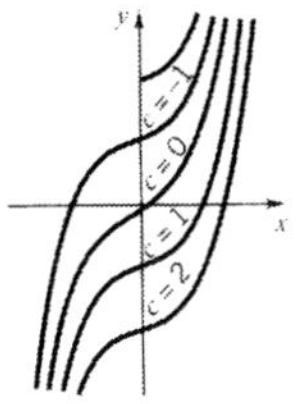

9. the lines $y = \pm x$ and the hyperbolas $x^2 - y^2 = c$

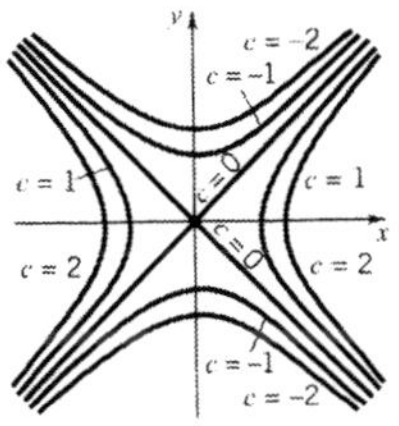

11. pairs of horizontal lines $y = \pm\sqrt{c}$ and the x-axis

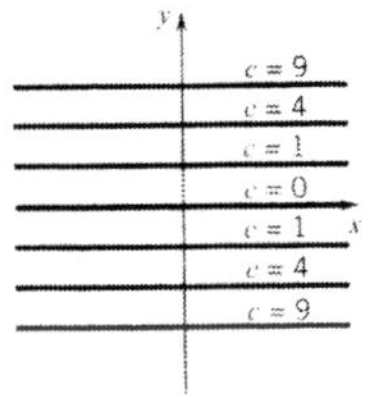

13. the circle $x^2 + y^2 = e^c$ with c real

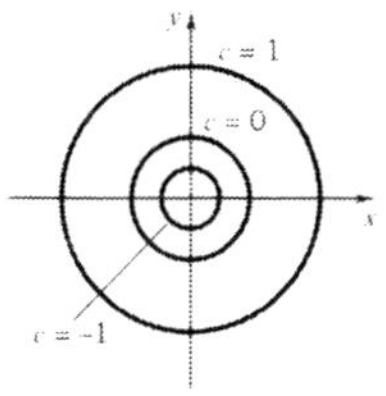

15. the curves $y = e^{cx^2}$ with the point (0, 1) omitted

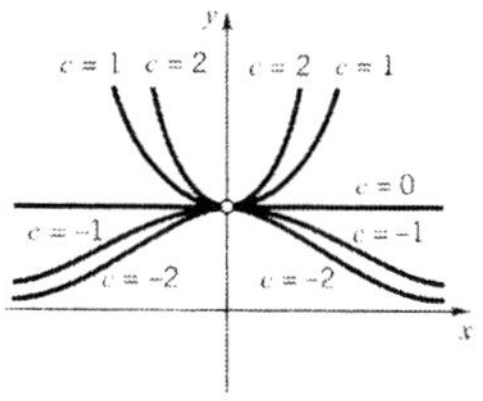

17. the coordinate axes and pairs of lines $y = \pm(\sqrt{1-c}/\sqrt{c})x$, the origin omitted throughout

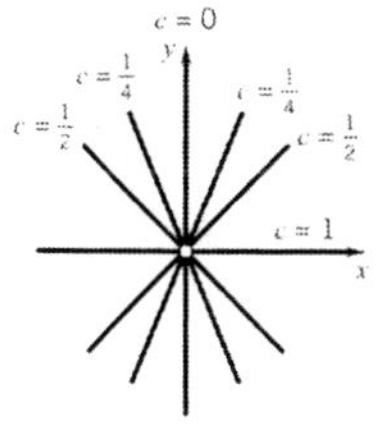

19. $x + 2y + 3z = 0$, plane through the origin

21. $z = \sqrt{x^2 + y^2}$, the upper nappe of the circular cone $z^2 = x^2 + y^2$; Figure 14.2.4

23. the elliptic paraboloid $\frac{x^2}{18} + \frac{y^2}{8} = z$ Figure 14.2.5

25. (i) hyperboloid of two sheets; Figure 14.2.3 (ii) circular cone; Figure 14.2.4 (iii) hyperboloid of one sheet; Figure 14.2.2

27. $4x^2 + y^2 = 1$

29. $y^2 \arctan x = \pi$

31. $x^2 + 2y^2 - 2xyz = 13$

35. (a) $\dfrac{3x+2y+1}{4x^2+9}=\dfrac{3}{5}$
(b) $x^2+2y^2-z^2=21$

37. $x^2+y^2+z^2=\dfrac{GmM}{c}$. The surfaces of constant gravitational force are concentric spheres.

39. (a) $T(x,y,z)=\dfrac{k}{\sqrt{x^2+y^2+z^2}}$ (b) $x^2+y^2+z^2=C$ constant, spheres.
(c) $T(4,0,3)=10\sqrt{6}$

41. F 43. A 45. E

SECTION 15.4

1. $\dfrac{\partial f}{\partial x}=6x-y,\quad \dfrac{\partial f}{\partial y}=1-x$

3. $\dfrac{\partial \rho}{\partial \phi}=\cos\phi\cos\theta,\quad \dfrac{\partial \rho}{\partial \theta}=-\sin\phi\sin\theta$

5. $\dfrac{\partial f}{\partial x}=e^{x-y}+e^{y-x},\quad \dfrac{\partial f}{\partial y}=-e^{x-y}-e^{y-x}$

7. $\dfrac{\partial g}{\partial x}=\dfrac{(AD-BC)y}{(Cx+Dy)^2},\quad \dfrac{\partial g}{\partial y}=\dfrac{(BC-AD)x}{(Cx+Dy)^2}$

9. $\dfrac{\partial u}{\partial x}=y+z,\quad \dfrac{\partial u}{\partial y}=x+z,\quad \dfrac{\partial u}{\partial z}=x+y$

11. $\dfrac{\partial f}{\partial x}=z\cos(x-y),\quad \dfrac{\partial f}{\partial y}=-z\cos(x-y),\quad \dfrac{\partial f}{\partial z}=\sin(x-y)$

13. $\dfrac{\partial \rho}{\partial \theta}=e^{\theta+\phi}[\cos(\theta-\phi)-\sin(\theta-\phi)],\quad \dfrac{\partial \rho}{\partial \phi}=e^{\theta+\phi}[\cos(\theta-\phi)+\sin(\theta-\phi)]$

15. $\dfrac{\partial f}{\partial x}=2xy\sec(xy)+x^2y^2\sec(xy)\tan(xy),\quad \dfrac{\partial f}{\partial y}=x^2\sec(xy)+x^3y\sec(xy)\tan(xy)$

17. $\dfrac{\partial h}{\partial x}=\dfrac{y^2-x^2}{(x^2+y^2)^2},\quad \dfrac{\partial h}{\partial y}=-\dfrac{2xy}{(x^2+y^2)^2}$

19. $\dfrac{\partial f}{\partial x}=\dfrac{\sin y(\cos x+x\sin x)}{y\cos^2 x},\quad \dfrac{\partial f}{\partial y}=\dfrac{x(y\cos y-\sin y)}{y^2\cos x}$

21. $\dfrac{\partial h}{\partial x}=2f(x)f'(x)g(y),\quad \dfrac{\partial h}{\partial y}=[f(x)]^2g'(y)$

23. $\dfrac{\partial f}{\partial x}=(y^2\ln z)z^{xy^2},\quad \dfrac{\partial f}{\partial y}=(2xy\ln z)z^{xy^2},\quad \dfrac{\partial f}{\partial z}=xy^2z^{xy^2-1}$

25. $\dfrac{\partial h}{\partial r}=2re^{2t}\cos(\theta-t),\quad \dfrac{\partial h}{\partial \theta}=-r^2e^{2t}\sin(\theta-t),\quad \dfrac{\partial h}{\partial t}=r^2e^{2t}[2\cos(\theta-t)+\sin(\theta-t)]$

27. $\dfrac{\partial f}{\partial x}=-\dfrac{yz}{x^2+y^2},\quad \dfrac{\partial f}{\partial y}=\dfrac{xz}{x^2+y^2},\quad \dfrac{\partial f}{\partial z}=\arctan(y/x)$

29. $f_x(0,e)=1,\quad f_y(0,e)=e^{-1}$

31. $f_x(1,2)=\frac{2}{9},\quad f_y(1,2)=-\frac{1}{9}$

33. $f_x(x,y)=2xy,\ f_y(x,y)=x^2$

35. $f_x(x,y)=\dfrac{2}{x},\ f_y(x,y)=\dfrac{1}{y}$

37. $f_x(x,y)=-\dfrac{1}{(x-y)^2},\quad f_y(x,y)=\dfrac{1}{(x-y)^2}$

39. $f_x(x,y,z)=y^2z,\quad f_y(x,y,z)=2xyz,\quad f_z(x,y,z)=xy^2$

41. (b) $x=x_0,\quad z-z_0=f_y(x_0,y_0)(y-y_0)$

43. $x=2,\quad z-5=2(y-1)$

45. $y=2,\quad z-9=6(x-3)$

47. (a) $m_x=-6$; tangent line: $y=2,\ z=-6x+13$
(b) $m_y=18$; tangent line: $x=1,\ z=18y-29$

53. (a) f depends only on y (b) f depends only on x

55. (a) $50\sqrt{3}$ in.^{2} (b) $5\sqrt{3}$ in.^{2} (c) 50 in.^{2} (d) $\frac{5}{18}\pi$ in.^{2} (e) -2

57. (a) y_0-section: $\mathbf{r}(x)=x\mathbf{i}+y_0\mathbf{j}+f(x_0,y_0)\,\mathbf{k}$

tangent line: $\mathbf{R}(t)=[x_0\mathbf{i}+y_0\mathbf{j}+f(x_0,y_0)\,\mathbf{k}]+t\left[\mathbf{i}+\dfrac{\partial f}{\partial x}(x_0,y_0)\,\mathbf{k}\right]$

(b) x_0-section: $\mathbf{r}(y)=x_0\mathbf{i}+y\mathbf{j}+f(x_0,y)\,\mathbf{k}$

tangent line: $\mathbf{R}(t)=[x_0\mathbf{i}+y_0\mathbf{j}+f(x_0,y_0)\,\mathbf{k}]+t\left[\mathbf{j}+\dfrac{\partial f}{\partial x}(x_0,y_0)\,\mathbf{k}\right]$

SECTION 15.5

1. interior $=\{(x,y): 2<x<4,\ 1<y<3\}$. (the inside of the rectangle)
boundary = the union of the four line segments that bound the rectangle;
set is closed

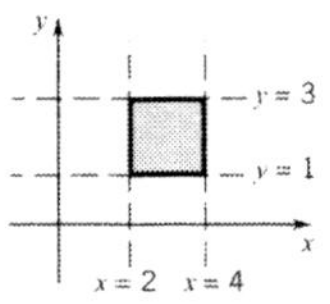

3. interior = the entire set (region between two concentric circles)
boundary = $\{(x, y) : x^2 + y^2 = 1 \text{ or } x^2 + y^2 = 4\}$ (the two circles);
set is open

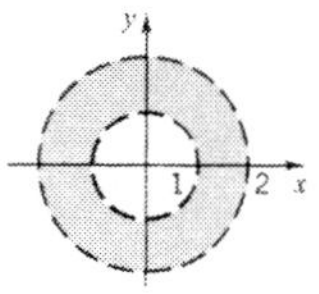

5. interior = $\{(x, y) : 1 < x^2 < 4\} = \{(x, y) : -2 < x < 1\} \cup \{(x, y) : 1 < x < 2\}$
(two vertical strips without the boundary lines)
boundary = $\{(x, y) : x = -2, x = -1, x = 1, \text{ or } x = 2\}$ (four vertical lines);
set is neither open nor closed

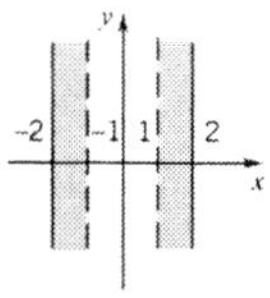

7. interior = $\{(x, y) : y < x^2\}$ (region below the parabola)
boundary = $\{(x, y) : y = x^2\}$ (the parabola);
set is closed

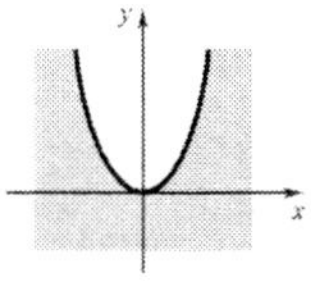

9. interior = $\{(x, y, z) : x^2 + y^2 < 1, 0 < z < 4\}$
(the inside of a cylinder)
boundary = the total surface of the cylinder
(the curved part, the top, the bottom);
set is closed

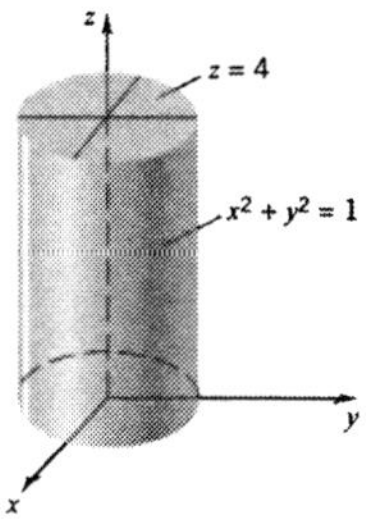

11. (a) ϕ (b) S (c) closed

13. interior = $\{x : 1 < x < 3\}$, boundary = $\{1, 3\}$; set is closed

15. interior = the entire set, boundary = $\{1\}$; set is open

17. interior = $\{x : |x| > 1\}$, boundary = $\{1, -1\}$; set is neither open nor closed

19. interior = ϕ, boundary = {the entire set} $\cup \{0\}$; the set is neither open nor closed

SECTION 15.6

1. $\dfrac{\partial^2 f}{\partial x^2} = 2A, \quad \dfrac{\partial^2 f}{\partial y^2} = 2C, \quad \dfrac{\partial^2 f}{\partial y \partial x} = \dfrac{\partial f}{\partial x \partial y} = 2B$

3. $\dfrac{\partial^2 f}{dx^2} = Cy^2 e^{xy}, \quad \dfrac{\partial^2 f}{\partial y^2} = Cx^2 e^{xy}, \quad \dfrac{\partial^2 f}{\partial y \partial x} = \dfrac{\partial^2 f}{\partial x \partial y} = Ce^{xy}(xy + 1)$

5. $\dfrac{\partial^2 f}{\partial x^2} = 2, \quad \dfrac{\partial^2 f}{\partial y^2} = 4(x + 3y^2 + z^3), \quad \dfrac{\partial^2 f}{\partial z^2} = 6z(2x + 2y^2 + 5z^3)$

$\dfrac{\partial^2 f}{\partial x \partial y} = \dfrac{\partial^2 f}{\partial y \partial x} = 4y, \quad \dfrac{\partial^2 f}{\partial z \partial x} = \dfrac{\partial^2 f}{\partial x \partial z} = 6z^2, \quad \dfrac{\partial^2 f}{\partial z \partial y} = \dfrac{\partial^2 f}{\partial y \partial z} = 12yz^2$

7. $\dfrac{\partial^2 f}{\partial x^2} = \dfrac{1}{(x + y)^2} - \dfrac{1}{x^2}, \quad \dfrac{\partial^2 f}{\partial y^2} = \dfrac{1}{(x + y)^2}, \quad \dfrac{\partial^2 f}{\partial y \partial x} = \dfrac{\partial^2 f}{\partial x \partial y} = \dfrac{1}{(x + y)^2}$

9. $\dfrac{\partial^2 f}{\partial x^2} = 2(y + z), \quad \dfrac{\partial^2 f}{\partial y^2} = 2(x + z), \quad \dfrac{\partial^2 f}{\partial z^2} = 2(x + y)$; the second mixed partials are all $2(x + y + z)$

11. $\dfrac{\partial^2 f}{\partial x^2} = y(y - 1)x^{y-2}, \quad \dfrac{\partial^2 f}{\partial y^2} = (\ln x)^2 x^y, \quad \dfrac{\partial^2 f}{\partial y \partial x} = \dfrac{\partial^2 f}{\partial x \partial y} = x^{y-1}(1 + y \ln x)$

13. $\dfrac{\partial^2 f}{\partial x^2} = ye^x, \quad \dfrac{\partial^2 f}{\partial y^2} = xe^y, \quad \dfrac{\partial^2 f}{\partial y \partial x} = e^y + e^x = \dfrac{\partial^2 f}{\partial x \partial y}$

15. $\dfrac{\partial^2 f}{\partial x^2} = \dfrac{y^2 - x^2}{(x^2 + y^2)^2}, \quad \dfrac{\partial^2 f}{\partial y^2} = \dfrac{x^2 - y^2}{(x^2 + y^2)^2}, \quad \dfrac{\partial^2 f}{\partial y \partial x} = -\dfrac{2xy}{(x^2 + y^2)^2} = \dfrac{\partial^2 f}{\partial x \partial y}$

17. $\dfrac{\partial^2 y}{\partial x^2} = -2y^2 \cos 2xy, \quad \dfrac{\partial^2 f}{\partial y^2} = -2x^2 \cos 2xy, \quad \dfrac{\partial^2 f}{\partial y \partial x} = -[\sin 2xy + 2xy \cos 2xy] = \dfrac{\partial^2 f}{\partial x \partial y}$

19. $\dfrac{\partial^2 f}{\partial x^2} = 0, \quad \dfrac{\partial^2 f}{\partial y^2} = xz \sin y, \quad \dfrac{\partial^2 f}{\partial z^2} = -xy \sin z$

$\dfrac{\partial^2 f}{\partial y \partial x} = \sin z - z \cos y = \dfrac{\partial^2 f}{\partial x \partial y}$

$\dfrac{\partial^2 f}{\partial z \partial x} = y \cos z - \sin y = \dfrac{\partial^2 f}{\partial x \partial z}$

$\dfrac{\partial^2 f}{\partial z \partial y} = x \cos z - x \cos y = \dfrac{\partial^2 f}{\partial y \partial z}$

23. (a) no, since $\dfrac{\partial^2 f}{\partial x \partial y} \neq \dfrac{\partial^2 f}{\partial y \partial x}$ (b) no, since $\dfrac{\partial^2 f}{\partial x \partial y} \neq \dfrac{\partial^2 f}{\partial y \partial x}$ for $x \neq y$

27. (a) 0 (b) 0 (c) $\dfrac{m}{1+m^2}$ (d) 0 (e) $\dfrac{f'(0)}{1+[f'(0)]^2}$ (f) $\dfrac{1}{4}\sqrt{3}$ (g) does not exist

29. (a) $\dfrac{\partial g}{\partial x}(0, 0) = \lim_{h \to 0} \dfrac{g(h, 0) - g(0, 0)}{h} = \lim_{h \to 0} 0 = 0, \quad \dfrac{\partial g}{\partial y}(0, 0) = \lim_{h \to 0} \dfrac{g(0, h) - g(0, 0)}{h} - \lim_{h \to 0} = 0$

(b) as (x, y) tends to $(0, 0)$ along the x-axis, $g(x, y) = g(x, 0) = 0$ tends to 0;

as (x, y) tends to $(0, 0)$ along the line $y = x$, $g(x, y) = g(x, x) = \frac{1}{2}$ tends to $\frac{1}{2}$

33. f must have the form: $f(x, y) = g(x) + h(y)$

Chapter 15 Review Exercises

1. domain: $\{(x, y) : y > x^2\}$; range: $(0, \infty)$

3. domain: $\{(x, y, z) : z \geq x^2 + y^2\}$; range: $[0, \infty)$

5. (a) $V = \frac{1}{3}\pi x^2 y$ (b) $V = 2x^2 y$ (c) $\theta = \arccos \dfrac{x + 2y}{\sqrt{5(x^2 + y^2)}}$

7. ellipsoid
xy-trace: the ellipse $4x^2 + 9y^2 = 36$
xz-trace: the ellipse $4x^2 + 36z^2 = 36$
yz-trace: the ellipse $9y^2 + 36z^2 = 36$

9. hyperbolic paraboloid
xy-trace; the lines $y = \pm x$
xz-trace; the parabola $z = -x^2$
yz-trace; the parabola $z = y^2$

11. circular cone
xy-trace: the lines $y = \pm x$
xz-trace: the lines $z = \pm x$
yz-trace: the origin

13. 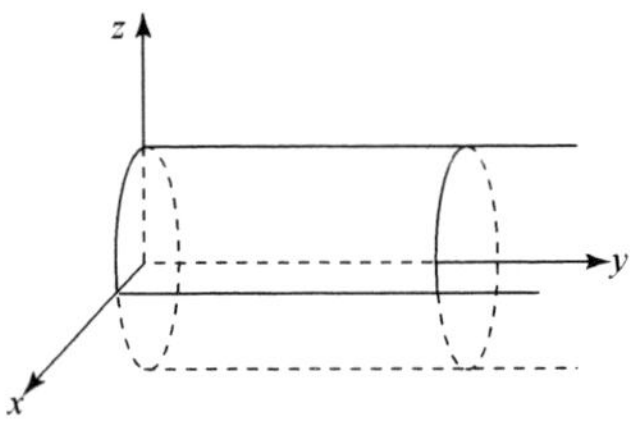

15. 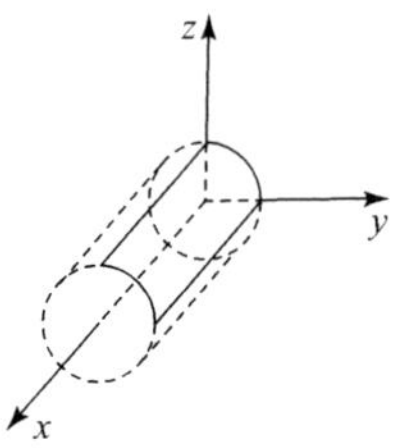

17. ellipses centered at the origin, major axes horizontal

19. parabolas with vertex at the origin, vertices and foci on the x-axis

21. the plane $2x + y + 3z = 6$

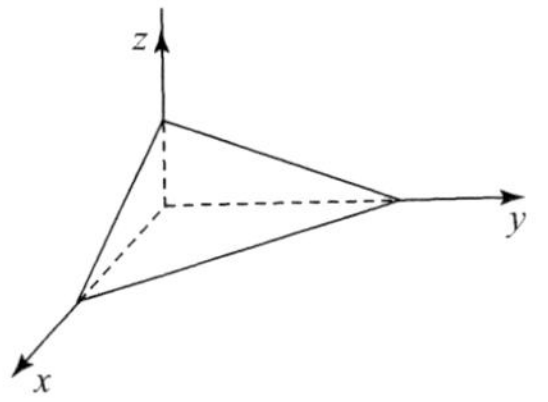

23. (a) $(y^2+1)e^x = 1$ (b) $(y^2+1)e^x = 4$ (c) $(y^2+1)e^x = 2e$

25. $f_x(x, y) = 2xy + 2y$ 27. $f_x(x, y) = 2xy - 2y^3$, $f_y(x, y) = x^2 - 6xy^2$

29. $\dfrac{\partial z}{\partial x} = 2x \sin xy^2 + x^2y^2 \cos xy^2$, $\dfrac{\partial z}{\partial y} = 2x^3 y \cos xy^2$

31. $h_x(x, y) = -2e^{-x} \sin(2x - y) - e^{-x} \cos(2x - y)$, $h_y(x, y) = e^{-x} \sin(2x - y)$

33. $f_x(x, y, z) = \dfrac{2y^2 + 2yz}{(x+y+z)^2}$, $f_y(x, y, z) = \dfrac{2x^2 + 2xz}{(x+y+z)^2}$, $f_x(x, y, z) = \dfrac{-2xy}{(x+y+z)^2}$

35. $f_x(x, y, z) = \dfrac{x}{x^2+y^2+z^2}$, $f_y(x, y, z) = \dfrac{y}{x^2+y^2+z^2}$ $f_z(x, y, z) = \dfrac{z}{x^2+y^2+z^2}$

37. $f_{xx}(x, y) = 6xy^2$, $f_{xy}(x, y) = 6x^2y - 12y^2$, $f_{yy}(x, y) = 2x^3 - 24xy$

39. $g_{xx}(x, y) = 2y^2 \cos xy - xy^3 \sin xy$,
$g_{xy}(x, y) = \sin xy + 3xy \cos xy - x^2y^2 \sin xy$
$g_{yy}(x, y) = 2x^2 \cos xy - x^3 y \sin xy$

41. $f_{xx}(x, y, z) = 2e^{2y} \cos(2z+1)$, $f_{xy}(x, y, z) = 4xe^{2y} \cos(2z+1)$
$f_{xz}(x, y, z) = -4x^2e^{2y} \sin(2z+1)$, $f_{yy}(x, y, z) = 4x^2e^{2y} \cos(2z+1)$,
$f_{yz}(x, y, z) = -8x^2e^{2y} \sin(2z+1)$, $f_{zz}(x, y, z) = -4x^2e^{2y} \cos(2z+1)$

43. $x = 1 + \frac{1}{10}t$, $y = 2$, $z = 8 + t$

45. (a) $x = 2$, $y = 1 - t$, $z = 3 + t$ (b) $x = 2 - \frac{3}{4}t$, $y = 1$, $z = 3 + t$ (c) $4x + 3y + 3z = 20$

47. interior: $\{(x, y) : 0 < x^2 + y^2 < 4\}$, boundary: $(0, 0)$, $x^2 + y^2 = 4$, open

49. interior: $\{(x, y, z) : 0 < x < 2, y^2 + z^2 < 4\}$
boundary: the square $0 \le x \le 2, 0 \le y \le 2$, the square $0 \le x \le 2, 0 \le z \le 2$,
the quarter disks $0 \le y^2 + z^2 \le 4, x = 0$, $0 \le y^2 + z^2 \le 4, x = 2$

53. no; $\dfrac{\partial^2 f}{\partial x \partial y} = x^2 e^{xy} \ne y^2 e^{xy} = \dfrac{\partial^2 f}{\partial y \partial x}$

CHAPTER 16

SECTION 16.1

1. $(6x - y)\mathbf{i} + (1 - x)\mathbf{j}$ 3. $e^{xy}[(xy+1)\mathbf{i} + x^2\mathbf{j}]$ 5. $[2y^2 \sin(x^2+1) + 4x^2y^2 \cos(x^2+1)]\mathbf{i} + 4xy \sin(x^2+1)\mathbf{j}$

7. $(e^{x-y} + e^{y-x})(\mathbf{i} - \mathbf{j})$ 9. $(z^2 + 2xy)\mathbf{i} + (x^2 + 2yz)\mathbf{j} + (y^2 + 2xz)\mathbf{k}$ 11. $e^{-z}(2xy\,\mathbf{i} + x^2\mathbf{j} - x^2y\,\mathbf{k})$

13. $e^{x+2y} \cos(z^2+1)\mathbf{i} + 2e^{x+2y} \cos(z^2+1)\mathbf{j} - 2ze^{x+2y} \sin(z^2+1)\mathbf{k}$ 15. $\left[2y \cos(2xy) + \dfrac{2}{x}\right]\mathbf{i} + 2x \cos(2xy)\mathbf{j} + \dfrac{1}{z}\mathbf{k}$

17. $\nabla f = -\mathbf{i} + 18\mathbf{j}$ 19. $\frac{4}{5}\mathbf{i} + \frac{2}{5}\mathbf{j}$ 21. $\mathbf{i}$ 23. $\nabla f = -\frac{1}{2}\sqrt{2}(\mathbf{i} + 2\mathbf{j} + \mathbf{k})$ 25. $\mathbf{i} + \frac{3}{5}\mathbf{j} - \frac{4}{5}\mathbf{k}$

27. (a) $\nabla f(0, 2) = 4\mathbf{i}$

(b) $\nabla f(\pi/4, \pi/6) = \left(-1 - \dfrac{-1+\sqrt{3}}{2\sqrt{2}}\right)\mathbf{i} + \left(-\dfrac{1}{2} + \dfrac{-1+\sqrt{3}}{\sqrt{2}}\right)\mathbf{j}$ (c) $\nabla f(1, e) = (1 - 2e)\mathbf{i} - 2\mathbf{j}$

29. $(6x - y)\mathbf{i} + (1 - x)\mathbf{j}$ 31. $(2xy + z^2)\mathbf{i} + (2yz + x^2)\mathbf{j} + (2xz + y^2)\mathbf{k}$

33. $f(x, y) = x^2y + y$ 35. $f(x, y) = \dfrac{x^2}{2} + x\sin y - y^2$ 37. (a) $(1/r^2)\mathbf{r}$ (b) $[(\cos r)/r]\mathbf{r}$ (c) $(e^r/r)\mathbf{r}$

39. (a) $(0, 0)$ (b)

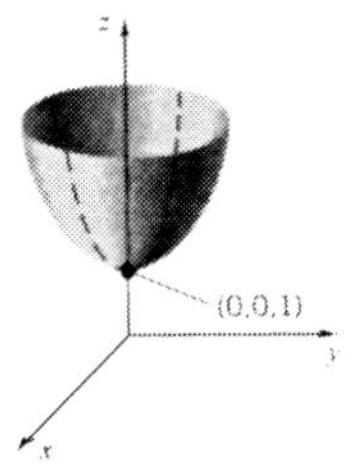

(c) f has an absolute minimum at $(0, 0)$

SECTION 16.2

1. $-2\sqrt{2}$ 3. $\frac{1}{5}(7 - 4e)$ 5. $\frac{1}{4}\sqrt{2}(a - b)$ 7. $\dfrac{2}{\sqrt{65}}$ 9. $\frac{2}{3}\sqrt{6}$ 11. $-3\sqrt{2}$ 13. $\dfrac{\sqrt{3}\pi}{12}$ 15. $-(x^2 + y^2)^{-1/2}$

17. (a) $\sqrt{2}[a(B - A) + b(C - B)]$ (b) $\sqrt{2}[a(A - B) + b(B - C)]$ 19. $-\frac{7}{5}\sqrt{5}$ 21. $\pm\frac{18}{\sqrt{14}}$

23. increases most rapidly in the direction of $\dfrac{1}{\sqrt{2}}\mathbf{i} + \dfrac{1}{\sqrt{2}}\mathbf{j}$, rate of change $2\sqrt{2}$; decreases most rapidly in the direction of $-\dfrac{1}{\sqrt{2}}\mathbf{i} - \dfrac{1}{\sqrt{2}}\mathbf{j}$, rate of change $-2\sqrt{2}$

25. increases most rapidly in the direction of $\dfrac{1}{\sqrt{6}}\mathbf{i} - \dfrac{2}{\sqrt{6}}\mathbf{j} + \dfrac{1}{\sqrt{6}}\mathbf{k}$, rate of change 1; decreases most rapidly in the direction of $-\dfrac{1}{\sqrt{6}}\mathbf{i} + \dfrac{2}{\sqrt{6}}\mathbf{j} - \dfrac{1}{\sqrt{6}}\mathbf{k}$, rate of change -1

27. $\nabla f = f'(x_0)\mathbf{i}$. If $f'(x_0) \neq 0$, the gradient points in the direction in which f increases: to the right if $f'(x_0) > 0$, to the left if $f'(x_0) < 0$.

29. (a) $\lim_{h\to 0} \dfrac{f(h, 0) - f(0, 0)}{h} = \lim_{h\to 0} \dfrac{\sqrt{h^2}}{h} = \lim_{h\to 0} \dfrac{|h|}{h}$ does not exist (b) no; by Theorem 16.2.5 f cannot be differentiable at $(0, 0)$

31. (a) $-\frac{2}{3}\sqrt{97}$ (b) $-\frac{8}{3}$ (c) $-\frac{26}{3}\sqrt{2}$ 33. (a) its projection onto the xy-plane is the curve $y = x^3$ from $(1, 1)$ to $(0, 0)$
(b) its projection onto the xy-plane is the curve $y = -2x^3$ from $(1, -2)$ to $(0, 0)$

35. its projection onto the xy-plane is the curve $(b^2)^{a^2}x^{b^2} = (a^2)^{b^2}y^{a^2}$ from (a^2, b^2) to $(0, 0)$

37. the curve $y = \ln|\sqrt{2}\sin x|$ in the direction of decreasing x

39. (a) 16 (b) 4 (c) $\frac{16}{17}\sqrt{17}$
(d) The limits computed in (a) and (b) are not directional derivatives. In (a) and (b) we have, in essence, computed $\nabla f(2, 4) \cdot \mathbf{r}_0$ taking $\mathbf{r}_0 = \mathbf{i} + 4\mathbf{j}$ in (a) and $\mathbf{r}_0 = \frac{1}{4}\mathbf{i} + \mathbf{j}$ in (b). In neither case is $\mathbf{r}_0$ a unit vector.

41. (b) $\dfrac{2\sqrt{3} - 3}{2}$

SECTION 16.3

1. $C = \left(\frac{1}{3}, \frac{5}{3}\right)$ 3. (a) $f(x, y, z) = a_1x + a_2y + a_3z + C$ (b) $f(x, y, z) = g(x, y, z) + a_1x + a_2y + a_3z + C$

5. (a) U is not connected (b) (i) $g(x) = f(x) - 1$ (ii) $g(x) = -f(x)$ 7. e^t 9. $\dfrac{-2\sin 2t}{1 + \cos^2 2t}$

11. $t^t\left[\dfrac{1}{t} + \ln t + (\ln t)^2\right] + \dfrac{1}{t}$ 13. $3t^2 - 5t^4$ 15. $2\omega(b^2 - a^2)\sin\omega t\cos\omega t + b\omega$ 17. $\sin 2t - 3\cos 2t$

19. $e^{t/2}\left(\frac{1}{2}\sin 2t + 2\cos 2t\right) + e^{2t}\left(2\sin\frac{1}{2}t + \frac{1}{2}\cos\frac{1}{2}t\right)$ 21. $e^{t^2}[2t\sin\pi t + \pi\cos\pi t]$ 23. $1 - 4t + 6t^2 - 4t^3$

25. increasing $\frac{1288}{3}\pi$ in.^{3}/sec 27. 41.34 sq in./sec 29. $\dfrac{\partial u}{\partial s} = 2s\cos^2 t - t\sin s\cos t - st\cos s\cos t$
$\dfrac{\partial u}{\partial t} = -2s^2\sin t\cos t + st\sin s\sin t - s\sin s\cos t$

31. $\dfrac{\partial u}{\partial s} = 4s^3t^2 \tan(s+t^2) + s^4t^2 \sec^2(s+t^2)$;
$\dfrac{\partial u}{\partial t} = 2s^4 t \tan(s+t^2) + 2s^4t^3 \sec^2(s+t^2)$

33. $\dfrac{\partial u}{\partial s} = 2s\cos^2 t - \sin(t-s)\cos t + s\cos t\cos(t-s) + 2t^2 \sin s\cos s$
$\dfrac{\partial u}{\partial t} = -2s^2 \sin t\cos t + s\sin(t-s)\sin t - s\cos t\cos(t-s) + 2t\sin^2 s$

35. $\dfrac{d}{dt}[f(\mathbf{r}(t))] = \left[\nabla f(\mathbf{r}(t)) \cdot \dfrac{\mathbf{r}'(t)}{\|\mathbf{r}'(t)\|}\right] \|\mathbf{r}'(t)\| = f'_{\mathbf{u}}(\mathbf{r}(t))\ \|\mathbf{r}'(t)\|$ where $\mathbf{u}(t) = \dfrac{\mathbf{r}'(t)}{\|\mathbf{r}'(t)\|}$

37. (a) $(\cos r)\dfrac{\mathbf{r}}{r}$ (b) $(r\cos r + \sin r)\dfrac{\mathbf{r}}{r}$ 39. (a) $(r\cos r - \sin r)\dfrac{\mathbf{r}}{r^3}$ (b) $\left(\dfrac{\sin r - r\cos r}{\sin^2 r}\right)\dfrac{\mathbf{r}}{r}$

41. (a) See the figure
(b) $\dfrac{\partial u}{\partial r} = \dfrac{\partial u}{\partial x}\left(\dfrac{\partial u}{\partial w}\dfrac{\partial w}{\partial r} + \dfrac{\partial x}{\partial t}\dfrac{\partial t}{\partial r}\right) + \dfrac{\partial u}{\partial y}\left(\dfrac{\partial y}{\partial w}\dfrac{\partial w}{\partial r} + \dfrac{\partial y}{\partial t}\dfrac{\partial t}{\partial r}\right) + \dfrac{\partial u}{\partial z}\left(\dfrac{\partial z}{\partial w}\dfrac{\partial w}{\partial r} + \dfrac{\partial z}{\partial t}\dfrac{\partial t}{\partial r}\right)$

To obtain $\dfrac{\partial u}{\partial s}$, replace each r by s.

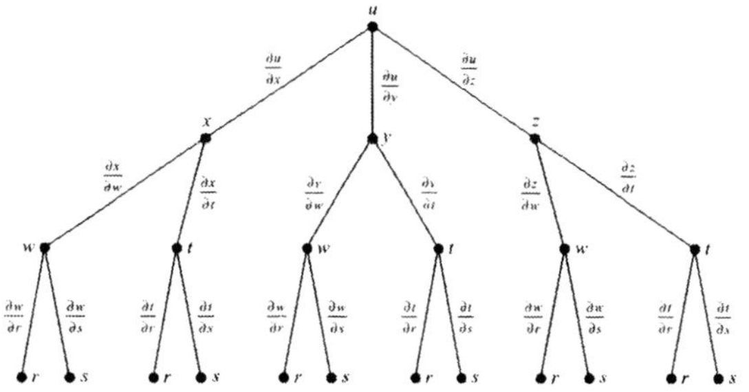

45. (b) $\left(\dfrac{\partial u}{\partial r}\right)^2 + \dfrac{1}{r^2}\left(\dfrac{\partial u}{\partial \theta}\right)^2 = \left(\dfrac{\partial u}{\partial x}\right)^2 + \left(\dfrac{\partial u}{\partial y}\right)^2$

49. $\nabla u = r(2 - \sin 2\theta)\,\mathbf{e}_r - r\cos 2\theta\ \mathbf{e}_\theta$

53. $\dfrac{dy}{dx} = -\dfrac{e^y + ye^x - 4xy}{xe^y + e^x - 2x^2}$

55. $\dfrac{dy}{dx} = \dfrac{\cos xy - xy\sin xy - y\sin x}{x^2 \sin xy - \cos x}$

57. $\dfrac{\partial z}{\partial x} = -\dfrac{2x - yz(x^2+y^2+z^2)\sin xyz}{2z - xy(x^2+y^2+z^2)\sin xyz}$; $\dfrac{\partial z}{\partial y} = -\dfrac{2y - xz(x^2+y^2+z^2)\sin xyz}{2z - xy(x^2+y^2+z^2)\sin xyz}$

59. $\dfrac{\partial \mathbf{u}}{\partial s} = \dfrac{\partial \mathbf{u}}{\partial x}\dfrac{\partial x}{\partial s} + \dfrac{\partial \mathbf{u}}{\partial y}\dfrac{\partial y}{\partial s}$, $\dfrac{\partial \mathbf{u}}{\partial t} = \dfrac{\partial \mathbf{u}}{\partial x}\dfrac{\partial x}{\partial t} + \dfrac{\partial \mathbf{u}}{\partial y}\dfrac{\partial y}{\partial t}$ where $\dfrac{\partial \mathbf{u}}{\partial x} = \dfrac{\partial u_1}{\partial x}\mathbf{i} + \dfrac{\partial u_2}{\partial x}\mathbf{j}$, $\dfrac{\partial \mathbf{u}}{\partial y} = \dfrac{\partial u_1}{\partial y}\mathbf{i} + \dfrac{\partial u_2}{\partial y}\mathbf{j}$

SECTION 16.4

1. normal vector $\mathbf{i} + \mathbf{j}$; tangent vector $\mathbf{i} - \mathbf{j}$
tangent line $x + y + 2 = 0$; normal line $x - y = 0$

3. normal vector $\sqrt{2}\,\mathbf{i} - 5\,\mathbf{j}$; tangent vector $5\,\mathbf{i} + \sqrt{2}\,\mathbf{j}$
tangent line $\sqrt{2}\,x - 5y + 3 = 0$; normal line $5x + \sqrt{2}\,y - 6\sqrt{2} = 0$

5. normal vector $7\,\mathbf{i} - 17\,\mathbf{j}$; tangent vector $17\,\mathbf{i} + 7\,\mathbf{j}$
tangent line $7x - 17y + 6 = 0$; normal line $17x + 7y - 82 = 0$

7. normal vector $\mathbf{i} - \mathbf{j}$; tangent vector $\mathbf{i} + \mathbf{j}$
tangent line $x - y - 3 = 0$; normal line $x + y + 1 = 0$

9. 0.

11. $4x - 5y + 4z = 0$; $x = 1 + 4t,\ y = 2 - 5t,\quad z = \frac{3}{2} + 4t$

13. $x + ay - z - 1 = 0$; $x = 1 + t,\ y = \frac{1}{a} + at,\quad z = 1 - t$

15. $2x + 2y - z = 0$; $x = 2t,\ y = 2t,\quad z = -t$

17. $b^2c^2x_0x - a^2c^2y_0y - a^2b^2z_0z - a^2 - b^2 - c^2 = 0$;
$x = x_0 + 2b^2c^2x_0t,\quad y = y_0 - 2a^2c^2y_0t,\quad z = z_0 - 2a^2b^2z_0t$

19. $(a^2/b,\ b^2/a,\ 3ab)$ 21. $(0, 0, 0)$ 23. $\left(\frac{1}{3}, \frac{11}{6}, -\frac{1}{12}\right)$

25. $\dfrac{x - x_0}{\partial f/\partial x(x_0, y_0, z_0)} = \dfrac{y - y_0}{\partial f/\partial y(x_0, y_0, z_0)} = \dfrac{z - z_0}{\partial f/\partial z(x_0, y_0, z_0)}$

27. the tangent planes meet at right angles and therefore the normals ∇F and ∇G must meet at right angles:

$$\frac{\partial F}{\partial x}\frac{\partial G}{\partial x}+\frac{\partial F}{\partial y}\frac{\partial G}{\partial y}+\frac{\partial F}{\partial z}\frac{\partial G}{\partial z}=0$$

29. $\frac{9}{2}a^3 (V=\frac{1}{3}Bh)$ 31. approx. 0.528 rad 33. $3x+4y+6z=22, \quad 6x+y-z=11$

35. $(1, 1, 2)$ lies on both surfaces and the normals at this point are perpendicular.

37. (a) $3x+4y+6=0$ (b) $\mathbf{r}(t)=(4t-2)\,\mathbf{i}-3t\,\mathbf{j}+(43t^2-16t+6)\,\mathbf{k}$ (c) $\mathbf{R}(s)=(2\,\mathbf{i}-3\,\mathbf{j}+33\,\mathbf{k})+s(4\,\mathbf{i}-3\,\mathbf{j}+70\,\mathbf{k})$
(d) $4x-18y-z=29$ (e) $\mathbf{r}(t)=t\,\mathbf{i}-\left(\frac{3}{4}t+\frac{3}{2}\right)\mathbf{j}+\left(\frac{35}{2}t-2\right)\mathbf{k}$; $l=l'$

39. (a) $2\,\mathbf{i}+2\,\mathbf{j}+4\,\mathbf{k}$; $x=1+2t, \quad y=2+2t, \quad z=2+4t$
(b) $x+y+2z-7=0$

41. (c) $\nabla f(x, y)=\mathbf{0}$ at $(0, 0), (\pm 1, 0), (0, \pm 1), (1, \pm 1), (-1, \pm 1)$

SECTION 16.5

1. $(1, 0)$ gives a local max of 1 3. $(-2, 1)$ gives a local min of -2 5. $(4, -2)$ gives a local min of -10

7. $(0, 0)$ is a saddle point; $(2, 2)$ gives a local min of -8 9. $\left(1, \frac{3}{2}\right)$ is a saddle point; $\left(5, \frac{27}{2}\right)$ gives a local min of $-\frac{117}{4}$

11. $(0, n\pi)$ for integral n are saddle points; no local extreme values 13. $(1, -1)$ and $(-1, 1)$ are saddle points; no local extreme values

15. $\left(\frac{1}{2}, 4\right)$ gives a local min of 6 17. $(1, 1)$ gives a local min of 3 19. $(1, 0)$ gives a local min of -1; $(-1, 0)$ gives a local max of 1

21. $(0, 0)$ is a saddle point; $(1, 0)$ and $(-1, 0)$ give a local min of -3

23. (π, π) is a saddle point; $\left(\frac{\pi}{2}, \frac{\pi}{2}\right)$ and $\left(\frac{3\pi}{2}, \frac{3\pi}{2}\right)$ give a local maximum of 1;
$\left(\frac{\pi}{2}, \frac{3\pi}{2}\right)$ and $\left(\frac{3\pi}{2}, \frac{\pi}{2}\right)$ give a local minimum of -1.

25. (a) $f_x=2x+ky, f_y=2y+kx$; $f_x(0, 0)=f_y(0, 0)=0$ independent of k (b) $|k|>2$ (c) $|k|<2$ (d) $|k|=2$

27. $\left(\frac{32}{9}, -\frac{16}{9}, \frac{32}{9}\right)$; $\frac{16}{3}$ 29. $\frac{\sqrt{114}}{6}$ 33. $(0, 0)$ is a saddle point; $(1, 1)$ gives a local maximum of 3.

35. $(-1, 0)$ gives a local maximum of 1; $(1, 0)$ gives a local minimum of -1.

SECTION 16.6

1. $(1, 1)$ gives absolute min of -1; $(2, 4)$ gives absolute max of 10

3. $(4, -2)$ gives absolute min of -13; $(0, -3)$ gives absolute max of 8

5. $(\sqrt{2}, -\sqrt{2})$ and $(-\sqrt{2}, \sqrt{2})$ give absolute min of 0; $(\sqrt{2}, \sqrt{2})$ and $(-\sqrt{2}, -\sqrt{2})$ give absolute max of 12

7. $(1, 1)$ gives absolute min of 0; $(-\sqrt{2}, -\sqrt{2})$ gives absolute max of $6+4\sqrt{2}$

9. $(1, 0)$ gives absolute min of -1; $(-1, 0)$ gives absolute max of 1

11. absolute min of 0 along the lines $x=0$ and $x=2$; $(1, 0)$ gives absolute max of 2

13. $(\sqrt{2}, 2)$ and $(-\sqrt{2}, -2)$ give absolute min of $-8-4\sqrt{2}$; $(-1, 1)$ gives absolute max of 1

15. $(0, 1)$ gives absolute min of -1; $(0, 1)$ gives absolute max of 1

17. absolute min of 0 along the line $y=x, 0\le x\le 4$; $(0, 12)$ gives absolute max of 144

19. $x=6, y=6, z=6$; maximum $=216$ 21. $\frac{1}{27}$

23. (a) $(0, 0)$ (b) no local extremes as $(0, 0)$ is a saddle point
(c) $(1, 0)$ and $(-1, 0)$ give absolute max of $\frac{1}{4}$; $(0, 1)$ and $(0, -1)$ give absolute min of $-\frac{1}{9}$

25. $V = \dfrac{xy(S-2xy)}{2(x+y)}$ has a maximum value when $x = y = z = \sqrt{\dfrac{S}{6}}$.

27. $\left(\dfrac{x_1+x_2+x_3}{3}, \dfrac{y_1+y_2+y_3}{3}\right)$ 29. $\theta = \frac{1}{6}\pi, x = (2-\sqrt{3})P, y = \frac{1}{6}(3-\sqrt{3})P$ 31. $\frac{2}{3}\sqrt{6}$

33. (a) cross section 18×18 inches; length 36 inches
(b) radius of cross section $36/\pi$ inches; length 36 inches

35. $x = 4$ in, $\theta = \dfrac{\pi}{3}$ 37. (a) $y = x - \frac{2}{3}$ (b) $y = \frac{14}{13}x^2 - \frac{19}{13}$

SECTION 16.7

1. 2 3. $-\frac{1}{2}ab$ 5. $\frac{2}{9}\sqrt{3}ab^2$ 7. 1 9. $\frac{1}{9}\sqrt{3}abc$ 11. $19\sqrt{2}$ 13. $\frac{1}{27}abc$ 15. 1

17. closest point $\left(\frac{2}{3}, \frac{1}{3}, \frac{2}{3}\right)$; furthest point $\left(-\frac{2}{3}, -\frac{1}{3}, -\frac{2}{3}\right)$ 19. $f(3, -2, 1) = 14$ 21. $|D|(A^2+B^2+C^2)^{-1/2}$

23. $4A^2(a^2+b^2+c^2)^{-1}$, where A is the area of the triangle and a, b, c, are the sides 25. $(2^{-1/3}, -2^{-1/3})$

29. (a) $f\left(\frac{k}{2}, \frac{k}{2}\right) = \frac{k}{2}$ is the maximum value (b) $(xy)^{1/2} = f(x, y) \le f\left(\frac{k}{2}, \frac{k}{2}\right) = \frac{k}{2} = \dfrac{x+y}{2}$

33. radius $\sqrt[3]{\dfrac{V}{2\pi}}$; height $2\sqrt[3]{\dfrac{V}{2\pi}}$ 35. $\dfrac{abc}{27}$

39. The optimal container is a sphere of radius $r = \dfrac{50\sqrt{3}}{\pi}$. 41. $\dfrac{16\sqrt{3}}{3}$ 43. $Q_1 = 10{,}000$, $Q_2 = 20{,}000$, $Q_3 = 30{,}000$

SECTION 16.8

1. $df = (3x^2y - 2xy^2)\Delta x + (x^3 - 2x^2y)\Delta y$ 3. $df = (\cos y + y\sin x)\Delta x - (x\sin y + \cos x)\Delta y$

5. $df = \Delta x - (\tan z)\Delta y - (y\sec^2 z)\Delta z$

7. $df = \dfrac{y(y^2+z^2-x^2)}{(x^2+y^2+z^2)^2}\Delta x + \dfrac{x(x^2+z^2-y^2)}{(x^2+y^2+z^2)^2}\Delta y - \dfrac{2xyz}{(x^2+y^2+z^2)^2}\Delta z$

9. $df = [\cos(x+y) + \cos(x-y)]\Delta x + [\cos(x+y) - \cos(x-y)]\Delta y$

11. $df = (y^2z\,e^{xz} + \ln z)\Delta x + 2y\,e^{xz}\Delta y + \left(xy^2\,e^{xz} + \dfrac{x}{z}\right)\Delta z$ 13. $\Delta u = -7.15, du = -7.50$ 15. $\Delta u = 2.896; du = 2.5$

17. $22\frac{249}{352}$ taking $u = x^{1/2}y^{1/4}$, $x = 121$, $y = 16$, $\Delta x = 4$, $\Delta y = 1$

19. $\frac{\pi}{14}\sqrt{2}$ taking $u = \sin x\cos y$, $x = \pi$, $y = \frac{1}{4}\pi$, $\Delta x = -\frac{1}{7}\pi$, $\Delta y = -\frac{1}{20}\pi$ 21. $f(2.9, 0.01) \cong 8.67$

23. $f(2.94, 1.1, 0.92) \cong 2.3391$ 25. $dz = -\frac{1}{90}, \Delta z = -\frac{1}{93}$ 27. decreases about 13.6π in.^{2} 29. $S \cong 246.8$

31. (a) $dv = 0.24$ (b) $\Delta V = 0.22077$ 33. $dT = 2.9$

35. (a) $\Delta h = -\dfrac{(2r+\Delta r)h}{(r+\Delta r)^2}\Delta r$, $\Delta h \cong -\left(\dfrac{2h}{r}\right)\Delta r$ (b) $\Delta h = -\dfrac{(2r+h+\Delta r)}{(r+\Delta r)}\Delta r$, $\Delta h \cong -\left(\dfrac{2r+h}{r}\right)\Delta r$

37. (a) $dA = x\sin\theta\Delta x + \frac{x^2}{2}\cos\theta\Delta\theta$ (b) The area is more affected by the change in θ. 39. $2.23 \le s \pm |\Delta s| \le 2.27$

SECTION 16.9

1. $f(x, y) = \frac{1}{2}x^2y^2 + C$ 3. $f(x, y) = xy + C$ 5. not a gradient 7. $f(x, y) = \sin x + y\cos x + C$

9. $f(x, y) = e^x\cos y^2 + C$ 11. $f(x, y) = xy\,e^x + e^{-y} + C$ 13. not a gradient

15. $f(x, y) = x + xy^2 + \frac{1}{2}x^2y^2 + \frac{1}{3}y^2 + y + C$ 17. $f(x, y) = \sqrt{x^2+y^2} + C$ 19. $f(x, y) = \frac{1}{3}x^3\arcsin y + y - y\ln y + C$

21. (a) yes (b) yes (c) no 23. $f(x, y) = Ce^{x+y}$ 25. (d) $f(x, y, z) = x^2 + yz + C$

27. $f(x, y, z) = x^2 + y^2 - z^2 + xy + yz + C$ 29. $f(x, y, z) = xy^2z^3 + x + \frac{1}{2}y^2 + z + C$ 31. $\mathbf{F}(\mathbf{r}) = \nabla\left(G\dfrac{mM}{r}\right)$

Chapter 16. Review Exercises

1. $\nabla f = (4x - 4y)\mathbf{i} + (-4x + 3y^2)\mathbf{j}$ 3. $\nabla f = (ye^{xy}\tan 2x + 2e^{xy}\sec^2 2x)\mathbf{i} + (xe^{xy}\tan 2x)\mathbf{j}$

5. $\nabla f = 2xe^{-yz}\sec z\,\mathbf{i} - x^2ze^{-yz}\sec z\,\mathbf{j} + (-x^2ye^{-yz}\sec z + x^2e^{-yz}\sec x\tan z)\mathbf{k}$ 7. $2/\sqrt{5}$ 9. $16/3$ 11. $18/\sqrt{13}$

13. $\pm 19/26$ 15. $\dfrac{\sqrt{39\pi^2+3}}{12}$ 17. $y = \ln(\sec x)$ 19. $\mathbf{u} = \dfrac{\pi}{\sqrt{\pi^2+4}}\mathbf{i} + \dfrac{2}{\sqrt{\pi^2+4}}\mathbf{j}$; $\dfrac{\sqrt{\pi^2+4}}{4}$ 21. $2 - 18e^{6t}$

23. $\dfrac{1-\sin t}{\cos^2 t}$ 25. $104t^3 + 150t^2 - 8t$ 27. $-\dfrac{9\sqrt{3}}{10}$ radians/sec

31. normal line: $x = 1 + 9t,\quad y = -1 - 5t$
tangent line: $x = 1 + 5t,\quad y = -1 + 9t$

33. tangent plane: $x + y - 2z + 2 = 0$
normal line: $x = 1 + t,\quad y = 1 + t,\quad z = 2 - 2t$

35. tangent plane: $x + y + 4z = 6$
normal line: $x = 1 + t,\quad y = 1 + t,\quad z = 1 + 4t$

39. $(5, 0)$ saddle, $(-3, 0)$ saddle, $(1, 4)$ local min. 41. $(0, 0)$ saddle, $(6, 6)$ local min. 43. $(1, 1)$ saddle, $(-1, -1)$ saddle

45. absolute max. $6 + 4\sqrt{2}$ at $(-\sqrt{2}, \sqrt{2})$, absolute min. 0 at $(1, -1)$

47. absolute max. $4 + \frac{3}{2}\sqrt{3}$ at $\left(-\frac{1}{2}, \sqrt{3}\right)$, absolute min. $-\frac{4}{15}$ at $\left(-\frac{1}{15}, -\frac{8}{15}\right)$ 49. $\left(\frac{41}{14}, -\frac{5}{7}, \frac{33}{14}\right)$; $9/\sqrt{14}$

51. absolute max. 3 at $\left(\frac{4}{3}, \frac{4}{3}, -\frac{1}{3}\right)$, absolute min. -3 at $\left(-\frac{4}{3}, -\frac{4}{3}, \frac{1}{3}\right)$ 53. $df = (9x^2 - 10xy^2 + 2)\,dx - (10x^2y + 1)\,dy$

55. $df = \dfrac{y^2z + yz^2}{(x+y+z)^2}dx + \dfrac{x^2z + xz^2}{(x+y+z)^2}dy + \dfrac{x^2y + xy^2}{(x+y+z)^2}dz$ 57. $\cong 4.1088$ 59. $\cong 4.8$ gallons

61. $f(x, y) = x^2y + 3x + y\cos x + y^2 + y + C$ 63. $f(x, y, z) = xe^y\sin z + x^2 - \frac{1}{3}y^3 + C$

CHAPTER 17

SECTION 17.1

1. 819 3. 0 5. $a_2 - a_1$ 7. $(a_2 - a_1)(b_2 - b_1)$ 9. $a_2^2 - a_1^2$ 11. $(a_2^2 - a_1^2)(b_2 - b_1)$

13. $2n(a_2 - a_1) - 3m(b_2 - b_1)$ 15. $(a_2 - a_1)(b_2 - b_1)(c_2 - c_1)$ 17. $a_{111} + a_{222} + \cdots + a_{nnn} = \sum_{p=1}^{n} a_{ppp}$

SECTION 17.2

1. $L_f(p) = 2\frac{1}{4},\quad U_f(p) = 5\frac{3}{4}$ 3. (a) $L_f(p) = \sum_{i=1}^{m}\sum_{j=1}^{n}(x_{i-1} + 2y_{i-1})\,\Delta x_i\,\Delta y_j,\quad U_f(p) = \sum_{i=1}^{m}\sum_{j=1}^{n}(x_i + 2y_j)\,\Delta x_i\,\Delta y_j$
(b) $I = 4$; the volume of the prism bounded above by the plane $z = x + 2y$ and below by R

5. $L_f(p) = -\frac{7}{24},\quad U_f(P) = \frac{7}{24}$ 7. (a) $L_f(p) = \sum_{i=1}^{m}\sum_{j=1}^{n} 4x_{i-1}y_{j-1}\,\Delta x_i\,\Delta y_j,\quad U_f(P) = \sum_{i=1}^{m}\sum_{j=1}^{n} 4x_iy_j\,\Delta x_i\,\Delta y_j$ (b) $I = b^2d^2$

9. (a) $L_f(p) = \sum_{i=1}^{m}\sum_{j=1}^{n} 3\left(x_{i-1}^2 - y_j^2\right)\Delta x_i\,\Delta y_j,\quad U_f p = \sum_{i=1}^{m}\sum_{j=1}^{n} 3\left(x_i^2 - y_{j-1}^2\right)\Delta x_i\,\Delta y_j$
(b) $I = bd(b^2 - d^2)$

11. $\displaystyle\iint_{\Omega} dx\,dy = \int_a^b \phi(x)\,dx$ 15. 6 19. $\frac{1}{8}$ of a sphere of radius 2; $\frac{4}{3}\pi$

21. tetrahedron bounded by the coordinate planes and the plane $\dfrac{x}{3} + \dfrac{y}{2} + \dfrac{z}{6} = 1$; 6

SECTION 17.3

1. 1 3. $\frac{9}{2}$ 5. $\frac{1}{24}$ 7. 2 9. $\frac{1}{4}\pi^2 + \frac{1}{64}\pi^4$ 11. $\frac{2}{27}$ 13. $\frac{512}{15}$ 15. 0 17. $\frac{1}{4}(e^4 - 1)$

19. $\int_0^1 \int_{y^{1/2}}^{y^{1/4}} f(x, y)\,dx\,dy$

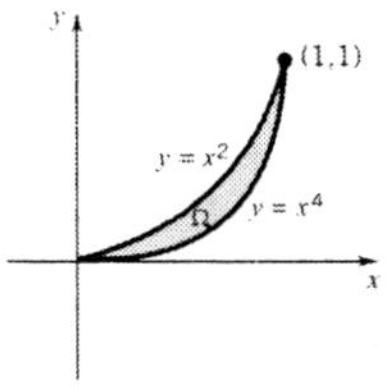

21. $\int_{-1}^{0} \int_{-x}^{1} f(x, y)\,dy\,dx + \int_0^1 \int_x^1 f(x, y)\,dy\,dx$

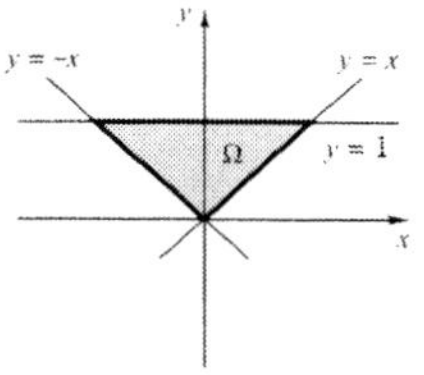

23. $\int_1^2 \int_1^y f(x, y)\,dx\,dy + \int_2^4 \int_{y/2}^{y} f(x, y)\,dx\,dy + \int_4^8 \int_{y/2}^{4} f(x, y)\,dx\,dy$ 25. 9 27. $\frac{1}{160}$

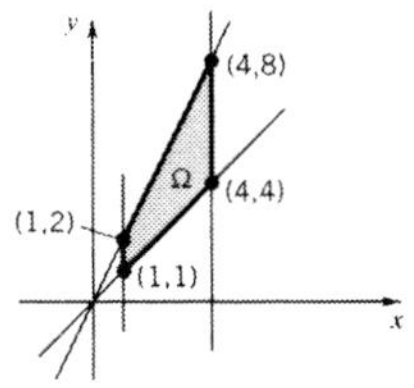

29. $\frac{2}{3}(\cos\frac{1}{2} - \cos 1)$

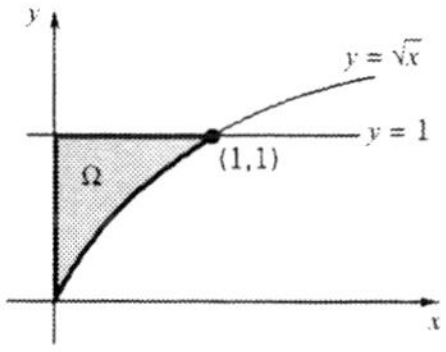

31. $1 - \ln 2$

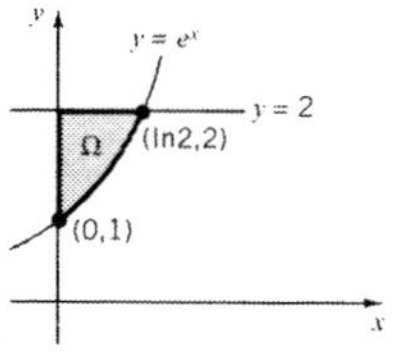

33. $\ln 4 - \frac{1}{2}$ 35. 4 37. $\frac{2}{15}$

39. 3π 41. $\frac{1}{6}$ 43. $\frac{11}{70}$ 45. $\frac{2}{3}a^3$ 47. $\frac{1}{2}(e - 1)$ 49. $\frac{1}{12}(e - 1)$ 51. $\frac{2}{3}$ 53. 1

61. (a) $\int_1^2 \int_{x^2-2x+2}^{1+\sqrt{x-1}} 1\,dy\,dx = \frac{1}{3}$ (b) $\int_1^2 \int_{y^2-2y+2}^{1+\sqrt{y-1}} 1\,dx\,dy = \frac{1}{3}$

SECTION 17.4

1. $\frac{1}{6}$ 3. 6 5. (a) $\pi \sin 1$ (b) $\pi(\sin 4 - \sin 1)$ 7. (a) $\frac{2}{3}$ (b) $\frac{14}{3}$ 9. $\frac{1}{3}\pi$ 11. $\frac{\pi}{6} - \frac{\sqrt{3}}{8}$ 13. $\frac{\pi}{2}(\sin 1 - \cos 1)$

15. $\frac{\pi}{2}$ 17. $\frac{3\pi}{4}$ 19. $\frac{4\pi}{3} + 2\sqrt{3}$ 21. 4 23. $b^3\pi$ 25. $\frac{16}{3}\sqrt{3}\pi$ 27. $\frac{2}{3}(8 - 3\sqrt{3})\pi$ 29. 2π 31. $\frac{1}{3}\pi a^2 b$ 33. $\frac{\pi}{2}$

SECTION 17.5

1. $M = \frac{2}{3}$, $x_M = 0$, $y_m = \frac{1}{2}$ 3. $M = \frac{1}{6}$, $x_M = \frac{4}{7}$, $y_M = \frac{3}{4}$ 5. $M = \frac{32}{3}$, $x_M = \frac{16}{3}$, $y_M = \frac{9}{7}$

7. $M = \frac{5}{8}$, $x_M = \frac{4}{5}$, $y_m = \frac{152}{75}$ 9. $M = \frac{5\pi}{3}$, $x_M = \frac{21}{20}$, $y_M = 0$

11. $I_x = \frac{1}{12}MW^2$, $I_y = \frac{1}{12}ML^2$, $I_z = \frac{1}{12}M(L^2 + W^2)$; $K_x = \frac{1}{6}\sqrt{3}W$, $K_y = \frac{1}{6}\sqrt{3}L$, $K_z = \frac{1}{6}\sqrt{3}\sqrt{L^2 + W^2}$

13. $x_M = \frac{1}{6}L$, $y_M = 0$ 15. $I_x = I_y = \frac{1}{4}MR^2$, $I_z = \frac{1}{2}MR^2$; $K_x = K_y = \frac{1}{2}R$, $K_z = \frac{1}{2}\sqrt{2}R$

17. center the disc at a distance $\sqrt{I_0 - \frac{1}{2}MR^2}\Big/\sqrt{M}$ from the origin 19. $I_x = \frac{1}{4}Mb^2$, $I_y = \frac{1}{4}Ma^2$, $I_z = \frac{1}{4}M(a^2 + b^2)$

21. $I_x = \frac{1}{10}$, $I_y = \frac{1}{16}$, $I_z = \frac{13}{80}$ 23. $I_x = \frac{33\pi}{40}$, $I_y = \frac{93\pi}{40}$, $I_z = \frac{63\pi}{20}$

25. (a) $\frac{1}{4}M\left(r_2^2+r_1^2\right)$ (b) $\frac{1}{4}M\left(r_2^2+5r_1^2\right)$ (c) $\frac{1}{4}M\left(5r_2^2+r_1^2\right)$ 27. $\frac{1}{2}M\left(r_2^2+r_1^2\right)$ 29. $x_M=0,\quad y_M=R/\pi$

31. on the diameter through P at a distance $\frac{6}{5}R$ from P

SECTION 17.6

1. they are equal 5. $\frac{1}{4}a^2b^2c$ 7. $\bar{x}=\dfrac{A^2BC-a^2bc}{ABC-abc},\quad \bar{y}=\dfrac{AB^2C-ab^2c}{ABC-abc},\quad \bar{z}=\dfrac{ABC^2-abc^2}{ABC-abc}$

9. $M=\frac{1}{2}Ka^4$ where K is the constant of proportionality for the density function 11. $I_z=\frac{2}{3}Ma^2$

SECTION 17.7

1. abc 3. $\frac{2}{3}$ 5. 16 7. $\frac{1}{3}$ 9. $\frac{47}{24}$

13. 8 15. $\left(\frac{2}{3}a,\frac{2}{3}b,\frac{2}{3}c\right)$ 17.

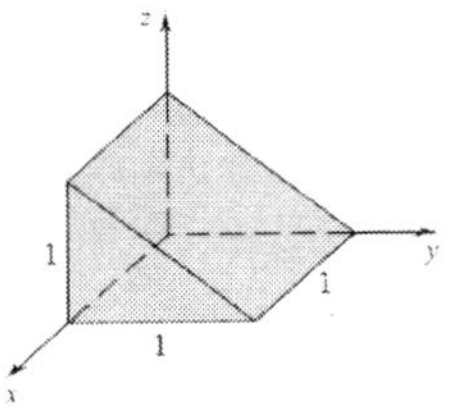

19. $\left(\frac{1}{2},\frac{1}{3},\frac{1}{3}\right)$

21. $$\int_{-r}^{r}\int_{-\sqrt{r^2-x^2}}^{\sqrt{r^2-x^2}}\int_{-\sqrt{r^2-(x^2+y^2)}}^{\sqrt{r^2-(x^2+y^2)}} k\left(r-\sqrt{x^2+y^2+z^2}\right)dz\,dy\,dx$$ 23. $$\int_0^1\int_{-\sqrt{x-x^2}}^{\sqrt{x-x^2}}\int_{-2x-3y-10}^{1-y^2}dz\,dy\,dx$$

25. $$\int_{-1}^{1}\int_{-2\sqrt{2-2x^2}}^{2\sqrt{2-2x^2}}\int_{3x^2+y^2/4}^{4-x^2-y^2/4}k\left(z-3x^2-\tfrac{1}{4}y^2\right)dz\,dy\,dx$$ 27. $\frac{28}{3}$ 29. $\frac{1}{270}$ 31. $\frac{12}{5}$ 33. $V=\frac{8}{3},\left(\frac{11}{10},\frac{9}{4},\frac{11}{20}\right)$

35. $V=\frac{27}{2},\left(\frac{1}{2},\frac{3}{2},\frac{12}{5}\right)$ 37. $V=\frac{1}{6}abc,\left(\frac{1}{4}a,\frac{1}{4}b,\frac{1}{4}c\right)$ 39. (a) $\frac{1}{3}M(a^2+b^2)$ (b) $\frac{1}{12}M(a^2+b^2)$ (c) $\frac{1}{3}Ma^2+\frac{1}{12}Mb^2$

41. $M=\frac{1}{2}k,\quad \left(\frac{7}{12},\frac{34}{45},\frac{37}{90}\right)$ 43. (a) 0 by symmetry (b) $\frac{4}{3}\pi a_4$ 45. $$8\int_0^a\int_0^{\sqrt{a^2-x^2}}\int_0^{\sqrt{a^2-x^2-y^2}}dz\,dy\,dz=\tfrac{4}{3}\pi a^3$$

47. $M=\frac{128}{15}k$

49. $M=\frac{135}{4}k,\left(\frac{1}{2},\frac{9}{5},\frac{12}{5}\right)$ 51. (a) $V=\displaystyle\int_0^6\int_{z/2}^{3}\int_x^{6-x}dy\,dx\,dz$

(b) $V=\displaystyle\int_0^3\int_0^{2x}\int_x^{6-x}dy\,dz\,dx$

(c) $V=\displaystyle\int_0^6\int_{z/2}^{3}\int_{z/2}^{y}dx\,dy\,dz+\int_0^6\int_3^{(12-z)/2}\int_{z/2}^{6-y}dx\,dy\,dz$

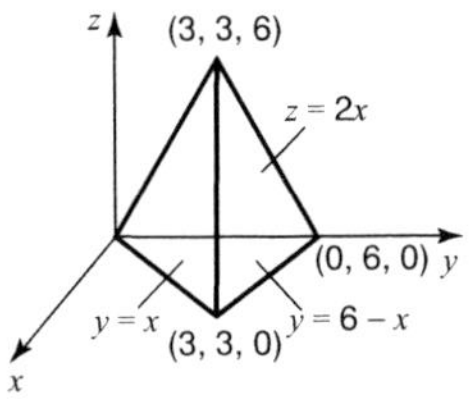

53. (a) $V=\displaystyle\iint_{\Omega_{yz}}2y\,dy\,dz$ (b) $V=\displaystyle\iint_{\Omega_{yz}}\left(\int_{-y}^{y}dx\right)dy\,dz$ (c) $V=\displaystyle\int_0^4\int_{-\sqrt{4-y}}^{\sqrt{4-y}}\int_{-y}^{y}dx\,dz\,dy$ (d) $V=\displaystyle\int_{-2}^{2}\int_0^{4-z^2}\int_{-y}^{y}dx\,dy\,dz$

55. (a) 6.80703 (b) $\frac{16\sqrt{3}}{3}(4\sqrt{2}-2)\cong 33.7801$

SECTION 17.8

1. $r^2+z^2=9$ 3. $z=2r$ 5. $4r^2=z^2$ 7. 2π 9. 8π

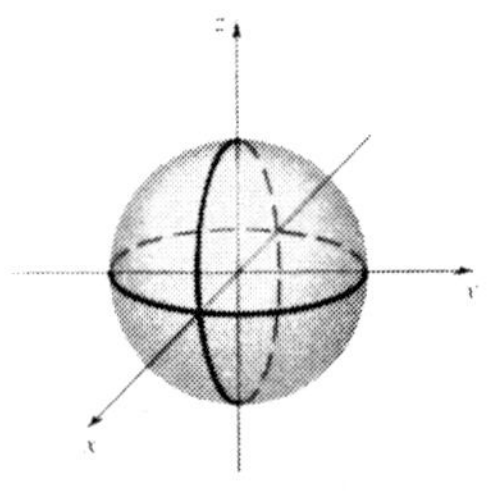

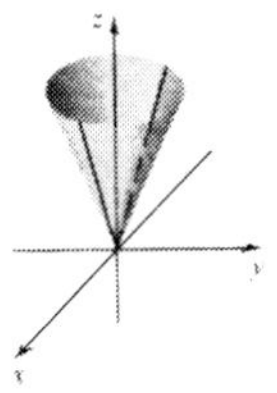

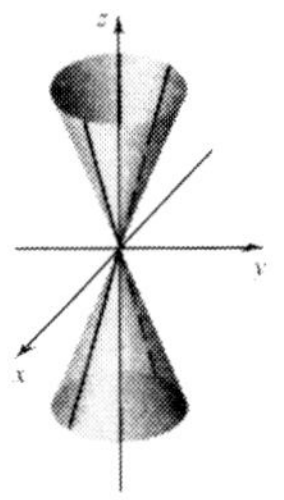

11. $\frac{1}{6}(8-3\sqrt{3})\pi$ 13. $\frac{9\pi^2}{8}$ 15. $\frac{\pi}{2}(1-\cos 1)\cong 0.7221$ 17. $r=1,\quad \theta=\frac{1}{2}\pi,\quad z=2$ 19. $r=1,\quad \theta=\frac{3}{2}\pi,\quad z=2$ 21. $\frac{32}{9}a^3$

23. $\frac{1}{36}a^3(9\pi-16)$ 25. $\frac{1}{32}\pi$ 27. $\frac{1}{3}\pi(2-\sqrt{3})$ 29. $\frac{32}{3}\pi\sqrt{2}$ 31. $M=\frac{1}{2}k\pi R^2h^2$ 33. $\frac{1}{2}MR^2$

37. $\frac{3}{10}MR^2$ 39. $\frac{1}{2}\pi$ 41. $\frac{1}{4}k\pi$

SECTION 17.9

1. $\left(\sqrt{3}, \frac{1}{4}\pi, \arccos\left[\frac{1}{3}\sqrt{3}\right]\right)$ 3. $\left(\frac{3}{4}, \frac{3}{4}, \sqrt{3}, \frac{3}{2}\sqrt{3}\right)$ 5. $(\rho,\theta,\phi)=\left(\frac{4\sqrt{6}}{3}, \frac{\pi}{4}, \frac{\pi}{3}\right)$ 7. $(x,y,z)=(0,0,3)$

9. the circular cylinder $x^2+y^2=1$; the radius of the cylinder is 1 and the axis is the z-axis 11. the lower nappe of the cone $z^2=x^2+y^2$

13. horizontal plane one unit above the xy-plane 15. T: sphere centered at the origin, radius 2; $\frac{32\pi}{3}$

17. T: the portion of the sphere $x^2+y^2+z^2=9$ that lies between the planes $z=0$ and $z=\frac{3}{2}\sqrt{3}$; $\frac{9}{4}\pi\sqrt{3}$ 19. $\frac{\pi}{3}(\sqrt{2}-1)$

21. $\frac{243\pi}{20}$ 23. $V=\frac{4}{3}\pi R^3$ 25. $V=\frac{2}{3}\alpha R^3$

27. $M=\frac{1}{6}k\pi h[(r^2+h^2)^{3/2}-h^3]$ 29. (a) $\frac{2}{5}MR^2$ (b) $\frac{7}{5}MR^2$ 31. (a) $\frac{2}{5}M\left(\frac{R_2^5-R_1^5}{R_2^3-R_1^3}\right)$ (b) $\frac{2}{3}MR^2$ (c) $\frac{5}{3}MR^2$

33. $V=\frac{2}{3}\pi(1-\cos\alpha)a^3$

35. (a) $\rho=2R\cos\phi$ (b) $0\le\theta\le 2\pi,\quad 0\le\phi\le\frac{1}{4}\pi,\quad R\sec\theta\le\rho\le 2R\cos\phi$ 37. $V=\frac{1}{3}(16-6\sqrt{2})\pi$

41. $\mathbf{F}=\frac{GmM}{R^2}(\sqrt{2}-1)\mathbf{k}$

SECTION 17.10

1. $ad-bc$ 3. $2(v^2-u^2)$ 5. $-3u^2v^2$ 7. abc 9. $w(1+w\cos v)$ 13. $\frac{1}{2}$ 15. 0 17. $\frac{2}{3}$

19. (a) $A=3\ln 2$ (b) $\bar{x}=\frac{7}{9\ln 2}, \bar{y}=\frac{14}{9\ln 2}$ 21. $I_x=\frac{4}{75}M,\ I_y=\frac{14}{75}M,\ I_z=\frac{18}{75}M$ 23. $A=\frac{32}{15}$ 25. $A=\pi/\sqrt{65}$

27. $V=\frac{4}{3}\pi abc$ 29. $I_x=\frac{1}{5}M(b^2+c^2),\ I_y=\frac{1}{5}M(a^2+c^2),\ I_z=\frac{1}{5}M(a^2+b^2)$

Chapter 17. Review Exercises

1. 1/40 3. $\frac{8}{3}(e-1)$ 5. $\frac{1}{3\sqrt{2}}$ 7. $-2/3$ 9. $-16/15$ 11. $\frac{1}{2}e-\frac{1}{2}$ 13. 1 15. 1/8 17. $-8/15$

19. 8/3 21. 32/15 23. $\frac{\pi}{2}(1+e^2)$ 25. $81\pi/2$ 27. 1/6 29. mass: $M=\frac{1}{4}\pi$; center of mass: $\left(0, \frac{16}{9}\pi\right)$

31. mass: $M=\frac{1}{8}\pi(R^4-r^4)$; center of mass: $\bar{x}=\bar{y}=\frac{8(R^5-r^5)}{5\pi(R^4-r^4)}$

33. (a) $(0, h/3)$ (b) $\frac{1}{6}Mh^2$ (c) $\frac{1}{24}Mb^2$ 35. 10 37. 24π 39. $5\pi/3$

41. $\pi\sqrt{2}/3$ 43. (a) $\left(\frac{9}{64}\pi, \frac{9}{64}\pi, \frac{3}{8}\right)$ (b) $\frac{3}{10}\lambda$ 45. (a) $\frac{\pi r^4 h}{2}$ (b) $(0, 0, \frac{1}{2}h)$

47. (a) $\frac{1}{6}\pi$ (b) $\left(0, 0, \frac{4}{5}\right)$ (c) $\frac{1}{15}\pi$ 49. e^{2u} 51. $\frac{3}{2}\sin 1$

CHAPTER 18

SECTION 18.1

1. (a) 1 (b) -2 3. 0 5. (a) $-\frac{17}{6}$ (b) $\frac{17}{6}$ 7. -8 9. $-\pi$ 11. (a) 1 (b) $\frac{23}{21}$

13. (a) $2+\sin 2-\cos 3$ (b) $\frac{4}{5}+\sin 1-\cos 1$ 15. 26 17. $\frac{1}{3}$ 19. $\dfrac{8\pi^3}{3}$

25. $|W|$ = area of ellipse

27. force at time $t=m\mathbf{r}''(t)=m(2\beta\mathbf{j}+6\gamma t\mathbf{k})$; $W=(2\beta^2+\frac{9}{2}\gamma^2)m$ 29. 0 31. (a) $\left(\dfrac{1}{\sqrt{5}}-\dfrac{1}{\sqrt{14}}\right)k$ (b) 0 33. $\alpha=\frac{5}{2}$

SECTION 18.2

1. 0 3. -1 5. 0 7. 0 9. 0 11. 4 13. e^3-2e^2+3 15. e^5-2e^2+1

17. 2π 19. 14 21. 0 25. $f(x,y,z)=\dfrac{k}{3}(x^2+y^2+z^2)^{3/2}$ 27. $W=mG\left(\dfrac{1}{r_2}-\dfrac{1}{r_1}\right)$ 29. $f(x,y,z)=\dfrac{mGr_0^2}{r_0+z}$

SECTION 18.3

3. The scalar field $U(x,y,z)=cz+d$ is a potential energy function for F. Since the total mechanical energy remains constant, for any times t_1 and t_2, $\frac{1}{2}m[v(t_1)]^2+cz(t_1)+d=\frac{1}{2}m[v(t_2)]^2+cz(t_2)+d$. Solve this equation for $v(t_2)$.

5. (b) At a point where U has a minimum, $\nabla U=0$ and therefore $\mathbf{F}=0$.

9. $f(x,y,z)=-\dfrac{k}{\sqrt{x^2+y^2+z^2}}$ is a potential function for $\mathbf{F}$.

SECTION 18.4

1. $\frac{1}{2}$ 3. $\frac{9}{2}$ 5. $\frac{11}{6}$ 7. 2 9. 16 11. $\frac{104}{5}$ 13. 4 15. 4 17. 2

19. 3 21. $\frac{176}{3}$ 23. 56 25. $\frac{1177}{30}$

27. (b) (i) 7, (ii) $\frac{-37}{3}$ 29. (a) $M=2ka^2$, $x_M=y_M=\frac{1}{8}a(\pi+2)$ (b) $I_x=ka^4=\frac{1}{2}Ma^2$

31. (a) $I_z=2ka^4=Ma^2$ (b) $I=\frac{1}{3}ka^4=\frac{1}{6}Ma^2$

33. (a) $L=2\pi\sqrt{a^2+b^2}$ (b) $x_M=y_M=0$, $z_M=\pi b$ (c) $I_x=I_y=\frac{1}{6}M(3a^2+8b^2\pi^2)$, $I_z=Ma^2$ 35. $M=\frac{2}{3}\pi k\sqrt{a^2+b^2}\,(3a^2+4\pi^2b^2)$

SECTION 18.5

1. $\frac{1}{6}$ 3. 6π 5. 2π 7. a^2b 9. 7π 11. $5a\pi r^2$ 13. 0 15. 0 17. πa^2

19. $\frac{15}{2}-4\ln 4$ 21. $(c-a)A$ 23. $3\pi R^2$ 29. $\oint_{C_1}=\oint_{C_2}+\oint_{C_3}$ 31. (a) 0 (b) 0

SECTION 18.6

1. $4[(u^2-v^2)\mathbf{i}-(u^2+v^2)\mathbf{j}+2uv\mathbf{k}]$ 3. $2(\mathbf{j}-\mathbf{i})$ 5. $\mathbf{r}(u,v)=3\cos u\cos v\,\mathbf{i}+2\sin u\cos v\,\mathbf{j}+6\sin v\,\mathbf{k}$, $u\in[0,2\pi]$, $v\in[0,\pi/2]$

7. $\mathbf{r}(u,v)=2\cos u\cos v\,\mathbf{i}+2\sin u\cos v\,\mathbf{j}+2\sin v\,\mathbf{k}$, $u\in[0,2\pi]$, $v\in(\pi/4,\pi/2]$ 9. $\mathbf{r}(u,v)=u\,\mathbf{i}+g(u,v)\,\mathbf{j}+v\,\mathbf{k}$, $(u,v)\in\Omega$

11. $x^2/a^2+y^2/b^2+z^2/c^2=1$; ellipsoid 13. $x^2/a^2-y^2/b^2=z$; hyperbolic paraboloid

15. $\mathbf{r}(u,v)=v\cos u\,\mathbf{i}+v\sin u\,\mathbf{j}+f(v)\,\mathbf{k}$; $0\le u\le 2\pi$, $a\le v\le b$ 17. area of $\Gamma=A_\Omega\sec\gamma$ 19. $\frac{1}{2}\sqrt{a^2b^2+a^2c^2+b^2c^2}$

21. $\frac{1}{6}\pi(17\sqrt{17}-1)$ 23. $\frac{1}{6}\pi[(4a^2+1)^{3/2}-(a^2+1)^{3/2}]$ 25. $\frac{1}{15}(36\sqrt{6}-50\sqrt{5}+32)$ 27. 4π

29. (a) $\iint_{\Omega} \sqrt{\left[\frac{\partial g}{\partial y}(y,z)\right]^2 + \left[\frac{\partial g}{\partial z}(y,z)\right]^2 + 1}\, dydz = \iint_{\Omega} \sec[\alpha(y,z)]\, dydz$

where α is the angle between the unit normal with positive **i** component and the x-axis

(b) $\iint_{\Omega} \sqrt{\left[\frac{\partial h}{\partial x}(x,z)\right]^2 + \left[\frac{\partial h}{\partial z}(x,z)\right]^2 + 1}\, dxdz = \iint_{\Omega} \sec[\beta(x,z)]\, dxdz$

where β is the angle between the unit normal with positive **j** component and the y-axis

31. (a) $\mathbf{N}(u,v) = v\cos u \sin\alpha\cos\alpha\,\mathbf{i} + v\sin u\sin\alpha\cos\alpha\,\mathbf{j} - v\sin^2\alpha\,\mathbf{k}$ (b) $A = \pi s^2 \sin\alpha$

33. (c) $A = \int_0^{2\pi}\int_{-\ln 2}^{\ln 2} \|\mathbf{N}(u,v)\|\, du dv$

$= \int_0^{2\pi}\int_{-\ln 2}^{\ln 2} \sqrt{64\cos^2 u\cosh^2 v + 144\sin^2 u\cosh^2 v + 36\cosh^2 v\sinh^2 v}\; du\, dv$

35. $A = \sqrt{A_1^2 + A_2^2 + A_3^2}$ 37. (a) $\frac{1}{4}\sqrt{2\pi}\left[\sqrt{6} + \ln(\sqrt{2}+\sqrt{3})\right]$ (b) $\frac{1}{2}a^2\left[\sqrt{2e^{4\pi}+1} - \sqrt{3} + 2\pi + \ln(1+\sqrt{3}) - \ln(1+\sqrt{2e^{4\pi}+1})\right]$

SECTION 18.7

1. $\frac{1}{2}\left[\sqrt{2} + \ln(1+\sqrt{2})\right]$ 3. $2\sqrt{2} - 1$ 5. $\frac{1}{3}[2\sqrt{2} - 1]$ 7. $\frac{9\sqrt{14}}{2}$ 9. $\frac{4}{3}$ 11. $\frac{4\pi}{3}$ 13. $\frac{1}{2}\sqrt{3}a^2k$

15. $\frac{1}{12}\sqrt{3}a^4k$ 17. $(0, 0, \frac{1}{2}a)$ 19. 2 21. $\frac{4}{3}\pi a^3$ 23. 0 25. $\frac{1}{2}\sqrt{3}a^3$ 27. 0 29. $-\frac{3}{2}$ 31. $2\pi a^2 l$

33. $\frac{8}{35}$ 35. $-\frac{4}{63}$ 37. $\bar{x} = \bar{y} = 0,\ \bar{z} = \frac{2}{3}s\cos\alpha$ 39. $x_M = y_M = 0,\ z_M = \frac{3}{4}$ 43. $x_M = \frac{11}{9}$ 45. 0

47. $(4\sqrt{2} - \frac{7}{2})\pi$

SECTION 18.8

1. $\nabla\cdot\mathbf{v} = 2,\ \nabla\times\mathbf{v} = \mathbf{0}$ 3. $\nabla\cdot\mathbf{v} = 0,\ \nabla\times\mathbf{v} = \mathbf{0}$ 5. $\nabla\cdot\mathbf{v} = 6,\ \nabla\times\mathbf{v} = \mathbf{0}$

7. $\nabla\cdot\mathbf{v} = yz + 1,\ \nabla\times\mathbf{v} = -x\,\mathbf{i} + xy\,\mathbf{j} + (1-x)z\,\mathbf{k}$ 9. $\nabla\cdot\mathbf{v} = 1/r^2,\ \nabla\times\mathbf{v} = \mathbf{0}$

11. $\nabla\cdot\mathbf{v} = 2(x+y+z)e^{r^2},\ \nabla\times\mathbf{v} = 2e^{r^2}[(y-z)\,\mathbf{i} - (x-z)\,\mathbf{j} + (x-y)\,\mathbf{k}]$ 13. $\nabla\cdot\mathbf{v} = f'(x),\ \nabla\times\mathbf{v} = \mathbf{0}$

17. $\nabla\cdot\mathbf{v} = 0$ 19. $\nabla\times\mathbf{v} = 0$ 21. $\nabla^2 f = 12(x^2+y^2+z^2)$

23. $\nabla^2 f = 2y^3z^4 + 6x^2yz^4 + 12x^2y^3z^2$ 25. $\nabla^2 f = e^r(1 + 2r^{-1})$ 27. (a) $2r^2$ (b) $-1/r$

33. $n = -1$

SECTION 18.9

1. 4π 3. 0 5. 3 7. 2 9. 36π 11. $\frac{1}{24}$ 13. 64π 15. 0 17. $(A+B+C)V$

SECTION 18.10

For Exercises 1 and 3: $\mathbf{n} = x\,\mathbf{i} + y\,\mathbf{j} + z\,\mathbf{k}$ and $C : \mathbf{r}(u) = \cos u\,\mathbf{i} + \sin u\,\mathbf{j},\ u \in [0, 2\pi]$.

1. (a) $\iint_S [(\nabla\times\mathbf{v})\cdot\mathbf{n}]\,d\sigma = \iint_S (\mathbf{0}\cdot\mathbf{n})\,d\sigma = 0.$

(b) S is bounded by the unit circle $C : \mathbf{r}(u) = \cos u\,\mathbf{i} + \sin u\,\mathbf{j},\ u \in [0, 2\pi]$.

$\oint_C \mathbf{v}(\mathbf{r})\cdot d\mathbf{r} = 0$ since $\mathbf{v}$ is a gradient.

3. (a) $\iint_S [(\nabla\times\mathrm{v})\cdot\mathrm{n}]\,d\sigma = 2\pi$

(b) $\oint_C \mathbf{v}(\mathbf{r})\cdot d\mathbf{r} = \oint_C z^2dx + 2x\,dy = \oint_C 2x\,dy = \int_0^{2\pi} 2\cos^2 u\,du = 2\pi$

For Exercises 5 and 7 take $S : z = 2 - x - y$ with $0 \le x \le 2,\ 0 \le y \le 2 - x$ and C as the triangle (2, 0, 0), (0, 2, 0), (0, 0, 2). $\mathbf{n} = \frac{1}{3}\sqrt{3}(\mathbf{i} + \mathbf{j} + \mathbf{k})$.

5. (a) $\iint_S [(\nabla \times \mathrm{v}) \cdot \mathbf{n}]\, d\sigma = \iint_S \frac{1}{3}\sqrt{3}\, d\sigma = \frac{1}{3}\sqrt{3}A = 2$

(b) $\oint_C \mathbf{v}(\mathbf{r}) \cdot \mathbf{dr} = \left(\int_{C_1} + \int_{C_2} + \int_{C_3}\right) \mathrm{v}(\mathbf{r}) \cdot d\mathbf{r} = -2 + 2 + 2 = 2$

7. (a) $\iint_S [(\nabla \times \mathrm{v}) \cdot \mathbf{n}]\, d\sigma = \frac{1}{3}\sqrt{3} \iint_S y\, d\sigma = \frac{1}{3}\sqrt{3}\bar{y}A = \frac{4}{3}$

(b) $\oint_C \mathrm{v}(\mathbf{r}) \cdot \mathbf{dr} = \left(\int_{C_1} + \int_{C_2} + \int_{C_3}\right) \mathbf{v}(\mathbf{r}) \cdot \mathbf{dr} = \left(\frac{4}{3} - \frac{32}{5}\right) + \frac{32}{5} + 0 = \frac{4}{3}$

9. 4π 11. 0 13. $\pm\frac{1}{8}\pi$ 15. $\pm\frac{1}{4}\pi$

Chapter 18. Review Exercises

1. (a) $-\frac{1}{12}$ (b) $-\frac{11}{72}$ 3. (a) $\frac{119}{2}$ (b) $\frac{119}{2}$ (c) $\frac{119}{2}$ 5. $-6\cos 3 + 2\sin 3 + \frac{1}{3}e^{27} - \cos 27 + \frac{2}{3}$ 7. $\frac{2685}{28}$

9. $4C$ 11. $\mathbf{e}^8 - 1$ 13. 1 15. (a) $-\frac{4}{15}$ (b) $-\frac{1}{2}$ (c) $-\frac{2}{5}$ 17. $\frac{1}{3}e^8 + \frac{17}{3} + 4\sin 2 + 2\cos 2$ 19. $-\frac{1}{3}$ 21. 6

23. -4 25. $-\frac{5}{2}\pi$ 27. $\frac{32}{3}$ 29. $8(\pi - 2)$ 31. $9\pi\sqrt{2}$ 33. $\frac{1}{4}\pi\sqrt{2}$ 35. $\frac{128}{3}\pi$ 37. $\nabla \cdot \mathbf{v} = 4x$, $\nabla \times \mathbf{v} = 2y\,\mathbf{k}$

39. $\nabla \cdot \mathbf{v} = 1 + xy$, $\nabla \times \mathbf{v} = (xz - x)\,\mathbf{i} - yz\,\mathbf{j} + z\,\mathbf{k}$ 41. $\frac{1}{2}$ 43. 324π 45. 4π

INDEX

D

TABLES OF INTEGRALS

POWERS

1. $\displaystyle\int u^n\,du = \frac{u^{n+1}}{n+1} + C, n \neq -1$

2. $\displaystyle\int \frac{du}{u} = \ln|u| + C$

EXPONENTIALS AND LOGARITHMS

3. $\displaystyle\int e^u\,du = e^u + C$

4. $\displaystyle\int p^u\,du = \frac{p^u}{\ln p} + C$

5. $\displaystyle\int ue^u\,du = ue^u - e^u + C$

6. $\displaystyle\int u^2e^u\,du = u^2e^u - 2ue^u + 2e^u + C$

7. $\displaystyle\int u^ne^u\,du = u^ne^u - n\int u^{n-1}e^u\,du$

8. $\displaystyle\int \ln u\,du = u\ln u - u + C$

9. $\displaystyle\int (\ln u)^2\,du = u(\ln u)^2 - 2u\ln u + 2u + C$

10. $\displaystyle\int u\ln u\,du = \tfrac{1}{2}u^2\ln u - \tfrac{1}{4}u^2 + C$

11. $\displaystyle\int u^n\ln u\,du = u^{n+1}\left[\frac{\ln u}{n+1} - \frac{1}{(n+1)^2}\right] + C$

12. $\displaystyle\int \frac{du}{u\ln u} = \ln|\ln u| + C$

SINES AND COSINES

13. $\displaystyle\int \sin u\,du = -\cos u + C$

14. $\displaystyle\int \cos u\,du = \sin u + C$

15. $\displaystyle\int \sin^2 u\,du = \tfrac{1}{2}u - \tfrac{1}{4}\sin 2u + C$

16. $\displaystyle\int \cos^2 u\,du = \tfrac{1}{2}u + \tfrac{1}{4}\sin 2u + C$

17. $\displaystyle\int \sin^3 u\,du = \tfrac{1}{3}\cos^3 u - \cos u + C$

18. $\displaystyle\int \cos^3 u\,du = \sin u - \tfrac{1}{3}\sin^3 u + C$

19. $\displaystyle\int \sin^n u\,du = -\frac{\sin^{n-1}u\cos u}{n} + \frac{n-1}{n}\int \sin^{n-2}u\,du$

20. $\displaystyle\int \cos^n u\,du = \frac{\cos^{n-1}u\sin u}{n} + \frac{n-1}{n}\int \cos^{n-2}u\,du$

21. $\displaystyle\int u\sin u\,du = -u\cos u + \sin u + C$

22. $\displaystyle\int \cos u\,du = u\sin u + \cos u + C$

23. $\displaystyle\int u^n\sin u\,du = -u^n\cos u + n\int u^{n-1}\cos u\,du$

24. $\displaystyle\int u^n\cos u\,du = u^n\sin u - n\int u^{n-1}\sin u\,du$

25. $\displaystyle\int \sin mu\sin nu\,du = \frac{\sin[(m-n)u]}{2(m-n)} - \frac{\sin[(m+n)u]}{2(m+n)} + C,\ m^2 \neq n^2$

26. $\displaystyle\int \cos mu\cos nu\,du = \frac{\sin[(m-n)u]}{2(m-n)} + \frac{\sin[(m+n)u]}{2(m+n)} + C,\ m^2 \neq n^2$

27. $\displaystyle\int \sin mu\cos nu\,du = -\frac{\cos[(m-n)u]}{2(m-n)} - \frac{\cos[(m+n)u]}{2(m+n)} + C,\ m^2 \neq n^2$

28. $\displaystyle\int e^{au}\sin bu\,du = \frac{e^{au}}{a^2+b^2}(a\sin bu - b\cos bu) + C$

29. $\displaystyle\int e^{au}\cos bu\,du = \frac{e^{au}}{a^2+b^2}(a\cos bu + b\sin bu) + C$

TANGENTS AND SECANTS

30. $\int \tan u\, du = \ln|\sec u| + C$

31. $\int \sec u\, du = \ln|\sec u + \tan u| + C$

32. $\int \tan^2 u\, du = \tan u - u + C$

33. $\int \sec^2 u\, du = \tan u + C$

34. $\int \sec u \tan u\, du = \sec u + C$

35. $\int \tan^3 u\, du = \frac{1}{2}\tan^2 u + \ln|\cos u| + C$

36. $\int \sec^3 u\, du = \frac{1}{2}\sec u \tan u + \frac{1}{2}\ln|\sec u + \tan u| + C$

37. $\int \tan^n u\, du = \dfrac{\tan^{n-1} u}{n-1} - \int \tan^{n-2} u\, du$

38. $\int \sec^n u\, du = \dfrac{\sec^{n-2} u \tan u}{n-1} + \dfrac{n-2}{n-1}\int \sec^{n-2} u\, du$

CONTANGENTS AND COSECANTS

39. $\int \cot u\, du = \ln|\sin u| + C$

40. $\int \csc u\, du = \ln|\csc u - \cot u| + C$

41. $\int \cot^2 u\, du = -\cot u - u + C$

42. $\int \csc^2 u\, du = -\cot u + C$

43. $\int \csc u \cot u\, du = -\csc u + C$

44. $\int \cot^3 u\, du = -\frac{1}{2}\cot^2 u - \ln|\sin u| + C$

45. $\int \csc^3 u\, du = -\frac{1}{2}\csc u \cot u + \frac{1}{2}\ln|\csc u - \cot u| + C$

46. $\int \cot^n u\, du = -\dfrac{\cot^{n-1} u}{n-1} - \int \cot^{n-2} u\, du$

47. $\int \csc^n u\, du = -\dfrac{\csc^{n-2} u \cot u}{n-1} + \dfrac{n-2}{n-1}\int \csc^{n-2} u\, du$

HYPERBOLIC FUNCTIONS

48. $\int \sinh u\, du = \cosh u + C$

49. $\int \cosh u\, du = \sinh u + C$

50. $\int \tanh u\, du = \ln(\cosh u) + C$

51. $\int \coth u\, du = \ln|\sinh u| + C$

52. $\int \operatorname{sech} u\, du = \arctan(\sinh u) + C$

53. $\int \operatorname{csch} u\, du = \ln|\tanh \frac{1}{2}u| + C$

54. $\int \operatorname{sech}^2 u\, du = \tanh u + C$

55. $\int \operatorname{csch}^2 u\, du = -\coth u + C$

56. $\int \operatorname{sech} u \tanh u\, du = -\operatorname{sech} u + C$

57. $\int \operatorname{csch} u \coth u\, du = -\operatorname{csch} u + C$

58. $\int \sinh^2 u\, du = \frac{1}{4}\sinh 2u - \frac{1}{2}u + C$

59. $\int \cosh^2 u\, du = \frac{1}{4}\sinh 2u + \frac{1}{2}u + C$

60. $\int \tanh^2 u\, du = u - \tanh u + C$

61. $\int \coth^2 u\, du = u - \coth u + C$

62. $\int u \sinh u\, du = u \cosh u - \sinh u + C$

63. $\int u \cosh u\, du = u \sinh u - \cosh u + C$

INVERSE TRIGONOMETRIC FUNCTIONS

64. $\int \arcsin u\, du = u \arcsin u + \sqrt{1-u^2} + C$

65. $\int \arccos u\, du = u \arccos u - \sqrt{1-u^2} + C$

66. $\int \arctan u\, du = u \arctan u - \frac{1}{2} \ln(1+u^2) + C$

67. $\int \operatorname{arccot} u\, du = u \operatorname{arccot} u + \frac{1}{2} \ln(1+u^2) + C$

68. $\int \operatorname{arcsec} u\, du = u \operatorname{arcsec} u - \ln|u + \sqrt{u^2-1}| + C$

69. $\int \operatorname{arccsc} u\, du = u \operatorname{arccsc} u + \ln\left|u + \sqrt{u^2-1}\right| + C$

70. $\int u \arcsin u\, du = \frac{1}{4}\left[(2u^2-1)\arcsin u + u\sqrt{1-u^2} + C\right]$

71. $\int u \arctan u\, du = \frac{1}{2}(u^2+1)\arctan u - \frac{1}{2}u + C$

72. $\int u \arccos u\, du = \frac{1}{4}\left[(2u^2-1)\arccos u - u\sqrt{1-u^2} + C\right]$

73. $\int u^n \arcsin u\, du = \frac{1}{n+1}\left[u^{n+1}\arcsin u - \int \frac{u^{n+1}}{\sqrt{1-u^2}}\, du\right],\ n \neq -1$

74. $\int u^n \arccos u\, du = \frac{1}{n+1}\left[u^{n+1}\arccos u + \int \frac{u^{n+1}}{\sqrt{1-u^2}}\, du\right],\ n \neq -1$

75. $\int u^n \arctan u\, du = \frac{1}{n+1}\left[u^{n+1}\arctan u - \int \frac{u^{n+1}}{1+u^2}\, du\right],\ n \neq -1$

$\sqrt{a^2+u^2},\ a > 0$

76. $\int \frac{du}{a^2+u^2} = \frac{1}{a}\arctan\frac{u}{a} + C$

77. $\int \frac{du}{\sqrt{a^2+u^2}} = \ln\left(u + \sqrt{a^2+u^2}\right) + C$

78. $\int \sqrt{a^2+u^2}\, du = \frac{u}{2}\sqrt{a^2+u^2} + \frac{a^2}{2}\ln\left(u + \sqrt{a^2+u^2}\right) + C$

79. $\int u^2\sqrt{a^2+u^2}\, du = \frac{u}{8}(a^2+2u^2)\sqrt{a^2+u^2} - \frac{a^4}{8}\ln\left(u + \sqrt{a^2+u^2}\right) + C$

80. $\int \frac{\sqrt{a^2+u^2}}{u}\, du = \sqrt{a^2+u^2} - a\ln\left|\frac{a+\sqrt{a^2+u^2}}{u}\right| + C$

81. $\int \frac{\sqrt{a^2+u^2}}{u^2}\, du = -\frac{\sqrt{a^2+u^2}}{u} + \ln\left(u + \sqrt{a^2+u^2}\right) + C$

82. $\int \frac{u^2\, du}{\sqrt{a^2+u^2}} = \frac{u}{2}\sqrt{a^2+u^2} - \frac{a^2}{2}\ln\left(u + \sqrt{a^2+u^2}\right) + C$

83. $\int \frac{du}{u\sqrt{a^2+u^2}} = -\frac{1}{a}\ln\left|\frac{a+\sqrt{a^2+u^2}}{u}\right| + C$

84. $\int \frac{du}{u^2\sqrt{a^2+u^2}} = -\frac{\sqrt{a^2+u^2}}{a^2u} + C$

85. $\int \frac{du}{(a^2+u^2)^{3/2}} = \frac{u}{a^2\sqrt{a^2+u^2}} + C$

$\sqrt{a^2-u^2},\ a > 0$

86. $\int \frac{du}{\sqrt{a^2-u^2}} = \arcsin\frac{u}{a} + C$

87. $\int \sqrt{a^2-u^2}\, du = \frac{u}{2}\sqrt{a^2-u^2} + \frac{a^2}{2}\arcsin\frac{u}{a} + C$

88. $\int u^2\sqrt{a^2-u^2}\, du = \frac{u}{8}(2u^2-a^2)\sqrt{a^2-u^2} + \frac{a^4}{8}\arcsin\frac{u}{a} + C$

89. $\displaystyle\int \frac{\sqrt{a^2-u^2}}{u}\,du = \sqrt{a^2-u^2} - a\ln\left|\frac{a+\sqrt{a^2-u^2}}{u}\right| + C$

90. $\displaystyle\int \frac{\sqrt{a^2-u^2}}{u^2}\,du = -\frac{1}{u}\sqrt{a^2-u^2} - \arcsin\frac{u}{a} + C$

91. $\displaystyle\int \frac{u^2\,du}{\sqrt{a^2-u^2}} = -\frac{u}{2}\sqrt{a^2-u^2} + \frac{a^2}{2}\arcsin\frac{u}{a} + C$

92. $\displaystyle\int \frac{du}{u\sqrt{a^2-u^2}} = -\frac{1}{a}\ln\left|\frac{a+\sqrt{a^2-u^2}}{u}\right| + C$

93. $\displaystyle\int \frac{du}{u^2\sqrt{a^2-u^2}} = -\frac{1}{a^2u}\sqrt{a^2-u^2} + C$

94. $\displaystyle\int (a^2-u^2)^{3/2}\,du = -\frac{u}{8}(2u^2-5a^2)\sqrt{a^2-u^2} + \frac{3a^4}{8}\arcsin\frac{u}{a} + C$

95. $\displaystyle\int \frac{du}{(a^2-u^2)^{3/2}} = \frac{u}{a^2\sqrt{a^2-u^2}} + C$

96. $\displaystyle\int \frac{du}{a^2-u^2} = \frac{1}{2a}\ln\left|\frac{a+u}{a-u}\right| + C$

$\sqrt{u^2-a^2},\ a>0$

97. $\displaystyle\int \frac{du}{u\sqrt{u^2-a^2}} = \frac{1}{a}\,\mathrm{arcsec}\,\frac{|u|}{a} + C$

98. $\displaystyle\int \frac{\sqrt{u^2-a^2}}{u}\,du = \sqrt{u^2-a^2} - a\,\mathrm{arcsec}\,\frac{u}{a} + C$

99. $\displaystyle\int \sqrt{u^2-a^2}\,du = \frac{u}{2}\sqrt{u^2-a^2} - \frac{a^2}{2}\ln\left|u+\sqrt{u^2-a^2}\right| + C$

100. $\displaystyle\int u^2\sqrt{u^2-a^2}\,du = \frac{u}{8}(2u^2-a^2)\sqrt{u^2-a^2} - \frac{a^4}{8}\ln\left|u+\sqrt{u^2-a^2}\right| + C$

101. $\displaystyle\int \frac{\sqrt{u^2-a^2}}{u^2}\,du = -\frac{\sqrt{u^2-a^2}}{u} + \ln\left|u+\sqrt{u^2-a^2}\right| + C$

102. $\displaystyle\int \frac{u^2\,du}{\sqrt{u^2-a^2}} = \frac{u}{2}\sqrt{u^2-a^2} + \frac{a^2}{2}\ln\left|u+\sqrt{u^2-a^2}\right| + C$

103. $\displaystyle\int \frac{du}{u^2\sqrt{u^2-a^2}} = \frac{\sqrt{u^2-a^2}}{a^2u} + C$

104. $\displaystyle\int \frac{du}{(u^2-a^2)^{3/2}} = -\frac{u}{a^2\sqrt{u^2-a^2}} + C$

105. $\displaystyle\int \frac{u^2\,du}{(u^2-a^2)^{3/2}} = \frac{-u}{\sqrt{u^2-a^2}} + \ln|u+\sqrt{u^2-a^2}| + C$

$a+bu,\ \sqrt{a+bu}$

106. $\displaystyle\int \frac{u\,du}{a+bu} = \frac{1}{b^2}(a+bu-a\ln|a+bu|) + C$

107. $\displaystyle\int \frac{u^2\,du}{a+bu} = \frac{1}{2b^3}[(a+bu)^2-4a(a+bu)+2a^2\ln|a+bu|] + C$

108. $\displaystyle\int \frac{du}{u(a+bu)} = \frac{1}{a}\ln\left|\frac{u}{a+bu}\right| + C$

109. $\displaystyle\int \frac{du}{u^2(a+bu)} = -\frac{1}{au} + \frac{b}{a^2}\ln\left|\frac{a+bu}{u}\right| + C$

110. $\displaystyle\int \frac{u\,du}{(a+bu)^2} = \frac{a}{b^2(a+bu)} + \frac{1}{b^2}\ln|a+bu| + C$

111. $\displaystyle\int \frac{du}{u(a+bu)^2} = \frac{1}{a(a+bu)} - \frac{1}{a^2}\ln\left|\frac{a+bu}{u}\right| + C$

112. $\displaystyle\int \frac{u^2\,du}{(a+bu)^2} = \frac{1}{b^3}\left(a+bu-\frac{a^2}{a+bu}-2a\ln|a+bu|\right) + C$

113. $\displaystyle\int \frac{u\,du}{\sqrt{a+bu}} = \frac{2}{3b^2}(bu-2a)\sqrt{a+bu} + C$

114. $\displaystyle\int u\sqrt{a+bu}\,du = \frac{2}{15b^2}(3bu-2a)(a+bu)^{3/2} + C$